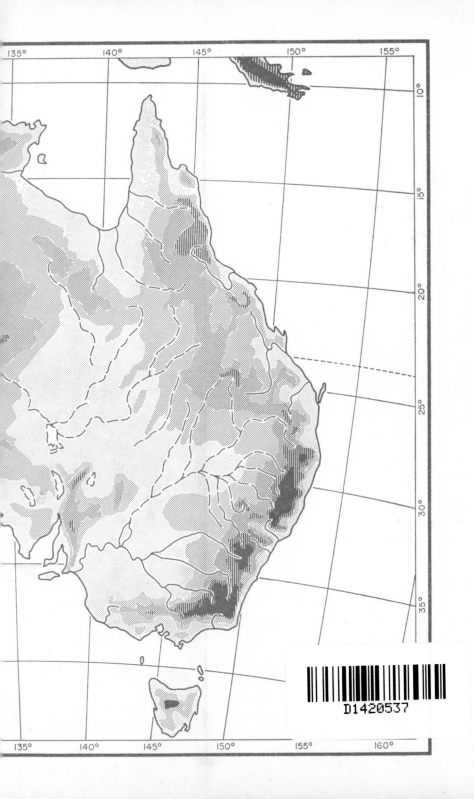

ARMS OF AUSTRALIA

THE QUEEN'S PERSONAL FLAG

NATIONAL FLAG

R.A.A.F. ENSIGN

CIVIL AIR ENSIGN

NAVAL ENSIGN

MERCHANT FLAG

PLATE 1: ARMS AND FLAGS OF AUSTRALIA

ENCYCLOPAEDIA OF
AUSTRALIA

Compiled by
ANDREW AND NANCY LEARMONTH

HICKS, SMITH & SONS PTY LTD
SYDNEY · BRISBANE · MELBOURNE

FREDERICK WARNE & CO LTD
LONDON · NEW YORK

ISBN 0 7232 1709 2

Made and printed in Great Britain by
William Clowes & Sons, Limited, London, Beccles and Colchester

526.673

FOREWORD

The fundamental problem of the encyclopaedist is one of selection. Inevitably, there is a subjective element in the choice, but, to make the coverage as representative as possible, formulae were devised to ensure fair shares to the major fields of biography, geography, natural history, literature, the arts, sport etc. This was followed by extensive reading of fundamental works acknowledged on page v. Not wishing to produce a yearbook, gazetteer, nor yet a *Who's Who*, we have set out to develop more interesting topics, not completely shunning interpretation; but very many items which would otherwise have been omitted have been classified in lists.

We hope that this book will be valuable as a family reference work, condensing material over a wide range. Sources are quoted, both general and particular, and these may lead readers to enrich their own bookshelves or open new doors through library borrowing or reference. We have tried to keep in mind the kind of enquiry likely to arise both among Australians, old and new, and among people overseas interested in this rapidly developing country.

Canberra

ANDREW LEARMONTH
NANCY LEARMONTH

Foreword to the Second Edition

The need for a complete revision has been evident for some time, but 1973 is a particularly fortunate year to be able to prepare this new edition for publication in Australia. The 1971 population census and the progressive metrication of measures have left barely a page unaffected. Hundreds more entries have been revised and rewritten and many new entries included. Book lists have been brought up to date and still we feel represent one of the encyclopaedia's major functions: to act as a point of entry to the literature available on a wide range of topics.

Shifting trade patterns, continued economic development, the move from old alliances to a new nationalism, and the change of government in December 1972 are all shaping a different Australia.

ANDREW LEARMONTH
NANCY LEARMONTH

January 1973

CONVENTIONS

Abbreviations Compass points are given in capitals without periods. For Australia and the States, abbreviations are used both as noun and adjective: Aus. (Australia, Australian), N.S.W. (New South Wales), N.T. (Northern Territory), Qld. (Queensland), S.A. (South Australia), Tas. (Tasmania), Vic. (Victoria), W.A. (Western Australia); also N.Z. (New Zealand), N.G. (New Guinea); also Eng. (England), U.K. (United Kingdom) and U.S. (United States). Other abbreviations used are: Mts. (Mountains), L. (Lake), Str. (Strait), mm. (millimetres), cm. (centimetres), m. (metres), km. (kilometres), ha. (hectares), g. (grammes), kg. (kilogrammes), l. (litres), b. (born), spp. (species).

Location of many places is given to the nearest degree, with the South latitude first, and the East longitude after an oblique line; the degree symbol is omitted. As many as possible are shown on the appropriate maps which have latitudes and longitudes along the margins. Thus Port Augusta S.A. 32S/138E will be found on Map 9, South Australia, at the end of the book. The position of places not shown on the maps can also be determined.

Population is given in brackets for each town after the location. All towns with 5,000 or more (1971) have separate entries, as have smaller towns for particular reasons. Every town of 1,000 or more will be found classified according to function in the State articles. If a town is declining, 2 or more census figures are given.

Cross Referencing has been carefully planned to lead the reader to other relevant entries, and is generally indicated by the use of an asterisk. Thus under **Platypus,** Monotreme* will clarify the distinctive characteristics of this unique animal order; under **Cunningham, Alan,** 'Oxley's* expedition' indicates further information of real relevance to Cunningham. Where lists are given, asterisks indicate the items having separate entries, e.g. under **Trees.**

Technical Terms are not obtrusively used, but access to a good dictionary is assumed.

Popular Names present a particular difficulty, for some plants and animals have 7 or 8 popular names, sometimes used quite locally, sometimes archaic. We did not wish to put the main entries under the technical Latin name, save in a few cases. Where possible, a widely used popular name has been selected, giving alternatives, but adding the Latin name in italics to allow precise identification. Lists have also been used to meet this problem, e.g. under **Wild Flowers** an alphabetical list of popular names is given, each having either a minimal description or an asterisk for a separate entry.

ACKNOWLEDGMENTS

First Edition In preparing line and colour illustrations Noela Young of Bayview, N.S.W., has combined artistry and accuracy. Peter Daniell of the Australian National University contributed both ideas and craftsmanship to the cartography, assisted by Petar Petrovich. The authors are responsible for the entire text, but called on a number of more expert critics to read particular sections: Dr. Nan Anderson (Botany), Mrs. Anne Gollan (Literature), Dr. D. Brook (Art), B. H. Crew (History and Queensland), B. R. Crouch (Victoria), P. Daniell (Western Australia), Mrs. Robin Grau (New South Wales), G. Kelly (Sport), Dr. J. G. Mosley (Conservation) and Dr. Patricia Woolley (Zoology). The typing of difficult manuscripts was handled mainly by Mrs. Sheila Arndt, Mrs. Elizabeth Brown and Mrs. M. Thornton.

Second Edition We owe a major debt of gratitude to Mrs. C. M. McArthur of Canberra, who has tirelessly pursued facts and figures to help up-date the work. Dr. D. Brook heavily revised the arts entries and Mrs. Gollan the literature and Mr. B. H. Crew the historical entries. In addition, Mr. P. Speelman and Mr. J. Stevens gave invaluable help on sport, Mr. T. W. Plumb and Mr. G. Parkinson on mapping and railways. Mr. J. Hunt re-drew some of the maps and revised others.

Sources A work of this nature depends heavily on existing publications. Outstanding general sources include: *Atlas of Australian Resources*, published with continuous revision by the Department of National Development; the *Official Yearbook of the Commonwealth of Australia*, Commonwealth Bureau of Census and Statistics, Canberra; *Australia in Facts and Figures*, News and Information Bureau, Canberra; J. Andrews, *Australia's Resources* (Sydney, 1972); *Longman's Australian Geographies*, General Editor G. H. Lawton (Melbourne, 1956–); Longman's *Industry in Australia*, General Editor G. J. R. Linge (Melbourne, 1967–); C.S.I.R.O., *The Australian Environment* (Melbourne, 1971); the *Australian Dictionary of Biography*, Vols. I to IV, 1788–1890, General Editor D. Pike (Melbourne, 1966–); many journals, notably *The Australian Geographer* (Sydney), *Australian Geographical Studies* (Melbourne), *Australian Natural History* (Australian Museum, Sydney), *The Australian Journal of Science* (Sydney), *Current Affairs Bulletin* (Sydney), *The Australian Journal of Politics and History* (Brisbane), *Hemisphere* (Sydney), *Walkabout* (Melbourne), *The Bulletin* (Sydney), *Nation* (Sydney), newspapers and *NatDev* quarterly from Department of National Development, *Australian News*. Aus. News and Information Bureau, London.

Sources and further reading on particular entries are listed with them.

While attempting a fresh compilation, we have, like many authors since its publication, leaned a good deal on the 10-volume *Australian Encyclopaedia*, Editor A. H. Chisholm (published by Grolier Society of Australia Pty. Ltd,

1963, revised 1965), to check items, fill gaps etc. We have made less but still grateful use of the *Modern Encyclopaedia of Australia and New Zealand* (Horwitz, Sydney, 1964), General Editor V. S. Barnes.

Grateful thanks are given to the Prime Minister's Department for kind permission to reproduce the Arms of Australia on the frontispiece.

LIST OF MAIN ARTICLES

LIST OF COLOUR PLATES

MAPS SECTION (pages 607–623)

A

ABALONE

Abalone A commercially important Gastropod*, in recent years a flourishing export to Asia as a food delicacy. The shellfish are obtained by skin-divers, earning very large sums when untapped colonies are found, sometimes on submerged shipwrecks; in 1972 restrictions were introduced off southern coasts.

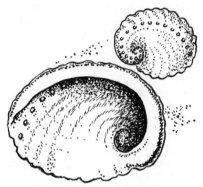

Abalone, about 12 cm. long

Abbott, Edward (1766–1832) b. Canada. He arrived in Aus. 1790 in N.S.W. Corps. Served in Norfolk Island 1791–4 and helped to suppress the Castle Hill Rising* in N.S.W. 1804. Although not actively concerned in the deposing of Bligh*, he supported it and was associated with Macarthur* and Johnston*. He served successfully, in spite of having no legal training, as deputy judge advocate of Van Diemen's Land 1814–24 and later as civil commandant, Launceston.

ABORIGINES (*Note*: usage varies between Aborigine and Aboriginal, but here the 2 forms are used for noun and adjective respectively.) Although Aborigines were enumerated at each

ABORIGINES

Commonwealth Census, results were inaccurate until 1966 when careful survey showed 80,207 people of over 50% Aboriginal blood. The Constitution precluded Aborigines from the published Census totals. This was amended in 1967, so the 1971 Census totals include Aborigines. Modern estimates are of some 47,000 'full blood' and 94,000 of mixed descent, comprising about 1% of the Aus. population. The estimated total in 1788, when white settlement began, was 300,000. They decreased rapidly owing to indiscriminate slaughter, including poisoning, punitive expeditions, and even more because of diseases such as smallpox and tuberculosis. The Tas. Aborigines, a distinctive negrito group of particularly simple culture, became extinct in 1888 owing to these factors and, it is said, because of a kind of death-wish sickness on separation from their ancestral lands. It appeared likely in the late 19th century that the mainland Aborigines would also become extinct, but they are now increasing.

Physical features include black skin, mainly black hair, curly but not frizzy, large brow-ridges, sloping forehead, large protruding jaws and a wide, flat nose, but with individual and regional variations. Blood group A predominates, with no group B except in the N, where some Melanesian influence is suspected; no Rh negative genes, high frequency of group N and therefore little group M. The blood group evidence strongly supports views of long genetic isolation since the Aboriginal immigration (bringing the dingo*) about 13–30,000 years ago (i.e. over the end of the Quaternary Ice Age). Affinities in general physique are with individuals among tribal groups in S

1

India, Ceylon and SE Asia, particularly among the taller Aborigines of NW Aus. (Carpentarians); the shorter stocky people of the S (Murrayians) have large faces and heads, with large teeth and fairly prominent jaws, while the rather rare distinctive groups of Qld. rain-forest refuge areas (Barrineans) are small, long-trunked, lighter in weight and perhaps with more negrito characteristics (raising the possibility of a negrito substratum in the mainland population, so that the negrito Tasmanians may have come by the mainland rather than from islands to the NE as is sometimes held). Quantitative data on intelligence are scarce or inaccessible (and tests notoriously culture-biased), but there is no evidence of any difference in range of intelligence as compared with other racial groups, despite the smaller average size of brain.

Languages may have numbered some 500 at the time of European contact; many survive and are still being studied and grouped linguistically. Broadly they are agglutinative languages, in which elements may be added to form long words expressing complex ideas. There is a quite subtle, though regionally varying, grammar. Distinctive groups include those of the Kimberleys and the NW, in which agglutination is largely by prefixes, the Western Desert group, with very early features linguistically, the Aranda group of W Central Aus., with distinctive combinations of consonants and rich combinations of verbs, and the Vic. group, possibly with primitive Tas. links and distinctive repetition of rather harsh syllables, e.g. *bidbidjerag*, an ibis.

Economy and Culture A Dutch report of 1623 spoke of the Aborigines as utter barbarians, Dampier in 1688 of the 'miserablest people in the whole world', yet Governor Phillip*, despite his spear-wound, set out with a commendably open and fair-minded attitude. Cook had been instructed to show 'every kind of courtesy and regard ... and with their consent ... to take possession. ...' Such provisions were eluded by the claim that, being nomadic, Aborigines had no land. Relations with Aborigines generally deteriorated as settlers pushed out to exploit what had been Aboriginal hunting grounds, except where individual settlers, policemen etc., had peculiar insight and imagination. An absurdly over-generalised and hostile stereotype came to be widely accepted as justifying the treatment of Aborigines as sub-human. Squalid peri-urban hutments, coupled with residual tribal brawls and mysterious disappearances from wage-labour to go 'walkabout', have not helped the image, which understandably still prevails in many communities where detribalised Aborigines in some numbers are in close and often sordid contact with rather small European communities—see Edward G. Docker's not unsympathetic vignette of Walgett in *Simply Human Beings*. As a reaction is an equally absurdly sentimental image, sometimes adjudged suitable for young children especially in predominantly European urban communities.

Primitive Aboriginal groups can be generalised as nomadic hunter-gatherers, with an intimate knowledge of the plants, animals and water resources of their territory, conservative of these resources but never reaching towards agriculture except possibly among some northern groups in former contact with island folk to the N. Their nomadism is linked to seasonal or sporadic changes in food resources, e.g. following rains in the desert, and with an extraordinary paucity of material possessions: they wear little or no clothing except for ornament (accentuated to bizarre proportions during religious tribal rituals); they lack protection even from cold desert nights, except for a small fire and a slight windbreak, having no housing except the flimsiest and most temporary shelters. This very simple economy demands deep and wide-ranging knowledge of the resources of the territory, and is linked with a complex web of religion and ritual, initiation and tabus. These cover: propitiation of spirits governing food supply; the organisation of hunting and gathering activities; the careful secreting of the *tjuringa* or roundish piece of wood or stone that becomes the abode of its owner's spirit after death; tribal and family movement; crimes and conduct; and even formalities in war and peace-making, including the well-known 'prostitution' of wives as a gesture of peace. Message sticks, carried by special messengers, often distinctively painted, were sent to arrange rituals, trade or other meetings. The carvings on the sticks are not the actual message,

Aboriginal Message Sticks, about 10 to 20 cm. long

which would be orally delivered; the sticks were a reminder, a token of the genuine nature of the message, even a kind of 'safe conduct' badge. Kinship laws are complex, a ritual web covering even attitudes and direction of conversation, as in the also well-known tabu on conversation between a husband (often much older than his wife) and his mother-in-law, which clearly has its own logic. Predominantly, it seems, there is lack of appreciation of the

connection between sexual intercourse and fertility and births, leading to acceptance of population control mainly by Malthusian checks of hunger and the abandonment of children (which still raises problems in settled areas fringing Central Aus.) There is a minimal range of stone-age tools, including the unique hunting and sporting boomerang* and the throwing-stick shared with a few other primitive groups. The whole culture is linked with primitive paintings varying from quick sketches, sometimes vividly life-like, sometimes formalised as in the X-ray paintings* of the E Alligator area of Arnhem Land, to highly finished works, including low-relief carved pictures made with a hammer and nail, and the bark paintings* from Alligator River to Groote Eylandt (*see also* ROCK ART). The music of both song and dance is mainly produced by the mouth and by rhythmic clapping of thighs or buttocks, but there are various simple drums and the well-known sustained but rhythmic use of the didjeridu* in the N, where music is at its most subtle; and A. P. Elkin believes he has found the art of counter-point in course of evolution. Ritual dance and mime have been shown to have a high potential for ballet and drama.

Such a stereotype must certainly be modified, in infinite detail for different tribes and kinship groups, and even regionally. The range of tools is greater among fishing groups, especially those constantly practising fishing as against seasonal gatherers of shellfish, along the Murray, on the SE coast and especially in Qld. where a large range of nets, fish-hooks and harpoons (for turtles and dugong) may have been enriched by contact with island groups farther N. The boomerang and the woomera are by no means universal. Kinship customs and tabus are almost as variable in detail as the languages; the music is proving susceptible to analysis, and strong regional variations are becoming known. Anthropological studies have greatly increased knowledge, especially since the 1920s, though in much of N.S.W. and Vic., and all Tas., virtually no Aboriginal life remains to observe, and contemporary accounts of varying accuracy and bias must be complemented by archaeological methods on cave deposits, shell middens etc.

Elkin pleads that to such a picture of externals we should add some understanding of the pre-existing spirits, human and animal in harmony, inhabiting the tribal territory. The father's spirit is put in touch with a pre-existing spirit which enters the mother's womb; her flesh and blood—and her animal totem—are equally essential. Away from the tribal territory, hostile spirits of unknown powers and propensities prevail. It is for this reason, not because of sentimentality, that it is often the professional anthropologist who pleads for clemency when a tribal Aborigine, perhaps involved in a murder of ritual or revenge, experiences a kind of spiritual rape and flaying by a cloud of alien spirits away from his territory, to sample white man's justice. Lacking knowledge of disease pathogens, illness is put down to witchcraft, and though herbal and other remedies of some efficacy are known, the medicine man also has to ward off witchcraft, or diagnose it in inquest after death—possibly leading to expeditions of revenge, though warfare may be formalised or warded off by balancing one injury against another (war for territorial aggrandisement is rare or unknown). Kinship is classificatory, and all within a local group are classified as brother, father, son, grandfather etc. Within the web of kinship are obligations to share the products of hunting etc.—hence what appears to the European to be the indiscriminate present-giving which rapidly wipes out temporary affluence in Aboriginal workers on stations etc. The seemingly feckless going walkabout, instead of sticking to regular station work, represents a sort of adjustment—possible only in the sparsely peopled outback—in which the white man's property rights and ways of work are, as it were, tolerated as a means of obtaining desirable items, e.g. tobacco and alcohol, but remain less important than tribal ways and spirits. But the elders may judge the young men unworthy to receive the tribal heritage and it may die—hence the marked and pathetic rootlessness of the fringe communities of Aborigines without tribal certainties, disillusioned too often with both Christianity and what the Australian way of life has to offer them.

Aborigines in the Community Some 45,000 Aborigines live on remote tribal reserves in northern and central Aus. in fairly primitive conditions of poverty and health. Most of the rest live on the fringes of country towns and depend on unskilled and seasonal labour. Only a small proportion live in cities and approach integration. From 1820 to about 1840, ruthless exploitation and extermination were pursued with few effective protests; from 1840 to about 1880 there were increasing pleas for more humanitarian treatment, and from 1880 onwards, the States—still the main authority—began to make various provisions for protection. Mission stations, some self-supporting economically, came to be accepted as a main instrument of assistance, though government stations were also set up. In 1967 the Aus. Council of Churches indicated a policy of progressively handing their Missions over to government control. Since 1945 there has been much more public conscience—partly, paradoxically, because of advances in the Trust Territory of Papua New Guinea. Aborigines now have voting and drinking rights, and are eligible for social services. In 1967 equal pay with white workers on pastoral properties was awarded, but is not always implemented. The issue of land rights came to a head with mineral development in the reserves. A Supreme Court Judgement in 1972 rejected such rights because 'their relationship with the land was not sufficiently economic to amount to a proprietary interest'. Militant reaction led to the setting up of a temporary, tented 'Aboriginal Embassy' opposite Parliament House in Canberra. The Labor Government elected in Dec. 1972 is pledged to grant Aborigines' land rights.

There is a Commonwealth Ministry of Aboriginal Affairs and an advisory Council. But most responsibility lies with the States, and legislation varies. Qld. is considered most discriminatory at present. The Federal Council for Advancement of Aborigines and Torres Strait Islanders is a private group. While the official policy aimed at assimilation, many thinking Aborigines saw this as virtually second-class citizenship, and express a wish to remain separate culturally but economically equal. Aborigines who have become well-known figures include Namatjira*, Harold Blair, a musician, Phillip Magalnir, a Methodist minister, Robert Tudawali, a film actor, Phillip Roberts, a medical assistant whose story is told by D. Lockwood in *I the Aboriginal* (Adelaide, 1962), E. Goolagong (tennis*) L. Rose (boxing*), Senator Bonner and Sir Douglas Nicholls (pastor), Kath Walker* (poet) and Bobbi Sykes (militant).

Early recording of the Aborigines was largely the work of dedicated amateurs: A. W. Howitt*, working with Lorimer Fison (1832–1907), a Wesleyan parson, made the first notable scientific contributions between 1880 and 1905 on the tribes of SE Aus. A later and equally remarkable partnership was that between Sir Walter Baldwin Spencer (1860–1929), Biology Professor at Melbourne, and F. J. Gillen (1856–1912), a postal official and sub-protector of Aborigines in S.A., in recording the Aranda and other tribes of the Centre and N (1910–30). Daisy Bates* was unique in her approach. Other early workers included W. Ridley (1819–1873), a Presbyterian minister who studied Aboriginal languages, R. B. Smyth (1830–1889), working with helpers and questionnaires in Vic., and W. E. Roth (1861–1933) in Qld.

The Social Science Research Council has a major project on Aborigines in Aus. Society (1964–). The Aus. Institute of Aboriginal Studies is concerned with culture and language. *For further reading see* A. P. Elkin (1891–): *The Australian Aborigines* (Sydney, 1954); F. W. Bleakley: *The Aborigines of Australia* (Brisbane, 1961); *The Australian Aborigines* (Department of Territories, 1967); I. G. Sharpe: *Aborigines in the Economy* (Melbourne, 1967); R. M. and C. H. Berndt: *Aboriginal Man in Australia* (Sydney, 1965); D. J. Mulvaney: *The Prehistory of Australia* (London, 1969); C. D. Rowley: *The Destruction of Aboriginal Society* (Vol. 1, Canberra, 1970).

Adaminaby N.S.W. 36S/149E A small town 52 km. NW of Cooma. The town was moved 11 km. NE to its present site in 1957, when the original site—dating from a pastoral station of 1848 and a gold-field period from 1860—was inundated by the rising waters of the artificial Lake Eucumbene*.

Adams, Arthur Henry (1872–1936) b. New Zealand. Arrived Aus. 1898, journalist, poet, playwright and writer of fiction who criticised the current Aus. scene with cultivated skill and acute observation. Although his work is little read today, his political farce *Mrs. Pretty and the Premier* was performed in London in 1916; his poems appeared in *Collected Verse* (Melbourne, 1913) and among a wide range of fiction the novel *Galahad Jones* is among the best.

Adams, Francis William Lauderdale (1862–1893) b. Malta. Lived in Aus. 1884–89. As a writer he was English rather than Aus., but his bitter verse influenced the Aus. 'poetry of revolt' of the turn of the century.

Adams, George (1839–1904) b. Hertfordshire, Eng. Arrived Aus. 1855, and was a sheephand and butcher before he leased Tattersall's Hotel, Sydney (1878), and organised sweepstakes on horse races for clients and then the general public. Anti-gambling legislation forced moves to Brisbane, then Hobart. (*See* GAMBLING.)

Adder The true adder or viper does not occur in Aus., but the names stone adder, rock adder, tree adder, pine adder are sometimes wrongly applied to the harmless Geckoes*. (*See also* DEATH ADDER.)

ADELAIDE S.A. 35S/138E (809,466 in 1971). The capital of S.A. and third Aus. city, has 65% of the State's population and was named after Queen Adelaide, the consort of William IV. The area had been traversed by Matthew Flinders in 1801–2, but settlement began in the mid-1830s under John Hindmarsh. After initial settlements on Kangaroo Island, and at Holdfast Bay (Glenelg), the present site was selected in the teeth of severe opposition by Colonel William Light, the first surveyor-general of S.A. His diary records that in his reasons for selecting the site he did not expect to be understood or calmly judged by his contemporaries, but that posterity would praise or blame. In fact the city owes a great deal to his selection of the site and initial plan, in recognition of which his statue gazes across parklands by the river Torrens to the variegated skyline of the central city today, from 'Light's Vision'. He placed the city centre about equidistant between the seashore and the fault-line scarp of the Mt. Lofty Range, both running about

N–S; it is in a mainly alluvial plain, but above floods and marshes, about 8 km. inland, and 16 km. SE of the small estuary of the Torrens (now diverted through an artificial outlet at Henley further S), which Light saw as a useful and sheltered seaport site. Light designed 2 central areas of grid-iron plan, one north and one south of the Torrens, with a belt of parklands flanking the ponded river. The whole was to be surrounded by a green belt, and this has been largely adhered to. This twin central core is now the focus of a widely spread city, linked by continuous development with Port Adelaide, Salisbury and the modern satellite town at Elizabeth, 24 km. N of the city, and S to Christie's Beach beyond Port Stanvac. The Mt. Lofty Range remains largely rural, as a national park or nature reserve, or for recreational uses or water catchments, though expensive housing is climbing up the lower slopes. E across the first range, Crafers-Bridgewater (5,301 in 1971) remains a separate entity of high-class housing, but naturally intimately linked with the city. Until the 1914–18 War, the city depended largely on its capital functions, along with commerce in the State's agricultural products, and there was a little processing industry, but now some 30% of the labour force is engaged in a wide variety of manufacturing industry. Heavy industry is located along the main railway axes and near the port: motor-body assembly at Woodville, Keswick and Tonsley Park, with associated steel tube and tyre works; abattoirs and fruit canning near the line from the stock lands to the N; rail workshops and household electrical appliances at Islington; chemicals based on salt pans at Osborne; sugar-refining at Port Adelaide; oil-refining at Port Stanvac; former munitions works at Henley make electrical equipment and were the nucleus of the Weapons Research Establishment at Salisbury to the N.

Winters are predominantly mild

with 53 cm. of rain and with occasional sharply cold spells; the summers are long, heat-waves with day after day over 37°C being not uncommon but relieved by cool changes. Water needs for domestic use are heavy, and rapidly growing industry also makes heavy demands on water. Light's siting in relation to water from the Torrens was for long adequate, with the use of reservoirs there and on the Onkaparinga and S Para and Myponga Rivers, constructed at different phases of growth; but large quantities of Murray River water now have to be pumped along a pipe-line from Mannum. (*See* MAP 10.)

Although increasingly varied in function and population, Adelaide retains much rather heavy dignity, an inheritance of its self-conscious origin as capital of a colony never associated with transportation. **Adelaide Festival of Arts** is a biennial function of international repute, with a fine Festival Theatre (1972). *See* M. Williams: *Adelaide* (Melbourne, 1966).

Adelaide River N.T. 13S/131E Flows permanently but with a big summer increase for 160 km. NE to Adam Bay, Van Diemen Gulf, 48 km. NE of Darwin. Much of the lower course is lined with fertile black-soil plain, from the 1890s the scene of several attempts at crop production and including successful vegetable growing for troops in the 1939–45 war, the unsuccessful post-war Humpty-Doo* rice project and present-day C.S.I.R.O.* experimental cattle and rice farms. The small township also called **Adelaide River** lies where the Stuart Highway* and N Aus. Railway cross the river. Near the mouth were the earlier unsuccessful settlements of Escape Cliffs* and Port Daly.

Aerial Agriculture In 1947 aerial fertilising and seeding was introduced to Aus. by D. M. Shand. The major use is for spreading superphosphate over large areas of pasture; with crop-dusting, seeding, bait-laying for pests, some 6 million ha. are treated every year, by over 150 light aircraft, mainly of American make.

Afghans (or **Ghans**) The name given to the several hundred Mohammedan camel drivers (*see* CAMELS) who came to Aus. between 1860 and the 1920s; in fact the majority came from the NW of the Indian subcontinent, now Pakistan, rather than Afghanistan. Many outback townships had roughly built 'Ghan Camps' on their outskirts: Bourke, N.S.W., Cloncurry, Qld., Marble Bar., W.A., and, Oodnadatta, S.A. (where some time ago one of the few surviving Afghans died, reputedly a hundred years old). Their nomadic tradition and skill in leading the strings of animals over otherwise inaccessible country, made them invaluable, although it led to bitter hatred by white bullock drivers who tried to have them banned in Qld. **Afghan Rocks,** 225 km. E of Norseman, W.A., 32S/122E, commemorates a fight with gold prospectors. The religious taboo on alcohol made Afghans in demand for carting it to thirsty camps. **The Ghan** is the train linking Port Augusta with Alice Springs.

Agents General Officials maintained in London by each State to supply information and encourage migration; before Federation they were more actively concerned than now in trade and financial promotion.

Agricultural Machinery Invention and manufacture were stimulated by the problems of opening up vast farmlands with a small labour force. Early Aus. products were a chaff-cutter (Bagshaw, 1837) and pumping equipment (Horwood, 1839) both in Adelaide, where Bagshaw-Horwood remains as the only major all-Aus. firm making agricultural machinery. The stripper-harvester* (1843) and stumpjump plough* (1876), Wolseley's shearing machine (patented 1877, in wide use after 1888) and the famous Sunshine Harvester of H. V. McKay* were major contributions. Today 80% of home demand, save for tractors which are largely imported ready for assembly, is met by 3 large integrated firms. International Harvesters make and assemble machinery and trucks and Massey-Ferguson assemble machines from huge earth-moving plants to small cultivators; both are in Melbourne. In addition numerous and widespread small works specialise in local needs, e.g. for sugar, rice and potato growing. Exports are about 5% of the total output by value and are mainly sent to SE Asia and N.Z. Farmers increasingly use contractors when heavy equipment is required.

A.I.F. Australian Imperial Force (*see* ARMY).

Air Beef Scheme (1949–62) The setting up of slaughter houses on Glenroy Station, W.A., 17S/126E, with chilling facilities and air-transported carcases to Wyndham and later to Derby meatworks. It proved uneconomic as an alternative to the long droving it sought to avoid, and has been replaced by road trains*.

Air Force The R.A.A.F., Royal Australian Air Force, dates from 1921, founded on the small but remarkable Australian Flying Corps of 1915–18 and post-war Australian Air Corps, and has built up a fine record of skill and courage. The R.A.A.F. now uses almost a third of the Defence budget, and has a complement of some 25,000. The strike reconnaissance force uses Canberra and Phantom aircraft; 24 new F111 fighter bombers bought from U.S. for $A300 million take over by late 1973. The R.A.A.F. also uses Mirage fighters (French), Hercules, Caribou, Dakota, Mystère 20 and B.A.C.111 for transport, Neptunes and Orions for maritime work, Iroquois helicopters, Macchi (Italian), Winjeel, Sabre and Mirage trainers.

The R.A.A.F. is administered by the Air Board. (*See also* DEFENCE.)

Air Races On 2 or 3 occasions these have brought home to Aus. the progressive shrinking of the world in the air age. The Commonwealth prize of £10,000 initiated by the air-minded Prime Minister W. M. Hughes in 1919, went to the first Aus. crew in a British-built machine to complete the Eng.–Aus. flight within 720 hours and by 31st December 1919; only in this sense was it a race. The successful crew consisted of Ross and Keith Smith, W. H. Shiers and J. M. Bennett in a Vickers Vimy bomber. Flying time of 135 hours for the 18,260 km. from Hounslow to Darwin was spread over 27 days and 20 hours. While preparing for a planned world flight not long before his death Sir Ross Smith predicted regular flights taking 10 days along his route. By 1934 when the Melbourne Centenary Air Race for prizes offered by Sir Macpherson Robertson took place, the time had shrunk further and C. W. A. Scott and T. Campbell Black in their De Havilland Comet took just under 3 days from London to Melbourne. By the time of the London–Aus.–Christchurch Air Race of 1953, the outright winners in a R.A.F. Canberra jet bomber took under 24 hours from London to Christchurch, and a British European Airways Viscount took under 36 hours from London to Melbourne.

Within Aus. an Aerial Derby was held at Adelaide in 1920, and several such were held in different places, but the Transcontinental Race of 1929, from Sydney to Perth was of real significance. It was won by Hereward de Havilland in one of the family firm's Gipsy Moths in 22 hours 50 minutes, and the handicap was won in a DH9 by H. C. Miller, co-founder of the MacRobertson-Miller Airline.

Aircraft Manufacture This is carried out by the Government Aircraft Factory, Fishermen's Bend, Vic. (1939), with final assembly and test field at Avalon, Vic., and the machine shop for repairs at Northfield, S.A.; by the Commonwealth Aircraft Corporation (formed from 6 companies in 1936) also near Fishermen's Bend; and by De Havilland, Sydney, which makes light aircraft frames, and was noted for the design and manufacture of the Drover, an outback plane capable of landing on short runways. Aircraft produced in Aus. during the war, included Beaufort and Lincoln bombers, Mustang and the Aus. designed Boomerang fighters. The French Mirage fighter and Italian Macchi trainer have been built in Vic. Parts of the Ikara anti-submarine missile are made at the Government Factory as is the Jindivik target aircraft which has some export. From the early 1970s a naval target aircraft, the *Turana*, with gas turbine engines, will be made. A new Aus. designed and built light aircraft, the Nomad, is in production. With STOL (short take off and landing) ability, it carries up to 12 passengers and may replace the widely used Cessna. The most notable designer was Sir Lawrence Wackett* (Widgeon flying boat, the Warbler, Warrigal (1928 for army work) and the trainer Wirraway, basis of the Boomerang fighter and Ceres crop duster). An Aus. designed Microwave Landing System (MLS) will be operational in 1973.

Airlines Australia's overseas airline is QANTAS*, entirely Commonwealth owned since 1947. It has a modern jet aircraft fleet adequate to operate a world-wide route network; from 1971 the fleet included Boeing 747 'jumbo' jets; over 6,000 inward and outward flights carry over 450,000 passengers, nearly half the total passenger flights to and from Aus., and a majority of freight and outward mail.

The inter-state airlines providing scheduled passenger and all-freight aircraft are: 1. The Commonwealth Government's Trans-Australia Airlines, established by the post-war Labor Government in 1945, after an attempt to nationalise all inter-state airlines had been declared unconstitutional. It carries some 52% of traffic. The first flight was Melbourne–Sydney, September 9th 1946. Today its less profitable country lines are being replaced by private 'feeder' services. 2. Ansett Airlines, a subsidiary of Ansett Transport Industries which acquired the second Australian National Airways Pty. Ltd. (*see* AVIATION) in 1957.

By the Government's two-airlines policy (for inter-state traffic) TAA and Ansett have comparable fleets and compete for the main inter-state routes and the N.G. traffic; each has also a non-competitive area—Ansett mainly from Melbourne, TAA mainly in Qld. Their main fleets include turbo-jets for the main inter-capital journeys like the Boeing 727 and D.C.9; other aircraft used include Electras, with small planes for outback routes.

Smaller intra-state airlines mainly bring local traffic to the State capitals: Sydney (Airlines of N.S.W. and East-West Airlines), Adelaide (Airlines of S.A.), and Perth (MacRobertson-Miller Airlines). From Alice Springs operates the subsidised Connellan Airways providing a remarkable service by circular routes linking outback cattle stations; MacRobertson-Miller has something of this character on some of its routes. Except for Connellan and East-West, these smaller lines are owned by Ansett Transport Industries. Except for the smaller planes used by Connellan, D.C.3s and the newer turbo-prop Fokker Fellowships are typical aircraft. By 1970 18 charter firms operated small aircraft on timetabled 'commuter services' connecting minor airfields with capital or major towns.

Passenger fares are relatively high in spite of competition, largely through taxation including heavy tax on fuel.

The Government restricts the development of new lines and charter companies. The safety record is one of the best in the world, partly through climatic factors, low density of route networks and lack of high jagged terrain; they also owe much to rigid department regulations developing from those set in the 1930s by A. G. Berg.

Aitken, John (?1792–1858) b. Scotland. Arrived Tas. about 1825 and became a much respected pioneer settler in the Port Phillip district from 1836. Noted for his fine Saxon, later Merino sheep.

Albacutya, Lake Vic. 36S/142E A frequently dry lacustrine surface of 9 by 5 km. sometimes receiving water from the Wimmera River in wet years when there is an overflow from L. Hindmarsh.*

Albany W.A. 35S/118E (13,055 in 1970) Port and regional centre for the SW of W.A. and site of the earliest white settlement in the State in 1826 under Lockyer*. It lies on King George Sound*. Port development was retarded after the Fremantle inner harbour was opened (1897), but is increasing again with land development in its hinterland. It now has bulk handling of wheat and meat, oil storage, a woollen mill, superphosphate factory and important wool sales. The Frenchmans Bay sperm whaling station on the W of the Sound is the only one in Aus. Originally named Frederickstown after the Duke of York and Albany, brother of George IV, it soon came to be called Albany. The population doubles with summer visitors, mainly Wheat Belt farmers, or fugitives from the Perth heat. **Albany Doctor** is a cool afternoon sea breeze felt 100 km. inland.

Albury N.S.W. 36S/147E City on Murray River (27,383 in 1971 with Wodonga, Vic.) lies near the site of crossing the Murray by Hume* and Hovell, in 1824. A small settlement grew round the police post at the river crossing. There was little growth until after 1855 when a steamer named after the town first opened up the river traffic which lasted until the rail links with Sydney and Melbourne were completed in 1883. The break of gauge at the border gave impetus to the town, until the standard-gauge was extended to Melbourne in 1962. Albury remains an important regional centre for a rich district; its wool sales, wool and clothing factories, abattoirs, honey processing, wholesale agricultural establishments and good shopping and professional services reflect the products and needs of the district. The Royal Commission appointed in 1903 to report on sites for the National Capital, visited Albury, but rejected it. A new city, Albury-Wodonga, for 300,000 is now planned. *See* W. A. Bayley: *Border City* (Albury, 1954).

Alexandrina, Lake S.A. 35S/139E At the mouth of the River Murray*; 32 km. E–W by 24 km. N–S, it is continued to the SE by the smaller L. Albert. Until the 5 barrages across its exit channels were built (1940) it was salty. Milang on the W shore, now a dairy and vegetable-growing centre for Adelaide, was an important river port until the railway (1884) killed the traffic. Sturt* named the lake in 1830, from the first name of the princess who became Queen Victoria.

Algae Simply constructed plants, somewhat comparable to fungi in gross morphology but able to photosynthesise. Aus. algae include: 1. Blue-Green Algae, Cyanophyceae, allied to bacteria, simple in structure and largely reproducing vegetatively by division, in long strings or tangled masses (*Oscillatoria*, able to move its filaments slowly) or in jelly-like masses (*Rivularia*). Some form nitrogen-fixing associations with the roots of Cycads*. 2. Green Algae, Chlorophyceae, seen in fresh water, damp soil and brackish sea water, of varying degrees of complexity: (a) the still simple but mobile *Chlamydomonas*; (b) the similar but colonial *Volvox*; (c) the single but symmetrically shaped cell form in free-floating freshwater Desmids; (d) *Ulva*, Sea Lettuce, in a flat membrane two cells thick; (e) forms such as marine *Caulerpa*, up to 30 cm. high and varied in shape (cypress-like in *C. cupressoides*, grape-like in *C. racemosa* in the Great Barrier Reef), but consisting of only one multi-nucleate cell; branched freshwater *Chara* and *Nitella* often with chalk encrustations, and seaweeds*, e.g. *Codium*; 3. Brown Algae, Phaeophyceae; and 4. Red Algae, Rhodophyceae, nearly all marine (*see* SEAWEEDS).

Alice Springs   N.T. 24S/134E (11,118 in 1971)   The chief town of 'The Centre'*. It lies on the Todd River* approached from the S by Heavitree Gap in the Macdonnell Ranges*. It was named Stuart until 1933; Alice Springs were waterholes used by the Overland Telegraph* workers nearby, named from the wife of Sir Charles Todd then S.A. Postmaster General. In 1929 the narrow-gauge rail from Oodnadatta made it a major cattle and mineral railing centre to Adelaide (1,594 km.); an oil refinery is planned to serve the Mereenie field to the W. Population increased by 74% 1966–71, and there is an ever growing number of tourists coming in the pleasant winter months.

Alligator River   N.T. 12S/132E   Three separate perennial rivers were erroneously named the W, S and E Alligator Rivers by P. P. King* in 1818, from the crocodiles infesting their lower mangrove- and jungle-fringed courses. The S and E Alligator Rivers rise in the rocky backbone of Arnhem Land and are some 325 km. long; the W Alligator is a coastal stream of 80 km. They widen greatly in the 'Wet' when their lower reaches are flanked by impenetrable swamp. A 250-m.-long bridge will carry the Arnhem Highway

by 1974. There is to be a wildlife sanctuary in the region.

Almond,   Red (*Alphitonia   excelsa*) Fine-grained red cabinet wood of E Aus. forests N from central N.S.W.

Alt, Augustus Theodore Henry   (1731– 1815)   Surveyor-general with First Fleet*. On Governor Phillip's instructions, he drafted a grandiose Sydney Plan with a 60-m. wide main street, but it was shelved.

Aluminium   Metal made from Bauxite* in two stages: refining of ore to produce alumina (Al_2O_3), and smelting of alumina to make aluminium. Refining is carried out at Gladstone, Qld. from Weipa ores (1967) with capacity now of 2,000,000 tonnes, at Gove, N.T. and at Kwinana and Pinjarra, W.A., from Darling Ranges ores; a new plant at Muchea will operate from 1977. Plants are planned at Weipa and Bunbury. Smelting requires 17,500 kW of electricity per ton of aluminium produced and must be located near power. Bell Bay, Tas. (1955), uses hydro-electricity and by 1971 had a capacity of 94,000 tonnes using some thermal power; Geelong, Vic. (1963), smelts Kwinana alumina with power from brown coal (capacity 90,000 tonnes); a third smelter at Kurri-Kurri* (1969) now smelts Gladstone alumina using power based on black coal (capacity 50,000 tonnes).

Amadeus Lake and **Basin**   N.T. 25S/ 131E   Salty mud flats extending for some 145 km. E–W (but all very shallow) in the centre of the sediment-filled trough between the Macdonnell and Musgrave Ranges and about 460 m. above sea level. L. Neale is a similar smaller patch 80 km. to the W. Amadeus L. was named by Giles* after the Spanish King (possibly at his patron Mueller's* suggestion). He described it as 'an infernal lake of mud and brine' when he was turned back by the waterless desert to the W in 1872. Natural gas* has been found in the

Amadeus Basin. The sand-hills and troughs have considerable vegetation cover of casuarina, kurrajong as well as spinifex, and there is underground water supply feeding the cattle of the 31,000 km². Angas Downs Station and several others such as Tempe Downs, Henbury and Erldunda.

America's Cup A silver trophy, valued at 100 guineas when it was presented for competition by the Royal Yacht Squadron, and known then as the Queen's Cup. In 1851, an American Schooner, the *America*, won it; the captain presented it in 1857 to the New York Yacht Club for an international challenge cup; it took its present name from the 1851 winner. The race, which takes place in the holder's country, specifies yachts of 12 m. size, and comprises up to 7 heats, the winner being the first to win 4. There are few other rules; the use of radar devices has caused recent controversy. Aus. first challenged in 1962 with the 12 m. *Gretel* designed by Alan Payne, winning 1 out of 5 heats; in 1967 *Dame Patty* was defeated in all 4 races; in 1970 *Gretel II* was defeated 4–1. Sir Frank Packer* is the leading sponsor.

Amphibia or **Amphibians** A Class of cold-blooded vertebrates, including in Aus. only the frogs and toads, well-known from the easy observation of hatching from the minute egg in a jelly-like sac, to gilled long-tailed tadpoles soon metamorphosed to lunged, legged, tail-less forms.

Aus. families are: 1. Ranidae, the 'typical' frogs of the world, with only one Aus. species, on present knowledge, the large long-legged *Rana papua* of N.G. and Cape York. 2. Leptodactylidae or Southern Frogs, such as: the Great Barred River Frog, *Mixophyes fasciolatus*, of coastal E Aus., 20 cm. from nose to extended hind feet; several *Limnodynastes*, e.g. the common but secretive *L. peronii* of the Sydney area, with white dorsal stripe and several very dark bands, and the small *L. tasmaniensis* which lays its eggs in a distinctively foamy jelly-like mass; the inland burrowing and water-holding *Cyclorana platycephalus* said to have been used by Aborigines to yield a little water on occasion; the mournful owl-like cry of the grey-brown *Heleioporus australiacus* is heard in the Sydney area, and the chirp-like call of the small grey-brown *Crinia signifera* is heard after rain over much of Aus.; the distinctive Cross-bearing Toad, *Notaden bennetti*, green with black warts in an irregular cross, with some small red and white spots giving off an irritant secretion when handled, the Crowned Toadlet, *Pseudophryne bibroni*, common under logs, stones or grass by streams from Qld. to S.A., and *P. australis* of the Sydney area with a well-marked red crown, black-brown warty back and white-mottled lower parts. 3. Hylidae or Tree-frogs, with 50–60 Aus. species, some with circular toe-discs adapted for tree-climbing; they include the Gold and Green Bell Frog, *Hyla aurea*, with reduced toe-discs and climbing powers and wide-spread in billabongs and irrigation ditches; the grey 'typical' tree-frog of the Sydney area *H. peronii*, active by night with a whirring call, rising to a crescendo, and hiding under loose tree-bark etc. by day; and the 7-cm.-long green (but changing) *H. caerulea* seen in damp places even in generally

Tree-frog (Hyla peronii), about 7 cm. long

dry areas over much of Aus. 4 Micro-
hylidae or Narrow-mouthed Frogs, on
present knowledge include relatively
few genera and species, such as
Sphenophryne spp., termite-eaters. The
introduced Giant Toad is noted under
Toad*.

Anabranch Probably a distinctively
Aus. word for an anastomosing river,
sending off distributaries which link up
again with each other and sometimes
with the parent stream. **The Great
Anabranch** leaves the Darling near
Menindee, 32S/142E, and flows S,
turning salt flats into salt lakes in wet
years, to join the Murray some miles
downstream from the Darling-Murray
confluence.

A.N.A.R.E. Aus. National Antarctic
Research Expeditions, organised 1947–
1968 under the Department of External
Affairs (now under the Department of
Supply), 'to maintain Aus. and British
interests in Antarctica, and to find a
suitable site for a base'. Bases include Casey*, Heard Island*, Macquarie Island*, Davis* and Mawson*.
P. G. Law was leader until 1966. There
was criticism of lack of Government
interest or support enough to make the
bases scientifically viable during the
1960s which led to enquiry, and in
1967 the Aus. Academy of Science
made a critical, constructive report.

Andamooka S.A. 30S/137E An opal
field N of the Andamooka Ranges, low
barren hills on the W shore of L.
Torrens*. Opals* were discovered by
S. Brooks in 1930, and several hundred
prospectors work the field in shallow
shafts which pit the barren landscape.
Yields are seldom revealed. The
Andamooka Opal, presented by S.A.
to Queen Elizabeth II in 1954, is
10 cm. by 6·4 cm.

Anderson, John (1893–1962) b. Lanarkshire, Scotland. Professor of Philosophy in Sydney University 1926–58,
profoundly influencing philosophical
thought and criticism through teaching

and writing, as in *Studies in Empirical
Philosophy* (Sydney, 1962).

Anderson, Keith Died in 1929 of thirst
after a forced landing in the Central
Aus. desert while on his way from
Sydney to join a search for his old
friend Kingsford Smith*, then lost in
Southern Cross near Wyndham. He
had been associated with Kingsford
Smith in West Australian Airways, and
in cattle trucking to finance long-
distance flights. He did the survey of
the route and landing places for the
1928 Pacific Flight in *Southern Cross*,
but withdrew from the actual flight. His
death was a factor in allegations that
Kingsford Smith had deliberately lost
himself as a publicity stunt; but a
Court of Enquiry found no truth in
this.

Angas, George Fife (1789–1879) b.
Newcastle, Eng. He became a leading
founder of S.A., after establishing
prosperous London shipping and
banking firms. As chairman of the
South Australian Company* he raised
capital and arranged the departure of
the first S.A. settlers in 1836, and, in
1838, of 300 dissident Lutherans from
Prussia to the Barossa Valley,* as
tenants on his property, then managed
by his son John. In 1851 he himself
settled in the region, becoming a
leading political and philanthropic
figure until his death. His son **George
French** (1822–1886) was a fine artist
and naturalist, and on explorations of
SE Aus. drew very detailed and accurate pictures of animals, Aborigines and
landscapes (*South Australia Illustrated*
re-published New Zealand, 1967).

Angaston S.A. 34S/139E (1,816 in
1971; 1,887 in 1966) On the E edge of
the Barossa Valley* with fruit canning,
wineries and cement—local limestone
is quarried also for Adelaide chemical
works.

Angler-fish Has a 'fishing rod' or lure,
an extended spine from the dorsal fin
waved in the water to attract smaller

fish within reach of its large mouth. Members of several families are found in Aus. Inshore species of 15–30 cm. long most often seen are of the family Antennariidae including the striped angler-fish, the Rags and Tatters, *Rhycherus*, named from the filaments and nodules all over its body and fins, the smooth-skinned Mouse-fish, *Ptero-phrynoides*, found climbing on floating weed, and the Black Angler of Sydney harbour and other estuaries, *Batra-chopus*. The primitive Hand-fish, *Brachionichthys hirsutus*, of SE Aus. and Tas. is well known because it is often caught by trawlers, where it walks on the deck on pectoral and ventral fins. *Lophiomus laticeps* of the family of the European angler-fish is trawled off the E coast. Various deep ocean species are usually dark in colour, with luminous lures. In some species parasitic males are attached to the females; they are small, almost eyeless and with vestigial 'fishing rods' and almost like outgrowths of the female's skin and tissue. Their sole function is to produce milt when the female is ready to spawn in response to hormone in the female's blood which is their only source of nourishment.

Angophora A genus of 6 or 7 trees in the Myrtaceae family, closely related to the eucalypts but lacking the tight-fitting flower cover from which *Eucalyptus** was named. The Smooth-bark Apple, *A. lanceolata*, produces tall timber but often with character-istically down-curved main branches, from apparently very poor sites with roots seeking out joints, e.g. in the Hawkesbury sandstones. The Smooth, summer-peeling bark is grey to pinkish-red, often with much exudate of 'gum' or kino, sometimes gathered for making astringents. (From the bark, the tree is also called Sydney Red Gum or Rusty Gum.) The red-tipped young foliage is used for indoor decoration, and its white or creamy clusters of blossom are much frequented by bees.

Other species include the Dwarf Apple, *A. cordifolia*; the Rough-bark Apple or Gum Myrtle, *A. intermedia*, used for rough timber construction and formerly for wheel hubs of carts; the inland Coolabah Apple, *A. melan-oxylon*; the Velvety Gum Myrtle, *A. subvelutina*, yielding fodder; the kino or gum of the Qld. *A. woodsiana* has been a remedy for diarrhoea.

Smooth-bark Apple (Angophora lanceolata)

Angry Penguins A literary movement and journal (1941–6) originally of Adelaide University, publishing and promoting *avant garde*, modern and largely incomprehensible verse which provoked the Ern Malley Hoax*; the name is from a line in a poem by Max Harris: 'Drunks, the angry penguins of the night'.

Angus, Samuel (1881–1943) b. N Ire-land. Professor of New Testament and Historical Theology, St. Andrew's Presbyterian College, Sydney Univer-sity 1914–43. He made widely recog-nised contributions on the origins of Christianity in *Religions and Chris-tianity* (London, 1925) and other works, and was the subject of heated Presbyterian controversy.

Anne, Mount Tas. 43S/146E A quartzite peak (1,426 m.) between the headwaters of Huon River* and Weld River, heavily eroded by ice.

Annear, Desbrowe Harold (1866–1933) b. Bendigo. The first significant Aus.-born architect, in the sense of rebellion from set, imported styles. He was the first to design functional homes, with features ahead of their time, in open plan, flush doors, ventilation features, built-in furniture and flat roofs. An existing example is Inglesby (1919, S Yarra, Melbourne).

Anstey, Frank (1865–1940) b. London. Arrived in Aus. as a stowaway 1876. Rough years in the Pacific Island trade set him against Blackbirding* and for White Australia. He entered Labor Party politics from the Seamen's Union, reaching Cabinet rank, and was a prolific and influential socialist writer.

Antarctic Territory, Australian In 1933 Britain transferred to Aus. claims to all the area S of 60S and between 160E and 45E, save for the narrow segment of the French claim, Adélie Land, 136E–142E. The claim was based on 19th-century British exploration, followed up by the notable work done by Mawson*, 1911–14 and 1929–31. The area is 6·4 million km². the largest national claim in the continent. Administration since 1968 has been by the Dept. of Supply, and where relevant, laws of the Australian Capital Territory apply. Since 1943 exploration and research has been undertaken by A.N.A.R.E.* Physically the Territory is part of the old Precambrian base of the E portion of Antarctica, covered with Palaeozoic sediments containing some coal; the whole largely submerged under ice. The coast has considerable ice-free areas of rocky islands and peninsulas, but with large ice tongues,

e.g. the Shackleton and Amery Ice Shelves, reaching the coast. The coast roughly follows the Antarctic Circle before dipping S in the N.Z. area to the E. The main Aus. base is at Mawson* with others at Davis* and Casey*, and on Macquarie Island*. The 2 Russian bases set up in the International Geophysical Year (1957), Mirnyy and Oazis, were on either side of the Shackleton Ice Shelf; Mirnyy has been maintained. Some Aus. anxiety on this score led to hesitation before agreeing to the Antarctic Treaty (1959) which provided for the peaceful use of all land S of 60S, and which involves Argentine, Belgium, Chile, Czechoslovakia, Denmark, France, Japan, N.Z., Norway, Poland, U.S., S Africa, U.S.S.R. and U.K. *Further reading* R. A. Swan: *Australia in the Antarctic* (Melbourne, 1961) and A. Grenfell Price: *The Winning of the Australian Antarctic* (Sydney, 1962).

Ant-eaters In Aus. these include the Monotreme* Spiny Ant-eater* (often called Echidna) and also the Marsupial* Banded Ant-eater or Termite-eater or Numbat*.

Anthony Lagoon N.T. 18S/135E Cattle station on the Barkly Tableland* and nearby permanent water sheet on the seasonal Creswell Creek. A new Beef Road* links it with the Barkly Highway.

Antill, John Henry (1904–   ) b. Sydney. A musician, whose successful works include the ballet *Corroboree* using Aboriginal material, and the opera *Endymion*.

Antipodean Group Artists who exhibited first in Melbourne in 1959, and issued a manifesto appealing for figurative art with Aus. subject matter. They included Arthur Boyd, who paints macabre and poetic figures and landscapes, John Perceval, noted for spontaneous views painted in the open, John Brack, with suburban satire,

Clifton Pugh, whose work includes scenes centred on weird but decoratively arranged animal corpses, as well as faithful portraiture, Bob Dickerson the only Sydney member, a self-taught former boxer, noted for lonely urban scenes, Charles Blackman, David Boyd, and as theorist for the group, the art historian Bernard Smith.

Ant-lions Insects of the family Myrmeleonidae, in the Order Neuroptera or Lace-wings*, several genera of which have larvae preying on ants and other insects; these are captured in pits, excavated in soft earth or sand in which the larva lies concealed. The adult is 4-winged, with brown or black markings, and short antennae, clubbed like a butterfly's.

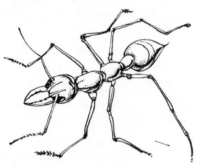

Bulldog Ant (Myrmecia)
about 2·5 cm. long

Ants Of the family Formicidae in the Order Hymenoptera*; together with the beetles, these are the dominant insects of Aus., with over 1,000 species; some species are unique and as elsewhere many species have a strongly social organisation of fertile males, fertile females and workers (infertile females). Their ceaseless activity seems well directed, and some form of communication seems beyond doubt. A new colony is formed after swarming of the fertile winged forms; the males die soon after. Many ants sting readily, including the large and uniquely Aus.

Bulldog Ant, *Myrmecia*, up to 2·5 cm. in length, which attacks spontaneously when the nest is approached, and has a very painful sting. A related group is the almost equally aggressive, stinging Jumper Ant, *Promyrmecia*. Sub-families include: 1. Ponerinae, stinging ants, e.g. the bright green-headed *Chalcopnera* spp. and long-jawed tropical *Odontomachus* spp. 2. Leptanillinae, small blind brown ants living underground in W.A. and also found in Mediterranean regions, Malaya and Java. 3. Eusphinctinae, also widespread, blind subterranean ants. 4. Cerapachyinae, noted for antiquity through fossil finds, includes the large, ferocious Robber Ants, *Phyracaces*, with over 40 species, which have nomadic habits and raid other ants' nests for larvae and pupae to feed their own larvae. 5. Myrmicinae, including the widespread genus *Pheidole* which builds craters over its ground nest; the family also includes introduced species, the House Ants, *Monomorium*, as well as native Tree Ants e.g. the widespread *Podomyrma* genus, occupying tunnels made by wood boring larvae. 6. Dolichoderinae, including the Racing Ants, *Leptomyrmex*, slender, rapidly moving and mobile ants of Qld. and N.S.W.; and the very common genus *Iridomyrmex*, with native species more common than any other in the country, and, even more important, the introduced small, brown Argentine Ant, *I. humilis*, which has become a serious pest, capable of destroying beneficial insects as well as other ants; *I. detectus* is the voracious meat ant, building huge nests. 7. Formicinae, including the Aborigines' delicacy, the black Honey-pot Ant, *Camponotus inflatus*, the abdomen of which is injected with honey to act as a store for the nest, until it protrudes as a yellow ball; and also the vicious Green Tree Ant noted by Joseph Banks, *Oecophylla virescens*, which builds intricate tree nests of leaves held by silk from the larvae, and will drop on to the unwary below, and sting fiercely. The Sugar Ant, *Campono-tus*, a non-stinging genus, is very wide-spread. **'Anting'** by birds is a much debated trait of some birds as in many parts of the world. The bird catches an ant in its beak and rubs it on its skin between the feathers, apparently as a massage and skin stimulus.

Anzac Initials, later the code name of Australia and New Zealand Army Corps, coined in 1915 when the troops were training in Egypt, but applied to all Aus. and N.Z. troops in the 1914–18, and to a lesser extent, the 1939–45 wars. Its chief association is with the campaign in Gallipoli* and the tenac-ity and heroism of Anzac troops. **Anzac Cove** lies on the W side of Gallipoli; it is N of the proposed landing place, but adverse currents pushed the craft off course; thus the troops were faced with steep rocky cliffs instead of a gentle sloping shore-line as they waded ashore under withering gunfire to establish a beach-head. **Anzac Day** April 25th, 1915 is commemorated by a public holiday each year, with solemn ceremonial marches, and less sober reunions of ex-servicemen of both wars. The 50th anniversary in 1965 saw a pilgrimage of surviving Anzacs to the beaches of Gallipoli.

A.N.Z.U.S. Mutual tri-partite security pact between Aus., New Zealand and United States, ratified April 1952 and having a council meeting periodically to discuss defence, political and eco-nomic developments in the Pacific area. Aus. and N.Z. recognition of Com-munist China (1972) weakened its purpose. *See* J. G. Starke: *The Anzus Treaty Alliance* (Melbourne, 1966).

Apostle-bird (from its flocking in groups of about a dozen, cf. the Babblers*) Also known as Grey Jumper (from its hopping from branch to branch to ascend a tree as if on a staircase). A common easily tamed species *Struthidea cinerea* (ashen bird),

of inland E and N Aus., making cup-shaped mud nests on groups of trees, lined with fine grass and containing 4–7 blue-white eggs. Grouped with the Mudlarks* and the White-winged Chough* as the Mudnesters. Apostle-bird is sometimes used for the Chough and the Grey-crowned Babbler.

Apostle-bird (Struthidea cinerea)
about 30 cm. long

Apple Name used in Aus., apart from the cultivated apple, for native trees in the Myrtaceae* family including the Apple Box* and *Angophora**, the former a Eucalypt, the latter a close relative, with opposite, not alternate, mature leaves. A relative of the Lilly-Pilly*, the Red Apple, *Acmena brachy-andra*, grows as a small tree of coastal Qld. and N N.S.W. with dark green oblong leaves to 12 cm. long, clusters of reddish flowers and 2 cm. red 'apples' in small clusters. Black Apple, Crab Apple, Black Plum, Wild Plum or Native Plum is *Planchonella australis*, a rough-barked small tree of the brush forests of humid coastal NE Aus., with thick broad leaves and dark red-black fruit 2 cm. long, plum-like but with one to five small seeds, and rather insipid to taste; it yields a fine yellow-grained timber. The name Apple is also used for fruits of species of *Solan-um*, the genus including the cultivated potato, particularly the Kangaroo Apple, *S. laciniatum*, with many edible fruits about 2 cm. across. The Emu Apple is *Owenia acidula*.

Apple Berries A common popular name for climbers of the genus *Billardiera*, in the largely Aus. family Pittosporaceae, especially *B. scandens*, which bears a pleasantly acidic cylindrical fruit sometimes called 'dumplings' by children and is widespread through E Aus. The flower is a 5-petalled bell; the leaves long and oval to pointed with notched edges.

Apple Box (*Eucalyptus bridgesiana*) A medium–small tree (12–21 m. by 0·5 to 1 m.) of 50–115 cm. rainfall, open woodland country W of the Great Divide in SE Aus., mainly on alluvial flats or fairly deep-soiled lower slopes. Juvenile and intermediate leaves are heart-shaped; adult leaves markedly lanceolate and 12–25 cm. long. Small pointed buds open to profuse inflorescence; hemispheric to conical fruit. The blossom is valuable to apiarists and it is a garden or park but not a timber tree.

Apples Grown in every State, with a total of 30,000 ha.; one third of the crop is exported. Output (33%) though not acreage is highest in Tas. in the Huon and Tamar valleys, mainly for overseas export which began when Tas. apples were barred from Vic. by tariff. The long journey is offset by cool storage (since 1886) and the demand created by the seasonal reversal of the hemispheres. Aus. apples are most important in UK from April to July, but there is concern over the adverse influence of UK entry into the Common Market through increased import tariffs. In Vic. (24%) growing areas are in the hills W of Melbourne; in N.S.W. (18%) on the Tablelands, e.g. round Bathurst and Orange; in W.A. (12%) in rolling hills from Bridgetown to Mt. Barker in the SW; at high altitudes round Stanthorpe in Qld. (7%) and in the Mt. Lofty Ranges in S.A. (6%). The long-keeping 'Granny Smith' is an Aus. variety, discovered accidentally from random planting of Tas. seeds by a farmer's wife near Sydney.

Arachnida (or **Arachnids**) Eight-legged invertebrates, a class in the Phylum Arthropoda*. Although from the Greek for spider, it includes also king-crabs (only as fossils in Aus.), scorpions*, whip-scorpions and false scorpions, spiders*, harvestmen* and the acarine mites* and ticks*.

Arafura Sea Lies N of Aus. It is relatively shallow and floored by an 'old-land' extension, the Sahul Shelf of the geologists, reaching towards Timor and S fringes of New Guinea.

Aranda, Aranta or **Arunta** A group of Aboriginal languages spoken by a number of tribes in Central Aus. Their terrain, which lies round and to the N of Alice Springs, is arid, rocky desert, especially in the S where the rainfall is most commonly some 5 to 10 cm. a year, with perhaps 100 cm. in a wet year like 1920–21. The hunter-gathering mode of life before European contact involved close knowledge of water, plants and animals in the tribal territory, ability to navigate by night in the cool, and adjustment of the population to the driest years. This mode of life maintains residually, with some employment for men on the few, very extensive cattle stations, and education at the main mission station at Hermannsburg, SW of Alice Springs.

Ararat Vic. 37S/143E (8,317 in 1971) A city just E of the Grampians, on the main Melbourne-Adelaide line. Now a major market and service centre with clothing, and industries and sawmilling, it grew on account of a brief but intensive gold-rush to the area in 1854-6.

Arbitration Began in industrial disputes in the 1890s: Vic. (1891) and S.A. (1894) had optional arbitration; in N.S.W. it was first voluntary (1892) then compulsory (1901). Arbitration by the Commonwealth was provided for in Section 51 of the Constitution, which empowered it to 'make laws with respect to conciliation and arbitration for the prevention and settlement of industrial disputes extending beyond the limits of any one State'. This was implemented by the creation in 1904 of the Conciliation and Arbitration Court with compulsory powers to intervene in the case of impasse between employer and employee groups registered with it (representing 80% of Trade Unionists). In 1956 it was supplemented by separating off an award-making Commission, and a judicial Industrial Court, to interpret and enforce the awards. Under Higgins*, the famous 1907 Harvester Judgment* initiated rulings by the Court on the Basic Wage*. Existing State courts overlapping the Federal body's functions have led to conflict, and a severe crisis which defeated Bruce* and Page* in 1929. While legally binding only on the parties to the dispute, in effect country-wide rulings are made, since a Union ensures that its 'log of claims' is served on as many employers as possible; if it is rejected, this constitutes a 'dispute'. An award may cover wages, hours, leave and detailed working conditions; strikes* have also been banned in an award. The discipline involved in the system was challenged from 1967 when the Commission allowed metal trades employers to absorb officially sanctioned wage rises in existing 'over award' payments; the decision was reversed. Conciliation and arbitration were separated in 1972 and economic consequences required to be taken into account when fixing wage levels in major cases. See J. E. Isaac and G. W. Ford: *Australian Labour Relations* (Melbourne, 1966) and K. W. Walker: *Australian Industrial Relations Systems* (Harvard, 1970).

Archer, Thomas, David and **John** Qld. pioneers who overlanded to Brisbane River (1841), opened up land in Burnett and Fitzroy Rivers and assisted Leichhardt*. **Archer River**, 13S/142E, flowing E-W for 272 km. in Cape York Peninsula, is named after them.

Archer Fish or **Rifle Fish** (genus *Toxotes*) Of tropical Aus. and SE Asia; this is a very deep-bodied, large-scaled fish with a continuous dorsal fin set well back, the front part spiny; it is yellow with broad brown side finger marks. It is named from its ability to bring down insects just above the surface with a jet of water. The Primitive Archer Fish, *Prototoxotes lorentzi*, may represent an ancestral type.

Archer, John Lee (1791-1852) b. Ireland. Arrived in Tas. 1827 as a civil engineer; he was responsible for many well-designed public buildings, including gaols, but notably Parliament House, Hobart, originally a Customs House. *For further reading see* R. S. Smith: *John Lee Archer, Tas. architect and engineer* (Hobart, 1962).

Archibald, John Feltham (Jules François) (1856-1919) b. Kildare, Vic. Co-founder (1880) with Haynes, of the *Bulletin** and editor from 1880-2 and 1886-1902. He had an important influence on Aus. writing by his selection, editing and encouragement of promising authors including Lawson* and Paterson*. His love of France is seen in his assumed Christian names and also in the **Archibald Memorial**, a bronze fountain in Hyde Park, Sydney, designed under his will by a French sculptor Sidard (1933) to commemorate the Aus.-French alliance in the 1914-18 War. He left the profits from one tenth of his estate for the **Archibald Prize** awarded annually for a portrait, 'preferentially' of a distinguished Australian.

ARCHITECTURE The Aborigines had no permanent structures and hence no architecture. The First Fleet brought no trained builders, nor materials and few tools, and the first European structures were crude palm-thatched huts, with walls made of clay between timber supports. Soon bricks were made and Macarthur described his

Elizabeth Farm (1794, the oldest extant building) as 'a most excellent brick house'. Lack of skill dictated the one-storey house which still dominates domestic architecture, and the verandah was a response to summer heat and glare, which has not been so universally retained.

Public building was almost equally rudimentary (although Bloodsworth, an emancipated bricklayer, had designed with ingenuity and skill) until Greenway* was appointed civil architect (1817–22) by Governor Macquarie*. A trained and sensitively artistic designer, he built what remain among the finest Aus. examples of architecture, with an individual interpretation of the prevailing English Georgian: Hyde Park Barracks (1817), St. Matthews, Windsor (1817); St. James, Sydney (1820). Bigge's criticisms of extravagance ended Macquarie's phase of dignified planning.

In the newly opened-up interior, the squatters* made do with earth-floored bark huts until prosperity and some security of tenure allowed more permanent homesteads. They were necessarily simple in material and plan; yet this Colonial Georgian style, with its long low white walls, a verandah that continues the line of the hipped roof, has since been seen as the first, possibly the best indigenous architectural style. Its urban counterpart was most successfully developed by Verge* in the 1830s. In Tas. abundant convict labour and good building stone allowed variants, often 2 storeyed and without verandahs. Early buildings in Tas. were influenced by Archer* and Blackburn*, many of them still extant.

On the mainland hotels and public buildings rose more than one storey; the familiar verandahed hotel developed early, the thin posts supporting the upper verandahs in contrast to the more pretentious columns on such public buildings as the famous Rum Hospital* in Sydney.

Gothic revival became dominant after the mid-19th century, and continued to dictate church architecture for 100 years. Blacket* was its major exponent, and Wardell's Roman Catholic Cathedrals (St. Patrick's, Melbourne, 1860 and St. Mary's, Sydney, 1855) are fine examples, as is Blacket's Great Hall of Sydney University (1854–60). In contrast, the design of many other public buildings responded to the affluence of the period of the gold-rushes, in neo-classical or Renaissance styles: in Melbourne, Parliament House (1856), the Treasury (1862) and Law Courts (1884) are examples. There were also many pretentious private mansions in Italianate styles, while the domestic versions of Gothic comprised steep gabled roofs decorated with carved 'Barge boards'. Ornamentation became increasingly fanciful. In the height of the Victorian period Aus. architecture was combined from many previous styles; there were a number of sincere and competent eclectic architects producing public buildings giving the rather pompous Victorian stamp to Aus. city centres that is only now yielding: Wardell in Melbourne and Sydney; Clark in Melbourne and Brisbane; Reed in Melbourne; Hennessy in Sydney.

Rising land costs squeezed houses on to narrower blocks of land. The verandah was retained across the narrow front only; about the mid 1880s, builders began to project a front room on one side of the door forwards, leaving the verandah reduced to a useless porch; sometimes it was left out altogether to give an 'L shape' or replaced by a 'terrace', and this pattern has persisted until today. The terraced houses of inner Sydney and Melbourne had their verandahs ornamented with cast-iron in various intricate designs, including Aus. themes of kookaburras and gum nuts; these are also now considered a specifically Aus. style to be prized.

The Depression of the 1890s halted the extravagant decoration of the now decadent Victorian styles, and some reversion to plainer surfaces followed, with decoration only in the form of 'naturalistic' flowing lines of so called *Art Nouveau*; it was successfully promoted by Haddon*. Bricks re-appeared from under cement and stucco, and the heavy roof tile, still the standard urban roofing material, was introduced. But in spite of Annear's* early functional attempts, the house styles soon became complex again, in the fussy spurious 'Queen Anne' of the early 1900s: roofs were broken by false gables, frilled ridges and fantastic terra-cotta ornaments; windows were lead-lighted and verandahs edged with ornamental wooden trellises. Inside, the same basic four-room design developed in the first houses remained largely unaltered.

In the 1920s two American house types appeared: the Californian Bunga-low, with a simple roof and pillared porches, and Spanish Mission, with cement walls and arcading. The idea that a Mediterranean architecture was more suitable than that of NW Europe, for most Aus. climates is a valid one, successfully expounded by Wilkinson* in Sydney, and seen at its best perhaps in the University of W.A. by Alsop and Sayce (1932). Griffin* introduced the idea of urban houses evolved for space, privacy and an 'organic' relationship with the setting. But the prevailing types of 'Modernistic' domestic archi-tecture in the 1920s ran to excessive use of geometric design, with some reaction to a brief period in the 1930s when a neo-Tudor fashion reigned (exemplified in the fantasy of Hay Court in Perth).

Public buildings in the 1930s went through periods of imported 'Modern Gothic' for office building, and gro-tesque, flamboyant picture palaces in every suburb. The first use of the genu-inely modern, international styles was seen after 1934 in schools, hospitals and factories, with Grounds* a pioneer. The suburban sprawl, following im-proved transport, had neither shape nor style. One of the few indigenous developments was the elevated Qld. house, with its screened-in space beneath, and most successfully expres-sed by Dod before being eclipsed by the universal types; it is now being re-discovered and put into modern guise. In the country, the old four-square weatherboard cottage, with corrugated iron roof and verandah is still very prevalent. The iron roof although ugly is fireproof, acts as a rainwater catchment, is easily put up and cools off quickly.

After the 1939–45 War, came Con-temporary styles, covering a wide and wild variety of roof and house shapes, new materials and a tendency to forget the climate again in excessive use of glass. Office blocks, freed at last from height restrictions imposed after the first multi-storey buildings were built in the 1880s, soared up in glass and concrete boxes, with extensive use of curtain (non-supporting) walls of metal and glass. These may now be modified by sun-screening devices. Churches broke from the Gothic tradition in the mid 1950s, with varying success.

Much hope for Aus. architecture as well as controversy is centred on two modern projects: the Sydney Opera House* by Utzon, and Roy Grounds's* Arts Centre in Melbourne which is built in volcanic blue-stone round a verandahed courtyard. *For further reading see* R. Boyd: *The Walls Around Us* (Melbourne, 1962). J. M. Freeland: *Architecture in Australia* (Melbourne, 1968).

Ardrossan S.A. 34S/138E A small port on the NE of Yorke Peninsula, handling wheat, dolomite and salt.

Area The total area of Aus. is 7,683,916 km².

Armidale N.S.W. 31S/152E (18,137 in 1971) A city on the New England* plateau (alt. 1,016 m.), on the gentle valley-slopes of the Dumaresq Creek, small and liable to flash floods. It is the centre for a rich agricultural area. It has 2 fine cathedrals and a largely residential university centred on the elaborate mansion of one of the early rich squatter families, which also specialises in correspondence courses. It is a regional centre for the press and radio and schools, and a main focus of the New State movement* for New England.

Army, Australian Various British Army regiments—along with naval personnel and marines—were intimately bound up with the convict phase from the First Fleet onwards, increasingly with local recruitment as the 19th century advanced. As the individual colonies gained self-government, their control over their troops increased; from 1850 onwards they were expected to meet defence costs; from 1870 British troops were withdrawn and each colony had its defence forces. Thanks to the 1877–83 reports of Major-General Sir William Jervois and Lieut-Colonel Peter Scratchley, the forces were organised in parallel in the separate colonies; this made for a smooth transition to the Commonwealth Army following Federation, under Major-General Sir Edward Hutton. Numbers and effectiveness had been stimulated by the Sudan campaign of 1885 and especially by the Boer War of 1899–1902, to which Aus. sent over 16,000 men. An Act for compulsory military training was passed in 1909, drafted by J. G. Legge, and in 1910 a report by Lord Kitchener led to some amendments. In the 1914–18 War the Australian Imperial Force (A.I.F.) was formed and there were bitter controversies over conscription*. The citizen force, the C.M.F.*, has been voluntary at times, linked at others with compulsory training in various ways; conscripts were used in operations overseas during the 1939–45 War and in the Vietnam War*. (*See* WORLD WAR, FIRST *and* SECOND.)

In 1970–1 the Army cost about $414 million, about 36% of the defence budget. Infantry battalions are being increased, along with high priority logistic units and airborne mobility appropriate to defensive and limited war situations (*see* DEFENCE). In 1972 the regular army had some 41,300 men, about 30% of them National Servicemen; the citizens forces totalled some 36,000 and the Pacific Islands Regiment 2,500. In 1972 the most radical changes since federation were announced: the former geographical Commands to be replaced over 5 years by 3 major Commands: Field, Training and Logistics. The main army camps are those of Puckapunyal, Vic., Holsworthy, N.S.W. and Enoggera and Townsville, Qld. Army establishments include the Apprentices' School at Balcombe, Vic., the Royal Military College at Duntroon, A.C.T., now with university status as part of the University of New South Wales, and the Staff College at Queenscliff, Vic.

Always noted for great courage and attack, Aus. troops now excel also in jungle warfare, from experience in N.G., Malaya and Vietnam. With the ending of conscription* (1972) the army is a volunteer force.

Arnhem Land N.T. This fills much of the central peninsula of the N Aus. coast, N and E of the Roper* and E Alligator Rivers*. It is the largest Aus. Aboriginal reserve, with some 4,000 tribal, formerly nomadic hunter-gatherers (Myowlie, Kakadu). The only permitted white settlement was in peripheral mission stations prior to the mineral discoveries of recent years. Traditional arts include bark paintings*. The heart of Arnhem Land is extremely rugged country over 300 m., rising in steep scarps on N and W, cut by forested ravines between flat-topped stony plateaux and ridges. Summer rains of up to 150 cm. feed rivers which flow N and E on to coastal plains along mangrove-fringed estuaries among paper-bark woodlands, with savannah especially in the W round Oenpelli*. The coast is fringed with numerous islands from Groote Eylandt* round to Melville* Island. The region was named from the Dutch ship *Arnhem*, which first described this coast in 1623. The first settlement was by garrisons on Cobourg Peninsula*. Development of the bauxite* in the NE at Gove* now affect the isolation and status of the reserve.

Arnold, Thomas (1823–1900) Son of Thomas Arnold of Rugby. He spent the years 1850–6 as inspector of schools in Tas., where he worked to improve the education system, in an era when religious and political conflicts were a drag on educational advance. *For further reading see* P. A. Howell: *Thomas Arnold the Younger in Van Diemen's Land* (Hobart, 1964).

Aroona Valley S.A. 31S/139E A starkly beautiful region N of Wilpena Pound in the Flinders Ranges*, widely known through Heysen's* paintings. In the 1850s it marked the most northerly pastoral settlement in the Ranges, the permanent springs giving the title 'Garden of the North' to the homestead. **Aroona Dam** 30S/138E, made in 1956 to supply Leigh Creek*, lies at the foot of Mt. Aroona confusingly named from the Aboriginal Alcaroona, but 480 km. N of Aroona Valley. The only permanent water surface in the Ranges, its evaporation rate can reach 230 cm. a year.

Arrow-worms With transparent arrow-shaped bodies from 8 to 60 mm. in length, they comprise an important component of plankton in many parts of the oceans; Aus. varieties include 14 spp. of *Sagitta*, and one each of *Pterosagitta*, *Krohnitta*, *Eukrohnia* and *Spadella*.

Art Education This began with Macquarie's worthy if premature sponsorship in 1812. The professional training of artists is almost the exclusive province of the State Departments of Technical Education. There are a few small, private or independent schools, such as the Mary White and Julian Ashton Schools in Sydney and the National Gallery School in Melbourne. There have been individual teachers of great influence, such as Desiderius Orban and Hirschfield Maek who brought new ideas to art for schoolchildren. The Power Institute of Fine Arts (1966) within the Sydney University Arts Faculty teaches art history, theory and criticism.

Art Galleries There are 5 major and 14 minor public galleries and a growing number of small commercial galleries, the main exhibitors of contemporary art. The Aus. National Gallery in Canberra is at an advanced planning stage. It will concentrate on contemporary and past Aus. art, art from Asia and the Pacific, and on worldwide 20th-century art to be exhibited in 12 galleries on 4 levels surrounded by large gardens containing sculptures. In Melbourne the National Gallery of Vic., now housed in the fine new Vic. Arts Centre, was founded in 1859 and has benefited from the Felton Bequest*. The State has public galleries (a number recently built) through local enterprise and Government help at Castlemaine, Geelong, Hamilton, Mildura, Sale, Shepperton, Swan Hill and Maryborough. In Sydney the Art Gallery of N.S.W. was founded in 1871 (built 1885) and the State has two others; outside the public galleries, the collection at Armidale Teachers College is very large, through the benefaction of H. Hinton (1867–1948). In Brisbane the Qld. Art Gallery was founded in 1895 in a concert hall; of the three others in the State, Toowoomba is notable. In Adelaide the National Gallery of S.A. was founded in 1881, and the State has one other public gallery. In Perth the W.A. Art Gallery was founded in 1895, and a new centre is now planned; there are 13 small public galleries, founded largely through C. Hotchin. In Hobart the Tas. Museum and Art Gallery was founded in 1887, and in Launceston, there is the Queen Victoria Museum and Art Gallery (1895).

Art Societies The oldest extant is the Royal Society of Artists of S.A. (1856). The most influential bodies are the Sydney Society of Artists (1895), the Contemporary Art Society (Sydney) and the groups associated with the public galleries. Important groups initiating changes in style have included the Contemporary Art Society in Melbourne (1939).

Arthropoda or **Arthropods** (i.e. jointed-legged) A large phylum including the following Classes: Crustacea* (crabs, shrimps etc.). Arachnida* (spiders, ticks, scorpions etc.). Myriapoda (i.e. many-legged; millipedes* and centipedes*). Insecta* (i.e. incised into distinct thorax and abdomen; bees, butterflies, beetles, fleas, flies, wasps etc.).

The Onychophora are worm-like animals with many short unjointed legs, with some worm-like or annelid characteristics, but with insect-like breathing apparatus and, in the Aus. genus *Ooperipatus*, laying insect-like eggs. They show features believed to be characteristic of early arthropods.

Arthur, Sir George (1784–1854) b. Plymouth, Eng. Lt.-Governor of Van Diemen's Land for 12 eventful and formative years (1824–36), covering separation from N.S.W. (1825), removal of the penal settlement from Port Macquarie to Port Arthur* (1832), the model prison for young convict boys at Point Puer* nearby (1835), the creation of the Van Diemen's Land Company* (1825) and the conclusion of the long Black War* with the Aborigines. Arthur was evangelistic, puritanical and humanitarian, but also extremely autocratic and intolerant (e.g. of Irish convicts who admittedly did dominate among the desperate cases sent from N.S.W., becoming the bushrangers* who caused many prob-

lems to the Colony); these characteristics involved him in the long fight to suppress freedom of the Press, against Andrew Bent*. He was not above making considerable moneys from land deals but was nevertheless a notable public servant of his day, serving also as governor in British Honduras (1814–22), Canada (1837–41) and Bombay (1842–6).

Arthur Range Tas. 43S/146E A NW-SE trending range, extending 32 km. largely forested and culminating in Federation Peak*. The whole region was heavily glaciated, and has been proposed as a Wilderness Area.

Arthur River Tas. 41S/145E This flows for about 160 km. from near Waratah, N then NW to the Indian Ocean at Gardiner Point. The upper course is in heavily dissected, glaciated rain-forest country, and is noted for its angling. The lower course is across button grass plains used for rough grazing.

Arthurs Lakes Tas. 42S/147E In spite of the plural name, this is one water surface of some 130 ha., on the unglaciated E part of the Central Plateau*; a dam at its W side with a conduit leading to Great Lake*, is part of the Great Lakes project (*see* TASMANIA, POWER).

Arts There is a considerable artistic heritage among at least some groups of the Aborigines*, notably in cave and bark paintings. European Aus. as a 19th-century creation, which began with a raw struggle for survival and a continual battle with the environment, has only slowly come to produce or even tolerate the arts. An initial phase of transplanted culture imitating English poetry and landscapes and importing English theatre, led to reaction at the end of the 19th century, in a swing towards nationalism: the *Bulletin* stories, the Heidelberg painters, the building of an 'Aus. tradition' of the bush democracy, mateship and the common man. In the 20th century a reaction is now being followed by striking a balance and great Aus. figures have appeared: Nolan* in painting and White* in literature. Pleas are still made against 'a cultural cringe', and as a reaction the Jindyworoboks* in writing and the Antipodean Group* in painting tried to stress an Aus. heritage. Creative activity is greatest in painting* and literature*, and least in music*. Sculpture*, drama*, architecture* and the theatre* have fine exponents who are reaching a stature great enough to join the world stream. In 1968 the **Australian Council for the Arts** was set up (*see* Elizabethan Theatre Trust*). In 1973 its functions were widened under 7 boards responsible for theatre, visual and plastic arts, music, literature, crafts, films, television and Aboriginal art. Other official agencies are the Music Board, Commonwealth Art Advisory Board, and Commonwealth Literary Fund*. There are divisions in N.S.W., Tas., Qld., S.A. and A.C.T., of the **Arts Council of Aus.** (1945), concerned with presenting the arts to young people through touring performances, exhibitions, summer schools etc. *For further reading see* A. L. McLeod ed. *The Pattern of Australian Culture* (Melbourne, 1963); A. McCulloch: *Encyclopaedia of Australian Art* (London, 1968); A. Davies and S. Encel eds. *Australian Society* (Melbourne, 1965).

Asbestos (meaning unquenchable) A fibrous rock resistant to fire and chemical action and used in a wide variety of products from brake linings to asbestos cement* and mainly imported before 1972. The stronger crocidolite or 'blue asbestos' was mined at Wittenoom*, W.A., until 1966; white chrysotile asbestos is mined open-cut at Baryulgil, 29S/151E, N.S.W. Much larger deposits are now worked at Woods Reef near Barraba, N.S.W., with export to Japan after processing in a fibre separation plant.

Asche, Oscar (1871–1936) b. Geelong, Vic. Son of a Norwegian, he became a well-known London actor and playwright. His biggest success *Chu-Chin-Chow* ran from 31st August 1916 to 22nd July 1921. He paid several return visits to Aus. with plays.

Ascidians Sea-squirts (including the cunjevoi*), marine animals of the Phylum Chordata. They are of interest as links between the invertebrates and the vertebrates. Most adult forms are sessile (stationary) usually with sac-like forms including water inlet and outlet valves—the outer sometimes taking discharge from the anus—and a sac-like form round a much-perforated pharynx with stigmata having a function analogous to gills in fish. Many species (there are over 100 species in Aus.) are hermaphrodite and some discharge eggs into the water; others retain the eggs until after hatching. It was close observation of the tadpole-like, free-swimming early stage by the Russian scientist Kowalevsky which established the relationship of the ascidians to the chordates.

Ash A northern hemisphere tree, genus *Fraxinus* (family Oleaceae), several of which are used in Aus. for ornamental or amenity trees, notably the English Ash, *F. excelsior*, with its pinnate leaf and rather smooth bark. The name ash is applied in Aus. to several different families.

1. It is given to a group of some 20 Eucalypts which are not particularly ash-like. They tend to have rather large, thick and asymmetric intermediate leaves and narrow usually curved adult leaves, glossy-green above and below, and usually with lateral veins at a very acute angle to the midrib. The buds are usually club-shaped, fruit pear-shaped and in bunches. In Mountain Ash and Brown Barrel there is a pair of bunches of buds at the base of leaf-stems. The bark varies from a small ground stocking of rough bark and long clean trunk in the Mountain

Ash, *Eucalyptus regnans* (the common name is given to other species also in parts of Aus.), to species reminiscent of Stringybark (the Messmate Stringybark, *E. obliqua*), and of the Ironbark (the Silvertop Ash, *E. sieberiana*). The Mountain Ash is an important hardwood timber, as is the Alpine Ash, *E. delegatensis*, found on higher slopes. *E. regnans* may be over 90 m. tall, and vies with Californian redwoods as the world's tallest tree (*see* PLATE 8).

2. Red Ash, *Alphitonia excelsa*, belongs to a quite different family, the Rhamnaceae, or Buckthorns. It is a tree of 30 m. by 0·6 m. found in coastal scrub forest and open forest in E Aus., with a hard, dark grey bark, oval to lanceolate leaves, whitish below and with prominent veins, and branched multiple heads of creamy, fragrant, 6 mm. flowers. The fruit are not unlike black cherries, the timber red and compact.

3. The Silver Ash, *Flindersia pubescens*, belongs to quite a different family again, the Meliaceae or Mahoganies. It has a pale grey bark, raspberry-scented and scaling in round patches. It has spear-shaped evergreen leaves of 23 cm. by 3 cm., arranged with an end leaf and 7 pairs along the branch, smooth and glossy above, pale and hairy below. There are upright multiple flower-heads, and spiny egg-shaped fruit with 5 boat-shaped segments containing 5-cm. winged seeds. The timber bends well and is used in tennis rackets etc.

4. The Blueberry Ash, Scrub Ash or Olive-berry of brush forest remnants in E Aus. is *Elaeocarpus reticulatus* (family Elaeocarpaceae, mainly tropical and sub-tropical), with long oval notched leaves, dark above and light below, small white bell flowers and beautiful light blue fruit.

Ashburton River W.A. 22S/115E Rises on the S slopes of the Ophthalmia Range SE of the Hamersley Range* and flows very sporadically SW then NW for 650 km. in a deep valley (cut in a wetter geological period) to mud-lined flats near Onslow. The **Ashburton Goldfield**, declared in 1890, led to ephemeral influxes of people, but has now ceased any production.

Ashes The Cricket* 'trophy' competed for in Test Matches* between Aus. and Eng. The term originated with a notice inserted in the *Sporting Times* in London on August 30th 1882, the day after Aus., largely through Spofforth's bowling, had defeated Eng. by 7 runs. It read: 'In affectionate memory of English Cricket which died at the Oval, 29th Aug 1882. Deeply lamented by a large circle of sorrowing friends and acquaintances. R.I.P. N.B. The body will be cremated and the ashes taken to Australia.' In Sydney the following year an urn, containing ashes of a burned stump, were presented to Ivo Bligh, captain of the victorious English team. Bligh (later Lord Darnley), who had done much to establish good will and respect in cricket internationals, later gave the urn to the Marylebone Cricket Club (M.C.C.) and it remains permanently in the pavilion at Lord's Cricket Ground.

Ashton, Julian Rossi (1851–1942) An artist, b. Eng., arrived in Sydney in 1878, where he founded an art school. It was through the integrity of his teaching rather than his own portraits and landscapes that he was most influential. His son **Julian Howard**, was an art critic of note.

Assignment System Convicts were first assigned to employers when Governor Phillip allotted convicts to civil and military officers in 1789, to grow food on land allocated to the officers, as a complement to the government farms —on the argument that an individual employer had a more material interest in the crops. Convict discipline remained. Though the system was subject to abuse, particularly in relation to female convicts, it continued until transportation* ceased. It reformed enough convicts to make some of the free settlers apprehensive that the social hierarchy was being undermined. The system played an important part in the adverse report by Commissioner Bigge* (1821) against Macquarie* who was trying to restrict the assignment to the towns as against dispersing the convicts to farms etc.

Astley, Thea Beatrice May (1925–   ) b. Brisbane. An important novelist and short story writer; among her novels is *The Well Dressed Explorer* (1962) and award-winning *The Acolyte* (Sydney, 1972).

Astley, William (Price Warung) (1854–1911) b. Liverpool, Eng. Arrived in Aus. in 1858 as a short story writer and journalist. Mainly described the convict system with a horror and realism based on careful study, as in *Tales of the Convict System* (Sydney, 1892).

ASTRONOMY Australia's position in astronomy is strong, being a large single political unit, with much clear sky, a stable government, and a position in the S hemisphere able to make observations complementary to those in the N hemisphere observatories on heavenly bodies and now on artificial earth satellites. The connection is long-established, for even Cook's voyage of 1769–70 was partly to observe the transit of Venus from Tahiti, and Lieut. Dawes of the First Fleet was commissioned to make observations on the voyage and to set up an observatory on arrival in the hope of observing a comet expected in 1788. From the wooden and then stone building on Dawes Point, where Flinders computed its longitude with an error of only 2 minutes, interest shifted for a period to Parramatta, where Governor Brisbane set up his own observatory after failing to get support from the government in London; though the instruments he bought for it have been described as 'large but faulty', many valuable observations were made by Rumker

and Dunlop. The present Sydney Observatory on Flagstaff Hill was built in 1856–8, and other State capitals built observatories at about the same time and up to the end of the century: Melbourne, Domain Park (1863), succeeding Williamstown (1853) and the magnetic and meteorological observatory on Flagstaff Hill; Brisbane (1879), after purchase of private instruments, moved to Wickham Terrace then George Street; Adelaide (1874), with a time-ball apparatus at the Semaphore, 14·5 km. away; Hobart (1840); Perth (1896) on Mount Eliza. Observations of longitude and of time (made available to ships by time-ball etc.) as well as triangulation and geodesy were important, but from the beginning there were contributions to astronomical knowledge, including both specific discoveries and patient cataloguing and astrographic work in many volumes. Significant work was done by individuals such as J. Tebbutt (1834–1916), W. F. Gale (1865–1945). Private observatories of note include Riverview College Observatory, founded by Father E. F. Pigot, S.J. The Commonwealth Observatory at Mount Stromlo was established in 1910, originally on a temporary basis to house a telescope presented by James Oddie of Ballarat, but proving suitable enough for more ambitious and permanent plans; these were interrupted by the 1914–18 War, but it was well developed by the 1920s under W. G. Duffield (1879–1929). Association with the Australian National University has brought further development notably under B. J. Bok from 1957–65, including the Observatory at Siding Spring Mt. in the Warrumbungles near Coonabarabran, which by 1974 will have a 3·8-m., $13-million optical telescope which is a British-Aus. undertaking. Other new developments include Sydney University's Mills Cross radio-telescope at Hoskingstown near Canberra, the radio-telescope at Parkes, N.S.W., and the C.S.I.R.O.

radio-heliograph at Culgoora, N.S.W. (between Wee Waa and Narrabri) with a 3·2 km. diameter circle and 96 radio-telescopes of 13·7 m. The American National Aeronautics and Space Administration (N.A.S.A.) have tracking stations at Island Lagoon and Red Lake near Woomera*, S.A., Carnarvon*, W.A. and Toowomba, Qld., and there are 3 installations in the Aus. Capital Territory. *For further reading see* W. J. Newell: *The Australian Sky* (Brisbane, 1965).

Atherton Tableland Distinctive region of NE Qld., 17S/145E, some 80 km. square, W of the Bellenden Ker Range and named after a local pastoralist, John Atherton (1837–1913). There are 3 levels, rising SW, with increasing rainfall, all built of Tertiary lava flows: the Mareeba-Dimbulah region at 390–600 m. with 90 cm. of rain (being in a rain shadow) is being increasingly developed from Barron River irrigation for tobacco and dairying; the region round **Atherton** (3,081 in 1971) at 732 m. and with 130–140 cm. of rain, has considerable cultivation of groundnuts, maize, vegetables, and with beef rearing: the Evelyn Tableland, which has 3 notable crater lakes (Eacham, Barrine, Euramoo) at 915 m. with about 250 cm. of rain, has the rainforest partially cleared for dairy farms, on rather poor natural pasture and supplies coastal towns as far as Townsville and Mt. Isa* (1,340 km.) on 'the longest milk run in the world'.

Athletics In recent years considerable international repute has been gained notably by Aus. sprinters including women; but amateur athletics do not have wide spectator interest. The Sydney Amateur Athletic Club (1872) was followed by State organisations by the 1890s and an Amateur Athletic Union of Australasia (1897), from which N.Z. seceded in 1927 when the Amateur Athletic Union of Aus. was formed. This body controls rules, inter-state fixtures, international liai-son, and Commonwealth and Empire Games representation of athletes. Olympic Gold Medallists or firsts have been: H. E. Flack (Athens, 1896, 800 and 1,500 m., not officially an Aus. representative as this was prior to Federation); A. W. Winter (1924, hop step and jump); J. Winter (1948, high jump); Marjorie Jackson (1952, 100 and 200 m.); Shirley Strickland (1952 and 1956, 80-m. hurdle); Betty Cuthbert (1956, 100 and 200 m.; 1964, 400 m. at Tokyo); H. Elliott (1960, 880 yd., 1 mile and 1,500 m.). Landy* was a famous miler, and R. W. Clarke* holds world records for the 2, 3 and 6 miles. D. Clayton holds an unofficial marathon record, R. Doubell (1968, 800 m., a shared record). Women champions have included: M. J. Mathews (Mrs. Willard) and M. M. Black (Mrs. Vasella) in 100 yd.; M. A. Burvill (220 yd.); J. F. Amoore (Mrs. Pollock) 440 yd.; D. I. Willis (880 yd.); P. Kilborn (80-m. hurdle), M. Caird (1968, 80-m. hurdle); Pam Ryan (100 m. hurdle). P. Cerutty and F. Stamfl have influenced coaching. J. Carlton and Decima Norton were earlier athletic idols. In the professional field, footracing remains important in Vic., with 3 major annual events, the Stawell and Wangaratta Gifts and the Bendigo Thousand. It was an active and very popular sport in the 1870s, and revived with the sprinting achievements of A. B. Postle and J. Donaldson early this century.

Atkins, Richard (1745–1820) b. Eng. as Richard Bowyer. Arrived in Aus. in 1791 and largely through influence was appointed Deputy Judge-Advocate (without legal training) in 1796–8 and 1800–2, then Judge-Advocate from 1802 until he was relieved by Ellis Bent on Macquarie's arrival in 1809, with an interval when he was supplanted by Abbott during the 'rebellion' against Governor Bligh. Constantly assailed by addiction to alcohol, insolvency, dissipation and living in squalor after his wife left him, he was the target of contemptuous abuse, yet was intimately a part of the long-drawn anti-Governor activities of Macarthur*. At first he was almost sycophantic in his support of Bligh; he was arrested with him by the dissidents, but later agreed to support the 'rebel' Major Johnston with evidence about misconduct of Bligh as Governor. Macquarie sent him to London as a witness for Bligh in the trial of Johnston, after which obscurity descended.

Atlas A weekly publication (1844–8) in Sydney, founded and edited by Lowe* and largely devoted to political controversies of the day, using satire as a weapon; contributions were of merit far beyond its contemporaries.

Atomic Energy (more correctly **Nuclear Energy**) The energy released by fission or fusion. The **Aus. Atomic Energy Commission** (1952) under the Minister for Minerals and Energy, has dual functions: in co-operation with the States, it controls prospecting for and mining of uranium*; it is also responsible for research into the practical uses of nuclear energy. The major centre is Lucas Heights just S of Sydney. Here the research reactor HIFAR (High Flux Aus. Reactor) produces radioisotopes (of which some are exported). There is also production of Cobalt 60 teletherapy sources for cancer treatment, and radio-active tracers used in coastal research on movements of sand and silt. Research into the development of high-temperature gas-cooled reactors may have practical applications in providing power possibly for mineral development in remote areas of the continent. There is also research on reactor fuels. Gamma radiation research in relation to crops is carried out, as well as the vital health aspects of radiation. **The Commonwealth X-ray and Radium Laboratory**, founded in Melbourne in 1929, on a basis of 10 g. of imported material, provides and controls distribution of radium needles to medical centres. Royal Adelaide

Hospital now has a Department of Nuclear Medicine. The **Aus. Institute of Nuclear Science** is mainly a liaison body between the A.A.E.C. and university research. The **Nuclear Research Foundation** (1954) is a largely privately financed body promoting research within the University of Sydney, under the Canadian-born Director, H. Messel (1922–). **Atomic weapons** have been tested on the Monte Bello Islands* and at Maralinga* in S.A., by joint U.K. and Aus. teams. **Atomic Scientists** of note working in Aus. include: Sir Mark Oliphant (1901–); J. N. Gregory (1920–); and the English-born Sir Ernest Titteron (1916–), Sir Philip Baxter (1905–). Sir Harrie Stewart Wilson Massey (b. Melbourne, 1908) works in U.K. The first Aus. nuclear power station proposed is at Jervis Bay, N.S.W.; but Aus. may not need nuclear power until the 1980s. In 1973 Aus. ratified the Nuclear Non-Proliferation Treaty.

Augustus, Mount W.A. 24S/117E 1,108 m. Stands above the surrounding plateau of the Gascoyne* valley, a pyramid of resistant conglomerate.

Aurora Australis or **Southern Lights** Patches of light in high-latitude night skies, corresponding to the aurora borealis in the northern hemisphere. They are visible in the extreme S of Aus. for a few nights each year at the equinoxes and in periods of sunspot activity. They vary from pale greenish-white to deep curtains of red and green; from vague patches to arcs or bands and the 'corona' display, in which rays of light radiate out from a focal light high in the sky. Causes are still the subject of research, but are probably associated with interaction between the earth's magnetic field (whose axis at present cuts the surface at 78° 38′S/111°E, and is the focal point of auroral activity in a circular zone 2,400 km. in radius) and the solar corpuscular streams of electrically charged particles, some of which penetrate to 105 km. from the earth's surface.

Austin, James (1810–1896) and **Thomas** (1815–1871) Successful early settlers on the Barwon (Vic.), nephews of James Austin (transported to Tas. from Somerset for honey-stealing, later becoming a successful farmer). Thomas successfully acclimatised sparrows and rabbits* from Glastonbury, the family home.

Australasia A term not clearly defined but generally used in reference to Aus., N.Z., N.G. and adjacent islands; it may even include the island groups of Oceania. It was widely used in the titles of Associations (e.g. for sport) which included both Aus. and N.Z. membership, in early Federation* proposals and is still used by some business concerns with interests in both countries.

Australia (the name) Derived from *australis*, southerly, which was used very early in reference to the supposed Southland, and in several linguistic forms after its discovery. The form Australia came into wide use especially in the colony itself, after the publication of Flinders's* *Voyages* in 1814; he had suggested its adoption, after it had been finally proved that the W section, New Holland, and the E section, N.S.W., were indeed one land mass. Macquarie* officially promoted it in 1817, but acceptance in London was slow.

Australia Day (26th January) Commemorates the landing of the First Fleet at Sydney Cove in 1788; the Monday following the 26th is a public holiday. First observed in N.S.W. in 1818, by order of Macquarie*, it was only adopted as a country-wide holiday after Federation, largely at the instigation of the Aus. Natives Association* in Vic. Known first as Foundation or Commemoration Day, the present name was adopted after 1931.

Australia House The Strand, London, completed 1918) The office of the Commonwealth and the Aus. High Commissioner in U.K. The States also have London offices: Vic. House, S.A. House, Savoy House (W.A.), Marble Hall (Qld.), Tas. at No. 457 and N.S.W. at Nos. 66–72 The Strand. (*See also* AGENTS GENERAL.)

Australian Academy of Science Incorporated by Royal Charter in 1954 to promote scientific knowledge and research in Aus. It organises symposia, lectures, congresses etc.; represents Aus. in international enterprises such as the International Geophysical Year; and, by the award of not more than 6 Fellowships (F.A.A.) a year, recognises outstanding contributions to science.

Australian Academy of Humanities. Founded 1969 with Prof. Sir Keith Hancock as President.

Australian Agricultural Company Chartered in 1825 in London, for the purpose of producing merino wool, vines and olives, in order to provide capital and skilled labour, as well as corrective work for convicts. The company, which now holds only a coal-mining interest in the Maitland field, began with a grant of 405,000 ha. in the Manning valley and later on the Peel River under its subsidiary Peel River Co. The N.S.W. Government gave it a monopoly over coal-mining in the Newcastle area 1830–45. Both land and mining ventures roused bitter criticism from the emancipists*. The family of John Macarthur* were leading promoters in the company and the first agents Robert Dawson (1782–1866) and Henry Dangar (1796–1861) surveyed much of its land, under the enterprising Commissioner (1829–34) Sir William Parry (1790–1855), a former Antarctic explorer; he was followed by Sir Henry Dumaresq* (1792–1838). The agricultural side did not thrive and lands were gradually sold off or resumed.

Australian Alps Name given to the SE and highest section of the Eastern Highlands; not clearly defined, it covers high country shared by Vic. and N.S.W. and including the Snowy Mountains*.

Australian Ballot Voting by secret ballot known by this name (mainly in U.S.), as it was used in Aus. earlier than elsewhere. It became the legal form in Vic. in March 1856 where W. Nicholson (1816–1865) was a major advocate; in S.A. in April 1856; in N.S.W. and Tas. 1858; Qld. 1859; W.A. 1879. Meanwhile N.Z. had adopted it in 1870 and Britain in 1872.

Australian Broadcasting Commission Established by the Federal Parliament in 1932. It comprises 9 members including the Chairman, all appointed on 3 year terms by the Government, and selected broadly to represent the States and diverse groups within the community; 1 member must be a woman. A General Manager controls the programmes through the Management Committee and, subject to the general policy of the Commission, can strongly influence the balance, quality and trend; Sir Charles Moses had this position from 1935–65. Sir Richard Boyer* was an influential Chairman from 1945–61. Headquarters are in Sydney, with managers in each State; the A.B.C. operates 78 radio and 41 television outlets in Aus. and N.G. (1970). Finance comes from Government funds, not directly from licences. The A.B.C. has a high reputation for its news services, children's educational programmes and its sponsorship and presentation of serious music*; the latter has led to the establishment of orchestras, and the sponsorship of 'Celebrity' concerts. There has been criticism of conservatism, especially in dodging the presentation of highly controversial topics but viewing ratings

are now increasing, and a modern image is sought.

AUSTRALIAN CAPITAL TERRITORY (A.C.T.) Defined in 1908, after surveys of various possible sites, for an area to be set aside from N.S.W., not less than 100 miles from Sydney, to include the future national capital (*see* CANBERRA). It forms an area of 2,357 km² in an irregularly shaped wedge pointed N–S, with a strong S–N grain in the pattern of hills and valleys. The S–N portion of the Murrumbidgee River* enters A.C.T. about half-way along its E edge, and then turns generally NNW towards Burrinjuck Reservoir and Yass, N.S.W., 35S/149E. Tributaries generally follow the S–N grain of the country very closely—from E to W the Naas, Gudgenby, Cotter (one main source for Canberra's water supply), and, just W of the boundary in N.S.W., the Goodradigbee. The Queanbeyan-Molonglo system, however, flows generally NW from the Great Divide, past Queanbeyan and Canberra (now ponded back by the Scrivener Dam as Lake Burley Griffin), to join the Murrumbidgee a few km. W of the city. The Canberra Basin at about 600 m. above sea-level, is part of a downfaulted strip between the higher land upfaulted to the E (the Greenock Highlands or Cullarin Horst) and the W (the Brindabella–Tidbinbilla Ranges running N from the Snowy massif). The Brindabella ridge on the W boundary includes Mt. Bimberi 1,913 m. and several other heights over 1,800 m., as well as the lower but impressive conical Mt. Coree (1,422 m.). The higher lands suggest more or less dissected plateau levels at various heights, the whole generally cut across fairly tightly folded and steeply dipping Ordovician and Silurian slates, schists and slaty shales and grits, with some Devonian intrusive or extrusive igneous rocks, such as the Red Hill-Mugga Mugga or Ainslie-Majura ridges rising, like the more resistant sandstones of Black Mt., above the alluvial flats of the Canberra basin.

The Canberra Basin is part of a marked rain-shadow area W of the Great Divide, with under 60 cm of mean annual rainfall, often described as well distributed throughout the year, but in fact quite variable from year to year and especially variable in the summer months; droughts of moderate severity are not uncommon and may come at almost any season, though commoner and more serious in the higher evaporation of summer. Temperatures are modified by altitude, especially in winter when low night temperatures are accentuated by frost hollow conditions, sometimes with shallow fogs. Mean maximum temperatures for January are about 27°C and minimum 18°C (periods of several weeks with day temperatures over 32°C being not uncommon), and in July 16·5°C and under 10°C. Under winter anticyclones there may be many nights under freezing point, and 7°C to − 8°C is by no means uncommon, but with afternoons over 10°C. The flats of the Basin were in savannah grassland with parkland trees, or even treeless grasslands locally, when the Europeans came in the 1820s, but most of the A.C.T. is under dry sclerophyll* forest, with wet sclerophyll on the wetter ridges (to 100–127 cm. mean annual rainfall). There has been much clearing for grazing and at times in some places for tillage.

The A.C.T. contains in the S and SW an area within the proposed Gudgenby National Park, and other mainly high steep areas remain forested to a great extent. The Cotter catchment and other substantial areas including the slopes now mirrored in the lower end of Lake Burley Griffin are under softwood plantings mainly of *Pinus radiata*, now being processed in Canberra. Freehold land occupies 17% only; all other holdings are leasehold, as a matter of policy for A.C.T. Except for limited areas of dairying and market-gardening on the Molonglo flood-plain and terraces, rather extensive mainly wool sheep grazing prevails, with rather less pasture improvement than in comparable areas of N.S.W. under freehold.

The rural population of A.C.T. is a rapidly diminishing proportion of the total and increasingly the land use of the area is dominated by the spread of Canberra as a planned process tightly controlled by the Commonwealth Government, and by the recreational needs of its rapidly growing population —for instance, in reserves along the banks of the Murrumbidgee, the lower Cotter and its tributary Paddy's River. The Fauna Reserve now developed at Tidbinbilla and farther afield the bushwalking of the Kosciusko National Park give outlets of a different kind. There is trout fishing in and around the A.C.T., and sailing on Lake Burley Griffin.

Apart from Canberra, the population of the A.C.T. is relatively sparse and static (2,716 in 1966). Total A.C.T. population in 1971 was 143,843.

Along with the A.C.T. the small piece of Commonwealth Territory at Jervis Bay* was vested in the Commonwealth in 1915, as a possible future port.

Australian Elizabethan Theatre Trust A body founded 1954, to sponsor Aus. theatrical development, instigated largely by H. C. Coombs*, and commemorating Queen Elizabeth's first visit to Aus. in 1954. It is financed by private donation and government subsidies, making a total annual income well over $1 million. After a period of indifferent success, in which permanent performing companies proved difficult to form or retain, the Trust met with success in establishing opera* and ballet* companies which are now autonomous. The Trust's main functions now are: the provision of financial guarantees to these companies; the maintenance of two orchestras serving the Aus. Ballet and Aus.

Opera Companies and administration of their subscription bookings; the execution of costume and scenery design; organising and instigating tours for Aus. and overseas companies; administration of the Aus. Marionette Theatre. The Trust is one of three federal co-ordinating organisations, supported by the Aus. Council for the Arts (1968).

Australian Inland Mission This grew from a special Home Mission Board section of the Presbyterian Church, set up in 1912 following a report by Flynn* on the needs of the remote inland settlers, both for spiritual and medical aid. Its first patrol padres used camel, horse and bullock transport. One of the major innovations of the A.I.M. was the famous Flying Doctor Service*.

Australian Labor Party (A.L.P.) *Note*: the Americanised spelling appeared early and may stem from widespread reading of American Socialist writing in the late 19th century. The Labor Party grew from the Trade Union Movement when it became clear that political action by a party in Parliament was needed to ensure the legislation unionists were working for. Labor Electoral Leagues were formed in N.S.W. in 1891 pledged to the 8-hour day, the single vote, manhood suffrage, factory legislation educational and agricultural progress; they were opposed to Federation.* In 1891 over 36 members were returned in the N.S.W. Legislative Assembly and immediately held a balance of power which in State and later Federal Governments was to pave the way to ascendancy in the early 20th century and force through much significant social legislation. In Qld. the movement was also very strong; initiated by Lane* it later trimmed its ideals and methods (as did all Labor Parties, of necessity) to political realities, and won 18 seats in 1893. The movement was less distinctive in Vic. and S.A., where platforms were shared and agreements made with the more progressive liberals. Labor Governments have had long and influential periods in power in almost all the States. From the beginning the Labor Party used the controversial 'Caucus' or pledge system to ensure solidarity: members promised to abide by the majority decisions of the party Caucus (i.e. meeting of Parliamentary Labor Party) when voting in the House.

There were brief Federal Labor Governments in 1904 under Watson* and 1908 under Fisher* but the first major period in power was 1910–13, again under Fisher, when Labor had 35 out of 72 seats in the House of Representatives and 23 out of 36 in the Senate. Growing more rigid and doctrinaire, however, the Labor Government achieved less real social advancement than it had done as an influential 'corner party' and was defeated by a majority of 1 in 1913, but resoundingly returned in September 1914, perhaps chiefly because of the instant committal to the 1914–18 War made by Fisher.

But as the war went on, the party lost faith in W. M. Hughes*, its fiery leader and Fisher's successor, mainly over conscription*; there were also growing doubts about the aims and length of the war and the involvement of Aus. With Hughes's defection at the historic Caucus of October 10th 1916 and the formation of the National Party, Labor went into virtual eclipse for many years. A further disastrous split, imminent in 1918 when an influential group wanted to press for peace negotiations, was avoided only by the ending of hostilities.

Between the wars Labor was in office only briefly, from 1929–32 under Scullin*; it was an unsuccessful administration because the Depression was rapidly worsening; there was a lack of experienced men and they had a minority in the Senate. So once more the party was split: in 1931 Lyons* and Fenton resigned over the re-instatement and financial proposals of Theodore, and supporters of Lang* (the Labor N.S.W. Premier) under Beasley brought about its fall by effectively splitting the Federal and N.S.W. Labor Parties. While there were undefined resolutions to 'socialise industry, production, distribution and exchange', the main concerns of the party remained the defence of White Australia, coupled with raising wages, reducing hours and improving conditions; but there were perennial suspicions between the political wing anxious for cautious advance and gaining power, and the militant left wing unions more concerned with concrete achievements. Any association with the Communist Party has always been shunned, but there was also a fear in the 1930s of Aus. involvement in a purely capitalist war. Under Curtin's* leadership (1935) solidarity was improved and the significance of world events more realistically assessed. In September 1939 he undertook to defend Aus., and the integrity of the British Commonwealth. In October 1941 Labor once more took charge of the country at war, with a remarkable team of outstanding men, remaining in power until 1949, under Curtin* then Chifley*. A landslide victory in 1943 gave a clear mandate, and social legislation was introduced or extended in the fields of unemployment, hospital benefits and education, allowances and scholarships. In the immediate post-war phase of optimism Labor Party planning was still acceptable: migration schemes largely under Calwell* reversed the old prejudices of the Party, Chifley's severe controls of imports allowed a building-up of assets against regression; development projects, notably in the Snowy Mountains* were matched with academic stimulus in the newly created Aus. National University* (1946). But the move to completely nationalise civil aviation was defeated by a High Court judgement and attempts at a complete bank

nationalisation and comprehensive health service also failed. The current of opinion began to turn in 1948 with resentment at continued controls and high taxation; and the party began once more to crack on issues such as Chifley's use of troops in the 1949 coal strike. The strikes themselves undermined Labor's position. In December 1949 Labor lost office, and was again defeated in 1954. In 1951 they fought vigorously to reject the Communist Party Dissolution Bill. The internal splits widened under Evatt's* leadership which was suspected of being too far to the left. There was disagreement on the recognition of Communist China and entry of other Communist countries to U.N. The strong Irish Roman Catholic vote was canalised under Santamaria* into a breakaway anti-Communist Labor Party in Vic., which fused with other groups to become the country-wide Democratic Labor Party* (1957). In 1969 a Labor resurgence began, winning 59 seats in Federal Parliament, and was returned in S.A. in 1970 and W. A. in 1971. Whitlam* succeeded Calwell in 1967 as leader. In Dec. 1972 after 23 years in opposition, Labor won the federal election with a majority of 9. Immediate steps were taken to complete withdrawal from Vietnam, to end conscription and recognise Communist China. Dollar revaluation, control of foreign investment on the economic front, condemnation of apartheid and proposed Aboriginal land rights on the racial front followed. But restricted immigration will maintain a white Australia. Domestic policy plans equal pay for women, urban renewal schemes, national health insurance, increased pensions, educational expansion. A historical study is L. F. Crisp: *The Aus. Labor Party 1901–1951* (London, 1955).

Australian National University Founded 1946 for research and reorganised in 1960 to incorporate

Canberra University College (until then part of Melbourne Univ.) The Institute of Advanced Studies concentrates on research, organised in schools of medicine, Pacific studies, chemistry and biological, social and physical sciences (over 500 postgraduate students in 1972). The School of General Studies has Faculties of Arts, Asian Studies, Economics, Law and Science (over 4,000 undergraduate and 500 postgraduates, 1972).

Australian Natives Association A patriotic non-sectarian association of native-born Australians, founded in Vic. in 1872 from an existing Patriotic Society, and today country wide. It has been an important political pressure group, constructively concerned in proposals for Federation and supporting compulsory military training, industrial and economic development and White Australia.

Australian Rules Football A unique development of Rugby*, and, it is believed, Gaelic football dating from the 1850s. The 18-a-side game makes winter use of the cricket ovals and the pitch may be any size within the limits of 137–183 m. by 110–155 m. There are 4 goal posts at each end 7 m. apart, the centre 2 at least 6·1 m. high, and 6 points are scored by a goal between the centre 2 and 1 for a 'behind' or goal between the outer posts. The oval ball is about 50 g. heavier than a rugby ball. The main characteristics of the game are speed and athletic skill; there are no scrums or line-outs, off-sides, or passing by throwing. The ball may be punched, and must be bounced within every 9 m. when carried. High leaping or 'marks' make spectacular play. The first Vic. League was played in 1897 and there have been inter-state carnivals every 3 years or so since 1908, dominated by Vic. wins.
One of the earliest games was an epic 40-a-side match between 2 Melbourne schools in 1856, with goal posts 6 km. apart. The evolution was influenced by T. W. Wills (also a cricketer) and H. C. A. Harrison. Although not a major code in N.S.W. and Qld., Aus. rules is Australia's leading spectator sport, finals matches attracting up to 120,000 in Melbourne. In all four southern states football, as it is called, dominates winter news and talk. Some of the many famous players include: pre-World War II, Jack Dyer, Bob Pratt, Laurie Nash, Haydn Bunton all of Vic.; Postwar, John Coleman, Ron Barassi, Ted Whitten (Vic.), Graham Farmer (W.A. and Vic.), Lindsay Head (S.A.) and Peter Hudson (Tas. and Vic.).

Australind W.A. 33S/116E A small resort N of Bunbury on the Leschenault Estuary, named from the abortive land settlement scheme attempted in 1841 on Wakefield* lines by the Western Aus. Land Co. The large land grant on Koombana Bay was subdivided and sold in London in 100-ac. lots (40·5 ha.) and proved quite uncultivable with existing techniques.

Australwinks Small shellfish of the periwinkle family Littorinidae, including the common Blue Australwink, *Melarapha unifasciata*, clustering in rock crevices etc. near high-water mark, and the Mangrove Australwink, *M. scabra*, found on the stems and leaves of mangroves.

Australwinks
about 1 cm. across

AVIATION Aus. is one of the most airminded countries in the world, with its great distances, largely anticyclonic weather and general affluence. Aviation is controlled with notably high safety standards by the Department of Civil Aviation. The 688 Commonwealth and local authority private aerodromes represent a high density for a large country with a relatively little developed centre, though many of the outback airstrips represent only a flat surface of a certain length, with few facilities beyond a wind-sock. Registered aircraft (1970) include 51 turbo-jets, 91 turbo-props, 67 large piston-engined aircraft (9,080 kg. and over all-up), 3,421 small piston aircraft, 99 helicopters and 264 gliders, making a total of 3,729 powered aircraft, with the Airlines* fleet at about 150, and light aircraft dominant and rapidly increasing with some 1,000 Cessnas, 500 Pipers and almost 300 De Havillands, but generally quite old machines. These smaller aircraft include the planes used for Aerial Agriculture*, and for the Flying Doctor Service*.

Aus. made its own contribution to the evolution of viable aeroplanes, notably through Lawrence Hargrave*. As elsewhere the first considerable impact came after the 1914–18 War, when pilots and machines became available for 'barn-storming' and joy-riding and itinerant air shows. Government policy favoured out-back air services, where other transport was deficient, and the valuable pioneering Geraldton–Derby service over 1,950 km. began on December 5th 1921, unfortunately with a fatal accident, while Fysh and McGuinness with 2 pastoralists formed the original QANTAS* (Qld. and N.T. Aerial Services Ltd.) in 1920, with the Charleville–Cloncurry service beginning in 1922. Guinea Airways (1927) did remarkable work in the transport of gold-mining equipment in N.G. Kingsford Smith* and Charles Ulm* had pioneered the Pacific crossing in 1926, and in 1930 Kingsford Smith began the Sydney–Brisbane service of the original Aus.

National Airways, soon extended to Melbourne–Launceston–Hobart. Despite the Depression, success seemed assured, but the tragic disappearance of the *Southern Cross* reduced confidence and traffic. The firm soon closed, and with it the barn-storming era.

Fresh development began in 1934 when QANTAS Empire Airways was formed to extend the 1933 Imperial Airways London–Singapore service to Sydney, and despite the 1939–45 War development continued, as in the remarkable flying-boat service Colombo–Perth of 1943–45. Equally significant was the new Aus. National Airways in 1936, with capital from Aus. and U.K. shipping interests, and soon the short SE Aus. air routes which they took over were consolidated and all-metal planes were effecting a revolution in comfort and reliability, the precursors of the DC3, the great aerial workhorse of the 1939–45 War. Remarkable work was accomplished in Aus. and N.G. despite the war.

The great post-war development of the industry brought new aircraft types—first the turbo-props and then the turbo-jets—and airline* consolidation into the present pattern.

Other notable figures in Aus. aviation history include: Bert Hinkler*; G. A. Taylor (1878–1928) who flew an engineless kite-like aircraft from Narrabeen beach in 1909; W. E. Hart who flew from Penrith to Parramatta and Sydney in 1911; Harry Hawker (1889–1921) who was a Sopwith racing and test pilot before and during the 1914–18 War, and who found by experiment how to get an aircraft out of a flat spin —a feat of great courage, also attempted to fly the Atlantic in 1919, leaving his name with Hawker Siddeley, makers of the Hurricane; R. Parer who with J. McIntosh flew a DH9 biplane from Eng. to Darwin in 1920; and Ross and Keith Smith who won the £10,000 prize for a flight from Eng.–Aus. in 1919. G. U. Allan, J. A. Mollison, P. G. Taylor* and E. H.

Aldis were important at home or overseas. (*See also* AIRCRAFT MANUFACTURE and AIR RACES.) *For further reading see* S. Brogden: *The History of Aus. Aviation* (Melbourne, 1960).

Avocet, Red-necked (*Recurvirostra novae-hollandiae*) A notably long-legged wading bird, with long narrow pointed beak curved upwards, and about 40 cm. from beak to tail, mainly white, with rich brownish-red head and neck. Found by streams and marshes in much of Aus., but rarer in N, in E coast areas, and Tas. Usually quiet, but gives a barking cry when disturbed at the nest (a hollow with a few twigs or pebbles, or built in shallow water from mud, reeds etc.).

Avon River and **Dam** N.S.W. A tributary of Nepean, on W slopes of Illawarra scarp, dammed as major water source for Sydney and 108 km. SW of the city, giving a long, narrow, twining and branched reservoir amid forests, a landmark on many flights from Canberra.

Avon River Vic. 38S/148E Flows for about 80 km. S then SE from the steep forested scarp of the E Highlands near Mt. Tamboritha (1,641 m.). It contributes irrigation water to the pastures and fodder crops of the Maffra-Stratford-Sale dairying flats, then enters the NW of L. Wellington in the Gippsland Lakes*.

Avon Valley W.A. 32S/117E Avon is the name of the upper course of the Swan; it flows for 320 km. NW behind the Darling Range* to Northam through this valley, one of the oldest established agricultural regions of the State. The mid section of the Swan-Avon runs for 32 km. through the scarp in gorges and over rapids.

Ayers Rock N.T. 25S/131E One of the world's great monoliths, an oval mass 9·7 km. in circumference rising 335·5 m. above the sand and gravel plains (860 m. above sea level). It is built of vertically dipping strata of pinkish-red conglomerate (water-worn pebbles of granites cemented by finer sands). The fluted effect of the steep lower slopes is the result of the wearing away of softer layers by seepage and sudden downpours; numerous rock holes retain storm water. Caves contain paintings by the Pitjantjatjara tribe, to whom the whole rock is of great religious-magical importance. It was named after the S.A. Premier by Gosse in 1873 although Giles* first reported it the year before.

Ayers Rock

Ayr Qld. 20S/147E (8,272 in 1971) On the Burdekin delta, founded in 1882 as the centre for rapidly increasing irrigated sugar-growing. A 1,104 m.-long bridge, 3 m. above the highest recorded flood level, links it with the other delta centre of Home Hill, 11 km. to the S.

B

Babbage, Benjamin Herschel (1815–1878) b. Eng. An explorer and scientist, he arrived in Aus. in 1851. Employed by the S.A. Government to survey for gold, he led two official explorations in 1856 and 1858 which helped to prove that Lakes Eyre and Torrens were separate; alleged incompetence led to his being superseded by Warburton*. He was involved in surveying the Overland Telegraph Line* and was an eccentric Adelaide character.

Babblers (*Pomatostomus*—lid-mouth) This genus comprises 5 Aus. species of mainly inland forest birds, about thrush-size, with large head and tail (often half-elevated) and a rather large, sharp, slightly downcurved beak. They are generally brown with whitish underparts, though some have some colour, and with a conspicuous white eye-stripe and tail-patch. They are highly social, usually seen in groups of about a dozen—hence one popular name, the Twelve Apostles—busily turning over forest litter etc. in search of grubs, and chattering loudly. Nests are large, superficially untidy, dome-shaped structures with a side entrance, often in a high fork in a tree, and there are 3–6 brownish eggs. The Grey-crowned Babbler, *P. temporalis*, is found from Cape York to the E of S.A., the Red-breasted Babbler, *P. rubeculus*, in much of tropical Aus., the White-browed Babbler, *P. superciliosus*, in much of the S of Aus., and the Chestnut-crowned Babbler, *P. ruficeps*, in much of E and SE Aus.

Bacchus Marsh Vic. 38S/144E (4,143 in 1971) It grew at a coach crossing of Werribee River on the route to the gold-fields and is now a dairying, orchard and market-gardening centre for Melbourne.

Bail up Colloquial verb used as the command in a hold-up, dating from the days of the rich gold escorts, and derived from *bail*, an English dialect word for the frame to which cows are tied for milking, hence to a command to stand still.

Bairnsdale Vic. 38S/148E (8,549 in 1971) A service centre on the Mitchell River in the E of Gippsland, 5 km. upstream from L. King*. The area was settled by cattle-men from N.S.W. but farming now also includes maize, sunflowers and beans. Bairnsdale initially was a port for Melbourne traffic. An important tourist trade, based on the Lakes holiday resorts, has been added to its timber industry.

Baitfish, Red or **Pearl Fish, Red Herring** or **Picarel** (*Emmelichthys nitidus*) A silvery fish with pink to beetroot tinge, apparently normally in schools in open temperate seas, but occasionally coming inshore in the S of Aus. (and other countries) in enormous numbers, perhaps in association with mackerel and pilchards. It is about 40 cm. long, good to eat, slender and graceful, with dorsal fins linked by spines.

Baker, Reginald Leslie ('Snowy') (1884–1953) b. Sydney. All-round athletic champion, and later a successful boxing promoter, branching out from the Sydney Stadium to other States. His achievements covered swimming, boxing, rugby and rowing and he spent the later part of his life, after he himself had appeared in films, coaching stars in California.

Ballarat Vic. 38S/144E (58,434 in 1971) Earlier called Ballaarat, once a gold-mining boom town and now a busy cathedral city and school and market centre in the Uplands, with a better balanced work force than most inland towns. The gently rolling countryside was opened by Thomas Learmonth* as emergency grazings in drought in 1837; by 1851, when gold was found, there were but a few scattered huts of squatters' workmen, yet by 1854 there were 27,000 people and by the 1870s 48,000 in a city with the fine substantial centre, boulevards, parks, art gallery, concert hall and recreation space which mark it today. L. Wendouree is near the city centre and L. Learmonth only 23 km. to the NW. Abandoned diggings, and more patchy development may be seen in the suburbs; also the memorial to Eureka Stockade*, as well as the varied factories (some in a converted munitions works) making engineering products, clothing, beer, paper, biscuits, brick and tiles, and timber products.

Ballet Now well established in Aus. The Aus. Ballet Foundation, with school and company, jointly formed by J. C. Williamson* and Aus. Elizabethan Theatre Trust*, gave its first season (1962–3) in Sydney, and has also toured overseas. Dancers have included Marilyn Jones, Kathleen Gorham, Garth Welch and Elaine Fifield*, with Peggy van Praagh an outstanding artistic director. Modern principals are Lucette Aldous and Alan Alder. Early interest followed the visits of Pavlova in 1926 and 1928, and de Basil's Ballet Russe and Ballet de Monte Carlo between 1936 and 1940. Members of these groups remained and founded several schools and companies. Burlakov's students in Sydney formed the first Aus. Ballet (1931). Madame Kirsova's company presented classical ballets in Sydney 1942–5; in Melbourne the Boranovsky Ballet (1940–60) was managed by J. C. Williamson, and the Polish-Aus. Ballet was founded in 1943 by Madame Koussnetovska. Modern ballet and dance interpretations have been pioneered in Aus. by the Bodenweiser Ballet in Sydney (1939).

Rex Reid's *Corroboree* (1950), with music by John Antill, which was inspired by Aboriginal themes, is the outstanding ballet created in Aus. Sir Robert Helpman is a famous expatriate. *For further reading see* I. Brown: *The Australian Ballet* (Melbourne, 1967).

Ballina N.S.W. 29S/154E (6,133 in 1971) A seaside resort and port with small coastal traffic and considerable fishing activity, at the mouth of the Richmond River; something of an outport for Lismore 32 km. upstream.

Ball's Pyramid N.S.W. 32S/158E A pinnacle of Tertiary basalt rising sheer for 550 m. from the Tasman Sea, 19 km. S of Lord Howe Island*.

Balmain, William (1762–1803) b. Perthshire, Scotland. Assistant surgeon to John White* with the First Fleet, serving on Norfolk Island 1791–5 and as White's successor in Sydney from 1795–1801. **Balmain** is a west-central south shore suburb of Sydney, the site of modern container-shipping port installations.

Balonne River Qld. A seasonally flowing 280-km.-long continuation of the Condamine* from Surat, 27S/149E, to the point where, after receiving the Maranoa from the N, it branches to the Culgoa, thence joining the Darling. The basin is used for sheep, dependent on bores, beef fattening on riverine lands, over 1,200 ha. irrigated fodder and cotton at St. George.

Balranald N.S.W. 35S/144E (1,425 in 1971) A former ferry point, important for stock, on the now bridged Murrumbidgee in the Lowbidgee* country near the confluence with the Murray. The old inn has been supplanted by motels etc.; the rail link is with Vic. When the early summer floods spread over the surrounding hollows the town is plagued by mosquitoes and graced by many beautiful waterfowl.

Bamaga The most northerly community on the Aus. mainland, 40 km. S of Cape York. Founded by Torres Str. Islanders who abandoned their home island of Saibai following a tidal wave in 1952, and named from their chief. It is now the centre of a Native Reserve of 6,775 km². Hardwood, coconuts and cattle industries are being developed and irrigation from the R. Jardine. There are some 1,200 people.

Bananas 95% of the total 11,000 ha. are in the N of N.S.W., on well-drained but rainy hill slopes and in the SE lowlands of Qld. Tariff protection and rapid rail transport, disease control and use of fertilisers offset soil erosion and competition. Ground water is used for bananas at Carnarvon*, W.A.

Bancroft, Joseph (1836–1894) b. Manchester, Eng. He and his son **Thomas Lane** (1860–1933) b. Nottingham, Eng., arrived in Qld. in 1864. Joseph was a medical practitioner who also did research on: 1. medical problems, discovering the adult female worm of *Filaria bancrofti* and the transmission of this filariasis by mosquitoes; 2. pharmacology, establishing the use of *Duboisia myoporoides*, a poisonous plant in the Solanaceae or potato family, to produce alkaloids containing atropine and other pupil-dilating drugs for ophthalmic purposes; and 3. experiments on rust-proof wheat, hybridisation, and diseases of sugar-cane and bananas.

The son also became a doctor, working in Qld. including research on: 1. the Qld. lungfish*; 2. filariasis, including its presence in many animals; 3. the transmission of the virus fever, dengue, by the mosquito *Aëdes aegypti*; 4. hybridisation in the peach, grapes, castor-oil and cotton plants.

Bandicoot (family Peramelidae) Small marsupials unique to the Australian region, nocturnal and omnivorous in habit, of the following genera: 1. the Long-nosed Bandicoot, *Perameles*, e.g. *P. nasuta* in E Aus. with other species in Tas., W.A., and Central Aus.; 2. the Short-nosed Bandicoot, *Isoodon*, e.g. *I. obesulus* in SE Aus., with other species in coastal areas around Aus.; 3. the Pig-footed Bandicoot, *Chaeropus*, e.g. *C. ecaudatus* of S.A., now probably extinct; and 4. the Rufescent Bandicoot, *Echymipera*, of N.G., of which *E. rufescens australis* has been seen in Qld. rain-forests. Named after but quite distinct from the Indian true rodent Bandicoots such as *Bandicota bengalensis*

Banfield, Edmund James (1852–1923) b. Liverpool, Eng. A journalist and writer about natural history, especially of Dunk Island* off the Qld. coast where he lived for 25 years. He wrote *The Confessions of a Beachcomber* (London, 1908) and *My Tropic Isle* (London, 1918).

BANKING Beginning with the Bank of New South Wales in 1817, there was early and widespread use of private sector banks, with practice modified from English and Scottish banking to suit the local circumstances; upon this foundation has been superimposed since Federation the Commonwealth banks, with clear-cut separation since 1960 of central banking functions to the **Reserve Bank of Australia,** the note-issuing authority. Most important for its central banking functions—as the bankers' bank and the Commonwealth Government's main agency for the control of the economy—it sets out to maintain full employment and general prosperity through a calculated degree of inflation or occasionally deflation by encouraging or discouraging the creation of money through credit facilities (much more significant than cash in the modern economy). It also has important rural credit functions. The Reserve Bank also controls the Development Finance Corporation (1967) aimed at preventing over-extension of individual banks in the financing of development operations, by refinancing them on such loans. The **Aus. Resources Development Bank** (1968) provides finance for major projects.

The **Commonwealth Banking Corporation** (1960) is the controlling body for: 1. **The Commonwealth Trading Bank** (included with the private-sector Trading Banks below). 2. **The Commonwealth Savings Bank of Australia** has deposits over $3,000 million, over 900 branches and over 8,000 agencies including many Post Offices. There are also State Savings Banks and, in Tas. 2 Trustee Savings Banks, all similarly aimed at safe investment for the small depositor. 3. **The Commonwealth Development Bank of Australia** was formed in the reorganisation of 1960 basically from the Mortgage Bank and Industrial Finance Departments of the former Commonwealth Bank structure; its function is the financing of worthwhile development projects in primary and secondary industries otherwise unable to get necessary finance on reasonable terms. Capital and reserve are over $90 million, deposits including other banks' balances over $170 million, loans over $260 million, and net profit over $2 million.

The **Trading Banks** are the main cheque-issuing deposit and overdraft and loan account banks dealing with the public and private sector industry etc., but some also operate Savings Banks. There are seven major trading banks: Bank of N.S.W.; Aus. and N.Z. Banking Group Ltd.; Commonwealth Trading Bank of Aus.; National Bank of Australasia; Commercial Bank of Aus. Ltd.; Commercial Banking Company of Sydney; and Bank of Adelaide.

Historical Development The early days of the colony in N.S.W. saw many problems of finance and currency—hence the use of the Holey Dollar*—and so Macquarie* encouraged a group of Sydney merchants to set up the Bank of New South Wales, at first as a partnership in 1817 which was converted to a company in 1828. By 1850 there were 18 banks, three formed in London and the rest in the largest towns in Aus. itself, but with only a handful of branches in the still small lesser centres. The gold-rush brought many new banks in the early 1850s, some involved in speculative land and building companies, and there was similar expansion in the mid 60s and the 80s. Aus. banking became more like that in America, with 34 private banks at one time, a large number in proportion to population. The collapse of export markets and withdrawals by overseas depositors in 1893 caused a sharp enough crisis which, combined with drought, cast something of a financial pall over the first few years of Federation. A few small banks had failed, and 12 of the 21 banks then operating had to suspend payment owing to involvement in the more speculative, sometimes badly run, building and land companies. Losses to shareholders and depositors are estimated at £21 million, and though most of the banks were able to reopen after a few months, reorganisation of the banking structure went on for 20 years. Even so, for a young country with several phases of economic ebullience, Aus. has seen remarkably few bank failures; mergers were more important—including some of the larger banks up to the National Bank-Queensland National Bank merger (1948), Bank of Australasia-Union Bank of Australia merger (1951), and (1970) the Aus. & N.Z. Bank and English, Scottish and Aus. Bank.

In 1911 came the Commonwealth Government's bank, the Commonwealth Bank of Australia. It was originally a trading and savings bank, but gradually by legislative measures acquired central banking functions (which up to Federation had been performed, though to a decreasing extent, by the Bank of England). The older, stable and experienced banks did not always respond to guidance from the younger Commonwealth Bank, and it was found invidious for the central bank to compete actively for ordinary business; it ceased to do this from 1928, and grew in prestige as a central bank through the Depression* of the 1930s. The Royal Commission on banking of 1935-7 recommended the licensing of trading banks and control by the central bank, and though there was no direct implementation of the report, partly because of the war, wartime controls gave much experience and the post-war Labor Government used it in framing the Banking Act of 1945. At this time, complete nationalisation was declared unconstitutional (1947). Apart from the Commonwealth Bank, 9 main trading banks were licensed (now 7, of which 2 are incorporated in London though with day-to-day management in Melbourne), 2 small banks (now only one, in Brisbane) and 3 foreign banks (from China, N.Z. and France). State banks in S.A., W.A. and N.S.W. operate within their own State. Special accounts proportional to deposits have to be maintained with the central bank; advances, foreign exchange transactions, investments and interest rates are all subject to control, and the principles remain despite the amending Act of 1953. In 1959 came the Acts setting up the Reserve Bank and Commonwealth Banks as outlined earlier.

At the end of the period of adjustment to Federation and of evolution of an independent policy of controlling the Aus. economy, the banking scene remains reminiscent of U.K. rather than U.S. Branch banking has re-expanded, after war-time contraction, to a total of over 4,500 branches proper and almost 1,800 agencies. The fluctuating overdraft remains the main means of lending, though there may be some trend towards the fixed-loan account which is slightly easier to control at a time of applying controls to credit. The unique importance of interest-bearing, fixed-term deposits remains, though of less relative importance. The century-old facility of loans on liens on wool is unfamiliar to a British banking eye. The share of the trading banks in the total financial structure of the country is relatively less than a generation ago. As elsewhere banks have met loss of business through hire purchase* development by seeking association with finance companies. Banks are being encouraged (1973) to be competitive in order to mobilize more Aus. investment. *For further reading see* H. W. Arndt and C. P. Harris: *The Australian Trading Banks* (Melbourne, 1957).

Banks, Sir Joseph (1743-1820) b. London. A great English naturalist (Fellow, later President of the Royal Society) who volunteered to join Cook on the *Endeavour's* voyage in 1768 at great personal expense. His initial descriptions of the Aus. coast were of a monotonous, barren land of little potential value; but after returning to Eng. he changed his views sufficiently to recommend Botany Bay strongly as a penal settlement on grounds of remoteness, paucity of natives, promising soil, climate, timber, water and grassland resources (and even trading potential) to the House of Commons committees on accommodation of prisoners (1779), and on transportation (1785). Subsequently he retained his interest in the colony, both its politics and natural history, and was frequently consulted. He supported both King* and Bligh* as Governors, influenced many minor appointments, and was instrumental in obtaining an Admiralty ship for Flinders's* expedition. Valuable original letters to Banks from Aus. are in the Mitchell Library in Sydney.

Banksia A genus of some 50 species of shrubs and trees, named after Sir Joseph Banks* who collected the first specimens from Botany Bay in 1770, in the mainly southern and largely Aus.

family Proteaceae. The popular name Bottlebrush is often applied to Banksias (as also to various species of *Callistemon*). Some Banksias are also called Honeysuckle*, from their nectar-rich qualities, e.g. *B. integrifolia*, the Coast Banksia or White Honeysuckle of E Aus. The cylindrical compound flowerhead is very distinctive and succeeded by thick woody cones bearing seed capsules, which release the seed eventually, notably after bush fires. The leaves are thick and leathery, narrow, often serrated, and white below. Banksias vary from 15-m. trees. e.g. *B. serrata* of E Aus., to under-storey species such as *B. grandis*, a tall bush growing under Jarrah* and Karri* in W.A., and small shrubs, e.g. the beautiful *B. coccinea* of W.A. with red and white spikes.

Bannerman, Charles (1851–1930) b. Woolwich, Eng. Arrived in Aus. as a boy. A cricketer and the first great Aus. batsman. He made the first Test century (165 not out Melbourne, 1877) and gained the Aus. victory. He had to retire because of ill health in 1880. His brother **A. C. Bannerman**, less outstanding, played 28 Tests, was a brilliant fielder and defensive batsman.

Baptist Church Now with some 177,000 adherents, it was introduced to Aus. in 1831 with services held in an inn until the first church was built in 1836. There have been relatively few splinter sects compared with U.S. Baptists engage in educational, health and publishing activities.

Barbed-wire Grass (*Cymbopogon refractus*) Has fairly short leaves in a small tuft, and a tall stem with groups of seed-heads at intervals from leafy sheaths, very suggestive of barbed wire. Like many of its genus it contains much aromatic essential oil, which in this species smells spicy or gingery when crushed.

Barcaldine Qld. 24S/145E (1,796 in 1966, 1,488 in 1971) A railing centre for stock on the Central line (1886)

and was the hub of Cobb and Co* coaching routes. It has kangaroo freezing works.

Barcoo River Qld. Headstream of Cooper Creek, 530 km. long, flowing intermittently through sheep country. The upper course was discovered by Mitchell* (1846), who wrongly thought it would continue as a 'great northern river'. 'Barcoo Rot' is probably scurvy.

Bardsley, Warren (1883–1954) b. Warren, N.S.W. Leading left-handed batsman who played with great care and precision. In 30 Tests against Eng. (1909–26) he averaged 33·4 with 6 centuries and was the first ever to score a century in both innings. In first-class cricket he totalled 16,707, averaging 49·63 with 52 centuries.

Bark Paintings Both sacred and secular, these paintings were and residually are still important to the Aborigines of Arnhem Land and Groote Eylandt; they are widely recognised as one of the most remarkable primitive art forms in the world. They often cover the whole of a sheet of bark, with designs in very detailed drawing and bright and harmonious colouring of both representational and purely decorative detail. In sacred paintings for rites on fertility and increase of food sources coastal tribes may portray fish, stingrays, sandbanks, clouds and rain; while an inland tribe may show emus, their nests, tracks in the bush, eucalypt foliage etc. In recent years commercial production has been started by missions etc. and more or less authentic designs may be bought in the area or even in the cities of the S, and a number of designs have been incorporated in the $1 note.

Barkly Tableland A distinctive region of 103,600 km². extending 485 km. NW–SE and 160–200 km. N–S, in the NE of N.T., extending in Qld. to Camooweal, 20S/138E. It is only a tableland when seen from the N where broken terrain drops to the Gulf Country* and the E, where it is edged by the tumbled N–S Selwyn Ranges.

To the W and S it is a very gently sloping basin, 230 m. in the centre, and is limited largely by rainfall and vegetation changes. Cambrian limestones and shales, undisturbed from their original horizontal beds laid down underwater then uplifted, have some of the world's oldest fossils. Sub-artesian water is pumped from 90 to 150 m.-deep bores often by windmills using the steady SE winds of the 'Dry'. In the 'Wet', rain averages 40 cm., decreasing southwards. The climax vegetation of tussocky Mitchell grass, interspersed with lower annual grasses, e.g. Flinders, gives an impression of an endless sea. The seasonal water courses make towards lower 'drybogs' (shown on maps as lakes: Corella, Sylvester, etc.) which may become lagoons in wet years, and are ringed by 'bluebush' swamps which contain some permanent water holes. Soils are heavy, dark coloured and slow-draining. Open-range cattle are bred on very large properties, over half managed on behalf of absentee owners and are sent, increasingly by 'road train' to railheads or directly for fattening near the Qld. coast and in the Channel Country*. Alexandria Station, over 28,000 km², is one of the biggest in the world; others are Brunette, Avon and Alroy Downs, Anthony Lagoon and Austral Downs. The area was named after a Vic. Governor by Landsborough in 1861. The **Barkly Highway**, a 650-km. link from Mt. Isa to the Stuart Highway 32 km. N of Tennant Creek* was sealed in the 1939–45 War and is an important Beef Road*.

Barklya (*Barklya syringifolia*) A tree of the Leguminaceae family, unique to rain-forest glades of NE N.S.W. and SE Qld., though now cultivated as a pleasant garden and shade tree. It reaches 19 m., and has glossy heart-shaped leaves about 8 cm. long, with a long conical apricot to golden yellow flower-head, succeeded by 5- to 8-cm.-long pods.

Barley This accounts for some 8% of cropland; while some is cut as 'hay', the bulk is divided between export to Europe and Japan, and malting (for which 2-row barley is grown). S.A. is the dominant producer, but it is also part of crop rotations in Vic. and N.S.W.

Barmera S.A. 34S/141E (1,683 in 1971) Service and irrigation centre on L. Bonney, a frequently dry flood-plain depression N of the Murray, originating with the post 1914–18 War Soldier Settlement here, and at Loveday nearby from 1948.

Barnacles The universal popular name for the Sub-Class Cirripedia (feather-footed) within the crustaceans*, particularly the immobile adult forms (with free-swimming larval forms). A barnacle lives as a small sessile crustacean in a conical structure of several calcareous plates, superficially like a very small limpet-shell. From this refuge it extends its feathery jointed limbs into the water in search of food. Common sessile barnacles in Aus. include the cosmopolitan *Balanus amphitrite*, to 2·5 cm. across, and its relative *B. nigrescens*, at or below low tide mark in S Aus. waters, which is the largest Aus. species, reaching 6·5 cm. high. The Honeycomb Barnacle is *Chamaesipho columna*; also common are the 4-plated *Tetraclita purpurescens* and *T. rosea*, and *Catophragmus polymerus* with 8 principal plates and several rings of small scale-like plates outside them. *Elminius modestus*, growing well above low water mark, is not among the most troublesome barnacles in its home in Aus. and N.Z., but it has become a serious fouling barnacle in W Europe since it suddenly appeared in Chichester Harbour in S Eng. in 1940.

Stalked barnacles are perhaps less often recognised as such by the layman, but are often seen swaying in masses on the end of stalks about 2·5 cm. long on driftwood, with shelly plates actually 5 in number but superficially like a very small Pipi* bivalve; inside is a small prawn-like crustacean, usually *Lepas anatifera*, or in W.A. perhaps the short-stalked reddish *Smilium peronii*, with 13 shell-valves. Several sessile and stalked barnacles are found attached to fish, whales etc., but the genus *Sacculina* is specialised to existence in a tumour-like mass near a crab's tail and is parasitic on it.

Barnes, Sydney (1918–   ) b. Qld. A cricketer noted for batting which was both controlled yet capable of very high scoring, and for brilliant close fielding. In 9 Tests against Eng. (1938 then 1946–48) he averaged 70·5. In first-class games he totalled 8,233, averaging 53·46, with 26 centuries.

Barney, George (1792–1862) b. Wolverhampton, Eng. Arrived in Aus. in 1835 as an army engineer. He was responsible for Circular Quay at Sydney, the Newcastle breakwater and notably the defences at Sydney including Fort Denison. He was in charge of the abortive convict settlement at Port Curtis (Gladstone) in 1847, and succeeded Mitchell as Surveyor-General (1855).

Barossa Valley S.A.   35S / 138E A shallow N–S depression 30 by 8–16 km. in the Mt. Lofty Ranges*, drained by the N Para River and named after a Spanish locality by Light*. It produces 50% of S.A. wines*. In 1842 the first Silesian Lutherans settled at Bethany, E of Tanunda; vines were grown from 1847, and the 3 major family wine firms were established by 1851. Reliable winter rains of 50 cm. and dry sunny summers, fairly poor soils suiting the vine, added to local skill, persistence and hard work, and supplementary farming of vegetables, fruit, pigs, poultry and sheep lie behind this unique landscape. Small hamlets cluster round the churches amid intensively used land; the 3 towns are Tanunda*, Nuriootpa and Angaston*.

Barrack for A verb, meaning to support, often vociferously as at football matches; without the preposition *for* it means to tease or to chaff or even jeer. The origin is controversial; possibly it is from similar N Irish word rather than the Aboriginal derivation previously suggested.

Barracouta (*Leionura atun*) Generally of about 76 cm. long and 1–3 kg. in weight, and the **King Barracouta**, Southern Kingfish, or 'Hake' of Sydney markets (*Rexea solandri*), of about 50 cm. long though sometimes up to 120 cm., are voracious strong-toothed fish lined in moderately deep temperate waters in many parts of the world, probably migratory over long distances, and grouped with the Snake Mackerels, the S African Snoek (cf. Snook). Both are steely blue above, with a silvery belly, the Barracouta with 1 line along its side, the King Barracouta with 2. The very long front back fin alone will distinguish it from the Barracuda (*see* DINGO-FISH), or the Snook*.

Barrallier, Francis Luis (1773–1853) b. Eng. Son of a French emigré, he arrived in Aus. in 1800 and joined N.S.W. Corps. He accompanied Grant in charting Bass Str. (1801); in 1802 Governor King* sent him to seek a route through the Blue Mountains. This he failed to do, reporting that W of Moss Vale they were impassable, and the Aborigines savage.

Barrington, George (real name probably Waldron) (?1755–1804) b. Ireland. He was educated for the Church, but became a notorious but charming thief and was transported (1791). Emancipated, he became Superintendent of Convicts, Parramatta (1796–1800), but went insane. He has been falsely credited with several accounts of the colony, and with the *Barrington Prologue*, supposedly written for the opening of the first theatre* (1796) which was in fact the work of H. Carter.

Barrington Tops N.S.W. 32S/152E A broad dissected dome at the S end of the Mt. Royal Range*, reaching 1,586 m. and formed from basaltic and slaty rocks. It is a tourist area noted for its snow gums and antarctic beeches.

Barron River Qld. About 112 km. long, it flows N then E from Atherton Tableland* to Trinity Bay just N of Cairns. Rich alluvial flats within the basalts are irrigated for tobacco, from Tinaroo Dam (1958). Where the Barron plunges 250 m. to the coastal plain, 1·6 km. from the sea a hydro-electric power station (60,000 kW) was completed in 1963 to supply Cairns.

Barrow Island W.A. 21S/115E 202 km². and 48 km. offshore, this is geologically part of the Carnarvon Basin* and the site of the first commercially producing oilfield in W.A. with a probable 15-year life (depth 732 m., in 240 wells employing 350 men). Oil shipments began in April 1967, and now provide some 7% of Aus. needs. Because of shallow water offshore a 10-km. submarine 50-cm. pipe takes the oil to a loading jetty. There are no derricks, but numerous 'Christmas Tree' pipe structures. Fracturing ('fraccing') of the rock to ease oil yield is necessary; power is from natural gas. The rainless island has some unique fauna. Oil has been found on Pasco Island 6.5 km S.

Bartle Frere, Mount 17S/146E The highest mountain in Qld. (1,612 m.) is a twin-peaked granite mass at the S end of the Bellenden Ker Range*.

Barton, Sir Edmund (1849–1920) First Aus. Prime Minister (1901–3), b. Sydney, entering politics from law in 1879. Barton inherited the political mantle of Parkes*, but was much more whole-hearted in the cause of Federation, serving on the drafting committee of 1891 and leading the elected delegates in the 1898 Conventions. He was asked to form the first Federal Ministry (Lyne having failed) and found himself with an 'army of generals', i.e. 5 former State Premiers as his Ministry. Barton disliked the emerging party strife and escaped to the newly formed High Court in 1903, which he served brilliantly with Griffith and O'Connor until his death. He coined the phrase White Australia Policy*. His elder brother **George** was a notable critic and the first literary historian of N.S.W.

Basic Wage Originated as a concept expressed by Higgins* in 1907 as supplying 'the normal needs of the average employee regarded as a human being in a civilised community', and then estimated as $4.40 a week in Melbourne for a man with 2 children. Gradually however the economic capacity of the community to pay became the decisive factor in arbitration* rulings. Later, the minimum wage was the basic wage plus a margin awarded according to skills, dangers or disagreeable factors in the occupation. Automatic quarterly adjustments based on cost of living indices operated 1921–53. Unions agitated for their renewal, while employers wanted a new 'total wage' declared and this was accepted by the Arbitration Commission in 1967, although unsuccessfully challenged in the High Court by the Trade Unions, since it would abolish hearings by separate benches for increases in basic wages and margins. Minimum wages are prescribed by industrial arbitration authorities. The 1971 minimum award averaged $58.00 for adult males (non professional or managerial). Female wages in general are 75% of male wages, but the concept of equal pay is gaining ground rapidly.

Bass, George (1771–1803) b. Lincolnshire, Eng. He became a naval surgeon, explorer and scientific observer of some merit. He arrived in N.S.W. on *Reliance* with Hunter* in 1795, making friends on board with Matthew Flinders*. With remarkable courage and seamanship they explored the coasts S of Sydney in tiny boats, and confirmed coal on the Illawarra coast (1796). In 1798 they proved the existence of the strait bearing his name and sailed round Van Diemen's Land. Bass disappeared without trace on a trading voyage to S America in 1803. *For further reading see* K. M. Bowden: *George Bass* (Melbourne, 1952).

Bass Strait 40S/146E Between Aus. mainland and Tas., this averages 240 km. in width and 60–100 m. in depth. It was originally formed by sedimentation in a Tertiary subsidence, which extended into the present Murray basin. Later uplift re-united it with the mainland, but final separation followed sea-level changes after the Ice Age. The Kent and Furneaux Islands and King Island are vestigial links between the older structures of the E Highlands and Tas. Highlands. The existence of a strait was confirmed by Flinders* and Bass* in 1798. The islands were occupied by the lawless 'Straitsmen' in the 19th century, many of them escaped convicts who lived from sealing. Today it is the scene of petroleum* and natural gas* exploration and development on the Gippsland Shelf, with further potential in Bass and Otway Basins. Natural gas is piped from Barracouta field (24 km. offshore) and Marlin field (48 km offshore). Oil in commercial quantities has been proved in Marlin field, and also some 80 km. offshore in the Halibut, Kingfish and Barracouta fields. In 1972 these 3 were producing 281,000 barrels per day.

Batchelor N.T. 13S/131E Mining town largely developed sine 1950 to house workers at the Rum Jungle* mines 6 km. to the N, although the original settlement (named after a S.A. Minister of Agriculture) was an important 1939–45 War air base.

Bates, Daisy (*née* **O'Dwyer Hunt**) (1861–1951) b. Tipperary, Ireland. First arrived in Aus. in 1884 for health reasons, marrying John Bates, and returning to Eng. 1894–9 when she was commissioned by *The Times* to investigate reports of cruelty to Aborigines in W.A. This was the beginning of her life's work with the Aborigines, with whom she lived almost all the time from 1912–46 notably near Ooldea S.A., becoming wholly accepted as 'Kabbarli' (grandmother). Her accumulated knowledge went into *The Passing of the Aborigines* (Adelaide, 1938, republished London, 1967). The title indicates her belief that they were dying out, which conditioned her views that neither proselytising nor white education were in their interest, and that the development of half-caste communities was to be avoided. The ignoring of the Aboriginal problem until recently has been attributed partly to her advocacy of this view. Much knowledge of tribal customs is due to her. *See* E. Salter: *Daisy Bates* (Sydney, 1971).

Bathurst N.S.W. 33S/150E (17,169 in 1971) One of the leading inland centres of N.S.W. in wheat and sheep country towards the W of the Central Tablelands, a regional educational and service centre, processing farming products (flour, vegetables and fruit canning and footwear), and with other small manufactures (light engineering and cement pipes). It was named after Henry Bathurst (1762–1834), Secretary of State for the Colonies (1812–27) soon after the first crossing of the Blue Mts. in 1813, and celebrated its 150th anniversary in 1965. The original site selected by Oxley* was changed in the 1830s and the town laid out along the present attractive lines of streets and gardens, with public buildings of impressive range and character, from rather heavy but not unpleasant 19th-century buildings, e.g. the post office, through the normal verandahs of inns and older shops to modern shopfronts and a fine modern Civic Centre building. Like many towns of the area, it was greatly stimulated by the gold-rush of the 1850s. In 1972, the Bathurst–Blayney–Orange region was designated as a growth region by N.S.W.

Bathurst Island N.T. 12S/130E A densely wooded, mangrove-fringed island of over 2,590 km.[2], W of Melville Island and separated by the narrow 80 km. by 1·6 km. Apsley Str. discovered by King* in 1819. A Roman Catholic Mission on the SE coast cares for Tiwi Aborigines for whom the island is a reserve. In 1967 a marooned French couple almost perished within 65 km. of the station lost and hemmed in by mangroves. Cypress pine is extracted and milled.

Bathurst, Lake N.S.W. About 13 km.[2] and up to 3 m. deep when full, and about 32 km. S of Goulburn, 35S/150E. It is less intermittent than L. George* a few miles to the W and its origin is different: a right bank tributary of the S–N Mulwaree Creek (an affluent of the Wollondilly*), has been dammed back by a gravel ridge deposited by the Mulwaree during a wetter climate than the present, possibly during or soon after the Quaternary glaciation.

Batman, John (1801–1839) Co-founder of Melbourne. b. Parramatta, son of a convict. Batman settled near Launceston in 1821. In 1830 he was granted further land in recognition of his capture of bushranger Brady and of his conciliation attempts with Aborigines. He unsuccessfully applied to Governor Darling to settle at Westernport, then formed the Port Phillip Association*. In June 1835 he landed and made a 'treaty' with the Dutigalla tribe of Aborigines, acquiring some 243,000 ha. in return for blankets, knives, mirrors, scissors, flour etc., alleging that the chiefs fully understood what they were doing. While he was back in Tas. Fawkner* landed and settled on the spot Batman had selected, which became the nucleus of Melbourne.

Claims for recognition of tenure were rejected and Batman had eventually to buy his land.

Bats Of the Order Chiroptera (hand-winged, for the wing-membrane is essentially stretched between long narrow fingers), these mammals are placed next to man and the other primates in respect of their highly organised auditory and nervous system. Their power of flight, quite as good as that of birds, has enabled them to be well represented in the native fauna of Aus., whereas terrestrial placental mammals were limited to the rodents until the advent of man and probably with him the ancestors of the dingo. Aus. bats include several of the larger, mainly fruit-eating Sub-Order Megachiroptera such as the Giant Fruit Bat or Flying Fox*, genus *Pteropus*, e.g. the Grey-headed Fruit Bat, *P. poliocephalus*, of much of coastal E Aus., and several other genera and species. Some of these live largely on eucalyptus blossoms but others cause damage to soft-fruit orchards. The nails are all long and hooked, to fasten round branches when the animal is at rest, upside-down with wings folded, especially by day, for feeding is crepuscular and nocturnal. Dentition is adapted to bulky vegetarian diet.

Insect-eating or Little Bats, Sub-Order Microchiroptera, are also represented in Aus. by several genera and many species. These are much smaller, swift-flying, nocturnal, and have the echo-sounding or almost radar-like mechanism to prevent collisions in flight; they also have a single lengthened claw by which they roost by day, again upside-down, and dentition adapted to grinding an insect diet (and in the False Vampire-bat to cannibalism, but there are no blood-sucking and potentially rabies-spreading bats in Aus.). Widespread genera and species include: Eastern Horseshoe Bat, *Rhinolophus megaphyllus*, with a horseshoe-shaped nose-leaf or membrane; Greater

Long-eared Bat, *Nyctophilus timoriensis*; the Little Brown (short-eared) Bat, *Vespadelus pumilus*; various Wattled bats, genus *Chalinolobus*, with fleshy lobes at the mouth-corners reminiscent of a turkey's wattles; the Large-footed Myotis, *Myotis macropus*, and Small-footed Myotis, *M. australis*, with very plain nose and muzzle; Broad-nosed bats, genus *Scoteanax*; the Bent-winged bats, genus *Miniopterus*, with long and very sharply jointed outer wing-digit and long tail embodied in the wing membrane; the Golden-tipped Bat, *Phoniscus papuensis*, of N.G. and Cape York; the Free-tailed (i.e. tail not in wing-membrane) or Sharp-nosed bats, genus *Saccolaimus* (referring to the pouch-like neck fold in males of most species), of Malaysia, N.G. and Aus.; and the Wrinkle-lipped or Mastiff bats, e.g. the White-striped Mastiff Bat, *Austronomus australis*. *For further reading see* F. Ratcliffe: *Flying Fox and Drifting Sand* (Sydney, 1963).

Baudin, Thomas Nicolas (1754-1803) Sailor, explorer, cartographer and naturalist in charge of a French scientific voyage to complete the charting of New Holland (1800). He commanded *le Géographe*, and Hamelin, a more capable if less charming commander, *le Naturaliste*. Peron and de Freycinet were also officers, and their record is the only one published. The voyage was hampered by illness, Baudin himself dying on the way home. After some charting of the W coast of Aus., then Tas., in April 1802, he met Flinders* making eastwards on his historic circumnavigation. Governor King* was suspicious of French intentions to annex Tas., but these seem to have been unfounded.

Bauxite Hydrous oxide of alumina and iron, the source of aluminium* (from Les Baux, France). Aus. has possibly the largest reserves in the world, only beginning to be fully developed. Weipa*, Qld. (1963), has probable reserves over 2,000 million tonnes; being developed by Comalco for export to Japan and to supply Gladstone refinery. Gove* N.T. has reserves over 250 million tonnes being developed for export by Nabalco. Reserves of 200 million tonnes have been proved on the Mitchell Plateau in the Kimberleys*. New developments include a proposed mine at Aurukun 72 km. S of Weipa and in the Hotham River region in the Darling Ranges* W.A.; here ore will be railed to Bunbury. Bauxite from Jarrahdale W.A. goes to Kwinana*. Only the Darling Ranges bauxites are in temperate latitudes.

Baylebridge, William (Charles William Blocksidge) (1883-1942) b. Brisbane. A poet, mainly writing philosophical and love poems, the best contained in *Selected Poems* (Sydney, 1919) and *Love Redeemed* (Sydney, 1934). Also a successful businessman, he published privately. There were fascist overtones in his philosophy.

Bayley's Reward The first quartz gold mine in the Coolgardie district, W.A., in 1892. Arthur Bayley (1866-1894) was a Qld. prospector, who with William Ford, followed up indications from a former companion, Macpherson, NE of Southern Cross*. They found alluvial gold at Fly Flat, then the rich quartz reef which gained him the government reward for the first payable gold in the region. Controversy still continues over the actual discovery since 3 young lads, Talbot, Baker and Fosser who followed them on their second journey, claimed that Bayley and Ford ordered them off a find they had made but were unable to peg legally, having no licences.

Baynton, Barbara (*née* **Kilpatrick**) (1862-1929) b. Scone, N.S.W., 6th child of immigrant settlers. After her second marriage (to Thomas Baynton) she wrote *Bush Studies* (London, 1902, republished 1966), which were grim even horrific and morbid tales. After her third marriage to an English Lord had failed, she returned to Aus. to become a notable Melbourne character.

Beaconsfield Tas. 41S/147E (950 in 1971; 1,028 in 1966) Near the W bank of the Tamar, was the site of the main Tas. gold-fields, operating 1877–1919 with a total extraction of 2,380 kg. from the Tasmanian Mine. There was also an early iron industry. It is now primarily a service centre in rich dairy and orchard country.

Beagle, **H.M.S.** Ship active in survey in S American waters under Fitzroy (1831–5). Her Pacific voyage (1835–6) was made famous by the scientist Darwin's writings. After surveying Cocos Keeling Islands (1836), sailing to England and returning (1837), *Beagle* carried survey parties, under commanders Wickham* and Stokes*, which filled in many details of the coastal waters of NW Aus. (1838–41) and Bass Str. (1842–3).

Bean, Charles Edwin Woodrow (1879–1968) b. Bathurst, N.S.W. Outback assignments as a journalist gave him material for his documentary *On the Wool Track* (Sydney, 1910) and a lesser volume *The Dreadnought of the Darling* (London, 1911). As war correspondent with the A.I.F., he gathered at first hand, material for the *Official History of Australia in the War, 1914–18* (Sydney, 1921–42), of which he wrote 6 of the 12 volumes and edited the others. He uncovered the true versions of several important actions, notably the Gallipoli* landings; a shorter history is *Anzac to Amiens* (Canberra, 1946).

Beaurepaire, Sir Frank (1891–1956) b. Melbourne. He was the first great international Aus. swimmer to sustain success over a period, appearing in the Olympic Games in 1908, 1920 and 1924. He used an individual stroke transitional between the old trudgen and the new crawl*, and at different times broke 14 world records. As Lord Mayor of Melbourne, he was influential

in bringing the 1956 Games to his city, but died just before they took place.

Becke, George Lewis (Louis) (1855–1913) b. Port Macquarie, N.S.W. A short story writer of the 1890s, mainly about the Pacific islands, where he was a trader, and on historical topics. *For further reading see* A. Grove Day: *Louis Becke* (Melbourne, 1967).

Beeby, Sir George Stephenson (1869–1942) b. Sydney, N.S.W. A judge and politician, first Labor then Progressive, serving under Holman*. He was also a playwright, using mainly social themes, with clever wit and dialogue as in *Concerning Ordinary People* (Sydney, 1923).

Beech In the world-wide Beech family, Fagaceae, Aus. has 3 species in the S temperate genus *Nothofagus* (counterparts of the N hemisphere genus *Fagus*); the name is used less accurately for the White Beech, *Gmelina leichhardtii*, in the tropical family Verbenaceae, and to several other trees of different families. The evergreen 30-m. Myrtle Beech, *Nothofagus cunninghami*, grows in mountain basins and gullies in Tas.; the 30-m. Antarctic Beech or Negro-head Beech, *N. moorei*, on the scarp-edge rain-forests of New England. Tas. has the deciduous bush *N. gunnii*. N.G. has 16 species. The leaves have a graceful broad spear shape, with finely serrated edge. The green male and female flowers and ovoid seed capsule with four sharp-edged boatlike seeds, are reminiscent of the northern beech, but the Antarctic Beech appears to reproduce vegetatively. *N. moorei* and *N. cunninghami* both yield commercial timber.

The White Beech (*see above*) is a 40-m. scrub and rain-forest tree of coastal NE Aus., with 13-cm. oval leaves, prominently veined and hairy below, small white and purple bell-shaped flowers in branched spikes at the end of branches, and a 4-celled, 4-seed blue fleshy fruit. The pale grey bark perhaps caused the popular name, and the timber is useful though now rare.

Beef Cattle Of the total of 18 million, 40% are bred on vast unfenced runs, grazing the natural Mitchell grass, mulga etc. in the 50–70-cm. summer rainfall regions of inland tropical Aus. The main areas are: Barkly Tableland*, notable stations being Alexandria, over 28,000 km.², Brunette, Avon and Alroy Downs and several others all with many thousands of head. In the NW, Kimberley* District, W.A., has Glenroy, Mount House, Fossil Downs on the Margaret River and Argyle, the famous Durack* station. The Ord and Victoria river basins are important. Aboriginal stockmen provide most of the labour. Cattle are driven on foot (increasingly by 'road trains'*) to railheads or directly, either for prior fattening at the coast or immediate slaughter at Brisbane, Rockhampton, Townsville (Qld.), and Wyndham and Derby, W.A. Some go S to the fattening pastures of the Channel Country* of SW Qld., thence to S.A. and N.S.W. Shorthorns are still the main breed, but the Zebu-Shorthorn and the American Santa Gertrudis (Brahmin-Shorthorn) crosses, as well as British Red Polls are important. Much tropical Aus. beef (which is of poor quality) is exported, largely to U.S. and Japan under trade agreements; with U.S., trade concentrates on boned beef for the beefburger market. Most is hard frozen, but a small proportion is chilled. The problem of Northern Development* is closely related to beef: difficulties are mainly of distance (see AIR BEEF and BEEF ROADS SCHEME), uncontrolled breeding, pests, especially the tick which is prevented from extending S by inspection at 'tick gates', high capital investment, risks specially of drought and uncertain leasehold conditions in Qld. Foreign capital and syndicates are both features with especially rapid American development in Cape York, Qld. and N.T. In the S beef cattle are bred mainly in areas too rugged or wet for sheep, e.g. the upper Hunter* or the Alpine snow leases, and sold for fattening on lowland farms in the wheat/sheep belt, the Western District* of Vic. or the recently developed Coonalpyn Downs* in S.A. Vic. is the main exporting state. The Meat Board (1964) controls external marketing and undertakes promotion. Aus. was the world's major beef exporter in 1972.

Beef Roads Scheme (1961) A shared Commonwealth-States Scheme to finance road construction of 4,000 km. and improvement of existing roads in W.A., Qld. and N.T. to carry 'road trains'* of linked trucks and thus ensure that cattle arrive at the railhead, fattening country or slaughter yards in better condition than by droving, and that drought losses are lessened by rapid removal of stock. The roads may incidentally assist the tourist traffic. A Commonwealth undertaking (1967) guaranteed Qld. and W.A. each $49 million over 7 years for development in Cape York, Gulf Country, Burdekin, Fitzroy, Pioneer Valleys in Qld. and the Kimberleys in W.A.

Beer Consumed at a rate of some 126 l. per head per year (Czechoslovakia 130; Germany 126; Belgium 117; N.Z. 107) with a peak in the hot dry summer months and increasing annually. Brewing is concentrated in the hands of 24 companies, dominated by a few giants, e.g. Carlton & United and (1968) Courage in Vic. or Tooth's and Toohey's in N.S.W. Hotels are mainly 'tied' to breweries. Malting barley* is sufficient for needs, but about 25% of the hops are imported, only being grown in Tas., a few in Vic. and at the foot of the Darling Scarp in W.A. Costs are high for such a staple drink, transport being a factor. Brewing was established early in the colony, encouraged by successive Governors in the hope of abating the excessive spirit demand.

Bees Nectar and pollen-gathering insects of the waisted Sub-Order Apocrita of the insect* Order Hymenoptera*. Among the bees are some social species with queens, drones and workers, and some species in which the females have the ovipositor specialised as a sting, carrying acid venom; in vegetarian insects, this is to paralyse enemies rather than prey. The sting is unpleasant to man, but rarely dangerous. The distinctive form and social organisation of the introduced Hive Bee, *Apis mellifera*, possibly a race of the rather formidable Indian Wild Bee, *Apis indica*, are sufficiently well known. The native Hive Bee, *Trigona carbonaria*, is easily recognised as an Aus. analogue. It is a small, stingless, thickset black bee with hairy legs, whose thin honey, varying in flavour with the bush flowers, was an important Aboriginal food. It often nests in treeholes, but so does the introduced honey-bee when swarms have gone wild and which of course does sting. The variety in native bees is such, many being flattened forms like wasps, that it seems best to regard them as differentiated largely by habit; wasps, as it were, specialised for a vegetarian and not a dominantly carnivorous diet; often with hairy legs for pollen gathering; sometimes hairy bodies; long tongue for sipping nectar, which is partly regurgitated after enzymic alteration to honey in some species; and usually feeding their larvae on honey or pollen (bee bread, sometimes a pollen and honey mixture). Many species are solitary, with a small burrow in earth or wood or a wasp-like mud or leaf case as a nest. Other native species representing different families include the Yellow-spotted Bee, genus *Prosopis*, the Golden-banded Burrowing Bee, *Nomia aurantifer*, the Silver-banded Leaf-cutting Bee, *Megachile chrysopyga*, the large humming bee of the warmer regions, genus *Xylocopa*, similar in appearance and comportment to the bumble-bee of Europe, and the related Carpenter Bee, *Lestis aerata*.

Bee farming is carried on by migratory apiarists following the biennial flowering of eucalypts in Vic., N.S.W. and Qld. The honey is collected from hives of *Apis mellifera*. There is a large export of honey, over 10 million kg.

Beetles These comprise the largest Order of insects*, the Coleoptera, and are the dominant insects of Aus. which has 20,000 of the world's several hundred thousand different beetles among its 50,000 insect species. Beetles generally have two pairs of wings, the front pair having developed as an opaque, sometimes ridged and ornamented, veinless wing-case, the rear pair remaining gauzy and veined and usually capable of effective flight. The jaws are predominantly of the biting and chewing type; some species are carnivorous, some vegetarian. They vary tremendously in size, shape, colour and habitat, with, for instance, some aquatic species. Larvae include both burrowing and surface feeders, both legless maggot-like and legged caterpillar-like forms. The pupa stage is often spent in a cocoon in an enclosed chamber in a tree or in the ground, and this is one way in which

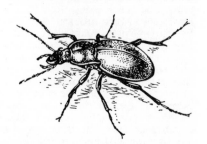

Carab Beetle, about 2 cm. long

over-wintering is accomplished in the colder climates. Some common Aus. families are: 1. Carab or Ground Beetles, Carabidae, which include a wide variety of common predatory beetles living under stones, logs etc., many emitting an unpleasant odour if threatened; 2. the shiny black or brown Passalidae, tunnelling in rotten logs; 3. the Darkling Beetles, Tenebrionidae, such as the ground beetle genus, *Cardiothorax*, but including the Rust-red Flour Beetle, *Tribolium castaneum*; 4. the Tiger Beetles, Cicindelidae, e.g. the handsome Velvet Green, *Cicindela* spp., of open sites such as riverside sand and mud banks, studied by a N.S.W. pastoralist, T. G. Sloane (1858–1932); 5. aquatic families which include the predatory Water Beetles, Dytiscidae; 6. the small Fruit Beetles, Nitidulidae, including the Kurrajong Fruit Beetle, *Circopes pilistriatus*, flat, hairy and reddish, with short clubbed antennae; 7. beetles boring in timber, including the Auger Beetles, Bostry-chidae, of which the largest and best-known is *Bostrychis jesuitica* (looks headless because the thorax conceals the head from above); Longicorn Beetles, Cerambycidae, which also lay eggs in cracks in bark or wood and the larvae tunnel in growing or dead timber and do much damage; and introduced pests including the Powder Post Beetle, *Lyctus brunneus*, and the Death Watch Beetle, *Anobium puncta-tum*; 8. the 75 species of Stag Beetles*, Lucanidae; 9. Scarabs or Cockchafers, Scarabaeidae (whose larvae, known as 'curl-grubs', in the roots of vegetation are sometimes a pest of pastures), which include the Christmas Beetle*; 10. the 1,000 species of colourful Jewel Beetles, Buprestidae, of various sizes including the genus *Stig-modera*, in brown, gold, yellow and blue; 11. the acrobatic, slim brown Click Bettles, Elateridae; 12. the Feather-horn Beetles, e.g. the white-spotted *Rhipidocera* spp. 13. the Lam-pyridae, Fireflies* and Soldier Beetles*; 14. the Cleridae, e.g. the black Yellow-horned Clerid, *Trogodendron fascicu-latum*, often seen rooting eagerly about a log for wood-boring larvae to eat; 15. the Rove Beetles, Staphylinidae, which look rather like earwigs without pincers (e.g. genus *Actinus*); adults and larvae are mainly scavengers, in-cluding some tolerated or kept in ants' nests; 16. Ladybirds*, Coccinellidae; 17. the Dermestidae, a family of hair and feather eaters, including the oval Black Carpet Beetle, *Attagenus piccus;* 18. the Leaf Beetles*, Chrysomelidae; 19. the Weevils*, Curculionidae.

Bega N.S.W. 37S/150E (4,146 in 1971) Despite its modest size, this is clearly a local, even regional centre for the S part of the dairying S Coast region, with a large milk-processing factory—supply-ing much fresh milk to Canberra by the steep road up Brown Mountain—and other agricultural market and service functions, e.g. for potatoes, agri-cultural machinery etc. It also has sawmilling, and furniture-making, brick, tile and fibrous plaster manu-facture etc. It is on the short Bega River 16 km. from the sea and the small fishing and holiday port of Tathra.

Bell, Archibald (1804–1883) b. Rich-mond, N.S.W. Son of a noted officer who was first magistrate of the district. His alternative Blue Mountain crossing (1823) N of the Grose Valley, 'Bell's Line of Road', had an easier western descent than Cox's road. It was not completely constructed and remained a stock route, but is now followed by a modern highway, begun for strategic purposes during the 1939–45 War and metalled later to relieve the pressure on the Western Highway from Sydney to Bathurst.

Bell Bay Tas. 41S/147E On the right bank of the Tamar, S of Georgetown, a modern mechanised port and the site of an aluminium smelter (1955 expanding to 74,460 tonnes capacity) using Qld. ore. Hydro-electric power from Treval-lyn is supplemented by oil. There is a new wood-chip plant.

Bell, George Henry Frederick (1878–1966) b. Vic. A rigorous and influential art teacher in Melbourne who led the newly formed Contemporary Art

Society of 1938 in a reaction against what they felt was the dead hand of established Aus. art at that time.

Bellbird (or **Bell-miner**) A smallish (18–20 cm. long) bird of the family of Honey-eaters*.

Bellbird A suburb of Cessnock* and fictional town in TV serial.

Bellenden Ker Range Qld. 17S/146E A granite massif, probably thrust upwards along fault lines. Its precipitous E face above the Mulgrave River and S face from the Innisfail plains rise to 1,525 m. through dense rain-forest to upland scrub, moss, lichen and orchids on the tumbled tors of the summits.

Ben Lomond Tas. 42S/148E A flat-topped mountain capped with dolerite; the top stretches 11 km. between Legges Tor (1,574 m.) at the NW edge, and Stack's Bluff (1,528 m.) on the SE. It lies in a National Park noted for winter sports. Tin and wolfram are mined on the SE slopes.

Benalla Vic. 37S/146E (8,235 in 1971) A market centre on the Broken River, a right-bank tributary of the Goulburn, with industry including railway workshops and a chain factory. It developed on an overlanding stock route after Mitchell's exploration in 1836 and was the scene of a savage attack by Aborigines, followed by an equally brutal reprisal in 1838.

Benaud, Richard (1930–) b. Penrith, N.S.W. A cricketer, notably a leg-spin bowler of great skill, who played in Tests since 1952. He is also a journalist.

Bendigo Vic. 37S/144E (45,860 in 1971) A former gold-mining boom town once known as Sandhurst, now an important local service centre in the Central Uplands, with considerable industry: armaments and other engineering products, a group processing varied foods (poultry and egg-pulp, meat, flour and bakeries, canning etc.), brickworks, woollen and clothing factories, eucalyptus oil and hardboard manufacture. The easily accessible alluvial gold, producing £1 million per month in the early 1850s, was soon exhausted, but deeper company mining continued until excessive water and high costs enforced the last closures in the 1950s; poppet-heads are still to be seen. As with Ballarat, gold rapidly produced an impressive city with tree-lined streets, and unlike, e.g. Coolgardie*, in harsher terrain, it has been able to adapt and remain prosperous beyond the gold era.

Bennelong (1764–1813) One of two Aborigines captured, befriended and trained by Phillip* who took them to London (1792). Bennelong returned with Hunter* (1795), living at the Governor's house, almost as an exhibit, but he returned often to the bush where he was rejected by his own people. Drink and degradation made him the first of many tragic failures to reconcile Aboriginal with European culture. **Bennelong Point** on S side of Port Jackson was where he lived in Phillip's time in a 4-m. square brick house later the site of Greenway's* Fort Macquarie and now of the Sydney Opera House*.

Bent, Andrew (1790–1851) A printer and journalist. He was convicted of burglary and transported to Tas. (1812). He published the official *Hobart Town Gazette and Southern Reporter* (1816–25) and later independent papers. Criticism of government led to his prosecution and persecution by Governor Arthur* but he is considered a major pioneer of a free press in Aus. He died in poverty in Sydney.

Bent, Ellis (1783–1815) b. Surrey, Eng. He arrived in Aus. in 1809 with Macquarie*, as Deputy Judge Advocate. He had accepted the position only because of family misfortunes. Disagreements developed over Bent's very commendable views on law reform and Macquarie's emancipist policy. He died while a letter recalling him was on its way. **Jeffrey Hart** (1781–1852) his brother, was in N.S.W. from 1814–17 as Judge of the newly created Supreme Court, and was even more vigorously opposed to Macquarie, especially over rights to practise of emancipist lawyers like George Crossley. For refusal to open the Supreme Court without English solicitors he was dismissed in 1817. *For further reading see* C. H. Currey: *The Brothers Bent* (Sydney, 1968).

Berri S.A. 34S/141E (2,712 in 1971) Irrigation centre on the right bank of the River Murray, dating from 1911. Of about 3,240 ha. irrigated, half are grapes; some of the wine is distilled locally for brandy. Fruits and juices are canned in the town.

Berry, Alexander (1781–1873) b. Fife, Scotland. He came to Aus. first in 1808 as a trader, and from 1822 developed land at the mouth of the Shoalhaven River, cutting a canal to give access which became the river mouth, growing crops and extracting cedar. He went into partnership with Wollstonecroft and they supplied their Sydney store with produce from the area. A small town bears his name.

Berry, Sir Graham (1822–1904) b. London. Vic. Premier 3 times between 1875–81. He arrived in Aus. in 1852 to become a merchant, newspaper owner then politician. He shared the views of David Syme* notably on curbing the powers of the Legislative Council. He succeeded in this by brilliant if dubious tactics (*see* BLACK WEDNESDAY). A constructive if extravagant coalition government (1883–6) with Service opened up the Mallee* and encouraged irrigation in the Riverina*.

B.H.P. (The Broken Hill Proprietary Co. Ltd.) A group of companies, based in Melbourne with some 21 subsidiaries, which dominates the private sector of Aus. industry. It has a near-monopoly of iron and steel production with integrated plants at Newcastle and Port Kembla in N.S.W., blast furnaces, electric steel-making and ship-yards at Whyalla in S.A., blast furnace etc. in Kwinana, W.A. It mines coal in N.S.W. and Qld., has iron interests at Iron Knob, S.A., and at Yampi Sound, Mt. Newman, Deepdale and Koolyanobbing, W.A., limestone at Marulan, N.S.W., Coffin Bay and Rapid Bay, S.A., and dolomite at Ardrossan, S.A., nickel leases near Rockhampton, Qld., manganese on Groote Eylandt, magnesite at Fifield, N.S.W., cement-making at Berrima, N.S.W., 8 water-side bulk-loading installations and a cargo fleet. There are wire product plants in Geelong, Hobart, Darwin, Sydney, Lae, and Malaysia, ferro-alloys at Bell Bay, Tas. Major associated groups extend its interests to tube-making, chemicals, fertiliser and mineral exploration, also association with Esso in Bass Str. oil and gas developments. B.H.P., with a mixed record of labour relations, employs some 55,000 people, a third of whom are migrants; 75% of the shareholders are Aus. It is a public, not a private company, the term 'Proprietary' being historical. B.H.P. was founded (1885) by C. Rasp and others to mine lead and silver at Broken Hill, N.S.W., then to smelt it at Port Pirie, S.A.; its peak profit there was £1·25 million in 1892. A lease of ironstone deposits for flux, only later found to be valuable for iron-smelting, and building of a rail and wharf at False Bay (named Whyalla*) was followed by evident decline in the mine and in prices. Under vigorous leadership by Darling (Chairman 1907–14), Delprat (Manager 1899–1921) and Baker an American adviser, B.H.P. reclaimed swamps at Newcastle and produced steel from 1915. It developed under Lewis (Manager 1921–40) to take over Aus. Iron and Steel (1935) and 5 other subsidiaries by 1939, when it finally left Broken Hill*. (*See also* IRON AND STEEL.)

Big and Little Deserts Vic. 35S/141E Mallee* regions respectively N and S of the Melbourne/Adelaide Highway merging into Coonalpyn Downs* of S.A. Formerly unproductive, it is now called Telopea Downs*.

Bigge, John Thomas (1780–1843) b. Northumberland, Eng. He was appointed (1819) Commissioner to enquire into the state of N.S.W., including an assessment of the effectiveness of transportation*, the conduct of officials, judicial systems, religion, education, revenue and trade. Bigge spent 17 months gathering evidence and travelling widely. He was soon at odds with Macquarie*, differing fundamentally though honestly with his views on emancipists*, the employment of convicts and industrial development. Bigge accepted Macarthur's* proposals for a large-scale pastoral economy using convict labour, while Macquarie envisaged more agricultural development. His reports had a profound influence on colonial policy in London.

Billabong A section of a river or creek, usually, although not originally applied to a cut-off meander, or anabranch. It was first recorded by T. L. Mitchell as 'Billabang' the local Aboriginal name for the Bell River in N.S.W.

Billiards Both amateur and professional, as well as snooker, have developed considerable popularity since their introduction in the second half of the 19th century, and have produced world champions, notably Walter Lindrum* in professional billiards, his nephew Horace Lindrum in snooker, and R. Marshall, amateur world record holder in billiards 4 times. There are State and national organisations and championships.

Billy (or **Billy Can**) A tin cooking utensil (originally improvised) with a wire handle, used for cooking in the open. The derivation is controversial: a Scots dialect word; the French

bouilli (beef, canned); Aboriginal *billa* (meaning water); or simply a man's name.

Bimberi, Mount (1,914 m.) The highest mountain in the A.C.T. on its W boundary and towards the S, in the forested ridge, largely accessible by a rough but fairly motorable road from the N, between the S–N valleys of the Cotter and the Goodradigbee. It is often snow-clad beneath the eucalyptus trees in winter, and gives skiing and sledging in severe winters.

Bindi-eye (*Calotis cuneifolia*) Common flower of the Compositae or daisy* family on the dry plains of Central and E Aus. One of the best known of an entirely Aus. genus, it grows in 30-cm. clumps, with notched wedge-shaped leaves, and a daisy-like flower, white, blue or lavender outside, yellow in the middle, succeeded by quite a prickly burr. In N Aus. the name is applied to various species of *Bassia* saltbush* also with long spiked burrs. A corruption of an Aboriginal name.

Bird-flower A popular name given to two somewhat laburnum-like N Aus. members of the Papilionaceae or pea family, from the very bird-like shape of the flower. Species are *Crotolaria laburnifolia* and *C. cunninghamii*. Also called Stuart's Pea or Parrot Flower.

BIRDS (of Aus.) These total about 650–700 species—almost the same, on present classifications, as those of N.G. Birds are not dependent on a land bridge as are most mammals, except the few flightless species, and as one would expect, there is a good deal of overlap between Aus. and N.G. species, and between both of these and the islands to the N and with S and SE Asia. This is even more pronounced with migratory land birds; while some sea-birds have very large ocean territories, some are seasonally migratory between the sub-Antarctic and the S of Aus., others between temperate and tropical latitudes, and a few migrate between the N and S hemisphere to have summer in each, e.g. the Arctic skua and the well-known mutton-bird. Even so, with over 400 species of birds endemic in Aus., there is a distinctively Aus. bird population, and some workers believe that despite repeated and presumably continuing waves of later-evolved birds, the Aus. birds largely represent an early separated and independently evolving group.

The uniquely Aus. birds include the emu and cassowary, the lyrebird and bower-bird, the Aus. magpies and butcher-birds, the frogmouths and mudlarks, the fly-catchers and Aus. chats, the scrub-birds, *Atrichornus* spp., and the fairy wrens, and along with N.G. the birds of paradise and their relatives, the rifle birds. There are also Aus. species of parrots, geese, finches, kingfishers (notably the kookaburra) and honey-eaters. Indeed, the dominant share of honey-eaters and the considerable share of the world's parrots and the weaver finches make a considerable contribution to the country's distinctiveness in bird life.

There are many black-and-white birds, many mimics, many song-birds —some with conventionally sweet songs, the most esteemed having a distinctive and non-saccharine flavour, such as the magpie's astringent roundel which means so much to most native-born Australians and not a few in-comers.

In thick bush many of the birds are not easy to observe, and song and call are difficult to link with their owners; but some representatives of the most distinctive genera will come to many a suburban garden, if there are not too many cats. Even there one may gain some flavour of the distinctive individual species. Perhaps more important, one may obtain some idea of the distinctive grouping in a largely eucalyptus-dominated woodland environment, along with an important and distinctive reptile and marsupial

population and limited placental fauna. As far as birds are concerned, this first acquaintance will surely include the magpies, the honey-eaters, the Willy Wagtail and perhaps Jacky Winter and robin, and in most parts of Aus. some at least of the parrots and perhaps also some of the introduced birds discussed in the next article.

Families missing from Aus. include the woodpeckers, vultures, titmice, gros-beaks and buntings, humming-birds, flamingoes and true pheasants.

Common or distinctive birds of Aus. include: Apostle Bird*; Red-necked Avocet*; Axe-bird or large-tailed Nightjar, *Caprimulgus macrurus*, of N Qld. and N.G. (and S and SE Asia); Babblers*; Bee-eater, *Merops ornatus*, a summer migrant from the tropics to the S of Aus.; Bellbird or Bell-miner, (*see* HONEY-EATERS); Bitterns*; Bower-birds*; Bristle-birds*; Brolga*; Budgerigar (*see* PARRAKEETS); Bustard*; Butcher-birds (*see* MAGPIES); Cassowary*; Catbird*; the robin-like Cave-bird, *Origmella solitaria*, of the Sydney area; Chats*; White-winged Chough*; Cockatiel*; Cockatoos* and other large Parrots; Cormorants*; Crane (*see* BROLGA); Crows*; Cuckoos*; Currawongs (*see* MAG-PIES); Diamond-birds (*see* PARDA-LOTES *below*); Doves (*see* PIGEONS); Ducks*; Eagles*; Emu*; Falcons (*see* HAWKS); Fantails, *Rhipidura* spp., widespread insect-catchers building cup-like nests in tree-forks; the oriole-like Fig-bird, *Sphecotheres* spp.; Finches*; Flycatchers*; Friar-birds (*see* HONEY-EATERS); Frogmouth*; Galah, Gang-Gang (*see* COCKATOOS); Geese*; Gibber-bird (*see* CHATS); Greenie*; Gulls (*see* SEA-BIRDS); Hawks*; Honey-eaters*; Jabiru*; Jacky Winter*; Kingfishers*; Kook-aburra* or Laughing Jackass; Lori-keets* or Honey-parrots; Lowan* or Mallee-fowl; Lyrebirds*; Magpie-Lark (*see* MUDLARK); Magpies*; Martins (*see Swallow*); Miner-birds (*see* HONEY-EATERS); Mistletoe-bird, *Dicaeum hir-*

undinaceum, common in suburban gardens and catching insects as well as eating mistletoe berries; Mocking-birds*, mimics of several species; Mousebird (*see* SCRUB-BIRD); Mudlark*; Mutton-bird*; Nightjar (*see* AXE-BIRD *above*); the handsome tropical Orioles, the Green, *Oriolus sagittatus,* and the Yellow, *O. flavocinctus;* Owls*, Pardalotes or Diamond-birds, *Pardalotus* spp., often with black-and-white, diamond-shaped markings but flashes of bright colours in different species, insectivores of outer tree foliage, with cup-shaped nests in tree-forks; Parrakeets or Grass Parrakeets*; Parrots*; Pelican*; Peewee (*see* MUDLARK); Penguins*; Petrels (*see* SEA-BIRDS); the short-tailed bright-coloured genus *Pitta,* of N and E Aus.; Pigeons*; the ground-dwelling sweet-songed Pilotbird, *Pycnoptilus floccosus* (downy, thick-feathered), found only from about Sydney to about Melbourne; Plovers including the migrant *Pluvialis dominica* and the resident genera *Zonifer* and *Lobibyx;* Quails of genera *Coturnix, Synoicus* and *Turnix* (the widespread Quail-thrush is *Cinclosoma* spp.); Rainbow-bird (*see* BEE-EATER *above*); Raven (*see* CROWS); the small Redthroat of the dry inland, *Pyrrholaemus brunneus;* the only Aus. Reedwarbler, and inter-state migrant, is *Acrocephalus australis;* Rifle-birds,

Little Quail (Turnix velox),
about 7 cm. long

Ptiloris spp., 30-cm. rain-forest birds of Qld., with showy plumage like a rifleman; Robins*; Rosellas*; Scrubbirds*; Sea-birds*; Shag (*see* CORMORANT); Shearwaters (*see* SEA-BIRDS); Shrike-thrush, *Colluricincla* spp., 23 cm. modestly coloured bush bird with a clear whistle, with a biggish cup-shaped nest in a tree-fork; the Shriketit, *Falcunculus,* spp., with striking black and white head-stripes; Silver-eyes*; Sittellas* or Tree-runners; Skuas (*see* SEA-BIRDS); Soldier-birds, Spinebills (*see* HONEY-EATERS); Stork (*see* JABIRU); Swallows*; Swan*; Swifts*; the Tailorbird, *Cisticola exilis,* with carefully stitched round nest in swamp vegetation; Terns (*see* SEA-BIRDS); Thornbills*; Thrushes*; Tree-creepers*; Waders*; the tiny leaf-haunting insectivorous Warblers, *Gerygone* spp., and even smaller Weebills, *Smicornis* spp.; Waterfowl*; Wattle-birds (*see* HONEY-EATERS); Whipbirds*; Whistlers, *Pachycephala* spp. (thick-headed), small, fairly long-tailed birds of upper tree foliage, building well-lined cuplike nests in tree-forks, mainly brown and buff with varied patches of bright colour in different species; White-eye (*see* SILVER-EYES); the small gregarious constantly foraging Whiteface, *Aphelocephala* spp.; Willy Wagtail*; Woodpeckers (*see* TREE-CREEPERS *and* SITTELLAS); Wood-swallows*; Wrens*.

Explorers (e.g. Sturt) and artists were important early observers and recorders of the rich world of Aus. bird-life. J. H. Lewins (1770–1819) wrote *Birds of N.S.W.* (1813), the first illustrated book printed in Aus. (it was printed by G. Howe*). The first great scientific worker was J. Gould* whose *Birds of Australia* was re-published in 1967 (London), followed by his former assistant J. Gilbert the explorer. Important early work was also done by T. J. Ewing (?1813–82) a Tas. clergyman, and by S. Diggles (1817–80) in Qld. who worked on an incomplete *Ornithology of Aus.* (1866–70). The monumental 13-volume *Birds* of *Australia* was the work of G. M. Matthews (1876–1949) and published in London between 1910 and 1927. G. J. Broinowski (1837–1913) was influential in his beautiful paintings of birds commissioned for use in schools; J. H. Leach (1870–1929), a Vic. school teacher, wrote and illustrated several successful works. The first Aus.-born ornithologist of stature was E. P. Ramsay (1842–1916). A standard work *Nests and Eggs of Australian Birds* (1900), was written by A. J. Campbell (1853–1929) and the major early work on W. A. birds was by H. M. Whittell (1883–1954). Societies existed from the mid-19th century. The Royal Aus. Ornithological Union was founded 1901, and the Gould League of Bird Lovers in 1909. N.H.P. Cayley and even more notably his son, N. W. Cayley (1870–1950) developed from painting to studying birds; *What Bird Is That?* (1931) has become a standard work (revised A. H. Chisholm, Sydney, 1971). *See also* A. Keast: *Bush Birds of Australia* (Melbourne, 1960); R. Hill: *Australian Birds* (Melbourne, 1967) and A. and S. Bell: *Common Aus. Birds* (London, 1971).

Birds, Introduced   At least 15 species of birds have become established in Aus. following deliberate introduction—usually ill-advised—or through escaping from cages and aviaries. These include the House-sparrow, *Passer domesticus*, and the slightly smaller and more definitely marked Tree Sparrow, *P. montanus*, cheerful enough in the suburban garden but on the whole a pest in the new environment and ruthlessly destroyed as a pest to wheat-farmers in W.A. The Starling, *Sturnus vulgaris*, about 20 cm. long, dark blue-black with some iridescence in the plumage, a walking bird constantly chattering and mimicking, is again a cheerful sight to the immigrant, but out of the European context is regarded almost universally as a vermin-harbouring pest. The not dissimilar Indian

Myna, *Acridotheres tristis*, brown with yellow cheeks and white on wing, does not seem to arouse such hostility, nor his fellow countryman the Red-whiskered Bulbul, *Pycnonotus jocosus*. The Song-thrush, *Turdus philomelos*, brown with lighter but dark-speckled breast, and the slightly larger Black-bird, *T. merula* (of which the hen is, confusingly, brown), were perhaps introduced for their songs—as were nightingales but without success. Indeed the exile may sometimes get a snatch of song which takes him to a very different spring in very different woods, but it seldom seems quite the same in depth and variety; and in places the Blackbird is a pest of orchards, etc. The introduced finches—of a different family from the indigenous weaver-finches—are on the whole successful introductions, including the Goldfinch, *Carduelis carduelis*, with brilliant markings in red, white, black, brown and bright yellow, and the more subdued green and yellowish Green-finch, *Chloris chloris*. The SE Asian Spice Finch, *Lonchura punctulata*, a dark brown, thick-billed bird with lighter but dark-speckled breast, is sometimes seen near Sydney. Two pigeons, the Senegal and Indian Turtle-doves, *Streptopelia senegalensis* and *S. chinensis*, the former smaller and purple, hazel and grey, the latter light to dark purplish-grey with black and white spotted nape, are regarded as fairly harmless introductions except for local raiding of poultry feed etc. Feral ostriches have been reported from S.A.

Birdsville   Qld.   26S/139E   A small settlement on the Diamantina River, some 32 km. N of the S.A./Qld. border, and at the head of the notorious **Birdsville Track**, a 520-km. stock route SW across Cooper Creek to Marree, motorable only in favourable conditions and with precautions, but being improved under the Beef Roads Scheme*. Intensive oil surveying has left deceptive tracks from the main one. Bores lie at 40-km. intervals, the water is hot; some give off gas.

Birdum N.T. 16S/133E A decaying settlement where the ill-fated N Aus. Railway* stops, although track foundations were continued further S. It lies 6·5 km. W of the Stuart Highway, where Larrimah is the effective terminus.

Bischoff, Mount Tas. 41S/145E (792 m.) The biggest known tin deposit in the world in the 1880s. Tin was discovered in 1871 by 'Philosopher' Smith and worked until 1945. The nearest settlement was Waratah*. Bischoff was chairman of the Van Diemen's Land Co*.

Bitterns Biggish wading birds, long-legged and long-necked, but commonly with the neck retracted except when alarmed, when they may stretch out neck and bill as camouflage to merge with the adjacent reeds of their swamp environment. As in Europe, some species have a booming call often associated with lonely swamps. Genera include *Ixobrychus* (reed-roarer), *Butorides*, *Dupetor* (roarer) and *Botaurus* (bull-like).

Bivalves (*Pelecypoda*—hatchet-footed) Molluscs*, mainly marine Shellfish*; the adults possess a shell in sections (valves), hinged at the 'beak', near which are interlocking teeth to keep the halves fitted together. The larval stage is shell-less and often rather differently shaped from the adult, sometimes living as gill-parasites on fish. Species representative of the main families of Aus. marine bivalves include: 1. the Date Shell, *Solemya australis*, family Solemyidae, with shell closed and date-like, with a shiny brown coat extending outward beyond the valves to form a slightly ragged 'skirt'; 2. the Nut Shells, family Nuculidae, also regarded as primitive, including the Superb Nut Shell, *Ennucula superba*, of Qld. with a more

rounded shell, with an olive-green outer skin on the shell in live specimens; and the distinctively shaped Spoon Shell, *Poroleda spathula*, of the S of Aus., a member of the Nuculanidae family; 3. the Dog Cockles, family Glycymeridae, including the Radiating Dog Cockle, *Veletuceta radians*, of much of the S of Aus.; there is a strong family resemblance but some species have more prominent concentric ridges; 4. the Heart Cockles, family Cardiidae, including the Southern Cockle, *Cardium racketti*, with its delicate, cream-pink shell with notched edge, very similar to the cockle of British shores; 5. the Ark Shells, family Arcidae, distinguished by a long straight hinge, as in the Noah's Ark Shell, *Arca pistachia*, of SE and S Aus.; other species vary a good deal in shape and size; 6. the Vulsellidae family, including the delicate Sponge Finger, *Vulsella vulsella*, which lives enveloped in living sponge, and the Hammer Oyster, *Malleus novelesianus*, which anchors in sand or mud below tide-level by a bunch of thread-like processes; 7. the fan-shaped Scallops family, Pectinidae, including the edible King Scallop of Tas., *Notovola meridionalis*; 8. the Carditidae family with several of the radial ribs on the shell much longer than the others, as in the Hollowed Cardita, *Cardita excavata*; 9. the Latticed Platter Shell, *Codakia rugifera*, saucer-shaped with marked radial and concentric ridges (family Lucinidae); 10. the well-known Jingle Shells, family Anomiidae, including the Orange Jingle Shell, *Anomia descripta*, of SE Aus.—translucent, orange, golden or silvery and irregularly shaped; 11. the brittle but sharp-shelled Razor Shells, family Pinnidae, including Menke's Razor Shell, *Pinna menkei*, often found anchored by threadlike processes and almost buried in mud or sand between tides or in shallow water in SE Aus., grey-brown with faint radial and concentric markings and occasional small spines; 12.

the Brooch Shell, *Neotrigonia margaritacea* (family Trigonidae), the deep cup and bedded radial ridges of which are well known over SE Aus., but especially in Tas.; 13. 10 species of File Shells (family Limidae) named from fine-toothed radial ridges, including Strange's File Shell, *Stabilima strangei*, found in shallow water along much of the S of Aus.; 14. the Edible Mussel, *Mytilus planulatus* (family Mytilidae), familiar along the same coasts and may be increasing in commercial importance; the pinkish Three-banded Mussel, *Musculus cumingianus*, of deep waters off E Aus. with 3 distinct bands, the middle smooth, the outer 2 ridged; 15. a distinctive Venus Shell, family Veneridae, the Frilled Venus Shell, *Callanaitis disjecta*, creamish with 7 pink concentric frills round the shell; other species brownish and sometimes called Biscuit Shells; 16. the delicate shallow Pink Butterfly Shell, *Tellinota albinella*, often washed up from deep water in the S of Aus. after a storm, with hinged shells which open like a butterfly, representing the sand-burrowing family Tellinidae; 17. the well-known Pipi, *Plebidonax deltoides*, family Donacidae (Wedge-shells), a somewhat stout surf-edge burrower, much 'fished for', by toe-wriggling, for bait and even for food; the shell is pinkish-white, with a greenish outer cover when alive, and a purplish interior; 18. in a different family, Mesodesmatidae, but of similar habits, the Little Wedge Shell, *Amesodesma angusta*, with a brown outer skin on a smaller white shell; 19. The Brown Trough Shell, *Austromactra rufescens*, family Mactridae, has a rougher, grooved shell, bluish with brown rings, purplish inside; 20. the Chinaman's Fingernail, *Solen correctus*, a common representative of the Finger Oysters or Fingernail Shells (family Solenidae); when closed like a cigar-case, a single valve like an over-curved cut-throat razor; the mollusc lies buried slanting in the sand; 21. the Boring Bivalves,

able to burrow in rock or wood with their shells, including the Angel's Wing, *Pholas australasiae* (family Pholadidae), and the Teredo, *Teredo austini*, with 2 small white burrowing shells at the front of a long wormlike body which leaves tunnels lined with a limy substance in driftwood etc.

Freshwater Bivalves include: 1. the Freshwater Mussells, family Prope-hydridellidae, such as the large *Alathyria jacksoni* of the Murray-Darling system and the small *Hydridella narracanensis*, with attractive mother-of-pearl insides to the shells and occasional pearls; 2. small clams, e.g. *Corbiculina australis*, family Corbiculidae, found in the rivers round Sydney; 3. the tiny pea-shells, such as various species of *Sphaerium* (family Sphaeriidae) often found as early invaders of newly dug dams.

Black Bean or **Moreton Bay Chestnut** (*Castanospermum australe*) A single-species genus of the Leguminosae, unique to NE Aus. and the New Hebrides. It grows to 21 m. by 1 m., and has dark grey, thin fairly smooth bark and there is a multiple leaf 60 cm. long bearing 13 cm. leaflets in opposed pairs. Flowers are somewhat pea-shaped, about 10 cm. by 2 cm., yellow, orange or red, and rather fleshy; the pods up to 25 cm. long contain 2–5 large spherical seeds, harmful if eaten raw but prepared as food by Aborigines Timber is excellent for cabinet-making, and the tree was early taken into cultivation.

Black Snake, Common or **Red-bellied** (*Pseudechis porphyriacus*) A large venomous snake haunting streams and swamps all over the wetter parts of E Aus. the venom mainly causes local, but sometimes more general, haemorrhage; only an injection into a main vein or artery is likely to cause death. Related species include the King Brown Snake, *P. australis*, Collett's Snake, *P. colletti colletti*, with its colourful pink, chocolate and black markings, and the Blue-bellied or Spotted Black Snake, *P. colletti guttatus.* (*See* PLATE 9.)

Black War The hostilities between Tas. settlers and Aborigines (1804–35), arising from brutal treatment of the negrito natives by bushrangers, sealers and farmers, and the blind savage revenge that was taken. Under Governor Arthur* an attempt, the **Black Drive**, was made in 1830 to sweep the survivors into the Tasman peninsula behind a **Black Line** using several thousand men; it captured a woman and boy sleeping behind a log; the others evaded and slipped through it. George Robinson* eventually persuaded the 200 surviving Aborigines to settle on Flinders Island, 1831–5; a residue of 44 were brought to Oyster Bay near Hobart, but the race became extinct.

Black Wednesday January 9th 1878 when over 200 Vic. civil servants were dismissed. It was named to parody 'Black Thursday' the 6th February 1851 bushfire. In order to force a deadlock between the Legislative Assembly and Council, Berry* tacked a bill he knew to be unacceptable to the Council, on to the normal Appropriations Bill which was then rejected. He then persuaded Governor Bowen that he had to dismiss the civil servants as they could not be paid (some were not reinstated for political reasons). The ensuing furore was such that the powers of the Legislative Council were curbed and its franchise increased.

Blackberry The name usually used for the introduced bramble *Rubus fruticosus* which has become a noxious weed in wetter and cooler parts of Aus. Related native Raspberries, e.g. *R. triphyllus, R. rosifolius* and *R. gunnianus* are unobtrusive members of the undergrowth.

Blackbirding Virtual slave raiding, rampant in the South Pacific 1860–90 to supply Qld. and Fiji sugar plantations with Kanakas*. Attempts to control the trade, by Qld. (1868–72) and by the British annexation of Fiji (1874) were only partly successful. William Hayes (1829–77) was a notorious blackbirder fictionalised by both Becke* and Boldrewood*.

Blackboys A mainly W.A. popular name for the peculiar, slow-growing, small, tree-like Grass-trees* of the *Xanthorrhoea* genus, closely allied to the Liliaceae or lily family, from a fancied resemblance to a grass-skirted figure flourishing a spear. (*See* PLATE 7.)

Blackburn, James (1803–1854) b. Eng. Deported to Tas. for forgery in 1833, pardoned 1841, and worked as engineer and architect. His churches in a wide variety of styles, built in the warm golden Tas. freestone, are small but very fine.

Blackbutt (*Eucalyptus pilularis*) An important hardwood tree growing on varied soils from sandy loams to clays residual from basalts, and particularly on shales, on hilly sites with 90–150 cm. mean annual rainfall between the sea and the E escarpment from Gippsland to central Qld. It has lanceolate juvenile and adult leaves, a rough grey-brown fibrous bark persistent over most of its trunk, though shed in strips in its upper part, and small groups of pointed buds and cup-shaped fruit about 1 cm. across. W.A. or Swan River Blackbutt, *E. patens*, is a good but not very widely available timber tree of 25–30 m. by 1–1·5 m., occurring mainly in small pure stands on deeper, fairly moist sandy soils in the 16–120 cm. rainfall belt of SW W.A. Juvenile leaves are a longish heart-shape and the grey-green; adult leaves are fairly narrowly lanceolate and dull green. There are small bunches of club-shaped to slightly pointed buds, and fruit are cup-shaped and about 1 cm. across. Bark is grey-brown, deeply furrowed, short-fibred and friable. The trunk is often about half the height, above which rather vertical main branches give a fairly narrow crown. The Dundas Blackbutt is *E. dundasi.*

Blacket, Edmund Thomas (1817–1883) b. Surrey, Eng. An architect although not formally trained. He arrived in Aus. in 1842 where he was a Church of England Schools Inspector, then Diocesan architect (1847), and Colonial architect (1849–54), thereafter concentrating on his practice. He was the leading Aus. architect of the second half of the 19th century, the chief and most successful exponent of the Gothic revival, seen in his many churches, such as St. Mark's, Darling Point, Sydney (1848), and the Great Hall of Sydney University (1854–60) echoing the medieval colleges of Oxford and Cambridge.

Blackthorn (*Bursaria spinosa*) Named from its masses of small white flowers which justify its other popular name, Christmas Bush. It belongs to the mainly southern family Pittosporaceae.

Blackwood, Hickory or **Sally Wattle** (*Acacia melanoxylon*) (meaning black wood) A valuable tree for decorative timber growing to 24–34 m. by 0·75–1.2 m. in coastal to hilly Tas. and Vic., and less in N.S.W. The juvenile leaves show the common *Acacia* pinnate form, with 15–20 pairs of leaflets, reducing in the upper leaves; the adult 'leaves', really flattened leaf stalks, are a narrow tongue shape, bluntly pointed but tapering to the base. Flowers are small globes, fruit in twining and curved pods. Bark is grey-brown, hard, furrowed and persistent to the lower branches. The dark timber is used in furniture-making.

Blackwood River W.A. 34S/115E Rises on the plateau and flows 320 km. SW, perennially only in its lower course, but sluggish and brackish there in summer. It passes from sheep country through the apple area of Bridgetown among the low forested hills of the scarp, to dairylands on the coastal plain behind Augusta.

Bladderwort A popular name for the carnivorous plants having some leaves developed with a bladder and sensitive lid to catch insects as prey, which are used as a supplementary source of nitrogen. Most are in the genus *Utricularia* (family Lentibulariaceae), of which the Purple Bladderwort, *U. dichotoma*, is common in shallow water and damp soils in SE Aus. The leaf is often elongated beyond the bladder. A group of very slender flower stems each carry 1–4 yellow-centred purple flowers, with small upper lip and fanlike lower lip.

Blady-grass Aus. popular name for *Imperata cylindrica*, the *kunai, kogon* or *lalang* grass of Polynesia and SE Asia where it invades clearings after shifting cultivation, particularly after fire, and may delay the secondary regrowth of forest cover; it is seen under woodland cover as far S as Central N.S.W. but does not appear to raise problems under Aus. conditions. Used for thatch in the early days of settlement.

Blair Athol Qld. 23S/148E A small mining town at 305 m., just NW of Clermont, with unusually thick coal seams, e.g. the 'Big Seam' is 21–24 m. under 46 m. of overburden.

Blamey, Sir Thomas Albert (1884–1951) First Aus. Field Marshal (1950). Born L. Albert, N.S.W., son of a Cornish migrant farmer. After teaching from 1889–1906 he entered the army, served in India 1911–13, at Gallipoli* and as an exceptionally efficient Chief of Staff in France to Monash*. He became Vic. Police Commissioner (1925–36); his resignation was forced following concealment of facts in a police shooting incident. He returned to public life in 1939 to survey manpower and then became G.O.C. of the new A.I.F., commanding the Anzac Corps in Greece, returning to command Aus. military forces under MacArthur's supreme command in 1942.

Bland, William (1789–1868) The most important early physician in N.S.W. Born London, transported to Sydney (1814) after a fatal duel in Bombay while in the Royal Navy. Emancipated (1815), he set up in private practice and, as a friend of Wentworth*, became increasingly involved in politics. A flamboyant, critical yet benevolent figure, he largely founded the Aus. Medical Association (1859) and was a founder of Sydney College. A small creek, town and stretch of fertile heavy soil country S of L. Cowal, N.S.W., 34S/147E, are named after him.

Blaxland, John (1769–1845) and **Gregory** (1778–1853) were Kentish gentleman farmers who, in straitened circumstances and on Sir Joseph Banks's advice, emigrated to N.S.W., 1806–7. They were the first free settlers under Castlereagh's scheme to give land and convict labour to desirable men of status and capital. While both became involved in political affairs, opposing Bligh, then Macquarie (John was obliged to spend 1808–11 in England over the Rum Rebellion* trials and Gregory took a colonists' petition for trial by jury to London in 1829), their contributions were to farming and exploration. Gregory developed winemaking, John cattle fattening. When insects, drought and land hunger made the discovery of fresh pastures essential after 1810, Gregory, with Lawson* and Wentworth*, made the first Blue Mountains crossing in 1813, by following the ridges. His journal is an imaginative if rather overstated record.

Bligh, William (1754–1817) b. Plymouth. Bligh's Governorship of N.S.W. (1806–10) was a stormy interlude in a successful and colourful naval career: he commanded the *Resolution* at 21, on Cook's last voyage (1776). In 1789 while commanding the *Bounty* his crew mutinied near Tonga, placing Bligh with 18 men in an open boat which he successfully navigated over 5,800 km. to Timor in 6 weeks.

Bligh's courage, seamanship and administrative ability are beyond dispute; his temper and character being more a matter of controversy as much among historians as among his contemporaries. For in spite of a severe reprimand for tyrannical treatment in 1805, Sir Joseph Banks strongly recommended him as Governor to replace King. He found the colony in a sorry state of chaos, debauchery and profiteering, especially by the officer élite of the N.S.W. Corps, whom he soon antagonised by stopping payments in spirits for services and goods. Matters came to a head in the Rum Rebellion* in January 1808 with the arrest and farcical trial of John Macarthur* who then with 6 others wrote to Major Johnston*, the senior officer, asking him to arrest Bligh and take over command. Bligh was kept under arrest for almost a year, attended chiefly by his daughter, Mary Putland, and refusing to leave for England as a prisoner, as his gaolers offered. Eventually he left in January 1810 in command of *Porpoise*, promising not to call at any other colony, but in fact making straight for Hobart where Collins* gave him little support. Returning to Sydney, where his successor Macquarie was already installed, Bligh spent several frantic weeks gathering evidence before sailing. At the subsequent trial of Johnston, Bligh was completely exonerated, and later promoted to Rear-Admiral. He did much for N.S.W. both in administration and agriculture which he favoured against grazing, encouraging new methods, improved seeds and even soil conservation. *For further reading see* G. Mackaness: *The Life of Vice-Admiral William Bligh* (Sydney, 1951).

Blind-grass or **Candyup Poison** Liliaceus flowers, *Stypandra imbricata* and *S. grandiflora*, of W.A., regarded as poisonous to stock. (*See* LILIES.)

Blind-your-eyes A popular name for the Aus. and SE Asian tree, genus

Excoecaria, e.g. the Milky Mangrove, *E. agallacha*, or the Scrub Poison-tree, *E. dallachyana*, of drier inland areas.

Blinman S.A. 31S/139E Now a very small centre for a pastoral area, but it was the main copper town of the N Flinders Ranges, operating sporadically between 1862 and 1908 and with smelters in its last years. The wood-driven steam traction engines which were unsuccessfully tried on the 200-km. haul to Port Augusta (1863–4) might rank as the first Aus. 'road trains'.

Bloodwoods A group of about 30 species of eucalypts with prominent members in extreme SW W.A. and in coastal E Aus. (not Vic., S.A. or Tas.) and some representatives in the monsoon forests of N Aus. (e.g. *Eucalyptus bleeseri*, *E. polycarpa*, *E. terminalis*, *E. nesophila*). They are named from the frequent veins of blood-red kino or 'gum', which reduces the value of most species as timber though some have specialised uses: the Spotted Gum, *E. maculata*, for tool-handles; the Lemon-scented Gum, *E. citriodora*, for the extraction of citronella oil etc. The bloodwoods of the E rain-forests are often on poor dry sites, stony, sandy or excessively drained and more lightly timbered than the rain-forests around. Juvenile and adult leaves tend to be moderately broad to fairly narrow lanceolates. Leaves are nearly always lighter on the undersides, and finely, regularly and closely veined; and they diverge at a wide angle from the twig. Forest specimens have long trunks, two-thirds of the height, and the bark is rough, persistent, short-stapled, rather scaly, in square or rectangular pieces and rather friable. Some species have smooth areas, and the Spotted Gum, *E. maculata*, and Lemon-scented Gum, *E. citriodora*, have smooth and attractively mottled trunks and branches. Buds are egg or club-shaped and when the flower emerges it is often large and showy, as in the small, straggling, many-branched Red-

flowering Gum, *E. ficifolia*, native to a coastal strip between Albany and Denmark, W.A., but now widely cultivated as an ornamental tree. Fruits are generally large, woody and egg or urn-shaped. The Marri or Red Gum, *E. calophylla*, is a tall forest tree of the SW of W.A., growing to 45 m. by 1·5 m., sometimes with dense and shady

Red-flowering Gum (*Eucalyptus ficifolia*), *about half life-size*

crown development. The Red Bloodwood, *E. gummifera*, of coastal forests from S Qld. to the S of N.S.W., is taller and straighter on good sites, but on typically poor sites 15–18 m. by 30–60 cm. with a rather short and twisted trunk. The Lemon-scented Gum of the Mackay-Maryborough and Atherton areas of Qld. is usually straight-trunked 24–40 m. by 60–120 cm., with light but regular crown; it is attractive and widely planted as an ornamental tree.

The leaves are strongly aromatic on crushing. The tall Spotted Gum of E Aus. grows to 24–35 m. by 70–120 cm. even on poorish sites, and the trunk is often straight and unbranched for ¾ of its height, yielding good timber.

Blown-grass Several species of *Agrostis*, slender tall grasses growing from a loose tuft of leaves. These bear large, widespread, delicate conical heads of small husked seeds, easily broken off and piled by the wind against fences, etc. (cf. Love-grass, Panic Grass). Their fodder value is minor.

Bludger Colloquial term for a cadger, or one who evades responsibility or work. Originally derived from an English dialect word for a low, often violent criminal, it acquired a specialised meaning in Aus. in the 19th century as a person living on the immoral earnings of women.

Blue Devil (*Eryngium rostratum*) A very attractive blue-flowered, thistle-like plant in the Umbelliferae family, a cosmopolitan genus with many S American members. Several of the Aus. species tend to become a pest in dry pastoral country.

Blue Gums 1. *Eastern Group* Related and fairly similar eucalypts, with foliage nearly always light under and dark above, having fine regular close veins like the bloodwoods and set at a high angle to the midrib; the leaves vary from ovoid-lanceolate to finely lanceolate, tending to lie horizontally; juvenile leaves are sometimes broad and oval. Most species tend to shed the bark in patches or totally except near the ground, the 3 'Mahoganies' being notable exceptions. Timber quality is variable in different species. Buds tend to be small and to occur in groups with a star-shaped cluster round a central bud, followed by small pear-shaped to cup-shaped fruit sometimes pointed, except for the Woollybutt which has groups of 2 or 3 large buds and fruit. The group occurs chiefly in wet sclerophyll* forest in the humid coastal belt of E Aus. The main group includes the clean-barked Deane's Gum, *Eucalyptus deanei*, the impressive Rose Gum, *E. grandis*, and Sydney Blue Gum, *E. saligna*, with increasing heights of bark 'stocking'; and the Southern Mahogany, *E. botryoides*, and Swamp Mahogany, *E. robusta*, both with thick short-fibred spongy bark persistent over much of the tree, especially the latter, and yielding good timber, especially the former. Closely related species here included in the group are the Red Mahogany or Red Messmate, *E. resinifera*, with rough stringy red-brown bark to the lower branches, the Grey Gum, *E. propinqua*, shedding its bark in patches in a pattern of pink, light grey and dark grey, and the Woollybutt, *E. longifolia*, which lacks the conspicuous difference between undersides and upper surfaces of leaves, and has an irregularly ridged and cracked or flaky grey bark to the large branches.

2. *Southern Group* Indigenous to the S and SE of Aus., they include: the Southern Blue Gum, *Eucalyptus globulus*, of SE Tas., Vic. and extreme S of N.S.W., 46–55 m. tall, early exported as timber and now forming major eucalypt forests in California and elsewhere, being relatively cold-resistant and fast-growing. The 30–43 m. Eurabbie or Victorian Blue Gum, *E. bicostata*, growing on the N side of the Aus. Alps and on Flinders Island, is also a good timber tree. The Mountain Grey or Spotted Grey Mountain Gum, *E. cypellocarpa*, growing at 900–1,220 m., is less important for timber. The Mountain Gum*, *E. dalrympleana*, is closely related, as is the medium-sized, profusely flowering Apple Box*, *E. bridgesiana*. The group as a whole has clean blotched bark shed in coarse ribbons, often seen caught up on a branch, and blue-green juvenile leaves giving the name Blue Gum, heart-shaped and opposite for many pairs. Adult leaves tend to be dark

green and lanceolate to strap-like, and the Blue Gum proper has a denser crown than in many eucalypts, and large warty buds and fruit; the Eurabbie has ribbed fruits in threes; the Mountain Grey Gum smaller fruits in clusters of about 7 rounded, rather than tulip-shaped; the Mountain Gum and Apple Box small clusters of small pointed buds and hemispheric to conical fruits.

Blue Lake S.A. 38S/141E Largest of the Mt. Gambier* crater lakes, named from its brilliant colour in the height of summer (although at other times it is grey). It is about 80 m. deep and covers 70 ha. and the 80-m. walls include limestone outcrops below ash and lava. Water levels seldom fluctuate here or in Valley L. (while they do in nearby Leg of Mutton L.) in spite of heavy summer usage for Mt. Gambier.

Blue Mountains N.S.W. A plateau of 600–1,100 m. around Katoomba, 34S/150E, dramatically dissected by the Grose and Cox's Rivers and their tributaries, the valleys of which are often steep-sided and crowned by precipices. The W edge of the plateau is the highest, and forms a very steep escarpment; the rocks dip to the E under Penrith, while the E edge also is very steep, owing to a sharp steepening in the angle of dip of rocks. The rocks are sedimentary, the uppermost a massive and resistant Triassic sandstone, underlain by much weaker Triassic shales and Permian coal measures. Erosion of these weaker substrata keeps the precipices fresh and steep, and large rock falls are not uncommon. The Blue Mts. were a barrier to expansion from Sydney until the pioneer crossing (in 1813), then the building of Cox's road, partly followed by the Western Highway today. The more accessible and extensive of the plateau fragments became at first a sort of 'hill station', almost after the Indian model. The switch of fashion to the beaches has caused elaborate hotels of last century to be outmoded, but given fast electric trains and motor traffic the area attracts the hardier commuters, and urban growth is rapid. **The City of Blue Mountains** (36,627 in 1971), 130 km long, but like a string of beads along the Highway with some gaps at the steepest parts, was formed in 1947 to attempt the difficult task of co-ordinating services and development from Emu Plains, through Glenbrook-Faulconbridge*, to Katoomba*-Wentworth Falls and on to Blackheath and Bell. Much tourist trade remains, often for shorter visits than in the earlier development, and a National Park on both sides of the Highway preserves much fine forest, cliff and river scenery. The N boundary of the Blue Mts. may be taken as the old coal and industrial area of Lithgow*.

Blue Tinsel Lily (*Calectasia cyanea*) A brilliantly metallic-blue liliaceous flower of the S of Aus., from W Vic. to W.A. (*See* LILIES.)

Bluebell In Aus. this name is perhaps best applied to species of *Wahlenbergia*, common in open country throughout E Aus. They have pairs of wavy-edged narrow leaves, and several slender flower stems on each main stem, bearing very delicate, partly cupped, 5-petalled flowers of pale to sky blue, purplish on the underside. There are several other Aus. species in a mainly S African genus, including the W.A. *W. gracilis* (*see* PLATE 6). The popular name is also applied to some Aus. plants in the closely related Lobelia family and to *Laurentia* species, e.g. the Rock and Swamp Isotomes of E Aus. Some species of *Lobelia* and *Laurentia* contain an alkaloid toxic to cattle.

Bluebottles The widely accepted Aus. term for certain marine Coelenterata* of genus *Physalia*, the Portuguese Man-O'-War of Europe. They have a distinctive blue air sac often 4 cm. long; though free-swimming rather than stationary, they are largely wind-blown and trailing tentacles of a few cm. to some m. long, some bearing the noxious stinging mechanism. They are quite often blown into surfing bays and on to the beaches by northerly onshore winds, and cause many painful stings to bathers—sometimes hundreds in a day on Sydney beaches despite warning flags etc. (the home first-aid measure traditionally used is a compress with a bag of washing blue). The species common in SE Aus. is *P. utriculus*.

Bluebottle (Physalia utriculus); the air sac is about 4 cm. long

Bluebush A popular name for several unrelated, shrubby, drought-resistant plants, some of which are important food for stock in low rainfall areas. The most important is *Kochia sedefolia* of the Chenopodiaceae (Goosefoot* or Fat Hen) family. It grows up to 1 m.

high, with small pointed leaves 6 mm. long, all covered with a dense mat of short white hairs, giving the characteristic blue effect at a distance. It is widespread in S and Central Aus. *Cratystylis conocephala*, of the Compositae of daisy family, is generally similar in appearance. It also grows in W.A.

Blue-grass A popular name for a valuable group of forage grasses of dry inland Aus., of the genera *Bothriochloa* and *Dichanthium* (the related genus *Capillipedium* being more often known as Scented-top). Some species will grow on light soils, though there stock tend to pull up the tussocks by the roots; but mainly they grow on clays in inland Aus. overlapping with Mitchell grass* and Flinders grass*. They are tufted grasses with prominent multiple heads falling, or the whole branch breaking when the seeds are ripe, as in Qld. Blue-grass, *B. sericeum*, or the less leafy Redleg-grass, *B. ambigua*. The Kentucky Blue-grass, a Fescue, has been introduced as a fodder grass.

Bluey The blanket or roll of blankets, carried as part or whole of a swag*, so called from the prevailing colour, popular, according to Henry Lawson, as it did not show the dirt.

Boake, Barcroft Henry (1866–1892) b. Sydney. Known for one ballad *Where the Dead Men Lie* (published Sydney, 1897), conveying the grim harshness of the outback, where he was a surveyor and boundary rider. He committed suicide at 26.

Boer War October 1899-May 1902. Aus. colonies made individual offers of forces prior to Federation becoming effective in January 1901; these were supplemented and unified as the Aus. Commonwealth Horse. Of a total of 16,175 men, 518 were killed. The bushcraft and tough courage of the Aus. contingents were valuable in the guerilla type of warfare: in turn Boer War veterans became an important element in the senior ranks of the A.I.F. in 1914.

Bogan River N.S.W. Rises in the Western Slopes NE of Parkes, 33S/148E, and flows generally WNW for 725 km. to join the Barwon. Its course, flowing only seasonally in most years, is through wheat-sheep country cleared from light woodlands, then more arid wool sheep country, then into heavy dark soils by the rivers, giving good fattening pastures in wetter years.

Bogong, Mount Vic. 37S/147E (1,987 m.) About 80 km. SW of Albury, the culmination of the Bogong High Country, undulating plateaux at 1,400 m. to 1,800 m. used, until recent controls protecting them from access, for summer grazing for beef cattle on the alpine pastures above the steep forested slopes. This is the only known area of occurrence of *Celmisia sericophylla*, a water-loving silky-leaved mountain daisy. The emphasis has now changed to winter sports, ski lifts and ski villages. **Bogong** township was built by Vic. State Electricity Commission during construction of the Kiewa* hydro-electric scheme. **Bogong Range**, N.S.W., including Bogong Peak (1,717) m.), is about 32 km. SE of Tumut and in the extreme N of the Kosciusko National Park.

Boldrewood, Rolf Pen-name of T. A. Browne*, best known for *Robbery Under Arms*.

Bonwick, James (1817–1906) b. London. Lived in Aus. from 1841–84 as teacher, digger, land agent, schools' inspector. He was a tireless, if untrained and not always reliable, researcher into historical records, and compiler and prolific writer of school texts, encyclopaedia articles and booklets on the colony.

Booby Island Qld. 10S/142E A minute island named (it is said independently) by Cook and Bligh from the nesting gannets (boobies). It lies at the

W end of Torres Str. A cave was used in sailing days as a 'post office' and emergency food stores. It now has the most northerly Aus. lighthouse.

Booklice Small pale insects of the Order Psocoptera, which gouge small pieces from plants and books. They include the native hairy-bodied Winged Booklouse, *Psocus* spp., normally found on tree foliage, and the introduced pest the Wingless Booklouse, *Atropos* spp., the most likely to be seen in houses.

Boomerang A curved, thin, flat, sharp-edged throwing stick with the property of returning to the thrower if it is thrown correctly. It is often thought of as the characteristic Aboriginal tool; it was indeed widespread but by no means universal, and it appears that its main use was as a toy or amusement. Throwing-sticks for hunting did not return to the thrower. The remarkable aerodynamics of the boomerang must have been accidentally discovered from these, then improved.

A *and* B *Returning Boomerangs;* C *and* D *Throwing Sticks*

Bordertown S.A. 36S/141E (1,977 in 1971) Actually 19 km. W of the Vic. border and originated as a gold escort depot from Vic. to Adelaide. A westerly extension of the Vic. Wimmera* red earths permitted early agricultural settlement in the surrounding Tatiara region.

Boronia Shrubs with 4-petalled flowers of an Aus. genus in the world-wide Rutaceae or Rue family, and sharing their aromatic leaves containing essential oils. There are about 90 species of boronias. Over half are in W.A., including the brown- and yellow-flowered Scented Boronia, *B. megastigma*, commercially exploited on a small scale for perfume, and the crimson-rose *B. heterophylla*. The mallee scrub country in the drier inland of SE Aus. has the attractive blue-flowered dwarf *B. caerulescens*, while in SE Aus. a common association on the coastal sandstone plateaux includes 3 pink-flowered boronias, the Feathery Boronia, *B. pinnata*, *B. ledifolia* which has groups of 3, strap-like leaves, and the Native Rose (*see* ROSES).

Borroloola N.T. 16S/136E A former port on the McArthur River* 81 km. from its mouth, with under 20 inhabitants, now reached by Beef Road from Anthony Lagoon and the Stuart Highway*; it has been called 'the end of the line'. Famed for its Carnegie Library astonishingly acquired by a local policeman, and now lost or eaten by white ants, and for its semi-recluses, it is also a Government Aboriginal welfare station. Supplies for the N Section of the Overland Telegraph* were landed here.

Botanic Gardens These now exist in all State capitals, and (since 1967) in Canberra. The oldest is in Sydney, at Farm Cove, in the heart of the city and on the site of the earliest farm in the colony; it covers 27 ha. The Royal Botanic Gardens in Melbourne (36 ha.) owe much to von Mueller*. Of the 49 ha. of the botanic gardens in Adelaide, 30 ha. form an arboretum; the 19 ha. of Brisbane's botanic gardens, on the river bank, have a wide tropical range, and so have Darwin's 32 ha. In Perth 10 ha. of gardens and 15 ha. of arboretum are now established in King's Park; the small Hobart botanic gardens are in the Queen's Domain. The new Canberra gardens will have the world's major collection of Aus. flora.

Botanists Apart from the observations of Banks* the first great figure was the Scot, Robert Browne (1773–1858), who accompanied Flinders* on his Aus. circumnavigation in 1801–3, and collected and described several thousand Aus. plants in a work published in 1810; on the same voyage the Austrian draughtsman F. Bauer prepared his illustrated work published in 1815, and now a rare collector's piece. Among the explorers with botanical training, Alan Cunningham* was outstanding; Leichhardt* was also a botanist. Von Mueller* was the major collector of the second half of the 19th century; but in scientific contribution he was perhaps overshadowed by Joseph Maiden (1859–1925), who produced classic although pioneer work on the eucalypts and acacias, among other major although not always finished writings. In Darwin M. W. Holtze (1840–1923) did important (often subsequently unheeded) work on potentially viable tropical plantation crops. As in other branches of natural history, the contributions of gifted, dedicated amateurs has been vital (*see* ORCHIDS). Other 19th-century botanists included: J. Drummond (1783–1863) in W.A.; R. C. Gunn (1808–1881) and L. Rodway (1853–1936) in Tas.; F. M. Bailey (1827–1915) and both his son and grandson, in Qld.; J. M. Black (1855–1951) and R. Tate (1840–1901) in S.A. (*See also* FLORA.)

Botany Bay N.S.W. 34S/151E Where Captain Cook* first landed in Aus.;

now surrounded by the airport and industrial Sydney. At first it was called Stingray Bay, but Cook altered it later to Botany Bay in honour of the plant collections made by Banks*. The **Botany Bay Project** (1973–77) is a multi-disciplinary investigation into urban polution problems and environmental policy in Aus.

Bottle Tree   A popular name for several Aus. trees, notably *Brachychiton rupestre*, a member of the pod-bearing family Sterculiaceae, very distinctive for its bottle-shaped trunk bearing green-brown fibrous and furrowed bark, up to 2 m. across at the base and narrowing to a neck bearing a dense crown of spear-shaped leaves, sometimes with 3 joined at the base. The compound flower-head is in the leaf-forks, and there are pods with 5–15 5-mm. seeds. The timber is soft, fibrous and contains a substance looking like paraffin wax; it is edible by stock and was used by Aborigines as a thirst-quencher. In the N the Aus. Baobab, *Adansonia gregorii*, with a similar swollen trunk, is found in many savannahs. (*See* VEGETATION.)

Bottlebrush   A popular name for various bushes and trees of 3 genera, *Melaleuca*, *Banksia* and *Callistemon* in the world-wide Myrtaceae family. The name is from the cylindrical composite flower-head, which does indeed closely resemble a bottlebrush in shape—though often very attractively coloured. There are some 20 species of *Callistemon*, mainly in N.S.W., with the distinctive flower-head succeeded at the tip by fresh growth and the next year's flower spike, and at the base of the individual flowers by hard cup-shaped seed capsules in which the seeds may mature for several years, successive years' capsules being identifiable on one branch. Leaves are narrowly lanceolate, sometimes stiff and flat, sometimes downy, sometimes fragrant on crushing. Habit varies greatly from a rough-barked

tough-timbered 18-m. tree such as the Weeping Bottlebrush, *C. viminalis*, named from its attractively pendent foliage, to riverside bushes such as *C. paludosus* and various species adapted to inland conditions, e.g. the red-flowered *C. teretifolius* of the Flinders Range, which has slender cylindrical leaves. Bottlebrush is also sometimes applied to some species of *Hakea** and *Grevillea**. The One-sided Bottlebrush of W.A. is the genus *Calothamnus* in the Myrtaceae family, e.g. the crimson Hairy Net-bush, *C. villosus*, of open bush.

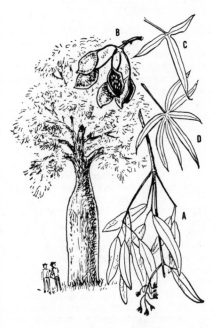

Bottle Tree (Brachychiton rupestre)

A *Branchlets bearing inflorescence;*

B *Fruit-bearing twig with 5 follicles;*

C *and* D *forms of leaves on young trees and sterile twigs*

Boulder W.A. 31S/121E A city, now part of the Kalgoorlie-Boulder municipality with a joint population of 20,784 (1971), developed first on the Golden Mile* and named from the Great Boulder lode. The town proper was laid out (1897) 1·6 km. to the W and 11 km. from Kalgoorlie, with which it has had continued rivalry.

Bourke N.S.W. 30S/146E (3,620 in 1971) On the River Darling, formerly a river port, now is an important wool railhead and pastoral centre. It was named from Fort Bourke, a stockade built by T. L. Mitchell* against the Aborigines. The phrase 'back o' Bourke' refers to the far outback country of N.S.W.

Bourke, Sir Richard (1777–1855) b. Dublin. N.S.W. Governor from 1831-8. Trained in law, Bourke had made an army career and acted as Lt.-Governor in the E District of Cape Colony before following Darling in N.S.W. He was one of a series of able governors unenviably placed between Colonial Office and colonists in the crucial developing years of 1820–50. During his term trial by jury was firmly established, land grants were replaced by sale in the Nineteen Counties and squatting regularised by licence; state aid to churches was begun, but he failed in getting elective government and his scheme of state-aided schools with denominational teaching accepted. Inevitably Bourke made enemies especially the exclusivists* and squatters*, but was popular among emancipists* whom he favoured, and the large Catholic population. He was accused of some nepotism; and resigned when his opposition to an appointment was not upheld in London.

Bowen Qld. 20S/148E (5,797 in 1971) Lies on Port Denison, a fine natural harbour in the NW of Edgecumbe Bay. Developed as an outlet for the N of Qld., it suffers from a more rugged immediate hinterland than Townsville*, but has meatworks (at Merinda, 6 km. to the W) a State coke plant (for Mt. Isa and Townsville metal plants) using Collinsville coal and solar salt evaporation. It exports tomatoes, bananas and mangoes, but the port is declining with the concentration of bulk sugar at Mackay and Townsville.

Bowen, Sir George Ferguson (1821–1899) b. Ireland. He arrived in Aus. in 1859 to be first Governor of the newly formed Queensland; Governor of N.Z. from 1868–73 (Maori Wars) and of Vic. 1873–9. His appointing Herbert* to the Premiership pending elections was critically received, but on the whole his governorship was capable and practical. In Vic. he was involved in bitter political controversy (*see* BLACK WEDNESDAY). Bowen was a fine classicist.

Bowen, John (1780–1827) Naval lieutenant sent by Governor King to establish a Van Diemen's Land Settlement (1803) at Risdon Cove, which was abandoned in favour of Hobart, when Collins superseded him in 1804.

Bower-birds (family Ptilonorhynchidae, meaning feather-bill) These are unique to Aus. and N.G., and though there are about 7 genera and 16 species (7 in Aus., 8 in N.G. and one in both), of widely differing physique, colour, habit etc., they have in common the unique display or release of nesting instinct, perhaps combined with some pleasure in ornamentation; this takes the form of building and sometimes painting a bower separate from the nest; or spreading a sort of carpet of leaves, though some species have seldom (some never) been seen to carry out this ritual (cf. the false nest of the Yellow-tailed Thornbill* of Qld. rain-forests). The general size is comparable with a pigeon and all the bower-birds hop and do not walk. All tend to mimic other birds, as well as having variable calls and alarm cries. The best-known bower-bird is the short-tailed, glossy blue-black Satin Bower-bird, *Ptilorhynchus violaceus*, of rain-forests in E Aus. (not Tas.). It eats forest berries and large insects, and builds a very simple stick nest about 5 m. up in a tree. The cock bird makes an almost tunnel-shaped grass bower, often lined with vertically placed sticks, and decorated with any blue or pale yellow objects that can be found. The bower is sometimes 'painted' with charcoal or dark fruits etc. mixed with saliva, sometimes while a piece of bark is held in the beak. Females and im-mature males are greenish on the back and head.

Other species show something of a spectrum in degree of elaboration of the bower: 1. the Regent Bower-bird, *Sericulus chrysocephalus* (silken, golden-headed, the cock being a spectacular gold and black) of E Aus. rain-forests; 2. the beautiful Golden Bower-bird, *Prionodura newtoniana* of NE Qld.; 3. the brown and buff-striped Tooth-billed Bower-bird, *Scenopoetes dentirostris* (tooth-billed tent-maker) of E Qld., a carpet-maker even if not a tent-maker. The miaowing Green Catbird* is a related bird in which bower-building has never been observed.

Bowls Lawn bowling is an increasingly popular pastime, for its social as much as its competitive functions; the num-ber of women's clubs, patronised largely by middle-aged members, has shown particularly rapid post-war growth. The earliest recorded Aus. game was in Hobart in 1845 and an inter-colony match was played in 1880 between Vic. and N.S.W. The Aus. Bowling Council (1911) and the Aus. Women's Bowling Council (1947) are the controlling bodies. **Ten-pin bowling** introduced from U.S. since the 1950s is also popular.

Bowral N.S.W. 34S/150E (5,913 in 1971) A tourist centre at 671 m. near the edge of the S Tablelands close to the Hume Highway. It is situated in pleasant green farming country near beauty spots such as the Fitzroy Falls.

Box This name was early applied in Aus. to certain eucalypts because their hard, close-fibred timber was reminis-cent of that of the European Box, *Buxus sempervirens*. The Box group includes some 60–70 species and varieties, mostly small mallees* of semi-arid hot summer areas of scrub and savannah woodland with 25–75 cm. mean annual rainfall. Bark is often rough, dark grey and a little fibrous, but persistent in some species and in others shed wholly or partly, leaving smooth branches and even trunks. Leaves are usually thick, but shapes are variable, from very narrowly lanceolate to oval or circular (as in the Poplar or Bimble Box, *E. populnea*). Buds are usually small and ovoid to pear-shaped, in bunches at the end of twigs, producing profuse blossom good for honey production. Fruit are usually small (Black Box, *E. largi-florens*, has fruit only 3mm. across), but very variable in shape. The flowering habit resembles the ironbarks*, closely related and sometimes hybridising. Despite their small size and commonly mallee form, timber is valued for special purposes like tool-making or even as fuel. Apple Box* is not a true box. The Black Box is important over a wide stretch of semi-arid SE Aus. The Coast or Gippsland Grey Box, *E. bosistoana*, of S N.S.W. and Vic. is the tallest box, often straight-trunked and growing to 30–55 m., sometimes in pure stands in valley bottoms, and is one of the best of the group as a timber tree. The Grey Box, *E. microcarpa*, of N coastal N.S.W. and SE Qld., reaches 20–27 m. by 60–90 cm. Both these boxes yield structural timber, railway sleepers etc. The Yellow Box, *E. mellio-dora*, the popular name from its yellow underbark, its Latin name meaning honey-scented, is often planted on the tablelands of SE Aus. for ornament, shade, honey, poles, structural timber and fuel. The small Red Box, *E. polyanthemos*, of open woodland to savannah conditions, in Vic. and S N.S.W., owes its common name to its red timber which is tough, durable but not seasoning readily and so best used for posts and firewood.

Boxing Bare-knuckle prize-fighting was widespread and popular although illegal, until finally banned in 1884. Scientific gloved boxing was introduced by the Englishman Mace, and was taken up by Larry Foley (1848–1917), a former prize fighter, who became a teacher and promoter; 2 of his pupils were the great heavyweight Peter Jackson and Albert Griffiths, 'Griffo' (1871–1927, lightweight). Organised promotion began with the building of Sydney Stadium (1908) by J. D. McIntosh, who was followed by R. L. Baker* in starting what was to become a near-monopoly of Aus. boxing promotion. A later important promoter was J. Wren. From 1910–20 or so, professional boxing in Sydney had larger gates and more prize money than anywhere in the world, and many international figures fought there, as well as the great Aus. idol Darcy*. A notable champion of the 1930s was Ron Richards. Bantam weight world championships were held by J. Carruthers (1952–4) and the young Aborigine Lionel Rose (1968–9). D. Sands, who died at 26, was potentially a world middleweight champion, and Rocky Gattellari a bantam weight champion 1961–5. Johnny Famechon won the world featherweight title in 1969.

Boyd, Benjamin (?1803–1851) b. Wigtonshire, Scotland. He arrived in Aus. in 1842, becoming a banker, squatter, shipping and whaling magnate. His Royal Bank of Aus. failed (1849). Boyd owned vast sheep runs in Monaro*, N.S.W. and Vic. and built **Boydtown** (1843) at Twofold Bay*, N.S.W., as a whaling station and port. In 1847 he began to import Pacific Islanders as station labour, but met so much opposition he had to give it up. Boyd's ventures failed, the town was abandoned (only one building and a ruined church remain) and he vanished in the Solomon Islands in 1851.

Boyd family They have contributed greatly to Aus. art and letters: **Arthur Merric** came to Aus. from N.Z. about 1866; he and his wife were landscape painters. Of his sons, **Theodore Penleigh** (1890–1923) was a noted artist and **Martin à Beckett** (1893–) an expatriate novelist. In the next generation **Arthur** (1920–) is an expatriate artist and **Robin** (1919–71) was one of the best known critics of the Aus. aesthetic scene, also a noted architect.

Boyer Tas. 43S/147E Newsprint mills established 1941 on the right bank of the Derwent River, and using 85% hardwood, mainly swamp gum (*Eucalyptus ovata*) and 15% New Zealand softwood. Timber comes from a 121,500-ha. concession in the Florentine and upper Derwent valleys, trucked to the railway at Maydena. The newsprint goes by barge to Hobart for export to the mainland. Capacity is 91,800 tonnes a year.

Boyer, Sir Richard (1891–1961) Chairman of the Australian Broadcasting Commission from 1945–61, the crucial formative post-war years which saw the introduction of television. He was a Methodist minister and later a Qld. grazier, a man of great personal courage, integrity and ideals. *For further reading see* G. C. Bolton: *Dick Boyer* (Canberra, 1966).

Brabham, John Arthur (Jack) (1926–) b. Sydney. World racing champion 1959, 1960 and 1966. A skilled motor mechanic, he began by racing midget cars, often home-built, after 1945. Later he changed to bigger cars, and won Aus. titles before going overseas, when he teamed successfully with the designer J. Cooper. His success is attributed to mechanical understanding, a carefully calculating approach and calm temperament. In 1966 he won with his own design, the Aus. Repco Brabham, the first racing driver to do so. He also has an Aus. motor accessories and design business.

Brachiopoda or **Brachiopods** A Phylum of marine animals, important in Palaeozoic and Mesozoic fossils, but with living representatives, often called Lamp-shells. Superficially they resemble Bivalve* Molluscs*, but their anatomy differs and they are usually anchored to the sea-floor by a peduncle. The Inarticulata, with more or less symmetrical but unhinged valves, include *Lingula* spp. along the coast of E Aus., and the Articulata, with asymmetrical, hinged valves, include 20 genera off the Aus. shores, e.g. *Crytopara brazieri* off E Aus. and the widespread *Cancellothyris australis*, as well as rocky shore species like *Megerlina lamarkinana* and *Magellania flavescens*.

Bradley, William (1757–1833) 1st Lieutenant on *Sirius* in the First Fleet*. His drawing of the entry into Botany Bay is the earliest such record of the colony. He did many of the first surveys, with Captain Hunter*, and his detailed journal covers 1786–92.

Bradman, Sir Donald George (1908–   ) b. Cootamundra, N.S.W. One of the 2 greatest Aus. cricketers (with Trumper*) and the most famous internationally. His career began in a country team at Bowral, N.S.W., through interstate to Test cricket, and like Trumper, his achievements came at a time of apathy, reviving the game. A unique bat grip, nimbleness and intelligent concentrated play gave him mastery. While not popular among all fellow players or critics, Bradman was always a great crowd-drawer. In 37 Tests against Eng. (1928–48), he averaged 89·78 with 19 centuries of which 2 were over 300 and 6 over 200. His overall Test average failed to reach 100 by 4 runs. His

record of 1448 runs in one season stood for 31 years until beaten in 1971 by Richards (S.A.). In first-class games he totalled 28,067, averaging 95·14 with 117 centuries, or almost 1 in every third innings.

Brady, Matthew (1799–1826) b. Manchester, Eng. Tasmania's most audacious bushranger. He escaped from Port Macquarie in 1824, and at his trial after capture by Batman* in April 1826, he faced over 300 charges, including many murders of stockmen and settlers; he had retorted to Arthur's offers of rewards with posters in Hobart offering rum in return for the capture of Arthur*.

Braidwood N.S.W. 35S/150E (1,086 in 1954; 1,052 in 1961; 959 in 1971). A declining town on a tributary of the Shoalhaven*, developed as a staging point near the brink of the E edge of the Southern Tablelands; formerly important for gold-mining (and bushrangers, the most notorious being the Clarkes), which was also carried out in the picturesque Araluen valley to the S.

Brampton Island Qld. 21S/149E A holiday resort in the hilly and forested Cumberland Islands, with its own air service from Mackay.

Bream These include some of the most prized sporting and commercial seafish of Aus. They are deep-bodied fish, mainly of temperate waters, though overlapping into the tropics. They often spawn in inshore and estuarine waters, though moving their feeding grounds at other times, some species to deeper offshore waters. The Bream is named from the European freshwater bream, a carp, but resemblances are superficial, differences fundamental (even the pronunciation 'brim' in Aus.) and families are widely separated. The bream include: 1. the Black or Silver Bream, *Acanthopagrus australis*, silvery olive-green from the open sea but darker from shady inshore waters, and with a sharp dip in the black line curving along the side, near the front; 2. the Bluenose or Southern Bream, *A. butcheri*, of Gippsland to the S of W.A. with a more continuous curve in the lateral line; 3. the Tropical or Pikey Bream, *A. berda*, in which the lateral line is arched farther back, about half-way along its length; the same names are used for the widely distributed *A. latus*, with a very long and strong spine in the anal fin; for 4. the Japanese or Hump-headed Bream, *A. palmaris*, also from tropical waters, which has slightly different markings and a slight bump on the forehead near the eye; 5. the Tarwhine, *Rhabdosargus sarba*, broadly similar, with a rounded snout profile, golden-bronze stripes along the body, and a notably large anal (rear belly) fin; it is widely known in the Indian and Pacific Oceans. (*See also* SNAPPER.)

Brennan, Christopher John (1870–1932) b. Sydney of Irish parents. He is considered by some as Australia's greatest poet. He was Associate Professor of German and Comparative Literature, Sydney University (1920–25), losing his post following separation from his wife and alleged intemperance. A large ebullient man, he was a leader of Sydney's intellectual life. His poems are short, philosophical and scholarly, often difficult and show more European than Aus. influences. A collection is: *The Verse of Christopher Brennan*, ed. A. R. Chisholm and J. J. Quinn (Sydney, 1960).

Brent of Bin Bin A pen-name used by the novelist Miles Franklin*, whose works include *Up the Country* (Edinburgh, 1928) a study of the 'squatto-cracy', *Back to Bool Bool* (Edinburgh, 1931), *Cockatoos* (Sydney, 1954) etc. The identification with Miles Franklin, long denied by the author, was only finally proved in 1966 with the publication of personal papers bequeathed by her to the Mitchell Library with a stipulated ten-year period before publication.

Brereton, John le Gay (1871–1933) b. Sydney, son of a poet-physician of the same name. As Professor of English Literature at Sydney University (1921–33) he was a notable Elizabethan scholar, and wrote a fine blank verse play about Robert Greene, playwright of that period, *Tomorrow* (1910). He was a minor mystic poet, and had an important influence on Aus. literature through his friendship with Lawson* and encouragement of many other writers.

Brethren The smallest defined Christian group for census purposes, with 22,963 adherents in 1971, mainly in 'open' groups which are widely tolerant, but small groups of Exclusive Brethren have received publicity. Stemming from Darby's original Plymouth groups, founded in Eng. in 1831, they first came to Tas. about the mid-19th century.

Bridges, Major-General Sir William Throsby (1861–1915) b. Greenock, Scotland, grandson of Throsby* the explorer. He arrived in Aus. in 1883. He served in the Boer War, represented Aus. at the Imperial General Staff (1909–10), was in charge of the new Duntroon Military College in 1911 and, as Inspector General of Commonwealth Forces, was responsible for the rapid organisation of the A.I.F.*, and insisted on its separate identity as a unit. He was fatally wounded at Gallipoli in May 1915. Widely read and very able, he was a sensitive and respected leader.

Bridgetown W.A. 34S/116E (1,531 in 1971; 1,877 in 1961) On the Blackwood River, a service centre for a cleared agricultural area on the plateau edge. Apple production here has suffered severe recent marketing and export setbacks.

Brigalow (*Acacia harpophylla*) A small tree of the Mimosaceae family, formerly dominant in inland scrub country over considerable areas of Qld., mainly on clay soil. Its ready suckering after felling has resisted widespread clearing until recent years which have brought new techniques. It grows to 12 m. by 30 cm., with a black, hard, fissured bark like ironbarks, containing tanning material now regarded as inferior. The 'leaves', blue-grey to silvery and scimitar-shaped, are flattened stalks structurally. There are globular compound flower-heads on short stems between the 'leaves', followed by narrow 4-seeded pods 10 cm. long. Timber is violet-scented, splits easily, e.g. for shingles, and was formerly used by Aborigines for spears and boomerangs. Young foliage is eaten by sheep, and adult foliage by stock in drought, but it is poor nutritionally. A useful grass of the Brigalow scrub is *Paspalidum caespitosum*.

The **Fitzroy Basin Brigalow Lands Development Scheme** started in 1962 aims at completion in 1975 when 4·8 million ha. will have been cleared by tractors and steel chain, and increasing the cattle capacity up to ten times. Blocks of 1,000–1,600 ha. are allotted by ballot. There is a research centre at Theodore, 25S/150E.

Bright Vic. 37S/147E (855 in 1971) Tourist centre at 305 m., formerly with gold dredging, on the upper valley of Ovens River.

BRISBANE   27S/153E   (816,987 in 1971) Capital, chief port and industrial centre of Qld. and third Aus. city, having just overtaken Adelaide in the 1971 census. It has 41% of the State's population. Metropolitan Brisbane includes Ipswich*, Redcliffe* and Pine Rivers outside the area controlled by the Brisbane City Council. This covers 993 km.², including 3,240 ha. of parks, and was formed (1925) from a number of small urban authorities. The Council has wider jurisdiction than any other single urban authority in Aus. It covers transport, electric power as well as natural gas, health, sewerage (so far about 70% of the city is sewered) and water, supplied from the Mt. Crosby and Manchester L. storages and Somerset Dam, which also mitigate the formerly devastating floods.

The general setting of Brisbane is one of natural beauty in an amphitheatre of lowland with low wooded ridges, between the 600 m. ramparts of the Main Range to the W and the island-studded Moreton Bay in the E. A warm temperate climate with 114 cm. of mainly summer rain, temperature range of 15°C–25°C, and high sunshine records make a pleasant environment, especially in the winter months. Humidity can be a summer trial, alleviated by the building on pillars of much of the older housing. Tropical trees line many streets; some coastal reaches retain the mangrove swamps which greeted the first settlers.

The heart of the city lies on the N bank of the Brisbane River within a great southward-looping meander. Residential suburbs spread concentrically and include bayside sections, expanding most rapidly; others border the rail and road to Ipswich, now almost linked by a continuous built-up area. On the S bank there are industrial areas, notably the Rocklea Estate, a wartime development now used by many firms concerned with engineering and consumer goods. The port and heavy industrial installations lie downstream along the 29 km. of Brisbane River below the city centre; the main wharves are developed as a deepwater outport. A fertiliser plant using piped natural gas has been built on Gibson 'Island'; an oil refinery has recently been established on Bulwer 'islands', reclaimed and linked to the shore and another on the opposite, S shore at Lytton. Dry dock facilities and a shipyard, both also legacies of 1939–45 wartime developments, are on the S bank, the latter in the heart of the city at Kangaroo Point.

History Brisbane was founded in 1824, when the initial penal settlement was moved from Redcliffe*. The early name of Edinglassie, chosen by Chief Justice Forbes, was officially replaced by that of Sir Thomas Brisbane*, the N.S.W. Governor, in 1834. The first stone buildings and basic layout were the work of Logan*. Free settlement began with land sales in 1842 and a steamer service to Sydney, but it was a period of depression and growth was slow in spite of much speculative buying. In 1846 when the newspaper the *Moreton Bay Courier* appeared, there were only 346 inhabitants, and Brisbane remained a rough frontier town for several decades, although the first bank appeared in 1851, and the district gained representation on the N.S.W. Legislative Council that year. The Darling Downs and local squatters shunned the town, pressing to have Ipswich their capital and Cleveland their port. The arrival of British immigrants, including J. D. Lang's* Scottish Presbyterian artisans after 1848, gave some impetus. In 1859 it was declared a municipality a few months before Qld. became a separate colony, with Brisbane its capital; the population was 5,000. In 1864 a fire devastated the central area; the following year Parliament House was begun. The first bridge (1865) was destroyed by flood in 1869, rebuilt 1874 and again swept away in the historic flood of 1893. There are now 4 bridges in Greater Brisbane, 7 including rail bridges.

By 1900 population was 101,000 and serious port development began, to deal with primary exports of wool, wheat, sugar, meat and fruit collected from the wide hinterland stretching into the N of N.S.W., and re-export of goods shipped from N Qld. ports.

The congestion of a grid-planned centre with narrow streets (named after English monarchs) on a river peninsula, and haphazard downstream industrial growth, have led to plans of varying imagination and practicability for redevelopment, including one to raise shops and offices above the traffic flow; these have so far been blocked largely for financial reasons. In the 1970s the city centre is being opened up with an ambitious road plan and there is further port development. **Brisbane River,** flowing 346 km. SE then NE to Moreton Bay, has good farmland in its valley; it is an important source of water, but subject to flooding.

Brisbane, Sir Thomas Makdougall (1773–1860) N.S.W. Governor 1821–5. He was born in Largs, Ayrshire, Scotland. After army service (1789–1805, 1810–18), Brisbane had returned to astronomical work at his Largs Observatory (elected F.R.S. 1810), when he was appointed to succeed Macquarie*. During his term N.S.W. made important progress: the 1823 Constitution, press freedom, currency stabilisation (including an attempt to use Spanish dollars), exploration, some limitation of land grants and the segregation of the worst types of convicts to Port Macquarie, Moreton Bay and Norfolk Island took place. He built and equipped Parramatta observatory. But Brisbane was not forceful enough to control the turbulent factions of the times, or his disloyal subordinates, notably Goulburn, N.S.W. Colonial Secretary. Both were recalled 1824.

Bristle-birds (genus *Dasyornis*) Small heath birds building a dome-shaped nest of grass near the ground. The Eastern Bristle-bird, *D. brachypterus*, is found in restricted areas from SE Qld. to E Vic., the Western Bristle-bird, *D. longirostris*, in the coastal heaths of SW W.A., and the Rufous Bristle-bird, *D. broadbenti*, in coastal Vic. and SE S.A. and SW W.A. This last may once have extended right across Aus. (cf. the discussion on the superficially similar *Atrichornis*—see SCRUB-BIRD).

Bristle-tails Jumping insects with a prominent three-fold tail, of the Order Thysanura and related to the Silverfish*. They are sometimes seen by the observant on a rocky beach or analogous inland sites in cool weather, but they retreat into shady crevices etc. in hot, dry weather.

Broadcasting Both sound Radio* and Television* are under the broad surveillance of the Aus. Broadcasting Control Board (1949) which issues the commercial licences for radio and television stations and has some control over advertising material used. It has subsidised surveys of the social effects of television.

Broad-headed Snake (*Hoplocephalus bungaroides*) Of coastal E Aus., it has venom which may cause a sharp neurotoxic illness. The genus includes the arboreal Pale-headed Snake, *H. bitorquatus*, and the Yellow-banded or Stephens's Yellow-banded Snake, *H. stephensii*, of coastal E Aus., an arboreal and aggressive species (sometimes wrongly referred to as Bandy Bandy). (*See* VENOMOUS SNAKES.)

Broken Bay N.S.W. An impressively steep-sided, drowned valley system at the mouth of the Hawkesbury River, 24 km. N of Sydney and larger than Port Jackson, on which stand substantial outer suburbs and resort towns, e.g. Woy Woy and Gosford, 33S/151E. It was named by Cook as it struck him as 'some broken land like a bay'. The main branches to the S are Pitt Water and Cowan Creek, to the N the broad and complex Brisbane Water. The relative freedom of Broken Bay from deltaic deposits is much discussed, for the Hawkesbury has a catchment comparable to that of the Hunter* and almost three-fourths of its average flow.

Broken Hill N.S.W. 32S/141E (29,743 in 1971; 31,267 in 1961; maximum in 1915 of 35,000) A mining town in the far W of the State, on one of the world's main deposits of lead-silver-zinc ores. It is 1,125 rail km. from Sydney by the standard-gauge line (1927), but only 410 km. from Port Pirie, S.A., by the 3-ft. 6-in. tramway and railway also now standardised. It retains close links with S.A., e.g. observing the Central Time Zone. It lies at 300 m. above sea level, on the broken hill giving it its name, a narrow ridge of Archaean metamorphic rock standing slightly above the gneissic plateau. This is semi-arid country, with only about 23 cm. mean annual rainfall; summers are hot, with heat-waves of up to 2 weeks in which 37°C is reached daily, occasional dust storms, and a semi-arid landscape of mulga, bluebush and saltbush; it is deforested in the mining area, though a half-mile strip around the town is being regenerated to reduce dust. The town is dominated by the pit-head gear and processing plant of the handful of large mining concerns along the ridge, with most of the town to the W and a smaller part to the E. The main streets contain some substantial public buildings and hotels, but like many mining towns it is dominantly of corrugated iron. This basic form has been modified by heat insulation with aluminium foil, and there are many modern homes of the materials and style common in other Aus. towns. The town has gained a great deal since ample water supplies have been ensured, and sewerage schemes completed.

The first mineral rushes followed silver-lead discoveries about 1875 at Thackaringa, 32 km. to the N, and later Silverton. In 1883 Charles Rasp, a boundary rider on the Mt. Gipps station, noted an iron-stained area, which he wrongly believed to be tin-bearing, on the present Block 12 of Broken Hill South mines. He pegged a lease with David James, and later the station manager became interested and the 'Syndicate of Seven' was formed, later enlarged, and much of the leased land taken over in 1885 by the original Broken Hill Proprietary Co. Ltd. (*see* B.H.P.) and some other companies. Up to 1897-8, the superficial oxidised ores yielded rich carbonate ores, smelted either at Broken Hill or in S.A., then until 1914 the deeper sulphide ores were concentrated for overseas treatment. Since then, the lead has been treated in Port Pirie*, the zinc at Risdon, Tas. Known reserves should last 50 years. Mining is highly mechanised, with techniques flexible enough to adjust to varying lead or zinc markets. The former dangers to health caused by dust are now controlled by water. Employment conditions are controlled by the Barrier Council. *For further reading see* G. Blainey: *The Rise of Broken Hill* (London, 1968).

Brolga, Australian Crane or **Native Companion** (*Grus rubicanda*—red crane) A long-legged grey bird standing about 1·5 m. tall, with a green and red head, longish sharp beak and long neck suited to its sudden movement, from frozen immobility, to catch frogs, small rodents, reptiles and insects in its swampy habitat, though it also eats some herbage, roots, bulbs etc. Its deep trumpeting call is distinctive, and the nest is usually a broad platform of reeds etc. built up from a swamp, with 2 whitish eggs. It is the only crane of Aus. and is widespread except in the SW and SE where it has been depleted by shooting. (*See* PLATE 5.)

Bromwich, John Edward (1918–) b. Sydney. One of the finest Aus. doubles tennis players, also noted for strokes using both hands. He played in Davis Cup* matches 1935–50 and won Wimbledon doubles in 1948 (with Sedgman*) and 1950 (with Quist*).

Brookes, Sir Norman Everard (1877–1968) b. Melbourne. A great left-handed tennis player, and the first Aus. to break into international tennis when he won at Wimbledon in 1905; he played in the Davis Cup between 1905 and 1920. He was president of the L.T.A.A. from 1926–55, and was a very influential selector and administrator in the game.

Broome W.A. 18S/122E (1,884 in 1971) On the N shore of Roebuck Bay, developed as an outlet for the W Kimberleys*; it became a pearling centre with over 300 luggers in the early 20th century; now less than 10 remain. A submarine cable reached Broome from Java in 1889. A meatworks built in 1940 exports chilled beef, bones and tallow. Citizens include many of Asian descent.

Broughton, William Grant (1788–1853) b. London. First Anglican Bishop in Aus. Succeeding Scott* as Archdeacon of N.S.W. in 1828, he was appointed Bishop of Aus. in 1836, but gradually shed the outer parts of his huge see. Broughton was sincere, gentle and well loved, yet also anti-democratic, fearing domination by Irish Catholic immigrants. He opposed non denominational state schooling, was responsible for founding of King's Schools at Parramatta and Sydney, and fought to uphold the Anglican's early established position of privilege and social prestige. *For further reading see* F. T. Whitington: *William Grant Broughton* (Sydney, 1936).

Brown Mallet (*Eucalyptus astringens*) A small tree of 9–24 m. by 30–76 cm., surviving often in pure stands on poor, uncleared, lateritic tabletops in W.A. on the drier inland side of the jarrah* belt with 35–56 cm. mean annual rainfall. Juvenile leaves are oval, adult leaves narrowly lanceolate and 10–15 cm. long, and there are small bunches of long tapering buds, succeeded by bell-shaped 5 mm. fruit. Bark is smooth brown or grey, impregnated with brown kino, but with patches of older and newer bark because of scaling; valuable for tanning.

Brown Snake (*Pseudonaja textilis textilis*) A venomous snake of up to 2 m. long, found all over Aus. except Tas. and the far NW, from woodlands and pastures to rice and wheat country. It is fast-moving, easily roused and with powerful neurotoxic and coagulant venom. The spring courtship includes fighting between males, perhaps to display rather than kill. Related species include the Peninsula Brown Snake, *P.t. inframacula*, the Western Brown Snake, *P. nuchalis nuchalis*, the Dugite, *P.n. affinis*, Tanner's Brown Snake, *P.n. tanneri*, the Collared Brown Snake, *P. modesta*, the Speckled Brown Snake, *P. guttata*, and the Sharp-snouted Brown Snake, *P. acutirostris*. (*See* PLATE 9.)

Brown Spider A popular name for many species mainly in the commonest genus *Ariadna*, family Dysderidae; under 6 mm. long, long-bodied and moderately long-legged with the first 3 pairs of legs pointing well forward, the last pair well backward so that the whole shape looks elongated. It builds a tube-like nest of silk in cracks in the ground or trees, often with radial 'trip-wires' of twigs or leaves arranged round the entrance.

Browne, Thomas Alexander (1826–1915) b. London. He arrived in Aus. in 1836. He wrote as Rolf Boldrewood (from Scott's *Marmion*) while working as a squatter, gold warden and magistrate. He is best known for *Robbery under Arms* (Sydney Mail Serial, 1882, published in book form, 1888) based on the exploit of the cattle stealer Redfern who overlanded 1,000 head of stolen animals from SW Qld. to Adelaide in 1870.

Bruce, Stanley Melbourne (1883–1967) b. Melbourne. Aus. Prime Minister from 1923–9. Wounded at Gallipoli and invalided out of the British Army, he entered the House of Representatives (1918), replacing Hughes* as Prime Minister (1923). Although he lost both Premiership and his own seat in 1929 as the result of mishandling of Arbitration*, his joint ministry with the Country Party* under Page* achieved much in the prosperous pre-depression years. Bruce's ability lay in seeing the need for overall planning: the C.S.I.R.O.*, created to solve problems of primary production, was tied to the export need; development and migration were seen as being complementary; the Tariff Board looked at wide aspects of the economy in relation to protection. He planned a comprehensive national insurance and rationalised the financial relationship of Commonwealth and States in 1927. As High Commissioner in London (1933–45), his shrewd financial mind, important contacts, and supreme confidence achieved much for Aus., e.g. interest reductions during the Depression. He remained in Eng., serving as Independent Chairman of the World Food Council of the Food and Agricultural Organisation; was first Chancellor of Aus. National University* (1951–61), Viscount Melbourne (1947) and became the first Aus. in the House of Lords. *For further reading see* C. Edwards: *Bruce of Melbourne* (London, 1966).

Brumby A wild horse, descended from escaped domesticated animals. Herds of brumbies roam the wilder outback, competing for grazing with station stock and are thus considered a pest and are now shot for pet meat. Name considered most likely to be a Qld. Aboriginal word for 'wild'.

Bruny D'Entrecasteaux, Joseph-Antoine Raymond (1739–1793) b. Aix, France. A sailor sent in charge of an expedition 1791–3 to look for La Perouse*, and carry out scientific research. The expedition charted the SW of Tas. and much of the S Aus. coast, E to Nuyt's Archipelago and later accomplished much Pacific investigation. Notable plant collections were made by La Billardière.

Bruny Island Tas. 43S/147E Off the S coast between D'Entrecasteaux Channel and Storm Bay, it extends 48 km. NE–SW, and comprises North and South Bruny, which are linked by a very narrow sand-spit 6 km. long, with Adventure Bay on its E side. It was named by Bruny D'Entrecasteaux* in 1792, but had been visited by Furneaux* in 1773, and Bligh* who planted fruit trees in 1788. From 1826 whaling was pioneered by Jorgensen*. Today its inhabitants (311 in 1971) cut timber, rear sheep and grow apples, but depopulation is continuous.

Brush Box (*Tristania conferta*) Of the myrtle family, Myrtaceae, this is a tree 37–43 m. by 1–2 m. of the 90–160 cm. rainfall belt of SE Qld. and NE N.S.W., growing best on fertile alluvium and often transitional between rain-forest and eucalypts. It has large glossy and pointed leaves, groups of about 7 buds fringed with pointed fingers, white feathery flower-heads, and conical 3-celled fruit not unlike those of many eucalypts. Timber is fairly good, but shrinks greatly.

Brush Cherry A white-flowered small tree of coastal NE Aus., bearing cherry-like fruit, of the Lilly-pilly* group.

Bryant, William (17 ? –1791) He and his wife Mary (b. Mary Broad, Cornwall 1765) were convicts who escaped from Sydney in March 1791 with their 2 children and 7 other convicts. Bryant was in charge of the colony's fishing boats. They stole a 6-oared boat (the Governor's cutter) which they navigated 5,240 km. to Timor in 10 weeks. All survived to this point but Bryant, the children and 3 convicts died there or on the voyage to Eng. where Mary and the others were leniently treated, then released largely through the efforts of James Boswell. One, Butcher, joined the N.S.W. Corps and settled in Aus. *For further reading see* C. H. Curry: *The Transportation, Escape and Pardoning of Mary Bryant* (Sydney, 1963).

Buccaneer Archipelago W.A. 16S/123E A large group of small islands off King Sound. Several are covered at high tide and only the iron-ore islands

of Cockatoo and Koolan are inhabited. The group was named by King after Dampier*.

Buckley, Vincent (1925–) b. Vic. A poet, critic and academic, whose poetry is of recognised stature, often concerned with current problems and events.

Buckley, William (1780–1856) A convict who escaped from Collins'* abortive settlement at Port Phillip in 1803 and lived with Aborigines in the Barwon area until 1835, when he gave himself up and acted as liaison and interpreter but not with great success for Batman*. *For further reading see* C. E. Sayer's edited version of the 1852 work by J. Morgan: *The Life and Times of William Buckley* (London, 1967).

Buckley's Chance An idiom often expressed as 'You haven't a Buckley's' meaning you have no chance at all. Origin may be from William Buckley*.

Budgerigah or **Budgerigar** (said to be from Aboriginal for good food in the New England area of N.S.W.) A small nomadic, seed-eating Parrakeet*. Green, yellow and blue, and well known as a cage-bird which will breed in captivity.

Buffalo First shipped from Timor to Melville Island in 1824 and later to Raffles Bay (1827) and Port Essington (1838). When these settlements were abandoned the buffalo were left and thrived in the swampy coastal plains. Some 200,000 are now estimated to wander in the region between the Adelaide River and E Alligator River. Since the 1880s they have been hunted for hides, which are very tough and were used for machine belting, and for sandal-making in the Middle East. Up to 16,000 hides a year have been exported, but the market collapsed after 1956, following the Suez crises and changing demands of quality. Abattoirs now process a few for meat. Licences are needed for shooting, a popular pastime in the region, and one in which Aborigines are very skilled. Domestication is being tried.

Buffalo

Buffalo, Mount Vic. 37S/147E (1,723 m.) A steep-sided craggy granite mountain, near the attractive township of Bright on the upper Ovens; not one of the highest summits but impressive because of its isolation.

Bugle, Australian (*Ajuga australis*) An Aus. representative of the European bugles in the Labiatae family, with coarse leaves, rounded and notched, near the ground, also small leaves close to the stem and dark groups of stalkless blue-purple lipped tubular flowers in the leaf axils. It is common on sandy and rocky terrain in SE Aus.

Bugs Insects with sucking beaks (mainly sap-sucking, but in some species blood-sucking) of the Order Hemiptera (i.e. half-wing). The Sub-Order Heteroptera (i.e. different wing), sometimes called the True Bugs, have indeed the different half-wing referred to in the 2 Latin names: the near part of the front wing is thickened as a wing cover like a beetle's, of which the introduced Green Vegetable Bug, *Nezara viridula*, is a common example; the sucking beak appears to rise from the front part of the underside of

the head. The True Bugs range very widely in appearance, habitat and food-source, from very varied vegetarian species including the Rutherglen Bug, *Nysius vinitor*, spreading from grasslands to gardens in a hot summer, to insectivorous species, e.g. the Assassin Bug, *Opistoplatys* spp., the Water Strider of SE Aus., *Gerris australis*, or the introduced Bed Bug, *Cimex lectularius*. In the Sub-Order Homoptera (same wing) the whole of the front wing is either thickened, as in the cockroaches, as a protection for the rear wing—or in some species entirely clear; and the sucking mouth appears to come from the rear part of the underside of the head. A common example is the Cicada*, such as the Yellow Monday Cicada. The Homoptera are sometimes referred to as the Leaf-hoppers, for they include species such as the Blue-winged Leaf Hopper, *Eurymela* spp., but they also include a considerable range of insects, from the Froghopper, *Philagra* spp. ('Cuckoo Spit' from the frothy slime between grass blades etc. in which the nymph stage lives), to the Aphids, e.g. the Green Peach Aphid, *Myzus persicae*, and the immobile Scale Insects, e.g. the genus *Eriococcus*, found beneath a protective waxy secretion on eucalypt twigs, and containing a deep purple pigment which stains the fingers if the insect is crushed.

Bulletin, The A weekly magazine founded in 1880. Today it is devoted largely to topical and political comment, with a large financial section. In its first 30 years it became the most widely read, influential journal of Australasia, forming a focus for the developing national consciousness and endeavouring to create a new nation and distinctive culture. Founded by J. Haynes, a Sydney journalist of Irish origin, and J. F. Archibald* then a 24-year-old cub reporter, it took its style from the San Francisco *News-letter*, the motto of which was 'Boil it down'. *The Bulletin* was put on its feet by W. H. Traill, proprietor 1881–7 (and editor in 1882 while its founders served a jail sentence for libel). Then W. Macleod bought the major interest, giving shares to Archibald whose brilliant editorship, chiefly a flair for selection, gave the paper its predominance, ably helped by A. G. Stephens's* literary criticism on the famous Red Page after 1896. During this time the Aus. short story—brief, episodic—was at its height with Lawson its chief exponent; Furphy's *Such is Life* was serialised and innumerable other writers encouraged, published and paid. In politics *The Bulletin* pursued protectionism, White Aus. policy, secular education, federation and republicanism (Australia for the Australians). Archibald was followed by Edmond whose style was heavier and lengthier, though he was more of a writer himself, and he fashioned the political side of the paper. From the 1920s *The Bulletin* lost its dominance, although remaining the chief literary forum, and became increasingly conservative. Its format and policy changed radically to emphasise finance and topical comment with new ownership in 1962.

Bulloo River Qld. An internal drainage basin of 71,460 km.² The intermittent river, 483 km. long, flows NE–SW from the E slopes of the Grey Range to L. Bulloo swamps, 29S/142E. The upper basin has poor sheep country and the lower basin has cattle fattening.

Bull-rout (*Notesthes robusta*) Of the spiny Scorpion-fish* family, an estuarine and freshwater fish, particularly poisonous because some of its spines have actual venom-glands. It is brown and black, with spines on snout, head and fins, up to 30 cm. long, and not uncommon in estuaries of N N.S.W. and Qld. Wounds should be treated by ligature and hot-water poultice etc.

Bulrushes (*Typha angustifolia* and *T. muelleri*) Native aquatic plants which are sometimes a nuisance in dams and irrigation areas.

Bunbury W.A. 33S/116E (17,762 in 1971) The major regional centre and port in the SW corner of the State, it was named after a Lieut. Bunbury who first explored the area. Traditionally a timber port, it is now sending jarrah sleepers to the Hamersley* ore railways, but rapid recent growth has been due to ilmenite sands. There is a woollen mill, superphosphate works and bulk wheat and oil installations. An alumina refinery using ores to be railed from the Hotham Valley area 128 km. to the NE and a new deep-water inner harbour are planned. The town has spread SE from its original peninsular site.

Bundaberg Qld. 25S/152E (26,570 in 1971) City on the S bank and 13 km. upstream on the Burnett River, the centre of a sugar area established from 1875 on large plantations, using Kanaka* labour. There are still several very large sugar estates. Millaquin refinery (1882) is served by pipes bringing juice from the crushing mills, 32 km. of them underground. A big deep-water bulk sugar terminal 1·5 km. from the mouth was built in 1958. Sugar harvesters are made for home and export; there are timber and butter factories.

Bunya Pine (or **Bunya-Bunya**) (*Araucaria bidwillii*) A good but slow growing softwood timber tree indigenous to low sites in parts of humid coastal Qld. It grows to 30–43 m. by 61–91 cm., with a long branchless trunk, and sharp hard green leaves in pairs, arranged in somewhat palm-like fronds, spirally and very symmetrically, though concentrated near the crown in the mature tree. The male flower is a long narrow spike at the end of branchlets; the female (on a separate tree) a cone of spirally arranged leaves at the end of short branchlets and bearing the sweetish seeds eaten by Aborigines.

Bunya Range Qld. 27S/152E Part of the Great Divide, in basaltic rock on the NE edge of the Darling Downs, reaching 1,100 m. in Mt. Mowbullan and dropping steeply on the E face. The forests include bunya pine*.

Bunyip A Vic. Aboriginal word for a legendary river creature described as 'amphibious and having a round head, an elongated neck, with a body and tail resembling an ox'. Seals provide a possible origin in the S, crocodiles in the N. It came by mid-19th century in Sydney to mean impostor, and hence the derisory term *Bunyip Aristocracy* applied to Wentworth's proposed Aus. peerage.

Burdekin Plum (*Pleiogynium solandri*) A tree of wet tropical Qld. and N.G., reaching 24 m. by 0·5 m. The timber is good for cabinet-making. It belongs to the widespread, chiefly tropical family Anacardiaceae. The compound leaf usually has 5 pairs of oval to lanceolate 9 cm. leaflets; there are male and female flower spikes, and the sparsely fleshed, 10 to 12-seeded 'plum' is edible fresh or after being buried in sand for a day or two. The tree is grown for ornament but is subject to scale insects and mould. Also called 'Tulip Plum', the Latin species name honours Solander, botanist on Cook's first voyage.

Burdekin River Qld. Discovered and named by Leichhardt (1845) after a woman patron, this rises within 72 km. of the Pacific in Seaview Ranges. It flows SW then SE, joined by the Clarke for 480 km. at low gradients, then after receiving the Suttor River which flows from the S through similar country, it turns sharply NE in a gorge section through the Leichhardt Range and crosses a 112-km. delta to the sea at Ayr-Home Hill, 20S/147E. The total catchment (130,500 km.^{2}) is second to the Fitzroy, of the Pacific rivers. It has a marked summer maximum. The upper basin with 64 cm. of summer rain has intensive beef production; delta gravels round Ayr provide underground water for crop irrigation. A large increase in irrigated land is planned from dams on the Broken R., a headwater; this will add to areas already irrigated for sugar, rice and seed beans round Clare, Mittaroo and Dalbeg and along the coast.

Burke, Robert O'Hara (1821–1861) Explorer. Born in Co. Galway, Ireland, he arrived in Aus. in 1853, after Army and Police service. Burke was a police inspector on the Vic. gold-fields when he was appointed to lead the Great Northern Exploration Expedition, aimed at a S–N continental crossing from Melbourne to the Gulf of Carpentaria. The lavishly equipped party left with much pomp in August 1861; the second in command, Landells, turned back after quarrelling with Burke, and Wills* took over. Leaving the heavy stores to follow from Menindee, Burke established a Base Camp on Cooper's Creek, in charge of Brahé, and set off with Gray, Wills and King on a rapid dash to the Gulf, reaching tidal waters in February. On the return Gray died. Brahé had given up and left Base Camp the day Burke got back; the leader found a message from him under a tree marked 'Dig', and left his reply saying he was making S towards Adelaide, but failed to alter the 'Dig' sign so that Brahé on his return never got it, and assumed Burke had not got back. Burke, Wills and King, ill and weak, failed to make any progress and Wills in turn went back to Base Camp, and in turn did not realise Brahé had been back. He and Burke died, but King was saved by the Aborigines. In the subsequent enquiry, Burke was described as having more zeal than prudence; it seems clear that his hasty unscientific temperament made him a tragic choice for work calling for these qualities as much as for the courage he certainly had in plenty. *For further reading see* A. Moorehead: *Cooper's Creek* (London, 1963).

Burketown Qld. 18S/139E On the Albert River, a distributary of the Gregory* and 32 km. inland, this is a small cattle centre in the Gulf Country*, the prototype for Nevil Shute's *A Town Like Alice*. The first recorded malaria epidemic in Aus. killed 50 out of the 76 inhabitants in 1866; the fever might have been typhoid.

Burn, David (1799–1875) b. Scotland. After a brief dramatic career in London, he farmed in Tas. (1826–45) where his mother was the first woman landholder. He wrote the first book of verse plays published (1842) in Aus. These were poor in quality, but he was an acutely observant journalist and also wrote the first Aus. drama performed on the stage, *The Bushrangers*, produced in Edinburgh in 1829.

Burnet, Sir (Frank) Macfarlane (1899–) b. Traralgon, Vic. An outstanding medical research worker, and Director of Walter and Eliza Hall Institute of Medical Research (1944–65). He was awarded a Nobel Prize in 1960 for his part in the discovery of immunology patterns in the human body.

Burnett River Qld. 435 km. long and perennial, with a catchment of 32,220 km.² E of the Divide; its basin includes beef lands on the inner slopes of the coast ranges and it reaches the sea 16 km. below Bundaberg, 25S/152E, in dairy and sugar country.

Burnie Tas. 41S/146E (20,088 in 1971 with Somerset) Third largest Tas. city; it lies on Emu Bay, and is spreading from a low sea-cut platform on to basaltic hills to the S. It is the major service centre for the NW, a port processing and exporting minerals from Rosebery and Mt. Lyell via the private Emu Bay railway. Writing and printing papers are made from *Eucalpytus delegatensis*, hard lining board largely from waste, also plywood (at Somerset 6·5 km. W of Burnie), from 'myrtlebeech' based on concessions originally made to the Van Diemen's Land Co*, of which Burnie was a Director. There are titanium dioxide works at Heybridge, 8 km. E. Recent port improvements include a breakwater and 'roll-on, roll-off' cargo installations, and an oil terminal.

Burns, Sir James (1846–1923) b. Scotland. Arrived in Aus. in 1862, and made a fortune largely as co-founder, with Robert Philps, of the Pacific shipping line, Burns, Philps & Co., based on Townsville. He founded the Presbyterian Burnside Homes, N.S.W., for children in 1910.

Burra S.A. 34S/139E (1,278 in 1971; 1,382 in 1961) Service centre for the drier sheep country on the E flanks of the N Mt. Lofty Ranges*, but originating with copper mining 1845–77; seven townships were collectively called The Burra. Renewed mining of low grade ore by open cut will last 10–15 years.

Burramundi (*Scleropages leichhardti*) A large-scaled, somewhat perch-like and very voracious freshwater fish of up to 1 m. and 14 kg., found in N Aus., N.G. and SE Asia. It is dark green with red spots and white belly.

Busby, John (1765–1857) Civil and mining engineer; born Alnwick, Eng. He arrived in Aus. in 1824 to supervise coal development at Newcastle and to devise a water supply for Sydney. Known as Busby's Bore, a 3,660-m.-long tunnel, 1·5 m. by 1·8 m., was cut (1827–37) from swamps (now Centennial Park) to the site of Hyde Park. **James** (1801–71), his second son, b. Edinburgh, was an early authority and influence on viticulture in N.S.W., touring Europe collecting cuttings and writing with style and great polish on the subject. He was the first British Resident in N.Z. (1833–40), and settled there.

Bush A term with varied meanings: forest or heavy wood and scrub; more widely it refers to the country as opposed to the city. It has many compounds: **bushranger***; **bush lawyer**, a glib persuader with fancied legal ability; **bushed**, lost either physically or intellectually; **bush telegraph**, originally the undercover information supplied to bushrangers by the populace, but extended to mean a 'grapevine' passage of news. The word is common to Africa and America, whence it reached Aus., and may derive from the Dutch *bosch*, meaning wood or forest.

Bushfires A serious dry season hazard, especially in the timbered or partially cleared areas of the SE and SW of the continent, in the tall timber stands S of the Dividing Range, in Vic.; less so in the summer rainfall forest zones of Qld. In the interior grass fires occur when rainy periods allowing lush growth are followed by hot dry conditions; in partially cleared grazing lands this can be the most hazardous type of season. Severity of bushfire danger depends on the development, strength and persistence of northerly winds and high temperatures. 2 seasons in 10 are expected to be severe, 4 average and 4 below average. The causes of outbreaks are estimated to be 90% human, including 30% from 'burning-off' operations, often illegally carried on out of the permitted season, or not sufficiently suppressed even in the season, and continuing to smoulder. Smokers have been blamed for up to 25% of fires in some areas, camp-fires and even over-heated exhaust pipes of tractors have been incriminated. Lightning is the major natural cause, setting off multiple outbreaks often in inaccessible areas. The eucalypt has remarkable regenerative powers after fire (but the wildlife is less easily replaced) and green shoots soon appear from seemingly dead, blackened trunks; not so the natural softwoods of Tas. or the planted conifers of the mainland. Apart from irreplaceable human losses, now into several hundreds, accountable loss lies in houses,

fences, sheds and immediate fodder (subterranean clover* survives). An estimate of loss over the last decade is $4 million a year. State forests are protected, where accessibility permits, by the forest authorities. Private property is protected by over 5,000 volunteer brigades, co-ordinated by Boards within the States. Many farms have a fire truck, with tanks of water, beaters etc. at the ready all summer; sworn enemies will share the task of beating, cutting firebreaks etc. in emergency. Yet there are cases of conflicting authority, overlap or worse, unprotected areas, which have led to demands for fuller co-ordination. Controlled burning of excess growth on the ground is increasingly being used to decrease fire hazards; air-dropped incendiary capsules are used. Although the Aborigines had clearly used fires deliberately, the most disastrous recorded fires date from the 1851 'Black Tuesday' in Vic. There were further bad years in Vic. in 1898 and 1919; in N.S.W. in 1926; and in N.S.W., Vic. and Tas. 1939 was exceptionally disastrous; in 1951–2 Qld. and S.A. were added to the records, having some of the most wide-spread fires known. In 1961 W.A. had severe fires in the jarrah forests; N.S.W. and Vic. had serious fires in 1964–5 and 1968–9 and in 1972. Tas. had its worst fire, with Hobart involved in 1967. Every year there are minor fires around the outskirts of Sydney.

BUSHRANGERS A term coined early in Aus. history for criminals basing their operations from the excellent concealment provided by the rough wooded terrain of the 'bush'. There were 4 contrasting phases and types of activity. 1. Escaped convicts were the first bushrangers, nicknamed Bolters. Van Diemen's Land (Tas.) had the worst of this phase, as Port Arthur and Macquarie Harbour received the worst criminals. An Act of 1830 allowed search and arrest by citizens as well as summary hanging without appeal, which, combined with the end of mainland transportation in 1842, brought about a decade of peace. 2. The gold-rush brought a resurgence in the 1850s in Vic. where the criminals were mainly ex-convicts from Van Diemen's Land (where transportation ended only in 1852). There was even a Chinese bushranger, San Poo, in N.S.W. 3. From 1860–80 was the heyday of bushranging in N.S.W., with a new type of man involved, the Aus.-born sons of convicts or poor settlers who found it more congenial to rob than work for a living. They roamed mainly in well-organised gangs, and like the terrorists of disturbed countries today, had the connivance, willing and unwilling, of the local people, who in general retained a hate of the law. An 1865 Act allowing the shooting at sight of an armed outlaw, combined with the fading gold-rushes and the increased use of non-negotiable cheques instead of cash, brought a further calm phase. 4. A final outburst in 1878–80 saw the exploits of Ned Kelly* with its roots not only in the convict past but in the transplanted hatred of the Irish Catholic for the English Protestant.

The major bushrangers (with active dates and separate entries for those with asterisks) were:

Tasmania: John Whitehead (1810–15), with a gang of 28; Michael Howe* (1814–18), 'Black Howe'; Musquito* (1818–25), an Aborigine; Tegg (1825), also an Aborigine who tracked Musquito, and turned bushranger when he did not receive the promised reward; Pierce (1822) who escaped from Macquarie Harbour with 8 companions, resorting to cannibalism (Marcus Clarke based Gabbett in '*For the term of his Natural Life*' on him); Brady* (1824–6); 'Gentleman Matt' Cash (1842–3), who escaped by swimming from Port Arthur*, and noted for his courteous manners, his top hat, and his final pardon and respectable end in charge of Hobart Botanical Gardens;

'Rocky' Whelan (1855), a brutal ex-Norfolk Island lone wolf.

N.S.W.: Black Caesar (1790–6), a negro convict on the First Fleet, and the earliest recorded bushranger; Knight, Warwick and Thrush (1804), noted for audacious holdups in Sydney area; 'Fox, Pitt and Burke', assumed names of a trio who had a perfect Blue Mts.* hideout complete with women and crops; 'Bold Jock Donahoe' (1827–30), the first popularly acclaimed bushranger, hero of song 'Wild Colonial Boy'; Darkey Underwood (1827–30), his accomplice, later with his own gang; Entwistle (1830), who escaped briefly with a band of 80 convicts; Jenkins (1834), who shot Wardell*, an influential barrister, leading to public outcry against rampant bushranging; 'Jewboy Gang' (1839–40) under Davis, who terrorised roads in Maitland region, but with grim humour; 'Scotchy' and Wilton in Weddin Mts. and Abercrombie Ranges (1830–9); Lynch (1840–1), ex-convict with religious mania, who murdered 9 people with an axe and left a lucid confession; 'Jackey Jackey*' (Westwood) (1840–2); Frank Gardiner* (1859–62); Ben Hall* (1862–5); John Gilbert, accomplice of Hall and Gardiner, with Dunn whose grandfather probably betrayed them; 'Mad Dan' Morgan (1862–5), assumed buccaneer name of Dan Owen, a vicious lone bushranger 'Terror of the Murrumbidgee'; 'Captain Thunderbolt'* (1863–8); Clarke Gang (1865–7), brothers of convict parentage, who robbed with impunity from their home in the forested ranges SE of the present Canberra; Governor brothers (1900), half-caste brothers goaded by racial prejudice, who killed 9 people and were hunted by over 2,000.

Victoria: Williams (1836), leader of an audacious gang, eventually besieged at a Yarraside homestead; Burgess (1852), who set himself up as a Melbourne dandy on stolen gold before being captured and later a notorious

PLATE 2: BUTTERFLIES AND MOTHS

1. Richmond Birdwing *(Ornithoptera priamus)*. 2. Fiery Jewel *(Hypochrysops ignita chrysonotus)*. 3. Common Oakblue *(Amblypodia amytis)*. 4. The Wanderer *(Danaida plexippus)*. 5. Bogong Moth *(Agrotis infusa)*. 6. Emperor Gum-moth *(Antheraea eucalypti)*.

N.Z. criminal; the McIvor Holdup (1853) at Kyneton, leader probably Grey who escaped with the £12,000 Eugowra theft (*see* GARDINER), the only successful robbery of the well-guarded gold escorts; Garrett (1854), who robbed a Melbourne bank of £14,000 before sailing to Eng. for a life of ease in London where only an unlucky coincidence betrayed him; 'Captain Melville' (1852) and 'Captain Moonlight'* (1869 in Vic., then 1879 in N.S.W.); and Ned Kelly* (1878–80), the most famous bushranger of all.

Bushrangers have been romanticised in story and song, but like the highwaymen they often imitated, their deeds were sordid and their lives in the main 'nasty, brutish and short'. *For further reading see* W. Joy and T. Prior: *Bushrangers* (Sydney, 1963); and T. Prior, B. Hannan and H. Nunn: *Plundering Sons* (Melbourne, 1966).

Busselton W.A. 34S/115E (5,020 in 1971) On Geographe Bay, a small timber port and a growing holiday centre. The town was named in 1837 after the local pioneering family of Bussell, a widow and 7 children who moved to the homestead 'Cattle Chosen' nearby, described in the book of that name by E. O. G. Shann (London, 1926).

Bustard or **Plain Turkey** (*Eupodotis australis*) A wary, ground-dwelling bird of inland Aus., with relatives in the Old World, reaching 1·2 m. tall and 14 kg. It has a black and yellow head and eye stripes, brown wings with blue and white flash, dark-mottled light buff breast and light underparts. It is now protected, after great reduction by shooting and foxes. The male breeding display is spectacular and includes a peculiar low roaring call. (*See* PLATE 5.)

Butcher-birds Smallish (about 33 cm. long), mainly pied birds of the Magpie* Group, familiar in bush and gardens in much of Aus. and with a highly esteemed song.

Buttercups Of the world-wide Ranunculaceae family, including in Aus. both native and introduced species, about a dozen of each. The Common or Burr Buttercup, *Ranunculus lappaceus*, with its attractive 5-petalled yellow flower, is often seen in high pastures in E Aus., and there are several swamp and floating species, some said to be poisonous to stock.

Butterfish (*Selenotoca multifasciatus*) A sea-fish of tropical waters of Aus. and farther N. It has a grey-green back and golden-silver belly, with brown vertical stripes above and spots below, very deep-bodied, almost rectangular, with front dorsal fin almost separate, fan-shaped and with sharp rather venomous spines. Fairly omnivorous.

BUTTERFLIES 4-winged, often brightly coloured insects of the Super-family Papilionoidea, which is one of the 14 Super-families of the Lepidoptera*, the others being Moths*. Butterflies are most readily distinguished by the clubbed antennae (though some moths have that), and by the wing co-ordination by means of the under-lapping of the rear pair under the front pair in almost all butterflies. They are often assumed to rest with wings erect as compared with moths, but there is in fact much variation in this. Though there are only some 360 butterfly species in the 10,000 named species of Aus. Lepidoptera, they attract a great deal of attention from their often bright colours and diurnal habits (though there are brilliantly coloured and diurnal moths also), particularly since they tend to be concentrated in the coastal regions where most people live and holiday.

The various species are grouped into 6 families, of which the first stands somewhat apart from all the others, so that it is sometimes classed as having Super-family status; with representative species, these are: 1. Family Hesperiidae, Skippers, distinguished from all other families by the wide separation of the antennae at the base, and by the unforked veins in the wings (only visible when the scales are removed). They are small to medium-sized, with broad head, short wings, and often with a male 'sex brand' in raised and differentiated wing scales. Flight is usually swift but jerky; resting position variable. The caterpillar, generally hairless, lives in a shelter formed by joining two leaves together, e.g. *Trapezites symmomus*, common in E Aus., dark brown, with a yellow spot on the forewings and an orange-brown patch on the rear wings. The larvae are found at the base of bunches of the Long Mat Rush, *Lomandra longifolia*. 2. Family Papilionidae, Swallowtails, large, high-flying and swift and often with a tail-like wing projection, common in the Tropics and best seen when feeding on blossom. The larvae have a hump behind the head, and some emit an unpleasant defensive odour when disturbed, e.g. the Richmond Birdwing, *Ornithoptera priamus*, less spectacular than its tropical cousins, but with 10-cm. wing-span, and the male particularly brilliant in iridescent green, yellow and black. 3. Family Pieridae, Whites and Yellows, of medium size often seen in bright sunshine and sometimes in flocks. The males often have sex brands, raised groups of scales towards the base of one or both pairs of wings. Caterpillars are generally cylindrical with dense short whitish hairs. The universal pest, Cabbage White, *Pieris rapae*, is a familiar example, and the attractive Grass Yellow, *Terias smilax*, over 2·5 cm. across and with dark-tipped forewings is also very widespread. 4. Family Nymphalidae, Danaids, Browns, Nymphs, vary in size, with 7 Sub-families, mainly tropical but one widespread, one favouring sunshine and one shade. To generalise, the front pair of legs is small and not used in walking; many are medium-sized, about 5 cm. across, yellow-brown with intricate patterns of brown and black spots, and often blue-centred 'eyes' on the wing, especially the rear wing, as in the Aus. Painted Lady, *Vanessa cardui kershawi*, which is both widespread and migratory; larvae are often seen on everlasting daisies, *Helichrysum* spp., Cape Weed, *Cryptostemma*, sometimes in a curled leaf by day. The large and powerful Wanderer, *Danaus plexippus*, orange-brown with attractively spotted black wing-edges, has spread naturally from N America; the larvae are brilliantly striped black and yellow, the pupa case jade green with rows of yellow spots. 5. Family Libytheidae, Beaks, a small family in Aus. somewhat similar, but with beak-like development of the mouth-parts, and the forelegs fully functional in the females, e.g. *Libythea geoffroyi genia*, a moderately sized brown butterfly with dark outer wings with spots in the forewing, sometimes seen sheltering under house verandahs in the heat of the day in N.T. and the far NW. 6. Family Lycaenidae, Blues, Coppers and Hairstreaks, variable in size and in colour but often blue-purple, with coppery tints, sometimes iridescent, sun-loving and commoner in the Tropics. Forelegs are slightly reduced in the males, the base of the antennae often causes a notch in the eye, and the rear wings often have a slight tail, as in the Common Oakblue, *Amblypodia amytis*, of Qld. Larvae of this family are often rather flat caterpillars, sometimes hairy; some species are remarkable for their symbiosis with ants which 'milk' them for secretions from special glands and some even feed on ant larvae, the larvae of Qld.'s Fiery Jewel, *Hypochrysops ignita chrysonotus*, for instance. *See* I. F. B. Common: *Australian Butterflies* (Brisbane, 1964). A recent work illustrating food plants, larvae and over 300 species is C. McCubbin: *Australian Butterflies* (Melbourne, 1971). (*See* PLATE 2.)

Butterfly Fish The term is used for fish of various families. (*See Chaetodon* *assarius* under FISHES, SEA, and Butter-fly Mackerel under MACKEREL.) The bizarrely spined Butterfly Cod is *Pterois volitans*; the bright tropical Butterfly Bream is *Nemipterus theodori.*

Button-grass A popular name for various species of *Dactyloctenium*, valuable forage grasses with tight finger-like heads.

Buttons or **Pink Buttons** A popular name for *Kunzea capitata* in the Myrtaceae family, a heath-like shrub of peaty patches in the E Aus. coastal sandstone, with small groups of globose compound crimson flowers, and many prominent stamens much longer than the 5 small petals (unlike *Leptos-permum—see* TEA-TREE). Related species include the spectacular rosy-red flowers of *K. baxteri* and the silver-leaved *K. sericea* in the coastal sand heaths E of Albany, W.A., 35S/118E, as well as the tick-bush *K. ambigua* of much of SE Aus. The name Buttons is sometimes used for *Pimelea* spp. (*see* RICE-FLOWER) in the Thymelaeaceae

family and for various Compositae (*see* DAISIES). Some have insignificant 'petals' (petal-like bracts).

Buvelot, Abram Louis (1814–1888) b. Switzerland. He arrived in Aus. in 1865, after living for 18 years in Brazil. He was the most important of a group of Continental artists who strongly affected the current trends in Aus. with truly Aus. interpretations and land-scapes. Buvelot painted mostly subur-ban or settled farming scenes.

Byron Bay N.S.W. 29S/154E (2,320 in 1971) A former coastal port, with residual whaling, sheltered by Cape Byron; it is quite an industrial town, with butter, bacon and meatworks and mineral sand processing. **Cape Byron,** N.S.W. 29S/154E, is the most E point in mainland Aus., named by Cook in 1770 after Commodore Byron, com-mander of another round-the-world survey ship a few years before (and the grandfather of the poet). It is about 90 m. high and carries a lighthouse.

C

CADDIS FLIES

Caddis Flies Insects of the Order Trichoptera (i.e. hair-wings), generally medium-sized, drab-coloured flies with 4 hairy wings. They are well known from their black-headed white-bodied larvae, which live in freshwater ponds and streams in a silk sheath attached to rocks or crawling about the bottom in a tube or spiral of gravel or slivers of wood cemented together. The enclosed case of the pupa is similar and the pupal stage is aquatic; the adult form breaks out of the case and crawls up a grass stem etc. to dry out and fly off. An Aus. genus is *Stenopsychodes*.

Cadell S.A. 34S/139E An irrigation area of about 400 ha. on the left bank of the Murray, over half in vines, and involving a lift of over 30 m. from the gorge. It was named after **Francis Cadell** (1822–79) b. Scotland. He arrived in Aus. in 1852 and won the government-sponsored race (but not the reward) for the first steam-boat up the Murray in 1853, in the *Lady Augusta*, and captained river boats until 1861.

Cahill, John Joseph (1891–1959). He was born in Redfern, N.S.W. Labor Premier of N.S.W. from 1952–9. His period in office saw considerable expansion of government-sponsored developments, including: 1. the **Cahill Expressway**, opened in 1958 (extended 1962), to free the approach to Sydney Harbour Bridge from the S, and 2. the plan for the Sydney Opera House*.

Cairn Curran Reservoir Vic. With up to 148 million m.³ held back by an earth-fill dam across the Loddon*, it provides irrigation downstream and helps to supplement the Goulburn River* in the W part of the large Goulburn irrigation system.

Cairns Qld. 17S/146E (32,570 in 1971)

CALLISTEMON

A city, bulk sugar port, tourist centre for Great Barrier Reef and rain-forested ranges, and outlet for Atherton Tableland*. It was built amid mud and mangrove on the W shore of a looping inlet of Trinity Bay in 1875 to serve the Hodgkinson gold-field, then the Herbertson tin mines.

Caley, George (1770–1829) b. Craven, Yorks., Eng. He trained as a farrier, but turned to botany and became a protégé of Banks* who secured him a free passage to N.S.W., where he stayed from 1800–8, as superintendent of the botanic garden at Parramatta, making journeys to collect plants; in 1801 he was with Grant, charting Westernport, and made several expeditions himself to the foot of the Blue Mts., but was unsuccessful in crossing them. Subsequently he worked in the W Indies. In *Reflections on the Colony of N.S.W.* (Melbourne, 1966), J. E. B. Currey has edited Caley's informative letters to Banks, linking them with a narrative of the botanist's period in Aus.

Callide Valley Qld. 24S/150E A SE–NW corridor W of the Calliope Range, about 113 km. long. Tertiary rocks include coal. Alluvial sub-artesian water used to irrigate dairy pastures; the black soils also support wheat- and cotton-growing. Open-cut coal (bituminous Triassic), developed since 1948 at **Callide** on the seasonal **Callide Creek** is supplied to a large power station (Cal Cap) nearby, and is railed to Rockhampton. Reserves are estimated at 235 million tonnes. Biloela (4,022 in 1971) is the main centre.

Callistemon An Aus. genus in the Myrtaceae family, many of which have attractive multiple, cylindrical flower-heads (*see* BOTTLEBRUSH).

Callop or **Yellowbelly** A commercially important freshwater fish* of E Aus., introduced into W.A.

Calwell, Arthur Augustus (1896–) b. Melbourne. Leader of the Parliamentary Labor Party (1960–7). He entered the House of Representatives in 1940 and held office as Minister of Information under Curtin*, and then as the first Minister for Immigration (1945–9). His able and active pursuit of increased immigration brought over 700,000 migrants whom he termed New Australians.

Camballin W.A. 18S/124E A small irrigation township on the Liveringa Station flood-plain of the lower Fitzroy River*. Rice has been grown since 1958, milled and exported as brown rice to U.K. Dry season sorghum* and, more promisingly, irrigated pasture are also being tried.

Cambridge, Ada (1844–1926) b. Norfolk, Eng. She arrived in Vic. in 1870 as the wife of a clergyman, G. F. Goss. She was a competent minor poet and a good novelist with a social conscience, as in *A Marked Man* (serial form, 1890); her autobiography, *Thirty Years in Australia* (London, 1903), is a useful period source.

Camels These played a very important part in the opening up of the arid interior of Aus. between the 1860s and 1920s. Apart from a few exhibits, the first camels imported were 6 small Arabian beasts for the Burke and Wills Expedition of 1862 (*see* EXPLORATION); they were replaced for the actual journey by 24 more sturdy Indian camels brought from Peshawar (Pakistan). With them came the first 3 'Afghans'*. The pastoralist Sir Thomas Elder imported camels in 1862, and in subsequent years many came back on ships that had taken Aus. horses for the use of the British Army in India. The Afghans mainly used camels as pack animals, carrying cleverly arranged loads up to 400 kg. of bore piping and mining machinery, copper ore in Qld. and S.A., gold, lead and asbestos in W.A., or poles for the Overland Telegraph*. They also carried supplies to stations and return-loads of wool to ports or more often railheads. Even bush patrols of the Aus. Inland Mission* used camels. White drivers, and some Afghans also, used them to pull drays which carried more, but were more dependent on roads or tracks, and were in often bitter competition with bullock teams. Explorers used them, up to Madigan's* Simpson Desert crossing in the 1930s. When finally ousted by motor lorries, many were turned loose in the desert where their descendants roam, sometimes to the extent of being considered pests. In *Camels and the Outback* (Melbourne, 1964), H. M. Barker, a N.Z.-born old-time camel contractor in W.A., writes in their defence. There is now some export of camels.

Campaspe River Vic. Rises in the Central Uplands some 80km NW of Melbourne, and flows N for 242 km. to the Murray near Echuca, 36S/145E. Its catchment area is small, about 3,885 km.^{2}, and though it floods severely and is dammed at several points for town water, it did not contribute much to the irrigation S of the Murray until the building of the Eppalock Reservoir with 308·5 million m.^{3} capacity, a project accompanied by remarkably thorough conservation measures to minimise silting.

Campbell, John Thomas (?1770–1830) b. Ireland. He arrived in Aus. in 1809. Secretary to Macquarie* (1810–20) whom he served with affection and loyalty, if without discretion as when he was successfully sued in 1817 for allowing a libel against Marsden* to appear in the *Sydney Gazette*, of which he was censor. He was elected President of the Board of Directors of the newly formed Bank of N.S.W. in 1817, and worked for the rights of emancipists.

Campbell, Robert (1769–1846) b. Greenock, Scotland. He joined his brother John in a Calcutta trading firm and from there visited Sydney (1798) to investigate trading possibilities. He bought land for a wharf and warehouses on the site of Circular Quay. Returning in 1800, he built Wharf House and settled to build up enterprises in trading, sealing, whaling, shipbuilding and farming. He fought the East India Company's monopoly (abolished 1813), visiting London (1805) over the seizure of his seal-oil ship *Lady Barlow*. In N.S.W. he fought the officers' trade monopoly, supporting Bligh in the rebellion (1808); the rebels arrested and abused him, and while he was reluctantly absent, as a witness at Johnston's court-martial (1811–15), his business was ruined. He rebuilt it, largely on his reputation for integrity and enterprise. In 1825 he bought land on the Molonglo, now the site of Canberra, with money received as compensation for the loss of his ship *Sydney*, which was requisitioned in 1806 to bring food to Hawkesbury flood victims, and wrecked. Here he built Duntroon. His public influence was great; he opposed transportation and the jury system; was a member of the first Legislative Council (1825–43); was co-founder of the first savings bank (1819–30) known as Campbell's Bank; supported the foundation of Bank of N.S.W. (1817) and King's School (1832). His 4 sons were all influential in trade, politics and farming. His grandson **Frederick** (1846–1928) built Yarralumla*. For further reading *see* M. Steven: *Merchant Campbell* (Melbourne, 1965); C. E. T. Newman: *Spirit of Wharf House* (Sydney, 1961).

Campbelltown 34S/151E (31,524 in 1971) A dairy and poultry centre, 52 km. SW of Sydney. Now recorded for census purposes as in the Metropolitan area and increasingly overwhelmed by urban growth, it has been proposed as a satellite city for Sydney. It was named by Macquarie in 1820 in honour of his wife's maiden name.

Camperdown Vic. 38S/143E (3,476 in 1971) In the rich volcanic Western District, with its crater lakes, e.g. Mt. Leura. It grew with the local squatters' wealth and development of the area in the late 19th century, and remains an important local centre of intensive onion and potato farming, with flour milling and a very large dairy factory.

Canary-grass (or **Toowoomba Canary-grass**) A popular name for the introduced pasture grass *Phalaris tuberosa*, and other species, but it is also widely known as Phalaris*.

CANBERRA A.C.T. 35S/149E (156,334 in 1971 with Queanbeyan) The Federal Capital of Aus. lies in the NE of the Australian Capital Territory* near the old-established N.S.W. market town of Queanbeyan* in the open landscape of the Limestone Plains, discovered in 1821 by Throsby.* The general location in the 'Yass-Canberry' area was chosen after 9 years of controversy (1899–1908), which included 2 Royal Commissions, Parliamentary Committees and site inspections of possibilities, ranging from Bathurst and Orange in the N, to Albury and Tumut and the Snowy foothill towns of Dalgety and Bombala in the S. The actual site was selected by Scrivener and a geological survey made by Griffith Taylor*. The original plan by Walter Burley Griffin* was as a result of an international competition (1911) which brought 137 entries, but was boycotted by the Royal Institute of British Architects because of objection to the lay adjudicator, King O'Malley*. The competitors were provided with a detailed contour map and cycloramic paintings of the attractively hill-studded basin traversed by the meanders and floodplain of the small Molonglo River*. Very much a child of its age, the new capital was to be a lease-hold city, like Howard's Garden Cities near London, to perpetuate control over standards and to reduce the unearned increment from inevitable land appreciation. Stately and elegant avenues and vistas were included, like those in Versailles and New Delhi. Designed at the same period by Lutyens, New Delhi has some similar features in the ground plan, but has more Imperial pomp in siting and architecture and was built more rapidly. The slower growth of Canberra resulted in only a small part of its Civic Centre bearing this imprint, and there are consequent unconformities of style. Only the inner suburbs have the circles and radii, as well as the major boulevards and vistas of Griffin's plan. Suburbs built between 1930–60 are still very different from the gridiron of so many Aus. towns, having crescents and flowing patterns to avoid monotony, and conform to the contours. Only the most recent and projected suburbs are becoming more adapted to the needs of a car-owning populace of a city with minimal public transport, by having major expressways, feeder roads, cul-de-sacs, and some rear-serviced houses and pedestrian enclaves to reduce the accidents, noise and fumes. Suburbs are mainly named after former Prime Ministers, but new ones include the imaginative Aboriginal Aranda. Over 2 million trees, many of them flowering exotics, have been planted.

The major vistas and landscape architecture of Griffin's plans are at least partly fulfilled and vindicated. Making full use of natural features, he envisaged a land axis from about the site of the present (provisional) Houses of Parliament to a major national monument below the commanding forested peak of Mt. Ainslie; though he could not have forseen the way in which, a few years later, the 1914–18 War and ANZAC* in particular would make it inevitably right that this site should be occupied by the combined shrine and war museum of the Aus. National War Memorial, and the vista along the axis towards Parliament by the wide ceremonial marching route of Anzac Parade, flanked by a growing avenue of native trees and beds of native shrubs. The new Parliament House will occupy a site on this axis, on Camp Hill. L. Burley Griffin created in 1964 has exceeded Griffin's vision of a main water axis for the capital city (he had envisaged rather a chain of lesser lakes). He also pictured a triangle of boulevards, with a major feature at each apex. The Parliamentary centre was to be on Capital Hill S of the lake (Capital Hill remains for future development, possibly as a major cultural centre or national monument.). This focal point is connected by Commonwealth Avenue to City Hill, both Hills being marked by tall flagstaffs carrying the Aus. flag, and flood-lit by night. King's Avenue connects Capital Hill with another visual focus at the small hill of Mt. Pleasant. Below this Griffin envisaged a large railway terminal and associated commercial and market development, but the railway station remains S of the lake, and the focal point is occupied by the large office blocks of the Defence Department, and more monumentally by the tall column of the Australian American War Memorial. Constitution Avenue, the third leg of Griffin's triangle, has not developed as a major boulevard; something of its function has been usurped by the expressway of Parkes Way.

The growth of Canberra at first was slow and episodic, interrupted by the 1914–18 War, the Depression of the early 1930s, the 1939–45 War, a recession in the early 1950s, and, in the early days by continued opposition and controversy. It is remarkable in the circumstances that so much of Burley Griffin's plan has survived, including some of its finest aspects. Building did not get under way until 1924 with the first leases and formation of the Federal Capital Commission which, while accused of unnecessary autocracy, achieved the building of Parliament House (1927) and the beginning of the still continuing process of transferring Government Departments from Melbourne. It was abolished in 1930 and Departmental control followed, with a National Capital Development Committee (1938), replaced (1957) by the present National Capital Development Commission (N.C.D.C.) with the consultancy of Sir William Holford. The subsequent detailed planning has gained much in sureness, in imagination and in appropriate evaluation of lessons from overseas. The Commission's slightly over-defensive attitude may seem outmoded and criticism of its unwillingness to admit error or react more to expressed needs of the people may be justified. Government is still through Ordinance, with only a partially elected local Advisory Council, and with a Parliamentary Representative; N.S.W. laws apply in the main but legal reform is under consideration. Architecturally, not much is outstanding by world standards but not much is outrageously bad, except perhaps some grandiose private houses. The 2 bridges taking King's Avenue and Commonwealth Avenue across L. Burley Griffin are very fine, with some of the city's better and more attractive street lighting. The War Memorial's clean lines against the bushland cone of Mt. Ainslie are impressive in vista from Anzac Parade, either by day or floodlit by night. The great National Library on the S lake shore is in classic style. Some school buildings are good. The shallow copper dome of the Academy of Sciences is one of the few daring buildings. The Civic Centre and the closely associated theatre and concert hall with fountains and statuary, make a satisfying complex. The Hobart Place tall office block group was successfully designed as a whole, with a shady—sometimes breezy—courtyard and fountain trough. One or two Embassy buildings are fine. The National Art Galley and High Court will be by the Lake.

By 1963 the city reached the stage of self-sustaining, even if still controlled growth, and is paying in revenue for the heavy capital expenditure lavished upon it, which is sometimes resented in the States. Its occupational structure remains biased towards the public service (38% in 1971). Building employment is high at 13% (as in nearby Queanbeyan). 25% are employed in state-backed institutions like C.S.I.R.O.* and the Aus. National University. Industry is only encouraged in the suburb of Fyshwick and employs under 10%. There is some overspill to Queanbeyan. Tertiary services (37%) have far outgrown the period of subordination to the older regional focus of Goulburn*. Tourist trade is considerable, and shared to some extent as nearby towns such as Yass*. Future development for half a million people will take place in new towns planned along arterial routes in a Y-shape. The most southerly Tuggeranong (begun in 1972) will take the city to the banks of the Murrumbidgee; the north-east and north-west 'arms' will extend to the N.S.W./A.C.T. border. *For further reading see* National Capital Development Commission: *Tomorrow's Canberra* (Canberra, 1970); G. J. R. Linge: *Canberra* (Melbourne, 1963); L. Wigmore: *The Long View* (Melbourne, 1963).

Candyup Poison The liliaceous flowers *Stypandra imbricata* and *S. grandiflora* of W.A., regarded as poisonous to stock. (*See* LILIES.)

Cane-grass A name used for several species of tall, hard-stemmed grasses, especially *Eragrostis australasica* in inland swamps, and sometimes *Leptochloa* spp., while the Sandhill Cane-grass is *Zygochloa paradoxa*. Sugar* cane is a large grass, *Saccharum officinarum*, cultivated in Qld.

Canning Basin or **Desert Basin** W.A. 20S/121E Covers some 400,000 km.^{2} of largely unexplored Great Sandy Desert*. Between parallel sand-dunes are clay pans and spinifex in the hollows. Strata of Permian-Cretaceous age dip SW from the Fitzroy Basin in the N, and NE from the De Gray River in the S, and contain artesian water. So far oil exploration has not yielded commercial quantities.

Canning Stock Route W.A. Pioneered by A. W. Canning (1861–1936) and Trotman in 1907–10, to give an outlet for Kimberley* cattle to the railhead then at Wiluna. Some 1,400 km. long, it is passable only in good years in spite of Canning's bores; reconstructed 1929 and in the 1939–45 War, when the bores were cleaned out, it was last used 1958. Canning also surveyed W.A.'s first rabbit-proof fence (1901–3). *For further reading see* E. Smith: *The Beckoning West* (Sydney, 1966).

Canobolas, Mount N.S.W. (1,395 m.) A very steep conical hill of Tertiary acid volcanic rock, rising dramatically from the almost level plains of basalt and recent deposits, about 13 km. SW of Orange. It is said to influence the climate of Orange, particularly by cold air drainage, lowering the night temperatures in the town in winter.

Cape Barren Island Tas. 40S/148E The central and second largest of the Furneaux Group*, 40 km. E–W and about 11 km. N–S, reaching 512 m. and clothed in heaths. There is a little alluvial tin. For **Cape Barren Geese**—*see* GEESE.

Cape Grim Tas. 41S/145E. The NW landfall of the State, named by Bass and Flinders (1798); it is cliff-edged heathland and the haunt of mutton-birds*.

Cape, William (1773–1847) b. Cumberland, Eng. He arrived in Aus. in 1822, in charge of the first Sydney public school (1824–7). His son **William Timothy** (1806–63), succeeded him and became a very notable educationist.

Cape York Qld. The most northerly point of mainland Aus. at 10°41′S, named by Cook in 1770. **Cape York Peninsula** widens S for 800 km. to its base which is 650 km. across from Cairns to the Gilbert River. The low granite ridge along the E is the beginning of the continental Divide. The Dutch seaman Jansz* touched the W coast in 1606, turning back at Cape Keerweer ('turn again'), reporting 'no good to be done there'. This remains largely true (although bauxite is now being developed at Weipa*) for the N part is barren sandstone, a quagmire in the 'Wet' and with poor grazing. Cattle stations increase southwards and there is considerable development by American interests, based on Townsville lucerne. fertilisers and the Brahman breed of cattle. It has several Aboriginal reservations, and in recent years important rock paintings have been discovered, over 100 galleries being observed from the air by a commercial pilot Captain Trezize, and followed up on the ground.

Capeweed (*Arctotheca calendula*) A widespread weed introduced from S Africa as early as the 1830s, with lemon-yellow, daisy-like flowers and a rosette form. In dry areas it gives some fodder but is a pest of dairy pastures, tainting milk.

Capital Punishment Abolished by law in Qld. in 1922, and in Tas. in 1968. In 1973 abolition was agreed by all the other states, and by the Commonwealth Govt. on behalf of A.C.T. and N.T. Until then it was very restricted in A.C.T. and N.S.W. The crimes subject to it varied in other States; in some it included rape. In effect the sentence was rarely carried out and usually only for murder; there were fewer than 10 executions in the last decade, and public opinion has been increasingly against it.

Capricorn-Bunker Islands Qld. 23S/152E At the S extremity of the Great Barrier Reef, these are built of sandy detritus on coral platforms revealed at low tide, and include among others Heron Island* and One Tree Island, named from the impression given by a large pandanus grove, typical of the vegetation.

Carabeen A popular name for several timber trees of Qld. rain-forests, especially the Red Carabeen, *Geissois benthamii*, and the Yellow Carabeen, *Sloanea woollsii*. (*See also* CARBEEN.)

Carbeen, Carbeen Bloodwood or **Moreton Bay Ash** (*Eucalyptus tessallatis*) Grows in E Qld., except Cape York and in extreme NE N.S.W. in rainfall of 38–150 cm.; also in very varied soils and terrain though best in deep sandy loam. Therefore it is very variable in size, growing 12–30 m. high and to 1 m. in diameter. Trunk, about half its height with dark grey bark, close and even, cracks into rectangular segments, then slender white upper branches with drooping twigs. Beyond seedling stage, leaves are narrow and lanceolate, up to 6–15 cm. Buds are very small, pear-shaped with pointed cover; fruit up to 1 cm. long, shaped like a beheaded egg and fragile. Used for timber, ornament and shelter-belt purposes.

Cargelligo, Lake N.S.W. An intermittent natural lake and town (1,095 in 1971) 80 km. WSW of Condobolin, 33S/147E. The lake is now regulated as part of the Lachlan control system, to accentuate its natural role of storing floodwater and releasing it slowly.

Carlton, James (1909–1951) b. Lismore, N.S.W. An athlete who became a national idol for a time, and centre of controversy over his attempt at the world 220-yd. record in 1932 when his record time of 20·6 seconds was disallowed on grounds of wind assistance. Carlton was a priest for a time, then a teacher and later an athletics coach.

Carnarvon W.A. 25S/114E (4,222 in 1971) At the mouth of the Gascoyne River, this is the centre for irrigated land growing bananas and beans along the river's banks and for a large pastoral hinterland. Whaling ceased in 1963 when an international embargo on killing hump-backed whales was agreed. A U.S. space-tracking station whose role will be reduced from 1973 is 12 km. from the town. Summer cyclones may cause serious damage. The **Carnarvon Basin** is a geological province of W-dipping Devonian-Permian sediments, extensively searched for oil in recent years. The coast is fringed with sand-dunes and lagoons such as L. Macleod to the S which has salt and potash deposits.

Carnarvon Range Qld. 25S/148E A section of the Great Divide in spectacular sandstones over 900 m. high and 160 km. long and containing Aboriginal animal paintings in caves.

Carstensz, Jan Captain of the Dutch ship *Pera* sent from Bantam, Java, in 1623 to seek gold in southern N.G., along with van Colster on *Arnhem*. They repeated Jansz'* error in striking Cape York peninsula, naming features but reporting very unfavourably on land and people.

Cartoons The first prolific period of cartoon and caricature appeared with the *Bulletin**: Over the period of Federation particularly there were plentiful characters and topics for the witty pen. Major *Bulletin* contributors included Phil May from 1885–8; Livingstone Hopkins, 'Hop', who drew for it for 30 years from 1883; David Souter, from 1892; G. W. Lambert and Norman Lindsay. The supreme cartoonist, David Low, worked for it from 1911–19. J. C. Bancks, whose street urchin 'Ginger Meggs' achieved fame overseas, worked for the *Sunday Sun*. *Smith's Weekly* (1919–50) also produced good cartooning, notably by George Finey. Some outstanding modern figures are George Molnar,

Emil Mercier, Bruce Petty and Tanner. *For further reading see* P. Coleman and L. Tanner: *Cartoons of Australian History* (Sydney, 1967).

Casey, Gavin Stodart (1907–1964) b. Kalgoorlie, W.A. A journalist, short story writer and novelist, his work concerns the Kalgoorlie gold-miners with whom he had worked.

Casey, Richard Gardiner (Lord Casey) (1890–) b. Brisbane. A politician and Governor General of Aus. (1965–69), following a long successful diplomatic career in service with both British and Aus. governments and including liaison duties between them. He was Governor of Bengal (1944–6) and was created a life peer 1960. His father, **Richard Gardiner Casey** (1846–1919), b. Tas., was a pastoralist in Qld. and later a city businessman. His grandfather **Cornelius Gavin Casey** (1811–1896), b. Liverpool, Eng., arrived in Aus. in 1833. A new Aus. base in the Antarctic near Wilkes* has been named after Lord Casey.

Casino N.S.W. 29S/153E (9,048 in 1971) A local road, rail and air point on the middle Richmond River and a centre for marketing, forestry, and butter and meat processing. Named after the town of Cassino in Italy, it was initially more important than Lismore*.

Cassia A genus of yellow-flowered, compound-leaved bushes widespread in the Tropics, in the mainly tropical pod-bearing family Caesalpinaceae, including 35 Aus. species. *C. laevigata*, of coastal Qld. and N.S.W. (and tropical America and Africa), has 4-cm. flowers with protruding curved stamens; the pods and leaves of *C. eremophila* are eaten by stock, while *C. brewsteri* is the Qld. Laburnum of popular usage. Senna and tanning bark are obtained from *Cassia* in some countries.

Cassilis Gap N.S.W. 32S/156E Lies W of the Goulburn-Hunter valley at about 490 m. It is the lowest pass across the E Highlands in N.S.W.

Cassowary (*Casuarius casuarius*) A large flightless bird of rain-forests in NE Qld. and N.G., comprising, with the Emu, Australia's Ratites, or large flightless birds. It stands over 1·2 m. high, and is mainly blue-black with vestigial wings and no real tail. The head has a large red-brown crest, said to function as a crash-helmet when the bird runs through thick forest. The featherless neck is bright blue, with bright red nape and front decorations. Its croaking and booming grunt recall the emu's cries. Its nest is a bed of forest litter at the foot of a forest tree; 3–5 light green eggs are laid from July–September. (*See* PLATE 5.)

Castle Hill Rising On 4th March 1804 some 300 Irish convicts led by William Johnston (transported 1798 for taking part in the Irish rebellion) and Philip Cunningham, set out to march from Castle Hill to the Hawkesbury, then to Sydney, vowing vengeance on their Protestant overlords and armed with pikes and rifles. They were betrayed by a fellow Irish convict, Keo, and met at Vinegar Hill after only 16 km. by Maj. George Johnston. The leaders were captured when they came forward to talk under a flag of truce: Maj. Johnston ordered his troops to charge, killing over a dozen and the rebels fled; 9 were hanged, many flogged, and others sent to Coal River (Newcastle) by Governor King.

Castlemaine Vic. 37S/144E (7,547 in 1971) Situated at 275 m. on a right-bank tributary 13 km. E of the Loddon River. It was the scene of one of the great gold-rushes, following the discovery in 1851 of rich alluvial deposits, and had as many as 30,000 people over the short period of easily won gold; the diggings were called Mt. Alexander. Farming development and early secondary industry (e.g. coachworks and tannery by 1860) saved it from becoming another ghost town. A quartz reef mine at Chewton 6·5 km. to the S was closed in 1964 and Castlemaine is primarily a market centre for a dairy/sheep region; it also has engineering and woollen industries.

Castlereagh River N.S.W. 550 km. long, it rises in the Warrumbungle Range, flows S past Coonabarabran, 31S/149E, through wheat-sheep country cleared from light woodland with some cypress pine, then turns W, entering drier and flatter country with heavy dark soils, to its confluence with the Darling. In its lower course, flow is normally seasonal.

Casuarina (often popularly called the **She-oak**) The only genus in the Casuarinaceae, a family of trees with over 40 species in Aus. and N.G., of which one extends to Asia and Africa. The Latin name is from a resemblance of its fronds to cassowary feathers. The male and female flowers are on separate trees. Pollen is dispersed by wind from the male spikelets on the end of branchlets, to the ovoid to globular female flowers between the base of branchlets and a main stem, producing an ovoid to cylindrical nut with flattish seeds, winged for aerial dispersion. The needle-like branchlets bear whorls of teeth representing reduced leaves, forming a collar around joints. (These are reminiscent of the horse-tails *Equisetum*, weeds common outside Aus. descended from forest trees preserved in Carboniferous fossils.) The handsome and widely known River She-oak, *C. cunninghamiana*, is common on river-banks, giving welcome shade in a great belt in the far E and N of Aus.; planted artificially it does well on quite dry sites, yielding fairly useful timber, fuel and emergency fodder in drought. The Forest Oak, *C. torulosa*, is a secondary tree in most eucalypt forests on undulating sites in the coastal belt of E Aus., yielding fuel, formerly shingles, turnery wood, and planted

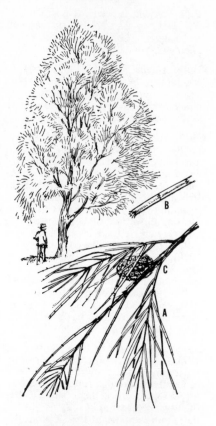

Casuarina cunninghamiana

for shelter. *C. equisetifolia* is used locally in parts of its very wide area for timber; its bark is used for astringents and dye, as well as being widely planted in India mainly for fuel. There are specialised species: in the desert (the termite-resistant Desert Oak, *C. decaisneana*, with very large fruit); in semi-arid gilgai basins inundated in occasional storms (the Belah, *C. cristata*, with prominent ovoid cones); in the sub-alpine zone (*C. nava* of Blue Mts. ridges); in the forests of SW W.A. (the useful furniture-timber tree *C. fraseriana* and the soft and yellow-barked *C. decussata* of the karri forests); and in dry scrubs and heaths *C. acuaria* and others.

Catagunya Tas. 42S/146E Dam and power station (av. annual 260 m. kWh) on River Derwent*, a very large pre-stressed concrete dam, made possible by high tensile steel cables anchoring it to rock base. It is 45·7 m. by 282·1 m. (*See* TAS., POWER.)

Catbird, Green (*Ailuroedus crassirostris*) A green-backed bird of E. Aus., with white blotched breast, about 28 cm. long, with large eyes and very deep longish bill, eating rain-forest berries and insects. It appears to be related to the bower-birds*, though it is not known to build a bower. The name is from its cat-like call.

Catchpole, Margaret (1762–1819) b. Suffolk, Eng. A colourful and courageous emancipated convict, transported in 1801 for escaping from prison while serving a horse-stealing sentence; pardoned in 1814. She lived in the Richmond area, acting as farm overseer and local midwife. Her letters home were grossly altered and published by Cobbold, an East Anglian parson, becoming a best-seller of 1845. The original letters are valuable contemporary material. *For further reading see* G. B. Barton: *The History of Margaret Catchpole* (Sydney, 1922).

Cats, Marsupial, Native or **Tiger**—*see* MARSUPIAL CATS. In places domestic cats have become wild or feral.

Cattle A gradually increasing but fluctuating total, now about 23 million, is distributed as follows: Qld. 35%; N.S.W. 25%; Vic. 21%; W.A. 8%; N.T. 5%; S.A. 4%; Tas. 2%. 17·5 million are beef cattle* and the remainder dairy cattle*. Broadly, beef cattle are grazed in the interior and dairy cattle in coastal areas. Governor Phillip brought cattle from Capetown with him in 1788, some of which escaped. Although not so important

as sheep, they provided milk, meat and traction to the early settlers.

Cattle-bush A popular name for 2 small trees of dry inland Aus. Their foliage gives useful fodder in drought periods: *Atalaya hemiglauca* (Whitewood) and *Heterodendron*, both in the mainly tropical family Sapindaceae.

Caustic Bush A popular name for *Sarcostemma australe*, a stemless trailing bush exuding a burning milky latex. It is widespread, except in Vic. and Tas., and a noxious weed in parts of Qld. It is a member of the mainly tropical and sub-tropical family Asclepiadaceae. In W.A. the prostrate annual Flat Spurge, *Euphorbia drummondii*, is called Caustic Weed.

Caves Many formed by solution of limestone are found in the Tertiary rocks of the Nullarbor* and in the Naracoorte* district of S.A. The coastal limestones of W.A. have over 120 known caves along a 100-km. stretch S from Cape Naturaliste, with especially fine drip formations in the humid climate. They include Mammoth Cave at Yallingup, 34S/115E, famed for deposits of marsupial bones, including extinct species. Caves in the E Highlands are found in Silurian and Devonian limestones and were formed by rivers during uplift. Among the best known are Jenolan, controlled as a N.S.W. Government tourist venture, Wombeyan to the S, and the unexploited Bungonia and Augusta caves; all are to the N and E of Goulburn, 35S/150E. Further W are the Yarrangobilly Caves, 36S/148E, on the NE edge of the Snowy Mts. In Vic. the most famous are the Buchan Caves, 38S/148E, N of the Gippsland lakes. In Tas. caves occur in limestones below the doleritic capping of the Central Plateau*: near Chudleigh in the N (Marakoopa and Mole Creek) and near Hastings (Nordegate Caves) in the S. In Qld. there are extensive cave formations in the region of Chillagoe, 17S/145E. Coastal caves resulting from marine erosion are not uncommon; there are spectacular 'blow holes' at Kiama, 35S/151E, in N.S.W., in W.A. near Albany. 35S/118E, and Geraldton 29S/115E, and along the Tasman peninsula in Tas.

Other shallower caves occur in horizontally bedded rocks such as the Blue Mts.* sandstones in N.S.W. or the quartzites of Arnhem Land* in N.T. Like the wind-eroded caves of the arid interior Macdonnell and Musgrave Ranges, these often contain examples of Aboriginal art.

Cavills A unique swimming family. **Frederick** (1839–1927) b. London, arrived in Aus. in 1879 with an established reputation and 2 near-successful English Channel attempts. As a self-styled 'Professor' he taught swimming in Sydney. Of his sons the eldest, **Ernest,** returned to Eng. and swam successfully there. **Charles** (1871–97) met a premature death exhibiting underwater swimming in U.S., after being the first to swim the Golden Gate at San Francisco in 1897. **Percy** (1875–1940) was a champion in N.S.W. and later coached professionally in U.S.; **Arthur** ('Tums') (1877–1914) also died tragically in the U.S. from exposure when trying to swim Seattle Harbour in midwinter, the culmination of a professional career which began when he was suspended for fouling Gromly in an attempt to assist Percy win the 1 mile in the Hawkesbury in 1896. He also demonstrated the new 'crawl'* by defeating S. Davis (with his legs tied loosely) in 1898. **Sydney** (1880–1945) claimed to have first taught the crawl in U.S. and originated the 'butterfly' stroke. **Richard** (1884–1938) first used the crawl competitively in 1902 when he was described as 'a screw propeller with a galvanic shock'. He had studied Wickham*, and benefited from his brothers' experience, although he failed to defeat his countryman F. C. V. Lane's

trudgen. In 1903 he took all the Aus. free-style titles.

Cedar Applied in Aus. mainly to 2 species in different genera of the widespread tropical and sub-tropical Meliaceae or Mahogany family. *Cedrela toona* var. *australis* (now *Toona australis*), the Red Cedar, is called as a variety of a species extending across SE Asia to India. It grows in the E Aus. rain-forests from Illawarra to Qld., up to 60 m. by 3 m., of valuable hardwood and historically important in opening up coastal tracts and ports, but now rare. Bark scales off the smooth red-brown trunk. It has up to 8 pairs of spear-shaped leaflets in the multiple leaf, branching flower-heads of 6 mm. blossom, and a small dry fruit capsule splitting to release 5 winged seeds. White Cedar, *Melia azedarach*, has serrated 8-cm. leaflets in multiple leaves, 2-cm. lilac flowers in many-branched multiple heads and 1-cm., oval berries with apricot-yellow pulp over a hard stone. The fruit are said to be poisonous to stock. A good cabinet timber.

Ceduna S.A. 32S/134E (2,056 in 1971) Service centre at NW corner of Eyre Peninsula* and on Eyre Highway. Its twin town Thevenard ships wheat and wool, and gypsum from L. Macdonnell to the W.

Celery Top Pine (*Phyllocladus asplenifolius*) A valuable but now scarce timber tree of W Tas., belonging to the Podocarpaceae*.

Celerywood (*Tieghemopanax elegans*) A tall tree of the family Araliaceae which consists mostly of tropical shrubs and climbers. It grows to 27 m. by 60 cm. in coastal scrubs of Qld., in sheltered valleys with good soil. It has 1 m. compound leaves of oval leaflets, and large numbers of small downy flowers in compound heads, producing small disc-like pods containing 2 seeds. As a garden tree it is well shaped and ornamental.

Cement or **Portland Cement** Made from limestone, clay and gypsum, cement is produced in all States, close to limestone and where possible, coal supplies. Over half the annual production, now well over 5 million tonnes a year, is in the hands of 3 major companies. Some 25% of the industry is foreign-owned. Vic. produces 32% at Fyansford (Geelong*) and Traralgon; N.S.W. 25% at Portland* and Kandos, 33S/150E; Qld. 16% near Brisbane, and using coral and shell; W.A. 12% at Perth and Kwinana*; S.A. 10% at Angaston* and Adelaide; Tas. 5% at Railton. **Asbestos cement** or 'fibro' is made from short-fibred chrysotile asbestos* in all capital cities and at Railton, Tas., in the form of flat and corrugated sheeting widely used in building. There are large numbers of small-scale works making cement products such as tiles and building blocks, and larger firms making pre-cast concrete materials.

Censorship (of literature and films) This operates at Commonwealth and State levels, and is a source of considerable controversy. The Minister of Customs and Excise is the final arbiter on all imported material. The States are responsible for censoring indigenous literature. A National Literature Board of Review set up in January 1968 comprises Commonwealth and State nominees to advise on all works of literary merit and is a step towards uniform censorship; but States retain the right to prosecute even if books are approved by the Board and Commonwealth, and the inter-state anomalies are likely to remain, both here and in low level magazine and cheap publications. A Film Censorship Board acts for the Commonwealth and all States except N.S.W. and S.A. *For further reading see* G. Dutton and M. Harris eds.: *Australia's Censorship Crisis* (Melbourne, 1970).

Census The Commonwealth Bureau of Census and Statistics was formed in 1906 and co-operated with State Statisticians to avoid duplication and ensure uniformity of data as far as possible. Tas. statistics are collected by the Commonwealth. Integration between Commonwealth and States was finally achieved in 1958 but an important earlier worker towards uniformity was H. H. Haytor (1821–1895) of Vic. A wide range of publications includes population, industry, prices, finance etc. 'Musters' of population were taken 1788–1828 but the first regular census of Aus. population was 1828, in N.S.W. Sporadic censuses were taken in the developing States, but the first Aus.-wide census on a specific date was in 1881, followed in 1891 and 1901 under State organisation, but by the Commonwealth Statistician in 1911, 1921, 1933, 1947, 1954, 1961, 1966 and 1971.

Centipedes The popular name for the Arthropod Class, Chilopoda, formerly classed with the Millipedes* in the Myriapoda. They are carnivorous on flies, cockroaches etc., and have segmented antennae, 19 or more body segments with 15 or more pairs of legs, and poison fangs on the first body segment. Aus. species include the long-legged *Allothereua maculata* and the yellowish, banded *Scolopendra morsitans*.

Central Mount Stuart N.T. 22S/134E Although 844·6 m., it rises about 300 m. above the surrounding country and is flat-topped. J. McDouall Stuart* named it Central Mt. Sturt as being almost the central point of Aus., on his expedition in 1860; it was later changed to his own name but it is uncertain whether by accident or design.

Central Plateau Tas. 42S/145E A distinctive region sloping gently southwards from 1,100 m. along its steep N edge to 600 m., and drained by the River Derwent*. Almost horizontal sediments were intruded by dolerite sheets which now form much of the surface and, with subsequent faulting give a stepped appearance to the landscape. The ice cap which formed on the Plateau, gouged the surface into hollows now filled with over 4,000 lakes. Summer pastures are used in the high regions; elsewhere rainforest grades eastwards into sclerophyll* woodland. The region is invaluable to Tas. as sources of recreation and water power.

Centre, The A term given to approximately 2·5 million km.² of central Aus. which includes true desert in the NW (Tanami*) and SE (Simpson*), the E-W rocky ridges of the Musgraves*, Mann and Petermann Ranges in the S, and the Macdonnell Ranges*, with the giant monoliths of Ayers Rock*, Mt. Olga* and Mt. Conner* between in the wide Amadeus Basin*. Big cattle stations at the mercy of the unreliable rainfall, and Aboriginal reserves are the main land use. Increasingly tourists visit the Centre, attracted by the fine weather in winter and the brilliant colouring of the rock structures made known through the works of Batterbee and his school of watercolourists from the Aborigines of the area. Alice Springs* is the main focus.

Cephalopoda or **Cephalopods** A Class within the Phylum Mollusca* in which the 'foot' has become modified into a number of sucker-bearing tentacles; the best known cephalopods are the octopuses, squids and cuttlefish. Oceanic floating and planktonic cephalopods with an external shell include the relatively large (15–18 cm.) *Nautilus alumnus* (family Nautilidae) with a beautiful whorled shell of cream, mottled with red-brown, and the smaller Ram's Horn Shell, *Spirula spirula* (family Spirulidae) with a small white shell; both are sometimes washed ashore in E Aus. and *N. pompilius* on the W Coast especially in the tropics. (The brittle Paper Nautilus is not a true shell but the egg-case of an octopus in the family Argonautidae.) Gould's Squid, *Nototodarus gouldi*, is a rapidly swimming Pacific squid whose slender internal bone-like shell is often washed ashore in E Aus., as is the broad flat oval cuttle-bone of Lilian's Cuttlefish, *Solitosepia liliana* (Sepiidae family), usually about 8 cm. long. Cuttle-bones of other squid reach about 38 cm. in length.

Cereals These occupy over 70% of the cropped area, dominated by the winter-grown wheat* (76%), oats* (11%), barley* (9%) and rye (·3%) Summer rainfall cereals are sorghum* (2%) and maize* (·5%), while rice is dependent on summer irrigation.

Cessnock N.S.W. 33S/151E (with Bellbird 16,141 in 1971) A coal-mining town in the important steam coal area of the Hunter Valley* coalfield and linked with Kurri Kurri and Weston as Greater Cessnock (35,003 in 1971). A substantial, modern Civic Centre contrasts with older public buildings and shops along the main street; the very mixed quality of housing offers a similar contrast. Coal was known from 1856, soon after a village was formed on an estate named by a settler from Ayrshire in Scotland; but development began only after Sir Edgeworth David* found the great Greta seam in 1886. Mining development here has seen all the stages: tunnels into outcrop, shallow to medium shaft, and deep shaft highly capitalised mines—including the Aberdare pit-head working near the centre of the town. This coalfield was hit by competitive use of petroleum in power and locomotion some years ago, but has recovered with export to Japan and increased mechanisation. Alternative employment is being found, new industries are being established, including clothing, electrical and aluminium factories. Commuting to Newcastle has developed.

Cessnock is close to the Pokolbin district, famed for its wines.

Chaffey, George (1848–1932) and **William** (1856–1926) Pioneers of irrigation in Aus. These Canadian-born irrigation engineers were working in California when Deakin* was there to investigate irrigation in 1885. In 1886 they selected the site of Mildura*, Vic., and began irrigation by pumping Murray River water on to the arid mallee country, using for the first time for this purpose a triple-expansion marine engine, which remained in operation until 1959. Some over-extension, lack of experienced settlers and transport problems, exacerbated by the Depression of the 1890s, led to the brothers' failure in 1895. George returned to continue a successful career in America, but William remained in Mildura as a leading citizen.

Chambers Pillar N.T. 25S/134E A residual sandstone pillar 46 m. high with surrounding scree slopes, 48 km. W of the Alice Springs–Adelaide Railway and 16 km. N of the Finke River*. Named after a friend by J. McDouall Stuart in 1860.

Channel Country A region of 155,400 km.² in SW Qld., named from the grooves cut into the wide flood-plains of Mulligan, Georgina, Diamantina*, Cooper* and Bulloo* by slowly spreading floods fed by summer rains in the upper catchments, and by rapid 'gutter floods' following occasional local storms. A usually dry brown landscape is then transformed to one of tangled silver braids among the brown-green of intervening spinifex and sand-hills, and as the water seeps into the heavy alluvium a wealth of nutritious grasses grows rapidly, to fatten large numbers of cattle for the next 8–10 months. Permanent waterholes, salt-bush and spinifex support mainly breeding in drier periods. Since its opening up in the mid-19th century there has been a constantly fluctuating occupancy with good and bad seasons. The tendency is towards large pastoral companies. The traditional role of the area is changing since cattle from N.T. now go to the E coast for fattening and 70% of holdings both breed and fatten; they are vulnerable to drought. *For further reading see* A. M. Duncan Kemp: *Our Channel Country* (Sydney, 1962).

Charleville Qld. 26S/146E (3,939 in 1971; 5,154 in 1961) On the Warrego River, a major service and collecting centre for the sheep belt, lying where the more densely stocked downland gives way to poorer spinifex land to the W. It developed rapidly even before the rail reached it (1888) with 500-600 registered bullock teams taking up to 15-ton loads E to the Roma railhead. The first regular Qantas service was Charleville–Cloncurry (1922), and it remains a major outback air centre, with a Flying Doctor Base.

Charlton, Andrew ('Boy') (b. 1908 N.S.W. now dead). World-class distance swimmer of the 1920s, appearing in the Olympic Games in 1924, 1928 and 1932; his major success was the 1,500 m. in 1924. He used a powerful trudgen-crawl and swam with what appears now to be a minimal amount of training.

Charters Towers Qld. 20S/146E (7,529 in 1971; 7,755 in 1966) A city in the upper Burdekin Basin. It was a gold boom town (1872–1909), during which period its population reached 30,000 and £30 million of gold was extracted from the reefs. Charters was local pastoralist and gold warden; Towers is corrupted from the original Tors, a name given to granite hills strewn with boulders in SW Eng. 'The Towers' is now a pastoral centre.

Chats Aus. species are unrelated to those of Europe and Africa; they are small (10–12 cm. long), rather short-tailed perching birds, mainly insectivorous and with a slender sharp beak, in contrast to the stout blunt beak of the seed-eating finches. The nest is a hair-lined grass cup in a low bush or tuft. The species of the drier N. Aus. are gorgeously coloured, mainly in yellow, including the Gibber-bird, *Ashbyia lovensis*, and several species of *Epthianura*, 2 of which are brown and crimson. The commonest chat in the more populated parts of Aus. is the White-fronted Chat, *E. albifrons*, with snow-white head, breast and belly cut by a black nape-to-breast band, light grey back and brown wing-edges and tail; it is often seen flocking over low bush or swamp country after insects, giving a sharp call from which it takes one popular name, Tang. (Also called Thistlebird and Nun—from its 'habit' rather than its habits.) 'The Orange Chat, *E. aurifrons*, is widespread in open country; it is sometimes called the Saltbush Canary (*see* PLATE 3).

Chauncey, Nancen Beryl (Nan) (1900–70) b. Eng. A writer of at least 12 well-known children's books, some translated into 14 languages, and with a number of awards (*Devil's Hill* (1958)) or filmed (*They Found a Cave* (1948)).

Chauvel, Charles Edward (1897–1959) b. Qld. An outstanding film producer, who introduced both Errol Flynn and Chips Rafferty* as stars. He made *Jedda* (1954), the story of an Aboriginal girl, and many other successful films such as *Forty Thousand Horsemen*.

Chauvel, General Sir Henry George (Harry) (1865–1945) b. Tabulum, N.S.W. Famous 1914–18 War cavalry leader. After the Gallipoli* campaign he took charge of the Anzac Mounted Division in Palestine and, in 1917, of the Desert Corps, including French, Indian and British troops as well as Anzacs, leading them brilliantly throughout the Middle East campaign. He was Inspector General of Commonwealth forces from 1919–30.

Cheese Tree (*Glochidion fernandini*) This tree, in the world-wide family Euphor-biaceae, is found in E Aus. and tropical SE Asia, usually up to 10 m. though occasionally 25 m. It is common in open woodland and in suburban gardens. It spreads widely from near the base, has fissured grey bark, spear-shaped leaves about 7 by 2 cm. Fruits are hollow discs reminiscent of Dutch cheeses.

Chemicals Chemicals, petroleum and coal products employ 70,000 in over 1,200 factories, predominantly Melbourne. Growth in recent years has been rapid and products range from cosmetics to industrial chemicals. The heavy chemicals industry, based on naturally occurring substances, evolved comparatively late—Mt. Lyell Chemicals producing caustic soda and chlorine by electrolysis of brine at Yarraville in 1919, and the ICIANZ ammonia-soda plant at Osborne near Adelaide, not producing until 1940. The importance of fertilisers makes sulphur vital (sulphuric acid is a component of superphosphate) and the post-war world shortage of natural sulphur (brimstone) made the Government give various encouragements to sulphur production from pyrites, now maintained residually with low world and import prices for sulphur. This traditional heavy chemicals industry, of less relative importance everywhere in recent years, is handicapped by lack of cheap salt and by distances, e.g. to get coking coal to Osborne. For the newer inorganic chemicals, on the world scale associated buoyantly though by no means exclusively with the petro-chemical industry, overseas oil companies have been willing to put in capital, initially to process imported petroleum, with hopes of substantial Aus. production to come. The Altona, Vic., petro-chemical complex leans towards the production of plastics and carbon black, the Botany group towards heavier chemicals and fertilisers.

Small firms are important and quite competitive in some branches of the industry. Product by product, however, there are signs of a quasi-monopolistic position. Yet prices on the whole are stable and moderate. Moderate protection is complicated by the pattern of subsidiaries of overseas firms—the parent firm is unlikely to import in competition with the subsidiary—but imports are still the main competitive element, and at times emergency protection has been necessary, e.g. of soda ash against Japanese competition in 1960. The larger units, being capital-intensive, are often installed by the overseas firm with excess capacity since the Aus. market though small is rapidly growing; this makes it difficult for the industry to compete at present with overseas firms commanding a large home market.

Cherry, Native or **Ballart** (*Exocarpus cupressiformis*) A graceful, small, cypress-like tree, in the Santalaceae family of semi-parasites, common in temperate Aus. It has a small nut resting on a fleshy red 'cherry'. The tree, like its relative the sandalwood, is a root parasite. **Brush Cherry** is often applied to a white-flowered Lillypilly*. The poisonous **Finger Cherry** of Qld. is *Rhodomyrtus macrocarpa*.

Chifley, Joseph Benedict (1885–1951) Aus. Labor Prime Minister 1945–9. b. Bathurst, N.S.W. Son of a blacksmith with Irish Catholic background. Chifley worked for N.S.W. railways, and was the youngest first-class locomotive driver in 1909, representing his union at arbitration, joining the 1917 strike for which he was demoted, and becoming increasingly concerned with Labor ideals. He was also studying finance and banking with the trained memory and the grasp of detail that made him an outstanding administrator, politician and planner. Bank nationalisation was one of his main aims. Elected M.H.R. (1928–31), he was Minister of Defence under Scullin*, but defeated by the Lang* faction, and was not re-elected until 1940 (re-

presenting Macquarie). Meantime he served on a Royal Commission on Banking (1935), built up a newspaper enterprise and fought Lang bitterly. Re-elected to Parliament in 1940, he became Federal Treasurer when Labor took over in 1941. He succeeded Curtin as Prime Minister. His famous 'light on the hill' of socialism seemingly attainable at last, he launched a full-scale realisation of the welfare and nationalisation aims of the Aus. Labor Party* which he succeeded in uniting. Obstinate single-mindedness lay behind the homely gentle exterior of this tall rugby player, who despised traditional pomp. The famous gravelly voice could produce fluent, compelling argument from a throat described by a specialist as resembling worn-out leather. *For further reading see* L. F. Crisp: *Ben Chifley* (Melbourne, 1961).

Childe, Vere Gordon (1892–1957) b. Sydney. An archaeologist of world repute who left Aus. in the 1920s, and was killed in the Blue Mts. on a return visit. His analytical *How Labour Governs* (London, 1923) used his experience as secretary to N.S.W. Labor Premier Storey.

Chinese The first Chinese in Aus., shepherds brought to replace convicts after transportation ended, were followed by many looking for gold. They were resented on the diggings largely because of their single-minded industry, with ugly incidents as at Lambing Flat* (1860–1). In Vic., however, at least one warden, W. H. Gaunt, insisted on their equality of treatment on the Ovens field. Uniform laws from 1855 in Vic., S.A., N.S.W. and Qld., followed by W.A. (1886), Tas. (1887), N.T. (1888), were among the earliest intercolonial agreements and the beginning of White Aus. as a policy. Many returned home; of those remaining of the peak total of 50,000 in 1888, some turned to small-holdings, and others to cabinet-making or rough labour. They are now well assimilated, with many in the professions, although a number of communal organisations remain.

Chisholm, Alexander Hugh (1890–) b. Victoria. A leading naturalist, notably on birds, and writer. Editor-in-chief of the 10-volume *Australian Encyclopaedia* (Sydney, 1st Edn., 1958). His *The Joy of the Earth* is autobiographical.

Chisholm, Caroline (1808–1877) b. Northampton, Eng. A remarkable philanthropist, who arrived in Aus. in 1838 from Madras with her husband on leave from the forces of the East India Co. Horrified by the squalor and neglect of immigrants, she met their ships, opened a reception home for females, found employment and personally escorted migrants into the country. In London (1846–54) she organised the Family Colonisation Loan Society, returning to Aus. (1854–66). *See* M. Kiddle: *Caroline Chisholm* (Melbourne, 1957).

Chitons Of the Class Amphineura within the Phylum Mollusca*, these are flat, rock-clinging molluscs with a tough carapace of 8 plates held together by ligaments and surrounded by a ring of leathery tissue. The separate plates are sometimes washed up as attractive blue or green 'butterfly shells'. Perhaps the commonest species

Chitons (Ischnoradsia australis), about 3 cm. long

in E Aus. is the Snake's Skin Chiton, *Sypharochiton pelliserpentis*, grey-green, about 3 cm. long and often seen in clefts in rock platforms about low tide level. The larger olive-green *Ischnoradsia australis* is sometimes seen in rock pools and under stones.

Chloanthes A genus of the large, widespread and varied Verbenaceae family, with rough coarse narrow leaves held close to the stem in a fashion reminiscent of some cacti, and bearing somewhat pitcher-like flowers. *C. stoechadis*, fairly common in the coastal sandstone country of E. Aus., has unusual greenish-yellow flowers and *C. coccinea* of W.A. has red flowers.

Chough, White-winged, Black Magpie or **Jay, Apostle-bird,** or **Mutton-bird** (both the latter names are confusing and better avoided). This species *Corcorax melanorhamphus* (black-billed crow), is a crow-like bird of inland E Aus., particularly the Murray basin forests. It is black with small white wing-patches, and with longish, slightly down-curved beak, eating insects and some forest or orchard fruit. It is sociable in small groups and sometimes in nesting, and because of its mud-nest it has sometimes been grouped with the mudlarks* and the apostle-birds*.

Chowilla Dam S.A. A projected dam and water storage on the Murray River, 10 km. below the N.S.W./S.A. border, which would hold 5,860 million m.^{3} and pond water for 193 km. upstream. Agreed in 1964, the project was shelved in 1967 and revived in 1970; costs, politics, potential evaporation and salinity rates are all involved. S. A. is particularly in need of the increased water storage.

Christesen, Clement Byrne (1912–) b. Townsville, Qld. Editor and founder of the literary quarterly *Meanjin*; also lyrical poet and author of *Australian Heritage* (Melbourne, 1949) which is a careful analysis of prose writings

showing the growth of Aus. characteristics.

Christian Science   A religion founded in
the U.S. by Mary Baker Eddy and
first established in Melbourne in 1898.
There are 53 Aus. branches affiliated
with the Mother Church in Boston,
Massachusetts. It is claimed by its
adherents that it is the reinstatement of
primitive Christianity. In practice, the
claim is that the understanding of truth
results in healing of sickness, disease
and sin.

Christmas Beetle (*Anoplagnathus* spp.)
Scarab beetles of greenish gold, about
2 cm. long, which blunder prodigally to
an early death, as it seems, in mid
summer, at or just after Christmas.

Christmas Beetle, about life size

Christmas Bells (*Blandfordia* spp.)   Brilliant red-and-yellow liliaceous plants
of swamps in the sandstone plateaux
of E. Aus. (*See* LILIES.)

Christmas Bush or **Tree**   Applied to the
white, purple-spotted *Prostanthera*
lasianthos in Vic.; in N.S.W. to the
holly-like trifoliate leaves and brilliant
red young fruit (flower-like from the
persistent calyx lobes) which follow
the masses of white flower-heads of
early summer on *Ceratopetalum gummi-
ferum* of the southern Cunoniaceae
family; in Tas. to the blackthorn-like
Bursaria spinosa, with its masses of

pretty small white flowers, of the southern family Pittosporaceae; and in W.A.
to the splendid pendent compound
heads with masses of golden orange-
yellow blossoms, each with 6 narrow
hanging petals, of *Nuytsia floribunda* of
the Loranthaceae or mistletoe family.
(*Nuytsia* is a root parasite on certain
banksias and other heath vegetation
and has caused problems by growing
round and cutting underground cables
etc.)

Christmas Island   10S/106E (3,361 in
1970, about one third European)   An
Aus. Territory (since 1958) in the
Indian Ocean. It extends about 18 by
8 km. From a volcanic base, coral
and phosphate-bearing rocks rise in
steps to a central plateau of about 180
m. rising to a maximum of 356 m.
and edged with cliffs. There are
equable temperatures about 26°C and
200 cm. of mainly summer rainfall. The
only resource is the phosphate in 3
main deposits, dried and exported
from the main settlement at Flying
Fish Cove, which dates from the first
settlement made there by G. Clunies
Ross* in 1888, when the Island was
annexed by Britain. The name possibly
commemorates its date of sighting by
the Dutch Sea Captain Mynors in
1643, although it was discovered earlier.

Chum, New   A newcomer, new settler or
migrant. A term dating from the prison
language recorded by Vaux* in 1812;
opposite is 'old hand' or 'old chum'.

Church of England in Australia   So
named in 1962, replacing Church of
England as the official title of the
Anglican community. There are current moves to change the name to
Anglican Church in Aus. There are
some 3,956,000 adherents in 25 dioceses, representing 38% of Aus. Christians. Recent Primates include Most
Rev. H. R. Gough, Most Rev. P. N. W.
Strong and Most Rev. Dr. Frank Woods
(1971–). A recent poll indicated 13%
of the total were regular church atten-
ders.

On February 3rd 1788, the second Sunday after the arrival of the First Fleet, the Rev. R. Johnson* held the first service in Aus. In 1793 he built the first church, and in 1794 was joined in N.S.W. by the Rev. S. Marsden*. Sydney was created an Archdeaconry under Rev. T. H. Scott* within the See of Calcutta in 1824, and in 1836 it became a Diocese with W. G. Broughton* the first Bishop, and Bishops were appointed in Tas. (1842), Melbourne and Adelaide (1847). The 'bush parson' was often a lonely but important figure in remote communities. Mission activity among Aborigines is strong especially in N.T. There are 2 Monastic and 3 Women's Anglican Orders, and many schools. The Bush Brotherhood is a bachelor order for outback mission work (described by I. Southall in *Parson on the Track*, Melbourne, 1967). An outstanding Anglican was Archdeacon R. B. S. Hammond (1870–1946) who did much for destitutes in Sydney in the 1930s. The Church of England has never been the legally established Church in Aus. although in the early years it had a monopoly in religion* and education*.

Churches of Christ These comprise independent congregations under varying names but with common aims, and numbering 97,426 in 1971. First founded in Adelaide in 1846, they are now particularly strong in Vic. Sir Douglas Nicholls (1906–), pastor of Fitzroy Aborigines Mission, was also a well-known footballer and runner.

Churchill Fellowships Awarded by the Winston Churchill Memorial Trust, established in 1965 from public donation and with capital of $4·4 million, these are available each year for Australians over 18. The object is to finance overseas study visits, either by promising young workers, or older people of proven achievement in any field, including primary and secondary industry, learning, education, public or community service or the arts. Indigenous residents of Territories other than A.C.T. may apply to study or work within Aus.

Cicadas Members of the family Cicadidae of the Order Hemiptera (*see* Bugs), sometimes wrongly termed Locusts. Their shrill chirping causes the popular confusion with the grasshopper family, but it is quite differently produced: male cicadas have a special vibrating membrane in 2 sound cavities behind rounded 'windows' on the underside of the abdomen. Common Aus. species bear picturesque popular names such as Green Grocer, Black Prince, Whisky Drinker etc. An example is the common Yellow Monday Cicada, *Cyclochila australiasiae*; the body is up to 4·5 cm. long, the wing-spread up to 12·5 cm., the wings gauzy and clear. The eggs are laid beneath tree bark, but the nymphs fall to the ground and burrow; climbing up tree trunks as maturity approaches, they slough the conspicuously hooked nymphal skin, often seen on lower trunks.

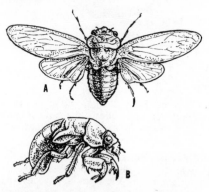

Yellow Monday Cicada (*Cyclochila australiasiae*), *about life size*

Circular Head Tas. 41S/145E. At the NE end of a low 8-km.-long peninsula. The core is a volcanic plug reaching 137 m., and locally called The Nut. The small cray-fishing and timber port of Stanley lies at its foot.

Citizenship The status of Aus. citizen dates from the Citizenship Act (1948–1969). Aus. citizens are, in common with those of other Commonwealth countries, designated British subjects, though not on passports from 1967. Citizenship is automatic if born in Aus., for those born outside Aus. of an Aus. father and registered at an Aus. consulate, those who had been resident for 5 years or more prior to 1948, and those whose fathers or husbands then qualified as citizens. In 1973, under a new Aus. Citizenship Act, all settlers, of whatever origin, can seek citizenship after 3 years residence.

Citrus Fruit Of some 30,000 ha., 85% is under oranges the main areas being in N.S.W., on the coast N of Sydney, in groves of navel oranges on sandy, irrigated soils of the Murrumbidgee Irrigation Area* and along the Murray, where much of the S.A. orange crop is grown round Renmark. Export is to N.Z. mainly. Lemons are irrigated in N.S.W. and rain-fed in Vic. W of Melbourne. There is some citrus on the coast plain S of Perth, W.A.

Clare S.A. 34S/139E (2,103 in 1971) A growing town W of the Mt. Lofty Ranges*, this is the service centre for the most northerly wine region of the State; solid and stone-built in its heyday in the great advance of wheat-growing into the Flinders Ranges 1860–85, for which it was a major centre.

Clarence River N.S.W. Flows for 395 km. from the McPherson Range on the Qld. border, through rain-forest and wet sclerophyll* to the coastal land, cleared for dairying, sugar and bananas, and a set of coastal lakes; then to the sea at Yamba, 29S/153E. Much of its basin is in 100–150 cm. rainfall country, and the flow at Newbold Crossing (catchment 1·7 million ha.), is 2,383 million m.³ River traffic, notably

for cedar in the past, has been important. There is minor port activity at Grafton, Yamba, Harwood and Maclean.

Clarke, Marcus Andrew Hislop (1846–1881) b. London. Arrived in Aus. in 1863, where, as a journalist he wrote numerous satirical newspaper sketches, lively historical essays, and some poor verse. He is best known for his novel *For the Term of His Natural Life*, published as a serial (1870–2, Australian Journal) after intensive study of the convict system, and in later revised book form. A lively, witty figure of the Melbourne scene, he was a co-founder of the literary Yorick Club.

Clarke, Ronald William (1937–) b. Melbourne. Considered one of the great distance runners of all time, ranking with Nurmi and Zatopek. In 1965 he held the world records for 3, 6 and 10 miles, 5,000, 10,000 and 20,000 m. and the 1 hour distance of 12 miles, 1,006 yd. 1 ft. 10 in. (19·657,889 km.) retaining (1973) the 2, 3 and 6 mile records.

Clarke, William Bramwhite (1798–1878) b. Sussex, Eng. Arrived in Aus. in 1839 for health reasons, and made the first scientific assessment of probable gold-bearing rocks in Aus. His academic training included geology before he became an Anglican minister and teacher. He travelled extensively, finding gold in 1841 in Hartley Valley and elsewhere in the area. Governor Gipps persuaded him to suppress his discoveries, but after the gold-rushes* began he was officially commissioned to make surveys. Clarke remained a leader of scientific life in N.S.W., and was created F.R.S. in 1876.

Clarke, William John Turner (?1801–1874) b. London. Arrived in Tas. in 1829, rapidly acquiring vast lands and money, there and on the mainland through ruthless, shrewd ability. Known as 'Big Clarke' or 'Van Diemen's Land Leviathan', he was a huge lame man, influential, respected and feared. He introduced Leicester sheep to Aus. **William John** (1831–1907), his eldest son, made philanthropic use of his father's fortune and received the first Aus. baronetcy (1862). He did much for shorthorn cattle-breeding and more scientific farming.

Cleary, Jon Stephen (1917–) b. Sydney, now living overseas. Writer of many best-selling novels such as *The Sundowners* and a grim study of city life, *You Can't See Round Corners* (Sydney, 1948), both filmed.

Clematis A climbing genus in the Ranunculaceae or Buttercup family. It includes 5 Aus. species, with 4 handsome calyx-lobes simulating petals, including the white Travellers' Joy or Old Man's Beard (from the mass of long, thin, feathery fruits). *C. aristata* and *C. pubescens* (*see* PLATE 6) are found in SW Aus. The leaf stalks are sensitive to contact, and twine round twigs, etc. supporting the plant.

CLIMATE Lat. 10°S passes through Torres Str., 40°S through Bass Str. The pattern of climate is set by position in relation to Polar Fronts, warm humid air of the Pacific and Tropics, and most of all the Sub-tropical High Pressure belt of W to E-moving anticyclonic cells promoting sunshine and drought. Though subject like all air masses to variations in flow and sway, the winter station of this belt lies across the continent, whose interior has much fine warm weather at this season while in summer it lies along the S fringes, bringing much fine hot weather to the S of Aus., though broken by sharp summer storms at times. Except for cooler and more equable Tas., Aus. is a warm to hot continent. Day temperatures in summer are quite commonly over 37°C over much of the continent, almost daily for much of the summer in a belt across Central Aus. just N of the Tropic, and in occasional heatwaves in most years even in the cooler coastal fringes.

The latitude, compact shape, and relationship with the global circulation also determine that much of Aus. has a desert or semi-arid climate, beyond the possibility of much improvement by rain-making* experiments. Ahead of a summer anticyclonic cell quite humid air moves N; on its trailing edge, air from the land moves S and with the 'cool change' sharp storms often develop along the low pressure troughs between the cells, as the television weather forecasters point out, sometimes ruefully. As the belt moves N in winter, the W–E depressions of the Polar Front are able to move northward, bringing storm after storm to the SW of W.A., the SE of S.A. and the S of Vic. Air moving E descends across the E facing scarp to the SE coastlands bringing crisp fine weather there, but there are also some winter storms, and since this area also gets rain from summer easterlies bringing humid maritime air, it has a good deal of rain, spread through the seasons though often with a dry spring. Farther inland, however, the area of transition between winter and summer rains, averaging out to show rain in every month, has moderate totals of rather low reliability; rain—or drought—may come in any season. NE coastal Aus. has ample to very heavy rains, coming in any month but rather less reliable than is often supposed, from tropical maritime air moving with the SE Trades system. Occasional hurricanes bring gales, heavy rains, with good and bad effects, and coastal erosion. W of the Great Divide west-moving air descending, forms a rainshadow, but like all the 2·5 million km.² to Broome and Port Hedland in W.A., this area is subject to summer monsoon storms, with moderate falls and reliability in the N, particularly the far NW, while the light and unreliable falls over the great N central belt include occasional torrential downpours. The NW is also subject to tropical hurricanes from the Timor Sea, which may bring in a single day falls much higher than the mean annual rainfall for the area. The summer monsoon rains are associated with a 'heat low' developing over the hot continent as the Sub-tropical high pressure belt moves to its southerly summer station, but also vary with upper air conditions, of which knowledge is steadily growing. In dry years the W–E 'zonal' (i.e. Sub-tropical high pressure zone) movement of upper air (3,000–6,000 m.) is dominant; in wet years the upper air has a big N–S component, perhaps several km. deep, of unstable tropical air. In some years some of the tropical storms link up with troughs between anticyclonic cells farther S, importing quite unusually heavy falls, and perhaps damaging crops particularly on flood-plains, as far S as Vic. Local factors can be important: orographic effects trigger off rain from unstable air and give local rainshadows. Local overheating of air may cause summer thunder, yet most thunder even in summer is associated with perturbations in warm humid air, or with sharply differentiated air in troughs. Winter thunder, by no means uncommon and sometimes accompanied by dangerous lightning and devastating hail storms, is often caused by the presence of cold air aloft, above relatively warm humid air, usually on the cold front of a Polar Front depression. (*See* MAP 1.) *See* J. Gentilli: *Aus. Climatic Patterns* (Melbourne, 1972).

Climbers Climbing plants of many families include in Aus. widely distributed genera like *Clematis**, Convolvulus* or Bindweed, and *Ipomaea**, and others including *Pandorea* (Wonga Wonga vine*), *Billardiera* (Apple Berries*), *Hardenbergia* (see Peas, Coral), *Smilax* (Sarsparilla*), *Passiflora* (Passion Fruit*), *Bredemeyera* or *Comesperma* (Love-creepers*), and several genera and species in the Vitaceae or vine family, e.g. *Cissus antarctica*, with tooth-edged, heart-shaped leaves and dark blue fruit, the Wild Grape of N.S.W. jungle country. The sweet-centred Doubah of SE Aus. is *Marsdonia suavolens*.

Cloncurry Qld. 21S/141E (2,190 in 1971; 2,438 in 1961) On the Cloncurry River, a tributary of the Flinders. It developed rapidly with the discovery of copper outcrops in the region by Henry (1867), although the railway dates only from 1908. It is a main railing point for cattle from the Gulf Country* but has lost most administrative functions for the NW to Mt. Isa*.

Clothing Manufacture This employs some 112,000 or 10% of workers, in over 6,000 establishments. Save for exotic and luxury imports production meets Aus. demand, and there is a little fashion export. Hosiery and other knitted goods are concentrated in Melbourne (60%) and Sydney (30%), and employ 22% of the total. The other groups, while largely in Melbourne and Sydney, are more widely dispersed in ratio to population distribution, with many small firms especially for women's clothing, medium-sized firms doing men's and boys' tailoring and employing 30% of the workers, and large factories dominating in production of pyjamas and foundation garments.

Clovers (*Trifolium* spp.) These are not indigenous but play a vital part in Aus. pasture management. Subterranean clover, *T. subterraneum*, introduced from the Mediterranean is named from the burying habit of the flowerhead. In the dry summer sheep nuzzle out the highly nutritious seeds. Clover root nodules fix atmospheric nitrogen in the soil. Along with superphosphate, subterranean clover has increased carrying capacity in the sheep areas, and the seed can form a useful cash crop. Pioneers in its use in Aus. were C. E. Prell in Vic. and A. W. Howard in S.A.

Clubmoss Moss-like plants allied to the ferns, of 2 families, Lycopodiaceae and Selaginellaceae, of which Aus. representatives are the large *Lycopodium deuterodensum* (somewhat like a 60-cm.-tall pine) and the moss-like *Selaginella australiensis*. The Skeleton Clubmoss, e.g. *Psilotum nudum*, is of the more primitive family Psilotaceae.

Clubs and Societies In Aus. these are legion. Membership of a social club is common, even assumed, through a wider social spectrum than in many countries, and the pioneering legacy that many social and public services are wholly or partly on a do-it-yourself basis, makes for innumerable *ad hoc* societies and committees, from the (Royal) Flying Doctor Service* to the local Bush Fire Brigades and learn-to-swim campaigns. Following the classification of a recent Department of the Interior publication dealing with the very club-minded national capital, examples show the range and importance of clubs, associations and committees:

Agricultural and Pastoral: Bush Fire Brigades; Junior Farmers' Clubs; specialist clubs, e.g. for poultry or bee farmers, graziers and more general bodies merging into scientific societies as one moves from the Aus. Primary Producers' Union to the National Agricultural Society and the Aus. Institute of Agricultural Science.

Churches: discussed as such under Religion, also have associated groups ranging from ministers' fraternals and missionary societies to clubs overlapping with sporting and youth clubs.

Clubs and Lodges (*Friendly Societies*) include general social, drinking and (in places) gambling clubs and the friendly societies changing in function with the trend towards the welfare state, some with leading roles in social services*.

Community and Welfare Organisations range from societies with international affiliations, e.g. the Red Cross Society or the St. John Ambulance Association, including some of the highly esteemed community service clubs. e.g. Rotary, Apex, Lions etc., to societies caring for Aborigines, Orphans (Legacy*), the Blind, Spastics etc., senior citizens clubs, local progress associations, and clubs to maintain overseas links from Caledonian to Maltese. There are 2 country-wide Humane Societies, one making gallantry awards and one for relief following shipwrecks.

Cultural and Scientific Bodies range from the Aus. and N.Z. Association for the Advancement of Science, the Arts Council and the Aus. Institute of Geographers, to local speleological, art and local history societies and societies to maintain links with the culture and literature of France, Germany etc., or Mensa, the society for the very intelligent.

Ex-Service Associations range from the large Returned Servicemen's League*, to the Rats of Tobruk.

Ex-Students' Associations include school as well as university and college bodies.

Political Clubs and Associations follow the main party lines (*see* POLITICS).

Professional, Trade and Employers' Associations range from the Aus. Medical Association to local groups of doctors, and similarly with science and language teachers and many others, though not always so well-organised nationally, lawyers, builders, electricians and so on.

School Parents' and Citizens' Associations and Pre-school Centre Committees attract much devoted public service (*see* EDUCATION).

Sporting and General Recreation Clubs, in addition to the major Sports, range from gliding to aquaria, from sailing to chess, from sheep dog trials to poodles, from gardening in general to native plants and African violets.

Statutory Bodies and Official Committees range from the various University Councils, or the War Memorial Trustees to Tourist Boards and advisory bodies from the Road Safety Council to the A.C.T. Advisory Council.

Industrial Groups include mainly the various Trade Unions*.

Women's Associations range from the powerful National Council of Women and the Country Women's Association to university women, war and civilian widows etc. Gatherings of witches appear to cover both sexes.

Youth Organisations include Aus. branches of world movements, e.g. the Boy Scouts and Girl Guides etc., Youth Hostels Association (rather weaker, except locally, than in smaller countries), the Y.M.C.A. and Y.W.C.A. (Young Men's and Women's Christian Associations) and various church youth groups. There are bodies such as the National Youth Council of Australia and the National Fitness Council. The Police and Citizens' Boys Clubs represent a remarkable effort to prevent juvenile delinquency etc. by well-placed sporting and recreational facilities, now trending towards more social activities, dancing and the like; N.S.W. Police Commissioner Mackay started the first such club in Woolloomooloo in 1937.

Clunies Ross family They were concerned with the settlement and development for copra of the Cocos (Keeling) Islands*. From 1827 as 'Kings of the Cocos' with a perpetual lease, first **John,** then his son **John George** and grandson **George** (who also founded a settlement on Christmas Island*) ruled paternally. **Sir Ian** (1899–1959) was an outstanding veterinary scientist, Chairman of C.S.I.R.O.* (1949); the family owns freehold of Home Island and other small islands but recognise Aus. sovereignty.

Clyde River N.S.W. Rises only some 24 km. inland near the E edge of the Southern Tablelands, NW of the seaside town of Ulladulla, 35S/150E. It flows about NNE–SSW with the grain of the Devonian and Permian sedimentary or slaty rocks, in wet sclerophyll* forest containing valuable timber, past the old ferry point at Nelligen, recently bridged, to turn E already as a small open estuary, i.e. not closed by a coastal sand barrier, like many other rivers.

C.M.F. Citizen Military Forces have a long ancestry in the separate colonies' defence forces of the 19th century and various schemes of compulsory military training of youth from 1908 onwards. In 1930 compulsory training was dropped and the term militia came into use; with the re-introduction of compulsory training in November 1939 the C.M.F. regiments became the home counterparts to the A.I.F. regiments, and after the war complemented the regular regiments. In the 1970s the 6 State regiments of the C.M.F. all bear the title Royal, e.g. Royal Queensland Regiment etc.

Coal Black coal is preserved in Permian sedimentary basins along the E flanks of the Great Divide; thus giving N.S.W. 76% and Qld. 15% of Aus. production. Isolated basins of sub-bituminous Permian coal lie in S.A. (producing 6% Aus. total) and W.A. (3%). Vic. and Tas. have only very small amounts of bituminous coal, compensated for in Vic. by her vast Tertiary brown coal resources and in Tas. by hydro-electric power. Total measured reserves in million tonnes are: N.S.W. 4,427; Qld. 1,928; S.A. 388 sub-bituminous, 630 lignite; W.A. 306 (sub-bituminous); Vic. 56,000 (lignite). Coal outcrops were discovered both N and S of Sydney in the very first years of the N.S.W. penal colony and a mining settlement was first established at Coal River in 1801, and re-opened in 1804, re-named Newcastle. Coal formed return cargoes to Britain and was sold in India as early as 1799. N.S.W. has remained the dominant coal-mining State, but mining began in Qld. in the 1840s. Development was slow until railways, ships and gas production stimulated the industry in the last quarter of the 19th century. Conditions were poor and there was a long history of industrial disputes especially in N.S.W. Output was 6·1 million tonnes in 1900, increasing to 12·24 million tonnes in 1913, but stagnating (until the 1939–45 War) as costs rose, and markets were lost during the Depression. It seemed that the wartime increase to 15·3 million tonnes in 1942 would again relapse in the 1950s when competition from oil was accompanied by a decrease in demand. But a recent upsurge has raised output from 21 million tonnes in 1957 to 46 million tonnes in 1970; this has been the result of increased demand from iron- and steel-making, thermal power plants and exports to Japan. Coal export was important in the early 20th century (reaching 2·04 million tonnes in 1921) to S America, N.Z. and SE Asia, but had fallen off. In 1955–70 exports of coal rose from 204,000 tonnes to 17·7 million tonnes, 97% to Japan. Coal is also being exported from Qld. to Europe including U.K. Cheaper open cut Qld. coal was causing disquiet to N.S.W. underground producers in 1973, when Japanese intake was lowered. Modernisation and mechanisation facilitated by relatively thick, level seams had reduced the number of miners to some 15,000 (1964) and there was some economic and social disolocation especially in the Northern field of N.S.W. Future development seems reasonably secure, but the home market must still compete with oil and natural gas (*see* GAS). Employment now exceeds 20,000.

COASTS The Aus. coasts, particularly in the more inhabited areas, are the focus of much attention as the most esteemed of recreation areas. The need for conservation of some parts of the inhabited coastlands is urgent, before the whole is completely transformed by the advancing tide of 'weekender', holiday and retirement homes. (*See* SURF, SWIMMING, SAILING.)

All over the world, a post-glacial rise in sea level followed Quaternary fluctuations with the waxing and waning of the major glaciations; one result in coastal landforms is the drowned valley, among mountains as at Hobart, Tas., or in plateau country with gentle slopes, e.g. Sydney Harbour, or steep sides, e.g. Middle Harbour. Botany Bay shows the contrasting shape between rocky headlands, such as Sydney Heads, kept steep by direct wave action, and muddy creeks of a flatter drowned area. See articles on the GIPPSLAND LAKES, L. ILLAWARRA, L. MACQUARIE, MANDURAH, COORONG, CLYDE RIVER and BROKEN BAY, and others, which bring out the varying degree of lagoon and delta formation under different conditions. A typical beach of much of the rural S of Aus. is backed by a platform of sand a little above most high tides, bound by *Spinifex**, convolvulus etc., then by sand-dunes, perhaps fixed by similar vegetation, but if much interfered with then probably wind-eroding and blowing inland. There may be several lines of dunes: the older ones with progressively more complex plant and animal associations, through Tea-trees* or, in W.A., the varied heathy associations, to Paperbarks*, on the flatter sand-apron beyond, with quite a high water-table, and so to swamp or lagoon conditions with Mangrove*.

This stereotype maintains with variations for much of the high wave-energy coasts—which also have rather low tidal ranges (mean spring tide 0·6–2·5 m.)—extending round the S of Aus. from Shark Bay, W.A., 25S/113E, to Fraser Island E of Maryborough, Qld., 25S/153E. The most powerful, long-fetch waves tend to be from the SW in the W coast of W.A., about SSW all along the S coast of the continent, and SSE to SE to ESE as one travels N from Cape Howe, 38S/150E, to Fraser Island. From Port Phillip Bay, 38S/145E, E into Gippsland and W and NW to Victor Harbour, S.A., 36S/

139E, the coast is in the only substantial part of the continent subject to much recent faulting and vulcanism, and there is greater importance than elsewhere in downfaulted basins such as Westernport* or upfaulted ridges as the Otway Range*. The hundreds of km. of cliffs, facing the Great Aus. Bight, are remarkable; chalky limestone below and hard limestone above, with the even low plateau skyline of the Nullarbor*. Beaches are mainly siliceous in SE Aus., with much more calcareous material in the S, SW and W. Within the protection of the Great Barrier Reef, the Qld. coast develops in response to local wind and wave action with much less marked smoothing by coastal sand barriers. Mangrove development is considerable.

The NW and N coasts are low wave-energy coasts for most of the year, while the NW coast in particular has much higher tidal ranges (mean spring tide ranges of 5 to 14 m. are recorded). The effect is to spread the impact of mainly lesser wave action over a wider zone of the shore, while in estuaries tidal scour is much more pronounced than in the low tidal range coasts. Again the effect is towards less coastal sand barrier formation, with more open estuaries. There is local mangrove development in very many places, but the whole coast, should not be thought of as a continuous mangrove swamp: there are many sandy beaches flanking the Gulf of Carpentaria and long stretches between Shark Bay and Broome, 18S/ 122E, with relatively little mangrove, and also with beaches and dunes tending to be calcareous. *For further reading see* E. C. F. Bird: *Coasts* (Cambridge, Mass., 1969).

Coastwatchers Civilian volunteer intelligence personnel, originally formed in 1919 to observe potential attackers off the Aus. coast, but they achieved most fame and note for their work behind Japanese lines in N.G. and the Pacific Islands from 1942, with great feats of courage and severe losses. *For further reading see* M. Murray: *Hunted* (Adelaide, 1967).

Coat of Arms or **The Commonwealth Arms** First granted in 1908; the Royal Warrant for the present Arms dates from 1912. A central shield contains the emblems of the 6 States (which have also their own Coats of Arms). On the top from left to right are: N.S.W., a white ground with a red cross, with a gold star on each limb and a central lion; Vic., a blue ground with 5 white stars (the Southern Cross) and a gold crown; Qld., a white ground, blue Maltese cross with a central gold Crown. On the lower row: S.A. a gold ground, with a black piping shrike on a red and green perch; W.A. a gold ground with a black swan; Tas., a red lion on a white ground. Above the shield a gold pointed star represents the States, and rests on a blue and gold wreath, and on the left a kangaroo and on the right an emu, support the shield. Although not on the Warrant a tradition developed of ornamenting the whole with intertwining wattle and a scroll with *Australia*. Recently a version in which the wattle is much reduced and stylised, has been used on many Government documents. (*See* PLATE 1.)

Cobar N.S.W. 32S/146E (3,744 in 1971) The terminal of a railway from Nyngan and on the Barrier Highway to Broken Hill, and a road focus and local centre of some importance in the E of the Western Plains region with sawmills serving a wide area. It was best known as a gold town (the largest mine in N.S.W. being closed only in 1953), and intermittently a copper-mining town. Formerly the Darling was used to ship the ores. Copper-mining was resumed in 1965 and ore is railed to Port Kembla. Further expansion in 1974 will add to growth of the town.

Cobb & Co. A coaching service (1853–1924) which dominated passenger transport throughout Vic., N.S.W. and Qld., and even after the railway era was established, continued as vital feeder and supplementary services until replaced by motor transport in the 20th century. The first Cobb & Co. service ran from Melbourne to Castlemaine in 1853 and the last from Yeulba to Surat (Qld.) in 1924. The founder was an American, Freeman Cobb, who with 3 fellow-countrymen, saw possibilities in the demand for transport to the goldfields; they used imported American Concord coaches, lightly built, swung on leather straps instead of the current steel springs, and capable of using the roughest tracks with reasonable speed and efficiency, thus earning Government contracts on an expanding Vic. network. Cobb left Aus. in 1856, and the original firm dissolved, but the name was retained. Expansion was greatest after 1860, under Rutherford who had ancillary hotel, pastoral and trading interests. He moved the headquarters from Bendigo to Bathurst in 1862, and had coaches built there; the Vic. firm became separate, and a Qld. branch began in 1865. In 1870 it is recorded that Cobb & Co. covered 45,000 km. a week and harnessed 6,000 horses every day. *For further reading see* K. A. Austin: *The Lights of Cobb and Co.* (Adelaide, 1967).

Cobber A friend, companion, workmate; its origin is uncertain but may well be an old Yorkshire dialect verb 'to cob' or take a liking to.

Cobourg Peninsula N.T. 11S/132E The NW extremity of Arnhem Land*, forming a narrow neck extending NW for 160 km. to Cape Don on Dundas Str. enclosing Van Diemen Gulf. The garrison settlement of Port Essington* (1838–49) was in a deep inlet on the N shore and that of Raffles Bay 24 km. NE (1827–9). Now the area has only nomadic Aborigines, and the wildlife includes wild ponies, goats, buffalo and Zebu cattle descended from those left when Port Essington was abandoned. It is a flora and fauna reserve.

Cockatiel (*Leptolophus hollandicus*) (delicate crested) A small red-brown Parrakeet*, with yellow cheeks and a

Cobb & Co. Coach

white crest; a seed-eater of open woods and grasslands, like a very miniature cockatoo.

Cockatoo Island W.A. 16S/124E In the Buccaneer Archipelago*, Yampi Sound, this is 31 km.^{2} in area and has large iron deposits. Acquired by Hoskins* in 1927 and inherited by B.H.P.*, it was not developed until after the 1939–45 War. The first shipment to the Newcastle, N.S.W., steelworks, 4,800 km. away, was in 1951. Returning ore ships bring steel for rolling at Kwinana*, and water to the island. Open-cut, highly mechanised methods are used and the wharf has to cope with a tidal range of 10·4 m. The fine powdery ore covers the island with red dust. The pre-fabricated township on hill slopes on the NW coast has some 350 people.

Cockatoos and other large Parrots* The grey-backed, pink-headed and pink-bellied Galah* (an Aboriginal name) or Pink Cockatoo, *Kakatoë tenuirostris*, is very common. The lemon-crested White Cockatoo, *K. galerita*, is common from Tas. and all mainland Aus. except the S of W.A. The Gang-gang or Red-headed Cockatoo, *Callocephalon fimbriatum*, of SE Aus., of which the cock has the beautiful red-fringed head of the Latin name, utters a wheezy call-note and a grumbling feeding noise. Darker-coloured species, include the 60-cm.-long Glossy Black Cockatoo, *Calyptorhynchus lathami*, with striking lemon-yellow patches, found in thick forests from Central Qld. to Vic. and Kangaroo Island, and the 60-cm.-long Palm Cockatoo, *Prosciger aterrimus*, of NE Qld. and N.G. Other large parrots include the Magnificent Parrots (*Polytelis* spp.): the Superb Parrot of E Aus. is *P. swainsoni*, slender, green, long-tailed, with yellow and red throat; the yellow-breasted Regent Parrot, *P. anthopeplus*, of all S Aus., and the Rose-throated Parrot, *P. alexandrae*, of Central to NW Aus.

The large sturdy, short-tailed Red-sided Parrot, *Lorius pectoralis*, of Qld. and N.G. is red, blue and black in the cock; green with blue shoulders and wing-edges in the hen. (*See* PLATE 4.)

Cockburn Sound W.A. 32S/116E A sheltered deep-water inlet, 23 km. N–S between the Swan River and Point Peron, with Garden Island and many reefs to the W. It is a major part of the outer Fremantle Harbour, becoming increasingly important to serve the coastal industrial strip. Development of a naval support facility at Garden Island in the Sound is planned to be in operation by 1975, and has been begun with a causeway across the southern end.

Cock-eye Bob Colloquial term for the summer cyclones of the tropical N of Aus.

Cockroaches Insects of the Order Dictyoptera, flattish, of variable size, usually with 2 pairs of wings, the front pair thickened almost like a wing-case for the rear pair, but often moving by swift running on long legs. They are commonest in tropical areas, where introduced species, e.g. the smaller, brown European Cockroach, *Blatella germanica*, and the larger, amber-brown American Cockroach, *Periplaneta americana*, are household pests, eating food left uncovered and clothes left in cupboards for long periods. Native Aus. species are mainly wingless and live under logs or burrow in damp soil, e.g. the largest living cockroach *Macropanesthia rhinoceros* of the Atherton Tableland. The genus *Panesthia* contains fairly typical Aus. species, rather hard-cased, stout cockroaches, with strong spiny legs which cut off the wings to make most of them wingless. The eggs of many cockroaches become fused into an egg-case, often carried about by the female.

Cocksfoot (*Dactylis glomerata*) A valuable European fodder grass widely introduced in Aus. It is a tall and vigorous, coarse grass with broad-keeled leaves and a slightly spread multiple seed-head, each spikelet in a compact ovoid cluster.

Cockspur Flower (*Plectranthus parviflora*) Of the world-wide Labiatae family, this is a succulent hairy herb 30–90 cm., with thick tooth-edged leaves up to 5 cm. long, and a multiple head of blue-purple spurred flowers 2 cm. long. It is common in E Aus. from the Great Divide to the coast.

Cocky A small farmer, often qualified, e.g. as in *Cow Cocky* for dairy farmers. Formerly *cockatoo*, the origin of this use is not certain; it may date from a convict term for the petty criminal, or refer to the birds of that name in a suggested likeness of habit, in that the smaller farmer, as opposed to the squatter*, had to scratch for his livelihood. Another explanation is that large numbers of cockatoos were attracted by grubs living in ring-barked trees.

Cocos (Keeling) Islands 12S/97E (611 in 1970, one third European) An Aus. Territory (from 1955) lying in the Indian Ocean. There are 27 islands in two atolls, 24 in the main group. The original settlement by the Clunies Ross family* was made on Home Island; the fuelling base and airstrip, developed on West Island in the 1939–45 War, are now a refuelling station on the Aus.–S Africa route; a cable station on Direction Island dates from 1901. The low coconut-clothed islands are fringed with gleaming beaches; SE winds prevail, rainfall averages 170 cm. and temperature range is 21°–32°C; there are occasional cyclones. Annexed by Britain in 1857 the islands were attached to Ceylon (1878), Straits Settlement (1886) and Singapore (1903). They were developed for copra under paternalistic rule by the Clunies Ross family, using mainly Javanese labour.

Coelenterata A Phylum of aquatic, mainly marine animals. Aus. has a great range including 4 Classes: Hydrozoa*, including freshwater polyps, 'hydroid zoophytes' and Bluebottles*; Scyphozoa, roughly coinciding with Jellyfish*; Actinozoa, including the Sea-anemones* and Corals*; and Ctenophora or Comb-jellies*.

The coelenterates are more or less radially symmetrical, of jelly-like consistency without blood or excretory system, the body cavity having only one opening. Most genera within these Classes have some form of tentacles, with stinging and grasping mechanism to paralyse and convey prey to the central mouth (some stings being harmful even to man), and there is a general tendency towards stages in the life-cycle involving a relatively or totally stationary polyp stage familiar from sea-anemones and coral polyps, and a much more mobile medusa stage of swimming by expansion and contraction of a cup-shaped body, familiar from the jellyfish.

Coffs Harbour N.S.W. 31S/153E (10,107 in 1971) A seaside resort, banana centre and important coastal shipping port until the railway siphoned off much of its trade; export of timber is residual from the early cedar exploitation which opened up the area.

Colac, Lake Vic. 38S/144E Shallow freshwater lake 8 by 5 km., one of many in depressions in the lava plains of the Western District*. The city of Colac (10,418 in 1971) lies on its southern shore; the city is a market centre for the surrounding dairy and potato- and onion-growing region, and has butter, clothing, flax, engineering and brick-making. It developed on a coaching route from Melbourne, now followed by Prince's Highway.

Coleambally Irrigation Area N.S.W. 35S/146E Lying on the left bank of the Murrumbidgee 32 km. SW of Leeton, this is an area under develop-

PLATE 3: BIRDS (SMALL)

1. Orange Chat *(Epthianura aurifrons),* male and female. 2. Blue Wren *(Malurus cyaneus),* male and female. 3. Scarlet Robin *(Petroica multicolor),* male and female. 4. Beautiful Firetail Finch *(Zonaeginthus bellus).* 5. Jacky Winter *(Microeca leucophaea).*

ment, watered from a new weir at Gogeldrie, to attain full development with the completion of certain parts of the Snowy Mts. Scheme*, particularly the Blowering Dam on the Tumut. Only some 2,800 ha. are irrigated, largely for rice—at present restricted to a limited number of years because of fear of water-logging and salinisation of the soil, but the command area will be about 30,000 ha. eventually. Holdings are rather large, and the scheme is held to be one of the most flexible of all the intensive irrigation schemes, in that intensive cropping, irrigated stock-farming, or integration with drier areas will all be possible according to the economics of irrigated crops in the coming decades. A new town is being built (population 245 in 1971).

Collie River W.A. 33S/116E Rises in plateau country and flows seasonally SW to the Darling Range* then perennially across the coastal plain to Koombana Bay, a total of some 112 km. The only coal-field of W.A. lies in the middle basin, covering 233 km.^{2} in 2 basins separated by a granitic ridge, with the town of **Collie** (6,802 in 1971) as the major centre. The grid pattern of streets spreads out into jarrah forest with much secondary growth and increasingly cleared for sheep, but still concealing the open cuts and the spoil heaps of the underground mines. The mines have operated since 1889 and produce about 4% of the Aus. total. The coal is sub-bituminous, friable and does not store well. Its main use is for power generation, including the Muja plant to the SE. Downstream the Wellington Dam (1934, enlarged 1960), in order to serve the 3,654 ha. of **Collie Irrigation District**, dairy land on the coast plain, and supplies water piped E to wheat belt* towns from Narrogin to Katanning. The town and river were named after **Alexander Collie** (1793–1835) a naval surgeon and explorer of the SW

of W.A. and first Government Resident at Albany (1831–1833).

Collins, David (1756–1810) A military officer who served as Deputy Judge-Advocate with the First Fleet* and acted as Governor's Secretary. He played a vital administrative part in the early days of the colony and wrote a detailed if rather dry description of it on his return to Eng. (1797–1803). In 1803 he was sent to establish a new settlement at Port Phillip, but selected the more unsuitable E shore, and obtained King's permission to move to Van Diemen's Land, where in 1804 he founded Hobart Town on the opposite shore to Bowen's original Risdon Cove settlement. He refused to support Bligh* (1809), who virtually blockaded Hobart for some months. His period of rule was one of difficulty and his administration and morals controversial. Although deeply religious, he treated offenders brutally; he inimicised the Aborigines. St. David's Cathedral was named after him.

Collinsville Qld. 21S/148E (2,146 in 1971; 2,122 in 1961) Coal is railed to Bowen for coking and once bunkering. Reserves will be important to Townsville for copper refining and in a new local power station to serve N Qld. (180,000 kW its eventual capacity) for which Eungella Dam on Broken River will supply cooling water with a surplus for irrigation in the Bowen and Burdekin valleys. Open-cut coal is obtained at Scottsville.

Colombo Plan This is for assisting the growth of the economy of under-developed countries, originating with a meeting suggested by Sir Percy Spender* of British Commonwealth Foreign Ministers in Colombo in 1950. A consultative committee which first met in Sydney in the same year subsequently grew to include: Aus., Canada, Ceylon, India, N.Z., Pakistan, U.K., Malaysia, U.S., Burma,

Cambodia, Indonesia, Japan, Laos, Nepal, Philippines, Thailand, Vietnam, Korea, Bhutan, Maldive Islands and Afghanistan. Aus. has contributed increasing amounts ($23 m. in 1970) in direct aid for economic development, technical co-operation and, since 1968, emergency aid to Indonesia. Economic development aid is either in the form of free equipment or commodities to be sold locally and the proceeds used to finance projects. The main recipients have been so far: India, Pakistan, Indonesia, Thailand, Burma, Vietnam and Cambodia.

Technical co-operation is through training in Aus. or correspondence courses, and includes medicine, engineering, administration and education. Main recipients have been Indonesia, Malaya, Pakistan, Thailand, Singapore, Vietnam and Philippines.

Colubrid Snakes The harmless and rear-fanged snakes, family Colubridae. This family includes all the snakes harmless to man except the rather distinct and specialised worm-snakes and pythons. The solid-toothed snakes, Aglypha, have been divided into the sub-families of Acrochordinae, the File Snakes*, or Harmless Water Snakes, truly aquatic and with file-like non-overlapping scales, and the Colubrinae or Harmless Land Snakes*, with overlapping scales, which include some semi-aquatic species. Similarly the Rear-fanged Snakes or Opisthoglypha, secreting venom but generally considered harmless to man, are divided into the Sub-families Boiginae, or Rear-fanged Land Snakes*, and Homalopsinae or Rear-fanged Water snakes*.

Comb-jellies A popular name for certain marine Coelenterata*. They are usually 1–2 cm. clear globular animals, drifting along in the surface waters of the sea, though with some powers of swimming in the 'combs', 8 rows of movable thread-like cilia; there are also 2 tentacles in pouches on opposite sides of the body. At times there are large numbers of *Pleurobranchia* spp. clogging shore seine or harbour nets, also of *Beroe* spp. (without tentacles). *Neis cordigera* at times produces colour spectra in the water in Sydney Harbour, and phosphorescence by night.

COMMONWEALTH CHRONOLOGY

1901 Proclamation of Commonwealth and first Parliament.
1902 Immigration Restriction Act.
1908 Canberra selected as national capital site.
1910 First Commonwealth bank notes.
1911 First Commonwealth census.
1913 Foundation of Canberra.
1914 First World War; formation and departure of Aus. Imperial Force.
1915 Gallipoli campaign. B.H.P.'s first steel-works opened.
1916 First Conscription Referendum defeated.
1917 Second Conscription Referendum defeated. Transcontinental Railway opened.
1918 Armistice, repatriation.
1919 First England/Aus. air flight, by Smiths.
1927 Federal Parliament met in Canberra for first time.
1928 First trans-Pacific flight by Kingsford Smith and Ulm.
1932 Sydney Harbour Bridge completed. Aus. Broadcasting Commission formed.
1939 Second World War; departure of troops for Middle East.
1941 War with Japan following Pearl Harbour.
1942 Darwin bombed; SW Pacific command under MacArthur, H.Q. Aus.
1944 Referendum on increased Commonwealth post-war powers defeated.
1945 Defeat of Germany and Japan: U.N. charter ratified.

1946 Referendum granting Commonwealth social service powers
successful.

1948 40-hour week throughout country.

1949 New Guinea under international trusteeship; Snowy Mts.
scheme begun.

1951 Transfer of Heard Island and
Macdonald Island to Aus.
Mawson Antarctic Base estab-
lished.

1954 Queen Elizabeth II makes first
tour by reigning monarch.

1955 Cocos (Keeling) Islands become
Commonwealth Territory.

1956 Olympic games in Melbourne.

1958 Christmas Island transferred to
Aus.

1961 First of U.S. tracking stations in
Aus.; first U.K.–Aus. non-
stop flight by R.A.F. Vulcan.

1962 Votes for Aborigines;

1965 Aus. troops sent to Vietnam.
Conscription for National Service.

1966 Decimal currency introduced.
First visit of an American President (Lyndon Johnson).

1967 Oil discoveries in Bass Str.,
nickel in W.A.

1970 Standard gauge rail link Sydney–Perth.

1972 Aus. completed withdrawal
from Vietnam. Aus. Labor
Party took office after 23 years.

Commonwealth Literary Fund Originated as a benevolent move by
Deakin* in 1908, for writers or their
families. Since 1939 its scope has been
enlarged to include: fellowships up to
$6,000 a year to selected applicant
writers; guarantees to publishers in
the case of outstanding manuscripts
of uncertain commercial viability;
grants for lectures on Aus. literature
in universities, colleges, schools and in
adult education centres; pensions;
assistance to literary periodicals. A
committee representing the 3 political
parties is chaired by a nominee of the
Prime Minister.

Commonwealth Serum Laboratory
Founded in Melbourne (1916), it produces penicillin, and poliomyelitis
vaccines, anti-venenes for snake bite,
smallpox, diphtheria and other pro-
phylactics. Materials are also produced
for prevention of contagious abortion
in cattle, pulpy kidney in sheep etc.

Communist Party In Aus. there are
some 4,500 members, the bulk of them
male manual workers although with a
significant minority of intellectuals.
Some 50% are in N.S.W., mainly the
industrial areas. The Party was established in 1920, absorbing the increasingly militant left-wing elements in the
Aus. Labor Party* which has subsequently bitterly opposed it. It has not
succeeded in winning Commonwealth
Parliamentary seats. Hughes* amended
immigration laws and passed the
Crimes Act specifically to suppress those
committed to forcible overthrow of the
state. In 1925–7 Bruce failed by a
High Court ruling to deport 2 Communist agitators, but gained more
strike-breaking power and in 1949
Chifley sent troops to cut coal when
convinced of Communist responsibility
for the strikes. Post-war Communist
expansion overseas and rise to 23,000
Aus. members in 1945 increased alarm,
but in 1951 Menzies's Communist Party
Dissolution Act was declared invalid
by the High Court; in the referendum
to amend the Constitution to permit
Anti-Communist legislation (1951) his
proposal was only narrowly defeated
(2,327,927 to 2,370,009). Alarm was
also caused by the 1954–5 Petrov
Affair* and subsequent Royal Commission. The Hungarian rising led to
resignations from the party. More splits
reflected the Moscow–Peking quarrel.

COMPANIES As compared with part-
nerships, these have a legal identity
separate from that of the individuals
comprising them, and continuing beyond the death of individuals, while
generally the liability of shareholders

in a company is limited to the paid-up value of his shares (all the assets of partners may be called on to meet partnership debts). **The Proprietary Company** (Private in Qld.) has been for long in Aus. the mark of a company registered under provisions of various Companies Acts intended to allow less stringent requirements in public filing of balance sheets and profit and loss accounts to companies with not more than 50 shareholders. In fact these are often holding companies for very large concerns, or a subsidiary with a new activity, formed for tax purposes or to gain Aus. registration for an overseas firm etc. Following Commonwealth and State ministerial meetings from 1959 to 1961, a draft Companies Bill was produced, virtually uniform Acts being passed in the various States in 1962 and 1963. Under these new provisions proprietary companies in which shares are held by public companies are no longer exempted from filing balance sheet and profit and loss account; only 'exempt' proprietary companies possess this privilege. Roughly these are companies with not more than 50 *individual* (i.e. not corporate) shareholders. Registration as proprietary companies is still sought for subsidiaries by large public and overseas companies because of other privileges—greater flexibility in commencing business in relation to filing of prospectuses, in numbers and appointments of directors etc. Public companies, on the other hand, are those entitled to appeal to the public for share capital and more likely to be quoted on the Stock Exchange and therefore subject to more rigorous formalities, auditing of accounts etc. *For further reading see* R. K. Yorston and S. R. Brown: *Company Law* (Sydney, 1964).

Overseas control of companies is an important feature. Over 80% overseas control is held in petroleum, chemicals, paint, agricultural equipment, motor vehicles and tobacco.

There is 50–80% overseas control in non-ferrous metals, excavating equipment and other heavy engineering, electric wires and cables, communications equipment, rubber tyres, textiles and pharmaceuticals, and 20–50% in cement, refrigerators, washing machines, radio and televisions, and food processing. The position is analysed in *Anatomy of Australian Manufacturing Industry* by E. L. Wheelwright and J. Miskelly (Sydney, 1967). In 1972 legislation 'froze' potential take-overs by foreign firms for a 3–5 month period of Govt. investigation.

Aus. has a high number of interlocking directorships, giving considerable concentration of power, analysed by H. Rolfe in *The Controllers*, Melbourne, 1967, indicating links between competitors, manufacturers and consumers, and family associations.

The last comprehensive survey (Aus. Financial Review, 1963) based on shareholders' funds gives companies in order; the following head the lists: *Manufacture, Mining, Primary:* Broken Hill Proprietary Ltd.*, General Motors Holden's Pty. Ltd., Colonial Sugar Refining Co. Ltd., Imperial Chemical Industries Aus. and N.Z. Ltd., Aus. Consolidated Industries Ltd., Mt. Isa Mines Ltd., Conzinc Rio Tinto of Aus. Ltd., Carlton and United Breweries Ltd., British Tobacco Co. (Aus.) Ltd., Aus. Paper Manufacturers Ltd. *Trading Companies:* G. J. Coles and Co. Ltd., Ampol Petroleum Ltd., Dalgety and N.Z. Loan Ltd., Elder Smith Goldsbrough Mort Ltd., Burns Philp and Co. Ltd., Myer Emporium Ltd., Woolworths Ltd., H. C. Sleigh Ltd. *Finance:* Commonwealth Banking Corporation, Bank of New South Wales, Aus. and N.Z. Bank Ltd., National Bank of Australasia, I.A.C. Holdings Ltd. *Non-Life Insurance:* State Government Insurance Office (Qld.), Government Insurance Office of N.S.W., South British Insurance Co. Ltd., Commercial Union Assurance Co. of Aus. Ltd. *Life Insurance:* Australian

Mutual Provident Society (A.M.P.), Colonial Mutual Life Assurance Society Ltd., National Mutual Life Association of Aus. Ltd., Mutual Life and Citizens' Assurance Co. Ltd. (M.L.C.), Temperance and General Mutual Life Association. *Utilities and Transport* (a) Without equity capital: State Electricity Commission Vic., Dept. of Railways N.S.W., Electricity Commission N.S.W., Victorian Railways, Tas. Hydro-Electric Commission. (b) With equity capital: Qantas Empire Airways Ltd., Gas and Fuel Corporation of Vic., Aus. Gas Light Co., Ansett Transport Industries Ltd., Commonwealth Railway. *Tertiary:* L. J. Hooker Investment Corporation Ltd. (Real Estate), Hoyts Theatre Ltd. (Sydney cinemas), Lend Lease Corporation (Building), Television Corporation Ltd., Federal Hotels Ltd. The 20 leading Aus. companies, from *The Times 1000* (1972–3) were: Broken Hill Proprietary, Conzinc Riotinto, Aus., Colonial Sugar Refining, I.C.I. Aus., Aus. Consolidated Industries, Myer Emporium, Aus. Paper Mfs., John Lysaght Aus., Dunlop Aus., British Tobacco Aus., Ampol, Woolworths, C. J. Coles, Carlton and United Breweries, Elder Smith Goldsbrough Mort, Ansett Transport Ind., David Jones, Burns, Philp, H. C. Sleigh, Boral.

Condamine River Qld. Part of the Darling* catchment, 692 km. long, rising W of the Divide, 28S/152E, flowing with a large summer maximum NW then W through the productive Darling Downs* to become the Balonne above Surat.

Conesticks A popular name for bushes of genus *Petrophila*, with a multiple head of tightly packed flowers simulating a cone growing from the stem. The pink-flowered *P. biloba* is mainly on granite country in W.A.; the white, downy *P. sessilis* on the sandstone plateaux of E Aus.

Congregational Church There are some 70,000 adherents. Possibly the first non-Anglican belief preached in Aus., by 2 Independents, as they were then called, in Sydney in 1798. The first organised group was formed in 1810 and the first church built in 1833. Congregations are completely autonomous.

Conner, Mount N.T. 21S/135E The most easterly of the 'Three Great Tors' of conglomerate, rising above the desert plain N of the Musgrave Range; the others are Mt. Olga* and Ayers Rock*. It differs in being a very flat-topped mesa, oval in shape and 5 km. by 1·6 km. in extent, with spinifex on the top. There is a sheer drop in cliffs for 120 m.; then steep scree slopes of rock form the lower 120 m. Ravines in the SW are the only accessible route up to it. Gosse named it in 1873 after a S.A. politician.

Conscription The compulsory call-up of selected age groups for military service. During the 1914–18 War* its use was rejected by 2 referenda. Initial voluntary enlistment was higher than requirements, but fell off in 1916–17. When Hughes* returned from England in 1916, pledged to find 16,500 men a month to replace the heavy Gallipoli and Western Front losses, there were already vociferous Universal Service Leagues pressing for conscription, and equally outspoken and consolidated opposition. Instead of using the wide wartime powers available, Hughes decided on a referendum; and was expelled from the Aus. Labor Party*. As Prime Minister in the succeeding National Coalition, he tried a second referendum in December 1917, to supply the estimated 7,000 per month needed, and again failed. It was subsequently proved that both estimates were unrealistically high. The campaigns, especially the second, saw unparalleled bitterness and venomous outbursts by Hughes and opponents, notably the Roman Catholic Bishop Mannix* (although other Roman Catholic clergy were in favour or uncommitted), and Ryan the Qld. Premier. The rejection reflected militant unionism, a growing war weariness and disillusion with its aims and progress, the traditional individualism and anti-government philosophy, and genuine reluctance to commit others by those unable by age or sex to fight themselves.

1st Referendum
Oct 28, 1916

	FOR	AGAINST
Over all	1,087,577	1,160,033
States	Vic., W.A., Tas.	Qld., S.A., N.S.W. (178,000 maj.)
Forces Overseas	72,399	58,894

2nd Referendum
Dec. 20, 1917

	FOR	AGAINST
Over all	1,015,159	1,181,747
States	W.A., Tas.	N.S.W., Vic., Qld., S.A.
Forces Overseas	103,789	93,910

In the 1939–45 War* compulsory military training and service in the Citizen Military Forces was introduced just after the war began. An amendment to the Defence Act in 1943 extended this to a defined SW Pacific area bounded by the Equator and between 110° and 159°E; there was little opposition save among diehard Labor adherents. There was no conscription for the Korean War*, but in 1965, conscription on a ballot of 20-year-olds

was introduced for the Vietnam War*, and was ended 1972. *See* R. Forward and B. Reece eds.: *Conscription in Australia* (Brisbane, 1968).

CONSERVATION (of flora, fauna, forests and soil) This has been neglected in Aus. in a similar way to other big countries opened up by pioneering settlement, and while the public conscience is now being stirred, much has already been lost. The early 'cedar getters' in the E coast rain-forest, and the loggers of Huon pine in Tas. almost eradicated both trees; on the dry inland margins, overgrazing has destroyed vegetation cover and led to wind erosion. Much unspoiled coast remains, but only where it is not accessible to developers of beach cottages or rich in mineral sands. Wheat and pasture land have replaced forest over 40·5 million ha. of SE Aus., substituting for a complex biological system a simple one, open to infestation by pests; these are eradicated by chemicals which have incidental effects on other forms of life, not yet fully studied, but which include the death of small birds.

Estimates of species now lost vary; but examples given to the International Biological Programme in 1967 were: in Vic. 12 plant species extinct, 36 probably extinct and 201 reduced to a few survivors; N.S.W. had 22 out of a former 52 marsupial species of open grazing land extinct or not recorded since 1944. Controversy rages over the kangaroo with a million shot in some years in E Aus. for pet food, hides and a meat export of 5 million kg.; yet numbers of kangaroos may be increasing with the land clearance going ahead in W.A. which yet threatens the unique flora. A Qld. experiment indicates that in the area studied, sheep and kangaroos are complementary and not normally competitive feeders in their selection of grasses, but kangaroos are more competitive in time of drought. Pleas for conservation are not new: in 1924 Sir James Barrett wrote *Save*

Australia; two later outcries are A. J. Marshall ed.: *The Great Extermination* (London, 1966) and V. Serventy: *Continent in Danger* (London, 1967).

The Australian Conservation Foundation (1966) is a non-government body working on an Aus.-wide collection of data and on publication, e.g. in its *Viewpoint Series*, and there are a number of localised societies of people concerned with conservation. State Governments may have departments concerned with conservation, but lack funds, and are often defeated by vested interests. N.S.W. has now a lead in conservation measures. In Vic. efforts are being made to re-introduce the Cape Barren goose, magpie goose, bustard and brolga to the mainland. State forests may have a temporary role in nature conservation through prevention of access, e.g. the upland rain-forests of Qld. are so far preserved, but the eventual aim is management (in which W.A. is especially efficient), but which results in a simpler complex of flora and fauna. It is unlikely that tragedies will recur on the scale of the slaughter of platypuses half a century ago, the near-extermination of the Bass Str. seals, or the infamous Qld. 'open seasons' for koala shooting which brought a million skins for export in 1924 alone. But with economic development paramount, there will be continuing heavy losses of plants and animals through clearing of land. (*See also* NATIONAL PARKS and POLLUTION).

Constitution With the benefit of all earlier federal experiments, in addition to the heritage of British parliamentary development to help them, the drafters of the Aus. constitution produced a remarkable compromise suited to the particular Aus. conditions. Passed by Parliament in London on July 9th 1900, the Constitution Act was effective from January 1st 1901.

The fundamental problem was one of combining the jealously guarded independence of the States, with a viable national Government. The result was the setting up of 2 Houses: the House of Representatives, elected for 3 years on universal suffrage (including women almost from the outset) by Preferential voting* and with members in proportion to population, but with a minimum of 5 per State to protect those less populated, and a Senate or States House, also elected by proportional representation, but with at first 6 members then 10, since 1949, from each State regardless of size and population, and for a term of 6 years. The Executive Ministers are chosen from members, and so are responsible to Parliament; in this respect the analogy is with Britain not the U.S. A High Court is the arbiter on interpretation of the Constitution; the ultimate appeal on Federal matters to the Privy Council was abolished in 1967. Deadlocks can lead to dissolution of both Houses by the Governor General, and to a new election. The Constitution can be altered by a Bill approved at a referendum* which must show an absolute majority, and a majority in the majority of States. The Governor General, appointed by the Crown, acting on advice from the Aus. Government since 1926, is the Sovereign's representative as ultimate head of state. The Federal powers cover defence, external affairs and treaties, customs and excise, communications including posts and telegraphs, banking, currency, insurance, marriage, immigration, certain industrial arbitration, weights and measures, copyright, fisheries, navigation (and effectively aviation), taxation, pensions, i.e. 'specific powers'. 'Residual' powers e.g. health, education, always remain with State parliaments. The Commonwealth has gradually attained dominance in the field of Finance*. In 1973 it was agreed that the last legal and constitutional ties with Britain should be cut.

Consumer Price Index Replacing a former 'C Series' Retail Price Index

(1921–60), a quarterly measure of variation in retail prices covering food, clothing, housing, housing supplies and equipment, and other goods and services. It is compiled for the State capitals and Canberra with a reference base 1966–7 of 100·0 and was introduced under Sir Stanley Carver as Commonwealth Statistician (1957–62). The average for the cities in 1969–70 was 109·4. Weighting is varied at intervals in response to changes in consumer expenditure. The Index is used in wage negotiation, and in economic assessments along with Wholesale and Export Price Indexes.

Convolvulus or **Bindweed** A genus of the mainly warm climate Convolvulaceae family, which includes the introduced *C. arvensis*, with white flowers and a poisonous seed, and also the native *C. erubescens*, with hairy trailing foliage and pale pink flower.

Coober Pedy S.A. 29S/135E Opal field in the low barren Stuart Range. Houses for the white population are often partly excavated to escape the intolerable heat. Opals are 'gouged' from shallow shafts and Aborigines also take part; yields are seldom revealed. Population 781 in 1971.

Coo-ee This was adopted as a call to attract attention by the early settlers from hearing it used by the Aborigines, and has spread to other countries.

Cook, James (1728–1779) 'I am one who has ambition not only to go further than any one has done before but as far as is possible for a man to go'. Cook, one of the great men of all time, was born at Marton, Yorkshire, Eng. and after being apprenticed to Whitby coal shippers, joined the navy as an able seaman in 1755. In the Seven Years War in Europe, and in America, his abilities as leader, cartographer, surveyor (especially of the St. Lawrence and Newfoundland after the war) and observer led to promotion and in 1769, in command of the *Endeavour*, he was

sent by the Admiralty and the Royal Society to the Pacific primarily to observe the 'passage of the planet Venus over the Disk of the Sun on 3rd June' along with Charles Green, Joseph Banks and Solander. Cook also had sealed orders 'whereas there is reason to imagine a Continent or land of great extent . . . to proceed southwards in order to make discovery of the Continent above mentioned'. Cook was himself sceptical of its existence; but having spent over 6 months charting the N.Z. coast, he decided to return home by Van Diemen's Land, N.G., and the Cape. The prevailing winds carried him N of his intended route and on April 17th land birds were seen and land sighted by Lieut. Hicks (and named Hick's Point) on the 19th. On the 28th he landed at Botany Bay, at first named Sting Ray Harbour. His first favourable reactions to the new land (although he did not consider it to be the great southland he was sent to look for), was 'rather low . . . the face of the country green and woody . . . great surf beats everywhere on the shore . . . a quantity of good grass . . . the soil a light white sand'. Elsewhere he noted black rich soil, and summed up the potentialities as being barren in its natural state but capable of producing roots, grain and fruit, and for pasturing cattle. He observed the Aborigines with sympathy, not the contempt of previous explorers. He proceeded northwards, charting the E coast and landing 3 more times: the *Endeavour* was careened at Endeavour Bay (site of Cooktown). In August he reached and named Possession Island and claimed all the land N of 38°S for King George, as N.S.W. In 1771 Cook made an even more remarkable voyage, again in search of *'terra australis incognita'* with Furneaux in *Adventure* and *Resolution*. Sailing in high latitudes to regions of perpetual snow and ice, he was separated from Furneaux near Van Diemen's Land. His third voyage in 1777–9 was to seek a northern passage between the Pacific and Atlantic: he sailed via the Cape and Van Diemen's Land, then across the Pacific to the N of Vancouver, but failed to find the passage. On a Hawaiian island in February 1779 a chief was shot, following the theft of a boat and in frenzied revenge the tribesmen attacked Cook's party. To the last Cook seemed unable to accept his real danger, and fell before their clubs. This tall, lean, dark, self-contained man apparently without strong religious beliefs, but with a passionate curiosity and dedication to work, left charts which remain valid today of the Pacific and its lands. That he discovered what was to become the focal area of a new continent was incidental—even accidental. **'Captain Cook's Cottage'** (in which actually his parents but not he himself lived) at Great Ayton, Yorks., was re-assembled in Fitzroy Gardens, Melbourne, in 1932. *For further reading see* J. C. Beaglehole ed.: *The Journals of Captain James Cook* (Cambridge, 1955); A. Villiers: *The Seaman's Seaman* (London, 1967).

Cook, Sir Joseph (1860–1947) b. Staffordshire, Eng. Liberal Prime Minister of Aus. 1913–14. He arrived in Aus. in 1885 to work at his coalmining trade, but quickly entered Labor politics in N.S.W. He left the Aus. Labor Party* over its Caucus system, and rose in Liberal ranks to succeed Reid in N.S.W. and later Deakin in Federal leadership. He became Prime Minister with a majority of 1 in the House of Representatives and a Senate minority, which led to a double dissolution in June 1914. The 1914–18 War broke out before the September elections, and Cook declared 'if the Empire is at war, Australia is at war'.

Cooktown Qld. 15S/145E At the mouth of the Endeavour River, named from Cook's ship being beached for careening there in 1770. Now a small port with 589 in 1971, it had a pros-

perous and literally riotous period during the Palmer River gold-rush with over 30,000 people, many of them Chinese, and 40 hotels. The railway to Laura (1885) now lifted was used weekly by a former London bus on bogie and wheels; Cooktown is reviving as tourism follows the opening of the Cairns–Cooktown Mulligan Highway.

Coolabah An Aboriginal and popular name for a form of box* eucalyptus, the Flooded Box, *Eucalyptus microtheca*. The Coolabah is medium-sized, with pale, narrow leaves up to 18 cm. long, growing widely on black soil plains and along watercourses of the interior, hence the reference in 'Waltzing Matilda'.

Coolabah
(*Eucalyptus microtheca*)

Coolangatta Qld. 28S/154E The S limit of the Gold Coast*, but older than most of it, it is a 'twin town' with the port of Tweed Heads over the N.S.W./Qld. border, but 1 hour different in time. (*See* DAYLIGHT SAVING).

Coolgardie W.A. 31S/121E (622 in 1971) Dates from the shanty and tent town of the Gnarlbine that sprung up following the discovery (1892) of Bayley's Reward*. Alluvial gold soon failed, but rich quartz reefs in the area gave rise to wild company promotion before they too failed at depth, and mining moved 40 km. E to the Golden Mile*, while Coolgardie struggled on as the 'Old Camp'. Each new report started a rush: the disastrous Siberia rush in 1893, 112 km. to the N, cost a number of lives from lack of water; the Wealth of Nations mine, 65 km. to the NW, uncovered a great fortune in 1894. In spite of acute water shortage causing disease and virtual summer evacuation, in its heyday Coolgardie had 15,000 people with a further 10,000 in nearby camps, 26 hotels and 3 breweries, a mosque, horse-racing and 7 newspapers. The pink sandstone public buildings still line the wide main street, and the town has escaped complete desertion by becoming a pastoral centre.

Cooma N.S.W. 36S/149E (7,784 in 1971; 9,106 in 1966) A railway town and road, market and service centre for the good Merino country on the rolling grassy Monaro* plateau in the Southern Tablelands. It has a hilly and attractive site at the junction of 2 creeks; it grew with the Kiandra goldrush in 1860, declined, rose for a time as a railhead, stagnated a little, and then enjoyed tremendous activity and stimulus as the headquarters of the Snowy Mts.* Authority. As the Snowy project passed its peak of activity after 1970, tourist traffic increased, but the town has lost in numbers.

Coombs, Herbert Cole (1906–) b. Kalamunda, W.A. A leading Aus. financial expert, Governor of the Commonwealth Bank of Aus. from 1949–60 and of the Reserve Bank from 1960–8, and Chancellor of the Aus. National University (1968–).

Coonabarabran N.S.W. 31S/149E (3,045 in 1971) A local market and service centre on the Castlereagh, near the Pilliga Scrub* (hence a sawmilling industry processing cypress pine) and

the Warrumbungles* (with a tourist potential). Diatomite (a chalk-like but siliceous deposit from freshwater algae) is mined for filtration and insulation purposes.

Coonalpyn Downs S.A. 36S/140E Some 24,000 km.^{2} of sandy mallee centred on Keith and formerly called The Ninety Mile Desert, a continuation of the Big and Little Deserts* of Vic. In the past 15 years over 100,000 ha. have been turned into sheep pasture lands by clearing cultivation with a modern stump-jump plough*, application of fertilisers and trace elements of zinc and copper, and also the use of subterranean clover and introduced grasses.

Coonawarra S.A. 37S/141E A small isolated region producing wines* in the SE on a patch of suitable red soils N of Penola, producing largely clarets and under 1% of the wines of the State but with a high reputation.

Cooper or **Cooper's Creek** Qld./S.A. An intermittent river of the L. Eyre* internal drainage catchment, formed by the confluence of the Thomson and Barcoo, 25S/142E, and flows SW for some 800 km., reaching L. Eyre only in occasional wet years. It is one of the main streams of the Channel Country*, discovered and named by Sturt (1845) and sometimes shown as the Barcoo. It was on its banks that Burke and Wills perished in 1861.

Coorong S.A. 36S/139E A narrow coastal lagoon stretching over 125 km. NW–SE behind the dunes of the Younghusband Peninsula which the Murray cuts at its W end to reach the sea.

Cootamundra N.S.W. 35S/148E (6,530 in 1971) Founded on a village which grew up on a large pastoral property; appropriately it remains a pastoral market and service centre centrally placed in the S part of the Western Slopes region, with one of the biggest sheep shows outside Sydney. There is a little gold-mining nearby, and manufactures are mainly processing agricultural products—butter, flour and rice. The concentration of road and rail routes is striking.

Copland, Sir Douglas Berry (1894–1971) b. Timaru, N.Z. An eminent economist, who had held government, advisory, academic, and political appointments including Aus. delegate to U.N. (1946, 1953) first Vice-Chancellor of the Australian National University*. He was particularly influential in analysing and advising measures to combat the 1930s Depression.

Copper This occurs in Pre-cambrian rocks at Mt. Isa*, Qld., which produces 75–80% of Aus. output. Large reserves exist there and in N.T. at Tennant Creek* and Rum Jungle*. It is also obtained with gold, in Palaeozoic rocks at Mt. Morgan*, Qld., and in Tas. at Mt. Lyell*. Former mines have been re-opened at Cobar*, N.S.W., and small quantities mined at Ravensthorpe, W.A. There is some export, fluctuating with world demand. Refineries are at Townsville, Qld. (for Mt. Isa) and at Port Kembla, N.S.W. Copper at Moonta* played an important part in early S.A. development and at Burra* S.A. Here are new open-cut workings. New mines are being opened at Mt. Gunsen 130 km. NW of Port Augusta*.

Copperhead Also called Superb Snake, Black Snake, Pink-bellied Black Snake, Yellow-bellied Black Snake, Tiger Snake and (Tas.) Diamond Snake, *Austrelaps superba* is a bulky snake, with head distinct from neck and body, reaching 1·5 m. in length widely distributed in SE Aus. often in tumbled boulders and under logs in mountain country, but also in open and coastal terrain. It is not aggressive, but a bite from a large specimen should be treated seriously.

Coppin, George Selth (1819–1906) b. Sussex, Eng. Theatrical entrepreneur. He arrived in Aus. about 1843. His first venture failed in Launceston and he opened theatres in Adelaide and later Melbourne, where he became very prosperous in the post-gold-rush theatrical boom, and brought leading artists to Aus., including G. V. Brooke (his partner for a time, who played Shakespeare) and the Keans. He was also an active politician. *For further reading see* A. Bagot: *Coppin the Great, Father of the Australian Theatre* (Melbourne, 1965).

Copyright In Aus. this was regulated by an Act of 1912 adopting British procedure. A report by a law committee under Sir John Spicer, tabled in 1959, is the basis for an Act, in force from 1969, designed to bring Aus. into agreement with the Berne and Universal Copyright conventions, and attain reciprocal rights with other countries.

Coral Fern A species of the fern* *Gleichenia*, scrambling in heaths and forests of wetter parts of Aus. It has a highly characteristic growth form, with repeatedly forked fronds.

Coral Sea, Battle of Took place on May 7th–8th 1942, when U.S. naval and carrier-based air forces with 2 Aus. light cruisers and Qld.-based U.S. and Aus. air squadrons engaged Japanese naval, carrier and Rabaul-based air forces aiming at a Port Moresby landing. It was a major turning point in the war.

Coral Sea Islands Territory Created 1969 because of anxiety over potential oil. It is administered from Norfolk Island, and comprises scattered unpeopled islands.

Coral Tree A widely popular name for flowering trees of the tropical genus *Erythrina* (Papilionaceae family) with about 35 species. There are groups of 3 ivy-like leaves, often shed in the winter or dry season; the branches have sharp prickles, and there are prominent pod-shaped, flame-coloured to red flowers, succeeded by thin pods bulging with large red-brown shiny seeds, sometimes poisonous. The wood is particularly light in weight. The most familiar Aus. species are the Indian Coral, *E. indica*, and the Bat's Wing Coral, *E. vespertilio*.

Corals A popular name for mainly colonial marine coelenterate polyps (*see* COELENTERATA). Aus. corals, mainly recorded from the Great Barrier Reef*, well studied in the last 40 years, include: 1. Alcyonarian or Soft Corals. These have 8 branched tentacles, some quite soft and yielding, e.g. the convoluted but cushion-like *Sacrophyton*, though with calcareous spicules within the tissues; some with more firm to massive skeletons in the colonies, which unlike the true or stone corals, retain their colouring after the death of the polyps, e.g. the red, orange or yellow dendritic patterns of *Mopsella*, the black branched *Antipathes*, *Tubipora* distinctive for its bright-red 'organ pipes', and blue *Heliopora*. 2. Scleractinian or Stony Corals. These have numerous tentacles, often in multiples of 6, and the characteristic hard skeleton of the colony's home, coloured by symbiotic algae in life, but pure white when cleaned or bleached. Common stony corals include: (a) solitary corals, like anemones with a calcareous skeleton, e.g. the Mushroom Coral, *Fungia* spp., the Fan-shaped Crisp Coral, *Flabellum* spp., of waters as far S as S Tas., and the conical *Conocyathus* of Sydney Harbour with the colonial *Flesiastraea*, like patches of green submarine moss on the rocks; (b) Star-Corals of genera *Goniastraea* and *Favia*, and Brain-Corals (*Meandrina* and *Coeloria*).

Corangamite, Lake. Vic. 38S/144E The largest lake in the State, a salt lake varying from about 230 km.² to about 300 km.² in a shallow depression in basalt lava flow country, rather than a crater like many of its smaller neighbours. A channel has been dug to the Barwon to reclaim some of the land submerged in flooding in 1956.

Corio Bay Vic. The bay on which stands Geelong. 38S/144E, rather cut off from the W arm of Port Phillip Bay by the promontory of Point Henry and by a baymouth sandbar which has necessitated the dredging of a channel to Geelong's port facilities. The shores are mainly occupied by the city and harbour works, oil refinery, aluminium smelter, salt pans etc., and pollution is becoming a problem, affecting fish life.

Corkscrew Grass A popular name for *Stipa* spp. (*See* SPEAR GRASS.)

Cormorants In Aus. these are primarily birds of coastal or inland lakes, swamps and streams, though like some of the waders they are familiar sights on some stretches of shore. They are large (from over 60 cm. to over 90 cm.) web-footed birds with long necks and beaks, good swimmers and divers, and sometimes persecuted by fishermen, though their diet consists primarily of non-commercial fish and yabbies etc. The birds are characteristically dark blue-black, though some have white breasts, and some yellow beaks. A typical sight is of a cormorant perched on a rock or tree-branch, for a post-prandial rest or ready to dive for prey. The largest is the Black Cormorant, *Phalacrocorax carbo*, (coal-black bald crow). The names of the others are fairly descriptive: the Little Black Cormorant, *P. sulcirostris*, the Black-faced Cormorant, *P. fuscescens*, the Yellow-faced Cormorant, *P. varius*, typically seen in quiet mangrove-fringed lagoons, and the Little Pied Cormorant, *P. melanoleucos*. All the species build large untidy communal nests, often in a tree above the swamp.

Corner Inlet Vic. 39S/147E An almost enclosed bay of over 260 km.² It is hemmed in by Wilsons Promontory* and the sandy Yanakie isthmus, while the mouth to the E is almost closed by a group of mainly sandy islands like Snake and Sunday Island and the long narrow Clonmel—really part of the

Ninety Mile Beach* system, shaped by wave refraction into the inlet.

Corowa Conference (July 1893) A historic turning point in the movement for Federation*, with delegates from several federalist associations, including Aus. Natives Association*, resolving that the time had come for enabling Acts in each State to allow elected, instead of nominated representatives to get down to the task, thus involving the people more directly.

Cotton A fluctuating but increasing acreage (now over 28,000 ha.) provides almost all the needs of Aus. manufacture. Over 70% is grown in N.S.W., on Namoi* and Macquarie and Murrumbidgee Irrigation Area, some 17% in Qld. mainly in the Callide valley, a little in Vic. and some on the Ord River W.A. As an annual shrub (*Gossypium*) needing high but seasonal rainfall or water supply, moisture-retentive soils and high temperatures it does not have ideal natural conditions in Aus., and labour costs make mechanised, irrigated farming necessary. The former Government Bounty was phased out by 1971. First grown in Qld. from 1852–7 cotton was exported in the American Civil War, but since then it was only grown sporadically until the 1960s.

Cotton-plants These include 2 native species, the beautiful Desert Rose*, *Gossypium sturtianum*, and *G. robinsonii* around Port Hedland, W.A., 20S/119E. Their seed capsules have little of the woolly covering of commercial cotton, to which they are related and which has run wild in parts of N Aus.

Cottonwood (*Hibiscus tiliaceus*) A 9-m. salt-tolerant tree of wet coastal NE N.S.W. and Qld. (and the SW Pacific), of the widespread Malvaceae or mallow family, including hibiscus and cotton plants. It has thin grey fibrous bark, evergreen heart-shaped leaves, and short-lived but long-flowering crimson-hearted yellow blossoms. There are about 10 seeds in a 2·5-cm. capsule.

Aborigines used bark fibre for fishing lines in some areas. Cottonwood is also applied to *Bedfordia salicina* (also called Blanket-leaf), in the Compositae or daisy family, common in SE Aus. fern gullies and yielding useful timber. Cottonwood is also a popular name for a N American poplar, generally their S Cottonwood, *Populus angulata*. It is a very rapid grower—faster even than coniferous softwoods, e.g. *Pinus radiata* —with very large leaves, growing well on deep fertile soils with ample water. It has recently been planted in thousands by the Snowy Mt. Authority on the flood-plains by the Tumut River near Tumut town, 35S/148E, made difficult for grazing etc. by the artificially induced fluctuations in river level, due to release of water for power generation from dams upstream. The main market is in match manufacture, but the tree has potential use in plywood and veneer production.

Couch-grass A popular name for prostrate grasses, rooting from joints along the creeping stalks, including: 1. Common Couch-grass or Bermuda Grass, *Cynodon dactylon*, the familiar pest of gardens but a fair forage plant, with 2–6 small-seeded spikelets spreading from the tip; 2. the Water Couch, *Paspalum distichum*, growing in shallow water or in clumps in damp places, with a smaller seed-head than the cultivated *Paspalum**, and narrower and more pointed seeds; 3. Saltwater or Coastal Couch, *Sporobolus virginicus*, a relative of the Rat's Tail Grass, *S. elongatus*, found in salt marshes in many countries; 4. the Couch Grass of N Europe, *Agropyron repens*, an introduced weed of heavy soils in the cooler parts of Aus. The first 3 species give useful forage.

Country Party The third political party with Federal representation (others are Liberal* and Aus. Labor*), and with influence disproportionate to its size, owing to its ability to hold the balance of power. The party has formed coalition governments with Nationalists (1922–9) and with Liberals (1949–72). Its origins lie in the group feeling among farmers and country-town dwellers of isolation, social, physical and economic, from the predominantly urban industrial population of Aus. Local organisations were strongest in the developing wheat lands of SW and SE Aus. from 1860, where marginal land, and precarious rainfall led to in-security and harsh conditions among 'Wheat Cockies' as distinct from the wealthy entrenched squatters*. W.A. pioneered political expression of these groups in the State Parliament. Tariff protection was sought and a com-pulsory minimum wage opposed. The first Federal break-through, giving 11 seats in 1919, was the result of graziers adding their support and financial backing as a reaction to Nationalist Government controls, and to the 1918 introduction of Preferential voting*. Since then many seats have been won on the second preferences of both Labor and Liberal voters. In the 1969 and 1972 elections the Country Party won 20 seats, but in 1972 Labor won the election. In the Liberal-Country Party coalition, 1949–72, a proportion of cabinet posts including that of Deputy Prime Minister went to the Party. But in opposition (1972–) the relationship is weakening. The Leader (1971–) is Douglas Anthony.

Court, Margaret (1942–) b. Al-bury. Leading woman tennis player from the age of 17. Wimbledon champion 1963, 65, 70; U.S. 1962, 65 and 69–71. Aus. champion 11 times to 1973.

Cowan, Peter Walkinshaw (1914–) b. Perth. Short-story writer and novelist.

Cowpastures A name long used for an area now centred on Camden, some 65 km. SW of Sydney, so named because of the herd of cattle found in the region in 1795, which were descen-ded from 4 escaped cows and 2 bulls of S African cattle brought to Sydney Cove by Governor Phillip in 1788. The herd exceeded 3,000 by 1806 and were protected for some years, before being dispersed, domesticated or killed.

Cowper, Sir Charles (1807–1875) b. Dryford, Lancs., Eng. Premier of N.S.W. 1857–9, 1861–3, 1865–6, 1870. Arrived in Sydney in 1809 with his father who was colonial chaplain under Marsden*. Cowper was an astute politician actively concerned in the transition to responsible government in N.S.W., problems of the gold-fields, land reform and rail development.

Cowra N.S.W. 34S/148E (7,282 in 1971) A growing local market, service and small manufacturing centre (food-processing, building materials, cordials, clothing etc.) in sheep-wheat country on the E edge of the Western Slopes region and on the N–S railway link line on the Lachlan*, whose river flats are now further diversified by irrigation from Wyangala Dam*. An agricultural ex-perimental station nearby carried on work on wheat breeding, and Farrer* worked there. In 1944 there was a mass outbreak of Japanese prisoners of war from a nearby camp. There is now a Japanese War Cemetery at Cowra.

Cox, William (1764–1837) b. Dorset, Eng. A pioneer in Windsor and later Bathurst districts. He arrived in Aus. in 1800 as paymaster in N.S.W. Corps and became a settler, noted for his super-vision of the first road over the Blue Mts*. His humanity was a major fac-tor in the building of 162 km. of road with over a dozen bridges by 30 men including convicts, from the Nepean to Bathurst, between July 1814 and Janu-ary 1815, with no loss of life or disci-plinary problems. The 12-ft. (3·7 m.) road, cut through forests, descended steeply from Mt. Yorke by Cox's Pass, following the exploratory routes of Wentworth*, Blaxland, Lawson, and was surveyed by Evans*.

Crab Spiders A popular name for the family Thomisidae, small forest spiders up to 1 cm. long, very crab-like with at least 2 front pairs of legs pointing well forward and the front pair used to seize prey. No snare web is used and a tunnel retreat rarely. There are many sub-families and species covering much of Aus.

Crabs Mainly short-tailed creeping and swimming aquatic crustaceans* of the Order Decapoda (10-footed), though popular usage includes the Hermit-crabs*. Aus. crabs belong mainly to 3 Tribes or groups of families.
1. The Sponge-crabs and their allies, Dromiacea, include the Sponge-crabs proper, family Dromiidae, e.g. the Bristled Sponge-crab, *Cryptodromia octodentata*, brown but often with marine debris in its hair bristles, and the somewhat similar Shaggy Sponge-crab, *Dromidiopsis excavata*; in tropical seas *Conchoecetes artificiosus* has a flat back often so covered with shells etc. that the crab is almost hidden.
2. The Tribe Oxystomata, with tri-angular mouth-opening, the point extending between the eyes, includes: (a) Box Crabs like *Calappa hepatica* which can burrow to hide with remark-able speed, its very broad flat pincer limbs being also used to protect its soft abdomen, and the Dawn Crab *Matuta* spp. with sharp projections on either side of the carapace, and very flat limb segments, adapted to fast swimming; (b) the Pebble Crabs, with very smooth rounded carapace, such as *Leucosides longifrons*.
3. The Tribe Brachygnatha (short-jawed crabs): (a) Sub-Tribe Oxy-rhyncha, with somewhat triangular carapace, includes the well-known Spider-crabs, e.g. *Hyastenus diacanthus*, often camouflaged with seaweed; the large tropical *Naxioides serpulifera* of somewhat similar habits; smaller Spider-crabs, e.g. the temperate-water crab *Halicarcinus ovatus*, usually brown and seen under rocks or in seaweed; and the striking Spider-crab, the Orna-mental Sea-toad, *Schizophrys dama*, with 'warty' and spectacularly spined,

almost antlered carapace, an inter-tidal crab.
(b) The Sub-Tribe Brachyrhyncha includes most and the most 'typical' of the world's crabs, with oval, round or squarish bodies. The Tas. *Pseudo-carcinus gigas*, up to 35 cm. across, is one of the largest crabs in the world. The Swimming Crabs with paddle-like rear feet include the well-known Blue Swimmer, *Portunus pelagicus*, and the Mangrove Crab, *Scylla serrata*. Tropi-cal species include the Periscope Crab, *Podophthalmus vigil*, and the colourful *Thalamita* spp.

Shore Crabs tend to have more de-veloped front claws as compared with the Swimming Crabs, as in the very common Steel-Backed Rock-Crab, *Lep-tograpsus variegatus*; the Ghost or Swift Crab, *Ocypode ceratophthalma*, of 5-cm. width, can be seen mainly at night scuttling on tropical or sub-tropical beaches, burrowing by day; Fiddler-Crabs, *Uca* spp., with one pincer much larger than the other, are seen on intertidal mangrove flats.

The Pea Crabs, e.g. *Pinnotheres vill-osulus*, depend for shelter and food on host molluscs, and have lost the hard carapace of the typical crab. Also living with a host is the very beautiful Retic-ulated Coral Crab, *Trapezia areolata*, living commensally with certain corals in the Great Barrier Reef; it has a red and white pattern on the carapace similar to that of the living coral polyps.

Of the Freshwater Crabs, the most widely distributed is the N Aus. *Para-telphusa leichhardti*.

Cradle Mountain-Lake St. Clair Nat-ional Park Tas. 42S/146E Covers 1,360 km.^{2} of uninhabited lake and mountain country, and originated in 1921 largely following the efforts of Weindorfer, an Austrian settler. There are 15 peaks over 1,200 m. Access is by a 85-km. foot track with regular shelters.

Crane, Australian, Brolga* or Native Companion A tall grey swamp bird.

Crapp, Lorraine (1939–) b. Bathurst, N.S.W. Champion swimmer, noted for a strongly individual crawl*, using a flexible leg action. She was Dawn Fraser's* early rival, and defeated her to win the 400 m. at the 1956 Olympic Games; she was the first woman to swim 440 yd. in under 5 minutes.

Crawford, Sir John Grenfell (1910–) b. Sydney. An outstanding modern economist, Vice-Chancellor of the Aus. National University (1968–73). He held high executive government positions including Secretary of the Department of Commerce and Agriculture (1950–6) and Trade (1956–60), and remains in demand overseas working with the World Bank on developing countries.

Crawford, John Herbert (1908–) b. Urangeline, N.S.W. A powerful tennis champion, noted for a great forehand, a slicing backhand, and stylish play. He played for Aus. in the Davis Cup 1928–39 and won at Wimbledon in 1933 in one of the greatest finals ever fought, against the American, Vines.

Crawl, Australian The basis of free style swimming, a double over-arm stroke, comprising drive and recovery and accompanied by carefully timed vertical leg movements. The modern version involves a rolling of the body about a shoulder axis; the extent of leg movement varies individually between champions. The origin is debated: an over-arm stroke was used by natives of N America, Africa and the Solomon Islands, and by the ancient Greeks and Assyrians, and was used competitively first by J. Trudgen in 1873 and gradually replaced the one-arm-over, sidestroke. The Aus. crawl was developed in Sydney from 1898, when it was used by Wickham* a Solomon Islander, and by the Cavills*. Its essential characteristic was the leg action which was minimal and vertical in contrast with the strong scissor kick of the trudgen (often spelled trudgeon).

Crayfish Aquatic, mainly marine crustaceans*; those with large nippers were formerly distinguished as Lobsters. **Marine Crayfish** of Aus. do not have large pincer development, unlike some Freshwater Crayfish and some prawns* and shrimps*. Most, including the main commercial species, have somewhat cylindrical bodies, with considerable power to curve and straighten them, using the broad tail as a powerful swimming tool; these are the family Palinuridae. There is also the Scyllaridae family of broad flat crayfish in which the antennae have become short but very broad and are used as shovels in burrowing into sandy or muddy sea-bottoms, as in the 30-cm. *Scyllarides sculptus* or the very common Flapjack or Prawn-killer, *Ibacus incisus*, red and 20 cm. long. The main commercial species are the Southern Crayfish, *Jasus lalandii*, from Tas. to the S of W.A., and the N.S.W. crayfish, *J. verreauxi*, important all along the E coast and reaching 90 cm. by 20 cm. and 8 kg. In W.A. *Panulirus longipes* is important for export as 'Lobster tails'. In tropical waters some are brilliantly coloured, e.g. the Painted Crayfish, *P. ornatus*.

  Freshwater Crayfish, found throughout Aus., include forms with well-developed pincers, the Lobsters of older usage, all of the family Parastacidae. The spiny Tas. genus *Astacopsis* inhabits clear mountain streams there, while the rest of Aus. has many species of smooth bodied *Cherax*, including the Yabbie. The Marron of W.A. is *C. tenuimanus*, and reaches 40 cm. *Cherax* spp. may be a pest in irrigation channels by burrowing in the banks, as is the large Murray River Lobster, *Euastacus armatus*. A few species of *Engaeus*, in the same family, have a limited terrestrial burrowing adaptation, but are confined to damp places in the S of E Aus. including Tas. All the Aus. Freshwater Crayfish can evade drought by burrowing in the beds of streams, lakes and dams.

Creepers Those native to Aus. include various *Convolvulus* and *Comesperma* species, e.g. the Love-creeper*. (*See also* CLIMBERS.)

Creswell, Sir William Rooke (1852–1933) b. Gibraltar. He arrived in Aus. in 1878 after retiring from the Royal Navy for health reasons. After a period of farming, he joined the S.A. State navy, commanding it and later the Qld. navy. His reports and work were strongly influential in the creation of the Royal Aus. Navy (1911) and he served as first Naval Member until 1919.

Creswick 38S/144E (1,786 in 1971) A former gold town lasting longer than Ballarat as such; 22 men were drowned when a mine was flooded in December 1882. It is now a forestry centre.

CRICKET Played from the earliest days of the colony, first by officers, then soon followed by civilian enthusiasts; each group had a club by 1826. Equipment was initially improvised. Melbourne had cricket almost as soon as it was founded and the first inter-colonial match between Vic. and N.S.W. was played in 1856. The now famous Melbourne Cricket Ground (centre for the 1960 Olympics) dates from 1861; that in Sydney, from about a decade later, has its own fame in the 'Hill', the slope noted for its noisy barrackers.

The first English team came out in 1861; it was professional, sponsored by a Melbourne catering firm, and was invariably victorious although always playing against sides of 18 or more men. But Lawrence, who remained behind from this tour, and Caffyn, who remained after the subsequent 1863 tour, as coaches began to build up Aus. cricket. In 1873 when W. G. Grace brought out a team for a personal fee of £1,500, paid by the Aus., there was evidence of emerging skill in Aus. In 1877 what is regarded as the first Test* Match was played in Melbourne, with both sides fielding 11 men. The Aus. team, mainly through Banner-man*, won the first and the English the second match. The first Aus. team to visit Eng. (1868) was entirely Aboriginal, a group assembled by W. R. Hayman, in the L. Wallace area in Vic., trained by the Aus. all-rounder T. W. Will and Lawrence and including a notable all-round player Johny Mullagh. In Eng. they won 14, lost 14 and drew 19 matches, described by D. J. Mulvany in *Cricket Walkabout* (Melbourne, 1967). There have been notable Aboriginal fast bowlers since, such as Marsh, Henry and Gilbert. In 1878 an Aus. team toured Eng. and first drew notice to the strength of Aus. cricket by the historic defeat of an MCC team by 9 wickets, with Spofforth* the bowler as the great star. In the following year Lord Harris's team in Aus. was largely successful, but was the cause of a near riot in Sydney over the dismissal of Murdoch by the umpire (who came from Vic.). There followed a decade of numerous exchange visits.

Within Aus. inter-state competition, especially for the Sheffield Shield*, is the invaluable proving and training ground of cricketers and there are many local clubs. Until 1832 bowling was underarm; over-arm bowling has provided the main controversies in the game, the most serious being in 1932 when the English team used so-called 'body line' attack in an attempt to defeat Bradman; angry cables were exchanged with the MCC, and feelings, exacerbated by the prevailing conditions of the Depression, ran high. There has been periodic controversy too over alleged 'throwing', now more easily checked with the use of film. 4 balls to the over were replaced first by 6 (1887 in Aus.) and later 8, first used in Test matches in 1924–5. The game has had periods of decline, notably in the 1890s, 1930s and 1950s when safety overruled adventure in the players' attitudes. The need for a more lively game has been met more recently in the West Indies' Test Matches, but there is a current Aus. decline in spectator interest. The speed and quality of

Aus. cricket may owe something to the use of concrete-based wickets in practice, and to the rule of covering all pitches; a reliable summer also helps. The Aus. Cricket Board of Control is the ruling and selection body for international games.

Among the great names of Aus. cricket the following must be included: *Batsmen to 1912:* Wills, C. Bannerman*, Horan, Bonnor, Bruce, S. Gregory*, McDonnell, Midwinter, Murdoch, Trumper*, Darling, Duff, Ransford, Hill*.
Inter-war: Macartney*, Collins, Bardsley*, Bradman*, Fingleton, Pellew, Ryder, Ponsford*, Richardson, Woodfull, Kippax, Jackson, McCabe.
Post-1945: Barnes*, Harvey*, Hassett*, Burge, Simpson MacKay, Morris*, Lawry, Walters, Stackpole, I. and G. Chappell.
Bowlers to 1912: Boyle, Spofforth*, Garrett, Ferris, Turner*, Trumble*, Cotter, Crawford, Saunders.
Inter-war: Macdonald, Kelleway, Grimmett, Blackie, Mailey, Fleetwood-Smith, O'Reilly*, Taylor.
Post-1945: Johnston, Benaud, Lindwall*, McKenzie, Lillee.
Wicket keepers to 1912: Blackham, Carter.
Inter-war: Oldfield.
Post-1945: Tallon, Langley, Grout, Marsh.
All-rounders to 1912: Giffen*, Noble*, Armstrong.
Inter-war: J. Gregory*.
Post-1945: Miller*, Davidson. *For further reading see* A. G. Moyes: *Australian Cricket* (Sydney, 1959).

Crickets Certain winged, jumping insects of the Order Orthoptera*, particularly those of 2–5 cm. long in which the stridulation is especially chirplike, produced by the scraping of one front wing-cover against tooth-like processes on the other wing.

Crinum A genus in the Amaryllidaceae family, mostly tropical and sub-tropical. *Crinum* has 11 Aus. species, including the Darling Lily, *C. flaccidum,* with a flower-stem crowned by a large white-pink 6-petalled flower, and bulbous roots from which arrowroot can be extracted, and the narrow-leaved *C. angustifolium* of Qld., believed to poison stock.

Crocodiles There are 2 Aus. species. The Estuarine or Salt-water crocodile, *Crocodilus porosus*, is also misnamed the alligator (several Aus. rivers have been named following wrong identification by early explorers or settlers); the alligator has a more rounded snout and lacks the long lower tooth near the snout which fits into an external notch in the upper jaw and therefore visible when the mouth is closed. *C. porosus* is found in northern estuaries and rivers. Some 40–80 eggs up to 8 cm. long are laid on a firm scrub-covered bank, in a leaf-mould nesting mound repaired by the female after damage; the young after hatching may stay with the mother for a day or so. The young make squeaky or frog-like sounds; adults make chiefly a hissing sound, with occasional growls or yelps—the bull-like roar of earlier reports seems to be exaggerated. The crocodile's normal lumbering amble can speed up to an alarmed fast run with body and tail raised, or a kind of glissade through the mud of a mangrove swamp. The prominent nostrils are connected to a tube coming well down the throat, while a valve at the base of the tongue enables it to swallow under water. Stomachs, on dissection, often contain stones—perhaps to aid digestion or act as ballast. The estuarine crocodile eats mainly fish, crabs, crayfish, water rats etc. and grows to 5 m. fairly commonly, exceptionally to 7 m. or more (some very large specimens being recorded in various parts of its range through S and SE Asia). It is normally shy, but it not uncommonly seizes cattle or horses by the nose when they are drinking, then drowning and eating its prey. Many Aborigines have been attacked or taken by a crocodile, usually after it has been wounded in a hunt, and occasionally white people have been lost. This crocodile has long been hunted for its leather by white hunters by day or by searchlight, and by Aboriginal spearmen; recently exceptionally successful hunters sometimes made considerable sums; near-extermination led to protection in W.A. and N.T. by 1971. Estuaries have such reduced populations of crocodiles that there is a plea for protection of small ones also in Qld. Demand was stimulated by the cutting off of supplies of skins to the world market from the chaotic Congo of the early 1960s, causing overshooting in Aus.

The Freshwater, or Johnstone's crocodile, *Crocodilus johnstoni*, with fewer teeth occurs in many freshwater streams, billabongs and lagoons of the far north, normally eating frogs, shrimps, crayfish, fish, insects and spiders, and grows to 3 m. It is extremely shy, harmless to man, and protected in W.A. and N.T., but poaching is serious.

Croker Island N.T. 11S/133E Off Cobourg Peninsula in Arnhem Land, this island is 48 km. N–S by 6 km. E–W and the site of a Methodist Mission caring for Aborigines and growing tropical fruit and vegetables.

Crookwell N.S.W. 35S/150E (2,340 in 1961; 2,120 in 1971) A local market and service centre on a branch railway and off the main highways. Situated at 885 m. and in part of the Southern Tablelands region, producing potatoes in addition to pastoral products. There are small but declining industries: processing plants for butter and meat, and manufacture of veterinary products.

Crows (genus *Corvus*) They include the large Raven, *C. coronoides* (raven-like crow), roosting in timbered country and feeding in more open country in E Aus.; the Crow, *C. cecilae*, of much of the tropical N, and the Little Crow, *C. bennetti*, of much of the interior.

These have the harsh croak of the crow family, and eat mainly insects, including blow-flies on sheep, but the raven is reputed also to prey on lambs, and sometimes to raid orchards.

Crow's Ash (*Flindersia australis*) In the world-wide Rutaceae (or Rue family, including *Boronia* and citrus fruits), this tree is up to 40 m. by 1·5 m., growing in coastal NE N.S.W. and Qld., giving good timber, sometimes called teak, and useful as a shade and shelter tree. There is a long trunk with brown, round-scaled bark, a multiple leaf with 3–13 10-cm. leaflets, much-branched compound flower-heads with 1-cm. individual blossoms, and woody, ovoid, prickly fruit with 5 boat-shaped segments, each containing 2–3 winged seeds.

Crustaceans The Class Crustacea in the Phylum Arthropoda (joint-footed) mostly with some form of horny carapace, 2 pairs of antennae and 2 pairs of mandibles. Many have eyes on stalks, and are aquatic (largely marine). Aus. has a very wide range in size, form and habitat and classification is complex. The following Sub-Classes and Orders include the Aus. crustaceans reviewed in separate articles.

The Sub-Class Malacostraca (soft-shelled) includes: 1. Amphipoda (with two kinds of feet, and sessile, i.e. unstalked, eyes)—Sandhoppers* and related species; 2. Isopoda (feet the same, and sessile eyes)—Wood-Lice* and Sea-Lice*; 3. Cumacea, with 160 Aus. species of very small sand and mud-burrowing crustaceans, with heavy fore-bodies and thin rear-quarters, the rear feet used for burrowing, and living on micro-organisms eaten from sand particles or by filtration; 4. Stomatopoda (mouth-footed, distinguished by eyes on separate movable segments) including Mantis-shrimps (*see* SHRIMPS); 5. Anaspidaceae, the Mountain-shrimps (*see* SHRIMPS) and Depoda (10-footed) including the Sub-Order Natantia (swimmers), the

Prawns* and Shrimps*, and the Sub-Order Reptantia (creeping), including Hermit-crabs*, Crayfish* and Crabs*.

The Sub-Class Cirripedia (feather-footed) includes the Barnacles*. Other Sub-Classes are Branchiopoda (gill-footed), Ostrapoda (plated feet) and Copepoda (oar-footed)—see WATER-FLEAS.

Crystal Brook S.A. 33S/138E (1,185 in 1971) Farming centre at the foot of the steep W edge of the main Flinders Range, developed as a wheat town from 1874, with a rail outlet to Port Pirie. The Crystal Brook itself had been named by Eyre in 1840.

C.S.I.R.O. Commonwealth Scientific and Industrial Research Organisation, a statutory body incorporated by Act of Parliament. Of the 6,400 employees, one third are professional scientists. Its functions are research in primary and secondary industry, training, testing and standardisation, publication and dissemination of scientific work, and subsidising further research. The governing Executive is responsible to the Minister for Education and Science for its policy and work. For research, C.S.I.R.O. is made into Divisions. Administration is through a Secretariat comprising an Administrative Branch, an Agricultural and Biological Sciences Branch, and an Industrial and Physical Sciences Branch.

The Head Office is in Canberra. The Research Divisions are in 5 main groups: Animal Research Laboratories comprising Animal Health (Melbourne), Nutritional Biochemistry (Adelaide), Animal Genetics and Animal Physiology (Sydney); the Environmental Physics Research Laboratories comprise Atmospheric Physics (Melbourne) and Environmental Mechanics (Canberra); Minerals Research Laboratories comprise Chemical Engineering (Melbourne), Mineral Chemistry (Melbourne and Sydney), Mineralogy (Perth, Canberra, Melbourne, Sydney); National Standards Laboratory comprises Applied Physics and Physics (both Sydney), Wool Research Laboratories comprise Protein Chemistry (Melbourne), Textile Industry (Geelong), Textile Physics (Sydney).

Other Divisions are: Applied Chemistry (Melbourne), Applied Geomechanics (Melbourne), Building Research (Melbourne), Chemical Physics (Melbourne), Computing Research (Canberra), Entomology (Canberra), Food Research (Sydney), Horticultural Research (Adelaide), Irrigation Research (Griffith), Land Research (Canberra), Mathematical Statistics (Adelaide), Mechanical Engineering (Melbourne), Plant Industry (Canberra), Radiophysics (Sydney and Parkes), Soils (Adelaide), Tribophysics (Melbourne), Tropical Pastures (Brisbane), Wildlife (Canberra). There are almost 100 branch laboratories and field stations ranging from Cattle Research (Rockhampton) to Forest Products (Melbourne) and Rangelands Research at Alice Springs.

Historical Development In spite of Parliamentary interest in the application of science to agriculture, expressed even before Federation, Bills to establish a Bureau of Agriculture were defeated in 1909 and 1913. In 1916, under wartime stimulus and influenced by British measures to organise scientific research and also the enthusiasm of W. M. Hughes*, an Advisory Council of Science and Industry was set up under Sir David Orme Masson, a distinguished chemist. In 1920 an Act established the Commonwealth Institute of Science and Industry, which laboured with lack of adequate funds until 1925. In 1926 the Council of Scientific and Industrial Research replaced it (C.S.I.R.). This was reorganised in 1949 under the present title with Sir Ian Clunies Ross* as the first Director. From 1939 research had widened to cover wool, mineral and other topics of industrial as well as agricultural concern. The present Chairman is Dr. J. R. Price (1970). *For* *further reading see* G. Currie & J. Graham: *The Origins of C.S.I.R.O.* (Canberra, 1966).

Cuckoos Over a dozen species are found in Aus. They are often migratory or semi-migratory and range in size from the Swamp Cuckoo, sometimes called Swamp Pheasant or Coucal, *Centropus phasianinus*, of much of N Aus., which is 60 cm. long with a black front and flecked-brown back—the only one that does not lay its eggs in other bird's nests—to the dainty (up to 15 cm.) Bronze Cuckoos, with green-bronze backs and brown-and-white striped breasts, of which the Golden Bronze Cuckoo, *Chalcitis plagosus*, of E and S Aus. lays bronze-brown eggs like that of its main host-species, but which are light blue-white when rubbed with a cloth. A typical medium-sized (to 25 cm.) species is the Fan-tailed Cuckoo, *Cacomantis pyrrhophanus* (bright-fire coloured, bad prophet-of spring) of many parts of Aus. and N.G. The mature bird has a slate-grey back and rich orange-buff breast, and lays a single purple-flecked egg in the domed nest of the small scrub-wren, thorn-bill etc., the young of which are often heaved from the nest by the lusty young cuckoos. The cuckoos are mainly insectivorous and their cries tend towards trilling. Many have the wave-like flight seen in jungle birds, and erect the tail on landing as if using a parachute-brake. (*See* PLATE 4.)

Culotta, Nino The pen-name of John O'Grady (1907–   ), born in Sydney. A pharmacist and linguist who wrote the highly successful *They're a Weird Mob* (Sydney, 1957), an idealised view of the Aus. way of life as seen by an Italian migrant.

Cumberland Islands Qld. 20S/150E Usually taken to include the Whitsun-day Islands*, these are a group of about 100 rocky islands of the inner 'continental' type. (*See* GREAT BARRIER REEF.)

Cunjevoi A name, derived from a N.S.W. Aboriginal language, for the sea-squirt. (*See* ASCIDIANS.)

Cunjevoi

Cunnamulla Qld. 28S/146E (1,806 in 1971; 2,234 in 1961) A railhead on the Warrego River and an important collecting and distributing point for the surrounding pastoral country. It de-veloped as a coaching centre from Bourke, N.S.W., by Cobb and Co.* (from 1879). Coaches survived in the area well into the 20th century. Bullock teams also assembled there to carry wool to the railway before it reached the town (1898).

Cunningham, Allan (1791–1839) b. Sur-rey, Eng. An outstanding botanist, sent as travelling collector for Kew Gardens to N.S.W. in 1816, where he joined Oxley's* expedition down the Lachlan. From 1817–22 he made valuable collections on coastal surveys under P. P. King*. Land exploration included finding a stock route to Liverpool Plains by Pandora's Pass (1823), and discovering the Darling Downs* (1827) and **Cunningham's Gap** through the Main Range, 29S/152E, down to Moreton Bay. His remains lie under an obelisk in the Botanic Gardens, Sydney, where for a short time (1837–9) he was Colonial Botanist, following his brother Richard. A number of Aus. plants bear his name.

Cupania, Tuckeroo or **Carrotwood** (*Cupaniopsis anacardioides*) Of the widespread tropical family Sapindaceae, growing well on sandy coastal ridges and tolerating salt-laden winds in NE N.S.W. and Qld. This tree yields useful pinkish timber though it is small, only exceptionally of 18 m. It has dark glossy, shady, 7-cm. oval to oblong leaves, multiple flowers spread along the branches, and showy, velvety, 3-lobed fruit capsules, 10 cm. long, which often split to reveal oval brown-black seeds in an orange-red covering.

Curl Snake (*Suta suta*) A small, venomous, nocturnal snake of inland Aus., with large flattened head and distinct broad snout. It is brown to red-brown with blackish head and white belly. On alarm it depresses and curls its body, sometimes in a knot. The neurotoxic venom from a large specimen would justify careful treatment.

Curr, Edward (1798–1850) b. Sheffield, Eng. He arrived in Tas. in 1820 and on his return to Eng. (1824) published *An Account of the Colony of Van Diemen's Land.* He was Agent of Van Diemen's Land Co.* (1826–41), and although efficient, was dismissed after prolonged disputes with the authorities and retired to Port Phillip. He became politically active, agitating for separation of Vic. from N.S.W. and continuation of transportation. 'Old Curr' became a controversial Melbourne character, whose election defeat caused riots in 1843. His son **Edward Micklethwaite** (1820–1889), became expert on stock as well as an amateur anthropologist and wrote *The Australian Race* (4 vols., Melbourne, 1886).

Currawongs Large pied magpies* about 45 cm. long with a name suggested by the cry, insectivorous but sometimes raiding orchards. (*See* PLATE 4.)

Currency Consists of decimal dollars and cents since changing progressively in 1966-7 from pounds, shillings and pence ($A2 = £1A).

Notes (F—Front; B—Back):
$1 F the Queen in Order of the Garter regalia and the Aus. Coat of Arms*; B Aboriginal Bark Paintings*, Rock Art*.
$2 F John Macarthur* and the wool industry; B William Farrer* and ears of wheat.
$5 F Joseph Banks* with Banksia*, Eucalyptus* fruit etc.; B Caroline Chisholm* with sailing ships, women and child migrants.
$10 F Francis Greenway* and some of his buildings; B Henry Lawson* with contemporary scenes, MSS etc.
$20 F Sir Charles Kingsford Smith and a pendulum design symbolic of wings; B Lawrence Hargrave* with some of his drawings of kites and aircraft.

All have a watermark of Captain Cook and an embedded metallic thread vertically near the centre. A $50 note was issued mid-1973.

Coins, designed by Devlin, bear on heads the Queen, head and shoulders and in profile, wearing a light crown. The tails are:

Cents: 1 Pigmy Possum*—bronze;
　　　 2 Frilled Lizard*—bronze;
　　　 5 Spiny Ant-eater*—cupro-nickel;
　　　10 Lyre-bird*—cupro-nickel;
　　　20 Duck-billed Platypus*—cupro-nickel;
　　　50 Coat-of-Arms of Aus.—silver (discontinued 1968). 12-sided cupro-nickel from 1969 with special Cook Commemoration issue for 1970.

Holey Dollars* were used in the early period of the colony. Prior to Federation English currency generally circulated, including the gold sovereign which up to 1931 was minted partly in Aus.; Aus. coins, at first minted overseas, were only introduced from 1910. Latterly there were only florins (2 shillings), shillings, sixpences, threepenny pieces, pennies and half-pennies, though a few crowns of 5 shillings were issued in the late 1930s.

The early shortage of cash was met

partly by the circulation of handwritten promissory notes; Governor King tried to control this private note-issue by demanding printed notes (printing being a government monopoly at the time) but he failed and some such notes were circulating as late as 1870. After the foundation of the Bank of New South Wales in 1817, however, notes were issued by it and other trading banks, and at Federation the note issue consisted of these and Qld. treasury notes. Note-issue was taken over by the Commonwealth Treasury in 1910, at first using overprinted trading bank notes. Treasury notes were issued in 1913. Aus. currency was at par with sterling until the depression year 1931, when Aus. devalued at £A125 = £100 sterling. The Commonwealth Bank took over the note issue in 1920 and the Reserve Bank in 1960. In November 1967 Aus. did not devalue along with sterling. In Dec. 1972 the dollar was revalued. $A1 was worth approximately 57p sterling and U.S. $1.4 in April 1973.

Currency Lads and Lasses A term widely used up to mid-19th century for Aus.-born as against British-born who were referred to as Sterling.

Curtin, John Joseph (1885–1945) b. Creswick, Vic. Son of an Irish Catholic police sergeant. Labor Prime Minister of Aus. 1941–5. He entered politics from Trade Union organisation and the editorship of the anti-conscription* *Westralian Worker* in Perth, where he had settled in 1916, entered Federal Parliament in 1928. He succeeded Scullin* in 1935 as leader of the Labor Party. Largely at Evatt's instigation he moved the no-confidence vote which brought down the Fadden Government in 1941, thus becoming almost reluctantly, a war-time Labor Prime Minister. He had won a personal battle over incipient alcoholism. Feeling the burden of responsibility deeply, he was quiet, persuasive, co-operative and accommodating, yet accomplished the necessary reorientation towards the

U.S. alliance brought about by the Japanese advance, and the acceptance of conscription for home and N.G. defence, although battling with his party die-hards on its extension to service in Dutch N.G. He died in office on the eve of victory.

Curtis Island Qld. 24S/151E Lies about 6 km. offshore just N of Gladstone. It is 40 km. long and 8–16 km. wide, with low hills of volcanic rocks in the S, mainly wooded but with some cattle.

Cusack, Ellen Dymphna b. Wyalong, N.S.W. She became a novelist and playwright after leaving N.S.W. teaching service which she indicts in her play *Morning Sacrifice* (Sydney, 1943). Several of her works have been translated into other languages.

Cuscus A popular name for large Possums* of the genus *Phalanger* found in the Cape York area.

Customs Duties Unified from separate codes for the 6 colonies at Federation, and administered by the Department of Customs and Excise at sea and airports, for both revenue and protection purposes. (*See also* TARIFFS.)

Cuthbert, Betty (1938–   ) b. Sydney. A sprinter, who won 3 gold medals in the 1956 Olympic Games (100 m., 200 m. and a relay); she broke records in the 200 m., 220 yd. and 60 m. also in 1956, still retaining the latter, and won the 400 m. in the Tokyo Olympics, 1964. Known as the 'Golden Girl', she became one of the most popular figures in Aus. sport.

Cycads Of the widespread tropical and sub-tropical family Cycadaceae or Cycadales, these are very slow-growing plants, like palms or tree-ferns in appearance, and are descendants of plants common in the Mesozoic, approximately 100 million years ago. (*See also* GYMNOSPERMS.) The genus *Cycas* has seeds in pairs on either side of the base of leafy scales which form a loose cone, while the 2 other Aus. genera *Macrozamia* and *Bowenia* have large cones weighing up to 25 kg. or more, the former resembling a large pineapple. Pollen is produced in sacs on the underside of scales in male cones. Seeds of several species are poisonous to man and stock, though after processing they were an important food for Aborigines. The roots form a nitrogen-fixing association with blue-green algae. Cycads are extraordinarily slow-growing and a 6-m. Qld. *Macrozamia*, felled by vandals, was estimated to be 1,000–1,500 years old. Smaller specimens are common in coastal woodlands N and S of Sydney.

Cycling Apart from racing, this is largely confined to children. The first recorded race was organised in 1869 by the Melbourne Boneshakers Club. Their wooden machines were soon replaced by Penny Farthings and many clubs were formed, following the Melbourne Bicycle Club of 1878. The change to the modern type of machine came in the 1890s.

Professional cycling, controlled by the Federal Cycling Union (1901), had a very prosperous period about 1890–1906 when large cash prizes, as in the Sydney Thousand (1903–6), drew famous American competitors, but then it declined. Aus. professionals who have achieved success overseas include Arnold, Strom, Opperman, and recently G. Johnson (world sprint champion 1970) and M. Walker. In Aus. the Austral Wheel Race (amateur 1886–90, then professional) is the main track race, and the Melbourne-Warrnambool and Sydney-Goulburn the main road races, with some long distance events.

Amateur cycling is controlled by the Amateur Cyclists Association of Aus. Olympic Medals were won:

1932	E. L. Grey (1,000 m. time trial);
1952	R. Mockridge, later a professional (1,000 m. time trial), and with L. Cox (2,000 m. tandem);
1956	Browne and Marchant (2,000 m. tandem).

Cyclones Tropical revolving storms developing over the Coral Sea and Indian Oceans Dec.–April and which can cause severe storms along the tropical NE and NW coasts. Bad years have included 1893, 1899, 1911, 1954. In 1970 (Whitsunday Is.), 1971 (Townsville), 1972 (Brisbane) cyclones caused damage. Advance warning centres are at Perth, Darwin and Brisbane.

Cypress Pines (*Callitris*) The chief Aus. members of the world-wide cypress family, Cupressaceae. They have little scale-leaves in whorls of 3 along the branches, and cones with 3 large and 3 small woody scales. There are about 20 species of various habitats. They range from the useful 18-m. Bribie Cypress Pine, *C. columellaris*, of NE N.S.W. and SE Qld., with its distinctive upright column rising from the centre of the cone, to mallee species, e.g. the warty-coned *C. verrucosa*, the Mallee or Scrub-pine. Widespread species yielding termite and teredo-resistant timber, workable and not shrinking much, but rather inflammable—as are the growing trees—include: the well-known White Cypress Pine, *C. hugelii*, found, often on sandy swellings, over a huge belt of the S two-thirds of Aus. with 35–70 cm. mean annual rainfall, and the Northern Cypress Pine, *C. intratropica*, important in a belt of 160–250 km. following the N coast from the Kimberley region of W.A. to Cape York, where it is invaluable but scarce because it is so liable to fire. There are also two endemic genera of shrubby cypresses, *Actinostrobus* (W.A.), and *Diselma* (W Tas.). (*See* PLATE 8.)

D

DAIRY CATTLE

Dairy Cattle Concentrated in SE Qld. (coastal lowlands and Darling Downs), the N and S coasts of N.S.W., Gippsland and the W District of Vic. (Vic. has 44% of the total dairy production), the hills E of Adelaide, S.A., the coast plain S of Perth, W.A., and on the plains of NE and NW Tas. Irrigation supports dairying along the Murray if water rates are low and there is an urban demand, and in Central Gippsland. Breeds are based on (often debased from) European Shorthorns (developed in the Aus. Illawarra Shorthorn), Friesians and Jerseys, with Ayrshires in rougher areas. Feed is almost entirely improved pasture of imported grasses (with fluctuations from seasonal rainfall incidence, drought and flood), or fodder crops, e.g. lucerne, legumes and sorghum. Farm units are small, usually family-run to avoid high labour costs; 60% of the milk is made into butter in 300 factories, a third in Vic.; 35–40% was exported, over 80% to U.K. under trade pact (to 1972), along with a similar proportion of the annual output of 90,000 tons of cheese (which uses 9% of the milk); together they comprise 5% of rural exports by value. Productivity, especially in butter-fat content, is relatively low, but efficiency of management, recording, breeding and marketing reflect economic as well as social factors and vary from well-organised units, such as many in Vic., to remote marginal units in the eastern belts. Dairying is the most highly subsidised and controversial rural industry; over $42 million of direct subsidy (1971), guaranteed prices and restriction of margarine production mean prosperity for productive units and a bare livelihood for many others none the less attached to their particular way of life. Some reorgan-

DALLEY

isation followed the 1967 sterling devaluation and U.K. entry to the Common Market in 1973.

Daisies Apart from the introduced *Bellis perennis* of many lawns etc., there are many native daisies also of the Compositae family, notably some 60 species of the genus *Brachycome*, such as the Swan River Daisy, *B. iberidifolia*, with blue or white flowers, and the light purple Narrow-leaf Daisy, *B. angustifolia*, of the N.S.W. coast and tablelands. There are some 80 Daisy Bushes, genus *Olearia*, including several in Tas., e.g. the Musk Daisy Bush, *O. argophylla*. The blue-flowered Forest Daisy Bush, *O. adenophora*, is common along the Great Divide, and the heath-like blue-flowered *O. ciliata* in many inland areas. The alpine *Celmisia*, with many species, e.g. the Snow or Silver Daisy, *C. longifolia*, have silvery hairs on the leaves. The downy-leaved Cudweed is *Gnaphalium* spp.

Dalby Qld. 27S/151E (8,890 in 1971) A growing service centre for the N half of the Darling Downs* in wheat-dairying country and dating from pastoral settlement in the area with the Ipswich rail link (1868). It is likely to increase with the development of the Moonie oilfield. Makes farm machinery.

Daley, (Victor) James William Patrick (1858–1905) b. Ireland. He arrived in Aus. about 1872, was a romantic poet, journalist and popular Sydney literary figure of the 1890s. *At Dawn and Dusk* (Sydney, 1898) contains his best poems and bears the name of a contemporary Sydney literary club.

Dalley, William Bede (1831–1888) b. Sydney, N.S.W. A politician and lawyer who, as Acting Premier of N.S.W.

(1884) sent Aus. troops to the Sudan, the first to serve overseas; he was the first Aus. member of Privy Council (1887). His second son **John Bede** (1878–1935) was a political and social satirist through *Bulletin* stories, and novels such as *Only the Morning* (Sydney, 1930).

Dalrymple, Alexander (1737–1808) b. Haddington, Scotland. Hydrographer to East India Company, later the Admiralty, he was intensely interested in exploration and convinced of the existence of the great Southland by analogy with the northern hemisphere. Although he was recommended by the Royal Society to go with the *Endeavour*, Cook gained the command and Dalrymple's lasting enmity and disparagement. He wrote valuable histories of exploratory voyages, bringing to English notice (1767) Torres's voyage of 1606, proving the existence of the strait between N.G. and New Holland; he also wrote strongly against the proposed convict settlement at Botany Bay.

Daly River N.T. 14S/131E Formed by the confluence of Katherine River* and King River and flows 320 km. NW to Anson Bay. Its basin of 58,600 km.² is generally flat or rolling lowland, becoming increasingly thickly wooded towards the wetter coast. Its total population is under 2,000 including Aborigines and the Roman Catholic Mission. Pioneer cattle stations developed 1911–20 were unprofitable through lack of markets, disease and the poor grazing in the 'Dry'; vast cattle stations belong to company-held chains; sorghum grown for fodder is now increasing yields. Peanut farms failed in the face of Qld.'s better yields and markets. C.S.I.R.O.* surveys of the area are valuable indicators of the potential for northern development*.

Daly Waters N.T. 16S/133E A small staging post on the Stuart Highway,

dating from an Overland Telegraph* Office, 1872. In 1862 J. McDouall Stuart left his initials on a tree when he conquered the fierce scrub belt that had repulsed him earlier.

Damper Bread cooked in the ashes of an outdoor fire, and comprising flour and water with or without a raising agent. The origin is a Lancashire dialect word for a snack between meals.

Dampier W.A. 21S/117E (3,558 in 1971) A completely new iron port built since 1965 on King Bay to export ore to Japan and Europe from Mt. Tom Price, 203 km. to the S. A pelletising plant treats the fine ores and dust. Water comes 24 km. from the Maitland River and from a desalinisation plant. Salt is exported. Workers also live at Karratha.*

Dampier, Alfred (1847–1908) b. London. Actor and theatrical entrepreneur. First toured Aus. as an actor in 1872 and 1877, returning permanently later. As well as much popular melodrama, he presented Shakespeare and stage versions of Aus. novels, notably *Robbery Under Arms*.

Dampier Land W.A. 17S/122E A low peninsula of red sand and gravels and poor scrub called 'pindan* country', between Roebuck Bay and King Sound. William Dampier's* last landing in 1699 was 80 km. to the SW. It is mainly an Aboriginal reserve served by Beagle Bay and Lombardina Missions.

Dampier, William (1651–1715) b. Somerset, Eng. He became a buccaneer in the West Indies. Later he joined the pirate ship *Cygnet* under Swan and later Read in the Philippines and in her sighted NW Aus. (1688) at Buccaneers Archipelago. His withering description of the barren land, the flies, and the natives 'the miserablest people on earth' was published in the highly popular *New Voyage Round the World* (1697). The book brought him fame and command of the *Roebuck*

(1699) with orders to explore New Holland further. He reached Shark Bay, W.A., after a 11,200-km. voyage from Brazil. A leaking boat and scurvy caused him to return after exploratory work NE from Shark Bay and in waters off the northern shores of N.G. Dampier was an adventurer and fine seaman, but a poor leader. *For further reading see* J. C. Shipman: *William Dampier, seaman-scientist* (Kansas, 1962); C. Lloyd: *William Dampier* (London, 1967).

Dampiera A genus of often hairy herbs and shrubs in the mainly Aus. Goodeniaceae family; most in W.A., including the leafless *D. alata* and the deep blue flowers of *D. linearis.* An E Aus. species common on poor sandy areas is the angular and erect herb *D. stricta,* with small spear-shaped leaves and yellow-hearted sky-blue flowers, the 5 petals split down one side and with rusty hairs on the underside.

Dandenong Ranges Vic. 38S/146E These reach 634 m. Forested reserves include Ferntree Gully National Park and Sherbrooke Forest, with its lyrebirds. Intensive market-gardening in the valleys, includes soft fruits round Monbulk, Sassifras and Olinda. There is increasing penetration by railserved commuter suburbs as far as Gembrook, and a new Melbourne water storage is planned. **Dandenong** a city (31,015 in 1966) on the SW slopes, combines traditional cattle-marketing for Gippsland with recent rapid industrial development of car, machinery, canning, rubber and glass factories and is now continuous with Melbourne.

Daphne, Native (*Pittosporum undulatum*) A 16-m. tree of coastal SE Aus.; *Pittosporum* is the only genus of the family Pittosporaceae which is also found outside Aus. in the tropics and sub-tropics. It has smooth grey-black bark, glossy, broadly lanceolate leaves making dense foliage, compound clusters of cream-white bells which are very strongly scented, hence 'mock orange', then a fruit capsule with 2 hard thick leafy covers opening to release many smallish dark red seeds. It is a popular garden and shade tree, but subject to wax and scale insects. Of the 100 or so species in the genus, about 12 are found in Aus., including the attractive Weeping Pittosporum, *P. phillyreoides,* of drier areas on the Western Slopes and Central Aus. and the Cheese-wood, *P. bicolor,* of the wet mountain gullies in Tas.

Darcy, James Leslie (Les) (1895–1917) b. Stradbroke, N.S.W. He was the greatest boxing idol Aus. has had. From a blacksmith's apprenticeship, he became Aus. lightweight, later middle- and heavy-weight champion, He stowed away to the U.S. in 1916, hoping to prove his world stature, but died of blood-poisoning the following year. In Aus. he had lost only 4 out of 50 fights (1911–16), including many against international boxers. *For further reading see* R. Swanwick: *Australia's Golden Boy of Boxing* (Sydney, 1965).

Dark, Eleanor (*née* O'Reilly) (1901–) b. Sydney. A leading novelist whose books fall into 2 groups: on human relationships, including 2 near-thrillers. *Prelude to Christopher* (Sydney, 1934) and *Return to Coolami* (London, 1936); and historical novels of considerable scholarship, of which *The Timeless Land* (London, 1941) is the best fictionalised portrayal of Governor Phillip* and the early colony.

Darling Downs A distinctive region of S Qld. with 21,000 km.^{2} and well over 100,000 people. Lying W of the Divide at 350–600 m., its rectangular shape follows the SE/NW course of the Condamine River* fed by short streams from the Main Range* and Bunya Range*. The W is bounded by poorer sandstone country, the S by the Granite Belt* and the N by the Great Divide, here a low plateau. Soils derived from basalt are the main factor in the rich agricultural development dominated by wheat, other grains and dairying, which followed the initial pastoral development and pioneer Scottish settlement after Cunningham's discovery (1827). There are prosperous market towns and industry at Too-woomba* and the other main centres which are growing at the expense of smaller towns and villages. *For further reading see* R. H. Greenwood: *The Darling Downs* (Melbourne, 1956).

Darling, Sir Ralph (1775–1858) Governor of N.S.W. 1825–31, succeeding Brisbane and having been a firm but unpopular military governor in Mauritius (1819–23). His term was much more turbulent, chiefly through his repeated clashes with the Emancipists*, led in vitriolic personal attacks by Wentworth*, which led to Darling's attempt to curb the press, defeated by Chief Justice Forbes*. The death, after punishment, of a defaulting but sick soldier, Sudds, added unjustly to his reputation for authoritarian brutality. Darling, backed by the rising 'Squattocracy', did not believe the colony was ready for a House of Assembly, and the 1828 Judicatory Act, extended membership of the Legislative Council and gave some qualified trial by jury. In 1829 Darling tried without success to contain settlement to within 240 km. of Sydney, fearing the difficulties of control over a wider area. He established a basic Public Service and re-organised the monetary and banking system and encouraged exploration.

Darling Range or **Scarp** W.A. 32/S 116E The most clearly defined section of the SW edge of the Great Plateau. It rises to an even skyline 240–300 m. above the coastal plain between Moora and Donnybrook, a distance of 225 km. and is locally called 'The Hills'. Short W-flowing rivers have dissected the scarp into a gently rolling topography of forested slopes and wide valleys. The highest point is Mt. Cook

(582·5 m.). Rainfall is over 120 cm. in parts, and the rivers are used for town and irrigation water supplies. Widespread bauxite deposits are worked at Jarrahdale and in the Hotham Valley.

Darling River N.S.W. Flows for some 1,900 km from the Barwon-Culgoa confluence (where it takes the name of Darling), 48 km. NE of Bourke, 30S/146E, to its junction with the Murray at Wentworth, 34S/142E. Above the Barwon-Culgoa confluence the longest of the group of headwaters (Condamine, Macintyre-Dumaresq*, Gwydir*, Namoi*, Castlereagh*, Macquarie* and Bogan*, are 800 km. long. Much of the Darling's course is through very extensive saltbush pastures in less than 25 cm. mean annual rainfall. Below Bourke only the Warrego and sometimes the Parroo succeed in getting right to the Darling; numerous distributaries set off from the Darling only to end in dry sandy channels flowing briefly in years of high flood, but the Talyawalka Creek flows for over 125 km. S of the river from near Wilcannia, 32S/143E, to near Menindee, 32S/142E, and the Great Anabranch* W of the lakes joins the Murray downstream from Wentworth. The headstreams were gradually discovered by graziers from 1815 on, and the Darling named a few years later by Sturt*. Legend has it that the first boat to reach Bourke in 1861, and the last boat in 1943 both carried 'grog'—the latter for troops in Qld. Weirs built under an Act of 1945 permit considerable use of Darling waters for domestic and stock use, particularly along the lower course, and the Menindee Lakes are now used to store floodwaters to help to maintain the agreed flow from N.S.W. to S.A., and to supplement the water supplies for Broken Hill*. Despite the aridity of its later course—'losement' rather than catchment—the flow at Menindee averages 3,600 million m.^{3} per annum; but this is from an enormous catchment of 57·5 million ha.

Darwin N.T. 12S/131E (36,828 in 1971) A city and administrative capital which spreads over and beyond a low peninsula edged with 15 to 30-m. cliffs on the N shore of **Port Darwin**, a deep NW–SE-trending inlet with a narrow entrance giving protection from the strong summer winds. It was found and named on the *Beagle** voyage which charted these coasts in 1838–41, but settlement did not follow until after the failure of the Escape Cliffs* venture in 1867. The town, surveyed by Goyder in 1869, was called Palmerston, and the name was changed to Darwin only when the N.T. passed from S.A. to Commonwealth administration in 1911. Short periods of impetus between long years of stagnation were given by the Overland Telegraph* (1870–2), the Pine Creek* gold-rush in 1873, the railway to Pine Creek (1889), the abortive meatworks (1917–20), pioneer air flights from Britain and later the flying boat service from Southampton to Sydney. In 1939 the population was only 6,000. In February 1942 Darwin was severely damaged by Japanese air attack; the civilian population were largely evacuated, and it became a garrison town. Growth has been more rapid in recent years with developing export of minerals from the hinterland, notably iron ore from Frances Creek. The rebuilt city has now more in common with suburbia anywhere than with its colourful, ramshackle past. The Chinese quarter has gone; and tertiary industry includes 2 breweries, ice cream and aerated water factories. Water is supplied from Manton Dam 68 km. away There are meatworks for the U.S. trade, port development and an International airport. *See* M. G. Kerr: *The Surveyors* (Adelaide, 1971).

Davey, Thomas (1758–1823) b. Devon, Eng. He succeeded Collins* as Lt.-Governor of Tas. (1812–6), having attained the post by influence rather than merit, for Goulburn warned Macquarie privately of his dubious honesty. Yet despite the debauchery of the private life of 'Mad Tom' as he was known, Davey made some considerable progress in bringing some order and prosperity to Tas., which he found in a state of chaos, terror from bushrangers, Aboriginal violence and poverty.

David, Sir Tannatt William Edgeworth (1858–1934) b. Wales. He arrived in Aus. in 1882. As surveyor with the N.S.W. Department of Mines, he traced the rich Greta coal seams. He became Professor of Geology and Physical Geography at Sydney University (1891–1924), carrying out fundamental work on Aus. geology. The first country-wide geological map appeared in 1932. David's *The Geology of the Commonwealth of Australia* (London, 1950) was completed by W. R. Browne. As a member of the Shackleton Antarctic Expedition (1907–9), he led the epic Magnetic Pole expedition and climbed Mt. Erebus. *For further reading see Professor David* (London, 1937) by his daughter, Mrs. M. E. McIntyre.

Davidson's Plum (*Davidsonia pruriens*) Found in the southern hemisphere, of the family Cunoniaceae, it grows in tropical rain-forests of Qld. and in many gardens, commonly to 12 m. by 30 cm. It has saw-edged leaflets of up to 30 cm. by 8 cm., in compound leaves 1 m. long, compound flowers up to 30 cm. long with small individual red blossoms, and a 7-cm. hairy purple fruit with rather bitter red flesh around 2 flat seeds, eaten by fruit-bats, and used for jams and jellies.

Davis 69S/78E An Antarctic research base on the shores of Princess Elizabeth Land, in the Vestfold Hills area, one of the largest ice-free sections of the continent, in an extensive area of boulder moraine. It was closed temporarily 1965–9. It was named after **J. K. Davis** (1884–1967), born in London, a navigator who relieved the Mawson* expedition in 1913 of which he was second in command; he was with Shackleton in 1907 and rescued his party in 1916. He discovered **Davis Sea** 1911. Davis was Director of Commonwealth Navigation Services (1920–49).

Davis, Arthur Hoey (1868–1935) b. Drayton, Qld. Writing as Steele Rudd, he was the creator of the *Dad and Dave* characters, which appear in films and comic strips; but originally in short, mainly humorous and caricatured studies of rough pioneering days on an outback 'selection' of S Qld., written for the *Bulletin*, and *On Our Selection* (Sydney, 1899), the first of a series.

Davis Cup A silver tennis trophy, weighing 6·07 kg. presented in 1900 by an American player and politician Dwight F. Davis, for international competition, and originally called the International Lawn Tennis Trophy. At first only U.S. and U.K. took part, but subsequently 35 nations have competed, although only 4 have won it: U.S., U.K., France and Aus. (with N.Z. until 1919). Regional elimination rounds determine the team which plays the Challenge Round against the holder, in the holder's country. Both doubles and singles matches are played, always by men, although women are not specifically precluded in the rules. Australasia won in 1907, 1908, 1909, 1911, 1914, 1919 and Aus. in 1939, then inclusively 1950–3, 1955–7, 1959–62, 1964–7.

Davison, Frank Dalby (1893–1970) b. Glenferne, Vic. A novelist and short-story writer. His stories, closely observed and written in almost lyrical prose, have a country background, often using insight into the 'minds' of animals as in *Dusty* (Sydney, 1946).

Dawson River Qld. A major but seasonal tributary of the Fitzroy*, rising in the Carnarvon Range and flowing 628 km. NE then N through a 80-km.-wide valley, floored with coal-bearing sediments and with rich

black earth under Brigalow* scrub, now being cleared for more intensive cattle rearing. Irrigation from 3 weirs (Theodore, Orange Creek and Moura) was developed from 1923, part of a larger scheme not realised.

Daylesford Vic. 37S/144E (2,946 in 1971) A former gold town at 610 m., known as Jim Crow Diggings, now a tourist centre of the volcanic Central Uplands region.

Daylight Saving The practice of advancing clocks one hour in summer was used in the World Wars. It was re-introduced in Tas. in 1967 and from 1972 in S.A., N.S.W., Vic. and A.C.T.

Deakin, Alfred (1856–1919) b. Fitzroy, Vic. Prime Minister of Aus. 3 times between 1903–10 and the outstanding political leader of the first years of the Commonwealth. A legal training was followed by journalism under Syme*. He entered the Vic. Legislative Assembly (1879) and soon achieved eminence through his power of advocacy and personality. He travelled widely: to study irrigation in California, in India and Europe; and to the London Colonial Conference (1887) where his outspoken defence of Aus. interests distinguished him. His great work in the Federation movement was one of negotiation, of persuasion, diplomacy and advocacy; and he played a major role in seeing the Bill accepted in London; his posthumously published *The Federal Story*, ed. H. Brookes (Melbourne, 1944) is a brilliantly analytical if sometimes biased account of the personalities involved. As Attorney General in the first Federal Parliament, he succeeded his friend Barton as Prime Minister for a first brief period 1903–4. His political aims had much in common with those of the emerging Labor party which supported him in his second and most constructive ministry (1905–8). It laid foundations for pensions, defence, protection and the broad bases of Aus. life for 30 years; yet in the kaleidoscope of developing party politics he formed the allegedly iniquitous Fusion with Reid's successor Cook (1909–10), and all his former enemies, to oust Labor briefly (*see* POLITICAL PARTIES). In England (1907) he campaigned vigorously for Imperial trade preferences. Deakin retired in 1913, having consistently refused all honours. His 2 biographers W. Murdoch: *Alfred Deakin—A Sketch* (London, 1923) and J. A. la Nauze: *Alfred Deakin* (Melbourne, 1965) concentrate respectively on the pre- and post-federal periods of his career.

Deane, John Phillip (1796–1849) b. London. A musician who became organist of St. David's Church, Hobart, 1826, and moved to Sydney in 1836 to open one of the first teaching studios. His son continued as an influential musical figure in Sydney.

Death Adder or **Deaf Adder** (*Acanthophis antarcticus antarcticus*) A short bulky grey or yellowish, venomous snake with darker bands, broad triangular head and notably small, thin tail with spiny end scales (used as a caterpillar-like lure for small lizards, birds etc. when the snake is lying buried in sand). It is widely distributed over Aus. except the interior and Tas.

Death Adder
(*Acanthophis antarcticus antarcticus*),
50–60 cm. nose to tail

It is sluggish to move on being approached, but bites very swiftly and effectively if harassed or trodden on. The venom is deadly and full first-aid treatment must be followed by prompt measures to get anti-venene treatment. The Desert Death Adder, *A. a. pyrrhus*, is a sub-species.

Defence Within the overall policy of the Government (*see* INTERNATIONAL RELATIONS), the Defence Department is responsible for defence policy, joint Service matters and financial and supply aspects, including research, operating through various high-level committees. The Department of Supply has important functions as in the Weapons Research Establishment Salisbury, S.A., and Woomera*. Facilities are given to friendly powers, e.g. the U.S. communications centre near North West Cape*, and exchanges of naval components and rocket facilities with Britain. Since 1945 Aus. commitments have been in Asia: support for Malaya against Communist terrorists and later Indonesian confrontation; the Korean War*; and 1962–72, the Vietnam War*. The present assumption is that deliberate global war is unlikely. The British withdrawal from South-East Asia and the Russian presence in the Indian Ocean influence present defence planning. Regional defence associations are sought. Strategy is based on strong maritime defence. The 24 swing-wing fighter-bomber F111s ordered from U.S. will provide the air 'umbrella' from 1973. Total annual defence spending exceeds $1,100 million; in 1970 an additional 5-year equipment programme costing $250 million was announced to include helicopters, submarines and a new aircraft carrier. The Army, Navy, Air Force and Civil Defence will be centralised by stages under the Ministry of Defence from 1973.

De Grey River W.A. 21S/120E Flows, very sporadically, N then NW (the main headwater is the Oakover River) from the Robertson Range to a mud-lined mouth S of the small settlement of the same name.

Deloraine Tas. 41S/147E (1,816 in 1971; 1,873 in 1961) On the Meander River, a tributary of the S Esk, and at the foot of the Great Western Tiers*, this is a service centre for productive dairy lands, and has a butter factory. Surveyor Scott named it from the *Lay of the Last Minstrel* by Sir Walter Scott.

Democratic Labor Party (D.L.P.) Formed 1955, from strongly anti-Communist, mainly Roman Catholic, Labor organisations in Vic. and N.S.W. (Industrial Groupers), thus splitting the Aus. Labor Party*. In 1958 they gained 9·4% of the total vote, 8·7% in 1961, and have continued to command a minority vote of great political importance since the D.L.P. 'second preference' goes to the Liberal-Country Party candidate. In 1973 there were no D.L.P. Members of the House of Representatives, but there were 5 Senators, who with the Independents held the balance.

Denham or **Shark Bay** W.A. 26S/113E Formerly a pearling port now with salt pans, freezing plants for crayfish, mullet and snapper trucked to Perth, whiting air freighted to the E states. The people are of Asian–Aus. descent.

Deniliquin N.S.W. 35S/145E (6,604 in 1971) A Riverina market and service centre of local importance on the Edwards River*, and branch of the Murray, and the local terminal of the Vic. railway line from Echuca, 36S/145E. Its hinterland includes long-famous merino stud country, and now the Berriquin fodder and cereal irrigation and Wakool rice project.

Denison, Sir William Thomas (1804–1871) b. London. Lt.-Governor, Tas. (1847–55), Governor of N.S.W. (1855–61), Governor of Madras (1861–3), Governor General of India (1863–4). Denison, an army engineer, was perhaps the last 'strong man' in the long line of Aus. governors. His transfer to N.S.W. coincided with self-government there. His Tas. term had been stormy for he favoured trans-portation against popular demand for abolition; he ruled without any council (1847–8) owing to resignations. In Sydney he fortified Port Jackson against possible Russian invasion in the Crimean War. **Fort Denison** is the small fortified island in Sydney Harbour once used for recalcitrant con-victs; though the appropriate early name Pinchgut was a sailors' word for narrows.

Dennis, Clare (1917–1971) b. Sydney. A champion woman breast-stroke swimmer winning the 200 m. in the 1932 Olympic Games. She began swimming reluctantly and using free-style. She became professional after 1936.

Dennis, Clarence Michael James (1876–1938) b. Auburn, S.A. He had various occupations, from barman to journal-ist, during which he wrote his famous humorous, slang-filled light verse of the wild Melbourne 'larrikin' redeemed by 'love of a pure woman': *The Songs of a Sentimental Bloke* (Sydney, 1915); with the sequel especially written for the A.I.F., *The Moods of Ginger Mick*. For further reading see A. H. Chis-holm: *The Making of a Sentimental Bloke* (Melbourne, 1946).

D'Entrecasteaux Channel Tas. 43S/147E Extends some 65 km. SW–NE between the mainland and Bruny Island and is locally called The Chan-nel. It has been a major centre of scallop-fishing (May-July), but sources are now declining.

Depression, The To living Australians this means the period 1929–35. Un-employment affected up to a third of the work force; hardship was universal in town and country; the country roads were thronged by swagmen and town street corners by out-of-work artisans and labourers. A legacy of bitterness remains and is still being worked off in 'depression novels' or in political factionalism.

World trends were responsible, but Aus. was particularly vulnerable because of her ultimate dependence on her primary exports whose prices fell drastically, and on foreign, notably British capital for her continuing development. Wheat and wool prices fell as much as 50% after 1929, loans floated in London failed, while interest on the existing £225 million loans had to be met; the unfavourable trade balance was £74 million in 1930; national income fell from £640 million in 1928–9 to £460 million in 1930–1.

The inexperienced, inward-looking Labor Government (1929–31), at something of a loss, accepted the proffered analysis by the Bank of England expert, Niemeyer, who pointed to the unpalatable truth that the high Aus. living standard had been artificially contrived behind protection and bore no relationship to productivity in a world context. The inevitable retrenchment advocated by the Loan Council*, on advice from a Committee under Sir Douglas Copland*, was agreed to by the State Premiers in June 1931, by reduction of expenditure and of interest rates and increased taxation. Meanwhile the wage earners had their real wage reduced by 10%. Other abortive plans were the work of Theodore*, Labor Treasurer, who advocated inflationary tactics implacably opposed by the banks and notably by Sir Robert Gibson, a leading financial figure, and Lang*, the rebellious N.S.W. Labor Premier who repudiated overseas interest payments. Rising prices for exports, devaluation of exchange rate, assisted by the stringent restriction of imports by tariffs and prohibitions, and a drop in purchasing power gave Aus. a seemingly more rapid recovery than many other countries achieved, but internally there resulted a long period of setback in economic development and social welfare.

The 2 earlier major depressions were in the 1840s, due to over-extension of wool production by the squatters*, and in the 1890s, following low wool prices and over-speculation by London in Argentine, and a consequent London financial crisis which led to withdrawal of capital from Aus. and the failure of many banks.

Derby W.A. 17S/124E (2,521 in 1971) On the W shore of a peninsula at the head of King Sound. As a port it suffers from severe tidal race and high range. It is now linked by Beef Road to Glenroy and exports chilled beef.

Derwent River Tas. 42S/147E Flows some 190 km. SE from L. St. Clair* to Storm Bay*. The upper course, joined from the Central Plateau* by the Nive, Dee, Ouse* and Clyde, and from the SW by the Florentine, is extensively developed for hydro-electricity (*see* TASMANIA, POWER). The lower course, in a fault-lined depression filled with sediments and carved into terraces by river action, is a rich farming area centred on New Norfolk*. Hobart lies 20 km. from the mouth, on the deep waters of the estuary.

Desert Rose or **Sturt's Desert Rose** Popular names for one of the Aus. Cotton Plants*, bearing a delicate blue-purple flower in the dry inland.

Devil's Marbles N.T. 20S/134E Some 46 km. S of Tennant Creek*, on either side of the Stuart Highway, are

Devil's Marbles

scattered or heaped granite boulders from 30 cm. to 3 m. in diameter, resting on quartz pebbles and outcrops over an area of several acres. They are the product of millennia of weathering and erosion of ancient jointed granitic intrusions, and are the subject of Aboriginal legends.

Devonport Tas. 41S/146E (18,150 in 1971) Fourth largest Tas. city which lies on both sides of the Mersey River* estuary and was formed by the joining of 2 settlements, Formby and Torquay, in 1890. The port has 2 basins, the upper forming a natural silt trap, the lower sheltered by the dolerite headland Mersey Bluff to the W. It is a major service centre, Melbourne ferry terminal and has canning, foundry, dairy and paper industries.

Deyeuxia A genus of grasses with about 30 Aus. species, including forest species, e.g. the tall, rough-leaved *D. brachyathera* of mountain gullies in SE Aus., which has a complex head like a single rather than a branched plume, and also several alpine species.

Diamantina River Qld./S.A. An intermittent river rising on the low Gulf-L. Eyre watershed, about 21S/142E, and flowing (seasonally) over 800 km. SW towards L. Eyre, through the Channel Country* and across the S.A. border, where its lower course is called the Warburton. It was named after the wife of Queensland's first Governor, Bowen.

Diamond-birds A popular name for the attractive, small spotted brown Pardalotes.

Diarists Those recording the life and scene in early Aus. have been numerous, leaving valuable contemporary records. First Fleet* journals include those of 3 officers, D. Southwell, W. Bradley, R. Clarke, and also Sgt. J. Scott, and Private J. Easty. Early days in Tas. were recorded by R. Knopwood and Anna Maria Dawbin; in Vic. by Georgiana McCrae; in W.A. by G. F.

Moore. The lives of squatters in the Canberra region were recorded by Samuel Shumack (first published Canberra, 1967).

Dibbs, Sir George (1834–1904) b. Sydney. Premier of N.S.W. 1885, 1889, 1891–4. A protectionist, opposed to Federation and an enemy of Parkes*. Dibbs probably saved N.S.W. from the worst of the 1890s' Depression by giving swift, firm Government backing to the banks.

Didjeridu An Aboriginal musical instrument consisting of a 1·2- to 1·5-m. hollow piece of bamboo or wood, about 5 cm. across the hollow, with a mouthpiece of wax or gum. It is blown trumpet-wise, with puffed out cheeks to sustain the note, sometimes a long booming like an organ bass, sometimes alternating rhythmically and sharply between 2 notes about a tenth apart.

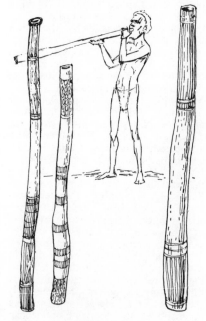

Didjeridu

Digger A word brought from U.S. to Aus. at the time of the first gold-rush and applied at first to all gold hunters, then specifically to those digging for alluvial gold. In the 1914–18 War it became the nickname of the Aus. soldier and has remained so since.

Dingo or **Warrigal** (*Canis antarticus*) The wild dog of Aus. except Tas., often yellowish-brown and resembling a large cattle dog, from which it is distinguished only by constantly erect ears, bushy tail and rather larger teeth on the average. The dingo may have come to Aus. with early man, but is now thoroughly wild and antipathetic with domestic dogs. Dingoes in many areas are a pest to sheep graziers; campaigns include shooting, trapping, poisoning and dingo-proof fences, but can lead to increased wild pigs and rabbits.

Dingo Fish, Sea-Pike or **Barracuda** (*Sphyraena*) (Not to be confused with the Barracouta*.) These are grey to greenish, white-bellied carnivorous fish with long strong teeth. Various species are netted or lined commercially in different parts of Aus.

Dinkum Genuine, authentic, true; most often applied to born and bred Aus. in the phrase 'dinkum Aussie', but also used in 'fair dinkum' which was originally an English dialect phrase meaning fair play, while 'dinkum' by itself meant hard work.

Diphtheria A virulent infection of mucous membranes, especially of the throat, by the bacillus *Corynebacterium diphtheriae*. It was one of a number of serious epidemic diseases of children in the late 19th century, reaching a peak in 1887–90. Antitoxin was introduced in 1895 and in recent years inoculation in infancy, which is so effective that the disease passed from popular consciousness; recently inoculation has been less used and diphtheria has had periods of increase.

Dirk Hartog Island W.A. 26S/113E

This forms the NW arm of Shark Bay. Overhanging limestone cliffs line the seaward edge, and sand dunes lie along the bay side. An automatic lighthouse stands at Point Inscription, where de Vlamingh found Hartog's pewter plate. The island is now a sheep station.

Disappointment, Lake W.A. 23S/123E A 160-km.-long salt encrustation, rarely with water, at the W edge of the Gibson Desert*, named in 1897 by the explorer F. H. Hann, while looking anxiously for fresh water. It is skirted by the Canning Stock Route*.

DISCOVERY Defined as the first incontrovertible recorded sightings. 1606 is given as the date, by the Dutch vessel *Duyfken*, under Jansz*. Prior to this it is certain that there was some knowledge of the N coast by the Malays, Chinese, Hindu and Buddhist colonists of the islands. Their Muslim successors, including the 18th-century Bugis trepang fishers, also had knowledge of the N coast. Europeans, from the Greeks onwards, conjectured the existence of a southland which appeared fancifully on their maps. Marco Polo alleged a land beyond Java (Java the Greater) and Mercator showed 'Beach' as the southern land. Navigational aids, pioneered by the Portuguese, gradually made it possible for a serious search for sea routes to the spice lands. By 1520 the South African route had been established by da Gama, and Magellan had made his incredible voyage round Cape Horn, but Aus. was completely missed, the prevailing winds and currents concentrating routes to the north. A series of French maps (1536–67) clearly based on Portuguese originals, and bearing remarkable correlations with the Aus. coast, which is called Jave le Grande, are contested by scholars as evidence of Portuguese discovery of the continent; but the case is not proven. The Spanish and Portuguese were motivated as much by religious zeal as by trading ambition, especially Mendaña who discovered the Solomons (1568), and Quiros* who found the New Hebrides in 1606, by sailing west from Peru. More significant however, was the voyage made by Quiros's companions, Torres* and Prado, who continued westwards, to be driven by adverse weather S of N.G. and through the Torres Str. The significance of this was not appreciated for 2 centuries, during which the Dutch assumed that there was no strait. Meanwhile Dutch and English mercantile interests became established through their respective East India Companies, and, devoid of proselytising zeal, were seeking trade and new lands. Thus a few months before Torres, the *Duyfken*, sent from Batavia for this purpose, had made the first historically proven landfall on the Aus. coast in 1606, on the W shore of Cape York, which they found to be 'for the greater part desert, with wild cruel black savages', and 'were constrained to return finding no good to be done there'. They did not observe Torres Str. The next discoveries were accidental but inevitable, following on the development of a route using the great Westerlies' belt by keeping due E from the Cape of Good Hope for 3,220 km., before northing to Java. Thus a series of landfalls were made along the W coast of Aus. (1616–28). First, Dirk Hartog* left his famous inscribed Pewter plate on Hartog Island (1616). Further sightings were made by the *Zeewolf* and *Mauritius* (1817) and the area became known as Eeendrachts Land, after Hartog's ship. In 1619 Houtman landed further S, at 32°S, on the Abrolhos Islands, and in 1621 shipwrecked Englishmen from the *Trial* saw the Monte Bello Islands and Barrow Island. In 1622 the *Leeuwin* (unknown master) discovered the SW tip of the continent and established the eastward set of the coast there.

These accidental discoveries were followed by a serious exploratory voyage to follow up that of the *Duyfken*; in 1623 Carstensz*, proceeding along the S N.G. coast, and again missing Torres Str., added to knowledge of the Cape York coastline; his companion Coolsteerdt, found the NE tip of Arnhem Land (named from his ship) on his way back to Java. In 1627 Nuyts and Thijjsen, continuing the *Leeuwin's* work, followed the S coast for some 1,500 km. eastwards, and an accidental discovery by de Witt sketched in more of the NW coast in 1628. There were a number of other sporadic sightings along the W coast, and when Pelsaart* made his great journey to Java, he finally established the suspected continuity of the continental coastline of the Southland as far as NW Cape. Pool and Pieterzoon, sent (1637) to the Carpentaria region, failed to establish whether this western region called New Holland was separated from the eastern land found by Jansz and Carstensz.

The Dutch East India Company commissioned Abel Tasman* to explore further (1642–3) 'for there must needs comprise well-populated districts in favourable climates' they argued, from analogy with Africa and S America. Sailing S from Mauritius, Tasman was turned back by weather at 50°S and on the advice of his pilot Visscher, then sailing eastwards from 44°S across the Bight, they sighted the W coast of Tas. and named it after Anthony van Diemen, the Dutch Governor General in Batavia. Tasman sailed E to discover N.Z., and complete what was in fact a circumnavigation of Aus. To the Dutch, the results were disappointing, and in 1644 Tasman was again despatched, this time to ascertain whether the 2 parts of the Southland were linked, or separated by sea, but failed to do so. Once again Torres Str. eluded the explorer.

This marked the end of all except more or less incidental sightings and charting by the Dutch navigators such as de Vlamingh who found Hartog's plate in 1696 and who named Swan River, which only seemed to prove further that this was a barren, unprofitable land, an impression which was confirmed by the observations of Dampier*, the English buccaneer who visited the NW coast in 1688 and in 1699.

Almost a hundred years later, James Cook* was sent to Tahiti in *Endeavour*, to observe a 'transit' of Venus and thence to proceed westwards to discover any new lands he might be able to. Thus, in April 1770, having rediscovered N.Z., and aiming for Tasman's Van Diemen's Land, he was edged northwards by the swell, and made the first recorded sighting of the E coast of Aus. so utterly different from the barren W and N, and claimed it for Eng., as New South Wales. With superb skill and seamanship, he sailed N from the first landfall at Cape Everard in Vic., landing first at Botany Bay, and charting the coast right round Cape York to Endeavour Str., proving the existence of a strait between N.G. and the mainland.

In 1788 the remaining problems of discovery were whether sea or land linked the 3 known segments, N.S.W., Van Diemen's Land and the western part of the continent (New Holland).

French exploration added knowledge of the SW corner: Baudin discovered some of the S coast W from Port Phillip, meeting Flinders* at Encounter Bay, coming from the W on his great circumnavigation in 1802, which had filled in the rest of the southern shore. By 1798 Bass and Flinders had established the probability of a str. between Aus. and Van Diemen's Land, further elucidated by Grant in 1800.

In 4 voyages from 1817 to 1821, P. P. King* greatly refined the charts, mainly by Tasman, of the NW coast, and by the time Wickham and Stokes on *Beagle** had filled in the Darwin–Victoria River stretch (1839), the discovery of Aus. might be said to be complete. The possibility of a vast inland sea was firmly believed because Flinders found no great river mouths, and was not disproved until the great period of land exploration*, about to begin, was complete. (*See* MAP 2.) *See* A. Sharp: *The Discovery of Australia* (Oxford, 1963); E. H. J. and E. E. Feeken, *The Discovery and Exploration of Australia* (Melbourne, 1970); and J. C. Beaglehole: *The Exploration of the Pacific* (London, 1934).

Discovery Bay S.A./Vic. 38S/141E A wide gently curved bay, stretching for almost 80 km. SE of Port McDonnell to Cape Bridgewater. The W part of the bay is more varied, the centre sandy—including the coastal sand barrier damming back the Glenelg River and the E which is particularly sandy and backed by tall dunes, some piled up on Cape Bridgewater.

Divorce The termination of marriages by the Supreme Courts of States or Territories by dissolution, annulment or judicial separation has rested, since the Commonwealth Matrimonial Causes Act (which came into force in 1961), on uniform legislation throughout Aus, simplified, 1973. Previously there were inter-state differences. Dissolutions total some 12,000 a year.

Dobell, William (1899–1970) b. Newcastle, N.S.W. One of the outstanding figures in Aus. art. His main contribution lay in forceful penetrating portraiture. His alleged caricature in the Archibald Prize painting of Joshua Smith in 1943, led to a law suit. From 1949–54 he painted New Guinea subjects returning to portraiture 1950–59. *See* V. Freeman *Dobell on Dobell* (Sydney 1970). Some 200 oils and sketches were found after his death.

Dobson, Rosemary de Brissac (Mrs. A. T. Bolton) (1920–) b. Sydney. A poet, a granddaughter of the English essayist Austin Dobson. Work as an art teacher reflects in her delicate, intellectual often unmistakably feminine verse, written with innate sureness and artistry, e.g. *Cock Crow* (Sydney, 1965).

Dogwood A popular name in Tas. for *Pomaderris apetala*, a member of the mainly tropical Rhamnaceae or Buckthorn family, growing to 9–12 m. on stream banks and in mountain gullies in SE Aus. It bears spikes of greenish-brown flowers, and has broad wrinkled leaves.

Dolphin Fish (*Coryphaena hippurus*) To be clearly distinguished from the mammalian dolphins*. It is a large, mainly blue, yellow and green oceanic fish widely distributed in the warmer waters of the world including much of Aus. It has a fin along the whole back and old male specimens have a blunt whale-like head. Grows to 1·2–1·8 m. but usually about 2–7 kg.

Dolphins A popular name for the whale* family Delphinidae, the smaller members of the Toothed Whales. Many dolphins are widely distributed, but species occurring in Aus. include: the 1·5-m. Common Dolphin, *Delphinus delphis*, the 3-m. Large Bottle-nosed Dolphin, *Tursiops catalania*, both protected in N.S.W., and the Grampus Dolphin, *Gramphidelphis exilis*.

Donahoe, John (1806–30) b. Ireland. Bushranger. Transported for life 1825, and escaping 1828, to live as a bush 'dandy', robbing mainly the rich. An intensive hunt ended at Campbelltown when Donahoe was shot. The song 'A Wild Colonial Boy', based on his exploits, was banned.

Donnybrook W.A. 34S/116E A minor industrial town at the foot of the Darling Range, noted in the past for its good building sandstone. Industries include cement and fruit canning. Apple-growing is important in the district. Population 1,002 in 1971.

Donkey Vote The name given to ballot papers filled in by apathetic ignorant voters, in the alphabetical order in which the candidates are placed. There is thus distinct advantage in having a surname beginning with a letter early in the alphabet; this has been proved statistically. The donkey vote has increased since compulsory voting was introduced in 1924. Selection of candidates by minor parties and in marginal seats is affected and Parliamentary membership shows a higher proportion of surnames in the first half of the alphabet than in the population at large.

Dorrigo N.S.W. 30S/153E (1,078 in 1971; 1,127 in 1961) A dairy and sawmilling centre in residual rain-forest country, the terminus of a branch railway twining spectacularly from the coast line at Glenreagh. It lies on the N slopes of the **Dorrigo Range**, a ridge of granite and basalt running from the New England plateau ENE from Point Lookout*, almost to the sea near Coffs Harbour*.

Doryanthes A genus in the Amaryllidaceae family. The Giant or Gymea Lily, *D. excelsa*, with a globular multiple head of red fleshy flowers, on a tall stem from a tuft of 1-m. leaves, is common on the coastal sandstone from Jervis Bay, 35S/151E, to Qld. The Spear Lily, *D. palmeri*, has a tall thick stem suggestive of a spear shaft, and flowers on one side of the stem, rather like gladioli.

Doves Those indigenous to Aus. include the widely known Bronzewing and some species rivalling the parrots in colour. (*See* PIGEONS *and* DOVES.) The Turtle Dove is introduced.

Dowling, Sir James (1787–1844) b. London. He arrived in Aus. in 1828 as a judge, succeeding Forbes* as Chief Justice 1837–44. His great contribution lay in painstakingly recording his notably impartial judgments in 14 hand-written volumes and 237 note-books of reports.

Dragon Lizards (family Agamidae) These are named from fancied comparability of their often bizarre appearance to the dragons of legend. The family includes 8 very diverse genera and over 40 species, but they usually have a very rough skin, often extended into tubercles, prickles or spines, and they may have an ability to puff out their throats or an erectile frill when threatened. They have teeth along the summit of the ridges of the jaw-bone, which are usually sharp. The eyes are small, with round pupils and movable lids, the tongue usually short and broad. Insectivorous habits are adapted to a very wide range of habitats; some are semi-aquatic, some semi-arboreal, some live largely on ants in the desert. Many are able to change colour to some extent, according to their surroundings. Some, when fleeing from an enemy, run (quite fast) on their hind feet in an erect position, and several different species are known as bicycle lizards in different parts of the country. Eggs are laid. Some species can cast the end of the tail, but most do not. Representative species are: 1. the 30- to 45-cm., dark-blotched grey-brown Tree Dragon, *Amphibolurus muricatus*, often seen running up trees in E Aus.; 2. the Common Bearded Dragon, *A. barbatus*, up to 60 cm. long, usually dark grey with whitish spots but yellowish when scared, common all over mainland Aus. and sometimes called Frill-neck in SE Aus. where the true Frill-neck does not occur; 3. the Military Dragon, *A. maculatus*, with sub-species in W.A. and in Central Aus., a swift, slender, long-tailed lizard up to 20 cm. long, reddish with black and cream spots and a yellow, black and white side stripe; 4. the 60- to 90-cm. Eastern Water Dragon, *Physignathus leseurii*, of coastal E Aus., a shy burrowing lizard eating small rodents, crustaceans, snails, worms etc.; 5. the very well-known 75-cm.-long Frill-neck or Blanket Lizard, *Chalmydosaurus kingii*, often seen rocking in an erect position when retreating back to a rough-barked tree, or turning to frighten an enemy by

hissing and erecting its 15- to 25-cm. frill which is red and yellow, grey and cream or grey and brown, and with cartilaginous supports like the ribs of an umbrella; 6. the Mountain Devil, *Moloch horridus*, of central Aus. deserts, a harmless lizard (observed to eat 1,800 ants in $1\frac{1}{2}$ hours) of formidable appearance 'like an animated cactus' with many spines and tubercles; red to yellow-brown in colour.

Mountain Devil
(*Moloch horridus*)

Dragonflies and **Damselflies**   Insects of the Order Odonata, carnivorous at all stages of the life cycle—as aquatic larvae or nymphs, with several moults, and as adult flies. Species are of varied sizes from under one to over 18 cm. in wing-spread, with long thin flexible bodies—often colourful—and clear but iridescent, veined wings. The damselflies are generally smaller, resting with wings folded over the abdomen, with rear and forward pairs similar; the dragonflies rest with wings outspread and tips low, the rear pair being broader than the front ones. *Austropetalia patricia*, of the Blue Mts. area in N.S.W., is a well-known dragonfly having distinctive brown or ruby spots near the edges of the wings. *Austrophlebia costalis*, found in the sub-alpine highlands, is one of the fastest insects in the world. Common damselfly genera include the slender metallic green *Synlestes* and the bronze and blue *Austrolestes*.

DRAMA   The writing of plays in Aus. or by Australians, was slower to develop than theatre* productions which flourished on largely imported material, but was, and is, reluctant to accept the inherent risk of trying new and local work.

Burn* a Scots farmer in Tas. had probably the first genuinely Aus.-based play, *The Bushrangers*, produced in Edinburgh in 1829. In 1835 Harpur's heavily literary verse-drama of the same name was published serially. There were a number of imitations of the current poor English comedies and melodramas. Gradually more Aus. themes emerged: Cooper's *Colonial Experience* (1869) and Sutherland's *Poetical Licence* (1884) had the now familiar characterisation of the rugged honest pioneer; often he was set against the devious affected migrant. There was also a flood of melodrama using the perennial themes of drought, flood, bushrangers and gold-rushes. Much was commissioned or even written by theatrical entrepreneurs, like Dampier* (*To the West*, 1896); but social or political comment was also appearing, as in Hoare's *Polling Day or Wooed and Won* (1883).

The 'little theatres' (*see* THEATRE) which emerged after about 1910, gave new scope and impetus for writers, and also educated a small but appreciative section of the middle class, most of whom, however, remained strongly oriented to Eng. for many more years. The melodramas disappeared; their audiences were now devoted to the film. Aus. playwriting had a nationalist phase equivalent to that of the literary field expressed through the *Bulletin* some 20 years earlier. William Moore's Aus. Drama Nights (Melbourne, 1909–12) and the Pioneer Players (Melbourne, 1922–6) were the longest-lived attempts to produce exclusively Aus. work, and introduced the works of Esson*, the first really outstanding Aus. playwright and of Vance Palmer*. Others of the period were A. H. Adams*, Tomholt, Dann and Katharine Prichard*.

Further stimulus was provided by radio from the 1930s and by the establishment of competitions, still an important feature and sponsored by widely varying groups, including business enterprises. They generally stipulated a 'national theme', which brought a plethora of works on topics from Bligh to Gallipoli; but they also encouraged better craftsmanship, convincing dialogue, realistic themes and settings and experimental forms. The voluntary Playwright's Advisory Board also now provides a critical forum. Douglas Stewart's verse-dramas were the major new development in the 1940s: *Fire on the Snow* (1941, for radio), *Ned Kelly* (1943) and *Shipwreck* (1947).

The majority of plays until about the mid 1950s at least, used working-class settings and vernacular speech, both indisputably Aus. in origins; bush settings were still commoner than urban. More recently urban settings and some more universal themes of human relationships and problems have been written, if not produced. Mature plays have contained pungent comment on and criticism of cherished myths: of mateship and the bush life in Lawler's *Summer of the Seventeenth Doll* (1955), the most successful Aus. play to date; of Anzac Day in Seymour's *The One Day of the Year* (1961); of xenophobia in Beynon's study of a migrant Italian family, *The Shifting Heart* (1957). Patrick White* has been the first successfully to probe suburbia with its materialist conformism in *The Season at Sarsaparilla* (1961), and his universally acclaimed *The Ham Funeral* (1961) is a social and psychological comment.

Modern playwrights include: Boddy, Buzo, Coburn, Collinson, Ellis, Hepworth, Ireland, Keneally*, McKinney, McNamara, Naish, Throssel, Tomholt, Williamson*; women writers Cusack, Drake-Brockman, Grey and Roland. A successful expatriate was Chambers, writing for the London West End until

1917; but others have had one or more successful London presentations, notably Hastings' *Seagulls over Sorrento* (1949). Among less serious drama, are Afford and Coppell's thrillers and the long-running radio serial *Blue Hills* by Gwen Meredith. The later 1960s show an increasing range in writing and performing of Aus. material. Peter O'Shaughnessy is a leading modern actor.

Dreyfus, George (1928–) b. Wuppertal, Germany. A composer. He arrived in Aus. in 1939. In 1967 he received a Creative Arts Fellowship at the Aus. National University.

Drought Severe water shortage due to unreliable rainfall. Research suggests that all Aus. will only escape drought in 20 out of 100 years; chances range from 46 years free in W.A. to 74 in Tas. The worst recorded period was 1902–3; 1957–66 was bad in inland Aus., 1964–8 in SE Aus.

Drummer, Silver, or Buffalo Bream (*Segutilum sydneyanum*) Fish of SE Aus. with a particularly oval body, and though the back fin is continuous the front part is differentiated as a fan of 10–12 strong spines. It eats seaweed largely though it has sometimes taken a fish bait.

Drumsticks or Narrow-leaf Conebush Popular names for bushes of the genus *Isopogon*, especially *I. anethifolius* which grows on the sandstone plateaux of E Aus. and has stiff leaves, a yellow globular flower and roundish cone.

Dry, Sir Richard (1815–1869) b. Tas. First Tas. knight (1858) and Tas. Premier (1866–9). A pastoralist and first Tas.-born politician of note, he was involved in the resignation of the Patriotic Six*, opposed transportation and encouraged rail building and immigration. *See* A. D. Baker: *Life and Times of Sir Richard Dry* (Hobart, 1951).

Drysdale, George Russell (1912–) b. Eng. A contemporary artist of high international repute. His interpretations of the harshness of the Aus. environment, full of reds and golds, and lean, almost surrealist forms, are yet done with intense compassion. This is seen for example in his commissioned work on the aftermath of drought in N.S.W., or his more recent preoccupations with the N of Aus. and the Aborigines.

Drysdale River W.A. 15S/127E The main N-flowing Kimberley* watercourse, active only in the 'Wet'. It is 437 km. long, running through poor cattle country from Mt. Hann to Napier-Broome Bay, a mangrove-fringed estuary, where Aborigines are cared for at the Roman Catholic Drysdale River Mission.

Dubbo N.S.W. 32S/149E (17,767 in 1971) A growing town on the Macquarie River, acting as a market, service and processing centre (timber, wool, flour, meatworks) for a large area central in the Western Slopes region; it is a busy railway junction, road and even air focus. It has a few other small but locally significant industries, e.g. clothing and packing postage stamps for collectors, and has several schools. Although the country is dominantly pastoral there is a large area of State forests nearby.

Duchess Qld. 21S/140E A mining settlement in the Selwyn Ranges on the Mt. Isa-Townsville railway; some copper is mined, but recent phosphate reserves are likely to stimulate further development.

Ducks Widespread in Aus., in suitable terrain usually with a nest of reeds etc. around swamps or on islands, though sometimes in tree-holes. They are much shot as game, and sometimes as pests of rice fields, but some rare varieties are protected. As elsewhere, ducks are seasonal migrants to some extent, and ringed birds are known to have moved up to 3,200 km. N–S and vice-versa. The very widespread Black Duck, *Anas superciliosa*, is a dark-flecked brown bird with a dark eye-stripe on a lighter brown head, and a little green on the wings. The body is almost a foot long. It is very like the female of the wild duck of the northern hemisphere *A. boschas*, but lacks the brilliant plumage in the drake (familiar in the domestic duck, derived from *A. boschas*). These 2 ducks interbreed freely in captivity, suggesting close relationship. Also widespread beyond Aus., or closely related to ducks seen over large parts of the world, are the rather similar Grey Teal, *A. gibberifrons* (humped forehead), the Chestnut Teal, *A. castanea*, with metallic-green head and neck, and the Blue-winged Shoveller or Spoonbill Duck, *A. rhynchotis*, with a whitish face and blue as well as green on the wing. Of the 2 handsome sheldrake or shelduck, the shy Chestnut-breasted Sheldrake or Mountain Duck, *Casarca tadarnoides* (duck-like goose), has a green head and neck, white collar, and a back which is dark and light brown below and green and white above save for a light chestnut breast and shoulders: while the White-headed Sheldrake or Burdekin Duck, *Tadorna radjah*, is predominantly a white duck with brown back and green wing-patch. Distinctively Aus. genera include the rare, light-brown Freckled or Monkey Duck, *Sticonetta naevosa* (spotted freckled duck), of much of the S of Aus.; the very prominently billed Pink-eared Zebra or Pink-eyed Duck, *Malacorhynchus membranaceus* (soft membrane-beak), sometimes seen in small groups sifting mud in a shallow inland lake or swamp-pool for insects etc., a mainly brown bird with lighter but dark-barred breast; and the Musk Duck, *Biziura lobata*, most often seen in the S of Aus., also a brown, with light breast crossed by lines of darker flecks, but very distinctive from its secretion of a strong musk-like odour in a sac hanging from its lower jaw. The

Whistling Tree-duck, *Dendrocygna arcuata* (curved tree-swan), is a more tropical duck, extending into SE Asia, with a notably red-brown breast, often seen flocking in inland lagoons, and commonly roosting, rather than nesting, in trees. The whistling or piping call is rather distinctive though not by any means unique among ducks. Some birds bearing popular names including the word duck are discussed under Geese*. *For further reading see* H. J. Frith: *Waterfowl in Australia* (Sydney, 1967).

Duffy, Sir Charles Gavan (1816–1903) b. Monaghen, Ireland. Premier of Vic. (1871–2), and notable Irish nationalist and federalist. He arrived in Aus. in 1855 after a turbulent period of involvement in Irish nationalism including an acquittal on a charge of treason, and membership of the House of Commons (1852–5). In Vic. he was responsible for the largely unsuccessful Duffy Land Act in 1862 in favour of selectors*. Duffy, as the champion of the small agriculturist, earned the hatred of the squatters*. **Sir Frank Gavan** (1852–1936), his second son, wrote brilliantly on law and was Chief Justice of Aus. 1930–6, succeeding Isaacs.

Dugong (from Malayan or Indonesian word) **Sea-Cow** or **Manatee** (Order Sirenia, from mythical sirens, mermaids) Aus. species, *Dugong australis*, a slow-breeding and vegetarian aquatic mammal 2·5–3 m. long and 400–550 kg. in weight, with a whale-like tail, hide and blubber, but more mobile front flippers. (The female is able, for instance, to hold the young to her nipple while suckling just above the water, while she floats on her side). The heavy blunt, rather oblong head is somewhat like a hippopotamus, lacking earlobes, with a slight narrowing in a short neck. It is regarded as having developed some whale-like characteristics, but from a different ancestral mammalian stock. Some features suggest a common ancestry with the elephant. The dugong frequents bays and estuaries, rather than the open sea, formerly as far south as Sydney, but it has been hunted to extinction except in the Great Barrier Reef and from the Qld. coast round to Broome in W.A. and N into SE Asia. Hunting the dugong from bark canoes, outriggers or platforms, by an ingenious harpoon with a detachable tip, was a main means of support for Aboriginal groups in the Cape York area. A period of commercial hunting for the oil for medicinal purposes brought heavy slaughter in the late 19th century. Today shark nets are killing dugong in Qld.

Dugong, about 2·5 m. long

Dumaresq The surname of 3 brothers **William, Henry** and **Edward**. They came to Aus. in 1825 with Governor Darling who had married their sister. Official appointments led to complaints of nepotism and censure of Darling. All became big landowners, respected for enlightened treatment of their convict labour. Major properties were held in the Hunter Valley and New England in N.S.W., and in 1827 Cunningham named the **Dumaresq River**, 29S/152E, after them; this Darling River headwater is the N.S.W./Qld. boundary for some 130 km.

Dumbleyung W.A. 33S/118E A small wheat belt* town on a feeder line to the Great Southern Railway at Wagin. The lake nearby was the scene of the late Donald Campbell's 1964 speed-boat record attempt.

Dunally Tas. 43S/148E A small fishing settlement on the narrow isthmus between Forestier Peninsula and the mainland, which is cut by a short canal for fishing boats; there is a fish cannery.

Dunk Island Qld. 17S/146E It consists of 7·7 km.[2] of forested granitic land fringed with coral, and made famous by the writings of E. J. Banfield*.

Dunstan, Sir Albert Arthur (1882–1950) b. Cape Cope, Vic. First Country Party* Premier of Vic. (1935–43 and 1943–45). He had led a radical splinter group in 1926, the Primary Producers' Union, concentrated in the Mallee wheat belt.

Durack family Pioneers of Irish origin who went from Goulburn, N.S.W., first to Qld. then the Kimberleys. Their history is chronicled by **Mary Durack** (1913–) in *Kings in Grass Castles* (London, 1959).

Durack, Fanny (1892–1956) b. Sydney. The first great competitive Aus. woman swimmer who between 1912–20 held every women's record. In the 1912 Olympic Games she won the first women's championships, the 100 m., the first Aus. woman gold medallist, followed to second place by her compatriot, Mina Wylie. She developed from a trudgen to crawl.

Durack River W.A. 17S/128E Flows about 240 km. in the 'Wet' only, through a 20,700-km.[2] catchment area, from the NE Kimberleys* to Cambridge Gulf, in deep sandstone gorges and poor savannah cattle country to a drowned estuary on which Wyndham stands.

Dutton, Geoffrey Piers (1922–) b. Kapunda, S.A. A poet, critic, travel writer and leading Aus. literary figure whose verse, stimulated by the Angry Penguin* movement, has now clarified, as in *Poems Soft and Loud* (Melbourne, 1968).

Dyson, William (1880–1938) b. Ballarat, Vic. He was a world-famed London cartoonist (1910–25 and 1930–8) who began in Aus. with *Lone Hand* and *Bulletin*, and was a dry-point artist of note. His poems *In Memory of a Wife* (London, 1919) contain beautiful lyric verse. His brother **Edward George** (1865–1931) was best known for mining ballads in *Rhymes from the Mines* (Sydney, 1896) and his humorous stories *Factr'y 'Ands* (Melbourne 1906).

E

EAGLEHAWK NECK

Eaglehawk Neck Tas. 43S/148E An isthmus, as narrow as 18 m. in parts, between Tasman and Forestier Peninsulas, notorious, in the days of the Port Arthur* penal station for the savage dogs chained across it to prevent escapes.

Eagles (the Eagle and Hawk* family, Accipitridae) They are adapted for catching and eating live prey, having a strong curved beak, sharp-clawed talons, and swift and manoeuvrable flight; of over 20 species a dozen or so are common. The large soaring eagles include the following.
1. The Wedge-tailed Eagle or Eagle-Hawk, *Aquila audax*, of all Aus. except Tas., is among the largest eagles in the world, with wing-span commonly over 2 m. and up to 2·75 m. with a large and distinctive diamond-shaped tail; rich brown and gingery

Wedge-tailed Eagle (Aquila audax), about 1 m. nose to tail

EARWIGS

neck darkening with age to dark brown or almost black. It lays 2 off-white eggs in 2- to 2·5 m. wide eyrie. Its food consists of small marsupials, rabbits, rats, perhaps young dingoes, but it is often shot—even from aircraft—because it may eat lambs.
2. The Whistling Eagle, *Haliastur sphenurus*, in flight has a long square-ended tail and T-shaped lighter colouring in belly and in light bands in dark wings.
3. The White-breasted Sea Eagle, *H. indus*, a predator of fish, sea-snakes etc., in flight shows a curved white patch continuing the white of the breast into the wings, and a curved fan-like tail with white tip.

Eardley-Wilmot, Sir John Eardley (1783–1847) Lt.-Governor of Tas. (1843–6). An English squire, with interests in penology, he was sent to administer the revised 'probationary' system of transportation*. He failed, in the hostile depression atmosphere prevailing, which was against transportation with its heavy costs, and which led to the incident of the Patriotic Six*. Gladstone's dismissal of him, for failure in his task and alleged immoral behaviour, was linked with the enmity of the Anglican Bishop Nixon.

Early Nancy (*Anguillaria dioica*) An attractive pink liliaceous, bulbous plant of good soils in all States. (*See* LILIES.)

Earwigs Leaf-eating and scavenging insects of the Order Dermaptera, distinctive for their rear pincers, probably defensive, including the common, but relatively little known, native species, e.g. the Banded Earwig, *Apachyus australiae*, to 4 cm. long, very flattened and usually found living under loose bark of eucalypts, and also the widely known introduced pest whose scavenging and predation on other insects is offset by damage to seedlings, the Common Earwig, *Forficula auricularia*. The largest earwig known is *Titanolabis colossea*, up to 5 cm. long and with formidable forceps, found in the N Tablelands of N.S.W.

Earthworms These are placed in the Oligochaeta (few-bristled) Class, as compared with the mainly marine Polychaeta (many-bristled), both within the Phylum Annelida along with the leeches*. The introduced European garden worms *Lumbricus terrestris* and *Allolobophora caliginosa* are often thought of as typical worms, but there is a rich native group of about 100 species of earthworms, and *Megascolex dorsalis*, for instance, is now commonly sold in bait-shops. A quick naked-eye identification is that if there are less than 18 segments from the nose to the raised reproductive gland belt it is probably in the Megascolecidae family. This includes 2 genera of giant earthworms: *Megascolides australis*, up to 3·6 m. by 1·3 cm. and so far reported from Gippsland, Vic., and the 2-gizzarded *Digaster longmani*, up to 1·7 m. by 2·5 cm., found in rain-forest country as far S as Kyogle, N.S.W., 29S/153E. The Squirter Earthworm, also with 2 gizzards, *Didymogaster sylvaticus*, is a stout 15-cm. long worm found in rotting logs etc., in cabbage tree palm rain-forest, well-known for its habit when disturbed, of squirting body fluid to a height of 30 cm. or more. The slender muscular light brown *Pheretina diffringens* is one native worm apparently able to compete in Sydney gardens with the introduced European species. The pink thread-like worm often seen in masses in silt heavily polluted with sullage water etc. is *Tubifex* spp.

East India Company Chartered in 1600, this had a trading monopoly, extending from the Cape of Good Hope to the Straits of Magellan, which lasted until 1813. The effects on the N.S.W. colony (to the formation of which the E.I.C. only grudgingly consented) were felt in the resulting prohibition of shipbuilding and consequent ability to trade independently. The whalers in the colony, seeing the rapid infiltration of American competitors, were largely responsible for the breaking of the monopoly. The case of the impounding of the *Lady Barlow*, owned by Robert Campbell* (1805), stimulated moves to end the monopoly of the Company. Many convict transports (including 3 of the First Fleet) were East Indiamen which took return cargoes from eastern ports. The *Dutch East India Co.* played a different role in Aus. history outlined under Discovery*.

Eastern Goldfields W.A. A Statistical Division in the SE, covering 645,580 km² with only 42,539 people (1971) of whom 20,784 are in Kalgoorlie-Boulder*. It is arid country with under 25 cm. rainfall, supporting only large sheep properties, but has contributed enormously to W.A. development through past and present gold-mining, and recent iron, nickel and lithium discovery. The granites and gneisses contain metamorphosed basalts called greenstones which are gold-bearing. Gold was mined in many areas now ghost towns* from 1888 when it was found at Southern Cross*. But by 1895 production was largely centred on the Golden Mile*. The Goldfields exercised considerable political influence at the time of Federation by threatening secession as the new State of Auralia. There was rivalry at first between the incomers from the E States (T'othersiders) and the W.A. 'Sandgropers'.

Ebor Falls N.S.W. 30S/152E Where the Guy Fawkes River in 3 main falls drops 150 m. down the E escarpment of the New England* plateau.

Eccles, Sir John Carew (1903–) b. Melbourne. An outstanding neurophysiologist awarded a Nobel prize in

1963, with Huxley and Hodgkin of U.K., for work in this field. He worked at the Kanematsu Memorial Institute of Pathology in Sydney (1937–43), overseas, then the Australian National University* (1951–66), and continued thereafter in the U.S.

Echidna A popular name for the Spiny Ant-eater, from an earlier zoological term for this monotreme*; it is also the present genus name for a marine eel of Aus. waters, with molar teeth.

Echinoderms The spiny-skinned sea creatures of the Phylum Echinodermata, including: 1. the Starfish* or Seastars, Class Asteroidea; 2. the Brittle-stars (*see* STARFISH), Class Ophiuroidea; 3. The Sea-urchins*, Class Echinoidea; 4. the Sea-lilies* and Feather-stars (*see* STARFISH), Class Crinoidea; and 5. Sea-cucumbers*, Class Holothuroidea. The common element in the Phylum is the reinforcing of the skin by limy plates, obvious in the sea-urchins, starfish and sea-lilies. Aus. has representatives (in some a wealth) of all these Classes.

Echo, Lake Tas. 42S/147E 11 km. N–S, narrowing from 6·5 to 3 km. E–W, it lies at 845 m. in a fairly shallow depression on dolerite plateau rocks; the level was raised by a 18·3-m. dam for hydro-electric power (L. Echo Power Station, annual average 76 million kWh, a diversion serves Tungatinah*) and it is supplemented by water diverted from the Ouse River by the 13-km. Monpeelyata Canal.

Echuca Vic. 36S/145E (8,636 in 1971 with Moama across the Murray) At the confluence of Murray and Campaspe Rivers, this was the greatest inland Aus. port for several decades after the Melbourne rail reached it in 1864. A settlement was already established there round a river crossing, and the enterprising Henry Hopwood, 'father of Echuca', had erected a pontoon bridge. The river boats brought wool, wheat and timber (£2·5 million worth in 1880) to the wharves, built high to cope with vagaries of river level, and now deserted save for an occasional tourist steamer or timber boat bringing red gum from the riverside forests. The rail extension into the Riverina in the 1880s killed the traffic, and the town dwindled until the Goulburn River Irrigation brought it new life as a market centre; a wartime ball-bearing factory, still surviving, was added to the small butter, flour and timber factories. *For further reading see* S. Priestley: *Echuca: A Centenary History* (Brisbane, 1965).

ECONOMY Gross national product (G.N.P.) has been steadily increasing, from $15·0 (1961–2) to $20·6 thousand million (1965–6) and $30·1 thousand million (1969–70), while population rose from 10·5 million to 12·7 million. With the lowest incomes protected by the minimum wage and by exemptions from direct taxation, this represents one of the highest standards of material living in the world, though there have been pockets of poverty and some financial hardship for families struck by illness beyond the provision of the health scheme. Personal disposable incomes (not allowing for price changes) increased from just over $1,000 to just over $1,500. Aus. has been defined as 'midway' between under-development and development, having a high living standard combined with primary export. Capital inflow has come increasingly from U.S. rather than U.K. as analysed by D. T. Brash in *American Investment in Australian Industry* (Canberra, 1967).

Manufacturing industries*, rather broadly defined, accounted for about 28% of the work force, but a rather smaller proportion of G.N.P. and only 12% of exports (though this is rising); thus the 10% in primary industry were responsible for 85% of the exports. Tertiary industries (distribution and services of all kinds) account for about

60% of employment and almost half the G.N.P.

The growth rate of the economy as a whole, at about 5-6% in recent years represents an increase in standards of living as compared with a population increase (including immigration) of about 2% per annum. There is widespread desire to control the economy in order to achieve growth at about this rate or a little higher, which is accentuated by the experience of the Depression* of the early 1930s, the post-war variations between the Korean War boom and the sharply deflationary measure of November 1960, coupled with anxieties about the future of the chief export, wool, and Britain's entry into the European Common Market in 1973. When Britain devalued sterling by 14·3% in November 1967, the Aus. Government did not devalue the dollar; the economy was judged sufficiently strong and independent (see TRADE, changed directions of). In the early 1970s Aus. was showing signs of the inflation afflicting all western economies: in 1971 cuts were proposed in public spending and private investment. In 1972 the 'floating, of the pound sterling had a disadvantageous effect on agricultural exports to U.K. which was further increased by British entry to the E.E.C. In Dec. 1972 the dollar was revalued by 4·85% in terms of the U.S. dollar, further affecting rural industry. Meanwhile exceptional wool prices in 1972-3 redressed some of the balance. A slight recession in mineral development linked with a dip in Japanese export and industry steadied, although mining and oil shares also suffered at revaluation, which had been brought about by the large trading surplus. The change from a conservative to a labour government in Dec. 1972 brought a shift in emphasis in policy, although no radical changes. Firmer control of potential takeovers by foreign capital is coupled with encouragement of Aus. investment to raise more of the vast amounts needed for mineral, transport and other development projects.

Unemployment rose in the late 1960s and early 70s to 2·4% in Dec. 1972 enough to lead to lower immigration* targets. The figure is relatively low, however, and inflation has been moderate, with periods of increased tempo. But growth has also been relatively slow. Reasons include the protection by tariffs* of some inefficient industries, the high transport costs of a large country, the low population preventing 'economies of scale' in the home market. A growth rate of 5–7% is forecast for the 1970s, giving a 3% increase in living standards if inflation is controlled. (*See also* ARBITRATION*.) *For further reading see* J. B. Condliffe, *The Development of Australia* (Sydney, 1964); B. D. Cameron: *The Theory of National Income and Employment* (Melbourne, 1966); B. D. Haig: *Real Product Income and Relative Prices in Australia and the United Kingdom* (Canberra, 1967); E. H. Boem: *20th Century Economic Development in Aus.* (Melbourne, 1971)

Eden N.S.W. 37S/150E (2,210 in 1971) Despite its modest size, this is a locally important trawl and line fishing port, with a substantial wharf in Twofold Bay*, a small boatyard, and fish, canning, freezing and packing facilities. It is a holiday centre, and will house over 250 new families brought by the wood plant at Twofold Bay. The port had a short-lived period of bustle to serve the Kiandra gold-rush.

EDUCATION From pre-school to university and other tertiary institutions, this is available to an extent varying with location, ability and to some degree finance; but primary and secondary schooling is compulsory for all from 6 to at least 15. The Aus. approach to education stems from its British origins and is formal, oriented to examinations and the hoped-for income and social status attainable from success; this latter is strongly developed and linked with the rather earlier moves towards equality of opportunity in education. There is increasing American influence on curricula and method, but discipline remains strongly authoritarian. There are 3 systems: State schools with 75% of the pupils, Roman Catholic Schools (20%) and private, mainly secondary denominational schools of high social prestige (5%). Religious teaching in State schools is handled in denominational groups by visiting clergy. Children living out of range of schools are served by 12 Schools of the Air*, and by correspondence schooling. Transfer from primary to secondary schools does not depend on examination. Selective academic, technical and practical schools remain in some metropolitan areas, but the trend is towards comprehensive area schools with a central core of studies and variations of grade and ability within the schools, as in the N.S.W. Wyndham Scheme (1962). State school administration is highly centralised under a Minister. Systems vary, leading to difficulties for families moving inter-state (see EDUCATION TABLE). Teachers are moved freely within the State, assuring an even spread between areas, but with the disadvantage that they are only transient members of a community. Books and equipment beyond basic needs are paid for by parents, directly and through fund-raising Parents and Citizens Associations. The Federal Government gives tax concessions, some 10,000 scholarships for upper secondary pupils and also university scholarships. A new co-ordinating body, the Federal Department of Education and Science was set up in 1966. Increased school population in the 1960s outstripped the supply of teachers, especially graduates. There are now 39 state-run teachers' colleges, 13 private colleges and courses in other tertiary institutions. A Commonwealth Teaching Service is being set up.

Historical Development No official provision was made for education in the early colony, but, moved by the crying needs of convicts' and settlers' children, there were some State-assisted schools under King, extended by Macquarie, as well as assorted private institutions. The Anglicans had a monopoly of Government aid for education until 1833. The Church and Schools Corporation (1826–33) marked its highest point. From 1836 denominational schools and Roman Catholics, Presbyterians and Methodists were also subsidised. Towards mid century each colony evolved a dual system of State-supported National and Denominational schools, the latter in prolific rivalry. National schools were committed to broad Christian but non-denominational principles of teaching. Growing 19th-century liberalism, dissatisfaction with the poor standards prevailing, and inter-denominational strife led to a series of State Acts creating central authorities (see EDUCATION TABLE, 5a). These (save in S.A.) continued State aid to Church schools under conditions of inspection, but were essentially compromise Acts leading to the final establishment of free compulsory and secular education and the withdrawal of State aid to Church schools (5b). This was maintained until 1964, since when Commonwealth subsidies have been introduced and steadily increased; in 1967 Tas., W.A. and N.S.W. re-introduced direct subsidisation.

Pre-school Education is very variable and is provided by the Federal Govt. in N.T. and Canberra. There is a model 'Lady Gowrie' pre-school in each capital as well as a number of private centres. In Tas. they are State run. The Aus. Pre-school Association is a co-ordinating promoting body. Some 15% of 3–5 year olds attend pre-school.

Technical Education stems from the work of Mechanics Institutes* from 1833 and is State run, either directly from State Departments of Education

EDUCATION TABLE

	N.S.W.	VIC.	QLD.	S.A.	W.A.	TAS.
1. Percentage in State schools	75	73	76	84	79	83
2. Leaving age	15	15	15	15	15	16
3. Title and year of secondary school external examinations	School Certificate (4) Higher School Certificate (6)	Intermediate (4) School Leaving (5) Higher School Certificate (6)	Junior Public (3) Senior Public (5) Note: Secondary intake is one year later than other States.	Intermediate (3) Leaving (4) Matriculation (5)	Achievement Certificate awarded on leaving school	Schools Board Certificate (4) Matriculation (5–6)
4. Universities* and date of founding (see also AUS. NATIONAL UNIVERSITY)	Sydney 1850 New England 1954 New South Wales (Sydney) 1958 Newcastle 1965 Univ. College Wollongong 1962 Macquarie (Sydney) 1967	Melbourne 1853 Monash (Melbourne) 1958 La Trobe (Melbourne) 1967 Univ. of Victoria (Geelong, Bendigo, Ballarat) planned for 1976– .	Queensland (Brisbane) 1909 James Cook University of North Queensland (Townsville) 1970 Griffith (Brisbane) 1971	Adelaide 1874 Flinders 1966	Western Australia (Perth) 1909 Murdoch (Perth) 1971	Tasmania (Hobart) 1890
19th-century legislation						
5 (a). Central Authority	1866 Public Schools Act	1862 Common Schools Act	1860 Primary Education Act	1851 Central Board established	1871 Elementary Education Act	1868 Public Schools Act (but effectively since 1854)
(b). Free secular compulsory schooling	1880	1872	1875	1875	1893	1885

Note Education in N.T. is the responsibility of the Commonwealth. A.C.T. education has now been separated from that of N.S.W.

(Qld., S.A., W.A., Tas.) or from a separate department (N.S.W.) or a dual State and college-council system in Vic. The Martin Report (1964) found technical education weak in relation to universities*; since then Vic. has established an Institute of Colleges to convert over 20 existing technical establishments into Colleges of Advanced Education; similar up-grading in other States has occurred. A feature of technical education by correspondence is the mobile workshop for practical work and there are now 45 Colleges of Advanced Education.

Agricultural Training is emphasised in a number of rural high schools. Tertiary courses are given in State-run colleges: 2 each in N.S.W. and Vic., 1 in Qld., S.A. and W.A. and the Burnley School of Horticulture in Vic.

Adult Education, in the sense of evening classes in widely varying subjects, is carried out by both universities and technical colleges and evening colleges of high schools in N.S.W. and S.A., and attracts a wide range of students. It too stems from the Mechanics Institutes of the late 19th century and the Workers' Educational Association (1913) formed in N.S.W. primarily for Unionists by David Stewart. Some notable contributors to education have included Peter Board (1858–1945) in N.S.W., Frank Tate (1863–1939) in Vic., P. R. Cole (1878–1948) in writing on education, Sir Frederick Schonell (1900–) in Qld. and A. S. Wyndham (1903–) in N.S.W. *For further reading see: Teachers in Australia* (Aus. College of Education, Melbourne, 1967); A. G. Austin: *Australian Education 1788–1900* (Melbourne, 1961); the *Melbourne Studies in Education* series and P. H. Partridge: *Society, Schools and Progress in Australia* (London 1969).

Edwards River N.S.W. A large anabranch* of the Murray; it leaves the Murray 48 km. upstream from Echuca, 36S/145E, and flows N,

receiving 2 smaller anabranches on the right. Passing through Deniliquin, 35S/145E, it splits, the Wakool flowing SW while the Edwards flows NW, joining the Yanco-Moulamein anabranch from the Murrumbidgee and flowing on as the Kyalite to rejoin the Murray some 80 km. downstream from Swan Hill*. Almost 28,500 ha. of rice, fodder and pastures of the Wakool project are fed from the Stevens Weir 25 km. downstream from Denilquin. A siphon under the Edwards brings water from the Mulwala Canal, after serving the Berriquin district, to the Deniboota district.

Eels (of Aus.) Fishes of the Order Apodes, which are mainly marine, totalling about 70 species, mainly the brightly coloured eels of coral reef and other tropical waters, e.g. the thick Moray or Reef Eel, *Verdithorax prasinus*, with fang-like teeth—it sometimes bites man—and very variable colours and markings. *Echidna* spp. have molar teeth. The banded Snake Eel of temperate waters is *Malvoliophis cyclorhinus*. There are 4 species of the Freshwater Eel, *Anguilla*, and as the eels of European rivers breed in the Sargasso Sea, so these may breed off Sumatra or New Caledonia. The larval 'glass eels' of the open oceans are little studied, and specimens stranded in storms are requested by museums.

Eggleston, Sir Frederick William (1875–1954) b. Melbourne. A diplomat and economist who served in the Vic. Parliament, and was Aus. Minister in China 1941–4, which involved isolated residence at Chungking. He later represented Aus. in U.S., and on his return wrote extensively on the place of Aus. in international, especially Asian affairs.

Eggs and Bacon A bizarre popular name in much of Aus. for various Bush Peas and related genera. (*See* PEAS.)

Eighty Mile Beach W.A. 20S–121E This marks the coastal edge of the Canning Basin*. It is lined by salt and samphire marsh, and extensive dunes in the Anna Plains stretch. Its dreary wastes are followed by the Great Northern Highway.

Eildon Reservoir Vic. On the Goulburn River, it now has a capacity of 3,392 million m.³, a dam 79·3 m. by 0·8 km. having superseded a smaller one a little upstream. The catchment is only 3,870 km.² but largely in the 100–127 cm. rainfall belt, making this reservoir among the most important in Aus., watering 145,000 ha. to the NE and linking up with the Campaspe and Loddon systems to the W, and ultimately with the Wimmera-Mallee* Domestic and Stock Supply system. Some hydro-electricity is generated. The small town of Eildon is a tourist resort.

Elcho Island N.T. 12S/136E A low narrow island some 48 km. SW–NE off the N coast of Arnhem Land*. A Methodist Mission cares for Aborigines and grows tropical crops which include rice. Cypress pine is extracted.

Elder, Sir Thomas (1818–1897) b. Kirkcaldy, Scotland. A pastoralist, businessman and Adelaide benefactor. He arrived in Aus. in 1840 to join his brother Alexander's wool and agricultural agency which was later joined by Robert Smith in 1863 to form Elder, Smith. In 1963 the firm amalgamated with Goldsbrough Mort to become the biggest wool-broking firm in Aus., with wide ancillary interests. Sir Thomas held extensive S.A. pastoral runs and introduced camels* to Aus. He financed exploration in search of new grazing lands, and gave money for the university, botanic gardens and a chair of Music, held in the **Elder Conservatorium of Music** (founded 1898).

Eldershaw, M. Barnard Pen-name of a very successful literary collaboration between **Marjorie Faith Barnard** (1897–), b. Sydney, a librarian, historian and short story writer, and **Flora Eldershaw** (1897–1956), b. Sydney, a teacher and industrial consultant. Of 5 jointly written novels the 2 most important are *A House is Built* (London, 1929), a saga of a Sydney business family, and *Tomorrow and Tomorrow* (Melbourne, 1947), set in the Depression.

Electorates *1. Federal* For the Senate the electorates are the 6 States, each electing 10 Senators. For the House of Representatives, States have members in proportion to population: N.S.W. 45; Vic. 34; Qld. 18; S.A. 12; W.A. 9; Tas. 5 (the minimum as laid down in the Constitution). The N.T. and A.C.T. each return 1 member. Electorates are based on 'community of interest, communications, physical features', and since 1965, area, population density and trends have been taken into account; they do not transgress State boundaries. A 20% deviation above or below the quota is legally allowed in any electorate. The Electoral Act requires post-census revision. There was a redistribution of electoral divisions in 1968. The 1967 Referendum* was aimed to overcome the constitutional link between the numbers in the 2 Houses by allowing increased membership of the Lower House; its rejection meant redistribution before 1969. The trend is towards reducing the historic disparity which gave more parliamentary strength per voter to rural than to city dwellers. Proposed increases of 4 Senators (2 for A.C.T, 2 for N.T.) and 2 M.H.R.s (1 for A.C.T., 1 for W.A.) were announced in 1973.

2. State Electorates Upper House electorates are: Vic. 18 2-member constituencies; S.A. 5 4-member constituencies; W.A. 15 2-member; Tas. 19 single-member. Qld. has no Upper House and that of N.S.W. is elected by both Houses. For the Lower

House, Tas. uses the Federal Electorates. All other States are divided into Regions, but with fewer people per region in country than city areas. This is especially marked in S.A. where city electorates average 26,000 and rural electorates 9,000 voters, and in W.A. where the North West Region has 4 electorates averaging only 1,450 voters; this is considerable weighting of the rural vote. There is continued controversy over the principle of one-vote, one value. (*See* GOVERNMENT.)

Electric Power   Aus. is 6th in the world in electricity consumed per head, following Norway, Canada, U.S., N.Z. and U.K. Demand is doubling every decade, and installations have quadrupled since 1945 to between 16 and 17 million kW (with annual generation of over 47,000 million kW hours in 1972), allowing the desired 10% margin between demand and capacity, and maintaining price levels. This has been achieved by building large new thermal power stations on the coal-fields, by increasing hydro-electric generation, by increasing the cover of long distance high voltage transmission lines and by integration of systems through grids, to spread peak loads.

Electricity is used in equal proportions (about 40%) by domestic and industrial consumers, the remainder by commercial undertakings and a small and decreasing amount for traction.

There is wide disparity between the States: N.S.W. dominates with 33% of the total capacity (1972) of 16,105,000 kW., followed by Vic. (18%). The Snowy Mountains Authority serving both States had 14%, Qld. 11%, Tas. 8%, S.A. 6%, W.A. 5%. The figures reflect population and industry. Metropolitan areas dominate, with secondary groups in industrial centres such as Newcastle and Wollongong or the Qld. ports of Rockhampton and Cairns. Areas served by reticulated supply follow the regions of settlement.

Thermal power supplies 74% of total Aus. electric power, and 85% in the mainland States: black coal in N.S.W. and Qld.; sub-bituminous in W.A. and S.A.; and brown coal in Vic. The remainder is hydro-electricity, save for 2–5% (varying with States) from oil-fired and internal combustion systems. Power in Tas is almost 100% hydro-electric based on high relief and rainfall and natural lakes. Natural gas is now an important source of power in S.A. which has little coal or water, and nuclear power stations are being discussed in States short of coal and water power (e.g. S.A.); these may be vital in exploiting remote mineral resources in the N. and W. The tidal power of the far NW coast may also play a part. The Snowy Mts.* and Kiewa* Schemes provide peak-load power to supplement thermal base-load stations in N.S.W. and Vic. through the only inter-state grid. Since 1900 control of electricity has been increasingly undertaken by public bodies: in Qld. the State Electricity Commission does not generate power, but in the other States it is the chief producer. Private firms still serve the remoter country towns, but to a decreasing extent, and many rural properties with their own plant are gradually being connected to a State grid. Several big mining and industrial concerns make their own power, as at Kalgoorlie, W.A., and Mt. Isa, Qld. Inter-state co-operation is increasing. Although constitutionally a State responsibility, Federal finance is increasingly needed for the high capital costs of expansion.

Electrona Tas. 43S/147E A carbide works unique in the S hemisphere, 32 km. S of Hobart, based on local limestone and hydro-electric power. Workers live at Snug, which, with the works, was severely damaged in the February 1967 bushfire.

Elephant Fish   A beaked species of the deep-sea Ghost Sharks, occasionally caught inshore. (*See* SHARKS.)

Elephant, Mount Vic. 38S/143E Only 395 m. above sea level, but is of interest as the highest of the volcanic cones standing above the basalt lava plateau of W Vic.

Elizabeth S.A. 35S/139E (33,363 in 1971) A city planned and built since 1954 as an independent residential and industrial town 27 km. N of Adelaide, although workers also travel to Adelaide factories, the Salisbury Weapons Research establishment and the coastal salt and chemical works. It was named after Queen Elizabeth II, and has a large, dominantly British, migrant element in its population.

Elliott, Herbert James (1938–) b. Perth. An athlete and one of the world's greatest middle-distance runners, retiring from the field in 1960 after winning the Rome Olympic 1,500 m. He held the 1 mile record 1958–62 and ran the mile in under 4 minutes 17 times: his last world record, the 1,500 m., was beaten in 1967. His outstanding physical ability was combined with an unusually developed, almost savage mental concentration on winning. He was trained by P. Cerutty. *For further reading: see The Golden Mile; the Herb Elliott Story as told to Allan Trengore* (London, 1961).

Elsey N.T. 15S/134E Cattle station on head waters of Roper River, which was made famous by Mrs. Aeneas Gunn's *We of the Never Never*. The old homestead lies just off the Stuart Highway, S of Mataranka, and the cemetery contains graves of some of the characters described in the book, including her husband 'The Maluka'.

El Sharana N.T. 13S/132E Mining base for uranium in the S Alligator valley, named from 3 daughters of one of the prospectors. The ore is obtained along a fault following the valley trend, usually in ridges well above the valley floor and making access difficult, especially in the 'Wet'. There is a treatment plant. A 976 kg. piece of pitchblende is probably the largest ever found. The main settlement is Moline.*

Emancipists Technically convicts fully or conditionally pardoned for conduct or service, but was a term applied (until about 1840) to time-expired convicts and also to a major pressure group campaigning vigorously under Wentworth* for emancipists' equality, for trial by jury and elected government. They were opposed by the 'exclusivist' faction of free settlers under Macarthur*, who feared their numerical superiority and considered them socially undesirable. Most governors, except Darling, favoured the emancipists, Macquarie to the extent of appointing them to high office. In 1821 1,367 emancipists signed a petition to the Crown pointing out that they comprised 7,556 adults compared with 1,558 free settlers, possessed 3 times as much land, had contributed greatly to the colony's development and held official positions, yet were being denied equal legal rights. A few attained wealth and position, notably Simeon Lord*, Andrew Thomson*, William Redfern*, Greenway*, Henry Kable and Henry Fulton*, but the children of emancipists were often more significant. The first emancipist was J. Irving, surgeon, freed in 1790.

Emerald Qld. 24S/148E (2,916 in 1971) On the Nogoa River, this is the focal point and main service centre for a wide NW/SE corridor or productive stock and grain land, and at the head of a new irrigation area of 130 farms on 35,640 ha. planned to grow lucerne, cotton, sorghum etc. Water stored by Fairbairn Dam 20 km. upstream impounding 1,443 million m.^{3}. It is the first major work under the National Water Resources Development Programme.

Emerson, Roy (1936–) b. Kingaroy, Qld. He developed from a brilliant schoolboy athlete to become a tennis champion, playing in Davis Cup matches from 1959, winning the Wimbledon Men's Singles 1964, 1965, the Wimbledon Doubles with Fraser (1959 and 1961) and the Aus. men's singles championship 1961–6. He turned professional in 1968.

Empire Games (or The British Empire and Commonwealth Games) They were held in Aus. in 1938 at Sydney, and 1962 at Perth.

Emu (*Dromaius novae-hollandiae*) Australia's largest bird, and of living birds second only to the ostrich. With the Cassowary* it makes up the Aus. Ratites or Giant Flightless Birds. It stands up to 1·5 m. high and weighs up to 55 kg., with fawn-brown feathers, twin flexible quills springing from each root. Vestigial wings, hardly visible on casual inspection, are held close to the body. The emu has bluish flesh on head and neck, short strong black bill and powerful black legs with large 3-toed feet, and is capable of running up to 48 km.p.h. There is no real tail. It has inhabited all of Aus., but is extinct in Tas., King Island and Kangaroo Island (perhaps there were insular species in the latter 2 islands). It is now seen mostly in open inland country; it prefers open grasslands, but since it competes for pasture, fouls land or damages wheat (though also eating caterpillars and grasshoppers) it is killed out—the flesh is sometimes used to feed dogs—or reduced to residual woodland refuges. The call is a resonant booming or drumming, with also lower throaty noises. The male makes the platform-like nest of trampled herbage, and incubates the eggs, stretching his long neck on the ground to escape detection if danger is sensed. There may be 7–10 greenish-black eggs, each of 0·5 kg. or so, laid April to November; the young hatch in about 2 months, and have brown and white stripes along their back and sides for 4–5 months. (*See* PLATE 5.)

Emu Bush A popular name for several species of the shrub genus *Eremophila*, in the mainly Aus. family Myoporaceae. The widespread Spotted Emu Bush, *E. maculata*, has broadly lanceolate, smooth 2·5 cm. leaves, a tubular lipped flower, brown and yellow or pink or whitish, with yellow, pink or red spots inside and markedly protruding stamens. The fruit is a smooth succulent sphere, eaten by emus, hence the popular name, though probably poisonous to stock in the fruiting season.

Emu Grass A popular name for the Scurf-Pea, *Psoralea tenax*. (*See* PEA.)

Emu-wren (*Stipiturus* spp.) This tiny bird has tail feathers reminiscent in structure of emu feathers.

Encephalitis This disease may be due to several causes; of the few score of cases in Aus. annually, a good many are probably 'Murray River fever', a virus disease, probably transmitted by a mosquito, causing a sharp illness.

Encounter Bay S.A. 36S/139E The shallow inlet W of the mouth of the Murray, named from the historic encounter in April 1802, of Flinders* and Baudin*. It became the site of whaling and sealing settlements.

Entrance, The N.S.W. 33S/152E (13,661 in 1971). A growing resort town at the entrance to Tuggerah L., grouped since the 1966 census with Bateau Bay, Berkeley Vale, part of Chittaway Point, Killarney Vale, Long Jetty, The Entrance North, Toowoon Bay and Tumbi Umbi.

Epidemics These have been remarkably few and light in Aus., especially in view of the difficulties of controlling standards of hygiene at times of rapid development during the gold-rushes etc., and of the frequent import of infections to a population of low immunity. The space and relative dispersion of population have saved many areas from involvement, through lack of close enough contact to maintain the infection. Cholera, malaria and yellow fever have been almost absent, but at different times plague*, smallpox* and tuberculosis* have all been severe. The influenza pandemic of 1919–20 was relatively light owing to Australia's almost unique ability to check it by quarantine. Children's diseases were very troublesome in the late 19th century, probably because infections brought in by immigrants severely affected local children of low immunity: the measles virus, the scarlet fever form of streptococcal infection, whooping-cough (from the bacillus *Haemophilus pertussis*) and diphtheria*; these are now of relatively little significance, either because of greatly improved treatment, or because artificial immunity can be given by inoculation, or sometimes both. Tuberculosis is still widespread as an infection but well under control. The virus disease rubella or German measles is normally trivial, but in 1941 Sir Norman Gregg showed its influence on congenital abnormalities, in a proportion of mothers infected during pregnancy. The virus disease poliomyelitis or infantile paralysis has been controlled by the mass administration of various vaccines, while the infective hepatitis virus, probably with a good deal in common in transmission by polluted water, flies or hands—occasionally no doubt by droplets in crowded places—remains as perhaps the most troublesome epidemic disease.

Eppalock Reservoir Vic. 37S/144E On the Campaspe River, with a 46-m. dam and a capacity of 308 million m.[3]. It is used to secure Bendigo town water and also for irrigation and water sports. The 2,000 km.[2] catchment has been the subject of an intensive and comprehensive campaign to reduce siltation through soil conservation measures, which may prove a model for other areas.

Eriachne A grass genus mainly of N Aus., with very varied species from small annuals to tall coarse perennials, and including the spiked cushions of *E. mucronata*, a rock-grass.

Ern Malley Hoax An experiment carried out in 1944 by writers James McAuley* and Harold Stewart*, in which they submitted poems to Max Harris, editor of *Angry Penguins**, as from the fictitious sister of a fictitious and deceased insurance agent; they had in fact been concocted from random selections of words. They were published, their spurious nature being only subsequently suggested by B. R. Elliott. Yet the poems have some fine imagery and effective lines. Harris was fined for publishing indecent material. *For further reading see: Ern Malley's Poems* with an introduction by M. Harris (Melbourne, 1961).

Ernabella Mission S.A. 26S/132E In the Musgrave Ranges. This is Presbyterian, and was founded in 1937 to provide a buffer between the remaining tribal Aborigines, both the local Pitjantjatjara and desert nomads further W, and European contact. It covers 1,300 km.[2] and has training and medical facilities.

Escape Cliffs N.T. 11S/131E On Adam Bay, this was one of the sites of attempted settlement in the Territory (1864–7) initially under Boyle Travers Finnis (1807–1893), a surveyor who had been the first Premier of S.A. under responsible government, in 1856. It had been named on the *Beagle* voyage of 1839 when 2 surveyors escaped from Aborigines by dancing to divert them until help arrived.

Esk Rivers Tas. 41S/148E The North Esk flows W along the N edge of the Ben Lomond* massif to join the South Esk, which rises within a few miles of it, but curves 240 km. SE then SW and NW round the same hill block. Below the confluence in Launceston, they form the drowned Tamar estuary.

The S Esk has tributaries from the Central Plateau and is important in hydro-electric development. (*See* TASMANIA, POWER.)

Esperance 34S/122E (4,860 in 1971) A port on the S coast of W.A., on **Esperance Bay**, a shallow inlet protected by the SW by Dempster Head, and named after his ship by Bruny D'Entrecasteaux* in 1792 when he sheltered there, as did subsequent whalers. The settlement grew with the E gold-fields as a resort and minor port and is expanding rapidly as a port for the nickel* fields to the N. Harbour improvements, a superphosphate factory, new shops etc. now reflect its function in serving **Esperance Plains.** This coastal strip 200 by 30 km. of sand plain, interspersed with rock outcrops and swampy creek basins, had reverted to scrub after sheep rearing failed. In 1949 a Government Research Station proved that only the addition of 'trace elements' copper, zinc, molybdenum and phosphatic fertiliser, followed by leguminous crops, was needed to make use of the 50 cm. of 'safe' winter rains. The land was opened for farming, but initial results were slow, and the 607,500 ha. option to the U.S. 'Chase Syndicate' failed. Since 1960 a further U.S. syndicate, which must sell half the land it develops in 810 ha. lots, and individual settlers have increased the developed area to 405,000 ha. in 600 properties with the main emphasis on wool and beef, although cereals and fodder crops are also successful.

Esson, Thomas Louis Buvelot (1879– 1943) b. Edinburgh. A playwright encouraged by Yeats and Synge to write Aus. plays of which the best are the one-act *The Drovers* and *Dead Timber*. He started the Pioneer Players in Melbourne (1922–6) with Vance Palmer, Win Moore and Stewart Mackay; together they were important founders of Aus. drama.

Eucalyptus (well-covered, referring to the tight covers remaining over the flowers until the mature stamens are ready to emerge) A large genus within the world-wide but mainly tropical family Myrtaceae, the myrtles.

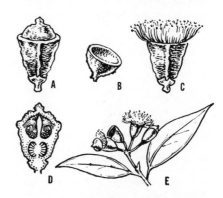

Eucalyptus
A *Flower bud;* B *Lid;* C *Flower;* D *Vertical section of flower;* E *Branch*

The genus contains between 400 and 600 species (classification is difficult because species hybridise freely), nearly all in Aus., half a dozen in N.G. and one species reaching N to the Philippines. They cover some 95% of the forested areas of Aus., and at lower densities much of the uncleared land between forested and desert areas. Ranging from rain-forest to semi-desert conditions, from temperate and sub-alpine conditions to hot wet and hot dry climates, they naturally have a wide range of form, size and adaptation, from the 90-m. Mountain Ash, *Eucalyptus regnans* (*see* PLATE 8) or the Great Karri of W.A., *E. diversicolor*, to the dwarf mallee* species with heavy rootstocks (lignotubers), e.g. *E. dumosa*. The name 'Gums' in many popular names is venerable, going back to Governor Phillip, but the sticky resinous exudate is more correctly kino as distinct from the true mucilage gums of various acacias and other species. Eucalyptus oil from some 20 species provides some export, but trade is declining; the main areas of distillation are in SE N.S.W. and in Vic. Eucalypts are unusual in being able to produce numerous fresh shoots, developed beneath the bark, after they have been scorched by fire. Because of their rapid growth and good timber, certain eucalypts are now very important planted forest trees in dry subtropical regions of the world, notably *E. globulus*, the Tas. Blue Gum in the Mediterranean, California and S America.

The popular names for eucalypts usually refer to their bark. Gums have smooth, grey or cream bark, shed in ribbons or large thin flakes, sometimes with a rough stocking at the base of the trunk. Boxes have hard durable wood; persistent scaly, flaky or slightly fibrous bark. Peppermints have leaves smelling strongly, when crushed, and persistent grey, finely interlaced bark. Stringybarks have thick long-fibred strands all over a long straight trunk. Ironbarks have a rough, thick, hard, very deeply fissured bark. Woollybutts have red or brown loose fibrous bark on the lower part of the trunk, smooth bark above. Mahoganies, largely found in rain-forests, are the eucalypts known for marked differences between the 2 leaf surfaces, and the leaves are generally horizontal, not hanging as in other species. Mallee eucalypts produce many trunks from a large underground woody tuber. Bloodwoods have deep red timber. Since a species may possess more than one of these characteristics, local names for a particular species vary.

Eucalypts are discussed in the following articles: Apple-box*, Ash*, Blackbutt*, Bloodwoods*, Blue Gums* (Eastern and Southern Groups), Box*, Brown Mallet*, Carbeen*, Coolabah*, Ghost Gum*, Gympie* or Yellow Messmate, Ironbark*, Jarrah*, Karri*, Mallee*, Manna Gum*, Mahogany*, Messmate*, Mountain Gum*,

Peppermint*, Red Gums*, Sallee*, Salmon Gum*, Scribbly Gum*, Snow Gum*, Stringybark*, Sugar Gum*, Swamp Gum*, Tallowwood*, Tingle* or Red Tingle, Tuart*, Wandoo*, White Gum*, Woollybutt*, Yate*.

Eucla W.A. 32S/129E On the Eyre Highway near the S.A. border, a former telegraph station linking Perth and Adelaide (1877) now sand-covered.

Eucla Basin The artesian basin underlying the Nullarbor Plain*, with highly mineralised water obtained in bores mainly along the railway.

Eucumbene, Lake Major storage in the Snowy Mt. Scheme*, completed 1958, with a capacity of 4,317 million m.^{3} and surface area of 145 km.^{2} The dam is 116 m. high and its earth core 0·8 km. thick at the base, flanked by rock and concrete. Stocked with rainbow trout, the lake is now a major tourist and fishing centre. (*See* ADAMINABY.)

Eureka Stockade Near Ballarat, the site of an armed rebellion or riot (1854), in which the most extreme of a much larger number of disaffected gold-miners drilled and gradually, though pathetically, armed themselves behind a stockade of slabs, and raised the new Aus. flag showing the Southern Cross against a blue ground. They were over-run by troops in 15 minutes in the early morning of December 3, 1854, with a loss of 22 miners, 1 officer and 5 troopers. The troops behaved badly until pulled up by their officers, destroying property and mutilating diggers; 128 prisoners were taken, some wounded, while others escaped, including the leader Peter Lalor*.

Black and Vern of the leaders also escaped, but 13 were tried for high treason (12 were acquitted and 1 prosecution was withdrawn), including the Italian Rafaello Carboni who wrote a narrative of events in vigorous broken English. *The Eureka Stockade: the consequences of some pirates wanting on Quarterdeck a Rebellion* (republished

Melbourne, 1942). Proximate causes were: indignation about the heavy charges for, and frequent inspections of, the flimsy mining licences (*see* MINER'S RIGHT); and resentment over police oppression and corruption, culminating in the burning down of the Eureka hotel after the acquittal (unjust and corrupt as the diggers saw it) of the proprietor, his wife and another man, on a charge of murdering a drunken miner by kicking him to death. But there were deeper and wider resentments: a delay in miners' franchise, Irish antagonism to the police and the English in general. The obelisk at the site salutes the martyrs of Eureka, and the incident, claimed as the birth of Aus. democracy, has become sentimentalised, enlarged and heroic. Consequent legislation gave cheaper licences, better gold-field administration, and miners' franchise, but also a poll tax on Chinese gold-seekers.

Euro A large kangaroo* or wallaroo of Central Aus., *Macropus erubescens*.

Evans, George Essex (1863–1909) b. London. He arrived in Aus. in 1881. A poet, living mainly in Toowoomba, Qld., where there is a memorial to him as a patriotic balladist.

Evans, George William (1780–1852) b. Warwick, Eng. He arrived in N.S.W. in 1802 from S Africa, and was appointed Acting Surveyor-General (1803–5). Governor King dismissed him, and he farmed on the Hawkesbury before re-joining the Survey Department as Deputy Surveyor for Van Diemen's Land (1810–25). Macquarie ordered his explorations in N.S.W.: in the Illawarra region (1812); to follow up the Blue Mts. Crossing (1813) in which he went much further than Blaxland* and was the first to cross the Dividing Range and find 'a fine plain of rich land, the handsomest country I ever saw' along the banks of the Macquarie River. He discovered the Lachlan River (1815); and was

Oxley's second in command (1817) when the great hopes of limitless pastures faded into the Macquarie swamps. He resigned following disputes with Governor Arthur* and died in obscurity. His place in Aus. exploration should be higher than it has been. *For further reading see* A. K. Weatherburn: *George William Evans* (Sydney, 1966).

Evatt, Herbert Vere (1894–1965) b. E Maitland, N.S.W. A brilliant but controversial Labor leader, who rose to legal eminence after a brilliant university career. He entered N.S.W. Legislative Assembly (1925), bitterly opposing Lang*, was High Court Justice (1930–40), the youngest ever, and was a noted constitutional authority. In Federal Parliament (1940–60) he was influential in the moves leading to Labor's period of office (1941–9), in which he served as Attorney General and Minister of External Affairs, and was responsible for many sharply worded despatches to London over war policies and tactics. He was President of the U.N. Assembly (1948–9). Succeeding to the Party Leadership (1951–60), his outspoken campaign against Menzies's moves to dissolve the Communist Party* in 1951 and his appearing for the men accused in the Petrov Affair* in 1954 brought suspicion of his left-wing views and at least influenced the 1955 split in the Labor Party. He wrote well and convincingly, notably in *Australian Labor Leader* (Sydney, 1940), a biography of Holman and study of the Labor Party. *For further reading see* A. Dalziel: *Evatt the Enigma* (Melbourne, 1967).

Everard Range S.A. 27S/132E An outlier, SE of the Musgrave Ranges, with bare rock and spinifex slopes rising abruptly to some 1,000 m. above the arid plain.

Everlastings or **Everlasting Daisies** The mainly yellow-flowered herbs of the Compositae family which have stiff papery bracts simulating petals, retaining their attractive form and colour for months after the brief flowering season, whether they are growing or in vases. The large genus *Helichrysum* with 500 species (240 in S Africa) includes some 75 Aus. species, mainly yellow-flowered. 1. The small-leaved Clustered Everlasting, *H. semipapposum*, of W.A. and the Western Plains of E. Aus. grows from 30–90 cm., with bell-shaped flowers. 2. The Golden Everlasting, *H. bracteatum*, of 30–60 cm., is found in grasslands in E Aus., with showy yellow bracts 2·5–5 cm. across, and the foundation of many garden everlastings. 3. Larger species include *H. dendroideum*, which grows as a small tree in mountain gullies in SE Aus. (*See also* SUNRAYS.)

Exclusivist A term coined by historians for the free settlers' faction bitterly opposed to the emancipists*.

Exmouth Gulf W.A. 22S/114E A shallow exposed inlet 80 km. N–S and 48 km. E–W between North West Cape and the mainland. A former pearling centre, it now has commercial prawn fisheries processed at Learmonth and a pearl culture farm. Salt obtained by solar evaporation is being developed for export.

EXPLORATION Land exploration began immediately the colony of N.S.W. was founded in 1788. Between Phillip's tentative forays and the complete modern aerial survey, the frontiers were pushed back gradually from the SE and SW corners towards the arid centre and tropical N. The map of phases (MAP 3, inset) resembles one of population density today, fanning out from the fertile fringes to the thinly peopled, least productive and last explored areas; it is also the reverse of the discovery map (MAP 2) starting from the SE instead of the N and W.

Exploration was motivated mainly by practical needs for more cropland to feed the isolated colony, then for pastures for increasing herds. Official expeditions were supplemented by shipwrecked sailors and escaped convicts, later by privately financed searches for fresh pastures, and by the overlanders*. Gold prospectors and, later, geologists looking for other minerals including oil, have filled in many blank corners.

Personal rewards varied, and tended to be in proportion to the value of the land discovered: Mitchell was knighted for discovering the grasslands of W Qld., and the fertile 'Australia Felix' of W Vic., accomplished with skill enough but no undue hardship; while Giles, whose desert exploits were epics of endurance, died a poor Coolgardie clerk. There was a spirit of adventure and a wish to serve, but there was also ambition, desire for recognition, and bitter personal rivalry involved between Sturt and Mitchell; Strzelecki and McMillan; Warburton and Giles. Inter-state rivalry, for honour and practical gain, inspired the S–N expedition of Burke and Wills in 1861, and the desert crossings of the 1870s. The first explorers were naval or military men, but later the majority were trained surveyors. The eccentricities of Leichhardt amd Burke, who both perished, showed that balance, observation and above all leadership, were as important as courage and vision.

Phase 1. To 1815 The Blue Mts. seemed at first an impassable barrier, for the early attempts to cross them followed the valleys and led only to precipitous sandstone scarps. But the need for new land increased, aggravated by drought in 1813, and a renewed attack succeeded by keeping to the watersheds. Macquarie wasted no time in following up Evans' discovery of the first W-flowing stream; a road was built and the settlement of the Western Slopes began. In Tas. exploration remained confined to the estuaries of Derwent and Tamar.

1788–9: Phillip* (Broken Bay, Hawkesbury River), Tench* (Nepean

River); 1791: Tench and Dawes* proved Nepean-Hawkesbury to be one; 1794: Hayes (Derwent River); 1798: Wilson (Wollondilly River); 1802: Barrallier* (Blue Mts.); 1804: Caley* (Blue Mts.); 1807: Laycock (N–S Tas.); 1813: Lawson*, Blaxland*, Wentworth* (Blue Mts.); 1814: Hume* (Berrima); 1815: Evans (Lachlan River).

Phase 2. 1815–27 The prospects of limitless room for expansion beyond the Blue Mts. faded with Oxley's report in 1827, that the W-flowing Macquarie and Lachlan Rivers ended in marshes, the edge, he suggested, of an inland sea. This belief influenced exploration for several decades. There was plenty of grazing land, however, south-westwards to the foothills of the Snowy Mts., and in 1824 the Murray was found and a route discovered to Port Phillip on the S coast. To the N land routes were being pioneered and in 1827 Cunningham found the Darling Downs. In Tas. the Van Diemen's Land Company* was opening up the NW, and the Tamar and Derwent settlements had been linked by land.

1817: White (Macleay River), Beaumont (Tas. Plateau), Oxley (Macquarie River); 1818: Throsby (Jervis Bay), Hume*, Meehan (L. Bathurst), Oxley*, Evans* (Castlereagh River); 1821: Throsby (Murrumbidgee River); 1822: Lawson (Goulburn River), Kearns (Molonglo River); 1823: Hardwick (NE Tas.), Ovens*, Currie (Monaro), Oxley (Moreton Bay); 1824: Hume, Hovell* (Murray River), Hobbs (W Tas.); 1826: Lockyer* (Kalgan River, W.A.); 1827: Cunningham* (Darling Downs).

Phase 3. 1828–40 The SE corner was now becoming known in broad outline, from Melbourne to Brisbane, including large areas W of the Divide. The fate of the W-flowing rivers remained a mystery until Sturt, giant among explorers, followed up his discovery of the Darling in 1828, by sailing down the Murrumbidgee to its confluences first with Murray, then Darling, and on to the dune-fringed lagoon, L. Alexandrina, where it reaches the sea hidden, from the coastal explorers who had looked for a major river mouth. Sturt's discoveries were largely confirmed by Mitchell, who traced the Darling further, and crossed the Murray to the fertile western district of Vic. Already, enterprising Tas. squatters in 1835 had crossed the Bass Str. to settle on its shores. Overlanders and squatters followed, literally in Mitchell's tracks and the frontier was pushed back to a line from Adelaide to Brisbane. The urgency, excitement and rivalry of the period were caught in Strzelecki's 'I'm off to the Snowies this minute' . . . before he traversed them, naming the highest mountain Kosciusko, and following McMillan down into eastern Vic. which he named Gipps Land. Meanwhile Grey's forced march down the coast of W.A. revealed its major river mouths.

1828: Sturt* (Bogan River, Darling River); 1830: Sturt (Murray); 1830: Dale (Swan-Avon River, W.A.); 1831: Bannister (Perth–Albany); 1832: Mitchell* (Macintyre River), Sharland (L. St. Clair, Tas.); 1836: Mitchell, Hawdon* (W. Vic.), Roe (SW of W.A.), Frankland (Central Tas.); 1837: Grey* (Glenelg River, W.A.); 1838: Eyre (Point Phillip–Adelaide); 1839: Grey (W.A. coast), McMillan (E Vic.); 1840: Strzelecki* (Snowy Mts.).

Phase 4. 1840–50 Attention now turned to the centre and N. Eyre, commissioned to find an overland route between S.A. and W.A., was consumed with curiosity about the heart of the continent. Turned back from this objective by L. Torrens (thought to be part of a great horseshoe lake barring the routes N), he went westwards, and crossed to King George Sound, finding no running water in 2,000 km. Sturt, also obsessed by the centre, but believing it contained a sea, spent 17 months in 1844–5 on a burning march and enforced encampment beside the only water in hundreds of km.; he was beaten back by the Simpson Desert. In the same year, an E–W continental crossing had been achieved by Leichhardt, from Qld. to Arnhem Land, and the rivers flowing to the Gulf of Carpentaria discovered. In 1846 Mitchell, whose obsession was a great NW-flowing river, persuaded himself that the wandering channels of the Barcoo were 'the river leading to India: the grand goal'. Leichhardt vanished on an attempted Qld.–W.A. crossing in 1847.

1841: Eyre (Adelaide–Esperance); 1843: Frome (L. Torrens), Lander, Lefroy (SW of W.A.); 1844–5: Sturt (Central Aus.), Leichhardt* (to Port Essington); 1846: Mitchell (Barcoo River); 1847: Kennedy* (Barcoo River), Gregory* (Murchison River W.A.), Roe (York–Esperance).

Phase 5. 1850–70 The discovery of gold, while encouraging prospecting journeys, also drew away many adventurous potential explorers; as did the Crimean War. There was plenty of good land, and what remained unknown was likely to be less valuable. Thus there was a slackening of the pace. Britain, still hoping for a new Ganges, sponsored exploration in the NW, and the rich Kimberley grasslands were found by Gregory, who then reversed Leichhardt's 1844 journey, with considerably more efficiency, and finally cleared up the problem of the river systems leading to L. Eyre. The lakes themselves were now outlined. Crossing the interior then became a race between S.A. and Vic., and was achieved by the 2 vastly contrasting expeditions of Burke and McDouall Stuart. The former, ending in disaster, was the first to reach tidal waters in the Gulf, but more by luck than management; while Stuart, after 3 dogged attempts, made the much longer Adelaide–Arnhem Land crossing through the real centre in 1861. Relief expeditions for Burke and Wills and for Leichhardt accomplished more than the original exploits. Landsborough,

for instance, reported so favourably on western Qld. that an influx of squatters followed him. Pastoralists were also penetrating into the SW corner of W.A. and into the best Tas. farmlands.

1850: Austin (W.A.); 1855: Babbage (S.A. Lakes); 1856: A. C. Gregory (N Aus.); 1857: Hack (Gawler Range); 1858: Warburton (S.A. lakes), F. Gregory (Gascoyne River), A. C. Gregory (Qld.–Adelaide); 1860: Buchanan (Thomson River); 1861: Burke*, Wills* (Vic.–Gulf of Carpentaria) with relief expeditions under Landsborough, Howitt*, Walker, McKinley, McdouallStuart* (Central Aus.); 1860–4: Cunningham, Dalrymple, (Burdekin River), McIntyre (W Qld.), Jardines (Cape York); 1869: Forrest (W.A. interior).

Phase 6. 1871–1939 The largest remaining blank was the W central desert. No sea or great river was expected now and the best that was hoped for was poor grazing on the margins of a desert. The Overland Telegraph (1871–3) provided a useful base and supply line for a number of E–W crossings of the desert in the 1870s, notably those of Forrest, Giles and Warburton. Meanwhile minor unknown areas were being opened up by smaller official expeditions, but more frequently by questing pastoralists whose overlanding feats were as great as many explorations.

The SW corner of Tas., along with parts of the eastern ranges, northern jungles, and much of the central desert remain areas of which considerable proportions have not been seen from the ground by white men.

An aerial survey of the Simpson Desert in 1929 was followed up in 1939 by the last great land exploration: Madigan*, using camels, which made so much of the previous exploration possible, traversed its northern fringes, from the SW and emerged near the point at which Sturt, almost a century before, had been beaten back across the stony desert that bears his name.

1870: Forrest (Perth–Adelaide), Ross (Central Aus.); 1872: Lewis (L. Eyre–Qld.), Giles* (L. Amadeus), Hann (Cape York); 1873: Giles (Gibson Desert), Warburton (Alice Springs–Oakover River); 1873–5: Mulligan, Hodgkinson, McCleod, Palmerston (N Qld.), Gosse finds Ayers Rock; 1874: Forrest, Ross (W.A.); 1875–6: Giles (W Desert), Hodgkinson (Diamantina River); 1877: Buchanan (Barkly Table-land); 1879: Favenc (Qld.–Central Aus.), Jackey Jackey (Cape York), A. Forrest (de Grey, Ord, Margaret Rivers), Lindsay (Arnhem Land); 1884: Stockdale (NW of W.A.); 1891–2: Lindsay, Wells (Central W.A.); 1894: Carnegie (W.A.); 1896: Mason (E of W.A.), Hubbe (Oodnadatta–Calgoorlie); 1896–8: Hann (Kimberleys); 1901: Canning (W.A. rabbit-proof fence), Muir (trans-continental rail survey); 1906: Canning (Kimberleys–Perth); 1923–36: Terry (centre and NW); 1931–5 Mackay (aerial surveys Central Aus.); 1939: Madigan (Simpson Desert). (*See* MAP 3.) *For further reading see* J. H. L. Cumpston: *The Inland Sea and the Great River* (Sydney, 1964); K. Fitzpatrick: *Australian Explorers* (London, 1958).

External Affairs, Department of The Department was set up with Federation—the first in the British Dominions with this title. In 1970 the name was changed to Department of Foreign Affairs in charge of a Minister of State for Foreign Affairs. For the Embassies etc. *see* INTERNATIONAL RELATIONS.

Eyre, Edward John (1815–1901) b. Yorkshire, Eng. The son of a clergy-man. He emigrated to Aus. in 1833. He overlanded cattle to Port Phillip and Adelaide and settled in S.A. where he made important exploratory jour-neys to seek new grazing lands in 1839, but was rebuffed by the seemingly impassable barrier of salt pans to the N, and the sterile Eyre peninsula to the W. In 1841, commissioned originally to find a land route to Perth, but personally drawn by curiosity about the interior, he again travelled north-wards; he was forced to turn W by the bogs round L. Torrens and so achieved the remarkable journey to Albany, surviving only by water collected from the dew and other Aboriginal devices, and by luckily falling in with a French whaler. His white companion Baxter was killed by 2 of his 3 Aborigines; the third, Wylie, loyally stayed with him. After a period as Protector of Aborig-ines in S.A., Eyre became Lt.-Governor of N.Z. and then held administra-tive posts in the West Indies. His allegedly brutal suppression of a rebellion while Jamaican Governor in 1864 led to prolonged enquiry, a Royal Commission and civil suits instigated by John Stuart Mill and Thomas Huxley; the defence com-mittee for him included Carlyle, Ruskin, Tennyson and Dickens. Eyre was exonerated. His journals were republished (1965) by the Libraries Board of S.A. *For further reading see* G. Dutton: *The Hero as Murderer* (Melbourne, 1967).

Eyre Highway S.A./W.A. A 1,900-km. road from Port Augusta to Norse-man and Coolgardie, where it joins the Kalgoorlie–Perth road. Sealing of the surface is progressing from both ends to improve conditions for the several hundred cars a week, which use it over holiday periods. Some semi-trailers use it, although most still go 'pick-a-back' on the Trans-continental Railway.

Eyre, Lake S.A. 28S/137E The largest of the Aus. salinas or salt 'lakes' covering 9,300 km.^{2} in 2 basins. L. Eyre N is 130 km. N–S by about 100 km. E–W and receives occasional Channel Country* waters from the Warburton and Cooper Creek, and even more rarely from the Macumba and Neale on the NW and the Frome on the SE. The bed slopes N–S to 12 m.

below sea level, and waters follow the Warburton Groove to fill the S embayments of Madigan Gulf and Belt Bay first. Goyder Channel links it with L. Eyre S, 65 km. E–W by 32 km. N–S, with its smaller catchment and rarer waters. In 1950 8,000 km.^{2} of water surface formed L. Eyre, the only recorded filling of the lake, which dried out in 2 years, although waters have been known to reach it in 1891, 1906, 1941 and 5 times since 1950, including 1963 when the late Donald Campbell was forced to abandon his land speed record attempt. Goyder named the lake in 1860, and following wet years brought pastoralists to its shores. Only a few stations survive on artesian water. Its origins lie in river systems of wet Tertiary times, followed by uplift to the S blocking the outlets and a subsequently arid climatic period lasting until today.

Eyre Peninsula S.A. 33S/135E This forms a triangle of low country stretching 320 km. S from a base along the Gawler Range, and underlain by Precambrian rocks covered in part by recent sands. Early pastoral settlement on open vegetation on limestones in the drier W and N has been followed since the 1914–18 War by clearing of the central mallee, partly for soldier settlement. Railways focusing on Port Lincoln, and water supply reticulated first from the Cleve Hills and Todd River (1922) and more recently from bores in the Uley-Wanila and Elliston-Locke areas, supply sheep/wheat/barley lands. In the NE are the iron-rich Middleback Ranges serving Whyalla.

F

Fadden, Sir Arthur William (1895-1973) b. Ingham, Qld. Leader of the Country Party* from 1941-58, becoming Prime Minister from August-October 1941, after the resignation of Menzies*, and Opposition Leader from 1941-3.

Fairfax, John (1804-1877) b. Warwick, Eng. He was a printer and bookseller who arrived in Aus. in 1838. In 1841 with Charles Kemp, he bought the *Sydney Herald* (*see* NEWSPAPERS), and after Kemp retired from the firm in 1853 it became the sole property of Fairfax and later his sons. The family still retain a major interest.

Fairweather, Ian b. 1890 in Scotland. He arrived in Aus. first in 1933 and then in 1942. A post-war artist of international repute now living on a Qld. island after much wandering in the East, which has influenced his abstract work.

Fairy Lantern A popular name for the almost leafless, glowing amber flower of *Thismia rodwayi*, in S Vic. and Tas., in the family Burmanniaceae, with flowers resembling Iris*. Like most of the family, the plant is a saprophyte, deriving much of its food from decaying organic material.

Fairy-grass Naturally is used to describe many grasses with delicate feathery flowerheads, but especially for various species of *Sporobolus*, a genus which includes very varied species, e.g. the Rat-tail Grass, *S. elongatus*, the creeping *S. mitchelli* of inland alluvial flats, and the introduced but naturalised Parramatta-grass, *S. capensis*.

Falcons (of Aus.) These include the swift Peregrine, *Falco peregrinus*, of medieval falconry. (*See* HAWKS.)

Fan Flower A popular name for various species of *Scaevola*, in the dominantly

Aus. family Goodeniaceae. They have strap-like succulent leaves and attractive flowers with 5 petals split to the base and arranged fan-like on one side on top of the ovary, often white or yellow near the base and shading into blue, purple or red. The widespread and attractive purple Fairy Fan Flower is *S. aemula*. The pale blue scented Fan Flower of E coast dunes is *S. calendulacea*. Plate 6 includes Royal Robe one of W.A.'s wealth of species which also include *S. pemescens*, under trial at one time as a cancer treatment.

Farm Cove A bay on the S shore of Port Jackson, N.S.W., just E of Bennelong Point, the site of Sydney Opera House. The first stock were grazed, and crops grown here in 1788. Today it forms the Botanic Gardens.

Farming Defined as the use of land to produce food and raw materials, directly by crop or grazing land, indirectly by fodder crop. Physical limitations of rainfall, soils, topography and distance have made Aus. basically a land of *extensive* farming; economic, historical and demographic factors have made it *commercial* and mechanised. These characteristics are the antithesis of the intensive subsistence farming of her Asian neighbours. Nor do they represent the optimum land use everywhere, and trends are towards intensification now that available farmland is mainly taken up, although it is not accompanied by closer settlement to any extent. There are some 252,000 rural holdings supporting just over 1 million people, predominantly as family farming units. Some 7% of the work force is engaged in farming but produces 18% of the gross national product. Rural industry has suffered recently from low world prices and high local costs but improved sharply by 10%, 1972–3. Total farmed area fluctuates with good and bad years, economic and climatic, but is in the region of 500,000 ha. Of this, 93% is grazing land, some of it improved by fertilisers, some spoiled by erosion, 4% is sown with exotic grasses and clovers, and only 3% is cropped. Production values are not proportionate: crops account for 45% and pastoral products 55% of net value. In exports wool dominates the Aus. list (20% of total export). It provides 33% of agricultural exports followed by cereals (20%), meats (20%), sugar (6%), dairy products (5%), hides and fruit (4% each).

In the early days farming in N.S.W. was inhibited by the leached soils and forests of the coastlands, and cultivated acreage climbed slowly, from 2,000 ha. in 1797 to 5,000 ha. by 1808; it did not reach 400,000 ha. until 1860 when increased population following the goldrushes had created a demand. Pastoral development followed introduction of the Merino* and discovery of the grazing lands beyond the mountains. Increase to present-day figures has been interrupted by Depressions*, notably in the 1840s, 1890s and 1930s, by world wars (depressing export through shipping problems) and the periodic droughts* which are a climatic feature of many parts of the country. Government protection, planning and development, e.g. in irrigation, has played an important part in many sectors. Major works are *Land Utilisation in Australia* (Melbourne, 1964) by a noted agriculturist Sir Samuel Wadham (1891–) with R. K. Wilson and G. L. Wood, and Sir Samuel Wadham, *Australian Farming* (Melbourne, 1967).

Farrer, William James (1845–1906) b. Westmorland, Eng. A farmer's son who trained in mathematics at Cambridge. He arrived in Aus. in 1870 for health reasons, hoping to farm. Finance prevented this, and he tutored, then became a surveyor until able to settle in 1885 at Lambrigg, 28 km. S of Canberra. Here he began scientific crossing, selection and fixing of wheat varieties for disease (notably 'bunt') and drought resistance; within 2 decades these varieties such as Federation, Bobs, Canberra etc. had expanded commercial wheat production into previously dry pastoral areas in SW and SE Aus.; they had greatly improved quality, notably gluten content, and so established the country as a major wheat exporter. He was appointed 'Wheat Experimentalist' in the N.S.W. Dept. of Agriculture (1898). There is an annual Farrer Oration on rural science.

Fauna (of Aus.) They include over 300 species of mammals* (about half marsupials*, with 3 species of monotremes*; the rest are placental mammals—*see* MAMMALS). There are about 650 species of birds*. Reptiles* include some 300 species of lizards*, 140 of snakes* and 2 crocodiles*. Aus. waters contain some 100 species of sharks*, 50 rays* and 2,000 of bony fishes*, as well as a number of species of mammalian whales*, dolphins*, dugong*, sealions and seals*. There are about 180 species of freshwater fishes*. Arthropods* include some 40,000 insects*, and 2,000 arachnids*. There are some 10,000 species of molluscs*, and worms* of many species, some universal, some unique. Amphibia* of Aus. are limited to frogs and toads.

The assemblage of fauna, like the vegetation*, is unique, and the ecological web of inter-relationships is of great beauty and fascination. Many species of plants and animals have become extinct in the European period, hence the modern emphasis on the need for conservation.* *For further reading see* D. Morgan et al. eds.: *Biological Science: The Web of Life* (Canberra, 1967); D. F. McMichael ed.: *A Treasury of Aus. Wildlife* (London, 1967); G. Pizzey: *Animals and Birds of Aus.* (Melbourne, 1966).

Favenc, Ernest (1845–1908) b. London. He arrived in Aus. in 1863. In 1878–9 he explored country NW of the Diamantina for a proposed Qld.–N.T. railway and later the Barkly Tableland and northern W.A. In his *History of Aus. Exploration* (Sydney, 1888) and his successful short stories, e.g. *The Last of Six* (Sydney, 1893), his accurate knowledge of the inland appears.

Fawkner, John Pascoe (1792–1869) b. London. He came with his mother and convict father to the abortive Port Phillip settlement of 1803, and later to Tas. where his enterprises included a nursery, bakery, newspaper and farming. He was transported to Newcastle (1816–17) for helping convicts to escape. In 1835 his party established a Port Phillip settlement (though Fawkner was delayed in Launceston over debts) on the exact site selected by Batman*, whom he long outlived, becoming a 'grand old man' in Vic. politics, aggressive and reactionary, but with ideals.

Feathertop, Mount Vic. 37S/147E, 1,924 m., the second highest summit in the Vic. Alps. It has a flat basalt top over Ordovician slates, fairly smooth slopes, good for skiing, and alpine grasslands rising above the tree-line, snow-covered in winter, long inaccessible but with some recent growth of winter sports.

Federation The ultimate union, in some form, of the Aus. colonies was inevitable but, in spite of precocious advocates as early as Wentworth* and the strong pleas of the British Prime Minister, Grey, at the time the States were given the power to draft their own constitutions in the 1850s, it was not until the last quarter of the 19th century that the drawbacks of separate development were sufficiently clear to a majority of the people. A convention in 1883 had included New Zealand and Fiji, but there were many setbacks, doubts and delays before the proclamation made by Queen Victoria from her Balmoral retreat on September 17th 1900, declared the birth of the Commonwealth of Aus. as from January 1st 1901.

The initial motivating force was one of fear: suspicions (justified in 1884) of German designs on N.G. and (unjustified) of French intentions to annex the New Hebrides emphasised the non-existence of effective defences. The result was the formation of a Federal Council meeting biennially 1886–1899, but without S.A. or N.S.W. participating, and with no power; yet it was an effective and influential forum in its early days.

Meanwhile economic factors were pointing towards union as trade was hampered by Vic. protective tariffs and discriminatory inter-state rail rates. The meeting at State borders of railways (albeit of different gauges) made the anomalous fiscal position very clear. Employers and Unions were already linked by country-wide organisations.

The third powerful influence was fear of coloured immigration bringing lowered standards and wages, and the need for uniform legislation. Parkes, at first hostile, was converted to federalism partly by the defence issue, partly by political acumen in realising its inevitability and a desire to take the credit; lending his political skill first to instigating the Ministers' Conference in Melbourne (1891), then to presiding over the ensuing Australasian Federal Convention in Sydney (1891), he became identified as the Father of Federation. As much, possibly more, credit belonged to Griffith and Barton, who at different stages were its chief architects, and to Deakin, its unswerving advocate in periods between 1891 and 1900 when the Federal prospect became shrouded in mists of personal and inter-state jealousy and distrust.

The work of the 1891 Convention, whose members were nominated by State parliaments, was to draw in bold outline, the shape of the proposed constitution of a Commonwealth of Australasia the name proposed by Parkes.

The main debating points were tariffs, financial residues and the relative power of the proposed 2 houses. There followed a period of stagnation on the issue in the State parliaments: N.S.W. rejected the constitution entirely, Vic. and S.A. passed it, Tas. and Qld. held back. Depression brought financial crises in the early 1890s, engrossing the governments. N.Z. dropped entirely from the stage. Now the popular agitation for unity became irresistible; sponsored by organisations like the Aus. Natives Association*, by the growing nationalist movements and by republican socialist periodicals such as *The Bulletin**, by business and professional leaders instigating public conferences, as at Corowa* (1893). A second Federal Convention, called by Reid, a vacillating federalist at best, but bowing again to the inevitable, met first in Adelaide in March 1897, then in Sydney and Melbourne after an adjournment for attendance at the Golden Jubilee in London. This time Qld., split by the Kanaka* problem, stayed away; W.A., split between the federalist gold-miners and the conservative coast farmers, appointed its 10 delegates, while in Vic., S.A., N.S.W. and Tas. they were elected by the people.

The 1891 draft was filled out and amended and the delegates went home to put it to a referendum*. Reid, by raising the agreed minimum in favour from 50,000 to 80,000, ensured its defeat in N.S.W., in order to pander to bitter Labor opposition and give him power to force amendments. In Vic. the powerful newspaper, the *Age* tried initially to wreck it. Re-convened late in 1898, amendments were made that finally brought acceptance by an average of 59% of those voting. W.A., after a threatened separatist movement by the gold-miners, yielded to a referendum. One amendment sought to satisfy the bedevilling N.S.W. –Vic. rivalry by providing for a Federal capital within N.S.W., but not less than 100 miles from Sydney. The draft

was approved in London after amendment, at the instigation of Joseph Chamberlain, extending the right of appeal to the Privy Council, which lasted until 1967. *For further reading see* R. R. Garran: *Prosper The Commonwealth* (Sydney, 1958).

Federation Peak Tas. 43S/147E 1,223 m., at the SE end of Arthur Range; this forms a gigantic amphitheatre round the corrie of L. Geeves on its E side.

Felton Bequest Made by Alfred Felton (1831–1904), a wealthy Melbourne dealer, druggist and investor, a frugal-living bachelor, interested in art. It was worth £378,000; half was left to charities, and half to the National Gallery of Vic., which is able to buy about $100,000 worth of art exhibits annually. While in the past this has allowed the acquisition of valuable overseas works, changing markets have reduced its relative purchasing powers; but it remains the major endowment of its type in Aus.

Female Factory At Parramatta, N.S.W. (1804–48), which housed female convicts; spinning and weaving were carried out there. It was over the gaol until a separate 3-storey building, also used for weaving, was designed by Greenway. It was later a lunatic and paupers' hospital.

Ferns (in Aus.) There are about 250 species of these cosmopolitan spore plants in the Group Pteridophyta (which has a long evolutionary history), a relatively small number compared with some other groups, but of great variety, especially in the rain-forests of E Aus. (and unlike so many botanical distributions poorest, not richest, in W.A.). Selected examples of the Class Filicinae, 'ferns' in the narrower sense of common use, show the range from rain-forest to quite arid and rocky sites, and terrestrial, climbing and epiphytic (but not parasitic) types.

The small terrestrial and epiphytic Adder's Tongue ferns, *Ophioglossum* spp., have a relative in the widespread Moonwort, *Botrychium australis*, with parsley-like fronds.

Among the tropical tree-ferns is the very large and handsome *Angiopteris erecta*.

The 'typical' ferns comprise many families, including the following genera and species. *Todea barbara* is a short-trunked tree-fern common along creeks in E Aus. *Schizeae rupestris* is a Blue Mts. fern with undivided frond, and its relative *S. bifida* occurs throughout Aus. *Lygodium scandens* is one of a genus of climbing ferns found in tropical and sub-tropical swamps, with attractive fan-like fronds. The widespread Nardoo*, *Marsilea* spp., with 4-leaf-clover fronds, occurs widely in Aus., in swamps, waterholes and grassy paddocks, coastal and inland. 2 well-known rain-forest tree-fern species of E Aus. are *Dicksonia antarctica* and *Cyathea australis*. The hairy creeping Lace-fern, *Dennstaedtia davallioides*, seen from Vic. to Qld., is one of the largest Aus. fern family, Polypodiaceae. An epiphyte growing on forest trees of humid E Aus. is *Arthropteris tenella*. The cosmopolitan Bracken species of Aus. is *Pteridium esculentum*, as elsewhere, a pest of pastures, rather poisonous to calves which eat young fronds; despite chemical weed-killers, frequent cutting or crushing may still be the best way of controlling bracken. The attractive Maidenhair-ferns include *Adiantum aethiopicum* and the giant form *A. formosum*. The xerophytic Rock Fern, *Cheilanthes tenuifolia*, has fine fronds, compared with shade-loving species in the genus. The Sickle-ferns include *Pellaea falcata*, seen in open forests and flanking the rain-forests of E Aus. An epiphyte seen on tropical trees is the grasslike *Vittoria elongata*. The Rasp-ferns, e.g. the terrestrial forest *Doodia aspera*, are named from their rough-textured fronds. The Bird's Nest Fern, named from its clump-like habit and seen in gardens—with other attractive members

of its genus—is *Asplenium nidus*. The distinctive fronds justify the popular names of Staghorn and Elkhorn for the 2 epiphytic ferns of logs and trees in E Aus. rain-forests, *Platycerium grande* and *P. bifurcatum*. Aus. has several interesting representatives of other orders of pteridophytes. The rootless, epiphytic *Psilotum* and *Tmesipteris* are the only genera of this peculiar order. *Tmesipteris*, growing on tree-fern trunks, is largely confined to Aus. and N.Z. The unique *Phylloglossum drummondi*, with a peculiar underground tuber, is confined to S Aus., Tas. and N.Z. The Clubmosses* *Lycopodium* and *Selaginella* occur as rain-forest epiphytes and in alpine meadows.

Finally, but not the least interesting, *Azolla filiculoides* is the more widely distributed of the 2 floating ferns of its genus and separate Sub-Order. (*See also* CORAL-FERN.)

Fescue A familiar introduced English grass of the genus *Festuca*, common in lawns and pastures. There are about 8 Aus. species, including the Snow Fescue, *F. eriopoda*, with a tuft of very slender blades often surrounded by old brown sheaths, and with a graceful widespread conical head of small seed spikelets. It is a forest grass, palatable to stock, often seen with Snow Grass*. Hooker's Fescue, *F. hookeriana*, gives useful forage in high swampy sites, while *F. littoralis* is a binding plant on coastal dunes.

Field, Barron (1786–1846) Judge of the Supreme Court, N.S.W. (1816–24), replacing J. H. Bent*; a direct descendant of Oliver Cromwell. He opposed the legal rights of the emancipists*, greatly influencing Bigge's* Report, and was a close associate of Marsden. He had been a member of London's literary circle and wrote *First Fruits of Australian Poetry* (Sydney, 1819), poor verse but Aus. in subject matter, and the first Aus. poetry to appear in book form.

Fifield, Elaine (1930–) b. Sydney. A ballerina. She largely trained and achieved success in London, before retiring from the stage to N.G. to join her husband in 1957. She returned to Aus. to work with the Aus. Ballet from 1963–6.

Fig Trees Fruit trees belonging to the genus *Ficus* in the tropical and subtropical family Moraceae. They are important in the vegetation of many tropical areas including N Aus. Figs produce an unusual fruit, from many fused flowers forming an almost closed cavity, male flowers near the mouth, female at the base. These are fertilised by a special type of wasp. The wasps develop in a sterile gall flower, where eggs are laid and develop without damage to the fertile flowers. As the young wasps emerge they brush against the male flowers, and carry pollen to fertilise other figs. Most plants produce buttress roots, spreading widely round the base. Some are trees, some climbers. The Moreton Bay Fig, *Ficus macrophylla*, is a tree of 50 m. by 2·5–3 m. with a smooth bark, containing juice (latex) like that of the rubber-producing fig of India, *F. elastica*. There is a very marked development of buttress roots. It has white-pink upright leaf buds, glossy green oval to pointed leaves 15–25 cm. long, and 2·5 cm.-long figs which are eaten by fruit-bats. Leaves and fruit are edible by cattle. The Port Jackson Fig, *F. rubiginosa*, with dense foliage and growing to 30 by 2 m., has a smooth buttressed trunk, 10–12-cm. oval leaves on hairy stalks (*see* PLATE 8); and produces 1·2-cm. figs similar to those of the Edible Fig, *F. carica*. The latter is often seen in gardens, with its deeply lobed leaves.

File Snakes or **Harmless Water Snakes** (family Acrochordinae) 2 species both found in estuaries in the far N of Aus. and into S and SE Asia are the stout baggy, Javan File Snake, *Acrochordus javanicus*, brown with darker veined back, reaching 2·75 m., which haunts overhanging banks, and the Little or Small File Snake, *A. granulatus*, also stout, only 90–120 cm. in length, and often seen on mud-flats. Both eat mainly fish. The Spotted Water-snake, *Enhydris punctata*, occurs in Cape York. Macleay's Water-snake, *E. Polyepis*, is found in NE Qld. The White-bellied Mangrove Snake, *Fordonia leucobalia* is seen along the coast of N. Aus., and Richardson's Mangrove Snake, *Myron richardsoni*, along the coast of NW Aus.

Films The first film show was in 1896; the first Aus.-made film was of the Melbourne Cup, also 1896. Joseph Perry's *Soldiers of the Cross* (1900) is claimed as the world's first full length feature film (now lost). The first 'talkie' was *The Lost Chord* (1907). *The Story of the Kelly Gang* (1906) cost $900 and made $50,000; many others followed. From 1905–30 some 255 silent films were made in Aus. which has great climatic advantages for outdoor filming. Most were based on Aus. characters, incidents or novels, e.g. *Mutiny on the Bounty*, *The Sentimental Bloke*, *Robbery under Arms* and a successful series of rural comedies. Stars included R. L. ('Snowy') Baker*, Roy René ('Mo'), Lottie Lyell and Shirley Ann Richards. Outstanding producers have included C. E. Chauvel*, Raymond Longford, K. G. Hall and J. W. Heyer (mainly for documentary work), while D. Parer was an outstanding war cameraman. Cinema was very popular between the wars and in the 1930s Aus. was said to have the world's biggest number of cinemas in relation to population; many have closed in face of television competition, others have been turned into 'little theatres'. There was less Aus. production after the introduction of sound films, but major productions were *Forty Thousand Horsemen* and *Jedda* (1955), starring Aborigine Robert Tudawali. Although about 60 have been produced, they decreased after the early 1950s when the current trends towards spectacular costly productions, using world famous stars, made an unsubsidised Aus. industry uneconomic, although television and documentary filming remain important. Several successful films have been made by overseas companies: *The Overlanders, Kangaroo, On the Beach, Summer of the Seventeenth Doll, The Sundowners, They're a Weird Mob* and in 1967 the first full-length colour feature produced and processed in Aus., *Journey out of Darkness. Ned Kelly*, Walkabout* and *Outback* are recent productions.

Aus. documentary work, especially of sociological and anthropological subjects, has achieved high standards: in 1967 a collection produced by the Commonwealth Film Unit (1945), ranging from film made in 1901 by Spencer, the anthropologist to Ian Dunlop's contemporary Aboriginal study *Desert People*, was acclaimed in Europe. The National Library film collection is one of the finest in the world. The Aus. National Film Board (1945) advises the Minister for the Interior on making and distributing educational, documentary and propaganda films. There is a National Film Development Corporation and a growing film and television school. Imported films are subject to Commonwealth censorship*. Expatriates successful in films include Merle Oberon, Errol Flynn, Peter Finch, Victoria Shaw, Ron Randall, Rod Steiger, and the director Robert Krasker.

Finance This has become increasingly controlled by the Commonwealth as against the States. Following Federation, the Commonwealth was constitutionally obliged, under the 'Braddon Clause', to return 75% of the customs and excise revenue it had taken over, to the States, and to share among them any surplus after meeting its own commitments. From 1911–27 this was replaced by a per capita payment to the States, and the Commonwealth assumed ultimate responsibility for State debts. By the Financial Agreement Bill of 1927, agreed by a referendum* (1928), the per capita payment ceased. The Loan Council*, formed to co-ordinate all government borrowing, was effectively dominated by the Commonwealth, which gave an agreed, limited but unconditional contribution towards State interest payments. The 'claimant States' of W.A., Tas., and, until 1959, S.A., were also assisted by special grants determined, from 1933, by the Grants Commission. In 1942 the Commonwealth raised war revenue through a uniform income tax, with some reimbursement to the States; this tax has remained as a permanent feature. States can legally charge income tax themselves, but as Commonwealth rates are high and have priority in collection, it is seldom politically expedient for them to do so. States may levy taxes on wages and salaries but not on money received for goods; in 1970 an important High Court ruling forbade taxation by W.A. of Hamersley iron sales. Borrowing for development projects is an important element in State finance. Grants for specific purposes became an increasingly important element and still account for 20% of all federal grants. In 1959 an attempt to formulate the annual general assistance grants on a percentage basis was made, to be adjusted annually in the light of wage increase and population changes: initially this was N.S.W. 34%, Vic. 25%, Qld. 15%, S.A. 11%, W.A. 10·5% and Tas. 4·5%. *For further reading see* J. A. Maxwell: *Commonwealth-State Financial Relations in Australia* (Melbourne, 1967).

Finches Indigenous finches of Aus. belong to the S and SE Asian family Ploceidae, the weaver finches, as distinct from the European finches, family Fringillidae, though some of these have become acclimatised (*see* BIRDS, INTRODUCED). They are small

(7–12 cm. long), often brightly coloured seed-eaters with stout blunt bills. Most construct a dome or bottle-shaped nest of woven grass, bark etc. lined with hair, feathers, fur etc., sometimes with a spout, and usually in thick grass or low bushes. There are over 20 species. The Zebra Finch, *Poëphila guttata* (spotted grass-lover), is widespread in Aus. except Tas., in savannah woodland to desert conditions, usually in flocks. It is about 10 cm. long, of which the tail is almost half, grey-brown with chestnut ear-patch and sides, the latter spotted with white, and narrow black bands on a pale grey throat and pale grey breast. The tail has black and white bars also. Bill and legs are orange. The female is more quietly coloured. The nest is bottle-shaped. The Banded Finch, *P. bichenovii*, of N and E Aus. is a small black-tailed white-rumped finch, with 2 prominent throat and breast crescents on its grey-brown plumage. It often nests near a wasps' nest. The Red-browed Finch or Sydney Waxbill, *Aegintha temporalis*, is an olive-green and light grey bird, with red bill, eye-stripe and rump, often seen in flocks, working over a stream-bank or garden for seeds and insects. The red rump is also prominent in flight in the slightly larger Spotted-side Finch or Diamond Firetail, *Zonaeginthus guttatus* (spotted banded bird) of SE Aus. which is quite distinctive because of its white diamonds on black sides, and almost blue-grey breast. The Beautiful Firetail, *Z. bellus*, of SE coastal Aus. and Tas. is about 13 cm. long with a white-on-black cross on the breast, and Western Firetail, *Z. oculatus*, of coastal SW Aus. has a white-on-black spotted breast and red ear. Among the most beautifully coloured finches are the Gouldian Finch, *P. gouldiae*, of the tropical N, in green, yellow and blue, the male sometimes with scarlet head, and the Crimson Finches, *Neochmia* spp., of the NW and NE. (*See* PLATE 3.) *Further reading* K. Immelmann: *Australian Finches in Bush and Aviary* (Sydney, 1967).

Fingal Tas. 42S/148E On a minor S Esk tributary, this has one of the 3 remaining Tas. coal-mines. Decreasing production has led to forestry schemes of softwood plantations to employ the displaced miners.

Finger Flower (*Cheiranthera linearis*) A member of the dominantly Aus. family Pittosporaceae, this is common in inland E Aus. and has small flat toothed leaves and 2 or 3 blue-purple flowers per stem, with 5 well spread and separated petals, and 5 stamens on one side of the flowers, whence the popular name.

Finke River N.T./S.A. 26S/135E Some 640 miles long, but only carries water in wet seasons although it has permanent waterholes and underground sources. It rises in the NW of the Macdonnell Range* which it leaves through the Glen Helen gorge, and wanders in a wide white sandy bed over Missionary Plain*, before plunging through 64 km. of gorge between Krichauff and James Ranges. Emerging on to widening mud and sand flats, it is joined by the Palmer River on its right bank and flows to the SE towards L. Eyre, which it only rarely reaches, along the Macumba Channel. The Finke was named after a patron by J. McDouall Stuart in 1860.

Fireflies Beetles of the family Lampyridae, their power to emit an intermittent glow from the end of the abdomen being probably to attract the opposite sex.

First Fleet The name given, after its arrival, to the 11 sailing ships which took the first convicts to Botany Bay in 1787–8. Ships, stores and crews were assembled during the 1786–7 winter. Preparations were disorganised until Phillip* took charge; his superb leadership undoubtedly accounted for the success of the hazardous voyage of over 24,000 km. in 8¼ months, often in unknown waters and rough weather, and accomplished with only 32 deaths from illness out of about 1,475 people on board, the credit being largely due to John White*. The total tonnage (3,892 tons) was less than a modest steamer, and that of the individual ships less than an average ferryboat today. The fleet sailed, almost unnoticed, from Portsmouth on the early morning of May 13th 1787, calling at Teneriffe on June 3rd. Some water shortage led to rationing and sickness between there and Rio de Janeiro, where it stayed from August 7th–September 4th, loading food and water as well as tropical plants and seeds, and rum. Crossing the S Atlantic, the Fleet stayed at Cape Town from October 13th–November 12th; further livestock were added to those brought from Eng., and more plants and seeds. Phillip changed from *Sirius* to *Supply* on November 26th and went ahead with the faster transports, *Alexander*, *Scarborough* and *Friendship*. In fact *Supply* was only 40 hours and the others only 20 hours ahead in arriving at Botany Bay by January 20th. The voyage is documented in many journals and letters by officers, seamen and at least one convict. Ships and tonnages were: *Sirius*, Royal Navy Convoy, 520; *Supply* Royal Navy armed tender, 170; transport ships: *Alexander*, 452, *Lady Penrhyn*, 333, *Charlotte*, 335, *Scarborough*, 430, *Friendship*, 274, *Prince of Wales*, 350; store ships: *Fishburn*, 378, *Golden Grove*, 375 and *Borrowdale*, 275. *For further reading see* C. Bateson: *The Convict Ships* (Glasgow, 1959).

Fisher, Andrew (1862–1928) b. Ayrshire, Scotland. Labor Prime Minister 1908, 1910–13, 1914–15. He arrived in Aus. in 1885 as a coal-miner. He entered the first Federal Parliament from Qld. politics, taking over the Labor Party Leadership (1907) and leading Labor's second brief rule in 1908. As Prime Minister (1910–13) he made his greatest mark, in the great heyday of the Aus. Labor Party*. Fisher's patent sincerity, integrity and tenacity lay behind a quiet personality, rather overshadowed by that of Hughes*, to whom he yielded leadership in 1915. At the beginning of the war he pledged Aus. to support the motherland to the last man and last shilling.

Fisheries Some 10,000–12,000 (about 2% of the total in primary industry and 0·3% of the work force) are employed, producing about 54 million kg. of fish worth about $62 million. This is only 4 kg. of fish per head (or 6 kg. allowing for imports), compared with Japan's 40 kg. and U.K.'s 15 kg. Though increasing in some sectors, the industry as a whole is small and ill-developed,

'Supply' at anchor in Botany Bay, with 'Sirius' and convoy coming into sight

even granting the greater availability of fish in the N hemisphere—on existing knowledge at least. Territorial waters extend 12 miles, the first 3 under State and the other 9 under Commonwealth control (12 miles = 19.3 km).

Pelagic fishing, of species caught near the surface in the open ocean, has recently become important for migratory fish, e.g. the tuna and Aus. salmon, and could be expanded. Estuarine fishing has been practised—Aborigines apart —almost from first settlement (*see* BRYANT), and now mullet, bream, prawns etc. are taken from small petrol- or diesel-powered boats in suitable waters from Port Douglas, Qld., 16S/145E, to Ceduna, S.A., 32S/134E (including Tas.), and in W.A. from Esperance, 34S/122E, to Exmouth Gulf, 22S/114E, more sporadically near Broome, 18S/122E, and northern waters near Darwin, N.T., 12S/131E, and Karumba, Qld., 17S/141E. Japanese fleets are active in N waters. Other areas may expand in future, e.g. potentially rich but very rough grounds at the exits of submarine canyons, 32–48 km. off the S coast of the continent, between Esperance and Kangaroo Island. Larger craft, 9–30 m. and diesel-powered, exploit the offshore reefs found off many coasts, mainly by line-fishing for snapper, and various species termed rock-cod. Steam trawlers operated (1915–60) off the SE, but soon overfished the limited area available and were unable to compete with smaller seiners whose catches improved when the trawlers left the field. Partly because of overfishing and partly because the seiners prefer shallower sea bottom, the public's favourite fish, the flathead, has become a rather small proportion of the catch, as against the morwong and other less popular fish. The seiners, in turn, have been finding it difficult to cope with rising costs and overseas competition, despite the considerable protection of distance alone.

Mullet is usually the leading fish,

caught by beach seine net and gill net; in occasional years it is led by similarly caught Aus. salmon or by tuna (by pole and livebait, trolling lines, gill net and purse seine, and important in S.A.). W.A. is the leading State with 30–45% of the Aus. total and over $20 per head of population (Aus. $5), with important catches of Aus. salmon, crayfish* (rock lobster) with export of tails worth $27 million (1972) mainly to U.S., requiring conservation by legislation on size, and prawns. There is a small pearling* industry in the N.

The barracouta, increasingly known by the S African name of snoek, is of growing importance (even being marketed by air from Karumba to Mt. Isa). Abalone* is an important export in SW and SE Aus. Oyster-fishing has been practised in SE Aus. from very early settlement, and after near-extinction through over-fishing, oyster-farming is now a prosperous business—not quite able to meet the large demand.

Fisher's Ghost Used in an opera by J. Gordon and a verse play by D. Stewart*, it relates to the ghost of a man murdered by a convict near Campbelltown, N.S.W., in 1826 and allegedly seen many times since it first appeared and led to discovery of the body.

FISHES, Freshwater Despite its relative poverty in rivers, Aus. has about 150 species of freshwater fish, of which we shall discuss examples of the main families. The Qld. Lungfish* has both gills and a lung-like structure and other features differentiating it from the bony fish; the Lampreys* are also placed in a different class. This is an early-evolved form of fish which has survived in a biologically relatively isolated environment. Some whole families of later-evolved Old World fish are missing from the native fish, such as the carp. (*See* FISHES, INTRODUCED.)

Representative species are listed as follows.

1. The Burramundi*. 2. The Freshwater Herring, *Potamalosa richmondia*, of coastal rivers of N.S.W. and Vic. is a greenish, silvery fish of about 30 cm. long, spawning in salt water in winter. 3. The Hairback Herring or Bony Bream, *Fluvialosa*, of different species in different parts of Aus. are silvery-blue school fish of up to 40 cm., with a distinctive thin spine projecting backward from the back of the dorsal fin. 4. The almost transparent Smelt of 3 species of *Retropinna*, up to 7 cm. long, may be seen in schools in many streams in SE Aus., feeding on mosquito larvae etc. 5. The Derwent Smelt or Tasmanian Troutlet, *Lovettia seallii*, 5 cm. long, is netted in the upper Derwent in autumn and canned. 6. The Australian Grayling, *Prototroctes maraena*, is a brown and yellow fish with a grey side-stripe, good to eat and to fish for, but in retreat before the larger introduced trout. 7. The Native or Mountain Trout, a small scaleless trout of 15–18 cm. long, lacking a fin in the centre of the back, is a representative of the genus *Galaxias* which is widespread from 30° to 60° S mainly in freshwater. 8. The E Aus. Freshwater Catfish, Tandan or Dew-fish, *Tandanus tandanus*, of up to 60 cm. and 3 kg. is one of a number of related genera, distinguished by the whiskers or barbels and long fringing fin uniting rear dorsal, tail and anal fins. 9. Forked-tailed catfishes, e.g. *Netuna*, have the barbels but separate tail, and include species of 60 and 90 cm. long. 10. There are several species of freshwater Eels*. 11. There is also the very thin One Gilled Eel, *Synbranchus gutturalis*, up to 60 cm. long, with a single gill-opening on the throat. 12. The 12-cm.-long, Small-headed Pipefish, *Oxleyana parviceps*, is a relative of the sea-horse and with a somewhat similar snout. 13. The River Garfish, *Reporhamphus ardelio*, of E Aus. has a beaklike lower jaw. 14. The Long Tom, *Stenocaulus krefftii*, of NE Aus. and N.G. has both jaws long, thin and toothed in a beaklike snout. 15. The

Freshwater Soles include the small *Trichobrachirus* of N. Qld. rivers. 16. The small silvery Hardyheads, genus *Atherinosoma*, of the W half of the S of Aus., have an orange yellow or black side stripe, more vivid during excitement; they are related to mullets and some species can move between fresh and salt water; most inland Hardyheads belong to the Line Eye, *Craterocephalus* genus, of which some though not all have a body line at eye level. 17. Several genera receive the popular name of Sunfish, mainly but not exclusively from tropical Aus. and N.G., e.g. the Striped Sunfish, *Rhombosoma trifasçiata*. 18. The Freshwater Mullet of E Aus., *Trachystoma petardi*, cultivated in farmers' dams, commonly reaches 30 cm. in length. 19. The Bass or Perch, *Percalates colonorum*, silvery-olive above and yellow-grey below and up to 58 cm. and 5 kg., is a good angling fish, with a fairly deep body and large scales, and a continuous dorsal fin, the front part fan-like and slightly spined; it is widespread in S and E Aus. and introduced into W.A. 20. The widespread Silver Perch or Bidyan, *Bidyanus bidyanus*, up to 60 cm. long is also a good food fish. 21. The Macquarie Perch of Silvereye, *Macquaria australasica*, and the commercially important Callop or Yellowbelly, *Plectroplites ambiguus*, are similar in formation to the above, but for a rather stumpy tail without the slight swallow-tail element; the former has a blue-grey to brownish back and reaches about 40 cm. long; the latter is warm yellow-brown with an olive-green back and up to 75 cm. long, weighing up to 27 kg. 23. There are several genera of very small perch-like fish, including the Pygmy Perch, genus *Nannoperca*, and the Westralian Pygmy Perch, *Edelia*, and tropical species in N Aus. and N.G., e.g. the Jungle Perch, *Dules rupestris haswelli*, silvery with dark tail markings. 24. The Flabby, Stinker or Qld. Mouthbreeder, genus *Glossamia*. 25. The large brown-spotted olive-green Murray

Cod*, the sporting and commercial king of Aus. freshwater fish. 26. There are several genera of Grunters*. 27. The Archer* or Rifle Fish. 28. The Nursery Fish or Humphead, *Kurtus gulliveri*, a purplish-silver fish with some black markings, has an unusual deep-bodied diamond shape with single deep dorsal fin and a long anal fin; the male has a forehead hump housing a bony cavity in which the female lays the eggs and in which they are incubated in conditions of water circulation and aeration not easy to secure in the muddy tropical waters they inhabit. 29. The Slippery or River Blackfish, *Gadopsis marmoratuş*, is a small but toothsome fish unique to SE Aus., yellow-bellied with green-brown black-blotched back and commonly up to 30 cm. long; it has a long dorsal fin deeper to the rear, a long anal fin and vestigial ventral fin under the gills. 30. The Congolli, Tupong or Sand Trout, *Pseudaphritis bursinus*, of up to 25 cm. long, is attractively spotted and marbled in reddish to greenish-browns; it flourishes in both fresh and salt water. 31. There are many genera of Gudgeon, of very varied size up 15–18 cm. or so, and varied habitats from streams to billabongs, including the Blind Gudgeon, *Milyeringa veritas*. 32. The Gobies are similar to Gudgeons but with the ventral fins fused to form a sucker-like anchor. The Tasman Goby, *Arenigobius tamarensi*, is mainly a saltwater species, contrasting with the isolated spring goby of the L. Eyre area, the Central Aus. Goby, *Chlamydogobius eremius*. 33. The poisonous-spined Bullrout* is found in NE Aus. 34. The small, squat-bodied, poisonous freshwater Toado* is *Aphanacanthus hamiltoni*.

Many saltwater species are recorded as entering freshwater rivers. These include the cartilaginous sharks and sawfish and many bony fishes, large and small, such as barramundi, mullet, threadfin, eels, lesser jewfish or mulloway, the deep-bodied and some-times spectacularly marked small bat-fish, the slender bramah or beach salmon, adults or young of more than one Scat, e.g. *Selenotoca* spp., and several gobies. Also the relative poverty of Aus. and Madagascar in freshwater species may have brought several genera into freshwater here which are marine elsewhere. *For further reading see* G. P. Whitley: *Native Freshwater Fishes of Australia* (Brisbane, 1960); A. H. Weatherley, ed.: *Australian Inland Waters and their Fauna* (Canberra, 1967). J. D. Ogilby's *Edible Fishes and Crustaceans of N.S.W.* (1893) was a landmark.

FISHES, Introduced Aus. freshwater streams and lakes contain introduced sporting and food fish. They include the Rainbow Trout from N America, *Salmo gairdneri*, and the European Brown Trout, *S. trutta*—the former is said to prefer swifter streams but also to be able to stand higher water temperatures. Food supply and rates of growth are great under Aus. conditions, so that experiments have been encouraged in the introduction of the Atlantic Salmon, *S. salar*. Introduced trout have tipped the ecological balance against some smaller but attractive indigenous fish, of the higher and cooler streams of SE Aus. and Tas. (*see* FISHES, FRESHWATER). The English Perch or Redfin, *Perca fluviatilis*, gives moderate sport and food, from many lakes and streams in the S of Aus. Carp, genera *Cyprinus* and *Carassius*, Silver, Golden, Red or White, have been introduced into many rivers of the S of Aus. They are of little use, and have doubtless been one factor in reducing the supply of excellent species for food and sport, such as the Murray Cod,* though silting, over-fishing and reservoirs (which lower water temperatures below the dam) play a part. The well-known mosquito-larvae-eating Topminnow, *Gambusia affinis*, has locally been useful. The Chinese introduced the Snake-head, *Channa striata*, as a food fish, and perhaps the Climbing Perch or Walking Fish, *Anabas testudinarius.*

FISHES, Sea   In Aus. waters there are over 2,000 species—many of course widely distributed over the oceans. Mainly following Whitley's illustrated guide (cited below), we have selected species representing some of the main families, to which Whitley will give further guidance to the interested reader; there are separate articles on the fish marked with an asterisk in the following list of popular names: Angler-Fish*; Baitfish, Pearl Fish, Red Herring or Picarel, *Emmelichthys nitidus*, an occasional visitor in schools to inshore waters of the S of Aus., up to 38 cm. long, silvery-tinged pink to beetroot, edible; Barracouta*; the numerous small, prominently finned Blennies, e.g. the Oyster Blenny, *Cyneichthys anolius*; Bonito, *Cybiosarda elegans* (*see also* MACKEREL); the Box-fish, e.g. *Ostracion tuberculatus* with its intricately ridged carapace, or the Horned Box-fish, *Lactoria cornutus*; Bream and Snapper*; tropical Butterfish or Scat, *Selenotoca multifasciatas*, a grey- green and golden-silver with brown stripes, deep-bodied, front dorsal fin slightly separated, omnivorous; Butterfly-fish, *Chaetodon assarius*, of coral reefs, very narrow but deep-bodied (almost disc-like), yellow with brown, black, white or red bars; Butterfly Mackerel (*see* MACKEREL); Dingo-fish, Sea-pike* or Barracuda*; Dolphin Fish*; Drummer, Silver Drummer or Buffalo Bream, *Segutilum sydneyanus*, very oval and deep-bodied, with continuous dorsal fin, spiny in front —normally vegetarian but takes a fish bait occasionally; Eels*; Flatheads*; Flounders, e.g., *Pseudorhombus anomalus;* the 15 cm. poisonous-spined Fortescue, *Centropogon australis;* the small, strong-jawed, crustacean-eating, spined but non-venomous Frog-fish, e.g. *Halophryne diemensis;* the bony but delicious and commercially important Garfish, e.g. *Reporhamphus australis,*

with beaklike lower jaw; the poisonous-spined Goblin-fish, *Glyptauchen* spp.; Gropers*; the large edible Hairfish, *Trichiurus coxii* of Broken Bay, N.S.W., silvery, ribbon-shaped, with whip-like tail; Herrings*; the snapper-like Hussar, *Lutjanus amabilis*; Jewfish*; John Dory*; Loo*; Luderick*, Nigger, Darkie or Dark-fish; the small deep-bodied Mado, *Atypichthys mado*, giving sport to children from wharves and estuary banks; Mackerel*; Marlins (*see* SWORDFISH *and* MARLINS); Morwong* and Jackass Fish; Mullet*; Mulloway* and Teraglin; Palmer* or Giant Perch; Parrot-fish*; Pennant-fish* or Diamond Trevally; the tough, spined Porcupine-fish, *Atopomycterus nichthemerus*, with poisonous flesh like its relative the Toado*; Rays*; Remoras* or Sucker-fish; Rock-cods*; the deep-sea Roughy, *Trachichthys australis*, with rasp-like scales, sometimes cast ashore in storms; Salmon* or Australian Salmon; Scorpion-fish*; Sea Perches*; Sea-pike*; Sergeant-fish or Black Kingfish, *Rachycentron pondicerianum*, an angling fish of E and SW Aus., growing to 1·8 m. and 68 kg., with hard, flattish head and stubby dorsal spines; Sharks*; Snapper*; Snook*; Sole, e.g. *Synclidopus macleayanus*; Sprats (small herrings), e.g. *Maugeclupea bassensis*; Spinefoot*; Stonefish*; Sucker-fish (*see* REMORAS); Sweet-lips*; Swordfish* and Marlins; Tailor*; Threadfins*; Toado*; Trevally*; Trumpeter Perch*; Trumpeters* and Bastard Trumpeters; Tuna (*see* MACKEREL); Turrum*; Wahoo*; Whitings*; the proverbially tough Wirrah *Acanthistius serratus*, which can intensify or subdue its black-edged blue spots; Wobbegong (*see* SHARKS); Wrasse*; Yellowtail* Kingfish. *For further reading see* G. P. Whitley: *Marine Fishes of Australia* Vols I and II (Brisbane, 1962).

Fishing Spiders   A popular name for the *Dolomedes*, often seen walking on the water to catch low-flying insects and diving for aquatic insects or larval stages, tadpoles etc. These are stalkers without burrows, aggressive and biting readily if provoked.

Fitton, Doris (1897–) b. N.S.W. A theatrical producer who founded the Independent Theatre, Sydney (1930), in a converted garage. It was responsible for introducing works by contemporary dramatists like Pinter, Wesker, Miller and Tennessee Williams to Aus. It provides training for actors, theatre for children and dramatic readings.

Fitzgerald, Charles (1798–1887) b. Ireland. He was the rather autocratic Lt.-Governor of W.A. from 1847–55, the period which sought to restore the flagging colony by transportation from 1850. Geraldton is named after him.

Fitzgerald, Robert David (1902–) b. Sydney. A leading modern poet. As a professional surveyor/engineer, he worked in Fiji, and with the Aus. Government. His verse has almost scientific precision, but often with philosophical, even metaphysical and narrative content, as in *Between Two Tides* (Sydney, 1952), and maturing from an early phase of fantasy to more reflective maturity.

Fitzroy (or **Fitz Roy**), **Sir Charles Augustus** (1796–1858) b. Derbyshire, Eng. Governor of N.S.W. (1845–1855), having governed in Prince Edward Island (1837–41) and the Leeward Islands (1841–5). He was also entitled Governor General of all Aus. colonies from 1851. His aristocratic birth tended his sympathies to the rich squatters, earning the enmity of Lang* and Lowe*, and an allegedly loose private life exacerbated popular criticism. Fitzroy's governorship, carried out with considerable powers of tact and conciliation, if with some lack of drive and efficiency, covered the end of transportation, changes in land tenure, the gold-rushes and self-government.

Fitzroy River Qld. Perennial and formed by the confluence (23S/150E) of the Dawson* and Mackenzie* Rivers; it then cuts NE through Broadsound Range, and turns sharply SE in to rolling dairy country to reach Keppel Bay by 2 main distributaries; above the fork is Rockhampton*. The catchment is 138,500 km². , the largest of the E coast rivers. It is now the subject of an intensive resources survey, covering beef-rearing potential, irrigation, coal, water and power development.

Fitzroy River W.A. 18S/124E Flows for 560 km. SW then NW from the Durack Range to King Sound. The catchment, with its main tributary the 160 km. Margaret River, is 117,000 km.². Both flow only in 'the Wet' and flood severely. The Fitzroy cuts through the spectacular limestone Geikie gorge, a potential dam site if irrigation, now experimental at Camballin* near the mouth, is developed. Much of the sedimentary basin shared with the Lennard River is in Permian rocks with residual hills, such as the Rough Range, coralline limestones (a Devonian 'barrier reef'), basaltic and alluvial soils. Sheep farming developed because of remoteness, but wool is below average on the large deteriorated runs. The Great Northern Highway, mainly sealed to **Fitzroy Crossing**, follows the N edge of the basin from Langi Crossing near the mouth.

Five-corners, Pink Five-corners, Green Five-corners etc. Popular names for the beautiful *Styphelia* genus in the southern heaths or Epacridaceae family, notably *S. triflora*, which grows on light soils in Qld. and N.S.W., and has stubby leaves sheathing the stems and solitary or clustered flowers, pale pink to yellow bells, with 5 groups of yellow hair-like processes inside the tube and very protruding stamens. One of the 4 W.A. species, *S. hainesii*, with long red flowers, extends on to the limestone country flanking the Great Australian Bight.

Flag A common popular name for garden irises or for native Iridaceae (*see* IRIS), e.g. the purple *Patersonia glabrata* or the white *Libertia paniculata*.

Flags The Commonwealth Flag, adopted in 1901 after a competition immediately after Federation, has the Union Jack in the upper hoist, a 7- (originally 6-) pointed star in the lower hoist to represent the 6 States and the Territories, and the Southern Cross* in the fly.

The R.A.A.F. Flag, the Aus. Red Ensign (merchant navy) and White Ensign (R.A.N.—adopted only in 1967) follow a similar motif. The States have individual flags, in each case the State's badge (*see* individual States) inserted in the fly of the plain Blue Ensign. (*See also* PLATE 1.)

Flake The name in the fish markets of E Aus. for the flesh of the edible shark, called the Gummy*—often sold in fish-and-chip shops.

Flame Tree (*Brachychiton acerifolius*) In the widespread pod-bearing family Sterculiaceae, and a relative of the Kurrajong* and the Bottle-tree*. It grows to 36 m. by 90 cm. in the coastal scrubs of E Aus. It has a long trunk bearing fibrous fissured grey bark, generally lobed but variably shaped leaves up to 18 cm. long, conspicuous red flowers in compound heads to 18 cm. long, and boat-like pods, generally grouped in fives. (*See* PLATE 8.)

Flannel-flower A popular name applied to various species of *Actinotus*, in the world-wide family Umbelliferae (with radiating stalked flowers). The small flowers are in a tight head like the centre of a daisy, surrounded by super-ficially petal-like velvety bracts which give the popular name. The white N.S.W. Flannel-flower, *A. helianthi*, is a hairy plant with grey-green to silvery, hairy parsley-shaped leaves; the attractive Pink Flannel-flower, *A forsythii*, of the Blue Mts. has more slender leaves. The W.A. *A. leucocephalus* and *A. superbus* have large, feathery bracts.

Flatheads A group of about 40 species of sea fish from mainly temperate waters, some of which are very important in commercial fisheries. They have a very depressed, flat head, long slender body, usually 30–60 cm. long but sometimes more, and very long and broad fins on the back, front and rear being just separated, and on the rear belly. The main species are the Sand Flatheads, *Platycephalus caerule-punctatus* and *P. arenarius*, the Dusky Flathead, *Planiprora fusca*, of many estuaries in Aus. except the N usually of 0·9–1·8 kg., and the Tiger Flathead, *Neoplatycephalus richardsoni*, which preys on other fish, and on crustaceans, shrimps and crabs and is caught in trawls in deeper water offshore. The Deepsea or Spook Flathead, *Oplichthys ogilbyi*, reaches 45 cm. or so, occurs in even deeper water and is even thinner in proportion to larger fins.

Flatworms—*see* HELMINTHS.

Flax Used for fibre; it is produced from *Linum usitatissimum* and was a winter crop not grown in Aus. since 1965, but widely grown in war-time in the E States. There is a considerable acreage of flax for oil (*see* OILSEEDS). The plant has run wild in places. It resembles the native flax *K. marginale* except that the former is annual, the latter perennial. Both are delicate herbs, with 5-petalled blue flowers and small pointed leaves. New Zealand Flax, *Phormium tenax* (also on Norfolk Island), is totally unrelated, a member of the lily* family. In the early 19th century it was cultivated round Sydney to provide cordage for ships and a possible export. The group of long fibrous sword-shaped leaves resembles the native Settler's Flax, *Gymnostachys anceps*, in the arum lily family, with small arum-like flowers on stalks about a foot long. Flax Lily or Smooth Flax Lily, *Dianella laevis*, is an attractive blue liliaceous flower of the better coastal soils of E Aus. (*see* LILIES).

Fleas Small, narrow-bodied, wingless, blood-sucking, jumping insects of the Order Siphonaptera. Eggs are laid in the ground, warm sandy soils being particularly favourable, sinking in a little to hatch, or hatching in cracks etc.; hence the occasional plagues of fleas in parts of W.A. Larvae are legless, with a distinct head, and live on organic matter in the soil, house dust etc. until they spin a cocoon for the pupa stage. Some species leave the host after a blood-meal, but some do not, including the Stickfast Flea, *Echidnophaga gallinacea*, a serious pest, clustering on poultry especially around the head. There is some interchange of hosts of the more mobile fleas, for instance a common human flea, *Pulex irritans*, is sometimes found on poultry and pigs (but rarely cats and dogs), while cat and dog fleas will bite man. A rat flea, e.g. the Indian *Xenopsylla cheopis*, is dangerous if rodent plague* is present.

Flies Insects distinguished as the True Flies, Order Diptera (i.e. 2-winged), have only the front pair of wings developed as such, the residuals of the rear pair being 2 clubbed stalks used to assist balance in flight. (Rarely, mainly in parasitic species, one or both these pairs may be vestigial or absent.) All True Flies have a sucking mouth, and consume liquid food, but blood-sucking species naturally have a piercing mechanism also. True Flies have 4 stages: egg, larva (often a legless maggot but in some families aquatic), pupa and adult, though the larvae of some are born alive. The 2,000 species of True Flies in Aus. may be classified in various ways; here, main families with representative species or genera, are grouped into 2 Sub-Orders.
I. Long-Antennae True Flies, Sub-Order Nematocera These are mainly rather small and delicate flies, such as the mosquitoes, often with aquatic larvae; the antennae are relatively long, with at least 7 segments. The main families are included in the following list.

1. The Mosquitoes* comprise the family Culicidae. 2. Gnats and non-biting Midges, Chironomidae, are similar in appearance to mosquitoes. They emerge, species after species, through the summer. The larvae of some species are red, especially in polluted water, and are sometimes called blood-worms. A typical genus of the Plumed Gnats is *Chironomus*. The Bibionidae are somewhat stouter gnats and breed in damp soils including gardens. 3. Biting Midges, Ceratopogonidae, e.g. genus *Culicoides*, are a great pest to man near swamps, especially mangrove swamps; sometimes wrongly known as sandflies. 4. Crane Flies or Daddy Longlegs, Tipulidae, e.g. the genus *Macromastix*, breed in damp places; the larvae are reputed to destroy lawns. 5. Moth-midges Psychodidae, like small 2-winged moths, often seen on windows, include the Sandflies, genus *Phlebotomus*, widespread but apparently with relatively little contact with man, fortunately, since they are known vectors of disease in other countries. 6. Fungus Flies, Mycetophilidae, are small delicate flies which, unusual for this Sub-Order, have maggot-like larvae living on the flesh of fungi (and often spoiling edible mushrooms); one of the remarkable Aus. species is the luminous cave Glow-worm, *Arachnocampa tasmaniensis*—mainland species exist, not yet identified. 7. Gall Midges, Cecidomyiidae, are minute delicate flies whose larvae live in small galls on eucalypts, tea-trees and some grasses.
II. Short-Antennae True Flies, Brachycera. These may be regarded as 'typical' flies, with short 3-segmented antennae ending in a feather-like or needle-like process in line with the other segments; all have maggot-like larvae, normally pupating in the soil. Families and representative species are included.

1. March-flies, Horse Flies or Horse Stingers of the family Tabanidae, such as *Tabanus indefinitus*, are large stout flies superficially like a blow-fly, but

with a disc-like head and strong straight jaws. Many species have nectar-eating males and blood-sucking females, the latter capable of inflicting a formidable bite, such as those which mar the pleasures of walking on the sub-alpine meadows on the Kosciusko summit plateau. There are also some beautifully marked vegetarian species. 2. Soldier Flies, Stratiomyiidae, such as *Neoexaireta spiniger* common in Sydney gardens, are rather slender shining flies, with long wings, one folding over the other, gauzy but with coloured patches on them. 3. Assassin Flies or Robber Flies, Asilidae, are medium to large (9-cm. wing-span in some *Blepharotes*), slender but with a stout rounded thorax, rather separate disc-like head, long stout proboscis, and bristly grasping legs. These are powerful flies able to catch other insects on the wing, even bees and dragonflies. 4. Bee Flies, Bombyliidae, are hovering and buzzing flies of which some genera have a close superficial resemblance to bees, notably the Golden Bee Fly, *Sisyromyia aurata*. 5. Water Cruisers, Empididae, include the Grey Water Cruiser, genus *Empis*, with grey- and black-banded, silvery-haired body and slender black legs with gingery hairs, often seen cruising above stream or pond. 6. Stilt Flies, Dolichopodidae, are small but long-legged metallic green-bronze-bodied flies often seen on or around trees, where they prey on small soft-bodied insects including aphids. 7. Hover-flies, Syrphidae, some of which are even more bee-like than the Bee Flies, hover and hum around garden or bush plants on a sunny day. Some foreign species are pests of garden bulbs etc., but Aus. species spend the larval stage in rotten wood or, as in the common Hover Fly or Drone Fly, *Eristalis tenax*, in polluted water, the long larval breathing-tube attracting the name of 'rat-tailed maggot'. 8. Fruit Flies, Trypetidae, are mainly small gauzy-winged flies with attractive bodies, striped in orange, brown and yellow. Native species include some so far living entirely apart from man, e.g. one found in the summer of 1964–5 in the fruit of mangroves in swamps near Sydney; another pest is the Qld. Fruit Fly, *Strumeta tryoni*. 9. Scavenger Flies, Sapromyzidae, e.g. the glossy-green-bodied *Lonchaea rugosifrons*, tend to lay their eggs in damaged fruit etc. (in this species, tomatoes and potatoes). 10. House-flies and Bush-flies, Muscidae, have a strong family resemblance and show, under a hand-lens, roundish white plates under the wing-fastenings. Common species include the introduced Common and Lesser House Fly, *Musca domestica* and *Fannia canicularis*, and the all-pervading Bush Fly, *Musca sorbens*, of open country, noted as settling on the eyes, mouth and nose from the very first Dutch landing. 11. Blowflies, Calliphoridae, include the small green blowfly *Lucilia cuprina*, which lays its eggs on fouled wool on sheep, from which maggot infestation begins, and the larger Lesser Brown Blowfly, *Calliphora augur*, with yellowish-brown abdomen and steel-blue tip, a common invader of houses. 12. Flesh Flies, Sarcophagidae, have bristly bodies, with longitudinal bands on the thorax and a chequered pattern on the abdomen, and lay living maggots on carcases. 13. Bristle-flies, Tachinidae, including the genus *Rutilia*, are large bristly, metallic blue, green, bronze or purple flies which parasitise caterpillars, saw-fly larvae, adult butterflies, grasshoppers etc. 14. Bot-flies, Oestridae, include introduced parasites of domestic stock. The eggs are licked up from the wool or fur of the animal, and the larval stage is spent in the intestines of the animal, passing out in the faeces to pupate in the ground. A native species *Tracheomyia macropi* is a parasite of kangaroos. 15. Louse-flies including Sheep Keds, Hippoboscidae, are wingless flattened insects with strong-clawed grasping legs, showing extreme adaptation to blood-sucking parasitism on particular hosts. The

Sheep Ked, *Melophagus ovinus*, causes irritation to the animal and damage to its fleece.

Flinders Chase S.A. 36S/137E A reserve of 550 km.² at the W tip of Kangaroo Island, where freedom from rabbits and foxes allows native flora and fauna to survive.

Flinders Grass A popular name for the 12 or so Aus. species of the genus *Iseilema*, found mainly in heavy soils in N inland Aus. along with Mitchell Grass*. Flinders Grass grows quickly after rains, giving valuable forage, green or dry, or even dry and shrivelled on the ground. The Small Flinders Grass, *I. membrenaceum*, has a branching, weak-stemmed habit, with many small seed-heads in leaf-axils. Other species are known as Red, Bull, Brittle and Scented Flinders Grass (*I. vaginiflorum, I. macratherum, I. fragile* and *I. windersii*).

Flinders Island Tas. 40S/148E The largest of the Furneaux Islands*, covering 2,000 km.². It is higher in the W and S, reaching 501 m. About a quarter is cleared for mixed livestock farming; the remainder is heath, especially along the swamps and lagoons of the E coast. Lady Barron on the S coast has a crayfish industry, and a little alluvial tin is found.

Flinders, Matthew (1774–1814) b. Lincolnshire, Eng. One of the greatest explorers who, but for his internment and early death, would certainly have contributed even more. He made friends with Bass* when both accompanied Hunter to N.S.W. in 1794. Together they examined the coasts S of Sydney soon after their arrival, in the tiny *Tom Thumb*. Convinced of the existence of a strait between Van Diemen's Land and N.S.W., they proved it in the *Norfolk* (1798) when, with Flinders in command, they sailed round Van Diemen's Land. He dedicated his valuable observations to Sir Joseph Banks* and interested him in a proposed circumnavigation

of the continent. The Admiralty equipped him with the *Investigator* for the purpose of charting the coast, but refused to allow his bride to accompany him: when he left Spithead in July 1801, he was not to see her again for 9½ years. From Cape Leeuwin he charted much of the S coast previously unknown, although he met with Baudin* at Encounter Bay. Keeping close inshore all the way, he was forced to return to Sydney with the leaky *Investigator*. On his way home again with his charts he was first shipwrecked on Porpoise Island, 1,127 km. N of Sydney, and later on calling at Mauritius, was detained on parole for 6½ years, in spite of having documents promising him safe passage and no molestation from the French. He was finally released, and reached London in 1810, broken in health but able to complete *A Voyage to Terra Australis*, published just before his death. His grandson was **Flinders Petrie**, the great Egyptologist. *For further reading see* E. Scott: *The life of Captain Matthew Flinders* (Sydney, 1914) and the facsimile of Flinders's *Observations on the coasts* (Adelaide, 1965).

Flinders Ranges S.A. 32–4S/138E A highland region reaching 1,189 m. which continues the Mt. Lofty Ranges beyond Peterborough, and shares their origin as Precambrian sediments uplifted along faults, but with an increasingly more barren and arid landscape northwards. The Flinders Range, described by Flinders in 1802 as 'a ridge of high rocky mountains', is the western edge, named in 1839 by Gawler, following Eyre's first inland journey. The discovery of further hills beyond the Willochra Plains* led to the plural form later. Pastoralists and wheat farmers have advanced and retreated with fluctuating periods of good rain and drought, and with copper-mining from 1860–1900. They have left evidence of greater settlement in abandoned homesteads, reduced townships, e.g. Blinman, Hammond, Orroroo, and ghost towns*. The stark beauty of vivid rocks and spring flowers has been painted by Heysen*; the geology was unravelled by Mawson. Increasingly travellers visit Wilpena Pound* and Aroona Valley*, though seldom penetrating to the N ramparts of the Gammon Range*. *For further reading see* H. Mincham: *The Story of the Flinders Ranges* (Adelaide, 1964).

Flinders River The longest river in Qld., rising on the SW slopes of the Gregory Range, 20S/143E, curving NW and flowing seasonally for 840 km. to the Gulf of Carpentaria. The catchment is 108,000 km.^{2}. Its main right-bank tributary, the Saxby, is linked with the Norman River by anabranches. Burke* reached tidal waters on the main of the 2 Flinders outlets in 1861. It had been discovered and named in 1841 by Stokes. The upper basin is sheep country, dependent on many bores, with emphasis changing to cattle as tussock grass is replaced by taller grasses and woodland near the Gulf.

Flindersia A genus of rain-forest trees in the world-wide Rutaceae family, found in sub-tropical and tropical Aus. and extending into SE Asia. It includes *F. australis*, the Crow's Ash or Flindowzee of Qld. and so-called Teak of N.S.W., the Yellowwood, *F. xanthoxyla*, of S Qld. and N.S.W., the Prickly Leopard-wood Tree or Prickly Pine, *F. strzeleckiana*, of the mid-west of Qld. and the more inland Leopard-wood, *F. maculosa*. Further N in Qld. are the Silver Silkwood, *F. acuminata*, Queensland Maple, *F. brayleyana*, Cairns Hickory, *F. ifflaiana*, and others.

FLORA Aus. is unusually rich in plant species, which number some 12,000 on present classification, with more in N.G. The individual flavour of many Aus. landscapes owes much to the trees, shrubs, herbs and grasses (*see also* VEGETATION), distinctive as compared with plants and plant associations in similar climates, soils and sites elsewhere; yet many Aus. plants are members of widespread or world-wide families. Thus the largely Aus. and distinctive *Eucalyptus** is a particularly large and complex genus in the tropical family Myrtaceae; the widespread Saltbush and Bluebush of inland Aus. belong to the cosmopolitan family Chenopodiaceae and even some of the main genera are also cosmopolitan. 4 uniquely Aus. families are small and relatively insignificant.

1. Akaniaceae has a single species *Alkania hillii*, a small rain-forest tree of NE N.S.W. and SE Qld., with 75-cm. multiple leaves, large pink-white multiple flower-heads and reddish 'turnipweed' timber, smelling as the name implies. 2. Brunoniaceae has a single species *Brunonia australis*, a blue-flowered herb common in inland E Aus. closely allied to the Goodeniaceae family see *Goodenia**. 3. Cephalotaceae has a single species *Cephalotus follicularis*, the Western Australian Pitcher-plant, with pitcher leaves in which insects are trapped and digested. 4. Tremandraceae has 22 species (13 in W.A.) of heath-like plants in 3 genera: *Tremandra* (W.A., with broad toothed leaves), *Platytheca* (W.A., blue-flowered) and *Tetratheca* including various pink-belled heaths of W.A. and E Aus., the latter including Black-eyed Susan. There are also wholly Aus. families of smaller plants, e.g. mosses. The genera *Byblis* (2 insectivorous spp.) and *Petermannia*, found only in Aus., are sometimes placed in separate families.

Families having a greater development in Aus. than elsewhere include those listed below.

1. Centrolepidaceae includes very small ground plants, e.g. the Tufted Centrolepis, *C. fasciata*, of SE Aus. 2. Proteaceae, a large southern family, includes Banksias* and Grevilleas*. 3. Epacridaceae, a family of shrubby, often sclerophyllous heaths* mostly of Aus. and N.Z., occupies a similar place in the vegetation to the family of true

heaths, Ericaceae, in the N hemisphere. 4. Stackhousiaceae, a family of 3 genera of flowering herbs, includes the creamy, fragrant upright Candles, *Stackhousia monogyna*, common in much of E Aus. 5. Myoporaceae has about 4 genera and 140 species of bushes or small trees in Aus., bearing dry or succulent stoned fruit, e.g. the brown-and-yellow tubular- to bell-flowered Spotted Emu Bush*. 6. Goodeniaceae, with 13 genera and 300 species, includes: *Dampiera* (attractive deep-blue flowering shrubs, e.g. *D. stricta* in E Aus. and *D. linearis* in W.A.); *Goodenia* (including yellow-flowering herbs such as the trumpet-bearing multiple head of *G. stelligera* in many coastal sites in E Aus.); the large-flowered heath-like *Leschenaultia*, mainly in W.A.; the widespread flowering herbs of *Scaevola* (e.g. the light-blue scented Fan Flower*); the two creeping perennial herbs of *Selliera*, one in W.A. and one in E Aus.; and the widespread mainly yellow *Velleia*, with a woody perennial rootstock. 7. An interesting and predominantly Aus. family is Stylidiaceae, mainly the genus *Stylidium*, the Trigger Plants*. 8. The Grass-tree* family, *Xanthorrhoeaceae*, formerly included with the Lily* family are largely Aus. 9. Several small families allied to the garden *Magnolia* are largely Aus. 10. The Casuarinaceae with only one genus *Casuarina* (the She-oaks) are largely Aus.

The Eucalypts* (Myrtaceae family) and the Wattles* (*Acacia*) each have about 600 Aus. species and contribute much to the distinctive character of the vegetation*, the former dominating over very large areas. The Wattles are members of the Mimosaceae family (formerly part of the Leguminosae) for they have much in common with the mimosas of N America.

In the divided Leguminosae, Aus. has also many of the great Papilionaceae or Pea* family—mainly climbers. —and many of the Caesalpinaceae family—mainly trees—with mimosa-like leaf and pea-like flowers. Distinctively Aus. Pea genera include *Daviesia*, *Dillwynia* and *Pultenaea*.

The *Callitris* genus, Cypress Pines* mainly Aus., belong to the world-wide Cupressaceae or Cypress family. There are many herbs, shrubs and trees of world-wide families, and only a few examples can be given. The Malvaceae or Mallows include the Cottonwood* as well as *Hibiscus** flowering creepers, and native Cotton-plants*. Urticaceae include native nettles*, some herbs and the well-known Nettle* or Stinging Tree, as well as the introduced 'domestic' nettle. Many distinctively Aus. flowers are in such families as the Liliaceae or Lilies*, the Compositae or Daisies* including, e.g., the blue Burr Daisy, *Calotis dentex*, whose burrs are a nuisance to wool-farmers, and the Everlastings*; the Ranunculaceae, or Buttercups, with *Clematis*, native and introduced; and many bulbous flowers of the Amaryllidaceae, including the garden narcissus and jonquil and distinctive flowers such as the Kangaroo Paw* and *Iridaceae*, the Iris family.

Mosses and lichens are mainly of cosmopolitan families and species, but there are purely Aus. mosses such as the single-species family Bryobartramiaceae of mountain terrain in Central Vic., and a characteristic association of mosses and lichens in the S of W.A.

Some tree genera have Antarctic affinities: the Southern Beeches* *Nothofagus*, very similar to the N hemisphere *Fagus* of the family Fagaceae; the Araucariaceae, important in the S of S America, include some Kauri Pines*, genus *Agathis*, of historic importance in N.Z., and the Bunya-bunya*, Hoop Pine* and Norfolk Island Pine*. The Podocarpaceae*, conifers with a seed exposed on a fleshy process, the usual cone being much reduced, include the Brown and Black Pines, the Celerytop* and Huon Pines* and various shrub-like forms. There are also mainly herb and bush families, e.g. the Pittosporaceae, which includes the

Native Frangipani* and the Sweet Bursaria (a rare instance of a native noxious weed).

On the tropical side, the rain-forests of E Aus. especially Qld. have Indo-Malayan affinities, while there are small residual occurrences in NW Aus. Examples are: the pod-bearing Sterculiaceae including the Bottle Tree*, Kurrajong* and certain Mangroves* (but also many trees in Central America, including *Theobroma*, the cultivated cocoa; the Moraceae, which includes many Figs*, widespread in many tropical areas; the Meliaceae or Mahoganies* including the so-called Cedars* of Aus.; the Verbenaceae, including the woolly shrubs of W.A., White Mangroves* and the introduced American flowering bush pest *Lantana**; and the Rhizophoraceae, including the tall Red Mangroves.

Thus, the flora has representatives of many widespread or world-wide families but is very rich in local genera. Many species have affinities with cooler S hemisphere regions, though the rain-forest species are mostly allied to those of the Indo-Malayan region. W.A. is unusually rich in local genera and species, families such as the Proteaceae being well represented. (*See also* BOTANISTS.) *For further reading see* A. M. Blombery: *A Guide to Native Australian Plants* (Sydney, 1968).

Flukes or **Trematodes** A Class of Flatworms or Platyhelminthes (*see* WORMS), somewhat similar to free-living Turbellaria, e.g. the Land Planarians, but with the sucker characteristic of parasitic worms. As a family they are mainly fish parasites with a simple cycle of aquatic eggs, aquatic free-swimming larvae, with a short larval life during which they must find a suitable host, and the adult phase hooked on to the host and obtaining sustenance from it. The well-known liver-fluke of sheep, *Fasciola hepatica*, is larger than most of the family and more complex in its cycle. The adult form may be seen in the liver like a white, slowly moving leaf. Enormous numbers of eggs are excreted, but only those reaching water have even a chance of continuing the cycle; the larvae are motile, and swim in search of a particular water-snail *Lymnaea tomentosa* (unlike other wet-pasture or swamp snails, the 'screw' on the shell is right-handed, looking down on the point). The larvae develop further in the snail, then emerge as free-swimming cercaria which then encyst on wet grass. Some are ingested by browsing sheep, the cyst cover is dissolved by the sheep's gastric juices, and the free larvae travel up the bile-duct to develop to adult form in the liver.

The somewhat comparable cycle of Bilharzia or Schistosomiasis has never developed to any extent in Aus., even following the return of servicemen with bilharzia from infected theatres of war, but the avian blood fluke cycle *Austrobilharzia terrigalensis* is maintained, and man is occasionally affected to the extent of developing swimmer's itch, but the swimming larval stage does not penetrate far or live long in man; dermatitis develops but not bilharzia.

Flycatchers A group of small perching insectivorous birds of Asia and Aus., with broad beaks with bristles round them. They include the Fantails and the Jacky Winter*. The Restless Flycatcher, *Seisura* (tail-shaker) *inquieta*, is about 15 cm. long, mostly tail, black above and white below though sometimes yellowish on the breast, often seen catching spiders from the corners of windows; its occasional nickname of Scissors-grinder comes from its single harsh call-note followed by a repeated grinding sound. (It somewhat resembles the Willy Wagtail* but the Wagtail has the black of head and back going right round the throat.) The beautiful grass and bark nest, cup-shaped and bound with cobweb and decorated with lichen, with 3 creamy eggs, is pugnaciously defended. Other species include the very broad-billed Boat-billed Flycatcher, *Machaerirhynchus flaviventer* (yellow-bellied swordbill), of N Qld., of which the cock bird is a spectacular black and golden yellow, and the ruff-necked black-and-white Pied Flycatcher, *Arses* (shouting) *kaupi*, often seen walking up tropical forest trees in search of insects.

Flying Doctor Service The Royal Flying Doctor Service to provide medical and dental service to outback areas is a non-profit-making organisation receiving Commonwealth financial assistance towards maintenance and capital costs. It is organised from 7 centres, covering sections with slightly different arrangements for charges for specific services, voluntary donations or fixed annual levies on graziers.

The service began with the remarkable Presbyterian minister the Rev. John Flynn*. He saw the need for a link between radio communications and air transport to relieve one of the most nagging fears of loneliness, that of illness or injury out of reach of medical help. With Alf Tregear he evolved the now famous 2-way pedal radio* used in every outback station or field survey party, and put his plan into action, at first with the help of QANTAS, from Cloncurry, Qld., in 1927. Standard first-aid sets are issued to isolated homesteads etc.; medical advice is given over the radio, and if need be, a doctor flies out to bring the patient back by air, saving time, often pain and even lives. A notable Qld. figure in the service was A. R. S. Vickers (1901–1967).

Flying Foxes or **Giant Fruit-bats** (*see* BATS) Large bats of which a few damage orchards in E Aus. in the course of very large migrations. *For further reading see* F. N. Ratcliffe: *Flying Fox and Drifting Sand* (London, 1938).

Flynn, John (1880–1951) b. Moliagul, Vic. He was a Presbyterian Minister, whose major interests lay with the needs of people of the outback. After a period of teaching, he took up missionary work, and in 1912 presented a vivid report to the Presbyterian Church which led to the establishment of the Aus. Inland Mission* which he organised until his death. One of its major contributions, and Flynn's best remembered achievement, was the (Royal) Flying Doctor Service*. Flynn was a true visionary, but also had the attributes of determination, persistence and administrative ability. The vivid book *Flynn of the Inland*, by I. L. Idriess (Sydney, 1932) gave him tremendous publicity, but is not very accurate. A more detailed and recent work is *John Flynn: Apostle to the Inland*, by W. S. McPheat (London, 1963).

Fodder Crops, apart from sown grasses, medick* and clovers, which are specifically grown to feed stock in 'off-seasons' for natural growth; they are important in the Vic. dairying area and increasingly for sheep and cattle-fattening elsewhere. They include hay* and green crops, the latter being second to wheat in crop acreage (18%) and including lucerne, oats, wheat, barley, sorghum, maize, rye, legumes,

Flying Fox, body about 30 cm. long

peas, beans, lupins (W.A.) and ground-nuts (Qld.). Commercial crops unlikely to yield highly in any year may also be cut or grazed as fodder. Ensilage is increasing, encouraged by subsidy and now exceeds 1 million tonnes a year.

Football This almost certainly arrived in Aus. very soon after the First Fleet, and was played by the garrison and soon the civilians. Development was rapid after the mid-19th century: Rugby* was introduced and gave rise to the unique Aus. version widely known as Australian Rules*; the break between amateur Rugby Union and professional League was in 1907. Soccer*, the fourth code played, was introduced in the 1880s but did not achieve wide popularity until after 1945.

Forbes N.S.W. 33S/148E (7,467 in 1971) On the Lachlan* and the railway to Cootamundra, it was a gold-rush town in the 1860s, surviving and now growing as a local service, market centre with small manufacturing (flour, dairy, canning, cement, timber and joinery). Its hinterland includes not only pastoral country in the Western Slopes region, but river flats now irrigated from Wyangala Dam*, including the large Jemalong district.

Forbes, Sir Francis (1784–1841) b. Bermuda. First Chief Justice, N.S.W. He arrived in Aus. in 1824. Having been involved in the drafting of the N.S.W. Judicature Act, while Chief Justice of Newfoundland, Forbes was keenly interested in its implementation, although he was unhappy about his supreme power of veto if legislation 'were repugnant to the laws of England'; he invoked it in his disagreement with Darling* to prevent press censorship. *For further reading see* C. H. Currey: *Sir Francis Forbes* (Sydney, 1968).

Forde, Francis Michael (1890–) b. Mitchell, Qld. Prime Minister of Aus. from 6th–13th July 1945.

Foreign Affairs, Department of Name given in 1970 to former Department of External Affairs*.

Forest Resources There is a timber production over 10 million m.³ (for sawing, peeling, slicing or pulping) —about 75% from hardwoods, valued at around $130 millions a year (about 0·25% of the gross national product). There is a small export of hardwoods, decreasing as local demand rises, and a considerable import of the easily worked softwoods in which Aus. forests are generally deficient. Employment in forestry (excluding sawmills) is only 9,000—under 2% of all primary industry. Over 200 million ha. (about 25%) of Aus. bear some kind of forest, but this includes scrub and savannah woodland only rarely of economic significance, and only about 6% carries substantial woodland (about the same proportion as U.K.), although it represents over 35% of the inhabited area, since people and trees are both concentrated in the wetter coastal belts. For the same reason there has been much ruthless clearing in cultivable areas, inevitable but wasteful, and early ruthless exploitation of timber species elsewhere, as settlement spread. Total State and other reserves of forestry value, at some 16 million ha., are probably satisfactory in relation to anticipated population, especially in view of the use of timber substitutes, but much of this is in poor condition, much of the rather scarce exploitable timber is inaccessible at present costs, and in places there is much need of forest expansion to combat soil erosion and conserve water (sometimes involving inter-state collaboration, as in the upper Murray area).

The very large forested area in Qld. includes relatively limited areas of tropical and sub-tropical rain-forests with many valuable cabinet woods scattered among their myriad species (*see* TREES). Only small resources remain of the native softwoods, hoop, bunya and kauri pines. Farther S on the E coast, mainly eucalypt forests of N.S.W. and Vic., the leading States in timber production, include valuable timber species such as ironbarks, various blue gums, blackbutt, and formerly the red cedar. The Gippsland forests have valuable stands of mountain ash. Farther inland the drier woodlands include valuable ironbarks and the workable yet hard and termite-resistant cypress pine, with tough, valuable red gum timber from the riverain forests. The forests of Tas., temperate and very dense and tall, include cabinet hardwoods and, using a special process, timber for pulp, with still some softwoods from the huon, celery-top and King William pines. The Tas. industry is over 12% of that of Aus. by value on under 1% of the land. The small wet area in the SW of W.A. yields the versatile jarrah and structural timber from the karri, as well as other timbers in small quantities; the industry is well organised.

Government and private plantations of mainly exotic conifers now total over 404,000 ha. and to reduce the deficieney in softwoods Commonwealth Government loans are used to encourage planting—it is hoped at the rate of 30,000 ha. per year. The N American *Pinus radiata* is very important, with *P. caribea* and *P. taeda* in more tropical areas, and *P. radiata* or *P. insignis* is the main tree in the important plantations of under-forested S.A. which date largely from the Depression of the 1930s. *For further reading see* A. Rule: *Forests of Australia* (Sydney, 1967).

Forgan Smith, William (1887–1953) b. Perthshire, Scotland. He arrived in Aus. in 1912 as a painter, rising to be Labor Premier of Qld. (1932–42). During the Depression he vigorously and imaginatively used State resources to counteract the worst effect of unemployment, by public works.

Forlonge (or **Forlong**) A family of remarkable pioneer settlers in Tas., Vic. and N.S.W. **William** (1811–1890) arrived in Tas. in 1829, with a flock of 76 Saxon sheep selected from German studs and driven on foot by himself, his brother Andrew and their mother Eliza, to Hamburg and then across Eng. to Liverpool. After a period in Tas., the brothers were among the early squatters in the Port Phillip area from 1838. A widowed aunt, Janet Templeton, had extensive properties in N.S.W. and Vic. from 1831. The family were descended from French Huguenots.

Forrest, Sir John (1847–1918) b. Bunbury, W.A. An explorer and statesman. Trained as a surveyor, he made his first exploratory journey to follow up a report of possible Leichhardt* remains in 1869, and later 2 well-organised W–E crossings of W.A. In 1870 he reversed Eyre's* route, and in 1874 explored the headwaters of Murchison River and thence over to the Musgrave Ranges. He was the first Premier of W.A. (1890–1901, a period which covered the gold-rushes) and he was concerned with the great water scheme to the gold-fields and railway and port construction. He had turbulent relations with the miners, and it has been suggested, introduced women's suffrage as a counterweight to their vote. During the Federal negotiations, realising the problems raised by W.A.'s isolation, he fought for and obtained the promise of the Trans-continental railway, and tariff benefits for W.A. as a price for joining the Commonwealth. He represented Swan in Federal Parliament from 1901–1918, and held several Cabinet posts, but was much less effective or popular than in his own State politics. He was created 1st Baron Forrest of Bunbury in 1918, the first Aus.-born peer. His brother, **Alexander** (1849–1901), acted as his second in command on his 1870 and 1874 journeys, and discovered the pastures of the NW of W.A. between the Fitzroy River and Leopold Ranges, Ord River and Victoria River in 1879.

Fortescue River W.A. 22S/117E Rises in the Ophthalmia Range E of the Hamersley Range* and flows very sporadically for 645 km. NE then NW through a rift valley to a mangrove and mud-lined mouth. Its tributaries, e.g. the Wittenoom, leave the bordering scarps in gorges.

Forth River Tas. 42S/146E Flows 97 km. N from Mt. Pelion West in the Central Plateau, falling steeply to the rich farmlands of the N coast plain, and forming the central stream in the Mersey–Forth power development. (*See* TASMANIA, POWER.)

Fossils Aus. fossils, while having unique elements, can, like the rock strata, be correlated with those elsewhere. The following time-scale gives **Eras**, subdivided into *Periods*, with age in brackets in million years, and major features of life development as recorded in fossils. (E) indicates types now extinct; others have modern forms.

Precambrian *Archaean* (2,000–3,000) and *Lower Proterozoic* (1,000–2,000): traces of primitive algae and worms. *Upper Proterozoic* (600–1,000): clear evidence of jellyfish.
Palaeozoic *Cambrian* (490–600): archaeocyathids, funnel-shaped sponge-like creatures (E); trilobites, marine crustaceans (E); brachiopods like modern lamp shells*; radiolaria, microscopic single-celled organisms. *Ordovician* (430–490): numerous graptolite fauna (E), whose development is used in dating strata; cephalopods*; gastropods*. *Silurian* (410–430): first land plants such as Baragwanathia (E); corals. *Devonian* (355–410): first vertebrates mainly fish; amphibian footprints found in Vic. (1972) oldest in world. *Carboniferous* (275–355): not the main coal era in Aus., though swamp plants like *Lepidodendroids* (E) reached tree size; moss animals*. *Permian* (220–275): brachiopods* the main fauna; crinoids (sea-lilies*); many insects; reptiles; coal-forming plants.
Mesozoic *Triassic* (180–220): flora better represented than fauna; reptile tracks in freshwater lake deposits. *Jurassic* (135–180): rich marine fauna including ammonites (E); dinosaur and and other footprints. *Cretaceous* (70–135): first flowering plants; dominance of marine fauna.
Cainozoic *Tertiary* (1–50): some species now extinct but also modern forms evolved, including many vertebrates, fish, reptiles, sharks, birds, marsupials and monotremes; abundant insects, shell and marine deposits. Pollen analysis is revealing much from the abundant fossil flora. *Quaternary* (the last million years): extinction of giant marsupials, e.g. *Diprotodon australis*, 3 m. long and 1·8 m. high over 15,000 years ago; other remains similar to modern flora and fauna. Notable workers have included H. A. Longman (1880–1954) in Qld., and Sir Frederick McCoy (1817–1899) in Vic. *For further reading see* H. Mincham: *Vanished Giants of Australia* (Adelaide, 1966).

Foveaux, Joseph (1765–1846) An officer of N.S.W. Corps sent by Governor King to administer Norfolk Island (1801–3) which he did with some brutality. On his way back after 4 years' sick leave (1808), he called at Sydney to find Bligh* under arrest, and being senior to Johnston*, he took over administration. In close association with Macarthur* he did much to improve the shocking state of the colony over the next 18 months, but was anxious to be rid of it to Paterson* who eventually arrived from Port Dalrymple. Foveaux remained until Macquarie was installed (1809), receiving much approbation for his actions from the new Governor, although on his return to Eng. (1810) he was censured for upholding Johnston against Bligh.

Fox, Emmanuel Phillips (1865–1915) b. Melbourne. He was one of the first Aus. artists to achieve recognition in Europe, mainly with his impressionist work. He lived in France from 1902, but had spent 10 influential years as director of a Melbourne art school before this; he also sent exhibitions home.

Frances Creek N.T. 14S/132E Iron ore mines linked by a spur line to Pine Creek on the N Aus. Railway, under contract for export to Japan from 1967.

Frangipani, Native A popular name for the attractive evergreen *Hymenosporum flavum* of coastal E Aus., in the mainly Aus. family Pittosporaceae. It has large widely spread 5-petalled yellow flowers, followed by 2·5-cm. hairy fruit.

Frankland River W.A. 35S/117E A 160-km.-long watercourse flowing from the plateau S to Denmark. In summer the water is brackish and slow. Rocky Gully on the upper Frankland is a post-war (1939–45) Land Settlement Community.

Franklin, Sir John (1786–1847) b. Spilsby, Eng. A polar explorer and Governor of Tas. (1837–43). He was with Flinders* on the *Investigator* and made 2 famous polar explorations in 1819–23 and 1825–7 before his appointment to Tas., which was not a success. Depression, anti-transportation movements, a recalcitrant council and subordinates, notably Montagu and Forster, and a vast influx of convicts now that none were being sent to N.S.W., were problems beyond the competence of this brilliant, liberal but gentle man, and he was recalled. He was lost on the greatest of his journeys (1845–7) in which he discovered the NW Passage. His wife **Jane,** made great impact in Tas., with her wide journeyings and social life, and educational interests. She founded Hobart's first museum. *For further reading see* K. Fitzpatrick: *Sir John Franklin in Tas. 1837–43* (Melbourne, 1949).

Franklin, Stella Maria Miles (1879–1954) b. Talbingo Station near Tumut, N.S.W. She was a major novelist. Her first published work was *My Brilliant Career* (Edinburgh, 1901, republished 1966), a combination of fiction and autobiography, set, like much of her work, in the upper Murrumbidgee area of her childhood. There was a long gap, when she worked as a journalist in Sydney, when she was in U.S. (1905–1914) associated with the women's socialist movement, and in war work in Europe. She returned permanently to Aus. in 1933. Meanwhile she had published *Old Blastus of Bandicoot* (London, 1931) to be followed by probably her best work *All That Swagger* (Sydney, 1936), a detailed saga of early settlement. The novels of 'Brent of Bin Bin'* were also by Miles Franklin. The *Miles Franklin Award* of $1,000 annually for a published novel 'of the highest literary merit which must present Australian life in any of its phases' was her bequest. *For further reading see* M. Barnard: *Miles Franklin* (Hill of Content, N.S.W., 1967).

Fraser, Dawn (1937–) b. Sydney. The world's greatest woman swimmer in her time. Asthmatic and youngest of 8 children, she grew up in a fairly poor Sydney suburb, enjoying swimming 'for fun' though winning many trophies in a professional club before she was 10, when she was found and trained by H. Gallagher. She won the 100 m. free-style in the 1956, 1960 and 1964 Olympic Games. Her 1964 100 m. free-style record was only equalled in 1971 by Shane Gould. A controversial and colourful sporting character, whom the Aus. Swimming Union, the controlling body, disciplined by banning from amateur swimming following incidents at the 1964 Olympic Games. *For further reading see* D. Fraser with H. Gordon: *Gold Medal Girl* (Melbourne, 1965).

Fraser Island Qld. 25S/153E An elongated, low, sandy, dune-fringed island, 130 km. N–S by 5–22 km. E–W, named after a sea captain shipwrecked on the Great Barrier Reef in 1836, who reached the island by ship's boat. Also known as Great Sandy Island, it formerly had ruthless timber extraction, now a Qld. Forestry Reserve. Sand mining leases are bringing opposition.

Fraser, Neale (1933–) b. Melbourne. A tennis player, representing Aus. in the Davis Cup* 1958–63, winning the Wimbledon Singles in 1960, and the Wimbledon Doubles with Emerson* in 1959 and 1961.

Fremantle W.A. 32S/116E (33,347 in 1971) A city (1929) and chief port of the State and the third Aus. port, now part of the Perth Metropolitan Area. It lies on both sides of the Swan River mouth. N Fremantle is smaller and declining, with industrial development of processing plants mainly in S and E Fremantle for wheat, hides and sugar; some boat-building, and a largely Italian fishing community. Oil, steel and phosphate ores are chief imports; refined oil, wheat and wool among the main exports. The development of container ships and a container terminal stimulated the port, along with the standard-gauge railway to the E (1968). 3 new ordinary berths have necessitated movement of the railway bridge. It is an important passenger port as the first and last Aus. port on the European run. The inner harbour, engineered by C. Y. O'Connor* and involving a breakwater and the blasting of a rock bar, was opened in 1897 when it superseded Albany as the main port. The outer harbour comprises Gage Roads, Owen Anchorage and Cockburn Sound* and serves Kwinana.* **Fremantle Doctor** is a welcome afternoon sea breeze which, in summer, brings relief many kilometres inland.

French, Leonard (1928–) A leading contemporary artist, noted especially for grand geometric abstractions, based often on heroic or religious themes, and for his glass ceiling in the Vic. Arts Centre in Melbourne (1967).

Frenchmans Cap National Park Tas. 42S/146E. This covers some 200 km.^{2} of wild glaciated mountain country,

reaching 1,445·4 m. in the quartzite-capped mountain which gives its name to the park.

Freycinet Peninsula Tas. 42S/148E On the E of Oyster Bay*, it is linked to the mainland by twin sand-spits, and reaches 614 m., with high granitic cliffs. It is a National Park.

Friarbirds Rather large (25–30 cm. long) Honey-eaters*, with much bare grey or black flesh on the head, hence the name.

Friend, Donald Stuart Leslie (1914–) b. N.S.W. An artist of international repute whose work was partly influenced by African experience. He was a leader of an artistic group in the former gold town of Hill End*, and of the Sydney Merioola Group, named from their base in an old mansion; now lives in Bali.

Froghoppers Small winged Bugs* of the Order Hemiptera, able to spring away when touched. The nymph stage is passed in a blob of slimy, bubbly matter called 'cuckoo spit' which may be in the junction between blades of grass. A common example is the Green Treehopper, *Sextius virescens*, which feeds on wattle trees and lays its eggs beneath the bark.

Frogmouth (genus *Podargus*—gouty foot) The commonest species is *P. strigoides* (owl-like), a nocturnal bird, widespread in Aus., up to 50 cm. long, grey, with very wide mouth, but long-headed compared with an owl. It sits very still awaiting prey, camouflaged as part of a bare branch, and nests on a small platform of twigs in a tree fork or stump, laying 2–3 roundish white eggs. It eats flying insects—including those round suburban street lights—but failing those, it will take ground insects, berries etc. One large species *P. papuensis* extends over N.G. and N Qld. The bird has often been confused with the owl, and also credited with the 'mopoke' hooting call. (*See* PLATE 4.)

Frogs and **Toads** As these cannot be equated with any scientific distinctions, they are treated under Amphibia*, where some of the numerous popular names are noted.

Frome, Lake S.A. 31S/140E A pear-shaped salina or salt 'lake' 100 km. N–S by up to 50 km. E–W, the largest and most southerly of an arc of such lakes NE of the Flinders Range; only rarely is there enough rainfall to supply the ephemeral watercourses which feed them. One of the coastal lakes of the SE of S.A. is also called L. Frome.

Fruit The total area (98,500 ha.) is diverse in location and type of fruit: from tropical pawpaws in Qld. to temperate berries and pome fruits in Tas. and irrigated citrus inland. The main fruit acreages are apples (30%), citrus (24%), peaches, pears and bananas (each 8–9%), pineapples (5%) and apricots (some 3%). Fruit exports earn $30 million having dropped in recent years: apples (66%), pears (20%), both to U.K., and citrus (10%) mainly to N.Z. Recently declining markets were blamed on over production and standards. Fresh or frozen, dried and tinned fruits are roughly equal in export value. The entry of Britain into the Common Market in 1973 means the loss of trade preference, further depressing the industry. Compensation to allow orchard reduction is being paid by the Government.

Fuchsia, Heath or **Native Fuchsia** (*Epacris longiflora*) A 1·5-m. heath of SE Aus. coastal sandstone country, with white-tipped red bells and small but quite broad spear-like leaves. In Vic. the term is used for *Correa reflexa*, a shrub with pairs of dark green and yellow-brown stemless leaves and tubular 4-petalled flowers, red with yellow tips and with protruding stamens—or sometimes purplish, yellow or green. Native Fuchsia is also applied to Aus.

plants of several genera, e.g. the White correa, *Correa alba*, the Emu Bush* and *Grevillea wilsoni* (*see* PLATE 6) and *G. bipinnatifida*.

Fulton, Henry (1761–1840) b. Eng. When serving as a minister of the Church of Ireland, he was implicated in the 1798 Irish rebellion and transported. Pardoned in 1805, he was an active influential minister and educationist. He supported Bligh in the Rum Rebellion.

Fungi Flowerless and leafless plants (spore-bearing and lacking chlorophyll) numbering some 100,000 in the world, and even the larger fungi of Aus. are over 1,000. These include: 1. the Ascomycetes, producing spores, usually in eights, from long flask-shaped cells (e.g. truffles, 'vegetable caterpillars' parasitic on larvae, such as *Cordyceps taylori*, and ergots); and 2. the Basidiomycetes bearing the spores, usually in fours, on rounded external cells (e.g. mushrooms* and toadstools, puffballs*, coral-fungi and bracket-fungi). The family Hymenogastraceae includes subterranean, often aromatic fungi eaten by burrowing marsupials, while the family Polysporaceae include Blackfellow's Bread, *Polyporus mylittae*, and the Stone-making Fungus, *P. basilapiloides*, forming hard masses underground in damp forests and mallee sand-hills respectively.

The small fungi include many food pests such as wheat rust and mildew, and human pathogens, e.g. that of 'ring-worm'. On the other hand penicillin was first observed on the common mould *Penicillium notatum*.

Funnelweb Spiders A popular name for several species of spiders, mainly in the Dipluridae family, e.g. the tree-nesting *Atrax formidabilis* and ground-nesting *A. robustus*, both very poisonous, and with carapace up to about 2·5 cm. long.

Funnelweb Spider (Atrax robustus)
about life size

Furneaux Islands Tas. 40S/148E. An island group in Bass Str. They were named by Cook. They extend 100 km. N–S and include Flinders*, Cape Barren* and Clarke Islands, and at least 20 smaller islands. Population totals about 1,000.

Furphy, Joseph (1843–1912) b. Yarra Glen, Vic. of migrant Irish parents. Writing as Tom Collins, a fictional minor official in the Riverina, Furphy produced the unique *Such is Life*
(Sydney, 1903), a kaleidoscopic study of country life in diary form, including description, serio-comic anecdote, pun and quotation, political and social comment, essay and satire. 2 sections, pruned at the suggestion of A. G. Stephens*, appeared as *Rigby's Romance* (Melbourne, 1921) and *The Buln Buln and the Brolga*, ed. R. G. Howarth (Sydney, 1948). After working on a poor selection and as a bullock teamster, he worked in his brother's foundry at Shepperton, Vic., before joining his sons in a similar business in Fremantle, W.A., in 1905. *For further reading see* K. Barker and Miles Franklin: *Joseph Furphy* (Sydney, 1944) and J. Barnes: *Joseph Furphy* (Melbourne, 1963).

Fyans, Foster (1790–1870) b. Ireland. He arrived in Aus. in 1833 as an army officer, and became first police magistrate and Crown Lands Commissioner, Port Phillip District (1837–53). His military posse of 'Border Police' was notoriously high-handed, ruthless but efficient and was at constant loggerheads with the squatters* of the Western District*.

G

GAIRDNER, LAKE

Gairdner, Lake S.A. 32S/136E A salina or salt 'lake', about 160 km. NW–SE and 48 km. E–W, very rarely with water and surrounded by large sheep stations among sand-hills, samphire and saltbush.

Galah Grey and pink Cockatoos* often seen flocking to an inland waterhole. 'Galah' is also used in slang for a loud-mouthed empty-headed person. (*See* PLATE 4.)

Gallipoli A rocky mountainous peninsula up to 50 km. wide and stretching 80 km. SW from the European mainland to form the W shore of the Dardanelles Straits, the narrow entrance to the Black Sea. From April–December 1915 it was the scene of an unsuccessful Allied campaign instigated by Winston Churchill (then First Lord of the Admiralty) to secure this route to the Russian grainlands, and open a front against Turkey; it involved British, Indian and French troops as well as the Anzacs*. Tenuous beachheads were made and held, but efforts to extend inland were defeated by the well-armed and trained Turkish Army. A secret withdrawal of 80,000 troops took place successfully between December 18th–20th 1915. Total killed 33,532: British and Indian 17,345, Anzacs 8,587, French 7,600.

Gambling The 'investment' per head of population is one of the world's highest. Of an estimated annual total of well over $2,500 million, two thirds is on horse-racing, some 25% on poker machines and 5% on lotteries; the rest on foot-racing, hounds, 'two-up', cards, etc. State Government Lotteries are run in Qld. (since 1916 when the Golden Casket began), N.S.W. (1930), W.A. (1932) and S.A.

GARDEN ISLAND

(1966); the proceeds, after 50–65% in prize money and expenses are paid, being channelled primarily into hospital funds. In Vic. considerable revenue (over 4% of tax receipts) are obtained from the privately run Tattersall's Lotteries, or 'Tatts', under Government licence, which was founded by G. Adams* in Sydney in 1881, and was later based first in Qld. then for over 30 years in Tas., until tempted to Vic. in 1954 by the Labor Premier John Cain. This caused a serious loss to Tas.'s revenues; a succeeding licensee operated there until 1961. Now Tattersall's sell tickets under licence in Tas. There are many other charitable lotteries, generally called Art Unions, a term deriving from the 19th-century custom of raffling paintings initiated by the artist J. Broinowski (1837–1913). One of the most famous is the Opera House Lottery, largely financing the Sydney Opera House*. Poker machines, legal only in N.S.W. which has over 20,000, partially finance the clubs which have them, and pay the State Government licence fees. Football pools began in Vic. in 1972.

Gammon Range S.A. 30S/138E A plateau 915 m. high and 32 km. long in horizontal sandstone strata, in the N Flinders Range. Periodic rumblings, the legendary indigestion of the snake Arkaroo after drinking L. Frome dry, are probably falls of rock broken off by excessive temperature ranges.

Gang-gang The Red-headed (in the male) Cockatoo*, *Callocephalon fimbriatum*, of SE Aus. (*See* PLATE 4.)

Garden Island W.A. 32S/116E To the W of Cockburn Sound*, 10 km. N–S and 1·6 km. wide. The first settlers had to stay here in temporary shelters when they arrived in May 1829, as weather was too rough to land on the mainland, so that the colony was first proclaimed here (and at Fremantle on June 18th 1829). Naval installations lie on the S tip, and there is much holiday development.

Garden Island N.S.W. 34S/151E On the S shore of Port Jackson. It was used to grow vegetables for ships of the First Fleet. It became first a N.S.W., then Commonwealth Naval Base, and was linked to the mainland at Potts Point by the 347 m.-long Captain Cook Graving Dock during the 1939–1945 War.

Gardiner, Frank (1830–1895) b. Boro Creek, N.S.W. A bushranger*, son of a Scottish migrant, Christie, and a half-caste girl, Clarke; he used both names but mainly the one he adopted from an employer, Gardiner. 2 convictions for horse-stealing were followed by a period (1859–62) as leader of a gang based in the Weddin Ranges, whose activities culminated in the hold-up in 1862 of the Forbes gold escort at Eugowra, the subject of the famous painting *Bailed up*, by Tom Roberts*. Gardiner escaped and was living as a storekeeper in Qld. when captured in 1864. He was released in 1872, on condition that he left the colony, an incident causing the downfall of Parkes*, and he died in U.S.

Garran, Sir Robert Randolph (1867–1957) b. Sydney. His long and distinguished legal career included active concern in Federation* and extensive drafting for Parliamentary legislation. *For further reading see* R. R. Garran: *Prosper the Commonwealth* (Sydney, 1958).

Gas Aus. has shared the European and American revolution in sources of raw material for gas production, but, save in Melbourne, not the associated rationalisation and integrated grid development. In 1950 black coal was the sole source; by 1966 it provided less than half of an increased gas output, the new sources being mainly derived from oil-refining and the Lurgi process of direct high-pressure brown coal gasification (also used for some black coals). The change was associated with high coal costs (including freight), a declining coke market, and development of natural gas.

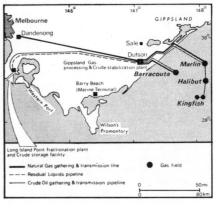

Natural Gas in Vic.
(with acknowledgment to NAT/DEV)

Natural gas will supply about 10% of primary energy consumption by 1974–1975. It has been known in Qld. since 1900, but was first commercially used in 1961. Widespread discoveries followed exploration in the 1960s; the major field is in Bass Strait*; new fields have been found in Qld.; at least 12 in the Cooper Basin in the NE of S.A. with production now at Gidgealpa and Moomba, at Mereenie and other sites in Palm Valley, southern N.T. In W.A. important fields are being developed several hundred km. N of Perth, at Dongara, Mondarra, Gin Gin and Yardarino. Brisbane, Melbourne and Adelaide had piped natural gas by 1970 with feeder lines to towns along the pipeline (Ipswich and Toowoomba in Qld., Latrobe valley towns in Vic., Whyalla and Port Pirie in S.A.). Pipelines from Dongara to Perth and Kwinana in W.A. and from Gidgealpa-Moomba in S.A. east into N.S.W. to serve Sydney with branches to Newcastle and Wollongong are being laid. A new field off NW W.A. will be producing by 1978.

Gascoyne River W.A. A sporadic 800-km.-long watercourse reaching the sea at Carnarvon, the catchment being 80,000 km.², with Lyons River flowing NW from the Collier Range. Irrigation from the stream-bed supports 500–800 ha. of bananas, tomatoes and beans grown in fairly small lots along the last 20 km. of the course. Floods, cyclones and, at other times, dropping water levels make it hazardous. Further development would involve upstream storage.

Gastropoda or **Gastropods** (stomach-footed) Of the Phylum Mollusca. Most adults have a shell which (except for the limpets) is in a spiral form. Larvae are usually free-swimming and hatch from jelly-like eggs. Species representative of the main families of Aus. are described. 1. True Limpets, family Patellidae, with a 'foot' specialised for suction on to rocks, include the Common or Colourful Limpet, *Cellana tramoserica*, of SE Aus., up to 5 cm. across and usually with alternate light and dark rays of yellow, orange, brown or black on the outside of the shell, silvery inside; the Giant Limpet, *C. laticostata*, of the rocky SW of W.A., the shell up to 10 cm. across, somewhat rounded with only faint ribs, orange-brown outside, usually orange inside; it often has a smaller species of limpet fastened on to its shell. 2. The False or Keyhole Limpets, family Fissurellidae, which have a small 'keyhole' near the top of the cone, include 2 species of SE Aus., the cream-brown Keyhole Limpet, *Elegidion audax*, and the Elephant Snail, *Scutus antipodes*, a black snail-like mollusc of rock pools, with long tentacles (hence Elephant) bearing a cream-brown broad shell of up to 8 cm. long and 2·5

cm. broad, one end squared and the other rounded, with the hole near the round end; the shells are known as Shield or Duck Bill shells. 3. The Abalones or Ear Shells, family Haliotidae, include the Red Ear Shell, *Haliotis ruber*, of SE Aus. which has a brick-red shell, sometimes variegated, on the outside, with pearly-white inside. There are many other species around the coasts such as the tropical *H. asinina*, whose shell is olive-brown suffused with pale green; the row of holes in the shell are outlets for water currents. It is prized and commercially exploited for food (including exports). 4. Top Shells, family Trochidae, varying widely in shape and colour, include the Zebra Top Shell, *Austrocochlea obtusa*, with varied black-and-white banding and even shape, found in different coasts from rocky to mangrove, the conical Comtesse's Top Shell, *Thalotia comtessei*, and the small banded Kelp Shell, *Bankivia fasciata*. 5. The Turban Shells, family Turbinidae, vary from those with flattened whorls as in the widespread Heavy Turban Shell, *Ninella torquata*, to the high-coned Bell Tent Shell, *Bellastraea sirius*, of N.S.W. 6. The Blue Australwink, *Melaphara unifasciata*, widespread and innumerable, may be taken as a typical Wink (family Littorinidae), but variations such as nodules, ridges and flattening may disguise the family shape somewhat; the Yellow Cluster Wink, *Hinea brasiliana*, is in a different family (Planaxidae), also the very common Black Nerita, *Melanerita atramentosa* (family Neritidae), with shell whorled but without a spire. 7. The Slipper Limpets, family Calyptraeidae, are only slightly whorled, e.g. the Prickly Slipper Limpet, *Crepidula aculeata*, of much of the S of Aus. and the Horse Hoof Limpet, family Hipponicidae, *Sabia conica*. 8. The Aus. Horn Shell, *Velacumantis australis*, of E Aus. is a medium-sized representative of the family Potamididae. 9. The Aus.

PLATE 4: BIRDS (MEDIUM)

1. Tawny Frogmouth *(Podargus strigoides)*. 2. Pied Currawong *(Strepera graculina)*. 3. Gang-gang Cockatoo *(Callocephalon fimbriatum)*. 4. Rainbow Lorikeet *(Trichoglossus moluccanus)*. 5. Galah *(Kakatoë tenuirostris)*. 6. Fan-tailed Cuckoo *(Cacomantis pyrrhophanus)*. 7. Kookaburra *(Dacelo novaeguineae)*. 8. Roseate Tern *(Sterna dougalli)*.

Wentletrap (family Epitoniidae), *Opalia australis*, is whorled with strong cross-ridges. 10. Gunn's Screw Shell, *Gazamedia gunni* (family Turritellidae), has slightly concave whorls; the deep-water Cox's Turrid, *Inquisitor coxi*, has some resemblance superficially but belongs to the family Turridae. 11. The Violet Snails, family Janthinidae, are open-sea, floating or planktonic molluscs which float with the pointed end down, their light purple bands facing down and dark purple upwards, as camouflage against enemies; they are blown inshore along with the less desirable Bluebottles*. The large Violet Snail, *Janthina violacea*, is quite common. 12. The Dog Whelks, family Nassariidae, e.g. the Handsome Dog Whelk, *Nassarius particeps*, and the False Buccinums, family Cominellidae, e.g. the Fern Shell, *Cominella filicinea*, both of N.S.W., are carnivores and scavengers. 13. The Pear Helmet, *Xenogalea pyrum*, family Cassididae, is superficially whelk-like, but strongly ridged and with dark markings; other shells with roughly whelk-like form include the beautiful purple and brown Slender Dove Shell, *Zemitrella* (family Pyrenidae), and the intricately frilled Pink Frilled Murex, *Torvamurex denudatus* (family Muricidae). 14. The Purples, family Thaisidae, include the Triton Purple, *Agnewia tritoniformis*, the deeply ridged Cart Rut Shell, *Dicathais orbita*, and the Mulberry Whelk, *Morula marginalba*, of E Aus., the shell of which is a dirty white with purplish-black rather rectangular tubercles. 15. Mitre Shells, family Mitridae, include mainly rather dull shells in the cooler waters of Aus., e.g. the Brown Mitre, *Vicimitra contermina*. 16. The Flower Cone, *Floraconus anemone* (family Conidae), is an attractive purple and brown. The tropical cones are brighter and include various poisonous species such as the Marbled Cone, *C. marmoreus*, of N Aus. and the rare and precious Glory of the Sea,

Conus gloriamaris, of SW Pacific waters. 17. The large Sand Snail, *Glossaulax aulocoglossa*, creamy-fawn and very globular, is widespread, and sometimes called the Moon Shell; related species, of family Naticidae, are smaller. 18. The Common Worm Shell, *Serpulorbis sipho*, often washed ashore in intertwined masses by storms, is typical of the family Siliquariidae. 19. The Tritons, or Rock Whelks, family Cymatiidae, range from the strongly ribbed brown-and-white Spengler's Triton, *Cymatilesta spengleri*, of much of the E and S of Aus., to the Hairy Oyster Borer, *Monoplex australasiae*. 20. Cowry Shells, family Cypraeidae, are common in tropical Aus. especially in the Great Barrier Reef, such as the handsome oval brown Arabian Cowry, *Arabica arabica*, but the small Bean Cowries, family Triviidae, include the Southern Bean Cowry, *Ellatrivia merces*, often seen on southern beaches. 21. The families Bullidae and Hydatinidae (Bubble Shells) differ from most other gastropods in being hermaphrodite (i.e. the individual has both male and female sex organs); both shells and the animals inside are commonly very beautiful, as in the Rose-petal Bubble Shell, *Hydatina physis*, which puts out billowing folds of pink membrane edged with iridescent blue, while its neat somewhat cowry-like shell is of a cream background with reddish and purplish stripes; the Pink Banded Bubble Shell, *Bullina lineata*, puts out similar whitish blue-edged folds, while the shell is creamy with red bands around its whorls and faint pink cross-stripes. Both species are quite common in E Aus. 22. The Sea Hares, family Aplysiidae, are slug-like marine molluscs with a fragile internal shell, including the Ringed Sea Hare, *Aplysia dactylomela*, which reaches 30 cm. long, widespread in Aus. and many other countries. It has 2 fleshy flaps on the back, with which it can swim, though it also crawls along in slug-like fashion with its tentacles out; the creamy roundish shell of a dead Sea Hare is sometimes found in pools. 23. Sea Slugs have no shell at all, e.g. the Red and Blue Sea Slug, *Glossodoris bennettii* (family Aglajidae, Order Nudibranchia); this brilliantly coloured mollusc is sometimes seen at about the low tide level in N.S.W.; other genera belong to the tropics or to the open oceans' plankton. 24. The Siphon Shells, family Siphonariidae, are a special group of marine molluscs which do not have gills but take up air between tides; they are rather like limpets with a groove down the inside of the cone from apex to edge, often differently coloured and appearing as a ridge on the outside. The Toothed Siphon Shell, *Siphonaria denticulata*, is common in much of Aus.

Land and Freshwater Molluscs total over 600 native Aus. species (Gastropods and Bivalves). Freshwater gastropods include some with gills, more closely related to marine types, e.g. *Plotiopsis balonnensis*, found in N N.S.W., and S Qld.—often evading droughts by burrowing into the mud and 'closing the lid' tight. Some might be potential alternate hosts for human diseases such as Chinese River Fluke and Oriental Lung Fluke, justifying careful quarantine regulations against these parasites. The lunged freshwater snails include larger species such as *Lymnaea lessoni*, and smaller, e.g. *L. tomentosa*. The native land snails and slugs also include some with gills akin to aquatic and marine types—mainly in the wet N, with many more in N.G., such as the slippery and glassy-shelled *Pupina* genus. The lunged land snails predominate; their drought-evading device is to seal off the outside world with mucous, the seal being discarded after the dry spell (up to several years in desert areas). They range from the carnivorous snail of some Sydney gardens *Strangesta capillacea* to the large Giant Panda Snail, *Hedleyella falconeri*, of the rain-forests of NE N.S.W. and SE Qld. The coastal forests of Qld. have many colourful banded snails, such as several species of *Bentosites*, banded in brown, yellow and white with quite an attractive shell. The Glass Snails of genus *Helicarion* have a very small transparent shell, while the shell has vanished in the slugs such as the Aus. Native Slug, *Triboniophorus graeffei*, whose pulmonary pore may be seen opening and shutting on its back. Many suburban gardens also include introduced snails and slugs.

Gawler S.A. 35S/139E (6,953 in 1971) Lies at the W foot of the Mt. Lofty Ranges, on a site selected by William Light who designed the town on a flat ridge where the N and S Para Rivers join to form the Gawler River. It commanded the Barossa Valley route through the hills and the main coastal plain routes to the N, and in the second half of the 19th century was a major industrial town with up to 8 foundry and machine workshops making farm machinery and locomotives of which only one remains. Gawler is being increasingly absorbed by Adelaide's advance, and becoming a dormitory town, with only food processing and a clothing factory.

Gawler, George (1795–1869) Second Governor of S.A. (1838–41), following Hindmarsh*. The positions of Governor and Commissioner were combined under Gawler, avoiding the quarrel causing Hindmarsh's downfall. But the principles on which the colony was founded were crumbling, and to provide employment for the disappointed immigrants, he launched a great scheme of public works, using first his own funds, then issuing bills in good faith on the London Headquarters of the Commission, which they refused to honour. His recall followed the consequent crash, and to his humiliation was delivered personally by Grey*, his successor and detractor in the ensuing criticism.

Gawler Ranges S.A. 32S/136E Low hills extending about 160 km. E–W across the N of Eyre Peninsula, rather higher in the W and reaching 475 m. in Mt. Bluff. They are thinly covered with vegetation, supporting only large cattle and sheep runs, but they include the iron-rich Middleback Range at their E end.

Geckoes (family Gekkonidae) There are almost 50 Aus. species, mainly nocturnal and insectivorous, some living among rocks, others darting from under tree-bark, and some house-haunting. Most have a soft granular skin, sometimes with wart-like tubercles, usually discarded on slough-ing as a single whitish fragile tissue.

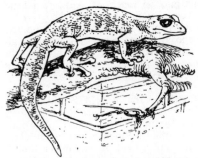

House Gecko (Gehyra variegata),
about life size

On handling or threat, they readily discard their tail, while some swell their body and some utter soft squeaky cries. Eggs, sometimes hard-shelled, sometimes soft, are laid, often 2 per year. The eyes are prominent, with a vertically elliptical pupil with a trans-parent cover but no movable lid. There are minute teeth on the inner side of the jawbone. The middle-ear membrane is visible on external inspection. Some have padded adhesive feet to assist in climbing. Some species attempt to bite on handling, but are harmless; their insect-eating habit is entirely beneficent

to man and it is unfortunate that the bizarre appearance of some species has led to their being attributed with veno-mous powers under names such as stone adder, rock adder, etc. Common spe-cies include: 1. the 10 cm. grey-white mottled or line-marked House Gecko, *Gehyra variegata*, also living in bark or rubble, and with distinctively padded claws; 2. the Common Barking Gecko, *Nephrurus laevis*, of C Aus., with tubercles on the back; 3. the Knob-tailed Barking Gecko, *N. asper*, of inland Qld.; 4. the Leaf-tailed Gecko, *Phyllurus cornutus*, of NE Aus.; the Thick-tailed Gecko, *Gymnodactylus milii*, brown with black lines and rows of white spots, of much of S and E Aus.; and 5. the Qld. rain-forest species *Carphodactylus laevis*, up to 23 cm. long with spectacular carrot-like tail, and 5 white stripes along a dark-brown back.

Geebungs The succulent, edible if astringent, fruit of some species of *Persoonia*, heaths, bushes or small trees in the Proteaceae family. The Willow Geebung, *P. laevis*, is a shrub with broad curved leaves, small 4-petalled open yellow flowers and single-seeded sticky fruit, edible but insipid, growing in coastal N.S.W., while the Fine-leaf Geebung, *P. pini-folia*, of the gullies in the Great Divide, has almost needle-like leaves, as its Latin name suggests.

Geelong Vic. 38S/144E (115,047 in 1971) A city 72 km. SW of Mel-bourne on Corio Bay*. Geelong grew as the port, social and market centre for the rich Western District*; its famous Anglican school (Geelong Grammar, 1854), exclusive residential areas to the W and the traditional boat-race reflect these functions, now rather overshadowed by industrial development which has spread the town along the bay sides from its nucleus between the shore and the steep Barwon Valley, and accounts for rapid population growth and large migrant intake. Woollens, agricultural machinery and superphosphates (the largest Aus. centre for these) still reflect the farming hinterland. The coastal position, cheap land and proximity to Melbourne have led to other developments. Oil-refining (1959) brings over half Geelong's imports in the form of crude oil, and has led to associated petro-chemicals. The motor industry began in 1925 with the assembly of the Model T Ford and now makes a 90% Aus. car. An aluminium smeltery has been built since 1960 on Point Henry E of the town. Glass (1937) and carpets (1960) have been established by parent British companies. The port covers 230 km.[2] and is reached by a 12-m. channel first dredged 1893. While still a major wool market, the wool is all exported from Melbourne. It has one of the world's largest bulk wheat stores and handles 25% of the Aus. wheat export. One campus of the new Univ. of Vic. will be at Geelong.

Geese Aus. geese include several distinct species. The Magpie or Semipalmated Goose, *Anseranas semipalmata* (half-webbed goose-duck), a large bird (over 90 cm. beak to tail) with black head and cranial knob, the bare skin on the head being reddish, black neck, forequarters, tail and rear wing-edges. It has yellowish legs and the half-webbed feet are distinctive. The strident call is ascribed to a trachea made much longer than the neck by convolutions. It was eradicated from N.S.W. in the early 1900s by drainage and poisoning, and is now common only in the N and NE of Aus. and into N.G., more rarely in the SE and SW. Recently it has been reported as damaging rice-fields, but normally searches for food in shallow natural swamp-pools. It has a broad nest of reeds etc., built up from the swamp, normally with 5–8 yellow-white eggs. The Cape Barren or Pig Goose, *Cereopsis novae-hollandiae* (wax-like), is found in coastal southern Aus. and offshore

islands where it breeds. It is largely vegetarian, feeding on salt-marsh grasses and sedges etc. In recent years the late Professor A. J. Marshall and others have expressed anxiety lest the species should be exterminated by shooting (*see* PLATE 5). The 2 pygmy geese, genus *Nettapus* (duck-footed), extending from SE Asia into NE Aus., are the Green Pygmy-goose or Goose-teal, *N. pulchellus* (pretty), and the White-quilled Pygmy Goose or Cotton Teal, *N. coromandelianus* (of SE India). Both are seen on inland streams and lakes, and are about 38–45 cm. beak to tail; and predominantly green and white in plumage. The Maned Goose or Wood Duck, *Chenonetta jubata* (maned goose-duck), a grass-eater of inland streams and timbered swamp-margins in much of Aus., is a little larger, mainly black-flecked white, with brown head and 'mane' on the nape, and nests in tree-holes, often high and far from water; it is duck-like in size and plumage, with a goose-like sharp beak.

Geeveston Tas. 43S/147E Just W of the lower Huon River*, this was an early apple-growing centre. A wood-pulp mill producing neutral sulphite pulp since 1961 is based on timber concessions along the Huon, on Bruny Island and Tasman Peninsula. Cutting is controlled and integrated with logging for sawn timber.

Gellibrand, Joseph Tice (1786–1837) First Tas. Attorney-General (1823–4). As a member of the Port Phillip Association, he probably drew up the 'treaty' Batman* made with the Aborigines. Gellibrand was killed by Aborigines with his companion Hesse on his second exploratory journey into the Port Phillip hinterland in 1837. His grandson, **Sir John** (1872–1945), was an outstanding First World War A.I.F. officer, having served in the British Army before returning to Tas. farming in 1912.

Geographe Bay W.A. 33S/115E A wide, exposed, sandy gulf curving S and W from Bunbury to Cape Naturaliste, and named, as was the latter, by Baudin in 1801.

GEOLOGY AND MAJOR LANDFORMS (*See* MAP 4 and for Geological Time Scale *see* FOSSILS)

The Great Plateau or Australian Shield is the framework and basement, formed of very ancient crystalline rocks, igneous or highly metamorphosed, at about 300 m. above sea level, covering well over 2·6 million km.². These Archaean rocks, (2,000–3,000 million years old) are largely of gneisses, with a prominent banded and foliated structure varying regionally in orientation, but generally planed across by the forces of erosion in the very ancient and monotonous surface. In places the 'strike' of the rocks becomes important topographically, as where a belt of resistant granite or other rock stands out above the general surface. The Archaean basement has for geological eras been relatively stable in structure, in that it has not been crumpled in fresh mountain-building, but it has been involved in downwarping of very different geological periods, and has almost certainly been involved in the horizontal (better tangential) movements of Continental Drift. The earliest downwarps accumulated Lower and Upper Proterozoic rocks. There are residual exposures sometimes in hills or plateaux of relatively little altered sedimentary rocks; the Lower Proterozoic, folded greywackes, sandstones and shales; and the Upper Proterozoic, mainly sandstones, lava flows, ironstones generally little contorted except in the much folded Yampi* area and in the faulted Shatter Belt flanking Spencer Gulf*. More recent downwarps have produced the sediment-filled basins noted below. In places there is very rich mineralisation, as in comparable structures in other continents, including much of the gold, lead, zinc, iron and uranium.

The Eastern Highlands Mainly marine but also some terrestrial, lacustrine and volcanic deposits were laid down mainly over E Aus., but also at some eras over what is now Central Aus. and on some basins now flanking the coast, during the successively younger geological eras. Mountain building occurred in each Period of the Palaeozoic era, at times including folding comparable at least to the Jura Mts. of modern Europe, at times rather as a gentle uplift which recurred during the Cretaceous, and to a slight extent during the Pliocene (late Tertiary) when the Kosciusko uplift occurred. The interplay of these various depositions and uplifts, and of varied exposure to weathering and erosion is responsible for the much more complex geological structures and landforms in the Eastern Highlands and coastal tracts, including Tas. Large tracts over 900 m. occur in SE Aus., where also are the highest uplifted blocks such as the Snowy Mts. and the Vic. Alps, and many miles of almost precipitous scarp edge lie above the low hills of the coastal belt. In places massive horizontal sandstones are prominent, e.g. the Blue Mts.; in places limestones with considerable cave development; in places folded somewhat slaty greywackes grits and shales, often in juxtaposition to tor-crowned granite ridges. Volcanic rocks of various ages are important, but with the plateau basalts of the quietly welling Cainozoic outbreaks prominent, as in the Atherton plateau, parts of New England, Monaro and W Vic. The older rocks, Cambrian, Ordovician and Silurian, contain metalliferous deposits, in association with igneous intrusions sometimes much younger, e.g. Cretaceous. Bituminous coals in Aus. come mainly from the Permian formation, while there are also some Jurassic coals, and the Tertiary brown coals are important particularly in Vic. The most important exploited coal-fields are preserved in strata relatively protected from erosion by downfolding or downfaulting within this region. The oil potential from the sedimentary rocks from the Palaeozoic onwards is in part within this region, but also in the great sedimentary basins. There are 250-million-year-old glacial deposits from the Permian glaciation, e.g. in parts of S.A., but the Quaternary glaciation which ceased only some 15,000 years ago, left much evidence in Tas. and the Snowy Mts., with wider peri-glacial weathering and soil-creep etc., still residually active. The Quaternary ice-caps lowered then raised sea level, drowning valleys in places, e.g. Sydney Harbour and much of the coast of Tas., and providing the ocean waves with much loose material still in evidence in coastal landform processes.

The Sedimentary Basins The Great Artesian Basin has alternations of aquifers and impermeable strata in sediments of Palaeozoic, Mesozoic and Tertiary ages, and many artesian bores of rather warm saline water suitable for stock. The surface is flat to gently undulating, but with low flat-topped hills with sharp edges imparted by a lateritic or siliceous capping or 'duricrust' (*see* SOILS). The Murray Artesian Basin contains considerable depths of Tertiary rocks from a former Murravian Gulf, including limestone aquifers yielding subartesian water, and marginal alternations of river deposits of now buried floodplains and terraces —sometimes even under basalt as in some gold-bearing gravels. Recent emergence of the area has left some landforms, such as the 80-km. wide belt of sand-dunes parallel to the coast near Mt. Gambier. The Eucla Basin is mainly of Tertiary limestone, the treeless Nullarbor plain extending above an artesian basin complicated by complex cave systems. The Desert Basin, the NW Basin, and the Coastal Plains Basin of W.A. include petroleum and natural gas; Permian coal is exploited at Collie; petroleum* at Barrow Island W.A.; and in Qld. and Bass Str. natural gas* and petroleum. There have been many notable geologists including amateurs; the most outstanding was T. W. Edgeworth David*. Although J. W. Gregory (1864–1932) was only in Aus. from 1899–1904, he made major contributions. In W.A. A. G. Maitland (1864–1951) was an important worker. *See* C. F. Laseron, revised J. N. Jennings: *The Face of Australia* (Sydney, 1972); J. N. Jennings and J. A. Mabbutt: *Landform Studies from Australia and New Guinea* (Canberra, 1967).

George Cross An award comprising a silver cross with a circular central medallion depicting St. George and the dragon, inscribed 'For Gallantry' and created in 1940 by King George VI for 'acts of the greatest heroism or of most conspicuous courage in circumstances of extreme danger'. Although primarily intended for civilians in response to the part they were playing in the 1939–45 War, it has a Military Division for actions not covered by military honours: these have mainly been associated with mine-laying and recovery, and prisoners of war. Aus. awards have included, 1 which superseded the former Empire Gallantry Medal held by P. G. Taylor* the aviator; 8 to military personnel; 1 to a policeman; 1 (posthumous) to the conductor of a Hobart tram involved in an accident. *For further reading see* L. Wigmore: *They Dared Mightily* (Aus. War Memorial, 1963).

George Gills Range N.T. 24S/132E A NW–SE range 300 m. above the Palmer River plain. It was discovered and named after a patron by Giles* who camped by King Creek, which has one of the most spectacular of the Central Aus. canyons, long a focus of Aboriginal pilgrimage.

George, Lake N.S.W. 35S/149E Alternately, for runs of years, a lake and valuable grazing flats. It is 24 by 10 km. and 7·6 m. deep when full. A small basin of internal drainage occupies a downfaulted valley in slaty Ordovician rocks, with a granite ridge to the E. Explanations of a romantic or bizarre variety for the vanishing and reappearing of the waters do not seem necessary: minor climate fluctuations, and runs of wetter years (mean annual rainfall 63 cm.) seem sufficient to explain the phenomenon. The lake was very full towards the end of the Quaternary glaciation, leaving large gravel ridges and terraces, especially at the N end.

George Town Tas. 41S/147E (6,027 in 1971) On the E bank of Port Dalrymple*, the mouth of the Tamar*, this is the residential centre for Bell Bay* aluminium works, and has a woollen industry. The original Port Dalrymple settlement was nearby, and Macquarie's scheme to make George Town the northern capital was tried (1819–24), but failed in face of Launceston's* development.

Georgina River N.T./Qld. Flows intermittently for some 1,130 km. SE from its source on the Barkly Tableland, 19S/138E, through the Channel Country*, then turns W as Eyre Creek and S, fed by the Mulligan, towards L. Eyre.

Geraldton W.A. 29S/115E (15,330 in 1971) The northern outlet for the Wheat Belt*, also shipping wool, manganese from Peak Hill and iron from Koolanooka for Japan. Crayfish for export to the U.S. have become important in recent years, and there is a superphosphate factory for the farming hinterland. Early tomatoes are sent as far as Melbourne. It began as a military post on the Murchison* Goldfield. Potash is to be extracted from a lake 32 km. N.

Geraniums Apart from imported garden varieties, there are several genera in the Geraniaceae family, true geraniums, such as the fodder-yielding crowfoot or Native Carrot *Geranium pilosum*, and the genus *Pelargonium*, with lipped flowers, e.g. the attractive pink *P. australe* on sandy soils in many parts of E Aus.

Ghans—*See* AFGHANS.

Ghost Gum, Moreton Bay Ash, White Gum, Cabbage Gum or **Pudding Gum** (*Eucalyptus papuana*) Grows in widely varied habitats, from 25–150 cm. monsoon rains in much of tropical N Aus. (and savannah country in the S of N.G.), and so varies from 6-18 m. and up to 45 cm. diameter, solitary in Central Aus. (in pictures by Namatjira and others), but with other monsoon forest species farther N. Short trunk then large spreading branches, smooth and white except near base where bark is thin, scaly, with irregular pattern, grey to rusty colour. Juvenile leaves are oblong to elliptical and 7·5 by 2·5 cm., intermediate leaves rather a broad lance-shape, adult narrow and lanceolate, 5–11 cm. long, and dull yellowish to light to dark green. Buds are small, egg- to club-shaped, fruit are small, like beheaded eggs on short stalks, and papery. Termite-resistant timber is used locally.

Ghost Sharks Somewhat shark-like, deep-water creatures, occasionally caught inshore and silvery when first caught. The Elephant Fish is a beaked species. (*See* SHARKS.)

Ghost Towns These are too numerous to list comprehensively: Many have vanished completely; others survive but truly as ghosts of their former selves, often by turning to another activity. The majority of Aus. ghost towns are relics of the gold-rushes*. In N.S.W. the Turon region, 33S/150E, is scattered with them: Summerhill Creek (later renamed Hargraves), Ophir, Tambaroora (formerly called Canton from the Chinese miners) are all gone; but Hill End survives as an artists' colony and Gulgong as a local service centre. Further N, Lawson's* country near Mudgee, 33S/150E, shows little evidence of the town of Pipeclay he described so clearly. In the far NW of the State, Milparinka has shrunk even further than Tibooburra, 30S/142E, from their great gold days of the 1880s. In S.A. Waukaringa is the main former gold town, only recently finally abandoned; it lies N of Yunta, 33S/140E, and the tall chimneys and batteries remain. In Qld. the Palmer River, 16S/143E, has a number of towns now almost swallowed by the bush; Laura survived as a minor centre, but Maytown and Palmerville have gone. Further W on the Gulf Plain, Croydon, 18S/143E, too is almost a ghost, its rail to Normanton now disused. In N.T. Tanami* and the Granites* are now dead, and 100 km. SE of Alice Springs, tourists chip hopefully among the solid stone ruins of Arltunga. In W.A. some of the most impressive relics of past grandeur are seen in the Eastern Goldfields, 31S/121E, especially in the sandstone buildings of Coolgardie*. But of the once flourishing Kanowna, N of Kalgoorlie, only the signposts erected by enthusiastic historians are to be seen. The other fields of the NW of W.A. are also dotted with ghost towns: Yinnitharra, 25S/116E, and Laverton, 29S/122E, now reviving with nickel discoveries; other towns are greatly shrunk, e.g. Cue, 27S/118E, or Daydream, just to the S of it. In Vic. Creswick* is now a forestry centre and Clunes, scene of the first gold discovery in the State, a thriving but small market town. Walhalla has almost gone and of many others there is little trace.

The Barrier Range in N.S.W., 32S/141E, had a number of silver towns before Broken Hill became preeminent: Thackaringa and the nearby Apollyon Valley mines are now only ruins; Silverton is merely an occasional halt for the ore trains to Port Pirie. Water shortage, and with it disease, were as much the enemy as dwindling

ores in this area and in many others. Just 48 km. SE of Canberra, Captain's Flat, also a lead–silver town is declining rapidly, following mine closure some years ago. Copper left ghost towns also, e.g. Chillagoe, 17S/145E, in Qld. where copper was smelted until 1943. In S.A. many solidly built batteries and sheds still stand, the work of the Cornish 'Cousin Jacks'; some of the towns survive as farming centres: Blinman*, Burra* and Moonta*. In Tas. some of the silver and later tin towns of the NW are reviving with new tin and iron workings, and Waratah, 41S/146E, survives as a small tourist centre; but Adamsfield in the rugged SW, 43S/146E, has died since osmiridium lost its market with the introduction of ball-point pens. In recent years uranium has left the ghost town of Radium Hill in S.A., 33S/141E, abandoned only in 1961, while in Qld. Mary Kathleen* was put in mothballs 1963-74. In W.A. the asbestos town of Wittenoom* was abandoned in 1966.

Apart from minerals, ghost towns mark former agricultural extension, as in the Willochra Plains* of S.A.; Cradock and Carrieton appear on maps but there is little there, Hammond just survives, but Gordon, Amyton and Eurelia have vanished. Numerous towns in E Aus. were surveyed and named in the anticipation of farming development that never came. There are ghost or semi-ghost towns that mark former customs posts on State borders: Innamincka*, now deserted, with Farina, further down the once bustling Strzelecki Track, Birdsville*, Oodnadatta*, Windorah, to name a few only. There are decayed ports along the S.A. coast, as at Robe; more notably, along the coasts of Qld. Cooktown* and Port Douglas survive now on the tourist trade; Bloomfield and Smithfield S of Cooktown are mere hamlets. Yet all 4 saw much activity as ports for the tin and goldfields of the interior. On the Gulf coast, sad relics are found in the rusty meatworks of Karumba, 18S/141E, once grandly planned as a major port; and to the W, Burketown and Borroloola* are in decline.

While populations into the thousands are quoted for many ghost towns in their heyday, the lack of remains is an indication of the flimsy, temporary nature of most of their buildings. The ruins that remain are most often those of the hotels, a courthouse or police station, and the minehead buildings themselves. *For further reading see* G. Farwell: *Ghost Towns of Australia* (Adelaide, 1965).

Gibber Stony desert in which wind erosion has removed loose particles, leaving a surface varying from boulders to small closely packed stones, on which a vehicle wheel leaves no trace. Gibber plains cover large areas of Gibson Desert* (W.A.) and the L. Eyre* basin (S.A. and SW of Qld.), including Sturt's Stony Desert*.

Gibber-bird The small grey-brown and yellow Aus. Chat of desert areas. (*See* CHATS.)

Giblin, Lyndhurst Falkiner (1872–1951) b. Hobart. Son of W. R. Giblin, who was Premier of Tas. from 1879–84. An outstanding economist who came to this work after extensive travel and political experience. He was an influential writer on the Depression, and Chairman of an economic advisory committee to the Federal Government (1939–46). A scholarship for Australians at King's College, Cambridge and annual lectures in Aus. both bear his name.

Gibson Desert W.A. A vast expanse of gibber plain and sand-dune country, N of the Warburton Range, and named by Giles* after the companion he lost there in 1874 when he crossed it from the E. It has been practically unvisited since, until, in the 1960s tracks adequate for 4-wheel-drive vehicles were marked across it, for weapon recovery from Woomera. *For further reading*

see L. Beadell: *Too Long in the Bush* (Adelaide, 1965).

Gidgealpa-Moomba S.A. 28S/140E A natural gas field in the SW of the Great Artesian Basin, in desert country between the Strzelecki and Cooper Greeks, with estimated reserves of 1 U.S. trillion m.^{3} and a life of at least 20 years. Exploitation is under way with a 800-km. pipeline to Adelaide (1969), with branches to the industrial towns at the head of Spencer Gulf, primarily for electricity generation at the Adelaide power station on Torrens Island. Further resources are reported from a separate structure at Daralingie, 32 km. S.

Gidgee (*Acacia cambagei*) A small shady tree of dry inland sandy soils, with grey to silvery phyllodes (twig tissue expanded to simulate leaves—the 'typical' pinnate acacia leaf is therefore not obvious). It reaches 7-9 m. and the timber, almost termite-proof, is locally useful.

Giffen, George (1859–1927) b. Adelaide. One of the best Aus. all-round cricketers, later serving as a selector. In 31 Tests against Eng. (1881–96) he scored 1,238, averaging 23 and including 4 centuries, and took 103 wickets for an average of 27, as a slow to medium bowler of great stamina.

Gilbert, John b. Eng. He arrived in Aus. in 1838 as field assistant to the ornithologist Gould. He worked in Tas. then W.A. (1839 and 1842), making major contributions to Gould's pioneer studies. In 1844 he joined Leichhardt* on his Port Essington expedition, and was killed by Aborigines in June 1845. His detailed diary, discovered in 1938, reveals many of Leichhardt's weaknesses. *For further reading see* A. H. Chisholm: *Strange New World* (Sydney, 1941).

Gilbert River Qld. 18S/143E Flows seasonally for 515 km. NW to the Gulf of Carpentaria. With its main (right-bank) tributary, the 420-km.-long Einasleigh, and the Staaten River to the N, with which it is linked by anabranches in the flood season, it has a catchment of 72,500 km.[2] mainly in tropical scrub with cattle stations.

Giles W.A. 25S/128E A Commonwealth meteorological station in the Rawlinson Range, with a staff of about 12 men.

Giles, William Ernest Powell (1835–1897) b. Bristol, Eng. He arrived in Aus. in 1851. He failed at the diggings and became a clerk in Melbourne, but, hating town life, turned to exploration and was financed in this by pastoralists seeking new land. In 1872 he found L. Amadeus; in 1874 he penetrated to the Gibson Desert, named after his companion who was lost; in 1875–6, backed by Elder and using camels, he crossed from S.A. to W.A., well N of Eyre's route, and returned by a route 644 km. N again—the only explorer to cross the worst of the western desert both ways. But Giles found little good land, and while fêted on his return was soon forgotten, and died when working as a clerk again, at Coolgardie. His *Australia Twice Traversed* was republished (1964) by the Libraries Board of S.A.

Gill, Samuel Thomas (1818–1880) b. Somerset, Eng. He arrived in Aus. in 1839, with his father, a minister. His prolific lithographed sketches, first of S.A., but notably of the Vic. goldfields, won him contemporary fame and a prosperity which did not last until his death, however. His lithographs provide a lively, often even humorous, but historically invaluable record and are of considerable artistic merit.

Gilmore, Dame Mary Jean (*née* Cameron) (1865–1962) b. Cottawalla, N.S.W. She was an important poet; her large output was dominated by a simple sincerity and devotion to humanity, though varying in quality. Many appear in *Selected Verse* (Sydney, 1948). After teaching, she joined the unsuccessful utopian New Australia* settlement, returning to Aus. in 1902, having married a fellow 'colonist'. As a journalist specialising in socialist causes, she encouraged many young writers and was created D.B.E. in 1936.

Gipps, Sir George (1791–1847) b. Kent, Eng. After an army career, successful work on an enquiry commission into West Indian slavery, parliamentary boundaries and Canadian problems, succeeded Bourke* as Governor of N.S.W. (1838–46). Able, conscientious and humane, he was yet extremely unpopular, with the squatters especially. He opposed moves to import Asians to replace convicts; he had 11 white men re-tried and 7 hanged after a group massacre of Aborigines (1838); his draft squatting and purchasing regulations (1844), aimed to give security of tenure, to raise revenue, and to balance large and small holdings by a licence system, was defeated after he retired, worn-out. He was also concerned to promote secular education* and agreed with moves to separate Port Phillip from N.S.W. He followed the official policy of suppressing gold discoveries in 1839 and 1841.

Gippsland A region of SE Vic. between Westernport and the N.S.W. border. It was discovered (1838) by McMillan*, but his name, Australia Caledonia, failed in favour of Strzelecki's*, after the N.S.W. Governor. Physically it comprises a forested northern hill area, the edge of the Vic. High Country and Aus. Alps, and a Tertiary sedimentary basin, which includes the now developed brown coal on the Latrobe River. In E Gippsland the plain reaches the sea (at Ninety Mile Beach*) and Gippsland Lakes, but in W Gippsland the low, rolling Strzelecki Ranges separate the Latrobe from a complex faulted coast of inlets and peninsulas (*see* WILSONS PROMONTORY, WESTERN PORT). Rainfall is over 125 cm. in the N; over 75 cm. in the extreme W and E; under 65 cm. in the central lowland which is irrigated from Glenmaggie Reservoir. Intensive dairying with associated pig-rearing and market-gardening for Melbourne and the Latrobe Valley towns has replaced roughly cleared cattle and sheep pastures. Forestry and coastal resorts are also important. *For further reading see* A. J. McIntyre: *Gippsland* (Melbourne).

Gippsland Lakes Vic. Near Lakes Entrance, 38S/148E, these are essentially shallow coastal lagoons, enclosed on the seaward side by a complex depositional barrier, the outer edge consisting of the Ninety Mile Beach and associated sand ridges and dunes, curved in consonance with SE ocean swell refracted into curves between Wilsons Promontory and Cape Everard. The main lines for the present coast took shape during the Tertiary era, but the details of the coastal barriers and lakes owe much to the Quaternary fall in sea level, when moisture was locked up in the ice caps, and to subsequent rises in sea level, notably during the last 15,000 years. Re-advancing across the former sea floor, the waves have been provided with ample material for coastal barrier construction, added to by wind-blown sand. There are 3 main and successive barriers, one N of L. King* and L. Victoria*, one to the S, and the outer barrier hemming in the long parallel lagoon of L. Reeve*. Wave action within the lagoon system has built up internal barriers, forming the separate lakes, Wellington, Victoria and King, e.g. the sandy deposits curved in consonance with local wave action E of L. Wellington, and in places delta formation, as where the long finger delta of the Mitchell River almost encloses Jones Bay from L. King. Erosion and deposition, effecting these

changes within the lagoon, are greater when the water is more salty, less when freshwater swamp vegetation acts as a stabilising influence. When Angus McMillan first found the lakes in 1839 and 1840, the natural entrance was at the far E near Red Bluff; the present artificial Lakes Entrance* was cut in 1889. The natural entrance has become sealed off near the small L. Bunga, To the E of Red Bluff, L. Tyres is a drowned valley system sealed off by a coastal barrier. *For further reading see* E. C. F. Bird: *A Geomorphological Study of the Gippsland Lakes* (Canberra, 1965).

Gippsland Shelf Vic. 38S/148E. Part of the Gippsland sedimentary basin of tertiary and Cretaceous rocks, which are reservoirs of large reserves of petroleum* and natural gas*.

Gladstone Qld. 24S/151E (15,365 in 1971) On the deep sound of Port Curtis, sheltered by Curtis Island, this town dates from the brief Gladstone Colony of 1847, a plan to settle N Qld. (as 'N Australia') with 'exiles' and time-expired convicts and initiated under W. E. Gladstone, then British Secretary of State for the Colonies. It was countermanded by his successor Grey, before getting under way from an unpromising start. Although serving small gold and copper fields, the port declined in the face of Rockhampton which was the rail terminal. Now rapid development is coming with the narrow-gauge diesel line bringing Kianga-Moura* coal for export to Japan from a new terminal; with the reduction of Weipa* bauxite to alumina for re-export, using thermal power from Callide and Kianga-Moura coal; there are also meatworks and dairy factories, and oil installations; a major sulphuric-acid plant, using pyrites from Mt. Morgan, and a 1,100-MW power station using coal from Bowen Basin.

Gladstone S.A. 33S/138E (926 in

1971; 1,053 in 1966). Town in wheat–sheep country at the rail-crossing of Port Pirie–Broken Hill, the narrow-gauge line N to the Willochra Plains, and the 5 ft. 3 in. line to Adelaide, all built in the era of wheat–mineral expansion to the N (1860–80). Until 1940 Booyoolie W of the line was a separate town.

Glass Manufacture Although widely distributed, this is in virtual control of one company. Silica sand, limestone and felspar deposits are adequate; soda ash is produced at Osborne near Adelaide, S.A. Plate glass is imported.

Glasshouse Mountains Qld. 27S/153E A group of 11 peaks rising dramatically from the coastal plain 80 km. N of Brisbane. They are 'volcanic plugs', the resistant (trachyte) rock which blocked the vents of Tertiary volcanoes, the outer ash layers having been eroded away. The highest is Mt. Beerwah (555 m.), and the most dramatic the sheer-sided Mt. Coonowrin (378 m.). Named by Cook, but whether because they shone, or resembled glass-making buildings is uncertain.

Glen Innes N.S.W. 30S/152E (5,771 in 1961; 5,673 in 1971) A rather stable and conservative local centre in the N of New England*, but with a considerable range of services and activities. It is a locally important crossroad, rail and air service centre, and shire headquarters.

Glenbawn N.S.W. A flood mitigation and irrigation reservoir on the Hunter River* upstream from Muswellbrook, 32S/151E. The earth dam is 76·5 m. high and the capacity 360 million m.[3] It has brought local benefits, and is part of a much larger scheme.

Glenbrook–Faulconbridge N.S.W. 34S/151E (9,640 in 1961; 13,722 in 1966) Part of the long twining ribbon of the City of the Blue Mts.*, grouped as an urban entity in the 1966 census, and rapidly growing, probably mainly with commuters to Sydney. The census

urban group includes Blaxland, Warrimoo, Valley Heights, Springwood and N Springwood.

Glenelg S.A. 35S/138E On Holdfast Bay and now incorporated in the Metropolitan Area of Adelaide, this was the site of the first S.A. settlement on the mainland. Here, Hindmarsh proclaimed the State on December 28th 1836.

Glenelg River Vic. 38S/141E Rises in the Grampians* and flows W then S for 470 km. to Discovery Bay where sand-dunes have deflected the mouth westward. Water for the Wimmera-Mallee is taken northwards from Rocklands Dam.

Glenmaggie Reservoir Vic. Has over 185 million m.[3], to irrigate dairy pastures etc. in good land in a rain shadow, W Gippsland. NW of Sale, 38S/147E, on the Macalister River.

Glenrowan Vic. 36S/146E A small rural centre at a gap in the Warby Ranges, followed by road and rail, and famous for the capture in 1880 of Ned Kelly*.

Glover, John (1767–1849) b. Leicestershire, Eng. After a successful artistic career, he emigrated from Cumberland, following his sons, to farm in Tas. in 1830, at 63. He bought some land, in exchange for paintings, from G. W. Evans, the surveyor. From his 2,800 ha. station near Ben Lomond* he sent back many landscapes, painted with a real appreciation of Aus. colour, landform and light.

Goannas (the term Iguanas is better avoided as referring properly to genera not found in Aus.) Also called Monitor Lizards, these are a one-genus family, the Varanidae, including some small forms under 23 cm. but also Australia's largest lizards of up to 2·5 m. The tongue is a distinguishing feature, being long, protrudable, and forked like a snake's. The tail is long, serrated and formidable; the claws strong, especially in tree-climbing species. Insects, lizards, small snakes, rabbits and sometimes carrion are eaten by the goannas. (In some areas this carrion-eating habit is regarded as entitling them to protection, though it is often said that a bite from a goanna is liable to serious sepsis because of bacteria from the teeth of carrion-eaters.) Eggs are laid. Teeth are long and powerful, and set on the

*Lace Monitor (Varanus varius),
about 2 m. long*

inner side of the jaw-bone. The goanna can run very fast on all fours, but may run on its hind legs if it wishes to observe its pursuers, say in long grass. The 20 Aus. species include: 1. the Common or Tree Goanna or Lace Monitor, *Varanus varius*, black with broad bands of yellow spots and may be 2 m. long; climbs and swims well and feeds on carrion, rabbits, possums, poultry, eggs etc.; 2. the Perenty Goanna, *V. giganteus*, 2–2·5 m., of central desert areas; 3. the 1 m. Water Monitor *V. mertensi*, of the rocky gorges of inland N Aus. and 4. *V. mitchelli* towards the N coast; 5. the Sand Goanna, *V. gouldii*, of many sandy areas all over mainland Aus., a burrowing species reaching 1·3 m; 6. the brown Black-headed Monitor, *V. tristis tristis*, up to 75 cm. long, common in open forests in many parts of Aus.; 7. one of the Pigmy Monitors, *V.*

gilleni, light brown with darker streaks and cross-bars, up to 36 cm., long, and common in Central Aus.

Gold Production varies; in the early 1970s it is rising with increasing prices; total value is $20–25 million. Over 90% comes from W.A. which has over 100 mines, most in the Kalgoorlie* Boulder region, and employing 3,000 people. Remaining production is from base metal concentrates, notably copper, at Mt. Lyell*, Tas., Mt. Morgan*, Qld., and Tennant Creek*, N.T. The world fixed price of U.S. $35 per oz. led to difficulties in face of post-war cost rises and resulted in Commonwealth assistance. All gold is bought initially by the Reserve Bank, but exports are through a producers' association.

Gold Coast Qld. 28S/154E (66,558 in 1971) A city lying along 32 km. of sandy coastline between Southport (the administrative centre) and Coolangatta on the N.S.W. border. Dependent almost entirely on tourists, the population trebles in summer, but it also attracts many southerners in the winter months. Growth has been especially rapid and continuous since building regulations were eased after 1952. In 1967 storms caused severe coastal erosion and subsequent decrease in tourist numbers, although a 34% increase in permanent population took place between 1966–71. The main centres are (from N–S) Southport, Surfers Paradise*, Broad Beach, Mermaid Beach, Miami, Burleigh Heads, Palm Beach, Currumbin Beach (and bird sanctuary), Tugun, Bilinga and Coolangatta*.

Golden Mile W.A. 31S/121E A series of mining leases operated by 4 main companies along the low ironstone ridge SE of Kalgoorlie*. In 1893, following Hannan's discovery, leased by 3 S.A. prospectors G. and W. G. Brookman, and S. Pearce, it was derisively known as Brookman's Sheep-run, until, following initial discoveries of unusual gold-bearing ores by a prospector Camilleri, the 3 found and named the Great Boulder lode after their former S.A. lease. The wealth of the 3-km. by 1·5-km. belt lies in the deep ores containing telluride of gold, requiring expensive methods of winning and processing. Some 3,000 men are employed in the 805 km. of mine-workings underground and surface plants for the crushing, flotation, roasting and cyaniding processes that leave ugly grey slime-heaps round the gaunt poppet-heads of the mines. But in 70 years 924,000 kg. of gold worth over $250 million has been extracted. Prosperity has fluctuated with rising costs and labour shortage against a fixed world price. Controlled production is worth an average of $16 million a year.

Goldfields and Agricultural Water Supply, W.A. This is the present development from the engineering masterpiece of 1896–1903, the Goldfields Water Supply Scheme. Water shortages were causing typhoid outbreaks in the Eastern Goldfields*, where water was obtained by condensers using the brackish lakes and ground water. The scheme to pump water from the Darling Range met much opposition which finally caused the suicide of its brilliant engineer C. Y. O'Connor*. From Mundaring Weir 550 km. of 30-in. (75 cm.) pipes and 8 steam pumping-stations raised 22,500 m.^{3} a day 396 m. to Bulla Bulling Reservoir, 34 km. W of Coolgardie, from where gravity led it to the gold-field. Here, on January 24th 1903, its arrival was greeted riotously. Now 6,279 km. of branch reticulation serve 88 towns in the wheat-sheep belts, and 1,822,500 ha. of farmland with stock and domestic supply; the daily total pumped (now by diesel stations) is 63,000 m.^{3}.

GOLD-RUSHES Through trebling the population (1851–61) and uncovering great wealth, gold discovery hastened constitutional development, economic growth and the dominance of urban over rural settlement. The first record of gold is in the 1823 notebook of a road surveyor working near Fish River in N.S.W. It is possible that Lhotsky found gold in 1834 and another more famous Pole, Strzelecki*, observed it in 1839; and Clarke* in 1841 had shown specimens to Governor Gipps, who said 'put it away . . . or we shall all have our throats cut'. Accidental discoveries were made by shepherds at different times. The Californian gold-rush of 1849 led to a reversal of the Government policy of suppressing the information, as the drift of men away from the colony was alarming. Hargraves*, a 'forty-niner', returned to his native Bathurst area, knowing of early discoveries there, and having learned the technique of panning, found gold at Summerhill Creek, a left-bank Macquarie tributary below Bathurst, in February 1851. His assistants, equipped with a 'cradle' which Hargraves left with them, found rich deposits downstream which led to the first gold-rush to Ophir, but they were much less handsomely rewarded than their tutor. A few months later, Ophir was deserted for Sofala on the Turon, a right-bank Macquarie tributary, and the hunt was on. In Vic., newly separated from N.S.W., employers, alarmed by the exodus of men and by a current depression, offered a reward for payable gold within 320 km. of Melbourne, which was won by Esmonds for his find in July 1851 at Clunes on Creswick Creek, a tributary valley of the Loddon, although his was by no means the first discovery in the area.

The erratic rivers draining the inland slopes of the Great Divide had for millennia been depositing alluvial gold, and the main fields were found along their valleys, from the Namoi in the N, S and W to the Wimmera.

Clunes was followed rapidly by Castlemaine (then called Mt. Alexander) in July 1851, by Ballarat (Ballaarat) in August 1851, and Bendigo, December 1851, and by the Ovens Valley fields to the NE in 1852. The Vic. fields were more compact, more rapidly discovered, and much richer than those of N.S.W., where, however, new finds were made up to the 1893 rush to Wyalong; Araluen in the scarp slope near the coast, 1851; New England near Tamworth and further N on the Gwydir, 1852; Kiandra on the Snowy River in 1859, and in a belt between the Murrumbidgee and Macquarie Rivers, Lambing Flat near Young, 1860; Grenfell, then Emu Creek, 1866). S.A. had only minor rushes (Echunga 1852, Gawler 1869). The first Qld. rush was an abortive one to Canoona W of Rockhampton in 1858, to be followed by minor finds in the area, and the great Gympie rush in 1867; Mt. Morgan, the 'mountain of gold', was developed from finds in 1882, and Charters Towers in 1872, the same year as a major, short-lived rush to the tropical Palmer River area. At about this time, gold was found in the course of the Overland Telegraph construction, and a disastrous rush to N.T. developed, to the alternately searing and steaming Pine Creek region, costing many their health and savings. In the 1890s there was a revival of Qld. discovery in the far N, but the main focus shifted to W.A., left behind so far, and discouraged by Hargraves's negative report in 1861. The Kimberley field, discovered by Hall and Slattery in 1885, had dwindled, but sporadic gold was being found in a 3,000 km. belt S to Norseman, and prospectors poured in, to rush on the Coolgardie discovery by Bayley in 1892, and Hannan's Find a few miles to the E in 1893, the beginnings of Kalgoorlie. Gold-rushes died out then, save for a few adventurous attempts in the Centre in the 1930s at Tanami, the Granites and Tennant Creek. A rare nugget is still to be picked up by the lucky or persevering, as at Wedderburn, Vic., in

1950 when over £5,000 worth was unearthed.

Surface gold was exhausted very soon; deeper 'leads' in old, buried alluvium were still accessible for some years to individuals or more commonly groups of 'diggers', but chance of finding such a 'gutter' was rare, and hard physical labour to sink and line the shafts and extract and wash the ore was involved. Crushing of gold-bearing rock was also possible for a time with primitive stamping and washing equipment but as the surface reefs gave out, deeper mining needed capital, and innumerable companies depending on small investors and employing labour were formed. The digger's day was over. Many made little; a number a working wage; a few a fortune (see Statistical Note, page 232).

The early gold-field scene was one of frantic activity by blue-shirted workers, in a lunar landscape of shafts, holes and heaps, shanties and tents, waterlogged in winter, saharan in summer. Yet there was considerable order, honesty and discipline between the diggers; contrasting with the hysterical urban scene where many squandered their finds. Violence did occur on the fields as a result of grievances over licences, leading to the Eureka Stockade* incident, from anti-Chinese feeling and from disputes over claims, as in the Tipperary Riots near Maryborough in 1855.

Until September 1852, migration was internal, including Tasmanians (Vandemonians), many of them recently expired convicts who contributed to much of the crime. Then came the overseas influx, 95,000 in 1852, of whom at least 80,000 stayed in Vic. Europeans predominated, but there were Americans, and from 1856, Chinese* who roused animosity. They were excluded by tax first in Vic., then in S.A. and N.S.W., but reappeared to constitute 90% of the Palmer River diggers in 1872 and in N.T.

It was in Vic., therefore, that the

wider effects of the gold-rushes were first demonstrated. Resentment at the licence, ruthlessly demanded regardless of a digger's success or failure, widened out to include demands along Chartist lines for suffrage so that diggers could be represented on the Legislative Council, then dominated by hostile squatters. Fear of the anarchy of the Californian fields, and possible revolution fanned by European hot heads, haunted both La Trobe* and Hotham*. As easy pickings disappeared, a drought and depression in 1864 turned ex-diggers' attention to the land, to find it locked also in the squatters' hands, and the demand for small selections was included. The final disappearance of transportation was hastened, since a penal colony with gold for the getting was ludicrous. The enrichment of S.A., by providing escorts and a good price for gold from Vic., was counterbalanced by losses in N.T. speculation; in W.A. it was the vote of the miners, largely 't'othersiders' (i.e. from the Eastern States) which pushed the colony into Federation.

Note: Holtermann's Nugget was a mass of pure gold (286 kg.), Hill End, N.S.W., 1872, as was *Kerr's Hundredweight* (48 kg), Turon, N.S.W., 1851. The largest nuggets were: *Welcome Stranger* (59 kg)., Moliagul, Vic., 1869; *Welcome* (55 kg.), Ballarat, Vic., 1858; *Blanche Barkley* (49 kg.), Kingover, Vic., 1857; *Precious* (45 kg.), Rheola, Vic., 1871. The richest 'gutters' were: *Blacksmith Claim*, Ballarat, 1 ton in 5 weeks worth £50,000; *Canadian Lead*, Ballarat, 1853, yielded £55,000 in a short time and more later. The artist S. T. Gill* recorded the gold-field scene; W. Howitt wrote *Land Labour and Gold* (1855) and there were many other contemporary accounts collected by N. Keesing in *Gold Fever* (Sydney, 1967). In fiction H. H. Richardson's *Fortunes of Richard Mahoney* is the finest evocation. *For further reading see also* N. Bartlett: *The Gold Seekers* (London, 1965); C. Barrett: *Gold in Australia* (Melbourne, 1951); and J. Monaghan: *Australians and the Gold Rush* (California, 1967). (*See* also GHOST TOWNS.)

Golf Increasingly popular in Aus., with many amateur clubs and a strong professional field, and opportunities, including the attraction of overseas talent to well-endowed tournaments sponsored by commercial firms. The Aus. Golf Union (1898) handles amateur inter-state and international arrangements, and there are controlling bodies in each State. It is probable that the game was introduced to Melbourne in 1847 by a settler from Fifeshire, Scotland, James Graham. In Adelaide Governor Sir James Ferguson had a 9-hole course laid out in 1869. Golf was started in Brisbane in 1880. The Royal Sydney and Royal Melbourne Clubs and the Aus. Golf Club (Sydney) dispute their respective claims as the oldest. The Aus. Open title has been played since 1904. Outstanding amateur players have been: Whitton (b. 1893) and Bachli (b. 1922). There are many first rank professionals: those mainly playing overseas include Kirkwood (b. 1898); Ferrier (b. 1915); Crampton (b. 1935); and others are Pickworth (b. 1918); Cremin (b. 1914); Von Nida (b. 1914), now a leading promoter; P. Thomson (b. 1929), the most famous to date, with 5 wins of the British Open 1954–8 and 1965; K. Nagle (b. 1920); B. Devlin (a highly successful professional) and D. Graham won the 18th World Cup at Buenos Aires in 1970, previously won by Aus. (Nagle and Thomson) in 1959.

Goodenia The largest genus in the mostly Aus. Goodeniaceae family. *G. stelligera*, common in coastal E Aus., has large dandelion-like, toothed leaves near the root and 30–45 cm. stem bearing many lipped and tubular yellow flowers. In Vic. *G. glauca* has profited from cultivation to become a weed. W.A. has showy species such as the blue *G. azurea*.

Goolagong, Evonne Fay (1951–) b. Barellan, N.S.W. A leading tennis player of Aboriginal birth, who won Wimbledon 1971.

Goolwa S.A. 36S/139E (680 in 1971) A dairy centre on the right bank of the Murray as it swings round the sandy Hindmarsh Island to its mouth; the channel is now crossed by **Goolwa Barrage** (1939), one of the 5 that prevent tidal inflow. The first public S.A. railway (horse-drawn) took produce from Goolwa to Victor Harbour (1856).

Goondiwindi Qld. 29S/150E (3,731 in 1971) On the Macintyre River* and N.S.W./Qld. border, this is an important crossing for cattle going S for fattening or slaughter.

Goonyella Qld. 21S/147E New coalfield linked by rail to Hay Point, and served by a new township Moranbah.

Goosefoot Widespread genus *Chenopodium*, with Aus. species of leafless, succulent herbs with jointed stems in the family Chenopodiaceae. Includes samphire or glasswort*, bluebush* and saltbush*.

Goossens, Sir Eugene (1893–1962) An Eng. conductor, first permanent conductor of Sydney Symphony Orchestra (1948–56) and given reputed credit for a suggestion that led to the Opera House*.

Gordon, Adam Lindsay (1833–1870) b. Azores. Of English parentage. Sent to S.A. in 1853 after a reckless youth, and became a police trooper, then horse-breaker and steeplechase rider. Proud, shy and melancholy, he shot himself after financial downfall and his daughter's death, just as his second and successful book was about to appear: *Bush Ballads and Galloping Rhymes* (Melbourne, 1870). While popular and spirited, his was mediocre verse: yet thought of as typifying the new, adventurous country. He is the only Aus. represented in Poets' Corner, Westminster Abbey.

Gordon River Tas. For 43S/146E runs S from King William Range then flows 200 km. NW to Macquarie Harbour, through formerly inaccessible mountain and rain-forest. The hydro-electric potential, to be developed by 1976, equals the Snowy Mts. Scheme*; a 500-km.[2] lake to flood the Serpentine Valley and L. Pedder* will be the largest Aus. water storage.

Gorton, John Grey (1911–) b. Melbourne. Liberal Party Leader and Prime Minister of Aus. from Jan. 1968–March 1971, following the death of Harold Holt*. He had held several Ministerial posts and was the first Minister for Education and Science (1966). Became Deputy Leader of the party under Mr McMahon* following a vote of no confidence by his party. Resigned Deputy Leadership 1971.

Gosford N.S.W. 33S/151E (with Woy Woy 38,093 in 1971) A resort and commuter town on Brisbane Water-Broken Bay, N of Sydney, with food processing and structural and building materials industries. The attractive local sandstone is valued for building or ornamental construction over a wide area. The electrification of the railway has greatly increased commuting to Sydney.

Goulburn N.S.W. 35S/150E (25,168 in 1971) A cathedral city and one of the larger inland service and market centres well placed to serve the NE part of the Southern Tablelands region, at the junction of the Wollondilly (Hawkesbury) and Mulwaree Rivers. It was a garrison and convict town, surveyed in 1828. The gaol remains, not unimportant. It is a general centre for education, professional services, important wool sales, stock sales, meatworks. etc. There are manufactures: chenille, knitting wool, and leather shoes. It is a local focus for sport, broadcasting and newspapers, and is a shire headquarters; the tree-lined streets justify the annual Lilac Festival. Until 1960 it provided some urban services for Canberra*, but the position is now reversed, and growth has slowed. Both the town and the Vic. Goulburn River* were named after **Henry Goulburn** (1784–1856), Under-Secretary for the Colonies (1812–21), serving in London under Bathurst. **Frederick Goulburn** (1788–1837), his youngest brother was first official Colonial Secretary in N.S.W. (1820–4).

Goulburn Islands N.T. 12S/133E 2 small islands each under 260 km.², off the N coast of Arnhem Land*; on the southern one is a Methodist Mission station which grows tropical fruit and vegetables and sends baskets and mats woven from pandanus leaf, tortoiseshell etc. to Darwin for the tourist trade.

Goulburn River Vic. Has a large catchment, including much in the 100–130 cm. rainfall belt, rising near the crest of the E Highlands about 130 km. NE of Melbourne and flowing NW, NE and NW in a great S bend—and in detail with spectacular meanders, many abandoned—to the Murray, 13 km. above Echuca, 36S/145E. Not much Goulburn water flows into the Murray. A little is diverted to Melbourne's system of reservoirs, but more important is its tapping for one of the country's biggest irrigation systems of 14,580 ha. The great Eildon Reservoir, and the Waranga Reservoir on the main channel leading from the Goulburn Weir, feed channels leading NW towards Shepparton, flanking the Campaspe River towards Echuca, E of the Loddon towards Kow Swamp Reservoir, and in the NW linking up with the Wimmera-Mallee domestic and stock water project.

Goulburn River. N.S.W. Important tributary of the Hunter River, its basin making a westerly embayment in the Great Divide. Rises about 32 km. NW of Mudgee, 33S/150E. Flows generally E to join the Hunter between Muswellbrook and Singleton, 33S/151E.

Gould, John (1804–1881) b. Dorset, Eng. Ornithologist, in Aus. 1838–40, who wrote *Birds of Australia* (London, 1848, in 36 parts and republished Melbourne, 1967 with text by A. Rutgers). Many illustrations were by his wife Elizabeth. **The Gould League of Bird-lovers** (1909) enrols schoolchildren to protect birds, and sponsors research.

Gould, Shane (1957–) b. Sydney. Brilliant woman swimmer who at 15 won 3 Olympic Gold Medals (all World Records) in 1972: 200 and 400 m. freestyle and 200 m. medley.

Gove Peninsula N.T. 12S/137E At the NE extremity of Arnhem Land*, with bauxite deposits now being developed. Nhulunbuy had 4,378 people and an alumina reduction plant in 1971. As it lies in a tribal reserve of the Yirrkala, there has been controversy over its development (as at Weipa*). A proportion of royalties will be devoted to problems associated with training and assimilation of the tribal people. In 1972 the Yirrkala lost their legal fight to ownership of tribal territories (*see under* ABORIGINES).

GOVERNMENT *Legislative* Since 1901 Aus. has had a Federal form of Government with 1 Commonwealth and 6 State Parliaments. In 1973 it was announced that 4 more Senators (2 for N.T. and 2 for A.C.T.) and 2 more M.H.R.s (1 each for A.C.T. and W.A.) were planned. Legislative power of the Commonwealth is vested in the Sovereign, represented by the Governor General, the Upper House or Senate, with 10 Members elected within each State, and the larger, Lower House of Representatives also elected by adult franchise, its numbers constitutionally required to be as near as possible twice those of the Senate. A referendum* to break this nexus was defeated in 1967.

The Commonwealth Government has grown in power and size over the years, and from 7 original Departments to 37 in the Labor Ministry of 1972– , looked after by 27 ministers of equal Cabinet rank. Five Cabinet committees 3 chaired by the Prime Minister will make recommendations. Cabinet Ministers control: Environment, Conservation, Overseas Trade, Secondary Industry, Science, External Territories, Repatriation, Works, Property, Services, Housing, Education, Health, Aboriginal Affairs, Postal Services, Media, Primary Industry, Immigration, Northern Development, Social Security, Treasury, Attorney General's Dept., Customs and Excise, Foreign Affairs, Defence, Labour, Tourism, Recreation, Minerals, Energy, Transport, Civil Aviation, Urban and Regional Development, Aus. Capital Territory, Northern Territory.

State Government departments include Education*, Police*, Transport, Water for power and irrigation, Industry, Housing, Mines, Decentralisation, Lands and Justice. Each State has a Governor representing the Sovereign. Qld. has only 1 House, the Legislative Assembly (since 1922). The other States have 2: the Upper House is the Legislative Council; the Lower House is the Legislative Assembly in N.S.W., Vic. and W.A., and the House of Assembly in S.A. and Tas. The Tas. Parliament has a 5-year maximum life, the others 3. All Lower Houses are elected by a universal adult franchise of British subjects, as is the Upper House in Vic. (1950), W.A. (1964) and Tas. (1969). But in S.A. a property qualification applies, and in N.S.W. the Upper House is elected by both Houses sitting together. The costs of 7 Parliaments, the duplication of effort, the difficulties over funds and the ease of modern communication are all factors accounting for signs of growing impatience with the Federal structure. (*See also* FINANCE; TAXATION.)

Executive power operates through a Public Service in each State and in the Commonwealth. While broadly similar to that of U.K., there has been more emphasis on professional specialist qualifications in high administrative posts as against the British tendency to use Arts graduates of the older universities. The employing body is the Board of Commissioners (or a similar group in the States) which is subject to Arbitration. Promotion is by merit, but with seniority, decisive in cases of 'equal merit' with systems of appeal, more often used. The growth of the Public Service since 1945 has led to reorganisation and innovation: attainment of degrees by part-time study and by cadetship is encouraged.

Historical Development In the early penal days legislative, executive and judiciary powers were wielded by the Governor alone, under orders from the Secretary of State in London. In effect, however, an embryo executive was formed with the dual functions of officers such as White as Surgeon General, or Alt as Surveyor, and of a Judiciary by making Collins* Judge Advocate. The Governor's rule by Proclamation was challenged effectively, if illegally, by the officers, and later by other factions such as exclusivists*, emancipists* and squatters*.

In 1814 the increasing friction between professional lawyers and military administration was partially resolved by the setting-up of a Supreme Court under a professional Judge. Criminal cases were still tried by the Judge Advocate and 6 officers; but there was continued confusion over applicability of English law in a penal settlement. The first major advance came with the N.S.W. Judicature Act of 1823. This recognised the emergence of a free settlement from a penal colony, by creating an advisory, nominated Legislative Council, enlarged and given greater power in 1828. It also created a Chief Justice, who in the person of Forbes* played a vital part in establishing English law and liberty. The Supreme Court was supplemented by Quarter Sessions and trial by jury could be requested in civil cases; the honorary magistrates (which had included almost every person of note) were gradually replaced by stipendiary magistrates. An Executive Council was also created in 1823, many of its officers also being on the Legislative Council; but a Colonial Secretary, and a number of administrators were appointed and sent from London, often with serious resulting conflicts with the Governors. A major attempt to organise the public service was made by Governor Darling* who organised local taxation to provide a police force, town water supply, postal service and introduced better pay conditions, pensions etc. for public servants. Appointments were still by patronage until almost the end of the 19th century, when the Vic. Public Service Act (1883) was followed by other States.

Meanwhile, however, the advance to self-government was marked by the 1842 Act for the Government of N.S.W. and Van Diemen's Land (Tas.), which made the Legislative Council two-thirds elective, although the high property qualifications vested most of this power in the hands of the squatters rather than the increasing urban populations. By this time, also, the N.S.W. Judiciary comprised a Supreme Court of 3 Judges, Circuit Courts at Bathurst, Maitland and Berrima, a Resident Judge at Port Phillip, Quarter Sessions at Sydney and 6 other centres with stipendiary chairmen, and trial by jury save for recharged convicts. This pattern was followed by the other colonies, until Federation (see LAW for subsequent development).

In 1850 the Aus. Colonies Government Act was the enabling Act which led to the separate self-governing colonies which were maintained until Federation. It separated Vic., giving it, with Tas. and S.A., a Legislative Council as in N.S.W. After petitions and near-rebellion over its restrictive phrasing, it was widened and virtually permitted the colonies to write and submit their own Constitutions. N.S.W., Vic., Tas. and S.A. had done so by 1855; Qld. was separated in 1859, but W.A. did not have its Constitution until 1890. It widened the franchise and allowed the charging of custom duties by the States. (See TABLE under HISTORY, pages 258–9.) For further reading see L. F. Crisp: Australian National Government (Melbourne, 1970); G. Sawer: Australian Government Today (Melbourne, 1970); J. D. B. Miller: Australian Government and Politics (London, 1959).

Governor In the early days of Aus. development, the administrator in charge of N.S.W. was the only Governor, while those of the other colonies were Lt.-Governors although they were frequently called Governor. Both were very powerful until the advent of responsible government in the 1850s, although their authority was increasingly curbed before then: unofficially by local groups such as the officers of the N.S.W. Corps or the squatters, and officially by the nominated Legislative Councils which preceded full self-government in the States. After this, they were much less influential, although many, through force of character, made important impact and may have influenced trends of development. After Federation the term **Governor General** was introduced for the Crown Representative in Aus. The term had been used without any underlying function in the period 1855–61 (Fitzroy and Denison). The Governor has residual powers under the Constitution* as well as having ceremonial and general leadership functions. Aus.-born Governor Generals, Isaacs, McKell, Casey and Hasluck have separate entries. A member of the Royal Family has twice been nominated: the Duke of Kent in 1939 was prevented from taking up office by the war, and by his death in 1942; the Duke of Gloucester was in office from 1945-7. Governor Generals were: Earl of Hopetoun (1901), Lord Tennyson (1903), Lord Northcote (1904), Earl of Dudley (1908), Lord Denman (1911), Sir Ronald Munro-Ferguson (1914), Lord Forster (1920), Lord Stonehaven (1925), Sir Isaac Isaacs (1931), Lord Gowrie (1936), The Duke of Gloucester (1945), Sir William McKell (1947), Sir William Slim (1953), Viscount Dunrossil (1960), Viscount de L'Isle (1961), Lord Casey (1965), Sir Paul Hasluck (1969). *For further reading see* H. V. Evatt: *The King and his Dominion Governors* (republished Melbourne, 1967).

Goyder's Line S.A. After disastrous droughts G. W. Goyder, Surveyor-General, was sent by the S.A. Government in 1865 to map 'the line of demarcation between that portion of the country where the rainfall has extended and that where the drought prevails', so that relief measures could be taken. Using the S limit of the saltbush, his 'Line of Rainfall' approximately delimits the area having 25 cm. mean annual rainfall and a growing season of 5 months, and was soon regarded as the limit of safe agriculture. (*See* MAP 10.)

Grafton N.S.W. 30S/153E (16,354 in 1971) Where road and rail cross a wide meander of the Clarence River*, 64 km. from the sea and the outport and resort of Yamba. It also has air connections with Sydney and Armidale and is an important focus of roads. Tertiary industries and services are important in a city commanding much local allegiance. It has manufactures, including matches, brewing and processing of butter, sugar, bacon, milk, timber and meat. The town has a boulevard main street and other avenues lined with jacarandas etc. The site, probably chosen at least partly as a cedar-exporting port, is liable to flooding.

Grampians Vic. 3 sandstone ranges forming a N-S arc, 145 km. long and pointing eastwards. Mt. William, named with the hills by Mitchell in 1836, reaches 1,168 km. They are the western termination of Australia's Eastern Highlands; the strata dip to the W, forming steep E-facing bluffs, e.g. Mt. Abrupt, the S end of the central Erra Range. Rainfall is 75 cm. Tourism is centred on Hall's Gap; about 800 flower species, natural woodland gorges and waterfalls make them a popular resort. Water catchments serve the Mallee and Wimmera to the N.

Granite Belt Qld. 29S/152E A distinctive region, 40 by 65 km. at 760-900 m., continuing the New England* Tableland and centred on Stanthorpe*. Alluvial tin was worked (1872-1900), but it is now famous for temperate fruits on some 6,000 ha. of orchards: apples and pears on higher ground; peaches, plums apricots and table grapes in sheltered valleys. Place names reflect the post-1914-18 War Soldier Settlement*: Amiens, Passchendaele etc.

Granites, The N.T. 21S/130E A rocky outcrop region above spinifex* and desert plains, which was the scene of the last great Aus. gold-rush in 1932; publicity given to finds attracted several hundreds, who battled through trackless, waterless wastes. The ores are there, but require large-scale costly operations, and many diggers were soon destitute; some settled to develop the Tennant Creek ores, but many were helped home.

Grant, James Macpherson (1822-1885) b. Scotland. He arrived in Aus. in 1836. He defended the Eureka* rebels and was deeply concerned to open the land for selectors*. The Grant Land Acts of 1865 and especially 1869 which insisted on occupation of selected land, foiled the notorious squatters'* evasions of previous legislation.

Grape, Wild (*Cissus antarctica*) A native member of the Vitaceae or vine family, with small rusty hairy flowers, blue-black edible fruit, and toothed heart-shaped leaves, found in the richer jungles of N.S.W. The Macquarie Harbour Grape of Tas., *Muehlenbeckia adpressa*, belongs to the dock family. The currant-like, acid fruits were used for tarts and preserves.

Grapes, cultivated—*see* VINES *and* WINES.

Grasses (in Aus.) These include some 140 genera and 700 species of the true grasses or Gramineae. (Sedges*, Cyperaceae, and Lilies, Liliaceae include some superficially grass-like members.) They are adapted to a very wide range of environments in a continent of wide contrasts from rain-forest to desert, including annual and perennial forms as elsewhere, creeping grasses such as Couch-grass* or true Spinifex*, many tufted rather than branched grasses, e.g. Serrated Tussock, and a few almost shrubby forms such as the waxy Cane-grass, *Eragrostis australasica*.

Significant forage grasses include: Blue-grass*; Button-grass*; Couch-grass*; Flinders-grass*; Kangaroo-grass*; Love-grass*; Millet, Native*; Minute-grass*;Mitchell-grass*;Mulga-grass*; Panic-grass*; Satin-top*; Scented-top*; Sorghum-grass*; Spear-grass*; Spinifex, as popularly used is Porcupine-grass* (cf. Spinifex proper); Wallaby-grass*; Warrego-grass*; Wheat-grass*; Windmill grass*.

Other prominent Aus. grasses are treated under the following popular or occasionally botanical names: Barbed-wire grass*; Blady-grass*; Blown-grass*; *Deyeuxia**; *Eriachne**; Fairy-grass*; Fescue*; Lemon-grass*; Rice-grass*; Snow-grass*; *Spinifex**; Tussock-grass*; Wire-grass*.

The many introduced fodder grasses —some naturalised, some pests locally —include: Cocksfoot*; Fescues*; Kikuyu*; Paspalum*; Phalaris or Canary-grass*; Rye-grasses*; *Sorghum* spp. *For further reading see* F. Turner: *Australian Grasses and Pasture Plants* (Melbourne, 1921). An important new work on wider aspects is: R. Milton Moore (ed.) *Australian Grasslands* (Canberra, 1970).

Grasshopper A popular name for certain winged, jumping insects of the Order Orthoptera* in Aus., the exceptions being the Crickets* and the Locusts* or Plague Locusts (though the latter are often classed as Short-horned Grasshoppers).

Grass-trees A widely accepted popular name for the Aus. genera *Xanthorrhoea*, Blackboys*, and *Kingia*. Some species have trunks. There is a crown of dense, rather tangled, strap-like to grass-like leaves, above which is a flower-head (for *Xanthorrhoea*) like a gigantic stiff grass-head, up to 3 m. long, and bearing densely packed white flowers in spring, or (for *Kingia*), a group of globular flower-heads like a crown of drumsticks. Growth is extraordinarily slow, perhaps 30 cm. a century, so that a 3-m. tree may be 1,000 years old. These plants have been taken as indicating very poor soil, the poverty now largely proved to be due to deficiencies in trace elements such as copper. The Aborigines ate the leaf bases, and early settlers extracted large amounts of sugar solution from the trunk. The resin-yielding *X. hastilis* is sometimes known as Spear Grass-tree (*see* PLATE 7).

Great Australian Bight The major indentation of the S coast of the continent, between 34S/124E and 34S/135E, a distance of some 1,125 km., and under 200 m. deep, being underlain by the continental shelf. The coast is lined evenly with the 75–90 m. cliffs of the Nullarbor Plain*.

Great Barrier Reef Stretches for 1,930 km. from 10°S–24°S with an area of 207,200 km.^{2} off the NE Aus. coast, and is the largest feature of its kind in the world. Reef-building corals consist mainly of numerous colonies of compound animals or polyps able to extract calcium carbonate from sea-water to form calcareous structures within and around their fleshy tissues. The living tissue in the 340 types of colony identified on the Barrier Reef are coloured by symbiotic algae living in them, and fade when the coral dies, leaving the hard structure which bleaches white. Coral only survives in clear salt shallow and moving water over 20° C. Dead corals get encrusted with calcareous seaweeds and are further cemented by coralline algae which also form calcium from the water, and are worn down to very fine particles which penetrate the interstices of the dead coral. Additional material contributing to the reef includes the single-celled Foraminifera (dyed and sold as 'coral flowers') and much general detritus of sands, remnants of molluscs etc. The 'Crown of Thorns' starfish* is causing considerable de-struction in some parts.

The origin of the reef is still debated but Darwin's theory (evolved on the *Beagle** voyage) is broadly accepted, with modifications: a reef is initially formed on a land margin which subsequently subsides, so that coral and ultimately the reef continue to grow upwards, always in shallow water, as sea level gradually rises. The Qld. Reef lies at the seaward margins of the continental shelf, and borings have failed to reach bedrock at 244 m. The reef is most continuous in the warmer N section, running N–S for 950 km. to Cape Melville, 14S/144E, where it is only 11 km. offshore, before swinging SE for 1,500 km. to its most E point in the maze of the Swain Reefs and most S point on Lady Elliot Island, 24S/153E, beyond the Capricorn-Bunker Group, becoming increasingly further from the coast, and more fragmented as the waters cool southwards. The seaward edge, marked by roaring surf, has a steep slope with living coral to 50 m., and landwards, cemented smooth dead coral, up to 800 m.

wide at low tide, sloping gently to the lagoon. Only some 10 navigable passages penetrate it, often opposite a river mouth where fresh water and silt inhibit coral, as in Flinders Passage, 19S/147E, off the Burdekin delta, and kept clear by tidal scour. On the land-ward side is the 2,000-km.-long lagoon, crystal clear, glassy smooth in the S, especially in 'winter', ruffled by the Trade Winds in the N and occasionally whipped by summer cyclones. It is floored with living reefs and sand, and studded with islands of 2 types: 200 or more 'cays' formed by deposition of detritus on a reef exposed at a low tide and anchored by vegetation, often now with mangroves on the leeward side (e.g. Low Island, 16S/145E), and the inshore coral-fringed hilly 'con-tinental islands', fragments of the drowned Qld. coastal mountains, e.g. Curtis, Magnetic, Hinchinbrook and The Cumberland Group. Conservation of the reef has become a controversial issue; modern dangers are from oil ex-ploration, pollution from pesticides etc. See P. Clare: *The Struggle for the Great Barrier Reef* (Melbourne, 1971).

Great Divide A term now preferred to the former **Great Dividing Range**, for the main watershed of E Aus. which only occasionally coincides with the highest sections of the E Highlands. From Cape York in Qld., the Divide runs S, and progressively inland to a maximum distance of over 480 km. from the coast between the Mackenzie and Barcoo basins, 24S/147E, then turns SE to within 80 km. near the Qld./N.S.W. border. Remaining within 160 km. of the coast, it then runs SSW and finally W in Vic., to culminate in the Grampians*. (*See* MAP 4.)

Great Lake Tas. 42S/147E Largest natural Aus. freshwater lake which runs 24 km. N–S, averaging 5–8 km. wide, in a shallow basin at 1,000 m. in the dolerite-capped Central Plateau, and within a few miles of its steep eastern scarp called the Great Western

Tiers*. Discovered by Toombs (1815), a kangaroo hunter, it is now a region of summer pasture, tourism and fishing, as well as being harnessed for hydro-electric development (see TASMANIA, POWER). The low level in not infrequent summer droughts is stabilised by water from L. Augusta and the River Ouse and Arthur Lakes, and the level is raised by Miena Dam at the southern outlet.

Great Northern Highway W.A. The major artery between the S and N of the State, especially after it joins the NW Coastal Highway S of the De Grey River. It runs from the Perth–Kalgoorlie road at Northam, 32S/117E, to Wyndham, 15S/128E, over 2,700 km. which is being surfaced to make it passable in bad conditions. The main sealed areas are in the S and along the Fitzroy Basin where it carries beef road-trains.

Great Sandy Desert W.A. Almost coincides with the sedimentary Canning Basin*. One of the least known and inhospitable regions in Aus., it was first crossed by Warburton from the E in 1873, when he found Joanna Springs in the centre; he nearly perished before reaching the Oakover River.

Great Victoria Desert W.A./S.A. A vast stretch of desert N of the Nullarbor Plain*, and is mainly a sur-face of parallel sand-dunes partly fixed by 'spinifex' (*Triodia*) and scattered mulga. The Laverton–Warburton Mis-sion track crosses its empty expanse, as do 4-wheel drive tracks for weapon recovery from Woomera*.

Great Western Tiers Tas. 42S/147E Basaltic cliffs towering up to 1,220 m. over the Midlands*, and forming the NE edge of the Central Plateau*. It was formed by faulting; the great fall is now used in both Great Lake–Esk River and the Mersey–Forth hydro-electric schemes (see TASMANIA, POWER). Tertiary sediments below the

basalt are weathered to gentler slopes and good farmland.

Greek Orthodox Church Much the largest of the Orthodox Churches*, with 154,924 adherents in 1961, this was first established in Sydney in 1897.

Green Island Qld. 16S/146E A tropi-cal coral island of some 12 ha., 26 km. from Cairns, famed for its underwater observatory.

Greenbushes W.A. 34S/116E A small alluvial tin-dredging centre just to the N of the Blackwood River, with a 100 km.^{2} field, but relatively low out-put.

Greenhood A popular name for *Ptero-stylis* orchids*.

Greenie The green-backed Western Silver-eye (see SILVER-EYES), an in-sectivorous and nectar-eating bush bird, which also unfortunately pecks ripe soft fruit and therefore is destroyed as a pest in W.A. orchard country. The term is also applied to the white-plumed Honey-eater, *Meliphaga peni-callata*, widespread except in SW Aus.

Greenway, Francis Howard (? 1777–1837) b. Bristol, Eng. The first and possibly greatest Aus. architect. He was deported to Aus. for forging a contract in connection with the build-ing firm he ran with his brothers. Phillips* gave him a commendation to Governor Macquarie* who released and, in 1817, pardoned him. He set up a practice in Sydney and from 1816–20 was Civil Architect. His major existing works include St. Matthews Church, Windsor (1817), and St. James, Sydney (1820); Hyde Park Barracks (1817), and the castellated stables of Govern-ment House, now the N.S.W. Conser-vatorium of Music. Working mainly within the Georgian style, Greenway added individual elements, revealing a sensitive talent. He was a short, red-haired arrogant man who clashed with many, including the civil engineer G.

Druitt, who supervised construction of a number of his buildings. After his dismissal by Governor Brisbane following the Bigge* Report, he lapsed into obscurity and died in some poverty, without, he said, adequate rewards for his work. (*See also* ARCHITECTURE.)

Gregory, Sir Augustus Charles (1819–1905) b. Nottinghamshire, Eng. He was brought to Aus. in 1829. An explorer and surveyor. In 1846 and 1848 he led official expeditions inland and N from Perth to the Gascoyne River. His major N Aus. expedition (1855–6) was financed by the British Government at the instigation of the Royal Geographical Society. Following up the Victoria River, Gregory was repulsed by desert and crossed the continent reversing Leichhardt's* 1844 route in a third of the time. In 1858, when sent to look for Leichhardt's lost expedition, he confirmed that Mitchell's 'Victoria River' was indeed a headwater of Cooper Creek, and proceeding S to Adelaide, solved the pattern of the S.A. salt lakes. His brother **Francis Thomas** (1821–88), also contributed to exploration*, notably in NW of W.A. in 1861.

Gregory family A famous Aus. cricketing family, founded by **Edward Gregory** who arrived in Aus. in 1813. Of his 7 sons, 5 played for N.S.W., and 2, **Edward** and **David**, in the first Test* Match, when David was captain. Edward's son **Sydney** (1870–1929) was a brilliant copybook batsman, playing 28 Tests against Eng. (1890–1912), scoring 2,193 with an average of 25·8. In first-class cricket he totalled 15,053, averaging 28·61 with 25 centuries. He was small, dark and very dynamic in play. **Jack Morrison** (1895–   ), his much younger taller cousin was an outstanding all-rounder who played in 21 Tests against Eng. as a left-handed batsman (1921–8) averaging 34·88; he took 70 wickets for an average of 33·77, and 70 catches.

Gregory Range Qld. The most westerly offshoot of the E Highlands, running SW–NW for 240 km. W of Gilberton, 19S/144E, and consisting largely of later sediments than most of the Highlands, uplifted with them to some 600 m.

Gregory River Qld. 290 km. long, with a perennial flow maintained by springs in the Barkly Tableland where it rises (20S/136E), and a total catchment, with the Nicholson which it joins near the Gulf, of 58,000 km.^{2} The Albert River is a major distributary.

Grevillea A genus of some 240 species of trees and shrubs, mostly in mainland Aus. in the large southern family Proteaceae. The genus may be divided in different ways, according to flowers or fruits. The Spider-flowers of the sandstone plateaux of coastal E Aus., are well-known for their round flower-cluster with projecting stalk-like processes suggestive of spiders' legs, e.g. the Grey Spider-flower, *G. buxifolia*, and the Red Spider-flower, *G. punicea*. The Silky Oak, *G. robusta*, a 37 m. tree of open or rain-forest in E Aus. may be taken as representing the grevilleas in which the flowers face one way on the spike, more like a toothbrush, producing woody capsules containing 1 or 2 thin papery seeds. There are somewhat feathery or fern-like multiple leaves, deep-green above and grey-silvery below. It was a useful cabinet timber now largely worked out, but is grown elsewhere in the tropics as a shade for tea plantations and for timber. The Beefwoods (from the red timber) of large areas in E Aus. include *G. striata*, with long narrow leaves and erect creamy spikes. From W.A. we may note the prickly leaved red-flowered *G. bipinnatifida* and *G. wilsonii*, and from father N the 60–90 cm. creamy spikes, loaded with flowers of *G. leucopteris*. (*See* PLATES 6 *and* 7.)

Grey, Sir George (1812–98) b. Portugal. Son of an army officer, he came first to Aus. in 1837 specifically to explore the NW coast for a great river outlet, but the expedition was cut short when he was wounded by Aborigines. He discovered the remarkable Kimberley rock paintings. In 1839 he landed much further S, at Shark Bay, lost first his stores then his whaleboats and made a forced overland march to Perth.

He was Governor of S.A. (1841–5) and rescued the bankrupt colony by stringent economic measures and persistence in obtaining honourable settlement for Gawler's* bills. He cut down relief work, thus forcing people out to work in the countryside. He had a great interest in Aboriginal welfare and culture. During his 2 periods of governing in N.Z. (1845–53 and 1861–8 and as Prime Minister 1877–9) he concerned himself primarily with Maori problems, and in Cape Colony (1854–61) it was in setting aside Kaffir reserves that he was most active. He represented N.Z. at the 1891 Federal Convention.

Grey Jumper—*See* APOSTLE-BIRD.

Grey Range Qld. This forms the low divide between the Bulloo River* and the L. Eyre basins. They are low hills trending NE–SW for 480 km. to the W of Quilpie, 27S/144E. Sturt was marooned by a waterhole for 6 months in 1845. The spinifex saltbush will support beef cattle. Opals and gold have been exploited.

Griffin, Walter Burley (1876–1937) b. Illinois U.S. An architect. He worked under Frank Lloyd Wright, and on his own until, in 1912 in collaboration with his future wife Marion Mahoney, he won the international competition for a plan for the new Federal Capital of Aus. The Griffins lived in Melbourne until 1928 then in Sydney until leaving for Lucknow to design university buildings in 1933; he died there. Griffin's plan, although modified, set the basic pattern for Canberra*. He ceased to be associated with it after

1920, frustrated and insulted by officialdom. He was equally influential in private practice: Newman College, Melbourne (1916), a Dance-Theatre complex at St. Kilda (1920–23, but later burned), Leonard House, a small office block, with a glass façade, the Capitol Theatre, Melbourne (1924), with its brilliant use of interior plaster work, and the town plan of Griffith, N.S.W., are diverse examples of his creative approach. In domestic architecture this was aimed at evolving houses for urban living with space, privacy and unobtrusive building; it is best seen in Castlecrag, Sydney, where he bought land and developed a small community of low stone or concrete flat roofed houses, in one of which he lived.

Griffith N.S.W. 34S/146E (11,015 in 1971) A railway junction and local service, market and fruit canning and processing centre in the Murrumbidgee Irrigation Area*. It was planned as a new town, to be the focus of intensive irrigation (rice, fruit, vines) within the project, and designed by Walter Burley Griffin*, the planner of Canberra, in 1914. The C.S.I.R.O.* irrigation research centre occupies a prominent place in the town. Gypsum is quarried nearby.

Griffith, Sir Samuel Walker (1845–1920) b. Merthyr Tydfil, Wales. Son of a Congregational Minister, he arrived in Aus. in 1854. He was Qld. Premier 1883–8 and 1890–3, Qld. Chief Justice 1893 and Lt.-Governor 1899–1903. In Qld. he was responsible for the abolition of Kanaka* labour and for free compulsory and secular education (1875). He was prominent in Federation* notably by his brilliant chairmanship of the Committee which, in 1891, made the first and basic draft of the Constitution, when his clear mind, scholarly leanings (he was a noted Italian translator) and legal training were combined with cool diplomacy. As first Chief Justice of Aus. 1903–19, his legal interpretations of the Constitution were very important.

Grimwade, Sir Wilfrid Russell (1879–1955) b. Caulfield, Vic. A manufacturing chemist and druggist and a great philanthropist, particularly in the fields of chemistry, bio-chemistry and conservation. He bought 'Captain Cook's Cottage' (see JAMES COOK) and had it rebuilt in Melbourne. *For further reading see* C. Turnbull: *Russell Grimwade* (Melbourne, 1967).

Groote Eylandt N.T. 14S/137E An island in the Gulf of Carpentaria, 65 km. N–S by 48 km. E–W, which shares the Precambrian rock structures of Arnhem Land* and contains large reserves of manganese*, exploitation of which is in progress by open cut; ore is loaded at Milner Bay; the township is Alyangula. A wide variety of tropical fruit, including citrus, is grown and cattle reared on planted lucerne. The name was given by Tasman in 1644.

Gropers This name is applied to mainly but not exclusively tropical fish of more than one family. 1. The large Blue and Red Gropers, *Achoerodus gouldii*, vary widely in colour, and reach over

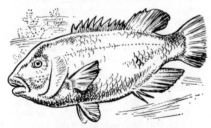

Red Groper (Achoerodus gouldii)
about 1 m. long

1 m. and over 45 kg.; they are bulky fish of the general wrasse shape, with very thick lips. 2. The rather sharp-snouted Pigfishes, such as *Verreo bellis*, are mainly pink with several dark interrupted lines along the sides,

and up to 45 cm. long. 3. The oval-bodied Macaw Fish, *Lienardella fasciata*, is a fish of coral reefs, gorgeously cross-striped in green, blue and scarlet. These fish have the teeth partly fused into a bony ridge (cf. the Parrot fishes*). For the large dangerous Queensland Groper *see* ROCK-COD.

Grose, Francis (? 1758–1814) b. Surrey, Eng. Appointed (1789) to form and command a special army corps, which became known as the New South Wales Corps*. He arrived in Sydney in February 1792, having meanwhile also been appointed Lt.-Governor of the colony so that when Phillip* left at the end of the year, Grose took charge. His short period of control (Dec. 1792–Dec. 1794) is controversial. He improved the staggering economy, but at the cost of disregarding Phillip's principles, by granting land, allowing the employment of convicts who were paid in rum, and trading by officers. Jovial, worldly and popular, his efforts were beneficial in the short term, but sowed the seeds of much of the subsequent dissipation and trouble in the colony.

Grounds, Roy Burman (1905–) An architect who, with G. H. Mewton, pioneered the Aus. interpretations of the modern international style in architecture after 1934: simple, functional lines were tempered with Aus. elements, verandahs, shutters, wide eaves, etc. His own Clendon Flats (1940) was imitated widely, but his most famous building, the domed Academy of Science, Canberra (1959), remains unique.

Groundsel The European name for *Senecio**, a yellow flower with downy seeds, introduced as a weed, but with Aus. relatives.

Group Settlement Scheme W.A. Devised in 1921 by the Premier Sir James Mitchell, to bring out British migrants and settle them in the SW of the State in loosely associated groups which would share the initial bush-clearing of a planned 6,000 holdings. It largely failed through lack of technical knowledge to cope with the difficult climate and terrain. There were some 10,000 'Groupies' and a maximum of 2,442 holdings, many later abandoned or amalgamated. *For further reading see* T. P. Field: *Post-war Land Settlement in W.A.* (Kentucky, 1963).

Gruner, Elioth (1882–1939) b. N.Z. He arrived in Aus. in childhood. An artist of the traditional landscape school, working under Ashton*. His work was popular as typifying the Aus. scene, but has been debased by imitation.

Grunters Freshwater fish mostly small, deep-bodied with large scales, and continuous dorsal fin, the front part spiny, e.g. the Sooty Grunters of the genus *Hephaestus*, warm-water species of tropical Aus. and Central Aus., including some able to live in warm borewater. The grunting noise from which they are named comes from expelling air from the swim-bladder.

Guinea Flower A popular name for *Hibbertia*, a largely Aus. genus of shrubs and trees in the Dilleniaceae family of tropics and sub-tropics. The Shiny Leaf Guinea Flower, *H. nitida*, is common in coastal Aus., especially in the E, and has small square-ended smooth glossy leaves and a 5-petalled yellow rose-like flower. The Twining Guinea Flower, *H. scandens*, has a showy 6-cm. yellow flower and shiny red berries in a dark brown calyx, with large dark green leaves.

Gulf of Carpentaria 14S/139E A 500 km-wide inlet between Arnhem Land*, N.T. and Cape York Peninsula*, Qld. It extends some 650 km. S to the shores of the Gulf Country*. Maximum known depth is 79 m. Islands are close inshore and include Groote Eylandt* and the Wellesley* and Sir Edward Pellew Islands. Carpentier was Governor General of the Dutch East Indies at the time of the early 17th-century Dutch voyages of discovery* in these waters.

Gulf Country A distinctive region of N Qld./N.T., comprising the lowlands round the Gulf of Carpentaria, where the rivers subdivide as they wander along tree-lined courses over flat savannah land. Rainfall of 75–100 cm. comes almost entirely in the 'Wet' (December–March). Temperatures are always high, and large cattle-breeding stations predominate, with outlets by beef roads, built or planned, to railheads further S and experimental coastal shipments replacing former droving to the E coast.

Gulls of Aus. coasts and seas include the medium-sized Silver Gull and the larger black-backed Pacific Gull. (*See* SEA-BIRDS.)

Gum A very widespread popular name for the Eucalypts* (probably extended at times to other superficially similar Myrtaceae). Governor Phillip himself seems to have coined the name in 1788, from the bitter, tannin-rich gum-like exudate or kino seen seeping on to the bark of many Eucalypts. Aus. does have resources of true, water-soluble gums, notably in certain Acacias, but only occasionally during war has exploitation been economic. Resins from the Grass-tree* or Blackboy, or from the Cypress-pine*, *Callitris* spp., have been used to a small extent from time to time.

Gum Vine (*Aphanopetalum resinosum*) A bush of rich coastal soils in E Aus. with 4-petalled white flowers, resembling the Christmas Bush*, *Ceratopetalum*, but lacking the large coloured sepals, also in the southern family Cunoniaceae.

Gummy The edible, crustacean-eating shark, *Emissolla antarctica*, lined for commercial marketing in the S waters of Aus., and named from the flat, crushing and grinding teeth. It is sometimes called 'Sweet William' from its unusual odour.

Gundagai 35S/148E (2,114 in 1966; 2,167 in 1971) A former mining centre and river steamer port, on the steep valley side of the Murrumbidgee. It is a local service and market centre on the railway and the Hume Highway, and centrally placed in the S part of the Western Slopes. The name is widely known from the ballad by Moses*, written when it was a notable centre for bullock teams. It retains some of this character as a staging post in its modern motels and cafés which cater for the passing motorists.

Gunn, Jeannie (née Taylor) (1870–1961) b. Melbourne. The wife of Aeneas Gunn, manager of Elsey Station*, N.T. She wrote the minor classic of outback life *We of the Never Never* (London, 1908). She was later a social worker in Melbourne.

Gunnedah N.S.W. 31S/150E (8,219 in 1971) A growing local service, market and processing centre (meatworks, milling cypress-pine) on the Namoi River, Newcastle–Walgett railway, and at an important road junction. It lies centrally in the rich fattening pastures on the black soils of the Liverpool Plains*.

Gunyah A roughly constructed and temporary Aboriginal bark shelter. The word derives from the dialect of the original Port Jackson natives. For a time in the mid-19th century it was applied to a digger's or stockman's crude shack.

Gwalia-Leonora W.A. 29S/121E Small twin towns. A former gold-mining centre and railhead N from Kalgoorlie; now a service centre for wool country.

Gwydir River N.S.W. Rises near Uralla, 31S/152E, in 75-cm. rainfall and dry sclerophyll* country in the New England* plateau, and flows W for 670 km. to the Darling River* through Moree, 29S/150E, into tree and shrub savannah and tussock grassland coun-try, where the slow, shallow, spreading river ceases to be perennial. The name, from N Wales, was named after Lord Gwydir by Allan Cunningham* in 1827. The Copeton Dam, to be built by 1976 on the upper Gwydir, will impound 1,356 million m.[3]

Gymnosperms (naked seeds) A major division of the plant kingdom, with a long fossil history and distinguished by the naked ovule. Pollen is produced in sacs, generally arranged in cones. Of 4 living Orders, 2 have members in Aus. The cycads*, with a palm-like growth habit, have 3 genera, *Macrozamia*, *Bowenia* and *Cycas*. The conifers include a number of families with members locally important in Aus. such as the Cypress* family, Cupressaceae, the Podocarpaceae*, the Araucariaceae, including Hoop Pine*. The N hemisphere Pine family includes *Pinus radiata*, a Californian species now widely planted in Aus. *Ginkgo*, the only living member of the third Order, is a native of China, but is sometimes planted in temperate Aus.

Gympie Qld. 26S/153E (11,131 in 1971) A city in the Mary River valley and the main service centre for land producing tropical fruits, especially pineapples*, with dairying and associated butter, and condensed and powdered milk factories. Its origin was due to gold, discovered in 1867 by James Nash, leading to a major gold-rush to the alluvial diggings, followed by 50 years of productive reef-mining lasting until the 1920s.

Gympie or **Yellow Messmate** (*Eucalyptus cloeziana*) A good timber tree of 40–45 m. by 90–150 cm., found in coastal to middle-belt Qld. from Gympie to Atherton, in scattered sites, the best often in pure stands on good loams on lower valley slopes. It has persistent brown bark on trunk and larger branches, much furrowed but rather soft and fibrous. Juvenile leaves are fairly broad, adult leaves lanceolate and often curved, paler on under side. There are large groups of fig-shaped buds and top-shaped fruit.

Gypsum Hydrous calcium sulphate, used in cement and plaster of Paris, is abundant in Aus. Of an annual total production of over 900,000 tonnes, two-thirds comes from the Yorke and Eyre Peninsulas and Kangaroo Island in S.A. It is used in fertilisers and cement.

H

HACKETT

Hackett, Sir John Winthrop (1848–1916) b. Ireland. W.A. politician, newspaper magnate and benefactor, who arrived in Aus. in 1875 to practise law, but turned to journalism in Sydney and later Perth. His large bequest to the University of W.A. and earlier endowment of a Chair of Agriculture have enormously benefited its development. He was a thoughtful and influential delegate to the Federal Conventions of 1891 and 1897. Hackett is also commemorated in a Canberra suburb.

Haddon Corner S.A. 26S/141E The NE corner of the State, surveyed and marked by Poeppel in 1879.

Haddon, Robert (1866–1929) b. Eng. An architect who arrived in Aus. in 1891, and lived in Melbourne from 1900 until his death. He was the most successful exponent of the *Art Nouveau* style through practice and teaching, in which he advocated a return to the plain surface, in reaction to the Victorian ornamentation. His own buildings always had some distinctive feature to break the plain wall.

Hairy-tails A popular name for some of the 150 Aus. species in the cosmopolitan Amarantaceae family, which includes many garden favourites and some imported weeds. In inland E Aus. the Hairy-tail is *Ptilotus semilanatus*, with leaves like rather broad grass, but obliquely veined, and pink and white flower spikes, like hairy clover-heads. (*See also* MULLA MULLA.)

Hakea An Aus., especially W.A., genus of shrubs and small trees in the southern family Proteaceae, mainly with lanceolate to needle-like leaves, and variable flowers, some like rather feathery and diffuse Bottlebrush* flower-heads, near

HALL

the ends of branches and among the foliage, some globular or pincushionlike, some almost like the spidery *Grevillea**; but the fruit is distinctive, a leathery structure often borne close to the branch, containing 2 winged seeds (often released after bushfires, making some species a pest in places). Well-known W.A. species include the red Pincushion Flower (with cream stigmas), *H. laurina*, with blunt, fairly broad leaves, turning red before they fall, the Broad-leaved Sea Urchin, *H. petiolaris*, while the Corkbark or Western Cork-tree, *H. lorea*, seen in many red sand areas of Central Aus., has leaves 60 cm. long and large yellow erect flower spikes. The crimson pink *H. gibbosa* is a common bush in W.A., while the spidery pink-white flowers of the Needlebush, *H. sericea*, are common on the less infertile soils of the coastal sandstone country of SE Aus.

Hall, Benjamin (1838–1865) b. Breeza, N.S.W. Said to have been driven to bushranging by the desertion of his wife when he was (possibly wrongly) accused of being an accomplice of Gardiner*. Between 1862 and 1865 he led a gang in the Forbes region which seemed immune to police action, robbing homesteads, banks and stage coaches, to the widespread admiration of all but the victims and police. Hall killed no one, but was not able to prevent his gang from doing so. He was shot after betrayal, while camped near Forbes.

Hall, Edward Smith (1786–1860) b. London. He arrived in Aus. in 1811. From 1826–38 he published the *Monitor*, which in spite of ensuing libel suits was very important in the struggle for a free press.

Hall, Rodney (1935–) b. Eng. arr. Aus. 1949. He is a leading modern poet.

Hall's Creek W.A. 18S/128E Developed on this Ord River headwater after alluvial gold was found by Hall and Slattery (1885), but soon faded from a shanty and tent town of several thousands to a small outback settlement. It has revived as an air and service centre for E Kimberleys* and on the Broome–Darwin section of the Great Northern Highway, and has been rebuilt 15 km. from the original site where the water supply is better.

Hamersley Range W.A. 22S/118E A NW–SE trending hill range above the wider Hamersley Plateau, and reaching 1,237 m. in Mt. Meharry. Horizontal Precambrian sediments, brilliantly coloured in reds and purples, are gashed by the deep gorges of the Fortescue and Ashburton Rivers and their tributaries. Even in dry periods, deep pools and rich green vegetation contrast strongly with the brown savannah of the plateau surface, and tourist development is likely to follow the opening up of the region for its vast iron* reserves that is now in progress.

Hamilton Vic. 38S/142E (9,662 in 1971; 10,062 in 1966) A city and market centre for a dairying, grazing region in the lava country of the Western District*. It grew round an inn at the crossing of the Grange Burn (named by Mitchell)* and was called The Grange.

Hammond, Joan Hood (1912–) b. N.Z. but arr. Aus. as an infant. From her operatic debut in Vienna in 1939 she achieved world fame as a dramatic soprano. She excelled too in golf and squash.

Hancock, Sir William Keith (1898–) b. Melbourne. An economic historian of high international repute, holding Chairs successively in Adelaide, Birmingham and Oxford. He edited the Civil Series of the U.K. War Histories, before joining the Aus. National University 1957–65; his *Australia* (London, 1930) is a classic. Recently he wrote *Discovering Monaro* (Cambridge, 1972).

Hanlon, Edward Michael (1887–1952) b. Brisbane. Labor Premier of Qld. 1946–1952, vigorously pressing development under State control, notably irrigation schemes like the Burdekin* and the health services.

Hann, Mount W.A. 16S/126E Highest point of the main Kimberley* Block. It rises 244 m. from the sandstone plateau to 854 m. above sea level.

Hardy, Francis Joseph (Frank) (1917–) b. near Warrnambool, Vic. A left-wing writer of stature, whose exposures of Vic. political shabbiness in *Power Without Glory* (Melbourne, 1950) led to an unsuccessful libel suit. He is also the creator of the *Yarns of Billy Borker*, many obtained from his father, which capture the spirit of the successful 'pub yarn' in describing Aus. characters and topics.

Hargrave, Lawrence (1850–1915) b. Greenwich, Eng. An engineering draftsman and later astronomical observer, who arrived in Aus. in 1866. He studied problems of flight, experimenting with kites on a N.S.W. beach (1892–4). An important early aviation pioneer; he is commemorated on the $20 note.

Hargraves, Edward Hammond (1816–1891) b. Gosport, Eng. He settled in N.S.W. in 1834, but went to the Californian gold-rush in 1849. On his return he used experience and local knowledge, and panned gold on February 12th 1851 at Summerhill Creek, with Tom and Lister. Officially regarded as the discoverer, he was awarded £1,000 and £250 by N.S.W. (1877). Only half the Vic. award of £5,000 was paid, following protests from Tom. He was unsuccessful in gold surveys in W.A. (1862) and Tas. (1864).

Harmless Land Snakes (Sub-family Colubrinae) 1. The attractive Common or Green Tree Snake, *Dendrelaphis punctulatus*, of N N.S.W. to the NW of

PLATE 5: BIRDS (LARGE)

1. Brolga *(Grus rubicanda)*. 2. Emu *(Dromaius novae-hollandiae)*.
3. Cassowary *(Casuarius casuarius)*. 4. Cape Barren Goose *(Cereopsis novae-hollandiae)*. 5. Bustard *(Eupodotis australis)*. 6. Superb Lyrebird *(Menura superba)*.

W.A., is not always arboreal nor always green (it may also be blue or yellowish to putty-coloured, and may have a crimson head and body lines, the colours flashing when it puffs out its neck when excited). The similar lighter-coloured but black-spotted Northern Tree Snake, *D. calligaster*, grows to 1-2 m. Both lay eggs, in forest litter. 2. The Common Keelback or Fresh-water Snake, *Natrix mairii*, of N Aus. is not dissimilar but semi-aquatic, slender, active and attractively coloured from grey to rich brown with pinkish belly; it lays eggs and eats mainly frogs. If caught by the tail, it may discard the end in the way common with lizards. 3. The entirely nocturnal Slaty-Grey Snake, *Stegonotus modestus*, up to 1·8 m. long, is found in crevices, climbs well, but lives near water and feeds largely on frogs, mice etc. All these snakes may bite on handling, but will hardly even draw blood.

Harpur, Charles (1813–1868) b. near Windsor, N.S.W., of formerly convict parents. He is considered the first important Aus. poet. Although strongly influenced by English poets, mainly Wordsworth and Milton, he wrote of the Aus. environment, its vastness and ever-changing light. No collection of his work has been made since 1883, but his poems are often in anthologies. His best work was blank narrative verse, but he also wrote verse drama, lyrical, satirical and political verse and prose criticism. He worked variously as clerk, farmer and gold commissioner.

Harris, Alexander (1805–1874) b. London. He was in Aus. from 1825–40, later going to America. He wrote extensively about the colony in *Settlers and Convicts* (1847) and *Testimony to the Truth* (1848), both autobiographical, and a novel, *The Emigrant Family* (1849); all have valuable social comment. His authorship was disputed until clarified by a Canadian grandson publishing *The Secrets of Alexander Harris* (Sydney, 1961).

Harris, Maxwell Hemby (1921–) b. Adelaide. A poet, critic, journalist and publisher, who was the central figure in the modern verse movement in Adelaide in the 1940s, focusing on the Angry Penguins* and the Ern Malley Hoax*.

Harrison, James (?1816–1893) b. near Ben Lomond, Scotland. He arrived in Aus. as a printer (1837) and became an influential journalist, notably with his *Geelong Almanac* (1842) and as editor of the *Age* (1867–73) supporting the squatters* and advocating trade protection. His greatest contribution was as a pioneer of refrigeration, beginning with the first Aus. ice plant at Geelong (1854); he patented processes and apparatus, and in 1873 as a result of a £2,500 award for proving the effectiveness of freezing meat, the first, though unsuccessful, refrigerated ship *Norfolk* sailed in 1873.

Hartog, Dirk An early 17th-century Dutch sea captain, the first recorded European to land in W.A. (*see* DISCOVERY). He left an inscribed pewter plate (now in Amsterdam), nailed to a post at the north end of Dirk Hartog Island*, later named Cape Inscription. Translated, it begins: '1616. On the 25th October there arrived here the ship *den Eendraght* of Amsterdam'. It was found in 1697 by de Vlamingh; and is Australia's earliest European relic.

Harts Range N.T. 23S/135E The NE limit of the Macdonnell Ranges*, lying E–W and reaching 872·3 m. in Mt. Palmer, N of the Plenty River basin. They are noted for the Stuart's Bean Tree, *Erythrina vespertilio*, up to 12 m. high, with bright scarlet beans. The rocks are granitic with mica beds.

Hartz Mountains Tas. 43S/147E A N–S range, extending 48 km., heavily glaciated, and reaching 1,254 m. in Hartz Mt. itself, the centre of a National Park. Further S is the spectacular Adamsons Peak (1,225 m.).

Harvester Case or Judgement Made by Justice Higgins in 1907, in defining 'fair and reasonable' wages as those adequate for an average man 'regarded as a human being in a civilised community', which he assessed at the time as 42 shillings per week for a man with 3 children. The judgement followed an application from Mackay* of Sunshine Harvesters for export excise exemption, then allowed to firms paying 'a fair and reasonable wage', part of the first Labor Government's attempt to link protection with wage standards. Mackay's application was refused. It marked the beginning of a basic wage*.

Harvestmen Arachnid* arthropods superficially resembling spiders, but with the cephalo-thorax and the abdomen fused together. About 60 species are known in Aus.

Harvey, Neil (1928–) b. Melbourne. An outstanding left-handed batsman of great power and attack, also a brilliant cover fielder. He scored a total of 6,149 (second only to D. G. Bradman*) in Tests for Aus., including 21 centuries. In 1967 he was elected an Aus. selector.

Harvey River W.A. 33S/116E A short but perennial river, rising behind the Darling Range* and flowing SW then NW across the coastal plain to the Peel Inlet, with a flood diversion channel cutting due W to the sea from the scarp foot. The first W.A. irrigation scheme began in 1916 with the Harvey Dam, greatly enlarged by the Stirling Dam upstream (1948). Citrus has given way to dairying supporting a cheese factory in the town of **Harvey** (2,329 in 1971), also the service centre for the **Harvey Irrigation District,** totalling 5,265 ha. and drawing water also from the Logue Brook Dam (1963).

Harwood, Gwen b. Tas. A modern poet of stature, writing sharply with wide knowledge as in *Poems* (Sydney, 1963 and 1968).

Hashemy A ship carrying probationary convicts, whose arrival caused such public outcry in Melbourne and Sydney in 1849, that with *Randolph*, arriving 2 months later, it was mainly discharged at Moreton Bay, Qld., though some convicts were sent up country in N.S.W. It was important in the final abolition of transportation*.

Hasluck, Sir Paul Meernaa Caedwalla (1905–) b. Fremantle, W.A. An academic, historian and poet as well as a distinguished politician, he succeeded Lord Casey as Governor General in 1969. Among other works he wrote *The Government and the People* 1939–45, a volume of the official War History. His wife **Alexandra Margaret Martin** is also a historian and biographer of note.

Hassett, Lindsay (1913–) b. Geelong, Vic. An outstanding batsman of solid defensive style especially in Tests. He played 24 Tests against Eng. (1938 and 1946–53), averaging 46·56. In first-class games he totalled 16,890, averaging 58·24 with 59 centuries.

Hastings River N.S.W. Flows for just over 160 km., but largely through 100–150 cm. rainfall country and rainforest on the E escarpment of New England*, then wet sclerophyll*, largely cleared for dairy farming in the lower basin, to the sea at Port Macquarie, 31S/153E. After only 72 km., at Kindee Bridge (catchment there 162,000 ha.), there is an average annual flow of 863 million m.^{3}.

Hawdon, Joseph (1813–71) b. Durham, Eng. He emigrated to Aus. in 1834, becoming a pioneer and overlander. In 1836-7 he made the first 'overlanding' journey, i.e. with flocks, from the Murray Valley to Port Phillip, along with J. Gardiner. In 1838, with Charles Bonney, he made a historic journey with animals to relieve Adelaide.

Hawker S.A. 32S/138E. A small pastoral centre and railhead in the Flinders Ranges, which has declined since the wheat frontier reached the area

(1860–80) and even further since the Port Augusta-Maree standard-gauge line (1956) by-passed it.

Hawke, Robert (1917–) b. Bordertown, S.A. A prominent Trade Union figure, President of the Aus. Council of Trade Unions* since 1970.

Hawkesbury River N.S.W. Rises as the Wollondilly near Crookwell, 35S/150E. It passes several stretches of gorge, including its middle course as the Warragamba River (now dammed as a chief source of Sydney's water supply), taking the name of a large right-bank affluent, the Nepean, and only after passing Camden, Penrith and Castlereagh and receiving the Grose from the left bank, does it become the Hawkesbury. Its main course has been about NE, but after receiving the Colo system from the left bank, it turns to flow SE, as a salt tidal stream, to enter Broken Bay*. The total course is almost 480 km. and the average annual discharge at Penrith (catchment 1·1 million ha.) is 1,356 million m³. It therefore has a large part of its course countersunk into the upland pastures of the Southern Tablelands; it emerges on to lowlands, returns to hill country cut in a gorge through the E edge of the Blue Mts. and then goes through rich vegetable-growing alluvial flats subject to occasional disastrous floods ever since the area was a granary for the young colony in 1806.

Hawks These are the medium to small members of the Eagle* family.
I *Medium-sized Hawks* 1. The worldwide Peregrine or Black-cheeked Falcon, *Falco peregrinus*, which may fly at 240–90 km. p.h which is essential for its aerial pursuit and the catching of very swift birds. It was the pride of medieval falconry. It is up to 50 cm. long (38 cm. the male) and nests, laying 2 buff eggs, on a cliff ledge or high tree hollow preferably in rugged timber country. 2. The Little Falcon, *F.*

Peregrine Falcon (Falco peregrinus), about 50 cm. long

Nankeen Kestrel (Falco cenchroides), about 33 cm. long

longipennis, reaches 30–35 cm. 3. The Brown Hawk, *F. berigora*, common over roads etc., is 40–48 cm. and less colourful. 4. The Brown Goshawk, *Accipiter fasciatus*, of 40–50 cm. has a streaked (in the immature bird) or banded (mature) red and white belly, and compared with the Peregrine it relies on ambush rather than very swift pursuit. 5. The Collared Sparrow Hawk, *Accipiter cirrocephalus*, is smaller, but with broadly similar markings, and there are very handsome Grey and White Goshawks, *Accipiter novaehollandiae*. 6. The Black-breasted Buzzard, *Hamirostra melanosterna*, is often seen soaring like the eagles. II *Small Hovering Hawks* 1. The Nankeen Kestrel, *Falco cenchroides*, is up to 33 cm. long (almost half tail), reddish-flecked, brown above and white-cream below (the male with grey tail). 2. Several kites often seen near inland farmsteads, preying on rats etc., include the handsome grey-white Black-shouldered Kite, *Elanus notatus*.

Hay Usage in Aus. includes meadow hay (about half), hay from lucerne and cereal hay. Together they account for 7% of the cropped area, with oaten and lucerne most important, the latter especially in more rainy or irrigated areas.

Hay N.S.W. 34S/145E (3,206 in 1971) A railhead and service, market and school centre for a wide area of the NW of the Riverina*, and for a limited area of fodder and pasture irrigation around the town.

Hay, William Gosse (1875–1945) b. Adelaide. Writer of 6 historical novels and 1 book of essays. Only *The Escape of the Notorious Sir William Heans* (London, 1918) is really notable, a melodramatic study of the convict system.

Hayman Island Qld. 20S/150E Most northerly of the Cumberland Islands*, with red granitic cliffs of over 60 m., dense tropical forest on hills up to 260 m. and a coral reef. Daylight saving* assists tourism. In January 1970 the island suffered severe cyclone damage.

Heard Island and McDonald Islands 53S/73E An uninhabited Aus. Territory 1,300 km. N of the Antarctic Circle, transferred from U.K. in 1947. Both the small rocky islets of the McDonald Group, and the larger NW–SE trend-

ing Heard Island, 44 by 19 km., are of volcanic rock, rising from the submarine Kerguelen Ridge; Big Benn, on Heard Island, has been historically active. The slopes above 300 m. have permanent snow. Named from an American sea captain and formerly a sealing base, Heard Island had an Aus. meteorological station there from 1947–55.

Hearn, William Edward (1826–88) b. Ireland. He arrived in Aus. in 1854 as one of 4 original Melbourne University Professors; he had a world reputation in economics and law. *For further reading see* D. B. Copland: *W. E. Hearn, First Australian Economist* (Melbourne, 1935).

Heaths Strictly members of the family **Ericaceae** of the N hemisphere, often used to describe other small, bushy shrubs with small leaves, or vegetation dominated by such plants. Aus. heaths, particularly rich in SW W.A., include mainly the Epacridaceae (*see* FLORA), such as the white-flowered Blunt-leaf Heath, *Epacris obtusifolia*, and Swamp Heath, *E. paludosa*; the Native Fuchsia*; Five Corners*; and *Sprengelia*, e.g. the beautiful white Rock Sprengelia, *S. monticola* and the Pink Swamp Heath, *S. incarnata*, of E Aus.; the widespread, dainty pink Fringe Myrtle, *Calythrix tetragona; Dracophyllum*, varying from *D. secundum*, like a narrow-leafed and cream-pink Lily of the Valley, growing by damp rocks in the Port Jackson area and the Blue Mts., to tree forms, e.g. *D. sayeri* and *D. fitzgeraldi* in Qld. and Lord Howe Island. The largest genus in the family is *Leucopogon*, Whitebeard. Other families include some heath-like forms; the Rutaceae family with genera such as the yellow-starred *Asterolasia* and the red-, pink- or purple-flowered *Philotheca*; several genera in the Myrtaceae, Tea-tree*, Pink Buttons*, Wax Plant* and the feathery flower masses of *Verticordia* on poor sands and gravels in W.A. Perhaps the most beautiful and distinctive heaths are the very varied species of *Leschenaultia** in the Goodenia* family mainly in W.A. (*See* PLATE 6.) Saline Heaths include many species of *Frankenia*, e.g. *F. connata*, with whitish leaves and rose-like flowers.

Heavitree Gap N.T. 24S/134E A low dip in the steep rampart of the Heavitree Range, the S wall of the Macdonnell Ranges*, rising sharply for some 475 m. from the plain to the S. The gap is used by both road and rail from S.A. to Alice Springs*, just to the N.

Heemskirk Mountain Tas. 42S/145E (747 m.) This was the scene of a tin-mining rush and boom in the 1880s, which came to nothing as the ore quality was low. Over 50 companies were promoted. It stimulated further, more successful discoveries, notably at Zeehan.

Heidelberg School A group of artists in Melbourne from 1888–90, who in their teaching camps at Heidelberg and other villages near Melbourne, initiated the first major Aus. painting school. They emphasised the recording of an impression, but not in the sense of 20th-century French Impressionism. An exhibition in 1889, called the 9 by 5, from its contents of 182 pictures on cigar-box lids of those inches, caused some shock at the exhibits' seeming sketchiness. The group was even more important in using really Aus. subject matter, and capturing some of the heat and light of the Aus. atmosphere. The leaders were Roberts*, Streeton*, Conder (who left Aus. soon after and achieved fame in Europe) and McCubbin*.

Heinze, Sir Bernard Thomas (1894–) b. Shepparton, Vic. A leading musical figure, violinist, conductor, teacher and former Director of the N.S.W. Conservatorium of Music.

Helminths A widely accepted semi-popular term for worm-like animals, often, but not invariably parasitic on animal hosts, frequently on particular species. The helminths are mainly of 2 Phyla, the Platyhelminthes or Flat-worms, and the Aschelminthes, a rather heterogeneous Phylum including the Nematodes or Roundworms.

Flatworms, usually flat on back and belly and thin laterally, and lacking a body cavity, include the Flukes* or Trematodes, and the Tapeworms or Cestodes. Numerous tapeworms may be found such as *Taenia pisiformis*, causing small spherical cysts in rabbit meat, or the long thread-like larval stage of *Dasyrhynchus pacificus* in the flesh of the Jewfish. The Dog Tapeworm causes Hydatid* disease. *T. saginata*, tapeworm of raw beef-eating and pol-luted-ground countries, is also harmful to man, and the cystal stage of the pig parasite *T. solium* sometimes causes serious illness to human beings eating infected pork too little cooked, but these 2 are rare.

Roundworms as a family are almost universal, including free-living forms in soil, swamps, lakes, rivers and the sea, but apparently almost interchangeable with parasitic species. The familiar threadworm of children, *Enterobius vermicularis*, has a simple cycle: ex-creted eggs ingested by the same or a fresh host, under conditions of poor hygiene; on the other hand the mos-quito-borne filarial worm, *Wuchereria bancrofti*, present in Qld. where it was discovered by Bancroft*, involves three factors, man, mosquito and the worm, developing in the mosquito as an alter-nate but obligate host after ingestion of the larval form by blood-sucking at a time when the larvae are in the peri-pheral bloodstream of the human host. Hookworms, both *Ancylostoma* and *Necator*, are also present in coastal NE Aus. and may cause some debility. But sheep parasites are probably of much greater economic significance: the Barber's Pole Worm, *Haemonchus contortus*, the Nodule Worm, *Oesopha-gostomum columbianum*, the Large-mouthed Bowel-worm, *Chabertia ovinum*, and others.

Henty family Important in early Tas. and Vic. as squatters*, bankers, merchants and whalers. As farmers and bankers in Sussex, Eng., they had Aus. connections through Merino breeding, and saw the colony as being able to 'do more for our family than Eng. ever will'. **Thomas** (1775–1839) and 7 sons migrated between 1829–37, first to W.A. where their grant proved useless land, next to Tas. where Thomas and several sons remained, then to Portland Bay, Vic., where **Edward** (1810–78) in 1834 became the first permanent settler preceding the 'discovery' of Western Vic. in 1835 by Mitchell*. *For further reading see* M. Bassett: *The Hentys* (London, 1954).

Herbert, Alfred Francis Xavier (1901–) b. Port Hedland, W.A. A novelist and short-story writer with experience and intimate knowledge of northern Aus. where he has spent most of his varied life partly as Protector of Aborigines. His major work is *Capricornia* (Sydney 1938), the story of a half-caste, in which he exposes and analyses the treatment of Aborigines, and the harshness yet humour of life in the north.

Herbert, Sir Robert George Wyndham (1831–1905) First Premier of Qld. 1859–66. He came out with Bowen* as his private secretary. As Premier he capably led the early development of the State and was popular in spite of his polished manner and aristocratic background.

Herberton River Qld. 240 km. long, perennial and with a catchment of 8,650 km.[2] with beef country round **Herberton**, 17S/145E, once a silver–lead–tin-mining centre, in the upper basin. There is dense rain-forest in the middle course, with intensive sugar-growing in the coastlands. On Stony Creek, a tributary, are the 296 m. Wallamon or Stony Creek Falls.

Herman, Sali (1898–) A contemporary artist, b. Switzerland. He arrived in Aus. in 1936 where he first studied under Bell and became noted for his atmospheric, crowded urban paintings of Sydney.

Hermannsburg Lutheran Mission Station N.T. 24S/133E Founded in 1877 by Pastors Schwartz and Kempe, sent from Tanunda*, S.A., with 3,100 sheep, in October 1875, but held up for 11 months by drought. The Mission was established on the banks of the Finke River* on Missionary Plains*, which were recommended by G. W. Goyder. It battled with disease and disaster, under its founders and later Pastor Strehlow (from 1894–1922), who gathered the lore of the Aranda tribes, and Pastor Allbrecht. Under Rex Batterbee a Watercolour School was developed after his discovery of Namatjira*. The Mission produces craft works, runs stock and grows vegetables etc. 2 outer stations, to the W at Haast's Bluff and S at Areyonga, help the nomadic tribes of the desert lands.

Hermit-crabs A tribe Paguridae belonging to the long-tailed Prawns*, adapted to using discarded Sea-snail Shells as additional protection, with corresponding modification of the tail and rear legs. Aus. species vary from the large Scaly-legged Hermit-crab, *Pagurus arrosor*, and the nipper scraping Stridulating Hermit-crab, *Trizopagurus strigimanus*, to the brilliant white-spotted red *Dardanus megistos* common all along the Great Barrier Reef and from Hawaii to the Red Sea, and to small burrow-inhabiting species such as the Miner Crab, *Cancellus typus*, seen in a few estuaries in SE Aus.

Related genera and species have forms and habits transitional to the Prawns, e.g. the Hairy Stone Crab of Tas., *Lomis hirta*, the mainly oceanic Whales Food, *Munida subrugosa*, or the burrowing Turtle and Mole Crabs, e.g. *Hippa adactyla* and *Albunea symnista*.

Heron Island Qld. 23S/152E 16 ha. in area in the Capricorn–Bunker Group, with a Marine Biological Station; it is a tourist resort. Turtle-catching, now illegal, supported a factory in the 1920s.

Herring, Lt.-Gen. Sir Edmund Francis (1892–) b. Maryborough, Vic. An outstanding military leader* and legal figure, who as Chief Justice of Vic. Supreme Court (1945–63) brought about considerable reform and expansion.

Herrings In Aus. are mainly in tropical inshore and estuarine waters, and include several families; representative species are: 1. the large-scaled silvery Ox-eye Herring, *Megalops cyprinoides*, up to 60 cm. long; 2. the Giant Herring, *Elops australis*, up to 1·2 m.; 3. the long, lean and voracious Wolf Herring, *Chirocentrus vorax*; and 4. a number of shoal herrings similar to those of Europe, such as *Maugeclupea novae-hollandiae*, and Pilchards, *Sardinops neopilchardus*, reaching 30 cm. or so, and often found in more temperate waters.

Hervey Bay Qld. 25S/153E Between Fraser Island and the mainland. This is also the name of a complex of bayside resorts (6,156 in 1971) including Pialba and Urangan (now the deep-water port for Maryborough).

Hessing, Leonard (1931–) b. Rumania. He arrived in Aus. in 1950. A contemporary artist of the Sydney school of landscape imagery.

Hetherington, John Aikman (1907–) b. Sandringham, Vic. A journalist and the author of a war novel of the Greek campaign of 1943, *The Winds are Still* (Melbourne, 1947). As a war-correspondent he wrote fine accounts of Aus. actions, and has since written profiles of many of his countrymen.

Heysen, Sir Hans (1877–1968) b. Germany. He arrived in Aus. in 1884, and grew up in S.A. to become a famous landscape artist, notably of the stark gum trees and vivid rocks of the Flinders Ranges*. Unfortunately the popularity of his work has led to endless and inferior imitation.

Hibiscus In the widespread Malvaceae or mallow family, this genus includes 40 Aus. species, from the Cotton Tree, *H. tiliacus*, to the fodder tree *H. heterophyllus*, the Green Kurrajong or Native Rosella, and various bushes bearing beautiful pink hibiscus flowers, often cultivated as Rose Mallows, e.g. the Rose of Sharon, *H. mutabilis* which turns from white to dark pink before falling. The widespread *H. heterophyllus* has toothed spear-shaped leaves; the yellow *H. diversifolius* of Qld. and N.S.W. has very varied leaves from oblong to slightly toothed and hairy. For *Cienfugosia hakeifolia*, or *Alyogyne hakeifolia*, of the NW of W.A., known as Red-centred Hibiscus, *see* PLATE 6.

Hickory The popular name of the N American tree, genus *Carya*, is used in Aus. for several kinds of timber trees, notably *Flindersia** and several Wattles*.

Higgins, Henry Bournes (1851–1929) b. Newtownards, N Ireland. He arrived in Aus. in 1870 with his family and entered law, becoming outstanding as High Court Judge from 1906. From 1907–21 he presided over the Conciliation and Arbitration Court, and here his humanity and sympathy with the worker led to his assessment of wages on the basis of average needs rather than economics, beginning with the Harvester Case*.

Highways The more important main routes are designated State Highways except in W.A. and S.A. where they are not distinguished from other main roads. Legally, the term Highway includes waterways. Many Highways are named from explorers whose routes they approximately follow: Eyre (Port Augusta–Kalgoorlie); Hume (Melbourne–Sydney); Stuart (Darwin–Alice

Springs); Mitchell (Bathurst–Cunnamulla); Mulligan (Cairns–Cooktown); Bass (along the N Tas. coast) are some examples. Prince's Highway is the main coastal route from Sydney to W Vic. through Melbourne. Qld. has 60 gazetted Highways, N.S.W. and Vic. each have 24, and Tas. 15.

Higinbotham, George (1826–1892) b. Dublin. He arrived in Aus. in 1854 as a barrister, but edited the Melbourne paper *Argus*, 1855–8, later becoming a politician and judge. His great contributions lay in clarifying and curbing the Governor's powers, and through them control from London; in consolidating Vic. law; in advocating the teaching of a 'common Christianity' in schools; and the support of workers, notably in the Maritime Strike*.

Hill, Alfred (1871–1960) b. Melbourne. A musician. After periods in Europe and N.Z., he returned to Sydney where he was a teacher, conductor and composer, notably of opera.

Hill, Clement (1877–1945) b. Adelaide. He is classed with Bradman*, Trumper* and Macartney* to make up the 4 leading Aus. batsmen; he was the finest left-hander. He had a short powerful build, nimbleness and incisive action. He played in 41 Tests against Eng. (1896–1912), averaging 35·4 with 4 centuries. In first-class cricket he totalled 1,720, averaging 43·56 with 45 centuries.

Hill, Ernestine (*née* **Hemmings**) b. Sydney. She is noted for her deep knowledge gained on much outback wandering, which she recorded in detailed works such as *The Great Australian Loneliness* (London, 1937).

Hill End N.S.W. 33S/149E Just N of the Turon River, this was a reef-gold-mining centre in the 1870s and had virtually become a ghost town* until it became something of an artists' colony in recent years and an officially preserved Historic Site. *For further*

reading see Donald Friend: *Hillendiana* (Sydney, 1956).

Hinchinbrook Island Qld. 18S/146E 32 km. N–S by 12–25 km. E–W, this is a spectacular rugged island clothed in varied vegetation from rain-forest to grassy tops and with rugged bluffs such as Mt. Bowen, its highest point, at 1,113 m. The **Hinchinbrook Channel** to the W is probably a drowned former extension of the Tully River, and was noted for its dugong and turtle.

Hindmarsh, Sir John (1785–1860) First Governor of S.A. (1836–8). When Charles Napier shrewdly refused the job, Hindmarsh, a brave and distinguished naval commander who had served with Nelson on the Nile and at Trafalgar, was appointed. Unfortunately he was neither politician nor administrator enough to cope with the complexities of founding a new colony, especially with the system of divided control between the Governor and Commissioner that was laid down for the settlement of S.A. He disagreed with the site chosen for Adelaide by Light* and was recalled when the quarrels with Commissioner Fisher reached unseemly proportions.

Hindmarsh, Lake Vic. About 40 km. NW of Warracknabeal, 36S/142E, this is in the Wimmera* basin of internal drainage. It takes water from the very variable Wimmera River and its Grampian affluents; in wet years it may cover 130 km.^{2}, and in drought years may dry up, endangering the pelican rookery on its islands.

Hinkler, Herbert John Louis (1892–1933) b. Bundaberg, Qld. As a youth, he made gliders which he modelled on the ibis. He went to Sydney then Eng. to learn to fly, served in 1914–18 War in the Royal Naval Air Service, and afterwards the Royal Flying Corps. He became a test pilot with A. V. Roe & Co., then he began a series of long-distance and record-breaking flights, including a record flight of 15½ days to

Darwin in 1928, for which he received awards and rewards. He designed a small amphibian touring plane, the *Ibis*, but was handicapped by lack of capital and, like many pioneers of his day, he was driven to more and more record-breaking attempts, though shy of publicity, until he crashed in the Apennines.

Hire-purchase A very important part of the modern Aus. way of life, and a major part of the work of various finance companies. Monthly bulletins on Instalment Credit for Retail Sales are among many published by the Bureau of Census and Statistics. Outstanding balances show steady increase each year and now exceed $20 million of which almost half is for motor vehicles.

Loans are generally advanced through retail shops, but the contract, collection etc. lies with a number of finance companies. Most of the banks have invested in large and reputable finance companies. The banks obtain a good profit without direct involvement, and the finance companies obtain an additional and highly respectable route of approach to prospective borrowers through branch banks. Conservative banks held off as long as possible from entering this relationship, and the criticism has been offered that in times of credit restriction the banks pass on custom rather freely to this very profitable high-interest lending. If need be the Government can control lending through varying the cash deposit required.

HISTORY Taken as beginning with the arrival in January 1788, of the First Fleet, Aus. has a relatively short, and by European standards, uneventful history. It is a story of expansion, from a half-starved penal colony living on the fringe of an alien land, hemmed in by seemingly impassable mountains and living in an atmosphere of fear, resentment and considerable brutality, to a thriving ebullient modern state, still clinging largely to the margins of the continent.

The transition from penal settlement to colony took the first 30 years, and was accomplished under a succession of governors whose authority was near-absolute, but was resisted with some success by the army officers with their rich rum traffic at stake, and later by the ambitious free settlers and emancipated convicts who, after the introduction of the Merino sheep, were anxious to exploit the grazing lands newly discovered beyond the Dividing Range. The initial settlement of N.S.W. had 3 offshoots: Van Diemen's Land (later Tas.), the Port Phillip District (Vic.) and Qld., which shared common penal origins. S.A. and W.A. were started as free settlements (the latter being driven to use transported convicts later, when it seemed the only way to avoid complete stagnation). N.T. was settled from S.A. and remained part of it until 1911 when it came under Commonwealth control. The Aus. Capital Territory was carved from N.S.W. to contain the national capital.

Until the mid-19th century, the main determining issues in the trends of development were: the spread of settlement by illegal squatting and consequent problems of controlling land tenure; an increasing restiveness among settlers and native-born alike for more freedom from the remote bureaucratic control of London. Associated with this resentment was the question of transportation; assigned convicts played an essential part in the economic and physical expansion, and squatters wished to retain the system. A growing urban proletariat felt the indignity of continued peopling by the rejects of Britain, and their agitation led to the ending of transportation by 1853 in eastern Aus. Even the diehard supporters of the system were convinced of its anachronistic nature, once the startling series of gold discoveries began in 1851. The following decade was one of accelerated growth both in wealth

State	Foundation	Sources of population
New South Wales	1788: Sydney Cove penal settlement. 1823: Created a Crown Colony.	Convicts 1788–1840. Free settlers especially after 1825. Gold-rushes 1851–60.
Tasmania (Van Diemen's Land until 1853).	1803: Risdon Cove. 1804: Hobart Town and Port Dalrymple penal settlements, united in 1812. 1825: Separation from N.S.W.	Convicts from N.S.W. and Norfolk Island initially, then direct from Britain until 1853. Free settlers after about 1820. Mineral rushes 1880–1900.
Victoria (Port Phillip District until 1851)	1803: Abortive Port Phillip* military settlement. 1826–8: Western Port military settlement. 1834: Hentys at Portland. 1835: Batman, Fawkner at Port Phillip. 1851: Vic. proclaimed.	Squatters from Tasmania, then N.S.W. Convicts until 1840. Tasmanian migrants. Free settlers from 1834. Gold-rush 1851–60 (about 400,000).
Queensland	1824–39: Moreton Bay penal colony. 1847: Jan.–Aug. abortive probationary penal settlement Point Curtis (Gladstone Colony). 1859: Separate State of Qld. proclaimed.	Intractable convicts from N.S.W. Convicts from Britain until 1849. Squatters overland from N.S.W. Free settlers after 1840. Gold and other minerals 1867–80.
South Australia	1834: Act establishing S.A. as non-convict, planned colony. 1836: Abortive Kangaroo Island settlement. 1837: Adelaide district successfully settled. 1863: N.T. under S.A.	Free settlers under assisted migrant schemes (including German Lutherans). Copper finds 1842, 1861.
Western Australia	1826: Albany military settlement. 1829: Swan River Free settlement. 1841: Australind, Bunbury. 1880–90: Kimberley area.	Free assisted migrants. 1849–68: Convicts in equal proportions to assisted migrants. Pastoralists from East. 1885–93 Gold-rushes.

Government	Governors	Premiers
1823: Judicature Act. Nominated L.C. 1841: One-third L.C. elected. 1855: Elected L.A. 1934: L.C. elected by both houses sitting together.	Phillip 1788; Hunter 1795; King 1800; Bligh 1806; Macquarie 1810; Brisbane 1822; Darling 1825; Bourke 1831; Gipps 1838; Fitzroy 1846–55. *See also* FOVEAUX and GROSE.	*Donaldson,* Cowper, *Parker, Forster,* Robertson, Martin, Parkes, *Farnell, Stuart,* Dibbs, *Jennings,* Reid, Lyne.
1825: Nominated L.C. 1850: Two-third elected L.C. 1855: Elected H.A. and L.C.	Collins 1804 (Hobart); Paterson 1804 (Launceston); Davey 1813; Sorrell 1817; Arthur 1824; Franklin 1837; Eardley-Wilmot 1843; Denison 1847–55.	*Champ, Gregson, Weston, Smith, Chapman, Whyte, Dry, Wilson, Innes, Kennerley, Reibey, Fysh, Giblin, Crowther, Douglas Agnew, Dobson.*
1842: 5 elected to N.S.W. L.C. 1850: 2/3 elected Vic. L.C. 1855: elected L.C. and L.A. 1954: electoral redistribution	La Trobe 1839. Hotham 1854–6.	*Haines, O'Shanassy, Nicholson, Heales, McCulloch, Sladen, Duffy, Francis, Kerford,* Berry, *Service, O'Loghlen, Gillies, Munro, Shiels, Patterson, Turner, McLean.*
1851–9 Elected members increasing to 9 in N.S.W. L.C. 1859 Qld. Parl. nominated L.C. elected L.A. 1922 L.C. abolished.	Bowen 1859 (inaugurated responsible government).	Herbert, *Macalister, Mackenzie, Lilley, Palmer, Thorn, Douglas,* McIlwraith, Griffith, *Morehead.*
1836 Gov. and Commissioners. 1842: Crown Colony L.C. of 7 1850: 2/3 elected L.C. 1856: Elected L.C. and H.A.	Hindmarsh 1835; Gawler 1838; Grey 1841; Robe 1845; Young 1848.	*Finniss, Baker,* Torrens, *Hanson, Reynolds, Waterhouse, Dutton, Ayers, Blyth, Hart, Boucat, Strangeways, Colton, Morgan, Bray, Downer, Mayford, Cockburn.*
1832: Nominated L.C. 1870: 2/3 elected L.C. 1890: Elected L.C. and L.A.	Stirling 1833; Hutt, 1839; Clarke 1846; Irwin 1847; Fitzgerald 1848; Kennedy 1855; Hampton 1862; Weld 1869; Robinson 1875 and 1880; Ord 1877; Broome 1883–90.	Forrest.

Note: L.C. Legislative Council (Upper)
H.A. House of Assembly (Lower)
L.A. Legislative Assembly (Lower)
Dates refer to passing of appropriate Acts; implementation was sometimes later.

and population, as thousands poured in to the 'diggings', of Vic. and to a lesser extent N.S.W. and later Qld. to seek their fortunes. A few found one; many more turned to other occupations, and finding the lands locked in huge runs in the hands of a few squatters, agitated for the break up of the large estates. The resulting turmoil of legislation led to wholesale abuse, and the desired closer settlement was achieved only in a few areas where soil, water and human conditions allowed it to survive.

Meanwhile, political advance, already well under way before the gold-rushes, was also accelerated. The States of N.S.W., Vic. and Qld. were separated in the 1850s (Tas. had been separated since 1825); and with S.A., these 5 attained responsible government during the decade, with broadly similar constitutions. W.A. was held back until 1890 by her retention of transportation.

The States, free to follow independent courses, committed sins of short-sighted self-interest which are not even yet remedied, notably in policies of trade and transport. Thus free trade N.S.W. faced a protectionist Vic. over a border running right through the middle of what was a clear natural region, the Murray valley. With S.A. joining in, the 3 States fought to draw off its rich resources to the rival ports of Melbourne, Adelaide and Sydney, via their differently gauged railways. There was a period of great boom in the 1870s and 80s. This was the heyday of the squatter in his stately country home, and of the city speculator in the increasing urban sprawls; the period of developing irrigation and of new mineral wealth. Almost the last of the continent was explored.

However, there had been over-extension, with excessive borrowing overseas, and the bubble burst in the early 1890s, when failures in the Argentine led to panic in London and consequent loss of confidence in overseas invest-

ment, including Aus., which was also suffering from drought. The ensuing depression was at its worst in Vic. where banks closed their doors, but unemployment was severe everywhere, and there was disillusion typified by the departure of William Lane's famous New Australia colonisers to Paraguay. There was also an increasing growth of unionism, and its political offspring the Labor Party, seen as little less than a cancer by the capitalist squatter and mine and factory owner; soon there were bitter struggles on the waterfront and in the shearing shed.

The need for closer association between the States was increasingly obvious as communications expanded to link them, and as Australians began to look a little to the world outside and to feel insecure in their small isolated State communities. Defence was an even more potent catalyst than economic forces, in the steps which led gradually to Federation in 1901, and the emergence of the Commonwealth of Aus. The Constitution of the united country was a masterly compromise, drawing from European and American models. The States fought vigorously to retain independent powers, at the same time bargaining for themselves. Thus W.A. achieved the trans-continental railway and Qld. a guarantee of protection for her sugar, as the price for joining the Federation. Since 1901 the Commonwealth has increasingly eroded and absorbed the State powers, largely through the 2 national emergency periods of the world wars when co-ordinated action became essential. The departure of the A.I.F. for Europe in September 1914, and the subsequent Gallipoli campaign, are seen by many Australians as the real point of emergence of the country as a nation. The war stimulated the economy but also brought a bitter division in the nation over conscription, and the loss of 60,000 men could be ill afforded.

Between the wars, Aus. came increasingly into the pattern of world events: a period of boom, which lasted longer because of the protection policies, was brutally ended as the general Depression developed in the world, and Aus. dependence on foreign capital led to the withdrawing of the underpinnings of her economy. However, the country was also one of the first to recover, and expansion was again under way when the 1939–45 War broke out.

This time also Aus. forces served in the Middle East and Europe, but the war suddenly came close to Aus. at home with the Japanese advance into S Asia. The bombing of Darwin in 1942 was a major shock to the previously isolated insular nation. The consequent reorientation from the traditional, wholly British links to a growing alliance with the U.S. was a trend which increased in the post-war era and became stronger than ever in the unsettled situation of the 1960s. The increasingly cosmopolitan origin of the population following the migration drives since the war has also served to loosen the links with Britain, whose own growing economic involvement with Europe is in turn bound to affect the relationship. Industrial and economic expansion has been fairly continuous, save for minor recessions as in 1970–1. By 1973 there was recovery in wool and beef and continued though decelerated mineral development. The 23 years of conservative rule had given way to Labor (Dec. 1972) which, although far from radical was tending towards more liberal policies, more rights for Aborigines, and a new nationalism. Not only the old tie with Britain, but more recent dependence on U.S. was loosening; China had been recognised and the realities of the Asian neighbour faced. (*See* Table, pp. 258–9, and Commonwealth Chronology, pp. 122–3.) *Note:* supplementary detail will be found under biographical entries for all Governors before the mid-19th century within the States, all Commonwealth Prime Ministers, those State Premiers not italicised in

the Table on page 259 and State Premiers after Federation as indicated in the articles on the States, and in the following entries: Assignment System*, Bushrangers*, Conscription*, Constitution*, Depression*, Discovery*, Emancipists*, Exploration*, Federation*, First Fleet*, Goldrushes*, Government*, Political Parties*, Rum Rebellion*, Second Fleet*, Selectors*, Squatters*, Trade Unions*, White Australia*, World Wars*. Specific sources are noted with relevant entries, but several major general works have been used in preparation of the main and many of the short entries. These are: C. M. H. Clark: *A History of Australia Vols. I and II* (Melbourne, 1962 and 1968); *A Short History of Australia* (New York, 1963) and (ed.) *Select Documents in Australian History* (Sydney, 1950); G. Greenwood ed.: *Australia, A Social and Political History* (Sydney, 1955); W. K. Hancock: *Australia* (London, 1930); D. H. Pike: *Australia, the Quiet Continent* (London, 1962); A. G. L. Shaw: *The Story of Australia* (New York, 1955); E. Scott, revised by H. Burton: *A Short History of Australia* (Oxford, 1961); M. Barnard: *A History of Australia* (Sydney, 1962); D. Pike, ed.: *Australian Dictionary of Biography* Vols I–IV (1788–1890) (Melbourne, 1967–72); B. C. Fitzpatrick: *The British Empire in Australia* (Melbourne, 1940); E. O'Brien: *The Foundation of Australia* (London, 1937). F. Alexander: *Australia since Federation* (1968).

Historical Records prior to self government, by the States, were in the form of Governors' Despatches to London, but after this the States retained their own. Valuable collation was done by F. Watson (1936). Microfilms of London-held records are now available.

Hoad, Lewis Allan (1934–   ) b. Sydney. He was considered among the world's great tennis players, especially noted for his power and top spin backhands. He had a long rivalry with Rosewall* from their first appearance together as 12-year-olds. He played in Davis Cup matches 1952–6, won at Wimbledon in 1956 and 1957, then turned professional for the biggest guarantee figure ever offered to any amateur sportsman at that date. He retired to Spain in 1967.

HOBART 43S/147E (129,808 in 1971) The capital of Tas., the eighth largest but second oldest Aus. city. It extends for 20 km. along the W bank of the Derwent estuary, and is confined by high country to the W including Mt. Wellington*. A smaller residential area on the E bank has grown since a pontoon bridge was built (1943), now replaced by the Tasman Bridge. The deep channel, gouged by the river when sea level was lower, provides one of the world's finest natural harbours. The temperature range from 8°C in July to 16°C in January indicates a climate different from any other Aus. capital. Rainfall averaging 76 cm. occurs all the year, but with maxima in spring and autumn. Long hot spells can develop in summer, but the late summer of 1966–7 saw an exceptionally prolonged period of high temperatures: on February 7th, there were hot swirling N winds, generated from a continental High Pressure and Tas. Low Pressure systems swept over the SE island. This is the season of normal burning off, with fires often left to be finally quenched by the autumn rains. Several small bushfires were whipped into uncontrollable infernos racing madly down the Derwent valley and on the slopes of Mt. Wellington. Within hours 62 people were killed, 1,313 houses destroyed, sheep losses estimated at over 20,000 and cattle over 1,000, almost 3,000 miles of fencing were burned. Apples burst prematurely into flower, cars melted, a brewery was gutted, carbide and newsprint works damaged, and $40–50 million of damage caused.

Hobart, named after the Secretary of State for the Colonies, Robert Hobart, was founded at Sullivan's Cove by Collins, in 1804, when he moved the Risdon Cove settlement, established by J. Bowen the previous year, upstream on the opposite bank, to a better water supply. The business heart remains within a few blocks of the wharves on the reclaimed foreshores of the cove; they are at their busiest in the apple season March–May. Much of the Georgian character and building remains in central Hobart. N of it the dolerite hill of Queen's Domain gives an open stretch. The heavier industry, copper-milling, zinc-refining and textiles, lies to the N between the river and Midland Highway. The zinc refinery, opposite Risdon Cove, has its own berths. Suburbs climb the lower slopes and there is considerable expansion along the estuary side to the S and on the E bank.

Hogan, Edmund John (1884–1964) b. Wallace, Vic. Labor Premier of Vic. 1927–8, and 1929–32. During the Depression he was expelled from his State party over the Premier's Plan for retrenchment in 1931. His appeal to law failed, establishing the voluntary nature and internal independence of political parties.

Holden, Sir Edward Wheewall (1885–1947) b. Adelaide. He was a manufacturer of motor car bodies (1917). Following amalgamation with General Motors in 1931, the name Holden was given to the first and subsequent cars they produced.

Holey Dollar The Spanish dollars in use during the Napoleonic War currency shortage, after Macquarie's proclamation of 1813 directing that a small circular piece of silver be cut from the centre of each coin; the smaller pieces were also used, attracting the name of dumps.

Hollingworth, May A pioneer of Sydney theatre production in the 1940s, upholding high quality and intimate presentation.

Holly, Native A popular name for the pea-like *Oxylobium trilobatum* (*see* PEA).

Holman, William Arthur (1871–1934) b. London. He arrived in Aus. in 1888. Premier of N.S.W. from 1913–20 and a very influential Labor politician and lawyer, a quick-witted, effective orator who introduced important social legislation and established State enterprises. He left the party in 1916 having supported conscription*. H. V. Evatt's *Australian Labour Leader* (Sydney, 1940) is an outstanding study of the Labor movement and also of Holman.

Holt, Harold Edward (1908–67) b. Sydney. Prime Minister of Aus. from 1965–7, formerly Leader of the House of Representatives. His Parliamentary career began in 1935 and included several Cabinet positions before he succeeded Sir Robert Menzies*. He was still in office when, in December 1967, he was drowned while bathing. He inherited and fostered the U.S. alliance notably in the Vietnam War and had been returned to office in the 1966 General Election.

Holtermann, Bernard Otto (1838–85) b. Germany. He arrived in Aus. in 1858. At Hill End* in N.S.W. the 'Holtermann Nugget' (actually a piece of reef-gold) was found in 1872, in a mine owned by Holtermann and Beyer (*see* GOLD-RUSHES). Later Holtermann, who settled in Sydney, organised the taking of a unique series of contemporary plate photographs of the gold-fields and N.S.W.

Honey Flower or **Mountain Devil** (*Lambertia formosa*) In the large southern family Proteaceae, this is perhaps the best known of its genus—a 80–95-cm. shrub with narrow, pungent leaves in bunches; striking red tubular flowers with protruding styles and full of honey

from which both popular names are derived. (*See* page 365 for sketch.)

Honey-eaters (family Meliphagidae) About a dozen genera and 70 species in Aus. extending also into the SW Pacific and SE Asia. They include mainly green-brown birds (though with bright colours in some species), of a wide range in size (10–38 cm. long), beak size and shape, habitat, habits, calls etc.; but the forked and bristly brush-tongue (for brushing out nectar) is characteristic. The most familiar species have a biggish downcurved beak and a bold and agile manner, and over half the species have either a white or yellow feather patch on the side of the head, or a brightly coloured piece of bare skin above the eye, or a fleshy wattle. All except 2 tropical species build cup-shaped nests of twigs, grass, bark etc. woven with cobwebs and lined with hair, moss etc. All eat nectar and it is the staple food for some, so that they tend to be migratory with the blossom, like the apiarist; but insects are probably the more important food over the whole group. Keast's list of the main types is useful (*see* BIRDS for source).
1. The typical green-olive-yellowish honey eaters, often with a pale streak below the eye, about 15–23 cm. long, include the White-plumed Honey-eater or Greenie, *Meliphaga penicillata*, of all Aus. (including suburban gardens) except the SW and Tas. 2. The Spinebills are only about 15 cm. long, with rather large heads and downward curved beaks about 2·5 cm. long: the Eastern, *Acanthorhynchus tenuirostris*, with blue head and lower back and the Western, *A. superciliosus*, with light stripes above and below the eye, much browner, with rust on breast and neck.
3. The Black-headed Honey-eaters of the genus *Melithreptus* (not in SW Aus.) include *M. affinis* with a very black head and neck and a small blue eye-stripe, but there are other species with a white crescent on the nape; all are smallish at 14–18 cm. long. 4. The Cres-

cent Honey-eater, genus *Meliornis*, with black and white head and a bold white eye-stripe, white body with bold black flecks, and yellow on tail and wing-edges, inhabits coastal areas of the E and S of Aus. including Tas. 5. The Soldier-birds, Miners and Bellbirds, genus *Myzantha* (flower-sucking), are biggish (about 30 cm. long), mainly light brown with darker flecks and back, with yellow or yellow-green on head, wings and tail, noisy and chattering (hence the idea of a soldier challenging an intruder, and perhaps the Miner from confusion with the chattering Indian Myna). The 3 species cover most of Aus., ranging widely in search of a varied diet of nectar, insects and berries. 6. The Friarbirds, genus *Philemon* (loving), the popular name from the bare head, are often grey or black-skinned, large (25–30 cm. long), slim, with large beak continuing the curve of the head, undulating flight, and chattering very noisily, not found in the SW of Aus. 7. The Wattle-birds, genus *Anthochaera* (rejoicing in flowers), large (30–38 cm.) of rather similar shape, but with red or yellow fleshy wattles on the lower cheeks, the light breast lined with dark flecks, and black back and tail with light flecks; also noisy, with a wide range of foods, and covering much of the country.

Honey-myrtles A popular name for the Melaleucas of bush form with attractively coloured and sometimes feathery flowers, including the swamp-dwelling Thyme Honey-myrtle, *M. thymifolia*, with almost heath-like small leaves and feathery pink flowers, the Oval-leaf Honey-myrtle, *M. elliptica*, of W.A., with crimson-pink 2·5 cm. flower-spikes, and the Rosy Honey-myrtle or Pink Paperbark, *M. erubescens*, of sandy coastal Qld., a heath-like bush of 60–120 cm. with light pink bottle-brushes. They are members of the Myrtaceae or Myrtle family.

Honeysuckle (*Lonicera* spp.) Has come to be used in Aus. also for nectar-rich *Banksia** and *Lambertia*, which are yellow-or-red-flowered shrubs with narrow leaves in the Proteaceae family and largely confined to W.A.

Hoop Pine (*Araucaria cunninghamii*) A valuable timber tree, 30–45 m. by 1·5–1·8 m., indigenous to upper slopes in a few areas of humid coastal NE N.S.W. and SE Qld., higher than Bunya Pine sites. Its timber is similar to the Bunya* and the Kauri*, but it is sufficiently fast-growing to make it an important tree for afforestation. The mature tree has the long branchless trunk of most *Araucaria* spp. The rough hard bark has horizontal cracks forming the hoops of the name, and a less symmetrical crown than in others of this genus, with pointed fronds of branchlets bearing hard straight pointed leaves over 5 mm. long. The male flower is a spike of pollen-bearing scales on the end of branchlets; the female is usually on separate trees, a cone of spirally arranged leaves, then woody scales each bearing a flat seed.

Hope, Alec Derwent (1907–   ) b. Cooma, N.S.W. Son of a Presbyterian minister, he grew up in Tas. He is a leading modern poet, writing brilliant, precise, controlled and often satirical verse full of astringent wit and observation often using several themes, and rich in allusion. He taught as a University Professor in Canberra 1951–69 and is a well-known critic. His works include *The Cave and the Spring* (Adelaide, 1967) and volumes of poems: *The Wandering Islands* (Sydney, 1955) and *Collected Poems* 1930–65 (London, 1966).

Hopegood, Cedric Peter (1891–   ) b. Essex, Eng. He arrived in Aus. in 1924. A poet of lyrical and ballad style, as in *Circus at World's End* (Sydney, 1967). His work has often a mythical base and symbolic purpose.

Hopman, Henry Cecil (1900–   ) b. Sydney. He developed from championship tennis-playing to become a very influential although controversial coach and non-playing captain and selector, notably for the Davis Cup*; he is often credited for its capture and retention, through his harsh training, discipline and judgment. He is also a former squash champion.

Hordern, Anthony (1789–1869) b. Retford, Eng. He arrived in Aus. in 1824; his wife first established the famous family drapery business in Sydney, which continued both there and in Melbourne. His grandson Anthony sponsored railway and immigration projects in W.A.

Horizontal The unusual but evocative popular name for the slender tree of wet mountain forests in Tas., *Anodopetalum biglandulosum*. Its stem, slender in proportion, bends easily and thickets of the horizontal stems form some of the most impenetrable and confusing jungles of the world.

Horne, Richard Henry (1803–84) b. London. During 17 years in Aus. (1852–69) he wrote the authoritative *Australian Facts and Prospects* (London, 1859). Known as 'Orion' from an epic poem he published in Eng., he was one of an active Melbourne literary group of the 1870s.

Horse-racing The early and continuing development of pastoral farming, combined with a national love of gambling, have made horse-racing the major Aus. sporting interest. There are some 4,000 race meetings a year, over 180 clubs, and 25,000 people professionally involved in what has become an industry. Bets placed with bookmakers and on the Totalisator amount to over 900 million dollars a year and are increasing. The automatic totalisator was evolved by G. A. Julius and installed in N.S.W. in 1917, having been first used in N.Z. in 1913. The bulk of interest and activity is in flat-racing, in which Aus. horses display great staying power. Steeple-chasing had great former popularity, but is now mainly confined to winter events in Vic. and

S.A. Aus. jockeys have often been successful overseas, and several have ridden English Derby winners. Some outstanding jockeys are Dempsey, Bullock, Wootten, Carslake, Johnstone, Breasley, Britt, Cook, Pike, D. and H. Munro, G. Moore, Williamson. Racing is carried on all the year in one or other centre, the focus shifting with season; thus horses can follow the major events, and interest and the industry are maintained. The major series are the spring and autumn meetings in Sydney and Melbourne; the spring races are earlier and the autumn races later in Sydney than in Melbourne with its longer winter. The main winter meetings are in Brisbane; Tas. and W.A. have their main racing season in summer. In S.A. the main races are in early spring and autumn. The Aus. Jockey Club (A.J.C.), begun in 1842, has met at Randwick since 1860; the Sydney Turf Club (S.T.C.), founded in 1943, meets at Rosehill; the Vic. Racing Club (V.R.C.), founded in 1864, meets at Flemington; the Vic. Amateur Turf Club (V.A.T.C.), 1875, meets at Caulfield and Sandown. M.V.R.C. is Moonee Valley Racing Club. The Qld. Turf Club (Q.T.C.), 1863, meets at Eagle Farm and the Brisbane Amateur Turf Club (B.A.T.C.), founded in 1923, meets at Doomben. The following are the races carrying over $10,000 stakes:

Spring, Sydney (early October) A.J.C.: Epsom Handicap;Metropolitan;A.J.C. Derby. *Melbourne* (October–November) V.A.T.C.: Caulfield Cup; Caulfield Guineas; Sandown Cup. V.R.C.: Fisher Plate; Vic. Derby; Melbourne Cup*. V.R.C.: Charen 'A' Stakes; George Adams Memorial Mile; Oaks Stakes. M.V.R.C.: Moonie Valley Cup and Stakes; W. S. Cox Plate.

Autumn, Melbourne V.R.C.: Newmarket Handicap; Queen Elizabeth Stakes; Aus. Cup. M.V.R.C.: Alister Clarke Stakes; Oakleigh Plate; Futurity Stakes. *Sydney* (Easter) A.J.C.: Sydney Cup; Doncaster Handicap; A.J.C.:

St. Leger; Sires Produce; Champagne Stakes. S.T.C.: Golden Slipper and Silver Slipper Stakes.
Winter, Melbourne (July) V.R.C.: Grand National Hurdle and Steeple. M.V.R.C.: A. V. Hiskins Steeple. *Brisbane* (June) Q.T.C.: Stradbroke Handicap; Brisbane Cup. (July) B.A.T.C. Doomben Ten Thousand; Doomben Cup.
Historical Development Racing followed almost immediately on settlement in each colony. The earliest meetings are recorded in N.S.W. (in Hyde Park, Sydney) in 1810; in Tas. in 1814; in W.A. in 1833; in Vic. and S.A. in 1838 and in Qld. in 1843. The economies following the Bigge* Report discouraged racing from 1821-5, but the interest and patronage of governors and leading citizens such as Wentworth* ensured its revival and the early development of clubs. The first was a former Sydney Turf Club (1825) which declined after a famous dinner in 1826 at which Wardell* allegedly criticised the absent Governor Darling, who withdrew his patronage. It was followed by the still extant Aus. Jockey Club (1842). A rapid spread of interest in racing and formation of clubs in country areas, followed the squatters into the interior in the 1830s. The first intercolony races were held in Melbourne in 1847; inter-state events are still held there. Since then English bloodstock has been imported, and there are many famous Aus. stud farms. In a long list of famous horses the following may be listed as representative of their period; the date of birth is given in brackets, but of course racing careers began 2 or more years later and varied greatly in length: 'Junius' (1819); 'Jorrocks' (c. 1834); 'Archer' (c. 1858); 'Tarragon' (1858); 'The Barb' (1863); 'Chester' (1874), whose son 'Kirkham' was the only Aus. horse to run in the English Derby; 'Grand Flaneur' (1877), who was never beaten; 'Carbine' (1885), claimed as one of the greatest Aus. horses of all (N.Z. bred); 'Poseidon' (1903);

'Desert Gold' (1912), a mare; 'Gloaming' (1915); 'Phar Lap' (1926) whose heart was heavier than that of an average horse, and is preserved in Canberra while the horse itself is stuffed and displayed in a Melbourne museum, and his skeleton in a Wellington (N.Z.) museum; 'Peter Pan' (1929); 'Bernborough' (1939); 'Flight' (1940); 'Tulloch' (1955), who became the first horse in Aus. racing to win over $200,000 ($220,247) in stakes. 'Phar Lap' and 'Tulloch' vie with 'Carbine' in racing legend, and were also bred in N.Z. 'Tobin Bronze' was sold to U.S. (1967) for an Aus. record price, $300,000 approx, 'Gunsynd' in 1972 was hailed as a new 'great'. *See* D. M. Barries: *Turf Cavalcade* (Sydney, 1960).

Horsham Vic. 37S/142E (11,046 in 1971) A city on the Wimmera River. It is a market, road and service centre for the Wimmera District* with some industry based on agriculture: machinery, butter, flour and meat freezing. It is stimulated by its position on the main Western Highway between Melbourne and Adelaide, and has a noted agricultural college specialising in the problems of the area.

Hoskins The early N.S.W. iron and steel firm headed first by **Charles Henry** (1851-1926) who arrived in Aus. in 1854. With his brother **George,** he developed a firm specialising in pipes (e.g. for Sydney water supply and W.A. Gold-fields Scheme) before buying Eskbank works at Lithgow (1908-30) and later starting coke ovens at Port Kembla (1927-35). Under his son, **Sir Cecil Harold** (1889-), the Lithgow works were dismantled and Aus. Iron and Steel formed at Port Kembla (1928) with 2 British firms. It was taken over by B.H.P.* in 1935.

Hospitals There were 768 public hospitals, 1,338 private hospitals and nursing homes, 63 mental institutions, 13 Repatriation* hospitals and 4 leper hospitals in Aus. in 1970. Control is a State responsibility, but with Commonwealth contributions at a fixed rate per patient. A major source of finance is from Lotteries* and patients' fees are partly met by Medical Benefit Funds (see SOCIAL SERVICES). Private contributions and fund-raising remain important. Administration varies between States; one centralised authority (except in Qld., which has several) generally controls the major metropolitan hospitals and regional base hospitals. Small district hospitals are usually run by elected boards, and partially elected boards are also used in the intermediate and base hospitals in some areas.

The first hospital was started under John White* on Sydney Cove within a month of the arrival of the First Fleet in 1788. This was followed by a better building on Dawes Point (1794), and then the famous Rum Hospital* (1817). When transportation ceased and the British Government was no longer responsible for convict hospitals, there was something of a hiatus, with only benevolent institutions to cater for the poor sick. The development of modern public training hospitals dates from the 1870s. Government control has steadily increased. The largest hospital in Aus. is the Royal Prince Alfred in Sydney.

Hotham, Sir Charles (1806–55) b. Suffolk, Eng. Governor of Vic. from 1854–5. He succeeded La Trobe* after naval and diplomatic service, and was faced with the gold-fields unrest, culminating in the Eureka Stockade*. While not unsympathetic, he blamed foreign subversive elements and handled the situation with naval discipline.

Hotham, Mount Vic. 37S/148E A mountain 1,861 m. in the Aus. Alps section of the Great Divide, with a road to a ski resort above the tree-line and near the summit, 695 km. from Melbourne. The flat top is of basalt, above fairly even slopes in Ordovician slates.

Housing (in Aus.) Mainly single-storey houses standing detached, each in its block of land. There is rapidly growing demand for flats, now making up over 12% of dwellings; many are available for purchase as 'home units'. Houses and blocks are not necessarily large, but ensure widely spread cities, increasing the pressure towards car-ownership, and largely explaining the limited extent of fully sewered suburbs. (See also ARCHITECTURE.) Over 70% are owned or in the course of purchase by instalments, and the rest tenanted in various ways. There is a Government Grant for young couples, of $1 for every $3 they have saved to buy a house (maximum on $1,500 saved). A Government scheme insures lenders against loss. Government houses comprise 20–30% in S.A. and W.A., 40% in A.C.T. and 75% in N.T. By a Commonwealth–State agreement of 1945 the Commonwealth provides most of the finance for the State Housing Commissions which undertake the building operations for housing very roughly comparable to council-housing in U.K. Many such houses are being or have been bought by the tenants. Building societies are increasing but are not as important in home purchase by instalments as in Britain. Trading and savings banks and insurance companies give advances on mortgage up to certain limits, but a second mortgage usually backed by a guarantee, e.g. from an employer, is often needed and interest rates for this part of the loan are usually rather high. Interest on housing loans is not deductible for income tax purposes (1973) but rates, land and property taxes are.

Houtman Abrolhos W.A. 29S/113E 3 groups of uninhabited islands, Pelsart, Easter and Wallabi, which extend over 80 km. They have a history of wrecks, including that of Pelsaert* in 1629. The Portuguese name, implying 'watch out', was given in 1598 by Houtman. Guano and phosphate have been quarried, and they are now a crayfish centre and holiday attraction, especially for ornithologists.

Hovea A genus of about 12 species in the Papilionaceae or Pea* family, including the tree-like *H. longipes* of Qld., the small purple-flowered and slender-leaved *H. linearis*, also of coastal Qld., and the *H. longifolia*, varying from an alpine compact bush with short broad leaves, to a tall form with narrow prickly leaves in mountain forests. *H. trisperma* is a spectacular W.A. species (*see* PLATE 6).

Hovell, William Hilton (1786–1875) b. Yarmouth, Eng. He migrated to N.S.W. (1813), and after serving on trading ships for Simeon Lord*, settled to farm. In 1824 he accompanied Hume* on an exploratory journey which found the Murray, and finished at Port Phillip Bay. Later there was bitter dispute, largely by Hume (the native-born), that Hovell (the immigrant) was at fault in their thinking that this was Western Port*.

Howe, Cape 38S/150E On the N.S.W./ Vic. border, this is a rather low headland with ocean swell licking up over the rocks, but with a 396-m. hill inland, a granite intrusion into the Ordovician slates and Devonian sandstones which here reach the coast.

Howe, George (1769–1821) b. West Indies. A London printer transported in 1800, and emancipated in 1806. He became Government Printer and in 1803 Governor King authorised his weekly *Sydney Gazette and N.S.W. Advertiser*, Australia's first newspaper, which he produced single-handed. Although a censored, official mouthpiece, it had critical, literary and improving aspirations. It was carried on after his death by his son **Robert** (1795–1829) and was freed of censorship after 1824. Howe also published the colony's first books. Another son **George Terry** (1806–63) started Launceston's first newspaper in 1825.

Howe, Michael (1787–1818) b. Pontefract, Eng. He was transported to Tas. for highway robbery (1811), and escaped to become the notorious audacious and brutal bushranger 'Black Howe' from 1814–18, making it a period of terror for settlers and travellers. He was killed near the Shannon River, having been decoyed after a year of hiding. *Michael Howe the last and worst of the Bushrangers of Van Diemen's Land* by Thomas Wells, published by Andrew Bent* (1818) was the first Aus. work of general literature, of which only 3 known copies survive.

Howitt, Alfred William (1830–1908) b. Nottingham, Eng. He arrived in Aus. gold-fields (1852) with his father William Howitt, author of a detailed gold-field novel *Land Labour and Gold* (London, 1855), and who returned to Eng. (1854). Alfred became a noted explorer, prospector, geologist, naturalist (making important contributions on eucalypts) and anthropologist, collaborating with Rev. Lorimer Fison, a digger and Wesleyan missionary, to write *Tribes of South East Australia* (London, 1904), a standard work. He led an expedition sent to trace Burke* and Wills.

Howse, Sir Neville Reginald (1863–1930) b. Somerset, Eng. He arrived in Aus. in 1889 and was the first Aus. winner of the Victoria Cross*, awarded for his rescue of a wounded man under fire in the Boer War. He practised medicine at Orange, N.S.W., and served with distinction also as a medical officer in the 1914–18 War and achieved Cabinet rank in a post-war political career.

Hughendon Qld. 21S/144E (1,924 in 1971; 2,329 in 1961) At the junction of the Winton link between the Great Northern and Central Lines, this is the main though declining service centre of a great stretch of sheep and cattle country, developing originally as a bullock-team centre.

Hughes, Enoch (1829–1893) b. Dudley, Eng. A pioneer ironmaster who opened the first Melbourne rolling mills in 1860. He was manager of the Fitzroy works at Mittagong (1862–5) and the Eskbank works, Lithgow (1874–83), which he initiated with Rutherford and Williams. Hughes had great pertinacity in the face of labour, capital and transport difficulties and saw the need for integrated production in Aus. isolated conditions.

Hughes, William Morris (1864–1952) b. London. He arrived in Aus. in 1884 after teaching for a short time, to become one of the most colourful and controversial political personalities and he was Prime Minister from 1915–23. His early jobs varied from Qld. shearer to Sydney bottle-washer, and he found his niche in the developing Labor politics, becoming a Member of N.S.W. Parliament in 1894, and of the Commonwealth Parliament from the first Federal elections until his death. Hughes was small in stature, and in compensation for this as well as the harsh conditions of his early life, he was hard, overbearing and arrogant. At the same time a brilliant political mind was accompanied by ready wit; and he was utterly single-minded in his pursuit of what he believed were Aus. interests. In 1916 he visited U.K. and the Western Front and was lionised as the 'Little Digger'; his consequent efforts to introduce conscription* led to his expulsion from the Labor Party. At Versailles in 1919 he fought pugnaciously for Aus. interests and his obsessive belief in White Australia* which he saw threatened by Wilson's idealism. The rising Country Party*, on whose support Hughes's Nationalist Government depended after 1920, insisted on his replacement in 1923 by Bruce*, and he joined the newly created United Australia Party* under Lyons*. In 1929 he was largely instrumental in bringing down Bruce's administration, but if he hoped to be rewarded by the new Labor Premiership, he was to be disappointed; and although serving in Lyons' Cabinet 1931–9 he had little real power. However, he continued to add spice to many debates and actively pursued defence campaigns and development of militia. At 74 he narrowly missed the Premiership to Menzies*, was Attorney General 1939–41, and served in the all-party War Advisory Council (1941–5). He was expelled from the U.A.P. in 1944 for refusing to withdraw from the Council when they did. The following year, however, he joined its successor, the Liberal Party. He left racy accounts of his early career in *Crusts and Crusades* (Sydney, 1947) and *Policies and Potentates* (Sydney, 1950). *For further reading see* L. F. Fitzhardinge: *William Morris Hughes* (Sydney, 1964).

Hume, Hamilton (1797–1873) b. Parramatta, N.S.W. Son of a convict superintendent of dubious character, he became 'one of the immortals of land exploration', particularly significant because he was native born. When only 16 he walked with his brother over the Berrima area; in 1818 he was a servant on the Throsby*-Meehan expedition; in 1822 he voyaged S and walked inland to the Braidwood area with Alexander Berry. His major contribution was to lead an expedition, accompanied by Hovell* (1824), originally intended to reach Spencer's Gulf, but turning S to reach Corio Bay on the western shore of Port Phillip, discovering en route the Upper Murray and naming it the Hume (Sturt, coming on it downstream unknowingly renamed it in 1829). Jealous incompatibility led to quarrels on the journey and to later acrimonious attacks on Hovell by Hume, over leadership and responsibility for their mistake in identifying Corio Bay as Western Port*. Hume accompanied Sturt to the Darling in 1828 and squatted in the Yass Plains which he had explored in 1821. He is commemorated in the **Hume Highway,** linking Melbourne and Sydney (900 km. long) and the Hume Reservoir*.

Hume Reservoir Vic. Completed in 1936 and expanded in 1961, with some hydro-electric generation in 1957. It dams back the Murray and lower Mitta Mitta, 16 km. upstream from Albury, 36S/147E, and on the N.S.W./ Vic. border. It now has a capacity of 3,084 million m.^{3}, and irrigates over 120,000 ha. through a complex system of weirs feeding canals and channels by gravity. The first weir, Yarrawonga, is 233 km. downstream.

Humpty Doo N.T. 12S/131E On Adelaide River 65 km. SE of Darwin, this was famed for the abortive attempt at large-scale rice-growing by Aus.–American capital from 1954–60. It failed in spite of early experimental success, through a combination of technical mistakes (e.g. insufficient land levelling), climatic hazards and pests, including wild buffalo, rats and geese.

Humpy Any roughly constructed small hut; originally *umpee*, an Aboriginal word from Moreton Bay, describing the crude branch and bark native shelters.

Hunter, John (1737–1821) b. Leith, Scotland. Second Governor of N.S.W. from 1795–1800. Although he was destined for the Ministry, he left Aberdeen University for the navy, following in his father's footsteps. He had risen to Captain when in 1788 he was appointed 'second captain' to Phillip* on the First Fleet*. Older than Phillip, he was more religious and equally upright, a meticulous observer and writer and with skills in both drawing and music, keenly interested in natural science, and incredibly tough physically. After charting Sydney Harbour, he sailed in *Sirius* via Cape Horn to get supplies from S Africa, returning via the Indian Ocean—a great pioneer circumnavigation. In 1790 he was stranded for 11 months on Norfolk Island after *Sirius* was wrecked. He published an account of the colony in 1792, and the following year he successfully applied to succeed Phillip as Governor. Before his arrival, however, under the interim control of Grose* and Paterson*, the trade monopolies of the N.S.W. Corps and many other evils were established. Hunter's integrity and efforts at reform, even though unsuccessful, made him many enemies, not least Macarthur*, and he was recalled largely through their slanderous accusations to London.

Hunter River N.S.W. Rises in the basalts of Mt. Royal Range*, rugged, wet and forested, flowing SW past Muswellbrook*, 32S/151E, with a marked elbow near Denman where it receives the main right-bank tributary the Goulburn River, adopting its direction of flow NW–SE to a lagoon-and-sandbar delta, then reaching the Pacific, near Newcastle*, 33S/152E. Its length is about 470 km., but in the 160 km. downstream from Singleton* it falls only 30 m. The fertile 8-km.-wide strip of alluvial silts, intensively used for dairying and for market-gardening near Maitland*, are subject to frequent flooding. The average flow at Singleton, from a catchment of 1·6 million ha., is only 740 million m.^{3}, but the flow is extraordinarily variable in volume. Tributaries from the wet Barrington Tops* area at times carry great volumes and at times pond back the spreading silt-laden waters of the Wollombi Brook, flowing N across sandstone country to the important Cessnock* coal-field. The widespread damage caused has made the Hunter Valley a field of intensive regional research. Glenbawn Dam* upstream from Muswellbrook, the first of 7 projected flood mitigation dams, already evens out flow for pump irrigation. The highly prized table wines are mainly grown on the lower slopes on the southern edge of the valley between Cessnock and Singleton, and include the famous Pokolbin vineyards. Several place names in the valley commemorate the Cornish family of Henry Dangar (1796–1861), an early surveyor. *See* A. Tweedie: *The Hunter Valley* (Melbourne, 1956); *The Hunter Valley Region* (Newcastle, 1968) by Hunter Valley Research Foundation.

Huntsmen Spiders A popular name for species mainly in the family Sparassidae, e.g. the widespread *Delena cancerides*, with body about 2·5 cm. long and long legs, the second pair of which may have a span of 5 cm. It is light brown with dark spots and cross-stripes on the back of the abdomen; and is found under stones etc. or in rubbish in outhouses, but may enter houses in search of prey. If it is disturbed it may assume an aggressive pose with front legs raised, and inflict a painful bite.

Huon Pine (*Dacrydium franklinii*) A valuable now scarce tree of SW Tas., in the Podocarpaceae* family. The timber has a high oil content, distilled for germicides, perfumes and soaps. A stand is preserved in the Denison Valley.

Huon River Tas. 43S/147E Rising on the slopes of Mt. Wedge and Mt. Bowen, it flows first S then E through upland forested and large inaccessible country for much of its 160-km. course, before turning SW into its tidal estuary below Huonville, then sharply SE at Geeveston, to the D'Entrecasteaux Channel. It was named after Bruny D'Entrecasteaux's* captain. The plains along the lower valley have the densest rural population in Tas. and 75% of the State's apple trees, as well as many sawmills and a pulp mill at Port Huon based on eucalypt, for cardboard, paper bags etc. Small settlements, of which Huonville on the main estuary and Cygnet on the Port Cygnet branch, are the chief, are served by boat, but road transport has replaced much of the formerly important shipping.

Hurley, James Francis (Frank) (1890–1962) b. Sydney. He became noted in later life as a photographer of the Aus. scene in 13 published books. Previously he had worked for 7 years in the Antarctic (1911–7 and 1932–4) with Shackleton and Mawson; was an official A.I.F. war photographer, 1917–1918. *For further reading see* F. Legg and T. Hurley: *Once More on My Adventure* (Sydney, 1967).

Hydatid Cyst-like structures occurring in animal tissues, but now especially the cysts of the larval stage of the dog tapeworm *Echinococcus granulosus* (*see also* HELMINTHS). The tapeworm eggs may be ingested by humans from handling fouled dog-fur and in salads from fouled soil or highly polluted water. Sheep particularly carry on the cycle, and it is a serious health hazard where sheep, men and dogs are in close association, also causing economic loss to graziers. In Aus. kangaroos and wallabies also carry on the cycle and the large bladder-like cysts may be seen in their flesh. Dogs are often fed sheep offal containing cysts; the larval cysts develop to adult tapeworms in the dog, eggs are excreted and so the cycle is maintained. It could be broken if offal were boiled before feeding, dogs were treated against tapeworm, and hands washed after handling dogs—most difficult with finger-sucking children.

Hydrozoa Class of aquatic, mainly marine animals, Phylum Coelenterata* including the following. 1. The simple freshwater *Hydra* spp. have small green to brown polyps with tentacles searching for prey on aquatic plants in ponds etc., or seasonally in mobile form; the colonial *Cordylophora* spp. occurs on submerged logs etc. in the Myall Lakes NE of Newcastle. 2. There are naked marine forms such as *Tubularia*, with a connecting stem along submerged rock and the polyp looking like separate flowers (hence the name zoophyte, animal flowers), or the tough branching stems and many polyps of *Pennaria*, common on rocks and wharves in Sydney Harbour. 3. There are covered polyps, e.g. the small moss-like tufts of *Obelia*, the cups of *Sertularia*, in pairs along the stem, often on the holdfast of kelp etc. below low tidal level, or *Plumularia*, with thick central stem and hair-like branches with stalkless polyp cups on one side of the branch. 4. Among the Hydrozoans where the free-swimming or medusa stage is dominant are the harmless By-the-Wind Sailor, *Velella* spp., with a buoyant sac like a Brazil nut, and the noxious Blue-bottle* with a rounder blue air-sac and tentacles; both are often blown into surfing bays and on to beaches in SE Aus. by the same NE storm. Some of the Hydrozoa bear a marked superficial resemblance to the more complex Moss-animals*.

Hymenoptera (membrane-winged) An Order of 4-winged insects, the front pair of wings larger than the rear pair and both pairs gauzy and veined; it includes the Sawflies*, Ants*, Bees* and Wasps* with over 6,000 Aus. species, many of which are beneficial in the pollination of plants, in control of other insects, in scavenging, and of course in the production of honey by the honey-bees. It includes the Sub-Order Symphyta with caterpillar-like larvae, and the Sub-Order Apocrita which has a 'waist' between thorax and abdomen (more accurately, between first and second segments of the abdomen, to the rear of which, in this Sub-Order, the abdomen is called the gaster). The females of some species of bees, wasps and ants have the egg-laying organ on the tail, specialised to function also as a sting carrying alkaline (wasps) or acid venom, usually mild to painful, but sometimes serious in its effects if there is multiple biting or individual allergy to the poison. The waistless Symphyta comprises chiefly the large Sawfly family, Tenthredinidae, and is discussed under Sawflies. The waisted Apocrita include the Ants*, Bees* and Wasps*. Species not treated in other articles include: the Cream-spotted Ichneumon-wasp, *Echthomorpha intricatoria*, the adult of which has a wing-span of up to 2·5 cm. across, a black body with cream side spots, long, bright orange antennae and a long sharp 'sting' which, however, does no more than prick human beings; the black Hatchet Wasp, *Evania appendigaster*, whose popular and Latin names have been given on account of its remarkably long and attenuated waist followed by the 'hatchet' with prominent ovipositor or 'sting', often raised above the thorax when seen perhaps on a house window; lastly the very large family of Chalcid Wasps, many species of which are very small and some of which have the rear pair of legs specialised for jumping; one of the families in this group includes the tiny *Pleistodontes imperialis* and *P. froggatti* one of whose functions is the pollination of the enclosed flowers of the native fig-trees*.

Cream-spotted Ichneumon Wasp
(Ecthomorpha intricatoria),
about twice life size

I

Idriess, Ion Llewellyn (1890–) b. Sydney. A journalistic writer of 54 books mainly about the Aus. inland which he knows intimately, such as *Flynn of the Inland* (Sydney, 1932), or *Lightning Ridge*, about opal-mining (Sydney, 1940).

Iguana A term sometimes used for Goannas*.

Illawarra, Lake N.S.W. A coastal lagoon SW of Wollongong, 34S/151E, formed by the blocking of 2 small drowned valleys and a rather broad embayment by a dune-crowned coastal sand-barrier; the narrow entrance is near Shellharbour, and the lake is ringed by other suburbs of Wollongong. The water is used by the Tallawarra power station (320,000 kW) which also uses Mt. Kembla coal. There is much dairying traditionally on lightly improved but fair quality pastures on basalt soils around the lake and the nearby lowlands; here, initially by accidental crossing, was evolved the **Australian Illawarra Shorthorn** or A.I.S. dairy breed, claimed to have inherited 'the vitality and high milk yield of the Ayrshire, the hardiness of the Devon, a beef animal, and the large bone-structure and ability to survive on poorer pastures of the Shorthorn'. *For further reading see* R. S. Mathieson: *Illawarra and the South Coast Region* (Melbourne, 1960).

Imlay family 3 brothers, **Peter, George** and **Alexander**, who were medical officers but became important settlers in the Bega area, N.S.W., from about 1830, developing whaling and trading in beef, wool, etc. with Tas., S.A. and N.Z.

IMMIGRATION Population increment in recent years due to net immigra-

tion (i.e. permanent arrivals from overseas, less returned migrants and Aus. emigrants) was about 100,000 people, or 0·8%, maintaining the total population increase at about 2% per annum in the face of a falling birth-rate. From 1945–66 there were 2·55 million permanent or long term arrivals, 1·26 million of them assisted; 1·36 British, 0·30 Italian, 0·15 Greek, 0·14 Dutch, 0·11 German, 0·08 Polish and 0·41 others. Almost 60% were in the age group 15–44, and over 30% up to 14, giving an access of both productive strength (about 65% with training), and of heavy consumer demand. About 75% of the 20,000 annual permanent departures were to U.K. (with N.Z. surprisingly high at almost 20%). About 33% of settlers intend to stay in N.S.W., 29% in Vic., 17% in S.A., and 8% in W.A., with about 1% for Tas. and A.C.T. and a few for N.T. Over half are destined for the State capitals, with under 30% for other towns, especially Newcastle, Wollongong and Geelong, and under 20% in rural areas. Agreements have been made since 1945 with various countries willing or anxious to foster emigration, often with a contribution to costs. The migrants make a small payment also. Assisted passages are dominantly from U.K., but with important streams from Germany, Italy, Greece, Netherlands, Malta and Austria; in the immediately post-war years a large number of refugees were absorbed. Private organisations to assist youthful migrants include Big Brother Movement (N.S.W., 1925), sponsoring boys, and Fairbridge Farm Schools (W.A., 1912), caring for orphans, both now with centres in other States. Only in the gold-rush years of the 1850s had a comparably cosmopolitan population been received. Though assimilation has

273

been successful and almost complete in the second generation, there have been some tendencies for national groups to dominate or at least strongly colour particular suburbs or shopping areas. Southern and East Europeans have partly replaced non-immigrant population moving out from central city areas, as in Sydney, Melbourne, Adelaide and Brisbane, or inner suburbs, e.g. Woollahra, North Sydney and Marrickville in Sydney; Collingwood, Richmond and Kew in Melbourne; South City and North City in Brisbane; and Kensington, Norwood and Hindmarsh in Adelaide. British, Dutch, and N.Z. immigrants have gathered in fair- to better-class suburbs or for instance in the new town of Elizabeth*, S.A., and Central and East Europeans in industrial suburbs such as those around Bankstown (Sydney) or Sunshine (Melbourne), with Southern Europeans in peri-urban market-gardening or irrigation areas. Such national associations have not been necessarily harmful to the process of assimilation, but rather may give a secure base from which it may be approached. There have been recurrent phases of activity and stagnation, the latter often connected with international monetary crises, as in the 1890s and the 1930s, sometimes with Aus. conditions, e.g. the post-Federation slump and drought years of 1901–6, and post-war minor recessions in 1952 and 1960. At the same time economic or political crises, even bad winters in U.K., increase the push element. British migrants are not necessarily or even usually from the least prosperous groups. The gold-rush period of the 1850s was a notable upsurge (population rose from 400,000 in 1850 to 1,100,000 in 1860), while the 1914–8 and 1939–45 wars brought periods of stagnation followed by great inflows. The 1960s saw anxiety when targets were not reached. But this has given way to an emphasis on consolidation, selection and reduced flow in the 1970s. This has resulted from the large

number of departures (44,719, 1971–2) and Aus. unemployment. The British quota has been reduced and Britain no longer contributes to the assisted passage scheme. Some 27,000 migrants of mixed descent were accepted 1966–72; about 400 Uganda Asians were admitted. The 1972–3 target for total immigrants was 110,000 with family reunion and sponsorship stressed. It was announced in 1973 that assisted passages would be available 'without regard to race, colour or nationality'. A source is, J. Jupp: *Arrivals and Departures* (Melbourne, 1967).

Indigo (*Indigofera*) Flowering shrub genus. *I. tinctoria*, formerly important for purple dye, grows in Qld. but may be introduced. The foliage may be poisonous to cattle.

Ingamells, Reginald Charles (Rex) (1913–1955) b. Orroroo, S.A. A poet, teacher and founder (1938) of *Jindyworobaks** literary movement. His poems often use Aboriginal themes and legends.

Ingham Qld. 19S/146E (5,797 in 1971) 30 km. up the Herbert River and vulnerable to its summer flooding. It serves both the surrounding canelands and the timber industry to the west.

Innamincka S.A. 28S/141E Cattle station and ghost township where the sporadic Cooper and Strzelecki Creeks separate. It originated as an inter-state Customs post before Federation. An Aus. Inland Mission* hostel was abandoned (1952), and little remains of the town, save part of its famous 200-m.-long and 15-m.-high heap of empty bottles.

Innisfail Qld. 17S/146E (7,475 in 1971) Formerly Geraldton, at the junction of N and S Johnstone Rivers, 8 km. from the coast, in the heart of sugar country, and linked by narrow-gauge rail to Mourilyan Harbour. Sugar lighters for Cairns reached the town at one time.

Insecta or Insects A class of the Phylum Arthropoda with 54,000 known species in Aus. One classification includes the following Sub-Classes and Orders.

I *Sub-Class Apterogyta*—primitively wingless Thysanura—Silverfish* and Bristletails*; Collembola—Springtails*.
II *Sub-Class Pterogyta*—winged or secondarily wingless.

A. *Series Palaeoptera*—wings folded over thorax: Ephemeroptera—Mayflies*; Odonata—Dragonflies* and Damselflies.

B. *Series Neoptera*—wings folded over abdomen: 1. *Division Exopterygota*—wings developing externally—includes Dictyoptera—Cockroaches* and Mantids*; Phasmodea—Stick and leaf insects; Orthoptera—Crickets*, Grasshoppers* and Locusts*; Isoptera —Termites*; Plecoptera—Stoneflies*; Dermaptera—Earwigs*; Embiaria—Web Spinners*; Psocoptera—Booklice*; Mallophaga—Chewing-lice (*see* Lice); Anoplura—Sucking-lice and Bird-lice (*see* Lice); Thysanoptera—Thrips*; Hemiptera—Bugs*, Cicadas*, Leaf-hoppers*, Froghoppers*, Scale-insects*, Water-bugs*. 2. *Division Endopterygota*—wings developing internally — includes Coleoptera—Beetles*; Mecoptera—Scorpion Flies; Neuroptera—Lacewings* and Ant-lions*; Diptera—Two-winged Flies (*see* Flies); Siphonaptera—Fleas*; Trichoptera—Caddis Flies*; Lepidoptera* —Moths* and Butterflies*; Hymenoptera*—Bees*, Wasps*, Ants*, Sawflies*.

C.S.I.R.O.* has a Division of Entomology. There were a number of important pioneer collectors, including Alexander Macleay* and W. W. Frogatt (1858–1937), author of the pioneer *Australian Insects* (1907); R. J. Tillyard: *Insects of Australia and New Zealand* (1926). A definitive work sponsored by C.S.I.R.O.* is *The Insects of Australia* (Melbourne, 1970). J. Child: *Aus. Insects* (Sydney, 1960) is introductory.

Insurance All undertakings except for friendly societies, superannuation schemes etc. (and under the Constitution, State insurance offices operating within their State), are required to lodge a deposit with the Commonwealth Treasurer (for investment in stocks selected by the insurer) as a security available to policy-holders in case of need. Of 46 Life Insurance Companies (1969), 9 were major mutual concerns and 33 were overseas companies*, but some of the Aus. companies have overseas interests.

The industry began with marine insurance in the 1830s, soon followed by fire and life business. The mutual life offices, from 1849 onwards, came to dominate the life insurance business. The important introduction of non-forfeiture in life assurance was made by J. M. Templeton (1840–1908). After a century of specialisation the last decade has seen many life companies forming subsidiaries to engage in general insurance.

Motor vehicle and compulsory third-party insurance for vehicles is now over 40% of general insurance business, and one which is unattractive to general companies because of heavy claims, at times exceeding incomes. Much of it, therefore, falls to State insurance offices and the specialist motoring organisations; young and accident-prone drivers now face very heavy premiums, while no-claims bonuses reduce motoring costs very considerably.

International Relations A Commonwealth Government responsibility since Federation, handled by the Department of Foreign Affairs*, though of course there is often a very close relationship with Defence* policy.

The British and British Commonwealth of Nations' connections remain close, friendly and valued, though diminishing in importance over the last 25 years or so. The fall of Singapore in 1941 brought great reliance on and co-partnership with the U.S. in the war in the Pacific. In the Suez crisis of 1956 the Aus. Government supported the U.K. Government of Sir Anthony

Eden; since then Britain's power and influence in Asia has been waning. The 1967 U.K. Labour Government announcement of withdrawal from the Far East was only modestly amended by the Conservatives in 1970. But U.K. continues to contribute to the Commonwealth Strategic Reserve, aimed at helping to maintain a balance of strength in SE Asia and the SW Pacific. These trends are coupled with economic changes following British entry to the European Common Market in 1973. The relationship with Britain has cooled further with the election of a Labor Government in 1972. More frequent and informal royal visits have not entirely offset a waning appeal of allegiance to the British Crown in an increasingly cosmopolitan Aus. Meanwhile the American connection strengthened, through A.N.Z.U.S.* and through Aus. participation in the Vietnam War. The growing importance of Asia and the Pacific was seen in S.E.A.T.O.*, A.S.P.A.C. (Asian and Pacific Council, 1966, with Aus. a foundation member), and in contributions to the Asian Development Bank, the Colombo Plan* and South Pacific Aid. Aus. participation in the United Nations has been active from the drafting of the charter in 1945, and she contributed as a member to the Korean War*, to peace-keeping in the Congo and Cyprus, and to various technical organisations and aid programmes. Foreign aid exceeded $220 million (1972–3, among the world's highest in proportion to population (0·75% of the national income): 65% of it, however, goes to Papua—N.G.*. As Senior Consultant to the U.N. Special Fund an Aus., Sir Robert Jackson (1911–) has advised on many Asian and African schemes. During the 1950s and 1960s Aus. was aligned with U.K. and U.S. in the anti-communist block. The new Labor Government from 1972 takes a more independent line, recognising China and establishing relations with E. Germany.

Aus. maintains overseas 45 Embassies, 18 High Commissions (i.e. to other British Commonwealth countries), and 16 other Missions including that to the United Nations in New York. In Aus. are 42 Embassies, 11 High Commissions, 60 other countries have consular representatives. See A. Watt: *The Evaluation of Aus. Foreign Policy 1938–65* (Cambridge, 1967); T. B. Millar: *Australia's Foreign Policy* (Sydney, 1968).

Inventions These may be patented under the 1952 Patents Act; an average of 5–6,000 Letters Patent are sealed each year. For major Aus. inventions *see* AGRICULTURAL MACHINERY, AVIATION, SCIENCE *and* REFRIGERATION.

Inverell N.S.W. 30S/151E (9,700 in 1971) A local service centre lying at just over 580 m. on the E edge of the wheat and fat-lamb country of the Western Slopes region, but including the NW part of the New England* plateau in its hinterland. It has been the centre for very varied mining including diamonds, and alluvial tin is still worked at Tingha, some 25 km. to the SE and sapphires from 1969.

Investigator Strait S.A. 36S/136E Between Yorke Peninsula and Kangaroo Island, it averages 56 m. in width.

Ipomaea A large genus in the Convolvulaceae family, including cosmopolitan species, e.g. the coastal *I. pes-caprae* common throughout the tropics and sub-tropics, the delicate mauve and deep purple Morning Glory, *I. cairica*, of the NE coast, Egyptian bindweed, *I. palmata*, its blue flowers often seen on the E coast, and many tropical Qld. species, some of which gave food to Aborigines. Introduced species include the sweet potato *I. batatas* and the American Morning Glory, *I. hederacea*.

Ipswich Qld. 28S/153E (60,017 in 1971)

A city on the Bremer River and now part of Metropolitan Brisbane. It dates from 1827, with Logan's* establishment of lime works for Brisbane buildings and was called Limestone until 1843. Later, as Ipswich, it became the 'Squatter's Capital' linked by Qld.'s first railway (1865) to Grandchester, then to Toowoomba (1867), and enjoyed a period as head of navigation until the railway killed the trade after 1876. Industries include large railway workshops, woollen mills, brickworks, butter, earthenware and hardboard factories (based on plantations); it is the centre of the W Moreton coal-field which, although with small-scale mines and variable faulted seams, has provided over half the State's coal, because of its proximity to markets.

Iris, Wild or **Leafy Purpleflag** Popular names for the small purple iris *Patersonia glabrata* with 3 delicate papery petals, narrow leaves, hairy at the base, and flowering on sunny spring days along the E Coast. There are many other species of *Patersonia*, as well as the elegant white *Libertia paniculata* and smaller sub-alpine *L. pulchella* of E Aus. in the Iridaceae family proper. There are also somewhat iris-like flowers in the Burmanniaceae, notably the rich purple *Burmannia disticha* of heath and swamp country in NE Aus.; and the almost leafless saprophyte, living on leaf-mould and decaying wood in S Vic. and Tas., *Thismia rodwayi*, called Fairy Lantern from its glowing amber trilobed flowers.

Iron Monarch S.A. The most productive of the iron ore mountains of the large Middleback Range*, being quarried in successively excavated benches.

Iron Ore Spectacular new developments since 1960, following the lifting of an export ban, have transformed Aus. from a position of self-sufficiency to a leading world exporter. Prior to 1966, S.A. produced 70% of the annual 5 million tons, from the Middleback Ranges, 33S/136E, the remainder coming from W.A., 28% from 2 Yampi Sound islands, 16S/124E, Cockatoo and Koolan, and 2% from Koolyanobbing 31S/119E. Reserves formerly reckoned under 204 million tonnes are now considered as being 20·4 thousand million tonnes 90% of this high-grade haematite, being in the Hamersley Ranges of W.A. Development is in train, with British, American, Japanese and Aus. interests, in various combinations of fiercely competitive companies, bargaining for mainly Japanese contracts. Commonwealth 'guidelines' on minimum prices had to be relaxed in 1967 in face of potential Brazilian and African competition. A major operational project, bringing ore from Mt. Tom Price (see map overleaf) by 294 km. of standard-gauge heavy duty railway to a new deep-water port Dampier, began exporting ore in 1966, as did Mt. Goldsworthy which depends on the recently deepened harbour at Port Hedland*, along with Mt. Newman mines (1969). Robe River limonite goes from a new port at Cape Lambert (1972). Deposits (McCamey's Monster) are to be mined near Mt. Newman for Japanese and European markets. Koolyanobbing expansion serves Kwinana* by the standard-guage line. In N.T. development of ores at Francis Creek, 320 km. SW of Darwin, required reconditioning of the 80-year-old narrow-gauge N Aus. Railway*. In Tas. formerly inaccessible ores on the Savage River* are piped as slurry to a pellet plant at Port Latta 24 k m. E of Smithton, 41S/145E. Although contracts promised $2,000 million a year by 1976 in iron export, Japanese cut-back was causing anxiety in 1972–3. Up to half Japanese iron import is from Aus., and some 5% world production. The Aus. economy will benefit in foreign exchange and to the extent that native capital is drawn in, and secondary processing developed here.

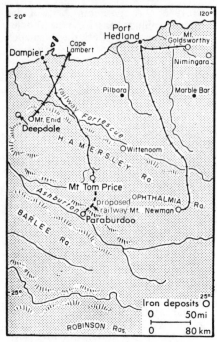

Paraburdoo–Tom Price is complete and a new line E from Mt. Goldsworthy under construction (Courtesy NAT/DEV)

Iron and Steel With annual output of 7 million tonnes of steel ingot (1972), Aus. ranks 14th in the world, making only 1% of the total steel, but lying sixth in per capita consumption. Domestic demand can be met except where type or price makes some import desirable; Aus. export may increase to N.Z. and SE Asia. There was a recession 1971–2.

About two-thirds of Aus. steel is made at Port Kembla*, N.S.W., almost one-third at Newcastle*, N.S.W., and a small amount at Whyalla*, S.A. All are controlled by the near-monopolistic B.H.P.* group. Expansion under way will give capacity of almost 9 million tonnes of raw steel. The Whyalla structural mill will rise to 490,000 tonnes. Kwinana, W.A. has a blast furnace

and a merchant mill and exports to China, Japan and Italy. There is demand for pipelines. Newcastle is the oldest extant centre (1915); modernisation has included development of the more rapid and economic Basic Oxygen processes (Linz–Donawitz), now producing 24% of Aus. steel. Port Kembla uses the open hearth method. Whyalla makes special steel by electric furnace, but will also make Basic Oxygen steel. Aus. is very well placed for raw materials: abundant coking coal, magnesite and some limestone in N.S.W.; vast haematite iron reserves in S.A. and W.A.; limestone and dolomite in S.A.; chromite in W.A., Qld. and New Caledonia (French). All are within reach of tidal waters, cutting transport costs.

The earliest foundry, in Sydney (1833), was followed by many others, using British pig iron cheaply imported as ballast in wool ships. The earliest iron smelting was near the present town of Mittagong*, N.S.W., producing the first Aus. pig iron (1864). Growing demands for rails, fences, roofing and machinery for mines and farms stimulated other unsuccessful attempts at smelting: in the Tamar Valley, Tas. in 1862, 1872 and 1874–96; near Ballarat, Vic. 1878–84; and in S.A. in the 1870s.

The only venture to survive into the 20th century was at Lithgow*, N.S.W., where the Eskbank works under the successive pioneers Hughes*, Sandford* and Hoskins* saw the first Aus. steel made in 1900. Lack of capital, experience and easy transport killed all the other attempts and Lithgow had a chequered career before Hoskins moved his steel-making to Port Kembla coal (1927–30) to form Aus. Iron and Steel with 2 British Companies. Meanwhile Federation (1901) was followed by protection in the form of bonuses (1908) and controversy over the need for a nationalised steel industry, for economic and defence reasons. At this point, B.H.P., hitherto concerned with extraction and smelting of silver–lead, entered steel-making, backed by its iron ore leases and port installation in S.A. (obtained for flux initially), its experience and reputation for profitability, and particularly its dynamic leadership. Newcastle began production in 1915; by 1935 it had expanded, recovered from the Depression, and bought the ordinary shares of Aus. Iron and Steel at Port Kembla. In 1939 output was 1 million tons. In 1941 B.H.P. first smelted iron and made ships at Whyalla: this was a result of S.A. bargaining before renewing the iron ore leases, but was made economically feasible by the advance in fuel technology which had reduced the coal needed to make a ton of steel from 3½ tons in 1915 to 1¼ tons; thus N.S.W. coal could now go to S.A. iron, as well as the reverse, in an economical 2-way traffic. Wartime expansion was followed by uncertainty in the 1950s and rapid subsequent growth: 1959 output was 3 million tons. Control of the basic industry of iron and steel by a profit-motivated monopoly rouses controversy, notably over potential export to help payment deficits, since this involves vast investment in capacity which may not be in constant use. *For further reading see* Helen Hughes: *The Australian Iron and Steel Industry* (Melbourne, 1964).

Ironbarks A group of Eucalypts, important timber trees of E and N Aus., most species having the dark, hard, deeply fissured persistent bark of the popular name, but some of the botanically related group have smooth upper branches (the Gum-top Ironbark, *E. decorticans*), while the Yellow Gum, *E. Leucoxylon*, has a bare trunk like the Red Gums. Some species have soft bark, as in young trees of the Broad-leaved Ironbark, *E. siderophloia*, and some quite thick cork as in the Grey Ironbark, *E. paniculata*. Different species cover a wide range of habitats from sandy soils in 35–40 cm. rainfall belt to deep loams in 150 cm. mean annual rainfall (though with smaller specimens on excessively drained stony ridges). Buds tend to be pointed, fruit conical to ovoid, and fairly small, about 6 mm. across. Some of the species with deeply furrowed bark have a white 'bloom' on leaves, buds and fruits: Blue Leaf Ironbark, *E. nubiles*, the small Silver-leaved Ironbark, *E. melanophloia*, with distinctive opposite and stalkless adult leaves and sometimes Red Ironbarks, *E. sideroxylon*. Others without this white bloom often have dull grey-green adult leaves including the Narrow-leaved Red Ironbark, *E. crebra*, and the Lemon-scented Ironbark, *E. staigeriana*, with rather broader round-tipped leaves containing the aromatic limonene. Some Ironbarks hybridise with Boxes. The Narrow-leaved Red Ironbark is important in a 320 to 500-km.-wide belt in NE N.S.W. and E. Qld., over a wide mean annual rainfall range from 60 to 150 cm.; the Broad-leaved Ironbark, *E. siderophloia*, with lanceolate adult and somewhat oval juvenile leaves in coastal N.S.W. and SE Qld. The Red Ironbark or Mugga, *E. sideroxylon*, with rather broadly lanceolate leaves of 6–12 cm. long, is important on the western slopes 35–60 cm. rainfall belt in N.S.W. and Vic.; the 25–30 m. straight-trunked Grey Ironbark, *E. paniculata*, in coastal N.S.W.; and the Grey Ironbark, *E. drepanophylla*, in Qld. The Yellow Gum, *E. leucoxylon*, often with bark scaled off to leave a yellow, white and blue-grey smooth mottled trunk, is common on undulating to hilly terrain with 50–75 cm. mean annual rainfall in W Vic.

Ironwood Applied in Aus. to hard timbers from several trees, including the poisonous *Erythrophloeum chlorostachys* in the tropical Caesalpinaceae family, several Acacias, and several in the Myrtaceae family, notably *Austromyrtus acmenioides, Choricarpia subargentea* and *Backhousia* spp.

Irrigation Some 1·5 million ha. are irrigated, about 0·2% of the surface.

Vic. leads with 40% of Aus. irrigated area (85% for pasture); N.S.W with 39% (50% for pasture) is next, followed by Qld. (12% of total, 88% of it for crops); S.A. (5% of total, 75% for crops); W.A. (just over 2% total, 50% for crops); and Tas. (under 2% total, 60% for crops). 40% of Aus. is arid, another 40% has considerable need for irrigation, but the total river run-off is small. Much is not available where it is needed, but irrigation can certainly be extended as the 'cost structure' justifies it. Except in limited areas, artesian water is useful for stock rather than irrigation. (*See also* CLIMATE *and* WATER RESOURCES.)

Apart from small local works, irrigation began with Acts in Vic. to set up irrigation trusts, following the severe drought of 1877–81. Wartook dam in the Grampians was built—the beginning of the Wimmera–Mallee network of today—but progress was slow until Deakin's* studies in U.S., Italy, Egypt and India, and his encouragement of the Chaffey* brothers to import techniques from California to the Mildura area. In N.S.W. interest dates from the 1880s, with surveys by F. J. Home, a retired irrigation engineer from Punjab, and McKinney, the State Engineer. McCaughey's* success with pump-fed channels from about 1900 encouraged the State Government to go ahead with the Burrinjuck Dam and Murrumbidgee canals. From these beginnings have spread the irrigation projects, intensive or extensive, and some domestic and stock watering projects, of the Murrumbidgee*, the Murray* itself, the Goulburn* valley, the Wimmera-Mallee*, the Snowy Mts. project* (partly for hydro-electricity), Gippsland (Glenmaggie*), the Lachlan*, major projects in Qld. such as Emerald*, in W.A. the Ord* project and the small coastal area of irrigation from the Harvey and Collie rivers. Notable engineers have included J. S. Dethridge (1865–1926) in Vic., who invented a now widely used metering device, and E. M. de Burgh (1863–1929) in N.S.W.

Isaacs, Sir Isaac Alfred (1855–1948) Although noted as the first native-born Governor General (1931–6)—a post opposed in London, particularly by George V—this great lawyer made lasting contributions throughout his long public career in law and politics. The son of a Jewish tailor from London, he was brought up frugally in Vic., working his way from teaching, to law clerk, to barrister, to become Attorney General, Justice of the High Court of Aus. (1906–30) and Chief Justice for one year before becoming Governor General. A passionate federalist, imperialist yet radical, he was an elected member of the Conventions framing the Constitution. *For further reading see* Max Gordon: *Sir Isaac Isaacs* (London, 1963); Z. Cowen: *Isaac Isaacs* (Melbourne, 1967).

J

Jabiru, Black-necked Stork or **Policeman Bird** (*Xenorhynchus asiaticus*—strange-beaked) Up to 1·5 m. tall, with black-grey beak, head and neck, white plumage with dark-green back, tail and wing-stripe, the last along with a purple stripe, and long red legs. From India to N and E Aus., it inhabits and fishes in swamp country for fish, crabs etc., though it also eats carrion; the nest, up to 2 m. broad, is in a tree or rarely on the ground, with 4–6 whitish eggs.

Jackass Fish A large deep-water fish of many Aus. temperate waters. (*See* MORWONGS *and* JACKASS FISH.)

Jackeroo A young man working on a sheep or cattle station and learning the job. The origin is uncertain, most probably a coined Aus.-sounding word based on a 'Jacky Raw', but an Aboriginal origin is also claimed. *Jillaroo* for a female land worker was coined in the 1939–45 War.

Jackey Jackey: Nickname of William Westwood, a bushranger, born in Kent, Eng. He was transported in 1836 and escaped in 1840 to become a legendary figure, a 'gentleman bushranger', allegedly even attending a Government House Ball, and making several escapes. Also the name of an Aboriginal guide with the explorer Kennedy*.

Jackson, Marjorie (1932–) b. Lithgow. A sprinter of world repute, winning gold medals at the Olympic Games in 1952 (100 and 220 m., which she also won in the 1954 Commonwealth Games).

Jacky Winter or **Brown Flycatcher** (*Microeca leucophaea*—fascinating small house bird). A familiar and well-

loved bird seen around houses in town and country in much of Aus., sitting on a favourite perch, repeatedly calling jacky-jacky or peter-peter according to 2 of its many popular names (also Post-sitter and Stump-bird). It takes off to catch insects in the air or on the ground (whereas the Robin is a ground-feeder exclusively). The small saucer-shaped nest, commented on in its Latin name, is beautifully finished with horse-hair, cobweb, lichen etc. and only about 5 cm. by 1 cm. deep, with 2 pale-blue eggs with some grey-brown spots. (*See* PLATE 3.)

James, Brian Pen-name of **John Lawrence Tierney** (1892–) b. Eurunderee near Mudgee, N.S.W. A short-story writer using small town themes and background for readable, racy tales, as in *Cookabundy Bridge* (Sydney, 1946). His novel *Advancement of Spencer Button* (Sydney, 1950) traces a State School teacher's career.

James Range N.T. 24S/133E Lies S of Missionaries Plain* and E of the spectacular Finke River gorge and Palm Valley, and cut by Ellery Creek and Hugh River gorges; some maps use this name also for the Krichauff Range W of the Finke.

Jansz (Janssen) Willem A Dutch sea captain, the first authenticated European to discover Aus. along with Rosengrin. (*See* DISCOVERY.) In the course of seeking trade on behalf of the Dutch East India Company, he sailed in the *Duyfken* along the S coast of N.G. in 1605. They struck a Cape they christened Keerweer, 14S/142E, 'Turn Again', not knowing it was on a peninsula (later called Cape York) of the great southland. They returned with

281

negative reports of the importance of their voyage.

Jarrah (*Eucalyptus marginata*) The famed hardwood timber of sandy lateritic soils in the 61–150 cm. rainfall belt of SW W.A. It is generally of 24–30 m. and 1–2 m. in diameter. Juvenile leaves are pale green, broad and pointed, adult leaves dark glossy green above, paler below, thick, leathery and rather broadly lanceolate. There are star-like clusters of long slender buds to 2·5 cm. long and ovoid fruit of about 1 cm. long. Bark is brown and stringy, and persistent to the lower branches.

Javelin Fish (*Pomadasys hasta*) A sea fish with straightish belly and curved, heavy back with a continuous fin, spiny in front. It is silver grey with 4–5 interrupted black lines along the upper sides, and up to 70 cm. long. Sometimes known as Qld. Trumpeter from the noise it makes out of water.

Jellyfish A popular name for certain aquatic, mainly marine Coelenterata*, though there are somewhat similar forms among the mobile members of other classes, e.g. Hydrozoa*. The commonest genus of Aus. coastal water is *Aurelia*, often with its umbrella-shaped form about 10 cm. across numerous fringing tentacles and 4 purple horseshoe markings in the jelly. Large jellyfish of SE Aus. waters include *Cyanea annaskala*, milky white-mauve, pink or brown, 60 cm. across and with tentacles to 4 m. long, and probably concerned in severe stinging of surfers in occasional years when it is blown close inshore in force; and *Catostylus*, clear blue or opaque yellow-brown, which is sometimes common in the drowned valley harbours of SE Aus. and also stings sharply on occasions.

Among the jellyfish seriously noxious to man, the chief are the rather oblong-bodied Box Jellyfish (known to have killed over 40 people in the N), Sea-wasps or Cubomedusans, including the S.A. *Carybdea rastonii*, with 15 cm. stinging tentacles causing sharp pain and illness but not fatal as yet, and the deadly Qld. *Chironex fleckeri* which has certainly caused several deaths, very rapidly, of both Europeans and Aborigines and often severe pain and temporary paralysis. These deadly species are clear and almost colourless, but very slightly blue, 15 cm. across the box or bell, with trailing tentacles up to 2 m. long, with some tendency to be in 3 hand-like groups on short arms below the bell. L. Burley Griffin (Canberra) has sporadic appearances of the freshwater jellyfish *Crespedacusta* spp., the only known place in E Aus.

Jervis Bay N.S.W. 35S/151E A broad but partly enclosed bay, with a small outlier of the A.C.T. on the S side, extending for 16 km. as far as Sussex Inlet and St. George's Basin. It was intended for port development for Canberra; there is a naval college and naval installations, and may be the site of the first (proposed) Aus. nuclear power station. Land has been leased by a U.S. steel company.

Jewfish or **Westralian Jew Fish** (*Glaucosoma hebraicum*) Silvery-grey sea fish with dark longitudinal bands (transverse in young fish), with spiny front fin on the back running to large back one which bears a single backward-curved spine. Pearl Perch of E. Aus. is *G. scapulare*, silvery with some pink and red, deep-bodied, with small front fin on the back running into large rear one. Both these fish are good to eat, reach 60–90 cm. long but are usually of about 1·3–2·2 kg. Jewfish is loosely applied to the Mulloway* and other fish.

Jews Classified officially by the census as Hebrews, and numbering 63,721 (1966), of whom over 90% are in Sydney and Melbourne. In Sydney organisation is fairly loose, and they are more of British, Austrian and

German origin; in Melbourne there are more S and SE European Jews, more closely knit, with more schools of their own. Some 40,000 foreign-born Jews have migrated to Aus. since the Nazi persecutions of the 1930s; the preponderance of older people and assimilation of younger ones to the general community give anxiety to the strongly orthodox. G. J. Cohen (1842–1937) was an outstanding layman and benefactor.

Jindabyne N.S.W. 36S/149E A small rural and holiday centre removed 1964–6 from its former site on the Snowy River to a new site on the W slope of the **Jindabyne Reservoir**, a storage regulator from the Snowy Mts. Scheme* from which water is pumped 200 m. up to Island Bend to the main Snowy–Murray tunnel.

Jindyworobaks A literary group (1938–53) founded in Adelaide by R. C. Ingamells* and Ian Mudie to encourage 'Australianism' in writing. It is an Aboriginal word meaning 'to join or to annexe' implying the need for writers to base their work on the Aus. environment.

John Dory (*Zeus australis*) A deep but thin oval fish, with prominent ragged fins, which approaches its prey stealthily and apparently camouflaged

John Dory (Zeus australis), about 60 cm. long

as a straggling vertical piece of seaweed. It is dark brown, though it may flush or pale, with lighter belly and the well-marked 'thumb-print' with lighter aureole on the side, and is netted commercially and lined for sport. Grows mostly to 30–40 cm. and 0·5–1 kg.

Johnson, Richard (1753–1827) b. Yorkshire, Eng. He was recommended by Wilberforce and appointed Chaplain with the First Fleet, thus Australia's first clergyman. He built the first church. His letters reveal his ardent faith, yet increasing despair both of his charges and of the colony's future. He started Sunday Schools to try to wean the convicts' children from their parental influences, and returned with Hunter* in 1800.

Johnston, George (1764–1823) b. Dumfriesshire, Scotland. A Major in N.S.W. Corps*, and one of the first officers to receive a land grant (1793) which he named Annandale after his birthplace. Johnston put down the Castle Hill Rising* with some brutality. In January 1808 Bligh's enemies under Macarthur wrote to 'implore you to place Governor Bligh under arrest and to assume command of the colony . . .'. This Johnston did, assuming the title of Lt.-Governor although this belonged to Paterson then in Tas. He ruled uneasily for 6 months, largely as Macarthur's tool, until Foveaux* arrived; he was court-martialled in London, cashiered in 1811 and returned to his extensive properties in N.S.W. in 1813.

Jones, David (1793–1873) b. Wales. He arrived in Aus. in 1835, founder of what has become a large department store business, in Sydney (1838). Jones accepted payment in kind (wool or wheat) from country customers and a large mail-order element remains in the business which is still in the hands of his descendants.

Jorgensen, Jorgen (1780–1841) b. Copenhagen. A versatile adventurer who visited Aus. as a sailor on survey and whaling ships (1801-5). He engineered an Icelandic revolution, acting as self-appointed Protector for 2 months in 1809. He was transported to Tas. (1826) for petty crime in Britain, induced by gambling. Pardoned (1833) after he had undertaken useful exploration, he turned to writing and studied the Aborigines. He wrote plays, an Aboriginal dictionary and an autobiography.

Joseph Bonaparte Gulf   N.T./W.A. 14S/ 128E   A wide inlet off the Timor Sea, into which flow the Ord and Victoria Rivers; named by the French explorer Baudin in 1803.

Jujube-tree (*Ziziphus jujuba*) A small prickly tree with orange-red fruit used in confectionery; its range extends from Qld. to India. It belongs to the mainly warm-climate Buckthorn family Rhamnaceae.

Jumbuck A sheep. The derivation is uncertain, but is not now considered Aboriginal; it may simply be a corruption of 'jump up'.

Jumping Spiders A popular name for species mainly in the family Salticidae with square-fronted heads and a heavy front pair of legs for jumping on prey after a successful stalk, often on foliage and often by day. There are many species, most in the N.

Junee   N.S.W. 35S/148E (3,765 in 1971; 3,980 in 1961)   A market and local service centre and shire headquarters in the S of and towards the W edge of the Western Slopes region. There were gold workings 1869-81. The town, proclaimed 1886, grew with the railway (1878) and a branch (1881) to serve the Riverina*, and with railway workshops. It is now developing as a dormitory town for Wagga*.

K

KADINA

Kadina S.A. 34S/138E (2,853 in 1971; 3,102 in 1961) A service centre at the N end of the Yorke Peninsula*, which developed with copper-mining from 1860–1923 in the Kadina–Wallaroo–Moonta* area, and has subsequently declined.

Kalgoorlie W.A. 31S/121E (20,784 in 1971, including Boulder) Developed as Hannan's Find in 1893, when diggers rushed E from the 'Old Camp' of Coolgardie* to work the alluvial and quartz reef deposits; it was later named Kalgurli. It escaped the ghost town fate of most of the Eastern Gold-fields* camps because of the rich deep ores of the Golden Mile* 5 km. to the S, for which, with its rival and now joint town of Boulder, it became the residential centre. By 1900 it was a wages town and small prospectors had moved on, although old-timers and lucky new-comers may still pick up a worth-while nugget or some black opal. The wide streets, now lined with supermarkets and milk bars, reflect the use of early camel and horse teams which needed to turn, until the railway came in 1896. It is isolated, in a harsh environment made more so by denudation of the woodland for fuel. Kalgoorlie has a strong local spirit, a devotion to sport, and an outspoken local press. The town is reviving and expanding as the centre for the developing nickel* fields, with a smelter planned along with standard-gauge rail links N to nickel mines and S to Kambalda and Esperance. *For further reading see* G. Casey and T. Mayman: *The Mile that Midas Touched* (Adelaide, 1964).

Kambalda W.A. 31S/122E A former gold-mining area (1898–1906) now being developed to exploit rich nickel* reserves for export from Esperance*

KANGAROO ISLAND

(1968). A treatment plant lies 3 km. NE on the shores of the salt lake Lefroy. Population 4,289 in 1971.

Kameruka N.S.W. 19 km. SW of Bega*, 37S/150E. An estate village, with dairy processing including a well-known cheese. It was founded on an estate which has been (larger or smaller) in the hands of the Sydney brewing family of Tooth and Tooth-Lucas since 1854. The planting of exotic trees in parklands to form a mildly post-feudal or 'squirearchy' atmosphere has caused the estate to be referred to as a 'transplanted English landscape'.

Kanaka Hawaiian word for 'man', but used for all South Sea Islanders brought to Qld. (1860–1900), first for cotton then sugar plantation labour, and often under the spurious 'contracts', of Blackbirding*. Legislation (1868–85) regulated conditions on the cane-fields but could not check abuses in recruiting; 50,000 had been brought by 1890. The abolition advocated by Griffith* to be effective from 1890 reflected growing Labor concern over jobs as well as humanitarian motives, but was repealed (1892) because of the prevailing Depression. The northern planters threatened secession on the issue. Meanwhile smaller holdings were replacing plantations, and mechanisation the need for so much labour. Abolition (1904) followed Federation pledged to a White Australia policy which brought a sugar subsidy, and all Kanakas were returned by 1907.

Kangaroo Island S.A. 36S/137E (3,380 in 1966) The third largest offshore island after Tas. and Melville Island, with an area of 4,308 km.^{2} It is a detached section of the Flinders-Mt. Lofty Ranges, here in the form of low hills. Poor soils have yielded to application of trace elements for sheep and barley in the E with considerable post-1948 clearance for soldier settlement. The original flora is preserved in Flinders Chase*. Tourist traffic and gypsum at Ballast Head add to the economy. The island was named in 1802 by Flinders whose crew had a 'regale' of its large fearless kangaroos; he found no humans. American sealers from 1803 had a rough lawless settlement at Pelican Lagoon (later named American River). In 1836 the pioneer whalers and the first S.A. settlers were established at Nepean Bay on the N coast, although Light chose Adelaide as the capital of the new colony within 6 months.

Kangaroo Paw A widely used popular name for the floral emblem of W.A., a bulbous plant of somewhat sedge-like habit, bearing 8–10 flowers with relatively small yellow-white recurved pointed petals and long stamens, protruding from tubes generally on one side of a stout stem; the whole is covered with velvety hair, green on the tubes and then red at the base and upper flower stem. The species described is *Anigozanthos manglesii*, common in King's Park, Perth, and many other places, but there are many other colourful species, for instance round Albany, 35S/118E. The genus, confined to W.A., is usually placed in the cosmopolitan Amaryllidaceae of bulbous flowering plants, particularly common in hot, dry areas. (*See* PLATE 6.)

Kangaroo-grass The widely used popular name for *Themeda australis*, a tall grass widespread in Aus. though commoner towards the coasts. It has keeled leaves, a series of broad spiked seedheads towards the top and several leafy spikelets protecting the fertile seed proper in the centre. The grass is nutritive and highly palatable to stock in the early summer, but easily grazed out and so most often seen in places protected from grazing.

KANGAROOS Including Rat-kangaroos, Wallabies, Wallaroos and the Kangaroos of popular usage, in the family Macropodidae (great-footed), these are among the more vegetarian marsupials. Within the family, 3 subfamilies may be distinguished: I the Hypsiprymnodontinae with dentition transitional between that of the other 2 sub-families and containing only the Musk Rat-kangaroo, *Hypsiprymnodon moschatus*; II the Rat-kangaroo subfamily Potoroinae; with canine teeth, though reduced in size, comparable to those of the carnivorous marsupials and III the Wallabies, Wallaroos and Kangaroos, sub-family Macropodinae, which sometimes have small canine teeth, but much smaller again than in the carnivorous marsupials.

I *Musk Rat-kangaroos* are found in forests of the Rockingham Bay area, Qld. They are up to 45 cm. long, from naked nose to scaly tail, run rather than hop, with only moderate enlargement of rear limbs, 5-toed front and rear, with second and third toes on hind foot joined and first toe opposable. Solitary, partly diurnal, terrestrial, can dig, eats insects, worms, tubers, nuts (sometimes holding them in forepaws).

II *Rat-kangaroos*, with more kangaroo-like feet and tail, but small rounded ears, were formerly found over much of Aus., but distribution is now greatly restricted. They make nests of grass and eat grasses, fungi etc. 1. The short-nosed genus *Bettongia* (Aboriginal) includes (a) Brush-tailed Rat-kangaroo, *Bettongia penicillata*, of N.S.W., rare, yet very widely distributed throughout Aus. except the extreme northern tips, though with regional races; the tail is prehensile; (b) Lesueur's Rat-kangaroo, *B. lesueur*, a burrowing species, of central to SW Aus., not dissimilar externally but with differences in skull etc.; (c) Tasmanian Rat-kangaroo, *B. cuniculus*, a rather large animal. 2. Rufous Rat-kangaroo, *Aepyprymnus rufescens*, is reddish-grey on the back, with whitish

Brown Hare-wallaby   *Whiptail Wallaby*   *Great Grey Kangaroo*
Rufous Rat-kangaroo   *Scale about 1/25th*

belly, the largest Rat-kangaroo, thick, coarse fur, tail tapering and not prehensile; it has a residual distribution in coastal eastern Aus. in open woodland where it nests under tussocks or bushes. 3. Potoroo or Long-nosed and broad-faced Rat-kangaroos, *Potorous*: (a) *P. tridactylus* with long foreclaws, relatively short hindfoot, naked top of muzzle, round ears, tapering prehensile tail, nests in forest litter in rainforest or wet sclerophyll woodland in SE Aus.; (b) the smaller Gilbert's Rat-kangaroo, *P. gilberti* and (c) the distinctive Broad-faced Rat-kangaroo, *P. platyops*, which may still exist in parts of SW W.A. 4. Desert or Bluff-nosed Rat-kangaroo, *Caloprymnus campestris*, is a nocturnal herbivorous species of attractive light colour, nesting below saltbush in sandflats or stony plains NE of L. Eyre. It has narrow ears, naked snout, tapering tail which is not prehensile; increases in numbers following wet seasons.
III *Wallabies, Wallaroos, 'Kangaroos'*, i.e. sub-family *Macropodinae*. Important genera and species are described. 1. Banded Hare-wallaby, *Lagostrophus fasciatus*, is about 75 cm. nose to tail-tip with naked snout, and thick fur, grey, black and white banding on rump

and grey-white belly; now rather rare on islands in Shark Bay. Its mainland relative is now restricted to SW of W.A. 2. (a) Brown Hare-wallaby, *Lagorchestes leporoides*, with hairy snout, reddish ring round eyes, and black patch on elbow, about 85 cm. total length, has a residual patchy distribution in inland SE Aus. Others in the genus are (b) Hare-wallaby, *L. hirsutus*, on islands in Shark Bay and residually in inland of W.A. and (c) Spectacled Hare-wallaby, *L. conspicillatus*, with various regional races on islands of W.A., patches on mainland, and in N.T. and north-central to coastal Qld; has reddish patches round the eyes, variable in colour from pale to dark fawn in different races. 3. Tree-kangaroos, genus *Dendrolagus* are typical of N.G. Aus. species are: (a) Lumholtz's Tree-kangaroo, *D. lumholtzi*, of N Qld., over 1·2 m. nose to tail, tip dark, grey-fawn with yellow-white belly, dark face with pale band on forehead, broad feet and long nails, short hindfoot and long tapering tail —balancing but not prehensile; (c) Dusky or Bennett's Tree-kangaroo, *D. bennettianus*, found in rain-forests between Cooktown, 15S/145E, and Daintree, 16S/145E; darker, with a dark reddish patch at the base of the tail. 4. Rock Wallabies are of genera *Petrogale* (10 species) and *Peradorcas* (1 species); modifications to tail and feet adapt them for their rock-dwelling habit. They eat grasses, leaves, bark and roots from which moisture is derived during droughts. Selected species are: (a) Blackflanked Rock Wallaby, *Petrogale lateralis*, with a marked black dorsal line widespread in W.A., but now much reduced by foxes; (b) the Plain or Qld. Rock Wallaby, *P. inornata*, of central to E Qld. and (c) Longman's Rock Wallaby, *P. longmani*, in the N of N.T.; (d) the single species of Little Rock Wallaby, *Peradorcas concinna*, under 75 cm. nose to tail-tip and is found in coastal tracts in N Aus. 5. Nail-tail Wallabies, genus *Onychogalea*, are all slender, about 100 cm. nose to tail-tip, about the size of a hare and with a small horny or nail-like extension beyond the tip of the tapering tail. The species are: (a) *O. unguifer*, the Northern or Sandy Nail-tail Wallaby, which is rather larger, fawn with a brown dorsal stripe, found in a belt along the coast of N Aus.; (b) the grey, white and black Bridled Nail-tail Wallaby, *O. fraenata*, found in residual patches in a mainly inland belt, from the Murray-Darling confluence to Rockhampton, Qld., 23S/151E; (c) the smaller Crescent Nail-tail Wallaby, *O. lunata*, which has the stripes from the armpit forming a crescent across the shoulder; it is found in patches in a belt from the SW of W.A. to the centre of Aus. 6. Pademelon (Aboriginal) or Scrub Wallabies of genera *Setonix* and *Thylogale* are simply the smallest of the many members of the Wallaby-kangaroo family, having hindfeet up to 15 cm. and skull up to 12 cm. long. They live in scrub, undergrowth and tall swamp or savannah grass, eating grass, leaves and shoots. Over much of their range they are greatly diminished because of clearing, hunting, feral cats and dogs, and foxes. Species include: (a) the

Red-legged Pademelon, *T. stigmatica*, with a patchy coastal distribution from Sydney to Cape York; it is 103 cm. nose to tail-tip, dark grey with reddish hindquarters and red heel, yellow hip stripe and dark neck stripe, naked snout. Broadly similar species are recorded near Melbourne and Mt. Gambier, S.A., and in Tas.; (b) the Quokka (Aboriginal) or Short-tailed Pademelon, *Setonix brachyurus*, rather smaller than a hare (body 58 cm., tapering tail only 25 cm.), with short, round ears and large permanent premolar teeth perhaps adapted to a diet including many tree-shoots; found in pockets in tea-tree scrub and thick sedge tussocks in coastal swamps and thickets of mainland and insular SW W.A., common on fox-free Rottnest and Bald Island. 7. Typical Brush Wallabies of genus *Wallabia* are the medium-sized species of the kangaroo family (hindfoot 16–25 cm., skull 11–15 cm. long). A Wallaby was observed by Pelsaert* in W.A. in 1629, and Captain Cook's kangaroo of the Cooktown landing in 1770 was also a Wallaby. Species include: (a) *Wallabia canguru*, Whiptail or Pretty-face Wallaby (up to 1·75 m. nose to tail-tip) with long, black-tipped, tapering tail, grey body, grey-white belly, dark brown ear-base, white face-stripe and naked snout, found in open woodland or sclerophyll* forest in coastal Qld. and N.S.W.; (b) the Swamp or Black-tailed Wallaby, *W. bicolor*, reddish-grey with reddish-orange belly, found in rain-forest or wet sclerophyll woodland of coastal E Aus.; (c) the Black-striped Wallaby, *W. dorsalis*, and (d) the Red-necked Wallaby, *W. rufogrisea*, distributions overlapping the other E Aus. species mentioned, the latter extending into Tas., (e) the brindled Toolache Wallaby, *W. greyi*, confined to the Eyre Peninsula and adjacent coastal patches; (f) the Black-gloved or Western Brush Wallaby, *W. irma*, of the SW of W.A. and (g) the Sandy or Agile Wallaby, *W. agilis*, of coastal N Aus. 8. The

Large Kangaroos and Wallaroos, genus *Macropus*, the largest living marsupials, with hind-feet over 25 cm. and skull over 14 cm. long, include 3 species: (a) the widespread sub-species of Euro or Hill Kangaroo, *M. robustus*, of up to 2·5 m. nose to tail-tip, dark grey to blackish with grey-white belly, thick coarse fur and naked snout; agile rock climbers; they use inaccessible hides in tumbled boulders, gorges etc., emerging at night to graze in open scrub country; (b) the widespread Great Grey, Grey or Forester Kangaroo, *M. giganteum*, up to 2·5 m. nose to tail-tip, grey-brown with white belly, short woolly fur, black tail-tip and hairy snout, of slender build; shelters by day at the base of rocks or trees, feeding at dusk; shy but inquisitive— sitting up on its haunches to gaze back at the pursuer—and therefore easily hunted; (c) Red or Plains Kangaroo, *Megaleia rufa*, the largest, up to 2·7 m. nose to tail-tip, with an almost continent-wide distribution over all the drier parts; it is of slender build, the female blue-grey, the male reddish (the young often mixed grey and reddish) with woolly fur; white face marks partly hairy snout and paler tail; they are gregarious, crepuscular-grazing, can hop up to 50 km.p.h., but like many of the family, stop, stand with head turned round to see the hunter, and are easy prey; as in most of the larger marsupials, births occur at any time of the year, with a preponderance of single births.

There is controversy over conservation* of kangaroos, views ranging from eradication as a pest to total protection; from indiscriminate shooting for pet meat and skins (1½ million a year until export of kangaroo products was banned in 1973), to management as an efficient grazing animal.

Kapunda S.A. 34S/138E (1,301 in 1971) A small service centre for wheat-sheep country in the Mt. Lofty Ranges, originating with the first S.A. copper-mining (1844–88), and mining may be resumed.

Karratha W.A. 26S/116E (1,823 in 1971) A new town built (1970) to house workers at Dampier* 20 km. away.

Karri (*Eucalyptus diversicolor*) The tallest tree of W.A. usually to 45–86 m., but exceptionally 76 m., and 1·5– 3 m. in diameter, with long straight branchless trunk to two-thirds of its length and strong even timber. Small outliers apart, it grows often in pure stands in a 16- to 25-km.-wide belt along the coast from Albany to Cape Leeuwin, in cool temperate conditions with 100– 150 cm. rainfall and on rolling hills—or lower valley sides on the drier side of its range. Thin bark is shed over the whole trunk in irregular patches, leaving an attractive pattern of yellow-brown and blue-grey. Juvenile leaves are oval, green with pale undersides, and adult leaves fairly broad lanceolates of 10–14 cm. long. Buds are rather long clubs of up to 2 cm., fruits pear-shaped to cup-like, on stalks of 6–12 mm. (*See* PLATE 8.)

Katanning W.A. 34S/118E (3,603 in 1971) A rail point and service centre for the S of the Wheat Belt*, and the more predominantly wool farms to the W of the main line.

Katherine N.T. 15S/132E (2,520 in 1971) Lies where the Stuart Highway, Overland Telegraph and N Aus. Railway cross the Katherine River, the main headwater of the Daly River*. The Katherine River flows seasonally for 240 km. SW from Arnhem Land*, passing through a gorge 32 km. from the town. Vegetable farms on the riverside levees, developed for troop supplies in the 1939–45 War, formed the basis for subsequent intensive C.S.I.R.O.* experiments in tropical cropping of sorghum, peanuts, cotton, fodder crops and improved pasture. Meatworks process beef for export to U.S. Katherine was the daughter of a patron of J. McDouall Stuart who found the river in 1862 on his continental crossing.

Katoomba N.S.W. 34S/150E (10,969 in 1961, with Wentworth Falls; 11,573 in 1971) A holiday resort at over 1,000 m. in the Blue Mts.*, the administrative headquarters of the City of Blue Mts.* The city grew from coal-mining, the railway and a now less fashionable Sydney summer resort function, away from the city heat, especially at Leura, nearby; now with commuting. It retains a much shorter-stay and day-tour traffic to see the cliffs and waterfalls nearby. There are small manufactures, e.g. leathergoods.

Kauri, South Qld. (*Agathis robusta*) The South Qld. Kauri is a useful softwood tree of the Araucaria family to 36–43 m. by 90–120 cm., growing on valley bottoms and lower slopes in the 100 to 150 cm. rainfall belt in parts of coastal Qld. It has a long straight trunk, with a rough scaly bark shed in round fragments, broad glossy pointed leaves in pairs and an ovoid fruit or cone about 1 cm. long. 2 other species of *Agathis* are indigenous to Aus.

Kavel, Augustus (1798–1860) b. Germany. Leader of German Lutheran settlers who arrived in S.A. in 1838. He sought and obtained financial advances from G. F. Angas* when they dissented from the Calvinistic impositions on forms of worship by King Frederick William III. Kavel remained a strong influence on the settlers although latterly he was involved in bitter doctrinal disputes.

Keepit Dam N.S.W. 31S/150E On the Namoi River*, it is 54 m. high and stores 425 million m.^{3} of water for rural water supplies, electricity generation and licensed private diversions including those for Wee-Waa* cotton.

Kellerman, Annette A swimming champion and exhibition swimmer and diver of the early 20th century who first took it up as a remedial exercise following poliomyelitis. She raced in marathons against men in the Yarra, the Seine and the Thames, reformed the style of women's swimming costumes, earned large sums in vaudeville and films, and is credited with the introduction of formation swimming.

Kelly, Edward (Ned) (1855–1880) b. Beveridge, Vic. Outlaw leader of a famous Vic. gang. He was the son of an Irish ex-convict 'Red' Kelly and Ellen Quinn. He grew up as one of a close-knit clan of Irish migrants in the Wangarratta-Beechworth area, which came to be called Kelly Country. The poor living of the Selections was supplemented by horse and cattle thieving from rich squatters, and there were continual police clashes. Ned alleged persecution of his family, and there is evidence of active police desire to reduce the Kelly prestige and arrogance. It is possible that neither the first police charge against him of assault nor the second of receiving a stolen horse (leading to 3 years in gaol 1871–4) was wholly justified. On release, Ned earned money as a timber-getter, but also as he later confessed to 'wholesale and retail horse and cattle dealing'; his brother Jim was gaoled for 10 years and brother Dan also charged. A dubious incident when Dan 'resisted arrest' led to the arrest of Mrs. Kelly for attempted murder of the policeman concerned, and to Ned and Dan 'going bush'. Superb bushmen, they were helped by their large clan to elude the intensive 18-month police hunt involving humiliating fiascos for the force. A police party camped near their hideout was 'bailed up' at Stringybark Creek by Kelly, who killed 3 of them. 2 audacious bank robberies, Euroa in December 1878 (when they held an entire station personnel hostage) and Jerilderie, N.S.W. (February 1879), when they imprisoned the 2 local policemen, increased their prestige and the reward money to £8,000. A former friend of Byrne (who with Hart had joined the gang) turned informer, and Byrne and Dan Kelly shot him. Ned planned to derail the trainload of special police reinforcements which this incident would bring, at Glenrowan, and they forced the townsfolk into the hotel. A schoolmaster managed to warn the train, and the police attacked the hotel. Ned, wounded, managed to limp into the bush. The others retreated inside where Byrne was shot dead, the other 2 probably killed themselves before the police fired the building the following afternoon, after the hostages had been allowed out. Meanwhile, at 7.00 a.m. Ned had returned and, weighed down by his 40 kg. of home-made armour, fell before police fire. He was hanged in Melbourne on November 11th 1880. Over 50 books as well as Douglas Stewart's play, several films and Nolan's paintings give the full range of opinions about Kelly, from murdering bushranger to a wronged hero who personified Aus. mateship, and deep Irish–English and selector-squatter hatreds of 19th-century Aus.

Kelpie An Aus.-developed breed of sheep and cattle dog, derived originally from Border collies, and named after one of the early champions, Kelpie. Theories of dingo blood are strongly held, but not substantiated. The kelpie is smooth haired with sharp nose and ears. *For further reading see* M. Hamilton-Wilkes and D. Cumming: *Kelpie and Cattle Dog* (Sydney, 1967).

Kempsey N.S.W. 31S/153E (8,867 in 1971) An important milk, butter, cheese and bacon processing centre amidst the dairy farms of the lower Macleay River*, 40 km. from its mouth; it is built on a river levee, and the lower parts are fairly frequently flooded. It was a centre of cedar exploited almost to extinction and vital in the early settlement; it retains a trade in other timbers, and a plywood factory.

Kendall, Henry Clarence (1839–1882) b. Ulladulla, N.S.W. A poet, whose work is represented in *The Golden Treasury* and *Oxford Book of English Verse*. His best work was lyrical (now rather unfashionable and considered derivative) description of the green sea-washed plains and forests of N.S.W. One of 5 children of drinking but educated and intellectually sympathetic parents, his life was harsh and he owed much to the charitable support of friends. His works can be found in T. I. Moore's *Selected Poems of Henry Kendall* (Sydney, 1957) and T. T. Reed ed.: *The Poetical Works of Henry Kendall* (Libraries Board of S.A., 1966).

Keneally, Thomas (1935–) b. Sydney. After preparation for the priesthood, he has become a leading novelist and playwright since publication of *Bring Larks and Heroes* (London, 1967); later works are: *Three Cheers for the Paraclete* (1968), *The Survivors* (1969) and *The Chant of Jimmy Blacksmith* (1972). Plays include *An Awful Rose* (1972).

Kennedy, Edmund Besley Court (1818–1848) b. Channel Islands. He arrived in Aus. in 1840. Surveyor and explorer, second in command to Mitchell on his 1845 expedition, and dispelled the hopes that they had found a great NW-flowing river next year. Killed by Aborigines in 1848 when he had nearly completed a journey through Cape York Peninsula, his fate was reported by his loyal and remarkable Aboriginal companion Jackey Jackey. *See* E. Beale: *Kennedy of Cape York* (Adelaide, 1970).

Kent Islands Tas. 40S/148E A small uninhabited group of 4 islands in the Bass Strait, named after a naval nephew of Governor Hunter.

Kent, Thomas (?–1832) He arrived in Sydney in 1808. He was an enterprising though rascally settler, with successive unsuccessful schemes for hemp, flax, coal, seaweed burning for alkali and finally, and at last with success, the first extraction of tanning material from wattle bark in 1819, at an establishment on the Huon River, Tas.

Kiama N.S.W. 35S/151E (4,706 in 1971, with Bombo and Minnamurra, a few miles off) A former cedar port, now holiday centre on a rocky coast, including a famous blow-hole, and with a prominent lighthouse nearby. The forested escarpment of the Southern Tablelands inland from Minnamurra has a very instructive and beautiful 'Nature trail'.

Kianga-Moura Qld. A coal-field in the Dawson* River valley, 900 km.[2] in extent, being exploited by an American/Aus./Japanese combine to export over 5 million tonnes of coking coal a year to Japan by a 185 km. electric, narrow-gauge railway to Gladstone* (1968). The open-cut workings are highly mechanised and include the world's largest walking dragline (American built), taking over 220 tonnes of overburden in each bite.

Kidman, Sir Sidney (1857–1935) The 'Cattle King'. He was born near Adelaide, and left home at 13. From his first property Owen Springs, N.T., 80 km. SW of Alice Springs, bought in 1880, he acquired by various means, chains of established properties exceeding 250,000 km.[2], which allowed him to move his stock according to grazing conditions and water supplies.

Kieran, Bernard Bene (Barney) (1886–1905) b. Sydney. A swimming champion, who using a trudgen stroke, broke every world record from 200 yd. to 1 mile in 1904–5. He died very young, following an appendix operation.

Kiewa River Vic. Left-bank Murray tributary about 110 km. long, joining near Albury, 36S/147E. Its headwaters rise in Vic. High Country near Mt. Bogong*, dropping over 1,300 m. in 25 km. This fact, along with winter snow and high annual rainfall, has been used in the **Kiewa Hydro-Electric Scheme** completed in 1958. 3 power stations are fed by diversion weirs and pipelines from the major Rocky Valley Storage Dam at 1,625 m., with a steep drop in penstocks down the side of Mt. McKay, part of the edge of the Bogong High Plains.

Kikuyu Named after the important tribe in Kenya, Africa, this is a valuable fodder grass, *Pennisetum clandestinum*, introduced only in the 1920s, but now widespread especially in the dairy country of NE N.S.W. and being a vigorous grower, is a pest of gardens there. It is a relative of Bullrush Millet. (*See* MILLET.)

Kimberley (The Kimberleys) W.A. A statistical Division of 356,500 km.[2] with 14,136 people (1971) almost 50% Aborigines. It contains the shires of E Kimberley-Wyndham, W Kimberley, Hall's Creek and Broome which cut across the clear physical divisions into Ord River Basin, Fitzroy River Basin and the **Kimberley Block**, 180,000 km.[2] of remote, almost empty land, averaging 610 m. and dipping NW to a drowned coast. It is bounded by steep faulted faces on the SW (King Leopold Range) and the NE (Durack Range and the basaltic Antrim plateau). Precambrian sandstones are cut deeply by rivers radiating from Mt. Hann plateau: Durack, Drysdale, King Edward, Prince Regent, Charnley, all with mangrove-lined estuaries edged with cliffs, and with power potential in the high tidal ranges. Following Sir John Forrest's* 1879 exploration, sheep farmers came from the S of W.A. to the Fitzroy, and cattlemen overlanded from Qld. and N.S.W. to E Kimberley; famous treks lasting several years were made by Macdonalds, Duracks, Pentons, Buchanan and others. Gold brought a brief rush to Hall's Creek* in 1885, and led to the building of Wyndham as a port. Mary Durack's *The Rock and the Sand* (London, 1970) tells much of the history.

Over-grazing, pests (wild donkeys, horses and pigs as well as kangaroo) and cattle disease plague the vast unfenced runs mainly managed for southern and overseas companies. Droving to coastal meatworks and ports or by the Canning Stock Route* to a railhead has been replaced by road trains on beef roads. Bauxite* deposits are to be developed round Admiralty Gulf.

King George Sound W.A. 35S/118E
Formerly King George III Sound, a magnificent sheltered natural harbour, of 90 km.², leading to the shallow but dredged Princess Royal Harbour, with the Albany* port installations. Discovered and named by George Vancouver on September 25th 1791, on his way to the Pacific; he also named the islands Breaksea and Michaelmas, and Oyster Harbour to the E. The Sound was the rendezvous for the convoys carrying the Aus. and N.Z. Expeditionary Force in 1914, and a replica of the destroyed Suez Anzac memorial statue overlooks it.

King Island Tas. 40S/144E (2,801 in 1971) A low island in Bass Strait extending 65 km. N–S and 25 km. E–W. About half has been cleared for mixed livestock farming in a broad central and smaller northern belt. The scheelite (tungsten*) deposits at Grassy in the SE have been worked sporadically since 1917 and currently produce 1,600 tonnes of 72% concentration, sent by road to Currie on the W coast, the main settlement. Underground extensions are being considered but are hampered by faulting. There are potentially valuable mineral sands. The wild storms from the W have caused 57 shipwrecks* along its shores in 160 years. Tourism is developing.

King, Lake Vic. 38S/148E A shallow (mainly under 6 m.) brackish to saline lagoon in the Gippsland Lakes*. It is almost split in 2 by the long but presently eroding finger delta of the Mitchell River, but the Tambo* delta is even more eroded.

King Leopold Ranges W.A. 17S/125E
These form the SW scarp edge of the Kimberley* highland, and trend NW–SE for 240 km., cut into flat-topped steep-sided sections by the Lennard, Fitzroy and other rivers. They average 600 m., but reach 900 m. in some peaks, and are scrub-covered. They were named by J. Forrest* after the Belgian King.

King, Philip Gidley (1758–1808) b. Cornwall, Eng. Third Governor of N.S.W. 1800–7, succeeding Hunter and preceding Bligh, having been aide to Phillip on the First Fleet. In February 1788 he was sent with 23 persons to found Norfolk Island* settlement; by 1793 there were 1,000 people and an export surplus of grain. His illegitimate son was the first child born there. With Banks's influences, he obtained a 'dormant commission' to act as substitute and eventual successor to Hunter; delay in departure until 1799 was followed by an awkward overlap with Hunter on arrival at Sydney before he could assume his Governorship. Able and conscientious, his period of control yet failed to curb the officers' trading monopoly; he encouraged exploration and emancipated convicts, and the development of whaling. The story of King and his lively wife is told by M. Bassett in The Governor's Lady (London, 1956). His son **Phillip Parker** (1791–1856), b. Norfolk Island, contributed notably to charting of the Aus. coast in 4 voyages (1817–22), particularly in the NW.

King River Tas. 42S/145E Rising on the E slopes of the Coast Range, it flows 80 km. S then W in a deep gorge to Macquarie Harbour. The highest recorded Tas. rainfall average (305 cm.) occurs on the bordering ridges, but the valley has 220 cm. The lower terraces are sedge-covered; the upper valley has residual rain-forest.

King William, Lake, Tas. 42S/146E An artificial lake 13 km. N–S on Derwent River, 6·5 km. SE of L. St. Clair, dammed (1952) by Clark Dam, raising its level 67 m. to augment hydro-electric storage (see TASMANIA, POWER).

King William Pine (*Arthrotaxis selaginoides*) This and 1 or 2 other species also of W Tas. are the only representatives of the Taxodiaceae family in the S hemisphere, far from the much taller *Sequoia* of California and *Cryptomeria* of Japan. It is a tree of 25–28 m. by 1–1·2 m., found in steep broken terrain with 150–250 cm. mean annual rainfall in SW Tas. It has red, fibrous spongy furrowed bark persistent to the lower branches, and the lower trunk is often buttressed or fluted. Leaves are leathery, lance-shaped, about 6–12 mm. long, curved inwards towards the branchlets, arranged spirally, thickly and slightly overlapping on the branchlets. Male catkins are on the same tree as the female flower which develops into a round scaly and partly spiny cone about 1 cm. across. The timber is useful but the tree is now scarce.

Kingaroy Qld. 27S/152E (4,931 in 1971) In the S Burnett district. The tall peanut silos and butter factory reflect its function as centre for the dairy lands to the E and the fertile volcanic soil to the W which grows wheat, maize and peanuts.

Kingfishers Include about a dozen species in Aus. sometimes divided into the true Kingfisher family Alcedinidae and the forest Kingfishers named (by anagram) Dacelonidae and including the Kookaburra*. The true Kingfishers include the Azure, Blue Water or Creek Kingfisher, *Alcyone azurea*, which shows its flashing blue wings and deep rust-red breast when diving for small fish from a stream-side branch in the N or E of Aus. or in Tas. It lays 5–6 roundish glossy white eggs in a nesting chamber at the end of a tunnel in a stream bank. The Little Kingfisher, *A. pusilla*, is a very small, more quietly coloured bird of the far N. The Sacred or Green Kingfisher, *Halcyon sanctus*, widespread and partly migratory throughout Aus. except the driest and wettest areas, and in the islands to the E and N, is much smaller (up to 20 cm.) with black and blue-green back, head and wings and yellowish-whitish collar, breast and belly. It is not unlike the Kookaburra in food and nesting habits; if disturbed, particularly near its nest, it dives at and scolds the intruder with raucous cries. (*Halcyon* means conceived on the sea, from the Greek idea that the kingfisher's nest floated on the sea which remained calm—hence halcyon-days—while the eggs were hatched.) The Red-backed Kingfisher, *H. pyrrhopygius*, is a summer migrant to much of the S of Aus.; it has a white breast and dark back and wings with a vivid red patch below the neck and above the tail. The Forest Kingfisher, *H. macleayi*, is cobalt to ultramarine on the back. The Whitetailed, Long-tailed, Silver-tailed or Racquet-tailed Kingfisher, *Tanysiptera sylvia*, is a small red-billed bird with a long tail (total length 30 cm., tail 18 cm.) with white tail and lower back, yellow belly and breast and blue-purple and black back, of fairly similar habits. It is a summer migrant, sometimes arriving exhausted in N Qld. from N.G. and the islands to the N.

King's Cross or **The Cross** An undefined central Sydney area centred on a major street-crossing in the Darlinghurst district, and originally named Queen's Cross. Closely built up, with a high percentage of hotels, flats, boarding and eating houses, it has a reputation for cosmopolitan and high living.

Kingscote S.A. 36S/138E (1,007 in 1971) On the W shore of Nepean Bay, Kangaroo Island*, the site of a pioneering but unsuccessful whaling settlement in 1836, and intended by some promoters as the focus of S.A. settlement. It is now a farming and holiday centre.

Kingsford Smith, Sir Charles (1897–1935) b. Brisbane. He was perhaps the greatest of the many notable pioneers of Aus. aviation*, knighted in 1932. In the 1914–18 War he won the M.C. in his first air action, but was wounded and became an instructor. In 1919 he was giving joy-rides in England, and preparing for an attempt to win the £10,000 prize for the first Eng.–Aus. flight by an Aus. (won by Ross and Keith Smith), until dissuaded by W. M. Hughes* on grounds of lack of navigation experience. He became a stunt pilot in Hollywood, joined Diggers Aviation for joy-riding and air-taxi work in 1921, then West Australian Airways in 1922. There he met Keith Anderson, and both met Charles Ulm in Sydney in 1925. All were interested in flying the Pacific, and to prove and improve their navigation they flew round Aus. in 1927 in 10 days and 6 hours, breaking the record. They bought the 3-engined Fokker, rechristened *Southern Cross*, from Sir Hubert Wilkins. Anderson surveyed the route then withdrew from the venture, and between May 31st and June 9th 1928 Kingsford Smith and Ulm with American navigator and radio operator (Lyon and Warner) made the first trans-Pacific flight, including the longest ocean crossing then made (Hawaii–Fiji). Honours and rewards flowed in and many other pioneer or record flights followed in *Southern Cross, Southern Cross Junior* and *Southern Cross Minor*. In 1931 came the loss of the *Southern Cloud** and the closure of the airline's internal routes. The same year he brought on the mail from the first Imperial Airways mail plane which crashed in Indonesia, and took the Christmas mail to Eng., bringing mail back to Aus. in 11 days. In 1935 came the King George V Silver Jubilee air mail flight across the Tasman in the ageing *Southern Cross*, in which the plane and crew, though not the mail, survived thanks to the amazing resource and courage of P. G. Taylor*. Kingsford Smith's last attempt to re-establish faith in aircraft speed with reliability through record-breaking, was when he set out with a co-pilot in *Lady Southern Cross* to break the London–Melbourne record of 73 hours set up by Scott and Black in the 1934 air race. The plane disappeared off the coast of Burma on November 8th 1935. **Kingsford Smith Airport** in Sydney bears a record of his journeys, and *Southern Cross* is preserved at the airport at Brisbane, where he was born. *For further reading see* F. Howard: *Charles Kingsford Smith* (Great Australians, Melbourne, 1962).

Kingsley, Henry (1830–1876) b. Northamptonshire, Eng. Younger brother of the novelist Charles Kingsley. He wandered in SE Aus. 1853–7 as digger, police trooper and on stations, and wrote *The Recollections of Geoffrey Hamlyn* (London, 1859), one of the best of romanticised novels of the squatter's life, and a major starting-point of Aus. fiction.

Kingston, Charles Cameron (1850–1908) b. Adelaide. Premier of S.A. from 1893–9. A sincere supporter of Federation, his ability in drafting was added to Griffith's skill in the 1891 draft Constitution; he presided over the 1898 Convention. In S.A. he brought in women's suffrage and arbitration measures, and in the first Federal Parliament, the earliest Protectionist measures.

Kingston Tas. 43S/147E (3,673 in 1971) A growing commuter town and holiday centre on the W bank of the Derwent estuary, 13 km. S of Hobart.

Kirkpatrick, John Simpson—*See* MAN WITH THE DONKEY.

Koala (*Phascolarctos cinereus*) The single living species of its genus; it is a heavily built, slow-moving, practically tail-less marsupial, furry, round-eared, and 'teddy-bear-like'. It is still fairly common in coastal Qld. S of Townsville, less common now in the belt farther S in N.S.W. and Vic. (apart from the spread of settlement, hunting etc., the koala population was swept by devastating epidemics in 1887–9 and 1900–3). It is arboreal, living largely on eucalyptus leaves, particularly of the manna gum in Vic. and the blue gum farther north. As an adaptation to the digestion of such a bulky diet, it has a very

Koala, about 1/12th scale

long caecum or blind gut (cf. the degenerate and apparently functionless appendix in man). The rudimentary but muscular tail and downward-pointing pouch with 2 teats, resemble the wombat's*, and argue a terrestrial and perhaps a burrowing phase, while the foot-structure with opposable thumb (first and second toe on forepaw) and the dentition resemble those of the Ringtailed Possum* and Greater Gliders. First reported from the Blue Mts. in 1798 as a sloth or monkey, the Koala was regarded as a bear until established as a marsupial. Its (Aboriginal) name is said to imply that it does not drink, deriving all its moisture from the leaves it eats.

Kokoda Trail In Papua, a 240-km. mountain track crossing the Owen Stanley Range and reaching over 1,800 m. In August 1942, Japanese forces began a landward attack on Port Moresby across the trail, but were held by Aus. forces who, in November 1942, began the offensive by pushing back the enemy over this high wet forested and rugged tropical terrain (*see* WORLD WAR, SECOND).

Konrads, John (1942–) b. Latvia. He arrived in Aus. from Germany in 1949. A swimming champion who, between 1958 and 1961, broke every world record from 200 m. to 1,500 m. and 220 to 1,650 yd. He won the 1,500 m. freestyle in the 1960 Olympic Games, and in 1959 every Aus. freestyle title. **Ilsa** (1944–), his sister, was trained with him by Don Talbot, and held 4 different world records.

Kookaburra, Laughing Jackass or **Great Brown Kingfisher** (*Dacelo novaeguineae*) The world's largest Kingfisher* at up to 40 cm. long (tail to almost 15 cm.), well-known from its chattering call like mocking human laughter. It is indigenous to E Aus. but introduced to Tas. and W.A. It nests, laying 2–4 roundish whitish eggs, in a tree-hollow or hollowed-out termite mound, and eats insects, lizards, small snakes, young birds and rats, and shows its relationship to Kingfishers generally by eating crabs and small fish. It occasionally raids garden ponds and chicken runs. It is off-white, with brown back, eye-bar and black-barred tail, with a flash of pale blue on the wing. A pair will maintain a fairly stable territory in open woodland or outer suburban landscape. The Blue-winged Kookaburra, *Dacelo leachi*, has more blue, including a blue tail in the female. (*See* PLATE 7.)

Koolan Island W.A. 16S/123E Iron mining township in Yampi Sound.

Koolanooka Hills W.A. 29S/116E Major iron field exporting through Geraldton*.

Koolyanobbing W.A. 31S/119E A mining town with high grade haematite and some limonite ores interbedded in the Precambrian base rocks; developed by B.H.P.*, and linked to the standard-gauge railway between Kwinana and Kalgoorlie (1968).

Koo-wee-rup Vic. 39S/146E (923 in 1971) A settlement and former swamp 60 km. SW of Melbourne. The 320 km.^{2} of rush-covered peat were reclaimed 1890–1900, and now grow potatoes and other vegetables and rear beef and dairy cattle for Melbourne.

Korean War June 25th 1950–July 27th 1953. Aus. naval and air squadrons were immediately put at the disposal of U.S. command, and an appeal made in July for enlistment. Aus. forces made distinguished rear-guard actions at Pakchon and in November 1950, at Kapyong. Casualties were 281 killed, 1,250 wounded. At home, the Government's anti-Communist moves were strengthened; there were vast wool profits; mineral prospecting was intensified.

Kosciusko, Mount N.S.W. (2,230 m.) Named by Strzelecki* from a fancied resemblance of summit tors on one of the Snowy Mts.* (possibly Mt. Townsend) to the grave of the Polish patriot Tadeusz Kosciusko. Rising above the rolling plateau, it is a great snowfield in winter when near-glacial processes are still at work, and in summer a broad alpine pasture of 'everlastings' and other attractive flowers. A road almost to the summit is motorable when clear of snow. Though there is much development of tourism and winter sports, land use is now controlled by the **Mount Kosciusko State Park Trust**—summer cattle grazing, for instance, is prohibited above 1,400 m. The **Kosciusko Lakes** in cirques or small ribbon form, with several morainic dams, are crucial for Aus. study of glacial geomorphology and alpine

flora and fauna, and are partly threatened by the Snowy Mts. Scheme*.

Krichauff Range or **Plateau** N.T. 24S/133E The W part of a spectacular E–W pitching anticline of brilliant red sandstone and quartzites lying in curving, curiously scalloped ranges. Areyonga Mission Station is on a headwater of the Palmer River which has the old Tempe Downs (1885) homestead on its banks. E of the Finke River and Palm Valley* the feature continues as the James Range.*

Kununurra W.A. 17S/129E (1,182 in 1971) An irrigation township, built as a service and residential centre for the Ord River* project. It lies E of the river and is linked to Wyndham by a sealed road which crosses the Bandicoot Bar diversion dam. A cotton ginnery processes the crop. Houses are designed for ventilation in the tropical climate.

Kurdaitcha Shoes Made of emu feathers, worn by Aborigines anxious to avoid leaving any tracks, e.g. to

Kurdaitcha Shoes

escape an avenging party. They were also worn by sorcerers. Arthur Upfield's* part-Aborigine detective makes use of them in *Bushranger of the Skies* (Sydney, 1940).

Kurrajong (*Brachychiton populneum*) A tree of the widespread pod-bearing family Sterculiaceae and a relative of the Flame* and Bottle Tree*. It grows 18 m. by 60 cm. in the 38 to 64 cm. rainfall belt of the western slopes of N.S.W. and Qld. and is invaluable to graziers for fodder, shade and shelter for their stock. It has oval to lanceolate lobed leaves 10–20 cm. long, green or whitish multiple nectar-rich flowers from leaf-forks near the ends of branches, succeeded by clusters of 10 cm. pods opening at one side and containing up to 30 1-cm. seeds. In Central Aus. and W.A. the Desert Kurrajong, *B. gregorii*, has much more deeply lobed leaves. The genus *Brachychiton* is confined to Aus.

In the same family *Commersonia bartramia* is sometimes called the Brown Kurrajong, and *Rulingia panosa*, the Black Kurrajong. In E Aus. Green Kurrajong is *Hibiscus heterophyllus*; the young shoots, leaves and bark are eaten by stock, and formerly by Aborigines who also used the gummy fibrous bark to make dilly bags; like the Kurrajong of Tas., *Plagianthus sidoides*, it is in the Mallow* family. (*See* FLORA.)

Kurri Kurri-Weston N.S.W. 33S/151E (11,624 i n 1971) Coal-mining towns in the lower Hunter Valley. An aluminium smelter uses Qld. bauxite*.

Kwinana W.A. An industrial area 19 km. S. of Perth* on Cockburn Sound*, developed to bring heavy industry to the State: oil-refining (1955), steel-rolling (1956), alumina reduction (1961), lubricant oil-refining (1963), a blast furnace (1968) using ores brought by the new standard-gauge railway from Koolyanobbing*, a 120,000 kW oil-fired power station (1971), a nickel refinery and a hoped-for integrated steel-works. Residential areas lies to the E on the limestone ridge (in Kwinana New Town) planned for 40,000 in 4 units. The 2 in existence are Medina and Calista (10,096 in 1971) named from ships which brought the 1829 settlers to this barren strip of coast. The *Kwinana* was a freighter wrecked there earlier this century.

L

LABOR PARTY

Labor Party—*see* AUSTRALIAN LABOR PARTY.

Labour Day A holiday celebrated in March in Tas., W.A. and Vic., May in Qld., and October in N.S.W. and S.A. It marks the achievement of a maximum 8-hour working day by Trade Unions*, although in some States it originated as a day of agitation for this goal, and was previously called Eight-Hour Day. While the building trades had achieved this early (Sydney and Melbourne by 1858 and many others by 1891), a 40-hour week was not universal in Aus. until 1948.

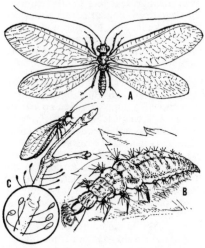

A *Golden Eyes Lacewing (Chrysopa ramburi)*
B *Larvae feeding on aphid*
C *Eggs on sticky stalks*

Lacewings (Order Neuroptera) Insects with 4 delicate gauzy wings and in many species generally rather delicate adult forms, but the larval stages are

LACEWINGS

active and carnivorous, some species biting and some sucking. The eggs are laid on the end of a sticky stalk on a twig etc., as a protection from predators, sometimes in groups. Lacewings include species of very variable size, from tiny Coniopterygidae to 10-cm.-long members of the large Ant-lion* family. Other distinctive species representative of families within the Order include: 1. the Alder Fly, *Austrosialis ignicollis*, of Tas., and the large Dobson-fly, *Archichaulioides gutteriferus*, which have aquatic larvae; 2. the superficially mantis-like Mantis Lacewing, *Mantispa australasiae*, the larvae of which are predators of spiders' eggs; 3. the small but very large-winged Golden Eyes, *Chrysopa ramburi*, the larvae feeding on aphids; 4. the large heavily built Moth Lacewings of family Ithonidae which are sometimes seen in mass migrations, occasionally blundering into houses; 5. the beautiful Silky Lacewing, *Megapsychopsis illidgei*, seen on the edges of Qld. rain-forests, its 7-cm. broad leaf-like wings covered with silky hairs; 6. the Brown Lacewings, family Hemerobiidae, several species of which are beneficial because the larvae prey on aphids etc., such as *Micromus tasmaniae* not uncommonly drawn to lights in houses of an evening; 7. *Acmonotus* spp. representing the family Ascaphilidae, the larvae living in forest litter, forming a cocoon of silk and leaf fragments, to emerge as adults rather like dragonflies with long clubbed antennae like butterflies; 8. *Stilboteryx napoleo*, a somewhat similar insect but with short antennae, seen in W.A. flying high at dusk; 9. Threadwing Lacewings, e.g. *Chasmopteryx hutti*, also found in W.A.; the rear wings have become extended into a thread-like then leaf-like 'tail'.

Lachlan River N.S.W. Flows for some 1,500 km. from a region with 75 cm. rainfall, first NW then W and SW, from W of Goulburn, 35S/150E, through Cowra, Forbes, Condobolin, Hillston and Booligal in increasingly arid country to its junction with the Murrumbidgee* W of Maude, 35S/144E (rainfall 25–38 cm.). At Forbes, after 400 km. and with a catchment of 1·9 million ha., the average annual flow is 987 million m.[3] Nevertheless there is a good deal of irrigation, and also occasional flooding now mitigated by Wyangala Dam*. Intensive irrigation for some cereals but mainly for fodder and pastures takes place in the Jemalong district between Forbes and Condobolin. Lakes Cargelligo* and Brewster are part of a domestic and stock water scheme, the command area of which extends mainly on the right bank downstream from Hillston.

Ladies Tresses, Austral (*Spiranthes sinensis*) A terrestrial orchid, widespread in damp coastal and upland sites except in W.A., some 30–40 cm. high, with a spiral multiple flowerhead of small crimson and white flowers.

Ladybirds Beetles of the family Coccinellidae with various numbers of spots; adults and larvae of most species eat aphids and other harmful insects, but some plant-eating species are occasional pests of vegetable gardens.

Lakes Entrance Vic. 38S/148E (2,581 in 1971) A fishing and resort town at the artificial entrance to the Gippsland Lakes*. The channel is maintained by tidal scour at a minimum depth of 6–9 m., but there is a troublesome offshore bar, less than 3 m. deep at low tides and preventing ships entering or leaving when waves break on it in stormy weather.

Lalor, Peter (1827–1889) b. Tinakill, Ireland. He arrived in Aus. in 1852. He was working on the Ballarat diggings, when his quiet, yet authoritative manner led to his selection as leader, albeit reluctantly, of the rebellious miners at Eureka Stockade*. He organised the stockade, and in the action received a wound leading to the loss of an arm. He escaped and was hidden until acquittal of other leaders made it safe to emerge. Elected later to the Legislative Council, he served in various posts, including that of Speaker (1880–7).

Lambert, George Washington Thomas (1873–1930) b. Russia of American parentage. He arrived in Aus. in 1887, and was very influential in art development especially after returning from 20 years in Europe in 1921. While his bush studies, portraits and fine drawing were well known, his major influence was through teaching and his support of the current contemporary group led by Wakelin, de Maistre and Grace Cossington Smith, attempting to break from tradition. His son **Constant** achieved overseas musical distinction.

Lambing Flat N.S.W. Gold-field discovered 1860, on Burrangong Creek, the site of Young*. It was so named because it was the sheltered river flat where sheep were brought in to lamb. It had considerable disorders 1860–1 when miners banded to deal with alleged thieves and then turned on the Chinese*, killing 2. Determined to drive them from the field, accusing them of wasting water, they destroyed the Chinese camp. From about 15,000 at its peak, the population dwindled as the alluvial gold gave out from 1865.

Lampreys While resembling eels superficially, they are placed in a separate Class Agnatha (jawless fish). They have a rasped sucker with which they may parasitically fasten on to larger fish. Aus. species are the Lamprey, *Geotria australia*, and the Murray or Shortheaded Lamprey, *Mordacia mordax*, both up to about 60 cm. long.

Lamp-shells A popular name for the shells of Brachiopods*, a Phylum of marine animals superficially like bivalve molluscs.

Lancewood This name is applied to several trees with hard durable wood: *Acacia doratoxylon, Dissiliaria baloghioides* in the widespread Euphorbiaceae family, *Albizzia basaltica* in the mainly tropical Mimosaceae family and *Harpullia pendula* in the tropical Sapindaceae family.

Land Tenure Types are complex and numerous, governed by Acts in each State and Ordinances for the Territories. There are 5 broad types: free grants and reservations for public purposes, including forest reserves, recreational areas etc.; purchase of freehold, conditionally or unconditionally; leases or licences in respect of land (much in the form of long term pastoral leases) and for mining; closer settlement, dating from earlier attempts to attain this and operating through Government purchase of Crown land and repayment by settlers over a period; settlement of returned personnel (i.e. servicemen) through loans. The percentages of alienated (purchased) land to leased or licensed land, and unoccupied and reserved land are: Aus. as a whole 10:57:33; N.S.W. 34:57:9; Vic. 61:11:28 (leases are mainly annual); Qld. 7:87:6; W.A. 7:40:53 (mainly unoccupied); Tas. 40:9:51; S.A. 7:60:33; A.C.T. 18:47:35 (where leasehold is encouraged). In N.T. only 0·1% is alienated, 57·5% leased and 42·4% reserved including 18% for Aborigines, defence and public use. The contrasts are thus evident: leasehold land varies from 87% of Qld. to 9% of Tas.; alienated from 61% of Vic. to 0·1% of N.T.; unoccupied or reserved from 6% of Qld. to 51% of Tas.
Historical Development The close settled farming community envisaged in London for the new colony proved unattainable. Repeated efforts at closer settlement began with small grants given by the early governors as rewards or bribes; free selection introduced from 1861, to provide for the population increased by the gold-rushes, was grossly abused by selectors* and squatters* alike and achieved very little expansion of ploughed land. Closer Settlement Acts in the 1890s were attempts to alleviate the Depression; of the Soldier Settlements* after 1918 and 1945, the former was almost a complete failure. Land was first sold in 1825 following the recommendation of the Bigge* Report; but survey was slow. A minimum price of £1 an acre was set in 1842, with auctioning of land; this was based on the S.A. experience of applying Wakefield's theories, but brought strong protest, as did the 1844 restrictions on the size of flocks and holdings. Squatters achieved security of tenure and first right to purchase, in 1847. The Torrens* Title, adopted by 1874, was a major contribution to the simplification of land purchase.

Landy, John (1930–   ) b. Melbourne. An athlete, specialising as a middle distance runner, the first Aus. and second runner in the world to cover a mile in under 4 minutes, when in June 1954 he topped Roger Bannister's achievement of 3 minutes, 59·6 seconds the previous month, by 1·7 seconds. He held the 1 mile record for 4 years; and barely lost to Bannister in the Vancouver 'Mile of the Century' at the 1954 Commonwealth Games. He was one of the first to undergo the rigorous modern training advocated by P. Cerutty.

Lane, William (1861–1917) b. Bristol, son of an Irish Conservative artisan. He arrived in Aus. in 1885, to become a Brisbane journalist. First writing in the *Courier* then in *Boomerang*, which he edited and part owned (1887–92), and the *Worker*, financed by the Unions which he was largely instrumental in organising, he spread socialist doctrines and was a major figure with Spence* behind the great strikes* of 1890-1. As labour moved into political power, he was disillusioned by the inevitable trimming and party manoeuvres involved, and organised the New Australian Settlement Association; £30,000 was subscribed, £1,000 by Lane. The Pioneers left Sydney (1893) to found New Australia*. His despotic tendencies were one reason for its failure. He lived mainly in N.Z. from 1900, becoming increasingly conservative and imperialistic in outlook.

Lang, John Dunmore (1799-1878) b. Scotland. He arrived in Aus. in 1823. Founder and Minister of Scots Church, Sydney (1826-76) although officially deposed by Synod (1842-63). Lang was involved in public affairs and politics from the outset. He was an outspoken vitriolic man, fearing no one, to the extent of libel suits being brought against him. His most important work was the development of family migration schemes; he bitterly opposed the Anglican domination of education, and as strongly proposed a republican, independent Aus. and the separation of the States.

Lang, John Thomas (1876-   ) b. Sydney. Labor Premier of N.S.W. from 1925-7 and 1930-2; the first period saw the first Aus. child endowment scheme, while the second, in the Depression, ended in his dismissal by the N.S.W. Governor, Sir Phillip Game, for unconstitutional action. Lang had said 'wages before dividends' and refused to honour overseas interest payments, and barricaded the Treasury. A tense situation developed and a semi-military New Guard* was formed. Lang's supporters brought down the Scullin Labor Government in 1931. Lang was expelled from the N.S.W. Labor Party in 1943; he was a controversial figure in politics, his enemies objecting to his dictatorial atti-

tudes. In 1967 he was still editing a turbulent weekly.

Langley, Eve (Mrs. Hilary Clark) (1908-1967) b. Forbes, N.S.W. Emigrated to N.Z. She is noted for one novel *The Pea Pickers* (Sydney, 1942), a long semi-autobiographical whimsical humorous work set in Vic. and considered a minor Aus. classic.

Language The great bulk of Aus. vocabulary and usage is common to British and, to a lesser extent, American English, but there is a considerable and distinctive Aus. English also, which had evolved sufficiently to lead to several published collections by the end of the 19th century. Although there are some regional variations, notably in climatic terms, or in relation to the size of containers for drink, Aus. English, like accent, is remarkably homogeneous over the continent.

Distinctively Aus. words can be grouped. Those borrowed from Aboriginal languages are most commonly flora and fauna (kangaroo*, budgerigar wombat*, bunya*) or natural features (gibber*) although unfortunately many English names were given to totally different species (ash, cedar, robin). Other words, quite new to English, were mostly made up from English words (outback*, offsider*, bluegum*, bottlebrush*, saltbush*), although a few were completely invented (jackeroo*). The greatest number, however, derive from English words of 2 categories: slang, either that specific to the convict language as recorded by Vaux* in 1812 (new chum*, swag*) or from regional dialects spoken by early convicts and settlers, some of which have died out in their place of origin: (ringer*, larrikin*) and standard English words which in Aus. acquired extended, often completely new meanings, (paddock, run, creek, mob, station). Some English words, at first transplanted, were soon completely replaced (meadow, field, wood and stream are not used). Words of American origin include a group associated with land survey (block, selection, township) probably imported via London directives, some associated with the land (bush*, squatter*, land-shark), and many associated with the gold-rushes (digger*, prospect, cradle). The early Aus. miners who went to California in 1849 also added to the American vocabulary, and there were indigenous Aus. gold period usages (gutter, reef, fossick). Words coined or acquired during the 2 world wars led to further American introductions but also to the spread of Aus. terms ('had it' is claimed as a N.T. phrase). European migrants, save for some influence on place names by the S.A. Germans, have had little linguistic impact; the migrants either assimilate quickly or tend to stay in national groups, and the second generation quickly loses the mother tongue. The present trend is to increased American usage and spelling (as in labor).

There is a distinctive, and regionally little varied **Australian accent** (although much that is claimed as such is common to slovenly speech anywhere, and while there is considerable gradation from 'educated' to broad speech, this is less marked than in U.K. The comparison to Cockney is only very partial. Typically, the Aus. voice is rather light, the intonation has little range, and delivery is slow and un-emphasised. Vowels show the most characteristic features: mate (meit), home (howm), too (tou), paint (pint) etc. There has been a recent rise of some pride in the Aus. accent, with popular publications and with directives to A.B.C. announcers to forsake B.B.C. English and use the more familiar interpretation.

For further reading see W.S.Ramson: *Australian English* (Canberra, 1966); G. W. Turner: *The English Language in Australia* (Melbourne, 1966); S. J. Baker: *Australia Speaks* (Sydney, London, New York, 1953) which supple-ments his *The Australian Language* (Sydney, 1945); and, more flippantly, 'Affableck Lauder': *Let's Talk Strine* (Sydney, 1965).

Lantana An odorous shrub genus in the Verbenaceae family; *L. camara* was introduced into Aus. as an ornamental shrub with varicoloured button-like heads succeeded by small black fruit; it became a pest in coastal Qld. and S at least to Nowra, 35S/151E. It can be controlled by cultivation, but chokes out other vegetation in clear-felled woodland for many years; it invades pastures where it is extremely harmful to dairy cattle. Biological control by insects has had limited success, but hormone sprays may be successful.

La Perouse, Jean-Françoise de Galaup, Compte de (1741–88) A French naval commander, who, after 5 years of Pacific exploration and charting, reached Botany Bay on January 24th 1788 with his 2 ships only a few days after the arrival of the First Fleet*, remaining 6 weeks.

Larrikin A high-spirited, mischievous, possibly even delinquent town youth. Originally it was a Warwickshire (Eng.) dialect word, although it has been claimed as being coined from a Melbourne Irish policeman's pronunciation of 'larking'. The modern word 'bodgie' has replaced larrikin.

Larrimah N.T. 15S/133E A small settlement on the Stuart Highway and N Aus. railway, of which it is the effective railhead for trans-shipment from road to rail.

Lasseter's Reef An alleged gold deposit reputedly worth $12 million which H. B. Lasseter claimed to have found in the Rawlinson Range* before becoming lost in 1897; he was rescued by an Afghan camel-driver. In 1930 he accompanied an expedition to find the reef, but left it in impatience and disappeared. A body found and buried in the Petermann Range* in 1931 was assumed to be his. A further expedition also failed in 1951, but in 1967 possibly large scale mineral resources of lead, silver and zinc as well as gold-bearing rocks in the Petermann Range area were reported by a well-equipped expedition using Lasseter's diaries and maps.

Latham, Sir John Greig (1877–1964) b. Ascot Vale, Vic. An outstanding lawyer who became Chief Justice of the High Court of Aus. 1935–52 after a distinguished political career (Deputy Prime Minister from 1931–4). He made several important contributions to the interpretation of the Constitution*.

Latrobe Tas. 42S/147E (2,451 in 1971) On the Mersey River, and a service centre for dairy and orchard farmlands and has had sporadic coal production since 1850.

La Trobe, Charles Joseph (1801–1875) Superintendent, Port Phillip District (1839–51), becoming first Lt.-Governor of Vic. (1851–4), making one of the longest periods of administration in Aus. at that time. He came from a musical family, and had taught, travelled and written reports on West Indian education, before he was appointed to the emerging settlement. He saw it through the early squatter phase, the attainment of separate statehood, and the early years of the gold-rush with considerable diplomacy and skill.

Latrobe River Vic. 38S/147E Flows for about 160 km., from the steep forested scarp edge of the E Highlands near Mt. Baw Baw at first SE towards the brown coal area, then with a meandering lowland course (the channel altered by the brown coal operations) for about 100 km. almost due E to a finger delta in L. Wellington*. The **Latrobe Valley** is almost synonymous with W Gippsland, with its cleared and improved dairy pastures, dwarfed since 1919 by the great inte-

grated development by the Vic. Government of the Tertiary brown coal deposits, for electricity generation, under the leadership of Sir John Monash*. It is also used for briquetting, for domestic burning important in the cool winter of Vic. and for a time for gas piped to Melbourne. The thick seams, shallow overburden and enormous deposits, the largest known in the world, have made operations simple and cheap enough to overcome the drawback of quality and high moisture content. Towns such as Yallourn*, Morwell*, Moe* and Traralgon* have been built or expanded and industries using female labour have come in to complement the fuel and power industries—textiles, clothing, shoes etc.—and Maryvale* has a large paper pulp mill. The present population in the valley is 105,000; it is expected to rise to 500,000 by 1980. Natural gas* from Bass Str. may compete with brown coal for power. Serious problems of air pollution may partly be due to the topography.

Laughing Jackass A term used perhaps decreasingly, for the Kookaburra* or Great Brown Kingfisher, *Dacelo novaeguineae*, from its call which resembles strident, mocking laughter, often so timed as to appear as just comment on human folly.

Launceston Tas. 41S/147E (62,181 in 1971) The eleventh largest Aus. city and major town in N Tas. It lies where the N and S Esk Rivers join to form the 65-km. tidal estuary of the Tamar. The S Esk enters through the wooded Cataract Gorge, developed for power by 1895; the N Esk from a meandering flood-plain which prevents settlements except on river terraces. The city is thus forced to expand N along the Tamar or S into the Midlands plain. Secondary industry employs 29% of the workforce and includes wool yarn (the major Aus. source) blankets, flannel and rayon, and engineering and motor-body building. Fruit, potatoes and dairy products are exported from the N farmlands. The name was taken from King's* birthplace. Larger shipping uses Beauty Point.

Laurel A popular name for *Anopterus*, a genus of shrubs or small trees in the Saxifrage family, with 2 species. *A. glandulosus*, the Tasmanian Laurel, with attractive leaves and white flowers, to be seen wild, e.g. in the Tas. National Park, or in many gardens, and *A. macleayanus*, often also called the Tasmanian Laurel, found in the rainforests around the Macleay basin in N.S.W. In N.S.W. and Qld. *Cryptocarya glaucescens* (also called Grey Sassafras, Beech or She-beech), a member of the Laurel family, is a small tree with elliptical leaves 5–10 cm. long, bluish below, white flowers and black globular fruit. Yields attractive but soft timber.

Laver, Rodney George (1938–   ) b. Rockhampton. Possibly the world's greatest tennis player. In 1962 and 1969 he won the Grand Slam of the Aus., French, U.S. and Wimbledon titles, adding the German and Italian. He won Wimbledon in 1961, 62, 68, 69.

LAW The Aus. legal system stems from the English but with important modifications inherent in a federal as against a unitary government, which give some aspects in common with U.S. (*See* GOVERNMENT for Historical Development of Judiciary.) The apex of the pyramid of courts until 1967 was the Judicial Committee of the Privy Council in London and abolition of all residual rights of appeal was proposed early in 1973. In Aus. the High Court, comprising a Chief Justice and 6 others, is the supreme federal court; its tasks are interpretation of the Constitution and some original jurisdiction, but mainly it is a court of appeal; there may be other federal courts created, e.g. the Courts of Conciliation and Arbitration. The Aus. High Court has rather more

flexibility than the House of Lords, being less bound by precedent.

In each State there are Supreme Courts, which have increased in power as a result of recent rulings to restrict the mass of appeals going to the High Court. The Supreme Court has civil and criminal, original and appellate functions; in N.S.W. the old division between Common Law and Equity are retained as separate jurisdictions. The 'inferior' courts vary between States: in N.S.W. and Vic. there are intermediate district or county courts respectively; the other States have nothing between the Supreme and the Magistrates Courts. There are always separate civil and criminal inferior courts, their limits set respectively by the amount of money or the seriousness of the crime involved. Legal education and professional organisation also vary between the States. Aus. innovations have most notably been in Arbitration* and in laws affecting family relationships, particularly divorce. The Constitution (sec. 51, xxii) gave the Federal Parliament the right to legislate in respect of 'Divorce and Matrimonial Causes; and in relation thereto, parental rights and the custody and guardianship of infants'. This was not taken up until recent federal Acts (1959 Matrimonial Causes Act and 1961 Marriage Act) have unified the varying State laws and virtually permitted divorce by consent. At the same time there is very strong emphasis on trying to retain the family unit, by reconciliation (marriage counselling is subsidised), and by strictly enforced provision for children in the event of divorce being inevitable.

While the legal framing of the Constitution has proved remarkably successful, one serious cause of disputes has arisen from Sec. 92: 'On the imposition of uniform duties of customs trade commerce and intercourse between the states . . . whether by means of internal carriage or ocean haulage, shall be absolutely free'. Interpretation of what this means, in terms of tariffs, road taxes and costs, has led more than once to appeals to the Privy Council. The Aus. attitude to the law is ambivalent: a deep respect for the higher legal authorities, a generally peaceable, law-abiding citizenry, is combined with some contempt for the lower courts, and for the police* force, stemming possibly from rebellious origins and pioneering independence. See E. Campbell and H. Whitmore: *Freedom in Australia* (Sydney, 1966) and H. A. Finlay and A. Bissett-Johnson: *Family Law in Aus.* (Melbourne, 1972).

Lawler, Raymond Evener A successful playwright who, after a long period of writing, achieved fame with *The Summer of the Seventeenth Doll*, set on the Qld. sugar coast (produced in Melbourne, 1955) and subsequently overseas, where he now lives.

Lawrence, David Herbert (1885–1930) English writer who, after spending some months in W.A. and N.S.W. in 1923, wrote *Kangaroo* (London, 1923) with its acute, if very personal obervation of the Aus. scene at that time.

Lawson, Henry Archibald (1867–1922) b. Grenfell, N.S.W. He was probably Australia's best-known writer. His short stories are of a very high standard and reflect the bush life of the period: harsh, often melancholy, but with dry country humour and rough comradeship. His poems were either ballads or verse which was rebellious and indignant against all inhumanity and this was more popular. His ballads do not match Paterson's*, and share the harsh melancholy background and unfortunate characters of his short stories. He was born in a gold-field tent, of a Norwegian father and a vigorous militant Aus. mother who was a powerful influence on him after his parents' separation (1883). His early boyhood was wretched, on a poor bush farm, then in Sydney. Growing increasingly

deaf from the age of 9, he failed to enter university. His first stories were for the *Bulletin** which sent him to walk and work in the bush in the 1892 drought. In 1967 his centenary brought a spate of re-appraisals: *Henry Lawson, Collected Verse 1885–1900*, ed. C. Roderick and *Henry Lawson's Humorous Stories* chosen by C. Mann (both Sydney, 1967).

Lawson, William (1774–1850) b. London. He arrived in Sydney in the N.S.W. Corps (1800), then served 6 years on Norfolk Island. Although involved in the quarrels leading to the Rum Rebellion*, he was more important as an explorer and farmer. With Wentworth* and Blaxland* on the historic Blue Mts. crossing, 1813, his surveying and recording were meticulously detailed. He was rewarded with land and the post of Commandant of Bathurst (1819–24). He carried out further exploration.

Lead The amount which is mined with Zinc* from Precambrian rocks at Broken Hill*, N.S.W., since 1883 still accounts for 62% of Aus. output. A further 17% comes from Mt. Isa, Qld., and the rest from the Read Rosebery mines. Tas., and Cobar, N.S.W. Aus. closely follows U.S. and U.S.S.R. in output and is the main exporter. Projected export value 1979–80 is $170 million, 10% of total mineral export. Further reserves are on McArthur River, N.T., Tarago, N.S.W. and Beltana, S.A. There are smelters at Port Pirie, S.A., and Cockle Creek in Newcastle, N.S.W., for Cobar and Broken Hills ores. Bullion from Mt. Isa goes to U.K. By-products include silver, antimony, cadmium, sulphur and cobalt. A **Lead Bonus** (1924) paid to all workers, is based on world prices and can add substantially to earnings.

Leaf Beetles A very large family of small to medium-sized beetles in the family Chrysomelidae, usually broad, oval to circular and shiny, often with rather brightly coloured caterpillar-like larvae, and including serious pests of forests (e.g. the Red-gum Beetle, *Paropsis* spp.), of Qld. pastures and sugar-cane (Black Grass Beetle, *Ryparida morosa*) or gardens (the Pumpkin Beetle, *Ceratia hilaris*). On the other hand some species have been used for biological control of weeds (e.g. *Chrysomela hyperici* to control St. John's Wort).

Leaf Hopper A common popular name for winged vegetarian Bugs* of the Order Hemiptera, often brightly coloured.

League of Rights, Australian An extremely conservative, mainly rural movement formed 1960 by federation of state leagues dating from the 1940s.

Learmonth family An early family of Vic. squatters*, both efficient and enlightened. Originally from Scotland, then Tas., settling first in Geelong, then the Ballarat district where they built the famous bluestone Scottish baronial mansion, Ercildoun. **Learmonth**, on the Exmouth Gulf in W.A., was named after **Charles Learmonth** (1917–44), a Second World War pilot. It is now an air base which is being expanded as part of the Aus. defence* strategy covering the Indian Ocean.

Leather A domestic and an export commodity from just over 100 factories, mainly in Sydney and Melbourne, but with others in major centres; it is only one-third as valuable an export as hides and skins untanned. Although wattle* is native to Aus., tanning material is largely imported from cultivated S African wattles.

Leeches Worm-like animals with suckers at nose and tail, or tail only, placed in the Class Hirudinea within the Phylum Annelida. Leeches of different species are adapted to salt and to fresh water and some to terrestrial life, though they require damp hiding places from which they can fan out in search of prey only in wet weather. The blood-sucking species are able to inject a local anaesthetic to avoid disturbing the victim, and also to put an anti-coagulant into the ingested blood to assist assimilation.

Largest and among the commonest of Aus. leeches is the Jawed Scrub Leech, *Limnobdella australis*, a freshwater species with black and yellow stripes along the back, formerly used for medicinal bleeding—and even occasionally today. It reaches 2–10 cm. long and in wet weather or damp gullies may fasten on to bush-walkers. Freshwater genera include the uniquely Aus. *Dineta* and *Semilageneta*, and the cosmopolitan *Herpobdella* and *Glossiphonia*, with prominent rear sucker and 3 pairs of eyes near the small nose sucker; *Glossiphonia* ranks as a Jawless Leech, the long proboscis and small nose sucker penetrating and sucking the victim's tissues, while *Dineta* also lacks the 3 skin-piercing jaws of the blood-sucking leeches and lives by swallowing worms whole. The marine Shark Leech, *Pontobdella raynerii*, is often seen by fishermen curled up tight on a captured shark. *Philaemon pungens*, uniquely Aus., is a terrestrial leech of SE Aus. including Tas., and there are several species of *Geobdella* in Aus. and N.G.; all of these live in damp places, *P. pungens* wandering fairly freely in search of an animal or man on which to fasten.

Leeton N.S.W. 35S/146E (6,638 in 1971) A busy market and service centre carrying out the function for which it was planned, as a new town and focus of intensive fruit and rice farming as part of the Murrumbidgee Irrigation Area*. It is the headquarters of the Rice Marketing Board which handles, mills and packs all marketable rice from the area, while nearby at Yanco, McCaughey's* old mansion is an agricultural high school and there is also an experimental irrigation farm.

Leeuwin, Cape W.A. 34S/115E A low rocky peninsula which is the first Aus. landfall from the SW, and named after a Dutch ship which was in the vicinity in 1622.

Legacy An organisation founded in Hobart by Maj. Gen. Sir John Gellibrand, an outstanding military leader, in 1922 and called Remembrance Club. Sir Stanley Savige founded the Melbourne Legacy Club in 1923. The object was to care for orphans of servicemen; there are now between 40 and 50 autonomous Legacy Clubs, and their wards are the widows and families of all Aus. servicemen dying in or as a result of war—over 60,000 wards in 1967. Apart from financial help, the great strength of Legacy lies in the closely maintained human relationships between members and the families concerned.

Legless Lizards, Snake-lizards or **Slowworms** Of the Aus./N.G. family Pygopididae, they are harmless nocturnal species eating mainly insects, termites, etc., except for the larger-toothed skink-eating *Lialis*, and are often killed because of their superficial resemblance to snakes. Teeth are on the inner side of the jaw and are very small and blunt for crushing, except for the longer, curved sharp teeth of *Lialis*. The tongue is broad and fleshy, there is an external ear (in contrast to snakes), and the tail is 3 or 4 times the body length, as against about a quarter in snakes. The tail, readily discarded, can be partly replaced, but this is always distinguishable by the structure and texture. The larger species live on the surface of the ground, the smaller live in crevices or termite mounds etc.; eggs are laid. There is no trace of forelegs, but vestigial hind legs remain as scaly flaps held close to the body on either side of the vent. The eye has no movable lid, but a fixed transparent scale; the pupil is vertical. There are also some legless skinks*, some with

stumps or vestigial limbs, some with none. Of 8 genera and 14 Aus. species, common species are: 1. the Common Scaly-foot, *Pygopus lepidopodus*, 30–75 cm. long, usually reddish or olive to dark brown with black spots, paler head and belly; 2. the Black-headed Scaly Foot, *P. nigriceps*, of inland S and E Aus.; 3. the long-nosed, slender Burton's Legless Lizard, *Lialis burtonis*, from putty-colour to brick-red, and black, sometimes striped; 4. Fraser's Legless Lizard, *Delma fraseri fraseri*, up to 45 cm. long, olive-brown, with circles of scales round the eyes, and widespread except in desert and coastal areas, with a sub-species in Qld. and another in SE Aus.

Leichhardt, Freidrich Wilhelm Ludwig (1813–1848) b. Prussia. The strangest character in Aus. exploration. Leichhardt arrived in Aus. in 1842, his fare out paid by William Nicholson who had financed him over 3 years of dilettante European wandering following his unfinished university career. He soon found Aus. patrons and in 1843, walked the 768 km. from Sydney to Moreton Bay. The following year he led a privately financed expedition N from Brisbane, W across the ranges to the Gulf of Carpentaria, thence over the Roper River and on to the coast at Port Essington. Although a great feat, it was a badly organised journey with grave miscalculations and side-tracking and suffered tragedy in the death of Gilbert*. On his return to Sydney Leichhardt was lionised, and inspired to attempt an E–W continental crossing in 1847, but the half-starved explorers returned after 8 months. He set off once more in 1848, from a station near Roma in Qld. and was never heard of again. The latest of many expeditions to solve the mystery failed in 1938. Contrasting views of this equivocal character are found in Patrick White's* *Voss* (London, 1957), in A. H. Chisholm's *Strange New World* (Sydney, 1941) and in M.

Aurousseau's collected and translated *Letters of F. W. Ludwig Leichhardt* (Cambridge, 1968).

Leichhardt River Qld. Flows seasonally for 320 km. N from Selwyn Range through Mt. Isa, 21S/139E. It was named by Gregory (1856).

Leichhardt Tree (*Nauclea orientalis*) A 24-m. tree of better-watered areas in the N Aus. scrub and rain-forests, in the largely tropical family Rubiaceae, the Madders, which includes the Gardenias, the Coffee Bush and Cinchona from which quinine is obtained—the last is interesting since the bark of the Leichhardt Tree has been used as a bush remedy for fevers, in common with that of many other trees of other families. It has heart-shaped to oval leaves to 25 cm. by 12 cm., yellow globular flower-heads 1 in. across, and a rough potted globular fruit containing 1–2 extremely bitter oblong seeds apparently formerly relished by Aborigines. The yellow wood smells of musk when freshly cut, and is good for cabinet work. Leichhardt Bean, *Entada scandens*, is a Qld. climber with Pea*-like flowers, and a pod up to 90 cm. long, carried long distances by ocean currents.

Leigh Creek S.A. 30S/138E (943 in 1971; 1,028 in 1966) Named from a normally dry creek in the W foothills of the N Flinders Range. Triassic, sub-bituminous coal was sporadically mined from 1899–1919; open-cut working, stimulated by wartime demands began in 1943, and has been operated since 1948 by the State Electricity Trust which has built a model town. The coal is railed by standard-gauge track (1956) to Port Augusta power stations, and electricity transmitted back to Leigh Creek (1961). Reserves are only enough for 15–20 years.

Lemon Grasses Contain essential oils smelling strongly of lemon-skins they are found in Aus., but not exploited.

They belong to the genus *Cymbopogon*. (*See* BARBED-WIRE GRASS.)

Lennox, David (1788–1833) b. Ayr, Scotland. He arrived in Aus. in 1832. He was a master mason and responsible for many of the colony's early bridges: **Lennox Bridge**, on the Western Road to Lithgow (1833), is the oldest extant in Aus. and only recently by-passed; **Lansdowne Bridge** (1836), near Liverpool, has a 33·5 m. span; **Lennox Bridge**, Parramatta (1839), is still in use; his largest, **Prince's Bridge** over the Yarra, Melbourne (1850–85), had a 45·7-m. span.

Lepidoptera (scale-winged) The Order of insects with 4 wings with a distinctive covering of overlapping rows of scales varying in colour (though females of some species have reduced wings or none), and undergoing a sudden metamorphosis from the caterpiller stage to the pupa and then the adult form, as compared with more gradual stages towards the adult form, e.g. in Mayflies. The Order is divided into 2 Sub-Orders, the Homoneura (with 2 super-families) in which the venation of fore and hind pairs of wings is similar, and the Heteroneura (with 12 super-families) in which the rear pair have fewer veins. The Butterflies*, the *Papilionidae*, are one of the 12 super-families within the Sub-Order Heteroneura, the rest being Moths*. The caterpillar's 3 pairs of legs on the thorax anticipate the legs on the 3 thoracic segments of the adult, but the varying numbers of pairs of abdominal legs disappear during the metamorphosis. The caterpillar's consumption of food—mainly vegetable and leafy, though some species are adapted to consume hair, wool etc., has to last through the pupa stage and in some species adult life also; in these last, the development of the mouth is poor or lacking, but adults of many species have a tube-like nectar-sucking mouth, coiled up between the jaws when not in use. There are at least 10,000 Aus.

species of Lepidoptera, about 95% moths and 5% butterflies, populations being largest in the wetter E and far SW, but the species are most varied in the N. Families of the E rainforests are fairly often in common with N.G., and those of the N with SE Asia, while the most distinctively Aus. butterflies and moths live in the dry and wet sclerophyll* woodlands. As a protection against predators Lepidopterans have evolved using 1. camouflage, 2. simulation of dangerous or unpleasant animals ('eye' markings on wings, body form like bees or wasps), and 3. sudden revealing of a startling colour especially in the rear pair of wings.

Leprosy A notifiable disease; a few score of new cases are notified annually and leprosaria exist in most States, and in Papua–N.G. It was introduced into Aus. in the 19th century, and spread rather rapidly among the Aborigines, probably especially those living in dirty crowded conditions fringing white settlement. A few cases occur in the white population, mainly in Qld. Treatment is now effective, but segregation of Aborigines for treatment is not easy, particularly in groups with a poor degree of assimilation. The causative agent is bacterial, *Mycobacterium leprae*, related to that of tuberculosis but not highly transmissible, certainly not by casual contact. Identification with the leprosy of the Bible is disputed by some authorities, and excessive horror and ostracism may well be a cause of its perpetuation through concealment of cases. A leading Aus. authority was J. A. Thompson (1848–1915), a N.S.W. medical officer and pioneer in public health.

Leptospermum A genus of trees including most of the species popularly called Tea-trees*.

Leptospirosis or **Weil's Disease** A serious jaundice, sometimes fatal, in which the pathogen from urine of rats, including the native species *Rattus*

conatus, is absorbed through cuts in the skin of people bathing in polluted water. In Qld. sugar-growing areas, the cane is burned off before cutting, to reduce the rat population and also to reduce the minor cuts from the leaves, in order to lessen incidence of this disease among workers.

Leschenaultia A most beautiful genus of heath plants in the mainly Aus. Goodeniaceae family. As in many of the distinctively Aus. flora, species are most numerous and varied in W.A., including the famed blue *L. biloba* around Northam, 32S/117E, the scarlet *L. formosa* around Esperance, 34S/122E, and the varied colours of *L. laricina* on the Darling Range near Perth. Other species extend across the N to NW N.S.W. and into S.A. (*See* PLATE 6.)

Levey, Barnett (1798–1837) b. London. He arrived in Aus. in 1821 to join his prosperous emanicipist brother Solomon. He became a merchant, banker and the first Aus. theatrical entrepreneur, advertising from 1829 for talent for his temporary theatre. This was closed in 1830 by Governor Darling. Levey was given permission to build the first Aus. theatre, the Royal, in 1833, seating 1,000 people.

Lewin, John William (1770–1819) b. Kent, Eng. He arrived in Aus. in 1800. A naturalist and artist; the first Aus. engravings appear in his book on entomology of N.S.W. (1805). His *Birds of N.S.W.* (London, 1808) has only 6 known copies.

Liberal Party As known today, was formed in 1944 from the discredited United Australia Party*, by Menzies's movement of opposition to Labor. In coalition with the Country Party*, it was in power 1949–72. Leadership passed from Menzies to Holt* (1965) to Gorton* (1968) to McMahon* (1971) and to Snedden in 1972.

The roots go back through the U.A.P. (1931–44) which in turn was formed from the Nationalist Party* (1917–31), both very strongly conservative and dependent on Country Party support. The earlier Liberals, who had more in common with Liberal aims in U.K., emerged as one of the 3 embryonic parties in the early days of Federal politics. Policy was based on trade protection, but committed also to advancing social welfare and with much in common with the emerging Labor Party, on whose support it relied when in power under Reid, Deakin and Fisher (1904–13). It was eclipsed more totally than the British Liberals as politics hardened after 1918 to divergent left and right wings. *For further reading see* K. West: *Power in the Liberal Party* (Melbourne, 1967).

Libraries The **National Library of Australia**, housed from 1968 in a marble-clad building on the lake shore in Canberra holds: over 1¼ million volumes; 27,000 paintings, pictures and prints, 18,000 films, air photographs and maps over a wide range, 54,000 microfilms, both Aus. and overseas, foreign material, newspapers and sound recordings and is strong in politics, economics and Aus. work. It has benefited from receipt of many notable collections (*see below*). The library developed from the Commonwealth Parliamentary Library (1901), but was separated from this in 1960. It is the national copyright library.
State Public Libraries have a total of well over 3 million volumes, of which half are in the N.S.W. (1869) and Vic. (1856) Public Libraries which are of international stature. They are, in the main, reference libraries, with extension services providing loans to country areas. Public Libraries were founded in Tas. (1870), S.A. (1884), Qld. (1896), and W.A. (1899); several have been associated with art galleries and museums.
University Libraries are growing most rapidly, with research and specialist material in addition to the normal requirements for undergraduates. The biggest is the **Fisher Library** of the University of Sydney, with almost 1 million volumes, and named in 1908 after Thomas Fisher (1820–1884), a Sydney merchant who left an endowment for a library of £30,000. The Baillieu Trust has greatly enhanced the library of the University of Melbourne which has some ½ million volumes. That of the Aus. National University is centred on the **R. G. Menzies Building**; the University of Adelaide has the **Barr-Smith Library**, named after a family of benefactors; it ranks in size with the libraries of Qld. University, the latter with a strong holding of tropical material. The Universities of W.A. and New England have libraries of about ¼ million and are followed in size by the new universities*.
Local Public Libraries are controlled by State Library Boards, which may subsidise rate-supported libraries. Many local authorities in N.S.W., Qld. and Vic. pool resources for library services. In S.A. the subscription library has remained the chief basis, with State Board subsidies. An outstanding service of the S.A. Libraries Board is the publication of facsimile editions of famous early Aus. writing.
Children's Libraries vary widely in quality, but are developing.
School Libraries are largely dependent on parental fund-raising and are therefore very variable in quality.
Specialist Libraries range in subject from the St. Mark's Anglican Library in Canberra, to the large scientific collections of the C.S.I.R.O.* in its various centres and the Royal Geographical Society of S.A. with its fine topography and historical geography; from the Commonwealth and State Archives and the War Memorial Library to the libraries of museums and industrial concerns.
Specific collections The N.S.W. Public Library in Sydney has 1. the **Mitchell Library**, which, since David Scott

Mitchell (1836-1907) left his 60,000 volumes of Australiana and £70,000 endowment, has trebled in size; 2. the **William Dixson Gallery** housing the historical pictures donated in 1929, and followed at the death of its donor, a merchant, in 1952, by an endowment of £113,000 and further books prints and pictures; 3. the **Shakespeare Tercentenary Memorial Library.** The Vic. Public Library contains among others **J. K. Moir** Australiana collection, **M. V. Anderson Chess** collection, **Brodie Shipping** collection. In the Qld. Public Library is the **Oxley Memorial Library** of historical Aus. and especially Qld. material. And the W.A. Public Library has the **J. S. Battye Library** of W.A. history. The National Library has the **Petherick** and **Ferguson collections** of Australiana, the **Cook Mss.**, the **Cumpston** collection on public health, the **Matthews Ornithological** collection, the **Rex Nan Kivell** collection of volumes and prints of Aus. and Pacific material, the **David Nicholl Smith** collection of 18th-century English literature, the collection of the **Clifford** family and the **Braga** collection of Portuguese material relating to Asia. This, with the Australiana, brings overseas scholars.

Library training is available for undergraduates in Colleges of Advanced Education in the capitals; postgraduate courses are run at Institutes of Technology in Vic. and W.A., the university of N.S.W. and the Canberra College of Advanced Education; more are likely.

Historical Development Only a few private libraries (first listed in 1821) existed for the first 50 years or so. A small Subscription Library and Reading Room was established in Sydney in 1827. Then the influence of the growing self-educative artisans' movement in Eng., with its Mechanics Institutes and Artisan Libraries, reached Aus., and the Sydney Mechanics School of Arts was founded in 1833. By 1900 there were over 1,000 in

Aus. But from a heyday in the 1880s, they had by then lost much of their cultural function and became more social clubs, with the libraries in a state of decay.

The modern era in library development did not begin until after a severely critical report on the backwardness of Aus. libraries was published in 1935, following a survey by an American librarian, Munn, with an Aus. colleague, Pitt. This stimulated Free Library movements, and between 1939-51 legislation was passed in all the States, establishing free libraries (except in S.A.) under Library Boards, permitting the taking over of old artisan libraries, subsidising subscription, rate-supported local libraries, and inter-library loan etc. Previous attempts to form inter-state library associations were in 1902 and 1934, but the Aus. Institute of Librarians (1937) has developed into the Library Association of Aus., and promotes better library services as well as raising and maintaining high professional standards. In 1948 the *McColvin Report*, by an English librarian, recorded progress and gave a clear outline of necessary development, and in 1963 the *Tauber Report*, by an American, found well-established services, but a need to keep up with the country's rapidly growing economy. *With acknowledgment for help given by the National Library of Aus.*

Lice Small, flattened wingless insects, including the Chewing Lice of the Order Mallophaga (in the world, as a whole, generally parasitic on birds, eating feathers and scales of skin, though some species parasitise mammals and live on hair), and the Sucking Lice, Order Siphunculata with a distinctive piercing and sucking mouthpiece (in the world as a whole, parasites of mammals). Most species of lice are specific to one species of host, bird or mammal (including the 3 species parasitic on man). Aus. native species of lice are predominantly Chewing Lice, parasitising not only birds as elsewhere but also many marsupials; one of the few native Sucking Lice occurs on the water-rat. Many species have been introduced, including Chewing Lice parasitic on poultry and cattle, and Sucking Lice parasitic on pigs, sheep, and at times man.

Lichens Spore-bearing green, grey or yellow plants forming an encrustation on rock, soil or wood, and comprising a remarkable symbiosis of blue-green or green algae* with the spore-bearing element, fungi of the Ascomycetes or cup fungi group. Lichens of Aus. include the leaf-dwelling *Strigula elegans* of Qld., many trunk lichens including *Usnea barbata*, and decaying log lichens including the scarlet-fruited *Cladonia macilenta. Thysanothecium hyalinum* is found on charred wood, and there are many soil-loving Cladonias including the coral-like *C. retipora.* The white antlers of *Thamnolia vermicularis* are seen in the Aus. Alps, *Parmelia conspersa* on bluestone, *Candelariella vitellina* on concrete, and *Lichina confinis* on inter-tidal shore rocks.

Liddell N.S.W. 33S/151E The biggest planned Aus. thermal power station lying on the Hunter River. Costing $200 million, with a designed capacity of 2 million kW in 4 stages by 1974, and fed by coal eventually at a rate over 5 million tonnes a year.

Light, William (1786–1839) b. Malaya. Son of an English trader and Malay or possibly Eurasian mother. Became Surveyor-General in S.A. (1836–8), following a picturesque career of travel and military service. He arrived before the Governor, but after the first ships had reached Kangaroo Island; using his authority to select a site, he choose the position of Adelaide. He had to defend his choice against bitter opposition, especially from Hindmarsh*, but it has proved itself over the years.

Light's imaginative layout, ahead of its time, has also worn well, and his meticulous survey was a model. Unfortunately he had neither enough time nor men, and refusing to lower his standards, resigned the post but remained in the colony. He was a talented water-colourist and musician.

Lilies Of the Liliaceae or Lily family, those in Aus. do not include the garden lilies, genus *Lilium*, but the name is often given to related genera in the Liliaceae including: 1. the 6-petalled, white or blue to deep purple *Stypandra*, on a grass-like plant, e.g. *S. glauca*, the Blue Lilly of E Aus., which like Blindgrass or Candyup Poison of W.A., *S. imbricata* and *S. grandiflora*, have been suspected of causing the blindness and death of stock; 2. the yellow-flowered Wild Onion or Bulbine Lily, *Bulbine bulbosa*, also reputedly poisonous to stock although prepared as food by Aborigines; 3. the flax lilies, such as *Dianella laevis* which grows on fertile coastal areas in E Aus., with white to mid-blue 6-petalled flowers, later an attractive blue berry, and very fibrous strap-like leaves; 4. the genus *Blandfordia*, particularly associated with the brilliant red and yellow Christmas Bells, *B. flammea*, growing in swampy spots in the sandstone plateaux of E Aus.; 5. the almost heath-like *Calectasia cyanea*, the Blue Tinsel or Star of Bethlehem of the S of W.A. to W Vic., brilliantly blue and metallic in bloom as the popular and Latin names suggest; 6. the Vanilla Lilly, *Sowerbaea juncea*, whose flowers of 3 petals and 3 sepals, pink-white to violet, have a faint vanilla scent, and which grows in poor swampy coastal sites, with narrow somewhat rush-like leaves as the species name suggests (the genus is named after a well-known naturalist and illustrator); 7. the bulbous Early Nancy, *Anguillaria dioica*, widespread on good soils in Aus., with 4–6 attractive pink flowers in line, with 6 widely open petals and sepals, on a tall stem rising from spear-like leaves; 8. the beautiful Fringed Lily or Fringed Violet, *Thysanotus tuberosus*, seen in grasslands in many parts of Aus. (*see* PLATE 6); 9. the attractive white and purple star of Milkmaid, *Burchardia umbellata*, a favourite with children in many parts of Aus.; 10. the Scrambling Lily, *Geitonolesium cymosum*, of E Aus. sandstone gullies; 11. the yellow Frogsmouth or Woolly Waterlily, *Philydrum lanuginosum*, of E Aus., or Yellow-eyes, *Xyris operculata*, extending with related species widely over Aus. and S and SE Asia; 12. the name lily is sometimes used for some *Doryanthes**, narcissus-like *Calostemma**, and others in the Amaryllidaceae family, to certain orchids*, and of course to Waterlilies*, and other swamp plants such as the Swamp Lily*.

Lillypilly (*Eugenia smithii* or *Acmena smithii*) (the generic name *Eugenia* is after Prince Eugene of Saxony) An 18-m. evergreen tree of coastal E Aus., in the world-wide Myrtaceae family and closely related to the clove of commerce. It has dark green broadly lanceolate leaves, clove-like buds, a spike of feathery blossom, and large bunches of attractive white to lilac, round fruit, 1 cm. across, with succulent edible pulp over a large seed, and eaten by Aborigines, small boys and birds. The tree is liable to infestation by scale insects and sooty mould. The Small-leaf Lillypilly, *E. luehmannii*, is a small tree with handsome red pear-shaped 1-cm. fruit.

Lindeman Island Qld. 20S/149E The first of the Cumberland Islands to be developed for tourists, in the 1920s—rocky, forested and coral-fringed.

Lindrum, Walter (1898–1960) b. Perth. Probably the world's greatest billiards* player to date. His father, sister and brother were Aus. champions and his nephew Horace a world snooker champion. Having defeated the English-man Joe Davis in 1934, he remained unrivalled until he retired in 1950. In 1932 he established a record break, scoring 4,137 points in 175 minutes; as a result of his complete mastery of the difficult long 'nursery cannon', new rules were introduced, but he overcame their challenge.

Lindsay family One of the most talented Aus. families, brought up in Creswick, Vic., where their Irish father was a doctor. Ballarat Art Gallery has a Lindsay Memorial Gallery. The most famous of the 10 children was Norman Lindsay* but **Percy** (1870–1952), **Lionel** (1874–1961), **Daryl** (b. 1890) and **Ruby** (1887–1919) have all been artists or illustrators of some note, and **Jack Lindsay** (b. 1900), Norman's son, is an expatriate author. *For further reading see* Sir Lionel Lindsay's autobiography: *The Leafy Tree* (Sydney, 1967).

Lindsay, Norman Alfred William (1879–1969) b. Creswick, Vic. One of the talented Lindsay family* and probably best known. He joined the *Bulletin* (1901) as artist and writer, with a strong vein of satire in both, and was a very influential, gay but arrogant Sydney literary figure of the 1920s. Children's stories, illustrated by himself, include *The Magic Pudding* (Sydney, 1918). His novels include *Saturdee* (Sydney, 1933), a study of tough boyhood, and novels of adolescence such as *Redheap* (London, 1930) and *Halfway to Anywhere* (Sydney, 1947). Their frankness on sex earned them Aus. censorship, as did his novels of adult social relationships which include *Pan in the Parlour* (London, 1934). He was a fine model maker of ships.

Lindwall, Ray (1921–) b. Sydney. An outstanding fast bowler, adding much, with Keith Miller*, to Aus. post-1945 cricket. He played in 55 tests (1946–56), taking 212 wickets for an average of 22·18. He captured 228 wickets in Test matches, average cost

23·05 runs. He played in 61 Tests from 1946–59, and scored Test centuries against Eng. (1946, 1949) and W Indies (1955).

Lismore N.S.W. 29S/153E (20,901 in 1971) A growing city on the N arm of the Richmond River*, 28 km. from the sea and its outport of Ballina. Lismore dominates the N Coast in secondary industry, producing about a third of the butter in N.S.W., bacon, sugar, textiles and clothing, and with considerable engineering and vehicle repairing etc. When the area was opened up Lismore outstripped Casino*, as it was the effective head of navigation during the important cedar extraction phase, the timber being floated down river. Parts of the town are liable to flooding.

LITERATURE *Note*: the main sources are H. M. Green: *A History of Australian Literature* (Sydney, 1961); C. Hadgraft: *Australian Literature* (London, 1960); G. Dutton ed.: *The Literature of Australia* (London, 1964). Literature is here defined as creative writing which stands the test of time, and includes substantially factual records written with imagination and skill. The modern period is difficult to assess, and a consensus of critical opinion has been used.

Aus. literature has to be judged, like that of all countries evolving from European origins, on 2 levels: work significant in the development of a national literature, and work which takes its place in the main stream of world literature. On both levels there has been considerable achievement, but as yet, only a few have produced creative writing which is both indisputably based on their own national origin, and also takes its place in the main stream; these great Aus. writers are, in prose, Henry Handel Richardson, Katherine Susannah Prichard, Patrick White; in poetry, Christopher Brennan, James Macauley, Kenneth

Slessor, R. D. Fitzgerald, A. D. Hope and Judith Wright. It is possible to define periods: Green gives 4, of which the years from 1923 take up the whole of his second volume. Hadgraft has 3: to 1880, 1880–1930, then to the present day; Dutton takes 1920 as the dividing point.

The earliest white arrivals, voluntary and involuntary, found a harsh environment in which the struggle to survive filled their lives. Yet some were able to record experiences and impressions. Of these, Watkins Tench's journals are outstanding in their detached observations and vivid evocation. The trained observational powers of other naval officers, including Phillips himself, make invaluable sources but are not literature. Similarly, the worm's eye view of the convicts, notably Vaux, which always found a ready market in Eng., had little lasting merit.

Nevertheless, the convicts, coming from a stratum of society in which song and story were still orally transmitted, provided the roots from which indigenous Aus. songs and ballads gradually developed. Verse took first the form of sycophantic public odes by M. M. Robinson, followed by the almost worthless *First Fruits of Australian Poetry* (1819) by Barron Field, and Wentworth's lengthy panegyric *Australasia* (1823).

As exploration widened the horizons, many descriptive works were produced; the explorers often being men of imagination, sometimes created in their journals works of enduring merit; this was true of Sturt, and to a lesser extent, of Mitchell, Eyre and, much later, of Giles. Another outstanding work of description was W. L. Ranken's *Dominion of Australia* (1874).

The first works of fiction based on Aus. environment flowed from the annalist tradition, with factual accounts but thinly disguised, and often pointed to the specific purpose of encouraging migrants from 'home'. These Hadgraft calls the 'guidebook' novels, with

Rowcroft and Harris giving the opposing viewpoints of romantic and realist. H. Savery's *Quintus Servinton* (Hobart, 1831), the first novel published in Aus., is the story of a convict, as is the more skilfully written *The Adventures of Ralph Rashleigh* (not published until 1929, but written in 1845–6), possibly by James Tucker.

Meanwhile the first real poet had appeared in Charles Harpur, publishing from 1833 and taking subjects and inspiration from the Aus. scene, though treating them in a very English lyrical manner. He was followed by Henry Kendall, writing lyrical verse from 1859 onwards, mainly about the soft coastal scene of S N.S.W.

The mid-19th century was a period of expansion to the frontiers and the turbulent days of the gold-rushes and the bushranger. In poetry this was reflected in the very popular, swinging verse of Adam Lindsay Gordon, foreshadowing the later ballads, of which the rough contemporary bush songs were also roots. Henry Kingsley wrote the first major work of fiction, *The Recollections of Geoffrey Hamlyn* (1859), about the adventures of pioneering life, and later came Rolf Boldrewood's *Robbery Under Arms* (1888) which survives today, in spite of its artificial contriving of plot and style. Transportation or 'the system' by now a thing of the past, provided material for one of the greatest Aus. novels, Marcus Clarke's *For the term of his Natural Life* (1874). In the 1870s there was an active literary group in Melbourne which included Clarke, A. L. Gordon and G. McCrae. At the same time, the rougher pioneering period was giving way to a more settled leisurely life on established farms, and 3 women novelists, 'Tasma', Ada Cambridge and Rosa Praed wrote of this life, although often with nostalgia and invidious comparisons with the greater refinement of 'home'. As a counterblast, there came the more popular, down-to-earth humour, in the squalor and realism of Steele Rudd's tales of the small Qld. farmer, which have survived in cartoon, serial and film.

The decades immediately before and after 1900 brought an upsurge of nationalism, a breakaway from the English heritage and a struggle for national identity. An important catalyst in both the literary and political field was the weekly magazine the *Bulletin* (founded 1880). Under its editor John Archibald, Aus. verse and fiction were encouraged. Much of it has been forgotten, but the works of Lawson, Paterson and Furphy were important milestones. Lawson, as the leader in the field of the short story and to a lesser extent as a balladist, wrote in brief, almost anecdotal style, of the harsh realities of the countryside. Paterson, leader of the ballad writers, had a less grim, more romantic view. There were also ballads of the sea, of the mines and of the city; all are more or less dismissed by the literary critic, yet they were very important as popular folk-expressions of the day.

Furphy was the first aggressively Aus. novelist with *Such is Life* (1903), which is unique in the literature in its mixture of documentary, anecdotal, philosophical and narrative topics, set in the Riverina district of N.S.W. Writing at about the same time, Miles Franklin gave a complementary view of station life in *My Brilliant Career* (1901), which threw off her predecessors' longings for 'home'. A. G. Stephens, literary editor of the *Bulletin* after 1896, did much to encourage both the Aus. writing of Furphy, Rudd and Franklin, as well as the more intellectual and lyrical poets. Here some important figures emerged, whose work begins to enter the main stream: Christopher Brennan (from 1897), a leading Sydney intellectual figure; Shaw Neilson whose modest, seemingly simple lyrical verse will perhaps survive much more recent poetry; Bernard O'Dowd and Mary Gilmore, writing poetry with an underlying social purpose.

Meanwhile, in Europe, Henry Handel Richardson was beginning a career of painstaking yet brilliant writing which gave her an international reputation. At the same time, she epitomises the ambivalent position of the Aus. critic, for only 2 of her novels have Aus. settings, although this includes *The Fortunes of Richard Mahoney* (published as a trilogy between 1917 and 1929, and her best work), and she lived in Europe from the age of 17. Is she thus an Aus. novelist?

The First World War had tremendous significance for Aus., and has often been taken as the true point of birth of the nation. Yet paradoxically, the period following 1920 saw an increasing emergence of her writers into the wider world of English literature. There has been far more good poetry than prose, and its prevailing note is one of gloom. In quantity there has been, of course, far more prose. Some, perhaps in order to take part more freely, live outside Aus. These include Christina Stead, Charles Cobb, Patrick White and Morris West; White is widely recognised as a major novelist, and generally uses Aus. settings.

The dominant literary influence in the 1920s was the group of Sydney writers and artists, centred round Norman Lindsay. Their creed was the need to pursue the gay life, with no inhibitions, and it gave rise to exotic works of prose, art and poetry. The writers (including Hugh McCrea, from 1909) who found impetus in this atmosphere, but whose writing will survive, have gone on from its limited field to develop their individual styles, so that it becomes impossible to place them in groups or schools. Kenneth Slessor (from 1926), one of the great Aus. poets, developed to write bitter commentaries on the condition of man. R. D. Fitzgerald (from 1929), developing later, turned more to mysticism and strong narrative. James McAuley used more traditional verse forms, brilliant narrative and descriptive powers. Two brief rebellious movements in Adelaide in the 1940s, one advocating more Aus. themes, the other a surrealist school, also produced poets who have gone on to find an individual form, e.g. Dutton. In recent years, 2 further major poets have emerged: A. D. Hope (from 1955, though much earlier in journals), writing astringent, often bitter, often humorous verse, rich in allusion, and Judith Wright (from 1946), whose work is universal in both emotional appeal and intellectual approach, yet nearly always using the Aus. image, and often clearly feminine in viewpoint. It is less necessary, it seems, for the poet to divorce himself from his land in order to find universal acceptance.

There has been, since 1920 an ever-increasing output of novels which can be grouped variously: there are sagas mining the endless lodes of pioneer days, of which Miles Franklin (*All That Swagger*, 1936) has written the finest example, but with a useful counter-balance in Penton's tale of the harsher realities of Qld. pioneering (*The Landtakers*, 1934). Historical novels, going back to the early days, are best represented by Eleanor Dark (*The Timeless Land*, 1941). Others continue the Lawson and Furphy tradition of using the Aus. countryside as settings. In this field Katherine Prichard has written of the karri forests of the SW (*Working Bullocks*, 1926), of opal miners, and a circus troup; and in a powerful novel of the cattle country of the far NW (*Coonardoo*, 1929) she introduces the problem of the Aborigines. But it was Xavier Herbert who exposed this particular aspect of contemporary Aus. in its rawest form, in *Capricornia* (1938). Kylie Tennant has also written of the countryside, in perhaps a lighter vein, but her best work spills over into the city scene.

Although the romance and the image of Aus. still lie in the outback, the preponderantly urban element in the population has been increasingly reflected in the literature. Louis Stone (*Jonah*, 1911) wrote the first important work with a town setting, in the Sydney slums. Later, the Depression period has been recorded by Barnard Eldershaw (*Tomorrow and Tomorrow*, 1947) as well as in Kylie Tennant's *Tiburon* (1935) and several others. The Second World War brought an inevitable if patchy crop of tales, George Johnston's *My Brother Jack* (1964) and sequel *Clean Straw for Nothing* (1969) follow through this period. A wide range of settings has been used by Thomas Keneally. An important new writer is Frank Moorhouse *The Americans, Baby* (1972).

Short story writers have tended to forsake the disciplined brevity of the *Bulletin* days. Katherine Prichard again was outstanding; but there has been worth-while work from Casey, writing about the W.A. gold-fields, and Dal Stivens, specialising in the 'tall story' while Hal Porter can reach higher levels than many.

It was still possible in 1962 for a leading critic to castigate his fellow Aus. writers for their 'cultural cringe' to Europe, in spite of the fierce attempts of the *Bulletin* between 1890 and 1910, and the later, less successful creations of the Jindyworobaks* in Adelaide in the 1940s. But in the 1970s Aus. writing is trending away from the parochial, and is concerned with problems of society everywhere. The increasing confidence of the nation in its own identity, an ability to laugh at itself, the watering down of old prejudices are all finding expression in the literature. *For further reading see* J. Wright: *Pre-occupations in Aus. Poetry* (Oxford, 1965); B. Elliott: *The landscapes of Aus. Poetry* (Melbourne, 1967); and the 2 volume *Poetry in Australia* (Sydney, 1964). An annual anthology (since 1942) is *Australian Poetry* and its companion annual selection of short stories, *Coast to Coast*. The first of 2

volumes of *The Short Stories of Australia* was published in Sydney, 1967 and there is the World's Classics *Australian Short Stories* (London, 1951). *Australian Writers and their Work* (Melbourne) is a series; and a recent survey is G. A. Wilkes: *Australian Literature: a Conspectus* (Sydney, 1969).

The main literary journals are: *Southerly* (1939), devoted largely to Aus. work; *Meanjin* (1940) looking within and beyond Aus. and taking its name from the Aboriginal 'spike' referring to the peninsular site of early Brisbane where it was founded; and *Quadrant* (1956).

The following list selecting some of the main writers of verse and fiction cannot claim to be exhaustive. Those with asterisks have separate entries, as do nearly all those mentioned in the main article above.

Mid to late 19th century 1. *Fiction:* J. Lang, J. Houlding, C. Spence*, R. Boldrewood*, G. Ranken, Caroline Leakey, H. Kingsley*, A. W. Howitt*, A. Cambridge*, J. B. O'Reilly, M. A. H. Clarke*, 2. *Verse:* A. L. Gordon*, R. H. Horne*, H. Halloran, J. L. Michael, D. H. Deniehy, G. G. McCrae*, J. B. Stephens*, H. C. Kendall*, A. P. Martin. *The Balladists* were Mary Foott, J. Farrell, J. Moses* (best known for the famous jingle *The Dog sat on the Tuckerbox*), Essex Evans*, A. B. Paterson*, G. H. Souter*, E. G. Dyson*, H. H. Morant* B. H. Boake*, H. A. Lawson*, W. H. Ogilvie*, E. J. Brady (sea ballads), W. Lawson, C. J. Dennis*, 'John O'Brien' (Rev. P. J. Hartigan).

Late 19th and early 20th century 1. *Fiction:* J. Furphy*, Catherine Martin, Tasma*, R. Praed*, Price Warung*, B. Baynton*, H. A. Lawson*, R. Bedford, Steel Rudd*, A. Dorrington, H. H. Richardson*, M. Franklin*, K. S. Prichard*. 2. *Verse:* J. Brereton*, J. Hebblethwaite, V. Daley*, F. W. L. Adams*, W. Gay, M. J. Gilmore*, B. P. O'Dowd*, R. J. Quinn, R. J.

Crawford, Marie Pitt, C. Brennan*, J. S. Neilson*, H. R. McCrae*, F. Maurice*, W. Baylebridge*, N. Palmer*, F. T. B. Macartney, L. M. Gellert. *Between the Wars* 1. *Fiction:* J. Hackston, N. Lindsay*, Vance Palmer*, H. Mathews, B. James*, F. D. Davidson*, L. Mann*, C. M. Mann*, B. Eldershaw*, E. Dark*, A. Marshall*, Ruth Park*, J. Morrison, B. C. Penton*, E. Langley*, K. Tennant*, D. G. Stivens*. 2. *Verse:* D. M. Wright, J. M. Devaney, C. P. Hopegood*, C. R. Jury, T. Inglis Moore*, J. Picot, K. Slessor*, J. A. R. McKellor, B. R. Elliott.

During and since the 1939-45 War 1. *Fiction:* A. F. X. Herbert*, T. M. Ronan, J. Waten*, J. L. Glassop, M. L. West*, P. W. Cowan*, D. Cusack*, J. Cleary*, H. Porter, F. J. Hardy*, G. H. Johnstone, O. Ruhen, Thea Astley*, J. R. Stow*, G. Taylor, G. McInnes, Elizabeth Harrower, P. Mathers, Tony Morphett, T. Keneally*, M. Trist. G. Johnston, F. Moorhouse, 2 *Verse*: Norma Davis, A. D. Hope*, R. McCuaig, I. M. Mudie, R. R. Robinson*, F. J. Blight, R. Ingamells*, R. D. Fitzgerald, D. A. Stewart*, K. I. Mackenzie*, J. Wright*, D. W. I. Campbell, J. Manifold*, H. F. Stewart, J. McAuley, Nancy Cato, Rosemary Dobson*, M. H. Harris*, Nan Macdonald, G. P. Dutton*, Nancy Keesing, F. C. Webb*, V. Buckley*, C. Thiele, B. Dawe, M. Lisle, C. Wallace-Crabbe*, H. Jones, E. Jones, N. Talbot, C. Higham, B. Beaver, R. A. Simpson, J. R. Rowland, Gwen Harwood*, Grace Perry, L. Collinson, E. C. Rolls, T. W. Shapcott, G. Lehmann, R. Mathew, R. Hall, L. A. Murray, V. Williams, V. Smith. *Expatriate writers* include M. Boyd*, C. F. Cobb, Christina Stead*, B. R. S. Close, P. V. M. White*, A. Moorehead*, E. G. Moll J. Aldridge, Shirley Hazzard, K. Harrison, P. Porter, J. Lindsay*, R. Braddon, P. Ritchie.

Lithgow N.S.W. 33S/150E (13,135 in 1971) A mining and manufacturing city at over 900 m. in the Central Tablelands W of the Blue Mts.* The coal industry grew with the difficult engineering of a railway line from Sydney in 1869, and there was iron or iron and steel making from Mort's venture of 1875 until the transfer of the Hoskins Plant to Port Kembla in 1928 (see IRON AND STEEL), and associated non-ferrous metals, refractories, technical education etc. The decline in population has steadied. There are woollen, textile and clothing industries.

Liverpool N.S.W. 34S/151E (82,270 in 1971) A city within the Metropolitan Area and 32 km. SW of Sydney. Residually a market and despatch and processing centre for dairy produce, poultry and grapes, but increasingly swamped by residential areas and by considerable local manufacturing (cables, electrical goods, woollens etc.).

Liverpool Plains N.S.W. A widely understood, but not precisely defined area N of the ridged volcanic and rocky Liverpool and Warrumbungle Ranges. Gunnedah*, 31S/150E, is usually accepted as its centre. This plain, developed over varied rocks in 50-75 cm. mean annual rainfall, has deep black earth soils of high inherent fertility. Squatters from 1833, and then the Aus. Agricultural Company* developed large-scale pastoral holdings, now much subdivided and a productive part of the sheep-wheat belt.

Lizards Along with the snakes*, they make up the Order Squamata or scaly reptiles. The Squamata share a movable quadrate bone (below the skull and the anchorage of the lower jaw), which is fixed in other reptiles and birds, and organs of copulation are paired. But lizards lack the remarkable elastic jaw ligament of the snakes. Lizards have ears, unlike snakes, and most have an ear opening. The lizards mainly have 4 prominent legs with clawed feet, though there are Legless

Lizards*. Only goannas have snake-like forked tongues. Lizards have teeth in a continuous longitudinal groove, or set in the edge of the jaw, as against the socketed teeth and aquatic breathing tubes of the crocodiles*. Lizards eat insects, and large ones also eat frogs, small snakes, and eggs of birds and other reptiles on occasion, and some ground vegetation. Many have a fairly elaborate mating dance or ritual; some bury eggs to incubate at ground temperature in suitable sites, others give birth to live young in an enclosed sac which is soon burst by the young who then eat the remains of the yolk. Some lizards are able to change colour and often enlarge parts of the body for camouflage, display, repelling of enemies etc. Aus. has about 300 of some 2,500 species in the world. No Aus. lizards are venomous, though bites from some, especially carrion-eaters, may carry bacteria causing septic wounds. The main ones are discussed under: Geckoes*, Legless Lizards*, Skinks*, Dragon Lizards* and Goannas*.

Loan Council A statutory body formed (1927) from earlier informal attempts to co-ordinate borrowing by the separate States. Each State and the Commonwealth has one representative, generally the Premier, but the Commonwealth has 2 votes and the casting vote. (*See* FINANCE.)

Lobelia Species native to Aus., *L. axillaris*, *L. concolor* and *L. tenuior* in the mainly tropical family Lobeliaceae, have milky alkaloid sap poisonous to cattle. (*See* PLATE 6.)

Lobethal S.A. 35S/139E (1,381 in 1971) A small service centre in the Mt. Lofty Range*, with woollen mills based originally on the local sheep farms. Founded by German Lutherans, the name was changed to Tweedvale 1917–35.

Lobster Originally applied to members of the Crayfish* family with enlarged claws. Rock lobster tails are a valuable export, often called crayfish.

Local Government There is not a uniform system throughout Aus., and no link between local and Federal government. The close network of fundraising autonomous local bodies envisaged in the 1842 Act and following the British pattern, proved quite inappropriate to the widely scattered Aus. population. Local responsibility has only been accepted with reluctance, since the costs of providing facilities in a new country are very high. There are 900 local government areas, covering all but the empty lands of N.S.W. and S.A., some offshore islands and the Territories*.

In N.S.W. the units are Cities, Municipalities and Shires. Councillors (Aldermen in some towns and cities) are elected on the Parliamentary franchise. The State is unique in also having County Councils, bodies of delegates from groups of local government units, which control specific services, such as electricity, the control of noxious weeds etc. The Cumberland County Council (1945–63) was created for planning in Greater Sydney which has no single Local Government equivalent to the Greater London Council. In Vic. the units are Cities, Towns, Boroughs and Shires, elected on a property franchise, allowing plural voting up to 3. In Qld. units are Cities, Towns and Shires. The State has unique features in that Brisbane has one Council and salaried Councillors. Election is on Parliamentary franchise. In S.A. units are Cities, Corporate Towns, District Councils, elected by a franchise based on rate payers and allowing a vote in each ward (or subdivision) in which rates are paid. There are also bodies similar to the N.S.W. County Councils. In W.A. units are Cities, Towns and Shires (where the authority is called the Road Board). Franchise is on a property basis with plural voting up to 4. In Tas. units are Municipalities save for the Cities of Hobart and Launceston; a property franchise allows plural voting up to 4. The urban Mayors (or Wardens, in Tas.) are elected by the voters in all but N.S.W. and Vic. where they are elected by the Councils. In Qld. the rural Chairmen are also elected by the voters. Thus there can be friction between the Mayor or Chairman and his Council. In addition to the general local bodies there are elected boards in some areas for specific functions such as roads, hospitals, fire-fighting etc.

Lockyer, Edmund (1784–1860) b. Devon, Eng. He arrived in Aus. in 1825, as an army officer, and was sent by Governor Brisbane to explore the Brisbane River in 1825, and to forestall possible French annexation of W.A. (New Holland) in 1826. He landed at King George Sound* December 25th 1826, formally declaring the territory a British possession.

Lockyer Valley Qld. 28S/153E A wide alluvial plain W of Brisbane, with soils derived from basalts, and containing underground water used intensively for onions, potatoes and other vegetables and for fodder crops for dairying for the Brisbane market. Gatton (3,546 in 1971) is the main centre.

Locusts Winged, jumping insects of the Order *Orthoptera**, of which the best known is the Plague Locust, *Chorotoicetes terminifera*, a green or brown locust with red hind legs and a black patch at the tip of the hind wing, spreading in great swarms as a serious pest of pastures in particular years when locust population has greatly multiplied in a particular area and the local supply of food has been eaten up. Scientific study of the movements and habits have made possible a considerable degree of control through careful surveillance of breeding areas.

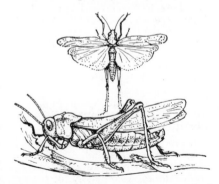

Plague Locust (Chorotoicetes terminifera) about life size

Loddon River Vic. Flows for over 320 km. NW and N from the crest of the Central Uplands about 80 km. NW of Melbourne, to join first an anabranch and then the Murray proper at Swan Hill, 35S/144E. It is variable in volume, but is dammed for several reservoirs, including Cairn Curran. The lower Loddon plains are in a rain-shadow with only 45 cm. mean annual rainfall, and the Goulburn River* irrigation water supplies much needed water along the valley.

Logan, Patrick (1791–1830) b. Berwickshire, Scotland. Commandant of Moreton Bay convict garrison from 1826–30. Little is known of the true personality of this hated commander except through official reports and the tales of floggings and escapes, and bitter ballads made by his convict charges whom he disciplined strictly and with some brutality. However, he laid out the beginnings of Brisbane systematically, and (partly with Cunningham*) explored into the ranges where he was killed by Aborigines. *For further reading see* C. Bateson: *Patrick Logan: Tyrant of Brisbane Town* (Sydney, 1966).

Logan River Flows 1,160 km. from the Macpherson Range to Moreton Bay.

Longford Tas. 42S/147E (1,712 in 1971) The service centre for a small dairying district on the banks of the S Esk River and a wider stock-rearing region on the N Midlands.

Longreach Qld. 23S/144E (3,453 in 1971) On the left bank of a straight 'reach' of the Thomson River, this is a major collecting and distributing centre for the pastoral district of Central and W Qld., developing from a camping site in the days of bullock teams, and linked to Rockhampton by rail in 1892.

Lonsdale, William (1800-1864) He was the first administrator of the Port Phillip District (1836-9), sent by Bourke* when he realised the illegal settlement by Batman, Fawkner and Aitken had to be accepted. As police magistrate, Lonsdale, a man of integrity and ability, had wide powers of surveillance and remained in important posts under La Trobe*.

Loo, Luvar or **Silver King** (*Luvarus imperialis*) A very rare but interesting fish in Aus., assuming 3 forms after hatching; the adult reaches 1·8 m. and has a blunt, almost whale-like head, a thin crescentic tail, and spiny fins along the rear of both back and belly. It is silvery-grey above with scarlet bands along the side, and has a silvery belly. It is a fish of open warm oceans, living on krill and other plankton.

Lord Howe Island N.S.W. 31S/159E (267 in 1966) An area of 825 ha. Lying in the Tasman Sea, 700 km. NE of Sydney, it forms a crescent 9·6 km. N-S and 1·6 km wide; the concave W coast has a shallow lagoon, fringed with the most southerly recorded true coral reef, explained by the warm sea current offshore. The flora and fauna have a considerable proportion unique to the island and show N.Z. and tropical rather than Aus. affinities, probably indicating ancient land bridges to N and S along the ocean rise on which the island lies. In the S are 2 precipitous mountains of Tertiary basalt, cloud-capped and forested: Mt. Gower (865·2 m.) and Mt. Lidgbird (763·4 m.). The island was discovered by Lieut. Lidgbird Ball in February 1788, and named after the British Admiral Howe; the first settlement was from N.Z. about 1834, but was replaced by a Sydney enterprise in settlement until 1847, after which the island was mainly a whaling base for many decades. The export of seeds of the Kentia palm, *Howea forsteriana*, has recently revived, but tourists brought by air from Sydney are now the main source of income. The Lord Howe Island Board manages the affairs of the islanders, who vote with a Sydney electorate.

Lord, Simeon (1771-1840) b. Leeds, Eng. He was transported in 1790 for stealing cloth. Lord is the outstanding example of an emancipist* who made good. A founder of Sydney's commercial class, he traded in coal, sealskins, whale oil, and later in wool, became a shipowner by 1806 and started a woollen goods factory in 1815. Macquarie gave him official positions of trust, thus causing controversy.

Lorikeets A group of nectar-eating parrots*, generally small, short-tailed mainly bright green, feeding boldly and greedily, darting swiftly from blossom to blossom, and moving through the forests as trees come into flower. The tongue is often hairy to assist in extracting the nectar. They range from the Red-cheeked Little Lorikeet, *Glossopsitta pusilla*, 15-18 cm. long, to the 30-cm. Rainbow Lorikeet, *Trichoglossus moluccanus*, with blue on the face and lower belly, red breast and yellow flanks. The Fig-parrots genus *Opopsitta*, are very small, 15 cm. or so long, generally green with red and blue faces and yellow on the flanks; they are somewhat similar except that they eat the fruit of figs and other trees deep in the Qld. rainforests. (*See* PLATE 4.)

Lotteries In addition to many privately organised lotteries, all States except Tas. and Vic. where Tattersall's operate, run lotteries, used mainly for hospital and charitable purposes. (*See* GAMBLING.)

Love-creeper (*Comesperma volubile*) A widespread climber with masses of bright blue flowers. Others of the genus are heath-like shrubs mainly in W.A., with pea-like flowers. The genus belongs to the cosmopolitan family Polygalaceae.

Love-grass A popular name for the attractive warm-climate grass genus *Eragrostis*, including native species, e.g. Brown's Love-grass, *E. brownii*, with several branches from a low tuft of foliage, each bearing a multiple seed-head, which matures to spread in almost fern-like form, each individual spikelet bearing many small, broad seed-husks in 2 neat rows. *E. trachycarpa* is one of the grasses which often lose their heads in the wind, which piles them against fences etc. Stinkgrass, strongly smelling when wet, is *E. cilianensis*. *E. australasica* is the waxy, almost shrubby Cane-grass*.

Lowan, Mallee-fowl or **Gnow** (*Leipoa ocellata*—egg-leaver with small eyemarks) A 50-cm.-long brown, grey and white speckled bird with light buff breast, of dry inland scrub, remarkable for its large nest-mound in which the eggs are buried and incubated by the heat of fermentation of the leaves etc. The male builds the mound and maintains the correct temperature.

Lowbidgee N.S.W. A district between Hay*, 34S/145E, and Balranald,* 35S/144E. It is the low-lying part of the Murrumbidgee alluvial tract where the river banks are low (not incised into the plain, as farther upstream) and therefore where there are widespread snowmelt floods every spring. The Lowbidgee gives excellent cattle grazing as the waters recede, and efforts are being made to control the flooding by weirs and channels to maximise the use of these flood plains.

Lowe, Robert (1811–1892) b. Bingham, Eng. He was in Aus. from 1842–50. An albino, Lowe's tormented school life embittered him, spurring on his intel-lectual development to brilliance at Oxford and in N.S.W., where he went, hoping to stave off blindness. There he vied with Wentworth* in politics, figured in famous law cases, antagonised everyone in turn with his vicious wit; but his oratory in such cases as land reform, transportation and secular education, was very influential. After his return to Eng. he became Chancellor of the Exchequer under Gladstone, and was created Viscount Sherbrooke in 1880. *For further reading see* Ruth Knight: *Robert Lowe; Illiberal Liberal* (Melbourne, 1965).

Loxton S.A. 34S/141E (2,658 in 1971) A town and irrigation area on the left bank of the Murray, and the chief service centre for the S.A. Mallee* area. About 2,400 ha. have been irrigated as Soldier Settlement* farms after the 1939–45 War but with severe problems of drainage.

Lucerne, Native A popular name for the native legume, Scurf-pea or Emu Grass, *Psoralea tenax*. The yellow-flowered Paddy's Lucerne of E Aus. is in the Mallow not the Pea family. Pasture lucerne like *Medicago sativa* is an introduced species. **Townsville Lucerne**, *Stylanthes humilis*, accidentally introduced in the early 1900s has recently been recognised and developed in tropical Aus. as a valuable, protein-rich, nitrogen-fixing fodder plant.

Luderick, Nigger, Darkie or **Blackfish** (*Girella tricuspidata*) A deep-bodied fish with a continuous back fin, and has about 10 dark, vertical stripes along its side; it is mainly vegetarian but sometimes takes a prawn or mussel bait; widely distributed in Aus. waters. The magnificent yellow-spotted sky-blue Bluefish, *Iredalella cyanea*, is related and similar in shape, but much more carnivorous. The Black Drummer, *Girellipiscis elevatus*, is a particularly deep-bodied fish, with coarse scales, a fine longitudinal line and a long back fin; it is long in the rear part and balanced by a large anal fin; although largely vegetarian, it will take shellfish etc. All of these fish are about 30–45 cm. long and edible particularly if eaten fresh, though some species grow much larger at which stage they may be less palatable.

Lungfish These have been placed in a Sub-Class Crossopterygii within the bony fishes. The Qld. lungfish *Neoceratodus forsteri*, large-scaled green white-bellied, has a bulky body running into a deep pointed tail and up to 1·8 m. long. Like other lungfish in other continents, it has gills, but also a swim-bladder modified into a lung, as compared with those of normal fish, by the development of breathing apparatus of veins and arteries. This adaptation enables the lungfish to survive better at times when the river is reduced to stagnant pools, but it soon dies out of water. Its flipper-like fins do not enable it to progress on land. It eats waterweed and small animals, and its eggs and young resemble frogspawn and tadpoles. It has been eaten by Aborigines and early settlers, but is now strictly preserved because of its great scientific interest. It is often referred to as a 'living fossil', meaning that the nearest related genera of fish are fossils from the Permian rocks of over 200 million years ago. The original range was restricted to the Burnett and Mary Rivers of Qld., but it has been introduced to a number of other rivers in S Qld.

Lungfish, about 1·8 m. long

Lutheran Church With 196,201 adherents in 1971, it is moving towards a union of the 2 factions which developed shortly after the arrival in S.A. in 1838 of German Lutherans opposed to enforced union with the Calvinistic churches in Germany (*see* BAROSSA VALLEY). Since 1945 migrants from Europe have swelled their numbers. The Hermannsburg Mission* is Lutheran.

Lycett, Joseph b. Staffordshire, Eng. He was a professional portraitist, transported in 1814 for forgery, a crime he repeated in Sydney in 1815, and was sent to Newcastle. His skill in church decoration and landscape painting brought ultimate pardon, and in 1825 he published *Views in Australia*. These are stereotyped and inferior to those of his other numerous landscapes and natural history sketches.

Lymburner, Francis (1916–1972) b. Brisbane. A contemporary artist especially influential in expressing the Sydney romanticism of the 1940s, before spending 10 years overseas.

Lyne, Sir William John (1844–1913) b. Apslawn, Tas. He was Premier of N.S.W. at the time of Federation*, and would have been the first Prime Minister of the Commonwealth, but failed to form a government.

Lyons, Joseph Aloysius (1879–1939) b. Circular Head, Tas. Prime Minister of Aus. from 1931–9. He gained his reputation as a very efficient Tas. Treasurer, becoming Premier from 1923–9. He then entered Federal Politics serving under Scullin*, before resigning from the Labor Party in 1931 over financial policy, doubts over the reinstatement of Theodore* and a revulsion against factionalism. He formed the United Aus. Party* with the Opposition, and on Labor's defeat in 1931, he became Prime Minister. Lyons's popularity was due not only to his patent sincerity but also in some measure to his lack of brilliance and hence identification by and with the 'man in the street'. He died in office. His widow, Dame Enid, became the first woman M.H.R. (Liberal for Darwin, Tas., in 1943), achieving Cabinet rank 1949–51.

Lyrebirds Two species, the Superb Lyrebird, *Menura superba* (proud mighty tail), found in wet sclerophyll forest from Stanthorpe Qld. to Dandenongs Vic., and the rather smaller and less spectacular Prince Albert Lyrebird, *M. alberti*, of the sub-tropical rain forests of NE N.S.W. and S Qld. are unique to Aus. The Superb Lyrebird is about 40 cm. long, beak to rump, with a long tail to 60 cm. which is brought right up over the back and spread fan-wise over the whole body during his remarkable courtship display and 'dance' on mounds of forest litter about 90 cm. in diameter. The female builds a large domed nest, lined with feathers from her breast, for the one grey-brown egg. The birds eat insects, snails etc., found by working over leaves and twigs, or by attacking touchwood logs etc.; they normally roost in forest tree-branches. The lyrebird's mimicry of other birds, especially in the male, is almost as remarkable as its plumage and display. (*See* PLATE 5.) *For further reading see* L. H. Smith: *The Lyrebird* (Melbourne, 1968).

M

MAATSUYKER ISLANDS

Maatsuyker Islands Tas. 44S/146E Fragments of Precambrian metamorphic rock forming an island group 16 km. offshore. The largest is De Witt Island (or Big Witch). On Maatsuyker Island (or Little Witch), the second largest, is the most southerly Aus. lighthouse. To the SE the remote Mewstone Rock is the home of the albatross, and the whole desolate uninhabited group, found and named by Tasman, is noted for its seals, penguins, sea-lions and mutton-birds.

Macadamia Nut Fruit of the trees *Macadamia tetraphylla* and *M. integrifolia*, an Aus. genus in the large southern family Proteaceae. A delicious nut, carried in long bunches, following flower-spikes at the end of the branches of large, toothed leaves. The nut is said to be more cultivated in Hawaii than in its native Qld., but it has economic potential here also.

Macaranga (*Macaranga tanarius*) A 6-m. tree of coastal E Qld. with 15-cm.-long leaves shaped like nasturtium leaves, pendent male catkins and longish ovoid female catkins, producing a 3-celled, 3-seed capsule. The timber is extraordinarily fibrous. It belongs to the cosmopolitan Euphorbiaceae or Spurge family.

Macarthur, John (1767–1834) b. Stoke Damerel, Devonshire, Eng. He had more influence than any other person, including the governors, on the political and economic development of N.S.W., 1790–1820. Arriving 1790 in the N.S.W. Corps*, he was granted 100 ac. at Parramatta and named it Elizabeth Farm after his courageous and energetic wife who played an important part in his success as a farmer, as well as in the social life of the colony. He played a leading role in the establishment of the

MACARTHUR

N.S.W. wool industry by the experiments, started in 1794, of crossing Bengal and Irish sheep and later by importing S African Merinos*. He introduced the first animal-drawn iron plough to the colony in 1795 and grew wheat and potatoes, but his vision of the colony was of landed pastoralist families, and he resented the successive efforts of Bligh and Macquarie to establish smaller scale agricultural communities; and especially the increasing favours given to emancipists*. Before long he had assumed the role of 'perturbator' by writing complaints to London, which led to the removal of Hunter*, and quarrelling with his successor King who sent him to London in 1801 to be tried for duelling. Macarthur escaped the charge by resigning from the Army, and used his time and influence to denigrate King and to further his interests, especially in the future of wool. He thus returned in triumph in 1805 with the promise of 10,000 ac. of his own selection, convict labour and more sheep from King George III's own flock, which he established at Camden Park. He was soon quarrelling with the new autocratic Governor Bligh who arrested him on a trivial charge in December 1807; the trial was chaotic and the tables were turned when Major Johnston* responded to Macarthur's appeal to arrest Bligh and take command in the so-called Rum Rebellion*. Again Macarthur went to Eng. (1811), this time as a witness at Johnston's trial and remained in exile until 1817. Elizabeth remained to look after and develop the farm; but he took his sons and during the 6 years they were educated and travelled Europe with their father, learning especially about wine production, which one of them, William, developed later. Meanwhile Macarthur's nephew Hannibal (1788-1861) was associated with his ventures. Macarthur, while superficially supporting Macquarie (who had treated his wife well and guarded his property in his absence), covertly set about undermining him, by gaining the ear of Commissioner Bigge* and by using his London contacts through his sons there, to vilify him. Increasingly weighed down by illness, his choleric and intemperate personality becoming more and more unpleasant, Macarthur continued to harass Governors Brisbane and Darling, but with less potency, until about 1832, when he lost his reason altogether. His fourth son James (1798-1867) was long an important public figure. *For further reading see* M. H. Ellis: *John Macarthur* (Sydney, 1955).

McArthur River N.T. 16S/136E Rises in the rugged N scarp edge of the Barkly Tableland* and flows (in summer only, in the upper course) for 240 km. NE to Port McArthur in the Gulf of Carpentaria, the lower reaches in swamp and jungle. There are rather poor cattle stations in its basin, but economic development is likely if exploitation proceeds of the large silver/lead/zinc deposits found recently in the valley, 80 km. from Borroloola*.

Macartney, Charles George (1886-1958) b. Maitland, N.S.W. One of the greatest Aus. batsmen with Trumper*, Hill* and Bradman*. He began as an all-rounder, with good slow left-arm bowling, developing after the 1914-18 War into an adventurous although not always consistent batsman. He played 32 Tests against Eng. (1909-26), averaging 43·15 with 5 centuries. In first-class games he totalled 14,217, averaging 47 with 48 centuries.

McAuley, James Phillip (1917-) b. Sydney. A leading modern poet, critic, essayist, Professor of English and editor of the literary journal *Quadrant* since its beginning. Lyricism and even romanticism are to be found, particularly

in McAuley's earlier work, but pellucid and distilled, yet inspired description remain among the happiest passages of even his epic *Captain Quiros* (1964); permeating and transcending these qualities are his constant challenges of sensual experience in the light of intellect, sharpened by empiricism, but deepened by his search for metaphysical values. He was converted to Roman Catholicism in 1952. Like Hope* and Stewart*, he follows the discipline of 18th-century verse forms and that of ancient classic poets. Examples of his work are: *Under Aldebaran* (1946) and *A Vision of Ceremony* (1956) and *Australian Poets: James McAuley* (Sydney, 1963) selected and introduced by McAuley himself. (*See also* ERN MALLEY.)

McCabe, Stanley Joseph (1910-68) b. near Grenfell, N.S.W. A cricketer noted for powerful well-placed batting, especially in 3 great Test innings: 1932 in Sydney against Larwood's 'bodyline' bowling; in 1935 in S Africa and 1938 in Eng. when his total of 232 was scored in one of the finest stands ever made. He played 36 Tests against Eng. (1930-8), averaging 48·27 with 4 centuries. In first-class matches he totalled 11,951, averaging 49·38 with 29 centuries.

McCaughey, Sir Samuel (1835-1919) b. Ballymena, N Ireland. He emigrated in 1856 with an uncle and became a jackeroo* and later acquired a share in Coonong station near Uralla 90 km. NE of Tamworth, where drought made him a pioneer in water conservation, sinking artesian bores and constructing large tanks. After an overseas visit in 1871-3, he experimented with selective breeding of sheep, at first for better wool, then for mutton. By 1880 he owned some 1·2 million ha., and on one of his properties near Bourke, N.S.W., in 1888 was held the first large-scale demonstration of shearing machines. In 1900 he bought Yanco on the Murrumbidgee and pioneered large-scale irrigation there, building 320 km. of channels to water 16,200 ha. In 1905 he consulted Pasteur on possible means of eliminating rabbits. He died a millionaire and a bachelor, leaving very large benefactions.

McCrae, George Gordon (1833–1927) b. Leith, Scotland. He arrived in Melbourne in 1841. His mother was an accomplished artist and a diarist (*Georgiana's Journals*, republished Sydney, 1966). He became a leading literary figure and patron, author of several long narrative poems unknown today. His son **Hugh Raymond** (1876–1958) b. Hawthorn, Vic., was a lyrical and descriptive poet whose work is full of vigour and colour, although based on English inheritance, with little that is intrinsically Aus. His much slighter short stories share a strong vein of humour. He was a lifelong friend of Norman Lindsay* who illustrated some of his poems. *For further reading see The Best Poems of Hugh McCrae* ed. Howarth (Sydney, 1961) and *Hugh McCrae: Selected Poems* (Sydney, 1966).

McCubbin, Frederick (1855–1917) b. Melbourne. A leading artist of the Heidelberg School*, influential through his teaching and noted for soft landscape studies.

Macdonnell Ranges N.T. 24S/133E Parallel ridges of bare red quartzites and sandstones, extending for 160 km. W and NE of Alice Springs. They were formed by pressure from N and S which caused the folds, but uplift has been slow enough for the rivers to keep pace, so that they cut transversely through them in deep spectacular gorges: e.g. Glen Helen, Ormiston Gorge (the Finke Basin), Simpson's Gap, Serpentine Slit (Ellery River) and Standley Chasm*. Rich flora in the gorges contrasts with the arid bare surrounding hills. The E Macdonnells are lower and separated into ranges by the E–W Hale Creek and Plenty River basins; they are more mineralised with gold, mica, beryl, garnet etc. The highest point is in the W Macdonnells: Mt. Zeil 1,511 m. one of a series of peaks in the NW. The ranges were found and named by J. McDouall Stuart in 1860 after the S.A. Governor.

Macedon, Mount Vic. 37S/144E (1,014 m.) A Tertiary volcanic peak, of which a crater to the NE is called the Camel's Hump, about 64 km. NW of Melbourne. At one time it had a summer residence for the Governor, and has fine gardens and homes.

McEwen, Sir John (1900–) b. Chiltern, Vic. Leader of the Country Party and Deputy Prime Minister 1958–71. He was Prime Minister of Aus. from December 1967 to January 1968 between the death of Harold Holt* and the Liberals' selection of John Gorton*. As Minister for Trade, McEwen worked intensively in the expanding field of Aus. trade, notably in international negotiation.

McGrath, Vivian (1918–) b. Mudgee, N.S.W. The first great double-handed tennis player in Aus., developing very young to international status, but retiring at 23. He played for Aus. in the Davis Cup from 1933–7.

McGregor, Kenneth (1929–) b. Adelaide. A tennis player who emerged after the 1939–45 War, using his great height and reach for brilliant shots. He played in Davis Cup* matches 1950–2, won the Wimbledon Doubles with Sedgman* in 1951–2, after which he turned professional. He was also a fine player of Aus. Rules football.

McIlwraith, Sir Thomas (1835–1900) b. Ayr, Scotland. He arrived in Aus. in 1854. Qld. Premier from 1879–83, 1888 and 1893–5. He was a masterful aggressive leader, responsible for an abortive attempt in 1883 to annex N.G.

McIntosh, Hugh Donald (1876–1942) b. Sydney. One of the most colourful Aus. business personalities, who rose from pie-selling to own a prosperous catering business. He became a boxing* promoter, theatre and newspaper-owner. He lived in grandeur in an English country mansion for some years before his empire crashed in the Depression. In 1935, at the suggestion of a fellow Aus., he opened Eng.'s first milk bar, in Fleet St., but died in poverty.

MacIntyre River N.S.W. With its main right-bank tributary the Dumaresq, forms the border with Qld. for 240 km. and is a main headwater of the Darling*. Rising on the granitic W slopes of the New England* plateau, it flows NW then W for 480 km. into 25–40 cm. rainfall country; it turns SW, receives the Weir on the right bank and changes its name to the Barwon*. The river is perennial to below Goondiwindi, Qld., 29S/150E, then sporadic —but flowing through good cattle country.

Mackay Qld. 21S/149E (28,416 in 1971) It lies on both banks and 4·8 km. from the mouth of the Pioneer River, discovered by John Mackay (1860). Within 10 years sugar-growing was firmly established in the district, and Mackay has one of the world's biggest bulk-handling installations at the artificial harbour, 5 km. N of the river mouth. Meat is exported and coal from the new port at Hay Point to the S from Goonyella*.

McKay, Hugh Victor (1865–1926) b. Raywood, Vic. The inventor and maker of Sunshine Harvester. As a boy he worked on combining stripper harvester and winnowing machines, in an old shed on his father's farm (Drummartin, Vic.), patenting his result in 1885; and with a Government Bounty he began production in 1894, first at Ballarat then Braybrook (renamed Sunshine), 16 km. W of Melbourne, exporting up to 9% in the 1900s. He also built an early disc cultivator (1909) and developed R. A. Squire's combined machine for cultivation, seed and fertiliser sowing (1917). He was industrious, persistent and independent, a good if demanding employer, and was the cause of the famous Harvester Judgment*, which in 1907 laid the principle of the Basic Wage.

McKell, Sir William John (1891–   ) b. Pambula, N.S.W. He was the second Aus.-born Governor General (1947–53). He worked as a boilermaker and rose in Labor politics to become N.S.W. Premier 1941–7, stabilising the State Labor Party after Lang*. *See also* V. Kelly: *A Man of the People* (Sydney, 1970).

Mackenzie, Kenneth Ivo (1913–1954) b. Perth. A poet and (as Seaforth Mackenzie) novelist. His work is richly sensual, as in the verse in *The Moonlit Doorway* (Sydney, 1944). He was strongly influenced by Norman Lindsay*.

Mackenzie River Qld. 23S/149E A major seasonal Fitzroy* tributary 275 km. long, formed at the confluence of the Nogoa and Comet Rivers, then cutting through the Expedition Range to receive the Isaacs from the N, and turning S through a wide scrub-covered beef-rearing valley.

Mackenzie, Stuart (1937–   ) b. Sydney. Champion at sculling*, winning the Diamond Sculls at Henley from 1957–62, many European titles and a 1954 Olympics silver medal. His brash flamboyant personality and prolonged rivalry with the Russian Ivanov made him a controversial sporting figure.

Mackerel and **Tuna** (familes Scombridae and Thunnidae, respectively) They form a group of voracious sea-fish, often travelling in schools. They are very swift swimmers, varying greatly in size, from species of 30 cm. to those of 1·2 m. or more, and are greatly esteemed as game-fish. They have in common a beautifully streamlined torpedo shape, generally well-separated back fins, a distinctive rather narrow and crescentic tail, and finlets between tail and rear fins (matched only in the Barracoutas and the Finny Scad in the Trevally group of fish). Most species of Mackerel have scales so fine as to be indistinguishable with the naked eye, and so have a rather slimy feel. Aus. species include: 1. the small iridescent green and deep blue Mackerel, *Pneumatophorus australasicus*; 2. the Qld. School Mackerel, *Scomberomorus queenslandicus*, often of 30–75 cm., the adult form with darker back and irregular rows of bronze-green side blotches; 3. the Spotted Spanish Mackerel, *S. niphonius*, of 55–100 cm. with definite side spots; 4. the Narrow-barred Spanish Mackerel or Qld. Kingfish, *Cybium commerson*, in which the dark iridescent blue-green back gives way to light grey sides and belly with irregular sub-vertical dark grey stripes, usually about 50–60 cm. and 4–4·5 kg. but quite commonly larger; 5. the Broad-banded Spanish Mackerel, *S. semifasciatus*, also a tropical fish, with shorter, well-marked stripes in the adult, and turning grey after death so that it appears in Qld. markets as the Grey Mackerel; 6. the Butterfly Mackerel, *Gasterochisma melampus*, named from the large front under fins of young fish, and in Latin from a special groove on the belly into which they fit; but of normal size in adults.

Aus. Tuna include: 1. the favourite sporting fish, the Southern Bluefin Tuna, *Thunnus maccoyii*, generally only of 3–16 kg., for the much larger adult specimens of 1·2–1·8 m. long probably do not appear much in coastal waters; migrations between Vic. and N.S.W. waters at different stages of maturity have also been proved; 2. the Northern Bluefin, *Kishinoella tonggol*, generally somewhat smaller; 3. the uniformly coloured Albacore, *Thunnus germo*, commonly up to 60–75 cm. and 4·5–8 kg. 4. the striped Tuna or Bonito, *Katsuwonus pelamis*, generally of 3–4·5 kg., with dark stripes along the lower sides and belly; 5. the Small Aus. Bonito or Horse-mackerel (used for bait for Marlin) with dark stripes along the dark back and upper sides.

McKinlay, John (1819–1872) b. Lanarkshire, Scotland. He emigrated to Aus. in 1836. He was sent by the S.A. Government to look for Burke* and Wills in 1861, having acquired a reputation for bushcraft and exploration. He found Grey's grave, then tried to push westwards, but was defeated by Sturt's Stony Desert, so he turned NE to the Gulf and thence the Qld. coast. In 1865 he reported on suitable settlement sites in the Adelaide-Roper River areas of N.T.

McLaren, Jack (1887–1954) b. Melbourne. He ran away to a varied, adventurous life at 17, finally settling in Eng. to write his experiences into adventure tales, notably in *My Crowded Life* (London, 1926, republished Adelaide, 1966), describing 8 years on the W coast of Cape York, trying to establish a coconut plantation with Aboriginal labour.

Macleay, Alexander (1767–1848) b. Ross-shire, Scotland. The very able Colonial Secretary in N.S.W. (1825–37) under Darling and Bourke, quarrelling bitterly with the latter mainly over exclusivist/emancipist disputes. He followed up early entomological interests and had many foreign plants in his ornamental garden at Elizabeth Bay House, built for him in 1832 by Verge*. **William Sharp** (1792–1865), his eldest son, came to Aus. 1838; he was an outstanding naturalist. His third son **Sir George** (1809–1891) accompanied Sturt* in 1829 to the Murray mouth (Rufus River commemorates his red hair). **William John** (1820–1891), his nephew, was a Murrumbidgee squatter who developed much further the Macleay entomological collection, now in Sydney University, adding to it from a N.G. expedition (1875). He also catalogued Aus. fishes (1881–4).

Macleay River N.S.W. 400 km. long, it starts as the Guyra River and topples 275 m. in cascades over the E escarpment of the New England* plateau, flowing S and receiving tributaries with famous waterfalls such as Wollomombi and Chandler, then mainly E, as the Macleay, to the sea in Trial Bay. Much of its catchment is 100–150 cm. rainfall country; its annual average flow at Turner's Flat, 72 km. from the sea, is 1,603 million m.^{3}, and it is liable to flooding, which has in the worst years caused considerable damage to the dairy farms using the lower flood-plains.

McMahon, William (1908–) b. Sydney. Prime Minister of Aus. 1971–2, succeeding Gorton*, having held Ministerial posts over 19 years including Treasury and Foreign Affairs.

McMillan, Angus (1810–1865) b. Skye. He emigrated to Aus. in 1837, to become an explorer and Vic. pioneer. Between 1838 and 1841 he established, with the aid of an Aboriginal guide Jimmy Gibber, a route from the Monaro plains to Bass Str., discovering the Gippsland* region.

Maconochie, Alexander (1787–1860) b. Edinburgh. He arrived in Tas. (1837) as secretary to Sir John Franklin, having been the first Professor of Geography in the University of London (1833–6). He wrote vigorously against the prevailing convict system, advocating the rehabilitation of convicts. He influenced English policy on transportation, but roused bitter opposition in Tas. In charge of Norfolk Island (1840–4) he put his theories into practice with some success. *For further reading see* J. V. Barry: *Alexander Maconochie of Norfolk Island* (Melbourne, 1958).

McPherson Range Qld. 28S/153E 130 km. from E–W, lava-topped, dissected and rain-forested. Its crest line, forming the Qld./N.S.W. border, is tunnelled at Richmond Gap; it contains the 16,000-ha. Lamington National Park, Mt. Lindesay (1,239 m.) and Mt. Barney (1,336 m.).

Macquarie Harbour Tas. 42S/145E An inlet extending 32 km. NW–SE, and

about 8 km. wide inside its narrow entrance at Hell's Gates, named from the strong tidal race. This remote forested W coast area was chosen for a penal settlement, replacing Norfolk Island* (1821–34). It was notorious for its attempted escapes. The inlet is a downfaulted trough, modified by glaciation.

Macquarie Island 54S/159E Extending 34 km. by 3 km., and with nearby rocky islets, this is a dependency of Tas. Members of an Aus. Antarctic Expedition lived there from 1911–15 and an A.N.A.R.E.* base has been maintained since 1948. It was officially discovered in 1810, and seals and penguins were slaughtered for oil until reserved from 1933.

Macquarie, Lachlan (1762–1824) b. Ulva, Scotland. N.S.W. Governor from 1810–22, after army service in America and India, becoming Major-General (1813). He lost his first wife at Macao (1796) and remarried (1807), having bought a Mull estate. In 1808 he was sent to N.S.W. to restore order, following the deposing of Bligh. During his period of office he reduced the use of rum for currency, introducing old Spanish dollars for this purpose, tried to improve the moral life of the colony by stern sabbatarian rules, set up the Bank of N.S.W., educational institutions, encouraged exploration beyond the Blue Mts., and had a road built within a year of their breaching. He envisaged a land of close settlement with small, agricultural holdings, and opposed large estates for wool growing. Under him the first fine buildings were erected, with many designs by Greenway*, and in general he believed in encouraging emancipists*. Thus he made enemies, notably of Marsden*, the Macarthurs* and Bents*. These powerful leaders sent complaints of extravagance, as well as against his emancipist and settlement policies to London, which resulted in the commissioning of Bigge* to report on the state of the colony. He resigned, leaving the colony in 1822 after a heart-warming farewell tour; for he almost pathetically sought approval. He was not permitted to publish any justification after the predominantly hostile Bigge Report came out, and retired to Mull, disillusioned and embittered. To many he was as much a father of Aus. as his arch-enemy Macarthur. *For further reading see* M. H. Ellis: *Lachlan Macquarie* (Sydney, 1952); M. Barnard: *Macquarie's World* (Melbourne, 1947).

Macquarie, Lake N.S.W. A branching coastal lagoon SW of Newcastle, 33S/152E, discovered in 1800. It is formed by the virtual blocking of 3 small branching estuaries by a dune-crowned coastal sand barrier. The fishing, holiday and small industrial town of Swansea is beside the narrow entrance, and the lake is ringed by suburbs of Newcastle and used by Vales Point and Pantaloon Bay power stations.

Macquarie River N.S.W. A headwater of the Darling* some 970 km. long, rising on the W slopes of the Dividing Range, cutting NW through the sheep and wheat lands of the plateau, past Bathurst*, 33S/150E, and Dubbo*. It becomes increasingly seasonal in régime, disappearing in the Macquarie Marshes which drain to the Barwon, and which deflected Oxley eastwards (1818) when he was following up its discovery by Evans (1813). He thought they marked the shore of a shallow inland sea. A major storage of 1,680 million m.³ behind Burrendong Dam, 24 km. from Wellington was completed in 1965, but did not fill until 1967 because of drought. Lions Island is a 80-ha. wildlife reserve.

Madigan, Cecil Thomas (1889–1947) b. Renmark, S.A. After serving with Mawson* in the Antarctic, and in the Sudan, Madigan, while teaching geology at Adelaide University, made an aerial reconnaissance of Central Aus. in 1929, followed by land exploration. In 1939 he traversed the Simpson Desert*.

Maffra Vic. 38S/147E (3,569 in 1971) On the lower Macalister River and heart of the irrigated dairy lands, this is primarily a rapidly growing service centre for the closely settled countryside, and has butter and cheese factories. It was named by a veteran of the Peninsular Wars after Mafra, Portugal.

Magnetic Island Qld. 19S/147E 64 km.² and 6·5 km. offshore from Townsville, it was named by Cook because of compass variations which he blamed (wrongly) on iron on the island; it is granitic, rising to 496 m. in Mt. Cook, now developing as a launch-commuter suburb of Townsville.

Magnetic Termite Mounds These are so called because they are oriented N–S; they are also wrongly called ant-hills. (*See* TERMITES.)

Magpie-lark A popular name for the familiar mud-nesting Mudlark* or Peewee.

Magpies, Currawongs and **Butcher-birds** (family Cracticidae) There are about 10 Aus. and N.G. species, crow-like birds, with long straight beaks, slightly downcurved at the end, pied, or predominantly black or grey, which build bowl-shaped nests of sticks, twigs etc. in trees, and eat mainly insects —the Currawong also eats fruit. They range in size from about 25–45 cm. and vary widely in habitat, but perhaps the most familiar species are birds of open forest and suburban gardens. The calls of the Currawong (contained in the name) and the curious rolling, twanging melody of the White-backed and Black-backed Magpies, are amongst the bird calls most prized and nostalgic to the Aus. of bush or town. The Magpie genus is *Gymnorhina* (bare-nosed), White-backed is *G. hypoleuca*, and the Black-backed, *G. tibicen* (flute-playing). The Pied Butcher-bird, *Cracticus* (loud-voiced) *nigrogularis* (black-throated), is smaller, with a white abdomen and rump, and a widely appreciated song. Related species have a more regional distribution. The Pied Currawong, *Strepera graculina* (jackdaw-like chatterer), is about 46 cm. long, a common visitor to gardens and an unwelcome one to orchards. Related species are more or less pied, grey or jet black, and between them cover much of Aus. (*See* PLATE 4.)

Mahogany The name is used in Aus. of various trees usually yielding good reddish timber, though some species are seldom of millable size and shape. The Red, Southern and Swamp Mahoganies, all Eucalypts of E and coastal Aus. are discussed under Blue Gums* (Eastern Group). White Mahogany or Yellow Stringybark, *Eucalyptus mantha*, is a good timber tree of 30–40 m. by 0·9–1·2 m., growing on varied sites under 300 m. altitude in the 60–125 cm. coastal rainfall belt of N N.S.W. and Qld. as far N as Atherton. It has a stringy close-grained persistent bark, broadly lanceolate seedling and intermediate leaves, and much narrower adult leaves, glossy green above, lighter below. There are small clusters of narrow pointed buds about 13 mm. long, and cup-shaped fruit about 6 mm. across. The Mahogany family proper, the Meliaceae, is represented among the tropical and sub-tropical broadleaved trees of Aus., e.g. by the Red Cedar*, *Cedrela australis*. The name Mahogany is also used for *Tristania conferta*, the Brush Box* of the Myrtle* family. The Dundas Mahogany is *Eucalyptus brockwayi*.

Main Range Qld. 28S/153E The chief part of the Qld. Eastern Highlands where the Great Divide coincides with the highest and most outstanding mountain range (over 1,200 m.). It is a NW–SE trending basaltic escarpment between the Moreton lowland and Darling Downs. Cunningham's* Gap (1828), a steep defile, has recently been developed into an important highway.

Maitland N.S.W. 33S/151E (24,530 in 1971) A city and main centre of the dairy lands of the lower Hunter River*

valley, 24 km. NW of Newcastle. Here, the river emerges on to the wide flood-plain, where the busy commercial centre and some suburbs are repeatedly isolated by flooding; it is the rail junction for Brisbane–Hunter Valley lines and the privately owned line to the South Maitland coal-field towns. Maitland includes older townships such as Morpeth, 8 km. E and head of Hunter Navigation, formerly an important river port; East Maitland, the original settlement; residential suburbs such as Largs and Telarah on higher ground; Lorn and the present central business districts on the flood-plain, from which houses are being gradually removed. West Maitland was earlier called Molly Morgan's* Plains. There are textile factories and farm-based industries.

Maize (*Zea mays*—Indian corn) It is relatively unimportant crop grown as fodder on the black soils of Darling Downs and Atherton Tableland in Qld. and alluvial flats in N.S.W. Primarily a pig food, it is given to sheep in droughts, and increasingly ensilaged, especially in the S.

Mallacoota Inlet Vic. 38S/150E 8 km. E of Genoa, this is a well-known system of drowned valleys in the Ordovician slate country W of Cape Howe, and in wet sclerophyll* forest. Boating, fishing and tourism are important. At times the mouth is closed by a sand bar.

Mallee An Aboriginal and popular Aus. word to describe many species of Eucalypts with a characteristic growth form. Several slender trunks arise from a large underground, woody lignotuber, which was a source of water to the Aborigines. When the lignotuber is poorly developed the tree is called a marlock. The name is also used for vegetation dominated by Mallee Eucalypts in 25 to 50-cm. mean annual rainfall belt of Aus. Of the numerous *Eucalyptus* species called 'Mallee', *E. oleosa*, Giant, Red or Oil Mallee, is one of the most widespread, growing on loam soils in the 30–40 cm. rainfall area. It may also form, like many Mallees, a single-trunked tree up to 12 m. high. The bark is rough at the base, smooth and ribbony above, the young leaves glaucous, lanceolate, in pairs, the adult thick, pale, glossy, alternate and rich in oil. The roots of some species, when dug up, cut in lengths and set on end, yield water in emergency. Mallee flowers include Daisy Bush *Olearia* spp. For Mallee Fowl *see* LOWAN.

Mallee Region The distinctive vegetation association has given its name to a region of NW Vic. covering about 40,000 km.^{2} between the Wimmera and Murray Rivers, and extending over the border into the SE of S.A. as far as the Mt. Lofty Range. Former extensive wheat-farming, based on the stump-jump plough, led to wind erosion of the rolling sand-hills which overlie limestone base rocks. The mallee is residual except where preserved as in Wyperfeld National Park. The low variable rainfall averages 25–30 cm., but the soils are rich although lacking nitrogen and phosphate. The region has been transformed by water brought to the southern half by the Wimmera*–Mallee Domestic and Stock Supply (1953), which feeds farm dams through 16,000 km. of channels; there are sub-artesian bores in the S and W, water from the Murray in the N obtained by lifting, and even some fed westwards from the Goulburn River*.

About 25,000 km.^{2} are supplied all together. Dry farming for wheat, with rotation to avoid leaving bare ground, is supplemented by irrigated fodder and stock-farming with lucerne and lupins on the sand-hills, while the mallee landscape has vanished completely along the Murray under the intensive irrigation of vine and citrus fruits of Sunraysia*, Renmark and on the lower Murray. Urban centres not on the river are small.

Mallow The popular name for the widespread Malvaceae family, is sometimes applied to various *Hibiscus* spp. in Aus.

Mammals Animals suckling their young, more or less hairy, and giving birth to active young except for the egg-laying Monotremes* (3 species unique to Aus.). There are some 150 species of native Aus. Placental Mammals (mainly Rodents* and Bats*, with the marine mammals, Whales* Dolphins*, Dugong*, Sea-lions and Seals*). The Dingo* may be the first of the introduced mammals*, but recent introductions include Deer (mainly Fallow Deer and Sambar, causing crop damage locally, but much less disastrous than the Red Deer introduced to N.Z.), the Fox (a new predator causing the extinction or near-extinction of several small marsupials), the Hare—a relatively harmless introduction compared with its relative the Rabbit*, and several species of Rats and Mice (*see* RODENTS). Several domestic animals have become feral including the Buffalo of N Aus., Cattle, Horses (Brumbies), Donkeys, Camels and Goats, and Dogs and Cats. Main source for mammals, E. Troughton: *Furred Animals of Australia* (Sydney, 1962).

Man with the Donkey (John Simpson Kirkpatrick) (1893–1915) b. Durham, Eng. He arrived in Aus. in 1910, enlisting as Private Simpson (1914). He became a legendary figure at Gallipoli* when, over 25 days until he was killed, he rescued an unknown but large number of wounded, using a stray donkey. *For further reading see* I. Benson: *Man with the Donkey* (London, 1965).

Mandurah W.A. 33S/116E (5,039 in 1971) Dating from Peel's* unsuccessful settlement in 1829, it lies at the narrow mouth of the Peel Inlet and is a service centre, fishing and holiday town.

Manganese Essential in the steel industry, it is mined in the Pilbara region, 21S/118E, and Peak Hill, 26S/119E., in W.A., Groote Eylandt*, N.T., now produces 85%. Some goes to Bell Bay, Tas. to make ferromanganese. Exports are estimated at $20 million in 1975.

Mangroves A group of bushes and trees, not all closely related botanically, which live in muddy coastal swamps and deltas in the tropics and sub-tropics. Adaptations to growth in airless mud and high salt contents include aerial stilt roots and surface roots, raft-like development of shallow roots in the mud, from which pneumatophores, 'breathing roots' or 'cobblers' pegs', are sent upwards to the surface. Seeds often germinate on the plant before being dropped into the tidal muds, ready to take root rapidly between tides. Most mangroves have rather small oval to lanceolate leaves, rather thick and leathery, and sometimes with glands which secrete salt, or with hairy undersides.

Aus. has 8 species of the mainly tropical Rhizophoraceae, including the Red Mangrove, *Rhizophora mangle*—exploited for fuel etc. in SE Asia, the Black Mangrove, *Bruguiera* spp., the small (90–120 cm.) Orange Mangrove, *Ceriops* spp., and *Carallia* spp. (one, *C. brachiata* is a rain-forest tree). The Grey or White Mangrove, *Avicennia marina*, belongs to the widespread tropical family Verbenaceae. It has not the stilt roots of the Red Mangrove, but sheds live seedlings and has shallow roots which send up cobblers' pegs; it is able to take root quickly, and therefore is the great coloniser of new mud-flats, seen in many extra-tropical muddy shores in Aus. The River Mangrove, *Aegiceras corniculatum*, again in a different family, the Myrsinaceae, widespread in warmer climates, has showy white flowers and sheds live seeds. Other species found in the mangrove vegetation association in Aus. though not to be classed as mangroves, include *Heriteria macrophylla*, in the Sterculia-

ceae family of pod-bearers, with very buoyant and therefore easily spread seeds—a buttressed tree, and the stemless palm *Nipa fruticans*. The Aus. Conservation Foundation has expressed concern over destruction of mangroves by coastal development.

Manifold, John (1915–) b. Melbourne. A journalist and poet who began with ballads; he is a leading folksong collector and singer, writes left-wing political poetry and edits 16th-century musical works.

Manjimup W.A. 34S/116E (3,523 in 1971) Sawmilling town and the market and service centre of a closely settled region cleared among karri forests. Tobacco growing (1930–65) has now been replaced by potatoes and dairying, with peach and apple orchards. It was the first, and a successful Group Settlement*.

Manly N.S.W. 34S/151E (39,250 in 1971) A Sydney dormitory and surfing suburb on a sand spit between North Head and the mainland. Manly Cove was named by Phillip, who was impressed by the bearing of the Aborigines; the ocean beaches lined with exotic Norfolk pines and over-looked by blocks of flats are liable to storm erosion.

Mann, Cecil McDonald (1896–) b. Cudgeon, N.S.W. A journalist and writer, mainly of small-town short stories of quiet skill and human penetration, as in *The River and Other Stories* (Sydney, 1945).

Mann, Leonard (1895–) b. Melbourne, A poet and novelist of considerable stature, writing with rough, sincere humanism and realism, with good characterisation, as in *Mountain Flat* (London, 1939), on family relationships set in a rural community, *The Go Getter* (Sydney, 1942,) set in Melbourne during the Depression, and his war novel *Flesh in Armour* (Melbourne, 1932).

Manna Gum (*Eucalyptus viminalis*) It is at its best a handsome tree of 30–36

m. or more, growing at its best on well-drained valley bottom podsols in hilly parts of N.S.W., Vic. and S.A., but yielding only fairly durable timber which is liable to warping. It has narrow juvenile leaves mostly in opposite pairs, narrowly lanceolate adult leaves, groups of 3 narrow ovoid buds and top-shaped fruit. The crown is open and spreading, with branchlets drooping. A favourite food of the koala.

Manning River N.S.W. Flows E for some 225 km. from the 100–150 cm. rainfall country of Barrington Tops (over 1,200 m. high) and Mt. Royal Range*, with many tributaries, and at Killawarra after 160 km. (catchment there 650,000 ha.) it has an average annual flow of 2,467 million m.[3]. Below Taree, 32S/152E, is a well-marked delta, the chief distributary being Harrington Inlet, with prosperous dairying for the Newcastle market on the deltaic islands.

Mannix, Most Rev. Daniel (1864–1963) b. Ireland. He arrived in Aus. in 1912. Roman Catholic Archbishop of Melbourne (1917–63). In a long career, this outspoken Irish churchman influenced the Irish Catholics of Vic., and all Aus. by his violently expressed views: in the 1914–18 War against conscription, and in later years in anti-Communist campaigns, a result of which was the 1955 split of the Aus. Labor Party*.

Mannum S.A. 35S/139E (2,036 in 1971) Developed as major river port of the lower Murray, and although bypassed by railways, it was revived later as the main service centre for the downstream dairy lands of Mypolonga and Jervois. Irrigation areas total 4,800 ha., with smaller schemes on floodplain swamps, which have been reclaimed and irrigated since 1881. Adelaide gets 60% of its water via the Mannum pipeline (1954) which rises to 450 m. over the Mt. Lofty Range on its 84-km. journey.

Mantids The bright green 3-cm.-long Praying Mantis, *Orthodera ministralis*, familiar in gardens, is placed in the Sub-Order Mantodea of the Order Dyctoptera (*see* COCKROACHES). This is a carnivorous insect, eating flies etc. The long body is well camouflaged, and it waits in the 'praying' position, upraised on the 2 rear pairs of long legs and with uplifted front legs armed with cutting edges and holding-hooks, ready to strike downwards to slash and hold the victim for leisurely consumption.

Manufacturing Industry (including repair and maintenance work, e.g. on shoes, cars etc.) This employs almost 25% of the work force in Aus., as compared with under 10% in rural industry. Though there are some differences and difficulties of classification, Aus. is one of the most highly industrial countries in the world; development is often ascribed to tariff* policy. It is a largely derivative industry in the sense of using mainly imported technology, and much of the capital and associated control is from overseas (*see* COMPANIES). Rates of growth and productivity are among the better, but not among the very highest in the world. There are disadvantages of the small population, its relative isolation, separation of the chief inhabited areas by long distances, the surplus capacity installed by foreign firms in order to get ahead of competitors, the high labour turnover, and complex arbitration* system, some restrictive trade practices and price-fixing. Advantages include importation of tried and proved techniques, perhaps even improved, and the high standards of the labour force. An increasing proportion of home demand can be met with products of good and improving quality, if rather high prices, accounting for 28% of the gross national product, but only about 12% (now increasing) of the exports.

Of the 1·3 million factory employees, 40% are in N.S.W., 34% in Vic., 9% in

Qld., 9% S.A., 5% W.A. and 3% Tas. Of the total employees, 45% are in industrial metals, machines and conveyances, 11% in food, drink and tobacco, 9% in clothing (other than knitted), 6% in textiles (not dresses etc.), 6% in paper, stationery, printing, 5% in sawmills, wood-turnery; 4% in chemicals, followed by bricks, pottery and glass, treatment of non-metalliferous ores, furniture, rubber, skins and leather, and miscellaneous manufactures.

In each State, high proportions of manufacturing industry are in the capitals: Adelaide and Melbourne 80%, Sydney 74%, Perth 69%, Brisbane 53% and Hobart 33% (much of the industry of Tas. is metal smelting, timber and pulp, using hydro-electric power and located away from Hobart). Despite varying encouragement to decentralisation in different States, by subsidy, preferential freight rates etc., industry as a whole is very strongly drawn to the metropolitan centres by the market, by their port function, the variety of labour available and by the advantages of association with other industries. However, some tend to be located at the source of materials (timber, fruit-canning, dairy factories), especially if there is loss of weight in processing; but changes occur with technological progress, as in iron* and steel. Grain milling is becoming more concentrated in metropolitan centres. Industries based on by-products are a special case, as are aluminium* smelting or carbide manufacture which use power almost as a raw material. At the other extreme are industries strongly attached to quite a local market and dispersed into almost every town of any size, especially if there is a gain in weight in the process or a bulky, heavy or fragile product. Despite the tendency towards factory production of bread, bakeries are still active in nearly every town, and aerated water and cordial factories almost as dispersed. The Aus. Industry Develop-

ment Corporation (1971) assists viable Aus. ventures in manufacturing, mining and processing. *See* A. Hunter, ed.: *The Economics of Australian Industry* (Melbourne, 1963), a major work used also for entries on individual industries.

Mapping The 540-sheet topographic series of Aus. at 1:250,000 scale was completed in 1968 by the Commonwealth Division of National Mapping. Topographic mapping is co-ordinated by the National Mapping Council representing the main mapping organisations: the Division of National Mapping, the Royal Aus. Survey Corps, Royal Aus. Navy Hydrographic Branch and Departments of Lands. Major topographic map series by Commonwealth mapping organisations are at scales of 1:1,000,000, 1:250,000, and 1:100,000. Whilst the aim for the 1:100,000 series is complete coverage of the continent by 1978, maps will be printed for only the more densely inhabited areas round the periphery, that is about half the total area. About 25% of this area were completed by 1972 The Royal Aus. Survey Corps also carries out some larger scale mapping of selected areas, mainly at scales of 1:50,000, 1:25,000 and 1:10,000.

State mapping is mainly at large scales e.g. 1:50,000 and 1:25,000 topographic and detailed cadastral maps at various scales. Before the introduction of metric scales, much State mapping was at 1:31,680. The Division of National Mapping is cooperating with States to produce urban maps 1:10,000 mainly for census purposes.

The Commonwealth Bureau of Mineral Resources, Geology and Geophysics and State Geological Surveys are responsible for systematic geological mapping. By 1972 80% of Aus. was covered at scale 1:250,000; completion is planned by 1979. Systematic regional gravity coverage based on readings at 11 km. grid intervals completed 1973 will be available at 1:500,000.

Land classification reconnaissance maps of large areas notably the sparsely peopled north, mainly at 1:1,000,000 have been made by C.S.I.R.O*. *The Atlas of Aus. Resources* has 30 progressively revised map sheets and commentaries by the former Dept. of National Development. All Aus. is covered by aerial photography 80% being super wide angle, each photo covering about 300 km.^{2} at scale 1:80,000. Most of Aus. is covered by mosaics at 1:250,000 or 1:63,360 and lithographed photo-indexes at 1:100,000. A 12-year project (1971) will cover bathymetric mapping of the continental shelf at scale 1:250,000. The Hydrographic Branch of the Royal Aus. Navy prepares coastal charts. The first of 170 maps of 2·4 million km^2 of Aus. continental shelf appeared in 1973.

Maralinga S.A. 30S/131E U.K. rocket-testing site on the N edge of the Nullarbor plain, and named from an Aboriginal word meaning thunder.

Marble Deposits are being worked in the Ashburton area of W.A. 23S/116E, for export to Italy and Israel from Port Hedland.

Marble Bar W.A. 21S/120E On the Coongan River, a sporadic left-bank tributary of the de Grey River*, and named from a bar of jasper in the creek bed, when a shanty town grew here round alluvial gold deposits in 1888. Allegedly the hottest Aus. town, it may have weeks of temperatures consistently over 37°C.

Mareeba Qld. 17S/145E (5,169 in 1971) A centre for irrigated tobacco and service centre on the Atherton Tableland.

Maria Island Tas. 43S/148E It extends 19 km. N–S and up to 8 km. E–W, and comprises 2 sections linked by a narrow sandy isthmus. It was named after the wife of Van Diemen. A penal colony at Darlington on the N coast (1825–32) had a clothing factory and farms; the island was also a sealing and whaling centre. In 1887 a

private company began development for vines and cement works, which closed in 1930. It is now run as a wildlife reserve.

Marine Worms (of Aus.) These include 3 Phyla. 1. Segmented or Annelid Worms, Phylum Annelida: (a) Lugworms, *Arenicola* spp., somewhat resembling earthworms, in wet beach sands; (b) Bristle-worms, with several antennae and bristles on each segment, include (i) wet sand species, e.g. the Surf Bait Worm, *Onuphis teres*, the formidably jawed beach worm often sought by the surf fisherman with a fish-bait and a pair of pliers to catch the worm behind the head when it extends it out of the sand towards the bait; (ii) Bristle-worms living in tubes fixed to rocks, such as the beautiful Feather-duster Worm, *Sabellastarte indica*; (iii) Free-living Bristle worms, such as the world-wide genus *Nereis*, with 2 tentacles, 2 feelers and 2 horny jaws, and the stinging *Eurythoe* of the Great Barrier Reef. 2. Flatworms of the Phylum Platyhelminthes, free-living relatives of the parasitic Flukes*, include the pests of oyster beds, the *Leptoplana* spp., and the coloured Banded Magic Carpet Worm, *Pseudoceros corralophilus* (white with an edge of orange-brown, black and yellow), named from its graceful gliding motion and seen in the Great Barrier Reef. 3. Ribbon Worms, Phylum Nemertea, like long narrow flatworms but with a long narrow sticky proboscis protruded and retracted in the search for food, almost like a lasso. The prey includes Bristle Worms. Ribbon Worms include the Orange Ribbon Worm, *Gorgonorhynchus repens*.

Marion or **Marion du Fresne, Nicholas** A French Captain and explorer, the first European after Tasman to visit Tas. (1772); he unintentionally clashed with the Aborigines.

Maritime Strike (August–November, 1890) This precipitated Australia's bitterest period of strikes*. The ship-owners refused wage negotiations to the Marine Officers Association if they affiliated with the Trades Hall Council (an association of small unions success-ful in negotiation before). Seamen supported the officers' strike, and it spread to miners, transport workers and, in September, to shearers who were trying to establish a 'closed shop'. Over 50,000 workers were 'out' over a 2 to 8-week period, and the eastern States were almost paralysed. Troops were out in Melbourne in August, and in Sydney, in November, they dispersed a crowd of 10,000 gathered when squatters tried to load non-union wool; the Riot Act was read. The £50,000 funds were not enough and the strikes failed. In March 1891, Qld. shearers gathered in strike camps flying the Eureka flag, but they too had to give in. (*See* TRADE UNIONS.)

Marlins Notable and large game-fish of SE Aus. and other waters. (*See* SWORD-FISHES AND MARLINS.)

Marree S.A. 30S/138E (683 in 1971) Settlement in thinly peopled pastoral country and desert at the point where the Birdsville Track* reaches the Alice Springs–Port Augusta railway. It was the main camel caravan centre and an inter-state Customs post. Since 1958 when the standard-gauge line from Port Augusta replaced the 3-ft. 6-in. line via Quorn, it has also been a gauge break and has grown.

Marsden, Samuel (1764–1838) b. Farsley, Yorkshire. Son of a black-smith. He arrived in N.S.W. (1794) as assistant to Chaplain Johnson and for 30 years was a colourful controversial and influential personality in the colony. As a priest, he was vitriolic in his condemnations, while apparently deeply sincere in his beliefs. From 1814 he was increasingly concerned with establishing N.Z. Missions, although doing little for Aus. Aborigines. As a magistrate, he was brutal in his sentences, earning criticism and hatred for the floggings he ordered. As a farmer, he pioneered sheep-breeding almost as much as Macarthur* and acquired a large property and fortune from this and from trading. In politics he wrote in support of Bligh* in 1808 (being in Eng. at the time), blaming Macarthur whom he hated. He quar-relled with Macquarie, especially over his emancipist policy (and with succeed-ing Governors Darling and Brisbane). His influence waned with the decline of the 'exclusivist'* faction. *For further reading see* S. M. Johnstone: *Samuel Marsden* (Sydney, 1932).

Marshall, Alan (1902–   ) b. Noorat, Vic. A journalist and writer of sensi-tivity, widely translated, mainly known for his courageous personality, humour and short stories, as in *Tell Us About the Turkey, Joe* (Sydney, 1946), and *I Can Jump Puddles* (1955).

MARSUPIAL ANIMALS Pouched mammals* of the Order Marsupiala, producing young at a very early stage of development and with special adap-tations, e.g. strong forepaws (even if rear paws are stronger in adult life as in the kangaroos) to enable them to crawl unaided to the mother's pouch in which they are suckled until they are viable in the outside world. Excep-tionally, some marsupials lack the pouch and the young adhere to a well-developed mammary area. (On the other hand the non-marsupial Spiny Ant-eater*, a Monotreme*, has a pouch for egg-brooding.) There are marsupials in the Americas, including the American Opossums, and there are fossil remains of marsupials in Europe; so it is held that the Marsupalia must have come to Aus. (and N.G., but not N.Z.) by a land bridge, as part of a fauna dominated by small marsupials and rodents, there to flourish and diversify in what became a relatively isolated realm, poor in later-evolved mammalian carnivores and herbivores which might have offered competition.

From ancestral stem-forms such as the insectivorous pouched mice or pigmy Possums, common descent is shown by a characteristic flanged lower jaw not found in higher animals, and there have evolved marsupials of a remarkable variety in size and habit, from as small as mice to kangaroos taller than a man, and including not only the hopping species commonly associated with the order but also burrowing, climbing and even gliding species; and not only the dominant herbivorous species but a minority of interesting insect- or flesh-eaters. These last include the insect and flesh-eating Marsupial Mice*, the Native Cats*, the Tasmanian Devil* and the Thylacine* (all in the family Dasyuridae); the Numbat* or Banded Termite-eater (Myrmecobiidae); the Marsupial Mole* (Noctoryctidae); the mixed-feeding Bandicoots (Peramelidae); and the American Opossums (family Didelphyidae). In contrast, are the Possums* and the Koala* (Phalangeridae), the Wombat* (Phascolomidae), and to conclude this distinctively Aus. and predominatly vegetarian Sub-Order, the species adapted to rapid hopping with great development of the rear paws, the Wallabies* and Kangaroos* (Macropodidae). For further reading see G. Lyne: Marsupials and Monotremes of Australia (Sydney, 1967); Part 5 of G. G. Simpson's The Geography of Evolution (Philadelphia, 1965); and B. J. Marlow: Marsupials of Australia (Brisbane, 1962).

Marsupial Cats or **Native** and **Tiger Cats** (family Dasyuridae) These include tree-climbing native and tiger cats, weasel-like to cat-like, of the following genera. 1. The Eastern Native Cat, Dasyurus, with only one species D. viverrinus, is superficially like a small light to dark brown domestic cat with white spots, having forefeet with 5 toes and hindfeet with 4 toes, but with an open pouch, at least when young are present, and up to 8 teats for

broods of up to 24, supernumerary young, which die at birth. It eats fish, insects, small lizards, birds and mammals, occasionally poultry, but also, it is believed, many rats and mice. It was formerly widespread in Tas. and

Little Northern Native Cat (Satanellus hallucatus), about 40 cm. nose to tail

coastal N.S.W., Vic. and S.A., but following disease in 1901–3, it has disappeared from much of its range though still found around Sydney. 2. the Western Native Cat, Dasyurinus geoffroii, now occurs only in W.A. and D. geoffroii fortis is not uncommon in SW of W.A., scavenging fish along the shore, sometimes raiding poultry and breeding in outer Perth suburbs, where the Aboriginal name Chuditch is often used. 3. The Little Northern Native Cat, Satanellus, again with only one species S. hallucatus though with several regional races, is a rather bushy-tailed and arboreal form, spread from Cape York and Groote Eylandt to the Kimberley area of W.A. 4. The largest of the marsupial cats, the Tiger Cat or Spotted-tailed Native Cat, genus Dasyurops, includes the larger species D. maculatus, which is over 100 cm. long, with the tail, and has serrated toe-pads well adapted to climbing; it is a skilful stalker and rather wasteful butcher, e.g. in a poultry-yard. It is found from about Cairns, Qld., to SE S.A., and fairly commonly in the Sydney region in recent years. The Little Spotted-tailed Native Cat, D. maculatus gracilis, from N Qld. is smaller.

Marsupial Mice and **Rats** Superficially they resemble various true rodents* but, pouch apart, they lack the rodents' opposed pairs of long incisors. The marsupial family *Dasyuridae* includes the Native Cats*, the Tasmanian Devil* and the Thylacine*, but the sub-family Phascogalinae or 'pouched-weasels', animals of sizes from about that of shrew or mouse to rat or weasel includes the following genera. 1. *Antechinus*, e.g. *A. flavipes*, the Yellow-footed Marsupial Mouse, is very widely endemic in Aus. 2. *Planigale* or Flat-skulled Marsupial Mice are adapted to sliding into cracks in rock or dried earth or between coarse tussocky grass stems; the W.A. species *P. subtilissima* is probably the smallest existing marsupial. 3. *Phascogale* spp. are the Brush-tailed Marsupial Rats (literally 'pouched weasels' which they resemble in lithe strength and blood-thirstiness), e.g. *P. tapoatafa*, a drawing of which appeared in John White's* journal of the Sydney Cove settlement in 1790

Yellow-footed Marsupial Mouse (Antechinus flavipes), about 5 cm. long

under the Aboriginal name of tapoa-tafa, which is now happily absorbed into the Latin zoological nomenclature; it eats farmyard mice but sometimes also poultry. W.A. species are known by the Aboriginal name of Wambenger. 4. *Dasycercus*, or Crest-tailed Marsu-pial Mice, are desert species: the Western Crest-tail, *D. blythi*, and the Mulgara, *D. cristicauda*, which has been observed to tolerate a mouse in its burrow, until hungry, then to kill and eat it. 5. *Dasyuroides byrnei* from SW Qld. is much larger with 5-toed forefeet and 4-toed hindfeet.

The genera listed as 1 to 4 comprise the broad-footed running or climbing species; No. 5 has some transitional characteristics, and the following gen-era 6 and 7 are narrow-footed and adapted to a more or less complete hopping action. 6. *Sminthopsis* or Narrow-footed Marsupial Mice com-prise numerous species in mainland Aus., one in Tas. and one in the Aru Islands and N.G., including Fat-tailed Sminthopsis, *S. crassicaudata*, once widely distributed from SW Aus. to S Qld., but probably now restricted by predation by domestic and feral cats. 7. *Antechinomys* or Jerboa-marsupials have greatly enlarged feet and pads to assist kangaroo-like hopping (forelimbs with 5 toes, hind-limbs with 4 toes), a rear-facing pouch and large ears. Superficially they resemble the placental Aus. Hopping-mice (*see under* RODENTS). There are only 2 species known, the Eastern, *A. laniger*, which is widely distributed in the interior of Vic., N.S.W. and Qld., but so nocturnal that it is seldom seen, and the somewhat larger Central desert species, *A. spenceri*, whose movements seen in the moonlight near Charlotte Waters, include leaps of almost 2 m. by animals only a few centimetres long.

Marsupial Mole A small, sightless, burrowing marsupial in the family Notoryctidae, of which only 2 species are known, *Notoryctes typhlops* (blind-eyed), found in a wide area of central and southern Aus. and *N. caurinus* found in the NW. The first specimen known to science was caught in 1888 on Idracowra station between Char-lotte Waters and Alice Springs. About 15 cm. long, including the short leathery tail used for leverage underground, the animal has a horny shield on the snout, used for pushing sandy soil aside, completely sightless lens-shaped residual eyes embodied in the face, slit-like nostrils, and small lobeless earopenings, beneath the white to goldenred fur, a marsupial pouch pointing backwards, and short stout limbs, with 5 digits on forepaw and hindpaw, of which the third and fourth on each paw have greatly enlarged nails to act as combined pick and shovel. Occasionally emerging above ground, the animal leaves a curious 3-fold track with its body and 2 trails from its paws. It has a strong superficial resemblance to the African Golden Moles (family Chrysochloridae), though these are evolved from much higher up the mammalian tree.

Martens, Conrad (1801–1878) b. Eng. An artist. He arrived in Aus. in 1835 after serving as a topographer on the survey vessel *Beagle**. He was the first settler to live mainly from painting and art-teaching. His watercolours of the Sydney area, including country houses, are of intrinsic merit and considerable historical value.

Martin, Sir James (1820–1886) b. County Cork, Ireland. He arrived in Aus. in 1821. Premier of N.S.W. from 1863–5, 1866–8 and 1870–2. He entered law and was also a noted journalist, author of youthful essays, editor of the newspaper *Atlas* and Chief Justice of N.S.W. from 1873–86. Martin was one of the key personalities (with Cowper, Robertson and Parkes) in the turbulent politics of N.S.W. in the later part of the 19th century.

Martins Birds of the swallow family (*see* SWALLOWS AND MARTINS).

Maryborough Qld. 26S/153E (19,962 in 1971) A city, port and industrial centre, 37 km. upstream on the Mary River; it is also the service and market centre for a wide farming area with beef and dairy cattle, sugar and fruit. Industry is dominated by manufacture of mining and sugar-mill machinery, locomotives and ships, and by saw-

mills. A deepsea port at Urangan handles larger ships.

Maryborough Vic. 37S/144E (7,469 in 1971) A city in the Central Uplands. Developed as a gold town, with 30,000 people in 1854, when it was named from the hometown of the Irish Police Commissioner. Now a cattle centre; also with woollen, engineering and dairy industries.

Mary Kathleen Qld. 21S/140E Uranium mining town in the Selwyn Range, midway between Cloncurry and Mt. Isa. The town was in 'mothballs' from 1964, was reopened 1972 to meet new overseas contracts. The name is that of the late wife of Norman McConachy who, with Clem Walton, found the ores in 1954; exploitation began in 1958. The well-planned garden city, in rough spinifex country, is watered from a dam on the nearby Corella River which flows N to the Cloncurry.

Mary River Qld. NE flowing, 320 km. long and perennial, draining 9,000 km.^{2} of wooded slopes and intensively used flats (sugar, fruit, dairying), it reaches the sea 37 km. below Maryborough, 26S/153E. In the 1860s giant cedar logs were floated down its waters and in 1964 Borumba Dam was completed to mitigate floods, to irrigate 7,250 ha. and supply Gympie.

Maryvale Vic. 38S/147E Between Morwell and Traralgon on the Latrobe River, the site of vast paper and pulp mills, using about 300,000 tonnes a year of small eucalypts from Gippsland forests to make cardboard; for papermaking the pulp is mixed with softwood from *Pinus radiata* plantations in Vic., S.A. and N.S.W.

Mathinna Tas. 42S/148E On the S Esk River*, second only to the Beaconsfield gold-field; it was in production from 1882–1912 and extracted 234,000 oz. It is now a minor service centre.

Matra, James Mario (1745–1806) An American loyalist after the War of

Independence, who, having been a midshipman on Cook's *Endeavour*, and much impressed by E Aus., put forward in 1783 a proposal for a colony at Botany Bay, not original in its ideas nor the only one, but the first publicised and with some influence.

Maurice, Furnley (1881–1942) Pen-name of Leslie Thompson Wilmot. b. Melbourne. A poet, critic and literary figure who wrote impassioned pacifist verses about the First World War, and lyrical and satirical poems.

Mawson 68S/63E An Antarctic meteorological, geophysical and geological research station, established in 1954 on the coast of MacRobertson Land in the Aus. Antarctic Territory* and continuously maintained since. It lies W of the great Amery Ice Shelf, in a region of relatively snow- and ice-free gently shelving rock, next to a fine deep harbour.

Mawson, Sir Douglas (1882–1958) b. Yorkshire, Eng. He arrived in Sydney in 1886. Professor of Geology in Adelaide and became renowned as explorer and scientist of the Antarctic. Trained as a geologist by Sir Edgeworth David*, he undertook the first intensive geological surveys in the New Hebrides (1903). On Shackleton's Antarctic expedition (1908), and with David and Mackay he climbed Mt. Erebus, the 4,000-m. complex, ice-covered volcanic cone, for the first time. Later the same party set out on foot, with stores and instruments on sledges for the magnetic pole, making first observation of its shifting position. In 1911–12 Mawson led the Aus. Antarctic expedition to survey the ice plateau W of the magnetic pole. After losing his 2 companions, Ninnis and Mertz, Mawson struggled the last 100 miles alone and on foot, in poor shape—the sole of one foot separated from the flesh—surviving falls down crevasses by amazing strength of body and will. In 1929–31, Mawson led a large British-Aus.-N.Z. research expedition in Scott's old ship *Discovery*. Using small aircraft, fresh knowledge of the shifting of the magnetic pole was obtained, and of the territories the expedition named Princess Elizabeth Land and MacRobertson Land (where Mawson* Base is now established); the voyage was also used to yield fresh knowledge about the Crozet, Kerguelen and Heard Islands, and to establish the shallowing of the ocean towards the Antarctic. Apart from expedition records and geological papers, Mawson has left a very vivid, straightforward account of his earlier Antarctic experiences in *The Land of the Blizzard*, Vols. I and II (London, 1915).

Mayflies Insects of the Order Ephemeroptera (referring to their very short adult life), of which Aus. has at least 60 species, including several of the

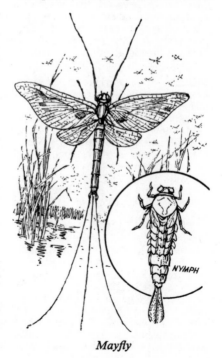

Mayfly

genus *Atalophlebia*. The aquatic nymph stage, with gills, roughly resembles a silverfish; different species live in unpolluted still or running water, free-swimming, burrowing or rock-clinging (using a sucker-like modification of the gills). The sub-imago, a pre-adult stage, on first emerging from the water, has dull opaque wings and is relatively inactive. The completely adult imago has no mouth, clear wings (the hind pair greatly reduced), and either 2 or 3 long caudal filaments or 'tails'; they only live for a few days, during which they are often seen dancing in swarms over water (a much prized food for freshwater fish), and mating and egg-laying are accomplished.

Mechanics' Institutes and/or Schools of Arts These are still seen as recreational halls, often in decline, in many Aus. towns. They are the legacy of a movement of great importance to adult education and Library facilities in the 19th century, beginning in Glasgow, Scotland, in 1800 and spreading in Aus. from the 1820s to the 1880s.

Medicine Aus. workers have made notable contributions from the early tropical work on filariasis by Bancroft* and plague* by J. A. Thompson (1848–1915) onwards. The prevalence of hydatid* disease led to early work, notably by Sir Joseph Verco (1851–1933), a great S.A. physician, A. Watson (1849–1940), an outstanding anatomist and teacher in S.A., C. H. Kellaway (1889–1952) in Melbourne and Sir Harold Dew (1891–1962) in Sydney. J. I. Hunter (1898–1924) achieved a world reputation as an anatomist in his short life. The formerly unidentified Q fever* was first scientifically recorded in Qld. in 1935 by E. H. Derrick (1898–) and named *Coxiella burneti*, after Sir Macfarlane Burnet* who isolated its causal virus; Burnet is one of the major Aus. medical scientists. The 1939–45 War gave impetus notably to research in

tropical diseases, and the control of malaria was advanced by the work directed by Sir Neil Hamilton Fairley (1891–1966); there was also important work on scrub typhus* by R. N. McCulloch.

In 1941 the link between rubella (German measles) in pregnancy and defects in babies was established by Sir Norman Gregg (1892–). Cancer research is active: Sir Herbert Schlink (1883–1962), who was also a pioneer of Aus. skiing, evolved internationally recognised systems of post-cancer checks; while the biochemist R. K. Morton (1920–1963) was tragically killed in the midst of fundamental work on the enzymes in relation to cancer. Sir John Eccles* is a world-wide figure in neuro-physiology. Other notable workers include: Sir Phillip Jones (1836–1918) on tuberculosis treatment, G. E. Phillips (1905–1952) in brain surgery, W. E. I. Summons (1881–) on miners' pthisis, J. A. H. McGeorge (1898–) in forensic medicine and psychiatry. Sir Charles James Martin (1866–1955), who was in Aus. from 1890–1903 and 1931-3, was profoundly influential in research and teaching. Among women, Dame Constance D'Arcy (1880–1950) in gynaecology, Charlotte Anderson (1915–) in coeliac disease, Ida Mann (1893–) on eye diseases, especially among Aborigines, are outstanding. The rehabilitation methods for poliomyelitis victims evolved by Sister Elizabeth Kenny (1886–1952), have been influential if controversial. Aus. medical scientists who achieved fame overseas include Sir Grafton Elliott Smith (1871–1937), the great anatomist and Egyptologist, Lord Florey (1898–1968) with his Nobel Prize-winning work on penicillin, M. Woodruff, designer and head of a pioneer human transplant centre in Edinburgh (1967), and Sir Hugh Cairns (1896–1952), brain surgeon. An Aus. developed heart pacemaker weighing only 120 g. won international orders from 1972.

The first medical school was founded in Melbourne in 1862, with the appointment of G. B. Halford as Professor of physiology and histology. In S.A. Sir Edward Stirling (1848–1919), a physiologist, was an important leader in medicine. Research Institutes date from the Walter and Eliza Hall* Institute founded in 1916, but mainly lacked funds until the last 3 decades. Among a number of private benefactors was the Polish-born jeweller Sir Adolph Basser (1887–   ). The John Curtin School of Medical Research in the Aus. National University, founded 1948, has attracted eminent workers. There are many specialist medical chairs in Aus.

Medick or **Medic**   A popular name for trifoliate plants of the genus *Medicago*, with 120 species of which several have long been naturalised in Aus., the most important being lucerne*.

Meehan, James   (1774–1826) A surveyor and explorer transported to Sydney in 1800 for a minor offence in the Irish rebellion of 1798. He was assigned to the Surveyor-General's department, and carried out very large amounts of land grant and town survey in some of the most formative years of the colony. He laid out Richmond, Windsor, Liverpool and others, and carried out exploration with Hume in the Hunter Valley (1801), the Lake Bathurst area and the Minnamurra–Shoalhaven area.

Meekatharra   W.A. 27S/118E   A railhead town, Flying Doctor and School of the Air centre for a wide pastoral area, with its origins in gold and copper in 1896.

Melaleuca   A mainly Aus. genus, in the Myrtaceae family, of some 150 species, mainly Aus. though with a few extending to Polynesia and SE Asia, notably the River Paperbark, *M. quinquenervia*. It includes the Paperbarks*, the Honeymyrtles*, some of the Bottlebrushes* and Tea-trees*. Leaves are very variable in shape and size, and in glossiness, hairiness etc., but most species have flower-spikes with long stamens in bottlebrush form and nutty fruit clusters. They flourish, sometimes in pure stands, in poor coastal sands and swampy saline sites. (*See* PLATE 8.)

Melba, Dame Nellie   (1861–1931) The great Aus. singer. She was born in Richmond, Melbourne, as Helen Porter Mitchell, the eldest of 8 children of a successful Scots contractor. She married C. F. N. Armstrong, engineer in a Qld. sugar plantation and son of an Irish baronet, in 1882, but she could neither settle nor sing in the oppressive Qld. climate and decided to take up a professional singing career from 1884. With her husband, small son and father she went to London in 1886. In Paris her great talent, and intelligence in the use of it, were recognised by Madame Marchesi who undertook her training. Her opera debut was in Brussels in 1887. She was not successful in her London debut of 1888, but was enthusiastically hailed the following year. She remained associated with Covent Garden until 1926. Hers was one of the greatest singing careers of all time, which included visits to Aus. and the founding of a singing school in Melbourne in 1915. Her marriage was dissolved in 1900; her husband had meanwhile been farming in Eng. Melba was an astute business woman and invested her money on the advice of Rothschild, one of the many admirers of this great and colourful personality. *For further reading see* J. Hetherington: *Melba* (Sydney, 1967).

MELBOURNE   Vic.   38S/145E 2,388,941 in 1971. The capital and containing over 60% of the State's population, it is centred on a rectangle of gridiron streets about 6·5 km. from the mouth of the Yarra River* and on its N or right bank; from this focal point it spreads to Port Melbourne, curves round the almost enclosed Port

Phillip Bay for some 65 km. and stretches out star-like—farthest along main roads and railways—from 12 to 25 km. The continuously built-up area is about 930 km.², covering gently undulating terrain, with attractive parks and gardens especially around the centre, and pleasant if unexciting beaches round the Bay. Mean monthly temperatures are from 10°C to 19°C, with occasional frosts and heatwaves over 37°C. The mean annual rainfall varies from 50 cm. just W of the city to 66 cm. in the centre and 88 cm. in the hillier country to the E. Most rain falls in winter, with a good deal of raw, blustery and drizzly weather, and the city experiences some sharp temperature drops, perhaps most disconcerting when a heat wave is ended by the arrival of a cold front from the Great Australian Bight.

The city began with the arrival of John Batman* in 1835, seeking fresh lands on behalf of a group of Tas. settlers; he 'purchased' some 240,000 ha. of land from Aborigines for some trade goods, but when he returned with the Port Phillip Association of business and professional men and pastoralists, they found another group of tradesmen, mechanics and labourers, under John Pascoe Fawkner*, camped on the future site of Melbourne. There was some disputation, and also the Governor of N.S.W. disallowed the 'purchase', but in 1836 sent Captain William Lonsdale as resident magistrate, with surveyors to map out streets and subdivisions. Governor Bourke authorised these steps on a visit in 1837, when the city was named Melbourne after the English Prime Minister. Batman and his associates aimed at a settlement of free settlers and petitioned against transportation. Wide streets and ample parklands (about a quarter of the central city area) were planned for from the outset, and by the 1840s the city and several of the suburbs, e.g. St. Kilda and Brighton, were developing to serve an easily accessible hinterland of pastoral country. But the separation of the new State, named Victoria in 1850, the discovery of gold in mid 1851, a few months after the exodus north to the Bathurst fields in N.S.W., brought great expansion, the foundation of the Cobb & Co.* coaching system, soon the railways; and then the great growth in numbers, wealth and development of both city and hinterland. Many of the older monumental buildings of central Melbourne belong to the period 1850-90: law courts, libraries, museums, the Royal Mint, the older part of the University, the domed Exhibition building and the 2 cathedrals. Already in 1861 Melbourne had 139,916 people (Sydney, 95,789), remaining larger until the 1911 census.

By 1871 manufacturing was already important, employing some 16,600 people in about 1,400 factories (total population 206,780), and the city was spreading out on the ground, widely and ever more widely in the tradition of the single-storey house on a plot of land. There has been continuous growth in the city, to 1 million during the Second World War and 2 million today, growth of the port, transport net by rail, tramway and road, the airport (Essendon NW of the city, now replaced by Tullamarine for international aircraft requiring long runways, 42 km. from the city-centre), and the constant enlargement of area to house a larger population dominantly in single houses. In the mid 1950s the planning restriction of building to 132 feet in height was removed, and the centre especially has been transformed by skyscrapers; the centre remains busy and important for many functions, but the pattern of retail shopping is changing under the impact of major suburban foci, e.g. those at Chadstone, Coburg, Morrabin and Ringwood, oriented to the motor-car. Some 12 ha. of former railway yards at Princess Gate are now replaced by shops and offices, as are the old Eastern and

Western Markets. Much industry remains central too, but larger factories are on areas such as reclaimed land at Fishermen's Bend obtained cheaply in the 1930s, or on large sites permitting modern one-storey construction and flow production, e.g. those along the Dandenong Road. Industrial production is 75% of Vic., even though Geelong is important, and 30% of Aus. including heavy engineering such as rolling stock, power-station gear, cars and agricultural and civil engineering machinery, clothing, textiles, paper, chemicals etc. Oil refineries at Altona on the W of the Bay are being supplemented by new installations at Westernport Bay*, SE of Port Phillip Bay, and on the other side of the city new bridges and freeways may increase the hitherto slower growth to the W. The possibilities of further growth seem limitless. Problems raised include: the formidable traffic snarls despite much thought on easing flow and much expenditure on, e.g. the King's Bridge across the Yarra, and on freeways; and, as in all but the most fortunate or far-seeing Aus. cities, the lack of universal sewerage systems in many suburbs. An Underground railway is planned for the central city. (*See* MAP 14.)

This is a city with a very rich hinterland reaching a little beyond the State boundary, of great intellectual vigour—its third university has been opened—active in the Press and in less ephemeral writing and publishing, in the arts, with a fine new Arts Centre almost complete, and in sport with an annual winter climax at the height of the season for the distinctive Australian Rules* Football.

Melbourne Cup A flat handicap horse-race run by the Vic. Racing Club at Flemington Race Course on the first Tuesday in November, over 3,200 m. (formerly 2 miles) and worth $100,000 (1972). The most important event in the Racing year, a public holiday in Vic. and the focus of national betting interest. It was first run in 1861, and has only been won twice by 3 horses: 'Archer' in 1861 and 1862, 'Peter Pan' in 1932 and 1934 and 'Rain Lover' (1968 and 1969). The record weight carried to victory was by 'Carbine' in 1890 (10st. 5lb.), while 'Phar Lap' in 1930 started on the shortest odds (11–8 on).

Meldrum, Duncan Max (1875–1955) b. Edinburgh, Scotland. An artist. He arrived in Aus. in 1888, and after a period in Europe, returned in 1913 to exert much influence on current art with insistence on accuracy in depicting the optical impression, but with minimal drawing. His successful, if near-photographic, portraiture led to much inferior imitation.

Melville Island N.T. 12S/131E 5,750 km. of low wooded hills and mangrove swamp off NW Arnhem Land*, and separated from Bathurst Island by the very narrow Apsley Str. Sighted by Tasman (1644), surveyed and named by Phillip Parker King (1818) after the First Lord of the Admiralty, it was the site of an ill-fated attempt at a convict settlement at Fort Dundas on Apsley Str. (1824–9) under Bremer, now the Roman Catholic mission, Garden Point. The island was infested by feral buffaloes until they were largely shot out. There is a Government Aboriginal settlement centred on Snake Bay in the N. A little trepang fishing and pearling goes on and there are 2 timber projects and sawmills at Snake Bay.

Menindee N.S.W. 32S/142E A small town and lakes, about 112 km. E of Broken Hill* which the lakes provide with drinking and industrial water and now also with water sports. This was Thomas Mitchell's* farthest point W (1835), a camp of Charles Sturt* (1844) and in 1860 the starting-point for the Burke* and Wills expedition. The lakes are primarily a natural feature, flooding through creeks connecting them with the Darling* at high water and then draining back to the river as the water-level falls. The Darling has been dammed back so that the whole system (completed 1960) can store some 2,470 million m.[3]; it is used to regulate the flow of the lower Darling, and so that water from L. Cawndilla can be sent down the Great Anabranch*. It is possible that local irrigation may greatly increase the intensity of land use in the area.

Menzies, Sir Robert Gordon (1894–) b. Jeparit, Vic. Prime Minister of Aus. from 1939–41 and 1949–65. A brilliant barrister, subsequently a dominant Liberal Party politician. His gifts of oratory, commanding voice and power-ful presence, made his manner memor-able; he carried much weight at home and abroad and had extraordinary political adroitness. Convincingly Aus., he had openly avowed attachment to the Crown and to some aspects of the link with Britain and the British Commonwealth of Nations, yet anti-colonial and pro-American in many contexts, conservative in domestic policies, but progressive particularly in developing the universities. His mem-oirs are *Afternoon Light* (London, 1967).

Dame Pattie Maie Menzies (maiden name Leckie) wife of Sir Robert, was created D.B.E. in 1954 for social work.

Meredith family An influential early Tas. family: **George** (1777–1856) b. Birmingham, Eng., arrived in Aus. (1821) in a ship chartered with partners. His son **Charles** (1811–1880) was notable as a Tas. Parliamentary figure for over 20 years from 1845; his wife **Louisa** was a writer.

Merino A breed of sheep noted for its fine wool, which contributes 75% of the Aus. wool clip. The merino was smuggled to other countries including Eng. where Sir Joseph Banks developed the royal flock described by H. B. Carter in *His Majesty's Flock* (Sydney, 1964). Macarthur* had imported 6 S

African merinos to N.S.W. in 1797 and improved their strain with 5 culled from the Royal flock in 1804. The Peppin family of Wanganella in the Riverina did much to improve the breed. There are now 120 million merinos with 35 million blood relatives in Aus.; 20 'parent' studs or breeding nuclei provide 22% of rams used; and a further 258 'daughter studs' provide another 25%. There are 685 'general' studs. Merinos differ from other sheep in having the wool-producing follicles in clusters of 20–5 instead of 3–7 as in other breeds. The export embargo on merino rams was eased in 1970, but led to union opposition as being against Aus. interests. *For further reading see* I. W. McDonald: *The Merino Sheep in Australia*.

Merredin W.A. 32S/118E (3,596 in 1971) A wheat belt* town on the Perth–Kalgoorlie line, developing by the end of the 19th century, and further stimulated by feeder loop lines to N and S.

Mersey River Tas. 42S/146E Flows 160 km. N from the lakes region of the Central Plateau, cutting deeply through the N edge, and crossing basaltic lowlands to its estuary at Devonport. Hydro-electric develop-ment is important (*see* TASMANIA, POWER). The lower valley is rich potato-, dairy- and apple-farming land.

Messmate A popular name for several Eucalypts usually seen along with other species, including *Eucalyptus obliqua* (Messmate Stringybark*), *E. cloeziana* (Gympie Messmate*) and *E. phellandra* (N.S.W. Messmate).

Meteorites Not including tektites*, there are at least 127 major finds in Aus. (The Tenham, Qld., 26S/143E, chondrite shower includes over 140 meteorites of graduated size found over an area of 20 by 5 km. (*see photograph in* A. A. Moss's book: *Meteorites*, London, 1967). Notable finds include: iron–nickel meteorites, Cranbourne, Vic., and Henbury on the Finke River (found 1931); pallasite (iron–nickel to stone) meteorite; Huckitta, N.T., 23S/136E (found 1937). The large crater at Wolf Creek, W.A., 19S/128E (found 1947), may not be due to a meteorite but to volcanic cauldron subsidence.

Methodist Church The third largest denomination, 1,151,989 adherents in 1971. Originating as a reform movement within the Church of England, separation came about 1795. Rev. R. Johnson*, the first clergyman in Aus. was an ordained Anglican, but was a convinced Methodist. The first meetings in Aus. were among laymen in 1812 in a cottage in the Rocks area, Sydney, and the first missionary was Samuel Leigh (1785–1852) in N.S.W. from 1815. The first church was built at Castlereagh in 1817 and an important early missionary in Vic. was J. R. Orton (1795–1842). There is a strong Methodist tradition in S.A., dating from the early days of settlement. The undenominational Far West Children's Health Scheme (1924) was initiated by a Methodist minister Stanley Drummond (1855–1943) for children of outback N.S.W.

Metrication of all Aus. measures will be 70–80% complete in 1976. Primary education (1973) and secondary education (1974) are in metric.

Michell, Anthony George Maldon (1870–) Vic. engineer and inventor of the Michell Thrust Bearing (patented 1905) which greatly increased the motive power of ocean-going screw steamships, by application of his research into the flow of lubricating oils. His elder brother **John Henry** (1863–1940) was a brilliant mathematician, the relevance of whose work to marine engineering was only turned to practical use from the 1930s.

Middleback Ranges S.A. 33S/137E The E extremity of the Gawler Ranges, in which high-grade haematite iron ore is quarried from the hills from Iron Monarch, Iron Knob, Iron Prince and Iron Baron, and railed to Whyalla

from Iron Knob mining settlement after crushing. It was the major Aus. source of iron before recent developments in W.A.

Midland W.A. 32S/116E (formerly Midland Junction) Now an industrial Perth suburb with railway workshops, stock-yards and abattoirs, which grew as the junction of the Kalgoorlie line and the line to the N. It was built in return for land grants by the Midland Railway Company which owned it until 1964.

Midlands Tas. 42S/147E A distinctive region lying E of the Central Plateau* between Hobart and Launceston. The N part is a fault-edged depression filled with Tertiary sediments, and is now productive farmland. Towards the S the Lower Midlands region comprises a higher, older landscape, with sclerophyll* forest and natural grazing. Early settlement, convict labour and abundant freestone allowed the building of some of the finest Aus. homesteads. The **Midland Highway**, 200 km. long, links Hobart with Launceston.

Mildura Vic. 34S/142E (13,190 in 1971) A fine, well laid-out city and the centre for the Mallee* wheat and grazing country. Formerly important for river traffic, now gone except for pleasure craft. Settlement at Mildura began with irrigation based on a pump designed by George Chaffey*. Now it is the centre for fruit growing and canning, grape and raisin packing and processing and winery (including some in greenhouses), and vegetables.

Military Leaders Since first engaging in overseas campaigns, Aus. has produced many outstanding military figures including those listed below. *1914–18 War Army* Generals: Sir Harry Chauvel*, Sir Brudenell White*, Sir John Monash*. Major-Generals: Sir William Bridges*, H. E. Elliot, Sir John Gellibrand, Sir Joseph Hobbs, W. Holmes, Sir Neville Howse*, J. H.

Legge, Sir Charles Rosenthal, Sir Granville Ryrie. Brigadier-General Sir Raymond Leane, Brigadier Sir Victor Windeyer, Col. A. J. Butler (Medical, officer and historian). *Navy:* Admiral Sir George Patey. Vice-Admirals: Sir William Creswell*, J. C. T. Glossop. Rear-Admirals: J. S. Dumaresq, H. J. Feakes.
1939–45 War Army Field-Marshal Sir Thomas Blamey*. Lt.-Generals: H. Gordon Bennett, Sir Frank Berriman, Sir William Bridford (also Korean War), R. Brierwith (also Korean War), Sir Edmund Herring*, Sir John Laverack, Sir Iven Mackay, Sir Leslie Morshead*, Sir John Northcott, Sir Sydney Rowell, Sir Stanley Savige, V. A. H. Sturdee. Major-Generals: A. S. Allen, C. A. Callaghan, E. W. C. Chaytor, B. M. Morris, Sir Frank Norris (medical, also Korea), G. A. Vasey. Brigadiers: Sir Neil Hamilton Fairley (malaria control), F. G. Gallaghan, A. A. L. Godfrey, M. J. Moten. *Navy* Vice-Admirals: H. J. Buchanan, Sir John Collins, Sir Roy Dowling (also post-war). Rear-Admirals: H. B. Farncomb, G. G. O. Gatacre (including post-war and Korea). Captain: H. M. L. Waller. *Air Force* Air Marshals: Sir George Jones, R. Williams, Sir Frederick Scherger (also Korean War). Air Vice-Marshals: F. M. Bladin, W. W. D. Bostock, C. E. Daley. Air Commodore A. H. Cobby; Group-Captain C. R. Caldwell a fighter-pilot. A number of Aus. airmen reached high rank in the R.A.F. Among well-known fighter-pilots were: Wing-Commander R. W. Bungey, Squadron Leaders J. F. Jackson, K. W. Truscott and Richard Hillary, an Aus. by birth, whose book *The Last Enemy* achieved much fame.

Milkmaid (*Burchardia umbellata*) In the Liliaceae family, an attractive white and purple star-like Lily* of sandy soils in many parts of Aus.

Milkwort or **Heath Milkwort** (*Comesperma ericinum*) A heath-like shrub of E Aus., with pea-like pink flowers. Like the Love-creeper, it is in the cosmopolitan Polygalaceae family. The Leafless Milkwort, *C. defoliatum* (actually with small leaves), has beautiful deep-blue, pea-like flowers, yellow-hearted, with rather small 'wings'.

Miller, Godfrey (1893–1964) b. N.Z. An artist, settled in Sydney in 1948, and subsequently influential both through teaching, and the imagery and experimental approach of his painting.

Miller, H. C. A pilot who became one of the first Aus. holders of flying and ground-engineer licences. He won the handicap prize in the Sydney–Perth Air Race in 1929 in a DH 9, set up an air service, at first in Adelaide, and then gained the contract for the service to the NW of W.A. from West Australian Airways in 1934, and with help from Sir Macpherson Robertson* started MacRobertson-Miller Airlines*.

Miller, Keith Ross (1919–) b. Melbourne. A cricket all-rounder, with the world record of 2,958 runs, averaging 36·9, and 170 wickets for an average of 22·97. He played in 55 Tests (1946–56), his brilliant performances being interspersed with erratic spells. His bowling is most memorable, delivered from the advantage of height and after a short run. He was also a successful Aus. Rules footballer.

Millet, Native A popular name for a widespread Aus. species of *Panicum* (*see* PANIC GRASSES). Bullrush Millet, *Pennisetum typhoideum*, is an introduced grass, now important in agriculture in tropical Aus., and used as human food in S Asia.

Millicent S.A. 38S/140E (5,075 in 1971) A growing service centre for the pastures of the drained SW swamplands, where the first drainage scheme of the region was carried out (1864–80). The town extends for 5 km. along a sandy ridge above the former flood levels. It has been stimulated by further drainage and land settlement since 1948, and by forest industries based on pine plantations at Snuggery and Mt. Burr.

Milingimbi Island N.T. 12S/135E The Headquarters of the Methodist Mission in N.T. on a small island off the N coast of Arnhem Land. Tropical fruit and vegetables are grown.

Millipedes Elongated slow-moving segmented arthropods, usually up to 2·5 cm. long of the Order Diplopoda, sometimes treated with the Centipedes*, Chilopoda, in one Class, Myriapoda. They live in soil, humus or under stones, eating mainly plant remains and gradually reducing them to humus. Unlike centipedes, they have more pairs of legs than they have segments, often 2 pairs to each of 11 to 22 segments. Aus. indigenous species include 4 species of relatively soft Diplopoda dwelling under stones, and many species of the more horny groups within the Diplopoda, some able to curl up as 'pill-millipedes' and some with spinning glands. The Symphyla, small, slender and relatively 'thin-skinned', include several species in the S of Aus. which are said to damage the roots of crops. There are 10 named species of the minute, whitish Pauropoda in the S of Aus. There are 2 introduced, almost cosmopolitan species, *Pauropus huxleyi lanceolatus* and *Stylopauropus pedunculatus*.

Mills Cross A form of radio-telescope named after its inventor Dr. B. Y. Mills, then of C.S.I.R.O. and later Head of the Astro-Physics Department of the University of Sydney. Multiple aerials in a cross, each arm about a mile long, pick up and record radio waves from deep in space. A Mills Cross radio-telescope under the control of Sydney University, partially financed from U.S., was opened in 1965 at Hoskinstown near Canberra.

Milparinka N.S.W. 30S/142E A small township in the arid far NW of the State near the boundary with Qld. and S.A., where towns are of importance locally out of proportion to size. Sturt* camped nearby for 6 hot months in 1845.

MINERALS Aus. is in a strong position in the diversity and size of its reserves of the basic minerals iron and coal, and many others needed in manufacturing industry, but so far is less strong in oil. Recent mineral discoveries on a vast scale have been compared in significance to the crossing of the Blue Mts. in 1913

Export surpluses exist in: Cadmium Copper*, Gold*, Lead*, Silver*, Zinc*, Barite, Bauxite*, Coal*, Gypsum*, Iron ore*, Mineral Sands*, Opal*, Salt*, Beryl, Manganese* (metallurgical), Tungsten*, Nickel*, Tin*, Asbestos* (chrysotile).

Minerals sufficient for Aus. needs include: Brown coal, most clays, Dolomite, Felspar and Limestone.

Production insufficient for Aus. needs: Lithium minerals, Sulphides, Antimony, Cobalt, Platinum, Abrasives, Bentonite, China Clay, Chromite, Diatomite, Fluorite, Magnesite, Manganese* (chemical), Petroleum*, Mineral pigments, Bismuth, Molybdenum, Asbestos* (crocidolite), Phosphate rock*.

No production at present: Arsenic, Diamonds, Graphite, Vermiculite, Mercury, Vanadium, Borates, Nitrates, Sulphur (which is made from pyrites).

Total mineral output in 1960 was worth $362 million and in 1970 $1,400 million; metals contribute 50% (dominated by iron ore and lead, silver and zinc ores), and fuel minerals 30% (with nine-tenths black coal), non-metals (e.g. limestone) 5% and quarried minerals largely for construction 15%. Mining employs 41,000 people or just under 1% of the total work force and 10·5% of the workers in all Primary Industry. Of the 3,000 or so undertakings, of which 40% are quarries and 60% mines, two-thirds employ 4 or fewer; but over half the miners are employed in 49 large-scale enterprises of over 200 workers. N.S.W. leads with 35% of total local value almost 50% from coal in the E, 20% from lead-silver-zinc in the extreme W, and the rest largely from coastal sands. Qld. produces 21·5% mainly from copper, lead-silver-zinc, but important coal also. W.A. (24%) is dominated by iron ore which has replaced gold. Vic. (7%) gets a third from brown coal and much of the rest from building materials; gold is now insignificant. S.A. (5%) is largely iron, with limestone, gypsum and salt. Tas. (4·5%) mainly the lead-silver-zinc ores and tin and developing iron. N.T. (3%) bauxite, iron and copper. Exports of minerals include both ores and concentrates as well as basic products such as pig-iron. Exports (1970): iron (30%), lead (15%), aluminium (15%), copper (8·6%), zinc (7%), mineral sands (5%), gold (3%), petroleum products (2·6%), tin (1·2%), tungsten (0·8%), silver (0·8%), salt (0·5%), others, mainly nickel (0·6%). Contracted sales will exceed $1,850 million by 1980. Japan is now the chief customer. Minerals have played an important part in the settlement and transport developments of Aus. from the gold-rushes of the 1850s, especially as deposits are often in remoter areas. A lull in the first half of the 20th century has been followed by eight-fold increase since 1950, discoveries of large-scale deposits of iron ore, bauxite, nickel and phosphate and intensive search for oil, rewarded by discovery of natural gas and major oilfields in Bass Str.* In 1973 the Govt. announced that foreign control would be restricted to its existing 62% of mining industry. A wide review is Sir Harold Raggatt's *Mountains of Ore* (Melbourne, 1968).

Mineral Sands These include titanium ores, rutile (90% world supply), and titanium metal, increasingly used in many supersonic aircraft components and in pigments, and ilmenite (22% world supply) for pigments, paper and textiles). Zircon (foundry sand ceramic glazes) 82% world supply; monazite (thorium ore) for lighter 'flints', glass-polishing and gas mantles is also exploited. These sands have been deposited from erosion of granites and sandstone in patches along the E coast from Brisbane, including the Moreton Bay* islands to Wollongong and in W.A. between Busselton and Bunbury and S from Geraldton. When the fluctuating market allows, exports are significant ($55 million in 1973), although spoliation, especially in the E, is severe.

Miner-birds Certain of the Honey-eaters*, not to be confused with the introduced Mynas, though the name may have originated from just such confusion.

Mint Bush A popular name for the *Prostanthera*+ genus of aromatic flowering shrubs.

Mints The Royal prerogative of minting coins through the Royal Mint in London (the Chancellor of the Exchequer being the Master of the Mint), had to be extended, at the maximum of direct influence of the British Empire, to branches in Canada, S Africa, India and Aus. Only the 2 Aus. branches in Melbourne and Perth survived until conversion to decimal currency; they have now been superseded by the Royal Australian Mint in Canberra (1965). Sydney had a mint in part of the old Rum Hospital (1855–1926), Adelaide's Assay Office operated as a sort of mint in 1852–3, Melbourne's dates from 1872, minting Aus. coins from 1916, and Perth's from 1899 (Aus. coins since 1940). Prior to this the Aus. mints refined and assayed gold, and minted gold sovereigns and half-sovereigns for the British Government until 1931.

Minute Grass or **Eight-Day Grass** Popular names for *Tripogon loliiformis*, a small leafy grass, from its rapid appearance after light rains, which makes it useful for forage in the inland.

Missionaries Plain N.T. 24S/133E A sandy mulga-dotted plain between the Macdonnell* and James Ranges*, crossed by the Finke River*. It was suggested by Goyder*, the S.A. Surveyor, as a suitable area for Aboriginal Mission work, with natural boundaries and a water supply, reported by Giles* in 1872, and was named from the Hermannsburg Lutheran Mission* established there in 1877.

Mistletoes (family Loranthaceae) Parasites very common in Aus. and are native, not introduced; they are parasitic on the sapwood of many eucalypts, apparently increasing towards pest proportions because of reduction of natural controls or increase in the spread of seeds, perhaps by introduced starlings. A common species of coastal E. Aus. is *Amyema congener*, with attractive yellow flowers like fringed bells, succulent, sticky greenish fruit and thick, opposite blunt-ended leaves. *A. miquelii* is in places a pest of box and mallee eucalypts, while other species are adapted to (and perhaps mimic the foliage of) wattle, casuarina, sandal etc.

Mitchell, James (1792–1869) b. Fife, Scotland. He arrived in Aus. in 1821, as a medical officer, and developed private practice. Later he settled in the Newcastle area where he was a pioneer of industry: copper-smelting (1846), using coal on his own property and successfully challenging the monopoly of the Aus. Agriculture Company*.

Mitchell, Sir James (1866–1951) b. Bunbury, W.A. Premier of W.A. from 1919–24, 1930–3, Lt.-Governor of W.A. from 1933–48, and Governor 1948–51, entering politics from banking. He was an important W.A. figure, concerned especially with developments in the wheat belt and dairy industry.

Mitchell, Sir Thomas Livingstone (1792–1855) b. Stirlingshire, Scotland, A surveyor and explorer. After working for a colliery-owning relative, Mitchell served with Wellington in the Peninsula, mainly as a surveyor and mapmaker. From 1828–55 he was Surveyor-General for N.S.W. He was faced with the enormous task of surveying the colony and planning roads, towns and bridges. In addition he wanted to explore, partly for its own sake, partly to achieve the fame an ambitious spirit craved. He led 4 expeditions. The first (1831) added little to existing knowledge of the Darling headwaters; nor did the second, in 1835, when he followed the Darling for 484 km., but not to the Murray confluence as instructed. The next year, however, he made the important discovery of the fertile Western District of Vic. (again when he had been instructed to verify Sturt's interpretation of the Murray–Darling system). 'The Major's Route', named after his military rank at the time, was immediately followed by overlanders and squatters and the Major himself was knighted in Eng. in 1837 for his exploit. He made a final expedition (1845), aiming to cross the continent to Port Essington, and hoping to establish his theory of a great NW-flowing river. Only wishful thinking explains his identification of the withering Cooper Creek (or Barcoo) as such a river, but he did so and named it Victoria, before turning back. Before his death, Mitchell's department came under censure. Never popular, he had been in open conflict with Darling, and made jealous attacks on Sturt and other explorers. Yet he was a gifted, artistic man of letters, devoted to his large family. He made large collections of natural history specimens, and several species, including the common wombat, bear his name. His expeditions had a military order, but lacked the humanity and loyalty that marked Sturt's relations with his companions. *For further reading see* J. H. L. Cumpston: *Thomas Mitchell* (Melbourne, 1954).

Mitchell River Qld. Rises 48 km. NW of Cairns (17S/146E) and flows (during 9 months only) 560 km. NW to the Gulf of Carpentaria through mainly wild scrub-covered cattle country. Anabranches diverge (e.g. Nassau River) 160 km. from the mouth. **Mitchell River Mission** (Anglican) serves the Aboriginal Reservation on the Gulf.

Mitchell, Sir William (1861–1962) b. Inveravon, Banffshire, Scotland. He was an outstanding philosopher, holding the Adelaide University Chair from 1894–1923. His *Structure and Growth of the Mind* (London, 1907) has remained a major contribution on philosophy/psychology.

Mitchell-grass A popular name after Sir Thomas Mitchell*, for 4 species of valuable forage grasses in the genus *Astrebla*, growing on heavy clay soils in the 25- to 65-cm. rainfall belt in much of inland Aus. The habit is branching and tussocky, the head compact and nutritious, in some almost wheat-like, in some one-sided like a tooth-brush, and the leaf-blades are nutritious and attractive to stock, even when hanging dry on the plant or detached and lying shrivelled on the ground, so that while this fodder lasts stock may do well even during drought. Forest Mitchell-grass is *Bothriochloa ewartiana*. Most of this genus are known as Blue-grass*.

Mites A popular name for the smaller acarine arachnid arthropods (*cf.* Ticks*). Aus. has many genera and species, some of which are actually or potentially involved in disease transmission. Some are vegetarian at all stages, including agricultural and horticultural pests, and others are partially parasitic on animals including man, usually at the larval stage, e.g. the adults and nymphs of the Trombiculidae family feed on the eggs of other small arthropods in the soil; their

larvae are important in the transmission of scrub typhus*.

Agricultural pests, mainly introduced, include the European Red Spider (misnamed), *Eotetranychus telarius*, in Qld. and N.S.W., the similar and more widespread *Tetranychus urticae*, *Metatetranychus ulmi* and *Bryobia praetiosa* on fruit trees, *Tenuialpus* spp. on vines, the Red-legged Earth-mite, *Halotydeus destructor*, on subterranean clover, and Pea-mite, *Penthaleus major*, on oat and pea crops. The Snout-mites, Bdelloidea family, however, help to control various smaller arthropods, including the Lucerne-flea or Springtail, *Sminthurus viridis*. The Eriophyidae family are responsible for big bud on blackcurrants and other gall-like swellings on fruit trees.

Among animal and human disease carriers are *Demodex* spp. (mange), *Sarcoptes scabei* (scabies in man, others affecting other animals), the native *Psorergates ovis* which eats wool on the sheep, the Beetle Mites of family Oribatidae (sheep tapeworm carrier), and *Trombicula akamushi* and *T. deliensis* (scrub typhus).

Mitta Mitta River Vic. Discovered by Hovell and Hume in 1824, it flows from the Great Divide E of Mt. Bogong, N for about 270 km. to join the Murray just above the Hume Reservoir, which occupies its lower valley. The alluvial plains of the middle basin contain some intensive farming of special crops, such as tobacco and hops. In the upper valley Dartmouth Dam (1973) is part of the Murray Waters system.

Mittagong N.S.W. 34S/150E (3,620 in 1971) The present town, a local dairying, market-garden centre, represents fusion of several villages associated with changes of the main road and with earlier industrialisation —the latter particularly linked with the first Aus. iron-smelting works at Fitzroy and a settlement of immigrant iron workers at New Sheffield.

Mock Orange (*Pittosporum undulatum*) A white-flowered shrub in the mainly southern family Pittosporaceae with dark strap-like leaves, common in E Aus.

Mocking-birds Mimicking birds, strictly the various species of *Mimus* of the Americas, but sometimes applied to various Aus. birds, including the Lyrebird* and *Atrichornis**, Scrub-bird*.

Moe Vic. 38S/146E (with Yallourn 20,764 in 1971) A service centre for part of the dairying and timber area of Gippsland, attracting custom even from the industrial town of Yallourn, but in recent years transformed, like Yallourn itself, through planned residential development in Moe and at Newborough on the E, by the State Electricity Commission, and growing very rapidly. Textile and clothing factories have come in to employ surplus female labour.

Moline N.T. 12S/132E The administrative centre and chief settlement for the S Alligator River* uranium field, 76 km. W of El Sharana* mine.

Molluscs or **Mollusca** A Phylum of the invertebrates, second in number only to the arthropods*. The molluscs are soft-bodied, and most secrete calcareous material to form a protective shell, usually external. Aus. has some 10,000 species of the 100,000 molluscs known in the world. For the Classes— *see* SHELLFISH, BIVALVES, GASTROPODS, CHITONS, TUSK SHELLS *and* CEPHALOPODS. The Class Monoplacophora, primitive deepsea shells, is not treated in this book.

Molonglo River N.S.W. A relatively minor tributary of the Murrumbidgee*, which acquired importance out of proportion to its size since Canberra* was planned in a basin in its middle course and since it was dammed to form L. Burley Griffin (1963). It flows for some 150 km. NW to Queanbeyan,

then WNW to its confluence with the Murrumbidgee about 25 km. WNW of Canberra. The outwash from spoil-heaps from the now defunct silver-lead zinc mine at Captain's Flat, has poisoned the flood-plain vegetation for some miles downstream, but, diluted by the Queanbeyan River, the water of L. Burley Griffin supports fish life well. It rises in attractive wet sclerophyll* forest country and there are pleasant, if relatively inaccessible gorge sections upstream from Queanbeyan, and near the Murrumbidgee confluence. It was discovered by Throsby* (1820).

Molucca Bramble (*Rubus* *moluccanus*) A native prickly scrambler with leaves, hooked spines and berries similar to the exotic blackberry, except that the fruit is red and somewhat tasteless. Common in E Aus.

Molvig, Jon (1923–1970) b. Newcastle, N.S.W. A leading contemporary artist living in Brisbane, noted for especially fine portraits, and outback paintings of savage intensity.

Monaro or **Monaro Plateau** Names often used for the S part of the Southern Tablelands of N.S.W. It is rolling country of natural tussock grassland, at about 900 m. above sea level, largely on deep red to blackish, in places peaty soil over Tertiary basalt, in a rain-shadow area of some 75 cm. between the wet coastal belt and the wet Snowy Mts. Wool and fat lamb production are on fairly large properties. Grasslands give way to mixed temperate eucalypt woodland, on the deeper granite soils. The main centres are Cooma*, 36S/149E, and Bombala, 37S/149E. *See* A. B. Costin: *A study of the Ecosystems of the Monaro Region with special reference to soil erosion* (Sydney, 1954); W. K. Hancock *Discovering Monaro* (Cambridge, 1972).

Monash, Sir John (1865–1931) b. Melbourne. Of Jewish parentage, he was an outstanding military leader in the

1914–18 War. Trained as a civil engineer, entering the army through long service in the citizens' militia, Monash served with distinction in Gallipoli and France, before succeeding Birdwood in command of the Aus. forces in France in May 1918. His analytical approach and plans were in no small measure responsible for the success of the 1918 offensive to break the Hindenberg Line. After the war, as General Manager of Vic. Electricity Commission, he planned and supervised the development of the Latrobe Valley brown coal resources, and is commemorated in Monash University.

Monkey Nut Applied in Aus. to *Hicksbeachia pinnatifolia,* a tall bush or small tree with very large notched and deeply lobed leaves, multiple flowers and orange-red edible nuts.

Monkey-flowers A common name for the genus *Mimulus.* (*See* WILD FLOWERS.)

Monotremes Animals with a single vent for excretion and reproduction: the egg-laying mammals, the Platypus and the Spiny Ant-eater, peculiar to Australasia. Their oviparous nature was first established by W. H. Caldwell, visiting Aus. in 1884. Within the Class Mammalia, they belong to a Sub-Class Prototheria (first beasts) or Ornithodelphia (bird-wombed), but the Order Monotremata is the only one with the 2 members noted. The monotremes are often assumed to represent a 'living fossil' stage of evolution between reptilian and placental mammalian forms; but most scientists believe that the monotremes are not closely related to the marsupials and higher mammals, and that they evolved from a distinct group of reptiles. There is barely a fossil record, but the first mammals were probably not toothless, as are adult monotremes, and since the young Platypus has 'milk teeth', replaced in adult life by flat horny plates used for crushing shells and insects, it appears that some features of these animals may be degenerative or adaptive.

However, the eggs have flexible shells, composed largely of keratin and similar to reptilian eggs; the shoulder girdle (in which shoulder joint, sternum and collar bones are linked) closely resembles that common in reptiles. On the other hand, the 'marsupial' or epipubic bones resemble those in marsupials, sometimes supposed to be related to supporting the marsupial pouch, now regarded as more probably related to supporting semi-erect reptilian ancestors.

Both the Platypus and the Spiny Ant-eater suckle their young, but teats are lacking: the milk oozes through enlarged pores to be licked up by the young. Adaptations to very different modes of life are seen in the Platypus* and the Spiny Ant-eater*. *For further reading see* G. Lyne: *Marsupials and Monotremes of Australia* (Sydney, 1967).

Montagu Island N.S.W. 36S/150E About 10 km. SE of Narooma and 290 km. S of Sydney (from which there is an annual yacht race around the island), with an important lighthouse visible for 32 km. It is a mere strip of granite, formerly quarried for important Sydney buildings including the G.P.O., but now a wildlife sanctuary. The surrounding waters are a recognised game-fishing ground. Captain Cook sighted the southern point in 1770 and named it Point Dromedary, without realising it was an island.

Monte Bello Islands W.A. 20S/115E An unnumbered group of small islets and rocks continuing a chain from NW Cape, uninhabited save for wildlife. They were used for the 1952 British atomic explosion and scientific follow-up investigations.

Moonbi Range N.S.W. A ridge of Permian granite on the SW edge of the New England plateau, a dramatic approach on the New England highway, NE of Tamworth, 31S/151E.

Moonie Qld. 27S/149E The first commercially exploited oilfield in Aus. (1964), with a pipeline to Brisbane (300 km.). A township is developing. Oil is also being commercially exploited at Alton, 97 km. to the SW in the same sedimentary basin. (*See* PETROLEUM.)

Moonlight, Captain (Andrew George Scott) (1842–1879) b. County Tyrone, Ireland. A parson's son. The most intriguing bushranger of all, Scott was also a superb confidence trickster; while a lay preacher at Mt. Egerton, Vic., he got away with holding up the bank manager, whom no one believed when he identified Scott as the 'Captain Moonlight' who had robbed him. After a gaol sentence for a false cheque in Sydney and the now discovered bank robbery, Scott had a brief preaching phase, then bushranging (1879–80), culminating in a brutal station hold-up, his capture and hanging.

Moonta S.A. 34S/137E (1,579 in 1971; 1,862 in 1961) At the NW end of the Yorke Peninsula, it developed, with Wallaroo and Kadina as a copper centre (1861–1923). W. H. Horn rode 265 km. to Adelaide in 22 hours to lodge a claim before rivals could do so. Moonta employed 1,800 in the 1870s, many of them Cornish Methodists; 10 chapels were recorded there in 1899. They were made famous in Oswald Pryor's *Bulletin* cartoons of 'Cousin Jacks'; the mining period is described in his book *Australia's Little Cornwall* (Adelaide, 1962).

Moore, Tom Inglis (1901–) b. Camden, N.S.W. A critic and poet, and formerly Professor of Aus. Literature in the Australian National University, Canberra. His poems of love and of war are found in *Adagio in Blue* (Sydney, 1938) and *Emu Parade* (Sydney, 1941), but he is also well known for critical work on Aus. poetry.

Moorehead, Alan (1910–) b. Melbourne. A very successful expatriate writer, a thorough researcher into his topic, as in *Cooper's Creek* (London, 1956) describing the Burke* and Wills expedition, *The Fatal Impact* (London, 1966), on white man in the Pacific region, and *Gallipoli* (London, 1956). *See also* A. Moorehead: *A Late Education* (London, 1970).

Mootwingie N.S.W. 31S/141E A small settlement and road junction from which the **Mootwingie Range,** of Devonian sandstone and conglomerates, runs NE for about 64 km., including about 8,000 ha. of reserve. This area contains very fine Aboriginal rock engravings, many of birds and animals, picked out with a hard stone on smooth rocks, and dating back probably 3,000 years.

Moran, Patrick Francis (1830–1911) b. Ireland. He arrived in Aus. in 1884 as Roman Catholic Archbishop of Sydney, becoming the first Aus. Cardinal (1885) and identifying himself wholly with Aus. He saw the importance of Irish migrants in the developing Labor movement, with which he sympathised, while working to keep it moderate and not too left wing.

Morant, Henry Harbord ('Breaker') (1865–1902) b. Devonshire, Eng. He arrived in Aus. in 1884. A horsebreaker and minor balladist, expressive in word, deed and character of the wildest days of the Aus. bush. He was executed during the Boer War for disobeying orders by killing prisoners.

Moree N.S.W. 29S/150E (9,114 in 1971) On the Gwydir River, a locally important route and service centre for the N part of the wheat and sheep country of the Western Slopes. It occasionally suffers from floods. A 915-m.-deep mineral-rich artesian bore made in 1895, has been utilised for medicinal baths. It has the Aboriginal fringe problem common in many towns of the Western Slopes and the W of N.S.W.

Moreton Bay Qld. 27S/153E A shallow inlet, on the shores of which the first Qld. settlement began (1824) at Redcliffe*. A crescent of sandy islands with dunes (up to 275 m. high on Moreton Island), which were wind-formed originally, but are now fixed by low vegetation, extends from Caloundra to Southport (Bribie, Moreton, Stradbroke Islands) and shelters the Bay from easterly storms.

Morgan S.A. 34S/139E The point at which the River Murray turns S, a railhead from Adelaide (1878) and the take-off point for the 360-km. pipeline to Whyalla (1944), later extended to Woomera, and now duplicated to extend the existing service to intervening farming areas.

Morgan, Molly (1762–1835) b. Shropshire, Eng. She was twice transported: for theft (1790) and arson (1804), and re-convicted in Aus. for cattle-stealing (1816). Given a few acres in the Maitland area in 1819, by 1830 she was the biggest landowner in the Hunter Valley.

Mormons Correctly they are members of the Church of Jesus Christ of Latter Day Saints, having some 15,000 Aus. adherents; a further 4,000 adhere to the dissident Reformed Church of the same name, which in U.S. was the legally recognised successor to the original foundation under Joseph Smith. The former group, stemming from Brigham Young's leadership to found Salt Lake City, Utah, was first established in Aus. in 1874. Both groups repudiate polygamy.

Mornington Vic. (7,349 in 1966) Some 48 km. S of Melbourne still with some functions as a market centre for the stud sheep and cattle district on the W (Port Phillip Bay) side of the **Mornington Peninsula**, a hilly tract (mainly a horst or upfaulted block of Devonian sandstones etc., and of granite and volcanic rocks), about 48 km. NE–SW by 24 km. NW–SE, and lying between Port Phillip Bay, Westernport and Cape Schanck in the S. The Port

Phillip Bay shore is almost continuously built up by seaside (now car-commuter dormitory) towns as far as Sorrento, 88 km. from Melbourne. The attractive bushland and orchard country of the interior of the peninsula is also the site of much peri-metropolitan development even on the slopes of Arthur's Seat (314 m.), and the E shore will be increasingly built up with the industrial development of Westernport.

Morris, Arthur Robert (1922–) b. Sydney. An outstanding left-handed batsman who added much to Aus. cricket after 1945. In 46 Tests to 1965 he scored 3,533, 12 centuries, average 46·48; in 24 Tests against Eng. he scored 2,080, averaging 50·78 with 8 centuries, including 2 in the 4th Test at Adelaide in 1947.

Morrison, George Ernest (1862–1920) b. Geelong, Vic., where his father (a Scot) was first headmaster of the now famous college. After attaining a medical degree he became a journalist with the *Age* under Syme*, and accomplished many journeys and adventures in Aus. and N.G. After a book on a Chinese journey he became *The Times* correspondent in China and was very widely known and read. From about 1900–19 he was a very powerful political influence, notably on the Dictator Yuan Sh-k'ai, in Peking and achieved the name 'Chinese Morrison'. He appreciated the dangers of Czarist Russian, and later Japanese military expansion in the East. The Morrison Papers held in the Mitchell Library, Sydney, are an unrivalled source on modern Chinese political and social history. *For further reading see* C. Pearl: *Morrison of Peking* (Sydney, 1966).

Morrison, John Gordon (1904–) b. Sunderland, Eng. He arrived in Aus. in 1923. He was the author of vigorous short stories, as in *Sailors Belong Ships* (Melbourne, 1947), also a novel about the urban spread of Melbourne, *The Creeping City* (Melbourne, 1949).

Morshead, Lt.-General Sir Leslie (1889–1959) b. Ballarat. After service at Gallipoli, he commanded the 33rd Battalion, A.I.F. (1916–19). Between the wars he was concerned in the militia, and his private interests were with a shipping line. He commanded the 9th Division in the siege of Tobruk in 1941, and at Alamein in 1942; was G.O.C. of the N.G. Force in 1944, and took a leading part in the Borneo campaign.

Morwell Vic. 38S/146E (16,827 in 1971) Transformed from a small rural centre in dairying country to one of the closely linked series of industrial towns by the great development of open-cut brown-coal mining and electric power industries based upon them, as well as briquetting the lignite. A high-speed conveyer belt 2 km. long carries coal to the new power station at Hazelwood and there is a major power station in Morwell. The briquetting plant uses Yallourn coal, the nearby sources being found unsuitable.

Morwong and **Jackass-fish** A group of edible sea fish of mainly temperate waters, offshore and fairly deep bottom feeders on crabs, shrimps, worms, sea urchins etc., taken mainly by trawl. They are deep-bodied fish, with a continuous dorsal fin, the front part slightly spiny; the pectoral fin has finger-like development of 1 or 2 rays. The plain olive-coloured Morwong, *Nemadactylus douglasii*, and the black-naped Jackass-fish, *N. macropterus*, both have almost rectangular anal fins, as compared with the Brown-banded Morwong, *Cheilodactylus spectabilis*, reddish brown with about 5 darker cross-bands, and the Red Morwong, *C. fuscus*, coppery-red with a dark mid-line along the side.

Moses, Jack (1860–1945) b. Sydney. A travelling wine-salesman, who wrote large numbers of jingles, ballads and stories about personalities and the Aus. bush, of which the best known is 'Nine Miles from Gundagai' (1923). A statue of a dog on a tuckerbox now marks the location of the tale.

Mosman Bay and **Mosman** N.S.W. On the N Shore of Port Jackson, 6·5 km. NE of central Sydney. The Bay was used for the shipping and whaling interests of Archibald and George Mosman (1828–39).

Mosquitoes (family Culicidae in the Order Diptera or Flies*) Include many species, adult females of which are blood-sucking—the males generally suck vegetable sap etc. Egg-laying occurs on water, different species preferring different types of water, and larval and pupal stages are aquatic; the up-and-down movement and head-touch-tail swimming motion of the 'wrigglers' is familiar to many. Aus. has over 100 species of mosquito, including many voracious feeders on man, but they also suck the blood of many other animals, and this is important to their potential as vectors of disease. Aus. *Anopheles* mosquitoes (feeding with head down and body tilted) include proven and occasional vectors of malaria, while *Culex* (feeding with body more or less horizontal) probably include potential vectors of filariasis, dengue and yellow fever. But the reservoir of infection so far appears to have been small, the numbers of mosquitoes large, and the numbers of alternate sources of blood-meals also large, so that after sucking infected human blood, the mosquito may bite a kangaroo at the crucial subsequent period so that the disease cycle is not maintained. A very common culicine species is the Common House Mosquito, *Culex fatigans*, the adult female biting nocturnally and laying eggs in small bodies of stagnant water near houses. A widespread anopheline is *Anopheles annulipes*, a proven malaria vector, breeding in a wide variety of water-bodies—ponds and pools, dams, swamps, rock-pools in mountain streams, and occasionally in brackish water.

Moss Vale N.S.W. 35S/150E (3,233 in 1971) Lies at 673 m. above sea level on the rolling plateau above the scarp, with 75 cm. mean annual rainfall. It is on the main Sydney–Melbourne railway, with an important link to the Wollongong area. It is one of a group of small service centres for a pleasant countryside of wool and fat-lamb production, with patches of market-gardening, and it has limestone quarries. Sutton Forest nearby still has a summer residence for the State Governor, and there is something of a 'hill station' function lingering, with holiday homes, waterfalls and fine view-points on the scarp edge.

Moss-animals Animalcules (Phylum Polyzoa, formerly Bryozoa) Colonial, aquatic, and mainly marine, tentacled animals superficially resembling the Hydrozoa*, but with a more complex structure, reproductive system etc. Each animal has an individual compartment in a colonial structure—branching, horny and plant-like, e.g. *Bugula* spp., a notable pest in fouling small craft in Sydney Harbour; branching but calcareous and somewhat coral-like, the Lace-coral, *Retepora* spp., often seen growing on Kelp, and other seaweeds; and more mat-like and gelatinous forms, e.g. *Membranipora membranacea*, which may also grow on kelp. There are over 3,000 species in the world, many of them widespread; over 100 have been recorded from Sydney Harbour alone.

Mosses Simple plants with over 600 species, include about 50 uniquely Aus., mainly in the moist SW of the continent, and as with other plants, some genera with mainly tropical affinities in the N, and some Antarctic species, mainly in the SW and in alpine environments. Characteristically, they lack true roots though some have hair-like processes underground, and they vary in size from mosses hard to observe with the naked eye to a 30-cm.-high rain-forest moss *Dawsonia superba*, the tallest moss known. There are 6 species of *Sphagnum*, spongy bog mosses, 4 of the red-purple-black, alpine-subalpine genus *Andreaea*, many *Bryales*, the order of mosses which are typical to the layman, including the mainly very small *Fissidens* spp., which grow in suitable sites even in quite arid climates, the *Bryum* spp., including *B. blandum*, an aquatic moss liable to grow on the sides of concrete hydro-electric channels, and *Campylopus*, also a large genus. The club-mosses* *Lycopodium* and *Selaginella* look superficially like mosses, but are in fact ferns* with a much more developed conducting system.

MOTHS These comprise 13 of the 14 super-families in 2 Sub-Orders, discussed under *Lepidoptera**, and summarised here in rough order of more primitive to later-evolved super-families (S.F.) with representative species:

I. Sub-Order Homoneura 1. S.F. Micropterygoidea, represented only by 2 species of minute moths in Qld., which are of interest as the most primitive moths known. 2. S.F. Hepialoidea, Swift or Ghost Moths, comprise 3 Families and some 40 species, including large moths such as the 20–25-cm. *Zelotypia stacyi* of N.S.W., the tawny Bent Wing Swift Moth, the larvae of which make large tunnels in some eucalypts; and *Trictena argentata* of much of the S of Aus. (wing-span 11 cm.), the adults of which are sometimes seen after heavy rains, while the larvae live in a silk-lined tunnel leading to their food source, the roots of certain eucalypts;

II. Sub-Order Heteroneura 1. S.F. Cossoidea, Wood Moths, stout, grey and attracted to light with short antennae often feathery, and larvae tunnelling beneath tree-bark, in the heartwood or in the roots. An example is the inland species *Xyleutes amphiplecta*, in which the adult female is short-winged and flightless, and whose larvae tunnel to feed from the roots of saltbush etc. 2. S.F. Castnioidea, includes 1 primitive family, mainly in W.A., of day-flying moths with clubbed antennae, e.g. *Synemon gerda*, a heath-country moth of almost 4 cm. wing-span, of which the female has bright hind-wings, probably to frighten predators, but the male is drab. 3. S.F. Tineoidea, with 20 families and some 4,000 species of mainly small moths, including the familiar Clothes Moth family Tineidae; the 'typical' family Tineodidae, however, is of small moths with long legs, narrow wings, sometimes deeply divided into plumes, as in the male of *Coenoloba obliteralis*. 4. S.F. Pterophoroidea includes 2 families of Plume moths, with deeply cleft wings forming varying numbers of plumes—24 in the 4 wings of *Orneodes phricodes*, of which the male has a wing-span of about 2 cm. and the larvae feed on the flowers of climbers, e.g. *Tecoma* spp., in humid bushland. 5. S.F. Pyraloidea includes 9 families and well over 1,000 species. The name-family Pyralidae includes mostly long-legged, small to medium-sized moths with rather beak-like and sometimes upward-inclined mouth-parts, often strong fliers and coming readily to light; the larvae are usually shiny and smooth, living between joined leaves, tunnels in various parts of plants, or silk tunnels in forest litter etc. *Tipanaea patulella* is a frail white, 2·5-cm.-long moth with slightly feathery wing edges, the larvae of which bore in rushes, sedge etc.; it is related to pests of rice plants. 6. S.F. Psychoidea includes 3 families, of which the name-family Psychidae includes small to medium moths, winged in both sexes or with a larva-like adult female which never leaves the larval case of silk, ornamented with fragments of sand, moss etc. The larval stage of *Trigonocyttara clandestina* attacks various eucalypts and wattles. 7. S.F. Lasiocampoidea in fact contains only one family of about 50 species, in which the

larvae are covered with soft woolly hairs, while the adults, swift-flying and light-responsive, have stout furry bodies, feathery antennae, and snout-like mouthparts, e.g. *Crexa acedesta* which feeds on mistletoe. 8. S.F. Noctuoidea includes some 1,300 species in 9 families, the larvae of many having stinging hairs, e.g. the Cut-worms of family Noctoidea, with usually sombre-coloured stout-bodied adults of small to medium size, with well-developed proboscis to suck nectar or in some species fermenting juices in over-ripe fruit. The Bogong Moth, *Agrotis infusa*, of SE Aus. is a well-known example; the larval cutworms are almost 4 cm. long; the adults are migratory in summer to the higher mountains, and pests in winter crops and pasture on the low ground. 9. S.F. Uranoidea includes 2 small families, of which the Uraniidea are medium to large broad-winged moths usually with simple antennae, e.g., the large black-and-green *Alcidas zodiaca* often seen feeding on lantana flowers in Qld. or the slender nocturnal *Aploschema discata*, also in rain-forest areas. The Eplemidae, such as *Balantiucha decorata* of Qld., rest with wings rolled and separate, forewings apart and reached forward, rear wings along the body. 10. S.F. Notodontoidae comprises 9 families and over 1,000 species. The family Notodontidae contains many large furry species, with broadly spread antennae, long proboscis and long forewings; they are swift flying and light-responsive, and include the various Hawk Moths, Loopers and species with highly communal larvae living in silk 'bag-shelters' on host trees, e.g. the myall and boree, and occasionally migrating in single file, e.g. the Aus. Puss Moth, *Cerura australis*, black and white spotted fore-wings and green larvae with purplish-brown back and 2 thread-like 'tails', or the Banksia Moth, *Danima banksiae*, with its 'plum-pudding caterpillars'. 11. S.F. Bombycoidea includes 2 notable families, Bombycidae which contains the silkworm moths, e.g. the Aus. Silkworm-moth *Lewinibombyx lewinae*, and the Saturniidae, the Emperor Moth family, e.g. the Emperor Gum-moth, *Antheraea eucalypti*, about 14 cm. across, fawn to red-brown, with pink eye-spots on forewings and orange eye-spots on rear wings—an example of colouration to frighten enemies by simulating the eyes of owls or lizards, not uncommon in large moths and butterflies. 12. The last and presumed to be the last-evolved S.F. is the Papilionoidea, the Butterflies*. (*See* PLATE 2.) *For further reading see* I. F. B. Common: *Australian Moths* (Brisbane, 1963).

Motor Vehicles Aus. is the 3rd most motorised nation, after U.S. and Canada, in terms of vehicles per population. Increase in car-ownership has been rapid in recent years (1945, 1 car to 8 people), although the rate is a rapid indicator of any recession period. Motor taxation supplies 25–35% of revenue to the States which have their own traffic laws. Accident rates averaging 8 killed per 10,000 vehicles, are among the world's highest; absolute numbers increase with registrations and were 3,502 killed, 87,164 injured (1969). Road accidents are the commonest cause of death among young men. The Aus. Safety Council is advisory and undertakes publicity. Wearing seat belts is compulsory in N.S.W. and Vic. They have reduced casualties. The metricated speed limit in built up areas will be 60 km.p.h.

The **motor industry** is one of the country's biggest employers with about 200,000 workers of whom two-thirds are in distribution and service. Manufacture dates from Tarrants' successful Aus.-designed and produced cars (Melbourne, 1901–6) which failed against cheap Ford imports. High tariff protection allowed the development of Aus. body-building and spare parts before 1939, notably in Vic. (which retains over 60% of the body industry). Government determination to foster Aus. manufacture led to the establishment here of foreign-owned companies. General Motors (U.S.) took over Holdens (originally an Adelaide saddlery, then body-works) and produced a specifically Aus. car, the Holden, in 1948, with mainly Aus. material. The stipulated Aus. content in all cars manufactured has been increased, and is a factor in high capital costs in the industry. The five dominant manufacturers are: General Motors-Holden (Adelaide and Melbourne) with some export, Ford of Canada (Geelong and Melbourne), Chrysler (Adelaide), Volkswagen (Melbourne), British Leyland Australia (Sydney). Japanese cars took over 18% of sales (1971): Nissan is planning a plant for engines in Melbourne and Toyota may also seek to satisfy the 85% local content requirement (1975) by local works. British Foden will assemble trucks for SE Asia in Perth; International Harvester in Melbourne makes heavy duty vehicles. Tariff protection for Aus. motor manufacture is about 67%. The small hand assembled Bolwell Nagari made in Melbourne is the only wholly Aus. owned firm. *See* P. Stubbs: *The Aus. Motor Industry: a study in protection and growth* (Melbourne, 1971).

Motor-racing There are circuits in all States, notably that of Warwick Farm in Sydney and Sandown Park in Melbourne. Hill and distance trials are widely sponsored by motor, oil and tyre firms. Racing was first recorded in Perth 1902; S.A. 1903; Vic. 1904; Sydney 1908. Outstanding drivers are the Geoghan brothers, Jack Brabham*, and Kevin Bartlett. Motor-cycling speedway racing has spread from N.S.W. where it was introduced at Maitland in the 1920s.

Mount Barker S.A. 35S/139E (2,340 in 1971) A farming centre in the Mt. Lofty Ranges with dairying and tanning. Mt. Barker subterranean clover is named from the pioneering of this plant by A. W. Howard in the area.

Mount Barker W.A. 35S/118E (1,595 in 1971) At the NW end of the Porongorups*, a service centre for wheat and sheep country. The apple industry centred on the town has suffered recent marketing setbacks.

Mount Beauty Vic. 37S/147E (1,569 in 1971) Formerly owned and built by Vic. State Electricity Commission for workers engaged in the Kiewa* hydro-electric scheme, largely sold for holiday homes on its completion.

Mount Burr S.A. 38S/140E (830 in 1961; 586 in 1971) A timber-milling township (from 1931) in pine plantations near the extinct Tertiary volcanic cone of the same name.

Mount Field National Park Tas. 43S/146E Covers almost 180 km.² of mountain, moorland and lake, easily accessible, 64 km. NW of Hobart, and well developed for winter sports. Mt. Field E is 1,270 m.

Mount Gambier S.A. 38S/141E (17,867 in 1971) The third largest city in the State and a growing service and industrial centre for the SE, with wood-processing based on planted pine forests, dairy produce, concrete pipes, woollen yarn, etc.; waste chips from the sawmill are fed by conveyor belt to a power station. The gridiron street plan is laid on the steeply rising slopes of a former Tertiary volcanic ash and lava cone, first sighted and named after an Admiral by Lieut. Grant from the *Lady Nelson*, in 1800. Lakes in the former craters indicate the water-table in a sub-artesian basin in corallian limestone, quarried elsewhere for its brilliant white smooth building stone. Water is pumped from Blue Lake*.

Mount Garnet Qld. 18S/145E (540 in 1971) On the Atherton Tableland; dredges alluvial tin which supplies some 10% of the Aus. total production. Formerly copper was mined.

Mount Goldsworthy W.A. 21S/120E An iron mine NE of the De Grey River in the Ellerine Hills; ore occurs in haematite lenses with 64% ore content, and is railed 113 km. to Port Hedland* for export.

Mount Isa Qld. 21S/139E (25,240 in 1971) In the Selwyn Range, the main Aus. copper town, with silver, lead and zinc for which the mines were first developed after the accidental discovery in 1923 of silver-lead ores by John Miles a prospector and odd job man (it is said while resting his horse near the Leichhardt River). Large-scale capital has been necessary to exploit the ores, and a history of uncertainty and near-closure has preceded the present prosperity. Copper, found in 1930, was worked from 1939. New discoveries of ore here and 19 km. N possibly mined by 1976 will make Mt. Isa the world's biggest producer of silver/lead/zinc. The ore is railed 970 km. by the reconstructed narrow-gauge rail to Townsville, some for refining there, the rest exported. Mt. Isa lies in harsh remote hills surrounded by spinifex country, but there is compensation in high wages, and amenities including L. Mondarra, dammed on the Leichhardt River (1958) (the projected Julius Dam is 64 km. N). The company is U.S.-controlled.

Mount Keira–Mount Kembla N.S.W. Adjacent bold, forested heights of about 610 m. in the E escarpment looking out over the green coastal belt and the great industrial and residential developments of Wollongong*–Port Kembla, about 10 km. to the E and to L. Illawarra. Beneath the great faces of Hawkesbury sandstone outcrop 3 seams of Permian coal. Mt. Keira had the first mine in the area, exporting to Sydney in 1849, while Mt. Kembla has the mine which suffered Australia's worst mining disaster in loss of life (95 men) in 1902, ascribed to the use of naked lights in the known presence of fire-damp and coal-dust. The 2 mines are now linked by a tunnel and worked as one.

Mount Lofty Ranges S.A. 33–6S/138E The southerly continuation, from about the Peterborough Gap, of the Flinders Ranges*, softer and more humid in landscape. They extend 325 km. S, curving SW in the Jervis Peninsula, and are divided at the Barossa Valley*, into N and S sections. Mt. Lofty (727 m.) was named by Flinders; the general height is 450 m. and the width 24–32 km. Their significance for water catchment and farming in a generally arid State is disproportionately high: a closely settled, intensively cultivated, yet green and wooded landscape gives Adelaide sources of food, water, wine and recreation. The Flinders–Mt. Lofty Highland is a relatively recently up-lifted block of previously folded and worn Precambrian sediments. Rivers form N–S valleys in softer beds, before flowing through defiles to the W coastal plain.

Mount Lyell Tas. 42S/146E A mining area, named like the Company ex-ploiting it, from a hill (844 m.) called after a geologist, in the rugged W Coast Range. Originally mined for gold (from 1881), silver (1893–5) and then copper (1897), the mine, in a saddle between Mt. Lyell and Mt. Owen, now provides over 90% of the State's copper, with silver and gold as by-products, from low grade open-cut deposits. Refining processes for ex-traction from pyrites were pioneered here. Fumes killed the mountain vege-tation, and subsequent erosion under rainfall exceeding 160 cm. a year has left a lunar landscape. New under-ground ore bodies are being developed. The copper goes by road to Hobart to the fabrication plant and for export to Port Kembla*. The original rack and pinion railway to Strahan has been dismantled. The workers live in Queenstown*.

Mount Morgan Qld. 24S/150E (3,733 in 1971) Named after the 3 Morgan brothers who, with 3 others began the exploitation of the 'mountain of gold' in 1882, which under 2 subsequent companies (1886–1927 and from 1929) has extracted over 100 tonnes of gold and 250,000 tonnes of copper. Open-cut excavation of the 230-m.-deep 'Glory Hole' has transformed the rocky mountain to a gaping terraced crater above the town on the Dee River flats below.

Mount Newman W.A. 23S/120E (3,889 in 1971) A new iron-ore town-ship in the Ophthalmia Range, built from 1967, along with 420 km. of rail to Port Hedland*, to exploit the enor-mous iron reserves of at least 1,000 million tonnes, in Mt. Whaleback a few kilometres to the S, discovered in 1956, Mt. Newman was named after Aubrey Newman, a West Australian surveyor, in 1896.

Mount Royal Range N.S.W. A N–S divide between the Hunter* and Manning* catchments, extending S from S of Tamworth, 31S/151E, with 125–180 cm. mean annual rainfall and culminating in the broad dissected dome of Barrington Tops*.

Mount Stromlo Observatory A.C.T. 11 km W of Canberra, from which domes of the telescope housing are visible on the top of the wooded hill. Established in 1911, it has 8 telescopes, from 5 to 74 in. (12·7 cm.–1·88 m.). In-corporated into the Australian National University in 1957, important work has been done on the Milky Way and Stars of the Southern Hemisphere.

Mount Tom Price W.A. 23S/117E (3,370 in 1971) An iron mine and town built since 1965 exploiting haema-tite by open cut. Highly mechanised methods are used for crushing, stock piling and loading over a tunnel: 166 trucks each over 100 tonnes are loaded in 70 minutes as a train creeps through, then taken by the new standard-gauge, 294-km. line to Dampier*. Thomas Price was vice-president of a U.S. steel corporation.

Mount Wells   N.T. 13S/132E   A small mining settlement with treatment battery near the Mary River. There are mainly tin ores but also some gold.

Mountain Devil A popular name for the E Aus. flowering shrub *Lambertia formosa* from its 'horned demon' fruit; and also for the small spiny lizard *Moloch horridus* (*see* LIZARDS).

Mountain Devil
(*Lambertia formosa*), *flower about 5 cm. tall*

Mountain Ebony (*Bauhinia hookeri*) A slow-growing 15-m. tree of the drier woodlands of Central and NW Qld., a member of the largely tropical family Caesalpinaceae. It has 2·5-cm. roundish but 2-lobed leaves, mid-green and slightly paler below, drooping white-pink flower-spikes, producing 2–4 curved seed pods of 10 by 2·5 cm. Its relative, *B. carroni*, with an over-lapping, but wider distribution, has striking red flowers. The wood is dark and good for cabinet-making.

Mountain Gum (*Eucalyptus dalrymple-ma*) A tree of 27–36 m. by 90–120 cm., found in reliable rainfalls of 90–140 cm. at 600–1,400 m. in Vic. and S N.S.W., and at 300–900 m. in Tas. Juvenile leaves are heart-shaped, adult leaves narrowly lanceolate and 15–25 cm. long. Buds are in small clusters, ovoid to pointed, fruit hemispheric to conic with several sharp points. The bark is fine and scales readily in strips to leave a

pattern of light and dark grey, white and pink.

Mouse-bird One popular name for the Rufous Scrub-bird*, from its mouse-like running along tunnel tracks in forest litter.

Mudgee N.S.W. 33S/150E (5,583 in 1971) A local road, rail and service centre with several small factories (textiles, timber, brewing and butter) in the wheat-sheep belt of the Central Tablelands region. It grew with the gold-fields in the 1850s. The boyhood home of Henry Lawson* was nearby at Eurunderee, and the district colours much of his writing.

Mudlark, Magpie Lark, Peewee or **Peewit** (*Grallina cyanoleuca*—black and-white stilted bird) A bird about 30 cm. long with longish legs and smallish beak, which is grouped with the White-winged Chough* and the Apostle Bird* as the Mud-nesters. The somewhat exhibitionist flying and calling *peewee* on being disturbed, particularly on taking off and landing, the rapid walk and the pied plumage

Mudlark (*Grallina cyanoleuca*), *about 30 cm. long*

are a little reminiscent of the European plover though there is no relationship; but the mud-nest is quite different; it is situated on the limb of a tree, preferably near water for the Mudlark builds with mud from a creek or dam etc., and also eats snails as well as insects; sometimes in quite a suburban area. There are 4–6 pinkish eggs with purplish and grey blotches. The bird will wait near a gardener turning over soil for a harvest of grubs etc.

Mueller, Sir Ferdinand von (1825–1896) b. Rostock, Germany. He came to Aus. in 1848 for health reasons, and became a great botanical collector and writer. As Vic. Government botanist from 1853, he organised Melbourne Botanic Gardens. He travelled widely in Vic. and was with A. C. Gregory* on his 1855–7 expedition across Northern Aus. He did much to encourage exploitation of the eucalypt for oil, and its planting abroad. For his work he received many honours, and was affectionately termed 'the Baron'. In 9 years he collected over 9,000 new Aus. plant specimens. 2 mountain ranges and 3 peaks bear his name.

Mulga An Aboriginal and popular name for some species of Wattle* (*Acacia*), widespread on sandy and loamy soils in the 12 to 25-cm. mean annual rainfall areas, of Aus. Particularly used for *A. aneura*, a shrub 2·5–6 m. high. The 'leaves' are flattened leaf stalks, about 5 cm. by 3 mm. The feathery yellow flower-spikes are about 20 mm. long, followed by flat, slightly sticky pods, 2·5 cm. by 6 mm. *A. cyperophylla*, Red Mulga, is similar, but has reddish bark and pods 5–7 cm. long, thickened and sticky at the edges. The leaves are eaten by stock, and insects sometimes form galls, 'Mulga Apples', which can provide water for travellers. The name is also used for scrub dominated by Mulga Bushes. Originally, the Aboriginal word mulga was used for a

long narrow shield of hard wood made from species of Myall*.

Mulga-grass A popular name for a number of genera and species of forage grasses including the small leafy tufts of *Aristida arenaria*, with the 3-awned seed-heads characteristic of a genus that also includes White Spear-grass, *A. leptotoda*, and Feathertop, *A. latifolia*. The term is also applied to *Danthonia bipartita*, with an almost bulbous woolly base, but in a genus treated under Wallaby-grass*, and for several Aus. species of the widespread tropical genus *Neurachne*, e.g. the Mulga Mitchell, *N. mitchelliana*, and the Foxtail Mulga, *N. alopecuroides*, of loose sandy soils in SE and SW Aus.

Mulla Mulla A W.A. name for various *Trichinium* species in the herbaceous flower family Amaranthaceae. (*See* HAIRY-TAILS.)

Mullet These fish inhabit warm fresh and salt waters of many countries; Aus. species are mainly grey to silver and normally 25–45 cm. long and 0·5–0·9 kg. in weight, different species having some distinctive colour in the fins. They are bottom feeders on organic material in muds etc. Several species are commercially important, notably the Sea Mullet, *Mugil dobula*, the Silver Mullet, *M. georgii*, the Yellow-eye, *Aldrichetta forsteri* (important in the Swan River fisheries), and the Flat-tail, *Moolgarda argentea*. Some species will occasionally take a bait.

Mullewa W.A. 29S/115E A small rural service centre at almost the NW limit of the wheat belt*, on the Northam–Geraldton line, developed also with Tallaring Peak iron, 42 km. to the N.

Mulligan, James Venture (1837–1907) b. County Down, Ireland. He arrived in Aus. in 1837. Following Hann's reports, he found Palmer River gold in 1873; in 1875 he found Hodgkinson River gold, and first reported silver W of Herberton. His incidental exploratory work was important in opening up this corner of Qld., including the Atherton Tableland*.

Mulloway and **Teraglin** (*Sciaena antarctica* and *Zeluco atelodus*) These are 2 related sea fish, the former very widely distributed and apparently unique to Aus. waters, the latter off E Aus. and it seems migrating N in winter. Both names are Aboriginal, and preferred to Jewfish and other popular names. The Mulloway is silvery-grey to greenish and up to 1·8 m. and 50 kg.; the Teraglin is bluish, smaller and more slender, often about 2·5 kg., though reaching 1 m. and 9 kg.

Mundaring Weir W.A. 32S/116E On the Helena River SE of Perth; it was built with a capacity of 20,000 m.³ (1898), for what is now the Goldfields and Agricultural Water Supply*. It was increased in 1951 and again recently to 77,000 m.³

Murchison River W.A. 28S/115E A sporadically flowing watercourse, fed mainly by winter rains, and 725 km. long, running W then S and W from the Robinson Range to Gantheaume Bay. It was named after an English scientist by Grey* on his heroic forced march from Shark Bay to the Swan in 1839. **Murchison Gold-field,** declared in 1891, and with ephemeral influxes to Nanine, Cue, Day Dawn, Peak Hill and other centres, still produces some 10% of the W.A. gold output.

Murdoch, Sir Keith Arthur (1885–1952) b. Melbourne. He was a vigorous and controversial war correspondent in the 1914–18 War, and from 1921 edited the Melbourne evening paper, the *Herald.* Later he built up the first major Aus. inter-state chain of newspaper interests. His son Rupert (b. 1931) founded the national daily *The Australian* (1964) and has extensive Aus. and U.K. newspaper and television interests.

Murdoch, Sir Walter Logie Forbes (1874–1970) b. Aberdeenshire, Scot-

land. He was the leading Aus. essayist and the first Professor of English Literature in the University of W.A. 1912–39, then Chancellor 1943–7. His style is light, unpretentious, deceptively simple and often humorous, as in *Speaking Personally* (1930). The second university of W.A. is named after him.

Murranji Track N.T. Once a notorious 400-km stock route from Newcastle Waters, 17S/133E, to Top Springs, 145 km. from the Victoria River*, skirting the Tanami Desert and going through thick scrub with only 3 unreliable waterholes. Now a graded beef road with regular bores runs a little to the N. It was pioneered by Nathaniel Buchanan for W-moving cattle to stock new properties in the 1880s, and later used for store cattle going E.

Murray A new city for 200,000 to be built near Murray Bridge* using world experts in city design.

Murray Bridge S.A. 35S/139E (7,400 in 1971) On the lower Murray, where the main Melbourne–Adelaide road and rail cross it, but originating on the overland route to Adelaide and with an important period as a river port.

Murray Cod (*Maccullochella macquariensis*) The sporting and commercial king of Aus. freshwater fish, it reaches 1·8 m. long and 80 kg. on its diet of Murray basin shrimps, mussels, crayfish, frogs etc. It is a large brown-spotted olive-green fish with rounded tail and continuous dorsal fin (the front part spined), very deep and broad bodied in large specimens. Its blue to white variant, said to frequent faster-running water and to be a better sporting fish, is now allotted to the same species, though popularly distinguished as the Trout-cod. It seems to be losing ground to the introduced perch and (useless) carp, and perhaps also because of alterations in the river ecology through human interference, including lower water temperatures through reservoir construction.

Murray Islands Qld. 10S/144E With Darnley Island, the most northerly outpost of Qld. There are 3 islands Dower, Wyder and Maer or Murray; the latter has most of the population, and striking extinct volcanic craters.

Murray River The principal river of Aus. flowing mainly W and NW over 2,580 km from the 100- to 130-cm. rainfall belt of the 900- to 1,800-m. Aus. Alps region into great riverine plains with only 25–40 cm. mean annual rainfall, then almost S through a terminal gorge in 60-m.-high Tertiary sediments, to enter the lagoon of L. Alexandrina, hemmed in by the multiple curved sand ridges enclosing the Coorong*. The setting is therefore a classic one for irrigation potential, now increased by the combined hydro-electric and irrigation Snowy Mts.* project. Its last 320 meandering km. are in S.A., but nearly all the rest of its long course forms the State boundary between N.S.W. and Vic., hence the need for the Murray River Commission responsible for equitable sharing of the waters since 1915. From its source among mountain ash forests, it drops about 900 m. in 50 km, flowing NE to Tom Groggin before turning NW into a gorge through the lowest ridge of the SW wall of the Snowy Mts., then falling gradually as it turns more westerly through the foothills to Albury at just over 150 m. where the Hume Reservoir* is one of a chain of works to secure perennial irrigation downstream. The plains course includes anabranches—the largest, the Edwards River, links up with the Murrumbidgee through Yanco Creek, itself regulated as part of the Murrumbidgee Irrigation Area* in N.S.W.—and billabongs or backwaters from former meander courses. These gave warm and insect-rich waters breeding the large, perch-like Murray cod*; round them were impressive swamps with many water-fowl and forests including the river red gum. Water temperature and water-levels are altered by the irrigation works, and these natural environments are only found residually. Flowing W, the Murray receives the rivers flowing N from the Aus. Alps—the Goulburn, Ovens, Campaspe, Loddon and Avoca, themselves important sources of irrigation. Kow Swamp, on an anabranch, has been turned into another storage reservoir, and a number of weirs, e.g. those at Yarrawonga and Torrumbarry raise the water-level sufficiently to feed it into distribution canals. Towns such as Echuca and Swan Hill have made the transition from river ports to service centres for irrigation districts. Some 80 km. NW of Swan Hill, the Murray receives the main Murrumbidgee waters. It turns more westerly near Mildura, 34S/142E, receives the sporadic Darling waters from the N near Wentworth, at a junction impressive for the roar and power of the waters surging controlled through the sluices, amid the quiet of the riverine forest here happily preserved. It flows W through Renmark, 34S/141E, all this having been classic country for pump irrigation from the days of Deakin and the Chaffey* brothers. The Chowilla Dam* site is 10 km. downstream from the S.A. border. Then comes the great elbow near Morgan, 34S/139E, and the southward course past holiday cottages and the cliffed bluffs through the rim of the basin to L. Alexandrina. There are 5 barrages (1940) linking islands, making a 24-km. barrier to prevent salt water penetrating the channel and maintain water-levels 80 km. upstream to permit gravity irrigation of dairy pastures along the reclaimed flood-plain. *For further reading see* J. Rutherford: *The Southern Murray Basin* (Melbourne, 1961).

Murrumbidgee River N.S.W. A major right-bank tributary of the Murray* which flows for 2,175 km. from alpine meadows NE of the Snowy

Mts.*, at first S and SE through the new reservoir at Tantangara, turning N at a marked elbow NW of Cooma, 36S/149E, flowing through the A.C.T. W of Canberra, turning westerly, dammed in the first great irrigation reservoir of Burrinjuck near Yass, 35S/149E, then through the rolling pastures of the Western Slopes, past Gundagai and Wagga Wagga. It leaves the 75 to 100-cm. rainfall belt to flow W into successively drier country, with 25–40 cm., where it receives the Lachlan* from the right and then joins the Murray. At first it is a little incised into older alluvial deposits of 'prior streams' which built up the plain, then in the annually inundated Lowbidgee* country. At Wagga Wagga, after 645 km. and 2·75 million ha. of its catchment, the average annual flow is almost 3,700 million m.³, with a marked early summer peak flow, including snowmelt from the Snowy Mts.

The Murrumbidgee Irrigation Area N.S.W., at present covers about 142,000 ha. of which some 70,850 ha. are irrigated, over a third intensively for rice, fruit etc., the rest for fodder and pastures. The basic system dates from 1912 with the Burrinjuck Dam ponding back the Murrumbidgee and its left-bank tributary, the Goodradigbee, near Yass, 35S/149E, and 390 km. downstream, the Berembed Weir, which lifts the water to feed the main canal by gravity, at first flowing near the river and then NW towards the Lachlan through the intensively irrigated areas round Leeton* and Griffith* to the stock irrigation area of Wah Wah. There are also weirs at Maude and Redbank, and new ones at Yanco and Gogeldrie, beginning the expansion permitted by part of the Snowy Mts. Scheme* project, mainly the Tantangara reservoir on the Murrumbidgee and the Blowering dam on the Tumut (*see also* COLEAMBALLY). A small area around Hay, 34S/145E, is irrigated by pumping

and there are various pumping agreements with individual riparian landholders. The main M.I.A. project was accomplished by means of widespread resumption of land by the N.S.W. Government, mainly from large pastoralists. Many opposed the scheme, urging that irrigation could be as well used by adaptation of existing land-use practices, but McCaughey* supported it even though much of his land was resumed, and many of the assumptions were based on the favourable results of cropping parts of his properties irrigated by pumping. The original scheme included concentric rings of different property sizes round the main towns of Leeton and Griffith—2 ac. (0·8 ha.), 5 ac. (2 ha.), 10 ac. (4 ha.), then 25–50 ac. (10–20 ha.), but modified to holdings of 0·8 ha. intended as part-time small-holdings for wage-earners, 4 ha. for horticulture, and 20 ha. for mixed farming, and all were varied according to the quality of land. The project can now claim some striking successes: the fruit farms, especially since many of the small-holdings have been taken over by families of Italian origin; some fine citrus orchards; rice in rotation with sheep pastures, producing the highest yields in the world on a highly mechanised system; and many irrigated stock farms. The suitability of particular qualities of land for particular purposes is now well understood, and control over heavy watering, e.g. for rice, is exercised in order to reduce risks of waterlogging and increasing salinity of the topsoil. However, many bankruptcies and much loss to government and individuals occurred, and the precise methods to be used in further extension of irrigation remain surprisingly controversial. *For further reading see* T. Langford-Smith and J. Rutherford: *Water and Land: two case studies in Irrigation* (Canberra, 1966).

Murwillumbah N.S.W. 28S/153E (7,374 in 1971) An important sugar- and butter-processing and service centre in the lower Tweed* basin, the terminus of the N Coast branch railway from Casino.

Museums For public use number 9 major and 18 smaller institutions, while 3 major and 4 smaller institutions combine the functions of Museums and Art Galleries* (1970). In the A.C.T. is the Australian War Memorial* and the Australian Institute of Anatomy with biological, anatomical and anthropological displays. In N.S.W. the Australian Museum, Sydney (1836), is the oldest in the country, with major natural history, ethnographic, geological and other collections, active research, educational activity and publication, including the quarterly *Australian Natural History*. The Museum of Applied Arts and Sciences, Sydney, has branches in Bathurst, Broken Hill and Goulburn. Also in Sydney is the only purely Geological and Mining Museum in Aus. Sydney University has the Macleay Museum of Natural History and the Nicholson Museum of Antiquities open to the public. In Vic. the National Museum (1854), Melbourne, has natural history and ethnographic collections, educational and research activities, and there is also the Institute of Applied Sciences. The Queensland Museum, Brisbane, dates from 1855. The South Australian Museum, Adelaide, which has outstanding Aboriginal collections, dates from 1862 and the West Australian Museum, Perth, from 1895. In Tas. Museum and Art Galleries are combined in Hobart and Launceston. A number of small museums have been established privately in or near historic sites, mainly to house local relics.

Musgrave Ranges S.A./N.T. border 26S/130E They extend for some 160 km. E–W and 16 km. N–S, rising to 1,525 m. in Mt. Woodruffe which does not stand out from the jumble of round-topped but steep-sided hills of red granite and gneiss which lie in short N–S ranges. Wide valley floors have richer saltbush than the prevailing mulga and the giant 'spinifex'*, but only occasional watercourses; there are Mission Stations, and it is an Aboriginal Reserve. They were sighted in 1873 by W. C. Gosse and named after the S.A. Governor.

Mushrooms and Toadstools Fungi* of the family Agaricaceae, with the well-known gilled formation of the head; they include many edible species though of varying flavour, and none of the most poisonous ones. The genus *Psalliota* includes the Field, Horse and Forest Mushrooms. The white-spored Parasol Mushroom is *Lepiota* spp., and there are many colourful species of *Cortinarius*, *Hygrophorus* etc. The luminous, 'Fairy Ring' and other Toadstools* and Horsehair fungi, belong to the same family. The most poisonous members of the genus *Amanita* are not met in Aus., though the white-flecked orange or red *A. muscaria* is sometimes seen under exotic trees in Vic.

Music Aus. has been slow to produce indigenous creative work of the international stature yet character, say, of Nolan's paintings, yet there is currently a strong demand for performed, particularly orchestral music. The country has produced a disproportionate number of singers of world repute: Melba*, Joan Sutherland*, Majorie Lawrence, June Bronhill, Sylvia Fisher, Frances Alda, Joan Hammond and Elizabeth Tippett; baritones Peter Dawson, David Brownlee and John Shaw; and the basses Stanley Clarkson and Lempriere Pringle. All live, or lived, and were trained overseas; Donald Smith (tenor) has now returned. (*For further reading see* B. and F. Mackenzie: *Singers of Australia*, Melbourne, 1967). The organist William McKie, pianists Eileen Joyce,

William Murdoch, Mewton-Wood and conductors Constant Lambert and Mackerras, and the composers Percy Grainger, Roy Agnew, Malcolm Williamson and Arthur Benjamin are also well-known musical expatriates. Permanent orchestras are maintained in the State capitals under the Australian Broadcasting Commission* which also invites overseas artists, organises schoolchildren and adult concerts and encourages Aus. composition. In many schools, however, music has a low priority in time and equipment. Conservatoria of music, in Sydney, Melbourne and Adelaide and the Canberra School of Music provide training, but do not have quite the status of similar American and European institutions.

Early instigators of performance and training include Deane* in Tas. (1826), Wallace in Sydney (1836–8), Nathan* in the 1840s and Levey*, the theatrical entrepreneur. Governor Bourke encouraged music and established the Sydney Philharmonic Society in 1833. From mid-19th century until the 1914–18 War there was a growing enthusiasm for amateur choral societies and for visiting operatic companies and stars, but between the wars there was a period of decline in musical interest within the country and an increasing exodus of talent. From 1945 there was revival, encouraged partly by European migrants increasing both artists and audiences, but Aus. suffered from lack of instrumentalists other than pianists. In the 1960s however there was a rapid development of performance of skill and variety, in which modern composition has been able to thrive. Modern composers include Meale, Butterley, Sculthorpe, le Galliene, Sitzky*, Dreyfus*, Hollier, Werder. Works are increasingly written on commision. The Commonwealth Assistance to Aus. Composers scheme guarantees publishers, and there is an increasing and appreciated flow of New Music, encouraged by the A.B.C.

and Musica Viva. *See* R. Covell: *Australia's Music* (Melbourne, 1967).

Muslims Although numbering only about 8,000, they are of interest in their origins in Aus. with the coming of the Afghan* camel-drivers and E European migrants. They had decreased considerably until stimulated by post-war temporary Asian student needs. There are Mosques in Canberra, Broken Hill, Shepparton (Vic.) and Perth. Turkish workers from 1968 have added to the Muslim total.

Musquito A N.S.W. Aborigine transported for murder to Tas. (1813), who tracked down Howe*, then turned bushranger himself, organising a native gang which he taught to farm and use the boomerang, and which savagely attacked settlements.

Muswellbrook or **Muscle Brook** N.S.W. 32S/151E (8,082 in 1971) A mining and local centre in the farming country in the upper Hunter* Valley. Thick coal seams are exploited by open cut (output being controlled as a matter of policy, to protect employment of skilled miners whose jobs were threatened), and by moderate-sized mechanised tunnels along the seams, including the State mine at Liddell* which also has a large power station. Its regional function in the upper valley suffices to give it some solidity and prosperity as against a certain seediness in many mining towns.

Mutton-bird or **Short-tailed Shearwater** (*Puffinus tenuirostris* — slender-billed) A migratory, oceanic, surface-feeding bird, about 38–45 cm. long, brown and inconspicuous, migrating to get 2 summers, from Japan to breeding sites in burrows in islands of SE Aus. It was an important food of certain Aboriginal groups who got to the islands at considerable risk, to collect an annual harvest of young birds from the burrows. There is now a considerable amount of commercial exploitation of the mutton-bird by the white man. The nesting areas are quiet by day but noisy by night, when parent birds change shifts, feed the young, and return or depart from fishing at sea.

Mutton-bird (Puffinus tenuirostris), about 45 cm. long

Myall, Weeping Myall, Bastard Gidgee or **Boree** (*Acacia pendula*) A 9-m. tree in the family Mimosaceae, growing in the drier parts of N.S.W. and Qld., often on occasionally inundated clay pans. A tree with coarse grey-black bark, and silver-grey foliage of narrow, lanceolate 'leaves', actually flattened leaf-stalks, hanging like a weeping willow, a valuable food for stock in drought. Single or bunched flowers are succeeded by crinkled 7-cm. seed pods. Timber is dark, fragrant and used for boomerangs by Aborigines and also for tool handles and fancy woodwork, particularly tobacco pipes. Myall is also used for other species of *Acacia* in other parts of Aus. (*See* PLATE 7.)

Myall Lakes. N.S.W. A complex system of coastal lagoons hemmed in by dune-crowned sand barriers about 64 km. NE of Newcastle, 33S/152E. A National Park of 34,000 ha. conflicts to some degree with mining of mineral sands*.

Myer, Sidney (1878–1934) b. Russia. He arrived in Aus. in 1898, where he developed the beginnings of the great department store bearing his name, from a drapery shop in Bendigo, Vic., in 1900. The **Myer Music Bowl** in Melbourne, modelled on that of Hollywood, is among many benefactions.

Myrtaceae (Myrtle family) Worldwide in the warmer climates, includes the 2 sub-families: 1. the dry-capsuled Leptospermoideae mostly Aus. and containing the *Eucalyptus**, *Angophora**, *Leptospermum* (*see* TEA-TREE), *Melaleuca* (*see* PAPERBARK), *Callistemon* (*see* BOTTLEBRUSH), *Syncarpia* (*see* TURPENTINE) and various heath-like genera such as the Fringe-myrtle, *Calytrix tetragona* (*see* MYRTLE); and 2. the Myrtoideae with fleshy berry-like fruits, including *Eugenia* spp. (e.g. the Lilly-pilly*, Weeping Myrtle) and the poisonous Finger Cherry, *Rhodomyrtus macrocarpa*, of E Aus.

Myrtle This name is applied in Aus. to many trees, some in the world-wide Myrtaceae* family, such as the Weeping Myrtle, *Eugenia ventinatii*, described below; others are not related, e.g. the so-called Myrtle Beech or Myrtle in the Antarctic Beech* genus *Nothofagus*. The Weeping Myrtle of N and E Aus. is named from its dense pendent evergreen foliage of 10 cm. dark glossy leaves. Small flowers in many branched multiple heads are succeeded by 1 cm. berries with a stone. It gives a good cabinet wood and is grown in many gardens. The Fringe Myrtle, *Calythrix tetragona*, in the Myrtaceae family, is a widespread heath-like plant with dainty pink stars with about 20 prominent stamens and a hairy fringe prolonged from the sepals.

Myxomatosis A virus disease of rabbits*—in Aus. chiefly mosquito-borne —by means of which rabbits have been much reduced in recent years in much of the country.

N

NAMATJIRA

Namatjira, Albert (1902–1959) b. N.T. Aboriginal artist. He was trained to paint in watercolour by Rex Batterbee (from 1936), who found that he had a great facility to depict the Central Aus. landscapes. He exhibited in Melbourne in 1938 and was widely acclaimed. Tragically, in spite of much well-meaning effort by many people, the publicity, agitation to grant him full citizenship (1957) and frank commercial exploitation, led to his drinking, and prosecution ensued from his sharing this privilege with his kinsmen. He died of heart disease, on the Hermannsburg Mission* where he was born.

Nambour Qld. 27S/153E (6,744 in 1971) 16 km. inland on the narrow coastal corridor E of the timbered Blackall Range, 112 km. N of Brisbane. It serves a sugar and tropical fruit area, and has sugar and timber works.

Namoi River N.S.W. A main headstream of the Darling*, rising as the Macdonald River in the S of the New England* plateau E of Tamworth, 31S/151E, flowing N and NW round the end of the Moonbi Range* to turn SW, then NW to join the Barwon (Darling) near Walgett, 30S/148E. Its course of 850 km. goes from 75–125 cm. rainfall country to 35 to 50 cm. in savannah and tussock grassland country now used for extensive wool-sheep grazing. It ceases to be perennial soon after Walgett, and on the whole is slow, shallow, spreading out in fairly sluggish sheets, even in floods. At Gunnedah, 31S/150E, after 350 km. and with a catchment of 1·7 million ha., it has an average annual flow of only 740 million m.³ (cf. short E-flowing rivers such as the Clarence* or Macleay*). Keepit Dam* irrigates cotton* along 50 km. of the N bank.

NARRAN

Naracoorte S.A. 37S/141E (4,399 in 1971) A service centre for the drained dairy and sheep pastures of the SE of the State; it developed early on the higher E rim of the region, and was stimulated by gold routes. It now has dairy factories, and caters for visitors to the nearby limestone caves.

Nardoo or **Clover Fern** (*Marsilea quadrifolia*) A creeping fern* with leaves like 4-leaved clovers, growing in swampy areas and eaten by stock. The fruiting bodies, like very hard oval peas, used to be an Aboriginal food, though not very nourishing . It saved the explorer King (*see* BURKE). The fruits were ground between stones, the lower with a channel, through which the watery paste ran off; it was cooked as a damper or eaten as it was. In Qld. the name Nardoo was used for a member of the Pea* family, *Sesbania aculeata*, apparently used similarly.

Narrabri N.S.W. 30S/150E (6,875 in 1971) An important and growing local centre of the W slopes region for marketing, services and processing agricultural and forest produce (flour, meat, sawmilling, joinery and oilseeds). The Pilliga Scrub* country lies to the SW, including much forest reserve, and the Nandewar Range (Mt. Kaputar, 1,524 m.), with a small National Park, stands out above the plain to the E. The town stands on an anabranch of the Namoi*. The C.S.I.R.O. radio heliograph is nearby.

Narran, Lake N.S.W. 30S/147E Alternatively called Terewah. It is 30 km. N–S by 10 km. wide, and the outlet of the Narran River, a 200-km.-long distributary of the Balonne-Culgoa headwaters of the Darling.

Narrandera N.S.W. 35S/147E (4,825 in 1971) A railway junction and local market centre, which shares in the prosperity brought by the Murrumbidgee Irrigation Area*—but remains a centre for a wide pastoral area more than the new towns of Leeton* and Griffith* to the NW. The fine courthouse is a reminder of its century of history.

Narrogin W.A. 33S/117E (4,843 in 1971) A major wheat belt* centre which developed with the Great Southern Railway, especially when it became the junction of lines both E into the wheat lands and W to the coastal plain. Water is piped 128 km. from the Wellington Dam on the Collie River, to be further distributed NE to Brookton and SE to Katanning.

Nathan, Isaac (1790–1864) b. Canterbury, Eng. A musician who moved among royal and literary circles in London before reaching Sydney in 1841. There he dominated the musical scene, through teaching and composition mainly of light opera. His *Don John of Austria* (1848) was the first opera to be written and performed in Aus.

National Parks They vary widely between States in administration, and equally widely in function, from accessible picnic areas to wide stretches of primitive country. The total area is 1·8% of Aus. (1970) and there is a continuous struggle between those concerned with conservation*, with public amenity and with exploitation of resources. Some States have established parks and reserves by means of National Parks legislation (Tas., Qld., Vic., S.A., N.S.W.). There are also many other reserves of National Park type, but not with that name. In addition nearly all States have separately administered systems of fauna reserves. The most advanced legislation is that of N.S.W., which centralised control in its National Parks and Wildlife Service in 1967. In the following list

the approximate percentage of reserved area (1970) is given in brackets for each State.
N.S.W. (1·3%). 12 National Parks, ranging from the 535,000-ha. Kosciusko National Park to the valuable recreational area of Royal National Park (1879) and Ku-ring-gai Chase near Sydney. Further inland are the Warrumbungle*, New England* and Blue Mts.* Parks, and in the far W Kinchega on the Darling River. There are also 4 State Parks, 6 Historic Sites, 63 Nature Reserves, 1 Game and 11 Flora.
Vic. (1·1%). The 2 largest of the 23 National Parks are the mallee* area of Wyperfeld* and the coasts and forests of Wilsons Promontory*. Others are Kinglake and Mt. Buffalo in the Highlands, and Mallacoota Inlet*. There are 33 Wildlife Reserves.
Qld. (0·6%). Of the 270 National Parks, 23 are islands, including Hinchinbrook* and Whitsunday*. The largest is the 505,000-ha. Simpson Desert* National Park. Others are the rain-forested Eungella Ranges behind Mackay, Bellenden Ker* Range in the N and Lamington in the McPherson Range* in the S. Many parks under 400 ha. are termed Scenic Areas; 5 Sanctuaries.
Tas. (6·7%) has 80 Scenic and Historic Reserves of which 9 are National Parks. They include Cradle Mt.-L. St. Clair* (135,000 ha.), L. Pedder*, Mt. Field*, Ben Lomond, Frenchmans Cap, Hartz Mts. and Freycinet Peninsula. 36 Sanctuaries.
S.A. (3·4%) has 67 National Parks. Hincks and Hambidge are large mallee reserves; others are Wilpena Pound*, Flinders Chase* and 57 other reserves.
W.A. (1·2%). The largest of 326 Reserves are Prince Regent River (634,000 ha.) and Kalbarri National Park. There are several along the SW coast, e.g. Nornalup and Cape le Grand.
N.T. (3·5%). The Tanami Desert* Sanctuary (3,756,000 ha.) is the largest wildlife reserve in Aus. Other important parks are Ayers Rock*-Mt. Olga National Park (134,000 ha.) and Co-

bourg Peninsula Sanctuary. There are
36 Reserves and 5 Sanctuaries.
A.C.T. (1·9%) has one 4,700 ha. fauna
reserve at Tidbinbilla.
   See V. Serventy: *Australia's National
Parks* (Sydney, 1969); M. Morcombe:
Australia's National Parks (Melbourne)
1969).

National Trusts   Beginning in N.S.W.
in 1945, there are now independent
organisations in each State, receiving
some Government grants, but largely
dependent on donations.

Nationalist Party   A right-wing political
party formed 1917 under Hughes*. It
continued in power under him until
1923 when the powerful Country Party*
interests on which it relied insisted on
Hughes's replacement by Bruce. The
party remained in power until 1929.
It re-appeared with the infusion of new
blood as the United Australia Party*
in 1931.

Naturalisation   The process by which
aliens become Aus. citizens. Appli-
cants of 5 years' residence, take the
oath of allegiance and are required to
show an adequate knowledge of the
responsibilities and privileges of citizenship. Public ceremonies with groups of
migrants receiving their certificates are
held locally, and presided over by the
head of the local Government authority.

Nauru Island   0S/167E   Only 22 km.^{2}
in area, is dependent on royalties
from its phosphate rocks which will be
exhausted by 1990. A joint U.K.-Aus.-
N.Z. Mandate took over from German
rule in 1919, and became a Trusteeship
in 1945 with complete independence in
1968 and control of the phosphate
industry from 1970. Of a population of 5,561 (1965) almost half are
Nauruans and 25% are other Pacific
Islanders, with 900 Chinese and 500
Europeans.

Nautilus   A floating oceanic Cephalo-
pod* such as the Pearly Nautilus, which
has a beautiful cream-and-brown mot-

*Nautilus,
about one-fifth life size*

tled shell and is sometimes blown
ashore in E Aus. from an easterly
storm.

Navy, Royal Australian   At present
takes almost 25% of the defence
budget and in June 1971 had 17,820
men with 5,128 reservists. It has
a small but well-balanced fleet ranging
from an aircraft-carrier and a fast
troop-transport, destroyers and guided
missile destroyers, minesweepers and
a boom defence ship with appropriate
support, training and survey vessels
and shore establishments. A submarine fleet is being built up, the anti-
submarine power strengthened and
patrol vessels built.
   The R.A.N. dates from 1910, building upon influential reports by Vice-
Admiral Sir William Creswell, and in
its short history has participated with
honour in notable naval battles and
exploits: in the 1914–18 War the destruction of the cruiser *Emden* and the
forcing of the Dardanelles by the submarine AE2, though the crew had to
sink her and surrender, and in the
1939–45 War the crucial Guadalcanal
landings in August 1942.
   Naval defence was in the hands of the
Royal Navy until 1887, with some
moves towards auxiliary naval brigades.
At one time it appeared that only
financial contributions would be made

from the colonies to the costs of naval defence, but a report by Admiral Sir George Tryon strongly urged that service by Australians should be encouraged even if for a time ships were provided by Britain. From then until Federation the separate colonies (except W.A. and for part of the period Tas.) had small auxiliary squadrons under Royal Navy command; 3 vessels and crews took part in the China War of 1900, raising problems of the use of Aus. ships and men which led after Federation to the separation of the R.A.N. Exchanges of vessels and facilities continue up to the present, though building of warships in Aus. and latterly in U.S. is increasing. The Royal Australian Naval College (1913) is at Jervis Bay, 35S/151E.

Neilson, John Shaw (1872–1942) b. Penola, S.A. A major lyrical poet. The son of humble Scottish parentage, he had a bush boyhood and little formal education although his father wrote verse. Drought drove him from the farm to various manual jobs. His sight began to fail. Through influence of friends, mainly A. G. Stephens who did much to publicise, mould and criticise his work, a humble Melbourne office job (1928–41) and a small pension were found for him. His poems, which had to be dictated, are deceptively simple in structure yet contain mysticism, insight and imagery of colour which make them universal, and the antithesis of the Aus. cult of tough masculinity.

Nelson, Cape Vic. 38S/142E Named after the *Lady Nelson* from which Bass Str. was surveyed in 1800. It is part of a complex headland including Cape Bridgewater and Point Danger, where a ridge of basalt outcrops between the beaches of Discovery Bay and Portland Bay. Dunes are piled up over Cape Bridgewater.

Nepean River N.S.W. Only 96 km. long, is an important catchment for Sydney's water supply (apart from the Nepean Dam, there are the Avon, Cordeaux and Cataract Dams on tributaries). It rises just W of the escarpment of the Southern Tablelands W of Wollongong, 34S/151E, and flows N past Picton and Camden; it receives the Wollondilly-Warragamba headwaters of the Hawkesbury, but remains the Nepean along the straight stretch well known for the Head of the River rowing contest, past Penrith, to become the Hawkesbury after receiving the Grose upstream from Richmond. (*See also* HAWKESBURY.)

Nettle or **Stinging Trees** Members of the mostly tropical nettle family Urticaceae, with a few genera having stinging hairs. There are 3 Aus. species. The Giant Stinging Tree, *Laportea gigas*, of rain-forests in E Aus., grows to 45 m. by 2 m., but with poor timber; it has grey fluted fibrous bark, large heart-shaped, saw-edged, semi-deciduous leaves clad with stinging hairs (especially in young leaves), branched and compound flower-heads (male and female on separate trees), and ovoid fruit about 1 cm. across. The root bark was an important source of fibres for the Aborigines.

New Australia An attempted utopian socialist settlement founded by 240 Australians on a 18,000-ha. grant by the Paraguayan Government. It was founded on the banks of a Plate River tributary, 24 km. from Asuncion in 1893 by William Lane* who, after the arrival of new recruits in 1894, led a group of 58 dissidents to found Cosme 32 km. away, on more Communistic lines. Both failed. Cosme had 131 people in 1897, only 15 in 1921 and descendants are now assimilated. *For further reading see* G. Souter: *A Peculiar People* (Sydney, 1968).

New Australians A term coined by Arthur Calwell* who promoted the great post-war drive for European migrants, in order to give them dignity, in place of a number of more careless or even derogatory terms.

PLATE 6: FLOWERS AND HERBS

1. Sand Hovea *(Hovea trisperma)*. 2. Royal Robe *(Scaevola striata)*. 3. Red-stemmed Green Kangaroo Paw *(Anigozanthos manglesii)*. 4. Slender Lobelia *(Lobelia tenuior)*. 5. Fringed Lily *(Thysanotus tuberosus)*. 6. White Spider Orchid *(Caladenia patersoni)*. 7. Bluebell *(Wahlenbergia gracilis)*. 8. Native Fuchsia *(Grevillea wilsonii)*. 9. Blue Leschenaultia *(Leschenaultia biloba)*. 10. Red-centred Hibiscus *(Cienfugosia hakeifolia)*. 11. White Clematis *(Clematis pubescens)*. 12. Sturt's Desert Pea *(Clianthus formosus)*.

New England N.S.W. A district roughly equated with the Northern Tablelands (see main article on N.S.W.), round Armidale, 31S/152E, and Glen Innes, 30S/152E, mainly rolling pastoral country at about 750–1,000 m. and about 320 km. N–S by 130 km. W–E. Considerable areas are over 1,200 m., along the E escarpment. The New State Movement*, seeking separation from N.S.W., uses somewhat larger boundaries if only to include the large urban centre of Newcastle and also Tamworth where the movement has its headquarters. The New England plateau is part of the escarpment-like E Highlands of Aus., the gentle dip slope to the W being the N part of the Western Slopes, while the E scarp face, often almost precipitous, varies from 15–30 km. from the Pacific in a few places to 65–80 km. in most. The Great Divide is not a well-marked feature here, but is important as the watershed between the short but powerful E rivers Richmond*, Clarence* and Macleay* and the W-flowing Darling affluents Gwydir*, Namoi* and Macintyre*. There is good (introduced) trout fishing in the headstreams. A complex structure of Palaeozoic metamorphic rocks and Devonian granites, acid lavas and sediments including glacial deposits, was worn down by erosion; renewed vulcanism, of gently welling Tertiary basalts, covered much of the area, followed by renewed uplift in a form antecedent to today's sharp E scarp and W dipslope. Meandering streams were able to keep pace with the uplift, leaving twisting incised gorges and scarp-face waterfalls, and viewpoints across the Coastal Belt such as Point Lookout*, now attractive to tourists. Mean annual rainfall is 190–230 cm. along the scarp edge, decreasing gradually to about 65 cm. on the W side of the region; summer temperatures are commonly 13–26°C, and in winter mainly 2–10°C, but with many frosts, up to 140 nights per year and severe in hollows. Snow lies

for a short time on the highest country. There is wet sclerophyll* forest in the wetter E and even some sub-tropical rain-forest. The plateau formerly carried temperate eucalypt woodland interdigitated with savannah, but there has been much clearing for more or less improved pastures, with much planting of exotics, elm and poplar, willow and pine, as well as orchards of the relatively frost-tolerant apples, pears and cherries. The still large properties (commonly 800–1,200 ha. with a few surviving large estates) carry 1,000–5,000 sheep and some beef cattle; beef cattle are fattened on the hillier more forested E, and maize is grown in the warmer N round Tenterfield, 29S/152E, and Glen Innes*. With only 4% of the N.S.W. area, New England carries 10% of the State's sheep, 20% of the beef cattle, 30% of the maize and 20% of the vegetables (on patches of rich soil developed from basalt—but the vegetables must be frost-tolerant). The native Wallaby Grass, Danthonia, and other grasses are nutritious, but the more palatable ones tend to die out with grazing. There has been much pasture improvement including fertilising and sowing of exotic grasses such as phalaris, cocksfoot, perennial rye grass and also various clovers. Hay has to be made to supplement the withered pastures of winter, and sheep-breeding is relatively less important than elsewhere so that the summer flush of growth is grazed by bought-in wethers, and cattle are used to keep the grass short enough for sheep to eat. Dairying is for local urban markets except for the rainy area with rich soils on basalts around the bacon-curing and butter centre of Dorrigo, 30S/153E. Mining, particularly for gold, was important in the development of the region, but has gone except for some alluvial tin dredging near Tingha, 30S/151E, and Emmaville, 29S/152E. Timber exploitation remains active in the E. About a third of New England's 60,000 people live from primary industry; the main towns are Armidale*, Glen Innes* and Tenterfield* with many smaller local centres (*see* N.S.W. Towns). *For further reading see* E. Thorpe: *The New England Plateau* (Melbourne, 1957).

New Guard An extreme, right-wing organisation in N.S.W. (1931–5) run on military lines under Campbell, a Sydney solicitor, avowedly to fight extreme socialism and Communism. It reflects the threatening situation of the Depression*. At the opening of Sydney Harbour Bridge a New Guard Officer, F. E. de Groot (an antique-dealer, Irish in origin), rode up and cut the ceremonial ribbon with his sword before the Premier (Lang*) could do it.

New Guinea An Aus. Trust Territory comprising the NE portion of the Island of New Guinea. The area of 237,793 km.[2] lies two-thirds on the mainland and one-third in the island arc looping round the Bismarck Sea, which includes the Admiralty Islands, New Ireland and New Britain, and the Solomon Islands stretching to the SE. There are 12 administrative Districts each with a Commissioner, and the administrative headquarters are at Port Moresby, capital of the single administrative unit of Papua–N.G.* Population (1966) was 1,562,153 indigenous people of mainly Melanesian stock, and 20,286 non-indigenous, mainly Aus. administrators, planters and missionaries.

New Holland The name given to the southern land mass by the Dutch, after Tasman's voyages (1842–6) believing Tas. (Van Diemen's Land) to be part of it. Cook specifically set out to find the eastern coast of New Holland in 1770, naming it New South Wales. It was not confirmed until the voyages of Flinders* that N.S.W. and the rest of New Holland were not separate islands, but Van Diemen's Land was.

New Norcia W.A. 31S/116E A Benedictine monastery, settlement and diocesan centre, founded in 1846 by Spanish Benedictines primarily to work with Aborigines. It is named after the Italian birthplace of St. Benedict. It now has also 2 secondary boarding schools serving a large area, and is a self-contained community.

New Norfolk Tas. 43S/147E (6,839 in 1971) The major service centre for the hop and apple farms of the lower Derwent River* and the residential centre for Boyer* newsprint works. The area was named when about a thousand free settlers were transferred there from Norfolk Island* (1807–8).

NEW SOUTH WALES The 4th largest State, lying in SE Aus., with 798,337 km.[2] and 4,589,556 people in 1971 (5·7 per km.[2]), and over 27% of Australia's population on 10·4% of her area, of whom over 60% live in metropolitan Sydney. The State forms a compact wedge-shaped quadrilateral, broader in the E and about 960 km. N–S and 1,200 km. E–W; the moderately indented coast is about 1,448 km. from Point Danger to Cape Howe. Aborigines totalled 12,213, of 50% or more Aboriginal blood, mainly in the W but with important groups in Sydney (1966).

Physical Geography and Land Use N.S.W. can be divided into the Coastal Belt; the Tablelands and the Great Divide; the Western Slopes; the Western Plains with the N Riverina and the Western Ridges.

The Coastal Belt is some 32 km. wide in the S and 80 km. in the N, though

Badge of New South Wales

stretching 160 km. farther W where the Hunter Valley* sets back the Great Divide*. River flats, deltas and infilled lagoons provide flat areas among predominantly undulating to hilly country with fairly reliable and well-distributed rainfall from over 75 cm. in the S to over 150 cm. in the N. It includes the lower plains of the Richmond*, Clarence*, Macleay*, Hastings*, Manning*, Nepean-Hawkesbury* and Shoalhaven* Rivers, and the major Hunter River* Valley— all fairly short rivers of 160–480 km. but with considerable discharges. Soils are poor leached podsols, especially on the coastal sands and the dry massive Triassic sandstones (e.g. the Hawkesbury and Narrabeen sandstones) still largely in poor, but not unattractive sclerophyll* forest. Meadow soils predominate wherever drainage is impeded on the lower and finer alluvial tracts, varying the main agricultural land use— dairying which varies in efficiency and prosperity (the N Coast with over 60% of the State's dairy cows, has mainly butter-production N of Kempsey*) and market-gardening on the lower Hunter flood-plain near Newcastle, along the Hawkesbury near Penrith and elsewhere within easy reach of the Sydney market and in parts of the Illawarra lowlands near Wollongong. There is a limited area of valuable banana-cultivation on small farms (the leading banana tract in Aus.), particularly on basalt soils in the far 'North Coast'*, sugar-cane on the lower plains of the Clarence, Richmond and Tweed, and a little pea-growing in the 'South Coast'. Mineral sands* are important in the N.

The Tablelands and the Great Divide are rolling plateau surfaces, largely cleared for wool-sheep or locally for fat-lamb or beef rearing and fattening, and generally at 600–900 m. Often the Great Divide is a rather insignificant watershed feature, but in places there are fairly rugged ridges of quartzite, schist, or tor-crowned granite—usually

forested with wet sclerophyll, but with dry sclerophyll in lower or rain-shadow areas in locally residual rain-forest, temperate in the S and sub-tropical in the N, on the scarp edge. The Tablelands rise almost precipitously from the Coastal Belt, with many waterfalls spectacular after rains, when, however, even the few tar-sealed roads may be awash with swiftly moving flash floods. Mean annual rainfall is 75–100 cm. in the S, up to 150 cm. in the N, and everywhere tending to be high near the E escarpment. The Tablelands extend almost continuously NNE–SSW for 960 km. through the State, but there are distinctive areas. (i) The New England* Tableland is rolling country at about 750 m. and some at 1,200 m. (ii) The Blue Mts.* and the Central Tablelands. The Central Tablelands have a rolling pastoral landscape notably round Bathurst*, grading gently W with the Western Slopes, with some striking residual ridges and peaks, notably Mt. Canobolas*. (iii) The S Tablelands, round Goulburn, 35S/150E, typically have wool-sheep or beef rearing on pastures rapidly improving on lower country, natural grassland or savannah in frost hollows, or cleared by ring-barking or felling and burning from dry sclerophyll woodland on lower slopes. The region includes the Australian Capital Territory*. Higher and steeper country is often still in bush, and there are considerable timber resources in the wetter E. There are limited areas of riverine irrigation, and of potato-growing, near Crookwell, 35S/150E, and on the black soils on basalt near Robertson, 34S/151E. S of Cooma, 36S/149E, lie the rolling treeless basalt pastures of Monaro*, and SW the forested sides and high rolling alpine meadows of the Snowy Mts.*

The Western Slopes, again a roughly NNE–SSW belt W of the Tablelands around 80 km. in width, have red-brown earths over gently rolling lower slopes developed in shales, sandstones, limestones, slates of varied ages, still with occasional ridges of granite breaking the skyline, and including the fertile Liverpool Plains*. Mean annual rainfall is variable, averaging 50–75 cm. and tending to a winter maximum in the the S and a summer maximum in the N. This is the wheat and sheep belt, and wheat silos at railing points are added to the wool-sheds of the Tablelands and the W plains. Again there are local specialisations, e.g. the small stone-fruit around Young and the orcharding, partly from 1918 soldier settlement, in the Tumut-Batlow area where there is also some dairying for the Canberra market.

The Western Plains are mainly in one of the great basin structures of Aus., with much Tertiary marine sedimentary infill of relatively horizontal and friable sandstones, limestones etc., but also a mantle of recent river deposits varying from successive layers of sands and gravels and low swelling ridges of aeolian sands often marked by the occurrence of cypress (*Callitris* spp.) as against prevailing eucalypts. Mean annual rainfall is 50 cm. in the E, decreasing to under 25 cm. of unreliable rain in the W, and this is extensive wool-sheep country. Bore wells, especially in the W, tap artesian or semi-artesian sources, often too saline for cropping or human consumption. Towards the SW there is some clearing of mallee* scrub for extensive wheat and sheep farming and local stock irrigation along the Darling. In the E central part of the Plains is a broad swelling of rocks similar to those of the Western Slopes, including ancient sandstones, shales and limestones with some granitic intrusions, roughly N from Narrandera, 35S/147E, towards Bourke. NE again a patch of younger Jurassic sandstones, shales and coal measures is broken by the dramatic felsite plugs of the Warrumbungles*. NE of Coonabarabran the Jurassic sands carry the poor Pilliga Scrub* with many cypress pines, and NE again are the distinctive black soils of the cotton area round Wee Waa*. The Riverina* is the south-central part of the Western Plains in which altitude, alluvial soils and the large perennial rivers, Murray* and Murrumbidgee* permit the development of the N.S.W. share of the largest irrigated tract of Aus.

The Western Ridges run NNE in the far W of the State, continuing from S.A., the Barrier Range; after a break there is the Grey Range, which runs NE into Qld. In the S there are large tracts of Archaean gneisses and schists, then Precambrian quartzites, sandstones etc.; farther N there are only small cores of the ancient basement rocks, lapped by younger rocks, Cretaceous sandstones and limestones and Tertiary clays, gravels and sands. Apart from Broken Hill*, 32S/141E, this is semi-arid shrub and saltbush country, giving very extensive grazing on large properties, subject to drought when grazing may cause permanent damage to vegetation and soil, and at best there is rather slow recovery after it so that careful control has to be applied.

Coal and Power The main bituminous coal-field of N.S.W. and of Aus. lies folded gently in a wedge-shaped gutter lying NW-SE, the wide part truncated by the coast between Newcastle and Ulladulla, and the narrower end to the NW between Coolah and Murrurundi. The coal measures and associated beds of sandstone and shale, of Permian age, outcrop on the E and W edges of the gutter, but dip towards the centre which is filled with later Triassic shales and considerable depths of hard, massive sandstones, giving the dry, barren plateaux, already noted, at a few hundred ft. round Sydney and W of the Hunter Valley, but raised to 600–900 m. and more in the Blue Mts. Distortion of the rim again brings coal to the surface at over 900 m. at Lithgow. The coal basin overlaps the Coastal Belt, including its westward sweep in the Hunter Valley, and the Central Tablelands. The main areas of exploitation are the Lithgow area in the west-centre (declining), the S area from Ulladulla to Wollongong, much of it by adits into the E-facing escarpment where thick seams outcrop, and the S side of the Hunter Valley, including the coking coals near Newcastle and the steam coals of the great Greta seam and others near Cessnock. The trend in power generation is away from the once dominant Sydney stations to large new ones on the coal-fields: Vales Point on L. Macquarie (875,000 kW), Munmorah (1,400,000 kW), Wangi and Tallawarra on L. Illawarra (320,000 kW). Some 16% of power is hydro-electric, with 70% of this from the Snowy Mts. Scheme.

Industry and Towns Primary industry remains important, as in Aus. as a whole, for exports especially, even though secondary and tertiary industry came to dominate both in value and employment, in the 1960s. Primary production in agriculture and forestry employ 9·5% of the work force of 1·3 million, and mining and quarrying only 1·7%, as against 35% for manufacturing and well over 50% for a very broadly defined tertiary group including power, transport and building industries. There are some 77,000 rural holdings, covering about 70 million ha., and varying in average size from about 160 ha. in the Coastal Belt, and 600 ha. on the Tablelands and Western Slopes, to over 1,200 ha. in the Central Plains and over 1,600 ha. in the arid western tracts. Of total primary plus factory production by value, rural industry accounts for 18% (pastoral 10%, dairying 3% and agriculture 5%). Of agricultural value, wheat is more than half, oats 3%, rice 3%, hay and green fodder 13%, citrus 4%, bananas only a little less, other fruit 3%, grapes 2½% and sugar-cane 2%, potatoes 2% and other vegetables 5%. Forestry is valued at just under 1% of the State total (primary plus manufacturing), fisheries only about ¼ as much. Mining and quarrying are 6% of value (of which metal-mining was 44%, fuel-

mining 42%, clay, gypsum, salt etc. 3% and quarrying of limestone, sandstone, road-metal etc. 11%). Factories account for over 75% of the total, but no value is imputed here for building, transport, services etc. In 1968 there were almost 25,000 factories employing over 530,000 workers, both showing steady increase since the slight setback of the minor recessions. They account for over 40% of Aus. factory employment, and 12% of the total N.S.W. population. The leading employers are: metals and vehicles (45%) food, drink and tobacco, textiles and clothing, followed by power, paper and printing, chemicals. Metals also lead in value (45%) followed by chemicals (11%) and food and drinks (10%). Well over 25% of the factories employed only 5–10 people, but just under 700 large factories (each with over 100 workers) employed over half the State total. The Sydney area has 72% of the factories, including over 80% of the larger units employing over 500, and 75% of the factory employment. Newcastle and Wollongong, with large steelworks etc., had 12% of the employees in only 5% of the factories (but 12% of the factories employing over 500). Women are largely in the clothing, textile and food-processing industries.

The concentration of heavy industry in Newcastle and Wollongong is clear, along with the great dominance of Sydney over a very wide range of engineering, electrical and electronic, clothing and food-processing industries, ranking almost equal with Melbourne and often capital-intensive rather than labour-intensive, though less in some growing industries such as car-manufacture. The 7,000 or so dispersed factories are mainly small, including many small units closely linked with primary production—with early and simple processing of agricultural and stock products (fruit- and juice-canning, abattoirs and meat-works, dairy factories, sugar mills in the N of the N coast, and the like), sawmills, industries tied to bulky raw materials or power-sources, e.g. power stations, brick and cement works etc. There are many small plants in country towns providing local needs. There are examples of larger industries in country centres through the official policy of decentralisation.

In the following classification (G) denotes former gold towns.

Coastal Belt Metropolitan Sydney is dominant (2,717,069).

150,000–260,000, steel towns: Newcastle, Wollongong.

20,000–30,000 regional centres: Maitland (Hunter), Lismore (Richmond), Gosford-Woy Woy (commutor).

10,000–20,000, coal centres: Cessnock, Kurri-Kurri-Weston; regional centres: Grafton (Clarence), Taree (Manning), industrial-resort of Nowra-Bomaderry; resorts: The Entrance, Coffs Harbour.

5,000–10,000, Port Macquarie, Ballina; river-valley rural centres: Casino (Richmond), Kempsey (Macleay), Murwillumbah (Tweed), Singleton, Raymond Terrace and Muswellbrook (Hunter), Bowral (plateau edge), Tweed Heads*; Thornton-Beresford, Richmond*, Windsor* peripheral to Sydney.

2,000–5,000, Camden*, resorts with some commuting and fishing: Forster-Tuncurry, Nambucca Heads, Macksville, Wangi-Rathmines, Nelson Bay, Terrigal-Wamberal and Kiama*; rural centres with timber, dairying etc.: Bega*, Wauchope (Hastings), Kyogle, Branxton-Greta (coal), Byron Bay, Wingham (Manning), Maclean (Clarence), Dungog (Williams), Gloucester, Scone (Hunter) and Moss Vale* and Mittagong* on the plateau edge; coastal resorts with fishing and often timber: Sawtell, Wyong, Davistown-Saratoga, Avondale, Ulladulla*, Batemans Bay, Eden*.

1,000–2,000, smaller coastal towns: Kingscliff, Woolgoolga, Smithton-Gladstone, Evans Head, Brunswick Head all on the 'North Coast', Camden Haven, Moruya, Narooma on the 'South Coast'.

Divide and Tablelands.
20,000–25,000, major regional centres: Orange, Goulburn.

10,000–20,000, regional centres: Bathurst, Armidale; City of the Blue Mts.* and resort: Katoomba-Wentworth Falls; Lithgow (coal) and Queanbeyan near Canberra*.

5,000–10,000, local centres of Cooma in the S, Wellington (G), Mudgee (G), in the centre, Glen Innes in New England.

2,000–5,000, regional centres: Yass*, Crookwell, Blue Mts. resorts: Lawson-Hazelbrook, Blackheath.

1,000–2,000, Blayney (rail centre), Oberon (forestry) in Central Tablelands; Guyra, Walcha, Uralla, Dorrigo in New England; Wallerawong (coal) near Lithgow. Portland and Kandos (limestone).

Western Slopes, Plains and Ridges.
15,000–30,000, Broken Hill (mining) and major regional centres of Wagga-Wagga, Albury, Tamworth, Dubbo.

5,000–10,000, Riverina irrigation centres: Griffith, Deniliquin, Leeton; major regional centres of Inverell (New England), Parkes (G), Forbes (G) in the central slopes, Moree, Gunnedah, Cowra, Narrabri in the N slopes and Cootamundra (G), Tumut*, Young (G) on the S.

2,000–5,000, Riverina centres: Narrandera*, Corowa-Wahgunya; Finlay; regional centres of the W slopes: Quirindi, Werris Creek on Liverpool Plains*, Temora (G), Junee*, West Wyalong (G), Murrumburrah, Grenfell, Gundagai*, Gilgandra, Narromine all on the Central and S slopes; and important centres, mainly on rivers in the far W Plains, Condobolin (Lachlan), Bourke (Darling), Coonamble, Coonabarabran (Castlereagh), Nyngan* (Bogan), Walgett* (Namoi), Cobar,* Warren (Macquarie),

1,000–2,000, Riverina centres: Tocumweal, Barham-Koondrook, Hillston, local centres on the W Slopes: Manilla, Barraba (asbestos), Warialda in the N, Kanoundra, Molong in the centre and Tumbarumbah (G), Batlow, Holbrook in the S; local centres mainly on rivers in the far W Plains: Wee Waa*, Brewarrina, Boggabri (Namoi), L. Cargelligo*, Wentworth (Darling), Balranald (Murrumbidgee). Jerilderie, Culcairn, Lockhart were just under 1,000 (1971).

Historical Development From Governor Phillip's bitter struggle for survival, developed the pastoral settlement dominated by the squatters*, once the Blue Mts. were crossed, and the interior grasslands settled after 1815. With the achievement of responsible government (1855), land tenure, franchise and education were the chief concerns, but politics were controlled by personalities rather than policies or parties for several decades. The Labor Party emerged after about 1880 and has remained very influential with a long period in office from 1941–64. N.S.W. was luke-warm about Federation, and supported Free Trade against Protectionism of Vic. The depression of the 1890s was less severe than in other States, but there was serious trouble in the 1930s' slump, with near-rebellion by the Premier, Lang*. The State has had considerable industrial unrest, notably in the coal and transport industries; but has also a record of enlightened social legislation such as the 40-hour week (1947) and the introduction of child allowances. A high share of migrant intake has been coupled with rapid industrial expansion since the 1939–45 War, but with an increasing tendency towards concentration in the coastal belt from Newcastle to Wollongong. Premiers since 1900: J. See (1901), T. Waddell (1904), J. H. Carruthers (1904), C. G. Wade (1907), J. S. T. McGowan (1910), W. A. Holman* (1913), J. Storey (1920), J. Dooley (1921 and 1922), G. W. Fuller

(1921 and 1922–5), J. T. Lang (1927, T. R. Bavin (1927), B. S. B. Stevens (1932), A. Mair (1939), W. J. McKell (1941), J. McGirr (1947), J. J. Cahill* (1952), R. J. Heffron (1959) and R. W. Askin (1965).

New South Wales Corps An infantry regiment specially recruited for garrison duties in N.S.W., the first detachment arriving with the Second Fleet in 1790 under Capt. Nicholas Nepean, and the second in 1792 under Grose*. The Corps returned to Eng. in 1810, having played a very important if not always creditable role in the colony's early days (*see* RUM REBELLION). Many officers received land grants and were the first free settlers. The total number averaged 500 and engaged in lucrative trading and, with time on their hands engaged in duels and feuds. There were constant arrogant disputes with the Governors. On the other hand, early explorations, land settlement, trade development and surveying owe much to the Corps.

New States These are provided for in the Constitution, sections 121–4, and though like many other sections these are subject to disputation, they are interpreted as requiring both the consent of the State legislature and of a majority of electors in the State by referendum. No new States have been set up, but quite serious movements for some have existed ever since Federation. In Qld. there was some agitation to have 3 separate States at the time of the moves towards Federation, and the Qld. legislature has passed resolutions on new States in 1910 and 1922, as did the N.S.W. legislature also in 1922. The post-Federation New England New State Movement has ancestry in a call by Earle Page made at Grafton, N.S.W., in 1915, for a Northern New South Wales, a movement revived after the 1914–18 War and again the 1939–45 War. Meanwhile, in 1935 a Royal Commission had recommended a tripartite division of

N.S.W. The New England movement was revived and renamed as such, following a conference on decentralisation convened by Dumaresq Shire and Armidale City Council. The movement adopted a provisional constitution in 1949 and formed a Constituent Assembly in 1954, following majorities of 71–88% in favour of the new State in a poll conducted along with local government elections in 16 Local Government Areas. In 1967 the N.S.W. Government held a referendum on the question in the area—including Tamworth, an important centre of the movement, and Newcastle, a possible seaport, capital and industrial balancer, as it were, for the proposed State. The result was a majority in favour, which fell short of the 60% specified by the 1929 recommendation noted in col. 2.

An untiring advocate of the New England New State has been Ulrich Ellis, who has also interested himself in the possible new State of Capricornia, and indeed in a tripartite division of Qld., somewhat as debated in the closing years of the 19th century, or earlier when J. D. Lang proposed 3 States. 1. Cooksland, S of the Tropic and including NE parts of N.S.W. (today quite strongly oriented towards Brisbane economically); 2. Leichartsland (sic) between the Tropic and the Gulf of Carpentaria; and 3. Flindersland or Cape York Peninsula. In a paper of 1959 Ellis argues that subdivision of a State without change of its boundary with other States does not require a referendum, and that petitions in favour of Capricornia bind the Government in terms of a policy statement by the Premier in 1957. He also examines its economic viability.

The Riverina District of New South Wales, conscious of its distinctiveness of interests, was somewhat swayed towards New Statism in the 1920s, and there is still a strong feeling of regionalism in relation to demands for decentralisation of industry, a new University of the Riverina etc.

A significant procedure was recommended by a Federal Royal Commission in 1929: the Commonwealth should, on receipt of a petition from not less than 20% of the electors of an area of not less than the population of Tas. (being the smallest state): (1) set up a Boundaries Commission; (2) call a Convention to draft a Constitution and (3) hold a referendum in the State concerned, and if 60% of the electors in the proposed new State and 40% of these in the undivided State approved the new State; then (4) the Commonwealth Parliament should have power to decide within a specified period, for or against the establishment of the new State (presumably on grounds of economic viability, all-Australia considerations, e.g. of Defence) etc.. *For further reading see* U. Ellis: *Capricornia New State Movement, Financial and Economic Aspects of New States* (Canberra, 1959).

Newcastle N.S.W. 33S/152E (249,962 in 1971) The largest city in Aus. outside the State capitals and, like the other big steel town Wollongong, it is bigger than Hobart. In origin it is an agglomeration of mining villages such as Waratah, Lambton and Merewether; some street alignments still follow long disused coal railways. It was used for a period after 1801 as a site of farther transportation for unruly convicts from Sydney. Metal-working using local coal came in with copper-smelting at Port Waratah in the 1860s, then processing of lead and zinc from Broken Hill at Cockle Creek. In 1915 B.H.P.* came into iron and steel production on a large wharf site at Port Waratah; this has now grown to a great integrated steelworks on a 120-ha. site, along with associated by-products: chemical production, sheet steel and wire production and many ancillary trades. Newcastle is also an important seaport, including the well-known and long-standing coal trade by the 'sixty milers' to Sydney.

Shipping is primarily concerned with coal, iron and steel and other local heavy industries. A new coal loading plant can handle over 2,000 tonnes an hour. Wool, wheat and frozen meat are shipped. The State dockyard with a floating dry dock can take ships of 15,000 tonnes. The heavy industry is balanced by factories employing much female labour, e.g. textiles. Moreover, despite its curiously long and straggling shopping centre and central district in Hunter Street, Newcastle is a regional centre of no mean order, and over half the income of the Hunter Valley region is generated by tertiary services, largely in the city. Though it bears the marks of heavy industry, the sea breezes, cliffs and beaches relieve the smoke pall even in the centre, while there are many pleasant areas in the suburbs spreading to L. Macquarie* and, almost in a conurbation, enveloping the now less exclusively coal-mining towns and villages of the lower Hunter Valley*. It is a University and Cathedral city, and has an impressive modern Cultural Centre.

Newcastle Waters N.T. 17S/133E Named by J. McDouall Stuart, after the Secretary of State for the Colonies, when he found the permanent waterholes of the Newcastle Creek in 1861; an important stock route stage.

Newcombe, John (1944–) b. Sydney Leading tennis player, now professional. Wimbledon champion 1967, 70, 71.

NEWSPAPERS There are 16 daily papers issued in the State capitals (9 morning and 7 evening), catering for over 90% of the country's population; there are 35 provincial dailies, and many more weeklies of small local circulation. Although having one of the world's highest rates of newspaper-buying per head, the general influence of Aus. newspapers is not considered to be high.

Only one daily, the *Australian* (1964), with different local editions, has a national circulation. The daily press in each State is likely to remain dominated by its metropolitan papers, concerned with politics, sport and news items within the State. Foreign news is mainly syndicated. Ownership of these papers is concentrated in few hands. Three-quarters of the papers printed belong either to the Melbourne-based *Herald* and *Weekly Times* group or to the Fairfax group in Sydney, now also controlling the *Age* (Melbourne). Rupert Murdoch and Sir Frank Packer* are also leading figures.

There is not the contrast between so-called 'quality' as against 'popular' press that is seen in other countries, partly because the market is not big enough to support such distinctions. Instead, within a narrower range, each paper attempts to cater for all tastes: high-grade articles (including some from U.S. and U.K. papers) and responsible editorials are found along with astrology, a great deal of sport and invariably a comic strip. While the tabloid format was adopted early, Aus. 'tabloids' are not quite so exclusively devoted to minimal news, sensation and illustration as overseas equivalents. The general attitude of the press is conservative, and while the Labor Party is well covered, there is no metropolitan Labor daily, and only 1 in the entire country, the *Barrier Daily Truth*, a subsidised Union paper in Broken Hill, N.S.W. With notable exceptions, there is little crusading or press vigilance on the activities of Governments compared with their 19th-century antecedents. Sunday and evening papers are of generally 'popular' standard; the *Bulletin*, *Nation* and *National Times* are main journals of comment. Since the national capital is even now relatively small, the *Canberra Times* ranks as a good provincial paper with a curious mixture of parish pump and national and overseas news. Newspapers have extensive control of commercial radio and television*.

Historical Development The earliest papers, while privately financed, were subject to official control and depended mainly on officially released information. The earliest were the *Sydney Gazette and N.S.W. Advertiser* (1803–42) published by Howe*, the short lived *Derwent Star* (1810), *Van Diemen's Land Gazette* (1814) and *Hobart Town Gazette* (1816–27) in Tas.

The first efforts to establish a free press were curtailed, by Governor Arthur* in Tas., who prosecuted and persecuted Andrew Bent* for his critical *Hobart Town Gazette* (the official organ, then produced privately 1824–5), and by Governor Darling* in N.S.W. where the *Australian* (1824) founded by Wentworth* and Wardell* was followed by Edward Hall's* *Monitor* (1826). While justifiably critical, all these papers also contained much that was scurrilous and vindictive. The principle of uncensored press was recognised by 1830, partly through Forbes's* legal rulings, partly because it was inevitably in a colony emerging from penal to free status.

The oldest extant newspaper was founded as a 4-page weekly called the *Sydney Herald* in 1831; it was issued daily from 1840 and became the *Sydney Morning Herald* in 1842; since 1853 it has been controlled by the family of John Fairfax*, and has retained throughout a sedate reputation. The *West Australian* (1833, but claiming a prior origin) became a daily in 1885; its most influential owner was Hackett*. In Melbourne the *Port Philip Herald* (1840) became the evening *Herald* (1869), and under Sir Keith Murdoch* extended to control of the biggest network in the country. The *Argus* (1846–1947), launched in support of land reform, became more conservative as Edward Wilson aged, and was the rival of the *Age* (1854), which under David Syme* was the most influential Vic. paper for many decades, in its radical and protectionist views. Today, it is a subsidiary of Fairfax (*Sydney Morning Herald*); the 2 are regarded as the doyens of the press, solid, staid, responsible and conservative, and battling with their less inhibited rivals, the *Daily Telegraph* (1879) in Sydney, and the *Sun-News Pictorial* (1922) in Melbourne (the *Herald's* morning paper). In Brisbane the *Courier Mail* (1933) was formed from 2 predecessors, one of which, the *Moreton Bay Courier*, dated from 1846. The only morning paper in Adelaide is the *Advertiser* (1858) and in Hobart the *Mercury* (1854), under the Davies family. The *Bulletin** (1888) has been completely metamorphosed from its radical, nationalist literary days to become a crisp, sophisticated, political and financial review.

Since 1920 the number of metropolitan dailies has been almost halved and proprietors cut by two-thirds.

Aus. has produced some notable war correspondents: C. E. W. Bean and Sir Keith Murdoch* in the 1914–18 War, Chester Wilmot (1911–1954) and the poet Kenneth Slessor, among many others in the 1939–45 War.

Newsprint The only newsprint mill in Aus. is at Boyer*, Tas. Use of hard wood eucalypts in paper making has been a notable Aus. innovation. Production over 205,000 tonnes is 50% Aus. requirements; it is owned by a group of Aus. newspaper companies.

Nickel A vital ferro alloy in steel making, which in the 1960s became the wonder mineral in the great Aus. mining boom, with unprecedented share trading, notably in Poseidon*. Proved nickel sulphide ore reserves exceed 30 million tonnes (30% non-Communist world total). Most lie in a 180,000 km.^{2} wedge of W.A. running NW from Norseman 32S/122E to Meekatharra 27S/118E, the E Goldfields nickel province. Mining began with Kambalda (1968); other projects include Mt. Windarra (Poseidon)

(1974), Carr Boyd Rocks, Widgiemool-tha, Mt. Keith, Ora Banda (lateritic), Wannaway, Scotia all in this province. Ores have been found (1972) at Nullagine*. Lateritic nickel ores are to be worked at Greenvale in Qld. Nickel is refined and exported at Kwinana*; there is a smelter at Kalgoorlie, and export from Esperance.

Nicotiana or **Tobacco Plants** Those native to Aus. include some 15 species, e.g. the white-flowered *N. suaveolens*; in the Potato family, Solanaceae.

Nightshade The popular name for many plants of the world-wide genus *Solanum*, which includes the Potato. Other *Solanum* species contain more or less belladonna (*see also* APPLE). A common native species in forests in E Aus. is the Tooth Nightshade, *S. xanthocarpum*, growing to 60–90 cm., leaves somewhat oak-like and to 10 cm. long, flowers light purple and potato-like; the fruit 1 cm. across and green-and-white mottled.

Niland, D'Arcy Francis (1919–1967) b. Glen Innes, N.S.W. Of Irish parents and named after Les Darcy*. He was a short-story writer and novelist whose best-known works are *The Shiralee* (Sydney, 1955) and *The Big Smoke* (Sydney, 1959). He shared some writing with his wife, Ruth Park.

Nineteen Counties Geographical units identified in 1829, following instructions that N.S.W. be divided into counties, hundreds and parishes, but with revision of boundaries and official Proclamation in 1835. They formed a semicircular area of 240-320 km. radius, centred on Sydney. Darling declared them the limit of legal settlement (already over-reached by the squatters*). They were Cumberland, Camden, St. Vincent, Argyle, Northumberland, Gloucester, Durham, Hunter, Cook, Westmoreland, Murray, King, Georgiana, Bathurst, Roxburgh, Phillip, Brisbane, Bligh and Welling-ton. The County in Aus. has no general administrative function. (*See* LOCAL GOVERNMENT.)

Ninety Mile Beach Vic. Extending from near Yarram, 39S/147E, to beyond Lakes Entrance, 38S/148E, this has been built in its great curve by calm weather SE swells which re-sorted sea-bottom material into a sand ridge. Above wave level there has been dune-building, partly fixed by coastal spinifex.

Ninety Mile Desert A region extending from S.A. to Vic. 35–6S/139–40E in the 42-cm. rainfall mallee area, trans-formed by addition of trace elements into grazing land (*see* COONALPYN DOWNS).

Noble, Montague Alfred (1873–1940) b. Sydney. One of the greatest Aus. all-round cricketers, with Giffen*, Greg-ory* and Miller*. A versatile medium-pace bowler and an effective batsman, most brilliant in defence.

Nolan, Sydney Robert (1917–) b. Melbourne. He is the most widely known Aus. artist, living mainly over-seas since 1953. He began with series of paintings based on the 19th cen-tury in Aus.: the famous Ned Kelly narrative (1948) followed by the Burke* and Wills expedition, and Eureka Stockade. His subjects include outback Qld., the Centre* and themes as far apart as Arizona and Antarctica, classical Greek myth and Gallipoli. He returns frequently to Aus. In 1972 a London exhibition included vast and vivid murals, *The Snake* and *Paradise Garden*, comprised of many individual panels.

Norfolk Island 29S/168E (1,152 in 1966) Covers 36 km.² and lies 1,655 km. NE of Sydney. It is about 8 km. E–W and 5 km. N–S. Basalt cliffs surround a low plateau at 90–120 m., rising to 316 m. in Mt. Pitt in the NW, where rain-forest scrub is a residual of a former dense forest cover including the Norfolk Island pine*. The rest of the island had eroded and deteriorated pasture land and small patches of intensive horticulture, wheat, maize and yams. Temperatures range from 8°C to 27°C and rainfall averages 142 cm. but is variable. Discovered in 1774 by Cook, the island was settled from Port Jackson in 1788, under King, who hoped to exploit its natural hemp and timber for the navy. It was a penal settlement until 1813 and again from 1826–55 (administered from Van Diemen's Land* 1844–56). During the later period it saw some of the worst brutalities of the convict system as well as Maconochie's* reform experiment. In 1856 it became a separate Crown colony and was settled by 194 descendants of the *Bounty* mutiny, from Pitcairn Island, who lived on a subsistence basis of wheat, maize etc. From 1896 it became a N.S.W. dependency, and in 1913 a Commonwealth Territory. Attempts to stimulate income and exports have largely failed, through distance from markets, poor quality, lack of harbours and uneconomic holdings, and have included bananas, passion fruit, French beans for seed, lemons, whaling. Tourism provides most of income today. The Norfolk Island Council comprises an appointed Administrator and 8 biennially elected members; its function is advisory. There are no taxes or social security benefits.

Norfolk Island Pine (*Araucaria heterophylla*) A softwood tree endemic in Norfolk Island, still prominent there and now in many coastal sites in E Aus. Both branches and leaves point upwards.

Norman, Decima (1916–) b. Perth, W.A. The first major woman athlete in Aus. who seemed set for an international reputation when, in the 1938 Empire Games in Sydney, she won 5 gold medals (100 yd., 220 yd., long-jump and 2 relays), but the 1939–45 War intervened.

Normanton Qld. 18S/141E On the Norman River 90 km. from its mouth. Attempts to ship cattle (which flourished 1868–90) have been revived from the Norman mouth where there is also prawn processing at Karumba.

Norseman W.A. 32S/122E (1,757 in 1971) Situated at the W end of the Eyre Highway*. Gold-mining continues today, but primarily for the extraction of pyrites as a source of sulphur for superphosphates.

North Australia Railway N.T. A 3-ft. 6-in. (1·07 m.) single track from Darwin to Birdum, 510 km. The effective railhead is Larrimah a few miles N, on the Stuart Highway*. The first section to Pine Creek* was built by imported Chinese labour (1886–9) to serve the gold-field there; it was extended to Katherine* in 1917 to serve the meatworks in Darwin, and to Birdum in 1929 and was taken over by Commonwealth Railways in 1918. Completion to meet the S.A. Railway at Alice Springs was planned but never carried out. The railway deteriorated, and reconstruction has been undertaken to allow haulage by diesel locomotives of iron ore* from Frances Creek to Darwin.

Norfolk Island Pine
(*Araucaria heterophylla*)

'North' Coast of N.S.W. In fact, part of the E coast of Aus., the part of the Coastal Belt lying NE of Newcastle, 33S/152E (*see under* NEW SOUTH WALES, main article). *For further reading see* J. Devery: *The North Coast of New South Wales* (Melbourne, 1963).

North West Cape W.A. 22S/114E A largely sand-dune peninsula forming the W shore of Exmouth Gulf*. Learmonth, a 1939–45 military base and modern air base, is on the bay side. A U.S. naval communication centre established in 1967 (renamed after Harold Holt* 1968) is near Exmouth (2,638, 1971) in which the streets are named after members of the famous 'Z Force*' exploit in the *Krait* which left from here. The centre has 13 towers reaching 387 m and the world's largest V.L.F. transmitter.

Northam W.A. 32S/117E (7,109 in 1971) One of the oldest towns of the State, in the productive Avon Valley*. It became the junction of the railways to Kalgoorlie, Geraldton and Albany, and has some secondary industry, (timber, metal-works). Iron ore deposits (magnetite) are to be mined for export.

Northampton W.A. 28S/114E Lying 40 km. inland, it was developed as the centre of a lead-copper field from 1848, and has had fluctuating but small production ever since.

Northern Development Some 39% of Aus. (2,695,246 km.²). lies N of the Tropic of Capricorn; this is roughly the area of India. It contains about 340,000 people, or 3% of the population. Of these 92% are in Qld., mainly along the Sugar Coast, 7% in N.T. and 1% in W.A. The North has widely varying topography, and while sharing a generally Monsoonal rainfall régime, totals vary from 250 cm on the Qld. coast to under 12 cm in the far interior. The emptiness of this vast tract has widely been thought undesirable strategically, politically and even morally, in relation to the relative proximity of the over-populated Asian fringe. Recurrent arguments range from wild journalistic claims of unlimited potential to careful analyses of facts and possibilities. The Commonwealth Department of National Development has a Northern Division; C.S.I.R.O.* maintain research centres; there is Government and private prospecting.

Production of beef cattle has dominated land use, much of it on large unfenced, unimproved and absentee-held runs. Transport development in the form of Beef Roads (although railways are also advocated), pasture and soil-erosion control, and expanding markets are all likely to maintain this as the economic base; reform of land tenure is also sought. Mineral resources include copper, lead, zinc, phosphates, manganese, nickel aluminium and iron. Extraction will be followed by at least some processing, but neither will lead to a great population increase. The close settlement brought by agricultural development is unlikely, save in very limited areas. A subsistence economy could perhaps support a good Asian living standard for considerable numbers at least for a time. But vast subsidisation and investment of capital more profitable elsewhere would be needed to support Aus. living standards over much of the North. The strategic desirability is no longer credible in present military contexts; the richer S would be the target of attack and capture. The issue is likely to remain a political and moral one, based ultimately on the retention or otherwise of a White Australia.

NORTHERN TERRITORY (N.T.) An Aus. internal Territory. Population 1971, 85,519, an increase of 8·6% from 1966. It lies between the N coast and the S.A. border along 26°S, and between W.A. along 129°E and Qld. along 138° E, 1,600 km. N–S and 934 km. E–W.

The area is 1,340,000 km. or 17·5% of Aus. 80% is N of the Tropic, 58% is leased (93% of this in pastoral lease); 18% is reserved, largely for Aborigines; 21% is unoccupied and unreserved. The population in 1971 was 85,591 including Aborigines of over half-blood who (in 1966) numbered 21,119, by far the greatest number of any State or Territory and under direct Commonwealth control. The population density at under 0·1 per km.² is the lowest in Aus.

Physical Geography and Land Use There are 3 broad physical regions: the northern coast plains and plateaux; the central lower sedimentary basins; and the southern mountain ranges and flanking basins. Climate is sub-tropical or tropical, with rainfall in the N of 130 cm., dominated by the summer Monsoon, giving distinct Dry and Wet seasons, but dropping to 12 cm. with increasing variability in the S, where diurnal and seasonal temperature ranges are greater.

The North, often referred to as 'The Top End', comprises a wet coastal belt of plains and offshore islands, and an inland region of low, but heavily dissected plateaux, including the N margins of the Barkly Tableland* behind the Gulf Country*, Arnhem Land* and the upper basins of Daly, Adelaide and Alligator Rivers. The rivers are seasonal in their upper courses, but perennial across the wet plains where rainfall is over 100 cm. Mangrove-lined estuaries, paperbark and pandanus woodland and swamp predominate. Only very limited agriculture on patches of more tractable black soil has developed in spite of repeated efforts, from the sugar and coffee plantations of the 1860s to the Humpty Doo* rice of the 1960s. In 1972, Americans controlled some 50% of pastoral land in the areas with over 60 cm. rainfall, on over 20 cattle stations averaging 400,000 ha. Soils are elsewhere skeletal and laterit-

ised. Cattle potential on the drier savannah belt is low because the level of nutrition in the rank, tall, tropical grasses drops in the dry season and cattle diseases are endemic.

The Central Belt Rainfall decreases S from 50 cm. to 25 cm. or less; tropical woodland gives way to grasslands, scrub and finally desert. In the W the Victoria River* savannahs and in the the E the Barkly Tableland* grasslands are major beef regions with good potential. Further S a low ridge followed by the Stuart Highway (Ashburton, Murchison, Davenport Ranges) forms a catchment for short sporadic streams, but like all others in the area they are lost in desert sands of the useless Tanami* Desert to the W, and the semi-desert flanking the Barkly Tableland to the E. Cattle stations lie along the central ridge and round the margins only.

The Mountains and Basin Region The S of the N.T. is the major part of the vast area of Aus. called 'The Centre'*. Rainfall is under 25 cm. and may be absent for years at a time; temperature ranges are high, especially between day and night. Ancient folds of Cambrian and older rocks form a series of E–W ranges often bare of vegetation: the Macdonnell*, James* and George Gills* Ranges are separated from the more southerly (and even older) Petermann* and Musgrave* Ranges, by the wide sedimentary Amadeus Basin* in which stand the 'Three Great Tors' of Mt. Olga*, Ayers Rock* and Mt. Conner*. The Finke* drains sporadically SE towards L. Eyre; all other watercourses vanish in desert sands. Yet the saltbush, mulga and spinifex*, supplemented by lower cover of grasses after rains and some underground water, support surprisingly good cattle feed in wetter periods. In the SE is the empty Simpson Desert*.

Industry and Population Minerals and beef cattle are the mainstay. Copper provides 60% of the mineral value:

over 80% of it from the Tennant Creek area which also produces all the silver and 80% of the gold. Until 1956 gold was the chief mineral; while production has remained steady, copper has increased, and gold is now 25% of mineral value. It is also obtained from uranium tailings in the S Alligator, and from small workings as at Pine Creek* or Love Creek. Uranium* is re-emerging in importance with new discoveries and exploration. The development of the Rum Jungle* mine and the S Alligator field took place in the 1950s. There is a little, small-scale tin-mining in the Darwin region encouraged by a Government crushing battery at Mt. Wells. Mica and wolfram have been obtained in the S but are now insignificant. Developments now advanced are Gove* bauxite, Groote Eylandt* manganese and Frances Creek* iron, but not McArthur River* lead and zinc. The cattle turnoff goes to Qld. through Camooweal and to S.A. through Alice Springs, with a small number to W.A. Boneless beef exports (including some buffalo) from processing plants at Montejinni (Victoria River* basin), Katherine and Darwin are increasing; hides (including crocodile) are less important than previously. Improvements in the cattle industry should stem from Beef Roads, pasture conservation and the use of introduced buffel grass and Townsville lucerne. The long leasehold by absentee holders without any stipulated improvements, is criticised as leading to over-exploitation of pasture lands which is causing erosion, and the poor level of quality and output. Agriculture is limited to some 1,600 ha. and comprises fruit and vegetables for local use round Darwin and the Mission Stations. Experimental farms near Katherine and Darwin also produce sorghum, pasture grasses and peanuts successfully.

Forest resources are confined to cypress pine and some other termite-resistant woods from the N areas, with a little planting now; but timber imports are needed. Only the N–S Stuart Highway and its W–E offshoot, the Barkly Highway, are sealed, but good graded gravel roads are extending into the cattle regions. There is a 970-km. gap between the Birdum and Alice Springs railheads on the once projected trans-continental line.

Secondary industry is confined to meatworks and sawmilling. Public administration dominates other employment, and Darwin has growing service industries and 2 breweries. Darwin (36,828 in 1971) is both the port and administrative centre. Tennant Creek* mining supports 1,789 (1971) and Alice Springs* service and tourist centre had 11,118 in 1971. Along the Stuart Highway, Katherine* is a growing centre (2,520), and Gove-Nhulunbuy the new bauxite town, (4,378.)

Many settlements shown on maps are little more than a police station and hotel. Cattle stations are often appreciable settlements in themselves, with homestead, workers' houses, Aboriginal encampments and perhaps a school. The other foci are small mining towns, e.g. Batchelor* or Moline*. The Mission Stations and Government Welfare/Training depots are each in touch with about a third of the Aboriginal population; most of the remaining third are on cattle stations and few if any have absolutely no contact with white settlement. However, contact may be sporadic for a number of Aborigines.

Historical Development Aboriginal tribes adapted to the contrasting environments of coast, range and desert met the early settlers with hostility. The first attempts made on the N coast to forestall possible French interest and to develop Asian trade, were failures: 1824–9 Fort Dundas; 1827–9 Raffles Bay*; 1838–49 Port Essington*.

After mid-19th century exploration revealed more of the region, S.A. sought and gained jurisdiction of it as its Northern Territory from 1862–1911. A new N coast settlement failed at Escape Cliffs* (1864–7), and was established at Palmerston on Port Darwin in 1868. Development was very slow in spite of the heroic Overland Telegraph* (1872), the brief gold-rush of the 1870s and the rail to Pine Creek from Darwin and to Oodnadatta from Adelaide (by 1889). Attempts to establish sugar, coffee and rubber plantations in the N all failed and pastoral development from the S was slow. Chinese arrived from 1875 and were long an important element in the population; the Japanese (ironically) declined an invitation to send settlers in 1877. In 1911 the Commonwealth paid £5,000,000 to take over. An initial impetus to develop took the form of pastoral leases to an overseas company which built a meatworks at Darwin and the rail was extended to Katherine (1917) and Birdum (1929), and the South Australia line N to Alice Springs (1929). The meat venture failed too, but big absentee leaseholds have remained. From 1926–31 the N.T. was divided into Central and Northern Australia, and a Northern Australian Development Commission was set up. The N.T. reverted to one unit in the Depression. The bombing of Darwin in 1942 shocked Aus. into the realities of the war, and road and garrison construction hastily followed. Government is by Administrator and Legislative Council of 6 official and 11 elected (formerly including 3 nominated members. There is one elected member to the House of Representatives, with full voting rights (1968). Future development is part of the broad problem of Northern Development*; it is significant that Commissions in 1913, 1924 and 1937 and several private experts have all agreed that increased cattle efficiency is the key rather than crop expansion. Now mineral exploitation for export is becoming even more important. Both depend on better transport. (See MAP 7.) For further

reading see C. L. A. Abbot: *Australia's Frontier Province* (Sydney, 1950); C. T. Madigan: *Crossing the Dead Heart* (Melbourne, 1946); E. Hill: *The Territory* (Sydney, 1951); A. H. Dyer: *The Northern Territory* (Melbourne, 1962); M. Bayne: *The Barkly Tableland* (Melbourne, 1957) and H. H. Finlayson: *The Red Centre* (Sydney, 1963).

Nowra-Bomaderry N.S.W. 35S/151E (12,866 in 1971) A rapidly growing local service, holiday and small industrial centre at the head of the Shoalhaven* delta with its rich dairy pastures. Bomaderry is the end of the South Coast railway from Sydney, and the dairy factory serves the fresh milk market, but also processes powdered and malted milk, taking Gippsland* milk when the reduced winter supply is fully used up by the Sydney market. There is also a large paper mill which was attracted here by the prospect of a stable labour force in a substantial country town with a good water supply, though raw material has to be imported through Port Kembla.

Nuclear Energy—*See* ATOMIC ENERGY.

Nullagine W.A. 22S/120E A small centre on the Nullagine Creek, a left-bank tributary of the De Grey* River. It was founded in a gold-rush in 1888 which soon faded, although a little shaft-mining survives. The **Nullagine Platform** or series covers a geological 'province' of 518,000 km² and comprises undisturbed Precambrian sediments overlying a crystalline base and including the iron, manganese, nickel and asbestos deposits of the Hamersley-Pilbara area.

Nullarbor Plain It lies equally in W.A. and S.A., some 725 km. E–W and 400 km. N–S, bordering the Great Aus. Bight, and rising gently inland from a cliffed coastline to 180 m. The name, coined from Latin in 1865 by Delisser, means 'no tree'. A vast slab of Tertiary limestone uplifted and undisturbed, perhaps the world's largest flat surface in bedrock, dips very slightly southwards. The uncertain winter rainfall, decreasing inland from 40 cm., seeps underground, leaving no surface streams. There are some 100 known caves, mainly in the wetter S. Shallow caves in the harder upper strata, and 14 known deep caves some 100 m. underground, spreading into chambers and tunnels, are the result of rock solution by percolating water in past periods of higher water tables; they lack stalactites or stalagmites as the water is scarce and seeps widely through the crumb structure and is not channelled by joints. The best-known caves are Abrakurrie, Koonalda, Mullamullang (5 km. long), Cocklebiddy and Weebubbie, most with watercourses or clear deep mineralised lakes. Acacia and eucalypt coastal scrub gives way to samphire, saltbush and ephemeral grasses inland. Apart from small settlements on the Transcontinental Railway* 160 km. inland, and the Eyre Highway* near the coast, there are only very scattered sheep stations on the margins, using subartesian water.

Numbat (Aboriginal) or **Banded Marsupial Termite-eater** (genus *Myrmecobius*) Has a brown back strikingly barred with white, white belly and pale dark-striped cheeks. It has numerous but degenerate teeth, assumed to be an adaptation to its diet very largely of termites, as is the very rapid extensile flicking of its tubular tongue. There are 2 species, the Numbat, *M. fasciatus*, of W.A. and the South-eastern or Rusty Numbat, *M. rufus*.

NURDA The National and Urban Regional Development Authority, formed 1972 to consider planning problems such as decentralisation and submetropolitan regional centres.

Nuyts Archipelago S.A. 33S/133E A group of at least 30 rocks and islands of which the largest is St. Peter Island (50 km.²) which is 16 km. offshore from Ceduna. Outer groups include Franklin and St. Francis Islands. They were named in 1802 by Flinders on the probably correct assumption that they were the islands recorded by Peter Nuijts during his voyage along the S coast in 1627.

Nyngan N.S.W. 32S/147E (2,478 in 1971) A railway junction and road focus in an east-central position in the Western Plains region, slowly increasing its population mainly as a service centre for a large wool-sheep area. It lies on the Bogan River*, to which water is diverted from the Macquarie.

O

OAKY FALLS

Oaky Falls N.S.W. Where the Oaky River cascades 274 m. down the E escarpment of the New England* plateau, to join the Macleay. They are now tapped by a small hydro-electric plant, about 48 km. E of Armidale, 31S/152E.

Oatlands Tas. 42S/147E A small but long-established service centre in the lower Midlands* on the shores of the shallow sandy L. Dulverton. It grew as a staging post between Hobart and Launceston and stretches along the Midland Highway.

Oats Cereal grown on 8% of cropped land, and in similar areas to wheat, being either cut and baled as 'oaten hay' or harvested for grain of which 15–20% is exported to Europe for animal feeds and to China for human consumption. W.A. has slightly more than the other main producers, N.S.W. and Vic.

Oceania A term varyingly used for the islands of the Pacific. In United Nations publications, among others, Aus. and N.Z. are included.

O'Connor, Charles Yelverton (1843–1902) b. Co. Meath, Ireland. He arrived in Aus. in 1891 as W.A. engineer-in-chief from N.Z., where he had worked since 1865. He was the engineer of Fremantle Harbour (1892–1900) and of the Gold-fields Water Supply* (1897–1903). He was accused and reviled by critics and enemies of this scheme, in which he was responsible not only for the huge engineering undertaking but also for associated land tenure and timber clearing problems. He shot himself, just before its inauguration.

O'Connor, Richard Edward (1851–1912) A leading architect of the Constitution, having served on the

OGILVIE

drafting committee of the Federal Convention (1897–8). He was appointed, with Sir Samuel Griffith* and Sir Edmund Barton*, one of the 3 first High Court Judges.

Octopuses The Order Octopoda, within the Class Cephalopoda*, represents the extreme case of molluscs with evolutionary development of the 'foot' into 8-tentacles round a 'head' or body, and no shell at all. They have a somewhat parrot-like 'beak' and can give a painfully venomous bite, occasionally fatal. A N Aus. species is *Octopus rugosus*. The dangerous 10-cm. *Hapalochlaena maculosa* is often seen in rock-pools, and the 60 to 90-cm. *Octopus cyaneus* inshore and in estuaries. The eye is the most highly developed among the invertebrates.

O'Dowd, Bernard Patrick (1866–1953) b. Beaufort, Vic. A leading intellectual socialist poet of Vic. in the 1890s, writing ardently radical political verse and pamphlets, idealistic yet socialistically militant on the future of Aus. He worked as a lawyer, Parliamentary draughtsman and librarian.

Oenpelli N.T. 12S/133E Anglican Mission station in the NW of Arnhem Land* on low land W of the great escarpment of the Spencer Range, the beginning of 'the stone country'. Tropical fruits and vegetables are grown and cattle are reared in the Mission lease of 500 km.² Buffalo* are hunted for hides. Aboriginal culture remains rich in this area.

Offsider Colloquial word for mate, or assistant, developed from the 'offside' bullocks in a team, on the driver's left.

Ogilvie, Albert George (1891–1939) b. Hobart. Labor Premier of Tas. 1934–9. He entered politics from law (1924) and succeeded Lyons* as Opposition Leader (1929). Ogilvie was a forceful effective Premier, concerned with development of Tas. industry and social welfare.

Ogilvie, William Henry (1869–1963) b. Kelso, Scotland. He was in Aus. from 1889–1901 as a drover, horse-breaker and station-hand. He wrote successful bush ballads for the *Bulletin*, with some hint of those of his native border country.

Oilseeds Largely a post-war development, following introduction of suitable varieties of linseed for Aus. conditions, and have increased to supply the domestic market for industrial uses (paints etc.) and to contribute towards margarine production. **Linseed,** mainly in the wheat belt of N.S.W., Esperance* area of W.A., Darling Downs* Qld., W. and NE Vic. **Safflower** (for cooking oils and margarine) is grown in the N.S.W. wheat belt, Callide-Dawson Valley, and Darling Downs in Qld. where **peanuts** and **cotton-seed** for oils are also important. The Mediterranean olive is now semi-wild in the Mt. Lofty Ranges of S.A., but some are collected for oil.

Olga, Mount N.T. 25S/131E The largest of a roughly circular group of monoliths of smoothly worn conglomerate, red in colour and rising abruptly for 457·5 m. (1,037 m. above sea level) from the mulga scrub and desert plain N of the Musgrave Range*. Deep chasms between the monoliths have very little sun, and retain moisture on their floors where there is a rich tropical flora and fauna even in prolonged drought. It is the most westerly of the 'Three Tors', Ayers Rock lying 48 km. to the E. Giles* named it in 1872 after the Spanish Queen (at his patron Mueller's* insistence).

Olive-wood (*Elaeodendron australe*) In the widespread family Celastraceae. It is a bush or small tree of coastal Qld. and N.S.W., with dark green oval leaves, inconspicuous flowers, but attractive red stoned fruit 1 cm. long.

Olsen, John (1928–) b. Newcastle, N.S.W. A leading contemporary artist of abstract work much of which is yet firmly based on the colour and form of the Aus. landscape. He instigated the Sydney 9, a Sydney focus similar to Melbourne's Antipodean Group*.

Olympic Games First held in Aus. 1956, the main stadium being at Melbourne Cricket Ground. Aus. achievements in Olympics are noted under relevant sports and individuals. In the 1972 Games, Aus. won 8 gold, 7 silver and 2 bronze medals, coming fifth in the world list. H. Flack was the first Aus. to attend Olympics (Athens, 1896).

Olympus, Mount Tas. 42S/146E 1,445 m. high. A flat-topped mountain rising steeply from the W side of L. St. Clair in the SW of the Central Plateau*. The whole region has been affected by ice. Forest cover extends up to the final steep cliffs below the dolerite capping.

O'Malley, King (1854–1953) b. in North America. He arrived in Aus. in 1901, and was a controversial political radical. A tendency to buffoonery and a flamboyant style earned O'Malley enemies, but also attention for his genuinely held beliefs: he was the chief driving-force behind the search for and acquisition of the site for a national capital. A play *The Legend of King O'Malley* by M. Boddy and R. Ellis was produced in 1970.

Onslow W.A. 22S/115E A decaying coastal town on a dreary salt-marsh stretch, owing its origin to the Ashburton gold-field in 1889. It now serves Barrow Island*, and may revive with the quickening development of the NW.

Oodnadatta S.A. 28S/136E On the Central Aus. Railway to Alice Springs. It was its railhead until 1929, and the starting-point of camel caravans, but has declined since. It lies in poor cattle country dependent on artesian bores.

Opals The best-known Aus. gem stones, supplying 95% of the world market. They are mainly milky white with vivid blues and greens and are found in Cretaceous sediments W of L. Torrens in S.A. round Coober Pedy* and Andamooka*. They are gouged from as much as 15 m. down by individual or small groups of white and Aboriginal miners who generally keep secret the details of their finds, and sell through dealers to the Japanese. Cutting, polishing and setting are carried out with low labour costs in Japan or Hong Kong and the main final market is U.S. There were 'opal-rushes' to the black opal-fields of Lightning Ridge, N.S.W., 29S/148E, and Quilpie district, Qld., 27S/144E, in the late 19th and early 20th century, and there are still pickings to be made there and in W.A. near Kalgoorlie. *For further reading see* I. Idriess: *Lightning Ridge* (Sydney, 1948).

Orange N.S.W. 33S/149E (24,154 in 1971) An attractive inland city at 855 m. with many parks and trees, especially ornamental cherries symbolic of the orcharding around. A village antedated the gold-rush of the 1850s which added greatly to it. The city is a considerable regional centre for professional services, stock-marketing, broadcasting, medical and other professional services, and has fruit-packing, meat, woollen, brick, cordial and confectionery works, and a large factory producing domestic electrical machines and a new Japanese wool textile mill (1973). In 1972 the Bathurst–Blayney–Orange region was designated a 'growth area'.

Oraparinna S.A. 31S/139E A barytes mining centre on the E edge of the Flinders Range. The mineral is in demand for drilling mud for oil exploration, and is treated at Quorn.

Orb-web Spiders A popular name for various species mainly in the family Argiopidae, such as the Garden or Orb-weaving Spiders of genus *Araneus*, often up to 2·5 cm. long with coarsely hairy legs. They spin a beautiful and complex symmetrical web, with main peripheral foundation lines, from which are non-sticky radial lines. At the core is a small closely woven hub, then non-sticky concentric lines in the attachment zone, a free space, followed by the sticky concentric lines in the large snare zone; this is constructed from the periphery and worked inwards by replacement of non-sticky lines, the inner attachment zone being a residual of the non-sticky lines.

Orchids Of the large and world-wide Orchidaceae family, those native to Aus. number over 70 genera and over 600 species, including both epiphytes and plants growing in the soil. Epiphytes outnumber terrestrial orchids in Qld., but terrestrial species have become adapted to very varying environments, right up to the desert margins. I. *Common epiphytes* 1. *Dendrobium beckleri*, the Pencil Orchid, has thin cylindrical, pendulous leaves, and white-green and purple flowers, often on riverside trees in N.S.W. and Qld., and others of the genus, mainly growing in damp E coast valleys, include the thick leaved Cucumber Orchid, *D. cucumerinum*, the yellow hyacinth-like Rock Lily, *D. speciosum*, the Tongue Orchid, *D. linguiforme*, with thick tongue-shaped leaves and very delicate white petals and sepals about 2·5 cm long, and the delicate white and red Ironbark Orchid, *D. aemulum*. 2. The genus *Bulbophyllum*, with one leaf growing from each pseudo-bulb, often has inconspicuous flowers, but some appear disproportionately large, e.g. the *B. weinthali*, growing high on Hoop Pines from Dorrigo, N.S.W., 30S/153E, and N into tropical Qld. 3. The genus *Sarcochilus*, often with short stems and broad, prominently veined leaves rather like an aspidistra, includes the olive-green, gold-and-red-flowered, *S. olivaceus*, of the brush forests of NE Aus.

and the Orange Blossom Orchid, *S. falcatus*, of dense forests from Qld. to Vic., with 8–10 flowers, snowy white except for orange-red streaked labellum. II. *Terrestrial orchids* 1. The genus *Prasophyllum*, the Leek Orchids, widespread in E Aus. forests, are often tiny, with inconspicuous flowers, green to purple-black, in a dense spike; but the largest species, *P. elatum*, is in 1 to 2 m. clumps. 2. The genus *Caladenia* includes the Finger Flower or Pinky, *C. carnea*, of poor sandy or stony depressions in the E coast lowlands, the white *C. alba*, the rich blue *C. caerulea*, and *C. patersoni* of W.A., the white Spider Orchid (*see* PLATE 6) and the Blood Spider Orchid. 3. The genus *Pterostylis* includes the nodding Greenhood, *P. nutans*, with a narrow, curved green and yellow 'hood', and the Red-

flowered Greenhood, *P. coccinea*, with a rather pitcher-like flower, common on the N.S.W. part of the Great Divide. 4. The genus *Thelymitra* includes the splendid deep blue Veined Sun Orchid, *T. venosa*, with the labellum little differentiated from other petals and sepals. 5. The Doubletails, genus *Diuris*, include the rich golden *D. aurea* of the E coastlands, the purple Dotted Doubletail, *D. punctata*, found from the E coast to the Western slopes and the widespread Spotted Doubletail, *D. maculata*, yellow with brown spots. 6. The genus *Cryptostylis*, the Tongue Orchids, has 13 species, including *C. erecta*, Striped Hood, growing on sandy coastal patches in E Aus. and have reddish flowers.

The study of Aus. orchids has largely been the work of amateurs: Rev. H. M. R. Rupp (1872–1956), R. D. Fitzgerald (1830–1892) a surveyor, R. S. Rogers (1862–1942) a doctor, W. H. Nicholls (1885–1951) a bookbinder turned gardener, and the Rev. W. Woolls (1814–1893) who also worked on wider aspects of the flora of Aus.

Ord River W.A. 15S/129E Rises in the E Kimberley* plateau, and flows seasonally E then N and NW to Cambridge Gulf, with a catchment of 41,500 km.[2] The upper basin in poor stony savannah is severely eroded by overgrazing and trampling near waterholes. 3,100 km.[2] have been resumed from absentee holders for rehabilitation. This has been necessitated by the downstream **Ord River Project** aimed at encouraging closer settlement by irrigated agriculture. Development of a projected 73,000-ha. area began in 1963 with a 18·3-m. diversion dam at Bandicoot Bar, based on a quartzite sill in the river-bed. The Kimberley Research Station nearby (1945) had proved the possibility of crop growing. The original 5 farms have increased to over 30, each about 250 ha. (not all irrigated yet); wet-season cotton is uneconomic without subsidy, dry-season

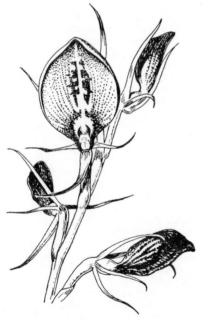

Striped Hood (*Cryptostylus erecta*), *about life size*

safflower is grown, Sorghum is promising, with potential Japanese export. It produces 3 crops a year, needs less water and labour and can be integrated as fodder with the Kimberley beef industry. A new town, Kununurra*, has been built. Further stages involve a main 5,920 million m³ storage dam with hydro-electric power in the Carr Boyd Range 48 km. upstream which was opened in 1972. A tourist complex, Lake Argyle, is planned on the largest man-made lake in Aus.

O'Reilly, William Joseph (1905–) b. White Cliffs, N.S.W. A cricketer, who ranked with Spofforth* and Turner* among the greatest Aus. bowlers; medium to fast and very versatile. He began his career in a country team at Wingello, N.S.W., meeting Bradman* and playing for the nearby Bowral team. In 19 Tests against Eng. (1932–8) he took 102 wickets for an average of 25·6, and in first-class games, 774 for an average of 16·5.

Ornamental and **Banded Snakes** (*Denisonia* spp.) Include *D. maculata*, a dark-mottled brown snake of Central and S Qld. with a broad head distinct from the neck and a rather thickset body of up to 50 cm. or so. The venom is neurotoxic and may cause rapid loss of consciousness, blindness etc., but with rapid recovery. De Vis's Banded Snake, *D. devisi*, occupies rather drier and more open country. The Little Spotted Snake, *D. punctata*, is found in Central Aus. and the Variegated Snake, *D. fasciata*, in parts of W.A.

Orthodox Churches There are 8 recognised branches in Aus. mainly dating from post-1945 immigration: Greek Orthodox*, Russian Orthodox*, Syrian, Rumanian, Bulgarian, Antiochian and 2 Ukrainian. The differences are of national tradition and language, rather than doctrine which stems from the great schism of Christendom in the 11th century. (About 335,000 in 1971.)

Orthoptera The Order of vegetarian, winged and jumping insects, mainly slender, including crickets*, grasshoppers* and locusts*. There are several ways of classifying the Orthoptera, but one is to separate off all the grasshoppers from the crickets. The grasshoppers are then divided simply into 2 groups. 1. The Short-horned (i.e. with short antennae), the Acridoidea, include as locusts only those species with the propensity to multiply greatly in a run of favourable years and then to fan out in swarms: the Plague Locust, *Chortoicetes terminifera*, the Yellow-winged Locust, *Gastrimargus musicus*, the Spur-throated Locust, *Austracris guttulosa*, and the migratory Locust, *Locusta migratoria*. Other species in the group include some that occasionally cause pasture damage, such as the small Plague Grasshopper, *Austroicetes cruciata*, in S.A. and W.A. and the Wingless Grasshopper, *Phaulacridium vittatum*. 2. The long-horned Grasshoppers, Tettigonidae, include: the graceful Gum Tree Grasshopper, *Caedicia olivacea*, with wings coloured and veined like leaves; the Crested Grasshopper, *Alectoria superba*; the blackish Mountain Grasshopper, *Acridopeza reticulata*, with red and blue back markings, displayed especially by the flightless female when she raises her front wings, rear wings being lacking; the wingless and formidably jawed Cave Cricket, *Anostostoma australasiae*, often seen near sandstone boulders from the great escarpments of SE Aus.; and the Brown Tree Cricket, *Paragryllacris combusta*, with soft gauzy wings and very long antennae, sometimes seen in Sydney houses.

The popular name Cricket has thus already been employed, and classification is both difficult and varying from time to time, but the Crickets proper may be said to include 2 families, the Mole Crickets, Gryllotalpidae, with front legs adapted for digging, such as the widely distributed introduced *Gryllotalpa africana*, its slightly raised tunnel-top ridge being seen by stream or lake-side, also some wingless burrowers; and the Field Crickets, Gryllidae, such as the Black Field Cricket, *Gryllus servillei*, often seen in gardens, under stones etc.

O'Shanassy, Sir John (1818–1883) b. Tipperary, Ireland. He arrived in Aus. in 1839. Premier of Vic. in 1857, 1858–9, 1861–3. He was active in the agitation for separation from N.S.W. and involved in the confused power struggles of the newly emerged State after 1851.

Ossa, Mount Tas. 42S/146E Rising to 1,619 m., the highest peak in the State, at the N end of the rugged, glaciated Du Cane Range and named like the adjacent Mt. Pelion and Mt. Achilles, from classical allusion. All are deeply gouged by corries.

O'Sullivan, Edward William (1846–1910) b. Launceston, Tas. An influential N.S.W. journalist and politician. As one of the 'wild men of Sydney', he advocated protection and closer settlement by selectors. *For further reading see* B. Mansfield: *Australian Democrat* (Sydney, 1965).

Otway, Cape and **Ranges** Vic. Near Apollo Bay, 39S/144E, part of a NE–SW upfaulted block of Cretaceous sandstones with some limestones, mudstones, etc. The hills are still partly forested with wet sclerophyll* woodlands in 75–100 cm mean annual rainfall. These rocks are truncated in the rugged cliffs of Cape Otway, called Cape Albany on the 1800 charting of Bass Str.

Ouse, River Tas. 42S/147E Flows S for 112 km. from the lakes region of the Central Plateau*, to join the Derwent near the small town of Ouse. The river has been diverted by canal twice: to Great Lake, and L. Echo, by the Monpeelyata Canal, 12 km. long. (*See* TASMANIA, POWER.)

Outback The name given to the inland rural areas far from close settlement;

it has had many compounds and derivatives, e.g. 'back of Bourke*' indicating really far-out primitive country.

Ovens River Vic. Flows generally NW for some 210 km. from the tall temperate rain-forests including the mountain ash, near Mt. Hotham (1,861 m.), receives the King River on the left bank at Wangarrata, 36S/146E, and joins the Murray W of Corowa. The valley was opened up by gold-mining in the 1850s, though it had been partly cleared by pastoralists, and routes through the steep forested hillsides used to take herds to the alpine summer pastures. Dredge-mining took place in the early decades of this century. Now the upper valleys are attractive holiday areas for anglers and bushwalkers, with access to winter snows from Bright*, while the broader lower valley has important hop, tobacco and vine cultivation and market towns such as Wangaratta, Beechworth and Myrtleford. Some hillsides formerly covered with St. John's wort have been forested with pines.

Overland Telegraph 2,900 km. of overhead cable, erected between Port Augusta, S.A., and Darwin, N.T., between June 1870 and October 1872, a magnificent achievement, since the only knowledge for much of the route was based on Stuart's* explorations 10 years before. Valuable survey work was done by J. Ross. There were 3 sections, the most northerly was delayed by the wet seasons and difficulties in sea transport of materials, and for some months the messages were carried by pony express over 480 km. between the unfinished ends. From Darwin a submarine link to Java was completed in 1871. Camels* were important in the supply trains, especially in the Central Desert section, and much incidental exploration was achieved. The line was duplicated in 1899, and further elaborated under great pressure in 1941. The link with the world provided in 1872 was important in decreasing the isolation of Aus. and was soon reflected in the changed function and format of the newspapers* with their 'Cable pages'. It was also a reflection of inter-state rivalry, with Qld. also bidding for the contract with the British Aus. Telegraph Co. Charles Todd was the leading engineer, as S.A. Postmaster-General.

Overlanders Drovers who broke new ground in driving stock to new stations, or from established stations to markets. The earliest overlanders, Gardiner, Ebden and Hawdon*, linked the Monaro Plain and Murray Valley with Port Phillip in 1837. In 1838 an overland route to Adelaide was found by Hawdon and Bonney in a race with Eyre by keeping to the certain water of the Murray as long as they could. Sturt* claimed that his overlanding trip to Adelaide in 1838 was more difficult than his explorations. Another pioneer of this route was the literary George Hamilton who recorded his experiences in *Experiences of a Colonist 40 years ago* (Adelaide, 1879). With the opening up of the western Qld. pastures, overlanding began to the N: to Moreton Bay, the Darling Downs, and later, the Jardines' famous trek into Cape York Peninsula (1864). Links between S.A. and W.A. were not established until the gold-fields era; but within W.A. Eyre pioneered a crossing from Perth–Albany. In the 1880s the greatest of overlanding exploits were carried out when Buchanan* (1881), and then the Duracks* (1883–6) overlanded cattle from N.S.W. to the Kimberleys and Arnhem Land. With the establishment of stock routes with permanent water, and of railheads, overlanding was replaced by droving along established routes. In *Droving Days* (London, 1966) H. M. Barker includes among outstanding drovers, J. Tyson, de Satgé, A. J. Cotton, R. Christison and G. Sutherland.

Owls Include the often brown and ear-tufted members of the family Strigidae, and the often whitish Barn Owls, family Tytonidae. All are adapted for a nocturnal and carnivorous life—on the whole, helping man by preying on insects and rodents—with large, sensitive eyes, powerful beaks and claws, noiseless flight and perhaps cries to 'freeze' the prey at times. These range from the hooting, familiar in many countries, of the fawn and white Barn Owl, *Tyto alba*, to the 'screaming-woman' cry of the E Aus. inland bush, now ascribed to the many-voiced Barking Owl, *Ninox connivens* (formerly to the 75-cm. forest-dwelling Powerful Owl, *N. strenua*, the largest Aus. owl). A common brown owl is the Boobook or Mopoke, *N. boobook*, a dainty white-flecked owl, 30 cm. long, which hides by day; it eats moths, mice etc. and lays 2–4 roundish eggs in tree hollows. *For further reading see* D. H. Fleay: *Nightwatchmen of Bush and Plain* (Brisbane, 1968).

Oxley, John Joseph William Molesworth (1785–1828) b. Westow, Yorkshire, Eng. He was appointed Surveyor-General of Lands in N.S.W. in 1812. Macquarie chose him to lead expeditions following up the crossing of the Blue Mts. In 1817, with George Evans and Allan Cunningham, he explored the Lachlan, and in 1818, the Macquarie. Both rivers disappeared in swamps and he believed they were 'in the vicinity of an inland lake or sea . . . gradually filling up with immense deposition from the higher lands . . .' a theory not disproved for many years. Turning E from the Macquarie Marshes, Oxley crossed the mountains and followed, and named, the fertile Hastings valley to the beautiful bay he named Port Macquarie, thence S along the coast. In 1819 he explored the south-coastal region of S N.S.W. and in 1823 the Moreton Bay area where he found 3 shipwrecked sailors (Finnegan, Pamphlett and Parsons) living with the Aborigines, who showed him a river he named the Brisbane. Oxley was unduly melancholy about the potentialities of the inland areas he explored, but he contributed much, not only to exploration but also as a pioneer settler in the Bowral area, and to early developments of banking, learned societies and libraries in the colony. He is commemorated in many place names. He opposed Macquarie's emancipist policy bitterly. *For further reading see* E. W. Dunlop: *John Oxley* (Melbourne, 1960).

Oyster Bay Tas. 42S/148E A fault-edged inlet on the E coast, 24 km. N–S by 8 km. E–W, the head heavily silted, and with residual lagoons behind Nine Mile Beach.

Oysters (*Ostrea*) About 10 species are found in Aus., the main commercial and cultivated one being the Rock Oyster, *O. commercialis*.

P

PACKER

Packer, Sir (Douglas), Frank, Hewson b. Sydney 1906. A leading figure in newspaper publication and a promotor of sport, notably sailing.

Pademelon A popular name for the smallish scrub Wallabies (*see* KANGAROOS.)

Page, Sir Earle Christmas Grafton (1880–1961) b. Grafton, N.S.W. A medical practitioner, who, entering politics in 1919, led the newly developed Country Party (1920–39). As a corner party, it supported the Bruce Government of 1923–9, and with Page as Treasurer this is often called the Bruce-Page Government. After its defeat in 1929 he held ministerial posts under Lyons, then Menzies until 1956 and was the first Chancellor of the University of New England.

PAINTING Aus. painting has emerged most distinctively among the creative arts in recent years. International attention has been particularly marked since the successful London exhibitions of the 1960s: San Francisco and Los Angeles (1959), Whitechapel Gallery, London (1962), the Tate (1963), European galleries (1965), Los Angeles (1966), Expo 67 Canada (1967), Mertz Collection (of 1964–6 Aus. work by 84 artists) on tour (1966–7). There is also a growing domestic appreciation and market for contemporary work and a number of travel scholarships, some included in the 60 or more annual art awards.
Historical Development The first European art in Aus. was either purely factual, valuable documentary recording of scenes or activities, as by Sydney Parkinson, who sailed with Cook, or highly romanticised views of the landscape as by John William

PAINTING

Lewin and Lycett* the convict. The oldest extant oil is the convict Thomas Watling's 'A View of Sydney Cove' (1794). Tas. had an early beginning in painting through the works of a visiting artist, John Skinner Prout, who organised Hobart's first exhibition in 1845, and of F. G. Simpkinson de Wesselow in the 1840s, by the fashionable portraits done by Wainewright* from 1837, and the landscapes of the early settler-artist Glover* from 1830 or the natural history paintings of W. B. Gould (1801–53), a convict at Macquarie Harbour. The first artist of high merit to settle in Aus. was Martens*, from 1835, and he was the first to support himself almost entirely from practising or teaching art. In the 1850s the contemporary scenes in S.A. and the Vic. gold-fields, were recorded with verve by Gill* whose work was widely circulated in lithographed form. About the same time some of the first attempts to capture the atmosphere of the outback were made by William Strutt. Melbourne, by then the largest city, was the major centre for art, dominated by a group of Continental artists, notably Buvelot*. It was here that the first coherent group of Aus. artists emerged as the Heidelberg School*, intent on conveying in their work some of the heat and light of the Aus. landscape, and using Aus. themes in a series of 'heroic pastorals'. This upsurge of nationalistic feeling was finding contemporary literary expression in the *Bulletin** which gave. an outlet for black and white cartoons*.

In the early 20th century many Aus. artists were working overseas, where John Russell, Rupert Bunny and Fox* especially gained recognition. In Aus. at the same time, Heysen's* landscapes and Meldrum's* portraits excelled in their fields but led to prolific and poor imitation. Sydney Long's landscapes and Blamire Young's watercolours were also notable influences, but Streeton's* work degenerated and his influence was to some extent stultifying. Post-impressionism developed in Sydney about 1913, with Roi de Maistre, Roland Wakelin and Grace Cossington-Smith, and then in Melbourne, with Arnold Shore and William Frater. In the 1920s Margaret Preston's work was outstanding in the field of non-figurative art. But in the 1930s, save for Norman Lindsay's* successful efforts to shock, Aus. art seemed fairly static, until shaken into life by the exhibition of contemporary European art, including the work of Matisse and Picasso and Dali, in 1938. This gave encouragement to an already restive group of young artists, but their work was scornfully received and caused much public controversy. Some of the new painters reacted in completely abstract or surrealist vein; others, who have emerged the more successful, tackled their Aus. environment with new interpretations and techniques of realist-expressionism. Among these are Nolan's* historical series, Tucker's* harsh almost surrealistic bush pictures, Sali Herman's* urban landscapes and Drysdale's* desert, outback and Aboriginal paintings, grim yet compassionate.

Since the 1950s, abstraction has grown more popular, especially among younger painters, although all degrees of figuration have persisted. The Melbourne Antipodean Group (1959) committed itself to a form of figurative expressionism that its leading participants still practise, although today some neo-realists are emerging. The Antipodean Group* includes some of the best Aus. artists of the 1960s. There is a common consent that there is an active creative Aus. contribution to the world of painting. The old account of Melbourne figurative realism against Sydney abstract romanticism is no longer helpful, and although the 2

centres still dominate, the other capitals all have artists, societies and patrons of influence. Towards the end of the 1960s, Antipodean figuration and School of Paris abstraction, as well as Abstract Expressionism and the tenuous Pop movement, were seriously challenged by American colour-field painting, strongly championed by the Central Street Gallery (an artists' co-operative) in Sydney. At the beginning of the 1970s post-object art of various kinds has been adopted by artists working outside the gallery system, and been tentatively institutionalised at the Inhibodress co-operative and the Pinacotheca Gallery in Melbourne. See B. W. Smith: *Australian Painting 1788–1960* (Melbourne, 1971); and the periodical *Art and Australia* (Sydney).

Palm Group Qld. Islands in Halifax Bay, 19S/147E, of which Great Palm Island, the largest, is 65 km.^{2} and reaches 549 m. in forested hills. It has an Aboriginal reserve and tropical cultivation. Orpheus Island is a tourist resort.

Palm Valley N.T. 24S/133E A short right-bank tributary of the Finke River* in Krichauff Ranges, accessible to tourists from Alice Springs. The steep red sandstone walls contrast with the dark depths of permanent waterholes, the rich tropical green vegetation, which includes the rare *Livistona mariae* palms, and the pale silvery ghost gums. Natural gas has been found.

Palmer, Edward Vance (1885–1959) b. Bundaberg, Qld. Of a literary family, he was a writer of novels, short stories, poems and plays. With Esson* he helped to establish Aus. drama with Pioneer Players (1922–6), and was an influential literary figure. His novels, notably *The Passage* (London, 1930) set in a Qld. fishing village, are works of craftsmanship, extolling an ethical code reflecting the writer's humanism. His wife **Janet Gertrude, 'Nettie',** *née*

Higgins (1885–), also wrote poems, short stories, criticism and biography.

Palmer, Giant Perch or **Barramundi** (*Lates calcarifer*) Sometimes called Burramundi (but cf. the Freshwater Burramundi*), this fish grows to 1·8 m. long and 55 kg. in weight. It is brown and silver, the front dorsal fin spiny and almost separated from a large rear one and the front gill-covers serrated and spiny.

Palmer River Qld. 16S/143E Flows for 320 km. E–W to the Mitchell. Alluvial gold, discovered by William Hann (1872), led to a rush in which Chinese and whites were decimated by malaria and Aboriginal cannibals; only ghost towns* remain. *For further reading see* H. Holthouse: *River of Gold* (Sydney, 1967).

Palms (family Palmae) Of 210 genera and 4,000 species in the world, tropical and sub-tropical Aus. has over 20 genera and over 40 species, mainly in the Tribe Areceae. They have berry fruits and include: Bangalow Palm, *Archontophoenix cunninghamiana*, of E Aus., tall with feathery leaves, the somewhat similar *Ptychosperma elegans*, the Black Palm of N. Qld., *Normanbya normanbyi*, with little-divided fronds, and well-developed adventitious roots around the base (as in all palms, replacing the primary root of the seedling stage), seen also in the short Walking-stick Palm, *Bacularia monostachya*. Kentia Palms, *Howea* spp., of Lord Howe Island are used as potplants.

The Tribe Coryphaea includes the well-known Cabbage Palm, *Livistona australis*, of E Aus.; in this genus are *L. alfredii* and *L. eastonii*, 2 of the rather limited palm flora of W.A., both in the monsoon belt of the N.

The Tribe Calameae includes the climbing rattans, e.g. the spiny Lawyer Vine, *Calamus muelleri*, of the rainforests of coastal NE Aus.

The Coconut Palm, *Cocos nucifera*, is naturalised along parts of the N coast. The Date Palm, *Phoenix dactylifera*, may have commercial potential; the stemless palm of the Asian deltas *Nipa fruticans* extends into N Qld.

Panic-grass A term spreading as a popular name from the cosmopolitan genus name *Panicum*. They are mainly tufted perennial grasses with rather graceful feathery conical heads of small soft seeds; they include the Native Millet, *P. decompositum*, the Hairy Panic Grass, *P. effusum*, the heads of which are often piled against fences by the wind, and the Sweet Panic Grass, *P. laevifolium*, probably an African species.

Paper and Pulp Industry Developed rapidly after processes were evolved, just before the 1939–45 War, for using the short-fibred eucalypt timber for pulping, notably by J. L. Somerville (1899–) and L. R. S. Benjamin (1892–), adding some imported and, increasingly, locally planted longfibred softwood pulp for paper-making. There are 21 paper mills, producing some 520 million tonnes a year, of which over 40% is board using a lot of waste, 25% wrapping, 15% fine writing and printing, and 13% newsprint* (this is entirely at one Tas. mill, Boyer*). Location of pulp mills must be near forests and a large water supply as at Port Huon in Tas; disposal of the unpleasant effluent creates problems. Vic. has 9 of the paper mills, dominated by Maryvale*. There are 3 in N.S.W. and 4 in Tas., with half Australia's needs in fine writing and printing made at Burnie*, although also recently developed in N.S.W. at Nowra*. There are 2 mills in Qld., 1 in W.A. and 2 in S.A., using planted *Pinus radiata*.

Paperbark or **Paperbark Tea-tree** (*Melaleuca quinquenervia*) Distinctive trees in the world-wide Myrtaceae* or Myrtle family; they grow in swampy terrain from Aus. to S and SE Asia, with readily peeling paper-like bark. Some species tend to branch from the ground. Leaves are spear-shaped and alternate flowers in yellow-green spikes which end branchlets and there are many small seeds in a globular fruit. Timber is grey with a pinkish tinge, termite-resistant and used for fencing in damp sites. Aborigines used sheets of bark for various purposes and some species yield aromatic oils, including the cajuput oil used in insecticides, from related species *M. alternifolia* and *M. linarifolia*. Related species are found in damp rather than swampy sites in E Aus., such as *M. ericofolia*. (*See* PLATE 8.)

Papua An Aus. Territory comprising the SE portion of the Island of N.G., extending from 5°S–11°S and 141°E to 154°E, some 1,450 km. The area is 223,000 km.², including over 5,000 km.² in the islands off the NE coast, the Trobriand, Woodlark and the D'Entrecasteaux groups. Population (1966) was 586,747 indigenous people of Melanesian stock in the E and Papuan in the W and inland, and 14,050 non-indigenous, including many Aus. administrators. There are 6 administrative districts. The capital is Port Moresby, which is also the administrative centre for the whole Territory of Papua–New Guinea*.

Papua–New Guinea, Territory of An administrative unit, comprising the Trust Territory of New Guinea* and the Territory of Papua*, and occupying the E half of the Island of N.G. Population (1966) was 2,148,300 indigenous, mainly Melanesian stock, and 34,736, non-indigenous, mostly Aus.-European expatriates, including administrators, planters and missionaries; a small Chinese trading community dates from the former importation of Asian labour.

Government has been through an Aus. Administrator with a Council of 11, of whom 7 come from the elected House of Assembly which in 1964 replaced the former Legislative Council. It had 64 Members, increased (1968) to 94; 10 official, 15 regional (on an educational qualification), and 69 open. Local Government Councils (1950) elected locally cover two-thirds of the people, and have considerable control in health, education, economic projects etc. With over 500 languages or diverse dialects, a pidgin English has developed. Education, with English the written medium, is still largely in Mission Schools. A university opened in 1966. Malaria eradication is well advanced in towns, and in progress in rural areas; other diseases are yaws, tropical ulcers, tuberculosis and scrub typhus. Medical aid posts in the villages are manned by trained indigenous personnel. The decreasing death-rate means an increasing and youthful population and some local population pressures, although in general there is enough potential farmland for some time; re-settlement schemes based on cash economies are encouraged.

The climate is equatorial, but with marked seasonal wind reversal between NW and SE, and maximum rainfall amounts and periods according to position and aspect; much of the Territory has over 250 cm. annually, but there is a drier region in the SE. Here grassland replaces the forest cover common to most of the island. A central mountain cordillera stretches NW–SE, built of folded sediments, but including extinct and active volcanoes, and reaching 4,491 m. in Mt. Wilhelm. Rain-forest is replaced by montane pines, laurels etc. at 900 m., and above 2,750 m. by moss-clothed myrtles etc. in almost perpetual mist. Intermont valleys have densely peopled pockets of intensively cultivated gardens, growing sweet potatoes; some groups (e.g. the Chimbu) were unknown until the 1930s. Mt. Hagen and Goroka are the main centres; Bulolo and Wau, formerly important mining areas, are now, respectively, centres of plywood production from kinki and hoop pine, and coffee plantations. In 1972 famine faced 130,000 when drought was followed by severe frost.

N of the mountains is a thinly peopled low trough through which the swamp-fringed and braided Markham and Sepik Rivers flow SE and NW respectively. Cattle have been introduced to some of the higher grasslands here. N again, a further, lower mountain region, reaching 1,525 m. lines the N coast; it is clothed in rain-forest. Towards the NW densely peopled areas are supported by shifting cultivation of yams, taro, bananas and tapioca, but villages are permanent, and fishing and sale of copra are supplements. S of the central mountains, the Fly River, 1,127 km. long, and others, have built out a swampy deltaic plain supporting sago-swamp inland, and mangrove nearer the low indented coast. SW of the Fly the low Omiara Plateau has ancient continental rocks supporting grassland, while to the SE, only a narrow plain lies between Port Moresby and the Owen Stanley Range. The rural peoples are thinly scattered, subsisting on sago palm, fish and gathered fruits, and living in elaborate stilted houses.

The offshore islands of the Admiralty, Bismarck Archipelago and Solomon Islands are submerged mountain chains. Large, low-grade copper deposits are being developed on Bougainville Is. The Gazelle Peninsula in the N of New Britain is one of the most densely peopled parts of N.G.; here the Tolai people have developed a successful cash economy based on copra and cocoa. Rabaul, on a fine natural harbour, is the Territory's main port.

Historical Development After early Spanish interest had waned and the Dutch annexation of W N.G. (1828), there was little European interest, save as a source of Kanaka* labour for Qld., until German annexation of the NE stimulated British acquisition of the

SE of the island in 1884; an abortive attempt by Qld. the previous year had been repudiated in London. In 1906 Aus. took over British N.G., renamed Papua, and in 1914 assumed control of German N.G., receiving a League of Nations Mandate for it in 1920. In 1942–5 the Japanese occupation led to some of the bitterest fighting of the Second World War* (*see also* KOKODA TRAIL, *and* COASTWATCHERS). In 1946 Aus. was given a United Nations Trusteeship of N.G., implying eventual self-determination; in 1949 a single administration of Papua–N.G. was set up. Self government is likely by the end of 1973, with full independence probable by 1974–5. A Constitutional Planning Committee was set up in 1972. *See* D. A. M. Lea and P. G. Irwin: *New Guinea* (Melbourne, 1967).

Paraburdoo W.A. 23S/117E Iron field and township 56 km from Mt. Tom Price planned for 2,500 people (1,778 in 1971).

Parakeelya An aboriginal name for an edible, fleshy desert herb *Calendrinia balonensis*. *C. polyandra* and *C. remota* provide food and moisture for stock.

Park, Ruth (Mrs. D'Arcy Niland) b. Auckland, N.Z. A successful popular children's writer and adult novelist, as in *Harp in the South* (Sydney, 1948), set in Sydney slums.

Parkes N.S.W. 33S/148E (8,489 in 1971) A reef and alluvial gold centre in the 1860s and 70s under the name of Bushman's, changed in 1873 in honour of Sir Henry Parkes*. It is now an important market, service, processing, local building and engineering centre for a central area of the Western Slopes region, holding its own although only 34 km. from the more rapidly growing Forbes*. It is a rail junction and is a striking focus of roads. Nearby is the impressive 64-m. revolving, bowl-shaped radio-telescope operated by C.S.I.R.O.*

Parkes, Sir Henry (1815–1896) b. Warwickshire, Eng. Premier of N.S.W. 5 times between 1872–91. The son of a poor farmer, he came to Aus. (1839) as a 'bounty migrant' after working in rope and brickworks and as an ivory turner's apprentice, meanwhile achieving self-education and Chartist views. Business ventures twice led to bankruptcy in 1858 and 1870; but a brilliant political instinct, a massively impressive physical appearance and clever if undistinguished oratory led him to gradual dominance of the confused N.S.W. political scene from 1854–91, culminating in defeat by Reid*. His work for Federation* was great though tempered by political expedience; thus, although instigating both, he prevented N.S.W. from joining the Federal Council in 1883, or passing the Draft Constitution of 1891. He suggested the name Commonwealth. Parkes was closely identified with the development of education*, introducing far-reaching bills in 1867 and 1880; he supported free trade and increased European migration and land selection, while curbing the Chinese influx. He wrote poor verse himself, but encouraged both Harpur* and Kendall*, and his *Fifty Years in the Making of Aus. History* (London, 1892) is heavy but valuable material. He died in some poverty.

Parrakeets or **Grass Parrakeets** They are generally green, long-tailed small Parrots*, flocking on grass-seeds etc. in open woodland or inland grass-lands, and typified by the well-known Budgerigah or Budgerigar, *Melopsittacus undulatus* (sweet-songed and marked with waves), with yellow head and wings, blue towards the tail, and up to 18–20 cm. long; it is found, now in much reduced flocks, all over Aus. except in rain-forests and Tas. Other important grass parrakeets include the Blue-winged Parrot, *Neophema chrysostoma* (the golden-mouthed new voice), of SE Aus. and several related

species; the Mulga Parrot, *Psephotus varius* (inlaid with variegated pebbles), with blue-edged wings and red and yellow on shoulder and lower belly, and several relatives including the Blue-bonnets, *P. narethae* and *P. haematogaster*, and the now rare Paradise Parrot, *P. pulcherrimus*, the cock bird being particularly handsome with yellow-green head grading into delicate blue body, with red shoulders, brown back and wings. The dainty crested Cockatiel, *Leptolophus hollandicus*, is also a grass-eater. A separate category might also be allotted to the Swamp Parrot, *Pezoporus wallicus* (pedestrian), which dwells much closer to the ground and is still seen in SE Aus., and the Night Parrot, *Geopsittacus occidentalis*, probably increasingly rare in the centre and N of Aus.; both are green flecked with black, the former with red brow, the latter yellow-faced.

Parramatta N.S.W. (110,717 in 1971) A city (since 1938) within Greater Sydney and about 24 km. W of Sydney Cove on the small creek and western branch of the drowned-valley system of Sydney Harbour. It was very early explored by Phillip himself on April 23rd 1788, was named at first Rose Hill after a British Treasury official, and was yielding crops by 1789; the first town was laid out in 1790, the name being changed to its present Aboriginal one the next year. There was a ferry to Sydney in 1793 and a road in 1794. A few historic buildings survive, such as Elizabeth Farm, built by John Macarthur* in 1793. The notable King's school dates from 1832. Today the gently undulating ground is mainly covered by suburban housing and industry.

Parramatta-grass A popular name for the naturalised species *Sporobolus capensis*, very similar in appearance to the native Rat-tail Grass, *S. elongatus*.

Parrot-fishes Named from the parrot-like beak formed by fusion of teeth. There are about 24 species, many brightly coloured and changing colours as they grow, in tropical Aus. waters, e.g. *Callyodon ghobban*. Pieces of dead coral are bitten off and ground to get food. A temperate relative is the Rainbow Fish, *Heteroscarus acroptilus*.

Parrots Including the Rosellas, Parrakeets (a popular name for small species), and the Cockatoos, they total over 50 Aus. species (about a fifth of those in the world mainly in the Tropics). Parrots are often brightly coloured, have a strong hooked bill for nut-eating etc. and have claws with a good grasp, 2 toes in front and 1 behind. They range very widely throughout the contrasting habitats of the whole country, from rain-forest to semi-desert, and from 60 to 20 cm. in length. Most nest in tree-holes, sometimes cliff-cavities, with 2-4 white eggs. They have varied calls, but in nature are not prominent as mimics. Classification is difficult and varies between different authorities, but a very rough, though overlapping classification by size would include the following groups and species. 1. Cockatoos* and other large Parrots. 2. The Rosellas*, cf. medium-size. 3. The nectar-eating Lorikeets*. 4. The generally small, green, long-tailed Grass Parrakeets*, typified by the well-known Budgerigah or Budgerigar. (*See* PLATE 4.)

Parsley, Wild (*Lomatia silaifolia*) A shrub in the large southern Proteaceae family, growing in sandstone and shale country, in both E and W Aus.; it has somewhat parsley-like branched foliage and pairs of very handsome white flowers with 4 spreading, but recurved tongue-like petals and a protruding style.

Paspalum Grass (*Paspalum dilatatum*) A valuable pasture grass especially for cattle, producing a luxuriant tussocky growth in summer, tending to become fibrous unless mixed with other fodder plants in the sward, but frost-sensitive and so contributing little or even dying

out in winter. It was introduced experimentally from S America in 1891, and spread accidentally about 1900.

Passion Fruit (*Passiflora* spp.) In the mainly tropical American family Passifloraceae. There are not only introduced fruit and flower species but also 4 native species, including the yellow-flowered ivy-type leaved *P. herbertiana* of rich damp areas in Qld. and N.S.W.

Passmore, John (1904–) b. Sydney. An artist who after a long period in Europe from 1933–50, returned to exert great influence on Sydney art students, notably Olsen*. His drawing is especially skilled, but he was in turn influenced by his pupil to new approaches in non-figurative work.

Paterson, Andrew Barton ('Banjo') (1864–1941) b. Narrambla, near Orange, N.S.W. Son of Scottish pioneer grazier and English mother; his boyhood near Yass gave him a lifelong love of the country. He began training as a solicitor, turning to journalism and was a correspondent in the Boer War, China and the Philippines. The name 'Banjo' was that of a racehorse. He published first in the *Bulletin* (1889); later his books of verse, largely bush ballads, achieved tremendous sales. Many aspects of bush life are described in racing evocative rhythms, capturing atmosphere and action (and the imagination of several Aus. generations whose ideal of 'the bush' they epitomise), in marked contrast with the depressing realism of Lawson's* verse. *The Man from Snowy River* is his most famous composition. His alleged authorship of *Waltzing Matilda** is uncertain. *For further reading see* C. Semmler: *The Banjo of the Bush* (Melbourne, 1966).

Paterson, William (1755–1810) b. Montrose, Scotland. Before arriving as a Captain in the N.S.W. Corps in 1791, Paterson had served in India and had made botanical explorations in S

PLATE 7: TREES AND SHRUBS

1. Red Spider-flower *(Grevillea punicea)*. 2. Spear Grass-tree *(Xanthorrhoea hastilis)*. 3. Cootamundra Wattle *(Acacia baileyana)*. 4. Tea-tree *(Leptospermum laevigatum)*. 5. Weeping Myall *(Acacia pendula)*.

Africa. As Senior Officer he took over the administration of the colony from Grose* for 9 months (1794–5) in the military interregnum between Governors Phillip and Hunter, and again, reluctantly, from Foveaux (January-December 1809) between Bligh and Macquarie. In the intervals he had plant-hunted for Banks, explored, and established Port Dalrymple (Launceston). A well-meaning character, he was too amiable and weak for his times and tasks, as well as being given to drink which led to the severe gout and illness, of which he died on his voyage home in 1810.

Paterson's Curse (*Echium plantagineum*) In the Boraginaceae family, a European flowering herb, Viper's Bugloss, which is said to have spread from one Paterson's garden in Albury, N.S.W., 36S/147E, to become a pest of pasture lands over much of SE Aus. In the semi-arid lands of S.A., however, it was regarded as good grazing, hence the contrasted local name of Salvation Jane. Between Adelaide and Elizabeth, and in many other S.A. landscapes, Paterson's Curse forms a purple carpet in the early summer.

Patriotic Six The name coined by the contemporary press for 6 Tas. members of the Legislative Assembly, led by Dry*, who resigned in October 1845 over the budget proposals to meet the heavy costs involved by the greatly increased numbers of convicts sent to Tas. when transportation was stopped to N.S.W. They were restored in 1846.

Patterson, Gerald Leighton (1895–1967) b. Melbourne. A nephew of Melba*, he was one of the greatest Aus. tennis players, representing the country in Davis Cup matches from 1919–28 and winning at Wimbledon in 1919 and 1922. His play was immensely powerful in forehand, volley and smash, but tended to be erratic.

Pea Strictly the garden pea *Pisum sativum* and extended to the sweet pea

Lathyrus odoratus, the name is also used in Aus. for a wide variety of plants, mainly of the world-wide Papilionaceae or Pea family. The plants of this family have the important agricultural ability to fix nitrogen by the activity of bacteria growing on the roots. Well-known wild flowers called Peas are listed here. 1. The Narrow-Leaf Bitter-Pea, *Daviesia corymbosa*, a dainty bush of the sandstone plateaux of the E coast, has small spear-shaped leaves almost hidden in spring by clusters of bright yellow flowers with dark red markings, followed by seeds in flat pods. 2. The Bush-Peas, genus *Pultenaea*, of stony or sandy E coast tracts, include the Hairy Bush Pea, *P. villosa*, orange and red, with red silk-haired pods, the Large-leaf Bush Pea, *P. daphnoides*, with dense compact multiple heads, the Fine-leaf Bush Pea, *P. stipularis*, with slender delicate leaves and even more compact compound heads of pea-like flowers grouped in a golden rosette, fringed by dark green, and various species, linked along with related genera by the popular name of Eggs and Bacon, some up to small tree size, such as the riverine *P. altissima* of N.S.W. 3. The Coral Pea, genus *Hardenbergia*, includes the violet-flowered *H. comptonia* of W.A. with fan-shaped leaves, the clover-leafed *H. retusa* of N Qld., and the simple-leafed false Sarsparilla, *H. violacea*, of E Aus. 4. The Cow-pea, genus *Vigna*, is most commonly applied to the trailing green manure plant *V. cylindrica*, probably introduced from Asia, but there are native species, e.g. the yellow-flowered *V. lutea* and *V. vexillata* of E Aus. 5. The Flame Pea, genus *Chorizema*, includes rather weak straggling shrubs with vivid orange-red short-keeled flowers, such as *C. cordatum* of W.A. 6. The Flat-peas, genus *Platylobium*, include the Handsome Flat-pea, *P. formosum*, of the E coast sandstone plateaux, which has broad spear-shaped leaves in pairs, with a magnificent blossom in each leaf axil, bright yellow, touched with deep red in keel, wings and standard. 7. The Parrot-peas, genus *Dillwynia*, include the Heathy Parrot-pea, *D. ericifolia*, whose foliage has indeed heath-like needles, the fine yellow flowers, profuse in spring, having a prominent red-marked standard or rear petal. 8. The Scurf-peas, from the black glands spotting the leaf, genus *Psoralea*, include the Native Lucerne or Emu Grass, *P. tenax* and the woolly blue-flowered *P. eriantha*. The Shaggy Peas, genus *Oxylobium*, include poisonous species such as *O. parviflorum* of W.A. and the yellow-flowered Native Holly, *O. trilobatum*, of damp gullies in E Aus. 10. The Wedge-peas, genus *Gompholobium*, include the Golden Glory or Broad Wedge-pea, *G. latifolium*, with soft broadly lanceolate leaves and magnificent yellow flowers almost 4 cm. across, quite common on the E coast sandstones. 11. The Darling or Broughton Pea, genus *Swainsona*, includes beautiful but poisonous species such as the snow-white White Darling Pea, *S. galegifolia*. 12. Sturt's Desert Pea, *Clianthus formosus*, growing over much of the dry inland if rain is suitable, has the magnificent white, red and purple blossoms of 7–10 cm long, which were first collected by Dampier in 1688 in NW Aus. 13. The Australian Pea is a misnomer sometimes used overseas for the common cultivated pulse of much of S Asia, of the genus *Dolichos*. 14. *Gastrolobium* is a genus with showy red, yellow or orange flowers, oval leathery pods and very varied leaves and habitats, very poisonous to cattle.

Peak Downs Qld. 23S/148E A distinctive district with peaks of volcanic rock (e.g. Wolfgang Peak, 305 m.), standing above rolling downland of natural light scrub and grass on black soils. Some 28,400 ha. were cleared (1948–53) by the British Qld. Food Corporation for sorghum mainly, then subdivided. The enterprise was not entirely successful, but has left a legacy of more diversified farming. Copper

and gold were mined for some years from 1862 at Copperfield and Clermont.

Peak Hill W.A. 26S/119E A gold and manganese centre in the Robinson Range, between Gascoyne and Murchison Rivers, but with only minor output.

Pearce, Sir George Foster (1870–1952) b. Mt. Barker, S.A. He went to W.A. (1892) and worked as a carpenter, rising through Trade Union organisation. He was a Member of the Senate for W.A. from 1901–38, holding ministerial office over 25 years. He left the Labor Party in 1917, being in favour of conscription. As Minister of Defence in several ministries between 1908–21, he was responsible for the Aus. military commitment in the 1914–18 War. *For further reading see* P. Heyden: *Quiet Decision* (Melbourne, 1965).

Pearling Mother of pearl, the shell of *Pinctada maxima*, is now, with Trochus*, only a very minor Aus. product since plastics took over the button market in the 1950s. Jewellery pearls, found incidentally, and traditionally the jealousy guarded property of the diver, are being produced in small but valuable amounts on 15 culture farms: 12 as joint Aus.-Japanese and 3 as purely Aus. enterprises. The first was in 1956 at Kuri Bay, W.A., 15S/124E. Pearl shells are found on the continental shelf from Cairns, Qld., and round to Broome, W.A., which was the biggest pearling centre in the heyday of the industry. In 1912 350 luggers operated from the town. There were high death-rates from paralysis among the Aboriginal, Torres Str. Islands, Malay, Filipino and Japanese divers until diving suits were used. Summer cyclones also led to severe losses among the ships. In 1935 20 luggers were lost in a cyclone in the Lacapedes Islands. The main market for oysters from the few remaining luggers is the culture farms, but there is some export to U.S., Japan and W Germany.

Pears Of a total of some 10,000 ha, some 68% are in Vic., in the hills W of Melbourne, and in the irrigated orchards of the Goulburn Valley, where canning of the Bartlett pear (along with peaches and apricots) is important at Shepparton*.

Pedal Radio A crystal radio powered by a pedal, invented in 1926 by Alfred Traeger, an electrician in Adelaide for the Flying Doctor Service*, and used for many years. It was compact and easily operated, and transmitted to 485 km.

Pedder, Lake Tas. 43S/146E Covers 23 km.² and feeds the Serpentine River and thence the Gordon River*. It was formed by damming with glacial outwash, and has a famous white sandy beach. Formerly inaccessible save to walkers, and sightseers brought by charter aircraft landing on the beach in summer low water, it is included as part of the Gordon River* hydro-electric scheme. Bitter controversy has been roused over the proposed flooding of the lake for this purpose.

Peel, Thomas (1793-1865) b. Lancashire, Eng. He arrived in Aus. in 1829. Peel was one of a rich cotton family and cousin of the British Prime Minister, Robert Peel. With partners, who later backed out, he formed a scheme for settlement in W.A., undertaking to send 10,000 settlers in return for 4 million ac.; this failed to be approved, but Peel accepted an offer of ½ million ac. on the Swan River, and was secretly backed by a returned, wealthy emancipist, Levey. However, he failed, through no fault of his own, to arrive in the stipulated time and had to take poorer land between Cockburn Sound and Murray River. The entire venture failed; his indentured labour left, stock and supplies failed to arrive, and the ground was found to be useless. Peel stayed on, though his family returned to Eng. after a short period with him, and he died proud, poor and forgotten. *For further reading see* A. Hasluck: *Thomas Peel of Swan River* (Melbourne, 1965).

Peewee A popular name for the pied Mudlark* from its call.

Pelican (*Pelecanus conspicillatus*—spectacled) Australia's only pelican and the largest in the world (over 1·2 m from tail to beak, itself over a foot long, and with the well-known pouch). It is webfooted and eats fish and shell-fish in fresh and salt-water, and though killed off by fishermen in the past, it is now protected in many of its breeding places in coastal or inland swamps, and appears to be holding its own. It is white, with black increasing towards the rear in body and wings. The tiny Walker's Island off the Nassau in the Gulf of Carpentaria has probably the world's biggest pelican rookery.

Pelsaert, Francois Commander of the Dutch East India Company ship *Batavia*, wrecked (1629) on the Abrolhos Islands*. Pelsaert, with a small group of the survivors, made the 3,200-km. journey to Batavia in a month, in an open boat. Landing frequently on the Aus. coast, they were appalled by the lack of water or vegetation, and by the flies. Returning with help, Pelsaert had to quell a mutiny and he marooned 2 of the culprits on shore, to become the first of Australia's involuntary white settlers. Tasman* was instructed to look for them in 1644 but found no trace. *For further reading see* H. Drake-Brockmann: *Voyage to Disaster* (Sydney, 1963); H. Edwards, in *Island of Angry Ghosts* (London, 1966), tells of the discovery of the wreck in 1963.

Pemberton W.A. 34S/116E A small sawmilling town in karri-jarrah forest, with some local potato- and hop-growing and dairying. The nearby **Gloucester Tree,** named after the Duke of Gloucester, is a 61-m. karri with a fire lookout on top reached by a 'peg' spiral staircase.

Penguin Tas. 41S/146E (2,287 in 1971) A service centre for the intensive potato, pea and dairy lands of the N coast plain, and residential centre for the ilmenite-processing for pigment at Blythe 11 km. to the W.

Penguins They nest in mainly insular sites off the S of Aus., and include the Thick-billed Penguin, *Eudyptes pachyrhynchus* (thick-billed expert diver), about 45 cm. tall, with the dark grey head and back, and white belly with yellow side-crests extending from an eye-stripe; and the much smaller, crestless Little or Fairy Penguin, *Eudyptula minor*. There are occasional chance visits from Antarctic penguins of various species.

Pennant-fish or **Diamond Trevally** (*Alectis ciliaris*) A 36-cm.-deep, thin, diamond-bodied fish, not in fact related to the Trevally. The young fish have long fin rays—'pennants'—waving behind them from back and belly fins. As the fish grow the pennants shorten or drop off.

Penrith N.S.W. 34S/151E (60,242 in 1971; 12,522 in 1961) A city near the Nepean River*, founded in 1815 and becoming the centre for a market-gardening and river resort area. The railway (1863) was electrified in 1955. As its enormous growth suggests, it is under strong metropolitan influence and is now recorded in the Sydney Metropolitan Area.

Penton, Brian Con (1904–1951) b. Brisbane. A novelist and journalist noted chiefly for his Qld. pioneering saga *Landtakers* (Sydney, 1934), followed by *Inheritors* (Sydney, 1936), portraying the brutalisation of the hero by the crude vicious realities of 19th-century Aus.

Peppermint The name applied in Aus. to a group of some 15 species and varieties of Eucalypts; leaves have few veins, many oil dots and enough oil for distillation. The timber is poor. Juvenile leaves in most species are opposite for many pairs, but vary in breadth, as do the adult leaves, notably between the

Narrow-leaved Peppermint, *Eucalyptus robertsoni*, and the Broad-leaved Peppermint, *E. dives*, both of high country in N.S.W. and Vic.—the former in higher, snowy country with 75–150 cm mean annual precipitation. *E. robertsoni* has pointed buds and pear-shaped fruit about 6 mm long, and *E. dives* has club-shaped buds and pear-shaped fruit. Bark in both is closely fibrous and persistent on the trunk and main branches. Other varieties are common from SE Qld. to Tas., generally on cool moist sites, but some on sandy soils. The River Peppermint, *E. andreana*, with only a short bark stocking, and the White Peppermint, *E. linearis*, are particularly attractive as ornamental trees. The Peppermints are related to Scribbly Gums, Snow Gums and Ashes and sometimes hybridise with these groups.

PERTH W.A. 32S/116E (664,426 in 1971). The capital and premier city of the State, with 68% of the population. It is the fifth city in Aus. The Metropolitan Area covers a region about 40 km. square, with fingers to the E beyond Midland and SE beyond Gosnells—towards Armadale. The total area is similar to that of Greater London, but the population only 6% of London's. The City of Perth, proclaimed in 1856, is some 62 km.².

Perth lies on the low plain between the coastal limestone and sand-dune belt and the Darling Range; it spreads along both banks of the lower Swan River, the centre being 19 km. from its mouth. The climate is equable and sunny for 8 months, but cold and damp in June and July, and uncomfortably hot in January and February, with many days over 32°C. Water supply is from the Serpentine and Canning Rivers, Munday and Churchman Brooks, all in the Darling Range, with occasional supplement from bores.

The core of the city forms a rectangular block between the N bank and the railway; tall concrete and glass buildings now tower over 19th-century Georgian and neo-Gothic. The business centre is St. George's Terrace; Hay Street is the main shopping focus. Industry, save for printing and clothing, has moved out along the rail and road arteries into a suburban zone. Heavy industry is concentrated in the area of Welshpool, S of the river, and close settlement in the S dates from 1939–45. Kwinana* is a major industrial complex to the S and a similar development is planned on the coast N of Perth. There is almost continuous building W to Fremantle*. Wealthier residential development extends NW towards the coast, and fringes the 403-ha. reserve of King's Park. More monotonous housing lies towards the N, E and S. Migrant and Aboriginal communities form important elements here and in S Perth. The Swan is crossed by a Causeway, using Heirisson Island, and by the Narrows Bridge (1959) crossing the strait between the wide Perth and Melville waters, linking the city S to Kwinana*, with a bold plan of approach roads and overpasses from the N and E just developing. The Stephenson Plan (1955) is the basis of future development envisaging a T-shaped urban area: the leg W–E from the Scarp, the arms N and S, parallel to the coast. The Metropolitan Region Authority has Parliamentary legislation behind it, unique so far in Aus.

Perth was named after the Scottish title of the Secretary of State for the Colonies in London at the time of its foundation. Growth was very slow and mainly on the N bank at Fremantle*, Perth and Guildford, a farming and trans-shipment point, until the goldrushes and Fremantle harbour works in the 1890s gave it impetus. Perth has a reputation as rigidly stratified socially, a result of its non-convict English origins, perhaps, as well as its isolation, but the spurt of W.A. development now in progress is bringing forces of change.

Peterborough S.A. 33S/139E (3,019 in 1971; 3,430 in 1961) A rail centre at the S of the Flinders Ranges, owing its origin and functions to the siting of the junction and workshops for the 3-ft. 6-in. gauge lines from Port Pirie and Terowie (thence broad-gauge to Adelaide) in 1881, Quorn (1882, later on to Alice Springs) and Broken Hill (1887). Originally called Petersburg from a local settler's name, it was changed with other German names in 1918. With completion of the standardisation of the Port Pirie line and extension of the 5-ft. 3-in. line from Terowie, it has 3 gauges.

Petermann Range W.A./N.T. 25S/129E Runs SE–NW for some 320 km. continuing the granite and gneisses of the Musgraves*. Separate E–W ridges became more haphazard towards the W. Rugged slopes include the Ruined Ramparts Cliff. It was in this country that Lasseter probably died in 1930, searching for the fabulous Lasseter's Reef*.

Petrels Medium to large sea-birds*, usually grey and white or brown.

Petroleum Aus. has producing oilfields at Moonie* in the Surat Basin of SE Qld., Barrow Island* field in W.A. which began production 1969 and the new Bass Strait* fields which raised indigenous oil production to 70% of needs by 1971–2. Total output 1971–2 was 120 million barrels, 88% from Bass Str. fields. About 70% of imported crude oil comes from the Middle East, the rest from Borneo. *Discovery* The survey ship *Beagle** used bitumen from the Victoria River estuary in W.A. to caulk her boards in 1839; the first exploratory oil-well was dug at Coorong, S.A., in 1892, based on an assumption that an algal scum on the lake was petroliferous. In 1900 an artesian bore at Roma, Qld., produced natural gas, and in 1919–20 discoveries of asphalt in the Kimberley region in

W.A. stimulated prospecting. Oil was also obtained in small quantities in the Lakes Entrance region of Vic. from 1930–41. But exploration was of sporadic, wild-catting character until after the 1939–45 War. Experts and capital were equally scarce until then. The creation of a Federal Bureau of Mineral Resources in 1948 saw the beginning of systematic survey of the extensive Palaeozoic-Tertiary sedimentary basins on the Aus. mainland and offshore, which are potential oil-bearing regions. Subsidies for private survey, along with Income Tax relief (until 1973) both for firms and private investors, have further stimulated exploration. Strategic and economic considerations are behind the national anxiety to reduce the reliance on imported oil. A 50% subsidy is paid on onshore oil exploration. Refiners refusing to use a share of native oil (more highly priced by the addition of a factor designed to stimulate further exploration) are penalised. The first important strike was made at Rough Range, Exmouth Gulf, in W.A. by WAPET (W Aus. Petroleum Ltd., an Ampol Caltex combine) in 1953, leading to excited speculation and renewed research which waned when further bores remained fruitless for 6 years. In 1960 a sub-commercial flow was produced at Cabawin in Qld. by Union Oil, followed in 1961 by the first commercial flow at Moonie and sent by the 320-km pipeline to Lytton refinery in Brisbane. In 1969 oil flow began from the Bass Strait field: Halibut (oil), Kingfish (oil) and Barracouta (gas and oil) and in 1972 were producing 280,000 barrels a day. Tirrawanna S.A. and Mereenie N.T. are new fields. *Legislation* for land survey and exploitation lies with the State Governments and therefore varies; as Crown property, rent as well as royalties (10%) may be charged and stipulations on bonds, length of tenure, minimum period within which operations must start etc. protect the Government

interest and control speculation. In 1967 pioneer legislation was tabled for offshore exploitation of oil and natural gas, to overcome the problems of Commonwealth and State rights. Offshore petroleum royalties are shared on the basis of 60% for the State and 40% for the Commonwealth Government. *Refining* 10 refineries are in operation: N.S.W. (Sydney), Clyde, Kurnell, Matraville; Qld. (Brisbane), Bulwer Island, Lytton; Vic., Westernport, Altona, Geelong; S.A., Port Stanvac, and W.A., Kwinana. Products already provide a surplus for export to N.Z. and SE Asia as well as a basis for a growing Aus. petrochemical industry (*see* CHEMICALS). Refineries are located near markets now (earlier, overseas refineries were near the source), and by-products are more used. Sea terminals are an important factor in siting. The economics of oil in Aus. are complicated by the predominance of international companies which export their profits and are anxious to send their own crude oil to Aus. refineries; this (especially Middle East oil) is heavy, and the residual oils from refining are unloaded on the Aus. fuel market at prices highly competitive with coal. Formation of a Govt. Authority to explore, produce, transport and refine petroleum is planned, with its own personnel and equipment.

Petrov Affair On April 3rd 1953, Petrov, third secretary of the Soviet Embassy in Canberra, asked for asylum, followed on the 20th by his wife who after leaving for Russia, turned back at Darwin. Petrov denounced alleged spies, and a Royal Commission reported (1955) on the existence of Soviet espionage in Aus. Evatt* alleged it was a pre-election anti-Labor plot, accepted Russian assurances and offered to defend the accused, which precipitated the 1955 split in the Labor Party.

Phalaris, Canary-grass or Toowoomba Canary-grass (*Phalaris tuberosa*) A very valuable introduced pasture grass, densely tufted, stout with a bulbous swelling at the stem base, and a compact but soft seed-head. With Subterranean Clover* in improved pastures it can transform the farm economy of the 40 to 65-cm. rainfall belt. Sirocco phalaris, developed in 1967 by C.S.I.R.O. from Moroccan species, will survive in under 42 cm. of rainfall, remaining dormant in summer. It could extend improved grasslands by 26,000 km.^{2} as well as increasing yields in existing sown pastures.

Phillip, Arthur (1738–1814) b. London. Son of a German father and English mother. Phillip became the first Governor of N.S.W., the paramount character in the colony's first perilous years and to whom it owed survival. Before his appointment as Captain General of the First Fleet by Lord Sydney in 1786, he had served in the English and Portuguese navies. From the outset, Phillip concerned himself energetically and persistently with the voyage preparations, with superb organisation and attention to detail. On reaching Botany Bay, he quickly dismissed it for the settlement. Within a few days he had explored the magnificent Port Jackson inlet, with deep anchorage and permanent water, and selected Sydney Cove, where, on the 7th February, before his assembled charges, official proclamations were read and he spoke firmly of the fair but rigorous discipline he intended to administer. He had almost absolute power, controlling law, finance, trade, defence, indeed every aspect of life in the settlement. Difficulties multiplied: the convicts were largely shiftless, lazy and debauched; the guards were jealous, homesick and unco-operative, the soil unyielding and food supplies dwindling. Phillip put his own rations into the common pool when starvation level was almost reached. He had sent King* with a group to settle on Norfolk Island, and ships to fetch supplies from the Cape. When the Second and Third

Fleets arrived they brought more convicts to eat the much needed supplies they carried. Meanwhile he had commissioned a fine town, had personally explored by land and water, and tried hard to establish good relations with the Aborigines. He had a missing front tooth which commended him to them. In spite of receiving a spear wound, he forbade retaliation (although later he was reluctantly forced to punish for murder of isolated whites). Envisaging a colony based on free settlers, he began land grants to ex-convicts and marines, and assigned convicts as labourers. His requests to be relieved as his health broke were finally granted, and he returned home in 1793, to serve further in the Navy until 1805 when he retired to Bath, retaining his interest in the colony until his death. *For further reading see* G. Mackaness: *Admiral Arthur Phillip* (Sydney, 1937).

Phillip Island Vic. An island of 155 km.^{2} miles about 22 km. NW of Wonthaggi, 39S/146E, accessible by bridge on the E and ferry on the NW, and a favourite holiday resort. Its reserves include a population of koala bears and a Fairy Penguin rookery. Chicory is grown.

Phosphate rock Mainly apatite, essential for making the fertiliser Superphosphate*. It is imported from Nauru*, Christmas Island and Ocean Island. Important Aus. discoveries were made in 1966–7 in a 24 by 5-km. belt near Duchess* and at Yelvertoft, 80 km. N of Mt. Isa, Qld. Exploitation by open cut is likely. There is also rock phosphate in the Rum Jungle* area of N.T.

Pichi Richi Pass S.A. 32S/138E   A 16-km. gorge SW from Quorn in the Flinders Range, pioneered by the wool drays of pastoralists, later followed by a now abandoned section of the 3-ft. 6-in. Port Augusta–Alice Springs railway line.

Pieman River Tas. 42S/145E   Flows 165 km. W then NW through wild mountain country from its birth at the confluence of 2 head streams E of Rosebery. There is a little timber extraction based on Corinna, a former gold township, but iron-ore development on its tributary, the Savage River, along with expansion at Mt. Lyell*, may stimulate exploitation of its large power potential. It bears the nickname of an infamous convict escapee from Port Macquarie.

Pigeons and **Doves** Excluding introduced species, Aus. has over 20 species in 3 families. 1. The Columbidae has 2 rain-forest species, the beautiful purple to green-backed Whiteheaded (and white-breasted) Pigeon, *Columba norfolciensis*, and Brown Pigeon, *Macropygia phasianella*, with its conspicuous tail. 2. In the family Turturidae the widely distributed Forest Bronze-wing, *Phaps chalcoptera*, up to 33 cm. long, is green and red, with a brown back and orange in the wings; it lives in open woodland and is much hunted—often too much—for its eating qualities. It has several close relatives, including the Brush Bronzewing, *P. elegans*, and the distinctive *Ocyphaps lophotes*, often seen near dams and homesteads. The Wonga Pigeon, *Leucosarcia melanoleuca*, named from its monotonous '*Wonk-wonk-wonk*', is the largest ground-pigeon, up to 38 cm. long, and found in rain-forests from Cape York to Vic.; it is grey with white stripes on its breast, brown wings, white-cream cap and belly, and a black and white herringbone pattern on the flanks. The small attractive Green-winged Pigeon, *Chalcophaps chrysochlora* extends into SE Asia; it has a pinkish-brown head and breast, and white patches on the wings. 3. The brilliantly coloured Fruit-Pigeons, family Treronidae, of S and SE Asia, extending into N and E Aus. with 8 species include the spectacular Topknot Pigeon, *Lopholaimus antarcticus*, crested blue in front, orange-brown behind, with red and green on its head, white breast and neck, grading to light blue-grey with dark blue-grey wing tips. The Purple-breasted Pigeon or Wompoo, *Megaloprepia magnifica*, rivals the parrots with its crimson-purple breast patch, yellow lower belly, green and yellow wings, and light blue-grey head. The Nutmeg Pigeon, *Myristicivora spilorrhoa*, migratory to Qld. from the N, is pure white with brown wingtips and tail, and grey-and-white flanks. These are largely in forests, being fruit and berry-eaters. Many species of pigeons are becoming rare because of excessive shooting.

Pigface (*Carpobrotus* spp.) A member of the Ficoidaceae family, it is a fleshy succulent plant with a bright red fruit accompanied by 2 ear-like floral leaves, fancied to resemble a pig's head. Garden varieties of Pigface are mainly African.

Pigs The total of about 2·5 million are reared as a sideline to dairying, and are orientated to exports. Wild pigs (descended from escaped domestic stock) are pests in Qld. and N.S.W. and are increasing in areas where dingoes* are being destroyed.

Pilbara W.A. A Statistical Division, forming an E–W belt. The Pilbara Gold-field, declared in 1888, had a short life. The crystalline base, which has manganese, nickel and iron deposits, is overlain by the Gibson Desert* sands to the E and Hamersley sediments to the W. The rolling country, at about, 300 m. with higher residual ridges, has low, variable rainfall and large sheep properties. Economic development is rapid. Iron ore* and offshore natural gas are the bases for a major future industrial region.

Pilliga Scrub N.S.W. About 5,000 km.² of low woodland on poor sandy soils over Jurassic sandstone and shales, with patches of grey and brown earths, now maintained largely in reserves and yielding considerable quantities of usable cypress pine. It lies between Narrabri, 30S/150E, and Coonabarabran, 31S/149E.

Pindan An Aboriginal name used in NW Aus. for a characteristic thicket vegetation of wattle* species growing on deep red sands in the 35-cm. mean annual rainfall area. Beneath the dense wattle or *Acacia* thicket there is a sparse layer of hummock or spinifex* grasses, while some eucalypt and other tree species project through the wattles.

Pine Creek N.T. 14S/132E A small settlement on the Stuart Highway and N Aus. Railway*, 240 km. from Darwin, which was the centre of the frantic 1871–4 gold-rush, afterwards declining almost to a ghost town. It is now growing with the iron-ore development to the E, and a branch line for it from Frances Creek*.

Pineapples Almost the entire acreage (5,200 ha.) is on acidic soils and sloping rainy land along the Qld. coast, stimulated by the canning industry in Woombye, Nambour and Palm Woods, but beset by erosion and technical problems. The so-called **Wild Pineapple** of N.S.W. and Qld. is *Macrozamia* (*see* CYCADS).

Pines The exotic genus *Pinus* was early introduced, especially *P. radiata* from California. In modern times this is a very important tree for softwood plantations in SE Aus. (For native pines *see* CYPRESS-PINE, KING WILLIAM PINE, HOOP PINE, KAURI PINE, *and* PODOCARPACEAE.)

Pinjarra W.A. 33S/116E A small settlement, the site of the so-called 'Battle of Pinjarra' in 1834, during a punitive expedition, following the killing of a soldier by Aborigines. An alumina plant was opened in 1972 using the port of Bunbury, Darling Range bauxite* and gas piped from the N.

Pink Foam Bark (*Jagera pseudorhus*) A 15-m. hardy evergreen tree of NE N.S.W. and E Qld., with distinctive soapy (saponin-rich) bark, smooth and grey but reddish when cut. Leaflets are 8 cm. by 2 cm., finely serrated, and in multiple leaves of up to 18 pairs, on hairy branchlets. There are many-branched mutliple heads of small flowers, and 6-mm. 3-celled hairy fruit capsules containing 3 black ovoid seeds. It yields useful hardwood timber.

Pinkeye, Heath A second popular name for the pink-flowered 4-petalled Blackeyed Susan of E Aus., *Tetrathica* spp.

Pioneer River and District Qld. 22S/149E The 'Midland Sugar Coast'. The river flows 80 km. E from forested Eungella Range National Park area, and with its tributary, Cattle Creek, forms an alluvial plain between the Clarke and O'Connor coastal ranges. The first development of centralised sugar-crushers replacing plantation mills, of distilling waste for industrial alcohol at Sarina (1937) and bulk-handling (at Mackay*) all took place in this district.

Pipi A marine shellfish*, often found by children when wiggling their toes down into wet sand. Used as bait.

Pipi, about half life size

Place-names About one-third of Aus. place-names are of Aboriginal origin; but often the authentic meaning is difficult to establish, and is therefore not given in this work. Transcription from oral to written form was difficult: the tribesmen may have deliberately misled the surveyor or settler who in turn may have misheard; or the native may not himself have known the meaning. There are often several meanings for one word; the proliferation of language and dialect and the lack of traditional knowledge among the present Aborigines make interpretation hazardous. Nevertheless the most successful and distinctive Aus. names are Aboriginal, such as Araluen, Barcoo, Kalgoorlie, Porongorup and many others. The bulk of the remaining names are English, but a sprinkling of Dutch names (e.g. Cape Keerweer, Qld., Arnhem Land, N.T.) and French names (Cape Naturaliste, W.A., D'Entrecasteaux Channel, Tas.) are reminders of early European navigators. The English names are largely places in Britain (Richmond, Liverpool and countless others); of contemporary notables in Eng., generally royalty (Victoria, Queensland, Adelaide), or politicians in London who were concerned with the colony (Sydney, Melbourne), and in Aus. (Port Phillip, Brisbane, or later, Parkes) or their wives (Blanchetown, S.A. Maryborough, Qld.). Explorers generally named features either after people, often their patrons (Port Jackson, N.S.W., Ashburton River, W.A.), or more imaginatively from an incident on the journey (Swan Hill), sometimes even an emotion (Mt. Hopeless, S.A., and L. Disappointment, W.A.), or coined a descriptive name (Mt. Prospect, N.S.W., Glass House Mts., Qld.). Apart from his use of people, Cook used evocative names (Botany Bay, Broken Bay, N.S.W., Possession Island, Qld.). The explorer T. E. Mitchell* emphasised the desirability of finding the native name where possible, and the redoubtable J. Dunmore Lang* pleaded for fewer Macquaries and more Aboriginal names. More recently, mining towns have been named from British coal-fields (Cessnock, Wallsend, Rhondda, all in Hunter Valley, N.S.W., are Scottish, English and

Welsh respectively). Many more local names have grown from common usage, and record some past owner or character or feature, such as a ferry. Most of the States now have a nomenclature board to supervise new names: E. H. J. Feeken and G. E. E. Feeken *The Discovery and Exploration of Australia* (Melbourne, 1970) records origins of over 4,000 names.

Plague A disease of rodents caused by *Pasteurella pestis*, transmitted by fleas parasitic on rodents, and in which man becomes involved. It reached Sydney in the late 1890s from China and affected the introduced urban rats, *Rattus rattus*, the Ship or Black Rat, and *R. norvegicus*, Brown or Sewer Rat. From the serious Sydney outbreak in 1900 until 1909 there were over 1,200 cases and 470 deaths. A leading Aus. figure was J. A. Thompson (1848–1915) who substantiated the existing French theory of transmission. Plague control in Aus. has been completely effective for many years.

Planarians, Land Free-living, land-dwelling, eyed and carnivorous flat-worms, of the family Turbellaria in the otherwise parasitic Phylum Platy-helminthes. They are often handsomely coloured, e.g. the cosmopolitan Shovel-headed Worm, *Bipalium kewense*, brown and yellow, 20–30 cm. long and the uniquely Aus. 9-cm. navy-blue and white *Geoplana caerulea*.

Plantain (*Plantago*) This genus has about 12 Aus. species of rosette-forming herbs. The introduced weeds of the genus show the rosette form and the characteristic rat-tail flower and fruit. Plantain is also applied to immature bananas cooked as vegetables in the tropics.

Plastics Materials which at some stage of production will flow, and can thus be shaped by heat or pressure. Plastic materials made in Aus. supply a half to two-thirds of the needs of the plastic products industry, which in turn supplies 80% of Aus. demand.

The materials are made by the foreign-owned major chemical firms in association with their other products, but suffer a cost disadvantage compared with imports even with protection, as demands are not high enough for 'scale economies'. Plastic products, which have less foreign ownership, employ over 15,000 people (55% in Vic. and 40% in N.S.W.) in 500 factories which belong to a small number of large firms and a large number of small firms, the latter with a little dispersion to country towns, and able to compete by specialising and using the less costly extrusion methods. All the machinery needed is now made in Aus.

Platypus (*Ornithorhynchus*—bird-beaked) It is a Monotreme*. Amphibious, it has a diaphragm between lungs and abdominal cavity, like all true mammals including the whale, and it can remain underwater only for some 3 minutes. Many of its characteristics appear to be close adaptations to its mode of life: its streamlined shape, its flat beaver-like tail, close fur and webbed feet to give great speed and manoeuvrability in the water; the retractibility of the web on its forepaws (the chief ones for swimming) to ease walking and especially burrowing, for digging is especially important to the female in the construction of the 5- to 15-m. breeding tunnel which gently rises and is stopped with earth banks against floods and intruders; and, not least, the duck-like bill and cheek-pouches to aid in sifting and masticating shells, prawns etc. There is only one species of Platypus, but there are regional variations in colouring etc. within Aus. Important work on the Platypus was done by: George Bennett (1804–1893), who contributed notably to the systematic description of Aus. natural history; C. J. Martin (1866–1955) and J. T. Wilson (1861–1945) on its embryology and H. J. Burrell (1873–1945), a

former comedian, who was the first to keep them in captivity and wrote the authoritative work *The Platypus* (Sydney, 1927), and D. H. Fleay (1907–   ) who bred them in captivity, and who has warned of their potential extinction through river pollution in E Aus.

Platypus, about 60 cm long

Playford, Sir Thomas (1896–   ) b. Norton's Summit, S.A. He was Liberal Premier of S.A. for the record term from 1938–65. His grandfather had been Premier from 1887–9 and 1892–3. He has much of the credit for the development of power and industry in S.A., following the Depression of the 1930s.

Plum, Native A popular name for several Aus. trees, including *Planchonella australis* (*see* APPLE), and *Endiandra sieberi*, a small tree of the rain-forests of Qld. and NE N.S.W., in the widespread Lauraceae family, which is also known as Pink Walnut and Moreton Bay Nutmeg. It has dark green glossy spear-shaped leaves, inconspicuous green-cream flowers and long oval berries with a nutmeg fragrance.

Plunkett, John Hubert (1802–1869) b. Ireland. He arrived in Aus. in 1832 as Solicitor-General; he was Attorney-

General from 1836–56, the first Roman Catholic to be appointed to high office. He was very influential in legal development: he regularised and drafted laws, e.g. the 1836 Church Act which gave religious equality; he worked for legal rights for emancipists*; successfully prosecuted in the retrial after the massacre of 28 Aborigines on Henry Dangar's Myall Creek Station in 1838 (*see* GIPPS). He supported the squatters* over land tenure, but opposed their wish for transportation to resume. Later he was an important political figure in the early days of self-government, opposing Parkes.

Poatina Tas. 42S/147E An underground power station (with annual output of 1,322 million kWh) fed by a 6·5-km. tunnel, 1·5-km. pressure pipeline and vertical shaft going 150 m. underground, a total head of 839 m. Tailrace water irrigates S of Longford*.

Poddy A hand-fed calf (or sometimes foal). The name comes from an English dialect word for fat. **Poddy dodger** is a cattle thief specialising in young unbranded calves (cleanskins).

Podocarpaceae (foot-fruited) A family of softwood trees widespread in the S hemisphere including SE Asia, of which the Aus. representatives are mainly in Tas. The cone is greatly modified so that the seed is borne exposed, and unlike most conifers is surrounded by a sometimes strikingly coloured fleshy process. Aus. genera include the shrubby *Pherosphaera* (2 species) and small creeping *Microcachtys* of Tas. and N.S.W., and several tall trees. Brown Pine, *Podocarpus elatus*, its bright yellow-green crown conspicuous in the dark green rain-forest foliage, and fleshy plum-like seed-holder, and Black Pine, *P. amarus*, yield a little golden-brown softwood timber (rare in the rain-forests of E Aus.). Huon Pine, *Dacrydium franklinii*, is a tree of 20–30 m. by 0·75–1·2 m., yielding very durable timber, but

now scarce, growing on lower slopes and alluvial flats in 150–250 cm. mean annual rainfall in the SW of Tas. It has very short, blunt, concave keeled and hairy-backed leaves which grow spirally and close to the branchlets, compact grey roughish bark persistent on trunk and branches, and small cones near the end of branchlets, bearing seeds under 2 mm. long on a fleshy membrane much less prominent than in other Podocarpaceae. The Celery Top Pine, *Phyllocladus asplennifolius*, is a tree of 18–30 m. by 0·5–0·9 m. growing over a wide range of slope and soil in 150–250 cm. mean annual rainfall in W Tas. The bark is red-brown with rectangular scales. The celery- or oak-like 'leaves' are in fact flattened branchlets; the edges bear true leaves of pine-needle type, which have been reduced in adult form to minute scales. The male flower is a cylindrical spike, and on the same tree the female flower spike develops into thick fleshy scales enclosing the base of an ovoid seed about 6 mm. long.

Poeppel's Corner 26S/138E The meeting point of the N.T./Qld. border with that of S.A.; it was marked by the S.A. Surveyor Poeppel in 1883 (and corrected by him 1884) with a 2-m. coolibah stump from Mulligan's Creek.

Point Hicks The name given by Cook to land sighted on April 19th 1770, and named after Lieut. Hicks 'who discovered this land'. It is fairly certainly identified as being Cape Everard, 16 km. E of the Cann River mouth in SE Vic., 38S/149E.

Point Lookout N.S.W. 31S/152E The highest point at 1,610 m., in the New England* plateau, giving a magnificent clear-weather view down the escarpment, across rain-forest (which includes the Antarctic Beech, *Nothofagus moorei*) to the Bellinger valley and the Pacific. The variety of plant and animal association in the **Point**

Lookout National Park prompted an intensive survey in the 1960s.

Point Puer Tas. 43S/148E On a rocky point in Port Arthur*, was a reformatory (1835–50) for boys of 11 to 18, where a serious attempt was made to train them usefully. *For further reading see* F. C. Hopper: *Prison Boys of Port Arthur* (Melbourne, 1967).

Point Sampson W.A. 21S/117E A small port developed to export Wittenoom asbestos, and which may revive with iron-ore export from the Hamersley* region.

Poison-bush A name applied to several quite different plants, notably the W.A. *Oxylobium* and *Gastrolobium* (*see* PEAS), Candyup Poison*, Dogwood* and others.

Poison-tree A popular name for certain trees, *Excoecaria* spp. *See* BLIND-YOUR-EYES.

Polding, John Bede (1794–1877) b. Liverpool, Eng. He arrived in Aus. in 1835, to be the first Roman Catholic Bishop in Aus. when it was detached from the See of Mauritius. In 1842 he was created Metropolitan of Aus. and Archbishop of Sydney, arousing the anxiety of the Anglican Church under Broughton, over its precedence. Polding travelled widely, building on the pioneer work of Therry* and Ullathorne* to build up his church, bring out priests and organise education, for which purposes he returned frequently to Europe.

Police Forces are organised by the States, except for Commonwealth responsibilities, in A.C.T. (since 1927), N.T. (since 1911), and the Commonwealth Police Force (1960) which is responsible for enforcement of Federal law, through the Investigations Service, with a uniformed branch to guard Commonwealth property. The Security Service, working under the Prime Minister, has specific functions. The States' Forces, broadly similar in organisation, stem from the British system. A Commissioner (formerly Inspector-General) heads the Force, Superintendents are in charge of Districts (Regions in S.A.), Inspectors of Sub-Districts, and Sergeants or Constables of Stations. Districts have developed on an *ad hoc* basis round growing population centres, and vary in number from 4 in Tas. to 17 in Qld. The national ratio of police to population is 1:600 (a desirable ratio is considered 1:530). Of the 50–60 black trackers (Aborigines attached to the police force, employed mainly for tracking criminals and lost persons in outlying districts), two-thirds are in N.T., most of the rest in Qld. and a few in W.A. and S.A. Separately administered branches control Traffic, Criminal Investigation and other specialist departments.

Historical Development The early policing was done by military personnel, gradually supplemented, then replaced by civilian recruitment. Material was poor, convicts often being used; funds were minimal and there was little pay; turnover was high, as was corruption. Crime was rampant. All this, combined with an inbuilt public resistance to any compulsion, has left a legacy of hostility or at best neutrality in the public attitude to the police, also associated with drinking and gambling laws. In N.S.W. and especially Tas., bushranging was widespread, with often overt public connivance. The use of mounted patrols of troopers to counter it spread from N.S.W. to other colonies. In N.S.W. and Vic. the gold-rushes* drained the police of manpower when most needed. English police were brought to N.S.W. in the 1830s, and to Vic. in the 1850s under S. Freeman, following strong public reaction to the Eureka* incident. He trained many successful officers: one was E. W. Fosbery, N.S.W. Inspector-General from 1874–1904, who consolidated the fine work done by J. McClerie, the first N.S.W. Inspector-General, appointed following the 1862 Police Act, which laid down the present basis of the State's Force. Public confidence in Vic. was further undermined by the manifest incompetence of the police at the time of the Kelly* gang. Reforms were repeatedly delayed and the culmination came in a Police Strike and near-anarchy in 1923, followed by Blamey's* re-organisation which also ended in unfortunate dispute, then a period of further stabilisation under an English officer, S. H. Porter. The gaol function of Tas. until 1853, the savage wars with the Aborigines, and the bushranging epidemics, all led to early police organisation under Governors Sorell and Arthur. A. W. Humphrey was appointed the first Police Magistrate then Police Superintendent in 1815. A unique feature in Tas. was the 'muster master' who organised convict records, complete population musters, lists of absconders and a 'black book'. Tas. forces were centralised in 1899.

In Qld. military policing operated until 1862. An early and important development was the Native Patrols under white officers, disbanded from 1899; these had also played an important role in the early days in Vic. In S.A. and W.A., the initially free settlement meant less lawlessness, but policing for protection from hostile natives led to the formation of military then civilian forces. N.T. was policed by S.A. until 1911, initially to protect the Overland Telegraph construction, then to maintain order in the northern gold-fields. The wide-ranging patrols, involving much contact with Aborigines, are a major feature today. Notable Chiefs have included D. T. Seymour in Qld. from 1864–95, and later, C. J. Carroll (1934–49), who introduced promotion by examination. Fairer promotion, as well as better relations with the public, were also promoted in N.S.W. under W. J.

MacKay, 1935–48, who also began Police Boys' Clubs, while his predecessor, J. Mitchell, between 1915–30 established the first soundly organised training of recruits. Since 1945 the Aus. police forces have shared the advances of other countries in method, technology, communication, and central record files. They joined Interpol in 1947. Current problems include a serious lack of recruits to deal with an increasing number of armed hold-ups and attacks. *For further reading see* G. M. O'Brien: *The Australian Police Forces* (Melbourne, 1960).

POLITICAL PARTIES In the 50 years of responsible government enjoyed by the States prior to Federation, the only cohesive party to emerge was Labor*. Politics revolved round personalities in a kaleidoscope of changing groups and issues: one of the most important was that of free trade as against protective tariffs.

The first Federal Parliaments had 3 parties: Liberal-Protectionist, Conservative-Free Trade, and Labor, with in 1903, 27, 24 and 24 members respectively, a situation described by Deakin as playing cricket with 3 elevens. The period 1904–10 was fluid as a 2-party system was evolved on the familiar right- and left-wing pattern, with the third, corner party wooed for support. In 1903–4 Labor supported the Liberal-Protectionists under Barton and Deakin, and again from 1905–8. In turn the Liberals supported Labor in 1908–9, but in 1909–10 a 'Fusion' of anti-Labor interests saw the end of the separate Liberal-Protectionist and Conservative Free Trade Parties. The present party system includes the Liberal* and Country* Parties, in power as a conservative coalition 1949–72, the Aus. Labor Party (in power 1972–), the Democratic Labor Party* and the recently formed Australia Party, liberal and reformist. (*See also* NATIONALIST PARTY, UNITED AUS. PARTY, COMMUNIST PARTY.) *See* L. Overacker:

The Australian Party System (Oxford, 1952); J. Jupp: *Australian Party Politics* (Melbourne, 1964).

Pollution Public disquiet led to the Senate Select Committee Report (1972) and the setting up of the Aus. Environment Council to provide co-ordination between States and Commonwealth. *See* A. Martin: *Pollution and Conservation in Australia* (Melbourne, 1971).

Pommy or **Pom** A generally derogatory term for an Englishman. The derivation is controversial; suggestions include: an abbreviation of Pomeranian, 'superior' dog; a blend of immigrant with pomegranate, referring to the red-cheeked Englishman; from Pompey, the slang term for Portsmouth; the old dialect English phrase 'all of a pom', deriving in turn from pomace the pulp stage of cider-making, and indicating an unpleasant state; and many others. It was first recorded in the 1914–18 War.

Pondweed Floating aquatic plants of the genus *Potamogeton*, e.g. *P. natans* with leaves just below the water surface, flower-heads just above.

Ponsford, William Harold (1900–   ) b. Vic. A cricketer noted for building up enormous scores including the world record of 2 over 400 (in Tas. and Qld.). His achievement was inevitably, although regrettably, eclipsed by the rise of Bradman*. He played in 20 Tests against Eng. (1924–34), averaging 47·21 with 5 centuries. In first-class games he totalled 13,819, averaging 65·18 with 47 centuries.

Poplars (genus *Populus*) Introduced trees. Ideal for landscaping and windbreaks, especially the Lombardy Poplar, *P. nigra*. (*See also* COTTONWOOD.) Poplar is also applied to the native tree *Homolanthus populifolius* in the world-wide Euphorbiaceae family, and to the bitter-leaved Mustard Tree of the mallee scrub, *Codonocarpus cotinifolius* (family Phytolaccaceae). The timber trade uses the name poplar for the wood of *Euroschinus falcatus*, a

rain-forest tree of coastal Qld. in the tropical Anacardaceae family.

POPULATION The 1971 Census showed a total of 12,728,461, an increase of 1·87% 1966–71. In Sep. 1972, the 13 million mark was passed. Aborigines were included in census totals for the first time in 1971. Male predominance is now very slight. Population is strikingly concentrated in the SW of W.A. and in a belt within 350 km of the coast from Port Pirie, S.A., 33S/138E, to Rockhampton, Qld., 23S/151E, with coastal patches northward to Cairns, 17S/146E. Even in this coastal belt many empty tracts remain; 2–4 people per km.^{2} is a relatively dense rural population, while 6 or more represents either particularly intensive, often irrigated agriculture, or peri-urban development. Inland, large tracts are empty, and 1 per 2 km.^{2} is relatively dense. The most sparsely peopled areas show a tendency to decrease with any increases usually linked with specific new developments, such as the Ord River project of W.A. or parts of the brigalow country of Qld. (e.g. the Taroom-Wandoan area, 26S/150E). The general picture is of rural population decrease of about 1–4% per annum and quite commonly higher. The population, then, is over 80% urban. Small towns in rural areas are tending to decrease as rapid transport encourages concentration of service functions in larger centres. Except in Qld. and Tas., well over half the States' population are in the capitals (S.A. 71%, Vic. 69%, W.A. 68%, N.S.W. 60%, Qld. 47%, Tas. 38%); the gap between the State capital and the next largest city is very large, still reflecting their marked dominance over the separate, pre-Federation colonies. Moreover, of the increase of just over 1 million in total population 1966–71, the 6 State Capitals took over 75%. Fastest growth was in N.T. (51·3%) followed by

A.C.T. (49·8%). Of the States, W.A. was far ahead of the others (21·1%). Qld. (8·9%), Vic. 8·6%) and N.S.W. (8·3%) were comparable; Tas. (7·1%), had the lowest rate of growth. *Historical and Demographic.* From about 1,000 arrivals with the First Fleet in 1788, the population fell in the first difficult years, but was reinforced to about 3,000 in the early 1790s. Increases fluctuating between 2·5 and 4% prevailed until about 1850; high birth-rates were accompanied by high but decreasing death-rates, and considerable natural increases were complemented by immigration mainly from Britain until the sharp increase, more cosmopolitan in composition, of the gold-rush period in the 1850s. The population exceeded a million before 1860. Thereafter the rates of increase were lower, but in relation to the larger total, absolute increases were commonly larger. Birth-rates gradually declined, with sharp decreases during the Depressions of the 1890s and the 1930s, but death-rates declined from about 14 per thousand in 1870 to about 9 in recent decades, and except in acute Depressions natural increase has remained well over 1% per annum, declining to just over 1% in the late 1960s. Natural increase accounted for some 55% of total increase. Immigration policies are changing in the 1970s and some slowing of growth is likely. (*See also* ABORIGINES, ECONOMY, IMMIGRATION *and* CENSUS.)

Porcupine-grass A popular name for the cushions of stiff spiny leaves of various species of *Triodia* grasses, often resinous, growing in inland Aus., sometimes with little or no soil and giving a little pasture. This is the plant popularly known as Spinifex*, wrongly but so persistently that it now seems pedantic to avoid the term 'Spinifex Country'.

Porongorup Range W.A. 35S/118E A small but conspicuous granitic group running NW–SE for 13 km. and rising sharply from the plain N of Albany*, to 607 m.; with karri* forest on the lower slopes and brilliant spring-flowering plants between the bare granite boulders of the tops.

Port Adelaide S.A. 35S/138E (39,038 in 1971) It was founded as the port for Adelaide* on the estuarine Port River, sheltered by a long N–S sandspit to the W. It is part of Adelaide-Metropolitan Area. An 8-m. dredged channel runs between the spit and Torrens Island and is being deepened. The Outer Harbour (1907), on reclaimed land at the NW tip of the sandspit, which takes all but the largest passenger ships and tankers, replaced the previous lightering at Glenelg and Largs.

Port Alma Qld. 23S/151E A cargo port at the mouth of the Fitzroy River created 1881, it handles exports of wool, wheat, refrigerated goods and minerals from the Fitzroy region. It is an oil terminal and refinery site, and has a new salt-extraction plant. Irrigation development in the Mackenzie Valley will lead to further expansion.

Port Arthur Tas. 43S/148E An inlet on the S of Tasman Peninsula, the penal settlement on its W shore (1830–77). Now a mellow, much visited ruin, it has been variously painted as a place of unlimited brutality and of enlightened reform, for its total of 30,000 convicts.

Port Augusta S.A. 32S/138E (12,095 in 1971) A city (1963), developing from 1854 as a port at the head of Spencer Gulf to serve pastoral, and for a time, wheat lands, when it was served by camel and bullock drays. Transport has continued to maintain it. The Central Aus. Railway (1878) and the Trans-continental Railway (1917) began here; rail workshops and housing are at Stirling, E of the town. The Eyre Highway begins from the bridge (1927). Recent growth has been due to power stations using Leigh Creek coal at Curlew Point, 6·5 km. to the S.

Port Dalrymple Tas. 41S/147E The entrance to the Tamar estuary, and the name applied for some years to the first settlements in N Tas. under Paterson in 1804. It was named by Bass and Flinders in 1798.

Port Davey Tas. 43S/146E A fiord on the SW coast, with 2 main arms at right angles, the longer reaching 32 km. inland along the narrow Bathurst Channel. The area is almost uninhabited mountain, forest and button-grass moors.

Port Essington N.T. 11S/132E An inlet penetrating 48 km. on the N coast of Cobourg Peninsula*, discovered by P.P. King* in 1818 and advocated by him as a settlement site. From 1838–49 an attempt was made to develop a trading centre at Victoria, on the SW shore, but was defeated by disease, remoteness and failure to attract any free settlement. Only ruins remain, including the small 'Government House' with 2 (unused) fireplaces! Pearl-culture experiments are being tried.

Port Fairy Vic. 38S/142E (2,440 in 1971) On the coast, and a railhead with fishing port functions, woollen, engineering and dairy industries. Named (1810) after the ship from which a landing was made, although it was called Belfast for some years.

Port Hacking N.S.W. 34S/151E A shallow inlet extending 24 km. inland, separated from Botany Bay* to the N by a narrow, largely built-up isthmus, but with the Royal National Park along its S shore. It was named after Henry Hacking (?1750–1831) an early seaman explorer.

Port Hedland W.A. 20S/119E (7,172 in 1971) On a tidal island reached by a causeway, it grew as the outlet for Pilbara gold and manganese with a railway from Marble Bar (1912–52). Camels were landed here from Karachi. It has become a leading Aus. port in tonnage and size of ship, with its vast iron ore export. The Mt. Goldsworthy*

ore is loaded from a jetty after crushing on Finucane Island and Mt. Newman* ore is loaded from Point Nelson on the inner harbour. Total port capacity will be over 30 million tonnes a year. Dredging and adequate storm warnings against summer cyclones are necessary. Development for a population of 12,000 by 1980 is planned, with a new town 8 km. inland, separated from the present focus by an industrial zone. Water is from bores in river basins up to 48 km. away. There is a solar salt evaporation plant exporting to Japan.

Port Jackson N.S.W. A drowned valley system including Sydney Harbour, 34S/151E, and Middle Harbour (a N branch), between the impressive sandstone cliffs of the N and S Heads (Sydney Heads). The growth of the city has not removed the beauty of this magnificent natural harbour. (*See* MAP 6, inset.)

Port Kembla N.S.W. 35S/151E Part of Greater Wollongong* with iron and steel, other metal and fertiliser plants, and port installations.

Port Latta Tas. 41S/145E On Brickmaker Bay, E of Stanley, is a new port with a pelletising plant now built to process and ship iron ore from Savage River*.

Port Lincoln S.A. 35S/136E (9,158 in 1971) On a fine natural harbour in the SE of Eyre Peninsula, it is the chief service, industrial and shipping centre for wheat, barley, wool and mutton which is railed from the peninsula farms. There is a fertiliser factory using imported phosphate, and tuna fishing, dairy produce and bulk loading, including limesand to Whyalla. The bay was named by Flinders in 1802 after his native county.

Port Macquarie N.S.W. 31S/153E (9,362 in 1971) A seaside and retirement resort at the mouth of the Hastings River, with residual port functions and some fishing, justifying small silt-control works. Found by Oxley in 1818, it was used, later than Newcastle, for further banishment even from Sydney Cove, but received free settlers from 1830. Export trade from New England developed after a road was built in 1830, but much of its hinterland went with the coming of the railway. A handsome church, designed by the convict architect Greenway*, dates from 1824.

Port Phillip Association Registered June 1835, with 15 members, led by Batman* in Launceston, Tas., to settle the Port Phillip area. It had dissolved by 1842. Its claim to legal ownership of the land was not recognised, although some adjustment was made in the purchase price in view of investment involved.

Port Phillip Bay Vic. 38S/145E A drowned basin, with Melbourne sited in the N and Geelong in the W, over 56 km. N–S and E–W, with a S entrance between Points Lonsdale and Nepean, only 1,092 m. wide, 13·7 m. deep, and with a very rapid tide race. The E shores are sandier and much more developed for holiday resorts which are now turned into commuter suburbs such as Dromana and Sorrento, backed by the attractive heights of Arthur's Seat (314 m.). *For further reading see* M. G. A. Wilson: *Port Phillip Bay* (Melbourne, 1965).

Port Pirie S.A. 33S/138E (15,506 in 1971) A city (1953) and second port of S.A. It was created by dredging a swamp-lined inlet in Germein Bay, Spencer Gulf, for wheat export in the 1870s, but it owes its development to the establishment in 1889 of lead-smelting and export of ores from Broken Hill*, N.S.W. It was unique in having 3 rail gauges: 3 ft. 6 in. from Broken Hill, now standardised, 5 ft. 3 in. from Adelaide, due for standardisation to link with the 4-ft. 8½-in. line to Port Augusta. Railways run down the main street to the factories and wharves

which now include bulk wheat loading.

Port Stanvac S.A. 35S/138E An oil refinery (1963) on Halletts Cove, 32 km. S of Adelaide, selected as the only available deep-water anchorage within reach of the city markets. Christies Beach to the S is the residential area.

Port Stephens N.S.W. A branching, drowned valley 44 km. NE of Newcastle, 33S/152E, partly closed off from the sea by a multiple coastal sand-barrier crowned by dunes, to form a lagoon. It is connected with the complex Myall Lakes system by the Myall River.

Port Welshpool Vic. A village 5 km. S of Welshpool, 48 km. S of Traralgon, 38S/147E. Until recently it has been a quiet fishing and cattle port (for Flinders Island), but is now developed as the base for service and maintenance of the Bass Str. natural gas field. Installations have been built at Barry's Beach along the foreshore of Corner Inlet to the W, and land reserved by the Government for industrial expansion, using the gas.

Porter, Hal (1917–) b. Melbourne. A short-story and play writer who was a former teacher and librarian; his highly stylised writing often concentrates on the eccentric misfit and attacks the mediocre and accepted, as in *The Cats of Venice* (Sydney, 1966) and his autobiographical *The Watcher on the Cast Iron Balcony* (Sydney, 1963) and *The Paper Chase* (Sydney, 1966).

Portland Vic. 38S/142E (8,212 in 1971) On the W, the sheltered side of **Portland Bay**, named by Lieut. Grant in 1800 after the Duke of Portland, although probably already known to the Bass Str. whalers and sealers. The Henty* brothers, Tas. squatters, established the first permanent settlement in Vic. there in 1834 and whaling continued until the 1860s; it is still a fishing port with a cannery. Since 1950 extensive harbour works, including a breakwater on the E point have allowed a 6-fold increase in trade, especially of oil imports for Western Vic., and direct overseas export of wool, wheat and frozen meat.

Ports The State capitals all developed as ports. The leading ports by tonnage handled (1971) are: Sydney (with Botany Bay), Port Hedland, Dampier, Newcastle, Port Kembla, Fremantle (with Kwinana), Whyalla, Geelong, Gladstone, Brisbane, Port Adelaide (with Port Stanvac), Port Latta, Westernport, Hobart, Darwin, Launceston, Burnie. Natural harbours are rare, but Sydney, Hobart and Albany are among the world's finest. A number of ports are on exposed deep-sea sites, with advantages of easy access and little dredging, but requiring expensive breakwaters; they include Port Kembla, Burnie, Portland, Townsville and Mackay. Ports at river mouths are sheltered, but require dredging, and with the increasing size of ships some have had to move downstream or be supplemented by deep-sea outports; they include Adelaide, Fremantle, Melbourne, Newcastle, Brisbane, Maryborough and Rockhampton. Tidal ranges and cyclones are important in the far NW. Trends are towards a steady reduction of small general cargo ports, formerly vital in development of coastal regions and river valleys. There is increasing concentration on specialised wharves within big ports, and on specialised minor ports handling sugar, grain, minerals, oil etc. Development of containerisation and in 'roll-on roll-off' methods are also leading to rapid change and big new investment. For overseas trade only Fremantle, Melbourne and Sydney are to be container terminals, with other Aus. ports serving as feeders. Mechanisation and redundancy cause some anxiety among stevedores or 'wharfies', but recent agreements have given them considerable security for the present.

N.S.W. ports are under the general supervision of the Maritime Services Board (1936), which is completely responsible for Sydney, Newcastle, Botany Bay and Port Kembla*. There are 29 minor ports many declining.

Vic. has individual Harbour Trusts. The Melbourne Harbour Trust (1877) has responsibility for general management, but private enterprise supplies stevedoring, bunkering, piloting etc. within its broad control. Geelong and Portland have Trusts. Port development on a large scale is under way at Westernport.

Qld. has no single centralised authority. The Department of Harbours and Marine supervises Brisbane port, but private companies control most of the individual wharves, sheds etc.; it also controls minor ports including Thursday Island, Weipa, Lucinda, Mourilyan, Maryborough-Urangan, Burketown and Normanton. The other deep-sea ports of Townsville, Cairns, Gladstone, Rockhampton (Port Alma), Bowen, Gladstone, Mackay and Bundaberg all have locally appointed Trusts.

In W.A. the Fremantle Port Authority controls this major Aus. port almost completely. Albany and Bunbury have local Boards, but the Harbour and Light Department controls Broome, Busselton Carnarvon Dampier, Derby, Esperance, Exmouth, Geraldton, Onslow, Point Sampson, Port Hedland, Wyndham and Yampi. The new iron-ore ports in the NW will outstrip all other Aus. ports in tonnage handled in the 1970s.

S.A. has a centralised authority in the S.A. Harbours Board, controlling all ports except the private ones of Whyalla, Rapid Bay and Ardrossan, and the railway-run Port Augusta. Deep-sea ports include Port Adelaide, Port Pirie, Wallaroo, Port Lincoln and Thevenard. The indented coast, forming isolated peninsulas, led to many minor ports now in decline.

Tas. has individual Autonomous

Boards for Hobart, Burnie, Devonport, Launceston Stanley, Wynyard, Ulverstone, Strahan, Currie and Whitemark (Flinders); Smithton has a Harbour Trust. *See* J. Bird: *Seaport Gateways of Australia* (London, 1968).

Poseidon A mining company owning Mt. Windarra mine, W.A. (production 1974) and gold mines in Kalgoorlie. Shares led the mining boom of the 1960s, reaching $280.

Possession Island Qld. 10S/142E A low uninhabited island 19 km. W of Cape York where Cook landed on August 22 1770, having been prevented by hostile Aborigines from landing on the mainland, and formally took possession of the E coast N from latitude 38°S.

Possums or **Phalangers** (family Phalangeridae) Arboreal Marsupials*, commonly taking a mixed diet of insects, nectar, blossom and pollen. Captain Cook noted the resemblance to the American Opossums in 1770, but omitted the initial O, and Possum is the widespread popular name. The possums range from small mouse-like animals to quite large gliding and brush-tailed forms, and the Cus-cus of 100 cm. nose to tail. A representative selection is given. 1. The Honey Possum, *Tarsipes spenserae*, is found from Geraldton to Esperance in coastal W.A. It has good climbing hands, a prehensile tail, proboscis-like snout, slender extensible tongue with bristles to gather sticky food from flowers, and flanges on the lips forming channels through which nectar or honey can be drawn; only soft bodied insects can be eaten. 2. The Pigmy or Feather-tail Glider, *Acrobates pygmaeus*, is found over the eucalypt forest zone from SE S.A. to N Qld. It has a feather-like tail which aids its gliding 'flight', and gliding membranes between front and back legs; it eats nectar from the ever-blossoming eucalypts, and builds—

Feather-tail Glider
(*Acrobates pygmaeus*), *about half life size*

and when alarmed sticks very close to— a globular nest of leaves etc. in a high tree-hole. It often stays in small family groups including immature young. 3. Pigmy Possums, *Cercartetus*, dormouse-like marsupials, are strongly nocturnal and hibernating (where the climate indicates), climbing actively at night and using the prehensile tail especially in descending, to gain a diet of insects, honey etc. *C. nanus* is widespread in Tas. and nearby islands and coastal S and E Aus., and *C. concinnus*, the South-western Pigmy Possum, is found from the S of W.A. and along the coast to S.A. into the orchards of the Mt. Lofty Ranges. 4. The Qld. Pigmy Possum, *Eudromicia macrura*, and Little Tasmanian Pigmy Possum, *E. lepida*, are placed in a different genus because of small anatomical differences mainly in dentition. 5. Striped Possums *Dactylopsila* (naked fingers), named by Wallace from a specimen from Aru Island, and with species in N.G., have powerful incisors and a long fourth finger suitable for getting insects out of hard wood (similar to adaptations in a Madagascar lemur of comparable diet); the single Aus. species is *D. picata* (pied). 6. Leadbeater's Possum,

Gymnobelideus leadbeateri (javelin), is a seldom-reported possum from SE Vic., living in tree hollows. 7. The Lesser Gliding Possums, *Petaurus* (i.e. tumbler or acrobat), are distributed in coastal bush in E Aus., e.g. the attractive vociferous Sugar Glider, *P. breviceps*, an insect and blossom-eater but capable of killing a mouse, nesting in tree hollows; the Squirrel Glider, *P. norfolcensis*; and the Yellow-bellied Glider, *P. australis*, described by Fleay and Brazenor as feeding on Manna Gum sap and blossom, and tender eucalypt suckers by night, using gliding flights of 27–36 m., climbing rather clumsily vertically but very agile on branches. 8. The Greater Glider, *Schoinobates volans* (flying rope-dancer), a blossom and leaf-eater, e.g. of narrow-leaved peppermint gums, is known to have covered 540 m. in 6 successive glides. 9. Ring-tailed Possums, *Pseudocheirus* (as if with hands), with very prehensile tail, i.e. in a ring round a branch, quarrelsome disposition, leaf and blossom diet, are widely distributed throughout coastal Aus. (and several species in N.G.), e.g. the South-eastern or Common Ringtail, *P. laniginosus* (woolly), the Tasmanian Ringtail, *P. convolutor*, the Western Ringtail, *P. occidentalis*, the Striped Ring-tail, *P. archeri*, of hilly areas in N Qld., which has a striped greenish fur unique in Aus., the colour of which is rare anywhere; and the Rock-haunting Ringtail, *P. dahli*, living in granite tor country in N.T. and showing adaptations from arboreal life, such as a shorter tail and less hand-like paws, though it does climb trees at night in search of food. 10. The Brush-tailed Ring-tail, *Hemibelideus lemuroides*, takes very long leaps between trees, using the bushy tail as a rudder; it is found in rain-forest and swamp-forest in N Qld. 11. Brush-tailed Possums, *Trichosurus* (hairy-tailed), have tails and a general appearance which made the naturalists of 1789 describe the specimen from Sydney Cove as vulpine (fox-like). They are much sought after

for their fur, and were de-restricted from protection in 1931–2 in order to help the heavy unemployment of the great slump period, which resulted in an export of over a million skins from N.S.W. These Possums have been shown to assist in controlling the spread of mistletoe*, thus benefiting hardwood forests and the honey industry. *T. vulpecula* (little fox) has a very wide distribution in mainland and insular Aus. from Melville and Bathurst Islands to Kangaroo Island, and shows remarkable adaptability, living in tree-holes, e.g. in box-gums by the creeks in the semi-arid inland, but also living in rock-holes, rabbit warrens, or burrows in creek banks; it is described as raucously quarrelsome with others of its kind, but silent on the approach of an enemy, including man, or the goanna, a particularly deadly natural foe. Mainly a leaf-eater (hence its control

Brush-tailed Possum
(*Trichosurus vulpecula*), *about 60 cm. long*

of mistletoe), it does damage single-stand plantations, e.g. of pines, and as an introduced animal has harmed forests in N.Z. It is known to eat flesh on occasions. 12. The Wyulda (Aboriginal) Scaly-tailed Possum, *Wyulda squamicaudata*, is adapted to dry and rocky conditions in NW W.A. 13. Cus-Cuses, *Phalanger* spp., are very large Possums with a wide range from Timor and Celebes, through N.G. to the Solomons and Cape York; the 2 Aus. species are Grey Cus-Cus, *Phalanger orientalis peninsulae*, of Cape York and N.G., and the Spotted Cus-Cus, *P. maculatus nudicaudatus*, brown, with creamy patches on the males low on the back, very nocturnal, leaf-eating, but does eat birds and small animals at times. 14. Specimens of ground-dwelling mountan pygmy possums *B. parvus* considered extinct were found in Vic. in 1966.

Postal Services Including telephones and mail contractors, employ over 100,000 and the Post Office is claimed as the largest single employer in Aus., with the largest vehicle fleet. There are over 7,000 post offices, ranging from 1 per 124 km.^{2} in Vic. to 1 per 4,170 km.^{2} in W.A., and serving an average of 1,049 people in Tas. to 1,999 in N.S.W. Over 2,000 billion letters are handled a year. Deliveries are mainly to household post-boxes placed between street and garden, or at farm road-ends; the use of numbered P.O. boxes is common. Many P.O.s act as agencies for the Commonwealth Savings Bank, and for the issuing of income tax rebate forms and other Government communications. In 1967 a Post Code System was introduced. New sorting devices include the Aus.-invented automatic electronic Redfern System (named after a Sydney sorting office), for letters of standard size. The Overseas Telecommunications Commission (1946) operates telegraph and telex services by cable and radio, and maintains and provides facilities for overseas telephone services operated by the Post Office. (*See* TELECOMMUNICATIONS.)

Potoroo A name for Rat-kangaroos dating back to the diary of John White* in 1790. (*See* KANGAROOS.)

Poultry The backyard 'chooks' are still important in rural and even suburban areas. Wartime stimulation for dried-egg export to U.K. was followed by depression but there is now some egg export to Hong Kong and the Middle East. Table-poultry rearing in batteries is a rapidly increasing industry. Leghorn, Rhode Island, Langshan and Australorp (a name adopted in 1930 for a locally developed Orpington) are the main breeds.

Praed, Rosa Caroline (*née* Murray-Prior) (1851–1935) b. Bromelton, Qld. She was a contemporarily successful novelist, writing as Mrs. Campbell Praed, mainly after leaving Aus. in 1876. About half her 37 novels have at least partial Aus. links, but conform to the contemporary view of a rough colonial environment as a setting for her romantic plots.

Prawns The popular name for many aquatic Crustaceans*. They have been netted by fine seine-nets etc. in coastal lagoons since the first European settlement (Botany Bay was important early), and trapped by Aborigines before that. They have long been known to migrate seaward on dark moonless summer nights and since large prawns were often caught by trawlers working offshore, it was reasoned that offshore trawling might bring good catches of large prawns. 2 progressive fishermen experimented off Broken Bay, N.S.W., 33S/151E, in 1945, and were successful, using a small otter-board trawl. Thus began the great post-war expansion of prawning, one of the most ebullient branches of a not always prosperous industry (*see* FISHERIES). Research has made it clear that further expansion is possible, including a substantial export to U.S., if fishing can be controlled and especially if the prawns, migrating seaward after an inshore maturing phase, can be given time offshore to grow further and, most important, to breed.

The main commercial prawns belong to the family Penaeidae (as do the well-studied and very valuable N American shrimps). The front 3 pairs of limbs have small nippers, quite short and placed under the mouth to convey food into it rather than reach out for it, as with genera with a pair of enlarged nippers. The principal commercial species are: 1. the King Prawn, *Penaeus plebejus* (N.S.W. and Qld.), to 30 cm. long, light-brown, with yellow legs and blue tail, and the slightly smaller W.A. King Prawn, *P. latisculatus*; 2. the School Prawn, *Metapenaeus macleayi* (N.S.W. and Qld.), to 15 cm., translucent, with green or red-brown spots; 3. Green-tail or Greasy-back, *M. mastersii* (N.S.W. and Qld.), to 12 cm. normally 8 cm., semi-transparent, speckled brown, greenish tail tip, normally non-migratory; 4. Banana or White Prawn, *P. merguiensis* (Qld. and W.A., potentially all tropical Aus. waters), semi-transparent cream, fine blue spots, to 23 cm.; 5. Common Tiger Prawn, *P. esculentus* (tropical Aus.), red-brown and light brown banding, red, yellow-tipped tail, to 23 cm.; and the Black or Giant Tiger, *P. monodon*, reaching 30 cm. Other Aus. prawn families are the Palaemonidae, (including the Transparent Ghost Shrimp, *Palaemon* spp.), Styidae (including *Atya* spp., *see* SHRIMPS), and Alpheidae (including the Nipper or Pistol Prawn, *Alpheus* spp.). In these the 2 front pairs of limbs have nippers (usually with one pair greatly enlarged); some of these are popularly called Shrimps*, as are some Stenopidae, also with 3 pairs of small nippers.

Preferential Voting The system was introduced by the Electoral Bill of 1918, and has been used in Federal and all State elections (except Qld. from 1942–62). The voter must arrange candidates in order of choice by placing his numbered order of preference against every name on the ballot paper. A candidate with an absolute majority of 'first preferences' wins, but if there is none, then the candidate with the lowest number of first preferences is eliminated and his second preferences are re-distributed among the relevant remaining candidates. This procedure continues until one candidate has half plus one of the valid votes. The system avoids the drawbacks of the 'first past the post' system of U.S. and U.K. in that a successful candidate will not have a minority of votes, but it leads to the election of members placed widely as second, not first preferences, and thus has helped the Country Party*; its complexity gives rise to the Donkey Vote*.

Premiers Conference While neither statutory nor executive, it has become a major factor in government. Convened generally by the Commonwealth Prime Minister in Canberra, it is a forum of debate, notably in Commonwealth–State relationships.

Presbyterian Church of Australia. The smallest of the 4 major denominations, and independent of, although sharing the traditions of the European and American Presbyterians. There were 1,028,654 adherents in 1971. There were gatherings of Scots in N.S.W. from 1803, and the first church was built at Ebenezer in 1809, the oldest Aus. church still in use. The first Minister did not arrive until 1822. In 1823 the great protagonist J. D. Lang* arrived to fight for and sometimes embarrass his fellow churchmen in his zeal. A dismissed former Presbyterian minister, C. Strong (1844–1942), founded the Australian Church in Melbourne in 1885, but it died with him. The 19th-century schism in the Scottish Church, resulting in Free Churches separate from the established Church of Scotland, was irrelevantly echoed in Aus., but the majority adhered to the latter. An important figure in healing the breach in 1865 was Rev. Robert Steel (1827–93). Only a small number of Free Churches remains. Post-1945 migration of Dutch and, later, Hungarians has increased the numbers. Influential schools, the original Flying Doctor Service* and Aus. Inland Mission* are among Presbyterian contributions.

Price, John Giles (1808–1857) b. Cornwall, Eng. He became a notoriously cruel prison supervisor, who was murdered by convicts on a prison hulk at Williamstown, Melbourne, for which 7 men were hanged. He was used as a literary prototype by both Marcus Clarke* and Price Warung*. *For further reading see* J. V. Barry: *The Life and Death of John Price* (Melbourne, 1964).

Prichard, Katherine Susannah (Mrs. H. Throssell) (1883–1969) b. Levuka, Fiji. The daughter of an Aus. journalist. She was a novelist of international repute, her work widely translated. She learned her trade through journalism, working freelance in Aus., London and U.S.; she has lived mainly in W.A. since establishing a reputation with *The Pioneers* (London, 1915). Her best works all have Aus. themes and strong tones of social protest, and cover the karri timber industry, opal-mining, cattle stations and circus life; all contain tragedy, especially poignant in the story of *Coonardoo* (London, 1929), an Aboriginal girl. Her culminating work, a W.A. gold-field trilogy, is less successful, though like her others, very carefully documented. Her short stories share the Lawson heritage. In her 80th year she published an autobiography *Child of the Hurricane* (Sydney, 1963). *For further reading see* H. Drake-Brockman: *Katherine Susannah Prichard* (Oxford, 1967).

Prickly Pear A popular name for the flat-stemmed members of the genus *Opuntia* in the Cactaceae or Cactus family. Captain Phillip seems to have brought *O. monacantha* (and some cochineal insects with them) from Brazil with the First Fleet, but the species, which later became outstanding pests, *O. inermis* from the Gulf of Mexico and *O. stricta* from Florida, can only be traced back to 1839 and 1870 respectively. Prickly pear covered 4 million ha. by 1900 and 24 million by 1920. A Prickly Pear Travelling Commission set out to find a combination of insects—it was hoped —to control the main pest species, after testing to ensure that fruit trees etc. would not also be attacked. The cochineal insects and several others were introduced and became established, with limited successes against the pest, but in 1925 2,750 eggs of *Cactoblastis cactorum*, a moth of S Brazil and N Argentine, were imported and bred, increasing tenfold by 1926 when the first releases were made. Except in a few cool areas, the larvae, tunnelling into the thick cactus leaves, have destroyed and successfully controlled the pest, allowing land to be redeveloped, and no further introductions have been necessary. Of the other insects, only the cochineal insects survive in any numbers.

Primary Industry Includes pastoral farming, agriculture, dairying, poultry, bee-farming, trapping, forestry, fishing, mining and quarrying and provides 35% of total production by value, and 85% of export value, with wool, wheat and minerals dominant. The Government includes a Department and Minister of Primary Industry. (*See also* FARMING, MINERALS, FORESTRY *and* SHEEP, WOOL, WHEAT, IRON, *etc.*)

Proserpine Qld. 20S/149E (2,955 in 1971) A sugar-milling centre on the lower Proserpine River, both named after the fertility goddess, a valid choice since this is highly productive sugar and banana land. The town also serves the tourist industry to the Cumberland Islands.

Prostanthera An E Aus. genus of over

60 species of shrubs and a few small trees in the Labiatae family, including the Christmas Bush* of Vic. and the strongly aromatic and purple-belled Oval Mint-bush of the Great Divide.

PUBLIC HEALTH In Aus. on the whole it has been good, right back to Phillip's remarkable record of preventive medicine during the voyage of the First Fleet and the first years at Sydney Cove. No doubt it owes much to space, sunshine, ample diets, especially in protein, and to the lack of population concentrations sufficient to maintain some of the infectious diseases, when they have been introduced to areas with the conditions needed for transmission. A stringent quarantine policy has been remarkably successful in virtually excluding Asian diseases such as cholera and plague, and the modern record is among the best in the world.

At birth in 1960–2, the expectation of life was 68 years for males, 74 years for females (U.K. 68 and 74, U.S. 67 and 74, Japan 68 and 73, and India 42 and 41). Infant mortality under one year was 18·5 in 1965; 25·2 in N.T., 19·1 in A.C.T. (cf. N.Z. 15·8 in A.C.T. (cf. N.Z. 19·5, U.K. 19·6, Japan 18·5, India 78). About 75% of the infant deaths were from pre-natal and natal causes, and well over half the rest from bronchitis and pneumonia. Gastroenteritis is not unimportant, and many deaths are presumed to be due to suffocation from vomit etc. Deaths from 1–4, when children are less tied to maternal care, are now often taken as an even better index of social conditions than infant mortality rates; in Aus. these are at present about 20% of the infant deaths (U.K. 14%; Japan, N.Z.: 25%; India 97%). The Aus. crude death-rate for 1966 was 9·0 per thousand people —males 9·9, females 8·0 (N.S.W. 9·3, A.C.T. 4·6, with rather small and youthful population; crude death-rates do not have adjustments to allow for different age structures).

Adjusted for age-structure, the 1965 rate was 14·9 for males and 13·8 for females, comparable to that in U.S., U.K., U.S.S.R. or Japan (cf. India 23·9, 24·7; Brazil 25·4, 22·0). After the relatively high death-rates of infancy and early childhood, rates naturally show a general decrease. There is, however, a sharp anomaly in deaths of young men, highest in the 20–4-year-olds compared with female death-rates; males show excess death-rates at up to 1 per thousand per annum, very largely due to motor accidents which accounted for over half the male death-rates in the 15–24-year-olds in 1965. The proportions of total male and female deaths due to particular causes in 1965 show interesting disparities: arteriorsclerotic heart disease 31·0 and 23·2%; other heart diseases 7·4 and 10·0%; arterosclerosis 2·0 and 2·8%; cerebral thrombosis etc. 10·4 and 17·8%; cancer of the stomach etc. 5·6 and 5·8%, lung 3·8 and 0·7% (breast 2·9%, womb etc. 2·3%); pneumonia 3·8 and 3·8%; bronchitis 3·8 and 0·8%; motor accidents 4·2 and 1·8%; other accidents 3·4 and 2·5%; suicide 1·9 and 1·4%.

A national survey of illness (morbidity) in 1962–3 in a sample of doctors' practices gave a complementary picture. The proportion of doctors' examinations due to different causes were: colds, influenza, pneumonia, bronchitis etc. 19·0%; pre-natal and other medical examinations 16·0%; accidents etc. 11·0%; boils and skin diseases 7·6%; digestive disorders 7·1%; disease of nervous system, eyes, ears, etc. 7·0%; ill-defined pains, senility etc. 5·1%; diseases of heart and circulation 5·0%; genito-urinary diseases 4·7%; diseases of bones and joints 4·2%; infective and parasitic diseases (bacteria, viruses, spirochaetes etc. with some overlap, e.g. with our first category) 3·7%; mental disorders etc. 3·6%; allergic disorders etc., including asthma 3·5%; cancers etc. 1·0%, and blood disorders 0·5%. Notifiable diseases are: anthrax, brucellosis, diphtheria, gonorrhoea, infective hepatitis, leprosy, leptospirosis, paratyphoid fever, poliomyelitis, syphilis, tetanus, tuberculosis, typhoid and typhus. Leading figures in establishment of public health measures include: J. H. L. Cumpston (1880–1954), first Commonwealth Director-General of Health, Sir Raphael Cilento (1893–), in tropical hygiene in Qld., J. A. Thompson (1848–1915) in N.S.W. and T. H. Lovegrove (1845–1928) in W.A.

Publishing Shows rapid increase by well-established firms, new companies and international firms operating in Aus. Some 55 companies belong to the Aus. Book Publishers Association. The National Library receives copies of all books and pamphlets published. In 1970 the total approached 5,000: over one third were government publications; one third were 'trade' (by publishing firms and widely available); 10% were by societies and institutions; the remainder were commercial or private. Some printing is done in Japan and Hong Kong. The oldest and still largest firm is Angus and Robertson (Sydney, 1884), developing from book-retailing. There are other major firms in Sydney, Melbourne, Adelaide and Brisbane, and in increasing output from University Presses.

Puffballs A large group of fungi called Gasteromycetes (stomach fungi), in which the spores are formed in the enclosed space within the round flesh or leathery sac, to be released in thousands of millions often suddenly when trodden on.

Pyrenees The name given by Mitchell*, from a fancied resemblance to the Franco-Spanish Pyrenees, to a range NE of Ararat*, Vic., 37S/143E. The highest point is Mt. Buangor (990 m.).

Pythons and **Rock Snakes** Members of the Sub-family Pythoninae which, with

the Boas (not found in Aus.), make up the family Boidae. They are non-poisonous snakes killing their prey by constriction, mainly by suffocation— the larger species being capable of overpowering and swallowing a wallaby. Most show vestigial hind limbs in scaly flaps held close to the body on either side of the vent. There are 4 genera, with selected species given here. 1. *Aspidites*. The Black-headed Python *A. melanocephalus* of the wetter part of N Aus., is up to 2·75 m., with black head, throat and neck, brown-cream body with bands of brick-red to dark brown, while the Woma, *A. ramsayi*, brown with darker bands and yellow-pink belly is found preying on lizards and birds in the drier inland. 2. *Chondropython*. The Green Tree-python or Green Python, *C. viridis*, of N.G. and (as was found early in the Second World War) of Cape York, grows up to 1·5–2 m. and lives on warm-blooded animals. 3. *Liasis*. The Scrub Python, N Qld. Python or Amethystine Python, *L. amethystinus*, is Australia's largest snake, up to 7 m. and perhaps more, ranking with the 8-m. Anaconda of S America and Regal Python of India. It is light brown with dark zigzag markings, being darker in colour in rain-forest, lighter in open woodland, and eats wallabies, rabbits, rats, bandicoots, birds etc. The small Children's Python, *L. childreni childreni*, a black-spotted light-brown snake with whitish belly, and up to 1–2 m. in length, is well-known N of a line from S of Brisbane to S of Perth. It lives in crevices in rocky country with access to water, living on lizards, birds and mice (rather than frogs); an overlapping variant near Perth apparently lives chiefly on termites etc. It may lay 25-30 eggs. The Olive Python *L. olivaceus*, of the coastal far N, reaches 4 m. or more, and is often killed on the Stuart Highway through fear because it is mistaken for a large Brown Snake. The Water Python, *L. fuscus*, of coastal streams and mangrove swamps in the far N is rich glossy brown with orange belly, semi-aquatic and living on birds, reptiles and small mammals. It reaches about 3 m. 4. *Morelia*. The dark olive and yellow diamond-patterned Diamond Snake or Diamond Python, *M. spilotes spilotes*, grows to 3 m., eats birds and small mammals, and is often kept semi-domesticated in barns to keep down rats and mice. It is normally quiet, but if harassed it is capable of giving a nasty though, of course, non-venomous bite. It is found E of the Divide from Coff's Harbour to Vic. It often lies in water for long periods, especially before sloughing, and in very hot weather tends to become nocturnal though it may be seen sun-basking in the early morning. It lays up to 35 eggs, and is one of the species which helps incubation by coiling round the eggs. The equally well-known and well-named Carpet Snake, *M. spilotes variegata*, a variant of olive to brown, with large line-and-square patterns of brown and black, lives a mainly nocturnal life in timbered or rocky country all over mainland Aus. except the N.S.W. coast. It also preys on small animals and may be used as a rat-catcher. It grows to 2–3 m. or even more, and also may give a nasty bite if harassed. It swims well, in inland waters. It also incubates a large clutch of eggs.

Q

Q FEVER

Q Fever An acute but not usually dangerous fever, first observed (1935) by Dr. E. H. Derrick in employees in Brisbane meatworks, and traced as a new disease to infection by the rickettsial *Coxiella burneti*. It appears to be a disease of the marsupial bandicoots, transmitted by ticks, which also bite and infect cattle, and thence man, by inhalation or handling of infective material, or through infected milk.

Qantas Australia's overseas airline, developed from Queensland and Northern Territory Aerial Services Ltd., founded in Qld. in 1920 with 2 small planes. The first regular service (1922) was between Charleville and Cloncurry. International flights began with the Brisbane–Singapore section of the London flight in 1934 and in 1947 the Aus. Government took major control. (*See* AIRLINES.)

Quakers Correctly the Religious Society of Friends, they have a small Aus. total around 1,000, with the main focus in Hobart. 2 Friends, Backhouse and Walker, arrived there in 1832, and became concerned in Aboriginal and convict welfare.

Quandong or **Native Peach** (*Eucarya acuminata*) A shrub or small tree of the widespread family Santalaceae. The edible red fruit has a fleshy outer part, eaten by Aborigines and settlers, covering a deeply pitted stony centre, very rich in oil, also used by Aborigines. The Bitter Quandong, *E. murrayana*, has a brownish-red, bitter, less fleshy fruit. Like most members of the family, they are root parasites on other plants. Brisbane Quandong or Blue Fig, *Elaeocarpus grandis*, belonging to the family of flowering limes, Tibaceae, is a timber tree of N.S.W. and Qld.,

QUEENSLAND

with blue fruits eaten by Aborigines, and soft easily worked timber.

Queanbeyan N.S.W 35S/149E (15,992 in 1971) A market and service centre for the central part of the Southern Tablelands. Its development was changed by the building of Canberra*, only 12 km. away in the Australian Capital Territory*. For a time its shops and facilities were better than Canberra's, and included alcohol in the early days of prohibition in the capital. Rapid growth owes much to residential provision, at times much cheaper than that in Canberra, and considerable industrial growth including building and constructional materials for the capital.

QUEENSLAND (Qld.) The second largest State after W.A. It has an area of 1,727,500 km.^{2} or 22% of Aus., and a population (1971) of 1,823,362, or 14% of the Aus. total, giving an average density of 1·06 per km.^{2} which is similar to S.A., higher than N.T. or W.A., but far below Vic., N.S.W. or Tas. The State extends some 2,000 km. N–S, between 10°S and 29°S, with 5,200 km. of coast; it extends to 1,500 km. E–W, reaching its widest along 26°S and tapering N to Cape York. The landward boundaries are with N.T. along 138°E, S.A. along 141°E and 26°N, and N.S.W. along 29°S, and by natural features.

Badge of Queensland

436

Physical Geography and Land Use There are 3 major regions: the tumbled ranges and basins E of the Great Divide*; the plateaux and slopes W of the Divide with the interior drainage basins of Bulloo and L. Eyre; and the edge of the great Aus. shield of Precambrian rocks in the far NW. Temperatures are sub-tropical, with frosts rare, save at high altitudes. Summer rainfall predominates, with totals decreasing from 250 cm. on the NE coast to under 12 cm. in the extreme SW. Rapid local climatic variations occur in the Eastern Basins and Ranges reflecting topographic influences.

The Eastern Ranges and Basins begin in the poor cattle country along the scrub-covered granitic spine near the E of Cape York Peninsula, where rainfall is 100–130 cm. The scarp edge reaches the coast N of Cairns, then swings inland to the towering Bellenden Ker Range, with its valuable rain-forest yielding cabinet woods. Behind this rampart (no longer the Great Divide, which sweeps inland through the lower ranges of the Chillagoe area) lies the sheltered Atherton Tableland. The narrow E coast plain is the 'Sugar Coast' with the highest rainfall in Aus., deep alluvial soils and perennial rivers. Inland, behind the ranges, rainfall drops to 75 cm. or less, scrub replaces trees, and large-scale cattle properties the small sugar farms. Rainfall also decreases sharply southwards where the coast swings SE, parallel to prevailing winds, and irrigation is used on the Burdekin delta. The upper Burdekin occupies the first of the NW–SE corridors which give a characteristic grain to much of the hill zone and its offshore islands; rivers cut through NW–SE-trending ranges, to reach restricted coast plains.

The belt of basins and ranges reaches a width of 650 km. in Central Qld., with Palaeozoic rocks capped in parts with Tertiary lavas. The Great Divide lies well to the W where younger sediments overlap, and is inconspicuous in rolling beef country among tropical woodland and savannah land with 50–75 cm. of rain, as in the Buckland Tableland. On the coast sugar gives way to dairying southwards. The Fitzroy* Basin echoes on a larger scale that of the Burdekin, with beef and wool in the interior and grain and cotton cultivation in the valleys. Brigalow* scrub is now being cleared to extend cultivation and stock farming. Rain-forest clothes the seaward slopes, and there are dairy, banana and pineapple farms on favoured coast lowlands.

In S Qld. the forested slopes of the Great Divide come to within 80 km. of the coast at Mt. Superbus, where the basaltic McPherson Range* carries the N.S.W./Qld. border towards the Pacific. The SE corner has the most varied and intensive farming of the State, reflecting the urban demands of the Metropolitan area and Gold Coast resorts, the early settlement and development, the overlapping of temperature conditions suitable for both sub-tropical and temperate crops, reliable rainfall of 100–150 cm and the convergence with the costal lowlands of the Brisbane and its tributary valleys of alluvial soils developed from Tertiary sediments, and the basalts of the Divide.

West of the Divide rainfall drops to the SW from 150 cm to under 12 cm. Landforms are gentle slopes and plateaux, except in the NW, underlain by the Tertiary sediments which include the aquifers of the Great Artesian Basin—vital to the life of farming and settlement in much of the area.

The N tip of Cape York* is agriculturally useless, but the SW of the peninsula, merging with the 'Gulf Country'*, and up to the Selwyn Range, supports taller woodland and tussock grass, and extensive cattle rearing. The main sheep belt (but with cattle too) lies in a broad region flanking both sides of the Divide in Central Qld., but more dependent on bores W of it in the 25- to 50-cm. rainfall zone where the tree-lined courses of the seasonal headwaters of the Darling system occupy wide basins. Another sheep belt borders the S of the Selwyn Range, where again artesian water is available. In the extreme SW is the unique Channel country*. The Darling Downs*, while W of the Divide and underlain by Tertiary and later rocks, share some of the intensive land use pattern of all SE Qld.

Industry and Towns Primary industry, and the secondary processing it entails, dominates the Qld. economy. The relative lack of other secondary industry is blamed for the comparatively slower economic growth in the State. Of primary products sugar and beef are equally valuable and between them provide nearly half the total. Minerals now led by coal, include copper, lead, zinc, gold, bauxite, the first Aus. commercial oil, and natural gas. The remaining primary products are vegetables and fruit (mainly pineapples, tomatoes and bananas), fodder crops, tobacco and oilseeds.

Processing industries of sugar, timber, meat, dairy produce and minerals are dispersed, depending on location of raw materials, so that Qld. has a bigger proportion of decentralised industry than other States. Engineering is important in the Metropolitan area, but also in Maryborough, Toowoomba and Townsville. The remaining secondary industry is concentrated in the SE and comprises clothing, textiles, furniture and electrical machinery. The tertiary industries generated by urban demand for food, drink, motor-vehicle servicing etc. again reflect the population concentration in the SE, but show more rapid growth in all towns over 10,000, notably on the Darling Downs and in the ports.

The remoteness of the capital, the need to move primary products destined for export from inland producing areas to the coast, and the physical nature of the country all contributed to the development of E–W railway links in the latter part of the 19th century, while the S–N coastal line was not built until the 1920s. Thus each of the ports of Cairns, Townsville and Rockhampton developed its hinterland stretching back beyond the Divide. The closest transport network is nevertheless in the SE. Unlike any other State, there is not a unified State Electricity Authority. Thermal power provides 80% and new plants have been built in the E. Hydro-electricity potential (with some development, e.g. the Barron River) is high only in the wet NE coastal ranges.

Eastern Ranges and Basins
1. *The North* is dominated by Townsville (71,109).

20,000–32,000, sugar ports: Cairns, Mackay.

4,000–10,000, sugar centres: Ayr*, Ingham*; Innisfail*; Bowen* (port); Charters Towers* (formerly gold), Mareeba* (market).

1,500–4,000 smaller sugar centres of Home Hill, Tully, Babinda, Gordonvale, Mossman, Proserpine*, Sarina; Collinsville* (coal).

Under 1,000, inter-state sugar ports: Mourilyan, Lucinda; former ports: Port Douglas, Cooktown*; dairy, timber and service centres: Daintree on the coast plain, Ravenshoe, Malanda, Millaa-Millaa, Yungaburra, Chillagoe, Atherton (Atherton Tableland); Mt. Garnet* (tin).

2. *The Centre* is dominated by Rockhampton (48,188).

5,000–10,000, Gladstone.

1,500–5,000, Mt. Morgan* (mining); Yeppoon, commuter-resort; service and market centres serving major valleys: Biloela (Callide Valley*), Emerald*, Clermont (Mackenzie Basin), Blackwater (coal).

Under 1,000, minor service centres: Rolleston, Capella and Springsure (Mackenzie Basin), Moura, Theodore (Dawson Basin); coal-mining at Blair Athol*, Baralaba and Styx;

formerly gold at Cracow. The Rock-hampton/Longreach railway is evenly strung with minor collecting-points.

3. *The South* Metropolitan Brisbane (816,987) which includes Ipswich and Redcliff, Lawton-Petrie and others is dominant, and the Gold Coast exceeds 65,000.

15,000–26,000, Bundaberg and Maryborough, industrial towns and sugar ports.

10,000–12,000, Gympie, former gold town. The remaining towns are predominantly service centres for farming regions, with secondary processing industries of timber, dairy produce, sugar and fruit according to district.

2,000–7,000, Kingaroy*, Murgon in the S Burnett basin, Nambour*, Caboolture, Beaudesert, Beenleigh and Gatton in the SE lowland, and the coasts resorts of Hervey Bay*, Caloundra and Maroochydore-Mooloolaba.

1,000–2,000, Monto, Mundubbera, Nanango in the Upper (N) Burnett, Wondai, Gayndah in the S Burnett; Childers, Cooroy on the coastal plain; Laidley, Kilcoy, Rosewood, Boonah in or flanking the Moreton lowlands; a number of important centres are under 1,000, e.g. Moore, Esk, Toogoolawah in the upper Brisbane Valley, or Howard (coal) near Hervey Bay and Cleveland on the plain.

West of the Divide The closely settled Darling Downs have a pattern more comparable with the E basins, but this thins rapidly westwards, and in the rest of the State, towns are small and widely spaced. Only Toowoomba is over 50,000.

10.000–20,000, Mt. Isa (mining).

5,000–10,000, major service centres: Dalby, Roma, Warwick.

2,000–5,000, service centres for areas marginal to the Downs: Goondiwindi*, Chinchilla, Stanthorpe*; and railing centres in the main pastoral belt: Charleville*, Longreach*, Cloncurry*, St. George*.

1,000–2,000, stock railing points:

Blackall, Hughenden*, Cunamulla*, Winton*, Barcaldine*; more closely placed service centres on agricultural land or the pastoral margins of the Downs, with processing industries: Milmerran, Miles, Texas, Mitchell, Pittsworth, Oakey and Weipa* on Cape York peninsula. In the thinly peopled country, centres with less than 1,000 may still exercise a vital function: Tara, Quilpie*, Birdsville, Windorah, Jundah, Boulia in the Channel Country, Burketown*, Croydon, Normanton* in the Gulf Country.

Historical Development The Qld. coast was charted by Cook in 1770, Flinders in 1802 and King in 1818. The Brisbane River was discovered in 1823 by Oxley, and Moreton Bay penal settlement established for escapees and second or recalcitrant offenders from Botany Bay in 1824. Harsh but efficient administration by Logan (1825–30) established Brisbane and saw exploration of the SE. Overland routes pioneered by Cunningham (1827) led to squatter settlement, prior to the official opening for free settlement in 1842. The N and W, explored by Leichhardt, Mitchell and Kennedy, disclosed natural grazing soon taken up by bold pastoralist settlement, but the unique white settlement N of the Tropic is due to abortive cotton and then successful sugar plantations after 1860. Aborigines, dependent on natural fruits and game, attacked and were counter-attacked brutally, until reserves were created after 1895.

Meanwhile, after increasing agitation and controversy over a border, Qld. was declared a separate colony with responsible government in 1859. Political confusion marked its early years, as in the other States; dominant groups were the pastoral squatters and the plantation owners; a major issue was land tenure. From 1867 mineral rushes brought new elements to the population. Growing opposition to the use of indentured Kanaka* labour on the cane-fields almost led to a secession of the North during Griffith's ministry. Qld. was reluctant to enter the Commonwealth until promised the tariff protection which would permit sugar-growing on small farms with white labour, in return for her promise to end Kanaka labour.

Because of the widespread and primary nature of the economy, the big depressions of the 1890s and 1930s were more easily weathered than in Vic. or N.S.W. The main feature since Federation has been the long period of Labor Government 1915–57, under notable leaders such as Ryan and Theodore. The Upper House was abolished in 1922, again a unique step in Aus. so far, preferential voting was re-introduced in 1962.

There has been more State involvement in social and economic spheres than in any other State. Although State industrial enterprises have not on the whole succeeded, there have been valuable irrigation and mining developments, and Qld. has the most comprehensive health service.

Future economic development in Qld. is likely to continue the present pattern, although the State would like more diversified secondary industry. Capital is difficult to draw from the existing industrial concentrations of the SE of Aus., and Qld. attracts a smaller share of migrants. Farming is expanding with Beef Roads, Brigalow clearing and irrigation. Mineral output, doubled in the last decade, will expand further with bauxite, coal export to Japan, phosphates and, less immediately, iron in the NW, oil and gas in the SE, already being piped to Brisbane. Rapid or extensive secondary industrial development seems less likely. (*See* MAP 8.)

Premiers since 1900: R. Philp (1899 and 1907–8), A. Morgan (1903), W. Kidston (1906 and 1908–11), D. F. Denham (1911), T. J. Ryan* (1915), E. G. Theodore* (1919), W. N. Gillies (1925), W. McCormack (1925), A. E. Moore (1929), W. Forgan Smith* (1932), F. A. Cooper (1942), E. M. Hanlon (1946), V. C. Gair (1952), G. F. R. Nicklin (1957), J. C. A. Pizzey (1968), J. Bjelke Peterson (1968–). *For further reading see* R. H. Greenwood: *Queensland, City, Coast and Country* (Brisbane, 1959); R. Cilento and C. Lack: *Triumph in the Tropics* (Brisbane, 1959); M. Gough, H. Hughes, B. J. Macfarlane and G. R. Palmer: *Queensland: Industrial Enigma* (Melbourne, 1964); G. C. Bolton: *A Thousand Miles Away* (Brisbane, 1963).

Queensland Nut (*Macadamia ternifolia*) In the S and largely Aus. family Proteaceae, which includes *Banksia*. It is a 20-m. evergreen coastal rainforest tree of NE N.S.W. and SE Qld. with stiff, hairy, strap-like prominently veined leaves in whorls along the branchlets, creamy hanging 25-cm. flower-spikes and 2-cm. round fruit, the green skin of which splits to reveal the tasty and marketable nut, grown commercially in Hawaii and elsewhere. It produces firm, reddish wood, easily polished.

Queenstown Tas. 42S/146E (4,984 in 1971) A mining town in the West coast ranges, 6 km from Mr. Lyell*. The notorious lunar landscape, caused by deforestation, smelter fumes killing vegetation and subsequent erosion, may be yielding to conservation efforts.

Quick, Sir John (1852–1923) b. Cornwall, Eng. He arrived in Aus. in 1854, his father going to the gold diggings at Bendigo. He became a key figure at the Corowa Conference on Federation*. With Garran*, wrote the monumental *Annotated Constitution of the Australian Commonwealth* (1901).

Quilpie Qld. 27S/144E A railhead, and although with less than 1,000 people, the main service and collecting centre for the Channel Country*. It lies on the intermittent Bulloo River*, and was reached by rail in 1917 from

Charleville*, and now by a Beef Road from Windorah.

Quiros, Pedro Fernandez de (1563–1615) b. Evora, Portugal A navigator of great skill and even greater religious zeal, dedicated to the salvation of the souls of the people of the undiscovered lands of the South Seas. In 1605, with Spanish support, he sailed from Peru and sighted land which he named *Austrialia del Espiritu Santo*, possibly after Phillip III of Spain, who was an Austrian Prince. It was later named by Cook the New Hebrides; but belief persisted even into this century, that he had found eastern Aus. Quiros turned back, but Torres* sailed on to make his important voyage. James McAuley's* narrative poem *Captain Quiros* (1964) is an imaginative evocation.

Quist, Adrian (1913–) b. Medindie, S.A. A great doubles tennis player, playing in Davis Cup* matches 1933–9, and winning the Wimbledon doubles in 1935 (with Crawford) and 1950 (with Bromwich).

Quokka (*Setonix brachyurus*) A small member of the Kangaroo*-wallaby family surviving in coastal swamps in SW W.A. and common on Rottnest Island.

Quorn S.A. 32S/138E It has declined to a small pastoral centre (but with treatment of Oraparinna barytes) since its great days as the major focus for the wheat expansion in the Willochra Plains* (1860–85), when flour mills and machine shops flourished. Its function as a rail junction with workshops declined when Port Adelaide traffic was diverted by the Port Augusta–Port Pirie Line (1937) and ceased when the 1956 standard-gauge line to Marree, replacing the old 3-ft. 6-in. line through Quorn, by-passed it to the W on the plain. Its frontier character made it an ideal location for part of the film *The Sundowners* (1960).

R

RABBITS

Rabbits The wild rabbit *Oryctolagus cuniculus* (digging hare), constitutes one of the great introduced animal pests of Aus. At times in recent years up to 100 million rabbit carcases and skins have found their way into the export market alone, for meat, as furs or for felt-making, but even allowing for domestic markets the damage done to pastures alone is regarded as far out-weighing the yields.

The history of rabbits in Aus. may be viewed in phases: 1. Caged rabbits were brought to Sydney Cove in 1788; some escaped, but the domesticated breed were only able to attain relatively local spread, but 'doing well' by 1825. 2. In Tas. the wild rabbit *O. cuniculus* was introduced by Crowther; widespread by 1827. 3. In 1859 Thomas Austin* released wild rabbits from Eng. at Barwon Park near Geelong, Vic.; they spread rapidly through parkland or savannahs, especially if burrowing was easy in alluvium or sandy soils (they avoided wet or clay areas), at about 120 km. a year (to inland Qld. by 1900 and the SW of W.A. shortly thereafter). 4. Increase was and is proverbially rapid (a gestation period of 28 days permits 4–5 litters a year, each of 6–7 kittens, despite short adult life, often lasting only a year though 3–4 years in individuals. 5. Commercial trapping for meat and skins does not aim at extinction, and varied legislation in the States found no effective measure, or combination of measures, in trapping, shooting, dogging, ripping burrows, poisoning, or fence construction (at heavy expense and sometimes hardship, often ineffective and too late, though in places modified against dingoes or kangaroos). 6. Germ warfare was considered by the Pasteur Institute of Paris in 1888, and

RADIO

myxomatosis, a virus disease of the S American 'rabbit' *Sylvilagus brasiliensis*, was suggested by Aragão of Brazil in 1919. C.S.I.R. did some work in 1936, and its successor C.S.I.R.O. in 1950–1. 7. Artificially introduced myxomatosis failed in dry areas, but almost eradicated rabbits in wetter tracts. Too late for efficient planning, it became clear that in Aus. the disease is mainly carried by 2 vector mosquitoes. 8. The present phase is of ebb and flow of myxomatosis in rabbit populations over millions of km.[2]; the likely result is a reduced population, but of immune or relatively immune rabbits. 9. With constant vigilance, and careful use of the new poisons, such as sodium fluoracetate (1080), rabbits should not attain their former plague proportions; but unfortunately 1080 kills other fauna.

Radio Began briefly in 1923, and more successfully in 1924; 2 groups of stations 'A' and 'B' later became the basis of the dual networks of Aus. Broadcasting Commission* (1932) and commercial stations, largely in the ownership of newspapers (licences are issued for 5 years at a time). In 1970 the National Broadcasting Service (programmes by A.B.C.) had 72 medium frequency and 18 high frequency stations (12 for the Overseas service 'Radio Australia'); there are 116 commercial stations. The A.B.C. must broadcast the proceedings of the Federal Parliament; it also gives much time to serious music. Commercial channels, dependent on advertising revenue, concentrate on local services, popular imported serial drama and music. The numbers listening to sound radio decreased sharply with the introduction of television, but licences rose again to 2,670,393 (1970). Frequency modulation (FM) is planned for 1975.

Radio Australia A high-frequency broadcasting system, run by the A.B.C. from 9 stations in Vic. with 3 repeater stations at Darwin and aimed mainly at SE Asia.

Rafferty, Chips (1909–71) b. Broken Hill, N.S.W. His real name was John William Goffage, a film actor and producer of mainly Aus. films, although starring also successfully in Hollywood.

Raffles Bay N.T. 11S/132E A short inlet on the N coast of Cobourg Peninsula*; in 1827 Fort Wellington was established on its E shore, after the failure of the Melville Island* settlement, but abandoned in 1829. In 1839 2 French ships anchored there were found by the Port Essington* garrison and seemed proof of the suspected French interest which had stimulated British attempts to settle the area.

Ragwort The popular name for a rosette-forming member of the Groundsel genus, *Senecio**, in the Compositae or Daisy family, which has become a serious pest of pastures in Vic. and elsewhere.

Railton Tas. 41S/146E A small service centre in the intensively farmed lower valley of the Mersey River, with limestone quarries producing over 275,000 tonnes a year, and cement works.

Railways They remain overwhelmingly State owned and run, though the initial steps in several States were taken by private companies, and were mainly taken over by the State after financial difficulties within a few years. The basic pattern, antedating Federation, is of State networks (and rating systems) designed to orient traffic towards the State capitals or major

State ports, and unfortunately historical accidents, probably assisted by interstate jealousies, have added differences of gauge (and some States, for cheapness in a big country, have added narrower, cheaper gauges in a fashion reminiscent of India). For a time in the early 1850s N.S.W., Vic. and S.A. agreed to use the Irish gauge of 5 ft. 3 in., but when the Irish engineer F. W. Shields resigned from the Sydney Railway Co., N.S.W. reversed its decision without consulting the other States, and they would not follow in changing back to the British standard gauge of 4 ft. 8½ in.

Agreements on the adoption of the 4-ft. 8½-in. standard-gauge was reached in 1921, but with little implementation except the Sydney–Brisbane link completed in 1930; the whole question was re-opened at the end of the 1939–45 War with fundamental work by Sir Harold Clapp (1875–1952). Marked progress seemed likely, but Qld. opposed completion of the Darwin–Port Augusta link on standard-gauge as likely to draw from the hinterland of her 3-ft. 6-in. network, and then a more limited Commonwealth agreement with N.S.W., Vic. and S.A. was not ratified by the N.S.W. Government. However, a standard-gauge line of 1962 parallels the 5-ft. 3-in. Vic. line from Melbourne to Wodonga on the Murray, to avoid the break of gauge on the Sydney–Melbourne run; a combined standardisation and developmental project has extended the transcontinental Port Pirie–Kalgoorlie standard-gauge line to East Perth–Fremantle and also links Koolyanobbing iron ore with Kwinana blast-furnaces. The S.A. Government has said that general conversion to standard-gauge must await similar conversion in Vic., but ever since 1923 3-ft. 6-in. lines in S.A. converted to 5 ft. 3 in. have been designed for the eventual change to standard-gauge. But the long-projected Broken Hill–Port Pirie standard-gauge line is now complete and the decision to develop the coalfield at Leigh Creek, 30S/138E, brought a new standard-gauge line west of the Flinders Range and now extended N to Marree. There is standard-gauge development, again, in new projects, e.g. the iron-ore railways in the Hamersley* area of W.A. By early 1970 the first transcontinental trains were running Sydney–Perth on standard-gauge in 65 hours. Standard-gauge lines are being built Whyalla–Port Augusta, Tarcoola–Alice Springs (830 km) and planned for Adelaide to the transcontinental. There are also private mineral lines in Qld., S.A., Tas., and N.S.W. mainly narrow gauge.

Historical Development There was a horse-drawn tramway from May 1854 in S.A. (to allow water-borne freight from the Murray River to Adelaide to avoid the treacherous Murray mouth), and in September the first steam train from Melbourne to Sandridge (Port Melbourne had a locomotive made locally as an emergency measure when the Stephenson engines from Eng. were held up). The Sydney–Parramatta line opened in 1855 and the Newcastle–E Maitland line in 1857. Railway history varies State by State, but there was a general tendency to slow development because of the high capital needed in a country of long distances, even though fairly easy for railway construction. As a response all States adopted American rather than British practices, e.g. in fastening rails directly to sleepers rather than in iron chairs, and soon adopted lighter rails and unballasted lines for less busy branch lines, while all States, except N.S.W. and Vic., did much of their building in 3-ft. 6-in. gauge, giving cheaper, lighter lines, locomotives, bridges etc.

Route-miles at selected dates were: 1861, 243; 1881, 4,192; 1901, 13,551; 1921, 26,202; 1941, 27,956; 1970, 25,060 (40,096 km). The last figure is for Government railways only).

During the growth of the railway systems the States had individualities. Vic. had its great expansion in the land boom era of the 1880s (even with some 2-ft. 6-in. lines, now closed), followed by closing uneconomic lines from the 1930s onwards, and complete reorganisation under Sir Harold Clapp, including Melbourne's electric suburban service and the 'Spirit of Progress', all-steel air-conditioned trains (1937). Qld. has its high route-mileage but relatively low freight totals, along with a relatively greater importance of the railcars important on quieter lines in all States. S.A. had its early horse-tram companies, then small railway companies mostly later absorbed by the State railway, its 2 main gauges of 5 ft. 3 in. and 3 ft. 6 in.; then came reorganisation largely on American lines in the 1920s by W. A. Webb, including the fine modern station in Adelaide. In W.A. the isolation, only broken by the Transcontinental* standard-gauge railway as part of the agreement to enter the Federation in 1901, encouraged the building of the light and cheap, if slow, 3-ft. 6-in. railways, and some important lines were developed on the basis of land grants either for timber exploitation or for disposal for farming purposes; e.g. the Midland region is closely associated with the railway company, which was only absorbed into the State system in 1964. Tas. has its neat little 500 miles (750 km.) of 3-ft. 6-in. line, after a period with some 5-ft. 3-in. lines including smaller-gauge operation over some broad-gauge routes on a third line, up to 1888. There was also a phase of 2-ft. gauge mineral line operation, even by the State railways, ending in 1932, and including some tiny 'Garratt' articulated locomotives—an extreme case of a fairly common use of these in Aus.—to minimise axle weight over light bridges while giving considerable power.

Commonwealth Railways operate the transcontinental standard-gauge line from Sydney to Perth with the *Indian Pacific* covering the 3,962 km. in under 70 hours, and the Central Aus. line, in standard-gauge to Marree and thence by 3-ft. 6-in. gauge to Alice Springs. From Darwin the North Australian Railway* (3 ft. 6 in.) to Larrimah may yet be superseded by a standard-gauge line to link with the line from the S to Alice Springs. There is also the 8-km. stretch from Canberra to Queanbeyan, with N.S.W. Railways rolling stock but Commonwealth station and line staff, which used to make the sixth change of railway and rate structure on a journey from Fremantle to the national capital.

As elsewhere, the 1950s in particular saw great modernisation, with diesel railcars and shunters and diesel-electric locomotives, suburban and even middle-distance electrification (Gippsland and Blue Mts.), improved rolling stock especially for freight, welding of rails with special provision for expansion on hot days, signalling, and more numerous signals and barriers at level-crossings.

Rainbow-bird (*Merops ornatus*) Australia's one immigrant species of Bee-eater; brightly coloured. (*See* BIRDS.)

Rain-making As the driest continent, Aus. was quick to follow up initial American experiments after 1945, and the first man-induced rain reached the ground in N.S.W. in February 1945. Further advances have been made, notably by C.S.I.R.O.* Where there are clouds of suitable moisture content but lacking nuclei needed for raindrops to form, they can be 'seeded', e.g. by silver iodide. However, in the prevailing conditions of the Aus. climate*, it is unlikely that rain-making will ever be of more than very local sporadic significance.

Rapotec, Stanislaus (1911–) b. Trieste, Italy. He arrived in Aus. in 1948. A contemporary artist, largely abstract, and not specifically Aus. in theme or interpretation.

Raspberry, Native This name may be applied to 3 indigenous species of Rubus, *R. triphyllus, R. rosifolius* and *R. gunnianus*. They are unobtrusive plants of undergrowth in the bush.

Raven The large tree-roosting but open-country feeding Crow* of E Aus.

Rawlinson Range W.A. 25S/128E The most westerly extension of the great granite-gneissic quartzite ranges which start with the Musgraves in S.A. Although only 250 m. above the plain, they are conspicuous ramparts and include the 1,220-m. Giles Pinnacle at the apex of a great crescentic range.

Raymond Terrace N.S.W. 33S/152E (6,001 in 1971) A former river port on the Hunter*, founded in the 1830s. It had a pottery in early years and is now a growing industrial town of the smaller sort, with a fibre-board factory and the Tomago rayon factory nearby.

Rays They are grouped with the Sharks* to comprise the Class Elasmobranchii (strap-gilled). Like the Sharks they are carnivorous and mainly large. The features differentiating them from the bony fish are broadly similar. Most Rays are born alive, but the Skates are oviparous. Rays tend to have blunt teeth, especially females. Aus. Rays, many widespread elsewhere, range from about 30 cm. to 3 m. or more in length. 1. The transitional forms, the Angel Shark or Monk-fish and Saw-sharks, are between sharks and rays, and are discussed under sharks. 2. Sawfish, genus *Pristis*, also show some transitional characteristics; they are mainly very large tropical creatures, up to 3 m. in smaller species, and 6–9 m. in large ones, with the long low side-lashing snout armed with saw-like teeth, but more wing-like development like that of the Rays. They are unlikely to pursue bathers, but accidental involvement with the saw might be very serious. 3. The Common Shovelnose or Guitar-fish, *Aptychotrema banksii*, shows some shark-like characteristics, but has marked wing-like lobes. It is of 0·9–1·2 m., a feeder on sandy bottoms, and of some market value. 4. The Great Northern Shovelnose, *Rhino batos granulatus*, reaches over 2 m.

5. The Great Shark Ray, *Rhino ancylostoma*, is much like a flattened Shark, with a sort of 'pavement' of small, rounded, roughish teeth mounted on 3 denture-like processes. 6. The Torpedoes or Electric Rays have electri-

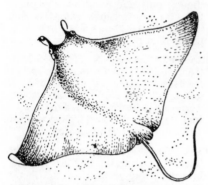

Whiptail Devil Ray (Mobula diabolus), about 3 m. long

cally charged organs on each side of the head; a shock of some volume can be put out, unpleasant to a fisherman, and presumably developed in order to stun prey; they include the Little Numbfish, *Narcine tasmaniensis*, the Short-tail Electric Ray or Large Numbfish, *Hypnos monopterygium*, and the Long-tail Electric Ray or Deep-water Numbfish, *Torpedo fairchildi*. 7. The True Skates—as distinct from fish marketed as Skate—have a very low flat head united with the pectoral fins and with most of the body to form the wing-like disc, with a quite small, separate and rather insignificant tail in proportion. They include the Large Thornback Skate, *Raja lemprieri*, and 2 others of that genus, and the distinctive Round Skate, *Psammobatis waitii*. 8. The Stingrays have the main part of the body and fins in the wing-like disc, and a longish thin tail armed with ivory-like backward-pointing venomous barbs, e.g. the large Black or Thorntail Stingray, *Dasyatis latus*, not infre-

quently trawled off N.S.W., but unlikely to be encountered inshore. If it is, it should not be taken into a small craft unless the tail can be cut off. Of the more tropical species, the rough-backed Cowtail Stingray, *D. sephen*, is usually only a few feet across. 9. The Eagle Rays, include the Duckbill or Beaked Eagle Ray, *Aetobatus narinari*, of up to 2 m. 10. The Devil Rays or Great Sea-Bats include the Whiptail Devil Ray, *Mobula diabolus*, of up to 3–4 m. and found off N.S.W. as well as in tropical waters.

Rear-fanged Land Snakes These include only the Brown or Red-banded Treesnake, Banana Snake and Salmon Snake, *Boiga irregularis*, found from the Kimberleys E to coastal N.S.W. (For classification *see under* SNAKES.) As the names imply their colours are variable, but usually pale brown to pinkish brown above, with thin bands of brown, red-brown or black, and a salmon-pink belly, and up to 1–2 m. They are fairly aggressive but the venom is not dangerous to man. They are nocturnal, living gregariously in hollow trees or crevices. Sometimes a specimen may be found in the morning coiled round a banana tree or in a birdcage, from which it cannot escape, having eaten the occupant. They normally eat geckoes, small birds, mammals and birds' eggs.

Rear-fanged Water Snakes (sub-family Homalopsinae) They include 4 genera, all producing young alive, almost entirely aquatic, and either diurnal or nocturnal, and recognisable by the valved nostrils on top of the snout. (For classification *see under* SNAKES.) Some tend to be aggressive, and to exude a smelly substance on handling, but their bite is only mildly harmful. Most occur in the far N in coastal tracts, and in the islands. 1. The Bockadam, *Cerberus rynchops australis*, has a broad head and is grey or olive with dark or black tiger-markings. 2. The Spotted Water-snake, *Enhydris punctata*, occurs in Cape York. 3. Macleay's Water-snake, *E. polyepis*, is found in NE Qld.; the White-bellied Mangrove Snake, *Fordonia leucobalia*, along the coast of N Aus.; and Richardson's Mangrove Snake, *Myron richardsoni*, along the coast of NW Aus.

Recherche, Archipelago of the W.A. 35S/123E Over 100 scattered, granitic and uninhabited islands extending 200 km. E–W, and formerly used by sealers and mainland graziers. They were named in 1792 by Bruny d'Entrecasteaux*, after one of his ships.

Red Gums A widespread group of some 30 species and varieties of Eucalypts*, with family resemblances: red timber and smooth bark peeling off in large strips or sheets to reveal red patches, broad juvenile and narrow to very narrow adult leaves, buds usually fairly sharply pointed at both ends and in bunches of up to 20, fruit usually about 6 mm. across and globular to bell-shaped, sometimes with points along the edges. They tend to have fairly specific habitats. The Forest Red Gum, *Eucalyptus tereticornis*, of wet areas from Gippsland, Vic., to N of Cairns, Qld., prefers rich alluvial flats, occasionally, but not frequently flooded. The very widespread River Red Gum, *E. camaldulensis*, grows on river flood-plains with high water-table over a great range of temperature and rainfall conditions from the Western Slopes of E Aus. to NW and SW W.A., interdigitating (and inter-breeding) in the far SW with the Flooded Gum, *E. rudis*, which retains the bark on trunk and larger branches. Blakely's Red Gum, *E. blakelyi*, is a tree of the better sandy loams of the savannah woodlands of the Western Slopes of N.S.W., not found along river courses, although sometimes on waterlogged flats; its timber is often used for construction purposes etc., being strong and durable, but much is split for fuel.

Red-back Spider (*Latrodectus mactans hasseltii*) In the Theridiidae family. Highly poisonous, small-bodied, with a globe-like abdomen and long thin legs. The adult female Red-back is black with 2 orange-red spots, or an 'hour-glass', on the back of the abdomen. The body is up to 6 mm. long, the first pair of legs spanning up to 2 cm. It is found in sheltered damp places in woodlands or houses, outhouses, basements etc., and has a tube-like retreat, an irregularly tangled snare, and vertical trap threads to the ground. The male is smaller. Not aggressive but will bite. A bite especially to a child, should have immediate treatment.

Red-back Spider, about 1½ times life size

Redcliffe Qld. 27S/153E (33,910 in 1971) A city on a peninsula 32 km. NE of Brisbane, but virtually continuous with it, and linked by a causeway over Bramble Bay. Oxley* selected this as the site of the first Qld. settlement (1824), but it was moved after a few months to the site of Brisbane, and the name 'Humpybong', implying deserted dwellings, was long applied to it. Now it is a growing commuter-holiday town.

Redfern, William (1774–1833) Transported (1801) for involvement in a British naval mutiny in 1797, was fully pardoned (1803) and after service on Norfolk Island was appointed assistant surgeon (1808) in the Sydney hospital. He established a considerable and popular private practice, until 1824, then farmed his 2,000 ac. (810 ha.) land grants near Liverpool. In 1821 he chaired an Emancipists'* meeting and, with Edward Eager, took the resulting successful petition to London in 1823. He was a friend of Macquarie, and Bigge was severely critical of his advancement. **Redfern,** a suburb of Sydney, was named after him.

Rees, Lloyd (1895–) b. Qld. An older but still admired contemporary artist, especially productive in Sydney in the 1940s, with a high level of achievement in his landscapes.

Reeve, Lake Vic. A long, narrow, shallow lagoon, between the intermediate and outermost coastal sandbarriers in the Gippsland Lakes*. It runs for about 64 km. behind the dunes of Ninety Mile Beach*, SW of Lakes Entrance, 38S/148E.

Referendum The Constitution* can only be amended by a Bill passed by both Houses, which has then been approved at a national referendum, showing an absolute majority, and a majority in the majority of States (i.e. at least 4). Voting has been compulsory since 1924. The device copies that of Switzerland (1874) where, however, referenda have been much more often affirmative than in Aus. Here, out of 25, only 4 have achieved affirmatives; a fifth, in 1967 with 2 sections was affirmed in 1 (giving the Commonwealth greater powers to legislate for Aborigines), but defeated over the amendment to alter the fixed relationship of numbers between the Senate and House of Representatives (*see* GOVERNMENT *and* ELECTORATES). Other successful referenda were: 1906 on detail of Senate elections; 1910, the taking over of public debts of States; 1928, to validate the important Financial Agreement with States (*see* FINANCE); 1946, to give the Commonwealth wide powers for social benefits (*see* SOCIAL SERVICES). The famous Conscription* Referenda were not on constitutional change. About two-thirds of the unsuccessful referenda concerned trade and commerce or industrial relations and employment.

Refrigeration and **Chilling Processes** These are important in the transport of perishable Aus. meat, dairy and fruit products to N hemisphere markets. Aus. contributors to the development include: James Harrison*, who built the first Aus. ice factory and sent the first (unsuccessful) shipment of frozen carcases in 1874; Norman Selfe (1839–1911), who designed ice-making machinery and worked for Thomas Sutcliffe Mort (1816–1878), an auctioneer and merchant who provided capital for refrigeration experiments carried out largely by Eugene Nicolle (1823–1902), a French migrant engineer who patented a number of ice-making machines from 1861–76. Augustus Morris (1820–1895) a pastoralist, tried hard to raise interest in Aus. and U.K. in refrigeration, and brought Mort and Nicolle together in about 1866. The first successful refrigerated cargo left Aus. in 1879.

Reibey, Mary (*née* **Haydock**) (1777–1855) b. Bury, Lancs. Eng. She was transported at the age of 13 for horse-stealing. She married Thomas Reibey (1769–1811), a soldier turned trader, and after his death continued to build up his business to become an extremely wealthy and admired citizen.

Reid, Sir George Houston (1845–1918) b. Johnstone, Lanarkshire, Scotland. He arrived in Aus. in 1852. Premier of N.S.W. (1894–9) and Prime Minister of Aus. (1904–5). He was particularly influential in having secondary and technical education measures passed, and pulled N.S.W. out of the 1890s' Depression by brilliant financial measures, including the first annual budgets. He was vigorously opposed to Federation*, protesting that it would damage N.S.W. free trade, and was dubbed 'Yes-No' Reid by the *Bulletin* in 1898 when an ambiguous, vacillating speech led to the initial defeat of the Federal Constitution Referendum in N.S.W. Reid led the Opposition in the first Federal Parliament and was Premier of a coalition briefly, after successively supporting Labor to defeat Deakin, and Deakin to defeat Labor in 1904. Later he was a British Member of Parliament (1916–18). Reid was physically gross but politically subtle, with plain but effective oratory.

RELIGIONS In 1971 86% of the populaation described itself as Christian, under 1% as having religions other than Christian (mainly Hebrew) and the remaining 13% gave no definite reply or stated that they had no religion. Within the Christians 31% were Church of England*, 28% Roman Catholic* (including those describing their religion as simply Catholic), 10% were Methodist* and about 9% Presbyterian*. Of the smaller remaining differentiated groups, the order was: Orthodox 3%, Baptist and Lutheran 1·5–2·0%, Churches of Christ 1%, Congregational 0·6% and small groups of Salvation Army*, Seventh Day Adventists* and Brethren*. In addition, a 1966 publication listed the following Aus. religious communities: Baha'i, Buddhists, Chinese Josshouses, Christadelphians, Christian Israelites, Christian Scientists*, Father Divine, Holiness Churches, House of David, Jehovah's Witnesses, Liberal Catholics, Mormons*, Meher Baba, Molokan Christian Holy Spiritual Jumpers, Muslims, 'New' Churches, New Apostolic Church, New Thought, Pentecostalists, People's Churches, Quakers*, Radio Church of God, Shalam, Sikhs*, Spiritualists, Templars Unitarians and Unity. The list testifies to great religious tolerance and an increasingly cosmopolitan population. The 2 major denominations, Anglican and Roman Catholic, are evenly spread throughout the social strata; this was not true in the 19th century when poorer communities were dominantly Catholic, and the richer, ruling group, Anglican. Protestants are a majority in rural areas. The early history of religion in Aus. was one of struggle for toleration and

church schools, especially by Roman Catholics, against the Church of Eng. which had some characteristics of an established Church until 1836 in N.S.W., including a monopoly of education*. This led to the unlikely but successful alliance of Irish Roman Catholics, Scots Presbyterians, and English Methodists. Other States began with the next phase in the parent colony, that of State aid for all denominations, which was first abrogated by S.A. in 1851. Increasing secularism and the Churches' fear of State intervention led to complete separation of Church and State by the time of Federation. Section 116 of the Constitution precludes any established Church, restrictions on religions or religious qualification for public employment. Since 1945 immigration has increased the membership of some groups, notably the strong Roman Catholic element. All the major Christian groups except Seventh Day Adventists and Mormons (from U.S.) and Lutherans and Orthodox (from Europe), are of British or Irish origin; few have a specifically Aus. character. Several are still directed from their original centres, but there is an increasing tendency towards autonomy. Aus. shares the general decay of the 20th-century Church as an influence on daily life or events and the modern ecumenical trends. Nevertheless, activity within missionary, educational and welfare spheres has been and remains important. *For further reading see* T. Van Sommers: *Religions in Australia* (Adelaide, 1966); L. Webb: *Churches in the Australian Community* (Melbourne Education Studies, 1958–9).

Remoras or **Suckerfish** Several species (genera *Echeneis* and *Remora*) are found in Aus. They are free-swimming or often attached to large sharks, marlin etc. by the powerful sucker on top of the head. There is fossil evidence that they have changed little over millions of years.

Renison Bell Tas. 42S/145E A tin-mining area worked since 1905, and now being greatly expanded, following major new discoveries of rich reserves, with new workings and separation plant and housing at Zeehan.

Renmark S.A. 34S/141E (3,277 in 1971) On the right bank of the Murray, the site of the first irrigation in S.A. (1877), managed since its near-failure in 1893 by an elected Irrigation Trust. Citrus, stone-fruit and vines are grown on 3,500 ha. of land irrigated by 4 main pumps. Packing of dried-fruit, canning, wine-making and distilling occupy a fluctuating labour-supply in the town, although grapes also go to the Barossa Valley* wineries.

Repatriation (of Servicemen) This also covers their rehabilitation, medical care, pensions, including those to surviving dependants, with educational help for children etc., and is controlled by the Commonwealth Repatriation Department, under the 1920 Repatriation Act. There are Repatriation hospitals in State capitals, and 6 auxiliary hospitals elsewhere, with Anzac Hostels in Qld. and Vic. for long term patients. Benefits cover Aus. service personnel of the Boer War, 1914–18 and 1939–45 Wars, Korean and Vietnam Wars, Malayan operations, Far East Strategic Reserve and Special Overseas Operations. Government assistance for Soldier Settlement* has also been important. Of many non-Government organisations, the R.S.L.* and Legacy* are notable.

Reptiles More technically the Class Reptilia. They include: Crocodiles*, Order Crocodylia (with 5-toed fore-feet and 4-toed, webbed hindfeet, as well as teeth in separate sockets, replaced on loss); Turtles* and Tortoises* Order Testudines, with their distinctive circular-plated carapace; the Lizards* and Snakes*, Order Squamata, or scaly reptiles; the lizard has teeth in a continuous groove or on the edge of the jaw (as distinct from the socketed teeth of the crocodiles), and most have well-marked legs and claws, whereas snakes are legless (though there are legless lizards and snakes—pythons—having vestigial legs). E. Worrell, *Reptiles of Aus.* (Sydney, 1964). H. Cogger, *Aus. Reptiles in Colour* (Sydney, 1967).

Returned Servicemen's League of Aus. The largest of the ex-service associations. With some 260,000 members recruited exclusively from men and women with overseas service, it is also a major pressure group, the only one with direct, formalised access to a Cabinet Committee. The motto is 'The price of liberty is eternal vigilance'. There are over 2,000 sub-branches, ranging from 30 or less members meeting in fairly crude premises, to palatial clubs run by sub-branches with 3,000 or more members. District branches may exist between the sub-branch and Branch level, the latter being the State organisation, with considerable autonomy. The National Congress, meeting annually, comprises 2 delegates from each Branch, except A.C.T. and Papua–N.G., who each send 1. The National Executive comprises the National President (elected), the full-time paid National Secretary, the Treasurer and the Branch Presidents. National Headquarters are in Canberra and are the source of most implementary and executive activity.

The functions of the R.S.L. are 3-fold: welfare, social and political. Much of the funds is used to provide housing and homes for ex-servicemen and their families, as well as medical help, clothing, funeral expenses, legal assistance etc. The local R.S.L. Club is a social focus with liquor licence and amusement facilities, particularly lavish in N.S.W. where poker machines provide finance. The political pressure group has 2 wings: problems relating to repatriated service personnel, notably pensions, land settlement etc. and broader issues of Aus. security, in which most attention is paid to defence, anti-Communism, immigration and a policy of self-sufficiency.

Historical Development In 1916 Returned Soldiers' associations in Vic., S.A., Tas. and Qld. federated, and were joined in 1917 by N.S.W. and in 1918 by W.A. The aims were to ensure fair treatment for returned men, to lend impetus to the war effort, and support conscription*. By 1919 it was a sufficiently consolidated body (then called the Returned Sailors', Soldiers' and Airmen's Imperial League of Aus.) and influential enough to attain the Government attention which it has retained. Between the Wars internal dissension, reaction against its militaristic image, and dwindling members caused some lessening of influence, but this was revived with the approach and outbreak of the 1939–45 War. Major success was achieved in repatriation problems after the 1914–18 War when Government acceptance of its responsibilities was less than it is now. Influence on national affairs has been less obviously successful. In addition to direct approach by written representation, deputation and personal interview, there is increasing indirect action through sympathetic politicians or organisations and by publicity. The declining numbers of 1914–18 War veterans is leading to slow change in the attitudes of the R.S.L., less devoted to 'Anzac'* memories; but the public image remains—a conservative, even reactionary and exclusive body as expressed by the expulsion in 1967 of 2 N.S.W. members for opposing the Aus. involvement in Vietnam—while the welfare work and moderate view of the majority are often overlooked. National Presidents: 1916 W. K. Bolton; 1919 Sir Gilbert Dyett, influential and controversial leader for 27 years; 1946 Sir Eric Millhouse; 1950 Sir George Holland; 1960 Sir Arthur Lee.

For further reading see G. L. Kristianson: *The Politics of Patriotism* (Canberra, 1966).

Reynella-Port Noarlunga S.A. 35S/138E (26,300 in 1971) A growing residential and service centre, with abattoirs and wine-making based on farming in the Mt. Lofty Range to the E.

Rice (*Oryza sativa*) It occupies about 32,000 ha., with among the highest yields in the world. First commercially grown at Yanco*, N.S.W., in 1925, it is now almost all produced as a rotation with wheat and pasture for fat lambs, in the irrigated lands of the Riverina*. Some is grown in the Townsville area, Qld. High water demands, drainage problems and dangers of over-production have led to controlled acreage and marketing. There is some export to Papua-New Guinea. Rice-growing in the N has not so far been encouraging (*see* ORD *and* FITZROY RIVERS *and* HUMPTY DOO).

Rice Flower A popular name for various species of *Pimelea* in the Thymelaeaceae family, mainly African, but including the garden *Daphne*. The Slender Rice Flower or Buttons, *P. linifolia*, grows on sandy country in coastal E Aus., has pairs of heath-like leaves and a compound flower-head of 4-petalled, pink-white small flowers with bright orange stamens in a sheath of 4 broad smooth green bracts.

Rice-grass (*Oryza australiensis*) A common swamp grass of N Aus. which is a rice botanically.

Richardson, Henry Handel (1870–1946) The pen-name of Mrs. Ethel Florence Robertson (née Richardson). She was born in Melbourne, the daughter of an Irish doctor. While acknowledging her a leading novelist, critics are uncertain of her place in Aus. literature, as she wrote entirely as an expatriate, and 2 only of her novels have Aus. settings. She spent an unhappy Aus. childhood, when her father, at first a failure and then successful, later became insane, and she spent unhappy years in a

Melbourne girls' school. She left for Europe at 17 and returned only once in 1912. Her husband was London University's first Professor of German. A slow painstaking writer, preoccupied with failure and tragedy, her work is detailed and relies on personal experience very largely, often backed with detailed historical research. Thus, *Maurice Guest* (1908) is an intense emotional tragedy based in Germany; *The Getting of Wisdom* (1910), on her unhappy schooldays; the monumental trilogy *The Fortunes of Richard Mahoney* (1917–1929), on her father as a failure who can fit into neither Aus. nor Eng. Her identity was only revealed with publication of its final volume.

Richmond N.S.W. 34S/151E (11,357 in 1971 with Windsor*) One of 5 towns founded by Macquarie in 1810 to be above the troublesome Hawkesbury* floods. For long a market-gardening centre, it is now within easy commuting distance of Sydney. There are food-processing and textile factories, and an agricultural college.

Richmond Qld. 21S/143E A small sheep and rail town on the W Slopes.

Richmond Tas. 43S/147E In a long-established farming area, it has one of the oldest bridges still extant (1823).

Richmond River N.S.W. 260 km. long, flowing through 100–150 cm. rainfall country, with an average annual flow of over 1,200 million m.^{3} at Casino, 29S/153E. It flows S then E from the McPherson Range* on the Qld. border to the sea at Ballina, from rain-forest country, then wet sclerophyll* to the Big Scrub* on basalt, now largely cleared for dairying, sugar and bananas. It carries river traffic residual of the formerly important trade (especially while cedar was being exploited) as far upstream as Casino.

Rickards, Harry (1845–1911) Stage name of a comedian and theatrical entrepreneur (his real name was Leete). He was born in London, Eng. He toured Aus. in 1871 and 1885, and stayed to develop the 'Tivoli Circuit' of music halls throughout all the States.

Ringbarking The process of killing trees by checking their sap-flow by cutting out a broad strip of bark. It has been used extensively to clear grazing land. The dead trees may later be felled and burned, but many Aus. landscapes have their skeletons.

Ringer The leading shearer in the wool shed, also an expert stockman. In general, something excellent of its kind, which is the meaning of the Yorkshire dialect word from which it has come.

Ripon Regulations (1831) Stopped free land grants, replacing them with a payment of 5 shillings per ac.

Risdon Cove Tas. 43S/147E On the E bank of the Derwent estuary, 10 km. above Hobart, was the site chosen by Bowen in 1803 for settlement, but in 1804 Collins changed it to Sullivan's Cove, now the heart of Hobart. Risdon Cove is now a wooded region, with Risdon Vale, a residential suburb, just inland.

Riverina, The N.S.W. The area between the Murray and the Lachlan, and W of a curving boundary varying, but not farther E than a belt connecting Condobolin, 33S/147E, Junee, 35S/148E, Wagga Wagga, 35S/147E, and Albury, 36S/147E. In the past it has been applied to the interfluve between the Murray and Darling. The origin of the name is ascribed to the Rev. John Dunmore Lang*. The region has some feeling of regional identity, finding expression in demands for a university. New State etc. Yet it is part of the great wheat-sheep belt, with increasing tendency towards more intensive rotations, and even for fat-lamb production to oust wheat production, in wetter E areas. Irrigation, mainly for wheat and sheep, with some rice production, extends along the N.S.W. side of the Murray from opposite Cobram to

Swan Hill*, Vic., 35S/144E. Farther N is the Murrumbidgee Irrigation Area*, and S of the Murrumbidgee lies the new irrigation area of Coleambally*. The region has seen all stages of settlement and all degrees of intensity of land use, from very large squatter properties for extensive grazing of fine wool sheep, to wheat-sheep production often on sub-divided properties, tending towards greater intensification, and irrigated properties of various degrees of intensity down to very small fruit- and vegetable-growing farms. *For further reading see* R. B. Ronald: *The Riverina: Land, People and Properties* (Melbourne, 1960).

Rivers Aus. rivers are very limited in proportion to the country's size, for the arid climate of the centre has only occasionally flowing desert watercourses leading to salt-flats seldom flooded as lakes. Resources are concentrated in the extreme SW of W.A. and in E Aus. In E Central and N Aus. flow is seasonal. (*See* WATER RESOURCES.)

Roads Aus. roads carry 80% of the passengers and 75% of the freight. They are good when total mileage is related to population, but not to the increasing number of vehicles, and vary from the beginnings of metropolitan and inter-metropolitan expressways and well-surfaced bitumen roads on most of the most important traffic flows, to all-weather gravel roads generally well bridged and culverted, and dirt roads of varying qualities, generally quite adequate in the prevailing climate and in mainly level country. The total Aus. road length in 1970 was 879,158 km.: bitumen or concrete 187,685; gravel

etc. 212,568; 478,905 formed or cleared only. Most are often fairly narrow in relation to characteristically high driving speeds and associated with heavy casualty rates, especially from head-on collisions. In addition to State management of main roads, Commonwealth grants are given in proportion to size, population and vehicles. Minor roads are a local authority responsibility.

Classification varies between States, as do the characteristics and problems of the road network. There is a rather intensive development in most of Vic. and much of Tas., a large variation between more and less developed areas in N.S.W., S.A. and especially W.A. Qld. has a fairly even network of moderate quality, mainly gravel roads. In N.T. the few tentacles of bitumen roads are supplemented by gravel Beef Roads.

The Aus. Road Research Board (1960) which became a public company in 1965, plans research and development and publishes *Aus. Road Research*.

Historical Development Convict labour built the first road systems and was in demand for this purpose by States without convicts (S.A. and W.A.) up to and even beyond the mid-19th century. As the use of convicts ceased, central control of roads lessened and some form of district board took over. The railways spread only tentacles, not a net, so only slightly damped the development of roads (and of coach services such as Cobb & Co.*). The motor age brought quickening of effort, with much Commonwealth help on through roads. With the 1939–45 War came strategic roads, in the central N

Roads in km. 1970	Qld.	N.S.W.	Vic.	S.A.	W.A.	Tas.	N.T.
Bitumen or concrete	32,197	53,590	50,273	15,174	23,358	6,229	3,712
Stone or gravel	30,021	66,654	46,011	29,925	23,916	13,691	1,946
Earth formation	64,267	45,070	33,126	12,219	43,692	} 2,134 {	2,923
Cleared only	64,266	42,277	32,272	63,147	62,576		10,890

(Darwin–Alice Springs, Mt. Isa–Tennant Creek), or a safe distance inland, as alternatives to vulnerable coast roads (e.g. the Putty road from the Hawkesbury River to the Hunter River, N.S.W.). Since the Second World War, numbers and speeds of private cars have greatly increased, along with freight movements by articulated 'semitrailers' (and in the N by road-trains). Inter-state movements are free of road tax, but not generally intra-state journeys (see TRANSPORT).

Governor Phillips had the first proper road made in the first year of settlement (1788), connecting his house (near the present Bridge Street–Phillip Street intersection) with Dawes Battery, and later that year the first road to Rose Hill (Parramatta). Phillip's enlightened ideas, including a network of 200-ft. (60 m.) streets for the infant city, were unfortunately not fulfilled, and Sydney's streets crowded in upon the first rough tracks inland from Sydney Cove. Roads gave continual trouble under Governor Hunter, and only under Macquarie* (1810–22) did real progress begin, while with the 1830s came many advances under the notable Surveyor-General T. L. Mitchell*. In 1858 in N.S.W. came the Main Roads Management Act and a great deal of improvement under Captain B. H. Martindale (actually engaged as Commissioner of Railways). In 1863 the Central Road Board gave way to local government control, but in 1925 came the motor-age reaction in the Department of Main Roads. In Tas. Macquarie sent Meehan* to construct a N–S highway, Lieutenant-Governor Arthur improved the system, and by 1850, Denison had bequeathed a Hobart–Launceston road, convict-built, which lasted apart from maintenance until the bitumen highway of 1934. In Vic., as elsewhere, the gold-rush showed the inadequacy of the roads and under La Trobe and the Act of 1853 improvements began. Later with local authority responsibility, conditions became more patchy. In S.A. road improvement progressed slowly for lack of a regular supply of convict labour, while the Central Road Board of 1848 was hamstrung by the labour shortage of the gold-rush period and in 1853 responsibility swung back to the District Road Boards with varying progress. In W.A. so few roads had been properly constructed by 1850 that the late convict phase of 1850–60 was largely actuated by the demand for a convict road labour-force. Then, as elsewhere, District Road Boards took over. In Qld. development came rather late, with only one road W from Brisbane in 1852, municipal action from 1864, and 74 District Boards from 1879, supplemented from 1920 by a Main Roads Board (later Department).

Road Trains, in which a prime mover heavy cattle truck pulls several more unpowered trucks, have along with Beef Roads revolutionised cattle transport in the last 20 years.

Robe S.A.37S/140E (440 in 1971). A wool port and society centre in the heyday of the squatters in the late 19th century; its trade was drawn off to Adelaide, Portland and Melbourne. Thousands of Chinese landed here and walked to the gold-fields to avoid Vic. poll tax.

Robe, Frederick Holt (1800–1871) Lt.-Governor of S.A. (1845–7), where his military autocratic rule provoked quarrels with the Council over State aid to religion, and mining royalties.

Roberts, Thomas William (Tom) (1856–1931) b. Dorchester, Eng. He arrived in Aus. in 1869. An artist. After studying art in Melbourne, he went to London from 1881–5 and returned to initiate a new approach to painting in Aus., of the Heidelberg School*. Famous works include 'Baled Up', a gold escort robbery, and 'Bourke Street, Melbourne', full of impressions of action and an Aus. atmosphere.

Robe River W.A. 22S/116E Major iron field (Mt. Enid) exporting to Japan (1972) from Cape Lambert.

Robertson, Sir John (1816–1891) b. London. He arrived in Aus. in 1820. Premier of N.S.W. from 1860–1, 1868–70, 1875–7 and 1885–6. Although becoming a wealthy squatter*, Robertson was convinced of the need for agricultural development and free selection (*see* LAND TENURE), and fought in both Houses for the passage of his Land Acts. His individual appearance and a speech defect made him a well-known figure in the noisy personal debates of the day. He was a rival of Parkes*; his reference to Vic. as a 'cabbage-garden' was long remembered with resentment.

Robertson, Sir Macpherson (1860–1945) b. Ballarat. He worked as a boy in confectionery in Scotland and Melbourne, during difficult family circumstances, and rose to make a great fortune from sweet manufacture. He became a benefactor of many charities and also of Antarctic exploration and in the cause of aviation. His gift of £100,000 for the centenary of Vic. in 1934 was accompanied by £15,000 for prizes in one of the most influential of the Air Races*, and with the pioneer airman H. C. Miller*, he initiated the MacRobertson-Miller air service (*see* AIRLINES).

Robins The Aus. species are not related to the European robin of the Christmas cards, but have something of the same appeal and peri-domestic association; there are a dozen or so species of several genera, mainly of quiet dark colours but with smart white patches, or yellow or reddish breasts. They are about 10–18 cm. long, somewhat stocky in shape, and often perch on a post or stump, flying down quickly to pick up insects from the ground. The red and yellow robins often hold their tails vertically, and the latter clings flat to a tree trunk if disturbed. The calls are mainly repeated single notes. Nests are well-finished small cups of grass, bark, horse-hair, cobwebs etc., often in a tree-fork. Species include: the Yellow Robin, *Eopsaltria* (dawn harpist) *australis*, of E and the S of Aus.; the Little Yellow Robin, *E. kempi*, of Qld., and the rather greyer Western Yellow Robin, *E. griseogularis* (grey-throated), of W.A. and the SW of S.A. The male of the Hooded, Pied or Black-and-white Robin, *Petroica cucullata* (hooded black dryad), shows his smart plumage over open woodland terrain in much of inland Aus.; his mate is relatively dowdy. The hen of the Scarlet Robin, *Petroica* (rock-house) *multicolor*, has a reddish breast, and the cock is black and white and bright red; this robin extends over the E and S of Aus., including Tas., and some SW Pacific Islands (*see* PLATE 3). The Red-capped Robin, *P. goodenovii*, of much of inland Aus. has a modest brown and brownish-white hen, but the cock is black-and-white with a bright red cap and upper breast. The White-breasted Robin of the S of W.A., *Quoyornis georgianus*, clings to tree trunks, while searching for insects. The Mangrove Robin, *Q. leucurus* (white-tailed), of the far N of Aus., is a modest little bird with a greenish-black back and white under-parts, introducing the habits and cup-nest of the group into the mangrove habitat.

Robinson, George Augustus (1789–1866) b. London. He arrived in Aus. in 1824, to follow his building trade, and was noted as conciliator and protector of Aborigines. A Methodist lay preacher, Robinson was appointed by Governor Arthur to look after the Bruny Island Aborigines (1829–30) and from 1830–4 to make a series of 6 unarmed missions which took him all over the island and succeeded in bringing a few hundred of the decimated tribes to the Bass Str. Islands reserves, where tragically they died out. Robinson kept meticulous field notes as he worked with evangelical zeal at his lost cause; they are edited by N. J. B. Plomley in *Friendly Mission* (Hobart, 1966). His term as Aborigine Protector, Port Phillip District (1839–49), had little impact.

Robinson, Sir Hercules George Robert (1824–1897) b. Rosmead, Co. Westmeath, Ireland. Created 1st Baron Rosmead in 1896, and Governor of N.S.W. from 1872–9. His period in N.S.W. was part of a long career in colonial governorship which included N.Z. and S Africa. His brother, **Sir William Cleaver Francis** (1834–1897), was an equally effective Governor, and was in W.A. from 1880–3 and 1890–5, and in S.A. 1883–9. He was popular in both States and also in an interim period in Vic.

Robinson, Michael Massey (1747–1826) b. Eng. He was transported in 1798 for blackmail, and served in important legal and clerical positions in N.S.W. dishonestly. He was half jestingly referred to as the colony's Poet Laureate, being the author of the first separately published Aus. verse (1810) which were odes of poor quality on people and events.

Robinson, Roland (1912–) b. Ireland. He arrived in Aus. in 1921, a poet of some stature, who had developed the Jindyworobak* theme by concentrating on Aus. landscapes and the Aborigines, whose legends appear in *Legend and Dreaming* (Sydney, 1952) and *Black-Feller, White-Feller* (Sydney, 1958). A collection of poems is *Tumult of the Swans* (Sydney, 1953).

Rock Art This work by Aus. Aborigines is found in many parts of the continent, often best preserved in caves or on overhanging precipices. It includes both paintings and punctured or grooved engravings of a wide variety of complexity from very simple and crude forms to highly complex representations—sometimes remarkable for breadth and sweep of colour,

sometimes for vigorous action, such as in a hunting scene, sometimes for elaborate and meticulous detail, representation or decoration reminiscent of the bark-paintings*. To sift out the successive cultures, usually progressing from simpler to more complex forms, in caves used—not always continuously —over many centuries, is a task for the skilled anthropologist or archaeologist and even so has a large and controversial literature of its own. Interestingly, the modern Aborigines of W Arnhem Land attribute distinctive single-line figures to a thin-bodied fairy people called Mimis, living in rock clefts.

The paintings and engravings include: 1. stencils, often of a hand (rarely decorated within the outline); 2. representations of human or anthropomorphic spiritual figures; 3. local animals of all kinds, but especially those of significance for totemism and (closely linked) food supply, often observed in relation to their habits, seasonal cycle and environment; 4. mythological resembling neither human nor animal forms; 5. material culture—implements, weapons, ritual objects etc.; 6. linear designs such as concentric circles or spirals; and 7. indeterminate figures identifiable only by local Aborigines where these still survive. *For further reading see* F. D. McCarthy: *Aboriginal Rock Art in Australia* (Sydney, 1962).

Rock-cods They include members of more than one family of fish, and are found mainly in tropical Aus. reefs, generally lying very still among rocks, ready to pounce on unwary fish, crabs etc.; they mostly have large mouths for this purpose, and are often able to change colour easily as camouflage. The family Epinephelidae includes several species of the genus *Epinephelus*, such as the Black Rock-cod, *E. dameli*, the Wire-netting Cod, *E. merra*, the proverbially almost inedible Wirrah, *Acanthistius serratus*, and the large and dangerous Queensland Groper, *Promicrops lanceolatus*; the Coral Cod, *Plectropomus maculatus*, of the Barrier Reef has beautiful blue spots on scarlet, pink, brown or grey sides. For the Red Rock-cod *see* SCORPION-FISH.

Rockhampton Qld. 23S/151E (48,188 in 1971) A city and port 80 km. upstream from the mouth of the Fitzroy River. It developed as a starting point for the abortive Canoona gold-rush (1858) and was further stimulated by the rush to Peak Downs (1861) and to Mt. Morgan (1882). The major factor, however, was the building (1867) of the railway, using easy gaps and gradients over the Divide out of the Fitzroy basin to tap the W pastoral lands. Port Alma* now handles all shipping. Industries include meatworks, cotton-ginning, railway workshops, fruit-canning and service industries. Exports are meat, wool and minerals (from Mt. Morgan). The town has a growth rate below the national average, owing to technical drawbacks of the port, the general decline of coastal shipping and to the development of Gladstone*.

Rocklands Dam Vic. On the zig-zag westerly course of the upper Glenelg* from the Grampians, before it turns S to Discovery Bay. It lies about 12 km. E of Balmoral, 37S/142E. The reservoir is of 65 km.^{2} and over 300 million m.^{3}, supplying the Wimmera-Mallee domestic and stock system, along with other reservoirs on the Wimmera River.

Rodents, Indigenous Native rodents are among the most numerous and important of the indigenous terrestrial mammalian fauna other than the Monotremes* and Marsupials*. Placental mammals, they have come to Aus. by sea—perhaps on driftwood or even in the boats of early man; some, such as the water-rats appear to have evolved important characteristics in the Aus. environment, so they are taken to be truly indigenous. The indigenous rodents are all of the family Muridae,

the rats and mice (cf. Marsupial Mice and Rats).

I The Sub-family Hydromyinae includes 2 genera. 1. The genus *Hydromys* has evolved aquatic characteristics in Aus.

Eastern Water-rat
(*Hydromys chrysogaster*), *about one-eighth scale*

This large burrowing animal (30 cm. head and body length) is well streamlined, particularly the flat head which is adapted to search for prey under stones in the water. The molars have concave crushing surfaces to deal with a diet of mussels, snails, crayfish etc. The fur is short, close and seal-like. The broad paddle-like feet are partly webbed and the toes modified. Large bivalves may be placed on 'tables' in the sun to open. Young duck and often small birds and occasionally larger adult birds are sometimes killed. At times there has been exterminatory trapping, especially when there is a fall in supplies of American muskrat skins. There are 2 species, the Eastern Water-rat, *Hydromys chrysogaster*, and the Western or Sooty Water-rat, *Hydromys fuliginosus*. 2. The False Water-rat, *Xeromys myoides*, reported from the Mackay area, Qld., 21S/149E, is described by Troughton as an aquatic-feeding land rat, the dentition of which shows evolution towards the concave molars of the true water-rats, and so helps to confirm the view that the genus *Hydromys* has evolved in Aus.

II The sub-family Murinae includes the more typical terrestrial or climbing rats and mice, with 3 ridged grinding molars on each side as against the 2 hollow molars of the Water-rats. 1. The genus *Rattus*, the typical rat of popular usage, includes some 16 indigenous species, normally open country animals, unobtrusive and usually harmless, often vegetarian. Though slower breeding than the introduced species, some indigenous species have been known to multiply to pest proportions, as in the Gulf Country in 1869–70, when continuous rains increased vegetation, and therefore rodent food, abnormally. The indigenous species the dusky Field Rat, *R. conatus*, is known to be implicated in the disease cycle of Leptospirosis*. The involvement of native rodents in the cycle causing Scrub Typhus* is important in N.G. and to a small extent in Qld.

Other rats in this genus include: 1. the Allied Rat, *R. assimilis*, so called from its general resemblance to the introduced urban rats, though slighter in build; widespread in hilly bush country in E Aus.; 2. the Western Swamp-rat, *R. fuscipes*, of the SW of Aus.; and the Eastern Swamp-rat, *R. lutreolus*, of S and E Aus., both vegetarian species maintaining tunnel-like runways through swamp vegetation.

A large number of species of more delicately built rodents from the size of small rats down to mice is now grouped in 4 genera: *Pseudomys*, *Thetomys*, *Leggadina* and *Gyomys*.

Other genera of native rodents include: 1. the Broad-toothed Rats, *Mastacomys*, of hill country in Tas. and SE Aus.; 2. the Thick-tailed Rats, *Laomys*, from the desert centre of Aus. (the tail does not store fatty tissue as was at first assumed); 3. *Mesembriomys* and *Conilurus*, perhaps better termed Rabbit-rats as a popular name, rather than Jerboa-rats as formerly, for they lack the very long hind feet and kangaroo-like gait of the foreign jerboas or of Aus. jerboa-like marsupials; 4. the Stick-nest Rats, *Leporillus*, described from the Murray-Darling

area, by Mitchell in 1838 and Sturt in 1844, but probably common now only in the Nullarbor; 5. *Notomys* and *Ascopharynx*, the smaller long-footed species which closely resemble the foreign jerboas, hopping very fast and nimbly in lightly wooded, often semi-arid country or actual desert, and digging tiny burrows, sometimes shared, surprisingly, with the superficially similar but carnivorous Marsupial Mouse*, *Antechinomys*; 6. the Naked-tailed Rats, genus *Melomys*, and the Giant Naked-tailed Rats, genus *Uromys*, of sub-tropical and especially tropical E Aus. and the islands, which are particularly adapted to climbing.

Rodents, Introduced They comprise the 2 rat species closely connected with man, his warehouses, houses and especially seaports, *Rattus rattus*, the Ship or Black Rat (often, in fact, brownish-grey), and *R. norvegicus*, the Sewer, Brown or Norway Rat; and also the familiar more or less domestic mouse *Mus musculus*, though it has, more than the rats, 'gone bush' to compete with indigenous species. No doubt these have come as stowaways on ships. Apart from the enormous damage they do to food every year, there are years of serious mouse plagues, as in the S.A. wheat country in 1916–17, and quite frequently on a more local scale.

Rodeos. Over 100 rough riding rodeos take place a year; riders follow a circuit which culminates in the National Finals Rodeo for the top 15.

Roebourne W.A. 21S/117E (1,395 in 1971). Established as a centre for copper-mining from 1872 and the Pilbra* gold-field, declared 1888, it lost its supremacy when a rail was built to its rival Port Hedland in 1912, but may be reviving. The small ghost town* port of Cossack, a former pearling centre, is N of it.

Roma Qld. 27S/149E (5,860 in 1971) Situated in stock-rearing country, but with local grapes and some wine-production, is famed for its natural gas, first known in 1900, used for local power generation, and now piped to Brisbane. Oil reserves in the Roma field are estimated at 5 million barrels. Oil is also piped to Brisbane.

Roman Catholic Church With some 3,443,000, this is the second largest denomination, and shows the most rapid increase, largely through immigration of Europeans, estimated at well over 500,000 since 1947. The hierarchy comprises 8 archbishops and 29 bishops. The early struggle for freedom to worship by the predominantly Roman Catholic Irish elements in N.S.W. (30% of the population in 1828) colouring the subsequent role the Church played, of generally anti-English, and pro-working class influence, led to support of the Aus. Labor Party* in its early days. Since 1950 the lay Catholic Social Movement under Santamaria has been directed against Communism and was partially instrumental in the formation of the Democratic Labor Party*. Catholic Action, with direct Church support publishes wide ranging guides on every-day issues.

The first Mass was held in 1803 by an emancipated Irish political prisoner priest; the Castle Hill Rising* led to withdrawal of the privilege, and until the arrival of the Rev. J. J. Therry* and Rev. P. Connolly in 1820 only clandestine celebrations were possible. Under direction from Cape Town, the first Aus. hierarchy was established in 1842; the first Aus. Cardinal (1885) was Rev. P. F. Moran*; the first Aus.-born Cardinal is the present Archbishop of Sydney, N. T. Gilroy (1896–). An Apostolic Delegate was first appointed in 1914. Still rated as a Mission Church in Rome, there are 25 Dioceses. Eminent figures are described in T. R. Luscombe's *Builders and Crusaders*

(Melbourne, 1967). *For further reading see* J. N. Moloney: *The Roman Mould of the Australian Catholic Church* (Melbourne, 1969) and P. O'Farrell: *The Catholic Church in Australia* (Sydney, 1969).

Roper River N.T. 15S/134E About 400 km. long and with a catchment of 60,000 km.², it forms the S boundary of Arnhem Land*. Its upper valley is followed for over 80 km. by the Stuart Highway* and the N Aus. Railway; it then turns E, flowing (with a large summer increase) to Limmen Bight in the Gulf of Carpentaria. Many N bank tributaries rise in the rugged Arnhem Land Plateaux in which they have cut steep forested groove-like valleys. There are several Mission Stations along the valley caring for Aborigines, for whom the region is a reserve. It is navigable by 200-ton motor vessels for 130 km.

Rose, Iain Murray (1939–) b. Birmingham, Eng. He arrived in Aus. in 1941. One of the world's greatest swimmers, using a very fast crawl with minimal leg movement. He won the 1,500 m. and 400 m. at the 1956 Olympic Games and retained the 400 m. in 1960. He was described as a great strategist with a versatile range; and was noted for his strictly vegetarian diet.

Rose Mallow or **Rose of Sharon** Names sometimes used for Aus. *Hibiscus*, especially garden varieties.

Rose, Mervyn (1933–) b. Coffs Harbour. A left-handed high-speed tennis player, outstanding during the 1950s, winning many European and U.S. singles and the Wimbledon doubles in 1954 with R. M. Hartwig, and playing in Davis Cup matches in 1951 and 1957. He turned professional in 1959.

Rosebery Tas. 42S/146E (2,381 in 1971) An expanding company mining town based on ores worked at Rosebery and Hercules mines and at Williamsford, 5 km. to the S, and Tullah to the NE for zinc (60%), lead

(20%) and silver-gold (20%). The zinc is refined at Risdon (Hobart) and the lead sent by the private Emu Bay railway to Burnie for export to U.S.

Rosella, Native A popular name for the fodder-yielding *Hibiscus* heterophyllus.*

Rosellas The medium-sized, long-tailed Parrots*, which live mainly in forest, eating seeds and berries, though some raid orchards. They include the Eastern Rosella, *Platycercus eximius,* with white-checked red head, green body with blue-edged wings and tail, with a red patch near the vent; the yellow-checked Western Rosella, *P. icterotis*; the blue-winged Yellow or Northern Rosella, *P. flaveolus,* of the NW, and the Pale-headed Rosella, *P. adscitus,* of E Qld. There are several Ring-necked Parrots of the genus *Barnardius,* mainly green with yellow collars. The name Rosella is said to be from Rosehill, an early name for Parramatta.

Rosemary, Coast (*Westringia rosmarinifolius*) In the world-wide Labiatae family. It is a narrow-leaved compact white-flowered shrub of the E Aus. coasts, quite similar in habit and appearance to the European Rosemary, *Rosmarinus officinalis.*

Roses They are not native to Aus. though some other Rosaceae are, e.g. *Acaena, Rubus* and *Geum.* However, an old-fashioned garden rose, the briar rose, has escaped and is a pest and in places has been declared a noxious weed. Native Rose is used for an almost heath-like Boronia* of SE Aus. The term Dog Rose, used for a hedge rose in Britain, but in Aus. for one of the Saxifragaceae family, *Bauera rubioides,* is a scrambling to erect shrub, to 2 m. high, with spreading hands of heath-like sharp leaves spaced along the branching stem, and many-petalled pink-white flowers.

Rosewall, Ken (1934–) b. Sydney. A tennis champion. He played for Aus. in Davis Cup matches from 1953–6, and won the Wimbledon doubles with

Hoad* in 1956, after which he turned professional. He won the Aus. Open in 1971 for the third time.

Rossarden Tas. 41S/148E Houses workers on the Aberfoyle tin-wolfram mine (1932) which is at 762 m. on Ben Lomond with works over 396 m. deep. There is a second mine at Storey's Creek nearby.

Rossi, Francis Nicholas (1776–1851) b. Corsica. He arrived in Aus. first in 1819, having joined the British Army after their capture of Corsica in 1795. He returned to N.S.W. from Mauritius when appointed Police Superintendent (1824–34). He was vigorous and efficient, but handicapped by lack of funds and recruits.

Rottnest Island W.A. A fragment of the coastal limestone with inland salt-lakes and sand-cover. It lies 20 km. NW of Fremantle and extends 11 km. E–W and up to 5 km. N–S. It was named Rottnest in 1696 by de Vlamingh from the small rat-like wallabies or quokkas* which abound, although it was known to earlier Dutch navigators. An Aboriginal penal settlement was followed by a children's reformatory and wartime military installations. Now a Board controls the island for limited holiday development, excluding the use of private vehicles.

Rough Riding or **Buck-jumping** This has become a popular spectator attraction at rodeos, with professional riders. It dates from the 1890s, centred on Warwick*, Qld., and the most famous family taking part was the Skuthorpes.

Rough-scaled or **Clarence River Snake** (*Tropidechis carinatus*) A large broad-headed snake of the central coast of E Aus. inland to the Great Divide, a partly nocturnal predator on frogs and mice, often found near water. A bite from a large specimen causes at least an acute illness.

Roundworms—*see* HELMINTHS.

Rowcroft, Charles (1781–1850) Was in Tas. from 1821–5 and wrote numerous poor novels, 3 with Aus. settings of which one was very popular in England: *Tales of the Colonies*, written as propaganda for emigration. It is an incident-packed success story which long coloured the English view of Aus.

Rowing A very popular sport with eight-oared championships for the Kings Cup held in each state in turn. The federal controlling body is the Aus. Rowing Council. (*See also* SCULLING.) Rowing dates from early in Aus. history; the first recorded race was in Sydney Harbour in 1818.

R.S.L. Returned Servicemen's League of Australia*.

R.S.S. and A.I.L.A. Returned Sailors', Soldiers' and Airmen's Imperial League of Aus., the name, until 1965 of the ex-service association, the Returned Servicemen's League of Aus.*, which is retained by some branches.

Rugby The game is played mainly in N.S.W. and Qld. It began with **Rugby Union,** played with 15 men a side, and started in Sydney University in 1864, followed by many clubs. There was a decline after the formation of the Rugby League in 1907, but with some inter-war and notably, post-1945 revival, especially in country areas. The first English team came in 1888, but an Aus. team did not visit Eng. until 1908; it is generally known as the Wallabies. Of 12 Test Series 1899–1959 Aus. won 2. In 5 exchanges with S Africa Aus. has won 5 out of 17 games, but no rubbers. Tests have been played against N.Z. since 1903. The Thornett brothers are leading names.

Rugby League dates from 1907 when a secession from Union, largely led by Trumper* the cricketer, sought to introduce payment for players. 2 forwards were dispensed with, making 13 players, and scrums replaced line-outs. The Test series with Eng. since 1908–9 have given (to 1973) 30 Aus. wins and 5 draws out of 79 games. Aus. won World Cup 1970. The overseas team is known as the Kangaroos. In Aus. it is the main football code in N.S.W., backed by social clubs financed by poker machines. Four great names are: H. H. (Dally) Messenger (d. 1959) and, post-war, Reg Gasnier, Johnny Raper and Graham Langlands.

Rum Hospital It was built in Macquarie Street, Sydney (1810–16), by contractors D'Arcy Wentworth and 2 prominent emancipists* William Broughton and Garnham Blaxcell, and Alexander Riley a wealthy landowning free settler, in return for a 3-year monopoly of rum-importing (other than Government import or by those licensed prior to 1810), extended to 1814. The long 2-storeyed building had a wide verandah supported by thick columns. Associated buildings have survived (part is incorporated in Parliament House), but the main site is occupied by Sydney Hospital.

Rum Jungle N.T. 13S/131E A mine and mining area opened for uranium, discovered in 1949 by J. M. White. Latterly production was stock piled then ceased. Deposits of silver/lead have been established and there is also copper. Workers live at Batchelor*. The name is said to date from the hectic rum-drinking gold-rush days.

Rum Rebellion A nickname given later to the events of January 1808, when Governor Bligh* was arrested and deposed from office by Major Johnston*, at the request of a number of officers of the N.S.W. Corps and settlers, led by John Macarthur*. The name derives from one of the immediate causes, the illegal importation of stills, and from the N.S.W. Corps' monopoly of all spirits, known indiscriminately as rum. Bligh had arrested Macarthur for failing to provision his ship *Parramatta*, thus forcing the sailors to come ashore, an illegal act; Macarthur's action had been a rejoinder to Bligh's demand of £900 bond for the earlier escape of a convict on the ship. Macarthur, with the support of 6 officers, questioned Atkins's* competence to try him; Bligh threatened them with treason charges; and Johnston ordered Macarthur's release. The N.S.W. Corps trained its guns on Government House and Johnston was petitioned to take over. Bligh refused to resign and was arrested, along with Robert Campbell* and Atkins. Bligh was upheld at Johnston's subsequent court martial in London, but the relatively light sentence indicated some sympathy with the rebels. *For further reading see* H. V. Evatt: *Rum Rebellion* (Sydney 1938).

Rusden, George William (1819–1903) b. Surrey, Eng. He arrived in Aus. in 1835. From 1849–51 he was the official Agent for promotion of the newly founded National Schools. He rode over 16,000 km., finding and building on widespread enthusiasm in spite of clerical opposition. Later, as a Vic. civil servant (1853–62), he largely saved the National Schools there from extinction. After returning to Eng. he published the first serious attempt at a history of Aus. which, although biased and not always accurate, was a major contribution. *For further reading see* C. G. Austin: *George William Rusden and National Education* (Melbourne, 1958).

Ruse, James (1760–1837) b. Launceston, Eng. He was transported with the First Fleet for burglary. Phillip* used his evident farming ability and industry to probe the possibilities of self-sufficient small-scale farming; this Ruse did by 1791, and was rewarded by being given the title to his 'Experimental Farm', the first land grant in the colony at Parramatta.

Rushes Swamp plants of the family Juncaceae, often grouped with the Sedges* (Cyperaceae), and the southern family Restionaceae. Common Aus. Rushes are the Basket Club-rush, *Scirpus validus*, the tall Spike-rush, *Eleocharis sphacelata*, and the Bulrush*. The Spiny Mat-rush is *Lomandra longifolia* in the Liliaceae family.

Russian Orthodox Church With some 20,000 adherents, it is the second largest of the Orthodox Churches* in Aus., and the most retentive of traditional dress for priests, outside ceremonial occasions.

Ryan, Thomas Joseph (1876–1921) b. Port Fairy, Vic. First Labor Premier of Qld. (1915–19), establishing State interests over a very wide field of public life.

Rye (*Secale cereali*) Although only grown on some 30,000 ha., it is of some importance in providing rye bread for European migrants, and as a soil-fixing crop in eroded areas such as the Vic. Mallee*. Historically it has been important for food and straw for stuffing horse collars.

Rye-grasses (*Lolium* spp.) These are among the most valuable fodder grasses of Europe, including both annual and perennial species of complementary quality in improved pastures. They have been introduced into Aus. and do well with good management.

S

SAGO-GRASS

Sago-grass A popular name for *Paspalidium globoideum*, an important forage grass, common in association with Blue-grass*, growing to 1 m. and stouter than relatives such as the Warrego-grass* and Brigalow-grass.

Sailing A very popular sport in summer, in sheltered coastal and some inland waters; weekend sailors are estimated at over 160,000. Racing dates from the 1820s, with the first recorded regatta at Hobart, followed by Sydney, in 1827. Yacht clubs, several now Royal, were formed, starting with the Vic. Yacht Club in 1856. A favourite family boat is the 11 ft. 3 in. *Heron* class. Some 5,000 new boats are built a year. Annual championships are held; a major trophy is the Savonara challenge cup (1904). Ocean racing has increased since the inauguration by John Illingworth of the 1,100-km. handicap from Sydney to Hobart in 1945; now a classic, this race attracts overseas entrants, and always starts on Boxing Day. There are major ocean races between Brisbane and Gladstone (Qld.), and Perth and Bunbury (W.A.). An Olympic Gold Medal was won in the 5·5-m. class by W. Northam in 1964. Three times Aus. has challenged unsuccessfully for the America's Cup*, in 1962 with *Gretel*, in 1967 with *Dame Pattie* and in 1970 with *Gretel II*.

St. Clair, Lake Tas. 42S/146E At 732 m., and the source of the Derwent River; it is used as storage for hydroelectric power (*see* TASMANIA, POWER). The lake runs for 15 km. NW/SE in dolerite tableland country overlooked by such flat-topped peaks as Mt. Olympus (1,448 m.); ice-excavated and moraine-dammed, it is at least 200 m. deep on the W side, the deepest Aus. lake.

SALE

Concentric wooded moraines are separated by shallow water and swamp on the SE shores.

St. George Qld. 28S/149E (2,184 in 1971) On the Balonne River , it is the centre of a small irrigation area (1,200 ha.) growing cotton and fodder for fat lambs, and a bridging point important on stock routes to the S.

St. George's Basin N.S.W. (and partly in A.C.T.) 24 km. S of Nowra, 35S/151E, it is a coastal lagoon shut off from the sea, except for Sussex Inlet, by the curved beaches and associated sand-barriers and dunes of Wreck Bay.

St. John's Wort The popular name for an almost world-wide genus of herbs, *Hypericum*, in the mainly tropical Hypericaceae family. Imported species of *Hypericum* have become noxious weeds in the wheatlands of E Aus. A native species is the Small St. John's Wort, *H. japonicum*, a small perennial with yellow flowers 1 cm. across, 5 petals and many stamens succeeded by a fruiting capsule, and small, oil-spotted, stem-clasping leaves. *Hypericum* contains a poison which causes cattle eating the plant to become light-sensitive with serious dermatitis.

St. Vincent Gulf S.A. 35S/138E A shallow triangular inlet 145 km. N–S, narrowing N from a width of 80 km. and formed by subsidence along faults between Yorke Peninsula and the Mt. Lofty Ranges. The high salinity and hot summer make it a major site for salt evaporation in Aus. It was named by Flinders in 1802, after a naval leader.

Sale Vic. 38S/147E (10,404 in 1971) A city and the major regional centre for the E part of Gippsland*, lying on the left bank of the Thomson River and at the S edge of the Macalister irrigation area serving cattle and cultivated land. Sale grew as an early port, and has grown rapidly as a major centre for oil and gas development in Bass Str.* Industries include plastics and engineering and a gas* absorption plant nearby at Dutsun which is piped to Melbourne.

Sallee, White or **Snow Gum*** (*Eucalyptus pauciflora*) A 9- to 18-m. tree, growing in cold, wet areas in SE Aus. from sea level to 600 m. in Tas. and 600–1,500 m. in Vic. and N.S.W. Its thin grey bark is shed in patches to leave a gleaming white trunk; it often forks from ground level and has twisted branches, particularly on exposed sites. Juvenile and intermediate leaves are broad, pointed and grey-green, the adult leaves broadly lanceolate, thick and bright green. There are star-shaped clusters of long buds and pear-shaped fruit about 6 mm. across. Black Sallee, *E. stellulata*, is a much more restricted sub-alpine species with dark persistent bark. It has a fairly dense crown.

Salmon, Australian (*Arripis trutta*) A large scaled, graceful, silver sea-fish, often about 75 cm. long and 3·5 kg., migrating seasonally and moving in schools between offshore and inshore waters, and perhaps also S–N and N–S. They are sometimes caught in large numbers by lines or beach nets. Young fish are green-backed with yellow spots, older black-backed without spots. The flesh is firm and dry, with a rather strong flavour when eaten fresh.

Salmon Gum (*Eucalyptus salmonophloia*) One of the larger and more widespread trees of the 20- to 50-cm. rainfall belt of inland SW W.A. growing on sandy loams to heavy clays, producing only fair but locally used timber, and planted for shade and ornament. It has a clean pinkish trunk and fairly dense crown of lanceolate glossy green

leaves. Pointed buds and cup-like fruit under 6 mm. across occur in bunches of 4–7; often several bunches are grouped along a stalk.

Salt No rock salt is exploited; the entire annual production of over 1 million tonnes, over half for the chemical industry, is from solar evaporation of sea or lake water. S.A. produced most at Lakes Fowler and Bumbunga and on the gulfs at Whyalla, Stenhouse, Price and the large ICIANZ beds at Dry Creek near Port Adelaide, developed to supply their alkali works (1940) and export to Japan. Salt is 'harvested' at the end of the summer, stacked, redissolved and piped to the factory. Dyes are added to the water to increase heat absorption. Increasing amounts of salt for export are being evaporated in W.A. at Dampier*, Port Hedland* and Exmouth Gulf*.

Saltbush A popular name for many salt-tolerant and salty-tasting plants, including many used for fodder in dry inland Aus.; easily grazed out, slow in regrowth but fire resistant. They belong mainly to the cosmopolitan halophytic Goosefoot, Fat Hen or Chenopodiaceae family, and to the genera *Atriplex* (cosmopolitan) and *Rhagodia*. The Old Man Saltbush, *A. nummularia*, reaches 3 m. and the Fragrant Saltbush, *R. parabolica*, 2·75-m. in sheltered rocky gullies (cf. Bluebush and Goosefoot).

Salvation Army Has some 66,500 adherents engaged in a wide variety of charitable and evangelical work. They were persecuted when first established in Adelaide (1881) and Melbourne (1882).

Salvation Jane Another name for Paterson's Curse*.

Sandalwood (*Santalum* spp.) A small tree yielding much-valued light and fragrant timber and essential oil, easily worked out and difficult to plant artificially because it is a root parasite, especially in early stages on other species of trees. There are 7 Aus. species in the genus, which extends to Hawaii and S and SE Asia. Timber and oil have had an extraordinary value (e.g. for incense and joss sticks) in many parts of monsoon Asia, and Aus. exports of timber and oil were considerable in the period 1910–30, and remain residually. The chief Aus. species are the Swan River Sandalwood, *S. spicatum*, and the Northern Sandalwood, *S. lanceolatum*. *Exocarpus latifolia* is also in the Santalaceae family, but the name is also applied to trees in quite different families: *Myoporum platycarpum* (Sugarwood) and *Eremophila mitchellii* in the mainly Aus. Myoporaceae family and the Tas. *Alyxia buxifolia* in the largely tropical Apocynaceae family.

Sandford, William (1840–1932) b. Torrington, Devon, Eng. An ironmaster. He arrived in Aus. in 1883 to open a wire-works for Lysaght of Bristol. He became interested in Aus. potential for iron production. He managed, leased, then bought Eskbank Works, Lithgow* (1886–1908), increasing production from 3,000 to 30,000 tons a year and installing the first open-hearth steel furnace in 1900.

Sandhoppers An evocative popular name for beach-dwelling species of Crustaceans*, of the Order Amphipoda. They have a distinct head, sessile (i.e. stalkless) eyes, and a curved body of 13 segments, the front part lacking the carapace of many crustaceans. The front legs are much shorter than those in the rear, and the sudden jump to recover after falling on their sides is by sudden straightening of the curved body. Aus. genera include *Orchestia* and *Talorchestia*. Marine species include *Caprella*, a predator on sea anemones, and *Chelura* which has been suspected as a borer of wharf timbers etc. Freshwater genera include the almost world-wide *Gammarus* and the Aus. *Neoniphargus*, some species of which have adapted to living in under-

ground water and are blind—these are the Well-shrimps sometimes found in borewater. *Talitrus* has become terrestrial, living on forest litter etc. Relatives such as *Euphausia superba* comprise the 'Krill' on which whales etc. feed in the cold Southern Ocean.

Sandover River N.T. 22S/135E Collects the very occasionally flowing waters from the creeks of the N slopes of the ranges E of Alice Springs. Its erratic course, generally a sandy indeterminate strip, makes NE towards the Georgina River* and is lost in almost unknown country.

Santamaria, Bartholomew Augustine (1915–) b. Brunswick, Vic. A leading Roman Catholic layman active and outspoken against the Communist Party in Aus.

Sarich, Ralph (1938–) Inventor of an 'orbital' engine, revolutionary in design, in W.A. in 1972 where it is being developed in association with B.H.P.* As a cheap, disposable unit it may be used in vehicle or industrial plant.

Sarsaparilla Climbers of the genus *Smilax* in the world-wide Liliaceae or Lily family, with 2 Aus. species: *S. glycophylla* in NE Aus. with broad alternate leaves, net-veined with tendrils at each leaf axil, rather insignificant flowers and dark round berries; and *S. australis* found farther S into Vic., with broad 5-veined leaves.

Sassafras A fragrant N American wood, from which the name has come to be applied to various Aus. genera and species with nutmeg-like scents in their bark, such as *Doryphora sassafras* found in Qld. and N.S.W., in the paired, fragrant and tooth-leafed Monimiaceae family, and the Black or Southern Sassafras, *Atherosperma moschatum*, found in mountain gullies throughout E Aus., with spear-shaped leaves, sometimes irregularly toothed, dark and glossy above and grey-green below, with small cream flowers in pink bracts, succeeded by red fruit. The barks are sometimes used for medicinal infusions.

Satintop A popular name for some grass species of the Blue-grass* group, mainly *Bothriochloa erianthoides*.

Savage River Tas. 42S/145E A right bank tributary of the Pieman River, where open-cut iron is being developed. Because of rough terrain it is crushed, mixed to form a slurry with water, and sent through a 22-cm. pipeline 85 km. to Port Latta for export to Japan. This permits exploitation of the low-grade ore.

Savery, Henry (1771–1842) b. Eng. He was transported to Tas. in 1825 for forgery and later sent to Port Arthur for further forgery. His writings, while revealing vain, snobbish, waspish characteristics and much that is apparently false, are valuable contemporary material, notably *Quintus Servinton* (Hobart, 1831), the first novel published in Aus. and largely autobiography.

Sawflies Leaf-eating insects of the Order Hymenoptera*, belonging to the Sub-Order Symphyta, lacking a 'waist' and with caterpillar-like larvae. Aus. has about 100 species, including the Steel-blue Sawfly, *Perga dorsalis*, up to 2 cm. long and with the saw-edged ovipositor or 'sting' used to cut slits in eucalypt leaves for egg-laying, and a large head and stout leaf-chewing jaws. The larvae of some species leave tunnels or blisters on eucalypt leaves, but others have become serious pests of orchards. The larvae of some species are extraordinarily gregarious, a system of tapping with the hardened tip of the abdomen being used to assist a 'lost' member to rejoin the group; and large masses of larvae are sometimes seen moving from a defoliated tree to 'fresh woods and pastures new'. Colony pupation occurs and is almost suggestive of a honeycomb.

Scaddan, John (1876–1934) b. Moonta, S.A. First Labor Premier of W.A.

(1911–6), entering politics from mining on the gold-fields, but leaving the Labor party over conscription.

Scale Insects Bugs* of the Order Hemiptera, difficult to recognise as insects at first sight because they are so immobile beneath some form of waxy cover, as in the Citrus Red Scale, *Aonidiella aurantii*: the family also includes the Mealy Bugs, e.g. *Callipappus australis*, and the Gall Formers; the male and female galls are often different, e.g. various species of *Apiomorpha* have usually tubular male galls and rounded female galls on eucalypt stems.

Scented-top A popular name for grasses of the genus *Capellipedium*, closely related to the Blue-grass* group.

Schools of the Air Link isolated children with their teacher, in lessons using 2-way radio, giving them some feeling of class participation to supplement correspondence teaching. There are 12 centres covering over 2·5 million km.^{2}: Alice Springs (1950) and Katherine, N.T., Broken Hill, N.S.W., Ceduna and Port Augusta in S.A., Charleville, Mt. Isa and Charters Towers in Qld., Meekatharra, Derby, Kalgoorlie and Port Hedland in W.A.

SCIENCE Scientific research in Aus. is carried out by Government agencies, universities, industrial concerns and private institutions usually founded through a benefactor. The major Government body is the Commonwealth Scientific and Industrial Research Organisation (C.S.I.R.O.*) with contributions in pasture improvement, rabbit control and in astronomy* etc. Research on problems of health is centred on Commonwealth Health Laboratories. The Bureaux of Meteorology and of Mineral Resources, Geology and Geophysics, are major centres, and in Defence* and Weapons Research, the Department of Supply, and the Atomic Energy* Commission each have laboratories. The States are concerned with research in agriculture, forestry, minerals, health, and the Snowy Mts. Authority has facilities at Cooma*.

University research is more in the fundamental or pure sciences; but the University of N.S.W. is more specifically concerned with applied science, and much university work has practical relevance. The Research Schools of the Aus. National University* have become foci. Among benefactors, important contributors include the Walter and Eliza Hall Trust*, the bequest of Peter Waite for founding the Waite Agricultural Institute*, that of pastoralist Sir Frederick McMaster (1873–1954) for the Animal Health Laboratory in Sydney University and of Winthrop Hackett* for agricultural research in the University of W.A.

Central organisations are the Aus. Academy of Science* and the Aus. and N.Z. Association for the Advancement of Science (A.N.Z.A.A.S.) founded 1887, and holding congresses about every 18 months in different centres. Each State has its Royal Society: Tas. (1844); Vic. (1859); N.S.W. (1866); S.A. (1880); Qld. (1884); W.A. (1913); Canberra (1930). Their functions lie largely in lectures and inter-disciplinary scientific exchange. There are over 200 specialised scientific societies, varying from those open to any interested persons to those with qualified entrance only, such as the Institute of Engineers, Aus.

Historical Development The discovery of Aus. followed from a primarily scientific expedition under Cook, and was the reason for the presence on board of Joseph Banks*, who was to sponsor so much of early scientific work in Aus., which was initially concerned with collecting, describing and classifying the new and excitingly strange natural phenomena, and included useful amateur anthropology. The need to introduce and acclimatise economically useful plants and animals led to further new work; and it is the biological sciences which have always

been most strongly represented. Royal Societies did much to encourage exploration and investigation in the 19th century before the many specialisms of today developed. The first Chair in Natural Science was held by F. McCoy in Melbourne from 1862. Prior to about 1914, Aus. scientific achievement was made only by isolated individuals. Organised and adequately financed research was only developed slowly, and the major growth has taken place since 1945, following the Murray Report on Universities* and the setting up of the A.N.U. Meanwhile many Aus. scientists had gone overseas; not a few achieved success, and of these some have returned to work in Aus.

Contributions have been considerable in proportion to population. Outstanding early work of world-wide significance included that of Farrer* in wheatbreeding, Hargrave* in aviation and Michell* in marine propulsion. More recently virus and neurological research in medicine* have won Nobel Prizes and the discoveries in flotation processes in mineral separation and in rain-making, in the links between presence or absence of trace elements in soils with pasture and animal health, in wool fibre technology and the structure of the tissues of timber, have all been recognised overseas. The southerly position and clear continental skies give Aus. a unique position for astronomy*. In addition, there have been many more locally applicable scientific advances: in the development of pulp-making from hardwoods, or the eradication of specific diseases, either pests or weeds, e.g. prickly pear*. Contributions were made by: H. J. Grayson (1856–1918) in microscopy; W. Sutherland (1859–1911) in physics; T. B. Robertson (1884–1930) in biochemistry; and J. Griffith (1905–69) in tropical pastures.

Sclerophyll A botanical term for plants with hard, scaly leaves, usually drought-resistant, and to associations of such plants (*see* VEGETATION). The term is now giving way to the more widely understood 'Open Forest'.

Scorpion Flies Insects of the Order Mecoptera, slender and rather delicate flies of small to medium size, superficially like Crane Flies (Daddy-long-legs) but with 4 wings. They are predators on other insects, mainly on True Flies, Diptera, holding on to grass or shrub twigs and catching passing insects with the long toothed hindlegs. Aus. species include *Harpobittacus tillyardi*, which is orange and brown with black markings and gauzy wings; the eggs are hard and cubical.

Scorpion-fish (family Scorpaenidae) Include the spiny Red Rock Cod, *Ruboralga jacksonensis*, and the Gurnet Perch, *Helicolenus* and *Neosebastes*. Many Scorpion-fish have venomous spines, especially the Bull-rout* of warm N estuaries.

Scorpions (Order Scorponidae, of the Class Arachnidae or arachnids*) They are well known by their slender, flexible segmented stinging tail and heavy and superficially nipper-like pedipalps

Large Brown Scorpion
(*Hormurus caudicula*), *slightly under life size*

attached to the maxilla or jaw (apparently a 'feeler'). Scorpions are shy and nocturnal, but will sting if molested. Only one death has been recorded from the sting, in a baby in W.A., where the small *Lychas marmoreus* appears to be more venomous than the larger common *Urodacus novae-hollandiae*. The small harmless (3 mm.) Pseudo-scorpion, with the pedipalp, but lacking the stinging tail, is in a little studied Order Chelonethi. The Large Brown Scorpion, *Hormurus caudicula*, is also found in N.G., the Philippines and Moluccas.

Scott, Andrew George The bushranger known as Captain Moonlight*.

Scott, Rose (1847–1925) b. Singleton, N.S.W. She was an important figure in the achievement of women's suffrage in N.S.W. (1902) and in subsequent reform of legislation especially in relation to women and children.

Scott, Thomas Hobbes (1783–1860) First Archdeacon of N.S.W. He was in Aus. (1819) as Secretary to Bigge*, his brother-in-law, and again as Archdeacon (1824–9). Scott's recommendations on education were largely responsible for the 1825 Act, giving the Anglicans a monopoly of primary education for a time, and arousing bitter controversy. He, himself, was arrogant and unpopular in office.

Scottish Martyrs 5 political offenders transported (1792–3) for alleged revolutionary speeches and publications; 1 escaped, 2 died very soon, 1 became a trader and farmer, and 1 led a very dubious life. In 1798 another political exile from Scotland, George Mealmaker, became Superintendent of a weaving factory employing about 100 women and old or sick convicts.

Scottsdale Tas. 41S/148E (1,800 in 1971) It is the most important service centre for the NE, in the heart of farmland on rich basaltic soils. There is a vegetable-processing factory.

Screw-pine A popular name for the somewhat palm-like genus *Pandanus*, from the fruit resembling a large cone or pineapple. *P. spiralis* is found across N Aus., as is the stream-side *P. aquaticus*; *P. pedunculatus* extends S into N.S.W. almost to Newcastle.

Scribbly Gum (*Eucalyptus micrantha*) A small tree of coastal N.S.W. and SE Qld. (9–18 m. by 30–75 cm. though larger on good sites towards the N). It grows mainly on poor sandstones from sea level to 600 m. and in 90–130 cm. mean annual rainfall. Juvenile leaves are broad, oblong to oval, and adult leaves narrowly lanceolate and often curved. Buds are narrow and cylindrical, fruit pear-shaped and up to 6 mm. across. The bark is shed in flakes leaving a smooth white surface, 'scribbled' on by insect larvae living under the bark. Its timber is only fair, but it is sometimes retained as an ornamental tree. Several related *Eucalyptus* spp. have bark 'scribbled' on by insect larvae tunnelling between layers of the bark, which then flakes off. *E. haemastoma* has a white trunk, often rather deformed, and thick lanceolate leaves, getting narrower and more curved in the adult. It grows on the poorer Hawkesbury Sandstone, and its brittle red timber is used for fuel. Further inland in N.S.W. *E. rossii* grows on poor acid soils, with thinner, more narrowly lanceolate leaves. It may reach 12 m. and the red timber is used for posts and fuel. At times *E. rossii* is hard to distinguish from *E. micrantha* (above) and from *E. maculosa*, the Red-spotted or White Gum, which, however, is never marked by insects.

Scrub The name in Aus. is usually applied to tall rain-forest, e.g. 'The Big Scrub', an example of understatement or meiosis.

Scrub-bird The uniquely Aus. genus *Atrichornis* including (1) the small Noisy or Western Scrub-bird, *A.*

clamosus, of SW W.A., a ground bird of thick bush, and (2) the Rufous Scrub-bird, *A. rufescens*, of rain-forest in SE Qld. and adjacent N.S.W. Both have loud but not always unpleasant calls, combined with ventriloquism.

Superficially they resemble the Bristle-birds, *Dasyornis*, except for the bristles round the bill from which the latter are named. (*Dasyornis* means hairy bird, *Atrichornis*—hairless bird). But *Atrichornis* has such distinctive anatomical features, e.g. lack of a wishbone, that it is placed in a family by itself, next to the much larger lyre-bird. The eastern species certainly, and the western species possibly, builds a quite remarkable nest in a sedge-clump or forest litter, made of dead leaves, grasses etc. outside, but lined with a cardboard-like dried wood-pulp (the drying time for which is so long that the nest takes a month to build). The bird's ventriloquism and almost mouse-like ability to run through forest litter make it difficult to observe, but the eastern species seems to be maintaining its numbers fairly well, though no doubt its specialised environment will make this more difficult as settlement proceeds. The western species was thought to be extinct, but has recently been observed in the coastal scrub near Albany.

Atrichornis has a very large literature (and, along with its discoverer John Gilbert, a memorial at Drakesbrook, W.A.) because of its distinctive anatomy and habits, but also because of the remarkable occurrence of the 2 species of this unique family at opposite sides of the Aus. continental mass. It is supposed that the family may once have spread right across the land mass, but that the 2 surviving species represent peripheral survivors when all the dry centre was cleared of such birds by adverse climatic conditions, probably marked aridity in post-glacial times.

Scullin, James Henry (1876–1953) b. Trawalla, Vic. Prime Minister (1929–

31), Leader of Labor Party (1928–35). He was self-educated, a Roman Catholic and a dedicated Labor worker. His Premiership was undermined by the difficulties of the Depression*, a Labor minority in the Senate, the lack of experienced Ministers, and the campaigns of J. T. Lang*, but his oratory and integrity left a lasting impression.

Sculling Single or double rowing events, in which Aus. has achieved international success from 1877, when E. Trickett went overseas, followed by P. Kemp, H. E. Searle and W. Beach who was the world professional champion from 1884–7. Outstanding scullers this century have been H. R. Pearce (Olympic Gold Medals 1928 and 1932 undefeated world champion), M. T. Wood (Olympic Gold Medal 1948) and S. A. Mackenzie*.

Sculpture Until quite recently Aus. sculpture was not comparable in quality and certainly not comparable in quantity, with painting. Sir Bertram Mackennal (1863–1931) was successful in England, and was the first Aus. to be elected to the Royal Academy. In this century academic naturalism was succeeded by a derivative biomorphism and vitalism only slightly stiffened by a Constructivist impulse (via the U.S.A.) represented by such artists as Frank Hinder (1906–). Robert Klippel has maintained a metamorphic style using junk until the late 1960s and Clement Meadmore has achieved a considerable reputation in the U.S.A. since 1968 with simple monumental welded constructions. In spite of the general deference to English art, Post-War Humanism did not flourish in Aus., nor has metal sculpture deriving from Caro in England and Smith in U.S.A. Instead, a motley of derivative styles have flourished until the recent adoption (in step with rather than deriving from overseas sources) of open form, systematic and serial sculpture as well as various post-object manifestations. The main centre and showplace of new Aus. sculpture is the triennial exhibition held at Mildura in Vic. since 1964.

Sea-anemones Marine animals of the Phylum Coelenterata*. The relatively sedentary tentacled polyp stage dominates the animal's way of life; many species can move appreciably by expansion and contraction of the base of the body, some by floating with the current, a few by use of the tentacles for crawling, and a few species, including some in N Aus. water, by actively swimming with their tentacles. Common small Aus. anemones include: 1. the Sea Waratah or Blood Red Anemone, *Actinia tenebrosa*, up to 2 cm. across and common on N.S.W. shore platforms; 2. the Speckled Anemone, *Oulactis muscosa*, often found in narrow rock gutters and crevices, and usually with fragments of shell-grit, gravel and coarse sand adhering to the body and tentacles; 3. Orange Anemone, *Corynactis australis*, found in the cunjevoi zone near low-tide level and capable of giving an adult a nasty sting; 4. Green Fingers, *Cnidopus verator*, about 4 cm. across, and often seen half-buried in sand in an intertidal rock pool; 5. Warty Anemone, *Phlyctenanthus australis*, yellow-brown, with blue-grey 'warts' and pink-brown tentacles. J. Child's *Aus. Seashore Life* (Sydney, 1962) describes common species.

Giant anemones of the Great Barrier Reef include: 1. *Physobranchia* spp. with long tentacles carrying conspicuous lobes when fully expanded, among which live messmate fish, 6 species of *Amphiprion* and *Actinocola percula*, which are unaffected by the stinging tentacles; 2. *Actinodendron* spp., one of the largest, with the disc developed into 6–8 permanent arm-like lobes armed with very numerous short, branched tentacles; the sting may cause severe skin irritation to human beings, and it may be encountered in wading across tidal flats; 3. the largest, *Discosoma* spp., embedded in the floor of tidal flats, and reaching 45 cm. across, the rather flattened expanded disc having a convoluted edge and, with numerous small bead-like tentacles in complex radial and arcuate patterns, giving it a certain coral-like appearance; again the sting may cause skin irritation.

Sea-birds Often whitish and all with webbed feet, are seen in Aus. waters, and many from Aus. shores. They total at least 60 species. They vary widely in size, form and habit, as our selected species show. The Snowy Albatross, *Diomedea chionoptera*, and the Wandering Albatross, *D. exulans* (with more brown on wings and body), have a wingspan of over 2 m. and sustain their large bulk by a diet mainly of squid, gathered over thousands of miles of patrolling the Southern Ocean. Related species tend to be smaller and browner and are often known by the Dutch name Mollymauk. The Shy or White-capped Albatross, *D. cauta*, nests on inaccessible islands in Tas. Gulls proper, genus *Larus*, are scavengers, with thickish, roundish beaks and rather rounded wings and tail, as compared with the sharp-beaked fish-hunting Terns or Swallow-tails, genus *Sterna*. The true gulls of Aus. are the widespread, medium-sized (up to 38 cm. long) Silver Gull, *L. novae-hollandiae*, and the larger (to 60 cm.) Pacific Gull, *L. pacificus*, with much more blackish-grey on the back, of the coasts of the SE. The terns include the Crested Tern, *S. bergii*, found over much of the Indian and Pacific Oceans, about 45 cm. long, grey and white with black head, with several more local species, the 25-cm. long, Fairy Tern, *S. nereis* (sea-nymph and the Roseate Tern, *S. dougalli* (*see* PLATE 4). The Caspian Tern is larger and allotted to a separate genus, *Hydroprogne caspia* (water-swallow); its total territory extends over much of the Old World, N America and Australasia. The Skuas, large stocky, often

quite dark-coloured birds, with stout often slightly down-curved beaks, pursue other birds which have fish and force them to relinquish or even disgorge them; species seen in Aus. waters include the Great or Antarctic Skua, *Catharacta skua* (bird of prey gull, from Greek and Norse), about 60 cm. long, and breeding in the Antarctic in summer, and the Arctic Skua, *Stercorarius parasiticus* (dung-coloured parasites), which breeds in the Arctic during the N hemisphere summer and then flies far S to summer again. The Gannets of Aus. include both subtropical species ('boobies'), e.g. the Brown Gannet or Booby, *Sula leucogaster* (white-bellied), or the Red-footed Gannet, *S. sula*, white with large red beak and feet and black wing-edges, and also temperate-zone species such as the Aus. Gannet, *S. serrator* (sawyer), which has very similar markings, but grey beak and feet. Gannets dive from considerable heights (15 m. or so), at particular fish, and have skulls adapted and strengthened for this form of fishing, and large beaks capable of dealing with sizable fish. The Petrels are a large group of birds including: 1. the Storm-Petrels or Mother Carey's Chickens, such as the small (15–17 cm.) Whitebacked Storm-Petrel, *Pelagodroma marina*, seen skimming across the waves in the wake of a ship, and nesting in burrows in sub-Antarctic islands; 2. the majority of the Petrels, quite small oceanic birds eating plankton or surface fish and coming to land only to breed in crevices or burrows, e.g. *Pterodroma* spp. along with the Shearwaters, *Puffinus*, spp. including Mutton-birds*; and 3. one Diving Petrel, *Pelecanoides urinatrix*, small, neat, white-bellied and grey-backed, which nests in islands in Bass Strait and nearby. Aus. has a few Penguins*. Distinctive sea-birds of the Aus. tropics include the long-tailed Red-tailed and White-tailed Tropic-birds, *Phaethon rubricaudus* and *P. lepturus*, and the Greater and

Lesser Frigate-birds, *Fregata minor* and *F. ariel*, about 1 m. long. (*See* D. L. Serventy, Vincent Serventy and J. Warham: *The Handbook of Australian Seabirds* (Sydney, 1971).

Seacom The South-East Asia Common wealth Cable, opened by the Queen on March 30, 1967. It provides the third link, with the Trans-Atlantic (Cantat) and Trans-Pacific (Compac) co-axial cable systems, 37,000 km. in length. Seacom links Singapore, Jesselton (Borneo), Guam (Philippines) and Madang (Java) with Cairns, Qld., and thence by micro-wave and co-axial land systems, to join Compac at Sydney. Aus. has a 28% share, and supplied over half the raw materials used.

Sea-cucumbers, Bêche-de-Mer or Trepang Sluggish sausage-shaped marine Echinoderms*, bottom-dwellers in mainly tropical seas. They have tentacles ex- tended at the front during feeding and travel by tube-feet below the body. The spiny echinoderm plates are reduced to small inclusions in the skin. Some species throw out thread-like material when disturbed (cotton-fish), and others break up or throw out certain organs. Several species have been caught, gutted, dried and marketed as trepang in E and SE Asia, but the Aus. trade has been small since the war. A common Aus. sea-cucumber is the rich red, *Holothuria edelis*, of about 20 cm. by 2 cm.

Sea-horses Of a distinctive family of fishes, they are common in Aus. waters, e.g. *Hippocampus whitei*; the Leafy Sea-horse, *Phycodurus* spp., and the Spiny Sea-horse, *Solegnathus* spp.

Sea-lice The marine genera of the Isopoda Order of the Crustaceans*, tending to be larger than the terrestrial forms, commonly to 5 cm. in Aus. waters and to 28 cm. in colder Antarctic seas. The Sea-slater, *Ligia oceanica*, is a relative and not unlike the terrestrial Slaters or Wood-lice*. *Ligia* are fairly often seen on beaches and estuaries in SE Aus. The world-wide Gribble, *Limnoria* spp., and the Marine Pill-bug, *Sphaeroma* spp., which rolls into a ball, are among the marine borers.

Sea-lilies With the Feather-stars (*see* STARFISH) they comprise the Class Crinoidea. They are marine animals superficially like feathery starfish, but relatively immobile at the end of a calcareous stalk, somewhat flower-like, hence the name. The stalk is often the part preserved in fossil crinoids from the Cambrian onwards. A modern Aus. crinoid is the fragile and colourless but attractive *Metacrinus cyaneus*, sometimes brought up from deep water off SE Aus.

Seals Semi-aquatic mammals, with webbed feet and stream-lined shape adapted for fast swimming to enable the animal to prey on fish. The earless true Seal is the most adapted, with hind

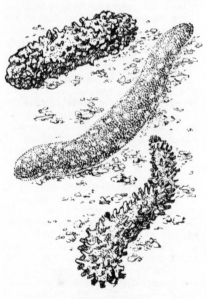

*Sea-cucumbers,
about a quarter life size*

flippers pointing back for swimming and little use ashore; the Arctic Walrus also without earlobes but with rear flippers able to act as supporting hind limbs is intermediate; and the Seal, Sea-lion or Sea-bear is least adapted, having not only lobes to the ear but also hind flippers able to make progress on land. Seal populations have been greatly depleted by hunting for the skins and blubber (used for curing the skins), but there are colonies, for instance on Seal Rocks, Port Stephen, N.S.W., Seal Rocks off Western Port, Vic., Lady Julia Percy Island, Port Fairy, Vic., and Macquarie Island. Claims of damage to fishing have been much over-stated, and with fairly successful protection the colonies are again increasing. Seals occasionally travel up inland rivers, and they, along with confusion with the crocodiles of the north, appear to have given rise to the bunyip legend.

Australian Fur-seal
(*Gypsophoca dorifera*), *about 2 m. long*

I *Sea-bears and Sea-lions* (family Otariidae, eared seal) include: 1. Australian Fur-Seal or Sea-bear, *Gypsophoca dorifera*, specimens from Kangaroo Island named by Peron in 1802; it is up to 2 m. in length, with reddish-brown fur; 2. the slightly larger Large or Tasmanian Fur Seal, *G. tasmanica*; and 3. White-capped Hair-seal or Sea-

lion, *Neophoca cinerea*, the largest seal of the S of Aus., from Bass Str. to the Geraldton area, up to 3·5 m., lacking the fine inner fur, and harmless, except for some male aggressiveness in the breeding season, polygynous and gregarious, especially in the crowded breeding beaches during the breeding season in spring.
II *Earless or True Seals* (family Phocidae) include: 1. Leopard Seal, *Hydrurga leptonyx*, a slim yellowish-white seal with black mottling and spots, found along the S of Aus. as a straggler from Macquarie Island and the Antarctic seas, where it feeds on penguins; 2. Crab-eater Seal, *Lobodon carcinophaga*, a silver-grey Antarctic seal similarly occurring as a straggler; and 3. Elephant Seal, *Macrorhinus proboscideus*, the only polygynous earless seal, its erectile proboscis justifying the popular name of Elephant Seal (but *not* Sea-elephant). This seal was formerly common around Tas. and the islands of the Bass Str. and as a visitor to the mainland; it has been protected on Macquarie Island through the efforts of Sir Douglas Mawson and is increasing, after a period of ruthless hunting for its oil.

Sea-perches A term best applied to the family Lutjanidae of deep-bodied mainly tropical inshore fish. They include: 1. the Red Emperor or King Snapper, *Lutjanus sebae* (to 105 cm. and 20 kg.), reddish with dark bands down the head, near the tail and across the midriff; 2. the Hussar, *L. amabilis*, which may be striped yellow or blue or silvery (when it is known as the Spanish Flag); it has a slightly spiny continuous back fin; 3. the Red Bass, *L. coatesi*, about 0·90 kg. and 35 cm. long; 4. the Chinaman Fish, *L. nematophorus*, pinkish with red bars along or across its sides, and sometimes long curved spines from the rear back fin; it reaches 0·9 m. and 14 kg. Red Bass and Chinaman Fish have been under suspicion of being poisonous to eat, if not fresh or sufficiently cooked.

Sea-pike The Long-finned Pike, *Dinolestes lewini*, generally reaches some 60 cm. long. Occasional attacks on bathers by the larger Sea-pikes are recorded. (*See* SNOOK *and* DINGO-FISH.)

Seas Bordering Aus. are the Tasman Sea between Aus. from 30S to Tas., and the W coast of N.Z.; the Coral Sea, between the NE coast of Aus. from 30S to the mouth of the Bensbach River in N.G., and the New Hebrides, and bordered by the Solomon Sea to the N; Arafura Sea between the N coast of Aus. from Cape York W to the NW of Arnhem Land, and N.G.; Timor Sea between the NW coast of Aus. from Arnhem Land to Cape Londonderry, and Timor. The Indian Ocean lies to W and S of Aus., the latter extending into the Great Aus. Bight*. An Aus.-Indonesian agreement (1972) shared the seabed half and half.

Sea-snakes The Front-fanged Sea-snakes, family Hydrophiidae, include 24 species found in Aus. (though some are widely dispersed in the oceans), in 2 sub-families and 12 genera. (For classification *see under* SNAKES.) The sea-snakes are venomous, some extremely so, weight for weight, though fangs tend to be short. Contact with Europeans is rare except for infrequent encounters with some species in rock pools or of fishermen handling one in mistake for an eel, but deaths from bites on bare skins in Asian fishermen have been common for centuries while anti-venene has only been available within the last few years. Sea-snakes are distinguished by several adaptations to an almost entirely marine life. Tails tend to be flattened for use as paddles in swimming, nostrils to be at the tip of the snout, shields to be developed interlocking across the front of the mouth so that it can be made waterproof when necessary (as against the grooved mouth of land snakes to allow

the tongue to flicker out constantly). The lung extends back to the alimentary tract, and serves as a float or as a reservoir of air while submerged. They feed on fish and eels. Most species occur in warmer seas of Aus., but some have been found as far S as Tas. Most produce live young, but a few lay eggs. The sub-family Hydrophiinae have very small belly scales, or none, suggesting the most complete marine adaptation; the sub-family Laticaudinae have broad ventral scales, suggesting less complete adaptation and some have been known to come ashore. Selected species of Hydrophiinae are as follows. 1. *Acalyptophis peronii* is a bulky grey or brown, white-bellied snake, up to 1·5 m. long with thorn-like projections from the scales over the eyes, smaller 'thorns' on body scales, and loose skin on the neck, found mainly in tropical Aus. waters. 2. *Astrotia stokesii* is one of the bulkiest sea-snakes, up to 2 m. long and 25 cm. girth, with a large head and little neck, light brown with darker blotches and yellow belly. Both these large snakes should be regarded as dangerous. 3. *Enhydrina schistosa* reaches over 1·5 m., but is relatively slender with rather a pointed snout and little neck, greyish above with darker cross-bands, with whitish belly; the venom is extraordinarily potent. 4. *Hydrelaps darwiniensis*, or Port Darwin Sea-snake, is a small (to 40 cm. long) but fairly bulky yellow-white snake with black cross-bands, sometimes with a yellow spot on each; it is found between Aus. and N.G., and is probably only mildly venomous to man. 5. *Hydrophis major* is a large (2 m.) and bulky snake found N of Shark Bay, W.A., and Moreton Bay, Qld. It is yellow to pale brown with broad and narrow crossbars alternating, and paler belly with brown or olive spots. Body scales overlap and bear a small tubercle. It is regarded as dangerous. 6. *H. elegans* grows to 2 m., slightly more slender in build, especially towards the tail, and with broad brown bands halfway down the sides. The venom is regarded as dangerous. 7. *H. ornatus* is dark grey with lighter sides and belly, it grows to 1·2 m. and the venom may be dangerous. 8. *H. inornatus* is of similar colouring, but with grey back and white belly demarcated clearly, up to 90 cm. long, with head and neck quite small and tapering; it is found from tropical Aus. to the Philippines, China and Java. 9. *H. fasciatus* grows to 1·2 m. and is an unusually elongate species, a dirty yellow with broad black bands, wedge-shaped at sides; has been found at Sydney, but mainly tropical. 10. *Lapemis hardwickii* is a large-headed, short (to 90 cm.) stout snake, dirty yellow with blurred broad brown cross-bands, found from N Aus. to Burma and Japan; venomous but not dangerous. 11. *Microcephalophis gracilis* is, as the name suggests, graceful in the water, it has a small head and neck, thick middle and tapering tail and reaches 1·2 m. in length; the head is olive-yellow, and the back greyish with darker grey-brown blurred cross-bands, the belly whitish. It is believed to be mildly venomous. It is rare from N. Aus. to Malaya, but commoner from the Persian Gulf to China. 12. The very striking Yellow-bellied Sea-snake, *Pelamis platurus*, is bright yellow below with a thick blue-black line along the back, sometimes clearly delimited. sometimes with blurred junction and duller colours. It reaches 75–100 cm., is not uncommonly washed ashore in storms, and has deadly venom but rather short fangs. It is the most widely distributed snake in the world, common in the Indian Ocean and Pacific waters, and may be washed ashore in Sydney at any season; it is fairly bulky, with a small and elongated head, and prominent flat tail, yellow with black spots. (*See* PLATE 9.)

Selected species of the Laticaudinae are as follows. 1. The Olive-Brown Sea-snake, *Aipysurus laevis*, a bulky snake up to 1·5 m. long, with tapered head and a flat front to its snout, little neck, a

keeled shape, and a ragged end to its flat tail. It is often stranded after storms on beaches on all Aus. coasts except the S, and occurs in N.G. It is venomous. 2. *A. duboisii* is rather small (up to 60–90 cm.) and also more slender in build, brown above and lighter below, with keeled body and a flat tail often with 1 or 2 spines. The venom is probably not deadly to man. 3. *Emydocephalus annulatus*, the Ringed Sea-snake, is up to 1·2 m. long, with a relatively slender yellowish body, ringed irregularly with rather ragged broad brown bands; the snout has a slight spine; the body scales overlap and are slightly ridged. The fangs are small and inclined inwards, so it is probably only mildly lethal to man, and there are no small teeth behind the fangs. It is distributed through the warmer waters of Aus. 4. *Ephalopis greyi* is an olive snake with 28 dark grey dorsal rings; it is notable for its broad belly scales suggestive of ability to progress on land. 5. The genus *Laticauda*, also with broad belly scales, comes ashore to lay its 20 or so eggs. 6. *L. colubrina* reaches 1·5 m. long and is slender, with bluish back and yellowish belly and numerous fairly broad black or dark brown bands; the head is black with yellow markings. It is widely distributed from Bengal to Japan and Aus. The venom is deadly, but the snake is very reluctant to bite man. 7. *L. laticaudata* is smaller, but similar in appearance and a very graceful swimmer; thought to be only mildly venomous to man. It is widely distributed from the Indian Ocean to the Pacific islands.

S.E.A.T.O. South East Asia Treaty Organisation evolved from the S.E. Asia collective defence pact, signed in October 1954, between U.S., Aus., France, N.Z., Thailand, Philippines, Pakistan and U.K. and extended to Cambodia, Laos and South Vietnam to take common action against Communist aggression and subversion, and to promote cultural, political and economic advancement in the area. In 1972 Pakistan withdrew. France remains an observer. The alliance has decreasing importance in the 1970s.

Sea-urchins Echinoderms*, with a 5-segmented spherical to cushion-shaped, calcareous external skeleton or test, armed with many small spines movable on ball-and-socket joints. Among the spines are a number of tube-feet, similar to those of the Starfish*. Centrally in the flattened bottom is a somewhat beak-like mouth, the anus being in the centre of the top. The test, smoothed of the spines by wave action, is often washed ashore as a 'sea-egg'. A common Aus. sea-urchin is the small purple to green-brown *Heliocidaris erythrogramma*, sometimes in a small cylindrical excavation or under a rock. The tropical species include the very large-spined Slate-Pencil Sea-urchin, *Heterocentrotus mammillatus*. The venomous *Toxopneustes pileolus*, distinguished by flower-like pedicellaria and long tube-feet, and known to have caused the deaths of several divers in Japan, has been recorded in Moreton Bay, Qld., 27S/153E, and from Sydney Harbour.

Sea-wasp A popular name for the Box Jellyfish, or Cubomedusans, some species of which sometimes sting bathers severely, causing intense pain, and temporary paralysis. Several deaths attributed to this in recent years are well authenticated. (*See* JELLYFISH.)

Seaweeds Marine plants of which the great majority are Algae*, but there are a few flowering plants such as Eelgrass, *Zostera* spp., the creeping rhizomes and leaves like coarse grass being sometimes exposed at very low tides, and Strapweed, *Posidonia* spp., a larger deeper-water plant with yellow flowers in spring.

1. Green Seaweeds, Chlorophyceae, include in Aus.: (a) the moss-like Baitweed or Greenweed, *Enteromorpha*, spp., and Sea Lettuce, *Ulva lactuca* (for structure *see* ALGAE); (b) Green Sea Velvet such as the antler-shaped *Codium fragile*; (c) the cactus-shaped *Halimeda opuntia* and related species, and (d) the remarkable single-celled *Caulerpa* spp., both of the Great Barrier Reef (*see* ALGAE).

2. Brown Seaweeds, Phaeophyceae. Aus. species include: (a) Necklace Seaweed or Neptune's Necklace, *Hormosira banksii*; (b) Bubble Weed, *Colpomenia sinuosa*; and rock pool species such as (c) Banded Fan Weed, *Padina commersoni*, with 5-cm. fronds contrasting with the irregular bunching of *Pocockiella* spp.; (d) Sausage Weed, *Splachnidium rugosum*, seen at mid-tide level in SE Aus.; (e) the broad and strap-like Kelp, *Ecklonia radiata*, living below low-tide level; and round S coasts of Aus. the giant Bull Kelp, *Durrillea potatorum*, 6 m. or more long; (f) *Sargassum*, comprising many of the attractively branched seaweeds of the Great Barrier Reef, and its relative, *Turbinaria ornata*, with a dome of buoyant trumpet-shaped branches.

3. Red Seaweeds, Rhodophyceae, generally in deeper water, include in Aus.: (a) *Claudea elegans*, a Bass Str. species claimed as the most beautiful of all seaweeds; (b) the regularly branched *Callithamnion* spp.; (c) the membranous red, green or purple *Porphyra* spp. seen on rocky coasts in winter, the algae cultivated as food by the Japanese; (d) various small red seaweeds of about the low-tide zone, with delicate fronds coated with lime; these often form a rough encrustation on the rocks at or below the cunjevoi* zone, and the building up of this crust is quite important in the maintenance of coral reefs once the polyps themselves are dead; the calcareous branching forms become whitish when the red seaweed dies, and are themselves reminiscent of coral, hence the genus name *Corallina*; unbranched forms, like a crust of thick pink lichen on the rock, are of genera such as *Melobesia* and *Lithothamnium*; and (e) nearer the high-

tide mark, the moss-like *Bangia* spp., threadlike *Polysiphonia*, spp., the fern-like *Pterocladia* and the Blue Glow Weed, *Champia compressa*, so striking in a rock pool.

Second Fleet The name given to the 6 ships comprising the transports *Lady Juliana* (which sailed from Eng. July 1789), *Surprise, Neptune* and *Scarborough* (December 1789); storeships *Guardian* (September 1789, damaged by ice and remaining at Cape Town) and *Justinian* (January 1790). 1,267 convicts and supplies were transported en route for Botany Bay, but in contrast with the care taken by Phillip over the First Fleet*, the contract system employed in victualling led to serious abuse, and 267 convicts died on the voyage. Half the survivors were sick on arrival, with scurvy, dysentery and fevers. The sighting of the *Lady Juliana* on June 3rd 1790, was wildly acclaimed by the starving colony, and in spite of its grim load of human misery, the stores it brought saved the settlement.

Sedge A popular name for a large group of grassy or rush-like plants in the cosmopolitan family Cyperaceae. Aus. has some 36 genera and over 400 species, growing chiefly in boggy or swampy sites, mainly in the genera *Cyperus, Fimbristylis, Schoenus, Carex, Lepidosperma* and *Scirpus*. (*See also* RUSHES.)

Sedgman, Francis (1927–   ), b. Albert, Vic. One of the first exponents of the 'power game' in Aus. tennis, with an aggressive, brilliant service. He was the first Aus. to win the U.S. singles (1951 and 1952). He also won at Wimbledon in 1952, after which he turned professional. He played in Davis Cup matches from 1949–52, becoming professional in 1953.

Selectors People who, through Land Acts in N.S.W. and Vic. after 1860, were able to 'select' holdings (N.S.W. up to 320 ac.; Vic. up to 640 ac). They mostly failed to make a living, lacking

capital and skill to combat flood, fire, drought and infertile soil. Failure to maintain the 3-year payment for the land and 'a simple system of corruption', led to many selections being taken over by squatters*. The squalid rural slums of earth-floored 'humpies' are the scene of writings by Lawson, Baynton and Rudd.

Senecio This genus in the Daisy or Compositae family, has over 2,000 species, more than any other flowering plant genus. Aus. has about 40 native species. The Saw Groundsel, *S. vagus*, of damp fertile coastal gullies in SE Aus., grows to 60–90 cm. high, with saw-edged leaves of 12–18 cm. by 7–10 cm. with yellow flowers 2·5 cm. across. The downy seeds of the genus *S. megaglossus*, of the Flinders Ranges, have heads over 5 cm. across. Introduced species include the European Groundsel, *S. vulgaris*, and the rosette-forming Ragwort, *S. jacobaea*, a serious pest in Vic. and elsewhere.

Seventh Day Adventist Reform Movement A religious group, with 41,621 adherents in 1971, stemming from U.S. influences and first founded in Aus. in Melbourne in 1885. The name derives from observance of Saturday as the Sabbath.

Seymour Vic. 37S/145E (5,761 in 1971) On the Goulburn River* plain, now a major service centre, with some textile and sawmilling industries. It grew at an important river-crossing, later used by the Melbourne–Sydney line.

Shag In Aus. it is synonomous with Cormorant*.

Shannon River Tas. 42S/147E It flows 24 km. S from Great Lake to join the Ouse at Waddamana, the site of an early power station now superseded. Until spoiled by power projects, the river was famous for its trout 'rise' in November.

Shark Bay W.A. 25S/113E An inlet 80 km. E–W and over 160 km. NW–SE in shallow waters, bisected by Peron Peninsula into 2 arms, Freycinet Estuary and Hamelin Pool. It was named by Dampier in 1699. Formerly a pearling area, it is now important for crayfish, prawns, whiting and snapper, and salt exported to Japan from Useless Loop.

SHARKS They are grouped with the Rays* in the Class Elasmobranchii (strap-gilled) as against the Bony Fish, Osteichthyes. The vital differences are in the skeleton, of cartilage not bone; the tough skin covered with denticles or minute teeth, appropriate members of which develop as the many sharp teeth lining both jaws of several species, and replaced as damaged; the gills, which have outlets through a series of slits on the side (of the neck behind the eye and mouth, instead of under gill-covers as in bony fish) and nostrils above the upper jaw for smelling, opening on the top of the head. The female's eggs are fertilised internally, the male having twin 'claspers' attached to the ventral fins (often about two-thirds along the shark from the snout) which, when erected and clasped together, convey the sperm, whereas bony fish discharge both eggs and sperm into the water where the eggs are fertilised. The young are generally born alive, though sometimes enclosed in a sac from which they soon break. Many sharks have a bird-like, whitish, movable membrane with which they can cover the eye, and they are said to pull this over as a protection when about to attack—or if they lack it, to roll back the eyes at the moment of impact.

Sharks as a group are major scavengers, slicing and swallowing whole all manner of marine carrion, but liable to attack living creatures, especially the old, wounded and weak, particularly if the victim has been wounded and is bleeding. Recent research by Hans Hass and other skin divers is very suggestive of this; perhaps the complicated organs of smell are involved and in-

flame both hunger and hunting instincts. Individuals of large species appear to extend this to the killing of a relatively inefficient swimmer—man—and even to attacking people who are wading rather than swimming, sometimes in fresh water at the head of estuaries particularly in tropical and subtropical areas including S Aus.

Adult sharks commonly vary in size from 30 cm. to 5 m., more rarely to 9–12 m. 1. The Bronze Whaler, *Eulamia ahenea*, and the Common or Grey Whaler, *Galeolamna greyi*, and several others of that genus are common as large and dangerous sharks off much of E Aus. and into estuaries and lower rivers even beyond tidal limits. The front dorsal fin is large and pointed, the rear small and obtuse angled. 2. The Grey Nurse, *Carcharias arenarius*, is most readily distinguished at sight from a Grey Whaler because both fins on the back are fairly large and sail-shaped; it preys on Aus. salmon and is described as a relatively sluggish shark, seldom a man-eater though often blamed for attacks on bathers in error for the Grey Whaler; it is a shark of temperate rather than tropical waters, though not unknown in Qld. 3. The Tiger Shark, *Galeocerdo rayneri*, is dark grey with darker stripes and blotches particularly in younger specimens; it grows to 4–6 m. and perhaps to 9 m. or so, and is feared as a man-eater in many tropical and sub-tropical waters. 4. The Mako or Blue Pointer, *Isuropsis mako*, beautifully streamlined, blue-backed and silvery-bellied, reaches 5 m. or so, and is regarded as a danger to surf-boards and small craft rather than to swimmers, for it seldom comes close inshore. It is a notable angling shark. 5. The swift Mackerel or Beaumaris Shark or Porbeagle, *Lamna whitleyi*, is up to 5 m. in length, also blue-backed, but shows rather porpoise-like deportment as it preys on schools of mackerel. 6. The Blue Whaler or Great Blue Shark, *Carcharhinus mackiei*, is relatively rare in

Aus., but grows up to 6 m., and is reputed to be a man-eater in other parts of the world including Europe. 7. The White Pointer, Great White Shark or White Death, *Carcharodon albimors*, of up to 12 m. long, grey or bronze-backed and white-bellied is perhaps the largest, most dangerous shark, quite common off the S of Aus. in summer, and off Qld. in winter as it moves north after the migrating Humpback Whales. It is relatively seldom inshore, but has probably carried off a few bathers. 8. The Thresher Shark, *Alopias caudatus*, is believed to use its extraordinarily long upper tail lobe to stun fish to eat. Legends of attacks on whales may be untrue, for its small mouth does not seem compatible with much whale eating (and also probably prevents it from being dangerous to man). 9. The Black-tipped Shark, *Mapolamia spallanzani*, is like a smaller and slimmer-built Whaler up to 2 m. long, with black tips on fins and tail. It is a tropical shark often persistent in following quite close to people visiting the Great Barrier Reef, and while too small to carry off an adult, it might well cause severe injury. A rounder-nosed variety

may be a separate species. 10. The Hammerhead Shark, *Sphyrna lewini*, carries the very distinctive hammerhead horizontally, with an eye at either end and the horseshoe-shaped mouth underneath; the front of the curved hammer carries very sensitive organs of smell. It is a voracious feeder on Aus. salmon, mullet and other fish mainly in open waters, and is potentially dangerous to man, but seldom inshore, as compared with the Whalers. 11. The Basking Shark, *Halsydrus maximus*, has a brown-black back and grows to 12 m. or more long. 12. The Whale or Checker-board Shark, *Rhincodon typus*, with white-spotted, bluish-green back and lighter belly, reaches 15 m. or more. It is rather blunt-headed like a whale. Both this and the preceding species have very small teeth and long vertical gill-slits; both, too, resemble the whalebone whales in living from the minute floating life of the open oceans, plankton, which they strain mainly by the gill-strainers and perhaps to a subsidiary extent by the small teeth. These very large sharks may cause alarm if encountered close to small craft, but are harmless. 13. There are numerous

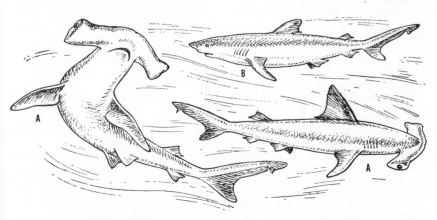

A *Hammerhead Shark*   B *Grey Whaler Shark*
  (*Sphyrna lewini*)   (*Galeolamna greyi*)
      The sharks shown are 4–5 m. long

small sharks, often seen inshore, in reef pools etc., such as the attractive brown-spotted Epaulette Shark, *Hemiscyllium ocellatum*, of the Great Barrier Reef, and various other Cat-sharks. 14. The largest Cat-shark, however, the Wobbegong or Carpet-shark, *Orectolobus ornatus*, is a rather broad flat shark, round-snouted from above, brown and patterned like a Paisley shawl or carpet. It lives in rocky weedy pools and crevices, normally sluggish, but is liable to bite severely if disturbed by skin-divers or wading fishermen, and though not a man-eating shark in the normal sense, it grows to 1–2·5 m. and should be treated with respect. 15. The Common or Piked Dogfish, *Squalus megalops*, may be taken as representative of several small (60–90 cm. long) sharks, harmless to man and indeed increasingly lined or trawled for the market. 16. The Angel Shark or Monk-fish, *Squatina australis*, also edible and marketed, sandy in colour and a bottom feeder. Commonly of 50–100 cm. long, it shows some shark-like features, but also wing-like flaps and other features transitional to the Rays*. 17. The Little Saw Sharks, *Pristiophorus cirratus*, and the Southern Saw Shark, *P. nudipinnis*, have a long low bony snout armed with saw-like teeth, with which they can inflict considerable wounds by thrashing sideways. In the Saw Sharks, unlike the Sawfishes discussed under Rays*, there are ribbon-like appendages halfway along the saw. Saw Sharks are mainly inshore, bottom feeders, of some commercial importance. 18. The Gummy* is commercially important. 19. The shellfish-eating Port Jackson Shark, *Heterodontus portusjacksoni*, reaches 1·2 m. and lays its eggs in a protective spiral of horn-like brown material.

The deep-sea Ghost Sharks such as *Chimaera ogilbyi* and the related Elephant Fish, *Callorhynchus milii*, with its distinctive beak or proboscis ending in a leaf-like process, reach 90 cm.–1·2 m. long, and show many shark-like features, e.g. the cartilage of the skeleton, but also some features like the bony fish, such as a single gill-opening. They show marked affinity with fossils as old as the Palaeozoic, and may represent an evolutionary branch which has survived but not developed further. Occasionally caught inshore.

A world authority on shark attack is V. M. Coppleson (1893–). *For further reading see* P. Goadby: *Sharks and other Predatory Fish of Australia* (Brisbane, 1959); and D. G. Stead: *Sharks and Rays of Australian Seas* (Sydney, 1963).

Shearwaters Medium-sized, generally brown sea-birds* of the Petrel group, including the well-known Mutton-birds*.

She-oak Very widely used in Aus. as a popular name for the Casuarina*.

Sheep Governor Phillip brought some Cape Fat-tailed sheep in 1788, but Macarthur's* Merinos* (1797) were the real start of the Aus. flocks, now amounting to 165 million sheep (N.S.W. 44%; Vic. 17·5%; Qld. 14%; W.A. 11·5%; S.A. 10·5%; Tas. 2·5%). Wool (75% from Merinos) comprises over a quarter of the total export value, while refrigerated mutton comprises 2% and is dominated by Vic. exports to U.K., Japan and Greece. Sheep-rearing has also played a vital part in the spread of settlement. Over half are reared on improved pastures in the 30- to 75-cm. rainfall belt S of the Tropic. This is also the optimum area for wheat* with medium-sized sheep-wheat farms (using rotation) and purely wheat or sheep properties, the latter including most of the famous Merino studs. On the drier margins some 25% of the total are carried on larger properties with capacity as low as 12–15 ha. per sheep and natural grazing of mulga, mallee, saltbush and Mitchell-grass perennials as staple, supplemented by annual grasses in wetter years. On the wetter margins (over 75 cm.) mutton, sheep and fat lambs reared on smaller farms are more important, as they are in areas of irrigated pasture and fodder crops. Crossbreds (10% of total) of Merino and English Leicesters, Lincolns, Romney Marsh or Southdowns yield coarse wool but also mutton, and the Comeback (5%) from Merino ram and Crossbred ewe, a better wool and mutton. The Aus. Polwarth derived originally from Merino/Lincoln crosses (2%) and Corriedale (6%) have medium wool and good mutton yield in areas too wet or cool for Merinos. All these are concentrated in the wheat-sheep and wetter regions. Merinos are completely dominant elsewhere.

Recent developments include intensified capacity and yield, since most available land has been taken up and much former sheep land changed over to crops. Subterranean clover, superphosphates and trace elements have improved pastures; predators (dingos, foxes) and competitors (rabbits, kangaroos) are the object of campaigns; parasites, both external (blowfly) and internal (liver-fluke), and diseases are guarded against by dipping, vaccination and injection. Problems include over-grazing, production costs in marginal areas, over-investment and price fluctuations notably of wool*. (*See also* TEXTILES.) *For further reading see* A. Barnard ed.: *The Simple Fleece* (Melbourne, 1962); R. Anderson: *On the Sheep's Back* (Melbourne, 1967).

Sheet Web Spider   A popular name for the Zodariidae family, hunting from terrestrial burrows, e.g. the widespread small shiny red-brown to black *Storena* genus.

Sheffield Shield   An inter-state cricket trophy, bought with a gift from Lord Sheffield, patron of the English touring team of 1892-3. Up to 1971 N.S.W. had been successful 36 times, including successive years 1953-62, Vic. has won 21, S.A. 9, W.A. 2 (fully participant only from 1956-7) and Qld. 0 (from 1926-7).

16*

Shells and **Shellfish**   Are found in great variety round the Aus. coasts. They are discussed, following a classification of the Phylum Mollusca* (not all of which have shells), under the following 5 separate articles: Bivalves*; Gastropoda*; Chitons*; Cephalopoda*; Tusk Shells*. 2 notable early conchologists were J. Brazier (1842-1930), working in the Aus. Museum and Sir Joseph Verco (1851-1933), a S.A. doctor who gathered many shells from the coast and Great Aus. Bight. *For further reading see also* D. F. McMichael: *Shells of the Australian Shore* (Brisbane, 1962); and J. Child: *Australian Sea Shells* (Sydney, 1963).

Shepparton   Vic. 36S/145E (19,409 in 1971)   A city on the E bank of the River Goulburn, and the headquarters of the Goulburn Irrigation area. It has grown from a river-crossing (originally called Macguire's Punt) on a sheep-run owned by a squatter called Sheppard, to become the service and commercial centre of a large orchard and vegetable-growing district. In addition to the soft fruit canneries (built 1917 and busy only from January-April) there is a new soup factory, older clothing and metal-works, a brick-works using local clay, and a woollen mill.

Shipping   Overseas shipping discharged and shipped in 1970 was over 90 million tonnes, a 42% increase since 1965. 8 ships were Aus. owned and registered, and 6 Aus. owned, overseas registered. The 3 major routes are: Europe with 30% more cargo cleared than entered; Middle East countries with much of the cleared tonnage as ballast in oil-tankers (this applies also to Indonesian routes) and Japan (over 50% total tonnage cleared) with ballast in entering ships which leave with ores, wool and coal. With Japanese trade increasing, the Aus. National Line (A.N.L.) along with a Japanese firm, is building up a cargo fleet.

Revolutionary changes are under way with the development of a 'round the world', containership service, operated jointly by Aus. National Lines and a British consortium, and also serving N.Z. About 27 sailings a year will go to Europe and N. America. The project includes highly mechanised dock facilities under way at Fremantle, Melbourne and Sydney.

Coastal shipping flourished in a continent of isolated coastal settlements, difficult terrain and barriers of rail-gauge and customs duties inland. These have been increasingly removed and, with rising shipping costs due to obsolescent ships, increased labour costs (especially in relation to short-haul, general cargo ships) there has been a marked decline in private coastal shipping where firms have sold out or diversified their interests. The Aus. Navigation Act (1912) inhibits operations by foreign vessels except where local lines cannot meet demands, as in oil-shipping between refineries; overseas vessels can carry inter-state passengers and frozen cargo only. The nationalised A.N.L. (1957) with 31 ships and gross tonnage 411,441 (1970) operates on private company lines, and handles 45% of coastal tonnage and the B.H.P.* another 25% (this being its own cargoes). The trend is to bulk handling 'roll-on roll-off' and container freight, and increased size of vessel as in the 1972 *Clutha Capricorn* of 84,660 tonnes deadweight built at Whyalla for the Weipa-Gladstone bauxite trade.

Shipbuilding There are 5 major merchant shipbuilding yards, all concerned with coastal vessels only: Whyalla, S.A., Cockatoo Dock, Sydney, Brisbane, Newcastle State Dockyard and Maryborough, Qld. Naval vessels are made in Sydney and at Williamstown, Melbourne, and many smaller yards make specialist and pleasure craft.

The early Governors were forbidden to allow building of ships which might interfere with the trade monopoly held until 1813 by the East India Company*; this restricted activities to small craft for local use. The earliest private shipyard was at the mouth of the Tank Stream and was owned by the emancipist James Underwood who joined with 2 other former convicts, Henry Kable and Simeon Lord, in a profitable sealing, trading and ship-building company. Whaling vessels were built later especially in Tas., but Aus. shipbuilding died with wooden ships until the native iron and steel industry, wartime needs and recent mineral discoveries stimulated its modern development. The Aus. Shipbuilding Board (1941) through which the industry is subsidised, arranged for the building of 214 ships, 1941–70; a further 24 were then on order.

Shipwrecks Off the Aus. coast, as elsewhere, these reflect not only the physical hazards of weather and rocks, but also the type and pace of ocean traffic. The earliest recorded wrecks were off the W.A. coast, and apart from the English ship *Tryal* (1822) on the Monte Bello Islands, were mainly Dutch merchantmen on their way, with the Trade Winds of the Indian Ocean, to the Spice Islands. The most famous was the *Batavia** (1629), but the *Vergulde Draak* —or Gilt Dragon (1656) and the *Zuytdorp* (1712) have left legends of treasure, which, with the later *Lancier* (1839), off Rottnest Island, and *Ocean Queen* (1842), on the Abrolhos Islands, keep skin-diving treasure-hunters busy today.

With the founding of N.S.W., the long history of wrecks along the E and SE coasts began. The greatest toll has been taken between Cape Howe and Newcastle (120); many of these have been small coastal vessels with coal, minerals and general cargo, and an average of 10 hands. The worst period was 1850–90 (50 ships lost), probably because of the quickening economic life, and a period of changeover from sail to the early uncertain days of steam. Sudden SE squalls can quickly blow ships on to the rocky headlands.

Major losses were: the *Dunbar* (1857) off Sydney Heads, with only 1 survivor from 123 people; the *Cawarra* (1860) with 60 drowned, only one of a long series of wrecks on the dreaded Oyster Bank off Newcastle, which began in 1805 with the collier *Francis*. Further S, Green Cape has had, among others, the wreck of the first steamship of the Australasian Steam Navigation Co., the *City of Sydney* (1862), and the *Ly-ee-Moon*, a passenger ship, with 76 lost (1886). Even in this century the N.S.W. coast has continued to have an average of 6 wrecks a decade. Today their discovery is prized by abalone* divers in SE Aus. Further out, the Tasman Sea has at least 25 recorded wrecks, and probably many others that just disappeared after leaving port.

To the S the Vic. coast is most dangerous in the region of Cape Otway. Wild westerly storms have blown many vessels on to the islands of the Bass Str., King Island in particular. Here, the migrant ship *Cataraqui* (1835) foundered with a loss of 406, probably the worst Aus. shipping disaster; in 1835 a convict ship *Neva* was also wrecked on the island and 200, mainly women convicts and their children, were drowned; the migrant ship *Netherby* (1866) was wrecked without loss of life, but *British Admiral* (1874) lost 79 from its 88 complement. Macquarie Island* has also seen many wrecks and castaways. The worst Tas. losses occurred when convict and migrant ships tried to beat their way up the D'Entrecasteaux Channel: the *Enchantress* (1835) lost 50 migrants and in the same year 134 convicts (about half the complement) were drowned in the wreck of the *George III*.

The coasts of the N half of Aus. have the serious hazard of summer cyclones; in addition, Qld. has the Great Barrier Reef, the intricate channels of which have bred some of the world's most skilful pilots. Pearling luggers lost in cyclones have been the major wrecks; some 55 in 2 days in March 1899 off the Qld. coast; and about 10 vessels off

Broome, W.A. in 1935. Off Qld. the biggest single disaster was the *Gothenberg* (1875), going from Darwin to Adelaide, with 102 people drowned. Individual reefs were notorious, Kenn Reef and Wreck Reef especially; the latter was named after the *Porpoise* (carrying Flinders) was wrecked there with the *Cato* in 1802. In Torres Str. the *Quetta* (1890) had at least 133 drowned. Wrecks today are relatively rare, with the development of safety devices, notably radar; the remaining dangers are of collision and the consequences of oil pollution.

Shiralee Another word for the swagman's bundle or bluey*.

Shoalhaven River N.S.W. Flows for over 320 km. largely S–N with the grain of the Southern Tablelands, between granite ridges, from its source just E of the Great Divide, 40 km. W of Moruya, 36S/150E. It flows through wet sclerophyll* forest in 75 to 100 cm. rainfall country, mainly in a precipitous gorge until it opens out into the open grazing of the Braidwood Basin, at about 600 m. It enters another precipitous gorge section E of Goulburn, known to tourists at Bungonia, turning E to leave the escarpment and to cross the levee and swampy silts of the delta, near Nowra, now highly developed for dairying, originally drained by a canal dug by convict labour, to the small Crookhaven River on its S edge. The Shoalhaven is to be developed to augment Sydney's water supply in 3 stages in the 1970s.

Shouting An Aus. term, now widely used, meaning to take a turn to pay for all the drinks, by shouting for the glasses to be filled.

Shrimps Aquatic Crustaceans* generally equated in Aus. with small members of the Prawns*, e.g. the Porcelain Shrimp, *Stenopus hispidus*, 10 cm. long, scarlet, white and blue, with lobster-like claws, seen in coral reef waters, or

Freshwater Shrimps, such as various members of the Atyidae family, with feeble pincer development on the 2 front pairs of legs, including a Mountain-shrimp, *Atya striolata*, and the common Freshwater Shrimp of the Murray-Darling system, *Paratya australiensis*. The name Mountain-shrimp is also applied to the interesting primitive *Anaspides tasmaniae* of the Mt. Wellington streams near Hobart and to 1 or 2 relatives, and to Brine and Fairy Shrimps (*see* WATER-FLEAS).

Shrubs Many Aus. species with attractive flowers are discussed from different viewpoints under Flora* and under Vegetation*, and in the following articles: Bird-flower*, Blackboys*, Blackthorn*, Bluebush*, Bottlebrush*, Callistemon*, Cassia*, Caustic Bush*, Christmas Bush*, Conesticks*, Drumsticks* or Narrow-Leaf Conebush, Emu Bush*, Frangipani*, Fuchsia* Heath, Geebungs*, Grass-trees*, Guinea-Flower*, Gum Vine*, Hakea*, Heaths*, Hibiscus*, Honey Flower*, Honey-myrtle*, Hovea*, Indigo*, Laurel or Tasmanian Laurel*, Mallow*, Milkwort*, Mint Bush*, Mistletoe*, Mock Orange*, Molucca Bramble*, Olive-wood*, Wild Parsley*, Passion Fruit*, Prostanthera*, Native Raspberry*, Saltbush*, Smoke Bush*, Stinkwood*, Velvet-bushes*, Verticordia*, Wax Plant*, Wedding Bush* Waratah*, Zieria*.

Shute, Nevil (1899–1960) b. London. He was an aviation engineer of some repute under his surname of Norway. He migrated to Aus. after the 1939–45 War, and using only his first 2 names became a best-selling novelist notably with *A Town Like Alice* and *On the Beach*.

Siding Spring Mountain N.S.W. 31S/149E (846 m.) A hill of volcanic rock in the Warrumbungle Range*, clad in dry sclerophyll* forest. Long regarded as a possible site for an astronomical observatory, this function came in the mid 1960s with development by the Australian National University. (Mt. Stromlo near Canberra had become more limited in use by the growth of the city's lights.) Initial development was crowned in 1967 by the announcement of an Aus.-British project for a 3·8-m. telescope, costing $13 million, and the second largest in the world (1974).

Sikhs Descended from 19th-century Punjabi migrants, they are found now in the banana-growing areas of N of N.S.W. and S of Qld. Few retain traditional dress or religious observance, although some recent revival has stemmed from Asian students in Sydney.

Silky Oak The name is often applied to the 36-m. *Grevillea* robusta of E Aus., but at present most timber of that name is from the Northern Silky Oak or Bull Oak, *Cardwellia sublimis*, an important Qld. timber tree; it is the only Aus. species of its genus, and is in the important southern hemisphere family Proteaceae.

Silver Obtained as a by-product mainly from lead* concentrates, with half the Aus. output at Broken Hill*, N.S.W., and from copper* concentrates at Mt. Isa* and Cobar*. Export, which is largely in the form of lead-silver bullion, is not large, but is expected to increase in the 1970s. Aus. is sixth in world production, accounting for 7% of the total.

Silver-eyes or White-eyes (genus *Zosterops*—belt-faced) Small insectivorous and nectar-eating birds of Africa, S Asia and Aus.; they are about 12 cm. long, with longish tails, mainly green-backed and buff-bellied, sometimes with some blue on back and breast, with the distinctive white around the eye. The nest is a well-made cup of grass, horsehair, moss, cobwebs etc., light enough to rest on comparatively slender twigs. The Grey-breasted Silver-eye, *Z. lateralis*, of E Aus. is often seen in gardens, eating greenfly, but exacting the price in ripe fruit; it has several calls and songs and also is a mimic. Those in Tas. largely migrate to the mainland in winter. It has recently become established in N.Z., presumably having been blown across 2,000 km. of the Tasman Sea. The 'greenie' of W.A., *Z. gouldi*, generally greenish with a flush of blue on the breast and buff belly, has at times been shot in large numbers in orchards. The Yellow Silver-eye, *Z. lutea*, lives in the mangrove swamps of the far N.

Silverfish Silvery insects of up to 2 cm. long, of the primitive Order Thysanura. The young are hatched directly into more or less the same form as the adults, but the skin is sloughed at least 12 times. Aus. native species are thought to be mainly parasitic in ants' nests, probably robbing them of nectar and other starchy food. Their rapid movement is compatible with this mode of life. The 2 most familiar species are both introduced, especially the nocturnal *Lepisma saccharina* which has adapted its tastes to food (such as wallpaper and bookbinding paste etc.) readily obtained in houses.

Simpson Desert A region of 145,000 km.², 23–27S/135–9E, mainly in N.T., but overlapping the Qld. and S.A. borders. It was named by Madigan, who examined the region from the air in 1929, after the President of the S.A. Geographical Society who later financed his camel-crossing in 1939, the first crossing made. It is a triangular area pointing to L. Eyre*, bordered by the Finke River* on the W, the Mulligan and Diamantina Rivers on the E and the Macdonnell Ranges and Plenty River on the N. The surface comprises thousands of NNW–SSE-trending sand-hills about 500 m. apart, with spinifex in the dips; Madigan crossed over 700. Paradoxically he was held up by rain twice on his 5 weeks' crossing in the cooler winter conditions of June/July. Sturt* was repulsed in 1845 by the ridges on the E 'stretching intermin-

ably . . . like waves of the sea'—but not the one he had come to seek. *See* C. T. Madigan; *Crossing the Dead Heart* (Melbourne, 1946).

Singleton N.S.W. 33S/151E (7,181 in 1971) A local market centre on the middle Hunter* Valley, in dairying, sheep and beef-cattle pastures and also in an area of viticulture for highly prized table wines. There are some interesting older buildings. Like Maitland*, it is liable to floods.

Sittellas or **Tree-runners** (genus *Neositta*) They are small, generally black and white birds with strong claws for vertical 'tree-running' in search of insects, and straight, very sharp beaks. They build cup-like nests in tree-forks, so camouflaged with bark as to be difficult to detect. (Contrast the slightly decurved beak and tree-hollow nests of the Tree-creepers*, which also more commonly run head-downwards.) There are slightly differing species in different parts of Aus. The Orange-winged Sittella, *N. chrysoptera* (golden-winged), is found in sclerophyll and savannah woodland in SE Aus. The White-headed Sittella, *N. leucocephala*, of the NE, is often seen in paperbarks. The Striated Sittella, *N. striata*, of NE Qld. is black-headed, the cock bird having a white eye-stripe; the Black-capped Sittella, *N. pileata*, of the SW, S and centre of Aus., with white face and breast; and the White-winged Sittella, *N. leucoptera* (really black-winged, but showing a white flash when it flies while the Orange-winged species flashes orange-red), seen high in trees in N Aus.

Sitsky, Larry (1934–) A leading Aus. musician and composer whose works include piano and chamber music and two operas (most recent is *Lenz*, 1970, librettto Gwen Harwood).

Skiing In Aus. it dates from the gold-rush period, when miners at Kiandra, N.S.W., organised races in 1862; then interest lapsed until early this century when some lodges were built. In the 1930s Austrian coaches were brought over, but the major development dates from the 1950s, when hydro-electric projects in the Aus. Alps and Snowy Mts. gave easier access to the snow-fields, and increasing affluence allowed wider participation. There are now considerable villages of ski lodges, notably in the Perisher and Thredbo Valleys flanking Mt. Kosciusko, and in the Vic. Alps. There are championships, attracting wide interest.

Skinks The largest family of Aus. lizards, Scincidae, with 9 genera and over 100 species; they range widely in size from 5 to over 50 cm., and in habitat from rain-forest and sub-alpine streams to desert rock crevices, small burrows in forest litter and suburban gardens. All are insectivorous and harmless, indeed, beneficent to man. Most have very smooth scales, with a smooth sheen and often handsome dark colouring. Nearly all are diurnal, among the larger skinks. Most are quick and active; all have movable eye-lids with the exception of one genus (*Ablepharus*), which have a fixed transparent scale; all produce their young alive except some of the smaller species which lay eggs. Some genera have only vestigial limbs, some mere stumps, some no trace of limbs and naturally their popular names overlap with the Legless Lizards and with snakes. 1. The Common Blue-tongue, *Tiliqua scincoides*, is widespread and adapted to suburban gardens, drain-pipes, rubbish tips etc. where it eats insects, snails and some berries; it is often 30–50 cm. long, grey to brown with dark cross-bands from head to tail; it swells the body, extends the cobalt blue tongue and hisses when harassed. The alpine form of SE Aus., black with pink-orange blotches and more robust, has been given separate species status as *T. nigrolutea*. 2. The largest skink, up to 60 cm. long, is the Land Mullet,

Egernia bungana; it is glossy brown-black, eats smaller skinks, snails, insects and some fruit, and lives in hollow logs or communal warrens in rain-forest in S Qld. and N N.S.W. 3. The Copper-tailed Skink, *Lygosoma taeniolatum*, with brilliant black and white side stripes, and up to 23 cm. long, lives under flat rocks in sandstone areas from Cape York to the SE of S.A. 4. The Water Skink, *L. quoyii quoyii*, also coppery but black-spotted, lives in and around streams in SE Aus. 5. The Common Grass Skink, *L. guichenoti*, only 5–10 cm. long and olive to bronze with black and cream side stripe, lives in communal nests in forest litter under low foliage, but has adapted to garden compost heaps, eating ants, termites, flies, moths, midges, mosquitoes, caterpillars and worms. 5. The Three-toed Skink, *L. aequale*, and 6. the Snake-lizard, *L. verrauxii*, are rain-forest species of E Aus., with a snake-like motion adapted to progress through leaf-mould etc. 7. *L. frontale*, in N Qld. rain-forests, is legless. 8. The 5-toed small Wall Lizard of W.A. is *Ablepharus boutonii plagiocephalus*. 9. *A. timidus* is a 3-toed burrowing skink living mostly underground in inland Aus., and insulated against the sharp daily changes of temperature.

Skuas Those seen in Aus. waters include 2 medium-sized brown birds, the Great or Antarctic Skua and the Arctic Skua. (*See* SEA-BIRDS.)

Slessor, Kenneth (1901–1971) b. Orange, N.S.W. A leading poet whose early verse was strongly influenced by the zestful Lindays*, as in *Earth Visitors*, but matured to a more bitter and individual style. Imagery is very strong; his major works include the elegy *Five Bells* and *Five Visions of Captain Cook* (1939). He was a journalist, editor and prose writer, a selection from which is *Bread and Wine* (Sydney, 1970). For further reading see C. Semmler: *Kenneth Slessor* (London, 1967).

Slow-worms The small, harmless Legless Lizards* with long discardable tails sometimes also called Worm-snakes*.

Smallpox A serious virus disease transmissible mainly by droplet, though treated as a contagious disease with strict isolation. At present parts of Asia, e.g. Bengal, are the main endemic home, from which it occasionally breaks out in epidemics elsewhere. Risks are increased by rapid modern transport which may take an infected person from an endemic area to a smallpox-free country within the incubation period of the virus, and for this reason the quarantine regulations are particularly stringent. Since Jenner's vaccination technique of 1798, using a cowpox virus, a reasonable degree of artificial immunity to the disease is available, at some, though relatively low, risk of disability or death following the vaccination itself, and compulsory vaccination of entrants to Aus. is an important part of quarantine regulations, failing which a quarantine period is enforced. In Aus. vaccination in infancy is not compulsory.

Smallpox seems to have swept through and decimated many Aboriginal populations soon after European settlement, but it is not clear whether the infection came from Sydney Cove or from Asian contacts with NW coastal groups. Serious epidemics in the 1880s affected white and black alike, in all colonies except Qld. and W.A., and were influential in creating a demand for better health conditions, including uniform quarantine regulations.

Smith Family A N.S.W. charitable organisation dating from 1922, when an anonymous group in Sydney began distributing to the poor. It has greatly increased through private giving and public appeals, and extends to pensioner housing and a children's convalescent home in N.S.W.

Smith, Isaac A seaman on the *Endeavour*. It was recorded that Cook, having decided on a landing at Botany Bay, said to him 'Isaac, you shall land first,' making him the first man ashore on the historic April 29th 1770.

Smith, Sir Keith Macpherson (1890–1955) b. Adelaide. He joined the Royal Flying Corps and served gallantly as an aerial gunnery officer; in 1919 he joined his brother Sir Ross Smith on the pioneer Eng.–Aus. flight in a Vickers Vimy bomber. Appropriately enough he served as Vickers representative in Aus. for many years.

Smith, Margaret (1942–) b. Albury, One of the greatest women tennis players (*see* COURT).

Smith, Sir Ross Macpherson (1892–1922) b. Adelaide. He served at Gallipoli and was transferred to No. 1 Squadron of the Aus. Flying Corps in 1916, where he served with extraordinary skill and courage. After the War he piloted the large Handley-Page bomber from Cairo to Calcutta with Sergeants J. M. Bennett and W. H. Shiers as mechanics. Vickers offered a Vimy bomber to bid for the Commonwealth Government's prize for an Eng.–Aus. flight (*see* AIR RACES) and with the same 2 mechanics and his brother Keith (later Sir Keith*) a remarkable pioneering flight was safely accomplished. With Bennett, Sir Ross was killed when preparing for a projected round-the-world flight in Eng., flying a Vickers Viking amphibian.

Smithton Tas. 41S/145E (3,203 in 1971) A port on Duck River serving the far NW of the State, and with butter-making and pea-canning.

Smoke Bush A popular W.A. name for *Conospermum stoechadis* and related species, with grass-like leaves (rejected by stock) and masses of woolly grey-white flowers (eaten by stock), giving the popular name. A related species of the barren sandstone of E Aus. is the recumbent, purple-flowered *C. tenuifolium*.

Snake-lizards The small, harmless Legless Lizards*, with long discardable tail. Saltbush Snake, Glass Snake and Jumping Snake are all popular names for the harmless Burton's Legless Lizard (*see under* LEGLESS LIZARDS). Glass Snake is also sometimes applied to the Legless Skink or Snake-Lizard, and both Glass Snake and Snake-lizard to the Three-toed Skink (*see* SKINKS). Glass Snake is also sometimes applied to the Worm Snakes.

SNAKES Long, smooth, scaly, limbless reptiles, of the Sub-Order Serpentes or Ophidia, which with the lizards* make up the Order Squamata or scaly reptiles. Compared with legless lizards*, snakes have the elastic ligament uniting the fronts of the jaw-bones, permitting them to swallow prey larger than the normal dimensions of the head. (Other differences are discussed under lizards). Of the snakes, only pythons have vestigial rear limbs. Some characteristics, e.g. the lidless eye with fixed, transparent scale, are shared with particular genera of lizards. Others are adaptations to legless existence, such as the wave-like muscular motion pushing the body forward, or the asymmetrical arrangement of paired organs, such as the lungs, liver and kidneys within the narrow tube-like body—rounded or 'keeled' (i.e. broad-based to grip tree-bark etc.).

Replaceable teeth, for gripping rather than cutting, are in shallow pits (not sockets) on the edges of the lower and upper jaw-bones, with additional teeth on the palate except in the blind worm snakes; some species also have teeth on the tip of the snout. The venomous species have venom glands and specialised fangs in the upper jaw—the more primitive and less poisonous with an enlarged rear fang, and the more poisonous, including the species dangerous to man, with a long recurved front fang—and sometimes with a reserve fang growing behind, so that 4 larger incisions may show to the front of the smaller toothmarks. A groove in front is fed with venom from an enclosed channel behind it. Compared with the vipers, family Viperidae, which are *not* found in Aus., the Aus. venomous snakes generally give a shallower wound and the venom is led on to the incision from the groove and channel, as compared with deeper injection from a longer hollow fang in the Vipers (much more liable to damage in striking, though the bone to which it is attached is hinged much more than in Aus. snakes to allow the fang to be folded back when the snake closes its mouth). Because of this difference, external cleaning of a bite, and relatively superficial swabbing and swilling, are often more efficacious in treatment than for Viper-bites (*see* FIRST AID FOR SNAKE-BITE, page 489). On the other hand the venom of some species such as the Tiger Snake and the Death Adder is several times more powerful than that of the Indian Cobra.

The harmless Aus. species, except the File Snakes, but including the Pythons, lay eggs; the venomous snakes mostly are born alive, directly from the vent or in a fine, often transparent sac from which the young soon break out, using their egg-tooth on the tip of the snout (but the Brown Snake and the Taipan lay eggs). Some species are believed to have placental apparatus so that the young may derive nourishment from the mother through the placenta, as in mammals, as distinct from being dependent on the store of nourishment in the egg. Eggs are laid in leaf-mould, decomposed log wood, or under a suitable turf; they are long, white and parchment-like, and laid over a period of 30 minutes to 2 days; they are left carefully covered to incubate in natural heat from the sun and forest litter. Snakes eat food ranging from the soft soil grubs of the worm snakes, to small furred animals, but seldom carrion. Some tree species eat birds' eggs, but most Aus. species do not.

Snake venom may be regarded as highly specialised saliva, produced from specially evolved salivary glands. Some are neuro-toxic, with a paralysing effect on the nervous system of the victim so that it cannot escape and can be eaten at leisure; these may kill because the victim cannot breathe. Some coagulate the victim's blood, and may cause heart failure. Many venoms contain digestive ferments, as does saliva, and a sort of pre-digestive process often breaks down the victim's blood cells or damages the linings of blood vessels, causing haemorrhage. Anti-venene is obtained by milking captive poisonous snakes of their venom into a vessel through a thin rubber cover. This is injected in gradually increasing doses into a horse, to stimulate the production of anti-venene in its blood. When the horse's blood serum contains a sufficiently high level of anti-venene, it can be bled, and the anti-venene concentrated and stored for injection into snake-bite victims.

Being cold-blooded, many snakes have to hibernate in winter, leading a sluggish existence at much reduced rates of metabolism in a burrow or hollow. Many snakes use a great deal of saliva in working their expanded jaw and head bones gradually over a large prey, but they do not cover it with saliva beforehand as has been thought. Other tall stories are of snakes milking cows, flying (though some arboreal species may flatten their bodies and glide a little), swallowing their young as a protection, taking revenge for a mate that has been killed, stinging with the tongue, being charmed by music (the Indian Cobra sways in rhythm with the flautist's movements, waiting to strike), failing to cross a horsehair or coir rope round a camp, and progressing by rolling rapidly, tail in mouth like a hoop.

Like many Aus. plants and animals, snakes have very confusing and often overlapping local, popular names, sometimes by application of names from Europe, e.g. Adder, sometimes by the use of terms such as Carpet Snake or Tiger Snake for somewhat similarly marked snakes in areas where the Carpet Snake or Tiger Snake proper is not found. As many local popular names as possible have been included in the main articles noted below on snakes, but we have not attempted to include separate articles under all the very numerous popular names.

Snakes may be classified as follows, and the selected species will be discussed in articles under the names marked with an asterisk. 1. Worm* or Blind Snakes, family Typhlopidae. 2. Pythons* and Rock Snakes, family Boidae. 3. Colubrid* Snakes, family Colubridae, including the sub-families: File Snakes* or Harmless Water Snakes, Acrochordinae; Harmless Land Snakes*, Colubrinae; Reared-fanged Water Snakes*, Homalopsinae; and Reared-fanged Land Snakes*, Boiginae (both sub-families are venomous, but unlikely to harm man). 4. Venomous or Front-fanged Land Snakes*, family Elapidae. 5. Sea-snakes*, the Front-fanged Sea-snakes, family Hydrophiidae.

Important work on snake venom has been done by: Sir Charles Martin (1866–1955) and C. H. Kellaway (1889–1952) in Melbourne, and E. Worrell (1924–), whose work *Reptiles of Australia* (Sydney, 1964) is a major source, has an Aus. Reptile Park at Gosford, N.S.W. *For further reading see also* J. R. Kinghorn: *The Snakes of Australia* (Sydney, 1956).

First Aid for Snake Bite 1. Assess quickly if the snake was identified as poisonous, or if the wound shows the deep front fang-marks of the species dangerous to man. 2. Apply a ligature or tourniquet between the wound and the heart (bandage, rubber tyre, webbing belt etc.), reducing, but not stopping the flow of blood, and releasing for 30 seconds after 20–25 minutes, and thereafter every 10 minutes. 3.

Wash any venom from the surface—in emergency even with urine. 4. Cut the wound with a sharp blade, in emergency with broken glass, to increase the flow of blood, to remove as much venom as possible. (As noted above, Aus. poisonous snakes inject the venom to only a shallow depth); if the tourniquet cannot be applied, e.g. to the buttocks, and if the wound is not near an artery, it is sometimes better to pinch up the skin and excise a small piece of flesh to the depth of the wound. 5. Suck the wound; unless there are open sores on the flesh of the mouth, this is quite safe. 6. Give only such stimulants as tea and coffee *not* alcohol. 7. Give reassurance—there are very few deaths from snake-bite since antivenene has been available. 8. Get the patient to hospital for anti-venene treatment, as quickly as possible and with identification of the snake concerned if at all possible. Treatment is generally by proportional dose of the Tiger Snake anti-venene, but Taipan anti-venene is also now available. 9. The rubbing in of Potassium Permanganate (Condy's crystals) is now *not* recommended, as tissue damage is likely to outweight any neutralising effect.

Snapper (*Chrysophrys guttulatus*) A pre-eminent commercial and sporting sea-fish related to the Black Bream and

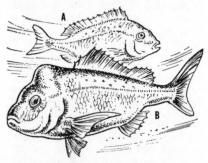

A *School Snapper*, B *Old Man Snapper, about 1·2 m. long*

Tarwine; it resembles these Bream until it develops the marked bulge above the eyes and gills in old age, but it grows commonly to 1·2 m. and over 18 kg. It is known by several names at different stages: the juvenile Cockney, to 12 cm. long; the Red Bream or Redfish to 0·5–0·7 kg.; the Squire at about 2·5 kg. and School Snapper at a little more, until it develops the bulging head and is Old Man Snapper. It eats mainly shellfish etc.

Snook (*Australuzza novae-hollandiae*) A grey to greenish fish with long strong teeth, which is netted or lined commercially, mainly in the S of Aus.

Snow Grass A popular name for various species of *Poa*, a grey-green fine-bladed montane forest grass of SE Aus., with a graceful spreading conical head of small seed spikelets, often seen with Snow Fescue (*see* FESCUE).

Snow Gum (*Eucalyptus pauciflora*) A small white-trunked tree of SE Aus. (*see* SALLEE). The name is also used for *E. niphophila*, often seen stunted and distorted by the wind in exposed sub-alpine sites. The Tasmanian Snow Gum, *E. coccifera*, with narrower intermediate leaves, broader buds, more conical fruit, and often a more straggling, white-limbed tree-form, grows in more alpine conditions than does *E. pauciflora*, in Tas. at about 700–1,300 m. and in 125–250 cm. mean annual precipitation.

Snowy Mountains, The N.S.W. They contain Australia's highest land and only extensive alpine area. The W face is dissected and steep, drained by the headwaters of the Murray River*, while the E has a more gentle slope, drained by the Snowy* and Murrumbidgee*. The highest point is Mt. Kosciusko* (2,230 m.). The highest peaks are merely residuals standing above a series of plateau levels; the most impressive is Jugengal (2,061 m.). Pleistocene glaciation has left cirques, moraine and erratic blocks. Snow lies for 3–6 months and may cover a greater area than in Switzerland; hotels for skiers in winter and sightseers in summer often copy the design of a Swiss chalet. The tree-line is at about 1,800 m.; above this is a rich carpet of alpine flowers in summer, below it the Snow Gums, *Eucalyptus niphophila*, and *E. pauciflora*, stunted and gnarled at first, then thickening and giving way to valuable stands of Alpine Ash, *E. gigantea*, and Mountain Ash, *E. regnans*. The 'Snow grass'. (*Poa* spp.), was valuable summer grazing for the pastoralist of the bordering regions. Too much use led to erosion and restriction. Much of the area is now under the control of the Kosciusko State Park Trust (1944) which covers 600,000 ha.

Snowy Mountains Scheme The Snowy Mountains Authority was established by Act of Parliament (1949), to develop the water resources of the only Aus. alpine area, for power and irrigation. There are 16 dams, the last (Talbingo on the Tumut River) completed in 1971. Tunnels total almost 150 km. and there are 80 km. of aqueduct. Peak power 4 million kW produced; 7 power stations. Total cost $800 million. High precipitation from winter depressions, including heavy snowfall, runs off to the S coast by the Snowy River, and inland by the Murrumbidgee, Murray and Tumut rivers which ultimately join. The W slope of the watershed is very abrupt. By diverting the water of the Snowy catchment through it in 2 main diversion systems, power is generated along this scarp foot before the water feeds irrigation schemes downstream. Power is also generated on Snowy tributaries falling sharply from the Kosciusko slopes. The main storage dams Eucumbene* and Jindabyne* are in the Snowy catchment, but the diversion tunnels are 2-way so that excess flow from one catchment can be diverted for storage in another. Construction of the Scheme

has employed large numbers of migrants as well as foreign experts; a special township (Cabramurra) was built and the main base is the foothill town of Cooma*. Doubts are expressed about the economic justification of high capital investment compared with thermal stations, of the potential markets for increased irrigation crops, and of the spoiling of a unique alpine ecology. On the other hand, the Snowy lies between the 2 industrial concentrations of Vic. and N.S.W., its power feeds both at peak times and running costs are low; access roads have permitted winter sports resorts to develop, and, not least, there is a considerable sense of achievement in this major engineering feat, which had been first discussed in the 1870s.

Snowy River 440 km. long, it rises on the E slopes of Mt. Kosciusko in the Snowy Mts. (N.S.W.), flowing to Bass Str. (Vic.) from alpine slopes and fed by heavy spring snow-melt. It runs through increasingly wooded gorges between cleared stretches of alluvial dairy land. Waters of the Snowy catchment are the main source for the Snowy Mountains Scheme*.

Snuggery S.A. 38S/140E A small timber processing centre, 10 km. SE of Millicent, with cellulose and tissue-paper-making, based on large pine plantations and using ample supplies of spring water.

Soccer or **Association Football** First recorded in Sydney in 1880, and a number of clubs developed in N.S.W. and Qld. The game has spread to all the States, much more rapidly in recent years with the arrival of British and European migrants. Teams based on European affiliations attract many Sunday spectators, unfortunately with some factional brawling. The Aus. Football League matches are used by Eng. Football Pools in the summer. Aus. teams play internationally.

SOCIAL SERVICES Some 40% of consolidated State and Commonwealth Revenue is devoted to a wide range of services. The Commonweath, empowered by the Constitution to award old age and invalid pensions, had its powers widened by the 1946 Referendum* to 'provision of maternity allowances, widows pensions, child endowment, unemployment, pharmaceutical and sickness and hospital benefits, medical and dental services (but not so as to authorise any form of civil conscription), benefits to students and family allowances'. These are financed from the National Welfare Fund (1943), a charge on Income Tax Revenue. Only maternity allowances and child endowment have been free of a means-test but in 1972, progressive abolition of means tested age pensions was announced. Subsidised health benefits are available to low income groups and migrants for their first 2 months in Aus. Income tax relief on medical costs is an additional Commonwealth contribution. The States are responsible for education*, public hospitals and many supplementary services. The operation of the medical and hospital benefits, dating from the National Health Act (1953), is a sophisticated, possibly unique system. The Commonwealth subsidises non-profit-making approved Societies or Funds (there are over 90) which, in return for subscriptions on varying scales, by largely voluntary members, reimburse a proportion of medical and hospital charges. Some 90% of the population is covered, 76% by voluntary schemes and 14% by Pensioner and other schemes. Pharmaceutical benefits are separately subsidised, as are the medical costs for old age pensioners and the chronically sick. In addition, the public hospitals provide free diagnostic and medical treatment, subject to a means-test, in outpatient departments. In outback areas district nursing is extended by **Bush Nursing Associations** (founded 1909) which maintain centres especially for mothers and children.

Historical Development (Dates are those of implementation) In the 19th century voluntary agencies, working with State Government funds supplementing charitable donations, provided a very minimal care for the utterly destitute. The social attitude echoed the current spirit of *laissez faire*. A strong fear of undermining self-reliance has been carried over to the present day. In 1900 N.S.W., then Vic. introduced non-contributory but means-tested old age pensions earlier than in U.K. or U.S., but following N.Z. and the Danes (1891). The Commonwealth superseded these (and the Qld. scheme, 1908) in 1909. Invalid pensions (1910) and maternity allowance (1912) followed. There was a long pause in further legislation, although in the 1920s a national insurance scheme reached the draft stage; the 1929–33 Depression led to relief works and food issues, but not cash doles. The 1939–45 War with its widespread impetus to ensure greater social security, coupled with a Labor Government, led to the next period of development: child endowment (1941, although pioneered in N.S.W. from 1927); widows' pensions (1942, although previous schemes existed in N.S.W. from 1925, and in Vic.)—they also apply to deserted wives and divorcees who have failed to secure maintenance, and to the wives of men in mental hospitals or gaoled for over 6 months; sickness and unemployment (1945), for which there had been no prior schemes save the 1923 Unemployment Insurance Act in Qld., although some industrial awards had included sick leave, and there were many Friendly Society benefits (*see* TRADE UNIONS); and rehabilitation (1948) for remediable cases. The 1953 National Health Act, introduced by a Liberal Government, expressly inhibited a comprehensive National Health Scheme. The Labor Party opposed contributory schemes for pensions or allowances and has supported the means-test in the past. There has now been successful pressure to abolish it from the growing numbers of pensioners who feel they are thus penalised for earlier thrift. Only in the last decade has there been much progress in social services that are not specifically aimed at remedying income losses. Mental health, marriage- and child-counselling, probationary and prisoner rehabilitation work all lack funds and, especially, adequate trained personnel. The Nimmo Report (1969) recommended improved health benefits for low income groups and in cases of prolonged illness. These were largely implemented under a National Health Insurance Commission (1970) with benefits based on a survey of 'most common fee charged'. By 1975 the Labor Govt. plans comprehensive schemes for health, superannuation and minimum guaranteed income.

Reciprocal agreements with N.Z. and U.K. effectively waive residential qualifications for most benefits which apply to people from other countries. T. H. Kewley's *Social Security in Australia* (Sydney, 1966) is an historical review.

SOIL AND SOIL TYPES In *The Aus. Environment* (1970) G. W. Leeper writes, 'The recurring theme in Aus. soils is age and poverty.' Climatic types, parent rocks, slope and drainage conditions and the related vegetation, natural or as affected by agricultural practices are all influences. These classifications are broadly based on repetitive patterns, not just at the surface but in section down to the solid rock or loose mantle not affected by soil-forming processes (plant roots, bacterial action, worms etc.). Layers from the surface are termed: *A* horizon, a leached layer, which may contain accumulated organic matter; *B* horizon, receiving clay and other material such as lime leached from above; *C* horizon, consisting mainly of products of weathering from parent rock; *D* horizon, parent rock or other material not related to the soil formation. Somewhat

apart, a *G* or 'gley' horizon is a layer mottled by chemical action associated with waterlogging. Soil sections or 'profiles', similar in crumb structure, texture, chemical composition etc., are grouped in great soil groups named or modified from pioneer research work, particularly in Russia and U.S. Detailed soil surveys over small areas use local names often from a 'type locality'. Major soil groups based on C.S.I.R.O.'s* *Aus. Environment* (1949) are:

1. *Fossil Soils* Aus. is so largely an ancient land surface that many plateau surfaces were subject to deep weathering and tropical soil-forming processes during the Tertiary era (*see* GEOLOGY), when hot humid conditions were much more widespread. Climatic change left deep tropical soils as fossils, while subsequent erosion has stripped off part of the living soil profile, in many places leaving either (a) Laterite (from the Latin, *later*, brick), a rather porous red clay, hardening on exposure, or (b) Pallid Zone soils, a greatly leached grey-white layer seen in many parts of Aus. as a sub-soil, and often in considerable depth (*see* SOIL EROSION).

2. *Humid Zone* (a) Podsols or grey-leached soils have an acid *A* horizon, often with some accumulation of organic matter, e.g. in a coniferous forest but otherwise ash-grey and heavily leached, while the *B* horizon again has a dark organic-rich upper layer, then yellowish clay; some podsols have an iron-oxide hard pan at the permanent top of the underground water table, sometimes quite difficult for roots or even implements to penetrate, and impeding drainage. These soils predominate over the humid E and SE of Aus., and the relatively small humid area in the SW of W.A. Within the zone, however, are residual stretches of 1 (a) and 1 (b) and also stretches of 2 (b)–2 (c). (b) Krasnozems or red loams, red-brown soils often on basalts, are well drained and loamy in crumb structure, yet with a high clay content, moderately acid to neutral, with little

development of layers except for surface organic matter. (c) Alpine and peaty podsols are found in the Aus. Alps and Snowy Mts. as well as very wet western hills in Tas.; acid peat accumulates in high rainfall conditions where the temperatures do not permit of rapid bacterial breakdown of organic material. (d) Rendzinas or limestone soils are residual clays from the solution of overlying limestone and include black soils with accumulation in *B* horizons related to the water table, and responding to drainage and superphosphates, as in the low belts, between sand-dunes in SE S.A.; and shallow stony and better-drained red soils (*terra rossa*), as in patches between limestone exposures in nearby parts of S.A. (e) Acid peaty swamp soils are relatively restricted in distribution.

3. *Seasonally Humid Zone* (a) Red-brown earths interdigitated with rendzinas on limestones are found in the 30- to 65-cm. winter rainfall belt of SW W.A., S of S.A., Vic. and in the wheatlands of the Western Slopes in N.S.W. They have a loamy, slightly acid *A* horizon, soluble salts having been leached out; lime concentrations may be deposited in a heavier, clay *B* horizon. There are large areas in SW Arnhem Land and Central Qld. (b) Black earths are deep grey-black clays, cracking in hot dry weather, and so 'self-mulching' as flakes and small clods drop from the edges down the deep cracks, but on the other hand extremely sticky in wet weather (one modern term 'grumosols' means viscous soils). The *A* horizon, often grey-black, turns mottled grey-brown lower down, with calcium concentration in the *B* horizon. The upper soil is neutral to alkaline. They are developed on volcanic or sometimes limestone areas so flat as to have impeded drainage; the dark colouring is due to particular clay minerals and not to organic matter which is quite low at 2–4%. The summer soil cracking is accompanied by the development of ridges and hollows called gilgai in Aus. Shallow black rendzinas interdigitate with these deep soils in limestone tracts.

4. *Semi-Arid Zone* (a) Solonised brown soils (mallee soils) and solonetz are mainly in the 20- to 40-cm. rainfall belt. The solonised soils are variable in colour and profile, but mainly grey-brown. The alkaline *A* horizons vary from deep sandy to shallow lime, rich loam over deep crusty to powdery clays in the *B* horizon, often highly saline. (b) Heavy grey-brown soils may replace 4 (a), particularly in the deep fine alluvium of old flood-plains, and are very important for good pasture country in the more easterly of the great river plains of E Aus. and in parts of N Aus. (c) Light-textured brown soils, porous, leached and acid, gradually increasing in clay content in depth, cover wide grazing areas in Central N.S.W. and SE Qld., interrupting the belt of 4 (b); they may represent fossil soils on an old land surface above the alluvial plains.

5. *Arid Zone* (a) Desert loams, mainly in the S, are deep soils, with high gypsum and salt content in a clayey *B* horizon, carrying saltbush and bluebush. (b) Arid red earths are slightly acid, deep porous soils carrying mulga woodland. (c) Other desert soils include calcareous powdery soils over limestone, sand-plains, sand-hills and stony deserts. Some of these might well be classified in 6.

6. *Skeletal Soils*, in which soil-forming processes have scarcely begun, include much material drifting downhill in hilly and mountainous tracts, probably many of the soils of 5 (c) and, on current soil maps, very large areas of 'tableland and ranges' in N Aus. where one would expect either laterites residual from earlier climates and landform development, or soils varying with humidity from red-brown earths to deep tropical podsols.

Soil Erosion This is quite severe for a continent only used for European cultivation and stock-rearing since 1788. On a state-wide basis, proportions now unusable because of soil erosion are relatively low, perhaps 1–3%, but over much, perhaps most, of the inhabited parts of the country some 50% of the land has been subject to moderate erosion and loss of topsoil, of which about half seems to be due to gully and stream erosion and half to wind erosion. Deforestation, overgrazing by stock animals and by the introduced rabbit, non-conservation cultivation practices, and the extension of cultivation in wet years into normally dry areas are all involved. Over semi-humid and semi-arid areas the variable rain, including the occasional torrential storm occurring after a drought, is particularly active in gully erosion of moderately sloping land. Under the natural vegetation of dry sclerophyll forest, lightly grazed by kangaroos etc., moisture interception by the trees, bushes and herbs, and moisture retention by the forest litter and humus-rich topsoil, were such that run-off was but slight. The increasingly sharp run-off with progressive human interference brought much more runnel formation and gully erosion began. Many soils* are developed on relic or fossil soils of past climates, notably tropical podsols with a pallid zone of grey-white clays, developing almost a viscous flow when thoroughly wet. Once gully erosion reaches this zone, it is extremely difficult to control. Over-extension of wheat cultivation, as in S.A., exposed large areas to equally gross wind erosion, again presenting difficult problems of rehabilitation.

Soil Conservation practices have been encouraged in all States since the 1930s: contour banks, contour ploughing, gully treatment with check-dams, net-wire, re-contouring (much easier since the development of the bulldozer), etc. Considerable success is attained in individual problem areas, and economically a case can be made —especially if posterity be considered.

In the 1970s the picture is one of increasingly stable soils round the humid margins, but of increasing erosion, exacerbated by severe drought in the late 1960s in the overgrazed rangelands towards the arid interior.

Soldier Beetles Of the family Cantharidae, e.g. *Cantharis lugubris*. In some years they are very numerous round Sydney; with short wing-case and black-and-yellow thorax; some species emit a substance which blisters the human skin, but the larvae eat Codling Moth larvae which are harmful to apples.

Soldier Settlement Schemes These were operated after both the 1914–18 and 1939–45 Wars, through Government loans to settlers. By 1924, 36,000 had taken up holdings, but over half gave them up over the next decade. Failure was because of unsuitable land which was expensive to clear, lack of farming experience, and the Depression*. The most successful were in irrigation areas. From 1940 some 10,000 have taken holdings with much greater success: more preliminary clearing, housing and fencing have been provided, and training schemes used. In Qld. the Scartwater Trust, formed from public subscription and organised by A. W. H. Cunningham (1879–1943), has a cattle-station run by ex-servicemen; the profits are used to benefit others of the area.

Soldier-birds Biggish (about 30 cm. long) Honey-eaters*, feeding on insects, pollen, fruit and berries, and named from their noisy challenge of intruders.

Sorell Tas. 43S/148E (2,010 in 1971 with Midway Point) On Pitt Water, a lagoon fed by the Coal River, it is one of the oldest Tas. towns, and the centre of the early wheat area, now a local service centre with fishing and tourism.

Sorell, Lake Tas. 42S/147E It covers about 50 km.² on the Central Plateau, and is separated from L. Crescent by a narrow isthmus on which stands the small settlement of Interlaken.

Sorell, William (1775–1848) A former soldier, who succeeded Davey as Lt.-Governor of Tas. (1816–24). Under his vigorous, able control, the island emerged from a period of terror by bushrangers to become relatively prosperous, attractive to free settlers and with a doubled population. He imported Merinos, encouraging wool production with a guaranteed price, as well as crop-growing (potatoes, hops and wheat). He attained a little independence from N.S.W. by using local Treasury Bills, and established a bank, schools and churches.

Sorghum (*Sorghum vulgare*) A tropical summer crop grown in Aus. for fodder, as grain, green feed or ensilage ('Sudan grass'), although in Asia it is a human staple in some areas. Main production is the Dawson-Callide area of Qld. (26S/150E) (*see also* EMERALD); varieties are grown for broom-making in Qld. and N N.S.W. A large-scale British Government scheme in Peak Downs, Qld. (1949–53), failed as such, but served to introduce the crop. It is now also being grown on the Ord River* in W.A. for cattle food and export.

Sorghum Grass The popular name for a valuable Aus. species of annual grass of the Channel Country*, *Echinochloa turneriana*, belonging to a cosmopolitan genus which includes the common Barnyard Grass, *E. crus-galli*, with coarse foliage and pyramidal multiple head. A number of true Sorghums*, mainly shared with Asia and Africa, also grow as native grasses (3 perennial, 11 annual species) mainly in N Aus. One African and one Mediterranean Sorghum have become naturalised in NE Aus., being a pest locally.

Sorrento Vic. 38S/145E A sandy peninsula almost enclosing Port Phillip Bay, the site of an abortive convict settlement (1803–4) under Collins*, the first Vic. settlement. Sorrento is a holiday/commuter town for Melbourne.

SOUTH AUSTRALIA (S.A.) It is the third largest State, covering 984,400 km.^{2}, 12·8% of Aus. The population (1,172,774 in 1971) is 9·2% of the Aus. total, less disproportionate to its area than that of W.A. and N.T., and the average density of 1·2 per km.^{2} is similar to that of Qld. However, 99% live in the southern 25% of the State,

Badge of South Australia

about the area of Vic. Of the Aboriginal population (5,505 in 1966) half are tribal full bloods, following a modified traditional way of life in the deserts, and half are mixed bloods. S.A. is unique in being the only State having a common border with all the other mainland States; only along the S there is a natural frontier, in the form of 2,500 km. of deeply indented coast.

Physical Geography and Land Use Part of the Precambrian rocks of the Great Plateau extend from the ranges of the NW to the Eyre Peninsula. In the NE is the SW limit of the Great Artesian sedimentary basin including the interior drainage areas of L. Eyre and L. Frome. The Flinders–Mt. Lofty Ranges form a N–S hill zone, part of a 'shatter belt' of relatively recent earth movements, still liable to occasional earth tremors in the Gulflands. To the E of this, the lower Murray basin lies in a Tertiary sea gulf, and has much limestone, as does the Eucla Basin of the far SW, underlying the Nullarbor Plain.

Climate ranges from the N deserts where prevailing high pressures are occasionally interrupted by summer thunderstorms or tropical depressions, and temperature ranges are high, through a semi-arid central zone, to the 'Mediterranean' régime of the S. Here, frontal rain from winter depressions becomes increasingly reliable towards the SE, exceeding 60 cm. there and in the Mt. Lofty Ranges. The long hot summers are tempered by brief 'cool changes' when tropical air is replaced by polar. The growing period, dependent on temperature-evaporation ratios, shortens northwards, and Goyder's Line* roughly divides agricultural from pastoral areas.

The Deserts and Sparselands A marginal area within the 25-cm. rainfall line is used mainly for stock, with wheat only in good years; the disastrous advance and retreat of wheat-growing (1860–85), has left a legacy in the substantial stone ruins of homesteads and railway stations. Sheep give way to cattle northwards beyond the 25-cm. isohyet, grazing the saltbush, bluebush and mulga, and dependent on water bores and adequate stock routes. There are large empty areas of sand and gibber desert, salinas and ranges of bare rock and 'spinifex'. The Yalata Aboriginal reserve covers 167,000 km.² in the far NW.

The Gulflands include the Eyre Peninsula, the Mt. Lofty Ranges, and the adjacent coastal plain on which S.A. settlement started. An established farming landscape reflects the early clearing for wheat, encouraged by reliable winter rain and summer sun, and proximity to sea transport. A cereal-sheep economy prevails, with barley in more humid coastal areas. Specialised agriculture is found in some areas: grapes in the Barossa Valley, Clare Hills, Reynella and McLaren Vale; vegetables near Adelaide in small artesian basins in the E hills and early

potatoes on the coast plain N of Port Pirie; almonds and stone fruit on the W foothills and dairying on the valley flats.

The South East Plains Much of the S.A. section of the Murray flows through limestone gorges, and its mouth lies among lagoons and sandhills. There are 2 irrigated zones: the fruit farms from Renmark to Waikerie and a belt of dairylands on reclaimed flood-plain swamps below Mannum. Away from the river, sandy Mallee continues the similar belt of NW Vic. and much has similarly been cleared, initially for wheat, but now with a sounder mixed sheep-cereal economy, and using underground water. The Coonalpyn Downs continue the Big and Little Deserts of Vic. and, like them, have responded in recent years to application of fertiliser and trace elements; they support sheep pastures. The extreme SE of the State is a unique region of parallel sandy ridges marking former shorelines, and intervening flats, waterlogged until drainage operations, started in 1863 (but continued more successfully since 1948), gave the basis for rich sheep pastures. The sandy regions have large areas of pine plantations. The volcanic plains of the Vic. W District*, and the red earths of the Wimmera* both overlap the border, the former round Mt. Gambier, the latter round Keith and Bordertown.

Industry and Towns. Primary industry provides 40% and factory industry 60% of production. Farm products supply 85% of primary production and 65% of the exports. Of rural output, wheat and wool each account for 25%, dairy and barley each 10%, wine and fruits each 5%, and fat lambs, oats and vegetables are significant. About two-thirds of the wheat is exported; the best areas are in Yorke and Eyre Peninsulas and N of Adelaide, and 75% of Aus. barley comes from these areas and the Mallee. Merino wool comes from the Mt. Lofty Ranges but more especially from the improved pastures of the SE. The unirrigated areas of the hills produce 75% of the wines, most of the rest coming from the Murray; S.A. makes 75% of Aus. wine and 90% of its brandy. Forestry is practically confined to the pine plantations of the SE, and is barely enough for local needs. The main fisheries are tuna and, increasingly, crayfish for export to U.S. Mining, accounting for 15% of primary production, is dominated by the iron ore of the Middleback Ranges; there are limestone and gypsum quarries in the S and opal fields in the desert. The formerly important copper industry is enjoying a revival with modern demands and techniques. Salt is evaporated from the shallow Gulf waters. Power resources were poor in the past from coal at Leigh Creek, timber in the SE. Now natural gas from the Gidgealpa-Moomba field in the NE reaches Adelaide by an 800-km. pipeline with branches to the industrial towns at the head of Spencer Gulf and to Angaston. S.A. gas will be piped to N.S.W. An oil strike at Tirrawanna near Moomba gas field was made in 1970.

Secondary industry Processing of primary products located in relation to raw materials, includes dairy factories, wineries, sawmills, meatworks and woollen mills. Processing of bulky minerals depends on transport: the Port Pirie lead-smelters for ores railed from Broken Hill, pig-iron at Whyalla, using coal back-loaded from N.S.W. by ore carriers, cement at Angaston and Adelaide, fertilisers at ports such as Port Lincoln and Wallaroo, and oil-refining at Port Stanvac. Apart from the important Whyalla shipyards, however, more complex assembly is concentrated in the Metropolitan area, dominated by motor-body assembly with associated plants, household electrical appliances, chemicals and electrical components.

It is not surprising therefore that Adelaide (809,466 in 1971) contains 69% of the population and that its

dominance is increasing at the expense of all save a few major provincial centres. The 1971 census showed 14 out of 44 centres of over 1,000 people listed below to have declined since 1966, and many others with insignificant increases or stagnation.

Over 30,000, Whyalla.

10,000–20,000, industrial centres of Port Augusta and Port Pirie; Mt. Gambier, centre for the SE; Noarlunga, residential/resort/industry.

5,000–10,000, Gawler, industrial/residential; Port Lincoln, prime centre of Eyre Peninsula; Murray Bridge, industrial and service centre; Crafers-Bridgewater, a commuter town; Millicent*.

2,000–5,000, Woomera-Maralinga*; Naracoorte* in SE, Renmark*, Berri*, Loxton*, Mannum* along the Murray, Nuriootpa (Barossa Valley), Peterborough* in the hills, Wallaroo* and Kadina* in Yorke Peninsula, Victor Harbour*, a resort, Mt. Barker*, Clare; *Eyre Peninsula*: Ceduna*-Thevenard.

1,000–2,000   Apart from Leigh Creek*, these are mainly service centres in the closely settled areas. *Hills*: Balaklava (dairy), Crystal Brook*, Jamestown (on the Port Pirie–Broken Hill railway), Kingscote* and Lobethal* (woollen mills), Burra* and Kapunda* (old copper towns), Strathalbyn. *South East*: Keith, Bordertown*, Penola, Kingstown. *Murray Valley*: Tailem Bend*, Barmera*. *Wine areas*: Tanunda*, Angaston* (with cement also). *Yorke Peninsula*: Maitland Moonta* (formerly copper). There are many centres under 1,000 of local importance or historical interest: the tiny settlements for railway 'fettlers' or local distribution, along the Transcontinental Railway, many bearing the august names of Commonwealth Prime Ministers; declining, almost ghost towns of the Flinders Ranges, relics of copper and wheat booms (e.g. Gladstone*); old ports of the SE coast.

Transport focuses on Adelaide, apart from mineral lines from Port Pirie and Whyalla, the Eyre Peninsula system from Port Lincoln, and Mallee wheat lines. Gauge-breaks from the original 5-ft. 3-in. lines of the S, to the cheaper 3-ft. 6-in. N network based on Peterborough are now at Port Pirie and Peterborough; standardisation of the Broken Hill–Port Pirie–Adelaide lines is projected; it already exists from Port Pirie to Port Augusta, and from there N to Marree and W to Kalgoorlie.

Historical Development Permanent settlement based on free but planned migration, stemming from the theories of Wakefield*, Gouger and others, began in 1836 under Hindmarsh, largely failed because initial control was shared by the conflicting Commissioner and Governor, surveying did not keep pace with arriving settlers, and speculation in land replaced development. S.A. became a Crown Colony in 1842. Exploration to the N revealed mainly barren land, and the belief in a Horseshoe Barrier of salt lakes persisted until 1858.

By 1844, following Grey's stringent measures, S.A. was more viable and self-sufficient. Copper (1845) gave considerable impetus, and the removal of restrictions on foreign shipping (1849) stimulated wheat-growing for export. German Lutherans (from 1838) brought zeal and industry, and there was increased British migration too. S.A. lost men to the gold-rushes of Vic. and N.S.W., but gained trade and gold by providing safe escorts to Adelaide. Again wheat was in demand.

Responsible Government (1857) was followed as in other States by confusion and personal rivalries, with bitter disputes over the extent of permissible State control leading notably to the dissociation of State and religion. Women's suffrage (1894) and the Torrens* Title land-tenure system were important S.A. contributions to Aus. as a whole, but education lagged.

A developing depression, following drought and farming retreats, in the 1860s was staved off by copper at Moonta (1865). Good years and easing of land-tenure laws (1869) tempted farmers too far N to grow wheat, and a boom lasted until further drought, over-borrowing and over-extension led to collapse in the mid 1880s. In spite of intensification of farming the State stagnated for 20 years, only entered Federation with some reluctance, and gained little from it initially. The Iron Knob iron exports began in 1915, but there was little secondary industry. Thus the State was very vulnerable to the 1930s Depression.

Since the 1939–45 War concerted efforts to attract secondary industry by the long Liberal Ministry under Playford (1938–65) and subsequent Labor Government successfully maintained fairly steady growth by lower wages, and concessions in transport, tax and housing, to compete with other States, although concentration on consumer industries makes the economy vulnerable to fluctuation. Immigration rates have been high, land-clearing and settlement very active. There was a slackening of pace in the 1960s aggravated by drought. In 1970 a Labor Government introduced some price controls against inflation. The basic problems of low mineral, power, land and water resources remain.

Premiers since 1900: J. G. Jenkins (1901); R. Butler (1905 and 1933–8); T. Price (1905); A. H. Peake (1909, 1912–15 and 1917–20); J. Verran (1910); C. Vaughan (1915); H. N. Barwell (1920); J. Gunn (1924); L. L. Hill (1926 and 1930–33); R. S. Richards (1933); T. Playford* (1938–65); F. H. Walsh (1965–6); D. Dunstan (1966–8 and 1970–), R. S. Hall (1968–70). *Sources:* A. Grenfell Price: *Pioneers and Founders of South Australia* (Adelaide, 1929); D. H. Pike: *Paradise of Dissent* (1957), D. D. Harris and D. A. M. Lea: *A Regional Geography of South Australia* (Melbourne, 1963). (*See* MAPS 9 and 10.)

South Australian Company (1836–59) Formed, with G. F. Angas* as Director, to buy land in S.A., which was not selling at the 20 shilling per ac. asked by the Commissioners in charge. The company acquired considerable areas at 12 shillings per ac., and financed port, banking and whaling facilities, all of which made the settlement viable; but it also joined the subsequent disastrous speculative boom. It should not be confused with the earlier South Australian Land Company of Gouger, whose application for a Charter to settle the area had been rejected by the Colonial Office in 1832.

South Pacific Commission It was set up in 1947 by Aus., N.Z., France, Netherlands, U.S. and U.K., and aimed at promoting economic, social and cultural advance in the South Pacific area, through advisory research and educational programmes.

Southerly Buster The name given to the sudden, strong, cold southerly winds which quite often end a hot spell along the SE coast of Aus., bringing temperature drops of up to 16°C in a few minutes. They are associated with frontal activity ahead of anticyclonic systems (*see* CLIMATE).

Southern Cloud A 3-engined Avro Fokker aircraft owned by the first Aus. National Airways which disappeared on Saturday, March 21st 1931 during a Sydney–Melbourne flight with two pilots and six passengers aboard. The cause was a severe storm of which the forecast was not available to the captain, Travis Shortridge, before leaving or by radio. Kingsford Smith* and Ulm* headed an intensive but unsuccessful search. On October 26th 1958 the wreckage was found half-buried in forest litter and charcoal in sapling growth recovering from several recent burnings, by a young carpenter from a Snowy Mountains Authority construction camp near Cabramurra, 36S/149E. Possibly Shortridge, known to prefer low flying, did not appreciate the effect of the gale-force headwinds and easterly drift which took him towards the mountains, and had turned back expecting to crash-land in level country.

It has been claimed that the crash, coinciding with the Depression, crippled the first Aus. National Airways, and doomed Kingsford Smith and Ulm to the renewed record-breaking attempts in which they were both lost at sea. Less speculatively, the loss of the *Southern Cloud* caused decisive Commonwealth intervention in the provisions of air-route communication and navigational aids. Parts of the wreck are preserved in a memorial bearing symbolic concrete wings at Cooma, N.S.W., 36S/149E. *For further reading see* I. R. Carter: *Southern Cloud* (Melbourne, 1963).

Southern Cross The constellation in the southern sky occupying something of the position of the Great Bear and the Pole Star in the northern hemisphere, and placed by Ptolemy in the constellation Centaurus in 140 A.D., but separated as Crux by Royer in 1679. It is visible S of 30° N in April and May, appearing fairly brilliant in a dark gap in the Milky Way. The head of the cross is found by pointing upwards from the 2 conspicuous stars in Centaurus. The 4 most conspicuous stars (used in the N.Z. flag) occupy the points of the cross; the less conspicuous fifth (included in the Aus. flag*) lies towards the lower right. The line connecting the top and bottom star, projected by 4 times its length towards the horizon, gives the bearing of the S celestial pole. The Southern Cross in October–November evenings is low in the heavens and invisible N of 28° S; in April–May it is high in the heavens.

Southern Cross appeared in the names of all the record-breaking planes of Kingsford Smith*, notably the 3-engined Dutch Fokker (now preserved in Brisbane airport) in which he flew the Pacific for the first time in 1928 with Ulm, Lyon and Warner.

Southern Cross W.A. 31S/119E (896 in 1961) Originated as centre of the Yilgarn gold-field declared in 1888. Laid out grandly with streets named from the constellations, it soon fell on bad days as the gold gave out, but survived as the starting point and railhead for the Coolgardie–Kalgoorlie rushes in 1892-3; and now as a pastoral and wheat service centre.

Southern Lights—*See* AURORA AUSTRALIS.

Spear-grass A popular name for various genera and species of grasses with sharp spear-like seeds; some give fair forage, but the seeds of many are troublesome to sheep. The *Stipa* genus, Corkscrew Grasses, includes the 1 to 1·5-m. Tall Spear-grass or Plains Grass, *S. aristiglumis*, rough and with a long loose conical seed-head with slender pointed husked seeds, common in ungrazed areas or woodlands, but easily grazed out. *S. elegantissima* is the feathery pinkish grass of the S of Aus. from W.A. to Vic. *Aristida* includes the useful Mulga-grass*, but also species such as White Spear-grass, *A. leptopoda* and Feathertop, *A. latifolia*, common on overgrazed pastures. Black Spear-grass or Bunch Spear-grass is *Heteropogon contortus*, a fair forage grass, but with damaging seeds. In the wetter parts of Qld. *Chrysopogon aciculatus* is a bad, creeping Spear-grass, but locally useful on lawns, and when young, as fodder.

Speedwell A common name for the 4-petalled *Veronica** genus of flowers, often blue.

Spence, Catherine Helen (1825–1910) b. Scotland. She arrived in Adelaide in 1839. A novelist with a background of socialist journalism, women's suffrage and political reform, notably campaigning for proportional representation. Her novels gave a woman's viewpoint of colonial life, as in *Clara Morrison* (London, 1854).

Spence, William Guthrie (1846–1926) b. Orkney, Scotland. He arrived in Aus. in 1853. The first Aus. professional union organiser. As a miner he saw the need for amalgamation of unions, which he achieved first of Vic. mining unions (1882) then the Amalgamated Shearers Union (1886) and Aus. Workers Union (1894). Spence, with Lane*, was a vital leader in the 1890-1 strikes* but was more practical and conciliatory where he saw any hope. He held office under Fisher and Hughes, with whom he was expelled from the Labor Party over conscription.

Spencer Gulf S.A. 34S/137E A shallow triangular inlet 320 km. N–S, narrowing N from a width of 80 km. between Eyre and Yorke Peninsulas, and formed by subsidence along faults. It was discovered and named after an Admiralty official by Flinders in 1802, who spelled it Gulph.

Spender, Sir Percy Claude (1897–   ) b. Sydney. A lawyer and statesman of high international repute, Judge of the International Court (1958-67). He describes his part in the Colombo Plan* and A.N.Z.U.S.* Treaty in *Exercises in Diplomacy* (Sydney, 1968).

Spiders The largest Order within the Arthropoda* Class, Arachnida. Spiders have 4 pairs of jointed legs, lay eggs, from which hatch young more or less similar to adult forms, and are distinguished from all other animals by their abdominal web-spinning glands and spinnerets, as well as by the female's sperm-storing sac attached to the palp or 'feeler', which is attached to the jaws (sperm-storage being associated with the eating of the male by the fertilised female of some, though by no means all species). Barbara Main's interesting classification of Aus. spiders distinguishes: 1. web-throwers; 2. snare-builders; and 3. hunters.

Primitive spiders with segmented abdomens are not found in Aus., and

the Sub-Orders may be thus arranged on anatomical and physiological grounds into 2 divergent groups.
I Mygalomorphae (i.e. mouse-shaped) The Trap-door* and Funnel-web* Spiders of popular usage, but they cover a wide range of nesting habits, and include: 1. a group of families with dense claw-tufts, able to climb well on smooth surfaces, even glass, (a) the Barychelidae, e.g. the hairy dry-country *Idiomatta blackwalli*, which does have a trap-door to its burrow and (b) the Theraphosidae which does not; 2. a group lacking the dense claw-tufts, e.g. (a) the Ctenizidae, the 'typical' Trap-door Spiders; (b) the Migidae of very varied size and nesting habit; and (c) the Dipluridae, usually with doorless tunnels and including the well-known Funnel-web Spiders; 3. the Araneomorphae (i.e. spider-shaped) or Dipneumonomorphae (i.e. 2-lunged), including most Aus. spiders, over 1,300 species, in some 35 families: (a) Daddy Longlegs, Pholcidae, e.g. *Pholcus phalangioides*; (b) Spitting Spiders, Sicariidae, e.g. *Scytodes thoracica*; (c) the Dysderidae, e.g. the Common Brown Spider*, *Ariadna* spp.; (d) the Jumping Spiders, Salticidae; (e) the 8-eyed spiders with crab-like posture and motion, Selenopidae, e.g. *Selenops australiensis*; (f) the Huntsmen Spiders, Sparassidae, e.g. *Delena cancerides*; (g) the Crab Spiders, Thomisidae; (h) the Theridiidae, including the well-known Red-back Spider*, *Latrodectus mectans hasselti*; (i) the Orb-web Spiders, Argiopidae, e.g. the Garden Orb-web Spiders, *Araneus* spp.; (j) the Web, Dome or Sheet Spiders, Linyphiidae, e.g. the Tent Spider, sub-family Linyphiinae, in forest litter; (k) Zodariidae, e.g. *Sorena* spp. which hunt from a terrestrial burrow without a snare-web, while Agelenidae, e.g. Platform Spiders, *Corasoides* spp., have a silk-lined burrow extending into a sheet-snare; (l) the Wolf Spiders, Lycosidae, e.g. *Lycosa* spp.; and (m) the Nursery Web

Spiders, Pisauridae, e.g. the Fishing Spiders, *Dolomedes* spp., often seen walking on ponds and billabongs; 4. the Apneumonomorphae (i.e. with no lungs, only trachea), of which the only Aus. species are very small spiders living in moss and forest litter in the E and SW of Aus.
II A more evolved group of Sub-Orders with varying degrees of evolution away from the primitive forms, e.g. with fewer lungs (or even no lungs, but only trachea), fewer spinnerets, etc. These include the Hypochilomorphae, relatively little modified and represented in Aus. by the long-legged *Ectatostricta troglodytes* of caves and cavities in Tas. and a leafmould spider of a different family in the Lamington Plateau, Qld. (*See* BROWN SPIDER, JUMPING SPIDER, HUNTSMEN SPIDER, CRAB SPIDER, RED-BACK SPIDER, ORB-WEB SPIDER, TENT SPIDER, SHEET WEB SPIDER, FISHING SPIDER.) *For further reading see* B. Y. Main: *Spiders of Australia* (Brisbane, 1964); K. C. McKeown: *Aus. Spiders* (Sydney, 1952).

Spinebills A genus of small Honey-eaters* with long downward-curved beaks.

Spinefoot (*Amphacanthus nebulosus*) An oval fish up to 34 cm. long of N Aus. and Indo-Pacific waters with a fringe of spines along the back and rear part of the belly, some of which are venomous.

Spinifex A grass genus of 3 species growing on sandy shores of Australasia and from Ceylon to Japan. They are creepers with long rhizomes very effective in binding sand. The spiny female flower and seed ball of *S. hirsutus* is familiar to many seaside holidaymakers in SE Aus.; the inflorescence on the male plants is less prominent. The term Spinifex is popularly applied to various inland species of *Triodia* and to *Plechtrachne schinzii*, with a distinctive, intertwined, hummocky growth, and stiff leaves sticking out, hence the popular name Porcupine Grass. The name Spinifex for these is apt and descriptive, but liable to cause confusion, and the term Hummock Grass is to be preferred.

Spiny Ant-eater (*Tachyglossus*—i.e. swift-tongued) It is a Monotreme*. Echidna, a former name for the genus meaning Viper, but resembling *Echinus*, the Hedgehog, is not now used because of possible confusion with a genus of eels, but is often heard as a popular name. Particular adaptations in the Ant-eater include: the long slender snout, with highly developed olfactory organs; the long slender sticky tongue for collecting ants etc.; the enlarged spade-like nails and probably the retention of the shoulder-girdle, to assist in the Spiny Ant-eater's remarkable defensive manoeuvre of digging itself into the ground vertically and *in situ*, when surprised on soft earth; the development of the hair into spines, again defensive, accounting for one popular but inaccurate name, the Aus. porcupine; the related enlargement of the second toenail to assist in scratching and cleaning between the spines; and the egg-pouch, which is lacking in the aquatic and burrowing Platypus, the other Monotreme. There are 2 species of *Tachyglossus*, the mainland *T. aucleatus* and the slightly larger Tas. *T. setosus* (also found on the Bass Str. Islands). The Spiny Ant-eater of N.G. is *Zaglossus*.

Spiny Ant-eater
about 50 cm. long

Spofforth, Frederick Robert (1853–1926) b. Sydney. A cricketer, the first great Aus. bowler and one of the greatest ever. His accuracy, speed and skill in disguising the type of ball he was going to deliver, allowed him to capture 1,146 wickets for an average of 13·55 runs in what would now count as first-class cricket. He played in 18 Tests against Eng. (from the second Test in 1877 to 1887) taking 94 wickets for an average of 18, and was nicknamed the Demon. He lived in Eng. from 1888.

Sponges Aquatic, mainly marine animals, the Phylum Porifera. Many species live in colonies sharing skeletons of spicules or fibres embedded in the tissues of the colony. The adult animal lives from oxygen and plankton circulating through its body with the aid of inflow and outflow pores in the hollows in the sponge. Aus. sponges include: 1. Limy Sponges, *Scypha* spp., white and vase-shaped, 2–3 cm. high, seen at low tide on exposed rocky coasts; 2. Heliotrope Sponge, genus *Haliclona*, of rock pools and crevices near low-tide level down to 3 m. and up to 30 cm. long; 3. Liver Sponge, *Chondrilla* spp., in similar sites; 4. Plum Sponge, *Tethya ingalli*, orange-red and about the size of a golf ball, found underneath stones and rock ledges: 5. potentially commercial species such as *Spongia officinalis*, found in the Great Barrier Reef and other tropical waters in sites overlapping with Sea-cucumbers*; 6. fresh-water Sponges in dams and reservoirs, of the genera *Spongilla* and *Ephydatia*.

SPORT Australians are sport lovers, as participators, spectators and gamblers. In competitive sport, Aus. emerged in the period from 1950, to an outstanding international position, especially considered in relation to population; this has been most marked in tennis and swimming, but there have also been record-breaking middle- and long-distance runners, women sprinters and hurdlers, golfers, world motor-racing, cycling and golf champions. Explanations vary, but the major factors include natural ability and the intensive application of coaching and training to young potential champions, selected through wide-spread club, State and national contests. A certain aggressiveness, expressed in a determined will to win, may be linked with the necessary toughness of migrant stock. The successful sportsman has a very high status in the community. All these have combined with an existing outdoor tradition, fine beaches, a pastoral and hence horse-using economy in the early days, long reliable summers and good diet to produce this great era of sporting achievement. But the educational function of sport for the average child has perhaps suffered in the concentration on winning talent.

Land Sports For spectator and gambling interests, horse-racing* is supreme, and there is a considerable history of trotting, and the old outback buckjumping has developed into the commercialised Rodeo*. Polo and its offshoot polocrosse are popular among the wealthier; 2 Olympic Gold Medals were won in the 1960 Games for equestrian events. Greyhound racing also caters for betting; the tin hare chase is popular in N.S.W. and Vic. Live hare coursing is legally curtailed in N.S.W. but is allowed in Vic. where the main trophy is the Waterloo Cup. The illegal Two Up* was another popular gambling game. In outdoor ball games tennis* and cricket* in summer, and football* in winter are commonest. Golf* is more easily accessible than in most countries other than Scotland. Baseball is played to inter-state championship level, for the Claxton Shield. Men's basketball is rapidly growing in popularity, and has produced Olympic teams; it is increasingly played in indoor stadia, with American coaching. Both men and women's hockey teams have had some overseas success. Softball, a version of baseball, is played in schools, along with vigaro, a cross between cricket and baseball. Lawn bowls* has a very large following, among older people especially.

Other outdoor sports range from wood-chopping, where Aus.–N.Z. champions approach supremacy, to motor-racing* among spectator sports; cycling* and athletics* for participants. Skiing* is restricted by income and access to snow-fields. Rifle-shooting is the competitive outlet for a wide-spread love of shooting that goes under the term of 'hunting', be it only for rabbits. Fishing, of both inland and coastal waters is also popular. Of the relatively few indoor sports, boxing* has waned, but wrestling is drawing large crowds after a decline from its heyday at the turn of the century; judo has been introduced with success. Billiards* is widely played and squash has grown rapidly since the 1939–45 War, with Heather McKay (née Blundell) and Ken Hiscoe becoming overseas champions. Tenpin bowling has developed rapidly in the past 5 years as a commercially run enterprise.

Water Sports Swimming* is most important for participation and spectator interest, followed by its offshoots of surf* sports, skindiving and water-skiing. Sailing* and rowing* races are as old as the arrival of the First Fleet, and there have been international sculling* champions. Inter-school Head-of-the-River, and an inter-state competition for the King's Cup are among major rowing events. In 1967 Aus. for the first time won a full international crew race (coxed fours) in U.S. In the 1972 Olympic Games Aus. won 8 gold medals 7 silver and 2 bronze medals. *See also* H. Gordon: *Young Men in a Hurry* (Melbourne, 1961).

Springtails A popular name for the insect Order Collembola, of which

PLATE 8: TREES
1. Mountain Ash *(Eucalyptus regnans)*. 2. Port Jackson Fig *(Ficus rubiginosa)*.
3. Bribie Cypress Pine *(Callitris columellaris)*. 4. Paperbark *(Melaleuca quinquenervia)*. 5. Flame Tree *(Brachychiton acerifolius)*. 6. Karri *(Eucalyptus diversicolor)*.

there are some 140 native and 60 introduced species in Aus., nearly all with a springing tail-like organ and living in damp soil, moss, fungi, compost heaps etc. The most familiar are introduced species such as the Lucerne 'Flea', *Sminthurus viridis*, a small dumpy green-coloured pest of clover and lucerne.

Squash First played in Aus. in the 1930s, it increased rapidly from the 1950s, with Heather McKay becoming a world champion.

Squatters A term originally used, as in America and Europe, for poor vagrants settling illegally on empty Crown Land. In Aus. a new class of squatter emerged as population increased, free land grants were abolished and new grasslands were discovered beyond the 'Nineteen Counties'*. Squatters were of every social origin from ex-convicts to elements of English aristocracy, initially sharing a 'sordid filthy' life, facing hazards of flood, drought, fire, dingoes and hostile Aborigines. A crude slab hut was put up by a waterhole, and they tended their flocks on free range. Many failed; others made fortunes before over-extension and drought led to a slump in the 1840s, when, following the initiative of O'Brien of Yass, squatters boiled their sheep down for tallow to realise a little of their value. They fought for security of tenure, enraged by Sir George Gipps's scheme (1844) of a licence of £10 for a maximum holding of 20 sq. miles and capable of holding 4,000 sheep or 500 cattle, with optional purchase of the homestead block at a minimum £1 per ac. after 5 years. In 1847 some security was given with longer licence periods and pre-emptive rights to buy. This allowed the setting up of more permanent homesteads. The loss of their shepherds to the diggings stimulated fencing, and better organisation to reduce labour needs encouraged itine-

rant shearing teams. Political power waned with responsible government in the 1850s, although the 'pure Merinos' or 'Squattocracy' continued to dominate the Upper Houses. They largely succeeded in ensuring the failure of the Land Acts, designed to 'unlock the land' after 1860 and put in the hands of small-scale farmers or selectors*, by employing 'dummies' at the sales or by bribery. A period of elegant prosperity lasted until the 1890s' Depression, after which closer settlement was more successful and application of capital allowed crop-growing alongside grazing. *For further reading see* S. H. Roberts: *The Squatting Age in Eastern Australia 1835–47* (Melbourne, 1935); and M. Kiddle: *Men of Yesterday* (Melbourne, 1961).

Squids 10-tentacled fast-swimming Cephalopods*, with eyes not dissimilar from those of vertebrates and beak-like tearing jaws.

Squid
about one-sixth life size

Stag-beetles Of the family Lucanidae, they include the golden-green *Lamprina* seen in both E and W States, as well as brown-red species such as *Rhyssonotus nebulosus*. The disproportionate growth of the male jaws, seen even in the larvae, seems to be a by-product of male sexual development rather than an essential for survival; the adults generally eat little, and the main nutrition takes place during wood-boring in rotten logs by the larvae.

Stamps Postage stamps were issued by the States until 1913 when the first Commonwealth series appeared, although 'Postage Due' stamps for under-paid postage were issued for all Aus., except Vic., from 1902. The lag between Federation and all-Aus. stamps resulted from the initial period when States retained their own accounting. The first Commonwealth stamps were the Kangaroo Series, with a kangaroo on a map of Aus., designed by Blamire Young, and approved by the Labor Government under Fisher; kangaroo stamps survived until 1945, the last issue being for 2 shillings. They were replaced by reigning monarchs for the main issues under succeeding Governments; the George V 1d stamp had a particularly long life (1914–37). From 1938 Aus. themes appeared more frequently: the koala (4d), merino (5d), kookaburra (6d), platypus (9d), and lyrebird (1/-). Commemorative stamps began with the opening of Parliament House (1927). In 1965 there were 6: 2 international topics (International Co-operation and Telecommunications) and issues showing Sir Winston Churchill, Hargrave*, Monash* and one for the 50th anniversary of Anzac*. In 1972, seven stamps honoured Aus. pioneers. On February 12th 1966 stamps with the new decimal units superseded all previous issues. On stamps up to 5 cents (which replaced the former 5d standard letter rate) the Queen's portrait appears. Aus. fauna were used for values up to 25 cents; higher values showed notable explorers. Stamps are all printed in Melbourne and recent technical progress includes the use of multicolour photogravure presses (1963), notably for the very fine bird series, and the addition of luminescent properties (1965) to help electronic cancellation. N.S.W. had stamped letter sheets at 1d from 1838, 18 months

earlier than in Eng. but they were little used; pre-payment became compulsory in 1850 and the famous 'Sydney Views' were the first adhesive stamps; the design was from the reverse of the Great Seal of George IV. Other States followed: Vic. in 1850 just prior to official separation, with a half-length portrait of the Queen; Tas., 1853 (as Van Diemen's Land), W.A., 1854 with a black swan, S.A., 1855 and Qld., 1860.

Philately is popular, with numerous societies and a number of journals, including a free bi-monthly bulletin from the Post Office. *For further reading see* A. R. Rosenblaum: *The Stamps of the Commonwealth of Australia* (Melbourne, 6th ed., 1966).

Standards Associations of Aus. Founded in 1929 by the amalgamation of 2 earlier bodies. It receives half its funds from the Commonwealth, the remainder from industrial and private subscription, publication etc. It is sub-divided into many specialised committees, whose function is to produce standards in specifications, test methods, codes of practice etc. which take into account both producer and consumer interests. Over 1,500 standards have been published.

Standley Chasm N.T. 24S/134E. A 150-m.-deep chasm in the Macdonnell Ranges, 64 km. W of Alice Springs; its red cliff walls are 3–9 m. apart. The name (also spelled Standly) was that of a pioneer woman schoolteacher of Alice Springs.

Stanthorpe Qld. 29S/152E (3,606 in 1971) At 800 m. in the Granite Belt* for which it is the service centre. Its former name of Stannum dated from its early development and rough days as a tin-mining region (1872–1900).

Star of Bethlehem A name applied to many wild flowers in Aus. and many other countries. (*See* LILIES.)

Starfish or **Sea Stars** Echinoderms*, generally with 5 arms but sometimes more, and very varied in size, form and colour. The arms carry many tube-feet used for travelling and sometimes for feeding and even opening shells to get food (though Aus. species are not reported as serious pests of oyster-beds, as in some countries). Starfish have considerable powers of regeneration of missing parts, which the 8-armed *Allostichaster polyplax* uses as a means of reproduction. A common sandy-shore species, often found stranded, is the Spiny Starfish, *Astropecten polyacanthus*. The small 8-armed *Patiriella calcar*, red, blue, orange, green or brown, is common in rock pools, and the cobalt-blue 30-cm. *Linckia laevigata* is readily seen in rock pools in the Great Barrier Reef. The very short-armed Biscuit Starfish, *Tosia australis*, is common in Vic. The tropical Crown-of-Thorns Starfish, *Acanthaster planci*, which can give an unpleasant sting, is a very serious predator of coral in the Great Barrier Reef.

The Brittle-stars are of a different Class, and have a well-marked, disc-like central body, and 5 long narrow arms, without obvious tube-feet and much more rapid and snake-like in their movements; they are found under rocks or at the base of kelp. Common Aus. species include *Ophiactis savignii*, the spotted purple *Ophiocoma pulchra* and the spotted green *Ophiarachna incrassata*. Brittle-stars with branched arms are sometimes hauled up round deep-sea bait, e.g. *Conocladus* spp. and *Euryale* spp.

The much more feathery and numerous arms distinguish the Feather-stars, which are mobile members of quite a different Class, the Crinoidea (*see* SEA-LILIES). *Cenolia trichoptera* is sometimes found in inter-tidal rocks in the S of Aus., but much more colourful species are found in tropical waters.

Station A rural grazing property, usually extensive and often, although not always, managed on behalf of the owner. It derives from the original military word for an outpost, and was used in 1815 by Macquarie* in reference to distant pasture lands he was establishing for Government cattle. It was soon adopted by private landholders, and led to many compounds: sheep station, cattle station, out station etc.

Stawell Vic. 37S/143E (5,826 in 1971) On the N flanks of the Grampians in the Wimmera; it was a former gold town with deep shafts, and supporting 30,000 or more people in the 1850s. It is now a farming centre, noted for the wines of Great Western to the SE and its famous Easter Gift footrace. *For further reading see* C. E. Sayers: *Shepherd's Gold* (Melbourne, 1966).

Stead, Christina Ellen (1902–) b. Sydney. Mrs. William Blake. She is an expatriate author of stature who left Aus. in 1928. She has worked in U.S. and settled in Eng. *Seven Poor Men of Sydney* (Sydney, 1934, re-published 1966) is her best-known work.

Steele Rudd The pen-name of Arthur Hoey Davis*, creator of 'Dad and Dave'.

Stephens, Alfred George (1865–1933) b. Toowoomba, Qld. After an early career as a Qld. and Fleet Street journalist, he joined the *Bulletin** (1896–1906) and instituted the famous Red Page (inside the red front cover) which became the focal point of the new aggressively Aus. literary upsurge of the period. He encouraged the major writers George McCrae, Joseph Furphy, John Shaw Neilson, and many others. His intuitive judgment was backed with practical experience and perspective as well as wide reading. As a literary biographer he left many important works on Chris Brennan, Victor Daley and Henry Kendall.

Stephens, James Brunton (1835–1902) b. Bo'ness, Scotland. A poet who arrived Qld. (1866) to tutor a squatter's family, later becoming a public servant. His lengthy narrative poems, with scholarly craftsmanship, notably *Convict Once* (London, 1871), patriotic verses, e.g. on Federation, humorous poems and ballads were notable at the time but little known now.

Sterculiaceae An important family of mainly tropical trees and shrubs, reaching Aus. and S Africa, of which the most widely known is perhaps the Cocoa Tree. Aus. genera and species include: the great buttressed Tulip Oaks of Qld. *Argyrodendron* spp.; the Bottle-trees*, *Brachychiton* spp; certain Mangroves*; the mainly W.A. Paperflowers, *Thomasia* spp.; Kurrajongs* of several genera; the Velvet-bushes*; and flowering shrubs such as *Keraudenia hillii*, seen in coastal NE Aus., a hairy plant with long tongue-like leaves and attractive purple flowers dominated by spreading sepals which remain as a sheath to the fruit.

Stewart, Douglas Alexander (1913–) b. Eltham, N.Z. A poet, dramatist and critic. He came to Aus. to join the *Bulletin* (1938) and was editor of its Red Page from 1941-6. Already an established writer when he came, he has become one of the most prolific, many-talented literary figures; his work includes highly regarded criticism, his folk ballad *Glencoe*, light-hearted and fine lyric verse, as in *The Seven Rivers* (Sydney, 1966), serious and effective radio and stage plays, some in verse such as *The Fire on the Snow* (Sydney, 1941) and *Ned Kelly* (Sydney, 1942), and anthologies. *For further reading see Collected Poems (1937-67)* (Sydney, 1967).

Stewart, Harold Frederick (1916–) b. Sydney. A poet and journalist who, with McAuley, perpetrated the Ern Malley* hoax. He finds much of his inspiration in Oriental subjects, often paintings.

Stewart, Nellie (1858-1931) b. Sydney. Of a theatrical family, she became a popular Aus. star of comic opera, and later an actress, over a long period from 1880 to the 1920s. She sang the memorial ode at the opening of the first Commonwealth Parliament in 1901.

Stick Insects Of the Order Phasmodea, they are slender but often quite large vegetarian insects, camouflaged as twigs or twigs with small leaves. The single eggs are dropped by the female, often from the tree-top where she has been feeding, to incubate on the ground. The 100 species in Aus. include varied forms, e.g. 1. the very twig-like Brown Stick Insect, *Acrophylla titan*; 2. the pale green body and delicate pink wings of intermediate forms, e.g. the Ringbarker, *Podocanthus wilkinsoni* (a gregarious species sometimes a forest pest damaging or even killing eucalypts); and 3. the considerable 'leaf' development of the 15-cm.-long Leaf Insect, *Extatosoma tiarartum*, often seen in gardens.

Stinkwood (*Zieria* smithii*) In the aromatic Rutaceae or Rue family, it has a strong to unpleasant odour from essential oils in the foliage etc., as the popular name suggests. The leaves are very variable, but may be narrowly lanceolate and radial round the branch, with clusters of small delicate white flowers from the leaf axillae; the bush is common on the better parts of coastal E Aus.

Stirling, Sir James (1791-1865) b. Lanarkshire, Scotland. The founder of Swan River Settlement, first Lt.-Governor then Governor of W.A. (1831-8). As a naval commander, Stirling surveyed and reported enthusiastically on the Swan River area, in the course of an assignment to remove the Melville Island* Settlement to Raffles Bay (1826-8). Pointing out the danger of French or even American interests in New Holland, he applied to supervise its colonisation; other schemes were being put forward, such as Peel's*. Stirling arrived (June 1829), a month after Fremantle formally annexed New Holland. He held the crumbling colony together through its initial serious difficulties of poor land, lack of supplies, unsuitable immigrants, hostile Aborigines and surveying problems, receiving little help from home in spite of personally returning to London to plead for it (1832–4). When he returned to naval service in 1839, he left it, if not prospering, at least fairly self-sufficient and with whaling, brewing, flour-milling, a newspaper and even a shipyard established.

Stirling Range W.A. 34S/118E It extends 80 km. E–W, rising abruptly from the low plateau N of Albany to 1,110 m. in Bluff Knoll, and to several other peaks. Composed of intensely folded Precambrian phyllites, the lower slopes have thick scrub, but the more open rocky tops are partly clothed in carpets of brilliant spring-flowering plants.

Stivens, Dallas George (1911–) b. Blayney, N.S.W. A writer and journalist, best known for 'tall stories' of the countryside and his novel *Jimmy Brocket* (London, 1951) about big business.

Stock Exchanges In Aus. these are self-governing bodies dealing with sales of Government stocks, and debentures, preference and ordinary shares of companies whose Articles of Association comply with the rules of the Associated Stock Exchanges of Aus. These rules, are intended to protect the public; occasionally worthless companies are quoted, particularly during phases of expansionism—in gold at various times and in nickel, petroleum, rutile and uranium in the last 20 years. Trading in stocks and shares began in Sydney in the 1840s and in Melbourne about 10 years later. The Sydney exchange was formed in 1872, Melbourne had successive associations, but the present

exchange dates from 1884 and those at Brisbane from 1889, Adelaide from 1887, Perth from 1889, Hobart from 1882. The Aus. Associated Stock Exchanges have a co-ordinating secretariat. A Senate committee followed spectacular collapses in 1970–71.

Stokes, John Lort (1812–1885) He served on *Beagle** from 1825–47 as an outstanding surveyor and succeeded Wickham in her command in 1841. He led exploratory parties inland, and was severely speared by Aborigines. He published *Discoveries in Australia* (London, 1840).

Stone, Louis (1871–1935) b. Leicester, Eng. He arrived in Aus. in 1885, becoming a Sydney schoolteacher and author of a major Aus. novel, *Jonah* (London, 1911) set in Sydney slums and full of detailed observation and characterisation.

Stone-fish (*Synanceja trachynis*). Highly poisonous, spined, rock-pool and coral-reef fish of N Aus. and the Indian and Pacific Oceans, up to 30–40 cm. long and remarkably camouflaged to resemble surrounding weathered rock. Their sting is extraordinarily painful, so that a victim may lose control and risk drowning even in shallow water. Palliatives are available, and research on the venom is in progress.

Stone-fish
(*Synanceja trachynis*), *about one-sixth life size*

Stoneflies Aquatic 4-winged insects of the Order Plecoptera, often cream to buff in colour and about 2·5 cm. long.

The gravid female may be seen dipping to wash the eggs into the water, where they sink and adhere to the bottom. The observant angler often sees the nymphs under stones in the stream, or more rarely swimming, or the sloughed skin discarded on a stone where the adult form has emerged, dried, stretched its wings and flown off. The Aus. Stonefly, *Stenoperla australis*, is common.

Storm Bay Tas. 43S/147E The wide inlet between North Bruny Island and the Tasman Peninsula, into which the River Derwent flows. It was named by Tasman in 1642 when a storm prevented his ships anchoring there.

Stow, Julian Randolph (1935–) b. Geraldton, W.A. An expatriate poet and novelist, who uses his W.A. background in his work. *To the Islands* (London, 1958); *The Merry-go-round in the Sea* (London, 1965). Collected poems are in *Counterfeit of Science* (1969).

Stradbroke Island Qld. 28S/153E Comprises 2 sandy islands in Moreton Bay*, separated by a storm in 1896: N Stradbroke is 39 by 11 km. and S Stradbroke 22 by 3 km. Mineral sands are exploited and holiday resorts have replaced timber villages.

Strahan Tas. 42S/145E Formerly the main outlet for Mt. Lyell* mines, now only exporting some copper to Port Kembla, brought by road since the dismantling of the famous rack and pinion railway. There is some fishing and sawmilling.

Strathbogie Range Vic. 37S/146E A SW–NE-trending hill region, reaching 861 m. in Mt. Wombat. Timbered and remote, the range formed a part of the so-called 'Kelly* Country'.

Streaky Bay S.A. 33S/134E The name of a sheltered inlet on the W coast of Eyre Peninsula and also the small port on its SE shore, which was at first called Flinders after the explorer

who named the bay from the discoloured streaks in its water.

Streeton, Sir Arthur Ernest (1867–1943) b. Vic. One of the artists of the Heidelberg School*, before moving to Sydney, and then mainly overseas (1898–1923) including a period as an official war artist. His early work was of very high quality, pioneering the new interpretation of raw Aus. landscapes, with their light, dust, heat and distances. After his return however, his influence was reactionary and his work stale.

Strickland, Shirley (Mrs. Delahunty) (1925–) b. Perth. A sprinter and hurdler. She broke the world record for the 80-m. hurdle in the Olympic Games in 1952 and again (her own record) in 1956, and has run very successfully in the 100 m. and in relays. She holds the most Olympic medals (7) of any woman athlete, and coaches in Perth.

Strikes They increased with the growth of Trade Unions*, especially after mid-19th century, over pay and conditions, and achieved considerable improvements. The Qld. dock strike (1889) against loading wool sheared by non-union labour was a first major inter-union success. But it was followed by a defeat for Unions in the serious strike wave started by the maritime strike* the following year: funds were inadequate, public hostility was loud, employers were well organised, and the prevailing Depression meant an abundance of unemployed to act as strike-breakers. A series of transport and mining strikes in the early years of the new century culminated in 1917 in a N.S.W. rail strike which spread to the mines and waterside over 8 weeks, affecting over 90,000 men. Militant elements were strengthened by the Labor Party split over conscription* at this time. Seamen, waterside workers, timbermen and coal-miners were affected in strikes from 1919–30, mainly on wages issues. In 1929 one miner was killed and several injured by police shooting in the 'Battle of Rothbury' near Maitland, N.S.W., in a strike over use of non-union labour. There was a lull until immediately after the 1939–45 War, when a series of outbreaks led to the major 1949 coal strike which evoked the use of troops in the mines by Chifley*. Increased left-wing control of Unions was regarded as the major factor exploiting an impatience with continued austerity and current wages. Since 1953 there has been a general decline in major strikes of long duration, save for the 1964 Mt. Isa* strike, but direct action remains a strong industrial weapon. In 1970 1·36 million were involved in disputes of over 10 man-days' duration, and 2·3 million working-days were lost, a sharp increase from 1968. *See* J. E. Isaac ed.: *Australian Labour Relations* (Melbourne, 1966).

Stringybark A term applied to many Eucalypts, not necessarily closely related, the bark of which peels off in long fibrous strips, but perhaps best kept for a large group of species with tufts of fine hairs on the juvenile leaves, rather thick, broadly lanceolate adult leaves, dark green above and lighter below. Buds are in biggish groups and are mainly small on short stalks, some blunt and fig-like, some pointed, and the fruit cup-shaped to globular, often with fine points, but sometimes so close together that the sides are flattened. Important timber species occur on varied but mainly well-drained soils in 60–150 cm. mean annual rainfall in a belt from the Great Divide to the sea in N.S.W. and Vic. These include the Red Stringybark, *Eucalyptus macrorrhyncha*, the Brown Stringybark, *E. baxteri*, the White Stringybarks, *E. scabra* and *E. globoidea*, and the Silvertop Stringy-bark, *E. laevopinea*, of New England. The popular names are mainly from timber colour. The Darwin Stringybark, *E. tetrodonta* is not closely related.

Stripper-harvester Invented in 1843 in S.A. by John Wrathall Bull, and improved but not patented, by flour-miller John Ridley, and commercially produced from 1850. Combs stripped, and beaters threshed the grain which was then winnowed. The machine played an important part in extending wheat-growing during and after the gold-rush.

Strzelecki Creek S.A. 29S/140E It was named by Sturt, and is one of the sporadic watercourses of the Channel Country*, leaving the course of Cooper Creek at Innamincka.

Strzelecki, Sir Paul Edmund de (1797–1873) b. near Poznan, Poland. He arrived in Aus. in 1839. He was an explorer, scientist and self-styled Count, having left his Prussian-dominated homeland in 1825 and wandered in Britain, the Americas and Pacific. He had no formal training, but absorbed enough science to become a notable mineralogist and collector, and so supported himself. His first Aus. journey was into the Blue Mts., where he discovered gold and reported it to Gipps, who suppressed the information. In 1840, with James, cousin of John Macarthur, he traversed the Snowy Mts., climbing Mt. Kosciusko* and naming it after a Polish patriot; thence he went S into the fertile E of Vic. which he called Gipps Land. He was preceded by McMillan, but went further. After 2 years of survey in Tas. he returned to Eng., where he wrote the detailed *Physical Description of N.S.W. and Van Diemen's Land*, published in London by public subscription in 1845. He was lionised and later knighted for his work in the Irish famine (1846–8). Perhaps the strangest feature of his life was the prolonged, intermittently passionate correspondence recounting his travels to Adyna Turno in Poland, with whom he had unsuccessfully tried to elope in 1819. *For further reading see* G. Rawson: *The Count* (London, 1954).

Stuart Highway N.T. A sealed road, 1,536 km. long, from Darwin to Alice Springs, completed in 1943 as a military priority, following a previous rough track and the line of the Overland Telegraph*.

Stuart, John McDouall (1815–1866) b. Fife, Scotland. He arrived in Aus. in 1838 and undertook a search for new pastures for pastoralists William Finke and James Chambers, and he accompanied Sturt* (1844–5). In 1860 he made the first of 3 attempts to cross the centre of Aus., but was turned back by illness, hostile Aborigines and failing supplies N of the site of Tennant Creek*. 4 months after his return, he set off again, but was defeated by impenetrable scrub 320 km. from the Victoria River. His third and successful journey began 10 weeks after his return, reaching Daly Waters and the Roper River, but he almost died on the hard return journey. Although Burke* and Wills had crossed the continent before him, Stuart's journeys were infinitely harder and are described by I. Stewart in *The Heroic Journey of John McDouall Stuart* (Sydney, 1968). Central Mt. Stuart was originally named Sturt by him, but was later changed to commemorate Stuart himself. He died in Eng. in some poverty.

Stump-jump Plough It was invented in 1876 by Richard Bower Smith in S.A.; it had 3 mould boards on a weighted, hinged beam, allowing them independently to 'jump' tree-stumps, so eliminating the costly 'grubbing' process. Particularly suited to smaller timber of mallee country, it was important in developing such areas in S.A. and Vic. in the 19th century; a modern 8-furrow version is still used in newly cleared mallee.

Sturt, Charles (1795–1869) b. India. Son of a Judge. After Army service in Spain, Canada, France and Ireland, he reached N.S.W. in 1827 and became A.D.C. to Darling. Fascinated by the problems of exploration, in 1827 he led his first expedition, with Hume, which discovered the River Darling. He made the greatest single contribution to Aus. exploration when, the following year, he unravelled the mystery of the W-flowing rivers by sailing down the Murrumbidgee to the mouth of the Murray in a whaleboat with 7 companions (3 of them convicts); the return journey against the current and with little food was an epic feat which temporarily blinded him. In 1838 he overlanded cattle to Adelaide, and then surveyed the proposed new site for a S.A. capital at Encounter Bay, advising against it. He accepted the Surveyor-Generalship of S.A., but had to yield to Frome, already appointed in London.

In 1844 he obtained permission to explore the interior, officially to find the main watershed, with a 16-man expedition, but Sturt was mainly motivated by his faith in a great inland sea. Drought, and searing temperatures which burst a thermometer at 52°C in the shade, turned him back, half blind and sick with scurvy after several abortive journeys from a base with water at Mount Poole. He had failed to penetrate the Simpson Desert, which lay beyond the stony desert plains that bear his name, between Cooper Creek and the Diamantina, 'the gloomy and burning deserts'. He died in Eng. before his nominated K.C.M.G. was gazetted and without political or financial reward of any measure. Yet he was perhaps the greatest of the explorers: a humble, intensely humane man of vision, inspiring deep love and loyalty which made his great journeys possible. He left these recorded in books published in 1833, vividly written and with his own gifted illustrations. *For further reading see* J. H. L. Cumpston: *Charles Sturt* (Melbourne, 1951).

Sturt's Desert Pea (*Clianthus formosus*) A magnificent crimson-, scarlet- (rarely white) flowered member of the Pea* family. The stems and pinnate leaves are covered with silky hairs. It grows wild throughout the drier parts of Aus., but is often grown in gardens. The name of the genus is taken from the Greek for 'glory flower'. (*See* PLATE 6.)

Sturt's Stony Desert S.A. 28S/138E In the NE corner of the State; it is a gibber* and sand-dune region between the Warburton River and Cooper Creek.

Subterranean Clover or **'Sub' Clover** (*Trifolium subterraneum*) A clover of European origin, now of great importance in Aus. in improved pastures. It has soft, strawberry-pink flower-heads, and derives its specific name from its habit of burying the fruiting pods underground, after which the plant dies. The seeds germinate later in the year, and the annual plant thus maintains itself in permanent pasture. Like other members of the Pea* family, Papilionaceae, the roots form an association with bacteria, fixing nitrogen and increasing fertility.

Subterranean Clover
(*Trifolium subterraneum*)

Sucker-fish or **Remoras*** Fish of various species, of 15 to 90 cm. long, with a sucker on top of the head, which they can fasten on to a shark or large fish to gain transport and food supply (from scraps), though they can swim.

17*

Sugar Aus. is fifth in world cane production and second in raw sugar export, earning over $100 million a year (almost 3% of total exports), 4th in farm exports after wool, wheat and meat. Cane, *Saccharum officinarum*, requires high temperatures, over 100 cm. rainfall, deep well-drained soil. Some 9,000 farms averaging 35 ha., lie in a discontinuous belt 5–50 km. wide along the NE coast, from Grafton, 30S/153E, N.S.W. to Mossman, 16S/145E, Qld. Qld. has 95% of the output. Mechanically planted 'setts' or cuttings throw up 8–12 shoots, to 4 m. tall during a growing period, which lengthens southwards from 12 to 24 months. 'Ratoon' crops then grow from the roots for 3–4 seasons, before fallowing is followed by new setts. After the burning-off of leaves and weeds, over 80% is mechanically harvested, the rest by hand, cane-cutters often being itinerant casual workers. Over 3,200 km. of 2-ft.-gauge railway carry the cane to 34 mills, for crushing, extraction and crystallising of 'raw sugar'; 'bagasse' (fibre) provides fuel. Two-thirds of the sugar is exported, by bulk-handling methods, under the International Sugar Agreement for 1969–74, reviewed 1972 (Aus. export quota is 1·1 million tonnes) and the British Commonwealth Sugar Agreement subject to triennial review on the basis of a Negotiated Price Quota. These are outside the International Sugar Agreement, as is the quota taken by U.S. Japan, Canada and N.Z. are also buyers. The remaining one-third of raw sugar is refined in Aus., 50% for domestic and 50% for concessional sale to preserving and canning factories; 95% is refined by the Colonial Sugar Refining Co. Ltd. (1855) in the State capitals and 5% by a Bundaberg* firm. Both buy from the Qld Government which (working with group associations shares proceeds between millers and growers, determines an annual 'mill peak' and assigns acreages to farmers.
    Sugar-cane was first grown and

milled successfully in 1862 by Captain the Hon. Louis Hope and John Buhot; but the first pioneer was T. A. Scott (?1777–1881) at Port Macquarie in 1823. The first refinery was in Sydney in 1842. A major figure in amalgamating refining companies to give C.S.R. a quasi-monopoly, was Sir Edward Knox (1819–1901). Early Qld. plantations were large and Kanaka* labour was used (1863–1906). Subsequent to tariff protection (Queensland's price for supporting Federation) and import embargoes (1915), expansion northwards and decreased farm-size ensued. In the 1970s U.K. entry into EEC and world prices are causing anxiety. The growing areas, ports and number of mills they serve are: N Qld., Cairns (4 mills), Mourilyan (4), Lucinda (2), Townsville (4); Central Qld., Mackay (8); S. Qld., Bundaberg (7), Brisbane (3) (including 1 in N.S.W.); N N.S.W. 2 sugar-mills sending direct to Brisbane or Sydney refineries.

Sugar Gum (*Eucalyptus cladocalyx*) A small tree of S.A. (often only 9 m. high though it can reach 30 m. by 0·9–1·5 m. in favourable conditions). It occurs: 1. on very poor skeletal soils in 3 main areas, with mean annual rainfall of 40–65 cm. in the southern Flinders Ranges, the N of Kangaroo Island and the E of Eyre Peninsula; 2. as a dominant in the dry sclerophyll forest of the wetter areas; and 3. as an element in savannah woodland in drier areas, with a broader tree shape. Juvenile leaves are broad, adult leaves narrowly lanceolate (8–15 cm. long); buds are in small bunches and rather long; fruit barrel-shaped and about 1 cm. long. The bark is fairly smooth and fine and scales in a pattern of white, grey and yellow-brown. It is widely planted for shelter, ornament and fence post production.

Sundew The popular name for carnivorous herbs of the genus *Drosera* in the family Droseraceae. The well-known Forked Sundew of tea-tree swamps from S.A. to Qld. (and N.Z.) has antler-like leaves bearing the sticky and sensitive glands used to capture and digest insects and extract nitrogen. The species was used by Darwin to demonstrate insectivorous powers in plants. It has attractive pink-white papery 5-petalled flowers. A small assassin bug, *Reduviidae* spp., often shares the captured insects. Other Aus. species are found in much drier environments than most Sundews, such as the rosette form and stemless *D. spathulata* of inland E Aus. and the rosy-pink *D. menziesii* of W.A., a climber with cymbal-shaped leaves with prominent tentacles. *D. arcturi* extends to alpine meadows in E Aus.; it has long strap-like leaves.

Sundowner A swagman* or wandering tramp who arrived as the sun set, to avoid having to work for the meal he begged.

Sunrays A common popular name for flowers of the genus *Helipterum* (similar to *Helichrysum*, but with plumed sepals), including the pink *H. roseum* and *H. manglesii* of the S of Aus. (the foundation for nursery flowers known as Acroclinium and Rhodanthe), and the white or yellow *H. albicans* seen in sheets in alpine and, after good rains, in mallee pastures.

Sunraysia The name given collectively to Vic. towns of Mildura, Red Cliffs, Merbein and Irymple, 34S/142E, the irrigation districts on the Murray, famous for dried vine fruits and citrus.

Superbus, Mount Qld. 29S/152E The highest point of S Qld. (1,380 m.), lying at the divergence of the McPherson and the Main Ranges; it is lava-topped and precipitous on its E face.

Superphosphate Often called 'super', it is the major fertiliser used in Aus. for both crops and pastures. It is made by the addition of sulphuric acid to imported rock phosphate*, and thus adds salts of sulphur and phosphorus to the soil. Considerable areas are treated by aerial agriculture*. Government subsidies encourage its use.

Surf The Aus. coast has many fine beaches on which waves, stirred by onshore winds blowing over vast ocean expanses, break in lines of surf. The beaches of the SE, bordering the Pacific, with its warm summer temperatures, are especially notable. The sport of **surf riding**, or **surfing** was first practised in Aus. by Tommy Tanna, a gardener's boy in Manly, N.S.W., who was a native of the South-Sea Islands, where Cook had noted the prowess of the people in riding the waves. Development of interest was especially rapid after 1902 when the archaic laws forbidding bathing during much of the day, were successfully defied by W. H. Gocher, a Manly newspaperman. Body-surfing was followed by **surf boards**, especially after the impressive demonstration of 1915, given by the Hawaiian Duke Kahanomoku. Early boards were solid, but to allow greater length, and scope, hollow plywood boards up to 5 m. long were developed. Since the mid 1950s these have been replaced by the 'zip' or Malibou board, 2·4–3 m. long, 51 cm. wide, 7 cm. deep and with an 18-cm. keel, made from balsa wood coated with fibre-glass. **Surf skis** are an Aus. variant, dating from 1933 almost a small canoe, on which the rider stands, kneels or sits and uses a paddle. The **surf boat** carrying 4 oarsmen is some 8 m. long, slim and very light. The rapid growth of surfing, a measure of affluence, has caused some controversy over its dangers to other bathers, and has led to segregation and even some banning by local authorities. In 1963 an Aus., B. Farrelly, won a world championship in Hawaii.

Surf life saving was uniquely developed in Aus., stimulated by the manifest dangers of the waters, including shark attack. Ropes and lifebelts placed at intervals, rescue by horseback and by human chain, were used. In 1906 the Bondi Surf Bathers Life Saving Club was formed, to be followed by others, which affiliated in 1907 as the N.S.W. Surf Bathers Association, later to become Surf Life Saving Association of N.S.W. and then of Aus. (S.L.S.A.A.). A noted early supporter was Judge A. H. Curlewis. In 1948 the various State organisations formed the National Council of Surf Life Saving.

Club subscriptions and functions support the purchase of equipment, and in recent years there has been some subsidy from Federal, State and local government bodies. The equipment used in over half the rescues comprises a length of waxed cotton or synthetic fibre rope on a revolving drum, and attached, with an emergency releasing device, to a light canvas belt, worn by the 'beltman'. He is the rescuer, swimming with a crawl stroke to the patient and both are hauled in. Earlier, buoyant cork- or kapok-filled life-jackets and belts were used, but defeated the need to plunge under the breakers in order to get a line out in heavy surf. Resuscitation, now mainly mouth to mouth, is also part of the training. Up to 1966, 144,115 people had been saved: more than the Aus. death-roll for both world wars.

Surf Carnivals have been held since 1908 to demonstrate, attract recruits and raise funds; they have increasingly become spectacular, competitive events. For conspicuously fine rescues there are Silver and Bronze Medals and certificates. One such rescue took place at Bondi on Feb. 6th 1938, called Black Sunday, when over 200 people were swept out by a fierce under-tow: 5 were killed, and 65 rescued by life-savers. The other major hazard is the Rip, an erratically flowing outward current, commonest at the ends of a short curved beach, and indicated often by flat water, and absence of regular and continuous lines of inflowing breakers. Long beaches may also be hazardous, the safest being about 1·5 km. in length. Waves of mixed direction or great height should also be avoided. The distress signal is a raised arm, and the swimmer's best asset is calmness: rips fade out beyond the breakers.

Rapidly increasing crowds at accessible beaches are now raising problems of finance and provision of sufficient life saving teams: motor surf boats, mobile patrols and professionals are likely to be used increasingly. But the image of the bronzed athletic amateur is likely to be retained. *For further reading see* J. Bloomfield: *Know How in the Surf* (Sydney, 1959).

Surfers Paradise Qld. 28S/154E Part of the Gold Coast*; the name dates from an hotel of that name built in the 1920s on a sand-spit between the Nerang River estuary to the W, and the surfing beaches of the Pacific on the E. There was a former cedar-cutters' settlement.

Sutherland, Joan (1928–) b. Sydney. An operatic soprano of high international repute, appearing in Europe and America, but with occasional returns to Aus.

Swag Originally part of convict language as recorded by Vaux*, meaning stolen 'wearing apparel, linen, piece goods etc.' It came to mean a bundle or parcel, then specifically the travelling worker's or tramp's bundle, comprising a calico strip (also providing shelter), blankets or blueys*, and clothing and possessions. **Swagman**, or **swaggie** are derived from it.

Swallows and **Martins** Of the family Hirundinidae, including summer migrants or semi-migratory species; they are swift and manoeuvrable fliers, streamlined with swept-back wing-position and forked tails, catching insects on the wing, perhaps flying higher in fine and lower in stormy weather. The swallow's bowl-shaped mud nest was originally built in a hole in the earth or rock, but the bird has now adopted the angle under house-eaves; some of the group nest in tunnels in stream-banks etc., some in tree-holes. Species seen in many parts of Aus. include: the Welcome Swallow, *Hirundo neoxena* (new, strange swallow), about 15 cm. long, half tail, with a bright rust flash on the head and breast upon trim brown and white plumage; the White-backed Swallow, *Cheramoeca leucosterna* (white-breasted cleft-house), nesting in burrows; the Fairy Martin or Bottle or Cliff Swallow, *Hylochelidon ariel* (woodsprite swallow), which makes a carefully lined bottle-shaped mud house; and the Tree Martin, *Hylochelidon nigricans* (blackish woodswallow), nesting in tree-holes or other cavities. (*See also* WOOD-SWALLOWS.)

Swamp Gum (*Eucalyptus ovata*) A small to medium-sized tree (20–30 m. by 60–90 cm.) of S Vic. and E Tas., in cool rainy conditions (mean annual rainfalls 50–100 cm., with many rainy days). It grows from coastal plains to well-drained foot-hill slopes, but tolerates and is commonest in swampy and frequently inundated sites. The leaves are generally ovate, increasing in size with age, though lanceolate adult leaves are found, up to 12 cm. long and very glossy. There are small bunches of pointed buds and conical fruit. The bark is rough, grey and stringy, peeling on upper butt and branches to reveal white-cream to pink patches. The crown is fairly dense. The wood is pale and only fairly durable.

Swamp Lily (*Ottelia ovalifolia*) In the aquatic, mainly tropical family Hydrocharitaceae. It grows on freshwater ponds in many parts of Aus. but not Tas.; it has rounded floating leaves and large white or pale yellow and red flowers with 3 petals and 3 papery sepals in a tubular bract about 4 cm. long.

Swamp Snake (*Austrelaps signata*) The brown-bellied black snake, yellow-lipped and up to 60–90 cm., of sheltered coastal swamps in SE Qld. and NE N.S.W. It is nocturnal in hot weather, and eats skinks and frogs. It is shy and reluctant to bite, but a bite from a large specimen might be quite serious, especially to a child, who should be treated quickly.

Swan, Black (*Cygnus atratus*) Can be found in suitable habitats in Aus. except the far N and Tas., the only Aus. and the only black swan, observed by de Vlamingh's Dutch expedition in 1697 on the Swan River which was then named from it. It has been the symbol of W.A. from pre-federation postage stamps until today. It is 90 cm. long, and makes a trumpet-like call as it moves in pairs or small flocks to a fresh feeding ground, often at dusk or by moonlight; the nest is a large open cup on a platform of reeds etc., built up from a swamp or on a small island.

Swan Hill Vic. 35S/144E (7,693 in 1971) A service and market centre for the Swan Hill Irrigation District, lying on the S bank of the Murray River at the E end of the Mallee* District. The name was given to the site by the explorer Mitchell in 1836 and it grew as a river-crossing and port in the days of the paddle-steamer. A moored steamer is now a museum and art gallery. Today its vegetable canneries and dairy factories reflect the intense land use of its irrigated countryside.

Swan River W.A. 32S/116E The lower 60–80 km. of the Avon*. Both were discovered independently, their common identity not being realised until 1834. The Swan River was named from its black swans. The linking section lies in the gorges and rapids of a 30-km. reach through the Darling Range. Above Perth the banks of the Swan are lined with market-gardens and vineyards producing currants for export and wines and grapes for local use. Within the city the river widens to 2 shallow tidal basins, Perth and Mel-

ville Waters, and is joined by the Canning from the S. The estuary narrows in its last few miles through the coastal limestones to the Indian Ocean at Fremantle. The **Swan River Settlement** was the name by which the early colonial settlement on its banks was known. The Helena and Canning are left-bank tributaries.

Sweetlips A name for mainly tropical fish of several species. It is best used for the genus *Plectorhinchus*, including the Golden Spotted (grey) Sweetlips, *P. pictus*, of which the juvenile form is orange with black stripes along the body. The Brown Sweetlips, *Pseudopristipoma nigra*, of 30–60 cm. long, is widespread in tropical seas; the larger Sweetlips Emperor, *Lethrinus chrysostomus*, is sharper-snouted, generally olive, but suffused, patched or striped with blue, scarlet, orange, yellow, pink and black.

Swifts (family Micropodidae) There are 2 species which are summer migrants to Aus. from Asia; they may be seen endlessly on the wing by day, catching insects—probably high in the air in fine weather, low before a storm as the weather adage suggests, and clinging to a cliff-face near a mud-and-saliva nest from the darkening to first light. They fly very fast, some species probably well over 160 km.p.h.; and are almost as manoeuvrable by day as bats are by night. They are generally brown and white birds, and share with the swallow and martins the mode of insect-catching and the characteristic stream-lined flight posture, with swept-back wings. But the swifts have structural differences, the most obvious, perhaps, is that all 4 toes point forward so that they cannot grasp a twig etc., and so will not be seen perched on telegraph wires. Swifts seen in Aus. are: the Fork-tailed Swift, *Apus* (footless) *pacificus*, and the Spine-tailed Swift, *Hirundapus* (footless swallow) *caudacutus* (sharp-tailed), which has small tail-spines to assist it in clinging to cliffs. These swifts reach 15–20 cm.

Swiftlet, Grey or **Moth-bird** (*Collocalia francica*—Mauritius glue-nest bird) A small brown and light buff bird, 10 cm. long and resembling a very small swift. Of NE Qld. and other oceanic areas.

Swimming A widespread and popular summer pastime, yet up to 500 deaths from drowning occur each year and have led to intensive learn-to-swim campaigns; only half the population can swim. There are surprisingly few heated indoor pools, although the southern half of the continent has several months of weather too cool for popular outdoor swimming. Competition is encouraged through clubs, inter-school events, State and national championships. In international competitive swimming Aus. was a dominant country a decade ago, with a peak achievement in the 1956 Olympic Games, of 5 individual gold medallists and 2 relay wins. In 1960 and 1964, there were 4 Aus. gold medallists. These achievements in relation to population were very great. They are credited to a deliberate policy, following the 1952 Olympics, when theorists and coaches introduced new, drastic but scientifically based training plans. These, involving strenuous, prolonged, rigidly disciplined training in and out of the water, over long periods and making use of a camp in the tropical north at Townsville, were applied to promising, and very young swimmers, training full-time; it succeeded in producing, in something of an assembly line, the champions listed in col. 2. More recently the approach has been used by other countries, notably America, on top since the 1960 Olympics.

Historical development Competitive swimming dates from 1846, the first inter-state meetings from 1858, the first regular championships from 1889 and the first Aus. championships from 1894 (which included N.Z.). The N.S.W. Amateur Swimming Association was founded in 1889, and the Amateur Swimming Union of Aus., still the central body, in 1909. The first Aus. competitors went overseas in 1900, and until 1930 a number of international champions were produced, including some notable women pioneer swimmers. There was a decline in the 1930s followed by a revival since the 1950s. A major contribution has been the stroke referred to as the Aus. Crawl*. Since 1945 skin-diving and water-skiing have become increasingly popular.

Outstanding swimmers (OG indicates an Olympic Games win) To 1910: W. J. Gormly; C. and J. Hellings; G. and T. Meadham; Cavill family*; J. Tooher; F. C. V. Lane, OG 1900; G. Read; B. B. Kieran; C. Healy; F. Beaurepaire*; A. Wickham*.

To 1920: W. Longworth; H. Hardwick; L. Boardman; M. Champion.

To 1939: A Charlton, OG 1924; W. Herald; K. Kirkland; I. Stedman; E. Henry; M. Christie; R. Ewe (diving); F. Doyle; N. Ryan; P. Oliver; H. R. Biddulph; W. Kendall; W. Green.

Since 1945: F. O'Neil; A. Beard; K. Stevens; J. Marshall; G. Agnew; D. Hawkins; B. Darke; J. Davies, OG 1952, butterfly-breast stroke; J. Henricks, OG 1956, 100 m.; G. Chapman; I. M. Rose*, OG 1956; K. Berry, OG 1964, butterfly; J. Devitt, OG 1960, 100 m. (disputed by U.S.); J. Konrads*, OG 1960; D. Thiele, OG 1956 and 1960, 100 m. back-stroke; T. Gathercole; N. Hayes; J. Monckton; I. O'Brien, OG 1964, 200 m. breaststroke; R. Windle, OG 1964, 1,500m.; M. Wendon, OG 1968 (100 m. and 200 m.); B. Cooper OG, 1972.

Women to 1910: A. Kellerman*. To 1920: F. Durack*, OG 1912; M. Wylie. 1920–39: C. Cauldwell; E. Davey; P. Mealing; C. Dennis*, OG 1932; E. de Lacey.

Since 1945: M. McQuade; J. J. Davies; N. Lyons; L. Crapp*, OG

1956; I. Konrads*; A. Colquhoun; L. McGill; D. Fraser*, OG 1956, 1960, 1964; B. McAuley (diving); B. Bainbridge; J. Andrews; L. McClements, OG, 1968; K. Moras; S. Gould* OG 1972; G. Neal OG, 1972; B. Whitfield. *Theorists and coaches* Professor Frank Cotton, S. Herford, Forbes Carlile, H. Gallagher, D. Talbot, F. Guthrie, A. Cusack, all operated since the 1950s. *See* J. Pollard: *Swimming Australian Style* (Melbourne, 1963); F. Carlile: *Forbes Carlile on Swimming* (London, 1963).

Swordfishes and **Marlins** Large carnivorous sea-fish of the families Xiphiidae and Istiophoridae; there are many species, of which at least 6 or 7 are found in Aus. waters. The strong sword, known to penetrate ship timbers etc., may be useful for defence against other predators, such as sharks, and for speed in swimming etc., but it is not essential for the procuring of its normal prey. Many of the group have a long triangular fin well forward on the back, rather reminiscent of that of many sharks. The Broadbill Swordfish, *Xiphias estara* or *X. gladius*, of tropical waters, has a long flattened sword and reaches 1–2 m. The tropical Sailfish, *Istiophorus ludibundus*, related to the Marlins, reaches 3 m. long, and is named from the very large and spreading front fin on the back. The Marlins have a circular sword and a triangular fin grading into a long low fin along the back, and include the Black Marlin, *Istiompax australis*, the slightly differing Blue Marlin, *I. ampla*, both with faint vertical bands on the sides, and the unbanded Howard's Marlin, *I. howardi*. The Striped Marlin, *Marlina audax zelandica* which, like the Black Marlin, is common in N.Z. seasonally, has quite distinct vertical bands with thin light stripes between.

SYDNEY N.S.W. 34S/151E (2,717,069 in 1971) The oldest and largest city in Aus. and capital of N.S.W. It was named after Thomas Townsend,

Lord Sydney (1733–1800), Home Secretary from 1784–9 and largely responsible for the establishment of a penal settlement in N.S.W. It contains almost 22% of the population of Aus. and 60% of that of N.S.W., and took almost 77% of the State's population increase from 1966–71. The convict settlement at Sydney Cove in 1788 was attracted from the site considered at first on Botany Bay by the water supply of the small Tank Stream, rather than by the magnificent natural harbour, but the latter has certainly had a crucial role in the city's later development. At the same time the regional situation is of constriction into the rather limited Cumberland Basin; the early settlers found this a disadvantage, especially in years of food shortage, until the route across the Blue Mts.* was found (*see* EXPLORATION), and even now the network of communications encounters some difficulties. The dominance of the capital over the State's trade, commerce and administration remains very strong and Sydney is 10 times larger than the next largest cities in the State, Newcastle and Wollongong, which some observers would already class as being within a Greater Sydney conurbation or urban sprawl along the coast.

By 1820 the convict settlement had given way to a small Regency city, with the main streets still traceable in the street names—but only a very occasional building remains, such as Bligh House or the Garrison Church in the modern Central Business District. The Governor's Domain E of Sydney Cove still has Government House and the Botanic Gardens*. The Rocks area SW of Sydney Cove is an enclave of old terraces with wrought iron verandahs, many restored in the last 20 years; there is opposition to proposed redevelopment. Ferry terminals and other special wharves include the overseas passenger terminal (Circular Quay) the interstate, N.Z. and general cargo facilities at Darling Harbour and new container facilities at White Bay.

Behind Darling harbour, warehousing has displaced some of the early 19th-century shopping streets, but others are incorporated in the fashionable shopping and entertainment area between Elizabeth and George Streets, from Martin Place S to Central Station. The great office blocks of the financial quarter between Martin Place and Sydney Cove have displaced early civic buildings, while the administrative and government offices lie to the E, between it and the parkland belt.

This core area occupies about 3 km.² of the 1,500–1,800 km.² of built-up area in the city, and there are many other specialised areas. The inner ring, within about 3·2 km. of the city centre, as in many cities, is subject to more or less urban blight, as in parts of King's Cross, an area of cosmopolitan eating-houses, and of urban adventure from spice to vice, or the many stretches of small terrace houses or ramshackle tenement houses in Redfern, Newtown, Surry Hills and Woolloomooloo. Within about 8 km. of the centre, an intermediate ring also contains rather poor, high-density housing, often with a mixture of factories, sometimes of noxious industry such as tanneries: Mascot, Botany, Kingsford, Marrickville, Stanmore, Petersham, Lewisham, Annandale and Balmain are examples. The middle belt also includes better suburbs with little industry, such as Randwick, Kensington, Waverley and Bondi, near the famous beach, while hilly sites overlooking the harbour, even quite close in, have some of the most esteemed areas for houses and luxury flats, e.g. Potts Point, Point Piper, Elizabeth Bay, Double Bay, Rose Bay and Bellevue Hill. From Bondi to Coogee and even Maroubra on the S, beaches are often foci of fairly high-density housing, including many flats, but the middle belt is dominated by small single-storey houses mainly on small blocks of land. Similar suburbs, but generally of higher quality, are found on the N side

of Sydney Harbour, e.g. Hunters Hill, Lane Cove, Greenwich, Waverley, Wollstonecraft, Cremorne, Neutral Bay, Mosman, Cammeray and Artarmon.

Beyond these, many suburbs date from the railway radial and loop lines rather than the motor age: Drummoyne, Concord, Ashfield, Croydon, Burwood, Strathfield, Flemington, Lidcombe and Auburn, linking with the several suburbs of the once agricultural focus of the city of Parramatta, 24 km. from Sydney, but continuous with it. The motor age has seen further expansion in the S and W, often in rather ill-planned and unsewered suburbs such as much of Bankstown, Canterbury, Hurstville, Rockdale and Kogarah. On the N side there are select areas: Lindfield, Killara, Gordon, Pymble, Turramurra, Warrawee, Wahroonga and the Ryde to Normanhurst area; resorts have become commuter suburbs: Manly, Harbord, Dee Why, Collaroy, Narrabeen and Mona Vale. Even these prosperous N suburbs have found that poorly maintained septic tanks in unsewered areas have been linked with sharp outbreaks of infective hepatitis.

The carefully delimited Metropolitan Statistical Division from the 1966 census shows tentacles of continuously urban building reaching out in Sutherland, Campbelltown, Penrith, Baulkham Hills, Hornsby and Warringah (including Palm Beach on Broken Bay). Beyond these, Sydney influence is certainly strong in partly commuter dormitory towns as far afield as Cronulla in the S, Liverpool in the W and Gosford in the N.

Into this complex pattern of Central Business District and spreading suburbs is insinuated not only the enormous commercial and financial business appropriate to a great seaport and the many tertiary services appropriate to a wealthy city of over 2½ million people, but also manufacturing industry employing 75% of the State's factory employees, or about 30% of that in Aus.

As it is near the steel cities of Newcastle and Wollongong, engineering and metal-processing are important and growing fast, and they tend to be capital-intensive rather than labour-intensive, and with high value added per worker, as compared with the great staple industries of Melbourne. The central city still dominates the industrial pattern, with over 140,000 employees there and in Leichhardt nearby, and naturally in high-value property on relatively small blocks of land, with much vertical development. Middle-belt suburbs, Marrickville, Canterbury and Concord have 10-20,000 employees, less intensively packed. Outer areas, such as Parramatta's outer suburbs and Bankstown, have 15,000-30,000 factory workers where cheaper land has allowed for more spreading, horizontal building.

This complex pattern under many city and municipal authorities has not grown without creating many planning problems of undesirable admixture of industry and housing, of lack of recreation space in some areas, of slums in others, of endless, shapeless sprawl and, particularly in the centre, of heavy, at times chaotic traffic conditions and on still nights of marked smog development. The 1951 Cumberland County Plan with its green belt concept was largely defeated by the very rapid city growth. In 1968 the Sydney Region Outline Plan envisaged new towns at Camden, Campbelltown and Appin in the SW, Blacktown, Mt. Druitt and Penrith in the W and in the Baulkham Hills area in the NW; all are to be 'visible entities' linked by rapid traffic arteries. Population is expected to reach 5½ million by 2,000 A.D. Water supplies will be augmented from the Southern Tablelands. The Outline Plan was prepared by the statutory State Planning Authority of N.S.W. (created 1964) and includes phasing proposals for expansion based on the provision of services along the major axes of growth.

Sydney Cove A ship bound from Calcutta-Sydney which was wrecked in February 1797, in Bass Str. 17 survivors in a whaleboat were wrecked again on Vic. coast and their forced walk towards Sydney (only 3 surviving) was the first lengthy piece of land exploration. They were rescued in May 1797 near Port Hacking by a fishing boat.

Sydney Ducks or **Sydney Coves** Names given in America to Aus. prospectors who arrived in the 'forty-nine' gold-rush and quickly established an unsavoury reputation. Although some persecution by vigilantes was motivated by xenophobia, the predominance of ex-convicts made them a dubious group, especially those congregating in the 'Sydney Town' area of San Francisco.

Sydney Harbour Bridge Built (1923-32) by Dorman Long Co. Ltd. of Middlesbrough, Eng.; the N.S.W. engineer most involved was J. J. C. Bradfield, an outstanding engineer concerned in many other projects. The design was by R. Freeman. The bridge links Dawes Point on the S with Milsons Point on the N shore; it is among the longest single-arch bridges in the world, the main span being 272·9 m.; the deck carries an 8-lane roadway (formerly included tramways); maximum clearance is 52·6 m. The cost was over £7 million, plus recent costly improvements to approaches. At the opening ceremony on March 19th 1932 by the N.S.W. Premier J. T. Lang*, the tape was unofficially cut by a horseman, a member of the New Guard*.

Sydney Opera House Opening October 1973 on the Harbour shore at Bennelong Point to a prize-winning design (1956) by the Danish architect Utzon who resigned from the project in 1967, in unfortunately hostile circumstances. The design uses difficult and revolutionary techniques, to which the engineer Ove Arup contributed, and the concept of interlocking shell vaults reflects the dancing harbour waves and sails. The present architect is Peter Hall. The cost ($100 million) trebled since building began in 1959, was met by lotteries. The Opera House is a source of pride and controversy; there was considerable dismay when, in 1967, it was decided to use the major hall (2,800 capacity) for concerts only, with opera relegated to the smaller hall (1,525), losing the functional reason for the shells (to contain stage machinery). There is a 550-seat drama theatre; this, like the opera theatre has rich tapestry curtains woven near Aubusson, France to a design by Aus. artist John Coburn. The concert hall has great acoustic properties of which the striking 'lifebelts' of clear perspex over the platform are a part. The walls and ceiling are of Aus. white birch. A fourth auditorium is for chamber music and cinema. M. Baume's *The Opera House Affair* (Sydney, 1967) is a commentary.

Syme, David (1827–1908) b. N. Ber-wick, Scotland. He arrived in Aus. to the gold-diggings, from California in 1853. In 1856, with his journalist brother Ebenezer who died in 1860, he bought the *Age*, already of some influence, and over 50 years built it up to be the most powerful Aus. newspaper. He used it to express his radical views, especially on protection of industry to foster self-sufficiency of Vic., but also on manhood suffrage, payment of Assembly members, curbing of squatter-dominated upper Legislative Council, and intensification and irrigation in farming (he sent his protégé Deakin* to study the latter in India). He answered advertising boycotts by reducing the price to 1d.; yet was astute enough in investment to die wealthy. He was called 'King David', was consulted by politicians and Governors, could make and break governments and wrote on evolution, philosophy and economics. His last son O. J. Syme died in 1967. *For further reading see* C. E. Sayers: *David Syme: A Life* (Melbourne, 1965).

T

TAILEM BEND

Tailem Bend S.A. 35S/139E (1,975 in 1971; 2,049 in 1961) On the right bank of the Murray in irrigated dairy pasture-land on the reclaimed flood-plain. It is the point where the Mallee railway system joins the main line and has rail workshops.

Tailor (*Pomatomus pedica*) An edible Aus. fish, widespread but mainly in estuaries and coastal waters of Qld. to Tas. and across to W.A.; the name is from the scissor-like jaws and teeth. It is grey-blue-olive, with silver belly and very good if eaten fresh. Grows to 75–125 cm. long and usually 1–2 kg.

Taipan (*Oxyuranus scutellatus scutellatus*) A large brown snake with orange-yellow-spotted belly of N Aus. and N.G. (which has the red-striped *O. s. canni*). It is the deadliest Aus. snake; only the very large Indian King Cobra carries more venom (though a little less venomous, weight for weight, than the Taipan, the venom of course being injected through the Cobra's hollow fang). The Taipan is not now regarded as naturally very aggressive, but if roused it may strike repeatedly from a considerable distance, chewing to increase the injection of extremely lethal neurotoxic and coagulant venom. Anti-venene is now available. (*See* PLATE 9.)

Talgai Skull An ancient cranium of a 14 to 15-year-old Aboriginal boy, thought to be an important link between *Homo erectus* and *Homo sapiens*. It was found 1886 on Talgai Station, Darling Downs, Qld. The precise site was established by Edgeworth David*, whose work was interrupted by the 1914–18 War, and only re-identified by K. W. G. MacIntosh in the mid 1960s. Modern radio-

TAMARIND

carbon dating permits a fresh estimate of the age of the cranium at 13,000–30,000 years. This new work affects interpretations of both descent and date of arrival of the Aborigines*.

Tallowwood (*Eucalyptus microcorys*) Growing to 36 m. by 2 m. and brittle-branched, but yielding easily worked timber, and found on the coastal belt with 90–150 cm. mean annual rainfall, and up to 750 m., in Southern Qld. and N N.S.W., in fertile depressions or on well-watered lighter soils. Juvenile leaves are ovoid; adult leaves broadly lanceolate, green above and pale below. There are small clusters of narrow club-shaped buds about 6 mm. long, and longish conical fruit of the same length. Bark is soft, brown, fibrous and corky, and persistent to the lower branches. It is one of the few Eucalypts found in rain-forests.

Tamar River Tas. 41S/147E The tidal estuary from the confluence of the N Esk and S Esk Rivers* at Launceston, extending 65 km. SE–NW and origi-nally named Port Dalrymple. Early but short-lived iron foundries were developed along its banks. The river terraces are among the most productive Tas. farmland. It is now crossed by the Batman* Bridge.

Tamarind, Native (*Diploglottis australis*) A 30-m. evergreen tree in the widespread tropical family Sapind-aceae, common in E coastal rain-forest with grey-brown bark, hairy younger branches, 60-cm. multiple leaves with up to 12 pairs of 20-cm. oak-like leaf-lets, smooth above and hairy below. There are many nectar-rich branched heads of 1-cm., 4-petalled flowers, and yellow fruit with 2–3 single seed-lobes with orange-red sweet but acid flesh, beloved by fruit-bats; they are also used for jams and jellies. Timber is good for cabinet-making and it makes a good garden tree.

Tamarisk (*Tamarix*) A genus of heathy shrubs in the Mediterranean and in central Asia; *T. aphylla*, the Athel Tree, has been introduced as a shade, windbreak and an amenity tree to Broken Hill and other dry parts of Aus. where it grows rapidly in poor sandy or calcareous soil and tolerates a wide range of shade temperatures from below freezing to over 48°C.

Tamarisk

Tambo River Vic. Flows SW from the steep forested scarp edge of the E Highlands NE of Omeo, 37S/148E, just across a ridge from the NE-flowing Murray headwaters, then turns mainly S, latterly through fertile alluvial pastures and maize fields, to a small finger delta in L. King, the easternmost of the lagoon system of Gippsland, NW of Lakes Entrance, 38S/148E.

Tamworth N.S.W. 31S/151E (24,649 in 1971) A growing city at a major focus of road and rail routes and the headquarters of one of the smaller airlines, on the Peel River tributary to the Namoi*. It is on the E side of the N part of the Western Slopes region, but serves a considerable part of the SW of the New England* plateau also, and was closely associated with the New State Movement*. Tamworth has long been one of the leading inland centres of N.S.W., a major focus of varied farming country, with processing as well as marketing (butter, flour, meat) and structural and building industries, a considerable range of professional and educational facilities, including an agricultural high school, and much agricultural engineering etc.

Tanami 20S/130E A desert area in the W of N.T. with E–W sand-dunes and isolated rocky mesas and ridges and fixed vegetation only in the hollows. One of the remotest, least-known regions of Aus. A minor gold-rush founded the small settlement of Tanami from 1909–11 in intolerably isolated and waterless conditions.

Tanunda S.A. 35S/138E (1,936 in 1971) A cultural and residential centre of the Barossa Valley*, retaining a distinctive air of German order.

Taree N.S.W. 32S/152E (11,914 in 1971) Where road and rail cross the Manning River* 16 km. from the sea; it is a growing local service centre with processing of dairy products, timber and fibre-boards, broom-making etc. Taree started as a 'private town' in 1854, to some extent displacing the government town at Wingham 16 km. upstream. It was at least partly built and sited as a river-port, and low-lying areas of the town are liable to flooding.

Tariffs They are widely regarded as essential for the stability and growth of Aus. industry, and only methods of assessment are actively debated. Vic. introduced protective tariffs to foster textile industries etc. when labour displaced from the gold-fields made this timely; it has been argued that Vic. industry also enjoyed natural protection due to distance, and that the effect of protection was a bias towards labour-intensive industry, since N.S.W., with free trade, made quite comparable industrial progress. Federation (1901) brought free trade internally, but protective duties against imports which were made more systematic under Deakin and Lyne in 1908, with the beginnings of a then unreciprocated preference towards U.K. The 1914–18 War gave stimulus and the post-war protective tariff of Greene was designed to consolidate the gains and encourage further expansion. The Tariff Board, a semi-government body of some, though sometimes disputed independence was set up to make detailed recommendations and with powers to take a much broader view. The Depression of 1929–31 brought devaluation and the Scullin revenue-protective duties ('primage', still residually in the tariff system). In 1932 came the Ottawa Agreement with Britain, giving reciprocal preferences, later extended in some degree to other Empire countries. The U.K.-Aus. Trade Agreement of 1957 ended in Feb. 1973 (see TRADE). The late 1930s were fairly stable in tariff policy, and the 1939–45 War renewed both stimulus and war-engendered 'protection'. The post-war consequences have been somewhat different. The General Agreement on Tariffs and Trade (G.A.T.T.) of 1948, as more and more countries became signatories, has given so many of them Most Favoured Nation status (with duties as low as possible, compatible with the then British preference rates) that the Most Favoured Nation rates were better referred to as Intermediate Tariff, leaving only a few important trading nations at the higher General Tariff, notably East Germany. Aus. negotiated other bilateral agreements with Canada, N.Z., Rhodesia, Malawi, Zambia and Malaysia (but not India) within the British Commonwealth, and outside it the important agreement with Japan of 1964, and others with Indonesia, the Philippines and U.S.S.R.

As in most countries there are revenue duties, mainly at very high rates on luxury goods such as liquor and tobacco. The protective duties, though adjudged item by item and forming a complex web of over 3,000 items usually at 3 different rates, are recommended by the Tariff Board following certain principles. 1. Only if an industry is actually established in Aus. and can prove the need, is it entitled to protection against foreign competition, until it is fully established. Any industry once started, often under licence from overseas, is fairly sure of protection. 2. Protective duties, if granted, are only at a minimum rate judged just sufficient to assist an efficient producer of a particular good, rather than a whole field of industry; this makes for a complex tariff pattern. 3. The industry must be economic, in terms of labour costs, though the Tariff Board is prepared to protect these to a large extent, but especially in terms of size of market. 4. If the Aus. industry is so small that large imports must continue even after protection, the additional costs to consumers will be weighed against the gain to the particular industry. 5. Protection is difficult to attain if it will raise costs to other manufacturers, especially for export.

Emergency duties may be imposed, to check dumping of foreign goods at lower prices than those prevailing in their country of origin. At the same time, if manufacturers of protected goods are unable to satisfy Aus. demand, duties may be waived under 'By-law admission', at the discretion of responsible Customs officers. A very large proportion of imports is in fact admitted free under this provision. Import control is retained for special items: ball-bearings, timber, aluminium and secondhand disposals goods. Only exceptionally is industry protected by bounty payments, rather than by tariff.

The basic tariff pattern is the *ad valorem* duty of the f.o.b. value of the goods (i.e. free on board, less than the c.i.f., or cost insurance freight basis used by many countries, thus favouring distant countries such as U.K. against nearer ones such as Japan); this percentage has been lowest for British preference countries, higher for intermediate tariff and highest for General tariff. Specific rates are a similarly varying flat rate per *item* of some goods; often these are rather high rates in relation to value, but are subject to erosion by inflation. Sometimes there are sliding scales, higher as a percentage on lower-priced consignments.

Reliable scholars believe that in relation to goods actually protected i.e. discounting free by-law imports, protective duties are about 30% of the value of the imports, the proportional protection to the actual manufacturing processing in Aus. being rather more. A comprehensive review under way will bring changes, consequent upon changing trends in the Economy* and Trade*.

Tarraleah Tas. 42S/146E A Hydro-electricity Commission village lying at 600 m. for operational staff, mainly at Tarraleah and Tungatinah* Power Station in the gorge of the Nive River, the water being brought 22 km. from the upper Derwent catchment (*see* TASMANIA, POWER).

Tasma (1848–1897) Pen-name of novelist Jessie Catherine Couvreur (*née* Huybers) b. London. She was twice married, taking her pen-name from Tasmania where she spent her childhood. She settled finally in Europe (1883) and married a Belgian politician. Her Aus. settings are well described, but her books little known today.

Tasman, Abel Janszoon (?1603–1659) b. Groningen, Holland. The Dutch Council in Batavia despatched him with 2 ships, the '*Heemskerck*' (60 tons) and '*Zeehan*' (100 tons) with 18 months provision, in August 1642 to make full exploration of the Southland (*see* DISCOVERY), and again in 1644. He discovered Tasmania, naming it Van Diemen's Land, in 1642. A skilled seaman, he was cruel, perhaps too unimaginative and even too timid for the almost superhuman tasks set him. His unfavourable reports helped·to quench the Dutch hopes of wealth in the S, and they lost interest.

Tasman Peninsula Tas. 43S/148E A 3-pronged area of some 500 km². on the E of Storm Bay and joined by the narrow Eaglehawk Neck to Forestier Peninsula. Cliffs and stacks in dolerite contain blow-holes. There are a number of small settlements serving fruit and sheep farming areas along the N coast and in the centre. The E and SW coasts are more exposed and wooded. Port Arthur is on the S side.

Tasman Sea The waters between 30°S on the E coast of Aus. as far S as the S of Tas. and the W coast of N.Z. Named in 1890 as recommended by Aus. and N.Z. Association for the Advancement of Science.

TASMANIA (Tas,) It is the smallest and only insular Aus. State, extending 290 km. N–S and 306 km. E–W, with an area of 48,200 km.² or 0·9% of the country, and population (1971) of 389,874 or 3% of the Aus. total. The average density is 8 per km.² (N.S.W. 5·7, Vic. 15), but as just over half the island is virtually uninhabited, the actual density of settled area is about 16 per km.² Truganini, the last of the distinctive Aborigines* on the island, died in 1876 (*see* GEORGE AUGUSTUS ROBINSON). The capital, Hobart, is much less dominant than in any other State, metropolitan functions being shared with Launceston.

Physical Geography and Land Use High-

Badge of Tasmania

lands, reaching over 1,500 m. in the W, dominate every landscape. High NW–SE ridges of Precambrian rock fill the western half of the island, numerous swift rivers flowing in wide valleys parallel to the ridges, but cutting through them in gorges to the cliffs of the W coast. In the NE is the isolated granitic mass of Ben Lomond*. Between, the Central Plateau* comprises Permian and later sediments, still horizontal and capped by sheets of intruded dolerite, which, along with subsequent faulting, gives a stepped landscape. Glaciation left steep-sided, flat-floored valleys in the W and, in the NW of the Central Plateau, gouged the beds of over 4,000 present-day lakes and dammed back many more. Post-glacial rises of sea level flooded the lower Tamar* and the faulted depressions of the Derwent*, Macquarie* and Oyster Harbours*, and separated Tas. finally from the mainland. The Midlands* S of Launceston are the only appreciable inland plain. Emerged marine platforms along the N coast, backed by low basaltic hills, provide the widest and most fertile farmland. Climate is governed by the island's position in the belt of permanent westerly influence, and the weather by the succession of low-pressure systems. Rainfall totals (including snow) drop sharply E of the Highlands, which have over 250 cm., and droughts are not uncommon in the E half where totals are under 75 cm., and hot northerly continental influences are felt in summer. The winter maximum of the W gives way to spring and autumn maxima in the E, when cyclones move in more from the NE. Maritime influences and altitude modify the normal temperatures of these latitudes ($40°S–43\frac{1}{2}°S$), with ranges quite high in interior valleys. The growing season is restricted by low winter temperatures and high summer evaporation. Forest cover, including some species also found in N.Z. and S America, covers much of the W half. Evergreen, broadleafed rain-forest be-

low 1,100 m. in areas with over 140 cm. of rain, is dominated by the beech myrtle, *Nothofagus cunninghamii*, and sassafras, *Atherosperma moschata*, with under-layers including the impenetrable horizontal scrub of the SW. Button grass, *Mesomelaena*, covers ill-drained valleys and slopes up to 1,100 m., especially where soils are poor, or fire has destroyed the rain-forest. Above 1,100 m. in the N and 600 m. in the S are 'australmontane' moorlands, with dwarf trees, shrubs and cushion plants. Towards the E, eucalypts appear, towering over the rain-forest canopy, and including valuable timber resources in the magnificent ashes *Eucalyptus regnans*, *E. delegatensis* and *E. obliqua*, variously and confusingly known as stringybarks and swamp gums. In the E half of Tas. mainland species dominate; the original open sclerophyll* woodland survives in parts, but is altered elsewhere by fire, especially by Aboriginal nomads, to give wide *Poa* grasslands, now used for rough grazing, as are the coastal heaths of the Bass Str. coast and islands. Rain-forest reappears, especially along gullies, in the NE hills. The land cleared for farming forms an arc from the N coast through the Midlands to the lower Derwent and Huon, and the SE. W of the Tamar intensive cultivation has been long established, and hedge-lined fields, reminiscent of Eng., grow potatoes, peas, clover hay and turnips, and support a mixed live-stock/arable economy, with an emphasis on dairying. The lower Tamar has fruit-growing and the N Midlands intensive cash cropping of oats, barley, peas and sheep-rearing, also found in the eastern half of the Derwent basin. The lower Derwent valley itself and the Huon have the island's most intensive farming of apples and other fruits, including hops, as well as dairy pastures.

Industry and Towns Factories contribute 62% and primary industry 38% to total production value. Within primary industry agriculture (26%) is followed by dairy, pastoral production and mining (each 20%) forestry (13%) and fishing (2%). Wool is the chief farm product, followed by dairy products; fruit, accounting for 35% of agricultural production, is the second main export, and the apples make up 75% of total Aus. output. Farming suffers from high costs of labour, distant fluctuating markets and physical limitations of climate and topography which inhibit large-scale operation. Trends are towards increased efficiency on more concentrated acreages, but retaining or introducing diversity for greater security. A third of the forests still covering 47% of Tas. are State Forests, with commercial concessions in 3 zones: the far NW and NE, and in the SW in a strip from L. St. Clair to the coast. Eucalypts comprise 90% of the cut, used for pulp, paper at Burnie, Boyer and Geeveston, as well as for furniture and building, but rain-forest species are used for plywood and boat-building; *Pinus radiata* supplements pulp supplies. Woodchips are exported to Japan.

Mineral output is dominated by Mt. Lyell* copper (25%) and Rosebery* zinc (20%), and lead, followed by tin from Rossarden on Ben Lomond* and Renison Bell*, alluvial tin in the NE region round Pioneer and scheelite (tungsten) on King Island*. The old mining region of the NW Highlands, which flourished in the late 19th and early 20th centuries, is undergoing a revival today with new ore bodies found at Renison Bell and Rosebery, and iron-ore exploitation at Savage River*. The only remaining coal-mines are at Kaoota, near Hobart, and in the NE at Fingal*. The limited continental shelf and relative lack of food keep the fishing industry fairly small. Crayfish or spiny lobster, *Jasus lalandii*, are now the main catch, followed by scallops, *Pecten meridionalis*, seasonally in Autumn, school shark, *Galeorhinus australis*, Aus. salmon, *Arripis trutta*, and 'Barracouta', *Leionura atun*.

Power (*see* MAP 12) Electricity is virtually all generated by water falling steeply from the Central Plateau*. An integrated transmission developed by the Hydro-electricity Commission (established 1939) supplies all the populated parts of the island, and cheap power has attracted several important industries.

There are 3 systems developed or in course of being developed, to be complete by 1974. 1. Derwent is the oldest and the catchment is now fully exploited. 3 tributary developments converge: in the W, the upper Derwent, stored in the natural L. St. Clair*, and the artificial L. King William which generates power in Butler's gorge and is then diverted E to use the steep drop to Tarraleah* in the Nive River gorge. On the opposite bank, Tungatinah* uses the Nive water, supplemented from the artificially raised L. Echo* which is fed by the diverted Ouse River*. In the main valley, the system has 6 dams: Wayatinah*, Catagunyah*, Repulse, Cluny, Meadowbank and Liapootah, which has the highly mechanised remote-control centre for all 6. 2. Great Lake-South Esk: earlier power stations on the natural S outlet (Shannon, now disused; Waddamana, peak use only) have been replaced by the spectacular diversion to the NE of the lake (supplemented from Arthurs Lakes* to the E and the small L. Augusta to the W) through the 600-m. scarp of the Western Tiers, to Poatina* underground power station, then by canal and Lake River to the South Esk* River where it is re-used at Trevallyn outside Launceston (a previous S Esk development for Bell Bay* aluminium-smelting). 3. Mersey-Forth-Wilmot, draining the northern slopes of the Central Plateau, are being united to feed 4 stations on the Forth (the central of the 3 rivers). The Mersey to the E has Rowallan Dam the main storage, and before diversion, is joined by L. Mackenzie water, falling from 1,118 m. to a power station on the Fisher River. The Wilmot is diverted from the W and below its junction with the Forth, Cethana (at 105 m. the highest Tas. dam), Devil's Gate and Paloona form a 40-km. stretch of 3-stepped lakes.

With the complete exploitation of the Central Plateau, development of the 2,400,000 kW potential of Gordon* and King* Rivers in the W is now well forward; anxiety over future power prices and availability were increased in droughts in the 1960s with power-rationing and daylight-saving* introduced as economies (the latter retained).

Transport Railways are 3-ft. 6-in. gauge and total some 930 km. Of a total of some 22,500 km. of road, 6,400 km. are sealed, making good tourist access to all except the SW of the island. Sea traffic remains vital, and has become increasingly concentrated in Hobart, Launceston, Devonport and Burnie, with recent developments of container and drive-on, drive-off facilities.

Secondary industry based on small workshops and consumer needs was stimulated early, by isolation, but the major factors in Tas. industry, which is highly developed in proportion to population, has been the availability of cheap water-power, timber and good harbours. Most important are the aluminium refinery at Bell Bay* in the N and the zinc refinery in Hobart. Timber processing is concentrated in pulp and paper-mills at Burnie*, Boyer* and Geeveston* but saw-milling is very widespread and small scale. Food-processing includes dairy and canning factories in the growing areas, as well as the Hobart chocolate factory. Tourism is a major industry, with about 120,000 mainlanders visiting the island every year. As yet there is no iron and steel industry, although there were foundries along the Tamar in the 19th century using local ores.

Urban Centres contain over 73% of 1971 population, many of them lying along the N coast plain W of the Tamar.

Over 120,000, Hobart.
60,000–70,000, Launceston.
15,000–25,000, Burnie, Devonport.
5,000–10,000, Ulverston, New Norfolk, service and residential.
2,500–5,000, Queenstown* (mining); George Town* (service-residential for industry); Wynyard*, Kingston*, Smithton* (major service with some industry), Rosebery*, Sorell*.
2,000–2,500, Latrobe* (service); Penguin* (service with residential).
1,000–2,000, Deloraine*, Scottsdale*, Longford* (N plain, service with locally based industry); Zeehan* (mining); Perth (minor service).
Under 1,000 but urban; Lauderdale, Beaconsfield* (minor service-commuter, Beaconsfield former gold); Beauty Point.

Many village-like centres have important local functions: Strahan*, Waratah in the NW mining area; Stanley, Sheffield, Railton on the N coast plain; St. Mary's, St. Helen's, Fingal*, Rossarden in the NE; Oatlands*, Campbell Town in the Midlands; Huonville, Cygnet, Geeveston* on the Huon; and the coastal fishing villages of Bicheno, Dunally*, Bridport and Triabunna. (*See* MAP 11.)

Historical Development Tas. was discovered by Tasman in 1642, who named it Van Diemen's Land*; its insularity was finally proved by Bass and Flinders in 1798. The initial settlements from N.S.W. on the Derwent (1803) and the Tamar (1804) were united, although rivalry has persisted, and the colony separated from N.S.W. in 1825. Rapid land development was based on cheap convict labour, but Tas. also saw the worst of the degradations and brutalities of transportation, and suffered from many bushranger escapees. Savage wars on the Aborigines* were followed by their ultimate extinction. Petitions to end transportation finally succeeded in 1853, and this was followed by responsible government in 1856. But the Vic. gold-fields drew off labour and there was severe depression until the silver, gold and tin discoveries of the 1870s led to a period of stability and agricultural expansion, notably under Giblin in the 1880s. The widespread Aus. Depression of the 1890s was severe and again emigration rose; the position was partially saved by development of apple-growing, following the introduction of refrigerated shipping and the Mt. Lyell copper from 1897. Tas. supported Federation as a solution to economic troubles, but at first suffered from cheap Vic. goods ruining local industry. Commonwealth grants remain necessary. The inter-war period was one of stagnation and migration, although high natural increase maintained totals. In the last 25 years hydro-electric development has led to industrial growth and there has been a sharp revival of mining in the NW. Even so, at 5% increase 1966–71 it remains the slowest growing state. Feelings of isolation persist in an environment unlike that of mainland Aus. Premiers since 1900: N. E. Lewis (1899 and 1909), W. B. Propsting (1903), J. W. Evans (1904), J. Earle (1909 and 1914–16), A. E. Solomon (1912), W. Lee (1916 and 1923), J. A. Lyons* (1923), J. McPhee (1928), A. G. Ogilvie (1934), E. Dwyer Gray (1939), R. Cosgrove (1939 and 1948), E. Brooker (1947), E. E. Reece (1958 and 1972–), W. A. Bethune (1969). *Sources*: J. L. Davies ed.: *Atlas of Tasmania* (Hobart, 1965); F. C. Green: *A Century of Responsible Government in Tasmania* (Hobart, 1956) and J. R. Skemp; *Tasmania Yesterday and Today* (Melbourne, 1959).

Tasmanian Devil (*Sarcophilus harrisi*— meaning flesh-loving) A carnivorous marsupial in the Marsupial Cat family, Dasyuridae, described as bear-like or like a large long-tailed Scotch terrier; it is over 1 m. long, including tail, and black with white patches on chest and rump. For a time these animals were restricted to the remoter parts of Tas. They may be extinct on the mainland,

but have recently increased in bush even near farmland, coming out by night to prey on rabbits, small wallabies and rat-kangaroos, smaller mammals, birds,

Tasmanian Devil
(*Sarcophilus harrisi*), *over 1 m. long*

lizards and probably frogs and crayfish; they are also scavengers of dead meat and also fish refuse. The marsupium opens backwards and contains 2 teats. They make a nest of leaves in hollow logs etc.

Taxation   Provides 95% of Commonwealth Consolidated Revenue of which 60% is from Income Tax, uniformly levied over the country since 1942; customs and excise provide about 25%, sales tax 10%, pay-roll tax 4%, and the remaining from such sources as estate duties, a small wool-sale tax and other levies on primary producers. In the States taxation provides under 20% of Consolidated Revenue, 30% from motor taxation, 20% from stamp duties, and most of the rest from taxation on lotteries, land, liquor, racing etc. Income Tax is generally subtracted from wages and salaries on a 'Pay-as-you-earn' basis, but Tax Returns must also be made each year, in which a number of deductible expenses, e.g. for education, medical costs and limited insurance are claimed and any refund is then paid. (*See also* FINANCE.)

Taylor, Sir Patrick Gordon (or **'Bill'**) (1896–1966) b. Sydney. He joined the

Royal Flying Corps and was awarded the M.C. in 1917. After the war he became associated with Kingsford Smith*, and in 1935 was co-pilot of *Southern Cross* on the attempted flight over the Tasman Sea with the King George V Jubilee Air Mail from N.Z. One of the side engines of the 3-motored plane was damaged and the wooden propeller broken, and had to be switched off. The other side engine overheated so badly that it seemed likely to seize up or go on fire. Walker performed the amazing feat of climbing out on the wing, removing oil from the silent engine and transferring it to the overheated engine by climbing out on the other wing. Kingsford Smith was able to nurse *Southern Cross* back to Sydney on 2 engines, but had to jettison the mail. Taylor was awarded the Empire Gallantry Medal (later changed to the George Cross) and went on to a long and notable career in aviation, including valuable survey flights by flying-boat in the Pacific in the early 1950s. *For further reading see* P. G. Taylor: *The Sky Beyond* (Melbourne, 1963).

Taylor, Thomas Griffith (1881–1963) b. London. He arrived in Aus. in 1893 and was one of the most dynamic and controversial Aus. scientific writers. Trained in science and mining, he developed interests in meteorology, anthropology and above all physiography, and was on Scott's Antarctic expedition (1910). As Professor of Geography in Sydney (1921–8), Chicago (1929–35) and Toronto (1935–50), he wrote and taught provocatively and widely, notably on Aus. to which he retired.

Tea-tree A popular name for various species of *Leptospermum* in the Myrtaceae family, named because Cook's crew made tea from the leaves in N.Z.; and was so used in the early days of settlement at Sydney. The name Tea-tree is also used for some Paperbarks*, *Melaleuca* spp. The 50 species of *Leptospermum* are mainly in Aus. with some in N.Z. and SE Asia; they vary in form from small trees to heath-like bushes. The familiar Tea-tree of coastal dunes and sand-apron, *L. laevigatum* (*see* PLATE 7), has small grey-green lanceolate leaves thickly clothing its flexible branchlets and often picturesquely twisted trunk and branches; its sand-binding qualities are important ecologically and in coastal conservation. Other Tea-trees found at many a stream-side camp site in E Aus. are the smaller 2 to 3-m. bushes, slightly lemon-scented and with small 5-petalled flowers of the common Tea-tree or the Tantoon, *L. flavescens*, or the rather similar *L. obovatum*. The Lemon-scented Tea-tree, *L. citratum*, yields citral oil, and *L. scoparium*, the white or pink-flowered tree common to Aus. and N.Z. (the Manuka of N.Z.), also contains essential oils.

Tektites The most generally accepted name for small pieces of volcanic glass, found in swarms in 9 or 10 large regions in the world, including SE

Tektites

Aus., hence the alternative local names of Australites, Black-fellows' Buttons (they were used for magical purposes by Aborigines), Button-stones and Emu Stones (they have been found in emus' crops). A theory, of growing acceptance, is that they represent debris from a comet swarm. Some 2 million may have fallen over S Aus.

Telecommunications The Overseas Telecommunications Commission (1964) provides telephone, telex and telegram services. Satellite earth stations are at Moree N.S.W. (1968), Ceduna, S.A. (1969), Carnarvon, W.A. (1969). Cables, part of the British Commonwealth system include COMPAC and SEACOM*; expansion is planned (1972).

Television Began in Sydney in 1956: commercial (September) Aus. Broadcasting Commission* (November), then Melbourne, and in all State capitals by 1960. 41 National and 45 commercial stations cover the more closely settled areas; colour TV is planned (1975). The line frequency used is 625. Aus. material is required to supply 50% of viewing time on commercial stations (August 1967), but for entertainment, the reliance on imported drama, panel games, quiz programmes and variety shows is still high; the A.B.C. uses more British and the commercial stations rather more American material. Surveys in Sydney and Melbourne show that adherence is approximately 80% to commercial and 20% to A.B.C.

Telopea Downs Vic. 36S/141E Named from the tree genus (*see* WARATAH). Continues the once barren Coonalpyn Downs* S.A., in 2 areas still sometimes significantly named the Big and Little Deserts. Much of this belt has good underground water supplies, but full development has only come following research work by C.S.I.R.O.* and the Waite Institute* in Adelaide, which established that soils were deficient in trace elements, remediable by the application of small quantities of copper, zinc and molybdenum sulphates as well as nitrogenous fertilisers and nitrogen-fixing crops, such as lupins and clover. This fundamental work has been followed by the financial initiative of a large insurance company which has here acted as a development agency. So far wool, fat lambs and some

beef are the main products of the new farm economy.

Temora N.S.W. 34S/148E (4,462 in 1971) A former gold-rush town and now a local service rail, road and market centre in the S part of the Western Slopes region and towards its W edge, with flour-milling, grain trade, meatworks and clothing manufacture.

Tench, Watkins (1758–1833) b. Chester, Eng. Marine captain-lieutenant with the First Fleet*, remaining in N.S.W. until 1792. He is best known for his keenly observed and well-written acounts of the first years of the colony, having undertaken several exploratory journeys which included the tracing of the Nepean-Hawkesbury River System. Tench later also wrote about France, when living there as a prisoner of war.

Tenison-Woods, Julian Edmund (1832–1889) b. London. He arrived in Tas. in 1853 for his health, having left Oxford for the priesthood. He was widely interested in science, especially geology and exploration on which he wrote important papers. On mission work he used to ride with Adam Lindsay Gordon*, and later wrote his biography.

Tennant Creek N.T. 20S/134E (1,789 in 1971) It lies at 450 m. in arid country of low, flat-topped hills. The settlement dates from the Overland Telegraph* station of 1872, but developed with the discovery of gold in lenses in hillocks in 1934 and large copper deposits in 1955. Gold, copper and silver are obtained from ores at 3 main mines: Peko to the SE, Ivanhoe and Orlando to the W of the Stuart Highway. They dominate the mineral output of the N.T. and go by road to the railhead at Alice Springs.

Tennant, Kylie (Mrs. L. C. Rodd) (1912–) b. Manly, N.S.W. A novelist using Aus. themes and settings, often based on the experiences of a varied life in both town and country, for stories which, although reflective of social conditions, have strong veins of humour, farce and satire; they are simply written and full of varying incident and vividly characterised as in *The Man on the Headland* (Sydney, 1971). See M. Dick: *The Novels of Kylie Tennant* (Adelaide, 1966).

Tennis Aus. players have held a leading, often dominant position in world lawn tennis over the last 20 years. This is accredited largely to a rigorous selection and disciplined training of young potential champions, from the 5,000 or more clubs existing in the country; to the development of a fast powerful game, largely on hard courts; to commercial sponsorship; and to a climate that allows year-round playing. The Davis Cup*, Wimbledon, U.S. and European titles are the goals of the succession of players winning the home championships; many of the most successful then turn professional.

The date of, and person responsible for the introduction of the game to Aus. are both unknown; it was probably returning Australians or new migrants in the 1870s. The first championships, and associations respectively were in Vic., 1885 and 1892; N.S.W., 1885 and 1890; Qld., 1889 and 1888; S.A., 1890 and 1889; Tas., 1893; W.A., 1895. The first inter-state championships were held in 1885. A national organisation was formed in 1904, largely through the efforts of T. L. Hicks, who wanted Aus. to have the necessary body to challenge for the Davis Cup. Until 1923 N.Z. belonged to it, after which it became the Lawn Tennis Association of Australia (L.T.A.A.). The first Aus. championship was held in 1905 and won by R. W. Heath. Royal Tennis (devised by Henry VIII) is played on one court in Hobart and one in Melbourne.

Although there were giants, notably Brookes* earlier, the development of Aus. tennis came after the 1914–18 War, and was most spectacular after the 1939–45 War. From 1910–72 an Aus. has won the Wimbledon men's singles 19 times, the bulk of the wins being since the early 1950s, and 1969 peaks were reached in Laver's achievement of the Grand Slam of Aus., U.S., French, Wimbledon and the Italian titles. There is some anxiety over a decline in spectator interest, and in the numbers of players. The introduction of 'open tennis' in recent years may resolve this to some extent, but there is also a feeling that as in cricket*, some new development is needed, in this case away from the service-dominated power game. The 1972 Wimbledon series lacked many Aus. players including the 1971 champion, owing to a dispute with professional sponsors.

Outstanding players are listed here (W indicates Wimbledon singles champion).

Before 1900: D. Webb, B. Green.
1900–20: R. Heath, L. Garden, A. Dunlop, H. Rice, N. E. Brookes* (W 1907; 1914), L. O. S. Pordevin.
1920s: G. L. Patterson (W 1919, 1922), J. O. Anderson, P. O'Hara Wood, J. B. Hawkes, C. Todd, S. Wertheim, R. Schlesinger, I. McInnes, F. Kalms, G. Moon, J. Willard, R. O. Cummings.
1930s and early 1940s: J. Crawford* (W 1933), V. McGrath*, A. Quist*, J. Bromwich*, J. Clemenger, D. Turnbull, L. Schwartz, C. Sproule (notably in administration and umpiring).
Since 1945: D. R. Pails, C. Long, G. Brown, O. W. T. (Bill) Sidwell, I. Ayre, F. Sedgman* (W 1952), G. Worthington, M. Rose*, K. McGregor*, K. Rosewall*, L. Hoad* (W 1956–7), R. Hewitt (now a S African), F. Stolle, R. Hartwig, R. Mark, A. Cooper (W 1958), M. Anderson, N. Fraser (W 1960), R. Laver* (W 1961–2, 1968–9), R. Emerson* (W 1964–5), J. Newcombe (W 1967, 70, 71), Tony Roche, W. Alexander, R. Ruffles.

Women players have been slower in international achievement.

Before 1930: P. A. Stewart, L. Addison, R. Payton, K. Baker (Mrs. Ford), F. St. George (Mrs. Conway), E. Boyd, D. Akhurst, Mrs. Molesworth.

1930–50s: N. Wynne (Mrs. Bolton), T. Coyne (Mrs. Long), J. Hartigan, M. Carter (Mrs. Reitano). Since 1960: M. Smith (Mrs. Court*) (W 1963, 65, 70), L. Turner, J. Lehane, R. Ebbern, J. Dalton, K. Melville, L. Bowrey, E. Goolagong* (W 1971). *See also* J. Pollard: *Tennis the Australian Way* (Melbourne, 1963).

Tent Spiders A popular name for the sub-family Linpyhiinae, living in forest litter where the distinctive trap is built.

Tenterfield N.S.W. 29S/152E (3,232 in 1971) An important service centre in the N of New England*, with meatworks, butter factory and sawmills; it was named from a mansion near Haddington, Scotland, by an early squatter. Here in 1889 Sir Henry Parkes made a speech claimed as crucial in the Federation movement.

Terminalia A genus of largely tropical trees in the mainly tropical family Combretaceae, with well-marked buttresses like many large tropical forest trees. Aus. species include *T. catappa,* Indian Almond (its range does indeed extend to India), and the endemic *T. oblongata, T. sericocarpa* and *T. muelleri.*

Winged Termite
(*Mastotermes darwiniensis*), *about life size*

Termites Colonial and wood-eating insects of the Order Isoptera, sometimes called White Ants in popular parlance, but not closely related to true ants, are primitive in structure (akin to cockroaches when in the winged condition), but with great modifications of body-shape and function in individuals, in accordance with their 'castes' and related function in the colony (numbering from hundreds to 1 or 2 million). The winged form has a long slender body and 2 pairs of long soft, transparent and gauzy wings, easily broken off. The 2 pairs are similar except in the large and destructive tropical species *Mastotermes darwiniensis,* where the rear wing has cockroach-like fan-shaped folds. A nuptial dance of these eyed and winged forms on a warm humid summer evening, perhaps clustered round a light with prodigal destruction of many, and the heap of discarded wings, tells of the climax of the work of one colony and of the kings and queens going off, now wingless, to form new colonies in a suitable site. Within the colony there is specialisation comparable to that in ants or bees. The queen, often a great white grub with abdomen so swollen that she cannot move, may go on producing eggs for many years, probably with periodic renewal of sperm by kings. The soldier termites are sterile and blind, with a long dark head and formidable jaws, often forming about 2–10% of the population. The workers are also sterile and blind, but specialised to the obtaining of food supplies from timber or growing trees, partly digesting it, with the aid of protozoa, the enzymes of which are essential for the assimilation of cellulose by the insects, and regurgitating it into the mouths of kings, queens, larval forms of these and soldiers; they also clean the tens of thousands of eggs from fungi which grow readily in the humid nest, and order and maintain the various tunnels of the colony. The black 'carton' material (in the core behind the clay exterior of a 'typical' termite mound of a soil-dwelling species, or inside a hollowed-out tree or timber) consists largely of the termites' own excreta. Apart from the tropical *Mastotermes* already noted, reputed to devour even rubber insulation on cables, a widespread timber-destroyer is *Copotermes acinaciformis.* The Magnetic or Meridional Termite, *Amitermes meridionalis,* builds the well-known N–S narrow mounds to minimise direct summer sun.

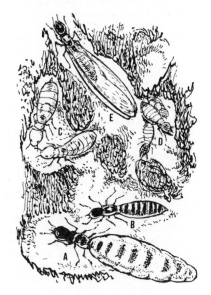

Termites (Coptotermes)
A   *Queen*
B   *Male (wingless)*
C   *Worker*
D   *Soldier*
E   *Winged sexual forms*

Terns or **Sea-swallows** Those seen in Aus. include about 16 species. Commonly seen are the large black-backed and black-capped Crested Tern, the small Fairy Terns, the Roseate or Graceful Tern (*see* PLATE 4), and more rarely the large, red-billed Caspian Tern. (*See also* SEA-BIRDS.)

Territories Federal Internal Territories are the Northern Territory* and Australian Capital Territory*. Federal External Territories are: Norfolk Island*, Papua*, Heard and McDonald Islands*, Australian Antarctic Territory*, Cocos (Keeling) Islands*, Christmas Island*, Ashmore and Cartier Island (administered with N.T.) and Coral Sea Islands Territory. In addition there were the Trust Territories of New Guinea (administered with Papua from 1949 to self-government in 1973) and Nauru* 1945–68.

Terry, Michael (1899–   ) b. Gateshead, Eng. He arrived in Aus. in 1918, and in 1922–3 made a first crossing by car from Winton, Qld., to Broome, W.A.; he made later pioneer trips in W and Central Aus. until 1933, using caterpillar or 6-wheel trucks, and has written extensively about them.

Test Matches A term applied mainly to cricket and rugby international matches. Cricket Tests have been played against Eng., W Indies, India, Pakistan and N.Z. The first Test is considered to have been the Eng.-Aus. match at Melbourne in March 1887 when the 2 sides first met on equal terms. The Aus. team, captained by D. Gregory*, with Bannerman* as the outstanding player, won this, but lost the return match. From 1876–1972 there have been 209 Tests of which Aus. won 82, England 69 and 58 were drawn. Tests are mainly played in 'rubbers' of 5, the winner getting the 'Ashes'*.

Matches with S Africa: 1910–11 (a draw); 1931–2, 1952–3 (both Aus. wins); 1963–4 (3 drawn, Aus. 1, S Africa 1); 1966–7 (Aus. 1, S Africa 3, 1 draw); 1970 (S Africa 4, Aus. 0).

W Indies: 1930–1 (Aus. 4, W.I. 1); 1951–2 (Aus. 4, W.I. 1); 1954–5 (Aus. 3, 2 draws); 1960–1 (Aus. 1, W.I. 1, 1 tie, 1 draw); 1965 (W.I. 2, Aus. 1, 2 draws); 1969 (Aus. 3, W.I. 1, 1 draw).

India: 1947–8 (Aus. 4, 1 draw); 1956 in India (Aus. 2, 1 draw); 1964 (Aus. 1, India 1, 1 draw); 1968 (Aus. 4, India 1); 1969–70 (Aus. 3, India 1, 1 drawn).

Pakistan: from 1956–73 there were 9 Tests of which Aus. won 5, lost 1 and drew 3.

Tewantin-Noosa Qld. 26S/153E (4,053 in 1971) In a region of coastal lagoons and sands, on the small Noosa River; now a holiday resort. Its development dates from cedar extraction, sawing and shipping to Brisbane in the 1870s.

Textile Manufacture Some 35,000 are employed in making wool (60%), cotton (30%) and man-made fibres (10%). While the bulk of the 250 factories are in N.S.W. and Vic., there is more dispersion among country towns than in any other industry, reflecting not only decentralisation policies but also the availability of labour and buildings for incoming manufacturers, and historical factors in the oldest established wool-mills.

Man-made fibres have been established since 1945 mainly by overseas companies. Two-thirds of the industry is in Vic. where much of the basic material is made (*see* CHEMICALS). They satisfy over half the Aus. demand, and are increasing in both metropolitan and dispersed factories.

Cotton Only 20% of Aus. demand is met, comprising the heavier qualities, and relying for two-thirds of its raw cotton on imports from U.S., Mexico, Brazil and Pakistan. Most of the output is in the hands of a few very large textile firms which also make wool, silk, etc., but there are smaller, more specialised firms in country towns.

Wool manufacture dates from the female convict blanket-factory at Parramatta (1801), and gradually developed in N.S.W., Vic. and Tas., with a major revival in the 1870s under Government protection in Vic., which retains over half the production. Development has been intermittent, and although enough is produced for most Aus. needs, there is some stagnation of demand with changing habits of dress, heating and with competition of man-made fibres. Characteristics of the industry are the degree of integration of several stages of production in single factories dispersed outside the capital cities, and of more specialised and mainly worsted metropolitan factories (although important exceptions occur), and the high proportion of virgin wool used, compared with European mills which mix waste rags etc.

Of every 500 tons of raw Aus. wool, 400 are exported directly. Of the remaining 100 tons which are cleaned, then scoured (for worsteds) or carbonised (for woollens), 57 tons are then exported, 1 goes to felt-making, and 12 (with shorter fibres) are spun for woollens, piecegoods, blankets and carpets (this latter also requires imported coarse woollens to mix). The longer fibred wools (accounting for 30 of the 100 tons) are the basis of worsteds, and are combed, carded and rolled into balls or 'tops'; 13 tons are exported in this form; this is an expanding and technically advanced sector. Some 4 tons, rejected for worsteds, return as 'noils' to the woollens sector, and of the remaining 13 tons, 6 will be woven for the clothing trade, 1 will make hand-knitting yarn and 6 provide a third of the raw material in machine-knitting plants. The preliminary processes and worsted spinning each employ a third of the work force; 'tops' woollen spinning, and dyeing and finishing share the other third almost equally.

THEATRE Like its literary counterpart, Drama*, it has seen little truly indigenous growth until the last decade, although theatrical entertainment based on imported productions, using visiting and some local artists, have had flourishing periods.

On June 4th 1789, in a mud hut at Sydney Cove, 11 convicts performed a farce, *The Recruiting Officer*, for the Governor. The first theatre (1796–8) was built in the present Bligh Street, Sydney, by a convict baker called Sidaway, and restoration comedies were staged. Levey* built the first professional theatre (1833–8), the Theatre Royal, with Conrad Knowles a leading actor along with John Lazar. Although

PLATE 9: SNAKES
1. Common Brown Snake *(Pseudonaja textilis textilis)*. 2. Common Black Snake *(Pseudechis porphyriacus)*. 3. Mainland Tiger Snake *(Notechis scutatus scutatus)*. 4. Taipan *(Oxyuranus scutellatus scutellatus)*. 5. Yellow-bellied Sea Snake *(Pelamis platurus)*.

the introduction of such a dubious activity to the colony caused some public demur, it was followed by the larger Royal Victoria (1838). In Tas. the first production was held in the Freemasons Tavern (1833), Hobart, and Coppin*, the first great entrepreneur of the Aus. theatre, began in Launceston before moving to the mainland. The Adelaide Theatre Royal (1838) was in the upper room of a tavern and was followed by Coppin's New Queens Theatre (1846). The wooden Theatre Royal in Melbourne (1842) was also followed by several of Coppin's enterprises. W.A. had a theatre in 1839, Brisbane not until 1850; and there were some itinerant companies under actor managers. A boom in theatrical production followed the gold-rushes, and by 1860 Coppin had opened 6 theatres in Melbourne, including the Olympic (1855), called the Iron Pot from its metal structure prefabricated in Eng. Several provincial theatres were opened. Visiting actors were brought from Eng. and vaudeville also flourished. Later in the century a middle-brow theatre, based largely on Gilbert and Sullivan, was developed by J. C. Williamson*, whose company grew to dominate this type of entertainment. Dampier* was one of a group of entrepreneurs mainly of melodrama and some good Shakespeare production; Bland Holt also commissioned, wrote and presented melodramas from 1876–1909, and the Boucicault and Brough families persevered with serious drama. Rickard's* musichalls led to the popular and widely spread Tivoli Circuit in all the States, and fostered an 'offensively Australian' brand of music-hall comedian, notably 'Mo' Wallace, and Jim Gerald. A. E. (Bert) Beuley (1872–1953) was a famous character actor.

A rapid decline in theatrical attendance, and consequently production, followed the 1914–18 War and persisted through the Depression in face of costs, taxes, competition from radio, and especially films*. Repertory was maintained, though with difficulty, e.g. under the actor-producer G. McMahon (1874–1941). The first major attempt at a modern theatre was the Minerva in Sydney (1940–50). This has been followed by a growth of mainly amateur 'little theatres' notably under Doris Fitton* and May Hollingworth*, introducing serious contemporary drama to Aus. as well as providing training grounds. The Union Theatre in Melbourne University has a professional core. The Phillip Street Theatre, Sydney, is noted for satiric reviews. Among modern directors Robin Lovejoy is highly rated. The larger concerns still produce the popular musicals that have replaced Gilbert and Sullivan. Visiting overseas companies, notably the Old Vic., are very well received. In 1954 the Aus. Elizabethan Theatre Trust* was formed to promote drama, opera and ballet, and Aus. writing and artists in the theatre, with moderate success, and television gives some attention to local sources. Criticism continues that the approach of enthusiastic amateurs, common to several facets of Aus. life, is not conducive to the 'solid roots' needed for an indigenous culture in theatre. Expatriate artists have included Oscar Asche*, Madge Elliot, Cyril Ritchard, Cicely Courtneidge, Judith Anderson, Diane Cilento and Zoe Caldwell and designer Kenneth Rowell. *For further reading see* H. Hunt: *The Making of an Australian Theatre* (Melbourne, 1960); and P. McGuire: *The Australian Theatre* (Melbourne, 1948).

Theodore, Edward Granville (1884–1950) b. Port Adelaide. Son of a Rumanian migrant, Qld. Premier from 1919–25, and Federal Labor politician. A former miner and Trade Unionist, he introduced far-reaching socialist legislation in Qld., including abolition of the Legislative Council in 1922. As member of the Commonwealth Parliament from 1927 he was charged with irregularity over his election, but rose to the Treasury under Scullin (1929–31), attempting to introduce radical cures for the Depression* which partially led to Labor's defeat in 1931. Meanwhile, a charge of fraud in relation to a mining sale in 1919 caused his resignation, but he was cleared and reinstated. Later he established successful business enterprises, including gold development in Fiji, and returned to a major wartime government post 1941–5.

Therry, John Joseph (1790–1864), b. Cork, Ireland. A Roman Catholic priest, one of 2 who arrived 1820. Therry was a man of deep compassion and vision, and worked untiringly under considerable restrictions and opposition. He established St. Mary's Cathedral, Sydney (1829), the first Roman Catholic Church in Aus.; the original building was burned down in 1865. *For further reading see* E. M. O'Brien: *Life and Letters of Archpriest John Joseph Therry* (Sydney, 1922).

Thistle Island S.A. 35S/136E Off Cape Catastrophe in the SW of Spencer Gulf, it is about 40 km.², and was named by Flinders in 1802 after the master of the *Investigator*, who was drowned here when a ship's boat was lost.

Thompson, Andrew (?1773–1810) b. Kirk Yetholm, Scotland. He was transported for theft (1792) with a 14-year sentence, but was pardoned (1797) for exemplary constabulary work. He became, like Simeon Lord, a very wealthy and influential emancipist* and a pioneer founder of Windsor. His interests included farming, salt-works and trading, and Macquarie gave him much friendship and trust.

Thomson, Sir Edward Deas (1800–1879) b. Edinburgh. He arrived in Aus. (1829) as clerk to the Legislative and Executive Council and succeeding Macleay as Colonial Secretary (1837–56). He was a loyal and efficient servant under successive Governors, estab-

lishing very high standards in the developing public service.

Thomson, Peter (1929–) b. Melbourne a leading golfer, winning the British Open 1954–56, 1958, 1965 and the Aus. Open 1951–67.

Thomson River Vic. Rising on the S-facing scarp of the Gippsland Highlands, it flows S in a forested upper valley round the E flank of Mt. Baw the Macalister River* and joins the Latrobe River. By 1975 the upper Thomson waters will be led through a 19-km. tunnel to the upper Yarra, to augment Melbourne's water supply.

Thornbills (genus *Acanthiza*—dweller in thorny brakes) A group of about a dozen uniquely Aus. birds (about 10 cm. long), generally warm-brown on the back, light on the front, often with a dark tail-band and a flash of bright colour about the rump, and sometimes with some smart flecking on head or breast feathers. They are often seen working over the outer and upper foliage of trees and shrubs, or with some species over grasslands, in search of insects; they have a pleasing chattering conversation. They are sometimes beneficent visitors to gardens and orchards. One Aus. popular name is Tit or Tom-tit, recalling the acrobatic insectivores of Europe. The nest is often domed and with a side entrance, despite which some species are parasitised by the egg-laying of cuckoos. The Yellow-tailed Thornbill, *A. chrysorrhoa* (golden-tail), of the S two-thirds of Aus. has such a nest, crowned with an open cup, sometimes interpreted as a resting place for the cock bird or as a decoy nest for the Bronze-wing cuckoo, but it is now thought to be an outlet for an excessive nest-building urge in the male. It is one of 6 or 7 mainly ground-feeding thornbills. One of the most distinctive is the Chestnut-tailed Thornbill, *A. uropygialis* (tail-rumped), with quite a bright red-brown rump and lower sides, and brown ribs and flecks on a light buff head and breast; it may be seen in pairs or flocks over much of inland Aus. in low scrub and grassy stretches. The Thornbills haunting outer foliage include the Striated Thornbill, *A. lineata*, with lines of dark brown flecks on its breast; it builds a much more bottle-shaped nest, with a hooded side entrance often seen in a small tree or sapling, of bark, grass, etc., well swathed in cobwebs etc., and lined with fur and feathers. There are regional variants, often given species status, such as the Brown Thornbill, *A. pusilla* (very small), of SE Aus., much like the Chestnut Thornbill already noted but without the vividly coloured rump, and the Broad-tailed Thornbill, *A. apicalis* (tipped), of SE Aus. very similar but with a more fan-like tail.

Threadfins (genus *Polydactylus*) They are mainly estuarine and tropical fish, blue or golden or greyish above, with silvery sides sometimes striped. The lower rays of the fins below the gills are separated as thread-like feelers for finding food. Species vary in size from a few cm. to a m. or so, the pink flesh is good to eat.

Thrips Small wingless or winged sap-sucking insects of the Order Thysanoptera, of which the brown-black, native Giant Thrips, *Idolothrips marginata*, at 12 mm. long, is the largest known; it normally lives under eucalyptus bark or leaf litter. Various introduced species are pests which cause drying up of foliage or galls on various commercial or garden plants, e.g. tobacco, pome and citrus fruit and gladioli.

Throsby, Charles (1777–1828) b. Leicester, Eng. He arrived in N.S.W. (1802) as surgeon on a convict ship. He was active in the colony as a doctor, a land agent and settler, but most importantly as an explorer. In 1818 he led an expedition southwards from Liverpool to Jervis Bay, on which Hume* was a servant; in 1819 he opened a new route across the Blue Mts. to Bathurst, finding good grazing land. In 1821 he followed the Molonglo to its junction with the Murrumbidgee, suggesting it would be joined by the Lachlan.

Thrushes Apart from the introduced thrush (*see* BIRDS, INTRODUCED), some native species have thrush as a popular name, such as the Grey Thrush. (*See* BIRDS.)

Thunderbolt, Captain (Frederick Ward) b. Windsor. A bushranger. He was gaoled for horse-stealing. He swam ashore from Cockatoo Island (1863) and became a 'gentleman' robber, specialising in courtesy, fast horses and highway robbery from Maitland to the New England plateau, until he was cornered and shot.

Thursday Island Qld. 10S/142E (2,216 in 1971; 2,655 in 1966) The navigation, administrative and quarantine centre for the Torres Str.* Islands, annexed to Qld. 1872. Only 3·25 km.^{2}, it is dwarfed by the much larger Prince of Wales and Horn Islands (the latter with the airstrip). A mixed population of Malay, Chinese, Japanese and local origin are engaged in pearl and trochus-shell diving; Port Kennedy harbour is on the E coast.

Thylacine, Tasmanian Wolf or Tasmanian Tiger (*Thylacinus cyanocephalus*) A single species of carnivorous marsupial, in the Dasyuridae family with

Tasmanian Wolf
(*Thylacinus cyanocephalus*), *almost 2 m. long*

the Marsupial Cats*. Through convergent evolution it has a remarkable resemblance, superficially and in many habits, to a wild dog, e.g. teeth adapted for meat-eating, but has a backward-opening pouch with 2 pairs of teats, and when hard-pressed, perhaps by dogs, or confronted with obstacles, it sometimes substitutes hopping on its kangaroo-like back legs, for its normal dog-like running on tip-toes. At such times it utters a guttural cough-like bark, with wheezing inbreath. The Thylacine is under 2 m. in length, nose to tail, generally resembling a rather powerfully built, short-legged dingo, the hindquarters tapering into an initially thick, but sharply pointed tail. It has a number of tapering stripes, longest over the hind legs and shortening to the middle of the back and the base of the tail (hence the name 'tiger', though not particularly cat-like in appearance or habit). Its natural diet includes wallabies and smaller marsupials, rats, birds, probably lizards and even spiny ant-eaters (tossed up until weakened by repeated falls, as a fox-terrier worries a hedgehog). Attacks on man are very rare indeed, but carnage among sheep (much easier hunting) caused the Tas. settlers to wage ruthless war on the Thylacine, so that it is seldom seen today, though it presumably survives in the remote tangled forests of SW Tas. Thylacine bones are found in cave deposits in W.A. In the Kingston area of SE of S.A. possible sightings of thylacines were reported in recent years, though repudiated by scientists.

Tichborne Case A famous legal case (1871–4), in which Arthur Orton, a Londoner who had settled in Wagga Wagga*, N.S.W., as a butcher, laid claim to the inheritance of the aristocratic Tichborne family in Eng. He convinced many people of his identity as Sir Roger Tichborne, including the Dowager, his alleged 'mother', but was convicted of perjury, released in 1884 and died in poverty in 1898. *For further reading see* M. Gilbert: *The Claimant* (London, 1957).

Ticket of Leave A certificate entitling a convict to work for himself within a specified area; conditions of attainment were regularised under Governor Brisbane.

Ticks Small flat parasites, 8-legged in adult life and parasitic on man, domestic and wild animals, belonging to the Acarina Order of the Arachnida.
    Aus. has over 40 species of Tick proper, 4 of which are introduced (the so-called Sheep Tick being in fact a Louse-fly—*see* FLIES). 1. Soft-bodied Ticks, family Argasidae, include the introduced Fowl-tick, *Argas persicus*, and the Kangaroo-tick, *Ornithodorus gurneyi* (causing intense irritation and temporary blindness in man). 2. Hard-bodies Ticks include the 6 mm. oval Dog Tick, *Ixodes holocyclus*, easily seen on careful search of the dog's fur, at least when swollen with engorged blood, and liable to cause respiratory paralysis leading to death in dogs and cats, and even in young children, and to sharp, if milder, symptoms in adults. The native Wallaby-tick, *Haemaphysalis* (blood-inflated) *bancrofti* (from the notable Aus. parasitologist Bancroft*), and Slender Possum-tick, *H. humerosa*, may feed on other hosts such as cattle and bandicoots. The Scrub-tick, *H. bispinosa* (from India), and another dog-tick, *H. leachi* (from Africa), have been introduced. Several of these have been incriminated, mainly overseas, in the transmission of rickettsial and other diseases. The introduced pale-coloured Cattle Tick, *Boophilus microplus*, of N Aus. hatches on the grass; the larval stage crawls up grasses etc. ready to fasten on to a passing host, and may cause Tick-fever and Tick-worry in cattle.

Tiger Snakes (genus *Notechis*) Large brown snakes with somewhat distinct head, round eye-pupils and 3–5 upper teeth behind the venom fang. The venom is highly lethal, neurotoxic and coagulant. Species include: 1. the Mainland Tiger Snake, *N. scutatus scutatus*, inhabiting rabbit burrows, hollow logs etc., on dry rather than swampy sites (*see* PLATE 9); 2. the Western Tiger Snake, *N. s. occidentalis*, steel-blue to blackish, sometimes with yellow-orange bands; 3. the Black Tiger Snake, *N. ater ater* of the Flinders Range; with or without bands; 4. the Peninsula Tiger Snake, *N. a. niger* of the Eyre Peninsula and islands nearby, very venomous for its smaller size; 5. the Chappell Island Tiger Snake, *N. a. serventyi*, of the E Bass Str. islands, very large but less venomous; and 6. the King Island Tiger Snake, *N. a. humphreysi*, of the islands off NW Tas., smaller and again less toxic.

Timber An industry of local and, in the strategic sense, of national importance, traditionally of hardwoods, mainly eucalypts, but increasingly from softwood plantations mainly of pines. (*See* FOREST RESOURCES *and* TREES— for a list mainly of timber trees.)

Time Zones There are 3 time zones based on the solar time at 120°E, 142° 30′E and 150°E. Eastern Aus. Standard Time is 10 hours ahead of Greenwich Mean Time and affects Qld., Vic., Tas., A.C.T. and N.S.W., except Broken Hill in the far W of the State which takes Central Aus. Standard Time, based on 142°30′E, 9½ hours ahead of G.M.T., along with S.A. and N.T. W.A. Time, based on 120°E, is 8 hours ahead of G.M.T. *See also* DAYLIGHT SAVING.

Tin As result of exploration and expansion of known deposits in recent years, Aus. is now a net exporter of tin. While in the past Aus. has been a signatory to the International Tin Agreement as a consumer, for the Fourth Agreement (1971–6) she became a producer and has to contribute to the 'buffer stock' which stabilises short term market fluctuations. Main mining areas are: the Herberton field

of NE Qld., Renison Bell and Mt. Cleveland in NW Tas., S Mt. Cameron near Gladstone, and Rossarden and Storey's Ck. on the slopes of Ben Lomond in NE Tas., Pilbara in NW of W.A. and Greenbushes in the SW of W.A., Mt. Tallebung, Gibsonvale and Ardlethen in New England area of N.S.W. There are 2 tin smelters in Sydney, and the tinplating industry at Port Kembla has expanded.

Tingle, Red (*Eucalyptus jacksoni*) A tall cool-temperate forest tree, with lanceolate leaves and cup-like fruit, growing in a small area near Nornalup Inlet, 100 km. W of Albany in SW W.A. It superficially resembles the jarrah, but tends to be taller, and yields similar, but rather lighter timber more suitable for furniture etc.

Toad A popular name used loosely and conflictingly for some Amphibia*, but perhaps especially for the Giant Toad, *Bufo marinus*, introduced to Qld. sugar areas in the hope of controlling greyback beetle.

Toado A popular name for small squat-bodied fish, marine and freshwater, the flesh of which is very poisonous to men and animals. The 4 teeth, forming a parrot-like beak in a blunt snout, are quite distinctive. There are some 30 Aus. species. A marine species with lines along the body and inflating to a pear shape is *Ovoides manillensis*. A species certainly living in fresh water is *Aphanacanthus hamiltoni*, dull greenish with dark blotches and cross-bars, very poisonous to eat, to men and animals, even in very small quantities; it ranges widely through the S of Aus.

Toadstools Aus. species include several luminous at night, e.g. *Pleurotus nidiformis*, and some forming 'fairy rings', e.g. *Marasmius oreades*. (*See also* MUSHROOMS.)

Tobacco It is grown on some 10,000 ha. and supplies 40% of Aus. consumption, manufactured in 16 factories mainly in Melbourne and Sydney which employ 4,800 people. It is blended with leaf imported with duty concession if a stipulated amount of Aus. leaf is also used (now 50% or more). Location of growing areas is limited by soil, available irrigation water and labour; many migrant share-croppers grow it. The main areas are Mareeba* with Albanian farmers, Beerwah and Texas in Qld. and the Italian farms of the Ovens Valley in Vic. Imports (1970) were $32 million and exports under $3 million worth.

Todd River N.T. 24S/134E It rises in the Macdonnell Ranges* and flows, in wet years only, SE for about 320 km. and into sand-hill country before losing itself in the Simpson Desert*. The dry bed through Alice Springs is occasion-ally the scene of a 'boat race', in which the boats are carried by runners, but it can be a considerable torrent. Water from its sands is pumped for use in the town. It was named after the S.A. Postmaster-General when the Overland Telegraph* was installed in 1870–2.

Tolpuddle Martyrs 6 Dorchester farm labourers led by George Loveless (1797–1874) who were transported under the 'Unlawful Oaths Act', but in reality for trying to form a Union to raise farm wages. In Aus. they were assigned to settlers as labourers. Par-doned in 1836 after agitation, they re-turned to Eng., 5 of them migrating to farm in Canada.

Tompson, Charles (1806–83) b. Sydney. The first Aus.-born poet to write a book of verse: *Wild Notes from the Lyre of a Native Minstrel* (1826); they are mediocre and highly derivative in style.

Toowoomba Qld. 28S/152E (57,543 in 1971) A city lying at 610 m. in a shallow gap in the Main Range*, at the eastern margin of the Darling Downs*, of which it is the major urban, service and route centre, with industries de-pending on the primary products of the region: dairy products, bacon, flour, food-processing and canning, brewing

and engineering, chiefly of agricultural machinery and engines. The original settlement of Drayton, 8 km. to the S ('The Springs'), was replaced by Too-woomba at the eastern side of 'The Swamp' and gained impetus with the Ipswich rail-link in 1867.

Torrens, Lake S.A. 31S/138E The second largest, after L. Eyre, of the great salinas or salt 'lakes' in S.A., extending over 160 km. N–S and 65 km. E–W, in the rift valley W of the Flinders Range; only rarely is there enough rain to send ephemeral waters to its salt- and bog-covered bed. Eyre was halted by it in 1839 and forced to turn W, and until 1858 it was thought to be the SW end of a great horseshoe barrier of lakes round the N end of the Flinders Range.

Torrens, River S.A. 35S/138E Flows 65 km. W from the Mt. Lofty Ranges to an artificial outlet (1937) W of Adelaide. The hill-gorge section has dams as part of the city's water supply; within Adelaide a weir creates a long, still stretch. Its reliable water supply was a major factor in Light's decision in siting Adelaide on the first non-flooded land upstream.

Torrens, Sir Robert (1780–1864) b. Ire-land. He was a colonial promoter and Chairman of the S.A. Commission to manage land sales and emigration (1835), but was dismissed when the scheme foundered. Both L. Torrens and River Torrens were named after him. His son **Robert Richard** (1814–1884) blended suggested tenure reforms in 1857 into the **Torrens Title**, later adop-ted by all the States. Torrens incor-porated the work of Ulrich Hubbe who had translated the laws of Paris and the towns of the Hanseatic League for him. The reform simplified procedures by eliminating the search for titles and combining all transactions in one, legally recognised certificate.

Torres, Luis Vaez de A Spanish sea-man who commanded the second of

Quiros's* ships in 1606. Carrying on westwards from the New Hebrides without Quiros, and nominally under Prado's command, bad weather prevented the 2 ships from rounding the eastern point of N.G., and they sailed along the S coast, the first Europeans to do so. The discovery of this vital strait was unknown in Eng. until published by Dalrymple* in 1764. Nothing else is known with certainty of his life.

Torres Strait 10S/142E 130 km. wide, it links the Arafura with the Coral Sea between Papua and Cape York. The main shipping route, the Prince of Wales Channel, lies between Good and Banks Islands and requires professional piloting to avoid shoals and reefs. The Endeavour Str. channel may be deepened. The Strait was named in 1767 by Dalrymple. The Torres Str. islands were annexed to Qld. (1872), the officially declared boundary (1879) including all islands within 100 km. of the coast. The **Torres Str. Islanders**, notorious for their earlier ferocity, were later arrivals than mainland Aborigines and have Malaysian affinities; there are some 6,000. They have some local autonomy through councils. They fought as T.S.I. Light Infantry in the 1939–45 War and were rehabilitated as pearlers. Racial mixture followed the development of pearling* after 1868. Some have become migratory workers on the mainland, e.g. on the W.A. iron ore railways.

Torrumbarry Weir Vic. On the Murray about 32 km. downstream from Echuca, 36S/145E, it raises the water to feed it into canals supplying the country from 80 to 160 km. downstream on the Vic. side of the river.

Tortoises In Aus. these are all aquatic, as distinct from the marine turtles*; the tortoises are generally smaller and have webbed, clawed feet, as compared with the turtle's flippers. Nostrils are on the tip of the snout, so that the tortoise can breathe when almost submerged. The head and feet can be retracted to some extent in time of danger, and scent glands on the side of the animal probably excrete enough odour to make the water around unpleasant to enemies. They are carnivorous (there are horny plates on the jaws, not teeth), the young tortoise graduating from mosquito larvae to tadpoles, frogs, insects, water plants etc., but rarely fish which are much faster than the tortoise. In turn they are preyed on by large fish, snakes, monitor lizards and hawks. The Aus. genera and species include: 1. the Long-necked Tortoise, *Chelodina (C. longicollis* in SE Aus.; the large *C. expansa* in Qld.; *C. oblonga* in NW Aus.; and the small rare *C. steindachneri* in SW W.A.); 2. the Short-necked Tortoise, *Emydura (E. macquarii* in the Murray basin; *E. australis* in the far N. of W.A.; the large, biting *E. latisternum* in NE Aus.); 3. the Aus. Snapping Tortoise, *Elseya dentata*, in N.T.; 4. the Western Swamp Tortoise, *Pseudemydura umbrina*, of the Perth area. *See* J. Goode: *Freshwater Tortoises of Aus. and N.G.* (Melbourne, 1967.)

Town Planning The first Aus. towns began with the grid-iron pattern common to colonial settlements from Roman times. While giving a moderately successful core on the flat sites of Perth and Melbourne, it was less satisfactory on the slopes of Brisbane River or the banks of the Derwent, on which Hobart was built; while in Sydney, the planned grid was soon modified by naturally developing tracks. In contrast, Adelaide adhered fairly closely to Light's vision of 2 grids separated by a green belt, a pattern copied in other S.A. towns. Elsewhere town sites were mainly surveyed on the grid pattern; many were never built, and those that were, soon escaped its rigidity. Laissez-faire 19th-century industrial and housing development caused congestion in central areas; in the 20th century the transport revolution allowed the equally undesirable, uncontrolled and largely unsewered suburban sprawl, with public works unable to keep pace with private development.

Although both W.A. and S.A. each appointed a Town Planner at State level in the 1920s, who was able to control further land use to some extent, the most active periods have been in the flush of post-war idealism from 1945, soon swamped by desperate housing needs and less worthy factors; and again from the early 1960s. In Sydney a master plan by the Cumberland County Council (1945–63) was followed in 1968 by the *Sydney Region Outline Plan*, by the State Planning Authority of N.S.W. A plan for Melbourne prepared by the Board of Works (1954) was followed (1967) by *The Future Growth of Melbourne* broadly advocating corridor growth of satellite towns. Brisbane benefits from its single City Council, but this in turn is limited by the ultimate planning authority held by the State Government. In Perth a plan accepted in 1960 is in the single hands of a Metropolitan Regional Planning Authority, and Adelaide's plan published in 1962, which was prepared by a State-appointed Committee under the Government Town Planner, was well received. The only 2 new planned cities in Aus. are Elizabeth*, S.A., and Canberra*. Major problems in controlling the urban explosion are: the reluctance of industrialists to accept decentralisation; the fragmentation of Local Government* leading to, at best, parochial planning and the sacrifice of overall thinking and implementation to local business interests; historical legacies, such as the flood-prone centres of former river ports, e.g. Grafton in N.S.W. *See also* NURDA. The Labor Govt. (1972–   ) has a Dept. of Urban and Regional Development. *See* P. N. Troy ed.: *Urban Redevelopment in Australia* (Canberra, 1968).

Townsend, Mount N.S.W. (2,211 m.) The second highest peak in Aus.,

4 km. NNW of Mt. Kosciusko and like it, a swelling above the rolling top of the Snowy Mountains* block.

Townsville Qld. 19S/147E (68,442 in 1971) A city and second largest port and town in the State; the most prominent and most rapidly growing northern town. It lies at the mouth of the Ross Creek and is dominated by the 290-m.-high craggy Castle Hill which looks over to Magnetic Island. It was founded (1864) by J. M. Black, who, commissioned by the merchant and pioneer cotton-grower R. Towns to find a port site for northern pastoralists, built a wool store and wharf here. Mineral discoveries in the 1870s and the Great Northern Railway (1899), now reconstructed, expanded the hinterland and made breakwaters and dredging necessary. Townsville chills, freezes and exports beef, stores sugar, refines copper (at Stuart 12 km. out), treats nickel, also exports wool, lead and zinc; makes railway rolling-stock and cement. It has the James Cook University of North Qld and the new Aus. Institute of Marine Science.

TRADE Aus. is a major trading nation, with large exports of primary products, and large imports both of consumer goods and of capital goods for its developing industries. While exports often exceed imports, Aus. long shared with underdeveloped countries, a tendency to have recurrent trade deficits, but differed from them in maintaining a high standard of living. Deficits were largely due to imports of capital goods, but overseas ownership of 25–33% of industrial capital also implies a continuing outflow as dividends and interest. Despite rising home demand higher rates of exports were attained by the early 1970s including minerals and more manufactured goods, notably in machinery and transport equipment. Trade and policy are in a phase of fluidity and adjustment. Trade surpluses caused upward revaluation of the $A in 1972.

The growth of mineral exports to Japan, made her the leading trading partner, followed by U.S. replacing Britain from 1972, and by the entry of Britain into the European Economic Community on Jan. 1, 1973. This means the phased withdrawal of the preferences Aus. goods have enjoyed in Britain and the application of EEC tariffs to them. The long standing trade agreement between Aus. and Britain, stemming from the Ottawa Agreement in 1932 ended in Feb. 1973. Preferences that British exports to Aus. have had, will therefore be ended. These changes, the floating of the £ sterling and $A revaluation in 1972 adversely affect some Aus. exports, notably fruit and dairy products.

On the wider front of world trade, Aus. is a contracting party to the General Agreement on Tariffs and Trade (GATT) which affects 80% of world trade, and recognises the problems of Aus. as a developed, industrialised country, yet dependent on primary raw materials for exports. Aus. operates preferences in favour of developing countries over a wide range of goods. In addition Aus. has bilateral agreements with at least 15 other countries, from Canada to Yugoslavia; Trade Commissioners numbered 53 posts in 40 countries (1973).

1972 saw a record in Aus. exports, valued at $A4,900 million from June 1971 to May 1972, giving a trading surplus of $A900 million. Pastoral products are still ahead, wool and beef having recovered in 1970–2 from the gradual reduction evident from the time of the Korean War boom in 1952. Iron ore export is growing, although there have been some cutbacks due to minor Japanese recession. Coal is increasing, machinery and transport equipment and chemicals (including salt), doubled 1967–70. W. Germany, Canada, N.Z. and China are important trading partners of Aus.

Imports are dominated by 'producers materials' including semi-finished goods (e.g. vehicle parts) and by capital equipment and consumer goods. Over 75% of imports are 'elaborately transformed 'while 78% of exports are unprocessed primary products. The imbalance of Aus. exports to over imports from Japan illustrates the problems. A basic work is by J. Crawford, with N. Anderson and M. G. N. Morris: *Aus. Trade Policy 1942–1966, A Documentary History* (Canberra, 1968).

Trade Unions In 1972 over 50% of the work-force were members of the 319 Trade Unions in Aus., which is one of the most highly unionised countries in the world. Over 50% are in only 5% of the total Unions, and over 90% in Unions with inter-state affiliations. Some remain branches of overseas parent organisations; the large Amalgamated Engineering Union only separated from its British parent in 1967. Unions have legal security and official encouragement through the machinery of Arbitration*; membership is often a condition of employment, or is strongly desirable for acceptability among workmates. Early craft associations, such as the Shipwrights' United Friendly Society in 1830, were mainly for benevolent purposes. With the influx of immigrants and their concentration in towns following the gold-rushes* and the legalisation of membership (1855), Unions developed rapidly. They extended their interests to combat competition by opposing assisted and coloured immigration; and began to associate inter-state, under the influence of Spence*. The first inter-state conference was held in 1879. Unions achieved legal protection of funds by 1886. In 1891 the formation of the Aus. Labor Party* provided the political arm necessary to achieve legislation. They supported protection and a White Australia Policy*, and achieved an 8-hour day: N.S.W., 1855; Vic., 1856; Qld., 1858; S.A., 1873; Tas., 1874; W.A., 1896. Less skilled workers began to unite after about 1885; the Shearers' Union, inter-state from its formation in 1886, was the precursor of the great Aus. Workers' Union (A.W.U.). There was a phase of rapid growth, with much idealistic discussion, influenced notably by Lane*. The Depression and strikes* of the 1890s were severe setbacks, however. In the new century membership again increased and there were major achievements. In 1927 the Aus. Council of Trade Unions (A.C.T.U.) was formed to promote closer association between Unions, and to speak generally for labour. With the affiliation in 1967 of the A.W.U., it became the supreme industrial labour organisation, with very powerful influence under Robert Hawke*, President 1970– . Union power is being strengthened under the Labor Govt. (1972–). See P. W. D. Matthews and G. W. Ford eds.: *Australian Trade Unions* (Melbourne, 1969).

Trains In Aus. they are not perhaps accorded the glamour they possess elsewhere. There is a poem on boyish train-spotting by the thoroughly Aus. J. B. McAuley, but on the other hand a stern suggestion from an author on Aus. successes in sport that if fewer British youths went train-spotting then Britain too might have a sparkling Olympic record! Yet Aus. possesses interesting problems of locomotive types (*see also* RAILWAYS) and some notable trains, including: *The Silver City Comet*, the first completely air-conditioned train in Aus., from Parkes to Broken Hill; *The Southern Aurora*, the through standard-gauge and air-conditioned Sydney–Melbourne express; *The Fish*, a commuting express between the Blue Mts. and Sydney, from a punning play on the name of an earlier driver called Heron; and *The Inlander* (Townsville–Mt. Isa), *The Westlander* (Brisbane–Cunnamulla), *The Midlander* (Rockhampton–Winton) and *The Sunlander* (Brisbane–Cairns), all comfortable air-conditioned Qld. expresses.

*The Australind** (non-stop Perth–Bunbury) commemorating the abortive settlement and the *Westlander* (Perth–Kalgoorlie). The *Indian Pacific* now runs from Sydney to Perth on the completed standard-gauge railway in under 70 hours of air conditioned luxury. This line has the world's longest straight of 478 km. across the Nullarbor. *The Tasmanian Limited* is drawn by 2 diesel-electric locomotives from Hobart to Wynyard. *The Ghan* runs to Alice Springs (*see* AFGHAN).

TRANSPORT Well developed in Aus. in relation to a relatively small and rather urban population, because of the cash-oriented and mainly and increasingly affluent economy which has dominated almost since the first European settlement in 1788. Except concerning exports, defence, safety etc. in the nation as a whole, transport is in the jurisdiction of the States, and this is important in practice. Of the total 'transport task' 4% is by air, 13% by rail and 83% by road. Shipping*, vital from the first, remains so for particular kinds of coastal traffic, e.g. the Newcastle–Sydney coal trade in the 'Sixty Milers', the long haul of iron ore from Yampi*, W.A., to Wollongong or Newcastle, and obviously the traffic to and from Tas. Climate, distances and temperament doubtless conspired to favour an early and large contribution to aviation*, while airlines* and aerial agriculture* are both well developed. Considerations of safety have given the Commonwealth considerable *de facto* control through the Department of Civil Aviation. Railways* began in 1854 and remain a vital, if so far largely State-oriented transport medium. Roads* are like railways, roughly in proportion to population, except for strategic roads and some to exploit a valuable resource in relatively empty country; main links are good for a large sparsely peopled country. Motor vehicles* per head are among the highest in the world, and passenger traffic by road is largely by private car. Freight traffic by road, however, is important by reason of its flexibility and convenience, even over long hauls with apparently heavy and expensive manpower in relation to limited load, and very important questions arise of real costs and of co-ordination of transport media.

On the whole the State railway rates are arranged (a) to maintain the importance of the State capitals and/or chief ports, and (b) to make a profit for a heavy State investment or at least avoid a loss, and to this end States exercise more or less effective control over intra-state freight movement by road. Inter-state control, after repeated testing by litigation, has proved illegal under the Constitution*. Controversy is inevitable. The road hauliers argue that the railways are being artificially maintained by socialistic measures as an inflexible and out-of-date transport medium. The proponents of railways rejoin that they excel in speed with safety over long hauls, that the use of containers with ancillary road-haulage imparts almost equal flexibility, and that the true costs of road-haulage are not met by haulier, consignor or consignee. Roads are subsidised by governments, it is argued, for many complex social and especially political reasons, and so the real cost of maintaining the roads which made road-haulage, especially long-distance haulage, so competitive with railways are not met by those concerned with the movement of the freight, but by other road users, e.g. private car owners, or by the community at large. In crowded urban centres, indeed, there is good evidence that neither commercial haulier nor car owner meets the real cost of his use of the roads.

The States' response varies somewhat. All have some form of licensing of road-hauliers. N.S.W. also imposes road tax, maintaining inspection stations for the purpose; this is levied in proportion to distance on the gross weight of vehicle and load, but is varied according to the degree of competition between rail and road on the particular journey. Qld. is similar, but road operators must charge at least the railway rate or where there is no railway rate for the journey, a rate based on road-operating costs. The other States nominally forbid journeys competitive with railways, and charge nominal tax on other journeys, but with many exceptions in practice. The tax is ultimately to compensate the railways for loss of custom. The Aus. Transport Advisory Council representing States and Commonwealth considers policy and problems and establishes specialised committees, e.g. on Road Safety or Air Pollution.

Transportation Punishment by exile to overseas prison settlements, awarded in Britain in the 18th and early 19th centuries, for over 200 crimes from petty thieving to crimes of violence, and including political offences. American Independence (1776) prevented further transportation there, and after a period of crowding in jails and old boat hulks, the suggestion of using Cook's newly discovered Botany Bay was seized on; the first consignment to Aus. was despatched under Phillip* in the First Fleet* in 1787. Transportation continued to N.S.W., which then included Moreton Bay and Port Phillip, until 1840; to Tas. until 1852; S.A. used some convict labour; the E States officially ended transportation in 1852, but the system was used in W.A. from 1850–68. A total of about 165,000 convicts were transported, the majority between 1820–40; in 1836, of the 14,000 convicted felons, 4,400 were transported. While a few were minor offenders, political exiles, e.g. 60 English Chartists (1842), Canadian rebels (1837), Scottish Martyrs* and Tolpuddle Martyrs*, and spirited rogues, the majority were the dregs of the urban, industrialising society: vicious, squalid, hopeless rejects. Contract payment per head to ships' masters led to appalling voyage conditions, until 1802 when more control was established.

Abolition of transportation was primarily stimulated from Britain, notably by Whately, Protestant Archbishop of Dublin, who pointed out that neither its deterrent nor reforming functions were demonstrable. Opposition developed in Aus. from the increasing numbers of free settlers, who resented the stigma of a penal colony and feared the labour competition. The squatters* found common ground in wishing to prolong it, for their prosperity depended on cheap labour under the Assignment System*. They only yielded when it was clear that transportation and self-government were incompatible. A Committee on Transportation (1837–8) revealed the sordid horrors of the system. A revised scheme of sending probationary prisoners was tried in the 1840s (Pentonvillians), but failed; attempts to re-introduce transportation met near-rebellion at Sydney and Melbourne in 1849, and the convicts had to be sent to Moreton Bay. Transportation finally ended in all eastern Aus. by 1852 and in W.A. in 1868.

Trap-door Spiders A popular name for many species, mainly in the family Ctenizidae, e.g. the widespread insect- and snail-eating *Missulena insignis* of which the female has a carapace 2 cm. long, red-brown and black with a red head, and the male 1·2 cm long, with blue rear and red head. Spiders of some other families also make trap-doors.

Traralgon Vic. 38S/147E (14,624 in 1971) Lies 8 km. S of the river, in the Latrobe Valley* E of the lignite field, but shares the industrial development of the region, with paper- and cement-works and a clothing factory built to absorb surplus female labour.

Tree-creepers (genus *Climacteris*—stair-case birds) They are small (about 15 cm. long), brown birds, often with some yellow or orange on the breast, white throats and black flecking and blackish tails; they have quite large and slightly down-curved beaks, and nest in tree-hollows, laying brown-spotted pinkish eggs unlike the white eggs found in most tree-hollow nests. The beaks and nesting habits distinguish them from the Sittellas* or Tree-runners. Both these genera are grouped as the family Sittidae (woodpecker-like), the true woodpecker not being found in Aus. Their claws are strong, adapted to much vertical crawling. The White-throated Tree-creeper, *C. leucophaea*, is common from the hilly rain-forests to the coastal woodlands and even the metropolitan outskirts of E. Aus., extending into N.G. It has a warbling call as well as a shrill repetitive alarm call like most of its relatives. The Brown Tree-creeper, *C. picumnus*, inhabits the drier parts, the Rufous Tree-creeper, *C. rufa*, SW Aus. from the Eyre Peninsula to Geraldton, W.A. The orange-red of the breast extends into a stripe above the eye.

Tree-ferns Ferns* of several Sub-Orders and genera with many species, including short-trunked species and some reaching the height of a small tree. They are mainly rain-forest plants, but reach out into coastal brush forests and inland into dry sclerophyll forests along gullies and in similar damp shady and sheltered sites.

Trees They are treated from different viewpoints under flora* and vegetation*. In alphabetical order of popular names, articles on Aus. trees include: Almond or Red Almond*, Angophora*, Apple*, Ash*, Banksia*, Barklya*, Beech*, Black Bean*, Blackwood*, Blind-your-eyes*, Boronia*, Bottle-tree*, Brigalow*, Brush Box*, Bunya Pine*, Burdekin Plum*, Carabeen*, Carbeen*, Cassia*, Casuarina*, Cedar*, Celery-top Pine*, Celerywood*, Cheese Tree*, Cherry*, Coolabah*, Coral Tree*, Cottonwood*, Crow's Ash*, Cupania*, Cycads*, Cypress*, Native Daphne*, Davidson's Plum*, Dogwood*, Eucalypts* Fig Trees*, Flame Tree*, Flindersia*, Grevillea*, Gymnosperms*, Hoop Pine*, Horizontal*, Huon Pine*, Ironwood*, Kauri* (South Qld. Kauri), King William Pine*, Kurrajong*, Leichhardt Tree*, Leptospermum*, Lillypilly*, Macaranga*, Mahogany*, Mallee*, Mangroves*, Melaleuca*, Mountain Ebony*, Mulga*, Myall*, Myrtaceae*, Myrtle*, Nettles*, Norfolk Island Pine*, Palms*, Paperbark*, Pink Foam Bark*, Plum or Native Plum*, Podocarpaceae*, Quandong*, Qld. Nut*, Sassafras*, Sclerophyll*, Screw-pine*, She-oak*, Silky Oak*, Sterculiaceae*, Sweet Verbena*, Tallowwood*, Tamarind*, Tamarisk* Teatree*, Telopea (see WARATAH), Treeferns*, Tuckeroo,* Tulip-wood*, Turpentine*, Umbrella Tree*, Water Gum*, Wattle*, Wheel of Fire*, (Native) Willow* and Woollybutt*. See Forest and Timber Bureau: *Forest Trees of Australia* (Canberra, 1957); H. Oakman: *Some Trees of Australia* (Brisbane, 1965). A recent well illustrated work is M. Miller: *Native Trees of Australia* (Melbourne, 1971).

Trevally A popular name for several important commercial and sporting fish. 1. King or Golden Trevally, Skipjack in W.A., *Caranx speciosus*, a swift, edible carnivore of Aus. reefs, beaches and estuaries, extending to Hawaii and the Red Sea; it has a fairly deep, narrow, oval body, and is typically 75–100 cm. long and up to 5 kg. in weight. 2. The Great Trevally, *C. sexfasciatus*, of Qld. may reach over 1 m. and 40 kg., and the Papuan Trevally, *C. papuensis*, is only slightly different. 3. The Trevally of the Sydney fish markets, *Usacaranx georgianus*, is a fish of more temperate waters, up to 75 cm. long, often in schools. 4. The Yellowtail Kingfish* ranges from S Qld., Tas. and N.Z. 5. The Turrum* is a fish of the Great Barrier Reef. 6. The Bludger, *Carangoides gymnostethoides*, is a longbodied fish with unattractive dark

flesh, named from its 'stealing' of bait intended for more desirable fish. 7. The cross-banded Pilot Fish, *Naucrates angeli*, of up to 60 cm. long, does not in fact herald a shark's attack, but often keeps company with one. For Diamond Trevally—*see* PENNANT-FISH; for Black Trevally—*see* SPINEFOOT.

Trigger Plants A popular name covering the 100 species in the genus *Stylidium*, the greater part of the mainly Aus. family Stylidiaceae; the Trigger Plants are small grass-like plants with a sensitive protruding fused style and stamens, curved down normally but erected on disturbance, spreading pollen on to the disturbing agent which distributes it. Most are in W.A., including *S. schoenoides*, with buff-pink flowers, and *S. breviscapum*, with yellow- and red-banded, boomerangshaped petals, but the grassy spike and pink wide-open lips of *S. laricifolium* are not uncommon in highland NE Aus. There are species right across the N.

Trochus (*Trochus niloticus*) A gastropod mollusc of some commercial importance for its shell, used formerly for buttons, but largely replaced by plastics. It is found off the coral reefs of Qld. Remaining small exports are to W Germany and Italy, and include re-export of SE Asian shell.

Trotting Dates from 1880, in Adelaide, and several Aus. horses have been successful in American events. Annual inter-Dominion championships include N.Z. In 1960 an Aus. team won the Equestrian Three-Day Military event in the Olympic Games, with L. Morgan also individually successful.

Trumble, Hugh (1867–1938) b. Melbourne. A cricketer; a very great medium-pace bowler, using the advantage of his height with skill. He was also a very sound batsman. In 31 Tests against Eng. (1894–1904) he took 141 wickets for an average of 20·8, including 2 'hat tricks', and in first-class cricket 929 for an average of 18.

Trumper, Victor Thomas (1877–1915) b. Sydney. He and Bradman* are famed as the greatest Aus. cricketers. He worked as a teacher, then a clerk and later owned a sports store. His unorthodox approach to batting made him slow to be recognised, but when he appeared in Tests and first-class cricket, his style and achievement lifted the game out of a period of near-decay. He was exceptionally clever in dealing with a wet wicket, as in Eng. in 1902 when he scored 11 centuries. He played 40 Tests (1899–1912) against Eng., averaging 32·89 and including 6 centuries. In first-class cricket he totalled 17,150, averaging 45 with 43 centuries.

Trumpeter Perch (*Pelates sexlineatus*). About 25 cm. long, a grunting fish of S and E Asia and Aus., with 4 brown to black lines along the dark-backed silver body. It is edible.

Trumpeters and **Bastard Trumpeters** Related fish, deep-bodied, the dorsal fin almost continuous (the front fin spiny) and netted for food seasonally in estuaries in temperate Aus., particularly Tas.; the preferred species is the yellow-bronze and white Striped or Hobart-town Trumpeter, *Latris lineata*, but the smaller Silver or Bastard Trumpeter, *Latridopsis forsteri*, is good when in season; it is silver in colour (the immature stage being reddish). It grows over 1 m. and 27 kg.

Tuart (*Eucalyptus gomphocephala*) A tree with very durable timber found in a 2 km. wide strip behind the sand-dunes of coastal SW W.A., from the Busselton area to N of Perth. Timber is used for railway carriages etc., but is of course in limited supply.

Tuberculosis An infectious disease caused by the bacillus *Mycobacterium tuberculosis*, usually affecting the lungs, but sometimes the lymph glands, gut, bones and joints, and central nervous system. Early diagnosis of pulmonary tuberculosis is possible, using mass radiography campaigns, while the the B.C.G. vaccine, containing tubercle of much reduced virulence, imparts considerable immunity; a joint Commonwealth and States campaign has been in progress since 1948, with considerable success. There are still almost 3,000 notifications a year, but there are very few deaths. Since 1950 allowances have been paid to patients to allow treatment.

Tucker, Albert (1914–) b. Melbourne. He is an artist of international repute. Before going abroad (1947–60), he made a name with his powerful 'Night Images' of wartime Aus. and had begun his series in Antipodean Heads, in which bushrangers, explorers and others are identified with their harsh desert and bush backgrounds.

Tuckeroo (*Cupaniopsis anacardioides*) A 12-m. brush forest tree of NE Aus., with dark green compound leaves, the leaflets oval, and inconspicuous flowers giving way to 3-chambered capsules opening to display 2 bright red fruit in each chamber. The timber is pink and tough. The genus is in the tropical family Sapindaceae.

Tuggerah Lakes N.S.W. E of Wyong, 33S/151E. 3 linked coastal lagoons (Tuggerah L., Budgewoi L. and Munmorah L.) formed by the almost complete enclosing of 3 small estuaries of drowned valleys, mainly by coastal sand-barriers crowned by dunes (there is a solid rock 'island' including Norah Point). The narrow entrance is in the S of the system, SE of Wyong. Like other lagoons, the system provides cooling water for a large power station at Munmorah.

Tulipwood (*Harpullia pendula*) In the widespread tropical family Sapindaceae. It is a 25-m. flowering and cabinet timber tree of coastal E Aus., N and S of Brisbane. It has 8-cm.-long oval leaflets in 3 pairs in a multiple leaf, small greenish-yellow compound flowers in the leaf-forks, and 1-cm. red to yellow fruit in twin round lobes, each containing 1–2 brown-black oval seeds. These berries are often in spectacular masses. The name is also used for other N.S.W. and Qld. trees producing hard, close-grained timber.

Tully River Qld. 113 km. long, flowing from Cardwell Range to Rockingham Bay about midway between Cairns and Townsville. There is over 250 cm. mean annual rainfall throughout the catchment. **Tully Falls,** where the river plunges off the tableland into a precipitous rain-forested gorge, is the site of Qld.'s largest hydro-electric station (Kareeya) completed in 1957, with 72,000 kW generated by water dropping about 475 m. from Koombooloomba Dam, and serving Townsville's industries and the Ayr-Cairns sugar-dairying coast. **Tully** (2,676 in 1971), 20 km. upstream, is a sugar centre and the wettest town in Aus. (average 455 cm. a year).

Tumut N.S.W. 35S/148E (5,525 in 1971) A growing local centre with dairy, saw-milling, pineboard and millet-broom industries in the pastoral and orcharding basin of the **Tumut River.** This flows in an impressive trough N from the N flanks of the Snowy Mts.* to join the Murrumbidgee near Gundagai, 35S/148E. The upper valley has 2 dams of the Snowy Mts. Scheme* and in the middle valley the Blowering and Talbingo Dams have been completed. A road is projected to Canberra through fine scenery by the Brindabella Range.

Tungatinah Tas. 42S/146E A power station (125,000 kW, completed in 1953) on the left bank of the Nive River gorge opposite Tarraleah*, and largest of the 10 Derwent system stations; main feeders are L. Echo, Pine Tier and Bronte Lagoons (*see* TASMANIA, POWER).

Tungsten An exportable surplus is obtained from tin-wolfram in the Avoca area in NE Tas. and from scheelite on King Island* in Bass Str., but trade is subject to severe fluctuations.

Turner, Charles Thomas Biass (1862–1944) b. Bathurst, N.S.W. A cricketer, notably a medium-pace, accurate bowler, nick-named the 'Terror', who followed the 'Demon' Spofforth* in 17 Tests against Eng. (1886–95), taking 101 wickets for an average of 16·53. In the equivalent of first-class cricket he took 1,061 wickets for an average of 13. Turner worked for Cobb & Co.*

Turner, Sir George (1851–1916) b. Melbourne. Vic. Premier from 1894–1901, and largely responsible for pulling Vic. out of the Depression of the early 1890s by rigorous economies; he introduced Income Tax (1894). He was later a greatly respected Federal Treasurer.

Turon River N.S.W. It rises near Portland, 33S/150E, and flows roughly NW then W through pleasant Central Tablelands scenery for 113 km., to join the Macquarie 80 km. NW of Bathurst. Its basin was the focus for many thousands of alluvial goldminers in the 1850s. Ghost towns* abound.

Turpentine The name is applied in Aus. to a tree of the Myrtaceae family, *Syncarpia glomulifera,* growing in the coastal 90 to 150-cm. rainfall belt from Atherton, Qld. to Batemans Bay, N.S.W. It grows to 40–50 m., and straight trunked, on good lowland sites, and as the timber is resistant to teredo, it is Australia's chief salt-water pile and quay timber. The leaves are ovate to pointed, glossy green above, lighter and hairy below, paired but whorled around the twigs. The buds are somewhat trumpet-like, 1 cm. long and in groups of about 7, the flowers in a dense globular head while the fruit are in tight bunches of 3-celled capsules. Bark is persistent, brown, fibrous, and deeply furrowed. The name is from the red-brown resinous exudate. The Brush Turpentine, *S. leptopetala*, is a much smaller tree with a smaller, though overlapping area.

Turrum (*Turrum emburyi*) A game-fish of the Great Barrier Reef, up to 1·5 m. long and 41 kg., with light blue, dark barred and yellow-spotted back, somewhat blunt-nosed in profile, narrow-bodied and related to the Trevally*.

Turtles In Aus. usage, they are the marine forms of the Order Testudines; they have flippers, as compared with the webbed clawed feet of the fresh-water tortoises*. Teeth are lacking, but a horny sheath to the jaw-bone per-forms almost the same functions. The carapace of horny plates has variations according to species. The females come ashore for egg-laying on particular beaches to which they instinctively re-turn; up to 200 eggs in up to 7 layings at about fortnightly intervals have been recorded for the Green Turtle. They are carefully laid in a bottle-shaped excavation which is subsequently filled in and its precise site concealed, hatching in 2 to 3 months according to the sand temperatures. But eggs and young are the prey of monitor lizards, and many of the young are also lost or eaten by predatory fish, birds etc. Pro-longed hunting is gradually giving way to conservation, led by Qld. Turtle farming is being tried by Torres Str. Islanders. The Leatherback, *Dermo-cheles coriacea schlegelli*, a fish-eating turtle, is the largest, up to 2·5 m. long and over half a tonne in weight. Its ridged carapace, a mosaic of small plates in a thick leathery skin, is separated from the vertebrae and ribs (whereas the skeleton is fused to the carapace in the other genera). The Green Turtle, *Chelonia mydas*, mottled green above and with greenish fatty tissue prized for turtle soup by Aborig-ines and island peoples, has 4 pairs of plates on each side of the central plates,

and half-grown specimens show a radial pattern, from which they are known as 'sun-ray turtles'. It is mainly vegetarian, living on seaweeds etc., but also eats shellfish and jellyfish. Num-bers and size have been savagely re-duced by hunting. Other species are the yellowish Flatback Turtle, *Chelonia japonica* probably restricted to Aus. waters; the Hawksbill Turtle, *Eret-mocheles imbricata bissa*, was fairly common as far S as Broken Bay*, N.S.W., but coastal development is alienating breeding grounds.

Tusk Shells A small group of molluscs (Scaphopoda class) narrow, curved and tapering, with shell after the fashion of an elephant's tusk. An Indo-Pacific species not uncommon in Aus. is the Elephant's Tusk Shell, *Dentalium ele-phantinum*, of 7–10 cm. long, grading from dark green to white at the point, with longitudinal ridges.

Tussock-grass This name is used for several grasses, including *Poa sieberiana* in forest grazings in SE Aus., the Snow-grass*, and *P. labillardieri* (often with Kangaroo-grass* on damper flats), and the introduced (S American) Serrated or Yass River Tussock, *Nassella tricho-toma*, a serious pest of overgrazed pastures in SE Aus., a tall tussock of tough thin blades, unpalatable to stock, with a loose purple-husked head.

Tweed Heads N.S.W. 28S/154E (3,828 in 1966) A rapidly growing seaside resort area on the Qld. border, now almost continuous with and classed as part of the City of Gold Coast*. **Tweed River,** only 80 km long, flows through wet country S of the McPher-son Range* into dairy, sugar and ba-nana lands on fertile soils based on lavas, to a considerable estuary S of Tweed Heads.

Two Up An illegal gambling game de-veloped from the old 'pitch and toss' in which the 'spinner', flicking 2 pennies from a small wooden bat or 'kip', backs the chances of their falling heads up. Another name is 'swy', probably from the German zwei meaning 2. Once widely played by working men and in the services, its popularity has waned because of changing social conditions and liberalised gambling laws. However it has found its way into Aus. literature and retains an affectionate place in folk tradition.

Twofold Bay N.S.W. As the name implies, it is a complex bay with curved beaches between several headlands, on which stand the fishing and former timber port of Eden*, 37S/150E (2,210 in 1971), and the few residuals of the ambitious projected port of Boydtown (*see* BOYD, BENJAMIN). From 1968 a new wood-chipping and pulping plant for export to Japan employs over 250 people.

Typhoid (Enteric or Enteric Fever in older literature) A serious bacterial infection of the gut with *Salmonella typhi*. It is spread by polluted water, flies or hands; a vaccine of killed bacteria gives moderate immunity for 2 years or so. Typhoid is not uncommon in Aus., though outbreaks are rapidly smothered by isolation, inoculation of contacts etc. In the 19th century it was a serious scourge at times, particularly on the gold-fields, from Vic. in the 1850s to Coolgardie in the 1890s.

Typhus A louse-borne rickettsial disease, common under conditions of over-crowding and dirt, brought to Aus. in the convict ships when several outbreaks were recorded from Tas., and again during the gold-rush. **Scrub typhus** is a rickettsial disease of wild and commensal rodents carried by acarine mites, particularly associated with the scrub-grassland or forest-grassland boundaries in various tropical and sub-tropical countries. It is a considerable health problem in N.G. and transmission occasionally occurs in Qld. Q fever* is another rickettsial disease.

Tyrrell, Lake Vic. A salt-encrusted surface, at times receiving water from the Tyrrell Creek, a branch of the Avoca River, in the internal drainage system of the Wimmera*. Salt is harvested.

U

ULLATHORNE

Ullathorne, William Bernard (1806–1889) b. Pocklington, Yorkshire, Eng. He was sent to Sydney as a vicar-general in the Roman Catholic see of Mauritius in 1833 and played a vital role under Polding* in establishing a Roman Catholic hierarchy in Aus. by 1842 and recruiting Irish priests. He wrote and spoke vigorously against transportation and returned to Eng. in 1845.

Ulm, Charles Thomas Phillipe (1897–1934) b. Melbourne. The son of Gustave Ulm of Paris and Melbourne. He qualified as a pilot towards the end of the 1914–18 War, having enlisted twice and being wounded 3 times. He set up one of the small, premature aviation* services of that era; he met Kingsford Smith*, joined him in record-breaking flights, including the 1928 trans-Pacific flight in *Southern Cross*, and in the first Aus. National Airways Pty. Ltd. until its liquidation in 1932. Record-breaking flights continued until he was lost in another trans-Pacific flight in December 1934.

Ulverstone Tas. 41S/146E (8,005 in 1971) At the mouth of the Leven River on the N coast; it is a major service and retirement town with some vegetable-canning.

Umbrella Bush A popular name for several small trees and bushes, particularly *Acacia oswaldi* in inland Aus. (also Umbrella Wattle).

Umbrella Tree (*Brassaia actinophylla*) In the mainly tropical Araliaceae family. It is often grown ornamentally in warmer parts of Aus.; it has hairy leaves and long composite flowers.

UNIVERSITIES

Umbrella Tree (*Brassaia actinophylla*), about 5 m. tall

United Australia Party (1931–1944) Formed under Lyons from the Nationalist Party and a small Labor group. The party won 37 seats in the House of Representatives and 22 in the Senate (1931) and was in power until 1941 with Lyons as Prime Minister until his death, then Menzies, who was forced to resign by personal and faction manoeuvres, in favour of Fadden. The period in office is alleged sometimes to have been too dominated by right-wing and financial interests. The essential Country Party support after 1934 also faded, and the 1943 Labor landslide led to the re-formation as the Liberal Party in 1944 under Menzies.

Universities (*see also* Table on page 170 under EDUCATION) There are 17 universities and 1 university college in Aus. Student enrolment is over 110,000, of whom about a third work either externally or part time. These numbers represent very rapid increase in the last three decades. The Universities are autonomous bodies established by Parliamentary Act, which stipulate

554

their own matriculation requirements; but 80% of their income is derived from Government grants. These are based on recommendations of the Aus. Universities Commission, established 1959 following the Murray Report, and comprise direct grants to the Australian National University* and grants to the States in relation to their universities. Entrance on matriculation is being increasingly modified by quota systems as demand outpaces supply of places. About half the students receive some type of aid; of these about 50% by Commonwealth Scholarships awarded on matriculation results and covering fees and, where a means-test indicates need, some living allowance; about 25% have State grants, and the rest of those assisted study under cadetships or bond agreements with their prospective employers (including State authorities of education). There is a strong tradition of making an attempt at a university course in the Aus. 'give it a go' belief, which results in a high proportion of failure and wastage; this also reflects the relative ease of entry up to now. Degree structures are broad and more flexible than in U.K., and specialists can acquire wide knowledge in associated or diverse disciplines from their own. Degrees are not on the U.S. pattern of a first pre-professional B.A. degree; they are regarded as a professional training and a gateway to desirable employment. There is an increasing introduction of voca-tional and practical courses: forestry, pharmacy, agricultural economics etc. and a swing towards science generally —e.g. the University of N.S.W. concentrates on basic and applied science. The Universities of New England and Qld. have well developed external courses by correspondence.

Upfield, Arthur William (1888–1964) b. Gosport, Hampshire, Eng. He arrived in Aus. in 1911, working as an estate agent until 1927, then as a full-time writer of highly successful detective fiction in which he created 'Napoleon Bonaparte', a Qld. half-caste detective. Upfield's work is notable for evocative backgrounds in contrasting parts of Aus.

Uranium Aus. has large reserves of uranium: the major area now is the E Alligator River region of N.T. Four major deposits are known: Ranger, Nabarlek, Jim Jim and Jabbalooks, all likely to be operating in the 1970s, Mary Kathleen, reopened 1972, made Aus. a producer for the first time since 1964. The former uranium area in the L. Frome area S.A. may be reactivated, and there are deposits at Westmoreland in NW Qld. 400 km. NW of Mt. Isa and at Yeelirrie, W.A. 450 km. NW of Kalgoorlie. Exploration is active and includes Japanese-Italian interests. Following a Japanese–Aus. treaty in 1972, Japan will import Aus. uranium as well as U.S. and W. Germany.

V

VAN DIEMEN GULF

Van Diemen Gulf N.T. 12S/132E It is 240 km. E–W and over 80 km. N–S, entered from the N by Dundas Str. and the W by Clarence Str. which lie between Melville Island* and the Mainland. It was discovered and named by Tasman in 1644.

Van Diemen's Land The name given by Tasman* in 1642, to his first landfall 'in the South Seas', and remaining the official name of Tas. until 1855, although almost out of use by then. Anthony Van Diemen was the Dutch Governor General at Batavia who commissioned Tasman's voyage.

Van Diemen's Land Company Chartered in London (1825), with Edward Curr* as local manager, it was largely responsible for the exploration and development for pasture, crops and later timber extraction of NW Tas., and still holds land in the area of its original grant at Circular Head.

Vanilla Plant (*Sowerbaea juncea*) A vanilla-scented, pink to white liliaceous plant of swamps in E Aus. (*See* LILIES.) Also called Rush Lily.

Vaux, James Hardy (1782–1853) b. Surrey, Eng. A petty but vicious, vain and unrepentant criminal, transported 3 times to N.S.W. and noted for his 2-volume memoir, chiefly written to his own glory and with a glossary of contemporary criminal slang (re-published London, 1964). Governor King pardoned and employed him as his secretary.

Vegetables Grown on some 120,000 ha.: potatoes (30%), green peas (20%) and tomatoes and beans 5% each; but there is important intensive production of many other table vegetables and salads. Production was formerly con-

VEGETATION

centrated round urban centres, where markets justified high costs of fertiliser, water and land. But irrigation, improved transport and increased population have allowed the use of more remote areas, and advantage is now taken of the wide disparity of seasons in the continent: Melbourne's tomatoes, for instance, come from Geraldton, W.A., in July, and subsequently Qld., S.A., and the Riverina. Canning and freezing have quadrupled since 1957, especially of peas and beans. Potatoes and onions are concentrated on the basaltic soils of the Western District* of Vic. and are exported to SE Asia, as well as inter-state. Potatoes are also grown in Tas., and on suitable soils in pockets on the N.S.W. and Qld. tablelands.

Vegetation The flora* may also be viewed in groups or associations of plants growing together under particular conditions of climate and soil. From arid to humid Aus. the vegetation progressively increases in height and leafiness from (1) the sparse association of specially adapted plants in the desert, through (2) grass-dominant associations (including herbs and scattered trees) to (3) shrub-dominant associations, then to (4) woodland and forest associations, culminating in rain-forest. There is an obvious relationship with rainfall, and very roughly, corresponding mean annual rainfall limits are: 1. under 20 cm. in the S and 30 cm. in the N; 2. 20–30 cm. in the S and 30–40 cm. in the N; 3. 30–40 cm. in the S and 40–45 cm. in the N; 4. over 40 cm. in the S and over 45 cm. in the N. Any refined statement requires careful assessment of the seasonal incidence, variability and effectiveness of the rainfall, and moreover soil factors—sometimes the result of past rather than present climates—are in Aus. at least as crucial as climate in controlling the vegetation in semi-arid conditions: saltbush and bluebush on clay pans, mallee and blackboys on nutrient-deficient soils. *Spinifex* holding loose coastal sands, and so on.

These 4 groups of vegetation associations may be briefly characterised.

1. *Desert plants* Sparse annual herbs (many growing, flowering and seeding within a few days following rain, perhaps after several years of drought and quiescence), low succulents, drought-resistant shrubs, and grasses in hummocks drawing on moisture from bare ground between.

2. *Grass-dominated vegetation* includes tropical and temperate savannahs, with scattered trees or shrubs, with many wattles*, and some coolabahs*, red gums*, bottle-trees*, kurrajong*, etc., and larger areas of more treeless tussock or hummock grassland, of layered grasses and sedges as in the Mitchell-grass* country of NE Aus., and herbaceous grasslands as in the alpine pastures of the Aus. Alps. Unlike similar formations in other parts of the world, the trees and shrubs are evergreen, not deciduous.

3. *The shrub-dominated vegetation* includes the association of tall shrubs with low shrub and heath of the mallee, the various sclerophyllous (leathery-leaved) shrub associations of the winter rainfall tracts comparable with the Mediterranean *maquis*, and various heath and tree-heath associations, e.g. in the SW of W.A.

4. *The woodland and forest vegetation* includes the layered monsoon woodlands of N Aus., the complex layered and liana-rich rain-forests of tropical Qld., rich in species, mostly related to Malayan ones, grading from large-leaved, tropical to temperate rain-forests with dominantly small-leaved and eucalypt species (but with Southern spp. of beech in New England, Vic. and Tas.); the moderate rainfall zones of E,

SE and far SW Aus. dominated by eucalypt species, in the wet sclerophyll and sparser and more drought-evading dry sclerophyll forests. A new and quantitative classification of vegetation by R. L. Specht (1971) replaced Rainforest by Closed Forest, Sclerophyll by Open Forest and Tree Savannah by Open Woodland.

Velvet-bushes (*Lasiopetalum* spp.) With hairy, often rusty covering on branches and leaves, they are in the tropical Sterculiaceae family, concentrated in W.A. and in S Africa. They include the pink-starred *L. behrii* of the mallee country, the lime-loving *L. discolor* of Bass Str. to W.A., and the Rust Plant or Red Velvet Bush, *L. rufum*, of N.S.W., with rusty-red undersides of leaves and capsule-like flowers.

Venereal Diseases Rank with infective hepatitis as the most common notifiable diseases at present—over 9,000 cases of gonorrhoea and over 900 cases of syphilis per annum. Incidence may be increasing despite more effective treatment since the late 1930s.

Venomous or **Front-fanged Land Snakes** (family Elapidae) They are distinguished primarily by the pair of enlarged and grooved venom fangs in the front of the upper jaw, often with one or even more pairs in reserve. (For classification *see* SNAKES.) They have nostrils on the side of the snout, broad belly-scales, and usually tails in pointed tube form (but see Death Adder*). Of some 30 Aus. genera and 70 species, only about 12 are dangerous to man (asterisked below, i.e. with separate entries), though a few more may cause sharp illness especially in children. Common species are: 1. Death Adder*, *Acanthophis antarcticus*; 2. Golden Crown or Red-bellied Snake, *Aspidomorphus squamulosus*, a mildly venomous brown snake, commonly seen under rocks in the coastal sandstone plateaux of E Aus.; 3. Red-naped Snake, *Brachysoma diadema*, a mildly venomous, 45-cm., white-bellied brown snake with very distinctive orange-scarlet nape, common under logs and in suburban gardens in N.S.W. and Qld.; 4. Bardick, *Brachyaspis curta*, of the S of Aus., up to 50 cm. long, red to dark brown to greenish with creamy-grey belly, with prominent head and teeth, normally eating lizards, frogs etc. and quite venomous; 5. the Aus. Coral Snake, *Brachyurophis australis*, of inland N.S.W. and coastal Qld., brick-crimson with black bands on head and neck, and up to 40 cm. long with sharp snout; nocturnal and harmless; 6. Half-girdled Snake, of W.A., *B. semifasciatus*, shy, burrowing and harmless; 7. Dwarf Crowned Snake, *Cacophis kreffti*, a 40-cm. snake of coastal E Aus., black with yellow head, harmless to man; 8. Copperhead*, *Austrelaps superba*; 9. the Little Whip Snake, *Cryptophis flagellum*, one of a genus of small, harmless snakes—up to 40 cm. long, white-bellied, brown with dark edges to the scales and black head, found in the E of S.A. and in Vic.; 10. Swamp Snake*, *A. signata*; 11. Whip Snakes*, *Demansia* spp.; 12. Ornamental* and Banded Snakes, *Denisonia* spp.; 13. the Grey Snake, *Drepanodontis daemelii*, of inland E Aus., a frog- and lizard-eating swamp snake of up to 75 cm. long, the young born jet black, the adult grey with black between scales and a cream, grey-spotted belly; 14. the Crowned Snake, *Drysdalia coronata*, grey-green to dark olive-brown with a dark cap and nape band, a predator on small lizards, frogs etc. across the S of Aus., only mildly venomous to man; the genus includes several small snakes with different markings; 15. the Little Brown Snake, *Elapognathus minor*, of the SW of S.A., up to 45 cm. long; and only mildly venomous to man; the upper jaw contains only the venomous fangs; 16. the White-Crowned Snake, *Glyphodon harriettae*, black with white head and neck markings, one of a genus of small, shy, nocturnal snakes of NE Aus., mildly venomous to man,

with varied markings; 17. the Broad-headed Snake*, *Hoplocephalus* spp.; 18. the Moon Snake, *Lunelaps christie-anus*, a very slender snake of up to 75 cm. long, seen in rotten logs etc. in tropical Aus., black with a red moon-shaped nape mark and white belly, not regarded as dangerous to man; 19. the Miniature Burrowing Snake, *Melwardia minima*, a 25-cm. pale brown desert snake, and the Beaded Snake, *M. calonota*, also small, red with black-edged blue vertebral scales looking not unlike beads; 20. Long-nosed Snake, *Narophis bimaculata*, a 50-cm., mildly venomous burrowing snake of W.A., pink-red with dark-edged back scales; 21. Tiger Snake*, *Notechis* spp.; 22. the Taipan*, *Oxyuranus scutellatus scutellatus*; 23. Gould's Snake, *Parasuta gouldii*, a small reddish-brown snake (darker brown in the E of W.A.), mildly venomous and living in termite mounds etc. over much of the S of Aus.; the genus includes the Black-striped Snake, *P. nigrostriata*, of E Aus., the large-headed Mitchell's Short-tailed snake, *P. brevicauda*, of rock and spinifex country in S.A., and the black and brown Dwyer's Snake, *P. dwyeri*, of inland Aus., a burrowing snake; 24. the Black Snake*, *Pseudechis porphyriacus*; 25. the Brown Snake*, *Pseudonaja textilis textilis*; 26. the Desert Banded Snake, *Rhynchoelaps bertholdi bertholdi*, one of several species in a genus of 30- to 40-cm. burrowing snakes, with rather flat heads, not very distinct from the neck, and round pupils; 27. the Narrow-banded Burrowing Snake, *Rhinelaps fasciolatus*, of the S of W.A., a sharp-snouted burrowing snake, probably only mildly venomous to man, up to 40 cm. long; the genus includes the Western Burrowing Snake, *R. approximans*, and the nocturnal De Vis' Burrowing Snake, *R. warro*, of the Qld. coastal ranges; 28. Miller's Snake, *Rhinhoplocephalus bicolor*, a rare olive-brown and white desert snake of the S of W.A., with a very square and blunt-ended snout; 29. the Curl Snake*, *Suta suta*; 30. the Rough-scaled* or Clarence River Snake, *Tropidechis carinatus*; 31. the Carpentaria (Whip) Snake, *Unechis carpentaria*, up to 60 cm. long, brown-black with light-tipped scales, reddish cheeks and cream belly, nocturnal, lizard-eating and probably only mildly venomous to man; 32. Bandy Bandy, *Vermicella annulata*, very well known all over mainland Aus., up to 75 cm. long, striking, banded white on black, nocturnal, normally inoffensive; the bite is mild except in cases of individual allergy etc. (*See* PLATE 9.)

Verbena, Sweet (*Backhousia citriodora*) A 12-m. tree of coastal E Qld. in the world-wide Myrtaceae family, with oval to pointed lemon-scented leaves with veins prominent below, hairy young branches, creamy nectar-rich cup-like flowers in small bunches, and small 2-seed fruit capsules.

Verge, John (1782–1861) b. Hampshire, Eng. An architect. He arrived in Aus. in 1828 to farm, but soon reverted to his profession, continuing until 1837. As well as a number of smaller churches, his 'Old Colonial' Georgian houses are fine examples of this early Aus. type. Camden Park (1831), built for the Macarthur* family, had the first bathroom, and with others, gas chandeliers. Mainly one-storeyed, with white stucco walls, French windows and pillared verandahs, they were carefully integrated with their settings; some still remain in Darlinghurst in Sydney.

Veronica A large genus of flowering herbs, often blue with multiple heads of 4-petalled flowers, including 10 Aus. species, such as Diggers' Speedwell, *V. perfoliata*, a slender plant of up to 91 cm., with pairs of prominently veined, broad leaves and purple-streaked blue flowers.

Verticordia A genus of flowering heath-like shrubs in the Myrtaceae family, with 50 species mainly in W.A.

sand plains, including the pale pink, fringed heads massed in the upper leaf axils of *V. insignis* and *V. pennigera*, and the 2-m. *V. grandis*, with broader, less heath-like leaves and magnificent scarlet flower-spikes 2·5 cm. across.

Victor Harbor S.A. 36S/139E (3,533 in 1971) Dates from whaling in Encounter Bay, and developed as a small port for the Murray Basin until railways took the trade to Adelaide and Melbourne. It is now a service centre for farmlands, with an important holiday trade. A causeway links it to Granite Island which was an early whaling station.

VICTORIA (Vic.) It is the smallest mainland State, with an area of 227,620 km.² (about that of Scotland, Eng. and Wales) in a compact block between Bass Str. and the Murray River. With a 1971 population of 3,496,161 it is the most densely peopled State (15 per km.²).

Badge of Victoria

Physical Geography and Land Use Port Phillip Bay lies centrally on the coast, with the Barwon lowlands to the W and the Gippsland lowlands to the E, behind which is the steep rise to the Central Highlands and Aus. Alps. N of Melbourne the Highlands grade into the volcanic plateau of W Vic., interrupted by the Grampians toward the W and sloping to plains N and S. The Wimmera internal-drainage area lies N of the Grampians, but much of the N is part of the Murray basin. Except for a small portion of W Vic., soils are deficient in phosphate and nitrogen.

The Central Highland is divided by the Kilmore Gap, at 360 m., N of Melbourne. The E section, reaching 1,800 m. in the Aus. Alps, include slaty Silurian and Ordovician rocks, Devonian sandstones and granitic intrusions. Above the steep S face and the stream gorges are wet sclerophyll* and rain-forest, including the tall mountain ash, and above that again alpine meadow and winter snowfields attracting tourists and with timber and water-power resources. The valleys opening N have vegetable-, tobacco- and hop-growing. Podsolic soils of varying quality, developed on the basalts, sandstones and shales at intermediate heights, support grazing, forestry and some specialised cropping such as potatoes.

W of Kilmore lies the hill country of the *Western District**, which also includes the section of the southern lowlands W of the Barwon River and the Grampians*. The plain to the S has been covered with Tertiary lava flows which have confused drainage and left a rolling landscape with lakes among volcanic cones and craters. Unimproved short grass supports merino sheep, with cross-breeds and merinos on improved pasture, and shelter belts planted against exposure. Block faulting has raised the Otway Ranges*, whereas on the limestone and clay lowlands near the coast, intensive dairying, potato and onion-growing has developed. Beyond the plain fringing Port Phillip Bay, the Southern Lowland is also broken by faulted blocks: the South Gippsland Hills, including the Strzelecki Ranges, are of sandstone similar to the Otways, and with the more complex Mornington* peninsula and granitic Wilsons Promontory*, retain residual sclerophyll woodland, tussock grass and improved pastures for fat lambs with intensive fruit and vegetable farms in some valleys. The Gippsland lowland from Westernport, a down-faulted basin, to the N.S.W. border, is filled with Tertiary limestones, sandstones, clays, and the important brown coal seams of the Latrobe Valley*. The wetter lowlands have prosperous dairy farms, helped in the drier central Gippsland region by irrigation; nearer Melbourne intensive market-gardens, orchards and stockholding paddocks compete with the increasing urban sprawl.

The land drops to the *Murray* Basin* N of the Central Uplands; the *N District* includes intervening uplands and the Goulburn, Ovens and Loddon valleys, with irrigated pastures for dairying, fruit, rice, hops and tobacco lands, but with unirrigable land still extensively farmed for winter wheat and wool, and residual woodland on the higher slopes. To the W are the Wimmera* and Mallee* regions merging into the formerly useless land of the Big and Little Deserts on the S.A. border. Both regions have been transformed from insecure extensive wheat-growing to well-planned stock/wheat farming based on water from the Grampians, the Murray, the Goulburn and artesian sources, and with intensive irrigated fruit-growing along the Murray itself.

Industries and Towns Primary industry supplies the urban needs and also a considerable export of canned and dried fruits, dairy products, egg pulp, beef, wool and wheat. Timber is extracted from the forests of the Central Uplands and Gippsland fringes and is processed at Maryvale pulp and paper mill and a number of increasingly centralised sawmills. The Latrobe Valley* brown coal feeds power, gas and briquette plants, but the only black coal mine, at Wonthaggi, is closed. The geological formations provide plentiful limestone, gypsum, diatomite, fluorite and building clays, as well as granite and basalt for road metal. The most important development is the oil and gas of the new offshore fields of Bass Str., the gas integrated by 1970 with the already well-rationalised gas supply to Melbourne by a 200-km pipeline from an absorption plant at Sale. Commercial oil comes from Kingfish, Barracouta and Halibut fields. Only a little gold-mining near Castlemaine remains of the great gold era of the 1850s.

Secondary industry, spreading out and diversifying from the early, protected textile and clothing plants, now employs over ½ million. Engineering includes car manufacture in Melbourne and Geelong; chemicals include fertilisers, plastics and pharmaceuticals; electrical and electronic products include radios, televisions and washing-machines, and there are big printing and publishing industries. About 75% of industrial employment is in the Melbourne area, but Geelong is expanding and decentralisation has led to establishment of engineering and clothing in the country towns, and the employment of surplus female labour in the Latrobe Valley.

Tertiary industries serve a hierarchy of towns along the network of road and rail which is focused on Melbourne and conditioned by gaps through the hill ranges, notably at Kilmore. A standard-gauge railway which has linked Melbourne with Sydney since 1962, overcame the old inhibiting gauge-break at the border and a 5-ft. 3-in. gauge line runs to Adelaide. The following table and Maps 13 and 14 show the size, position, function and relationships of the main centres, from the overwhelming dominance of the Melbourne conurbation, stretching 30 km. or more, to the moderately sized inland towns such as Ballarat, down to small local foci of 1,000 people or so. Some towns were born of the gold-rushes; some developed with the clearing and settling of the land, usually at a route-crossing; some have grown only with recent development for tourism, coal or water power. (G denotes a former gold town).

Central Highland
Over 40,000, Ballarat, Bendigo.

5,000–16,000, service and industrial towns: Wangaratta, Benalla, Maryborough (G), Castlemaine (G), Seymour.

2,000–5,000, service towns with smaller industrial development and tourism in the hills: Beechworth (G), Yarrawonga, Daylesford* (G), Euroa, Myrtleford.

1,000–2,000, local service, timber or tourist centres: Creswick* (G), Broadford, Corryong, Yea, Beaufort, Kilmore, Mt. Beauty*, Rutherglen, Woodend, Heathcote (G), Alexandra, Mansfield.

Grampians and Western District
Over 15,000, Warrnambool, main service centre with industry.

5,000–12,000, market and service centres with farm-based industry and tourism: Hamilton, Colac, Ararat (G), Portland.

1,000–5,000, Smaller centres with similar functions: Camperdown*, Casterton, Port Fairy*, Terang, Cobden, Coleraine, Koroit, Mortlake, Heywood.

Southern Lowlands Melbourne Metropolitan Area (2,388,941) is dominant, followed by Geelong (115,047) and the Latrobe Valley complex of Moe, Yallourn, Morwell, with over 35,000.

5,000–15,000, Werribee, peripheral to Melbourne*; Traralgon in the Latrobe Valley; Gippsland service, timber, dairy centres: Sale, Bairnsdale, Warragul; commuter towns on Port Phillip*: Dromana-Sorrento (with Rye and Rosebud), Mornington, Balcombe, Sunbury, W of Melbourne.

2,000–5,000, service and market centres with dairying or other industry: Wonthaggi*, Bacchus Marsh*, Maffra*, Korumburra, Leongatha, Orbost, Healesville, Drouin, Yarram; commuter-resort of Queenscliff on Port Phillip, and the resort of Ocean Grove-Barwon Heads in E Gippsland.

1,000–2,000, Gippsland dairy centres: Trafalgar, Heyfield; seaside towns: Lakes Entrance*, Torquay, Lorne, Portarlington; centres peripheral to Melbourne: Hastings, Yarra Junction; and Crib Point on Westernport Bay*.

Mallee, Wimmera and the North
10,000–20,000, the 2 major irrigation centres of Mildura and Shepparton; Horsham in the Wimmera, Echuca-Moama on the Murray.

5,000–10,000, Stawell*, the former river port Swan Hill, and Kyabram.

2,000–5,000, irrigation centres with canning industries and the larger non-irrigation area service centres: Cobram, Kerang, Kyneton (G), Mooroopna, Red Cliffs, Tatura, Cohuna, Numurkah, Rochester; the flour-milling service centres of Wimmera: St. Arnaud, Warracknabeal, Nhill; small service centres of Wimmera or Mallee: Dimboola, Charlton, Donald, Hopetoun, Avoca, Murtoa; others throughout the region include: Robinvale, Ouyen, Merbein (irrigation), Rushworth (G), Nathalie, Birchip.

Historical Development The permanent settlement of Vic., which remained the Port Phillip District of N.S.W. until 1851, began in 1834, although abortive attempts had been made in 1803 and 1828. Squatters from Tas. were followed by others from N.S.W. in illegally establishing themselves, and the Government was forced to provide an administration in 1836. In 1851 the discovery of gold inaugurated a decade of rapid population increase, political and economic development, including responsible government. When gold-mining declined after 1865 agricultural and industrial expansion absorbed the surplus 'diggers'; while the firmly entrenched 'Squattocracy' (*see* SQUATTERS) retained and increased their estates, new wheat-lands were opened in the drier N and W; factories flourished on the large home market and on the tariff protection, which was carried by Victorians (who were ardent Federalists) into Commonwealth policy after Federation*. But over-expansion and speculation based on foreign borrowings led to a disastrous

slump after 1891, when many banks failed. Vic. only fully recovered from this in the industrial production stimulated by the First World War. However, the financial dominance of Melbourne has been retained. Widespread State undertakings were established by Liberal Governments after 1902 and Labor, deprived of this platform, and competing with the strong Country Party in rural areas, has been less powerful than in other States, although Premier John Cain played an important role in post-war development. Industrial expansion, based on brown coal deposits, augmented by natural gas and oil, and accompanied by a drift to the towns and a large share of the migrant intake, has continued since the 1939–45 War.

Premiers since 1900: A. McLean (1900); G. Turner (1901); A. J. Peacock (1901); W. H. Irvine (1902); T. Bent (1904); J. Murray (1909); W. A. Watt (1912); G. A. Elmslie (1913); W. A. Watt (1913); A. J. Peacock (1914 and 1924); J. Bowser (1917); H. S. W. Lawson (1918); G. M. Prendergast (1924); J. Allan (1924); E. J. Hogan (1927 and 1929–32); W. M. McPherson (1928); S. S. Argyle (1932); A. A. Dunstan (1935–43 and 1943–5); J. Cain, a notable Labor Premier (1943, 1945–7 and 1952–5); I. Macfarlan (1945); T. T. Hollway (1950 and 1952); J. G. B. McDonald (1950); H. E. Bolte (1955–72); R. J. Hamer (1972–)
Sources: G. W. Leeper ed.: *Introducing Victoria* (Melbourne, 1955); K. J. Collins and D. D. Harris: *A Regional Geography of Victoria* (Melbourne, 1964).

Victoria Cross Created (1856) by Queen Victoria, and awarded, in the words of the 1961 consolidating warrant, 'for most conspicuous bravery, or some daring or pre-eminent act of valour or self-sacrifice or extreme devotion to duty in the presence of the enemy'. The Maltese cross, inscribed 'For Valour', is fashioned of bronze from Turkish guns captured at Sebastopol. To 1967, 94 Australians received it, 28 of them posthumously. There were 6 in the Boer War, including Howse* the first Aus. to receive the award; all were soldiers. In the 1914–18 War there were 66, of whom 65 were soldiers and 1 was an airman (in Palestine); 53 were won in France or Belgium, 9 at Gallipoli*, 2 in N Russia (1919) and 1 in E Africa. In the 1939–45 War, 17 soldiers and 3 airmen became V.C.s, 12 in the Pacific theatre, 6 in N Africa and 2 in Europe; and in the Vietnam war 4 VCs (2 posthumous) were awarded. The dominance of awards in the First World War reflects the type of warfare in relation to observed bravery. The individual exploits of Aus. V.C.s are recorded in *They Dared Mightily* by L. Wigmore (Aus. War Memorial, 1963). Probably the first V.C. to be seen in Aus. belonged to Timothy O'Hea (1846–74) who died on a search for Leichhardt*; he had won the award in Canada in 1866 for quenching a fire on an ammunition train.

Victoria, Lake Vic. A narrow and relatively deep lagoon in the Gippsland Lakes*, stretching SW from Lakes Entrance, 38S/148E, for some 56 km, much of it about 9 m. deep and reaching 17 m. near Metung about 11 km. from Lakes Entrance. The connection with L. King is about 3 km. wide. The lakes are influenced by the tide from the artificial Lakes Entrance and locally by ocean swells and by waves within the lakes from local winds. Salinity varies seasonally with the inflow from the rivers, Mitchell, Nicholson and Tambo, and by the 9-m.-deep McLennon's Str. from L. Wellington. Off river-mouths during floods there are currents up to 7 knots. True tides occur, but oscillations called tides are due to local winds. **Lake Victoria** S.A. 34S/141E is a Murray storage.

Victoria River N.T. 15S/130E It flows (seasonally in the upper course) for 650 km. N then NW, from its source at 365 m. in low sand-hills, through alternating basins and hills to Queen's Channel in Joseph Bonaparte Gulf; its basin covers 70,000 km.². It is only 150 m. above sea level 480 km. upstream; the last 160 km. are tidal and the last 80 navigable to 3-m. draught boats. Rainfall decreases from 100 cm. at the coast to 35 cm. at the source; vegetation changes southwards from tropical woodland to Mitchell-grass* downs and savannah, and then to spinifex.* The main left-bank tributary, the Wickham, flows from limestone ranges. The river was discovered, named and explored for some 145 km. by the *Beagle** expedition in 1839. In 1855–6 A. C. Gregory* traced its upper course and later unsuccessfully advocated settlement which did not materialise, however, until pastoralists took up the land in the 1880s, several of them after epic overland journeys of 3,225 km. from N.S.W. and Qld. There are now over 20 stations, averaging 2,600 km.² and 8,000 head of beef cattle. The largest, Wave Hill in the S, and Victoria River in the Wickham Valley in the Central basin, are over 13,000 km.². Cattle are sent overland to fatten in Qld. or increasingly by the big pastoral companies which dominate the leases to their meatworks at Darwin, Montejinni and Katherine for export. A new Beef Road from Top Springs to Katherine is accentuating this trend. Over-grazing in the drier headwater zones has led to soil erosion, aggravated by wild (feral) donkeys, scrub cattle and minimal fencing. *See* J. Makin: *The Big Run* (Adelaide, 1970)

Vidal, Mary Theresa (*née* Johnson) (1815–1869) She lived in N.S.W. with her clergyman husband from 1840–5. She was one of the earliest fiction writers, mainly of moral tales, but with the beginnings of Aus. background, especially in *Bengala* (London, 1860).

Vietnam War Aus. involvement began in July 1962 with an army training team of 30 advisers, increased to 90 in May 1964, having permission to go on operations with Vietnamese units. The first combat troops were sent in June 1965, with a total force of 1,100. The total was successively raised to 5,750 in 1966 and to a maximum of 8,500 in 1968 including some air and naval support. In 1970, in consonance with U.S. policy of 'Vietnamisation' the first Aus. troops were withdrawn from Phuoc Tuy Province; withdrawal was complete by Dec. 1972. Conscription based on a ballot of 20-year-olds was used 1965–72. This and the general involvement in the war had many critics in Aus. Total killed was 474. Anxiety over Chinese expansion and the need to retain the U.S. alliance were behind Aus. policy in the 1960s.

Vines There are several genera and species of native Vitaceae, including the Wild Grape*. The distribution and uses of the cultivated exotic plants from the 60,000 ha. of bearing vineyards are tabulated.

State	Total Aus. Vineyards Percentages	Percentage of the State Total for		
		Wine	Dried fruits	Table grapes
S.A.	43	65	35	—	100
Vic.	33	3	91	6	100
N.S.W.	16	40	53	7	100
W.A.	4	31	57	12	100
Qld.	4	—	4	96	100
Aus.	100				

Irrigated land bordering the Murray in N.S.W., Vic. and S.A. dominates in output of dried fruit; wines* are more esteemed where vines depend on rainfall. Here, winter pruning is followed by alternative cultivation and controlled irrigation; picking begins with currants in February and drying is complete by April; a cold potash dip, making skins less resistant to evaporation, precedes the spreading of fruit on racks. Grading and packing, which is increasingly quality-controlled, is done in central sheds serving several of the small property units which prevail; much labour is casual. Exports account for two-thirds of output, with sultanas most important. U.K. entry to EEC may adversely affect exports. International stability is assisted by agreements with Greece and Turkey (1963) and, internally, prices are guaranteed by a contributory fund with Commonwealth help in unfavourable years. Qld. grapes are from Roma, in W.A. from the Darling Ranges and Swan Valley, and in S.A. from the Adelaide Hills and hillfoot and coastal Regions. Apart from the Murray and Murrumbidgee areas, N.S.W. output is from the Hunter Valley, and Vic. production is from Stawell and Rutherglen.

Violets The native species of the widespread Violaceae family. The genus *Viola* includes several herbs of SE Aus., e.g. Purple Violet, *V. betonicifolia*, and the Ivy-leaf Violet, *V. hederacea*, with small, purple flowers and round or heart-shaped leaves. The genus *Hybanthus* includes the small and delicate Lady's Slipper or Slender Violet, *H. monopetalus*, with 4 short petals and 1 long, curved in a slipper shape, and the bushy blue-flowered, *H. floribundus*, of the mallee* country. The Tree-violet, *Hymenanthera dentata*, is stunted in alpine sites in SE Aus., but reaches 5 m. in valley sites, bearing many scented, creamy, bell-shaped flowers, then purplish berries. The Fringed Violet of N.S.W. is a straggling climber of the Lily* family, *Thysanotus* *tuberosus*, with fringed purple petals, on the bunches of flowers. It is common in most of Aus. (*See* PLATE 6.)

Vlamingh Plate   A pewter plate, now in the W.A. Museum, Perth; it dates from 1697, when a Dutch sea captain, Willem de Vlamingh, left it in place of Dirk Hartog's* plate on Dirk Hartog Island. The inscription records both landings.

Voting   In Federal and State elections it has been compulsory since 1924. Compulsion was introduced in Qld. in 1915. Enrolment of voters is compulsory save for the S.A. Lower House, and for Aborigines in Federal, Qld. and W.A. elections. Once enrolled, voting is compulsory; evasion is punishable by a relatively light fine or imprisonment. **Informal Votes** are those in which the ballot paper is spoiled, incomplete or wrongly used. Qualifications for Commonwealth franchise are possessed by any British subject (*see* CITIZENSHIP) over 18 with a minimum of 6 months residence, unless disentitled on specific grounds. In 1970 W.A., S.A. and Tas. lowered the voting age (for State elections) to 18. In 1972 the High Court rejected voting rights for 18 year olds in Federal elections as being a legislative not judicial matter, and in 1973 the Labor Government lowered the minimum age for both voters and candidates to 18. The remaining states agreed to do so also. Election results are based on the system of Preferential Voting*. (*See also* GOVERNMENT *and* DONKEY VOTE.)

Voyager, **H.M.A.S.**   A destroyer sunk with heavy loss of life on the night of February 10 1964, during night manoeuvres requiring steering in close unison, as 'plane guard destroyer', when she sailed on a collision course with the much larger aircraft-carrier H.M.A.S. *Melbourne* and was cut in two, sinking very rapidly. A Royal Commission of enquiry reached only inconclusive results, and Captain R. J. Robertson of the *Melbourne* resigned after being posted to a shore establishment. Public disquiet continued; a second Royal Commission in 1967 exonerated Robertson and his officers.

W

WACKETT

Wackett, Sir Lawrence James (1896–) b. Townsville, Qld. His service with the Royal Flying Corps, and then the R.A.A.F. included development work. He was pre-eminent among Aus. aircraft designers, and was head of the Commonwealth Aircraft Corporation from 1936–60 (see AIRCRAFT MANU-FACTURE).

Waders A very large group of birds, very variable in size, length of leg and neck, and habits, though most are birds of swamps or of the very fringe of land and sea. Many waders are seasonal migrants over long distances sometimes including long sea crossings, even small and apparently frail birds such as the Dotterels *Charadrius* spp., some of which cross from N.Z. and some from Asia. Such far-travelling birds tend not to belong to one country or even continent, but Aus. genera and species include: the tall Jabiru* and Brolga*, several species of the beautiful White Egret, genus *Egretta*; the Great-billed Heron, *Ardea sumatrana*, extending into N.G. and SE Asia as the Latin name suggests, and several species of *Notophoyx* (southern heron), with bulky high nests often seen on coastal swamps and laboured but speedy flight; the Ibis, with long down-curved bill, of genera *Plegadis* (sickle-bill) and *Threskiornis* (sacred bird); several Spoonbills, genus *Plata-lea*, like plainer egrets with the spoon-shaped bill for sifting mud for insects etc.; the smaller (about 30 cm. long) but still relatively long-legged Avocets*, genus *Recurvirostra* with the distinctively long, curved beak of the Latin name, and the straight-beaked and—as it seems—almost incredibly fragile Stilts, genera *Himantopus* (water-bird) and *Cladorhynchos* ((beak like curved

WAGGA WAGGA

twig); the very long-toed Lotusbird, *Irediparra gallinacea*, adapted to walk lightly, in spreading its weight, across the large floating leaves of the lotus or water-lily. And so to the waders of the shore, such as the red-beaked and red-legged Oyster-catchers, genus *Haematopus* (blood-footed), the Beach Curlew, genus *Orthorhamphus* (straight-billed), the migrants from N Asia. e.g. the Greenshank, *Tringa nebularia* (cloudy—from its large flocks), Sand-piper, *T. hypoleucos* (white-bellied), Sanderling, *Crocethia alba* (white shore-runner), Red-necked Stint, *Erolia rufi-collis*, and Plover of genera *Squatarola* and *Pluvialis*. Inland are waders such as Native Hens, genus *Tribonyx* (three-clawed), the Crakes, genus *Porzana*, the Rails and Bush-hens, genera *Rallus*, *Rallina* and *Amaurornis* (dark bird), Inland Dotterel, *Peltohyas australis* (shield-plover), Stint, *Erolia* spp. and Snipe, genera *Gallinago* and *Rostratula*.

Wagga Wagga N.S.W. 35S/147E (27,636 in 1971) Often abbreviated to Wagga. A city on the Murrumbidgee River; standing on the E edge of the Riverina* and the W edge of the Western Slopes regions, it acts as a regional market, service, educational, and processing centre for a considerable tract of country in both regions. Factories include dairy, meat, flour, timber, bacon-processing, foundries and rubber manufacture, and the saleyards are among the leading ones inland. A teachers' college, technical college and agricultural college and also research station (earlier associated with work on wheat breeding by Farrer*) illustrate its role. The courthouse was built by 1847, and soon a town was marked out and the essential urban service buildings—an inn, stores etc.—appeared, but with slow growth until the railway came in 1878. The main new growth of the town is in West Wagga, spreading S from the flood-plain; E of this, Willans Hill gives a site for a 'look-out' and nature reserve, while beyond is high-class housing development pointing to rapid growth in population.

Wahoo (*Acanthocybium solandri*) A fish of tropical, including N Aus., waters, distinctive for its long slender shape, long front and dorsal fin, speed and size (up to 2 m. or so).

Waikerie S.A. 34S/140E An irrigation area of some 1,620 ha. in vines and citrus mainly, dating from 1908, but with recent co-operative expansion, and involving a lift of 46 m. from the Murray on to limestone country which provides good natural drainage.

Wainewright, Thomas Griffiths (1794– 1847) b. London. He was of some note as an essayist and artist, but was transported to Tas. (1837) for forgery; it was widely believed that he had also poisoned at least one wealthy relative. Allowed some freedom, he painted several Tas. watercolours and portraits.

Waite Agricultural Research Institute S.A. Founded 1924 as part of the University of Adelaide at Glen Osmond, E of the city, and named after a pastoralist benefactor of the University. The Institute, along with C.S.I.R.O.*, has made fundamental contributions to agricultural development, notably in plant introduction, e.g. clovers, and in soil research, especially in the study of trace elements.

Wakefield, Edward Gibbon (1796– 1862) English theorist on colonisation whose ideas had an important influence on settlement, especially of S.A. While in jail in London for abduction and a run-away marriage (his second), he wrote *A Letter from Sydney* (1829), propounding a system of colonisation of ingenious yet practical simplicity:

broadly it rested on ensuring that land should not be freely or cheaply available, but sold at 'sufficient price' so that it was attainable only by men of capital, the proceeds to be used to pay the passages of selected free migrants, preferably young couples who would provide labour but also have the incentive of saving for their own land in turn. In fact Wakefield disassociated himself from the compromise system laid down for S.A., and turned to Canada, then N.Z. where he settled, as outlets for his plans.

Wakool River N.S.W. An anabranch linking the Murray and Murrumbidgee systems, leaving the Edwards River downstream from Deniliquin, 35S/145E, and flowing W then NW for some 145 km., before rejoining the Edwards-Kyalite and then the Murray. A weir near Deniliquin feeds water into the Wakool as the basis of an important irrigation district, with 28,000 ha. of rice and other cereals, fodder and irrigated pasture.

Walgett N.S.W. 30S/148E (2,284 in 1971) An important cattle railhead, road junction and bridge town near the junction of the Namoi and Barwon, supplied by artesian wells as is most of its hinterland. Like many towns on the Western Plains, it has numbers of Aborigines living on the fringe of the town.

Walker, Sir Edward Ronald (1907–) b. Cobar, N.S.W. An economist/diplomat who has represented Aus. at the United Nations and served on the Security and Trusteeship Councils. His writing on economics stresses the importance of human motives and influences behind the economic facts.

Walker, Kath A Qld. Aborigine who has published successful volumes of verse: *We are Going* (Brisbane, 1963) and *The Dawn is at Hand* (Brisbane, 1967); the theme of protest at the Aboriginal condition is more marked in the first volume.

Wallaby A widely accepted name for the smaller members of the Kangaroo* family.

Wallaby-grass A popular name for a group of about 30 species in the genus *Danthonia*, generally 15- to 25-cm. tufted perennials, with short dense plump spikelets. Wallaby-grass is a common pasture grass in the S half of Aus., for while it is not of very high nutritive value it does give green feed for much of most years on varied terrain though better on deeper soils. Common species include Short Wallaby-grass, *D. carphoides*, the large-headed Lobed Wallaby-grass, *D. auriculata*, and the tall Silvertop, *D. pallida*, of stony slopes in dry forest areas.

Wallace-Crabbe, Chris (1934–) b. Melbourne. A poet of stature, writing mainly short, often cynical poems, e.g. *The Music of Division* (Sydney, 1959).

Wallace's Line A name used for the fairly clearly demarcated boundary between the distinctive Australasian fauna (notably monotremes, marsupials and marine species) and that of Asia. A. R. Wallace was an English scientist who indicated this distinction in 1860. There have been important subsequent modifications.

Wallaroo S.A. 34S/138E (2,092 in 1971; 2,237 in 1961) Now a service centre and bulk grain exporter for the Yorke Peninsula, with a clothing and a fertiliser factory. It developed with copper-mining (1860–1923), which supported up to 20,000 people in the Wallaroo-Moonta*-Kadina triangle, and had copper smelters.

Wallum (*Banksia aemula*) From Aboriginal. A Banksia with large fruiting cones which has given its name to a rather infertile coastal heath tract in SE Qld.

Walter and Eliza Hall Trust Founded in 1912 by Eliza Hall (1847–1916), with money left by her husband Walter (1831–1911), which was made largely from Cobb and Co*, and Mt. Morgan* gold. A philanthropic interest in social work led Mrs. Hall to stipulate one third of the income to be used for the benefit of women and children, education, religion and social work, one half of the income being spent in N.S.W. and a quarter each in Qld. and Vic. The most famous beneficiary has been the **Walter and Eliza Hall Institute of Medical Research** (1916), attached to the Royal Melbourne Hospital, and now largely financed from other sources, including overseas foundations and Vic. and Commonwealth Governments. Directors have been S. W. Patterson (1919–23), C. H. Kellaway (1923–43), Sir Macfarlane Burnet* (1944–65), and G. J. V. Nossal (1965–). The 2 main wings are clinical research in association with the hospital, and wider medical research, in which notable contributions have been made in virus research, including Murray Valley Encephalitis* and the rickettsial scrub typhus*.

Waltzing Matilda Widely accepted as the national song of Aus., though hardly suitable as its national anthem, as was once mooted. It is a simple but attractive ballad of a swagman, a stolen sheep, a camp by a billabong and a coolabah tree, and characteristically anti-police sentiment with the swagman's drowning rather than be arrested. The tune so often boomed out from bar-rooms at Anzac Day reunions, or on the public address system as migrant-ships pull out from Southampton, or Naples or Malta, is inferior to a version in a minor key much more apposite to the sad little tale. Its origin is disputed. Winton, Qld., 22S/143E, confidently asserts that the song was written about 1898 by A. B. (Banjo) Paterson* at Dagworth Station nearby, and that his host's niece, Miss Christina Macpherson, wrote the music; a memorial includes a statue of Paterson and a billabong-shaped swimming pool. The music is also attributed to Mrs. Marie

Cowan, wife of the accountant of the Sydney tea firm of James Inglis & Co. who gave away copies of the words and music in 1906 as appropriate advertising for their 'Billy Tea'. Oscar Mendelsohn in *A Waltz with Matilda* (Melbourne, 1966) produces evidence that the original music was by Harry Nathan, sometime organist of the Anglican Cathedral in Townsville and music teacher in Toowoomba, who died an alcoholic in 1906. The words, he thinks, are unlikely to be by Paterson.

Wandering Jew (*Commelina cyanea*) A very pretty creeping herb of N.T., Qld. and N.S.W., with soft, light green, parallel-veined leaves, 2-7 cm. long, narrowly ovate, and forming a pinkish sheath round the stem at the base. The flowers are clear deep blue with 3 triangular petals. The name is also given to introduced and escaped species of the related genus *Tradescantia*.

Wandoo (*Eucalyptus wandoo*) A generally small tree usually 15–21 m. by 60–90 cm.) growing up to 35 m., occurring mainly in SW W.A. on the drier inland side of jarrah* belt (mean annual rainfall 40–50 cm.), though there is also a small coastal area N of Busselton. The timber is heavy and durable, and the tree yields tannin. Juvenile leaves are broad, adult leaves narrow and lanceolate (8–15 cm. long); buds are in small bunches, long and pointed, fruit pear-shaped and 8 mm. long. Bark is smooth yellowish-white with red patches, tending to scale off in strips.

Wangaratta Vic. 36S/146E (15,535 in 1971) A city, now a major regional centre, developed at a river-crossing below the confluence of Ovens and King Rivers (which can cause damage by flash floods) and on an early overlanding stock route which used the Glenrowan Gap (now followed by the railway and N.S.W.–Vic. Hume Highway), through the steep scarp of the

Warby Range a few miles W of the town. Industrial development, including nylon and woollen factories, is the result of Vic. attempts to decentralise, and uses the plentiful local water and power from the N.S.W.–Vic. grid.

Waranga Reservoir Vic. Built 1905, and enlarged 1936, it is on canals going W from Goulburn Weir, to store supplies for the W part of the Goulburn River* irrigation system, with a capacity of over 370 million m.^{3}.

Waratah The Aboriginal and popular name of *Telopea speciosissima* (most beautiful) in the Proteaceae Family; a shrub bearing magnificent deep crimson multiple flower-heads, the blossom sheathed by deep crimson bracts; the leaves are dark green, lighter below, and often toothed, while the fruit is a leathery capsule up to 10 cm. long, the seeds flat and winged. It was described in 1793 as the most magnificent plant in New Holland, and is the floral emblem of N.S.W. Related species occur over SE Aus.

Warburton, Peter Egerton (1813–89) b. Cheshire, Eng. He arrived in Aus. in 1853 on his retirement after 24 years in the Indian Army. He was Police Commissioner until 1867, and took up exploration*; his journeys helped to clarify the pattern of the great S.A. salt lakes. In 1873, privately equipped by Elder* and other pastoralists, he crossed from Alice Springs to the De Grey River, a journey through the worst of the desert country, which nearly ended in disaster from lack of water.

Warburton Range W.A. 26S/126E Trends E–W at 475–610 m., marking the W extremity of the crystalline ranges of Central Aus., and forming part of a low swelling separating the Gibson Desert to the N and the Great Victoria Desert to the S; the slightly better vegetation and water support scattered Aboriginal nomads now mainly in some contact with the

Warburton Mission. The region is being prospected for minerals, and nickel at Wingella and vanadium in the Jameson Range have been found, while Aborigines are mining copper which is bought by an Aus. mining company.

Wardell, Robert (1793–1834) He arrived in Aus. in 1824, and established a legal practice with Wentworth, with whom he published the *Australian*, editing it until 1828 and incurring a libel action by Governor Darling. He was an efficient lawyer and satirical trenchant writer. He was shot by bushrangers.

Wardell, William Wilkinson (1823–1899) b. London. An architect. He arrived in Aus. in 1858 after practising in London, and was architect to the Vic. Government 1859–78. His best-known building is St. Patrick's Cathedral, Melbourne (1860–97), with spires added (1936), in dark igneous bluestone, massive Gothic style, and with a particularly fine interior; he also designed the sandstone St. Mary's Cathedral, Sydney (1855). Wardell was a fine and discriminating copyist rather than an original designer; for example his Vic. Government House (1872–6) imitated Osborne House, Queen Victoria's Isle of Wight residence.

War Memorials Mainly to commemorate the dead of the 1914–18 War*, with those who died in 1939–45 and later added, they are found in most centres of any size. There are also a number of plaques and memorials dating from the Sudan and Boer Wars. Canberra has the Aus. War Memorial (1941), which houses over 4,000 paintings, sculptures and reliefs, over 40,000 actual war relics, as varied as Victoria Crosses, aeroplanes, submarines, tanks, and library and photographic records. It is built round a central courtyard and pool, flanked by 2-storey galleries containing the exhibits, and with the casualty lists along arched cloisters leading to the dome of the Hall of Memory. Over half a million visit the Memorial every year which is owned and run by the Commonwealth. Under 1 km. to the E is the Australian-American War Memorial, a 67-m. aluminium sheathed column (1954). In Sydney the Anzac Memorial (1934) is in Hyde Park, and the Cenotaph (1927) in Martin Place, which is the focal point of Anzac and Remembrance Day services. Melbourne has a Shrine of Remembrance (1934) in the Domain, and Adelaide the National War Memorial (1931). In Perth the State War Memorial (1929) is in King's Park, and in Brisbane the Qld. National Anzac Memorial (1930) is in Anzac Square. There is a State Memorial in Hobart (1925). In addition there are many Memorial Driveways (officially part of the Canberra–Sydney Highway is one, and some planting follows the roadsides for 16 km. out of Canberra) as well as many practically expressed memorials in the form of parks, swimming pools, playgrounds, etc.

Warning, Mount N.S.W. (1,125 m.) About 35 km. SW of Coolangatta and Point Danger, named by Cook in 1770 at the same time that the *Endeavour* was in hazard off the Point.

Warragamba River N.S.W. The name given to part of the middle course of the Wollondilly–Warragamba – Nepean – Hawkesbury (*see* HAWKESBURY). The **Warragamba Dam**, 25 km. upstream from Penrith, 34S/151E, is a main source of Sydney's water supply, yielding some hydro-electricity and flood mitigation also; the Dam is 116 m. high, storage 2,100 million m.^{3} and the reservoir is named L. Burragorang.

Warragul Vic 38S/146E (7,193 in 1971) A market and service centre in dairying, and one time thickly wooded, country in W Gippsland*, lying at 116 m. on a Tertiary basalt cap. Secondary industry includes dairy products, rope and clothing.

Warrego Grass (*Paspalidium jubiflorum*) A valuable pasture grass of inland Aus., with many small flattish heads bearing heavy seeds which often bend the plants to the ground. Also called Yellow-flowered Panic or Vandyke Grass.

Warrigal A corruption from an Aboriginal language, as an alternative name for the Dingo* or wild dog; hence anything wild, e.g. a wild horse or wild Aborigine (and the name given by Boldrewood* to the Aboriginal tracker in *Robbery under Arms*). Warrigal Cabbage is a Pigface*.

Warrnambool Vic. 38S/142E (18,663 in 1971) A city on fairly rugged coast near the mouth of the Hopkins River and sometimes claimed as the capital of the Western District* which lies to the N. It is a service centre for the rich dairying and vegetable-growing coastal low plateau, with butter factories, and also woollen and clothing mills, timber trades, plastics, plaster sheet and foundry works, engineering both agricultural and general, and an increasing tourist trade. Yet industry remains

Warrumbungles

small, and growth slow though fairly steady.

Warrumbungle Range N.S.W. A massif W of Coonabarabran, reaching 1,228 m. in Mt. Exmouth, 31S/149E, and including Siding Spring Mountain* and a National Park of 34 km.[2]. The mountains include the trachyte cores of Tertiary volcanoes, forming vertical spires and turrets comparable with the Glasshouse Mountains* in Qld. The Range extends dry sclerophyll forest into lower woodlands and savannah country.

Warung, Price The pen-name of a short-story writer of the 19th century, William Astley*.

Warwick Qld. 28S/152E (9,356 in 1971; 10,075 in 1966) At 458 m. on the Condamine River* this city is the main centre for the S part of the Darling Downs*. Dairy produce and wheat-farming have replaced the original pastoral economy established by the first Qld. settlers from N.S.W. (1840), led by Patrick Leslie. The Leslie Dam on Sandy Creek supplies the town and some irrigation along the Condamine.

Wasps Insects, mainly winged, of the waisted Sub-Order Apocrita of the Order Hymenoptera*. The females of some species have the ovipositor adapted as a sting, carrying alkaline poison as a defence and to paralyse prey (for larvae to eat), but also quite painful to man. The females of certain species are wingless. Adults of many species eat nectar and pollen (like bees), or fruit, especially rotten fruit, but the larvae tend to be carnivorous on stored food or parasitic on the larvae of other insects, including other wasps, e.g. in the green or blue Emerald or Cuckoo Wasps, of Family Chrysididae, of very varying sizes. The females of some species lay the eggs in the clay-walled nest of Mason Wasps (genus *Odynerus*), or in a bees' nest. The Yellow-banded Club Wasp, *Sceliphron laetum*, with its quite distinctive body shape, is an example of a clay cell builder where the female stocks the larder for the hatching larvæ with paralysed spiders. The 'Solitary Ant' is in fact the wingless female of smaller winged males, e.g. the black-and-white wasp *Ephutomorpha rugicollis*, and the 'Blue Ant' is also a winged female of the large black-winged Flower Wasp, *Diamma bicolor*, sometimes seen carrying the female in flight. Social Wasps are less important (and obtrusive) in Aus. than in Europe; their wings are folded along the body at rest; they have banded bodies. The common species, the Paper Wasp, *Polistes variabilis*, is of a rather dull red-brown, and has rather long legs trailed when in flight; this wasp stings readily. The somewhat hexagonal comb 'chewed-cellulose paper', often in a rather shallow dome suspended from a branch or rock overhang, is built up by an over-wintering queen who herself feeds the first summer generation of workers on regurgitated caterpillars; the workers, on hatching, take on the duty of feeding the succeeding batches, and before the winter desertion of the nest, the males fertilise the females who then hibernate. The very large orange and black Cicada Hunter, *Exeirus lateritus*, has strong spined clasping legs. (For Ichneumon Wasps—*see* HYMENOPTERA.)

Water Gum (*Tristania neriifolia*) A tree in the Myrtaceae family related to the Brush Box*; in a mainly tropical genus, the Water Gum is found by rocky creek-banks in coastal N.S.W. and the Blue Mts., usually as a bush, with dark green broadly lanceolate leaves and masses of small 5-petalled flowers on ends of branches.

Water Hyacinth (*Eichhornia crassipes*) An aquatic plant in the family Ponteriaceae, introduced from tropical and sub-tropical America as a garden plant, probably in the late 19th century and, as in other tropical countries, spreading as a serious pest, by 1920 impeding water transport and domestic water supplies along N.S.W. rivers. Until the introduction of the new effective hormone weed-killers, the only treatment was to chop rafts of the weed and float it downstream to salt water where it died.

WATER RESOURCES 1. *Rainfall and its use* Over 40% of Aus. is arid, and another 40% has under 75 cm. mean annual rainfall, mostly seasonal, variable and subject to strong evaporation. Average estimated run-off, spread over the land surface, would be only 3·3 cm. deep, and only 6·8 cm. even of the 48% drained by rivers reaching the ocean (U.S., 22 cm.). The total Aus. river run-off has been estimated at 345,380 million m.³ (Amazon, 3,638,825, Volga, 252,868). In most of Aus. water-supply is a problem for domestic use, stock-watering, irrigation and industrial purposes; some urban and industrial units cause problems downstream through water pollution. Storage of roof water is a standard rural source—a 45,000-litre tank will feed a family's taps over a dry summer, especially if water from an earthen excavated and embanked dam can be used for toilets and gardens.

2. *Underground water* includes free or ground water and confined, pressure or artesian water. In humid areas the ground water forms a continuous body between the water table and the uppermost impervious rocks; there is a slow movement downhill to points where the water table comes to the surface in a spring or seepage (sometimes under a river or lake or under the sea, as off the Nullarbor coast) and wells are useful. In arid areas ground water is found sporadically, in river gravels such as those feeding Alice Springs, in joint-planes, solution cavities in rock or along a fault-plane. Pressure or artesian water fed by rain on a surface aquifer is confined between 2 impermeable strata and is under hydraulic pressure from an uphill direction, sufficient to bring it to the surface at a bore. The

strata may be in basin form, or the water trapped in rocks dipping towards a fault bringing impermeable rock against the aquifer. If the pressure is insufficient to bring the water right to the surface, the bore is called sub-artesian, and pumping may be used. Artesian water is important in parts of the basins shown on Map 4, but in places, e.g. the N of the Murray artesian basin, it is too saline even for stock. At great depths it is often at or over the surface boiling point, and salinity varies widely with the rocks and conditions in the intake area. Recommended salinity limits in grains per litre are: for human use and all agricultural purposes, to 20; lucerne irrigation, 30–45; but no irrigation, over 70; stock, 70–150, and sheep have lived on water up to 200. Water from the hundreds of bores in the Great Artesian Basin in Qld. supplies most of the sheep and cattle in the State, but bores have used past accumulations; many have dried up, more become sub-artesian, and control measures are needed. New sources in the Centre* are under study.

Surface Water is important in the wetter coastal tracts, but even here there is enormous variability seasonally and towards the arid margins, between flood and drought years—the Darling has fluctuated from 1·25 million to 14,000 million m.^{3} (average 3,000 million m.^{3} per annum).

The great Murray Basin covers about 14% of Aus., and has a discharge of about 10,000 million m.^{3} (15,000 million but for storage, diversion for irrigation and losses; cf. Danube 28,000, Ganges 180,000).

The rivers of the E slopes are relatively short. Total discharges are some 100,000 million m.^{3}, the northern rivers with a marked summer maximum flow, a winter or spring maximum in Vic., and a double maximum in winter and summer in the N of N.S.W. Streams with average flow over 1,200 million m.^{3} with uses (U = urban, I =

Irrigation,   HE = hydro-electricity) are: Snowy I and HE, Hawkesbury U, Manning, Macleay, Clarence, Richmond. In the N Fitzroy, Herbert and Burdekin I (all over 4,900 million), Burnett and Johnstone. In the SE Yarra U, Latrobe U, Shoalhaven and Tweed are over 600 million.

The Gulf of Carpentaria rivers have total estimated discharges averaging 58,000 million m.^{3}, but varying from summer monsoon flood to little or no winter flow except for the spring-fed Gregory. In order of flow they are: Mitchell, Gilbert-Staaten, Flinders, Leichhardt, Gregory-Nicholson and Roper. Similar conditions prevail in the Timor Sea group of rivers, estimated at 53,000 million m.^{3} average flow: Daly, Victoria, Ord I and Fitzroy I.

The Indian ocean rivers, De Grey, Fortescue, Ashburton, Gascoyne and Murchison, have the intermittent or ephemeral flow of a hot desert region, alternating with occasional years of overwhelming floods; the estimated average flow of 3,700 million m.^{3} is rather meaningless.

The SW W.A. system, estimated average flow 12,000 million m.^{3}, has few perennial rivers—Swan-Avon U, Blackwood, Warren and Frankland (each over 185 million m.^{3} per annum) and some spring-fed streams from the Darling Scarp. The Adelaide coastal drainage system has small seasonal rivers: Onkaparinga and Torrens U, and Yorke and Eyre Peninsulas have rural supply schemes based on small catchments with some underground water.

In Tas., with more ample reliable rains and natural lake storage, only small works have been necessary until quite recent years for urban supplies, such as the small storages from springs on Mt. Wellington to supply Hobart. Rivers exceeding 1,200 million m.^{3} are: Derwent HE, S Esk HE, Mersey HE, Arthur, Pieman, King, Gordon and Huon.

L. Eyre, 12 m. below sea level, and

the associated system of seldom-flooded desert salt-lakes, are the focus of one of the world's greatest basins of internal drainage, $1\frac{1}{4}$ million km.[2] in area. Much of the rest of the continent has unco-ordinated drainage—over 2·5 million km.[2] of the Great Western Plateau, the Simpson Desert area, and W Vic. (where the drainage lines are upset by lava flows in a semi-arid climate). There might be some surface drainage in the Desert Basin of W.A. but for a sandy mantle over a porous aquifer, and in parts of the Nullarbor Desert but for the underlying limestone strata containing cave systems which are partly a legacy of past climates.

Water Conservation, obviously of importance, is implicit in all storage and irrigation works. Evaporation can be reduced from suitable water-bodies, by chemical applications evolved by C.S.I.R.O. in 1956 (evaporation exceeds rainfall over about half of Aus. and exceeds 250 cm. per annum in much of the Centre and NW).

The often advocated planting of trees in water catchment areas prolongs the life of the reservoir by reducing accelerated soil erosion and silting, but the effect on run-off is controversial.

Other land-use programmes have been suggested to increase the benefits from holding local rain on the land on which it falls. H. G. Geddes, with experience on an experimental dairy farm on poor soils, advocates farm-by-farm storage of irrigation water. P. A. Yeomans (*The Challenge of Landscape,* Sydney, 1958) urges that there is a vital break of slope, the keyline, along every valley, and that a system of excavated dams, contour channels, and cultivation carefully chosen in relation to absorption of rainfall into the subsoil can be so related to the keyline as to build up a whole complex of better pastures, more absorbent topsoils and subsoils with indefinite and to some extent cumulative effects in storing moisture from wet years against dry.

Waten, Judah (1911–) b. Odessa, Russia. He arrived in Aus. in 1914. He is an important novelist, portraying city life especially in his own Jewish community. One of his finest works is *Season of Youth* (Melbourne, 1966), set in the Depression period.

Water-bugs An expression loosely used to cover a number of aquatic insects or stages of insects, but the true Water-bugs belong to the Sub-Order Heteroptera of the Order Hemiptera (*see* BUGS). They are mainly carnivorous, sucking

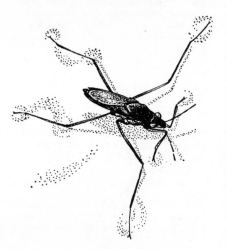

Water Strider (Gerris australis), about 3 times life size

the body fluids from other insects, and include the Water Strider of SE Aus., *Gerris australis,* the Water Measurer, *Hydrometra* spp., like stick insects walking on the water, the 7·5-cm.-long Giant Water Bug, *Lethocerus* spp., the Back Swimmers such as the *Anisops* spp., the Water Scorpions such as the Aus. toe-biter *Laccotrephes tristis,* living in pond-bottom debris, and the Water Boatmen, e.g. *Arctocorisa australis* often seen diving and coming up for air alternately.

Waterfalls They are fairly common along the coastward edge of the E Highlands of Aus., but have great seasonal flow variation. The highest are: Wollomombi on a Macleay River tributary, N.S.W., 31S/152E, with a sheer drop of 336 m. and total of 480 m., and Wallaman Falls on Stony Creek, a tributary of the Herbert River, Qld., 18S/146E, 280 m. sheer, 350 m. total. In Qld. the Barron* and Tully* Rivers have spectacular wet season falls. The Wentworth Falls over the sandstone cliffs of the Blue Mountains*, the upper reaches of Shoalhaven (Fitzroy Falls) and Macleay (Ebor Falls) in N.S.W. have drops of 150 m. or over. Tas. waterfalls, while not generally so high, are more perennial.

Water-fleas A popular name for a number of species of aquatic crustaceans*; the name is applied most appropriately to small branchipod (gill-footed) crustaceans of jumping habit, and genus *Daphnia*, but extended to the Copepoda and Ostracoda Orders.

These predominantly freshwater animals are world-wide, flourishing in warm equable waters, but with eggs able to withstand great cold or drought and able to repopulate the water with adult crustaceans with seemingly miraculous speed when warm or wet conditions return. There is some form of shell, often of bivalve type, antennae, often the chief means of swimming and jumping, and in some species leaf-like appendages simulating feet, while sometimes there is a tail also assisting locomotion.

In Aus. the Water-fleas in the large sense include Tadpole-shrimps, genera *Triops* and *Lepidurus* in temporary high mountain pools, Fairy Shrimps, *Chirocephalus* and *Branchipus*, and Clam Shrimps, *Conchostraca*, in temporary shallow river backwaters, Brine Shrimps, *Artemia*, in inland salt lakes and pools, the very small *Cypris*, in tiny bivalve shells, in many fresh and salt waters, and the important plankton crustacean *Cyclops*, like several of these genera, with a single eye, but notable for translucent and sometimes beautifully coloured body forms.

Waterfowl As well as ducks*, geese*, and cormorants*, waterfowl of Aus. include the Coot, *Fulica atra*, black with white horny shield above the beak, and notable for its rhythmic head-movements while swimming, its easy diving, and open bulky nest on top of a clump of reeds, etc.; and the large and extraordinarily thin-necked Darter or Snake-bird, *Anhinga novae-hollandiae*, which dives well and often swims with only its small head and long neck above water, looking like a water-snake—the generic name is from Brazil, the specific from Aus. *For further reading see* H. J. Frith: *Waterfowl in Australia* (Sydney, 1967).

Waterhouse Range N.T. 14S/133E An oval dome of quartzite rising 150 m. above Missionaries Plain*, for some 48 km. E–W and 8 km. N–S, with a slight central depression eroded in shales. Owen Springs cattle station is on its N slopes.

Water-lilies In the family Nymphaeaceae; they include 2 Aus. genera and 4 species, notably the Giant Blue Water-lily, *Nymphaea gigantea*.

Watson, John Christian (1867–1941) b. Chile. He arrived in Aus. from N.Z. (1886). He became first Labor Prime Minister of Aus. April–August 1904, having risen from Union work in his trade as compositor, to membership of the first Federal Parliament and leadership of the Labor Party from 1901–7.

Wattle This is widely accepted as the Aus. popular name for a large number of bushes and small trees, nearly all *Acacia* in the Mimosaceae family. They yield local timber for fencing, tools, small turnery etc., rather than commercial timbers, some species for fodder especially in drought years, and some species for bark for tanning purposes. The 600 Aus. species are, at least locally, almost co-dominants with the eucalypts in the Aus. flora. The Aus. name comes from the use made of the shrubby stems and branches for weaving into wattle-and-daub hut walls, in the very first days of the settlement at Sydney Cove. The fluffy and often fragrant compound flower-spikes of many species have become the Aus. floral emblem, appearing on the Commonwealth coat of arms and on postage stamps. Species common in the more humid and inhabited areas have compound leaves with leaflets in pairs, e.g. the tall Black Wattle or Sydney Green Wattle, *Acacia decurrens*. Pods are often long, narrow and thin, cracking in hot weather to release the seeds, chiefly on dry sandy sites and in semi-arid and arid areas. Several species have the leaf-stalk enlarged and flattened to resemble a leaf; except in seedlings the true leaves are reduced to small marginal leaflets or scale-like processes as in the Coastal Myall, *A. glaucescens*, with 10- to 15-cm. sickle-shaped 'leaves', or the Prickly Moses, *A. juniperina*, of coastal sands in E Aus. with short, sharp, prickly 'leaves', attractive golden balls in flower, and long thin pods.

Species yielding tanning material include the S.A. Golden Wattle, *A. pycnantha*, Black Wattle, *A. mollissima*, and the Black or Sydney Green Wattle. (Some species are widely grown for tanning etc. in S Africa and India.) The Cootamundra Wattle, *A. baileyana*, is particularly esteemed for its blossom (*see* PLATE 7). Blackwood, *A. melanoxylon*, yields useful cabinet and cooper's timber; Mulga, *A. aneura*, and the scented Raspberry Jam, *A. acuminata*, good small timber. The Mulga* also gives fodder, as does the Weeping Myall* and Cooba or Native Willow*, *A. salacina*. The Brigalow* Scrub is dominated by *A. harpophylla*.

Wattle-birds Birds of several species (30 to 40 cm. long) with red or yellow fleshy wattles behind the beak; among the largest of the Honey-eaters*.

Wax Flowers A popular name for various species of the shrub genus *Eriostemon* in the Rutaceae or Rue family, common in poor sandy or rocky country mainly in temperate Aus. They have thick waxy 5-petalled flowers, mainly pink-white. The Pink Wax Flower, *E. lanceolatus*, of sandy coastal E Aus. has handsome flowers and slender grey-green leaves. The Fairy Wax Flower, *E. obovalis*, grows in barren mountain ridges in SE Aus., with small pink stars on thick short leaves close to the stem. In W.A. *E. spicatus* is common on sandy heath country near Albany, with lavender flower-heads, and inland sand-heaths near Kalgoorlie have the scarlet-flowered *E. coccineus*. A somewhat similar bush of wet gullies in E Aus. is *Phebalium dentatum*, with masses of white and yellow small flowers along the branches, and in W.A. *P. argenteum* the oily 'blister plant'. In sub-tropical E Aus. there are 6 spp. of *Hoya australis*, commonly called Wax Flower, highly poisonous and especially dangerous to cattle.

Wax Plant A popular name for the genus *Chamelaucium*, in the family Myrtaceae, heath-like in habit, with fine and narrow leaves, including some of the most esteemed of the heath shrubs of W.A., e.g. the pink-white flowered Geraldton Wax Plant, *C. uncinatum*, and the Esperance Wax Plant, *C. megalopetalum*, with large white flowers.

Wayatinah Tas. 42S/146E Hydro-Electricity Commission village, Dam, lagoon and Power Station (38,250 kW, completed 1957) at the confluence of Nive and Derwent Rivers. Liapootah Power Station (83,700 kW) upstream on the lagoon shore was part of this development, and is fed by its own dam. (*See* TASMANIA, POWER.)

Webb, Francis Charles (1925–) b. Adelaide. A poet noted for historic narrative, as in *A Drum for Ben Boyd* (Sydney, 1948), as well as a poetic drama on Leichhardt.

Web-spinners They are long, slender, 4-winged, vegetarian insects of the Order Embiaria, superficially like winged termites, but with a web-spinning organ on the front legs, with which they spin the silk tunnels in which they live in forest litter, e.g. under Casuarinas.

Wedding Bush A popular name for the mainly Aus. flowering shrub genus *Ricinocarpos* in the world-wide Spurge family of mainly milky-sapped climbers and trees, the Euphorbiaceae. An attractive yellow-flowered W.A. species is *R. glauca*, growing under the karri forest. The popular name comes from *R. pinifolius*, common in heaths on deep sandy soils in E. Aus., with masses of snowy white flowers with 5 open, slender petals; there is a prickly fruit like that of the castor-oil plant. The Pink Wedding Bush, *R. bowmanii*, common on inland hillsides in Qld. and N.S.W., has hairy narrow leaves up to 3 cm. long and attractive clusters of pink star-like flowers.

Wee Waa N.S.W. 30S/149E (1,840 in 1971) A small but rapidly growing local service centre on the Namoi River. It has been greatly stimulated by irrigation under licence since the building of the Keepit Dam*, largely for cotton-growing on fertile grey loams, with American growers as innovators. There is a cotton ginnery.

Weeds, mainly Introduced Most of the most objectionable weeds in Aus. have been introduced, adventitiously with crop-seed, or as deliberate introductions to gardens, mainly from Europe, but some of the worst from S Africa or Latin America. In the quite different ecology of their new environment, many have proved very difficult to con-

trol, though biological control has had some notable victories, e.g. *Cactoblastis* larvae against Prickly Pear*, and recently hormone weed-killers, e.g. against Water Hyacinth*. Examples are: Brassica or Cabbage family (Charlock, Wild Turnip or Mediterranean Mustard), Compositae or Daisy family (Skeleton Weed, *Chondrilla juncea*), various Thistles, especially Shore Thistle, *Carduus*, Saffron, *Carthamus*, Star, *Centaurea*, Stemless, *Onopordon* and Perennial, *Cirsium*; Dock or Polygoneaceae family (Middle East Pink Dock, *Rumex roseus*); twiners of several families including *Convolvulus* and various members of the Cucumber-Melon family, Cucurbitaceae; annuals, e.g. poppies, are pests in cereal fields, in damp areas the Sedge*, *Cyperus rotundus* (Nut-grass), and the thorny Giant Sensitive Plant, *Mimosa invisa* (from Brazil), in the Qld. sugar areas. The Prickly Pear* is perhaps the classic case of a campaign against an officially proscribed noxious weed, but various plants are outlawed in different areas at different times, e.g. the Blackberry*, the Briar Rose (spread in the dung of horses browsing on hips in urban gardens), and Lantana*.

Weevils Beetles of the very large family Curculionidae of small beetles, most of which have a very distinctive long, hard snout, hence Elephant Beetle; most larvae are legless maggots feeding on all kinds of vegetable matter, though some form galls in flower-buds or tunnel in eucalypt leaves. The Sapphire Weevil, *Chrysolophos spectabilis*, lives on wattles, but some native species have become pests of orchards, while the introduced pests of grain stores are universal, such as the Granary Weevil, *Sitophilus granaria*.

Weipa Qld. 13S/142E A former Presbyterian Mission Station, in the NW of Cape York, and the site of vast bauxite* deposits along 160 km. of coastline, the development of which has involved a new (Dutch-built) port and a town (2,129 in 1971). A shipping channel has been dredged to the mouth of the Embley River; some bauxite goes to Japan and Europe, but most goes to Gladstone*. A refinery is planned. Devices to make tropical living comfortable characterise the pinkish brick houses. Aboriginal workers have the same wage and live in new aluminium houses at the Reserve. Flinders noted the 'red cliffs' in 1803; their potential was recognised in 1955 as the largest known economic deposit of the raw material for aluminium* in the world.

Wellesley Islands Qld., 16S/139E In the S of the Gulf of Carpentaria are 2 groups of scrub- and tree-covered low islands. The 2 largest are Mornington (650 km.²), which has a settlement of about 600 Aborigines, making tourist souvenirs. Bentinck (160 km.²) is uninhabited.

Wellington N.S.W. 33S/149E (5,534 in 1971; 5,929 in 1961) A local service market and processing centre on the Macquarie River (butter, meat, flour, timber) with considerable tourist traffic. There are limestone caves and old gold-workings (the State's one large gold-dredging plant ceased work only in 1958).

Wellington, Lake Vic. The innermost and least saline of the Gippsland Lakes*. It is oval, about 16 by 12 km. mostly under 4 m. deep, and receiving the Latrobe and Avon Rivers, while draining to L. Victoria by McLennan's Str. which is deeper, up to 11 m.

Wellington, Mount Tas. 43S/147E 1,270 m., and named to commemorate the Battle of Waterloo, it rises steeply from the Derwent estuary behind Hobart. Suburbs climbing its lower slopes were burned in the severe February 1967 bushfire. Forest gives way to beetling dolerite crags at the summit, with montane vegetation and long periods of snow cover. It is reached by a 19-km. road.

Wentworth, D'Arcy (?1762–1827) b. County Down, Ireland. A colourful character with aristocratic connections He was acquitted of charges of highway robbery, while supposedly studying surgery. He sailed with the Second Fleet in 1790. After 6 years on Norfolk Island he brought his mistress (a former convict) and family to Sydney where he rose to many official positions, including the Supreme Court, and achieved great wealth and honour. His son **William Charles** (1790–1872), b. Norfolk Island, was the first Aus.-born citizen to achieve important office. In 1813 he crossed the Blue Mts. with Lawson* and Blaxland*. In Eng. again (1816–24), studying law, he wrote and spoke on the potentialities of Aus. including a long poem *Australasia*. Except for a journey to see the N.S.W. Constitution through Parliament in 1855, he was in Aus. from 1824–62, returning to spend his last 10 years in Eng. The most influential politician of his day, his views, like those of many statesmen changed with the years. At first he was a radical, opposed to exclusivists, violently campaigning for emancipists' rights, freedom of press (founding the *Australian* with Wardell in 1824), and self-government, forming the Australian Patriotic Association for this purpose in 1835. He was also a precocious federalist. Later he came to favour more conservative views, supporting squatters and landed interests, continued transportation and even proposing a peerage (brilliantly ridiculed by the satirist, D. H. Deniehy), and only limited franchise based on property, thus losing the support of the increasing urban proletariat. *Source:* A. C. V. Melbourne: *William Charles Wentworth* (Brisbane, 1934). His great grandson, **W. C. Wentworth IV**, (1907–) is a politician of note.

Wessel Islands N.T. 11S/136E A chain of small islands extending NE from the Napier Peninsula in Arnhem Land*, and part of the Aborigine reserve. The largest, Marchinbar, has bauxite deposits, not scheduled so far for development.

West, John (1809–1873) b. London. He arrived in Aus. in 1838. As a minister and newspaper owner, with James Aikenhead, in Launceston, and later the first official editor of the *Sydney Morning Herald* (1854–73), he wrote vigorously against transportation and the cruelty of Price* and others; initiated the formation of the Australian Anti-Transportation League (1851–54).

West, Morris (1916–) b. St. Kilda, Vic. He is a successful modern novelist, formerly a teacher and secretary to W. M. Hughes*. His main works include *The Devil's Advocate* (London, 1959), *The Shoes of the Fisherman* (London, 1963), *The Ambassador* (New York, 1965), set in SE Asia, and *Tower of Babel* (London, 1968) in the Middle East.

WESTERN AUSTRALIA (W.A.) The largest Aus. State, with an area of 2,515,552 km.², a third of it N of the Tropic. It is bounded by sea on the NW and S, and on the E by 129°E longitude, with N.T. to the N and S.A. to the S of 26°S latitude. The population in 1971 was 1,027,372 including Aborigines, 21·4% increase from 1966, and a rate of growth twice any other state. Only a few thousand full-blood Aborigines remain and even fewer follow their traditional ways of life in the N and in the deserts. Most of the half-bloods are

*Badge of
Western Australia*

poor citizens of the SW. The average density of 0·41 per km.² is higher than the N.T., but in the tropical third of W.A., which only has 2% of the State's people, it is similar. Three-quarters live SW of a line from Geraldton to Albany.

Physical Geography and Land Use Over 90% lies at about 300 m. on the Great Plateau; Precambrian igneous and metamorphic rocks have been worn to even surfaces on which rather younger, undisturbed sandstones form the higher blocks. The highest point, Mt. Meharry in the Hamersley*, is only 1,217 m. Coastal plains are narrow, and occur where basins filled by younger sediments are truncated by the shore-line. Between plateau and coast is a scarp zone dissected by rivers that are mainly seasonal in flow. Climates range from the sub-tropical summer Monsoon of the N, through an intermediate zone in which scanty and unreliable rain may come in any month and where summer cyclones sweep the coast, to the typically 'Mediterranean' regime of the SW with its cool rainy winter and hot arid summer. Rainfall is over 100 cm. only in the extreme N and SW, decreasing rapidly inland to the vast interior deserts.

The Far North The stony Kimberleys* block is bordered to the E by the Ord River* and to the S by the wider valleys of the Fitzroy* Basin. Large unfenced cattle properties predominate, but there are sheep in the central Fitzroy Valley and some irrigated agricultural lands in the lower Ord and Fitzroy Valleys. Along the NW is an unused belt of tropical woodland and poor grass, edged by drowned estuaries lined with swamp and mangrove. The Canning Basin* to the S, with under 35 cm. of rain, is largely empty except for some cattle properties along the coastal margin.

The North-west The Hamersley Range* sediments and Pilbara* crystalline rocks provide some of the roughest country in the State. They are separated by the Fortescue River*, in a rift valley, and edged along the coast by the younger sediments of the Carnarvon Basin*. Rainfall is erratic and the summers extremely hot; tropical cyclones are liable to cause severe coastal damage about once in 5 years. Scrub and savannah support large sheep and cattle properties, but pasture deterioration and competition from kangaroos, wild horses, donkeys and pigs are major problems. There is a little irrigated agriculture along the lower Gascoyne*, and some stimulus to farming may be expected from the major mineral development now under way.

Murchison-Kalgoorlie This wide inland region between the desert and the Wheat Belt* is a gently rolling granitic surface, with innumerable salt-lakes in shallow depressions. Its gold-bearing rocks brought influxes of people in the 1890s to this harsh waterless environment. Rainfall increases towards the S, where a winter maximum and greater reliability support eucalypt woodland in place of the Northern mulga and scrub. Exploitation for fuel for the Kalgoorlie mines has caused wind erosion. Large sheep-runs dominate, although the extension of wheat-growing is possible, using modern techniques.

*The Wheat Belt**, distinguished from the previous area by climate and not topography, shares its gently rolling character, developed on a crystalline rock base, with salt-lakes and sandplains. But the winter rainfall, increasing to 50 cm. in the SW, and the easily cleared mallee and eucalypt woodland encouraged wheat-growing with sheep-rearing towards the wetter SW.

The South West The Plateau edge is dissected to form a hill belt with winter rainfall up to 150 cm. in the S. Tall jarrah and karri forests are interspersed with land cleared for stone and pome fruits, cereals and sheep. The coast plain has a clay strip along the hillfoot and a seaward belt of low limestone ridges. Rainfall is under 35 cm. N of Perth and E of Esperance, and here wheat reaches towards the coast.

Irrigated citrus, vines and dairy pastures use scarp river storages from the Swan to the Harvey. Poorer unirrigated dairy and potato farms survive in the damp clay soils and prolonged wet season of the extreme SW.

Industry and Towns Primary industry provides 55% of Aus. primary production and 51% of the State's total export value, accounting for an overseas trading surplus and invaluable to the country as a whole. Pastoral and agricultural products are of roughly equal importance, dominated by wheat and wool, but with significant amounts of oats, barley, beef, fat lambs and fruit. Present trends are to increased specialisation and efficiency in optimum areas to overcome marketing problems of quality, but clearing of timber and the use of new breeds and of 'trace elements' is extending farmland, especially in the Esperance* area. Minerals supply 56% of primary production worth $A 646 million (1971). The dominance of gold has changed with iron and nickel shipments from 1967. The Barrow Island* oilfield is second in Aus. and vast reserves of natural gas* off the NW coast may power heavy industry in Pilbara* region. Timber extraction from the forests of the SW, controlled since 1918, provides 2–3% of production, dairying 2% and fishing 2%.

Heavy secondary industry was lacking until the establishment, mainly since 1950, of steel-rolling, alumina, cement, oil-refining and paper in the region bordering Cockburn Sound*. Integrated iron and steel works in the next 2 decades are part of the agreements with iron-ore extracting companies. These all increase the existing concentration of industry in the Perth area which has 75% of the factory workers. Planned development of the NW region could add oil-refining, and asbestos plants there to the existing iron-pelletiser works. Elsewhere, fertilisers are made in the ports serving farming areas, sawmills and dairy produce factories are important in the SW which has also titanium-processing at Bunbury. There are meatworks at Broome, Derby and Wyndham, and a cotton ginnery on the Ord. Food processing, printing and most other tertiary industries are concentrated in Perth.

The transport network is closest in the SW, radiating from Perth. Early timber railways were followed by several built in exchange for land grants and Government lines to the gold-fields and Wheat Belt. Air transport began with the first regular Aus. service in 1921 (Geraldton–Derby) and is essential to the mining towns and rural areas of the N. Sealed roads are scarce N of 26°S, but Beef Roads are improving access to the ports in the Kimberleys.

The Metropolitan area contains 68% of the population and urbanisation is increasing, though, as elsewhere, some small towns are declining.

Over 20,000, Kalgoorlie-Boulder (Mining).

10,000–18,000, Albany, Bunbury, Geraldton are ports with farming hinterlands and some industry. Rockingham (resort), Kwinana*.

5,000–10,000, Collie (coal), Northam (agricultural centre), Port Hedland*, Busselton*, Mandurah*.

2,000–5,000, Esperance* (port and resort); Wheat Belt service and rail towns: Narrogin*, Merredin*, Katanning*; coast belt farming centre: Manjimup* and Harvey (irrigation); ports of Exmouth*, Carnarvon*, Dampier*, Derby*; iron ore towns: Tom Price, Newman; Kambalda (nickel).

1,000–2,000, irrigation centre: Waroona; valley or hillfoot farming centres: Bridgetown*, Mt. Barker*; smaller ports: Broome*, Wyndham*; Wheat Belt service centres: Norseman*, Kellerberrin, Wagin, Moora, York*, Gnowangerup; iron-smelting at Wundowie*; iron ore towns: Goldsworthy, Paraburdoo*; coastal towns: Pinjarra*, Roebourne*; new towns: Karratha*, Kununurra*; Donnybrook (local centre).

Many local centres under 1,000 of importance, e.g. Pemberton*. Many lie along the railways fanning out through the Wheat Belt and to Kalgoorlie. Sequences along the 3 main lines are: (E) Cunderdin, Merredin, Southern Cross; (S) Beverley, Brookton, Pingelly; (W) Morawa-Mullewa. Bullfinch, Gwalia-Leonara, Quairading, Corrigin, Wickipin, Dumbleyung, Ongerup, Pingrup and L. Grace are all on feeder lines. Sawmilling centres include jarrah mills at Jarrahdale, Banksiadale, Yarloop, Mornington, Kirup, Jarrahwood, Nannup, Yornup, Palgarup, and jarrah/karri mills at Deanmill, Manjimup, Jardee, Donkelly, Quinninup, Northcliffe and Shannon. Dairy factories are the main function of Boyanup, Brunswick, Capel, Margaret River and Balingup. Gold is still mined at Bullfinch, Mt. Magnet. (*See* MAPS 15 and 16.)

Historical Development   Fear of French interest led to the first settlement at Albany in 1827, but it was Stirling's glowing reports of the Swan River* area that brought free settlement and the 1829 proclamation of the colony of W.A., thus completing British annexation of the continent. Early pioneers had to battle with poor land, lack of skill, labour and adequate survey, and by 1840 population had dropped to 1,139; the situation worsened with the Depression of the 1840s. From 1850–68 transportation, petitioned in desperation, brought some 10,000 convicts and some economic expansion, followed by stagnation from 1860–70, a decade when population rose only by 4,035, to 29,019. Exploration revealed new pasture lands in the N, but progress remained slow until the gold-rushes of 1885–95; by 1900 population had jumped to 179,967, a 270% increase since 1890. The gold-miners and the old established coastal farmers formed antagonistic groups, especially over Federation into which Forrest* took the colony with some reluctance. He bargained, in return, for the transcontinental railway (opened 1917) and for 5 years in which W.A. could continue to levy its own customs. The feeling of isolation from the E States and neglect by the Commonwealth reached a peak when, in 1933, at the depth of the Depression a referendum brought a 3:1 vote in favour of secession, which however was rejected in London.

Meanwhile agricultural extension had successfully developed the Wheat Belt* and the less successful Group Settlement* Scheme had cleared dairyland in the SW. Increased immigration after 1945 and world demand for primary products (notably the Korean War wool boom and Communist China's wheat demands) led to further clearing and development of farmland. The vast iron deposits of the NW and nickel field of the E Goldfields are yielding high export values in the 1970s, and wool and wheat recovered in the early 1970s after decline. But low population density and great distances lead to high costs. Special financial concessions and a special Minister show the interest in Northern Development*.

Premiers since 1900: G. Throssell, G. Leake, A. E. Morgan (all 1901), F. Illingworth, W. H. James (1902), H. Daglish (1904), C. H. Rason (1905), N. J. Moore (1906), F. Wilson (1910 & 1916), J. Scaddan (1911), H. B. Lefroy (1917), H. P. Colebatch (1919), J. Mitchell (1919 & 1930), P. Collier (1924, 1933-6), J. C. Willcock (1936), F. J. S. Wise (1945), D. R. McClarty (1947), A. R. G. Hawke (1953), D. Brand (1959-71), J. Tonkin (1971-). See F. K. Crowley: *A Short History of W.A.* (Melbourne, 1959); A. M. Kerr: *Australia's North-West* (Perth, 1967); and *The South-West of W.A.* (Perth, 1965).

Western District Vic. A region (not administrative) between Port Phillip and the S.A. border, separated from the Wimmera* by the Grampians* and with the Otway Ranges* in the S.E. Settled by Tas. squatters from 1834, it

was also reached in 1836 by Mitchell*, followed by squatters overland from N.S.W.; his names predominate in the region, which he called 'Australia Felix'. It was developed for wool by famous squatter families and personalities, such as the Learmonths* and Neil Black (1804-1880), who built up wealth and stately mansions centred on local towns, e.g. Hamilton, in the second half of the 19th century. Today more intensive arable farming has been developed. The Heywood-Dartmoor area has the most extensive pine plantations in Vic. and there is a Soldier Land Settlement Scheme at Heylesbury. *For further reading see* M. Kiddle: *Men of Yesterday, A Social History of the Western District of Victoria, 1834-90* (Melbourne, 1961).

Western Port Bay Vic. 38S/145E Now commonly called Westernport, this is a circular bay about 50 km. across. The low hills of French Island (218 km.²) which is used as a gaol, lie in the centre; Phillip Island in the S is 155 km.². It is a drowned downfaulted area between the upfaulted Mornington Peninsula and the Strzelecki Ranges, and with much sand and mudflat siltation in the N. The Bay was named in 1798 by Bass*. An abortive attempt at settlement, to forestall possible French interests, took place on the E shore (1826-8). Industrial development is now taking place along the W shore: an oil-refinery at Crib Point is to be followed by a fully integrated iron and steel works; a cold strip mill is operating and the full works scheduled for completion 1985; ancillary industries are growing, with reclamation of 29 km. of foreshore for port development on Hastings Bay. Bay pollution will be minimised but is inevitable.

Whales With the Dolphins*, and with the northern hemisphere porpoises, comprise the Order Cetacea, mammals with lungs and diaphragm for breathing, necessarily at the surface, but otherwise very completely adapted to a wholly aquatic existence. Whale species most likely to be seen in Aus. waters, or occasionally stranded on the shore, include members of the 2 main Sub-Orders, the Toothless, Baleen or Whale-bone Whales and the Toothed Whales. *I Whalebone Whales* Mystacoceti (moustached whales) engulf huge mouthfuls of water, then filter it very efficiently through the whalebone screen, for krill and other plankton. 1. Southern Right Whale, *Balaena australis*, the 'right whale' to yield formerly valuable whalebone, is up to 18 m. long, and lacks dorsal fin and external throat-furrows. 2. Blue Whale, *Balaenoptera musculus*, or 'sulphur-bottom' from the yellowish film of diatoms common on the throat, usually grows up to 30 m. although it has been recorded up to 40 m., the largest mammal ever known, even the calf at birth being 7-8 m.; the mouth is cavernous, the throat only 30 cm. across. 3. The Finback or Rorqual, *Balaenoptera physalus*, is smaller and faster. 4. The Little Piked Whale, *Balaenoptera acutorostrata*, is still a smaller relative. 5. Pygmy Whale, *Neobalaena marginata*,

of up to 6 m. in length, has a dorsal fin, but lacks throat furrows (hence Pigmy Right Whale as one popular name) 6. The Humpback Whale, *Megaptera nodosa*, is the commonest and most exploited whale in Aus. waters, with a marked hump of thick blubber and very long flippers (5 m. in a 14-m. whale).
II Toothed Whales have ivory-like teeth, at least in the lower jaw, adapted to chopping up much larger food than that of the Whalebone Whales, such as fish, squid and, in the Killer Whale, preying on other whales. 1. The Sperm Whale, *Physeter catodon*, the largest and most important commercially of the Toothed Whales, with the enormous square-fronted head with numerous large peg-teeth often seen in pictures of whaling from small boats. It feeds on giant octopuses and squids, and stomach irritation from some element in this diet is believed to stimulate the formation of ambergris, a waxy substance sometimes found on Aus. beaches and of value in the perfume trade as a vehicle assisting the lingering qualities of delicate perfumes (though prices have been reduced by substitutes). The Sperm Whales, however, were hunted almost to extinction last

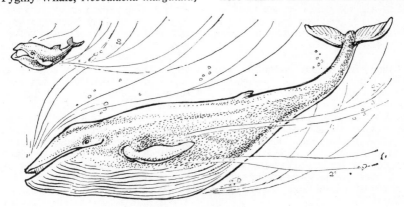

Pygmy and Blue Whales
(Neobalaena marginata; Balaenoptera musculus)

century, for spermaceti oil, used for clear-burning candles. Reservoirs of the oil in the whale's body are believed to have a function in assisting it to remain stable at the very great depth to which it dives. 2. The Pygmy Sperm Whale, *Kogia breviceps*, is 3–4 m. long. 3. Killer Whale or Grampus, *Orcinus orca*, is a black whale with white patches, the male reaching 9 m., the female 5–6 m. in length, with scythe-like dorsal fin, and 40–52 stout peg-like teeth. They hunt in packs of 40 or more, preying on other whales (particularly the tongue), dolphins, seals and penguins. 4. False Killer, *Pseudorca crassidens*, grows up to 6 m. (male) and 3 m. (female). Occasionally whole packs become stranded on shores widely dispersed over the world (Dornoch Firth, Scotland, 1927, and Stanley, Tas., 1936). 5. Beaked Whales of several different genera are sometimes stranded on Aus. shores. These are whales in which the upper jaw has evolved into a beak of ivory-like substance, though non-functional teeth may be embodied in it; on the lower jaw are usually 2 teeth of different types in different genera or species, e.g. the Strap-toothed Whale, *Mesoplodon layardi*, is up to 5 m., with 2 flattened tusks growing up from the middle of the lower jaw, sometimes crossing so as to prevent full opening of the mouth.

Whaling In Aus. at present it is of slight importance, owing to overfishing followed by international control to prevent extinction of species—humpback whales were fished in W.A. from 1949 and off the E coast from 1952, but E coast stations were closed in 1962 and all fishing of this species S of the equator in 1963. The Albany station still operates, handling sperm whales Whale oil exports 1969–70 were about $500,000.

It is difficult from this modern picture to envisage the historical importance of whaling. In 1791 5 whaling ships, after carrying convicts and stores to Sydney, killed 7 whales off SE Aus., but lost 5 owing to bad weather. The East India Company* monopoly restricted whaling. Although there were some relaxations in 1795, 1797 and 1801, and bases at Sydney, Hobart and Norfolk Island had established a Tasman Sea whaling ground by 1803, American whalers and sealers and whalers from Nantucket (from 1792 onwards), unrestricted by the monopoly, creamed off much of both trade and skilled labour. After cessation of the monopoly in 1813 and of heavy duties on oil in 1828, Sydney and especially Hobart whaling flourished, initially Bay whaling, towing the carcases to several stations from Twofold Bay, N.S.W., 37S/150E, to the Swan River, W.A., 32S/116E. Then deep-sea whaling developed.

Mitchell* in his exploration of SW Vic. found that a whaling station at Portland Bay, 41S/148E, and settlement based on it had anticipated him. Whaling was significant in the first settlement of both W.A. and S.A.

The industry, including sealing, declined in the second half of the 19th century, with occasional revivals. Renewed activity in the 20th century has several times been associated with foreign, particularly Norwegian interests, and the Commonwealth Government took Norwegian advice before setting up the Whaling Commission in 1949. The Commission actually engaged in operations for a few years, setting up the station at Babbage Island near Carnarvon, W.A., 25S/114E, which was sold in 1956 to a private company transferring its activities from another station. Other stations of the 1950s were at Moreton Bay, Qld., 27S/153E, Frenchman Bay near Albany, W.A., 35S/118E, Byron Bay, N.S.W., 29S/153E, and Norfolk Island. The Whaling Commission, operating within the International Whaling Convention of 1946, allots quotas aimed at conservation of the different species.

Japanese whalers operate off the Aus. sector of Antarctic territory.

Wheat The most important single crop in Aus., occupying half the cropland, and is second only to wool in the country's exports. Over two-thirds of the crop is exported, comprising 15% of the world export of wheat from 4% of the wheat acreage. After rapid increases in acreages 1956–8, overproduction led to a quota system on growers. Acreages increased again 1960–72. Exports first grew after the repeal of the British Corn Laws (1845) and extensive wheat-growing developed first in S.A. where suitable land lay near the ports; railways later opened up the other areas. The International Grains Arrangement (1967) ensures the price range and, within Aus., the Wheat Board (1939) guarantees the price for Aus. consumed wheat on a 'cost of production' basis (higher than actual costs) which is also guaranteed on the first 200 million bushels for export. In the 1960s China was taking up to 65% of exports, but ceased to buy 1969–72 causing a serious setback, before returning to the market. Japan, U.K., Malaysia and Russia are important buyers. Flour, though whiter is less protein-rich than the N American type. Wheat is grown mainly with the winter rains (25–65 cm.) in an inland belt in the SW of W.A. (29%); in the Eyre and Yorke Peninsulas of S.A. (14%); on the inner slopes and plains of Vic. (14%) and N.S.W. (36%); increasing summer rains limit this belt on the N, but wheat is grown on the Darling Downs* in Qld. (6%). The Central lowland of Tas., once a granary for the colony, is now insignificant. Good wheat soils include the black earths of Qld. and N N.S.W., and red-brown soils, both formerly supporting grass, open bushland or mallee*, not difficult to clear and fairly easily worked. The topography has also favoured mechanisation which, coupled with labour shortage, stimulated Aus.

inventions such as the stump-jump plough and harvesters (*see* AGRICULTURAL MACHINERY). The grain, harvested in early summer is dry enough to store immediately, and is increasingly bulk-handled both at railheads and ports. Yield per ha. is improving, now averaging 35–50 bushels, compared with 25 earlier this century, but varies seasonally and regionally: the Wimmera* can produce 100 or more, but W.A. under 35. The commonest breeds are Insignia, Heron, Falcon, Olympic, Gabo, but over 40 are in common use, following the work of Farrer* and subsequent research on disease-resistant varieties. Trends are towards intensification of farming within the wheat belts, and retraction from marginal areas, except in W.A. where new land is still being developed. 'Ley farming' with 4–6 year rotations, including sown pasture and stock, is replacing the former wheat/fallow rotation.

Wheat Belt W.A. A distinctive crop region forming a crescent based along the Perth–Albany railway between Northam and Katanning, bulging E to Southern Cross and covering some 150,000 km². The rapid development of the area after 1905, when gold declined, was due to Government loans, surveys and the building of 3,200 km. of feeder railways, to superphosphates and to special breeds based on Farrer's* research, immigration, Soldier Settlement Schemes and mechanisation. Oats, barley and wool are now produced on wheat-belt farms. The grain, harvested November–December, is loaded from storage bins at sidings: the bulk is exported. Rainfall decreases inland from 50 cm. to 25 cm. and the eucalypt vegetation (e.g. salmon gums) was not hard to clear. **The Wheat Belt of E Aus.** is discussed under Wheat* and under New South Wales*, Victoria* and South Australia*.

Wheat Grass (*Agropyron scabrum*) A widespread grassland and open forest grass with a short leafy tuft in winter, but a tall summer seed-head with groups of about 6 spiked seed-heads spaced along it, like barley or spiked wheat. It is palatable to stock, but easily grazed out.

Wheel of Fire (*Stenocarpus sinuatus*) A slender 30-m. tree of deep soil and sheltered sites within the rain-forests of coastal NE Aus. in the largely southern family Proteaceae with the *Banksia, Grevillia* etc. It has coarse, grey bark, 18-cm. deeply lobed leaves, glossy green above and paler below, and the distinctive wheel-like flowers clustered on branchlets in the leaf-forks. The pods are boat-shaped with 2 thin seeds. The timber is useful, and sometimes called White Beef-wood or White Oak.

Whipbirds (genus *Psophodes*—noisy) 2 uniquely Aus. species of generally dark green and black birds with a black, white-edged throat; they roughly resemble large crested thrushes, some 23 cm. long and named from their remarkable call of 2 soft whistles, an explosive whip-like crack and 2 melodious cheeps. The tail is large, and the flight is in short bursts, as in many jungle birds. The Eastern Whipbird, *P. olivaceus*, has more black markings than the comparatively drab Western Whipbird, *P. nigrogularis* (black-throated), which also has a less distinctive call. Whipbirds are usually seen in pairs. The nest is cup-like, but more loosely constructed than in the Shrike-thrushes and the smaller Robins and Flycatchers.

Whip-snakes Include the Yellow-faced Whip-snake of sandstone terrain in E Aus., *Demansia psammophis*, and the Black Whip-snake, *D. olivacea*, of coastal and riverine sands of the far N and N.G. A bite, particularly in the case of a child, from a large specimen, should receive treatment.

White Australia Policy The unofficial term for an early stated Government policy, legalised in the 1901 Restrictive Immigration Act, of maintaining a predominantly European cultural and racial pattern. Based, at least originally, on the concept of racial superiority, it has been and still is defended on the economic need to maintain living standards by preventing cheap labour, and to avoid racial conflicts. Agitation against a potential plantation economy began when squatters tried to replace convicts with coolies in the 1840s; and was exacerbated by the influx of Chinese* to the gold-fields and Kanaka* labour to Qld. The 1901 Act avoided overt exclusion of Asiatics, but effectively prohibited all but a very few from entry by dictation test, now discontinued of 50 words in a 'prescribed language'. The policy has been supported by all parties, including the Aus. Labor Party. The term was unashamedly used and defended by great politicians such as Deakin and Hughes. Attitudes have been conditioned by the proximity of a near-empty continent to the overcrowded Asian plains. The Labor Govt. (1972–) states that 'race will play no part in the selection of new Australians'.

White, General Sir Cyril Brudenell Bingham (1876–1940) b. St. Arnaud,

Eastern Whipbird (Psophodes olivaceus), about quarter life size

Vic. An outstanding military organiser; he served in the Boer War. As Chief of Staff to Bridges*, he helped to organise the A.I.F. and at Gallipoli was largely responsible for the success of the secret Anzac withdrawal and subsequent re-organisation. He served with Lord Birdwood in France and remained Chief of General Staff until 1923. He was recalled to be C.G.S. again in March 1940, but was killed in the disastrous Canberra air-crash of 1940, in which other important leaders were also lost.

White, John (1756–1832) He worked with Phillip in preparation of the First Fleet and as chief surgeon to the Botany Bay settlement. His success in obtaining suitable food and ensuring some hygiene and exercise was largely responsible for the remarkable health of the convicts. In his journal of a *Voyage to New South Wales* (London, 1790) he described it as 'a place so forbidding and hateful as only to merit curses', and resigned rather than return after his leave in 1796.

White, Patrick (Victor Martindale) (1912–) b. London of Aus. parents. He is widely recognised as the major Aus. novelist, taking his place in the mainstream of English literature. His stature lies in the size of his canvas and brilliant craftsmanship with language. He has lived mainly overseas, apart from a brief early period as a jackeroo, and later as a farmer near Sydney. Major works include: *The Tree of Man* (New York, 1955), *Voss* (London and New York, 1957), *Riders in the Chariot* (London, 1961), *The Silver Mandala* (London, 1966) and *The Vivisector* (London, 1970).

White Gum or Poplar Gum (*Eucalyptus alba*) A medium to small tree (to 25 m.) of tropical Aus. It grows in E Qld., and is an important tree of flat to gently undulating terrain in the wetter parts of N.T. and N W.A. along watercourses, and as a stunted 3-m. tree in

drier areas or on very poor skeletal soils. The seedling leaves are somewhat diamond-shaped; the intermediate leaves broadly diamond-shaped and up to 30 cm. long, the adult leaves somewhat narrower and 6–23 cm. long. There are small bunches of ovoid to pointed buds, and rather conical fruit. Bark is smooth, dull and with a powdery bloom, and has white, cream or pink patches. The tree is attractive, the timber fair and used locally.

White-eye An alternative name for the small greenish Silver-eyes*, insect- and nectar-eating birds, sometimes eating orchard fruit.

Whitings The term is used in Aus. for fish not related to English Whitings of the true Cod family, nor to the Aus. Rock Whitings of the Parrot-fish family. They are fairly slender sandy-brown estuarine fish. The jaw is horseshoe-shaped with small teeth. The main species are the small (250–450 g.) Trumpeter Whiting, *Sillago maculata*, with some lines along sides, back fins and tail, the Sand Whiting, *S. ciliata*, about the same size, but only lightly marked, the School Whiting, *S. bassensis*, with rusty blotches and found in rather deeper water, and the rather larger Spotted or King George Whiting, *Sillaginodes punctatus*, found all along the S of Aus. in suitable estuaries and bays.

Whitlam, Edward Gough (1916–) b. Kew, Vic. Prime Minister of Aus., Dec. 1972– . He became Leader of the Federal Labor Party in 1967, and hence of the Opposition, succeeding Arthur Calwell*, and has been M.H.R. for Werriwa, N.S.W. since 1952.

Whyalla S.A. 33S/138E (32,085 in 1971) A rapidly growing industrial city, now the second largest in S.A., with 2 blast furnaces (1941 and 1965), 5 ship-building yards N of the town, making tankers and bulk ore and grain carriers and (recently) an offshore oil-rig, and also electric generator manu-

facture. Iron ore is shipped by B.H.P.*
to N.S.W. and over 10 million tonnes of
iron pellets will go to Japan from 1968–
76. Integrated iron and steel, using the
Basic Oxygen method has been developed. A jetty (1902) from Hummock
Hill was built to send Middleback
Ranges ironstone over to Port Pirie as
flux for lead-smelting. But finding the
ore of high quality, Whyalla was developed by B.H.P. as a company town,
shipping ore to its N.S.W. steelworks.
Concern for industry in the State led
the S.A. Government to stipulate
manufacture in return for leases, and
the 1939–45 War gave the impetus. The
desert environment is ameliorated by
water piped 374 km. from the Murray
(1943) for irrigated dairy pastures and
gardens. Labour turnover among a
largely migrant population is high.

Wickham, Alick A Solomon Islander,
b. 1891, son of a trader, schooled and
employed in Sydney, where later, he
astonished spectators with his double
over-arm swimming stroke, described
by an onlooker as 'crawling' and one
suggested origin of the Aus. Crawl*.
He later undertook stunt diving.

Wickham, John Clements (1798–1864)
b. Leith, Scotland. He was a naval
surveyor and first Moreton Bay Resident (1852–9), where he had the confidence and respect of the settlers. He
had commanded the *Beagle** (1837–41)
on notable survey work.

Wilcannia N.S.W. 32S/143E (936 in
1971) A small, widely important service centre on the Darling in the
Western Plains region, in which residues of its former river-port activity can
still be seen. It is on the Barrier Highway and is a road focus.

WILD FLOWERS They are discussed
from different viewpoints under Flora*
and under Vegetation*. Species likely
to be met in the country and suburbs
are listed by popular names; those with
an asterisk have separate articles, while

the others have popular name, genus
and species names in italics, then the
family name in brackets: Apple Berries,
Billardiera scandens (Pittosporaceae),
climbers with 5-petalled bell, and acidic
edible cylindrical fruit—'dumplings';
Bindi-eye*; Black-eyed Susan (*see*
Heath Pinkeye, below); Bladderwort*;
Blind-grass—*see* LILIES; Bluebell*;
Blue Devil*; Blue Tinsel Lily—*see*
LILIES; Bugle or Australian Bugle,
Ajuga australis (Labiatae), of sandstone
terrain in SE Aus., with coarse rounded
notched leaves near the ground, small
leaves close to the stem, and dark blue-
purple lipped tubular flowers in the leaf
axillae; Buttercups*; Buttons*; Candyup Poison*—*see* LILIES; Chloanthes,
Chloanthes stoechadis (Verbenaceae),
with greenish-yellow flowers, *C. parviflora* (bluish)—both on E Aus. coastal
sandstones, and *C. coccinea* (red) in
W.A.; Christmas Bells*; Christmas
Bush*; Clematis*; Climbers*; Cockspur Flower, *Plectranthus parviflorus*
(Labiatae), a succulent, hairy, toothed-
leaved herb of coastal E Aus., with a
head of blue-purple spurred flowers;
Convolvulus*; Cotton-plants*; Creepers*; Crinum*; Daisies*; Dampiera*;
Desert Rose*; Doryanthes*; Early
Nancy*; Eggs and Bacon—*see* PEAS;
Emu Grass—*see* PEAS; Fairy Lantern*—
see IRIS; Fan Flower*; Finger Flower*;
Five-corners*; Flag—*see* IRIS; Flannel-
flower*; Flax Lily—*see* LILIES; Geraniums*; Goodenia*; Grape*, Wild;
Greenhood—*see* ORCHIDS; Hairy-
tails*; Heath Pinkeye or Black-eyed
Susan, *Tetratheca* spp. (Tremandraceae), a heath with 4-petalled pink
flowers; Helichrysum—*see* EVERLAST-
INGS; Holly, Native—*see* PEAS; Howittia, *Howittia trilocularis* (Malvaceae), of
damp shady gullies in SE Aus., with
dark green heart-shaped leaves and
masses of 2·5-cm. purple flowers; Ipomaea*; Iris*; Kangaroo Paw*; Ladies
Tresses, *Spiranthes sinensis* (Orchidaceae), a terrestrial orchid of damp
coastal and upland sites, except in
W.A., with head of small crimson-and-

white flowers; Leschenaultia*; Lilies*; Love-creepers*; Lucerne, Native—*see* PEAS; Marsh-flower, or Yellow Marsh-flower, *Villarsia exaltata* (Gentian-aceae), with coarse dark leaves and yellow, open, star-shaped flowers on a separate stem; Milkmaid*; Mimulus or Monkey Flowers, *Mimulus repens* (Scrophulariaceae), a low, broad-leaved swamp plant with yellow and blue-purple bells, while *M. gracilis* is more upright; Mirbelia, *Mirbelia speciosa* (Papilionaceae), a small-leaved crim-son-flowered heath plant of E Aus., while the blue-flowered Wedge-leaved Mirbelia, *M. dilatata*, is one of many W.A. species; Mulla Mulla—*see* HAIRY-TAILS; Nightshade*; Orchids*; Pea*; Pigface*; Pincushion, Aus. or Blue Pincushion, *Brunonia australia* (Good-eniaceae), with roundish leaves near the root and cushion-like multiple head of blue-purple flowers with 3 petals and 3 petal-like sepals; Rice Flower*; Rosella*; Native Rosella; Rose Mallow, Rose of Sharon—*see* HIBIS-CUS; Rosemary, Coast Rosemary, *West-ringia rosmariniformis* (Labiatae), a nar-row-leaved compact white-flowered heath resembling European Rosemary; Roses*; St. John's Wort*; Sarsaparilla*; Speedwell, see Veronica below; Star of Bethlehem*; Sturt's Desert Pea*; Sun-dew*; Swamp Lily, *Ottelia ovalifolia* (Hydrocharitaceae), of much of Aus., with rounded floating leaves and large cream-white and red flowers with 3 petals and 3 papery sepals; Trigger Plants*; Vanilla Plant*—*see* LILIES; Veronica or Digger's Speedwell, *Veron-ica perfoliata* (Scrophulariaceae), up to 90 cm., with pairs of prominently veined broad leaves and purple-streaked blue flowers; Violets*; Wandering Jew*; Water-hyacinth*; Water-lilies*; Wax-flowers*; Wonga Wonga Vine, *Pandorea pandorana* (Bignoniaceae), a climber with long heart-shaped leaves, cream-and-red trumpet flowers and long tapering pods; Yellow-eye, *Xyris operculata* (Xyridaceae), rush-like swamp herbs of E and S Aus., with

2·5-cm. yellow papery flowers. (*See also* SHRUBS.) *For further reading see* T. Y. Harris: *Wild Flowers of Aus.* (Sydney, 5th edn., 1962); Nuri Mass: *Australian Wild Flower Magic* (Summer Hill, N.S.W., 1967); C. Barrett: *An Australian Wild Flower Book* (Melbourne, 1942); and the *Jacaranda Wild Flower Guides* (Brisbane, 1967–).

Wilkes 66S/110E An Antarctic Re-search station replaced 1969 by a more modern installation nearby (Casey*). It lay on Vincennes Bay, and was estab-lished by U.S. in 1957; Aus. took over custody and shared scientific work, from 1959.

Willandra Creek or **Billabong** N.S.W. An intermittent distributary of the Lachlan*, leaving the main river about 120 km. SW from Condobolin, 33S/147E, and flowing for over 160 km. roughly W to lose itself in salt-lakes or salt-pans in semi-arid country S of Ivanhoe, 33S/144E. The summer flow has been partly regulated through flood storage in Lake Cargelligo*.

Williamson, David (1942–) b. Mel-bourne. A writer earning widespread recognition in Aus. and overseas with work including the plays *Don's Party* and *The Removalist* (1971).

Williamson, James Cassius (1845–1913) b. Pennsylvania, U.S. He arrived in Aus. in 1874 as an actor in a comic melodrama, *Struck Oil*, with his wife Maggie Moore (1851–1926) a popular actress for many years. He acquired the sole Aus. rights to Gilbert and Sullivan operas from 1879. His Comic Opera Company became J. C. William-son Theatres Ltd. in 1904 ('The Firm') which, with control by Taits after 1931 came to dominate the popular Aus. theatre. *See* V. Tait: *A Family of Brothers* (Melbourne, 1970).

Williamson, Malcolm (1931–) b. Syd-ney. A composer, living overseas, with a worldwide reputation, notably in opera with audience participation, such as *The Stone Wall* (1971).

Willochra Plains S.A. 32S/138E A depression at 300 m., 95 km. N–S by 30 km. E–W, E of the towering Flinders Range. The salty Willochra Creek, usually dry, is capable of dangerous flash floods. Formerly wheat country (1860–80) it is now marginal grazing land.

Willow (*Salix* spp.) A moisture-loving tree which was very early introduced, and is now naturalised along many watercourses in Aus., especially the Weeping Willow, *S. babylonica*, which gives welcome shade by many a swimming hole.

Willow, Native, Butterbush or **Weeping Pittosporum** Popular names for *Pittosporum phyllyroides*, a graceful narrow-leaved yellow-flowered and rather birch-like tree of Central Aus., now reduced through browsing by stock; it belongs to the largely southern family *Pittosporaceae*. Like related species in wetter areas, its fruit capsule carries sticky orange-red seeds.

Wills, William John (1834–1861) b. Devon, Eng. He emigrated in 1852, and was appointed third in command of the Great Northern Exploration Expedition (1860–1) under Burke*, later becoming second-in-command. Wills's journal is the only record of this tragic journey during which he died, with Burke and Grey.

Willy Wagtail (*Rhipidura leucophrys*), *about quarter life size*

Willy Wagtail (*Rhipidura leucophrys* —white-browed fantail) A Flycatcher* familiar in most parts of Aus. in town and country, sallying forth from a perch or a bullock's back to catch an insect with well-judged aerobatics. It has a pleasant repetitive call, sometimes represented as 'sweet pretty creature', at times nocturnal. Like other Flycatchers, it makes a well-finished cup-like nest which is often completed with cobwebs and lichen.

Willy Willy A fierce brief squall or very localised small whirlwind.

Wilpena Pound S.A. 31S/139E An isolated quartzite plateau in the N Flinders Range; the surface dips to a central depression of 57 km.[2] from an encircling escarpment, following the rock strata. St. Mary's Peak on the E rim is 1,189 m. The only access is by the 1·6 km. gorge of the sporadic Wilpena Creek, on the E. Sugar gum, *Eucalyptus cladocalyx*, acacia and grass support pastoral properties and there is increasing tourist traffic.

Wilson, John (died 1800) He was transported with First Fleet for theft; on expiry of his term he 'went bush' and was accepted by the Aborigines. His acquired bushcraft was put to use by Governor Hunter who put him in charge of 2 expeditions into the mountains in 1798. During the first, when he was in charge of 4 Irish convicts looking for an alleged Chinese civilisation in which they believed, he found the first lyrebirds and koala. The second penetrated to the Berrima region. Wilson was killed by Aborigines with whom he had returned to live.

Wilson or **Wilson's Promontory** Vic. 39S/147E The southernmost point of the Aus. mainland; it is a granite peninsula very literally almost an island, for it is linked to the mainland by the multiple beach ridges of Yanakie, now much overgrazed and eroding. The bare granite flanks below the lighthouse on its S tip plunge straight into the sea, often with ocean swell licking far up the slopes. There are several hills of 600 m. in the area, and since 1908 it has been a National Park of over 40,000 ha., a fine association of mainly dry sclerophyll* forest and little altered fauna. However, in places it is degraded by fire and overgrazing, and now threatened by difficult problems of tourist access.

Wilson, William Hardy (1881–1955) b. Sydney. An architect. He recorded and wrote up the old Colonial period of architecture and became the most successful exponent of its revival in the 1920s.

Wiluna W.A. 27S/120E A declining town, originally a railhead and gold settlement. Both functions having ceased, it remains the service centre for a wide pastoral area; its fine stone buildings are a record of past prosperity.

Wimmera A region of about 24,000 km.² in NW Vic. centred on Horsham, 37S/142E, lying between the Loddon River and the S.A. border, and sloping N from the Grampians* to the Mallee*. Rich Chernozem soils* cover wide areas, but variable winter rainfall of about 45 cm. made it an uncertain farming area in the basin of internal drainage of the N-flowing **Wimmera River,** which dissipates in anabranches, and Lakes Hindmarsh and Albacutya*. But the **Wimmera Mallee Domestic and Stock Supply System,** largely developed since the opening of Rockland Dam* (1953), uses the water thus diverted from the S-flowing Glenelg, along with water from the Murray and from subartesian bores. Intensive cropping for wheat has been carried on for over a century, with the highest yields in Aus. Identification of a zinc deficiency in the 1930s allowed rapid expansion.

Windmill Grass (*Chloris truncata*) An evocative popular name for an Aus. representative of a warm country genus with several stems spreading round a circular tuft of low foliage, each bearing 6–9 seed stems, the seeds angled below the stem, well spread like windmill sails or an open umbrella. It gives some fodder in early summer.

Windsor N.S.W. 34S/151E (11,357 in 1971 now including Richmond) One of 5 towns, sited by Macquarie in 1810 in the area previously known and farmed as Green Hills, to be above the troublesome Hawkesbury* floods (in fact inundating low parts of the modern town after exceptional storms). The church, built 1817–22, was designed by Greenway*. There are some manufactures (food-processing, plastics, clothing) and many commuters to Sydney in recent years.

WINES All types, including brandy, are made in Aus. with a total of 150–180 million litres a year; consumption is about 5·4 litres a head. The main contrasts with European wines are: fewer varieties since growing districts are fewer; quality is more stable from year to year, since summer sunshine is more reliable, which also makes the majority of wines sweeter and heavier; and the average quality must be reasonable as there is no large-scale market for cheap *vin ordinaire*. Organisation is mainly in the hands of large companies, including Penfolds, Seppelts, McWilliam, Lindeman, Hardy, Gramp, Wynn, Mildara, Smith (Yalumba), Reynell, Hamilton, Martin, Angove and Leo Buring. They own their own vineyards in different parts of the country and also buy from small growers. Blending is a major Aus. characteristic in winemaking, in general with good results, although it may be sometimes concealed by deceptive labelling. There are also many long established family wineries, a few attached to monasteries, and some Co-operatives; all these use local grapes only. City wholesalers may also undertake their own blending. Nomenclature is confused, for European terms used may have varying connotations. Broadly: *sherries* are dry, medium (called amontillado) or sweet, the latter very similar to the fortified dessert wines, muscats, ports and madeiras that were long the main Aus. wines; *white wines* marketed young, include acidic types called riesling (less commonly hock or moselle) and non-acid types called chablis or white burgundy, and on the whole more successful; sauternes are sweeter yet and are achieved by later picking, or by blending. Of the *red wines*, clarets are the astringent acidic variety, often with distinct flavours, while softer fuller reds are the burgundies. *Sparkling wines*, carbonated by natural-tank or bottle-fermentation or by artificial methods, are called pearl, champagne, sparkling burgundy, moselle or hock.

In S.A., which produces 75% of Aus. wines, the main region is along the Mt. Lofty Ranges*; soils are often calcareous and thin, summers long and hot. 1. Clare-Watervale, 34S/139E, makes acidic table wines; there is a Co-operative winery, and families include Birks, Buring, Sobels, Knappstein. 2. Barossa Valley*, 35S/139E, has major company wineries and old German family names, including Henschke, Falkenburg, Thumm. Fortified wines in the main valley contrast with the dry white wines from the podsolic upland soils nearby in the Eden-Springfield area. 3. Adelaide environs include the home of Penfold's at Magill. 4. Southern Vales where, as in the Adelaide region, urban encroachment is reducing the area; but famous families include Ingoldby and Robertson, and the Reynella Co. is centred here; astringent firm red and white table wines are made. 5. Coonawarra, 37S/143E, in the SE of the State (Wynn, Mildara, Lindeman) produces very acidic, distinctly flavoured red wines on pockets of soil derived from limestone. 6. The Murray irrigation areas in S.A. and Vic. and on the Murrumbidgee* in N.S.W. grow vines mainly for dried fruit, but also produce the bulk of Aus. brandy, and heavy mediocre table wines, sold cheaply or used in blending.

Vic. has two main areas. 1. Great Western (N of Ararat, 37S/143E) where the Thomson family and Seppelts produce acidic red wines, and sparkling burgundies and champagne on poor granitic gravels. 2. NE Vic. between Rutherglen and Milawa, 36S/146E, has many old family wineries, including Sutherland Smith, Buller and Booth, producing heavy red and fortified wines on gravelly soils derived from igneous rocks. There are new vineyards near Portland, 38S/142E.

N.S.W., apart from the irrigated areas, wineries became concentrated round Pokolbin, 33S/151E, S of the Hunter River and, more recently, upstream at Muswellbrook. Soils are alluvials flanking poor sandstone uplands. Families include Drayton, Tulloch, Elliott, Tyrrell and big company wineries. The main wines are heavy soft burgundies, and much goes for blending.

W.A. produces sweet fortified wines and a very fine white burgundy along the Swan River.

Historical Development Captain Phillip brought vines from S Africa in 1788 and Macarthur* used his European exile to study viticulture as well as sheep, and had planted the first commercial vineyards by 1827 near Penrith. The real father of the industry was James Busby, who in 1832 at the instigation of the British Government, brought out 20,000 cuttings and began wine-making in the Hunter Valley. Vineyards were widespread in the following decades when it was hoped to establish Aus. as England's main source of wines. Reduction, by economic factors and *Phylloxera*, drastically reduced acreages by the end of the century; S.A. escaped the disease. There was a further period of over-planting in the early 20th century, followed by rapid reduction in the 1930s and 1940s, and a resurgence since the early 1950s when home demand in-

creased. The mainstay has been fortified sweet dessert wines, cheap and
strong and nicknamed variously 'Red
Ned' or 'Plonk' (probably a soldier's
version of *vin blanc* from the 1914–18
War). But in the last 2 decades table
wines have risen from 4% to 40% of the
market. The Aus. Wine Research
Institute (1955) is based at Glen Osmond, S.A. The Aus. Wine Board
co-ordinates exports, now in the region
of 9 million litres a year, and runs
the Aus. Wine Centre in London. *For
further reading see* D. F. Murphy:
The Australian Wine Guide (Melbourne,
1966); M. Lake: *Classic Wines of
Australia* (Melbourne, 1966); and A.
Simon: *The Wines, Vineyards and
Vignerons of Australia* (Melbourne,
1967).

Wingen, Mount or **Burning Mountain**
N.S.W. 32S/151E (549 m.) It rises
about 244 m. above the Page River, a
right-bank tributary of the Hunter*.
From its first observation in 1828,
smoke—at first taken as volcanic—has
been emitted from a long cleft in the
hillside. This arises from slow combustion of Permian coal of the Greta
seam deep underground, perhaps at
some 475 m. down, probably by
spontaneous combustion and quite
possibly started thousands of years ago,
though likely to be restricted in the
future by a fault a few miles to the S
which cuts off the coal-seam (however,
the leading edge of the fire is only
moving S at about 10 cm. a year).

Winstanley, Eliza (1818–1882) b. Eng.
She arrived in Aus. in 1828 and became
the dominant actress in Aus. (1834–48).
She played successfully in Eng. (including Windsor Castle), before turning
to writing popular novelettes and an
autobiography.

Winton Qld. 22S/143E (1,307 in 1971;
A railhead and cattle centre between
the Channel Country* and the main
Qld. pastoral belt bordering the Divide,
with rail access to both Townsville and

Rockhampton. It is also the terminus
of a main Beef Road from Boulia.

Wire-grass, Tangle Grass or **Wiry Rice-
grass** Popular names for *Tetrarrhena
juncea*, a scrambling grass of N.S.W.,
Vic. and Tas. forests, with small sharp
barbs along the stems.

Wittenoom W.A. 22S/118E An asbestos mine and town, active from 1938
until 1966 when low prices and high
costs forced its closure. Bought by
local pastoralist-prospecting partners,
it is likely to revive with development of
large iron-ore resources nearby; access
roads have been built and export from
Cape Lambert to Europe is planned.

Wobbegong or **Carpet Shark** A rather
flat, broad Shark*, round-snouted from
above, its brown body patterned like a
Paisley shawl or a carpet.

Wobblies The nickname for the small
left-wing political movement, Industrial
Workers of the World, which reached
Aus. from America in 1907. They agi-
tated against the war and conscription.
In 1916 12 were imprisoned on charges
of sedition and conspiracy to burn
Sydney buildings. I. Turner, in *Sydney's
Burning* (London, 1967), deduces that
the trial, which led to 2 later Royal
Commissions, was a 'frame-up' to
discredit the movement at the time of
W. M. Hughes's conscription* cam-
paign.

Wodonga Vic. 36S/147E (10,533 in
1971, part of Albury*, N.S.W.) In the
Murray flood-plain on the opposite
bank from Albury*; it was once a
customs post. In addition to important
stock markets, there has been recent
industrial and population growth;
there are sawmills, concrete and fertiliser works.

Wolf Spiders A popular name for the
family Lycosidae, with carapace high in
front, and conspicuous patterns, such
as the genus *Lycosa*, which has radial
patterns of grey, or black and white on

the carapace, and white bands on the back of the abdomen. The Wolf Spiders include some species found in wet places; others hunt from burrows in arid areas, which have a lightly-hinged door folding flat on the ground when opened, in contrast with the Trap-door Spiders*.

Wollomombi Falls N.S.W. 31S/152E One of the world's great falls though normally of small volume except after heavy rains. Here the Wollomombi River has a sheer drop of over 336 m. and a total drop of 480 m. down the E escarpment of the New England* plateau; the Chandler River nearby falls by smaller steps, to join and ultimately flow into the Macleay.

Wollondilly River N.S.W. The upper course of the Hawkesbury*.

Wollongong N.S.W. 34S/151E (185,890 in 1971, Greater Wollongong with Port Kembla and Shellharbour) A rapidly growing steel-making city. Early export trade in cedar timber (*Toona australis*) started small port activity from arti-ficial harbours at both Wollongong and Port Kembla, and this was transformed to coal export for a more populous hinterland, with the exploitation of the thick high-quality seams such as the Bulli (named from a seaside mining village just N of the city). The structure of this S part of the Wollongong-Lith-gow-Newcastle coal-field can largely be exploited by adits driven into the E-facing escarpment behind the narrow coastal belt. Breakwaters and wharves at Port Kembla were the more de-veloped, and it became the dominant port, selected in 1896 for the provision of coal-exporting facilities. In 1928 came the long-foreshadowed develop-ment of steelworks (*see* IRON AND STEEL *and* B.H.P.); and from 1955 the dredging of the Inner Harbour from Tom Thumb's Lagoon to extend the facilities needed for a major centre of integrated iron and steel production, expanding to a capacity of over 6 million tonnes a year, with associated heavy and ancil-lary industries, copper-refining, refrac-tories and other bricks, chemicals, fertilisers etc. Industries using female labour have at times been less than the demand, but include textiles, clothing, knitwear, shoes, confectionery and other food-processing, and costume jewellery, as well as a set of tertiary industries, large and growing, though it is perhaps less of a regional centre than is Newcastle*. A largely technical col-lege has developed into the Wollongong University College of the University of N.S.W. The city's growth has extended until its suburbs embrace former mining villages, e.g. Thirroul (the 'Mullumimby' of D. H. Lawrence's *Kangaroo*), the former port of Shell-harbour across the bridged mouth of Lake Illawarra*, and lakeside ex-tensions, e.g. Dapto and Oak Flats. *For further reading see Sublime Vision* (Council of Greater Wollongong, 1963); and R. S. Mathieson: *Illawarra and the South Coast Region* (Melbourne, 1960).

Wombats (family Phascolomidae) With 2 living genera *Phascolomis* and *Lasior-hinus* they are burrowing marsupials of bear-like or badger-like appearance, and belong to the more vegetarian of the Marsupials*. *P. ursinus*, a smallish species of Tas. and the Bass Str. Islands, was reported in 1797, and the popular name Wombat was adopted from an Aboriginal name near the Nepean River in 1798. All the wombats have a

Common Wombat
(*Phascolomis mitchelli*), *over 1 m. long*

heavy compact build, a rudimentary tail, short head and small eyes, stout legs and broad clawed feet well adapted for digging; their chisel-like incisors, easily capable of cutting tree-roots, and grinding molars all grow continually (a recent observer points out remarkable superficial resemblance to the teeth of the Ground-squirrel or Marmot of Central Asia). The female has a pouch containing 2 teats. The young, usually a single one, is born in autumn, is nourished in the pouch over the winter, and is weaned in the spring. Though seeming slow-moving and slow-thinking, wombats can move at a fast shuffle, or clumsy but effective gallop.

The Common Wombat, *P. mitchelli*, the largest, is up to 1·2 m. in length; it is found in residual forests in SE Aus. The Wombat is not protected; in fact there is a scalp bounty in places. It may burrow under rabbit or dingo fences, and the burrows may harbour rabbits during extermination campaigns or can be dangerous to horses. As they are graminivorous, Wombats raid crops. The Common Wombat has very coarse hair, and makes a burrow of 3–5 m. long from the base of a rock or tree, ending in a leaf-lined nest.

The softer furred Hairy-nosed Wombat, *Lasiorhinus latifrons* (hairy-nosed, broad-fronted), was formerly widespread in drier, savannah woodland country from S.A. to Qld., but now only in patches, e.g. the Blanchetown area W of the lower Murray where a sanctuary is being developed. They use communal warrens, some very long.

Wonga Wonga Vine A widely used popular name for climbers of the genus *Pandorea* in the Trumpet-flower family Bignoniaceae, especially *P. pandorana*, which has long heart-shaped leaves, cream-and-red flowers and long tapering pods to 8 cm. long. *Pandorea* is also called Bower Plant.

Wonthaggi Vic. 39S/146E (4,436 in 1971) 8 km. inland, it developed after 1908 when the Vic. Government opened up Jurassic black coal for railway use, to overcome the need to import N.S.W. coal held up by a strike. Thin faulted seams, and competition from brown coal for power and diesel oil for trains led to closure (1968), with replacement by clothing and engineering industries.

Wood, George Arnold (1865–1928) b. Salford, Lancashire. He arrived in Sydney in 1891 to take up the first Chair in History. His *Discovery of Australia* (London, 1922) is a classic and still a standard, though controversial text.

Wood-lice The terrestrial genera of the Isopoda Order of the Crustaceans*, often also known as Slaters, Carpenters and Sow-bugs. Garden Wood-lice or Slaters, slate-grey above and yellow-green below, may be the introduced *Porcellio scaber* or *Metaporthus pruinosus*, but there are also native species. Despite their broad back and numerous legs, they can roll into a ball with great speed. There are freshwater Isopods, including some blind subterranean species and some with eyes living in borewaters in Central Aus. For marine genera—*see* SEA-LICE.

Woodpeckers A popular name sometimes given to the small brown-black Tree-creepers* and Sittellas*, often seen crawling up tree-trunks in search of insects. The true woodpecker is not found in Aus.

Woods, Lake N.T. 18S/133E In the centre of a small internal drainage area in the W of the Barkly Tableland, fed by Newcastle Creek seasonally, but generally dry.

Wood-swallows Of 5 or 6 species, they are found in open woodland to savannah country in various parts of Aus, and the islands to the N. They are medium-sized birds (15–23 cm. long), not related to swallows, but superficially resembling them in their swift graceful flight to catch insects on the wing, though some also eat nectar; they alight much more often than swallows or swifts. Sociable, they sometimes cluster close to a tree almost like a swarm of bees. The grey-winged, brown Dusky Wood-swallow, *Artamus cyanopterus* (blue-winged butcher), inhabits much of the S of Aus., the white-breasted Black-faced Wood-swallow much of inland Aus., extending into SE Asia; it overlaps with the masked Wood-swallow, *A. personatus*, which is grey and buff with a black face edged with white, the White-browed Wood-swallow, *A. superciliosus*, black-faced and orange-rust breasted, and the quiet-hued grey and orange-brown Little Wood-swallow, *A. minor.*

Wool Aus. produces over 900 million kg. of (greasy) wool a year, about one third of the world total and half of its fine merino wool. The main buyer is Japan, followed by U.K., U.S., Italy, France and W Germany. China has also recently bought Aus. wool. Wool is sheared by well-organised itinerant teams, often living in special 'quarters' and working in large sheds on an agreed rate per 100 sheep; an average sheared is 100–120 per day, but the record (1972) is 347. Shearers have been important in the Aus. 'image' and the Labor and Trade Union* movements.

After 'skirting' to remove poor, dirty 'crutchings', the wool is classed—by the farmer on smaller farms, by professional classers on large ones—according to its fineness. Grading is based on the estimated number of 'hanks' from a given weight. It is then compressed into bales of about 135 kg. of 20–30 fleeces, the average per fleece being a little over 4·5 kg. (highest in S.A., lowest in Tas.).

Over 90% is auctioned, but private buying has been important in W.A. There are 14 centres with large stores, and an annual programme is agreed in advance. Buyers assemble from 50 countries. Price fluctuation and sus-

pected manipulation among brokers led to investigation and the establishment of the Aus. Wool Board (1963), financed by a 2% levy on growers, to promote sales and research. In Nov. 1970 the Aus. Wool Commission was set up to operate a 'flexible reserve price scheme' as a buyer at wool auctions, the Government meeting any losses incurred. In 1972 the Wool Board and the Wool Commission were amalgamated as the Aus. Wool Marketing Corporation, which may in time acquire the total wool crop. Unexpectedly competitive bidding, mainly by Japan, emerging from a recession with low stocks in 1972, led to boom prices: the record of 501 cents a kg. beat the 1951 record price of 440. Average prices were over 50% higher than 1971 and the export value four times higher in spite of 164 million fewer sheep and 78 million kg. less wool which reflected widespread slaughtering following very low prices 1970–2. (*See* SHEEP, MERINO *and* TEXTILES.)

Woollybutts A name given to species of *Eucalyptus** with smooth flaking bark on the upper parts of the trunk, and rough, finely fibrous, loose bark below. In Vic. it is used for *E. delegatensis*, Alpine Ash, a tall tree with open crown, on well-drained soils in mountain areas. In N.S.W. *E. longifolia* is a coastal tree, with dense crown and hanging branches, on deep alluvium (*see also* BLUE GUMS, EASTERN GROUP). Darwin Woollybutt, *E. miniata*, is not closely related; it grows to 15–25 m. on sandy to laterite soils in the 75- to 150-cm. monsoon rain belt; yielding timber of local importance.

Woomera S.A. 31S/137E (4,069 in 1971, with Maralinga*) A town established in 1947, housing workers associated with the test-firing of rockets by the Weapons Research Establishment which is based at Salisbury, N of Adelaide. It is a joint Aus.–U.K. enterprise, set up in 1946–7 under

Sir John Evatts and W. A. S. Butement. A U.S. space tracking station is at Island Lagoon 22 km. away. Water is pumped along a branch pipe of the Morgan-Whyalla pipeline from Port Augusta, and every effort is made to make desert living tolerable. The range crosses an Aboriginal reserve and the name was taken from a type of throwing-stick; recovery tracks now cross the desert.

WORLD WAR, FIRST As part of the British Empire, Aus. was immediately committed to a state of war when it was declared at midnight, August 4th 1914, although most Australians were largely unaware of the sequence or significance of European events leading to the outbreak. There was instant wholehearted and enthusiastic response by both political parties, and by the people, followed by organisation of an expeditionary force of 20,000 by Bridges* and White*. Volunteers far exceeded this, allowing rigorous selection and so a very impressive degree of fitness in the force, which was trained initially on improvised drilling grounds, and in main centres at Liverpool and Melbourne. It embarked (with N.Z. troops) on 38 (including 10 N.Z.) transports at Albany, W.A., on November 1st. Later the name Anzacs was used. The escort included the battle cruiser *Sydney* which destroyed the German raider *Emden* at Cocos Islands on November 9th.

Campaigns After further training in Egypt, the Anzacs with Birdwood as G.O.C., embarked in early April for the Dardanelles, to take part in the doomed Gallipoli* Campaign. After the withdrawal, they were divided: 4 infantry divisions went to the Western Front and 3 brigades of the mounted troops, under Chauvel*, went to Sinai. Before Allenby's forces arrived in 1917, the Anzacs were the main Middle-East force, clearing the Turks from Sinai. Their bushcraft, horsemanship and dash made them excellent desert troops; particular exploits included

Beersheba oasis, Romani (1916) and Damascus (1918), and they took part in over 30 other major engagements, losing over 1,000 men. In France the Anzacs were recognised as invaluable shock troops, often spear-heading attacks: July–October 1916, on the Somme, 21,000 men were lost in 9 weeks in actions such as the capture of Pozières; 1917: the April–June offensive saw Anzacs at famous actions of Bullecourt, Messine, Hill 60, Polygon Wood; autumn, the Passchendaele and Ypres battles made up a total of 20,000 Aus. dead for the year, from a total of 120,000 Anzacs on the Western Front at the beginning of 1917. 1918: in the March spring offensive (in the planning of which Monash* was prominent) Anzacs were outstanding at Amiens; and in holding the German counter offensive at Villes Bretonneux (where the Aus. war memorial stands), but, most important, they were in the spearhead of the final push from August 8th, notably capturing Mont St. Quentin, and at the breaking of the Hindenberg Line. Losses (10,000) were less in 1918 because of better shelling preparation before infantry attacks, again due, partly at least, to Monash.

The Navy, in addition to the *Emden* sinking, and working with the Royal Navy, took part in patrol and escort duty, and at the outset was responsible for taking over the German Pacific possessions in N.G. and Samoa. There were Aus. airmen in Mesopotamia and in France. The total enlistment was 416,809: overseas service, 331,781; killed 59,342; wounded, 152,171; total casualties of 226,000 included victims of malaria in the Middle East, trench fever, dysentery etc. in France and were the highest in proportion to population in the Empire.

Domestic Affairs were affected radically: a general election (September 1914) resolved the current political deadlock, returning the Labor Government which passed a widely enabling War Precautions Act, introduced censorship, alien internment, and tried to establish industries to make Aus. self-sufficient in producing uniforms and ammunition, although this proved impossible in the case of heavy shells and guns; 42 S.A. place names were changed from the German. Hughes* succeeded Fisher* and became the dominant Aus. personality of the war. Having visited U.K. in 1916, he was convinced of the need for conscription*, which became the major domestic issue, leading in 1916 to the splitting of the Labor Party and the formation of a fusion of former Labor and Liberal Parties in a National Party committed to all-out war efforts. By 1917, however, war-weariness, disillusionment, lowered living standards and militant unionism led to a series of grave industrial disputes. Guaranteed Government purchases of wool, wheat, butter and beef gave security for development of primary industry in spite of severe storage and shipping problems (Hughes bought a Government fleet to overcome this). B.H.P.* opened its blast furnaces at Newcastle in April 1915; previous German domination of the metals industry was replaced by domestic smelting, notably the Risdon (Tas.) zinc smelter; secondary industry added 400 articles to its list of manufactures. Loss of overseas markets outside the Empire, and drying up of external capital investment were adverse factors. Most important was the increased Commonwealth power vis-à-vis the States—Commonwealth Income Tax (1915), and country-wide price and profiteering controls (not entirely successful). The war cost Aus. £364 million and a subsequent £270 million in pensions up to 1939; most of it was raised by loans rather than taxation. The results of the war for Aus. were serious in the big loss of men in their prime, and in the domestic strife, notably over conscription, which left a long-lasting bitterness still evident, and the problems of rehabilitation and soldier settlement. But there was posi-

tive gain too: the intangible, but very real 'proving' of nationhood in the Anzac exploits; the tangible boost to economic growth both in primary and secondary industry; and the pugnaciously fought-for concessions Hughes achieved at Versailles, where he resisted Wilson's idealism with stern outspoken realism, and gained Aus. a 'C' Mandate over N.G., amounting to indefinite and complete control, including N.G. immigration policy, and in the defeat of the Japanese-sponsored Racial Equality Clause—both ultimately in defence of a White Australia*.

WORLD WAR, SECOND Aus. was at war immediately it was declared; the Menzies Government with no hesitation, and Labor under Curtin, pledging defence of Aus. and the integrity of the British Commonwealth, although Labor was more whole-hearted after the German invasion of Russia in 1941. *Campaigns* A second A.I.F. was formed under Blamey* and sent to the Middle East, followed by the 7th division in May 1940, where they were involved against unsuccessful Italian thrusts toward Suez. In April–May 1941 Aus. forces suffered heavily as rear-guards in the Greece–Crete campaigns, and in the successful operations in Syria in June that year. Aus. cruisers were important in the vital Cape Matapan battle to hold open the eastern Mediterranean in March 1941. The beleaguered Tobruk 'Rats', cut off by German advances in mid year, included 4 Aus. brigades and were relieved by largely Aus. forces in December 1941, only to be pushed rapidly eastwards in the first half of 1942 by Rommel. In October 1942 the 9th division served under Montgomery and took part in the Alamein victory and final defeat of N African Axis forces in January 1943. The R.A.A.F. had 17 squadrons in U.K. in 1942.

Meanwhile, the Japanese attack on Pearl Harbour and Asian landings on

December 7th 1941, brought close and vital involvement of Aus. troops near home. Over 15,000 were captured at Singapore in February 1942, and on February 19th the bombing of Darwin (and later Broome and Wyndham) led the Government to refuse the diversion of the 7th Division, on its way back from the Middle East, to Burma as requested from London. By March 1942 Japanese land forces were within reach of Port Moresby and the final isolation of Aus. Their sea expedition to capture the town turned back after the engagement with Aus. and U.S. forces in the Coral Sea Battle*. There were submarine attacks off the E coast and 2 midget submarines in Sydney Harbour. The turning-point came at the end of 1942, but the long slow war of attrition until 1944 involved many casualties in the vicious guerilla and mopping-up operations which fell to Aus. forces under MacArthur's island-hopping strategy. The campaigns speeded up after European victory in 1944, and ended with the atomic bombs on Japan in 1945. Aus. forces comprised much of the British Commonwealth Occupation Force in Japan.

Total enlistment:	691,400
Killed:	29,400
Prisoners (of the Japanese, nearly 8,000 died):	22,000

Domestic Affairs There was a repeated historical pattern when a Labor Prime Minister emerged as a leader of great stature: Curtin with a notable team, including Chifley and Evatt, was able to have unpalatable curtailments of individual liberty accepted. These included man-power direction, rationing of petrol and some foodstuffs, restrictions on travel, investment, building and the extension of conscription. These were combined with the beginning of the socialist programme of legislation which came in a spate after 1945. The economy again received a stimulus in the manufacturing industry, but while farmers were given guaranteed sales and prices, drought, labour and fertiliser shortage (notably Nauru Island phosphates) offset these to some extent. The cost of the war (£1,200 million) was met, two-thirds by taxation and one-third by internally raised loans, and supplemented by lend-lease arrangements with U.S. (the £8 million owing was largely absorbed in Fulbright scholarships after the war). The Commonwealth invasion of States' powers, evident in the First War, was even more marked, with ultimate financial control established in 1942, when a uniform income tax replaced varying States taxation, and in return the States received a negotiated grant.

The manpower loss was less severe; the economic results were, on the whole, favourable; the national maturity increased by the needs, as the leaders saw it, to re-orientate to Pacific alliances. An official War History, *Aus. in the War of 1939-45*, has been written.

Worm Snake, Blind Snake, Glass Snake Slow Worm or Glow Worm (family Typhlopidae) These are completely harmless snakes, superficially like very large worms and preying on worms, larvae, pupae and adult insects; they are mainly underground though often emerging at night. They have only rudimentary eyes, seen as bluish marks under transparent scales, no fangs, and small teeth only on the upper jaw; they have highly polished scales and often a sharpish nose adapted to pushing through the earth—and sometimes a tail spine with which to push forward. There are over 20 species in Aus., but many have only been identified a few times. The dark brown to pinkish-backed, pink-bellied *Typhlops nigrescens*, of up to 30-40 cm., exceptionally 75 cm., is common under rotting logs and leaf-mould from S Qld. to Vic.; it is slender in youth, thicker in old age. Similar species are found in N Aus. *T. proximus* is found in E Aus., in woodlands or under compost-heaps etc.; it is bulbous-nosed and reaches 50 cm. *T. bituberculatus* is common all over the southern half of Aus.; it grows to 38 cm., and has a very distinctive nose, showing a main ridge from above like a fingernail, with 2 smaller side ridges, while from the side it has something of a hooked-beak appearance. *T. australis* also extends right across the S of the continent; the nose shows a single central ridge from above, a blunter hooked snout from the side, and though growing only to 50 cm. it has a particularly long and slender appearance, for it may be 12 mm. or even less in diameter.

Worms A popular name for long soft-bodied animals classified in quite different Classes and even Phyla, and also much more loosely of insect larvae, small snakes and even skin fungi such as in 'ringworm'. (*See* EARTHWORMS; FLUKES; HELMINTHS; HYDATIDS; LAND PLANARIANS; LEECHES; *and* MARINE WORMS.)

Wowser A person who is piously and puritanically opposed to any activities giving joy or pleasure. The term is claimed by John Norton, an editor of the 1890s, as his invention to describe a kill-joy counsellor, but based on a widely used verb 'to wow', meaning to whine and complain. It has been adopted into American and British English.

Woy Woy N.S.W. 34S/152E (Part of Gosford*, with Umina, Blackwell, Booker Bay, Ettalong and Pearl Beach) A resort and commuter town N of Sydney, with recent manufactures, mainly of clothing.

Wrasse A mainly tropical family of medium-sized sea-fish. 1. *Tiricoris sandeyeri rex*, has a blunt snout and tail, the latter fanning out a little from a thick base, and notably a long dorsal fin and rear belly fin; colours may be brilliant reds, greens and blues but variable with age. 2. The Combfish or Banana fish, *Ctenocorissa picta*, is rather long and graceful, cream with a broad black mid-stripe along its side, with downward strokes like a comb; it reaches 25 cm. 3. The Maori, *Ophthalmolepis lineolatus*, is rather larger, silvery, and yellow-bellied, with a pink or black side stripe. 4. The very small Cleaner, *Labroides dimidiatus*, has striking blue and black stripes and white belly, and quite specialised to its tasks of freeing larger fish of food debris, parasites etc., which gain it such tolerance from larger species that it has been worth the while of a carnivorous blenny to imitate its colouring in order to prey on larger fish. 5. The Doubleheader, *Coris cyanea*, is large blue to greenish fish; the large hump, like a forehead, is absent in the brown-and-yellow juvenile form. 6. The Jawslinger, Sling-jaw or Telescope-fish, *Epibulus insidiator*, has, as its name implies, rather protruding lips, extensible to catch its prey. 7. The Keelheaded Wrasse, *Novaculichthys jacksoniensis*, has an extremely blunt snout, but a thin keel to enable it to burrow rapidly in sand.

Wrens In Aus. this is a term perhaps most appropriately applied to the *Malurus* spp. (soft-tailed), sometimes distinguished as Fairy Wrens. There are about a dozen species of Fairy Wrens, small, sharp-beaked insectivorous birds of heath and shrubs (and of suburban gardens for some species). They have slender legs, a small rounded body and a long, frequently erect tail; they are perpetually alert and moving the head, ready to fuss and scold and give the first alert of an enemy. The cock birds have bright plumage during the breeding season, in many species often blue, blue and white, or blue and red, fading in brilliance in winter. The females are predominantly a modest dark brown with light brown-white underparts, but often with a bluish tail. The normal call is a thin but vigorous warble. The nests are often fur- or feather-lined domes of grass, bark etc in a low bush or tall grass, with a side or top entrance. The Blue Wren, *M. cyaneus*, of S Qld. to Tas. and the S of S.A., may be taken as representative of several species of mainly blue-coloured wrens (*see* PLATE 3). The Variegated Wren, *M. lamberti*, of E Aus. has red upper wings, as also has the Blue-breasted Wren, *M. pulcherrimus*, of S.A. to SW Aus. The Red-backed Wren, *M. melanocephalus*, of much of tropical Aus. is very black in general appearance, but with a brilliant crescent of red across the back.

The popular name 'wren' is extended to include several birds not very closely related including the Emu-wren, *Stipiturus* (stem-tailed) *malachurus*, of coastal E Aus. with the smallest body of any Aus. bird and a long gauzy tail erected almost over its head, often hopping almost mouse-like through grass tunnels, flying only short distances, very shy, and building a small dome-shaped nest on or near the ground. The Striated Field-wren, *Calamanthus* (reed-bird) *fuliginosus* (sooty), of SE Aus., is somewhat lark-like in appearance, and several related species cover most of the country. The Chestnut-tailed Heath or Ground Wren, *Hylacola* (wood-dwelling) *pyrrhopygia* (fire-tailed), and Mallee Heath-wren, *H. cauta* (shy), of E and S Aus. are very similar, but with a bright red or red-brown rump. Several species of Grass-wrens, of genus *Amytornis*, are seen in Central and N Aus., running rapidly to hide among rocks, and with rather bulky dome or globe-shaped nests in spinifex etc.; several have black and white flecking in lines on the fore-part, whitish breasts, and mainly brown body and tail. The Scrub-wrens, of genus *Sericornis* (silken bird), have substantial, blunt and less erectile tails, are generally brown with lighter, sometimes brown-flecked breasts, and often a dark face-patch, contrasting with light eyelines; slightly differing species cover much of the country. Generally they live off terrestrial insects and in undergrowth, building a dome-shaped

nest with a side entrance on or near the ground.

Wright, Judith (Mrs. J. P. McKinney (1915–   ) b. near Armidale, N.S.W. A fifth-generation Aus. of pioneering ancestry. She is one of Australia's leading poets. After secretarial work, she married and now lives in Qld. Her first book of poems, *The Moving Image* (Melbourne, 1946), immediately claimed her a place in world literature; it has been followed by several more. The second, *Woman to Man* (Sydney, 1949), states the feminine viewpoint on love; many of her poems are on Aus. subjects and settings, yet they remain universal in their emotional appeal, evocation and clear precise economical style. She is also a critic and writes for children.

Wundowie W.A. 32S/116E (1,042 in 1971) A small, State-owned iron-smelting centre operating since 1948. Local limonite has been replaced by haematite ore from Koolyanobbing. Fuel is from an integrated wood-distillation and charcoal plant, using eucalypts of the surrounding Darling Range. Annual production is about 50,000 tonnes of pig-iron.

Wyangala Dam N.S.W. 34S/149E On the Lachlan*, it is 61 m. high and stores 310 million m.³ of water for domestic and stock water, irrigation and some hydro-electricity. It is now being raised 21 m. to store 1,200 million m.³ in all.

Wyndham W.A. 15S/128E (1,496 in 1971) It lies 80 km. from the mouth of the Durack River and is hemmed in by mud-flats and the sandstone 'Bastion' hill. It was founded as a port for E Kimberleys gold-field, declared in 1885 but short-lived. Meat-works, recently taken over from the Government by private enterprise, have operated since 1919, and from 1949–62 handled 'Airbeef', as well as cattle driven in from the stations. The season is May–September and vessels loading the chilled beef, tallow, bones etc. require careful pilotage in the channel. Temporary labour swells the population. Competition from Broome, Derby, Katherine and Darwin meatworks has caused a decrease in carcases handled.

Wynyard Tas., 41S/146E (4,013 in 1971) A service centre with vegetable canning and dairy factories, on the N coast at the mouth of the Inglis River.

Wyperfeld National Park Vic. 560 km.^{2} W of Hopetoun, 36S/142E, in the Mallee*, with untouched vegetation cover and lowan* or mallee-fowl.

X

XANTHORRHOEA

Xanthorrhoea A uniquely Aus. genus of the Liliaceae or Lily family, commonly known as Grass-trees*. Their grass-like leaves spring from a tuft at the top of a thick, often trunk-like stem. They grow in dry sclerophyll* woodland and are highly resistant to bushfires: the colour of the charred but surviving trunks partly explains their W.A. name of Blackboys*.

Xenophon A naval sloop of 334 tons, of which Matthew Flinders* took command in 1801. She had been overhauled and re-coppered, and he changed her name to *Investigator*, before setting out on his famous voyages round the Aus. coast.

X-Ray Paintings By Aborigines of W

X-RAY LABORATORY

Arnhem Land, showing internal organs such as the heart, and sometimes the skeleton, executed both on bark and in caves. This form of representation is more highly developed than in any other primitive art.

X-Ray and Radium Laboratory, Commonwealth (Melbourne) Re-named (1935) from the Commonwealth Radium Laboratory (1929) when its scope was extended to include physical aspects of X-Ray therapy. In addition to controlling import and distribution of radium for medical use, the Laboratory investigates all safety aspects of radiation, including safe degrees of dosage, protection of employees, and the monitoring of radio-active fall-out.

Y

YABBIE

Yabbie A popular name, especially in inland E Aus., for freshwater Crayfish*, now a gourmet delicacy.

Yagan An outstanding W.A. Aborigine at the time of the Swan River Settlement, who led a number of attacks on the settlers generally in reprisal for wrongs, and was killed as an outlaw in 1833.

Yallourn Vic. 38S/147E (Moe-Yallourn, 20,764 in 1971; 23,222 in 1966) On the S bank of the Latrobe River*, it was built from 1921 by the State Electricity Commission of Vic. along with the development of vast brown coal deposits. Removal of the town is planned for the 1980s to allow exploitation of seams under it. The open cut covers over 5 km.^{2} and is being extended S and W, and at Yallourn North over the river, where the earliest mining took place in 1887. The coal excavated at rates of up to 1,785 tonnes an hour by bucket-and-chain scoops on crawlers, is tipped into trucks and conveyed to the briquette works between the cut and the town, and the power station on the river-bank to the N. The overburden (about 12 m. over seams of 60–90 m.) is deposited in the exploited area.

Yampi Sound W.A. 16S/123E An island-studded water between the Buccaneer Archipelago and Dampier Land, with severe shipping hazards in tidal race and range. It contains the iron-ore islands Cockatoo* and Koolan*.

Yanchep W.A. 32S/116E A National Park of 245 ha. in the coastal limestone country, 50 km. N of Perth. Over 60 caves are known, notably the Yonderup and Crystal, discovered in 1838 by Grey. Relief works in the 1930s' Depression improved access and facilities.

YARRALUMLA

Koalas were introduced in 1938. The lakes, nearby beaches and fine tuart* trees all make a fine amenity for Perth.

Yanco (earlier Yanko) N.S.W. 35S/146E A creek and small town; Yanco Creek is the only anabranch* of the Murrumbidgee, flowing for over 322 km. through the alluvial plains to join the Wakool River, an anabranch of the Murray. Yanco Creek changes its name to Moulamein or Billabong Creek and Kyalite River. Control of the river for irrigation makes Yanco Creek perennial, providing domestic and stock water to a broad belt of country along its course, and new weirs at Yanco and Gogeldrie will intensify irrigation in this tract. (*See also* COLEAMBALLY.)

Yarra River Vic. It rises near Mt. Baw Baw, and not far from the sources of the Goulburn and Thomson, about 120 km. NE of Melbourne, but its course to the small dredged estuary in Port Phillip Bay is about 240 km. Its water supply was crucial from the first settlement of Melbourne, and the catchment, with some supplementation from that of the Goulburn, still supplies a large part of the city's water. Some flood protection and reclamation works from billabongs etc. have been necessary as the city has grown.

Yarralumla Residence of the Governor General in Canberra; originally the name of a property of 10,530 ha. largely developed by Frederick Campbell, grandson of Robert Campbell*, from 1881. He built much of the existing house after 1891; it was taken over by the Government in 1913 and Lord Stonehaven was the first Governor General to occupy it, in 1927. It has given its name to a Canberra suburb.

Yarrawonga Weir 233 km. downstream from the great storage of the Hume Reservoir* on the Murray; it raises the water enough to gravity-feed some 121,000 ha. through the Mulwala Canal in N.S.W. (Berriquin Irrigation District) and, after crossing under the Edwards River by siphon feeds the Deniboota district, and on the Vic. side another 101,250 ha. between the Murray and Broken Rivers.

Yass N.S.W. 35S/149E (4,240 in 1971) On the Yass River, a tributary to the Murrumbidgee; it was established in the 1830s and is the focus of a long-settled grazing area. Yass Junction is on the main Melbourne–Sydney line, the Hume Highway passes through the town, and tourism is being developed.

Yate (*Eucalyptus cornuta*) A relatively small but thick-trunked tree (15–20 m. by 90 cm.) of the Albany-Busselton area, yielding very hard timber almost as strong as wrought iron. It grows on swampy ground near Albany, W.A., with the Flooded Gum, *E. rudis*, on moderately fertile river terraces with Tuart, *E. gomphocephala*, etc., and in places in pure stands but in stunted form. It is sometimes seen on hillsides.

Yellowbelly or **Callop** A commercially important freshwater fish* of E Aus. introduced to W.A.

Yellow-eye (*Xyris operculata*) A rush-like herb of swamps in E and S Aus., bearing 2·5-cm. bright yellow papery flowers with dark bracts. There are some 15 Aus. species in the widespread genus, which with a tropical S American genus makes up the Xyridaceae family.

Yellowtail Kingfish (*Regificola grandis*) Dark blue with silvery belly and usually a yellow side stripe, it reaches 2·5 m. and 70 kg. and is one of the most esteemed of sea angling fish from S Qld. to Tas. and N.Z.; related to the Trevally*.

Yirrkala N.T. 12S/137E A Methodist Mission for Aborigines on Gove Peninsula* in Arnhem Land*, some 32 km.

S of the present bauxite development. Its people were involved in the controversy over resumption of the region for this purpose (*see* ABORIGINES).

Yorick Club Possibly the oldest literary society of status in Aus., founded in Melbourne 1868, with notable members including Marcus Clarke*, Adam Lindsay Gordon*, Henry Kendall* and Joseph Furphy*.

York W.A. 32S/116E (1,176 in 1971; 1,435 in 1966) In the Avon Valley*; it is one of the State's oldest towns, in early developed farming country and on the Great Southern Railway.

Yorke Peninsula S.A. 34S/138E A fault-lined, but lowland block, between the rift valleys of Spencer and St. Vincent Gulfs, extending NE–SW. for 160 km. from Moonta* to Cape Spencer, and averaging 40 km. in width. Settlement began with Moonta copper; now there is a long-established landscape of mixed farms edged with sheltered belts and rectangular road patterns. Field dams for sheep are augmented for domestic water by Mt. Lofty Range reservoirs. Malting barley is important and there are gypsum, dolomite and salt exports from small ports. Flinders named it after the First Lord of the Admiralty.

Young N.S.W. 34S/148E (6,062 in 1971) In gently rolling cherry-orchard country towards the E edge of the S part of the Western Slopes region. Renamed after a Governor of N.S.W., it was formerly called Lambing Flat. It became a large gold-rush town, and saw sharp anti-Chinese riots. There is wheat and fruit trade, storage and processing.

Young, Sir Henry Edward Fox (1808–1870) b. Kent, Eng. Lieutenant-Governor of S.A. (1848–55), and Governor of Tas. (1855–61). The first civilian Governor of S.A. and a trained diplomat, he saw the colony through self-government negotiations, then transferred to the already self-governing Tas.

Z

Z FORCE

Z Force A Commando group in the 1939–45 War, in the form of small volunteer raiding forces, particularly against Japanese shipping. *For further reading see* R. McKie: *The Heroes* (Sydney, 1960).

Zamia Fern Sometimes used as a popular name for the Cycads*, especially *Macrozamia* spp.

Zeehan 42S/145E (1,476 in 1971) Formerly a mining centre based on silver-lead discovered in 1882, with wild company promotion and over 160 companies in 1891 and peak silver production in 1894. No mines operate now, but the town serves the tin mines at Renison Bell, 19 km. to the NE. Rainfall is 250 cm. a year. Zeehan is the railhead for the narrow-gauge line to Burnie. **Mt. Zeehan** (700 m.) about 6 km. to the SW was sighted by Tasman in 1642 and later named after one of his ships.

Zeil, Mount N.T. 24S/133E The highest point of the Macdonnell Ranges and of the N.T.; it is 1,510 m. and lies at the NW end of the ranges.

ZOOLOGICAL GARDENS

Zieria An Aus. genus of about 16 aromatic shrubs in the world-wide Rutaceae or Rue family; the aroma from essential oils in the foliage may be strong, even unpleasant (*see* STINK-WOOD).

Zinc Obtained from the same ore concentrate as lead*, at Broken Hill*, N.S.W., (70%) Mt. Read-Rosebery, Tas. (10%) and Mt. Isa, Qld. (20%). With 9–10% of world output, Aus. is 3rd after U.S. and Canada as a zinc producer. Prices fluctuate but in 1969–1970 were worth $69 million. Refined zinc (some $\frac{1}{4}$ million tonnes a year) is from plants at Risdon (Tas.), Cockle Creek (N.S.W.) and Port Pirie (S.A.). New deposits may be developed in S.A. at Beltana and Aroona and at Tarago, N.S.W.

Zoological Gardens Established in Sydney (Taronga Park, 1912, on the N shore of the harbour), Melbourne Royal Park (1862), Adelaide (1883) and a smaller one in S Perth. There are a number of private zoos and sanctuaries for Aus. wildlife, notably koalas.

MAP SECTION

THE CLIMATE OF AUSTRALIA

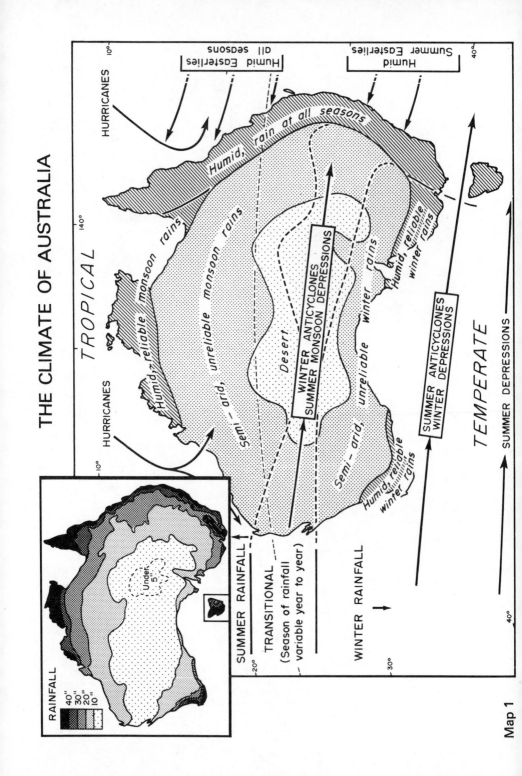

Map 1

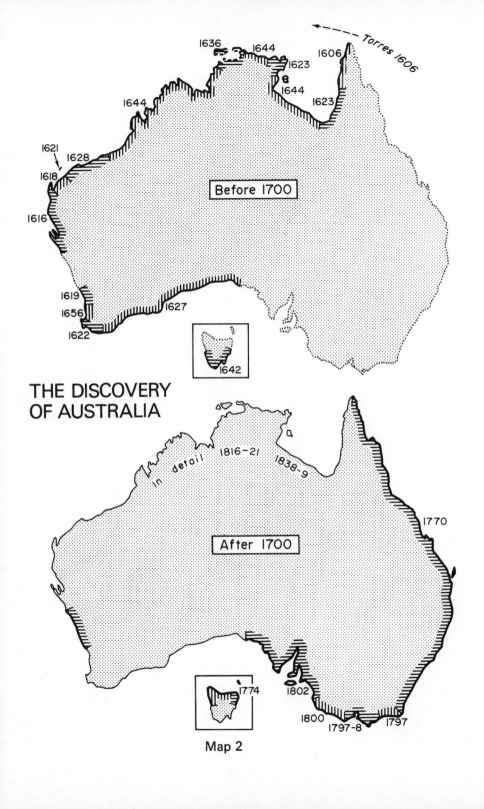

Torres 1606

1636   1644   1606
        1623
1644
            1644
        1623

Before 1700

1621
1628
1618

1616

1619
1656   1627
1622
        1642

THE DISCOVERY
OF AUSTRALIA

In detail   1816-21   1838-9

1770

After 1700

1774
    1802
1800   1797
1797-8

Map 2

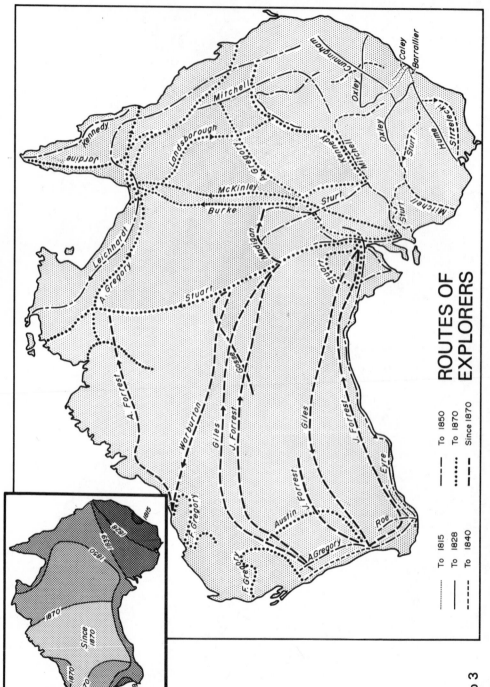

ROUTES OF EXPLORERS

To 1815	....
To 1828	———
To 1840	– – –
To 1850	—— —
To 1870	·········
Since 1870	— — —

Map 3

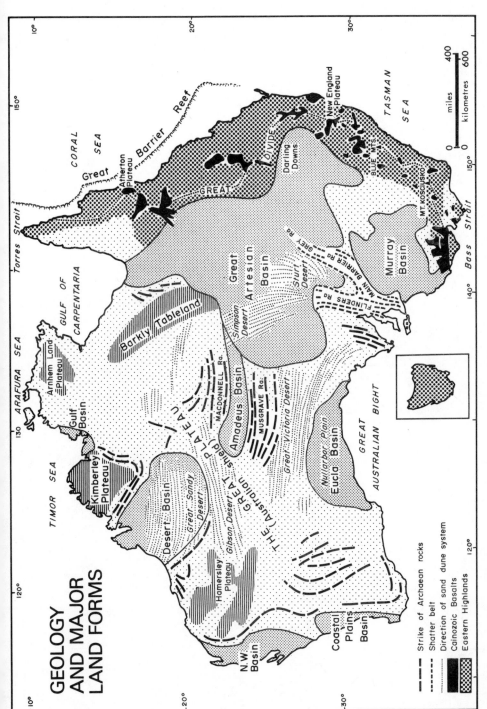

GEOLOGY AND MAJOR LAND FORMS

Map 4

TIMOR SEA

ARAFURA SEA

Torres Strait

GULF OF CARPENTARIA

CORAL SEA

Great Barrier Reef

Atherton Plateau

Arnhem Land Plateau

Gulf Basin

Kimberley Plateau

Barkly Tableland

GREAT

Great Artesian Basin

New England Plateau

DIVIDE

Darling Downs

TASMAN SEA

Desert Basin

Great Sandy Desert

Hamersley Plateau

Gibson Desert

Amadeus Basin

GREAT (THE AUSTRALIAN) PLATEAU

MACDONNELL Ra.

MUSGRAVE Ra.

Great Victoria Desert

Simpson Desert

Sturt Desert

GREY Rd

FLINDERS Rd

MAIN BARRIER Rd

Murray Basin

BLUE MTS.

MT KOSCIUSKO

Bass Strait

N.W. Basin

Coastal Plains Basin

Nullarbor Plain

Eucla Basin

GREAT AUSTRALIAN BIGHT

Legend:
- ─ ─ ─ Strike of Archaean rocks
- ─ ─ ─ Shatter belt
- :::::::: Direction of sand dune system
- ■ Cainozoic Basalts
- ▨ Eastern Highlands

Scale: miles 0 — 400 ; kilometres 0 — 600

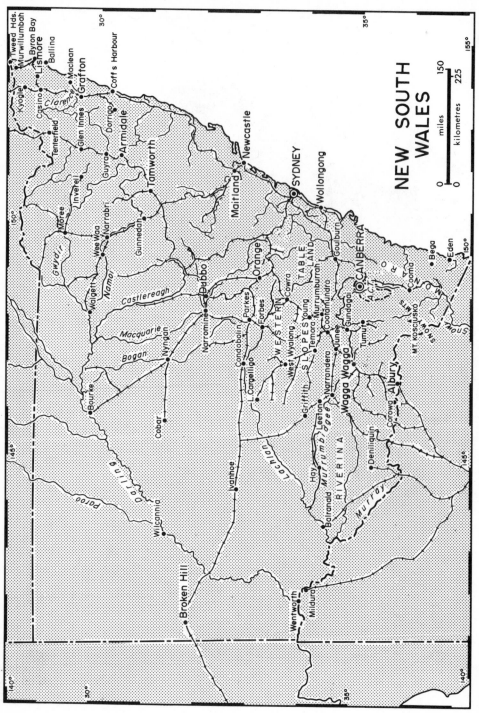

NEW SOUTH WALES

miles 0 150
kilometres 0 225

Map 5

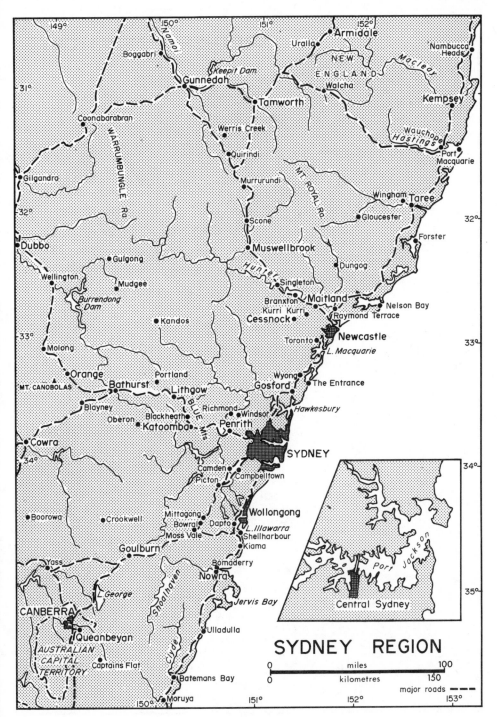

SYDNEY REGION

major roads ▬ ▬ ▬

Map 6

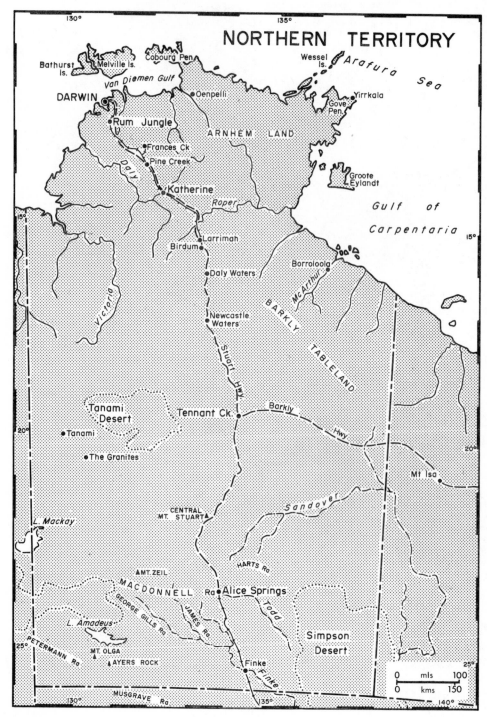

Map 7

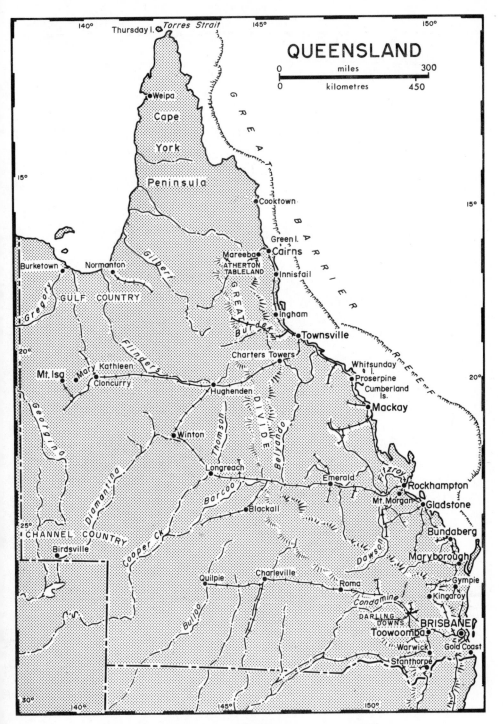

Map 8

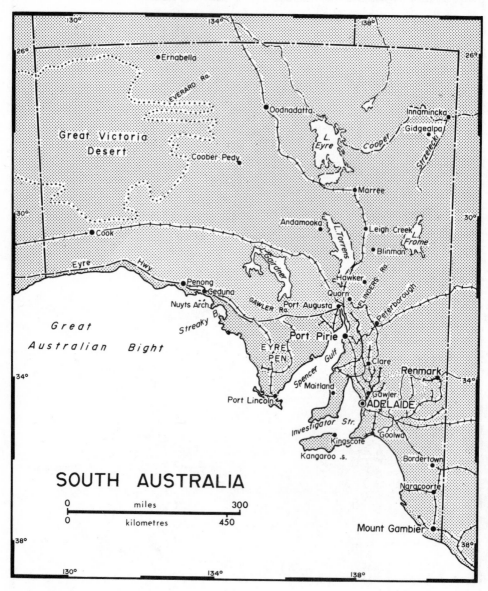

Great Victoria
Desert

•Ernabella

EVERARD Ra.

•Oodnadatta

L.
Eyre

Cooper

Innamincka
•
Gidgealpa

Strzelecki

•Coober Pedy

•Marree

•Cook

Andamooka
•

L. Torrens

Leigh Creek

L.
Frome

•Blinman

Eyre   Hwy.

Penong
•Geduna

Nuyts Arch.

Streaky B.

Gardner

GAWLER   Ra.

•Hawker

Quorn

FLINDERS Ra.

Port Augusta

Peterborough

Great

Australian   Bight

EYRE
PEN.

Port Pirie •

Spencer Gulf

•Clare

Renmark
•

Port Lincoln •

Maitland

•Gawler

◎ADELAIDE

Investigator Str.

Goolwa

Kingscote

Bordertown
•

Kangaroo .s.

Naracoorte
•

SOUTH AUSTRALIA

0	miles	300
0	kilometres	450

Mount Gambier •

Map 9

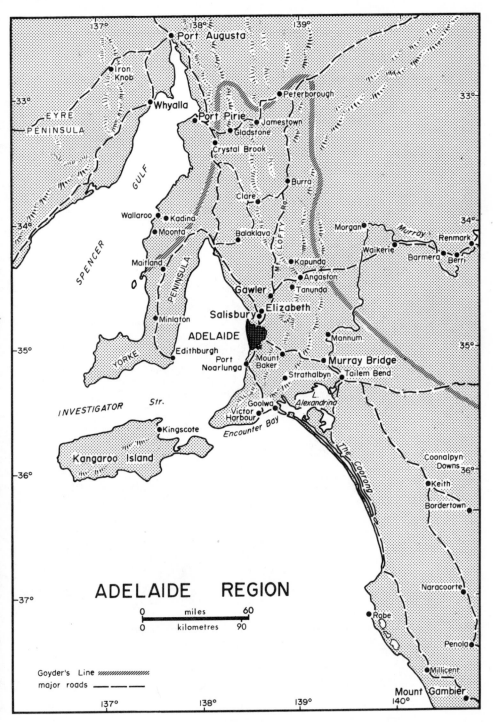

ADELAIDE REGION

```
0          miles         60
0        kilometres       90
```

Goyder's Line //////////////
major roads ———— ————

Map 10

TASMANIA

miles 0 — 60
kilometres 0 — 90

144° 146° 148°

King Island

Kent Group

Furneaux

B A S S   S T R A I T

Group

Flinders Island

40°

Cape Barren Island

Cape Grim

Circular Head

Smithton Wynyard
Penguin Ulverstone
Burnie Devonport GeorgeTown
Bell Bay Scottsdale

Arthur

Latrobe Beauty Pt Beaconsfield
Railton Launceston

MT. BISCHOFF

Forth Deloraine Longford Mathinna
BEN LOMOND St. Marys
Rossarden Fingal

Pieman Rosebery
MT. HEEMSKIRK Renison Bell
Zeehan

Savage

Mersey GREAT WESTERN TIERS
Great Lake

South Esk

Campbell Town

Queenstown MT. OLYMPUS L. St.Clair L. Echo

42° Strahan MT. OLYMPUS 42°
King FRENCHMANS CAP L. King William Oatlands
Wayatinah Swansea Freycinet Pen.

Macquarie

Huon Ouse Oyster Bay

MT. FIELD Derwent Triabunna

Gordon MT. ANNE New Norfolk Bridgewater Maria I.
L. Pedder MT. WELLINGTON Sorell
Kingston HOBART Dunalley

Huon Geeveston Eaglehawk Neck
HARTZ MTS. Port Arthur
FEDERATION PEAK Tasman Pen.

Port Davey Bruny I. Storm Bay
Hythe

major roads ———

D'Entrecasteaux Channel

Maatsuyker I.

144° 146° 148°

Map 11

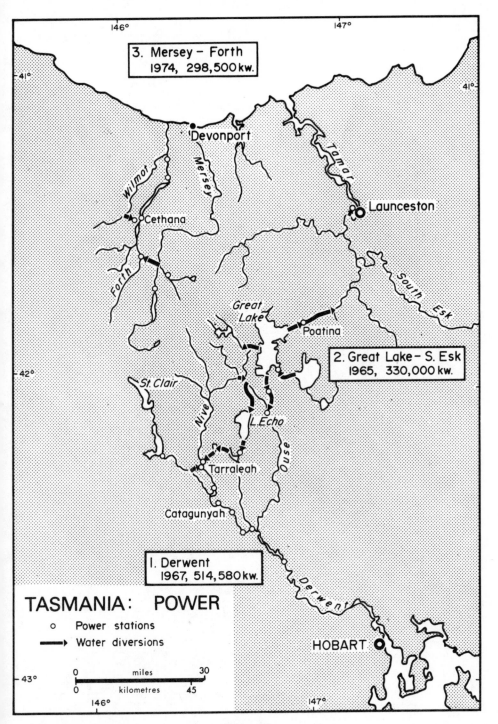

3. Mersey – Forth
1974, 298,500 kw.

Devonport

Launceston

Cethana

Great
Lake

Poatina

2. Great Lake – S. Esk
1965, 330,000 kw.

St. Clair

L. Echo

Tarraleah

Catagunyah

1. Derwent
1967, 514,580 kw.

TASMANIA: POWER

o   Power stations
➤   Water diversions

0   miles   30
0   kilometres   45

HOBART

Map 12

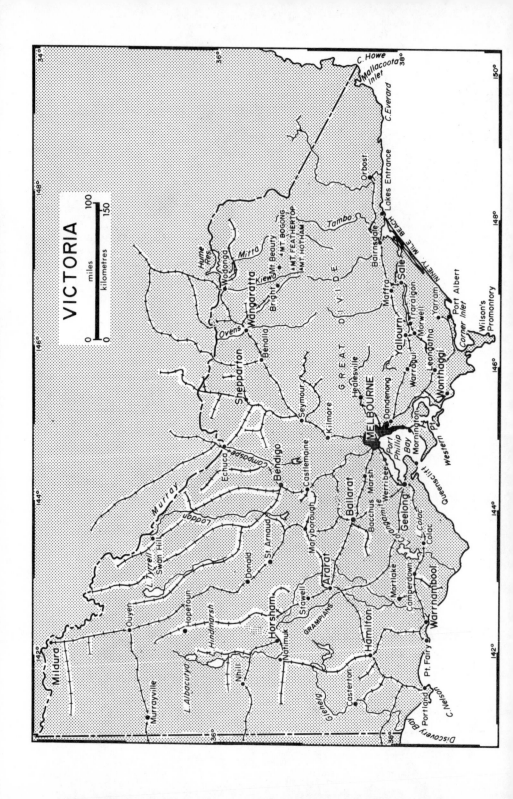